W9-BIV-614

— Edited by —
WOLFGANG BEINERT and
FRANCIS SCHÜSSLER FIORENZA

Handbook of
CATHOLIC
THEOLOGY

A Herder & Herder Book
The Crossroad Publishing Company
New York

This printing: 2000

The Crossroad Publishing Company
370 Lexington Avenue, New York, NY 10017

Original edition: *Lexikon der katholischen Dogmatik*, Wolfgang Beinert, edit(
©1987 by Verlag Herder, Freiburg im Breisgau

English-language edition, with new materials, © 1995 by The Crossroad
Publishing Company

Printed in the United States of America

Library of Congress Cataloging-in-Publication Data

Lexikon der katholischen Dogmatik. English.
   Handbook of Catholic theology / edited by Wolfgang Beinert,
Francis Schüssler Fiorenza.
      p.   cm.
   Includes bibliographical references and index.
   ISBN 0-8245-1423-8 (hard); 0-8245-1854-3 (pbk.)
   1. Catholic Church—Doctrines—Dictionaries.   2. Theology,
Doctrinal—Dictionaries.   I. Beinert, Wolfgang.   II. Fiorenza, Franci:
Schüssler.   III. Title.
BX1745.5.L4913   1995
230'.2'03—dc20   95-1216
                                                    CIP

Handbook of
CATHOLIC
THEOLOGY

Contents

List of Tables

Preface

Our time is one of theological change. New ideas circulate in the marketplace. New theological viewpoints are widely discussed. The flood of theological diversity and innovation overwhelms many. At the same time, an increasing lack of theological literacy characterizes our situation. Traditional religious education has become less prevalent. Many lack training and knowledge in the fundamentals of Roman Catholic theology and its tradition. What are the basic topics and categories of Roman Catholic theology? What are the central teachings of the Roman Catholic Church? What are their meaning and significance? What are the biblical texts at the roots or origin of the development of Catholic beliefs? What are the decisive church councils and their precise teaching? What are the major controversies and differences of opinion within traditional as well as contemporary theology?

In a time of change and transition, it becomes important to know both traditional as well as new categories of theology. It becomes important to relate contemporary theological issues to classical problems and formulations so that one can understand the ground and nature of the shifts to new categories and ideas within theology. Such knowledge is helpful not only to students of theology, be they seminarians or laypersons, but also for the educated adult who in reading theology comes across terms and definitions with which he or she is not familiar. Many adult Roman Catholics seeking understanding and knowledge about their Catholic faith may pick up theology books but may lack a rudimentary theological background. Students majoring in theology, whether entering a seminary or taking master's level courses in theology, encounter lectures, articles, and books that presuppose a basic knowledge of the elements of Catholic theology.

To meet these needs this handbook focuses on Roman Catholic systematic theology. Many introductions or dictionaries are either too broad or too narrow. Many encyclopedias of religion discuss the world religions in their diversity; many dictionaries cover either specialized areas within theology or all aspects of religion. The *Handbook of Catholic Theology* concentrates on Catholic systematic theology and thereby fulfills an urgent need. It seeks to present an objective and balanced introduction to the basic notions of Catholic theology. Sometimes handbooks of theology are written by one person. They may serve as an excellent introduction to that individual theologian's thought but fail to introduce other directions within theology. Sometimes handbooks or dictionaries have hundreds of authors, each writing his or her own articles.

They present a plethora of viewpoints but often lack the consistency and development that a more focused approach can give. This handbook has sought a middle path. Several leading theologians present diverse articles and topics but within the framework of specific theological treatises. Such an approach allows consistency and depth in the treatment of a topic and at the same time provides the necessary diversity and balance. As a complement, several North American theologians have been asked specifically not only to provide additional perspectives but also to discuss contemporary issues.

The structure of the articles seeks to serve these diverse functions. Each article is divided into five sections: the first section, *Biblical Background,* points to the importance of the Scriptures for contemporary Catholic theology. Catholic theology has come a long way from when Scripture served as a proof-text for particular doctrinal positions in debates. Nevertheless, it is important to understand the biblical roots of Roman Catholic beliefs and practices from which particular traditions have developed. The second section, *History of Theology,* seeks to show that theological concepts and religious belief are not static but undergo change and development. Many doctrines have been formulated within the context of specific controversies and against the background of a specific social and cultural milieu. To understand them, it is necessary to view them within their historical context and to grasp their particular presuppositions. A third section, *Church Teaching,* tries to clarify what exactly has been the teaching of the church. In many cases, there have been no explicit pronouncements. In other cases, such pronouncements have been limited. Quite often what is presumed as defined has not been defined, or what is regarded as a certain is merely a theological opinion. For these reasons, this third section seeks to clarify and to delineate quite carefully what is the official teaching of the Roman Catholic Church on issues of Catholic belief. A fourth section, *Ecumenical Perspectives,* deals with the relation between Roman Catholic teachings and those of other Christian churches. This section attempts not only to lay out the historical differences between a Roman Catholic and a Lutheran or Calvinist position but also to point out and describe some of the ecumenical consensus statements and developments that have emerged in the last decades. The final section, *Systematic Reflections,* presents a systematic exposition of the topic. These reflections strive to clarify the meaning of Roman Catholic belief and doctrines. They survey diverse contemporary theological directions, and they develop specific systematic proposals and constructive interpretations.

One of the outstanding features of this handbook is its charts and tables. These present a visually clear overview of important theological notions, topics, and events. They provide an invaluable assistance for any student of theology seeking to grasp the essential contours of significant theological controversies, doctrines, conciliar statements, ecumenical agreements, and so on. What is described in detail in the articles is crystalized in the charts. In my opinion, they alone make this handbook very useful for students of theology.

Several theologians were asked to analyze the major theological treatises in relation to contemporary and debated issues. Their essays survey the latest currents and directions of theology. They therefore provide background and contours to some current issues or offer different and additional perspectives to the initial treatment in the handbook. These essays thereby present both a diversity of opinion as well as an insight into present directions of Catholic theology.

Finally, the bibliographies have been created specially for this English edition. Since the book is a handbook, the bibliographies refer primarily to English works. Some of these are modern "classics" of Catholic theology that have decisively contributed to our knowledge of the topics or have significantly influenced modern theology. Others are the basic works in the fields that provide the reader with a general introduction. Other bibliographic references point to additional important essays, monographs, or special studies that can provide the reader with guidance for further study on the subject, either deepening the viewpoint of the individual article or offering alternative perspectives.

Several persons have contributed significantly to the publication of this handbook. Frank Oveis, formerly of Crossroad/Continuum and now with Continuum, initiated the idea for an English edition of this volume. He orchestrated the team of translators and oversaw the translations. I want to thank Dr. Gwendolyn Herder and Michael Leach of Crossroad/Herder for their support of the project. The *Handbook of Catholic Theology* appears in print exactly at the time the Catholic Theological Society of America is celebrating its fiftieth anniversary. As I reflect on the history of Roman Catholic theology in the United States, it is evident that Crossroad and Herder have played a significant role during this half-century in the formation of the English-speaking theological community. Their encyclopedias, dictionaries, histories, and handbooks have become standard works over the past years. Through their translations, many of the leading European theologians have become well known in English-speaking countries: one thinks of Karl Rahner, Edward Schillebeeckx, Yves Congar, Henri de Lubac, Hans Urs von Balthasar, Joseph Ratzinger, Hans Küng, Walter Kasper, Johann B. Metz — to mention just a few of the theologians published by Herder and Crossroad. At the same time they have published many Anglo-Saxon and American authors who have now become established theologians. The publication of this handbook continues this tradition of the Crossroad/Herder commitment to Catholic theological scholarship and education.

A very special word of thanks goes to Michael Leach, the publisher of Crossroad/Herder. He not only supported the project during a transition period but exercised hands-on guidance and leadership in seeing the project to publication. His friendly and persistent encouragement has been much appreciated. Hank Schlau of EdiType is to be thanked not only for his careful copyediting but also for the format and layout of the book. I am also especially thankful for the assistance of two doctoral assistants at Harvard Divinity School. Elizabeth A. Pritchard helped in the initial preparation of the English bibliographies. Julie B. Miller's assistance in the final preparation and editing of the manuscript has been invaluable. I am also grateful to the librarians of Harvard's Andover Library for their help in tracking down bibliographical sources.

FRANCIS SCHÜSSLER FIORENZA

Harvard University

HANDBOOK
OF
CATHOLIC
THEOLOGY

A a

Absolution. In the doctrine of the sacraments, absolution means the release of repentant sinners from their sins in the sacrament of reconciliation. Absolution is given by a priest who has jurisdiction to hear confessions and derives its efficacy from the power of the church to forgive sins.

(1) *Biblical Background.* In the New Testament this power to forgive sins is granted to the community as a whole and, at the same time, to its official representatives who are commissioned by Christ (Mt 18:18; Jn 20:23). Absolution by a priest represents an obligatory concretization of this power to forgive sins.

(2) *History of Theology.* In the period when canonical penance was practiced in the church, absolution was to a great extent identical with the reconciliation of sinners with the church (*reconciliatio cum ecclesia*); this in turn was an affair of the bishop, and to it was ascribed a simultaneous complete reconciliation with God. For a lengthy period during the Middle Ages, the question was debated whether the forgiveness of serious sins comes about through the contrition of the sinner and, if it does, what significance the absolution (for example, one that is purely declaratory) still has. On the other hand, Hugh of St. Victor, for example, insisted that only absolution by a priest brings forgiveness. Thomas Aquinas effected a synthesis: perfect contrition justifies the baptized sinner, but not unless the sinner has (at least implicitly) the intention of receiving the sacrament of reconciliation and therefore absolution. In the sacrament of reconciliation itself the acts of the penitent and the absolution are related to each other as matter and form, so that here again the subjective cooperation of the recipient clearly plays a part in obtaining the gracious forgiveness of God through the sacrament. In its essentials, this synthesis has stood down to the present time.

(3) *Church Teaching.* In a doctrinal passage the Council of Trent says that "the form of the sacrament of penance, in which its power principally resides, consists in these words of the minister: I absolve you..." (DS 1673). The council condemns the assertion that "the sacramental absolution of the priest is not a judicial act but a mere ministry of pronouncing and declaring to him who confesses that his sins are forgiven" (DS 1709). When Trent prescribes that the formula of absolution is to be indicative in form (as opposed to the deprecative form used even in the early Roman Church), it does not mean that the deprecative form used in the Eastern churches is invalid. The new Rite of Penance of 1973 combines various types of statements in a single formula: "God, the Father of mercies, through the death and resurrection of his Son has reconciled the world to himself and sent the Holy Spirit among us for the forgiveness of

sins; through the ministry of the church may God give you pardon and peace, and I absolve you from your sins in the name … "

(4) *Ecumenical Perspectives.* The churches of the Reformation acknowledge an authoritative grant of reconciliation with God in Jesus Christ, but deny judicial absolution by a priest. In dialogue with them, the emphasis needs to be placed, in accordance with the new formula of absolution, on the ministerial character of absolution, while showing that this ministry can definitely be an exercise of authority and (in an analogous sense) judicial.

(5) *Systematic Reflections.* This last statement shows the most important theological approach to be taken today: absolution is a concrete form of the church's servant ministry. Its purpose (and that of the sacrament of reconciliation as a whole) is the authoritative granting of God's forgiveness to penitent sinners, and not their condemnation. The refusal of absolution is a possibility only when the penitent does not bring the required dispositions to the sacrament of reconciliation (or when absolution is reserved to a higher ecclesiastical authority). There is need of further theological reflection, in the light of the tradition, on the relationship between absolution and the forgiveness of sins on the basis of the sinner's contrition.

See also FORGIVENESS OF SIN: THE CHURCH AND THE; REPENTANCE; SACRAMENT OF RECONCILIATION.

Bibliography

Dease, Dennis J. "General Confession and Absolution." *Worship* 51 (1977) 536–45.
Dudley, Martin, and Geoffrey Rowell, eds. *Confession and Absolution.* London: SPCK, 1990.
Gallen, John. "General Sacramental Absolution: Pastoral Remarks on Pastoral Norms [Issued by Sacred Congregation for the Doctrine of the Faith, 1972]." *ThS* 34 (1977) 114–21.
Garafalo, Robert C. "Reconciliation and Celebration: A Pastoral Case for General Absolution." *Worship* 63 (1989) 447–56.
Orsy, Ladislas. "General Absolution: New Law, Old Traditions, Some Questions." *ThS* 45 (1984) 676–89.
Perales, Jorge. "The Service of the Indulgentia: Light on the Rite of General Confession and Absolution." *Worship* 62 (1989) 138–53.
Rahner, Karl. "Forgotten Truths concerning the Sacrament of Penance." In *Theological Investigations,* 2:140–49. Baltimore: Helicon, 1963.
———. "Penance as an Additional Act of Reconciliation with the Church." *Theological Investigations,* 10:125–49. New York: Herder and Herder, 1973.
Vorgrimler, Herbert. *Sacramental Theology.* Collegeville, Minn.: Liturgical Press, 1992.

GÜNTER KOCH

Agnosticism. The term *agnosticism* refers to the standpoint that denies God's knowability on the grounds that everything beyond the reach of the senses is unknowable. It involves either a materialistic attitude centered on this world or a state of uneasy doubt.

(1) *Biblical Background.* Holy Scripture stresses that God's knowability is a basic human belief while at the same time affirming its rootedness in mystery.

(2) *History of Theology.* Tradition reasserts that position in the context of negative theology (Anselm of Canterbury, Thomas Aquinas, Nicholas of

Cusa): God is knowable as God precisely in that the divine essence remains inscrutable.

(3) *Church Teaching.* Against agnosticism, Vatican I stresses God's knowability through reason and revelation (DS 3004); Vatican II (*DV,* chap. 1) puts the accent on God's self-communication in Jesus Christ.

(4) *Ecumenical Perspectives.* Since the Protestant Reformation emphasized that human beings are in bondage to sin, that is, they live in a state of remoteness from God from which they cannot free themselves, it was skeptical about the possibility of any "natural" knowledge of God.

(5) *Systematic Reflections.* Theology always has the task, and especially so today, to establish the link between the human question about God and the initiative of God, who desires, by means of love, to overcome the darkness that surrounds God. Therefore, theology must come to terms both with an "aporetic" agnosticism, which draws from that darkness the conclusion that the world is absurd, and with an everyday agnosticism, which acknowledges the existence of a "higher being" but does not relate this belief to concrete life decisions. Here, theology refrains (in appreciation of Kant's critique) from overvaluing reason and knows that communion with God can sustain even our falling silent before God.

See also ANALOGY; GOD: POSSIBILITY OF KNOWLEDGE OF.

Bibliography
Huxley, Thomas Henry. *Science and Christian Tradition: Essays H. Huxley.* New York: D. Appleton, 1897.

WILHELM BREUNING

Analogy. In theology, the term *analogy* signifies the mode and manner in which we can use human words to speak pertinently about God.

(1) *Biblical Background.* In Holy Scripture, Wis 13:15 uses the notion of analogy to express that the knowledge of the greatness and beauty of created things leads to knowledge of the Creator. Rom 12:6 refers to the correspondence between prophetic utterance and faith. These biblical statements reflect the basic characteristic of biblical language that seeks to lead humans from the reality of creation to the reality of God's rule. The parables of Jesus are to be understood similarly. According to Jn 14:9, Jesus himself makes the reality of God visible in his personality. Rom 1:18–20 refers to the possibility of drawing conclusions about God from God's created works, though in a context dealing with humans' having shut themselves off from God.

(2) *History of Theology.* That discourse about God is at the same time both necessary and impossible was summed up by classic Christian theology with the term "negative theology" and with the formula: "Regarding things divine, negations are true and affirmations inadequate" (Dionysius the Areopagite, *De coel. hier.* 2.3). In early Scholasticism, Anselm of Canterbury refers to God both as "something than which nothing greater can be conceived" and as something that is greater than everything that can be conceived. Scholasticism links

negative and affirmative theology through trinitarian theology: God can become human and die on the cross because God is self-renouncing love. With his theological emphasis on creation, Thomas Aquinas concludes that God is not called good inasmuch as God is the cause of the good, but rather, "Inasmuch as he is good, he imparts goodness to things" (*STh* 1, q. 13, a. 2). God's freely self-disclosing love thereby becomes a means of making analogy possible as a path leading from created things to an incomparable and absolutely transcendent God.

(3) *Church Teaching.* The church's official teaching on analogy is: "No similarity between Creator and creature can be asserted without its implying a greater dissimilarity between the two" (Fourth Lateran Council [DS 860]).

(4) *Ecumenical Perspectives.* The Reformation opposed an almost exclusively philosophical understanding of the doctrine of analogy. Luther therefore stressed the "theology of the cross" (*theologia crucis*), that is, seeing God "in terms of the contrary" (*sub contrario*), that is, in the form of death, a principle alien to God. Such a theory of the cross is a very concrete negative theology. Its aim is to make God's incomprehensible nearness understandable to believers in the sense of an analogy of belief. In the twentieth century, K. Barth's debate with E. Przywara and G. Söhngen has shown that the theology of the cross does not eliminate the analogy of creation: the analogy does not place God at the disposal of human thinking, but refers only to the basis of God's "graspability" — human beings, too, as creatures, have always been "grasped" by God.

(5) *Systematic Reflections.* Analogy has its foundation in the peculiarity of language that enables concepts to be used to designate not only self-contained realities (univocal concepts) but also interrelationships and similarities between things (analogical concepts, e.g., healthy as said of a person, a food, or a medicine) (see table). Theologically, analogy makes possible language about God,

---

Concepts can be univocal (e.g., "automobile"): the concept corresponds to the object in reality and is clearly unambiguous; equivocal (e.g., "bank"): it refers to completely different objects ("edge of river," "financial institution," etc.); or analogical (e.g., "healthy"): the concept refers to what is partly similar and partly dissimilar; it is partly equivocal because those entities that it signifies are not fully identical (healthy can designate "organism," "complexion," or "medicine"). The relationship of similarity can take varied forms: a distinction is made between (a) *analogy of proportion (of attribution)* (*analogia proportionis [attributionis]*): based on a central concept (the principal analogue [*analogatum princeps*]: the healthy organism), the conceptual content is transferred to other realities that have a proportional similarity to it (the healthy skin color indicates the health of the organism; the medicine helps bring about a healthy organism); and (b) *analogy of proportionality* (*analogia proportionalitatis*): both similarity and difference in the relationships between two things are signified ("body" as an image of social realities: just as the one body has many members, so the one church has many charismata).

which is based upon God's self-mediation as Creator, redeemer, and fulfiller. It enables humans to perceive (created) reality as a symbol of God, and it thereby sets them on the path of movement toward the Creator. However, above all, it is in the incarnation of the second divine person that God becomes present in history in such a way that God's innermost nature opens itself to humans and thereby makes them aware of God as an enduring mystery. Analogy is thus a mode of communication that leads into the depths of the divine mystery. This mystery, though remaining a mystery, is disclosed to us, through the Son in the Spirit, as the mystery of love. Analogy implies a three-stage process for theological knowledge: (a) Some positive aspect of created reality (e.g., wisdom) must, because of the way that the creature is related to the Creator, also be positively predicable of God. (b) Its concrete creaturely form must, however, be denied of God because of God's transcendence (God is not wise, i.e., not in the way that creatures are). (c) Nevertheless, this negation is intended only to direct attention to the infinite reality that transcends everything created (God is infinitely wise). These three steps, comprising the affirmative way, the negative way, and the way of eminence (via affirmativa, negativa, and eminentiae), are always taken together. The negative way is thereby the soul of the process insofar as it points toward the fulfillment that is characteristic of God alone. Hence, analogy does not exactly allow us to take hold of God, but it draws us closer to God. The analogy in creation thus leads into the analogy of the path of belief, upon which the Father leads human beings toward him through the Son in the Holy Spirit: the Son is the path, while the Spirit provides the communion.

See also GOD: ATTRIBUTES OF; DISCOURSE ABOUT GOD; MYSTERY OF FAITH; THEOLOGY; TRINITY.

Bibliography

Burrell, David. Knowing the Unknowable God: Ibn-Sina, Maimonides, Aquinas. Notre Dame, Ind.: University of Notre Dame Press, 1986.

Hill, William J. Knowing the Unknown God. New York: Philosophical Library, 1971.

Klubertanz, George P. St. Thomas Aquinas on Analogy: A Textual and Systematic Analysis. Chicago: Loyola University Press, 1960.

Lyttkens, Hampus. The Analogy between God and the World: An Investigation of Its Background and Interpretation of Its Use by Thomas of Aquino. Uppsala: Almqvist and Wiksell, 1952.

Preller, Victor. Divine Science and the Science of God. Princeton, N.J.: Princeton University Press, 1967.

WILHELM BREUNING

Angel. This concept refers to spiritual beings who, according to many biblical texts, perform a function of mediation under commission from God or, more precisely, one of conveying messages from God (Greek: ángelos; Hebrew: malak = messenger).

(1) *Biblical Background.* The Old Testament, primarily in texts handed down from earlier times and following a notion from "popular culture," speaks of

"the angel of Yahweh." He is a helpful messenger (2 Sm 14:17, 20; 1 Kgs 19:7), protects Israel at the Red Sea (Ex 14:19), strikes down its enemies (2 Kgs 19:35), guides it (Ex 23:20), and communicates things to be done (Jgs 6:11–13). Thus he shows himself to be an instrument of the grace of the covenant, the personified figure of divine readiness to help. In some texts, he can hardly be distinguished from Yahweh, who speaks and appears (Gn 16:7–9; 21:17–19; 22:11–13). Whenever he plainly functions as a figure in which God appears, mention of him serves to make clear God's transcendence and concealedness (see Ex 33:2f.). Other heavenly beings are known to the Old Testament, even a "royal court" that the Creator utilizes in governing the world. In the postexile period, when there was less threat of derailment into polytheism, a full-blown angelology was developed. According to it, God has many angels, who had acclaimed God already at the creation of the earthly world (Jb 38:7), are instructors and advocates to human beings (Jb 33:23), and "come to collect" the dying (Jb 33:22; cf. Pss 78:49; 89:6, 8). Some are given personal names related to their function, for example, Michael ("Who is like God?" [Dn 10:13, 21]) and Gabriel ("man of God" [Dn 8:15f.]). In the New Testament, the Baptist is once equated with Yahweh's messenger who prepares the way (Mt 11:10 par. Mk 1:2). Otherwise, as in the Old Testament, the angels represent that other world that surrounds and approaches our world, that mysterious sphere of reality, governed wholly by God, that can also be called "heaven," and out of which Christ comes (cf. Gal 4:14; 1 Tm 5:21; Heb 12:22). The angels contemplate God, but at the same time they perform services in relation to the life of Jesus, primarily at its beginning (Mt 1:20, 24; 2:13: the angel of Yahweh addresses Joseph in a dream) and glorious end (Mt 28:2–7), as well as in moments of crisis (Mt 4:11; Lk 22:43). Their actions are never independent; their essence exhausts itself totally in being instruments in God's hands. That also applies when, on the eschatological day of judgment, they stand by the Judge (Lk 12:8f.; 2 Thes 1:7; Rv 5:11–13; 19:1–3). The angel of Yahweh also accompanies the original community (Acts 5:19; 8:26; 10:3–5; 12:7–9). In Paul, Christ is so predominant, as the liberating presence of God in the world, that the significance of the angels greatly recedes. Within the school of Paul, gnostically tinged mythologizing about angels is opposed (Col 2:18; cf. 1:16).

(2) *History of Theology.* Among the Fathers, mention must be made of Augustine, with his reservation: "For angel is a name based on function, and not on nature" ("Angelus enim officii nomen est, non naturae" [*Sermo* 7.3]; cf. Gregory the Great, *Hom. in Ev.* 34.8), and Dionysius the Areopagite, with his elaborate doctrine of "the celestial hierarchy."

(3) *Church Teaching.* Teaching office has rested content with declaring that "at the beginning of time" God created "angelic creatures" (*creatura angelica*) as well as "earthly" (*mundana*) and "human" (*humana*) ones (Fourth Lateran Council, 1215 [DS 800]). Vatican I, in view of modern materialism, repeated this doctrine literally (DS 3002).

(4) *Ecumenical Perspectives.* M. Luther "sees angels as having been sup-

planted — with the advent of the New Testament — by Christ in the role of mediators of redemption, but as participating instead, by acting as coagents of God's 'officiary power,' in the governing of the world and of individual lives" (Gloege, *RGG* 2:468). J. Calvin stresses that biblical discourse about angels had origins in popular culture, reviews this in detail, and notes that angels are not just manifestations of divine force or stirrings that God has inspired in humans, as the Sadducees thought, but rather "ministering spirits sent to serve" (Heb 1:14) (*Inst.* 1.14.9; cf. 3–12).

(5) *Systematic Reflections.* Present-day dogmatics is forced to take a position on R. Bultmann's radical proposition that, for scientifically "enlightened" minds, the New Testament notion of an angel is "finished." It concedes that doctrinal office gave no definition of the nature of angels and nowhere discussed the manner and degree in which an analogy with persons might be applied to them. The doctrine of angels does not belong, in the sense of the HIERARCHY OF TRUTHS, among those that are central for believers. Nevertheless, it is meaningful as an elucidation of God's will to engage, right from the very beginning of creation, in communication with humans through spiritual means. Discourse about angels also challenges our belief to acknowledge "how limited is the reality seen by us, and the fact that God's kingdom embraces more than the reality knowable to us" (C. Westermann, *Gottes Engel brauchen keine Flügel* [Stuttgart-Berlin, 1978], 125f.).

See also HEAVEN.

Bibliography
Schlier, Heinrich. *Principalities and Powers in the New Testament.* New York: Herder and Herder, 1961.
Westermann, Claus. *God's Angels Need No Wings.* Philadelphia: Fortress, 1979.

ALEXANDRE GANOCZY

Anointing of the Sick. The anointing of the sick, which from about the twelfth century until well into the twentieth was also called extreme unction or the last anointing, is one of the seven sacraments of the Catholic Church. Through this sacrament God wills to grant salvation to those who have fallen seriously ill.

(1) *Biblical Background.* In the background of the anointing of the sick is the fact that Jesus sent out his disciples not only to preach but also to heal the sick; this healing evidently took the form of an anointing with oil (see Mk 6:13). The classical New Testament passage showing the existence, rite of administration, and saving effect of the anointing of the sick is Jas 5:14f. The setting is a series of instructions for certain situations: suffering, joy (5:13), and sickness (nothing is said of a sickness leading to death): "Are any among you sick? They should call for the elders of the church and have them pray over them, anointing them with oil in the name of the Lord. The prayer of faith will save the sick, and the Lord will raise them up; and anyone who has committed sins will

be forgiven." The elders are not charismatics but officials whose ministry has already acquired an institutional form at this late New Testament period. It is exegetically debatable whether the promised effect of the anointing and prayer is a present reality or whether the eschatological future is meant. The majority of exegetes today see an effect in the present or near future. The Lord will save and raise up the sick through prayer and anointing. What kind of "saving" is meant? The Middle Ages unequivocally emphasized the spiritual and mental effect. Today this is almost universally regarded as incorrect. The immediate context shows that the salvation is one that affects the entire person; Jas 5:13 looks upon the human person as a unity, one that brings all its distresses, bodily and spiritual, to God in petition and praise. More specifically, when seen against the background of Late Jewish views, "save" refers to a beneficial effect on the body of the sick person; "raise up" refers in addition to a simultaneous spiritual effect, the spiritual "raising up" of the sick person by the Lord. The Lord helps the sick to overcome their distress interiorly. A further effect of the anointing, accompanied by prayer, that is done in the name, that is, in the power and by commission of the Lord, is the forgiveness of sins, although only conditionally. This means that the forgiveness of sins is not the primary focus of the anointing of the sick in the New Testament. The positive effect of the anointing is the salvation of the sick person, and this in every dimension of the person's existence; in addition, there is the overcoming of sin, which has a radically detrimental influence on the person's life. Nothing is said, however, of a causal link between sin and sickness. The completely natural way in which Jas 5:14f. attests the "sacramental" practice of anointing the sick shows that it was familiar to the New Testament communities. This must be due to the fact that in the final analysis the practice had its origin and therefore its basis in a practice for which Jesus commissioned his disciples. He called the Twelve and gave them "authority to expel unclean spirits" (Mk 6:7). "The Twelve went out and called men and women to repentance. They expelled many demons and anointed many sick persons with oil and healed them" (Mk 6:12f.).

(2) *History of Theology.* We know little about the development of the anointing of the sick in the centuries that followed. What has come down to us is chiefly prayers of consecration of the oil for the sick. This consecration was increasingly reserved to bishops and for a while, especially in the West, was regarded as the properly sacramental action. The few texts that have been preserved from the early centuries of the church, outstanding among which is the prayer for the consecration of the oil in the *Euchologion* of Serapion of Thmuis in Lower Egypt (fourth century), present the following picture: the potential recipients of the anointing of the sick are all the sick who suffer from illnesses and handicaps, including those that are mental, be these less severe or more severe. Immediate help and alleviation are expected. Not only bishops and priests but laypersons, and even the sick themselves, are the ministers. The forgiveness of sins is rarely emphasized. Beginning in the early Middle Ages there is a significant shift: the anointing of the sick becomes the sacrament of the dying,

a sacramental consecration of the final hour. The practice of lay administration ceases from the beginning of the Middle Ages; in the ninth century it is forbidden (this prohibition is connected with the fact that the episcopal consecration of the oil for the sick is no longer regarded as the sacramental act). More specifically, from the early Middle Ages on, the liturgical rituals (*ordines*) almost without exception connect the anointing of the sick with the confession of the critically ill and with viaticum, or eucharistic Communion administered to strengthen the dying for their "passing." At the same time, the anointing is made more solemn (e.g., usually an anointing on seven places of the body); it becomes expensive, and, above all, it is linked to difficult conditions that to some extent remove the anointed from normal life (they may, e.g., no longer eat meat or have marital intercourse or dance). All these changes brought about a restructuring of consciousness: the anointing of the sick, the saving effect of which on the body now plays only a subordinate role, is put off to the final hour, spiritualized, and at the same time made an individual concern (whereas according to what we see in the Bible, the anointing of the sick not only was administered in sickness, regarded as a "normal situation" in human life, but was at the same time a normal event in the life of the church, an event in which the community probably took part not only by calling in its presbyters but also by conscious participation). Medieval theology reflected on this transformed and restrictive practice and gave it a theological justification. Thus Thomas Aquinas (d. 1274) calls the anointing of the sick a sacrament of healing, but he has in mind principally a spiritual healing, the overcoming of sin and its consequences, although he does not completely exclude a bodily healing. In his view, this sacrament is first and foremost a preparation for entrance into the fulfillment of heaven.

(3) *Church Teaching.* On the one hand, the statements of the magisterium (see table, p. 12) reflect the dominant practice, while, on the other, they consolidate and confirm this practice; Vatican II is the first to hark back to the New Testament and shift the emphases. The earliest magisterial document is a letter of Innocent I to Bishop Decentius of Gubbio (416). Asked about the meaning of the passage in James, the pope replied: "This must undoubtedly be accepted and understood as referring to the oil of Chrism, prepared by the bishop, which can be used for anointing not only by priests but also by all Christians whenever they themselves or their people are in need of it." Innocent goes on to say that this anointing with oil is one of the sacraments (DS 216). He thus locates the anointing of the sick in the "normal situation" of human illness. The effect is seen to be an inclusive one: the overcoming of the distress caused by illness (which is to be understood as affecting the whole person). The Council of Florence (1439) confirms (in a noninfallible doctrinal decree) the theory and practice that predominated in the Middle Ages: "This sacrament may not be given except to a sick person whose life is feared for" (DS 1324). "The minister of this sacrament is the priest" (DS 1325). "Its matter is olive oil blessed by the bishop" (DS 1325), which is used to anoint the five senses. The form of

KEY STATEMENTS ON THE ANOINTING OF THE SICK

Document of the Magisterium	Recipient	Minister	Effect
Letter of Innocent I (416)	The sick (not penitents)	Consecration of oil by bishop; administration by priests and laity, including self-administration	Overcoming distress of illness
Council of Florence (1439)	The sick in danger of death	Consecration of oil by bishop; administration only by priests	Healing of soul, possibly of body
Council of Trent (1551)	The seriously ill	Consecration of oil by bishop; administration only by priests	Grace of Holy Spirit to remove sin and the remains of sin, to strengthen the soul in trust in God, and possibly to heal body
Vatican II apostolic constitution	The seriously ill and the weak (also numerous recipients at same time)	Consecration of oil by bishop, or by priest in case of need; administration by priests	Union with Christ and church by faith for raising up and saving whole person, and for good of the church, in the power of the Holy Spirit and the church's intercession; possibly the forgiveness of sins

the sacrament is the one that was current until 1972: "May the Lord forgive you by this holy anointing and his most loving mercy whatever sins you have committed by the use of your sight, hearing..." (DS 1324). "The effect is the healing of the mind and, as far as it is good for the soul, of the body as well" (DS 1325). The Council of Trent (1551) confirmed this teaching in its essentials (see DS 1694–1700, 1716–19). The recipient, however, was no longer a dying person but one dangerously ill. Furthermore, Trent specifically defined that the "last anointing" is a true and proper sacrament instituted by Christ and promulgated by James; it communicates grace, takes away sins, and puts new heart into the sick. The council makes careful distinctions when speaking of the effect: the latter marks the completion of the penitential process and of the whole Christian life; the anointing "very aptly represents the grace of the Holy Spirit with which the soul of the sick is invisibly anointed" (DS 1695). "For the reality [res = effect] is the grace of the Holy Spirit, whose anointing takes away the sins if there be any still to be expiated, and also the remains of sin; it comforts and strengthens the soul of the sick person by awakening in him great confidence in the divine mercy; supported by this, the sick bears more lightly the inconveniences and trials of his illness...; at times it also restores bodily health when it is expedient for the salvation of the soul" (DS 1696). In contrast, Vatican II emphasizes the ecclesiological and christological dimensions: "By the sacred anointing of the sick and the prayer of the priests the whole Church commends those who are ill to the suffering and glorified Lord that he may raise them up and save them.... And indeed she exhorts them to contribute to the good of the People of God by freely uniting themselves to the passion and death of Christ" (LG 11). The sacrament is to be administered any time there is danger of death "from sickness or old age" (SC 73), and the rite is to be adapted to the varying conditions of the sick (SC 75). These principles were applied in a new rite, which, when published in 1972, was accompanied by an apostolic constitution of Paul VI and introductions of a pastoral kind. In the new rite, only the forehead and hands are anointed with vegetable oil that has been blessed (in case of necessity, by the priest himself). There is a new formula for administration: "Through this holy anointing may the Lord in his love and mercy help you with the grace of the Holy Spirit. Amen. May the Lord who frees you from sin save you and raise you up. Amen." Moreover, the anointing of the sick may be administered to a large number of the sick at a communal celebration (e.g., in connection with a celebration of the Eucharist).

(4) *Ecumenical Perspectives.* Since Luther had no high regard for the Letter of James, he could not adopt a positive attitude to the anointing of the sick. Along with the other Reformers he denied the sacramentality of this anointing. The contemporary ecumenical dialogue on the anointing of the sick is still only beginning (although in some churches of the Reformation the anointing of the sick is again being practiced). Any dialogue must begin with the results of exegesis, including that of Protestant scholars, that takes seriously once again the widespread practice in the early church of a rite that was meant to affect the whole person and that also required faith. At the same time, it must respect the anthropological insight that only the whole person can be saved and that Christian soteriology must therefore take the bodily dimension of the person into account, a point to which the Protestant understanding of the person must in particular be open. If possible, charismatic and pietist experiences of healing must also be given a place in the dialogue. In any case, one presupposition of a fruitful dialogue is the Catholic understanding of the anointing of the sick as now renewed in accordance with Vatican II.

(5) *Systematic Reflections.* Those who seek a renewed understanding of the anointing of the sick must do so in the context of modern thought and the modern longing for life, while at the same time harking back to the witness of the Scriptures; in this return to the Scriptures they will also accept the guidance of the tradition, even while trying to break free of its restrictive vision. Vatican II

has basically gone before them in this direction. With its statements as points of departure, dogmatic and pastoral theology must further clarify the anthropological, christological, and ecclesiological dimensions of the anointing of the sick. Anthropological: human beings, and especially the sick, must be seen as looking not for an isolated salvation of the soul but for a salvation that affects the entire person and discloses at least the meaning of sickness. This is something that the anointing of the sick can effectively address in its sacramental sign: the anointing, because it is a sign that the Holy Spirit, once again exerting an invigorating power, lays hold of and transforms the special situation of the sick and establishes a new bond between the sick person and the suffering and risen Christ and between the sick person and the community of Christ; the formula of administration or "prayer of faith," because it is an efficacious sign of the encounter of faith with God in Jesus Christ and his church. The sick will thus be able to realize with an existential faith that their situation has been made to serve their salvation (part of their "situation" is also, and specifically, the efforts — by no means excluded by the sacrament — of physicians and their medications to obtain healing) and that in this situation they can encounter the God of their salvation. These remarks point simultaneously to the christological and ecclesiological dimensions that need to be clarified: in the anointing of the sick the latter are once again placed under the saving dominion of Christ as the sole Lord. The idols that can find a place for themselves in the situation of illness are stripped of their power, and the sick are united to Christ in a new way. At the same time, they are united to the church and experience the service of their fellow Christians, who in the celebration of the anointing of the sick should not be represented solely by the priest, and who are also called to be of further service to the sick; the sick can learn experientially that their special situation, when accepted in faith, can indeed "contribute to the good of the People of God." For the rest, many theologians regard it as possible for the anointing of the sick to be once against administered by laypersons who are specially commissioned for this. Vatican II did not contemplate such a solution, probably because it had Jas 5:14 in mind.

   See also SACRAMENT; SALVATION.

Bibliography

Fink, Peter, ed. *Anointing of the Sick*. Vol. 7 of *Alternative Future for Worship*. Collegeville, Minn.: Liturgical Press, 1987.

Gusmer, Charles. *And You Visited Me: Sacramental Ministry to the Sick and Dying*. New York: Pueblo, 1984.

Knauber, Adolf. *Pastoral Theology of the Anointing of the Sick*. Collegeville, Minn.: Liturgical Press, 1975.

Poschmann, Bernhard. *Penance and the Anointing of the Sick*. New York: Herder and Herder, 1964.

Rahner, Karl. *The Anointing of the Sick*. Collegeville, Minn.: Liturgical Press, 1975.

                                                                          GÜNTER KOCH

Anthropocentrism. Anthropocentrism is in the first place a methodological concept. An anthropocentric theology starts out fundamentally from the human person's own experience of self and world and therefore allows only those theological statements that have a demonstrable relation to the human person. In certain contexts anthropocentrism takes on a polemical meaning. In these cases, specific theologies are suspected of making human experience and the human capacity for understanding the standard for what God can be and do.

(1) *Biblical Background.* The main biblical argument for an anthropocentric approach in theology is the fact that the Bible as a whole seeks to be the message of salvation for the human person. The New Testament message especially is the "word of salvation" (Acts 13:26). A message that seeks to save human persons or to open up the way to salvation must directly touch human persons as they experience themselves in the world.

(2) *History of Theology.* The origin of the concept of anthropocentrism is closely linked in intellectual history with the coming of modernity, which can also be described as the anthropological turn or the turn to the subject. This move was already anticipated in Scholasticism when, for example, Thomas Aquinas saw the meaning of all material reality in that the knowing person takes it up in his or her spiritual relationship with God (CREATURE-LINESS OF THE HUMAN PERSON). In modernity, then, God was conceived as the necessary presupposition for the human person to be a subject and to have a world. In this view, the object of theological knowledge seemed to be only religious consciousness, the person's experience of God. In the nineteenth century, anthropocentric theology became dominant above all in Protestantism (F. Schleiermacher). Around the turn of the century in Catholic theology the ecclesial magisterium also saw itself confronted with anthropocentric tendencies, especially in relation to the origin of dogmas (DOGMAS/DOGMATIC STATEMENTS). In the so-called "Oath against Modernism" (DS 3541f.), Pius X condemned this trend together with other new teachings. In Protestantism at the beginning of the twentieth century, dialectical theology (K. Barth) proposed against anthropocentrism the program of a strictly theocentric theology. Yet within this new theology there soon arose again a fierce controversy over the anthropological starting point for this theology (R. Bultmann, E. Brunner), which later also flowed over into Catholic theology (K. Rahner).

(3) *Church Teaching.* Vatican II did not take up the concept of anthropocentrism; it presumed, however, a relative anthropocentrism as the general view of Christians and non-Christians (GS 12).

(4) *Ecumenical Perspectives.* Apart from some extreme anthropocentric interpretations of Christian faith (e.g., F. Buri), which also represent extreme positions in Protestant theology, the concept of anthropocentrism today no longer marks confessional boundaries. The discussion about the proper relationship between theocentrism and anthropocentrism cuts across denominational lines.

(5) *Systematic Reflections.* Anthropocentrism and theocentrism do not exclude each other when it is recognized that the human person in his or her experience of self and world inevitably raises the question of the ultimate "whence" and "whereto." That is, human beings ask about what they cannot determine from themselves, about that from which their existence and world first receive their encompassing determination and goal. In the places where this is found in the basic approach of theology, it is better, thus, not to speak of anthropocentrism, but rather of the anthropological approach in theology.

See also HUMAN PERSON; SALVATION; THEOLOGICAL ANTHROPOLOGY.

Bibliography
Metz, Johannes Baptist. *Christliche Anthropozentrik über die Denkform des Thomas von Aquin.* Munich: Kösel, 1962.
———. *Theology of the World.* New York: Herder and Herder, 1969.
Rahner, Karl. "Christian Humanism." In *Theological Investigations,* 9:64–82. New York: Herder and Herder, 1972.
———. "Theology and Anthropology." In *Theological Investigations,* 9:28–45. New York: Herder and Herder, 1972.
Snyder, Dale Norman. *Karl Barth's Struggle with Anthropocentric Theology.* The Hague: Boekhandel Wattez, 1966.

GEORG LANGEMEYER

Anthropology

Contemporary Issues

Anthropology addresses the question: What does it mean to be human? In many respects, this question has become the lens through which most theologians view theological topics today. Although theology cannot be reduced to anthropology, the perspective, widely shared by contemporary theologians, is that whatever contributes to an understanding of human existence potentially contributes to the theological enterprise. The anthropological emphasis is characterized by an explicit turn from classical cosmocentric metaphysics and a turn to human subjectivity with an emphasis on human experience. The "turn to the subject" has been further complemented by a "social turn" with emphasis on liberating (liberation theology) and emancipatory (political theology) praxis, and most recently by a further "ecological turn" to restore health to the complex ecosystems of the earth.

Christian anthropology, as a distinct area of theology, explores the meaning of human existence in relationship to God in the doctrines of IMAGE OF GOD, GRACE, and ESCHATOLOGY. Since grace and eschatology are treated elsewhere in this volume, "image of God" will be the focus of this article. A full contemporary understanding of *imago Dei*, however, is impossible unless the relationship of this symbol to grace and eschatology is noted. What God set in motion with creation, especially with the creation of the human as *imago Dei*, God brings to fulfillment in the eschaton. In the in-between-time, we are called to communion with God by the free offer of the grace of Jesus Christ through the Holy Spirit.

1. *Archetypal Symbols: Imago Dei and Imago Christi.* "Let us make humanity in our image, after our likeness" (Gn 1:26) is the symbolic biblical response to the question: What does it mean to be human? In the Christian tradition *imago Dei* has become the defining symbol for humans as those creatures who are uniquely gifted with a relationship with God and the foundational symbol for the inviolable dignity of all persons. In contemporary theological anthropology, understandings of human existence are grounded not only in *imago Dei* but also in *imago Christi*. For the Christian, the meaning of human existence in relationship to God is found in Jesus Christ. The attention given to CHRISTOLOGY since the fifteen-hundredth anniversary of the Council of Chalcedon (451) has contributed to an explicit Christocentric perspective in theological anthropology. Jesus Christ, at once truly divine and truly human, is the only fully adequate image of God. Image of the invisible God and firstborn of all creation (Col 1:15), Jesus Christ reveals to us, in a unique and ultimate manner, God, a mystery that the human mind can never penetrate. Jesus as truly human also reveals what humans are called to be and do, to love God and one's neighbor as oneself.

Imago Christi is not without problems where feminist theological anthropology is concerned. Christological symbols have served to support male dominance of women and the exclusion of women from church polity. However, what is important about the *imago Christi* symbol is not that Jesus was a historical male, but that he was human. The Council of Chalcedon makes this distinction explicit by confessing Jesus Christ to be *vere homo* and not *vere vir.* A naive physicalism where Jesus Christ is concerned ignores the profound meaning of incarnation for faith and excludes women from the mystery of redemption. *Imago Christi*, rightly understood, symbolizes a call from God to all men and women of every age and culture to be conformed to the image of Christ (Rom 8:29).

2. *Christian Existence.* The classical orthodox explanation of *imago Dei* was expressed in essentialist categories adapted from Greek metaphysics. A major characteristic of contemporary theological anthropology is the abandonment of classical conceptions of human nature and the adoption of historical, personalist, and phenomenological analysis and reflection on Christian existence. *Gaudium et spes,* the only document of Vatican II that explicitly addresses theological anthropology, presents a biblically rooted description of humans as spiritual and embodied creatures gifted with intellect, conscience, and freedom (*GS* 12–17). The phenomenological description of human activity and the historical consciousness evident in *Gaudium et spes* are representative of the contemporary trend to speak about humanity in nonmetaphysical terms. The

emphasis is on Christian existence in the world, not on essentialist definitions of the unchanging nature of being human.

3. *Search for Adequate Typologies and Descriptive Categories.* The pitfalls of traditional metaphysical definitions of human nature in body and soul categories have been given a great deal of attention by contemporary theologians. In particular, the dualism of classical metaphysical theology has been rejected by feminist theologians because of the ways in which it has contributed to the diminishment of the dignity of women. An influential source for classical orthodox anthropology has been the writings of Augustine. His Neoplatonic, dualistic, and hierarchical interpretation of *imago Dei* contributed to the legitimation of the subordinate role of women in church and society. Augustine ascribed to a hierarchical conception of mind over body and reason over passions. He correlated maleness with the mind and reason, and femaleness with the body and passions. This is clearly illustrated in a prayer of praise for God's creation in the *Confessions*. Augustine declares that humanity (*hominem*), made to God's image and likeness, is set over all nonrational animals by the power of reason. It is reason that also rules the body. In like manner, although woman has equality in nature with man because of her rational mind, in her bodily sex she is subject to the male sex (*Confessions* 13.32.47). Woman as an embodied self, therefore, is not equivalent to man in her image of God. In her essential nature woman is depicted as having less of the higher spiritual nature and more of the lower physical nature than man. In the course of the development of the Christian tradition male theologians, such as Thomas Aquinas, contributed further to the position that it is males who are normatively human. Women are "other" than the norm.

In this era of heightened historical consciousness, the dualistic interpretation of *imago Dei* is recognized to be a product of patriarchal culture. The rationalized myth of female subordination to males on the basis of a hierarchical dualism of soul over body is widely rejected in contemporary Christian anthropology, as are all forms of female subordination to males. A dual anthropology, rooted in cultural and religious attitudes of the past, assumed the subordination of women as a class. One of the distinctive elements of contemporary theological anthropology is that it not only seeks out and analyzes structures that oppress women but also seeks to transform them for the good of women and men.

In the effort to affirm the full dignity of women and men, one contemporary perspective is the affirmation of the complementarity of the sexes by arguing that males and females are different, but equal. In this typology the duality of males and females is presented as part of the divine plan for creation and therefore unchangeable. Such a position lends itself to a two-nature anthropology that treats gender differences as unchanging, rather than as the result of historically conditioned cultural attitudes. Some feminist theologians are critical of complementarity on the grounds that it does not remedy the subordination of women in Christian polity and praxis, because by definition women are relegated to the realm of the private and passive.

A diametrically opposite typology is a single-nature th
ogy reflective of the biblical affirmation that in Christ the
nor females, and that all are one (Gal 3:28). In this conte
sexual difference is recognized to be biologically importa
but is not viewed as determinative of a person's life ch
terminism of gender roles in church and society is rejecte
anthropology presents an androgynous ideal for being
growing consensus that this typology is inadequate becaus
ticularity of experience rooted in human bodiliness and
about gender, race, and class.

To remedy the impasse of two natures versus andro
theologians are offering new proposals in which the pa
and social experience is given full attention. Steps towarc
evident in the attention currently being given to human coi
porary theologies of the body. Humans are not souls clot
a body-self — male and female — is constitutive of our be
It follows that a christological-incarnational anthropolog
tian existence as a sacrament of God becoming embodied i
common flesh in creative, saving, and liberating ways.

Sexuality, however, is obviously not the only factor that
human. Sexuality is one among many anthropological con:
personal identity within a particular culture. Intrinsic to hi
relationship we have to the ecological systems of the earth;
individual persons; the relation to social, political, and (
the conditioning of persons and cultures by historical tin
terrelationship of theory and praxis in a culture as oppose
orientation to hope and the pull of the future (E. Schillebe
of these constants results in an acknowledgment of differe
tic of the human condition. Attention to the pluralism in
our human existence as a participant in societies with di
titudes about gender, race, and class moves theological a
the contrasting typologies of sexual dualism and of same
logical horizon in which the acknowledgment of differer
affirmation of the human dignity of all persons.

4. *Ecological Consciousness.* One of the anthropolog
above is the relationship of humans to the ecological sys
dominant characteristic of modern Western culture is an ai
views the earth and its resources as the building materia
ploitative and utilitarian attitudes toward the earth have
ecological crisis. Contemporary theological responses to
two major forms: stewardship of the environment and e
for a revisionist theological anthropology. In the first, the l
a "steward" or caretaker of the earth. Many biblical scho
tion of human creation in the image and likeness of God a

:ly author of Genesis 1 depicts the human creature as God's representative,
.s a steward represented his ruler in his absence in ancient Middle Eastern
:y. It follows that the directive to exercise dominion means that humans
) provide responsible care for the earth in the manner in which God, the
eign ruler of creation, would.
ofeminism stresses the problem with dominion as it has been histori-
exercised and argues that the dominations of nature and of women are
ately connected and mutually reinforcing. Ecofeminist theological anthro-
,y, unlike theologies of stewardship, does not regard the environment as
ist arena of nature outside ourselves that we humans are to repair and re-
. True to the ecological paradigm, which by its very nature stresses the
iic wholeness and interconnectedness of all forms of life, ecofeminism
es the earthliness of human existence. An ecofeminist perspective on be-
uman calls for a radical conversion of mind and heart from hierarchical
sm to egalitarian holism.
. ecofeminist perspective on *imago Dei* is critical of a God imaged after the
; class. A patriarchal God rules over nature as man rules woman. This hi-
nical dualism is of one piece with the dualism that separates humans from
uman nature. Ecofeminist understandings of God place emphasis on the
nence of God as the ground of being and source of creation, rather than
od as a transcendent power over creation. In an ecofeminist theological an-
ology the solidarity of humans with nonhuman nature is stressed. Humans
iade from the same materials as the rest of creation — the same elements
.re in the rocks of the hills, the birds of the air, and the fish of the seas are in
ur relationship to all the other creatures of the earth is one of interdepen-
kinship with respect for the diversity God has created. In an ecofeminist
ogical anthropology, mutuality is regarded as central to a relationship of
ns with the rest of creation that sustains, rather than destroys, life.

;raphy
\nne E. *Transforming Grace: Christian Tradition and Women's Experience*, 118–33.
n Francisco: Harper and Row, 1988.
\nne E., and Elisabeth Schüssler Fiorenza, eds. *The Special Nature of Women?* Vol. 6
Concilium. Philadelphia: Trinity, 1991.
'aul II. *Mulieris Dignitatem* (On the Dignity and Vocation of Women). August 15,
•88.
:, Karl. *Foundations of Christian Faith: An Introduction to the Idea of Christianity.*
ew York: Seabury, 1978.
r, Rosemary Radford. *Gaia and God: An Ecofeminist Theology of Earth Healing.*
ew York: HarperCollins, 1992.
. *Sexism and God-Talk: Toward a Feminist Theology.* Boston: Beacon, 1983.
peeckx, Edward. *Christ: The Experience of Jesus as Lord,* 731–43. New York: Seabury,
80.

ANNE M. CLIFFORD

Antichrist. According to the evidence of the New Testament and Christian tradition, the Antichrist (antagonist of Christ) is an individual person, or an institution connected with an individual person, that militates against the order established by God and the message of Christ.

(1) *Biblical Background.* In the New Testament the word *Antichrist* occurs only in 1 and 2 John, whereas the reality meant by it is described in various New Testament books, especially Revelation. The appearance of the Antichrist is regarded as one of the signs preceding the parousia. The question of whether the Antichrist is to be understood primarily as an individual or as a collectivity cannot be answered with certainty. The way is prepared for New Testament statements about the Antichrist by the expectation found in the Old Testament and early Judaism of a power that is hostile to God or kingdoms that are hostile to God and rise up against Israel (see, e.g., Ezekiel 38; Dn 2:31–45; 7:7f.) and of the embodiment of this power or these kingdoms in a godless individual, especially Antiochus IV Epiphanes, who desecrated the temple (Dn 7:19–25; 8:11f.; 9:26f.), or one of the Roman emperors (Revelation 13 and 17). In the Synoptic discourse on the final days (Mt 24:15; Mk 13:14; see Lk 21:20) there occurs the phrase "abomination of desolation" (an expression based on Dn 9:27; 11:31; 12:11), but its interpretation in terms of contemporary history remains unclear. Likewise uncertain is the interpretation of another image based on the Old Testament (Dn 11:36; Ez 28:2; Is 11:4), that of the "lawless one" in 2 Thes 2:3–12, whom Christ will kill with the breath of his mouth at the parousia. Unambiguous, on the other hand, are the statements about the Antichrist in 1 John (1:22–23; 2:18; 4:3) and 2 John 7, where the Antichrist, who is spoken of in both the singular and the plural, is to be understood as a theological and not a political figure, and more specifically as the seducer and false teacher of the community of the last hour. The most detailed description of the Antichrist is given in Revelation, where the adversary of Christ and the church is depicted in two forms: as a beast from the sea (13:1–10) and a beast from the earth (13:11–18). According to one common interpretation, the first beast symbolizes the power of the Roman Empire, which is the backdrop for an imperial figure, while the second beast symbolizes the pseudoprophets and propagandists of the cult of the emperors.

(2) *History of Theology.* The idea of the Antichrist has varied in the course of history, where it has not been understood primarily as a figure in the future but has been identified with particular persons in the church and the state. Especially in the early church, due to the impact of persecution, the Antichrist was identified with the Roman Empire and was at times understood to be Nero returning. In the early Middle Ages, history was interpreted as a continuing struggle between Christ and the Antichrist, as in the theology of history of Rupert of Deutz (d. 1229/30) or Gerhoh of Reichersberg (d. 1175). In the high Middle Ages, the theology and philosophy of history of Joachim of Fiore (d. 1202), in which the images of the Apocalypse were interpreted as referring to contemporary events, became widely influential. In the Franciscan poverty

movement, which had ties with Joachim, the Antichrist was equated with the papacy in general, which rejected the movement's inflexible demands, and was later identified especially with John XXII. In the late Middle Ages, and under the influence still of the poverty movement, Wycliffe and Hus continued the attack on the papacy as the Antichrist. From 1518 on, and with great clarity and harshness from 1522 on, Luther called the papacy the Antichrist because it set its own authority over that of God's word and adulterated the gospel. In his treatise *De potestate et primatu papae,* Melanchthon sees the papal temporal kingdom as the sign of the Antichrist. Luther also regards the theology of the Catholic controversialists as a forerunner of the Antichrist. For the Pietists every kind of dead Christianity is a form of Antichrist. Since the Enlightenment, which rejected the Antichrist along with the devil, the concept of Antichrist has lost its importance.

(3) *Church Teaching.* The ecclesial magisterium has not taken an explicit position on the question of the Antichrist, unless one cites the rejection of the eschatological views of the Fraticelli by John XXII in 1318, inasmuch as this mentions the doctrine of the Antichrist (DS 916).

(4) *Ecumenical Perspectives.* On the ecumenical scene, the Antichrist idea is hardly mentioned any longer, although the concept has not yet been eliminated from the Reformed confessional documents as a description of the papacy.

(5) *Systematic Reflections.* Although secularist and atheistic interpretations of history find the biblical concept of Antichrist to be an oddity, it has occasionally been taken up in very recent times as a description of inhuman systems.

See also CHILIASM; EXPECTATION OF AN IMMINENT END; HISTORY/HISTORICITY; PAROUSIA.

Bibliography
Bousset, Wilhelm. *The Antichrist Legend: A Chapter in Christian and Jewish Folklore.* London: Hutchinson, 1896.
Jenks, Gregory C. *The Origins and Early Development of the Antichrist Myth.* Berlin and New York: de Gruyter, 1991.

JOSEF FINKENZELLER

Apocatastasis. Apocatastasis (universal reconciliation) is the definitive restoration of the entire creation, including sinners, the damned, and demons, to a state of perfect blessedness at the end of time.

(1) *Biblical Background.* The word *apocatastasis* occurs in the New Testament only in Acts 3:21, where Peter, in a sermon to Jews, describes as a messianic hope the universal restoration that God has proclaimed through the mouths of the holy prophets.

(2) *History of Theology.* A first theological development of a doctrine of apocatastasis took place in the school of Alexandria. Clement of Alexandria suggested a temporal limitation of the pains of hell; Origen (whose views are still the subject of debate) developed a doctrine of a future dominion of Christ

over the whole of creation (in accordance with Ps 110:1; 1 Cor 15:25–28; and Phil 2:5–11), that is, the subjection of all enemies to Christ and, through Christ, to the Father. The apocatastasis will mark the beginning of the new heavens and the new earth (Is 66:22) and the effective union of all things with God for which Christ prayed (Jn 17:21–23) and to which Paul alludes (Eph 4:13). In the spirit of Origen important theologians of the patristic period taught the apocatastasis: for example, Gregory of Nazianzus, Gregory of Nyssa, Didymus the Blind, Diodorus of Tarsus, Theodore of Mopsuestia, and, initially, Jerome as well. After a condemnation of apocatastasis by the church the idea lived on in various theories about the mitigation of the pains of hell. It was also occasionally defended even in the Middle Ages.

(3) *Church Teaching.* Since apocatastasis is incompatible with the doctrine of the eternity of hell, it was rejected by the church in a number of doctrinal decrees. At the provincial Council of Constantinople in 543 the following statement of the Origenists was condemned: "The punishment of evil spirits and wicked human beings is only temporary and after a certain period will come to an end; then there will be a complete restoration (*apokatastasis*) of evil spirits and wicked human beings" (DS 411). Apocatastasis is condemned by implication in doctrinal decrees on the eternity of hell.

(4) *Ecumenical Perspectives.* During the Reformation, ideas that surfaced now and then of a complete restoration (apocatastasis) were rejected in the Augsburg Confession (CA 17), and the eternity of hell was stressed. In the second half of the seventeenth century the doctrine of apocatastasis was to be found in mystico-theosophical movements and among rationalists. In the ensuing period Evangelical theologians (F. Schleiermacher, E. Troeltsch, J. Weiss, E. Lietzmann) wavered in their support of the doctrine. In our own century respected Evangelical theologians have rejected an apocatastasis in principle, but speak of an open area between God's election and rejection (K. Barth) or allow for two possible outcomes (P. Althaus, E. Brunner). The statements on judgment must be adapted to the paramount proclamation of grace in such a way that the latter can become a proclamation of universal restoration (W. Michaelis).

(5) *Systematic Reflections.* After the teaching of H. Schell on the possibility of a qualified apocatastasis was condemned, the substantive issue has taken on new meaning in recent decades in the question of the possibility or actuality of a hell.

See also HELL.

Bibliography
Davis, Stephen T. "Universalism, Hell, and the Fate of the Ignorant." *MT* 6 (1990) 173–86.
Robinson, James A. T. *In the End, God.* London: James Clarke, 1950.
Torrance, Thomas F. "Universalism or Election?" *SJT* 2 (1949) 310–18.

JOSEF FINKENZELLER

Apostle. Apostle is the name given to those who founded or governed the first Christian communities in virtue of the mission given to them by the risen Christ.

(1) *Biblical Background.* The Greek word *apostolos* is probably a translation of the Hebrew *šalíaḥ* and therefore means a legally and personally authorized representative. The concept derives its concrete content, however, from its christological and ecclesiological context. According to Gal 1:17ff. and 1 Cor 15:1–11, there was a permanent group of apostles in Jerusalem who were responsible for the governance of the first community there. Peter and James certainly belonged to this group, as did, probably, the "Twelve" who had accompanied Jesus as disciples. According to Acts 13:1–3 and 14:4, 14, a different form of apostleship developed in Antioch: the "charismatic itinerant apostle." Paul combined both forms. He did not, of course, belong to the preresurrection group of disciples; all the more important in his case, therefore, was an encounter granted him with the risen Christ. The importance of the apostles, especially in the case of Paul, was due, on the one hand, to their activity as founders and leaders of the communities and, on the other, to the fact that they were the first to give expression to the gospel of the grace that God communicated to us in Jesus Christ and that they did so in a way valid for all future ages.

(2) *History of Theology.* At a very early date, and especially in the context of the clash with gnosticism, links with the apostles became the criterion of orthodoxy in the church. Irenaeus and Tertullian are the most important witnesses to this development. In the course of the centuries the special importance of the holder of the "Chair of Peter" (*cathedra Petri*), that is, of the pope as successor of Peter, was increasingly emphasized. Peter was given special attention and veneration in the Catholic Church. The founding of the church by Jesus Christ was associated with Peter's confession of Jesus as messiah and with the promise given to him in response (Mt 16:16–18). The churches of the Reformation thought of themselves as linked rather to Paul as the great preacher of the grace of God. The apostles have always been, and still are today, venerated as the "pillars" and "foundation" of the church (Eph 2:20; Mt 16:18; Rv 21:14).

(3) *Church Teaching.* The place of the apostles in the church is explained at length in *LG* 19. Several points made there deserve to be noted: the group of apostles emerges from the larger group of disciples; the apostles form a college; Peter is given a special role among the apostles; the apostles are sent to preach the gospel and spread the church; the activity of the apostles is guided by the Holy Spirit; the group of the apostles is continued by the college of bishops with the pope at its head; and the activity of the apostles remains normative through all periods of the church's existence.

(4) *Ecumenical Perspectives.* In the ecumenical dialogue it is chiefly the exegetes who have discussed the place and role of the apostles. It has been and still is a matter of dispute whether the apostles are to be regarded as holders of an ecclesiastical office or possessors of a charism. At times, these two views

have been considered mutually exclusive. Another subject of discussion, past and present, is whether and how the functions of the apostles in the church can and must be passed on to others.

(5) *Systematic Reflections.* The church thinks of itself as "apostolic," that is, in terms (among others) of its continuity with the apostles. If it is to have a correct understanding of this self-description, it must focus on the biblical testimony regarding the call and mission of the apostles.

See also APOSTOLICITY OF THE CHURCH; APOSTOLIC SUCCESSION; COLLE-GIALITY; MINISTRY IN THE CHURCH; POPE.

Bibliography
Barrett, C. K. *The Signs of an Apostle.* Philadelphia: Fortress, 1970.
Campenhausen, Hans von. *Ecclesiastical Authority and Spiritual Power in the Church of the First Three Centuries.* Stanford, Calif.: Stanford University Press, 1969.
Schmithals, Walter. *The Office of Apostle in the Early Church.* Nashville: Abingdon, 1969.

WERNER LÖSER

Apostolicity of the Church. By the apostolicity of the church is meant the oneness of the present-day church with the original apostolic church. Due to its apostolicity the church remains identical through all places and times.

(1) *Biblical Background.* The concept is not in the New Testament, but the reality it defines is. The New Testament writings (e.g., the Pastoral Letters) that originated in the "second generation" of the very early church bear witness to the ways in which the church remained apostolic as it advanced in time. Among these ways, the faithful preservation and transmission of teaching and ministry are especially emphasized (1 Tm 1:3–5; 2 Tm 1:13; 2:2; 3:14f.; 4:5; Ti 1:5). When the New Testament describes the apostles as the "pillars" and "foundation" of the church (Eph 2:20; Mt 16:18; Rv 21:14), it is implicitly asserting also the apostolicity of the church.

(2) *History of Theology.* At an early date apostolicity was already being regarded as a criterion of the true church (Irenaeus and Tertullian, among others). In the Nicene-Constantinopolitan Creed apostolicity appears as an attribute of the church. It plays an important role in the controversies of the Reformation period, with the theologians of the Reformation emphasizing apostolicity of doctrine and the Catholic theologians the apostolicity of ministry or office that is manifested by an unbroken succession. In the Catholic Church it is recognized today that the apostolicity of the church requires both apostolic tradition and apostolic succession.

(3) *Church Teaching.* The combination of apostolic succession in office and apostolic preaching finds expression in the documents of Vatican II. In *LG* 20 transmission of office and transmission of the gospel are seen as going together. Especially important is *DV* 7f. Here it is said that apostolic tradition includes everything that Jesus Christ handed on as essential to the apostolic church so that it in turn might hand it on to all later generations. "The Church in her

doctrine, life, and worship, perpetuates and transmits to every generation all that she herself is, all that she believes" (*DV* 8). Apostolic succession is at the service of apostolic tradition. "In order that the full and living gospel might always be preserved in the Church the apostles left bishops as their successors. They gave them 'their own position of teaching authority' " (*DV* 7).

(4) *Ecumenical Perspectives.* The churches are in agreement that the church of Jesus Christ is to be regarded as apostolic, but there are different views as to the elements in which apostolicity must manifest itself and how the church of any given age can be sure of its apostolicity. The apostolicity of the church has been the subject of a dialogue of the Joint Working Group of the Roman Catholic Church and the World Council of Churches.

(5) *Systematic Reflections.* The church is true to its nature and mission only if it is apostolic. Its apostolicity ensures its continuity with its normative original stage and preserves its identity. The apostolicity of the church finds expression in a broad network of structures and activities that in their substance are already attested as apostolic in the New Testament and are now being transmitted through history. Thus the apostolicity of the church becomes evident when the doctrine preached by the apostles is handed on, when the sacraments are celebrated, when the apostolic ministry is transmitted and performs its service, when Sunday is kept as the Lord's Day, and when Christians give active witness and service to the world.

See also APOSTLE; APOSTOLIC SUCCESSION; TRADITION.

Bibliography
Brown, Raymond E. *The Churches the Apostles Left Behind.* New York: Paulist, 1984.
———. *Priest and Bishop: Biblical Reflections.* New York: Paulist, 1970.
Brown, Raymond, and John P. Meier. *Antioch and Rome: New Testament Cradles of Catholic Christianity.* New York: Paulist, 1983.
Cwiekowski, Frederick J. *The Beginnings of the Church.* New York: Paulist, 1988.
Harrington, Daniel J. *The Light of All Nations: Essays on the Church in New Testament Research.* Good News Studies, vol. 3. Wilmington, Del.: Glazier, 1982.
Schnackenburg, Rudolf. "Apostolicity: The Present Position of Studies." *One in Christ* 6 (1970) 243–73.

WERNER LÖSER

Apostolic Succession. Apostolic succession means the integration, effected through ordination, of bishops (and, by derivation through them, of priests and deacons) into the college of bishops, which is one and goes back to the apostles. The chain or network of layings on of hands is a sensible element in the complete sacramental process whereby a ministry, thus understood, is transmitted.

(1) *Biblical Background.* There is no developed doctrine of apostolic succession in the New Testament, but the reality behind the doctrine is clearly present in an inchoative form. Paul appointed Timothy to be his representative (1 Cor 4:7). According to Acts, the Twelve appointed seven "deacons." Paul and Barnabas appointed "presbyters." According to the Pastoral Letters,

appointment to ecclesiastical ministries is done by imposition of hands and a prayer. According to Acts 15, the presbyters collaborate with the apostles in a kind of "college."

(2) *History of Theology.* A clear witness to apostolic succession is given in 1 Clement. Those having an ecclesiastical ministry can exercise it legitimately only if they have received it in a line from the apostles. Irenaeus stresses the importance of apostolic succession in his dealings with heretical gnosis. In Catholic theology there has never been any serious doubt that apostolic succession is a constitutive factor in ecclesiastical ministry. As understood by the Reformers, however, the apostolicity of the church depends not on the apostolic succession of ecclesiastical officeholders but on the church's remaining faithful to the apostolic message and teaching. It is becoming increasingly clear to Catholic theologians that apostolic succession must not be taken in isolation but connected with other factors that also make up the apostolicity of the church.

(3) *Church Teaching.* In various papal or conciliar documents the bishops are called the successors of the apostles and the pope the successor of Peter (see, e.g., DS 379, 697, 766, 960, 1824, 1828, 2287). Vatican II explains at some length that the college of apostles is continued by the college of bishops and the office of Peter by the office of the pope. The council speaks of apostolic succession as of "divine institution" and declares it to be therefore a constitutive element of the church. *LG* 20 says: "Just as the office which the Lord confided to Peter alone, as first of the apostles, destined to be transmitted to his successors, is a permanent one, so also endures the office, which the apostles received, of shepherding the Church, a charge destined to be exercised without interruption by the sacred order of bishops. The sacred synod consequently teaches that the bishops have by divine institution taken the place of the apostles as pastors of the Church."

(4) *Ecumenical Perspectives.* In ecumenical dialogue on ministry in the church the subject of apostolic succession always comes up. The question arises whether with a view to the reciprocal recognition of ministries that is so often called for, a succession at the presbyterial level (as distinct from a succession at the episcopal level) can be regarded as adequate.

(5) *Systematic Reflections.* The importance of apostolic succession becomes clear when one takes into consideration the sacramentality of the church. The church is the one body of Christ; just as there is therefore only *one* faith and *one* baptism, so too there is but *one* office. This becomes visible in the one college of bishops, to which the colleges of priests and deacons are related. The individual bishop is incorporated into this college by his ordination, and as a result of the incorporation he receives the authority for episcopal activities. In this way he is in the line of apostolic succession.

See also APOSTLE; APOSTOLICITY OF THE CHURCH; COLLEGIALITY; MINISTRY IN THE CHURCH.

Bibliography

Brown, Raymond E. *The Critical Meaning of the Bible,* 121–46. New York: Paulist, 1981.

Brown, Raymond E., and John P. Meier. *Antioch and Rome: New Testament Cradles of Catholic Christianity.* New York: Paulist, 1983.

Küng, Hans, ed. *Apostolic Succession: Rethinking a Barrier to Unity.* Vol. 34 of *Concilium.* Glen Rock, N.J.: Paulist, 1968.

Lohfink, Gerhard. *Jesus and Community: The Social Dimension of Christian Faith.* New York: Paulist; Philadelphia: Fortress, 1984.

Rahner, Karl. *Bishops: Their Status and Function.* Baltimore: Helicon, 1964.

Rahner, Karl, and Joseph Ratzinger. *The Episcopate and the Primacy.* New York: Herder and Herder, 1962.

Ratzinger, Joseph. "The Key Question in the Catholic–Protestant Dialogue: Tradition and Successio Apostolica." In *Principles of Catholic Theology,* 239–84. San Francisco: Ignatius, 1987.

WERNER LÖSER

Appropriations. In trinitarian theology the term *appropriations* refers to statements that predicate certain qualities or activities of a single divine person that are undoubtedly common to all the divine persons, but regarding which the uniqueness of the persons nevertheless plays a role because their concretely given reciprocal relations have a relevant bearing.

(1) *Biblical Background.* The New Testament describes Christ as wisdom from God (1 Cor 1:30). "Wisdom" links Christ and the Father most closely, but it also affirms and characterizes the uniqueness of the person of the Incarnate Son. Phil 2:9–11 directs our attention to the loving power of the Father. The Holy Spirit appears as an absolute gift of God when "love, joy, peace, patience, kindness, generosity, faithfulness, gentleness, and self-control" are attributed to the Spirit as its "fruit" (Gal 5:22–23).

(2) *History of Theology.* Scholasticism (Bonaventure) developed the notion of appropriations into a subtle category of trinitarian theology.

(3) *Church Teaching.* Church teaching has sought to prevent any misuse of the doctrine of appropriations in the sense of a tritheism by emphasizing that God's external action and causality are strictly common to all three persons (DS 1330).

(4) *Ecumenical Perspectives.* The doctrine of appropriations is not a subject of interconfessional controversy.

(5) *Systematic Reflections.* Without impugning the external unity of effective causation in God's activity, one must still ask whether God's nature, as God's personal, relational love, is not thoroughly stamped on the being of creatures. The appropriations, then, as ascriptions of certain qualities or activities to one divine person, can also state something about the interrelated way in which the three persons act, and thus about the inner life of the Trinity. More than ever, the encounter with the self-communicating God must become lively, experienced as a movement in the Holy Spirit, through Christ, and toward the

Father. In that way, creation and salvation become "areas of application" for the doctrine of appropriations.

See also TRINITY.

Bibliography
Kasper, Walter. *The God of Jesus Christ*. New York: Crossroad, 1984.

WILHELM BREUNING

Ascension of Christ. The ascension of Christ is an intrinsic moment within belief in Jesus' resurrection, since through it the glorification or exaltation of Jesus (the incarnate Son of the Father) and his eschatological reign (as messiah and Lord) become manifest, even though he always remains salvifically present to his church (through the mediation of the Holy Spirit) until he comes again to judge.

(1) *Biblical Background.* In the New Testament, belief in the ascension of Christ is expressed through various images or ideas: "exaltation" (Acts 2:33; 5:31; Phil 2:9; referred to in Jn 3:14; 8:28; 12:32, 34 as the Son of Man's being "lifted up" on the cross); "glorification" (Jn 7:39; 12:16, 23; 17:1); "being taken up in glory" (1 Tm 3:16); "entering into his glory" (Lk 24:26); "going to/returning to the Father/God" (Jn 13:1, 3); "the ascension of the Son of Man" (which corresponds to "descending" [Jn 3:13; 6:62]); "going to the Father" (which corresponds to "coming from the Father" [Jn 16:28]; cf. "ascending to the Father" [Jn 20:17]). Alluding to Ps 68:19 or 110:1, the glorification or exaltation of Jesus is described as a triumphal entry into heaven or enthronement at God's right hand by which the resurrected one begins his powerful rule "high above all" or "over all" (Eph 1:20f.; 4:8–10; see Mk 16:19; 1 Pt 3:22). The exaltation of Jesus as Lord, messiah, and Son (Acts 2:36; Rom 1:4; 14:19) and as intercessor, leader, and savior (Acts 5:31) is linked with the resurrection and refers eschatologically to the parousia and judgment (Acts 10:40–42; 17:31; 1 Thes 1:10). According to Mt 28:18ff., "all power in heaven and on earth" is given to the resurrected one, and he remains with his community "always, to the end of the age." In Acts 1:9–11 (see Lk 24:50ff.; Mk 16:19) Luke alone, in accordance with his theology of salvation-history, presents the ascension narratively, although he does not actually depict it. For "clouds" (= the dimension of power and God's reign) "lifted him up, out of their sight"; that is, in this last appearance the "apostles" who were present as "witnesses" (see Acts 1:8, 22; 10:41) experienced the crucified and resurrected Christ as the one who definitively "goes" to God or is with God. The message of an angel reveals to them the relationship of Christ's ascension to his parousia. The expectation of the parousia, the content of the (theologically developed) image of exaltation, and consciousness of the living presence of the resurrected one — all these are the basic data of the earliest post-Easter Christology. The expectation of the Son of Man is (perhaps) based on what the earthly Jesus proclaimed. The early community apparently used the notion to express its faith in the living

crucified one who was now in heaven and who would return as eschatological judge in the parousia (see Mk 13:26 par.; 14:62 par.; Lk 12:8f. par.). The early Jewish-Christian confession of faith used by Paul (Rom 1:3f.) indicates a similar horizon of expectation. The salvific meaning of the ascension of Christ is described variously: his "departure" or "glorification" is necessary so that he can send the Spirit and the church can be founded (Lk 24:49; Jn 7:39; 16:7; Acts 1:8; 2:32; Eph 4:8–12); a "dwelling place" is to be prepared (Jn 14:2); the resurrection of Jesus will become efficacious in believers (in baptism) so that their lives will become "hidden in God" (Col 3:1) and they themselves will become "a house in heaven" (Eph 2:22). Hebrews, alluding to Ps 110:1, describes the oblation on the cross accomplished by Christ as the entrance of the high priest into the holy of holies of heaven (4:14; 6:20; 7:25–27; 9:11f., 23–26). Thus he has become the "pioneer and perfecter of faith," who "has taken his seat at the right hand of the throne of God" (12:2; see 1:3, 13; 8:1; 10:12f.).

(2) *History of Theology.* Melito of Sardis (*Hom. in Pascha* 100–105) sees the resurrection, the ascension, and the presence of the exalted Christ and his enthronement at the right hand of the Father as belonging together. Irenaeus includes the "bodily ascension" as part of the faith received by the church from the apostles and their successors (*Adv. haer.* 1.10.1). Augustine (*De civ. Dei* 22.8.1; *In Ps.* 132.2) and Leo I (*Serm.* 73f.) also emphasize the bodiliness of the glorification of the human nature of Jesus Christ. The fact that the "forty days" were not at first understood by the early church as a period of time is seen in the practice of adding the celebration of the ascension to the feast of the Pentecost (the fiftieth day). Only around 370 did it become a separate feast (*Apost. const.* 8.33). An echo of New Testament exaltation-Christology is found in Polycarp and again in two anti-Arians, Marcellus of Ancyra and Hilary of Poitiers. Following Phil 2:11, Polycarp links the titles Kyrios and Son of God to the exaltation (2 Phil 1:2; 2:1; 12:2) and to Christ as judge (6:2f.; 11:2). Marcellus speaks of the "glorious" or "glorified man" (*kyriakòs ánthropos*), a state that begins with the incarnation, ends with his suffering, and is related to the exalted Lord. He thereby keeps the expressions of his humiliation separate from the Logos and can ascribe them to the assumed human nature. According to Hilary, the incarnation is already humanity's ascension to God, but only with the exaltation is the divinity of Christ fully effective in humanity. In the resurrection the fullness of glory is bestowed on the body of Christ; with the final glorification the resurrected Christ enters into the glory of God and rules forever "in this same glorified body" (*De Trin.* 11). In his sermons on Christ's ascension (*Serm.* 73f.), Leo I paraphrases the story in Acts 1 but clarifies its soteriological content: because the head has preceded us, the ascension of Christ is our own elevation; since that time "what was visible in the Redeemer has passed over into the sacraments." For this reason the bodily eye can no longer remain fixed on the man, Jesus, but faith knows more deeply the nature of the Son as consubstantial with the Father. In his view — referring to Phil 2:9ff. —

the exaltation happens to the human nature "which was to be enriched by the addition of such a glorification" (cf. the so-called Tom. II, ep. 165, 115). At the end of the patristic period, John Damascene emphasizes (as had Athanasius, *Or. c. Arianos* 1.6) that Christ sits bodily at God's right hand. However, this does not mean a "localized right hand," but the glory and honor of the divinity, in which the Son of God, as divine and as consubstantial with the Father, exists eternally; here too his flesh is glorified (*De fid. orth.* 4.2). Thomas Aquinas accepts this interpretation (*STh* 3, q. 1, ad 1) and, with Augustine, understands the "right hand of God" metaphorically as the blessedness of the Father and his power to rule and judge (a. 1), in which Christ participates (a. 4). His medieval worldview is apparent, however, when he considers the ascension as "local movement" and describes the "ascension above the heavens" as a "localizing" (3, q. 57, a. 2 and 4). We see the intrinsic limitation of this thought-form from natural philosophy in his references to the exalted one as "above every spiritual creature" (q. 5), as revealed in the ascension of Christ. Thomas considers the ascension of Christ as a basic fact of our salvation because it directs faith, hope, and love to the exalted Christ, who has established himself as our forerunner and intercessor before the Father (57, 6). There were also other attempts in the Middle Ages to find a "cosmological place" for the ascension of Christ, including those by John Scotus Erigena (*De div. nat.* 1.5.38), Albert the Great (*De resurr. tr.* 2.9.3), and Nicolas of Cusa (*Doct. ignor.* 3.8).

(3) *Church Teaching*. The councils clearly testify to belief in the ascension of Christ (DS 11–30, 72, 76, 125, 150, 189, 502, 1338). They emphasize his *bodily* ascension (DS 44, 681, 801, 852). Being "seated at the right hand of the Father" is also considered fundamental to faith (DS 11–30, 44, 72, 150, 502, 681, 852, 1338). Trent specifies *iuxta modum naturalem* (according to the natural mode of existing) (DS 1636) to distinguish his glorified existence with the Father from his sacramental presence.

(4) *Ecumenical Perspectives*. In recent Evangelical theology, wherever the ascension of Christ is not considered a "later, secondary legend" added to the original faith in the resurrection, there are two tendencies within the theological and systematic understanding of the ascension; these still reveal traces of the Lutheran doctrine of *ubiquitas* (because of the *unio hypostatica,* the humanity of Christ is "everywhere") and the *extra calvinisticum* (the finite humanity is continually with the infinite divinity, but not vice versa — i.e., the Logos assumed a complete human nature but remains "outside" it). Dogmaticians of the Lutheran tradition do not treat the ascension of Christ as a separate theme, but explain it in connection with the resurrection, as the glory of the exalted Christ. Thus, for W. Elert the ascension of Christ is an explanation of the resurrection, which only had meaning for the disciples. P. Althaus speaks of it as a legend that expresses the fact that Jesus has been exalted to God. Resurrection and exaltation are a single process. E. Schlink sees in the reports on the ascension a definitive concentration of the essential "disappearance" of all the appearance stories, and he understands the appearances, the glorification of

the exalted Christ, and the parousia as "an urgent, world-penetrating movement of God's power" (*Ökumenische Dogmatik* [Göttingen, 1983], 398). For
W. Joest the proclamation of the ascension of Christ is the Easter message in
its full significance. According to G. Ebeling, the "ascent to the right hand of
God" is closely joined with the resurrection, but adds nuances to it. It deals
with Christ's presence, for in the language of the councils, the "entrance into
God's revealed presence and dominion" is explained temporally, locally, and
humanly. It is not an end but a beginning; not distant but near; he is not a
private person but a *person publica*. For theologians of the Reformed tradition (especially disciples of K. Barth), the "history" of the forty days (between
the resurrection and the ascension) thematizes withdrawal from and association with human time. K. Barth emphasizes Jesus' being as a historical "event."
"He is the history of God with humankind" (*KD* 4/1:172) whereby this history is accomplished not in the relationship of humiliation and elevation, but
in the conjunction of both these orientations, and as an act of God it has never
ceased happening (*KD* 4/2:119). The resurrection did not eliminate Jesus' historicity but opened it to time for all human beings (*KD* 4/1:348). Therefore,
the forty days have a fundamental significance: here the "real act of revelation
as such" takes place (*KD* 1/2:101). This christological (and pneumatological)
understanding is clear in Barth's thesis on the three periods of the parousia: the
resurrection, the coming (as Spirit) after the ascension, and the final coming (as
judge of the world). These three are "forms of one and the same event" (*KD*
4/3:340). O. Weber speaks of an "eschatological history," which is determined
by Jesus' origin (in the Spirit) and goal (the ascension) and has its middle in the
Easter-event. H. Vogel speaks of the exaltation as a "history determined by the
acts of rising, ascending, and returning" (*Gott in Christo* [Berlin, 1952], 734),
so that "the one who was exalted for us still has a history," which reaches its
goal in the Second Coming by means of our human history. The ascension of
Christ ends the forty days, which are a time of revelation, and makes possible
the church, which is grounded in the hidden presence of the exalted one.

(5) *Systematic Reflections.* The various New Testament images and ideas of
the ascension of Christ are mutually limiting. They enable the main fact to appear and go beyond any idea of spatiality. The crucified and resurrected one is
definitively with God, his Father, and nevertheless present (through the Spirit)
in a new way to the church and the world. This new presence is the beginning
of the parousia (in hidden form). Since the Son who became *man* was exalted
only in the ascension, humanity is with God through him as its head, and the
eschatological reality of HEAVEN becomes a reality; in other words, the dimension of God is basically open to humankind. In this sense the ascension points
"upward." It also points to the "here and now": the beginning of the time of
the church, when the Lord is sending out his witnesses on mission. Now his humanly visible presence is in the sacraments, especially in his sacramental (given
and transfigured) body, by means of the church as the very body of Christ. The
real though hidden glory of Christ, which will be definitively revealed in the

parousia, pertains also to the world. Therefore the ascension of Christ points "by anticipation" to the future and inspires us to active abandonment. We must also reflect on the relationship between history and salvation in reference to the resurrection *and* ascension of Christ. Any explanation of Luke's theology of the forty days must, on the one hand, take into account the unity of the two and, on the other hand, give a suitable explanation of their difference. For Luke, the time of Jesus is "superimposed" on the time of the church during the forty days. This "superimposition of times" expresses the continuity between Jesus and the church. The ascension is the last appearance of the resurrected Christ. Does this lead to the idea of "various stages" in Jesus' glorification, a step-by-step way to the Father, a "history of the exalted Christ"? This does not have to be imaged, only understood — namely, by reconsidering the relationship between eternity and time. If we include God's power over time within God's eternity, and if we understand this power as that of God's presence in time, then the resurrection of Jesus is significant not as the disappearance of temporality but as its fulfillment. It is "the intrinsic historicity of transfigured existence" (W. Kasper). The one transcendent event of the paschal mystery would thus allow for historical differentiation, as developed by the death, descent into hell, resurrection, ascension, sending of the Spirit, and the parousia.

See also CHRIST'S DESCENT INTO HELL; PAROUSIA; RESURRECTION NARRATIVES; RESURRECTION OF JESUS.

Bibliography
Fitzmyer, Joseph A. "The Ascension of Christ and Pentecost." *ThS* 45 (1984) 409–40.
Grillmeier, Alois. *Christ in Christian Tradition.* 2d rev. ed. London: Mowbray, 1975.
Kasper, Walter. *Jesus the Christ.* New York: Paulist, 1976.
O'Toole, Robert F. "Luke's Understanding of Jesus' Resurrection–Ascension–Exaltation." *BTB* 9 (1984) 106–14.
Parsons, Mikeal C. "The Text of Acts 1:2 Reconsidered." *CBQ* 50 (1988) 58–71.
Schillebeeckx, Edward C. "Ascension and Pentecost." *Worship* 35 (1961) 336–63.
Wilson, S. G. "The Ascension: A Critique and an Interpretation." *ZNW* 59 (1968) 269–81.

LOTHAR ULLRICH

Assumption of Mary. At the end of her life, Mary was assumed *entirely* and *without division* into the glory of God, the fulfillment of every earthly thing.

(1) *Biblical Background.* We cannot point to any explicit scriptural texts as the foundation for this faith conviction; as with the doctrine of faith concerning Mary's freedom from original sin, the only testimonies that can be mentioned are those that comprise this dogma at an undeveloped level. First of all is the belief that God "is God, not of the dead, but of the living" (Mk 12:27); further, there is the proclamation of the risen Christ, the firstfruits of those who have fallen asleep (1 Cor 15:23). One's participation in Christ establishes *immediately* an identity with his death, resurrection, and ascension into heaven (see Eph 2:5f.; Col 3:3). The earthly union with Christ finds its fulfillment in the beatific vision of God face-to-face (1 Cor 13:12). The texts revolving around

Mary's motherhood, which show her faith-filled closeness to Christ and to his mission, contributed to the later application of the biblical belief in election and resurrection to the person of Mary. Thus, we have Elizabeth's greeting: "Blessed is she who believed" (Lk 1:45); likewise, the verse from the Magnificat: "Yes, from this day forward all generations will call me blessed" (Lk 1:48); and other similar texts that recognize the intrinsic connection among election, blessedness, and glorification (Rom 8:30; Eph 1:3–6). Mary's exalting praise will endure throughout all ages, since her son is Lord forever over the house of Jacob (Lk 1:33). From the standpoint of the history of tradition, these verses are an early echo of the primitive church's high esteem for Mary; however, they do not yet have in view Mary's eschatological fulfillment.

(2) *History of Theology.* This step was taken when people began, following upon the cult of the martyrs, to praise Mary in hymns and to call upon her in prayer as one living in eternal communion with Christ. Similar to the martyrs, the glorified Mother of the Lord was believed in and celebrated as devoted to helping the church evermore. The question regarding the end of Mary's life and the specific mode of her fulfillment was not raised at that time: the worshiper knew simply that she is in ultimate communion with Christ. From the sixth century, the Eastern Church has celebrated on August 15 the feast of the passing of Mary; the Western Church then became familiar with the feast of the dormition of Mary, attested since 430 in Jerusalem; in the eighth century, however, the Western Church settled on the designation of *Assumptio.* The content of this feast was adorned with legends (as in the apocrypha of Mary's Ascent) by preachers both in the East and in the West (not without contradiction: e.g., Paschasius Radbertus, *PL* 30, 122–42; Ps.-Augustine, *PL* 40, 1141–48). On theological grounds, reference was made to the election by grace and the divine maternity, through which Mary was and remains physically bound to Christ. He, the fulfiller of the law, complied with the fourth commandment precisely through her physical glorification. Influential on this point is the text of Jn 12:26: "Wherever I am, my servant will be there too" (see also Jn 17:24). Related to these texts and notions is the concept that Mary can act out her motherhood by praying for the church, a role that stems from her fulfillment in Christ. The concept of *body and soul* employed in Scholastic anthropology signifies the one entire human being, who exists as both a physical and a spiritual being. With this same wholeness in mind, the goal of earthly pilgrimage is also recognized: the fulfillment of both body and soul. Neither of these two components is excluded. On this account, Bonaventure makes this argument with respect to the glorification of Mary: since the soul separated by death from the body is not a person, Mary's fulfillment would be apersonal and not completely beatific if she were taken to be only a soul (*De Assumptione B.M.V.,* serm. 2, ed. Quaracchi IX 690a). Thomas Aquinas thinks along similar lines (*STh* 1, q. 29, a. 1, ad 5). On the basis, then, of *body and soul,* the conclusion for High Scholasticism is: Mary is wholly and undivided, precisely as a person, with Christ.

(3) *Church Teaching.* Accordingly, Pius XII, in his bull *Munificentissimus Deus* (November 1, 1950), formulated the definition of the assumption of Mary in Scholastic terms of thought and speech, proclaiming that part of the revealed deposit of faith is that Mary "in body *and* soul" had been "assumed into heavenly glory" (DS 3903). By the expressed will of the pope, this act of definition was intended to serve the "glorification of Almighty God" and "the honor of his Son"; yet it was also intended to increase "the glories of the exalted Mother of God" and to contribute to the joy of the whole church. This latreutic framework is significant for the comprehension of this dogma. Its proclamation was not especially a decision of the magisterium on a disputed question. This conviction was firmly anchored in the church's pious sense of belief. As in the case of the dogma of Mary's freedom from original sin, here it is a matter of giving glory to God and of proclaiming Mary's praise.

(4) *Ecumenical Perspectives.* There are three critical reasons why this dogma in particular is in need of penetrating ecumenical discourse. First, it raises the question: To what extent might specific Marian consequences be drawn from general biblical premises through the so-called conclusion process? Is not the exclusive terrain of revelation thereby left behind? Second, alongside these hermeneutic questions, there is the substantive objection that the unique position of Christ is touched upon here, insofar as Mary is placed into an exceptional position at his side and with regard to humanity. Third, the protest is also heard that here, as in the instance of the dogma of Mary's freedom from original sin, the church has glorified itself: it is no longer the lowly handmaid in Mary, but rather the institution of salvation mediating grace. In point of fact, the Catholic understanding of the exaltation of the Mother of the Lord expresses that salvation is not just promised to the church, but rather is already fulfilled and present in Mary. Mary is the symbol of what the Christian hopes for: to be fulfilled by grace, regardless of one's limitations.

(5) *Systematic Reflections.* For the systematic communication of this dogma, it is proper first to call to mind that the definition should be a worshipful act that in its very language bears traces of hymns. The act of definition does not involve solely the establishment of historical facts, but rather also involves homage to that woman who has "won God's favor" (Lk 1:30), "who believed" (Lk 1:45), and therefore in whom the goal of all discipleship has been totally fulfilled (Jn 17:25; 12:26). Mary is celebrated as the one in whom the words of Paul are manifest, for she is one of "those [whom God] called [that] he intended for this; those he called he justified, and with those he justified he shared his glory" (Rom 8:30). For a deeper substantive definition, one must bear in mind the principle of eschatological statements: they are analogical and imaginal in character. As consoling utterances, they are a hopeful preview of humankind's earthly situation in salvation-history; however, they do not have the purpose of imparting information on clearly definable and settled facts with unvarying terminology. "The things that no eye has seen and no ear has heard" (1 Cor 2:9) cannot be adequately grasped by us *in their essence,* but only by approximation

and with the images of *our* experience of salvation within history: these images render, although *not immediately,* the things unseen and unheard that we hope and wait for in their own particular kind. This means, when applied to Mary, that her ultimate goal is to be determined from her close sharing with Christ in salvation-history; a consequence of this is that Mary was "bound most intimately with her divine Son" during her lifetime and always shared his lot (DS 3900). *How* the identity and continuity of historical discipleship and eschatological "being with the Lord" (1 Thes 4:16) are to be thought of in Mary's case, *how* the fulfillment of Mary's earthly life finally appears, can be suitably answered only in the Pauline antitheses (1 Cor 15:36–38, 39–41, 42–50, 51–57): "The thing that is sown is perishable, but what is raised is imperishable; the thing that is sown is contemptible, but what is raised is glorious" (1 Cor 15:42f.). These series of images, approaching one another yet constantly correcting one another, might be *the* appropriate aid for understanding and the appropriate form of expression for asserting Mary's bodily glorification. In current discussion the question is raised whether this glorification as a personal privilege signifies more than what can be hoped for in the case of other faithful who have died. The specific background for this question is the thesis on the resurrection of the dead. If the new existence is to be determined from earthly being-with-Christ, then Mary's personality within salvation-history is established precisely in her fulfillment through her divine motherhood. The hermeneutic for eschatological statements requires that the question raised concerning Mary's personal distinction be approached from this aspect and that one be clearly aware that it is *only* an analogous form of knowing and saying. The question whether other human beings have, like Mary, found full personal perfection ("with body and soul") in God, or whether they await it until the last day, may remain open because of the unimaginable difference between the present and the future life.

See also DOGMA/DOGMATIC STATEMENT; ESCHATOLOGY; GRACE; HEAVEN; IMMACULATE CONCEPTION.

Bibliography

Duggan, Paul E. *The Assumption Dogma: Some Reactions and Ecumenical Implications in the Thought of English-Speaking Theologians.* Cleveland: Emerson, 1989.
Rahner, Karl. "The Interpretation of the Dogma of the Assumption." In *Theological Investigations,* 1:201–13. Baltimore: Helicon, 1954.

FRANZ COURTH

Atheism. The term *atheism* refers to the denial that God exists or to the rejection of any possibility of knowing God (theoretical atheism) or to the claim that God is not significant for practical life (practical atheism). It is decisive for any consideration of theoretical atheism to determine just which idea of God is being presupposed or rejected.

(1) *Biblical Background.* The Bible assumes the existence of God as self-evident. It looks upon the denial of divine governance of the universe as

foolishness (Pss 10:4; 14:1; 53:2). The crucial question in the Bible regards the search for the true God, in the contest with the gods of the other religions. Human beings are so much creatures of God that they live in constant relationship with God (Acts 17:27–29).

(2) *History of Theology.* Up to modern times, those who were seen as worshipers of false gods were often called atheists (as were Christians themselves early on). Once Christianity became Christendom and had established itself as the foundation of culture, atheism became, at most, the lot of a few individuals. It is only since the nineteenth century that atheism has become a mass phenomenon and a theological problem of the first order.

(3) *Church Teaching.* The church's teaching therefore took its first stance on atheism at Vatican I (DS 3021f.) and then more intensively at Vatican II. Despite ample rejection of atheism, Vatican II affirmed that an atheist who strives after truth is not excluded from salvation (*LG* 16). It taught that misunderstandings about God can also arise, in part, through incorrect religious practices. Positively, Vatican II sought to make clear that God's existence does not render humans unfree, but rather grounds their dignity and constitutes their hope (*GS* 19–21).

(4) *Ecumenical Perspectives.* A more radical confrontation with atheism has taken place in Protestant than in Catholic theology. For Protestant theology atheism is the result of those modern currents of thought that turn God into a function of human self-grounding. On the other hand, as K. Rahner has agreed, the modern emphasis on human subjectivity can provide a point of entry into the problem of God.

(5) *Systematic Reflections.* The need to come to terms with modern atheism has led to important nuances in theology. Whereas in the natural sciences one has begun to realize that not all the questions that the sciences raise are solvable, in theology one realizes that God cannot simply be brought in as a stopgap to explain such riddles. These two tendencies have overcome the atheism occasioned by the natural sciences. Moreover, the humanistic objection that the existence of God precludes real human freedom has lost its force, especially since today experience of the totalitarian threat to humanity by humans themselves has become worldwide. The suffering in the world, as the "rock of atheism," cannot, it is true, be cleared away speculatively by some theoretical "justification of God" (THEODICY). However, if God is seen in the light of the cross of the Son, whose suffering affects God's own self, then God becomes "conceivable" as the vanquisher of human suffering and hence as the object of human hope. Conversely, it has become clear today that Christians have a responsibility to ensure that the line of sight to the "true" God does not become blocked by themselves. The problem of atheism, then, is not primarily a theoretical but a practical problem. What needs to be overcome is the attitude of indifference as a loss of sensitivity to God; what needs to be proclaimed is that persons are called to friendship with God. Further, what needs to be critically

questioned is the superficial, this-worldly ideal of emancipation that often lies behind practical atheism.

See also AGNOSTICISM; GOD: POSSIBILITY OF KNOWLEDGE OF; GOD: PROOFS OF EXISTENCE OF.

Bibliography
Buckley, Michael J. *At the Origins of Modern Atheism.* New Haven: Yale University Press, 1987.
Lubac, Henri de. *The Drama of Atheistic Humanism.* Cleveland: World, 1963.
Kasper, Walter. *The God of Jesus Christ,* 16–115. New York: Crossroad, 1984.
Küng, Hans. *Does God Exist? An Answer for Today.* New York: Doubleday, 1980.

WILHELM BREUNING

Attributes of the Church. The properties of unity, holiness, catholicity, and apostolicity as predicated of the church are usually called the attributes of the church.

(1) *Biblical Background.* The New Testament starting points for the doctrine of the attributes of the church are described under the four relevant entries.

(2) *History of Theology.* The four attributes are taken from the Nicene-Constantinopolitan Creed (DS 150). The Middle Ages saw the beginnings of a doctrine of the four attributes in the context of an apologetic ECCLESIOLOGY, while in the course of the Reformation the four attributes were explicitly called "marks" by which the true church is to be known (N. Herborn, *De notis Ecclesiae* [1529]; S. Hosius, *Confessio catholicae fidei christianae* [1550]). The argument was that these "marks of the church" were given to it by Christ and that therefore the true church is the one in which they are found without diminution; this is the case, however, only with the Roman Catholic Church. The number "four," by the way, was only gradually accepted by all; at times, as many as one hundred "marks" were listed. Today the "marks approach" (*via notarum*) has been largely abandoned; instead, the attributes of the church have been given a new dogmatic and spiritual interpretation.

(3) *Church Teaching.* The "marks approach" was still being followed by Pius IX (DS 2888). In *Lumen gentium,* Vatican II develops a rich variety of dogmatic and spiritual approaches to the attributes of the church (see the relevant entries).

(4) *Ecumenical Perspectives.* The doctrine of the "marks of the church" has always played an important role in Evangelical theology. According to CA 7, the true church manifests itself wherever the gospel is correctly preached and the sacraments correctly administered. Both are necessary, but they also suffice. In the Reformed tradition, however, a third "mark" is given: obedience to those in office, and church discipline. The attributes of the church in the creed are thus rejected, not as properties, however, but only as marks. The question of principle that is at issue in the distinction between properties and marks was recognized as important in the conflict with National Socialism (Barmen Declaration [1934]).

(5) *Systematic Reflections.* The significance of the attributes of the church and their interrelationship becomes clear especially in view of the inculturation process, as, for example, when unity and catholicity or the institutional (apostolicity) and charismatic (holiness) elements in the church have to be balanced and combined.

See also APOSTOLICITY OF THE CHURCH; CATHOLICITY OF THE CHURCH; HOLINESS AND SINFULNESS OF THE CHURCH; UNITY OF THE CHURCH.

Bibliography
Vorgrimler, Herbert. *One, Holy, Catholic and Apostolic.* London: Sheed and Ward, 1968.
See also the bibliography under SACRAMENT OF ORDERS.

WERNER LÖSER

Authority in the Church. Whoever or whatever is empowered to organize the concrete reality of the church in accordance with the will of Jesus Christ has authority in the church. This authority is derived and transmitted by appointment, whereas the original authority resides ultimately in the triune God, who is the source and ground not only of the church but of all authority in it. In different ways the following have authority in the church: Sacred Scripture, ecclesiastical traditions (among them, the profession of faith and dogma), the pope and councils, appointees to ministry in the church, the saints, the people of God who make known the "sense of the faithful" (sensus fidelium), and the consensus of theologians. Authority in the church is limited. It is subject to the standard of the word of God as attested in Sacred Scripture (*norma normans,* "a norm that is the source of normativeness for other norms") and must serve the building up of the church, the faith of the faithful, and the good of the human race. The following discussion is limited to the authority actually exercised at any given time by persons and institutions in the church.

(1) *Biblical Background.* The concept of authority is not found in the Scriptures. The term that best expresses the reality in question is *exousia* (Greek: "right to act; might, power"): Jesus acted with "full power." He gave a share in this to the disciples whom he chose and sent out. In the Easter appearances the risen Christ gave the disciples apostolic power for the time of the church's existence (Mt 28:18–20; John 21).

(2) *History of Theology.* The concept of authority comes from Roman private and public law. Tertullian already makes it part of the ecclesiastical vocabulary. According to him and other writers of the early church, the apostles and the traditions that go back to them have authority. In the course of the centuries the concept of authority has increasingly been applied to persons — pope, bishops, council — who possess the power to make decisions in the church. In the Reformation of the sixteenth century one of the radical issues was a new conception of the structures of authority in the church. When the Reformers rejected papal authority, the Roman Catholic Church responded by emphasizing this authority all the more. For centuries, the church has wrestled with the question of how papal, episcopal, and conciliar authority are interrelated.

(3) *Church Teaching*. The ecclesial magisterium has defined the "highest authority in the church." This resides in the pope. Vatican I defined the content of the papal primacy of jurisdiction: by the will of Jesus Christ the pope possesses ordinary, immediate, and supreme jurisdiction over the entire church (DS 3059–64), as well as, under certain conditions, INFALLIBILITY (DS 3065–75). Vatican II confirmed these decrees, but at the same time strengthened the position and authority of the bishops (*LG,* chap. 3). This most recent council speaks frequently in its documents of the authority of the pope, the bishops, and the council (e.g., *LG* 22–24, 27; *CD*).

(4) *Ecumenical Perspectives*. What and who possess authority in the church and how the exercise of authority in the church is grounded and limited are two of the most discussed questions in ecumenical dialogue. They are always raised when the subject of MINISTRY IN THE CHURCH is brought up. At times they are also the express subject of ecumenical conversations (e.g., the Anglican–Roman Catholic Venice Statement on "Authority in the Church"). The Faith and Order Commission of the World Council of Churches produced a study titled "How Does the Church Teach with Authority Today?" (*Ecumenical Review* 31 [1979] 77–93).

(5) *Systematic Reflections*. Like all other forms of authority, authority in the church runs up against many reservations nowadays. It must therefore be exercised and justified in a correspondingly more responsible way. It is not enough to argue that the church is an earthly society and as such needs governors who possess authority (*LG* 8). It must be added that authority is exercised in the church because the authority of Jesus is to be made present therein.

See also COUNCIL; ECCLESIAL MAGISTERIUM; POPE; SCRIPTURE.

Bibliography
Lash, Nicolas. *Voices of Authority*. Shepherdstown, W.Va.: Patmos, 1976.
Lytle, Guy F. *Reform and Authority in the Medieval and Reformation Church*. Washington, D.C.: Catholic University of America, 1981.
Stanks, Howland. *Authority in the Church: A Study of Changing Paradigms*. Missoula, Mont.: Scholars Press, 1974.
Todd, John M. *Problems of Authority*. Baltimore: Helicon, 1962.

WERNER LÖSER

Autonomy and Theonomy of the Human Person. This pair of concepts points toward a theological problem that arises from, on the one hand, the relation between human reason and freedom and, on the other, the dependence upon the divine creative will. That human beings are determined in the present and future by God seems to contradict the free self-determination of human beings in their thinking and acting.

(1) *Biblical Background*. A central theme in the Pauline letters is that Christian faith liberates a person from external powers and inner constraints and encourages independent judging and action (Rom 14:22f.; 1 Thes 5:21; 1 Corinthians 8; 10:15, 29). "Why should my freedom depend on the judgment of

conscience of others?" (1 Cor 10:29). Yet this autonomy of judgment and action won through faith in Christ is itself oriented to love as God's law (Rom 13:8; 14:15; 1 Cor 8:1f.). It is theonomous autonomy.

(2) *History of Theology*. In contrast to this theonomy of the rational and free human person as put forth in Christian tradition, in modernity the Enlightenment elevated reason to be the final arbitrator over all religious and moral traditions. The historical occasion for this was the inhumanity of the wars of religion and their religious and political consequences.

(3) *Church Teaching*. A concept of autonomy that reduces the Christian faith to what human reason by itself can know about God and the ethical obligation of human beings is in conflict with the Catholic teaching on faith (DS 3031; cf. DS 3008). The church acknowledges, however, the relative autonomy of reason in the realms of science, of culture, and of the temporal order, as long as these realms do not oppose the religious calling of the human person (GS 36, 56; AA 1 passim).

(4) *Ecumenical Perspectives*. Protestant theology was able to be more receptive than Catholic theology to the modern striving toward autonomy because Luther clearly distinguished between the bondage of the human person before God and his or her freedom in the world. Still, the influence of the Reformation interpretation of freedom upon the Enlightenment interpretation of autonomy is nowadays a subject of dispute.

(5) *Systematic Reflections*. The insights of the human sciences (biology, depth psychology, sociology, cultural anthropology, etc.) as well as the experience of the ecological crisis have made clear the limits of the autonomous self-determination of the human person. For the cosmic-evolutive, depth psychological, and social predeterminations of human reason and freedom cannot be totally transformed by self-determination. This goal could not even be the content of Christian hope, since this hope concerns the salvation and perfection of the whole human person especially in view of a heteronomy that is beyond rational grasp. At the same time, the external determination of the person through heredity and through cultural, early childhood, and social forces cannot be directly understood theologically as theonomy. This remains primarily an area for critical reason and liberating action. Theology cannot be allowed to fall back to a pre-Enlightenment attitude. But the limits to autonomous reason and freedom point toward a theonomy that encompasses both the human person and his or her world.

See also ANTHROPOCENTRISM; SALVATION.

Bibliography
Schillebeeckx, Edward, and Bas van Israel. *Jesus Christ and Human Freedom*. Vol. 93 of *Concilium*. New York: Herder and Herder, 1974.

GEORG LANGEMEYER

Bb

Baptism. Baptism is the most fundamental of the seven sacraments.

(1) *Biblical Background.* Apart from Rom 6:1–11 there are no extended treatments of baptism in the New Testament; there are, however, numerous isolated statements. These are at one in showing that after Easter baptism was a universal practice (see Acts 2:38, 41; 8:12), probably taking the form, in the beginning, of immersion in running water (see Acts 8:36–39). Baptism was baptism in the name or into the name of Jesus (see Acts 2:38), but soon the baptismal formula acquired the trinitarian form it still has (see Mt 28:18f.). The formula signifies a new and especially close relationship with Jesus Christ, a submission to his saving rule as Kyrios (Lord) (see Rom 10:9, which is probably a baptismal confession of faith). In Rom 6:1–11 Paul interprets this turning point in the life of the baptized as their union with the death and resurrection of Jesus. Baptism and conversion go together, as do baptism and faith (see Mk 16:16; Acts 2:36). Baptism does not replace the personal response of faith; it is a dialogical event and is meant to establish a dialogue. It is through baptism that the church, which is the communion of those united to Christ, comes into being (see Acts 2:41f.; Eph 5:25f.). Further important New Testament developments of the theme of baptism can be summed up as follows: (*a*) Baptism creates a new beginning for human beings; it is a new birth, a rebirth (see Jn 3:5; Ti 3:5). It is the grace of a new beginning. (*b*) Baptism makes human beings members of a new community; it makes them all one and equal by uniting them with Christ (see 1 Cor 12:13f.; Gal 3:26–28; Eph 4:5). (*c*) Baptism delivers them from the dominion of sin (see Rom 5:12–6:11); it brings the forgiveness of sin and a new, unending life by the power of the Holy Spirit (see Acts 2:38; Gal 3:27; Col 2:12). (*d*) Baptism gives a new direction; it enlightens; and it makes possible and promotes a new activity. Eph 5:14 may be assumed to be a hymn from a primitive Christian baptismal liturgy. (*e*) Baptism is the divinely willed way to salvation; it is (for those who know of it) necessary for salvation (see Mt 16:16; Jn 3:5). The origin of baptism in an express act of Jesus' will can, at most, be deduced from the universality of the practice of baptism. In any case, the disciples had before them the great model of Jesus' own baptism by John (see Mk 1:9–11 par.) and, for example, the stimulus of proselyte baptism that was common in Judaism.

(2) *History of Theology.* The liturgy of baptism underwent further development in the early church: the catechumenate as preparation for baptism became a universal practice, and for adults baptism continued to be the great turning point. Theological clarifications soon followed, but so did imbalances: (*a*) Attention shifted to the minister of baptism. The third-century dispute over

baptism by heretics led to the realization that the validity of baptism does not depend on the orthodoxy of the minister. In the fourth century, Augustine also made it clear (against the Donatists) that neither does the efficacy of baptism depend on the holiness of the minister, since Christ himself is the primary baptizer. (b) Augustine laid special emphasis on one effect of baptism: it sets human beings free from the original sin that makes it impossible for them to be saved. Even children who have not reached the use of reason and who die unbaptized are lost. (c) From the Middle Ages on, baptism (like all the sacraments) was regarded as an instrument used by God to effect grace, rather than as an encounter. The response of the recipient was now easily neglected.

(3) *Church Teaching*. The Council of Trent emphasized once more those aspects of the doctrine of baptism that had been the object of special hostility in the history of the faith (see DS 1614–27). It stressed, above all else, the saving effect in the individual (liberation from original sin, grace, divine filiation) in a somewhat "instrumental" sense. Vatican II changed the emphasis. It stressed the following points (*LG* 11; *SC* 65–70, 59–61): (a) not only the saving effect in the individual, but also the incorporation into the church and its work that baptism brings; (b) not only the "objective effect," but also the dialogical nature of the sacrament as an encounter with Christ and thus an encounter with God in faith; this encounter takes place in a symbolic action that is at once efficacious and didactic; (c) not only the foundation laid by the administration of the sacrament, but also the character of baptism as the beginning of a new journey of faith that the sacrament both enables and obliges its recipients to undertake.

(4) *Ecumenical Perspectives*. There is no fundamental disagreement on baptism among the Christian churches. All the more, then, is it necessary to be clear on the demand that the sacrament makes of patiently bringing to fruition in individual and ecclesial life the unity of all the baptized that it establishes (see *UR* 3, 22).

(5) *Systematic Reflections*. The sacrament of baptism sets a variety of tasks for contemporary theology on the basis of Vatican II: (a) The symbolic nature of baptism must be more fully developed: not only the sacramental action proper (the pouring or sprinkling with water, or immersion, and the formula of administration: "N., I baptize you in the name of the Father and of the Son and of the Holy Spirit"), but also its liturgical setting. (b) Also to be emphasized is the interpersonal nature of the sacrament. Baptism is an event involving the minister (in case of necessity, anyone who intends "to do what the church does"), who represents Christ and his church, and the recipient or those responsible for the recipient as representatives of the community. (c) The dialogical aspect of baptism must be developed. God in Christ calls the baptizands by their individual names and, at the same time, as members of the church. Human beings may and must initially and repeatedly respond to the call in faith. Because they respond, there is given to them the grace of baptism that is guaranteed by the indelible seal or character of baptism (a seal that is

itself a gift). The baptismal character is the effect of the abiding readiness of God to be found by this particular individual and to be given in grace to the believer. For the sacrament is fruitful only when the human being properly responds. (*d*) The realization that human beings can also obtain salvation in other ways raises the question of the inner meaning of the New Testament command of baptism. The incorporation into the church that takes place in baptism is a dimension of salvation itself. God's yes to human beings is meant to be mediated concretely through their fellow believers. The decisive, concrete form of grace and of the victory over sin is the inclusion, which takes place in baptism, in the visible communion of those who have been accepted by God and who accept one another in Christ.

See also BAPTISM OF DESIRE; INDELIBLE CHARACTER; INFANT BAPTISM; SACRAMENTS OF INITIATION.

Bibliography
Beasley-Murray, George. *Baptism in the New Testament*. Grand Rapids: Eerdmans, 1962.
Brown, Raymond E. "We Profess One Baptism for the Forgiveness of Sins." *Worship* 40 (1966) 260–71.
Cullmann, Oscar. *Baptism in the New Testament*. London: SCM, 1950.
Dunn, James. *Baptism in the Holy Spirit*. London: SCM, 1970.
Ganoczy, Alexandre. *Becoming Christian: A Theology of Baptism as the Sacrament of Human History*. Ramsey, N.J.: Paulist, 1976.
Kavanagh, Aidan. *The Shape of Baptism: The Rite of Christian Initiation*. New York: Pueblo, 1978.
Neunheuser, Burkhard. *Baptism and Confirmation*. New York: Herder and Herder, 1964.
Rite of Baptism for Children. Washington, D.C.: United States Catholic Conference, 1969.
Schnackenburg, Rudolf. *Baptism in the Thought of St. Paul*. New York: Herder and Herder, 1964.

GÜNTER KOCH

Baptism of Desire. Baptism of desire (*votum baptismi*) is the (at least implicit) desire to receive water baptism and thereby to participate in the justification it effects.

(1) *Biblical Background*. The doctrine of baptism of desire can be inferred from some complementary biblical truths: the necessity of baptism for salvation (Mk 16:16; Jn 3:5) and the UNIVERSAL SALVIFIC WILL OF GOD (1 Tm 2:4ff.). There is also the fact that according to the New Testament salvation and healing are granted to those who have not received water baptism: Acts 10:47 (Cornelius receives the Holy Spirit before baptism) and Lk 23:43 (Jesus promises the good thief entrance into the fulfillment of heaven).

(2) *History of Theology*. Testimonies to baptism of desire in the early centuries of the church are not numerous. The most important is from Ambrose (ca. 339–97). In his funeral oration for Emperor Valentinian II, who had died as a catechumen, he refers to the desire for baptism and ascribes to it, as to baptism by blood, the wiping away of sin (*De obitu Valent.* 51; 53). From the Middle Ages on, and especially from the age of discoveries on, it became a universal conviction that human beings can be justified by baptism of desire,

without the actual reception of water baptism. Relatively recent, however, is the clear understanding that the desire for baptism may also be only implicit (*votum implicitum*).

(3) *Church Teaching*. Since the Middle Ages there have been several magisterial testimonies to baptism of desire (e.g., Innocent II [DS 741]; Innocent III [DS 788]; Council of Trent [DS 1524]), so that this doctrine must be regarded as part of the church's teaching on the faith. According to a letter of the Holy Office to Archbishop Cushing of Boston (1949), it is also to be regarded as church teaching that an implicit desire of baptism ("I want to do all that God wishes me to do") is enough for justification (DS 3866–73).

(4) *Ecumenical Perspectives*. Although the theology of the Reformation has held strongly to the importance of baptism, it has maintained no less strongly that what really justifies is faith in the God who is revealed in Christ. Objectively, therefore, it need have no difficulty about baptism of desire.

(5) *Systematic Reflections*. The doctrine of baptism by desire is an auxiliary theological construct that arises with a certain inner logic from the necessity of baptism for salvation, on the one hand, and God's universal saving will, on the other; all who are ready to obey the will of God — and therefore to receive baptism, if it becomes clear that this is God's will for them — can receive decisive parts of the total effect of baptism: liberation and salvation (but not full membership in the church). According to Vatican II, it is probably no longer unconditionally necessary to fall back on the theological construct that is baptism of desire, since the readiness of human beings to follow the will of God — even if this is found only in the voice of their own consciences — unites them in a mysterious way to Christ and his church, which is the universal sacrament, and thus opens the way of salvation to them.

See also BAPTISM; CHURCH; INFANT BAPTISM.

Bibliography

Fahey, Michael, ed. *Catholic Perspectives on Baptism, Eucharist, and Ministry: CTSA Study.* Lanham, Md.: University Press of America, 1986.

Rahner, Karl. "Membership of the Church according to the Teaching of Pius XII's Encyclical 'Mystici Corporis Christi.'" In *Theological Investigations,* 2:1–88. Baltimore: Helicon, 1962.

GÜNTER KOCH

Beginning. Humans, as historical beings, exist within time and thus cannot evade the question about their beginning and their end. They are conscious that they — or more broadly, the entire human race — had a beginning "at some point in time." But this beginning does not permit of being explained as just the first moment in a succession of later moments; rather, it is understood as an act that both enables and commences an entire process, an act that always, from the start, sets the temporal chain of events in motion toward its end. Aristotle had already occupied himself intensively with the notion of "beginning" in a cosmological context, as the *arché* of all things. He perceived this in *noûs*, the "intelligence" that pervades the world and makes it understandable. For human beings, the *arché* discloses itself in moments of wonderment, uncertainty, or extreme experience. According to classical philosophy, the beginning is determinative for any being; according to mythological thought, it is usually the locus of the good and the true, whereas, for the scientific understanding of the world, it tends to be that of the crude and underdeveloped.

(1) *Biblical Background.* The Bible begins with the sentence: "In the beginning...God created the heavens and the earth" (Gn 1:1). That is no philosophical assertion but a praiseful acknowledgment that God is the Creator of the universe — which implies the idea that God existed when there was still no world or history. God, as the one who creates "in the beginning," is *the* beginning for all things. God's eternity is thereby conceived as the comprehensive sphere within which time and space are able to arise at all. God's comprehensiveness is best expressed through Old Testament phraseology, in which God is addressed as the first *and* the last (Is 44:6; 48:12). Particularly indicative is Is 41:4: "Who has performed these deeds? He who has called forth the generations since the beginning. I, the Lord, am the first, and with the last I will also be." The New Testament extends this divine predicate to Christ as well, of whom Jn 1:1 says: "In the beginning was the Word" (cf. 1 Jn 2:13), and whom the Apocalypse records (Rv 22:13) as affirming: "I am the Alpha and the Omega, the first and the last, the beginning and the end" (cf. Rv 1:17; 2:8; as self-description by God: 1:8; 21:6). In the view of Paul, Christ is the first to be resurrected among "those who have fallen asleep" (1 Cor 15:20, 23) and hence the beginning of the new creation, who can therefore also be called the "last" — that is, the "eschatological," new, second — Adam (1 Cor 15:45). For the author of Colossians, Christ is present not only in the new creation, as its beginning, but also in the old: "For in him were created all things.... [A]ll things were created through him and for him. He is before all things, and in him all things hold together" (Col 1:16f.). He is the *arché* (Col 1:18). Beginning and new beginning in one, Christ thus serves as the revelation and embodiment of God's plan for salvation (cf. Eph 1:3–2:22).

(5) *Systematic Reflections.* Accordingly, the following can hold valid as a philosophico-theological statement: "The beginning...draws its life from the process of movement toward the culmination, the unfolding of which is sustained by God, who alone is both beginning and end at once and thus, as transcendental unity, keeps the beginning and the end apart while also tying them together within the finite" (Darlapp, *LThK*² 1:528).

See also CHRISTOLOGICAL TITLES; CREATION; CREATION OUT OF NOTHING.

Bibliography

Doria, Charles, and Harris Lenowitz, eds. *Origins: Creation Texts from the Ancient Mediterranean.* Garden City, N.Y.: Doubleday, 1976.

ALEXANDRE GANOCZY

Bishop. Bishop is the name given to the holder of the highest ecclesiastical office or ministry that is transmitted through ordination. In virtue of his membership in the college of bishops, a bishop shares in the governance of the universal church. At the same time, he governs the LOCAL CHURCH to which he is assigned. He is supported by priests and deacons.

(1) *Biblical Background.* The governance of the first Christian communities was in the hands of elders (*presbyteroi*) (Acts 20:17, 28). They continued the ministry of the apostles and acquired their office through the laying on of hands and prayer. In the first century, the relation of the several ministries to one another was still unsettled.

(2) *History of Theology.* In the letters of Ignatius of Antioch the three grades of ecclesiastical ministry (episcopate, presbyterate, diaconate) are already clearly distinguished. The *Apostolic Tradition* of Hippolytus of Rome contains ordination liturgies that certify their existence. In his commentary on the Letter to Titus, Jerome takes the view that the episcopate had been instituted by the church. Therefore the precedence of bishops is due "more to custom than to the authority of an arrangement made by the Lord"; consequently, "A presbyter is the same as a bishop." In the ensuing period, the understanding of the independent sacramental quality of the episcopal office disappeared. Power to ordain and confirm, as well as jurisdiction over a diocese, were still reserved to him; his authority to govern, however, was thought of as transmitted to him by the pope, while the powers of orders (*potestas ordinis*) that he possessed came to him from his ordination to the priesthood. A complete clarification of the sacramental foundation of the episcopal office was achieved again only at Vatican II.

(3) *Church Teaching.* This most recent council restored the three levels of ecclesiastical ministry that the early church had recognized, and it determined that the ministry in its fullness is conferred by episcopal ordination (*LG 21*). The source of both jurisdictional and sacramental power is episcopal ordination. In virtue of this ordination the bishops are the successors of the apostles and continue the latter's pastoral ministry. They form a college that manifests itself in councils and similar assemblies (e.g., the synod of bishops). The bishops are not representatives of the pope but, in virtue of their ordination, act in the person of Christ (*in persona Christi*). Of course, they exercise their office in a legitimate way only when they are in communion with the college of bishops and the pope (*LG 27*). In describing the tasks of a bishop the council makes use of the "doctrine of the three offices": a bishop has the offices of preaching, sanctifying (through the celebration of the sacraments), and governing. The council did not make any definitive statement on how the ministries of bishop, presbyter, and deacon are related to one another. It says only that the degrees of ministry have been distinguished from one another "from ancient times" (*LG 28*).

(4) *Ecumenical Perspectives.* In the churches of the Reformation the office of bishop, or at least the sacramental interpretation of it, was lost in the sixteenth

century. Efforts to restore it are observable today, although there are also reservations regarding these efforts. See the statement on convergence in the area of ecclesiastical ministry that was issued by the Faith and Order Commission of the World Council of Churches (Lima Report, 1982); it is said there that all churches need a ministry of "supervision" (*episkopē*). This is a starting point that can lead to further development.

(5) *Systematic Reflections.* In the Catholic view, the episcopate continues the apostolic ministry (*LG* 20–21). The episcopal ministry is one of the most concrete ways in which the apostolicity of the church finds expression.

See also APOSTLE; APOSTOLICITY OF THE CHURCH; APOSTOLIC SUCCESSION; DEACON; MINISTRY IN THE CHURCH; POPE; PRIEST.

Bibliography
Betrams, Williams. *The Papacy, the Episcopacy, and Collegiality.* Westminster, Md.: Newman, 1964.
Brown, Raymond E. *Priest and Bishop: Biblical Reflections.* New York: Paulist, 1970.
Moore, Peter, ed. *Bishops, but What Kind? Reflections on Episcopacy.* London: SPCK, 1982.
Swidler, Leonard, ed. *Bishops and People.* Philadelphia: Westminster, 1970.

WERNER LÖSER

Body of Christ. "Body of Christ" is one of the most commonly used descriptions of the church. Together with the terms "people of God" and "temple of the Holy Spirit," it asserts the origin of the church in the triune God.

(1) *Biblical Background.* The concept of body of Christ is attested in the letters of Paul; the exegetes disagree on where Paul found it and how he changed it. Influences from other religions need not be excluded, provided they are critically evaluated. The concept of body of Christ is found in a developed form in Ephesians and Colossians, where the relation between the church as body and Jesus Christ as its head is the focus of attention (see Eph 1:22ff.; 4:12, 16; 5:23–30; Col 1:18–24; 2:19). Head and body belong together: as the head is one, so the body with its global dimensions is one. In the theology of the body of Christ as found in Romans and 1 Corinthians, which are earlier, Paul is thinking not of the universal church but of the individual community. In such a community the faithful are linked to one another like the members of a body (Romans 12; 1 Cor 12:12ff.). They place their spiritual gifts at the service of the entire community.

(2) *History of Theology.* Throughout the entire history of theology, body of Christ has been a constant image for the church, but the emphases have differed at different times. From the Middle Ages on, the stress was on the connection between the church as the "true" body of Christ and the Eucharist as the "mystical" body of Christ. Then, in the nineteenth century, the adjectives were interchanged: emphasis on the Real Presence caused "true" or "real" to be predicated of the eucharistic body of the Lord, while "mystical" was predicated of the church as the "mysterious organism of divine grace," which was identified with the Roman Catholic Church.

(3) *Church Teaching.* Although the idea of the church as body of Christ played no role at Vatican I, it became absolutely central in the first half of the twentieth century (Pius XII, *Mystici corporis* [1943]; *Humani generis* [1950]). Vatican II took over the idea with considerable modifications (*LG* 7); it is bunched together with the other images of the church, and the unqualified identification with the Roman Catholic Church is abandoned (see *LG* 8).

(4) *Ecumenical Perspectives.* In Evangelical theology the concept of body of Christ as applied to the church is quite customary. In developing the concept, this theology emphasizes the inalienable difference between the church and Jesus Christ, its head and Lord. The church is always a recipient; never does it collaborate with and under him. The body of Christ is manifested where the gospel of God is preached in its purity and the sacraments are administered in accordance with the gospel (CA 7). Beyond this, the body of Christ is not at our disposal.

(5) *Systematic Reflections.* The one body of Christ has a threefold form. The first and original is Jesus Christ himself in his historical body in which "he bore our sins on the wood of the cross" (1 Pt 2:24). He has bequeathed us his body in the form of his eucharistic flesh and blood, so that we might be "assimilated" to him and so be built up ever anew into the body of Christ that is the church. Seen in this light, an ecclesiology based on the concept of the body of Christ is the center of a eucharistic understanding of the church as "communion."

See also CHURCH; EUCHARIST; PEOPLE OF GOD.

Bibliography
Best, Ernest. *One Body in Christ.* London: SPCK, 1955.
Cerfaux, Lucien. *Christ in the Theology of Saint Paul.* New York: Herder and Herder, 1959.
———. *The Church in the Theology of Saint Paul.* New York: Herder and Herder, 1959.
Schnackenburg, Rudolf. *The Church in the New Testament.* New York: Herder and Herder, 1965.

WERNER LÖSER

Cc

Canon. The term *canon* (Greek: *kánon* = guiding rule, standard, criterion) denotes the collection of those writings that are normative for the Christian faith as Scripture. Books whose membership in the canon was never contested are called protocanonical books or Homologumena. If their membership was put into question at certain times or in certain areas, one speaks of deuterocanonical writings or Antilegomena (in Protestant linguistic usage they are also called the Apocrypha; in Catholic terminology this word marks the early Christian writings that did not come from the apostles; Protestants speak here of the Pseudepigrapha).

(1) *Biblical Background.* Ancient Israel had already had the experience that there is a written word of God that is valid and effective in the present (Neh 8:1–12; 2 Mc 2:13f.; 8:23). The early Christian community acknowledged such writings as being valid for itself (Acts 1:16; 17:2, 11; 18:28) and as God's word (Gal 3:8). To those books that were later called the Old Testament, whose authority was unquestioned, were joined the writings of what is today called the New Testament. This occurred because the church recognized that these writings, which arose from specific occasions, pass on the words of Jesus or interpret them with apostolic authority.

(2) *History of Theology.* The chronology of the formation of the canon — the term used since the fourth century (Council of Laodicea) — has not been fully clarified in detail (see outline). The reason for the collection arose from the necessity to complete the Jewish Scripture through the tradition of the events concerning Jesus, a tradition that was first of all transmitted orally, then taken down in writing. At the same time, it was necessary to protect this tradition against attempts at correction (Marcion, Montanists, Apocrypha). The criteria for the reception of a writing into the canon are *apostolicity* (origin from the apostles or their disciples), *liturgical use* (indication of its existential meaning), and *ecclesial reception* (correspondence to the rule of faith [*kánon tès písteos*], i.e., to the early Christian creeds).

(3) *Church Teaching.* In reaction to the Reformers, and taking over the tradition (Council of Florence [DS 1334f.]), the Council of Trent (DS 1501–5) gave the final magisterial definition of the canon.

(4) *Ecumenical Perspectives.* Basically, all Christian churches know and acknowledge the binding character of the canon. There are differences concerning the extent of the canon, but these are not significant enough to divide the churches. After a long period of fluctuation (partly because of the Protestant influence: Cyril Lucaris and Russian theology of the nineteenth century) regarding the canonicity of the deuterocanonical books, the Orthodox churches today

50

OUTLINE OF THE ORIGIN OF THE BIBLICAL CANON

The dating of the individual events is partly a matter of conjecture. The history of the canon is still quite obscure.

Old Testament

Time	Event
B.C.E. 13th/ 12th cents.	Origin of the oldest literary documents that were received into the canon.
8th cent.	First collections of prophetic writings.
5th cent.	Conclusion of the Pentateuch.
3rd cent.	Conclusion of the Prophetic Books.
250–150	Origin of the Septuagint (LXX): it becomes the OT of early Christianity.
mid–1st cent.	Dn and Wis, the most recent writings of the canon, are composed.
ca. 130	Sir, preface: arrangement of the canon in Law — Prophets — other books.
C.E. 1st cent.	Flavius Josephus makes up a list of 22 books (= protocanonical writings).
90	Synod of Jamnia/Jabneh(?): Hebrew canon (without the deuterocanonical books; the 12 Minor Prophets = 1 book).
4th cent.	The Christian church generally also acknowledges the deuterocanonical books.
1442	The Council of Florence defines the OT canon.
1546	Definitive official definition of the canon at the Council of Trent.

To the deuterocanonical books belong: Tb, Jdt, Bar, Wis, Sir, 1 and 2 Mc, the Greek sections of Dn and Est.

New Testament

C.E.	Event
after 33	Q sayings (inferable from Mt and Lk).
ca. 50–ca. 110	Origin of the writings of the NT.
around 110	2 Pt 3:15: a collection of Pauline letters exists.
around 140	Marcion acknowledges only Lk and 10 Pauline (reedited) letters; the OT is rejected.
2nd half 2nd cent.	Muratorian canon: all NT writings except for Heb, Jas, 1 and 2 Pt, 3 Jn, with other writings instead.
367	Athanasius, 39th Easter letter: all the writings of the modern canon are listed.
393, 397, 419	African synods take over the listing of Athanasius.
405	Pope Innocent I takes over the listing of Athanasius.
1442	Council of Florence: all the books of the canon are acknowledged.
1546	Council of Trent: definitive official definition of the canon.

To the deuterocanonical books belong: Heb, Jas, 2 Pt, 2 and 3 Jn, Jude, Rv.

CANON OF THE OLD TESTAMENT

Hebrew description	Hebrew Bible	Septuagint	Luther Bible	Ecumenical translation
TORAH		Historical books	Historical books	The 5 books of Moses
	Gn	Gn	1st–5th Book	Gn
	Ex	Ex	of Moses	Ex
	Lv	Lv		Lv
	Nm	Nm		Nm
	Dt	Dt		Dt
NEBIIM	Early prophets			The books of the history of the people of God
	Jos	Jos	Jos	Jos
	Jgs	Jgs	Jgs	Jgs
		Ru	Ru	Ru
	1–2 Sm	{ 1–4 Kgs	1–2 Sm	1–2 Sm
	1–2 Kgs		1–2 Kgs	1–2 Kgs
	Later prophets			
	Is	1–2 Chr	1–2 Chr	1–2 Chr
	Jer	Ezr	Ezr	Ezr
	Ez	Neh	Neh	Neh
	Book of			
	12 prophets	Est	Est	Tb
	(Hos–Mal)	Jdt		Jdt
		Tb		Est
		1–4 Mc		1–2 Mc
KETUBIM		Instructional books	Instructional books	Wisdom books and Psalms
	Ps			
	Jb		Jb	Jb
	Prv	Ps	Ps	Ps
	Ruth	Odes		
	Song(Sg)			
	Eccl	Prv	Prv	Prv
		Eccl	Eccl (Preacher)	Eccl
	Lam	Song(Sg)	Song(Sg)	Song(Sg)
	Est			
		Jb		
	Dn			
		Wis		Wis
	Ezr	Sir		Sir
	Neh			
	1–2 Chr	Ps of Sol		
			Is	Is
			Jer + Lam	Jer + Lam
				Bar
			Ez	Ez
			Dn	Dn
		Book of the	Book of the	Book of the
		12 Prophets	12 Prophets	12 Prophets
		(Hos–Mal)	(Hos–Mal)	(Hos–Mal)
			Apocrypha	
		Is	Jdt	
		Jer	Wis	
		Bar	Tb	
		Lam		
			Sir	
		Epis Jer	Bar	
		Ez	1–2 Mc	
		Sus	and smaller	
		Dn	Greek sections	
		Bel		

THEOLOGICAL EXPLANATION OF THE FORMATION
OF THE CANON

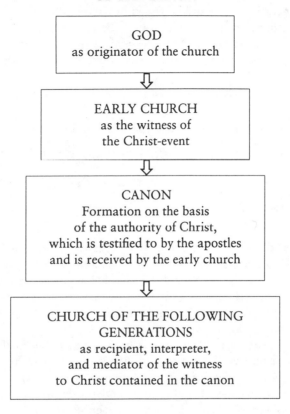

consider all the books as having the same rank. A definitive authoritative demarcation has never been undertaken. In Protestantism the deuterocanonical books are not usually fully acknowledged as Holy Scripture. Luther himself for a period of time considered James as noncanonical.

(5) *Systematic Reflections.* In the theological and spiritual sense, the authority of the canon is based on the fact that all the writings belonging to it — and only these — are regarded as inspired. In a material sense, it is founded on the fact that in them — and only in them — the authority of Christ, which is based on God's authority, can be historically grasped through the apostolic witness. The ground for the binding character of the canon is, thus, neither the ecclesial magisterium (which then would be the supreme norm for faith instead of the Bible) nor an inner-biblical "core of Scripture" (which as such would then itself have to be grounded) but rather the authority of Christ that the early church since Easter experienced as divine authority. Through the process of the formation of the canon in the early church, the Bible becomes the book of the church, which thereby has made an infallible and irreversible de-

cision. To justify this one can state with K. Rahner that the early church as a church of the witnesses of the Easter-event has a norm-giving significance for all further generations. Its faith is passed on historically in Scripture whereby it becomes the normative objectification of the faith of the early church. Inasmuch as the church witnesses to and recognizes this norm, the church defines the canon. The canon then becomes the supreme norm of faith for the whole postapostolic church.

See also HERMENEUTICS; INERRANCY; INSPIRATION; SCRIPTURE.

Bibliography
Barr, James. *Holy Scripture: Canon, Authority, and Criticism.* Philadelphia: Westminster, 1983.
Campenhausen, Hans von. *The Formation of the Christian Bible.* Philadelphia: Fortress, 1972.
Sanders, James. *Canon and Community: A Guide to Canonical Criticism.* Philadelphia: Fortress, 1984.

WOLFGANG BEINERT

Catholicity of the Church.

Catholicity is an essential attribute of the church. "Catholic," however, also serves as a specific confessional designation of the "Roman" Church that is united under the pope. Finally, and in a broader sense, those churches are called "Catholic" that are at one in having an episcopal ministry with apostolic succession and attaching importance to the sacramental mode of communicating salvation.

(1) *Biblical Background.* The term *catholic* is not found in the New Testament, but the reality is. It finds its strongest expression in Ephesians, which speaks of the global dimensions of the church as the body of Christ to which Jews and Gentiles belong. In Luke, Acts, and the Pastoral Letters there is a great deal about ecclesiastical ministries and other "catholic" institutions. This "early catholic" theology of the church has at times (e.g., E. Käsemann) been criticized in light of the Pauline doctrine of justification.

(2) *History of Theology.* Ignatius of Antioch inferred the catholicity of the church from Christ, "for, where Jesus Christ is, the Catholic Church also is" (*Smyrn.* 8.2). In the Nicene-Constantinopolitan Creed catholicity is listed among the essential attributes of the church. The entire history of theology has wrestled with the meaning of the term *catholic.* It took on a special character in the various churches once they became aware of their limitations, which were a consequence of the divisions of the church.

(3) *Church Teaching.* The Roman Catholic Church gained a new awareness of its catholicity at Vatican II (*LG* 8, 13; see *AG* 4; *UR* 4, 17). The catholicity shows itself in the fact that all nations are called to join the people of God and that they can contribute all their talents and abilities, insofar as these are good. The catholicity of the church is also proved by the fact that all human beings belong to the church, even if in different ways (see *LG* 14–16: Catholics, other Christians, all human beings called to salvation).

(4) *Ecumenical Perspectives.* Once "Catholic" became a confessional designation of the Roman Church, many Evangelical churches replaced the term *catholic* with *universal.* Today the discussion of the meaning of catholicity has gained in importance in the ecumenical movement. In 1970 the World Council of Churches and Roman Catholic Joint Theological Commission produced a study document entitled *Catholicity and Apostolicity.*

(5) *Systematic Reflections.* At the end of the second millennium of its history the church has rapidly, and decisively, taken on the characteristics of a worldwide church. The particular churches project their own distinctive image. Thus the catholicity of the church can be experienced in a new way.

See also CHURCH; LOCAL CHURCH; PROFESSION OF FAITH.

Bibliography

Catholicity and Apostolicity. Special issue of *One in Christ* 6, no. 3 (1970). Report of the World Council of Churches and Roman Catholic Joint Theological Commission.

Dulles, Avery. *The Catholicity of the Church.* Oxford: Oxford University Press, 1985.

———. *The Reshaping of Catholicism: Current Challenges in the Theology of Church.* San Francisco: Harper and Row, 1988.

Lubac, Henri de. *Catholicism: A Study of Dogma in Relation to the Corporate Destiny of Mankind.* New York: Longman, 1950.

Vorgrimler, Herbert. *One, Holy, Catholic and Apostolic.* London: Sheed and Ward, 1968.

WERNER LÖSER

Causality. The term *causality,* or *causation,* designates the relationship between an effecting principle and that which it effects. The concept results from general awareness that the phenomenon of becoming or changing implies a transition from possibility to reality, from potentiality to actuality, that presupposes the influence of a single or multiple cause. The knowledge based on experience is regarded as obvious: nothing comes to be, nothing takes place or changes, without a cause. Viewed in this way, *cause* and *reason* are related concepts.

(1) *Biblical Background.* Holy Scripture sees God as the Creator, sustainer, and consummator of history and the world, but without drawing upon a philosophy of causes to express this.

(2) *History of Theology.* Anaxagoras, through his analysis of nature, came to realize that matter, of itself, was by no means enough to enable the assumption of self-transcending, constantly higher forms of development; for that, matter depends on an effective force different from itself, namely, "intelligence" (*noûs*). For Plato, this causality was achieved through the ideas, without whose example the demiurge is unable to create. Aristotle distinguished four causes (*aitíai*): two internal ones, matter (*hýle*) and form (*morphé*), along with two external ones, efficacy (*hóthen hè kínesis*) and purpose (*télos*). All beings are internally constituted by matter and form (hence the term HYLOMORPHISM) and require, for their spatio-temporal movement within the realm of being, an efficient and final cause (*Ph.* 1.3–5; *Meta.* 1.2–10; 5.1–4). Thomas Aqui-

nas adopted the Aristotelian doctrine of four causes and spoke of a material, formal, efficient, and final cause (*De princ. naturae; Ph.* 2.5f.; *Meta.* 1.4; 5.1–4). However, he enriches his understanding of causality through concepts like *exemplary cause* (*causa exemplaris*), which is reminiscent of the way Platonic ideas function as models, and *instrumental cause* (*causa instrumentalis*), which designates the instrumental use of one cause by another, higher cause. As a matter of supreme self-evidence, he equates God with the first cause of all beings (*STh* 1, q. 44, a. 1). God is the "absolute being who exists in and through himself [*ipsum esse per se subsistens*]," and who causes God's creatures as "beings through participation [*entes per participationem*]" (*STh* 1, q. 44, a. 1). The Creator is the total and universal cause of all creatures; for the Creator, the triune God, omnipotence serves as efficient cause (*STh* 1, q. 45, a. 6f.), wisdom as exemplary cause (*STh* 1, q. 44, a. 3), and goodness as final cause, since it aims at guiding creatures to their perfection (*STh* 1, q. 44, a. 4). In addition, God also permits secondary and particular causes, such as, for example, the reproductive act, which therefore deserves the name *procreation* (*procreatio*) (*STh* 1, q. 103, a. 3). Finally, God's providence is also to be understood as causality (*STh* 1, q. 22, a. 2).

(3) *Church Teaching.* Doctrinal office has made repeated use of the Thomist teaching on causality, probably most clearly at the Council of Trent: "The causes of justification are: The final cause: the glory of God and Christ as well as eternal life. The efficient cause: merciful God ... The meritorious cause, however, being his beloved, only begotten Son ... The instrumental cause is the sacrament of baptism" (DS 1529). Divine causality is also invoked, of course, for creation itself (DS 3326).

(4) *Ecumenical Perspectives.* Protestant dogmatics generally shows an aversion to using causal concepts.

(5) *Systematic Reflections.* Even at the linguistic level, present-day theology must take account of how the concept of causality has changed in modern times or of criticisms made of it. Since the seventeenth century, our Western WORLDVIEW has become strongly mechanized. In this context, talk of material, formal, and final causes was no longer meaningful. The notion of "efficient cause" — which in fact remained and was described as causality and deterministically interpreted — was soon itself dislodged by the concept of "function," which refers to the directional relationship of interdependency between two processes of change. In place of causality, the category of "law" then became central and, indeed, usually in the sense of interrelational laws according to which a whole system of experimentally disclosable, interactive effects is to be regarded as the change-generating factor. The latest nuclear physics, as influenced by quantum mechanics, recognizes that, along with determined processes, there are also undetermined processes — at least at the microphysical level — that cannot be described with strict precision, so that nothing more than a high-percentage probability calculation is possible regarding them. This sort of perspective on matter opens up new possibilities for dialogue with a

theology of creation that is prepared to recognize an interplay of necessary and contingent processes.

See also CONTINGENCY; CREATION: THEOLOGY OF.

Bibliography
Heidegger, Martin. *The Principle of Reason.* Bloomington: Indiana University Press, 1991.
Owens, David. *Causes and Coincidences.* New York: Cambridge University Press, 1992.
Sosa, Ernst, and Michael Tooley. *Causation.* New York: Oxford University Press, 1993.

ALEXANDRE GANOCZY

Celibacy. Celibacy means the unmarried state as the way of life proper to priests.

(1) *Biblical Background.* A biblical basis can be shown for the evangelical counsels of poverty, abstinence from marriage, and obedience (see the scriptural references in *PC* 12–14), but only an indirect basis can be given for celibacy as the way of life of ordained ministers. According to the Pastoral Letters, ministers are expected to lead an exemplary life and to have been married only once (1 Tm 3:12; Ti 1:6).

(2) *History of Theology.* The first legislative requirements regarding celibacy came at the beginning of the fourth century. In the West, the Synod of Elvira (can. 306) forbade bishops, priests, and deacons to have marital intercourse with their wives (can. 33 [DS 119]). In the ensuing period the popes repeatedly emphasized this regulation, and on an increasingly wider scale; in the process it met with considerable opposition in some places. In the eleventh century, Gregory VII forbade the participation of married priests in liturgical activities. In 1139, Innocent II declared episcopal, priestly, and diaconal ordination to be diriment impediments to marriage. Despite these regulations the discipline of celibacy remained in a highly unsatisfactory state even in the high and late Middle Ages. The reform decrees of the Council of Trent, one of which was the introduction of the requirement of form for a valid marriage, contributed to an improved observance of the obligation of celibacy. A wave of resistance to the law of celibacy arose in the period of the Enlightenment. Despite all difficulties, the Latin Church has held unwaveringly to its regulations. On many continents and in many cultures it is admittedly still difficult to make priestly celibacy a plausible value. In many countries celibacy is probably one of the reasons for the paucity of candidates for the priesthood.

(3) *Church Teaching.* Despite these rather major problems, Vatican II reaffirmed the unmarried state as the way of life for the priests of the Latin Church. In *PO* 15–17 it speaks of the three evangelical counsels insofar as these should mold the spiritual life of priests. Number 16 begins by describing the inner harmony between priestly ministry and the celibate way of life. This harmony shows the appropriateness, though not the necessity, of the customary rule in the Latin Church. The council then expressly adds that in the future the Roman Catholic Church will continue to uphold the law of celibacy for its priests.

The new Code of Canon Law reflects this decision: "Clerics are obliged to observe perfect and perpetual continence for the sake of the kingdom of heaven and therefore are obliged to observe celibacy, which is a special gift of God, by which sacred ministers can adhere more easily to Christ with an undivided heart and can more freely dedicate themselves to the service of God and humankind" (can. 277).

(4) *Ecumenical Perspectives.* The Orthodox churches have retained the rule of celibacy only for their bishops; the churches of the Reformation have abolished it for their ministers.

(5) *Systematic Reflections.* While celibacy is often experienced as a form of loneliness, even here it can become a way of following Jesus, who in his own way experienced loneliness. When the celibate way of life is adopted as a call, the loneliness, should God allow it, that is shared with Jesus can become a shared fruitfulness as well.

See also DISCIPLESHIP, CHRISTIAN; PRIEST; SACRAMENT OF ORDERS.

Bibliography
Bassett, William, and Peter Huizing, eds. *Celibacy in the Church.* Vol. 78 of *Concilium.* New York: Herder and Herder, 1972.
Schillebeeckx, Edward. *Celibacy.* New York: Sheed and Ward, 1968.
Vogels, Heinz-Jürgen. *Celibacy: Gift or Law? A Critical Investigation.* Tunbridge Wells, England: Burns and Oates, 1992.

WERNER LÖSER

Certitude concerning Salvation.

Certitude concerning salvation refers to the unshakable conviction a person has regarding his or her own salvation.

(1) *Biblical Background.* In Scripture there is an indicative certitude concerning salvation that is the consequence of fidelity to the love of God (Rom 5:1–11; 8:31–39; 1 Jn 3:14, 19–24), but there are also threats to salvation brought about by human weakness (Phil 2:12f.). Thus God's fidelity is not unrelated to exhortations regarding human fidelity to God (1 Cor 10:12f.).

(2) *History of Theology.* In Augustine, certitude concerning salvation coincides with a certitude about predestination: no one predestined to be saved will be lost (*De corr. et grat.* 7.14). Thomas Aquinas rejects the idea of certitude concerning grace, but allows a presumption of grace based on signs (the joy in God, awareness of being guiltless [*STh* 1–2, q. 112, a. 5]). He knows however that in trusting God the believer hopes for salvation with absolute certainty (*STh* 1–2, q. 18, a. 4).

(3) *Church Teaching.* The position of Trent regarding certitude of salvation was developed in opposition to M. Luther and J. Calvin: no one can know with the certainty of faith that cannot be subject to error that he or she has obtained the grace of God (DS 1534). In opposition to Calvin it was affirmed that no one can be certain about whether he or she is predestined to be saved or has certainly been granted the gift of final perseverance (DS 1565f.).

(4) *Ecumenical Perspectives.* On the basis of his interpretation of Paul's mes-

sage of justification, Luther considers certitude concerning salvation to be the same thing as faith (*WA* 18:783). However, he distinguishes certitude (*certitudo*) from assurance about salvation (*securitas*): the latter is excluded because of the precariousness of faith. The doctrine of predestination leads Calvin to accept an absolute certitude concerning salvation. Since God's salvific will always remains unchanged, those predestined possess infallibly the gift of final perseverance (*perseverantia*) (CF 36.260f., 275; OS 4.388, 393). Today the various churches are no longer divided over this question. The Thomistic certitude of hope takes into account the Reformed claim concerning certitude of faith. The Reformed teaching on the precariousness of faith implies the Catholic claim that the salvific event should make allowance for human weaknesses.

(5) *Systematic Reflections.* Certitude concerning salvation, an unshakable conviction about it, is intrinsically connected with the two major problems of justification (righteousness) and predestination. Our answer to the question of how our salvific communion with God, established by justification, will reach completion must take into account God's side and humankind's side. From the side of God, there is an unconditional certitude concerning salvation because God remains absolutely faithful to a love for humankind that wills the salvation of every individual human being. From the side of individual human beings, however, there is only a conditional certitude of salvation because individual faith, which is based on each person's humanly conditioned weakness, is continually subject to the danger of falling away from God. This unavoidable tension during life on earth between unconditional certitude given by God and the fragility of salvation due to the human condition must be taken into account and accepted. The overcoming of this tension takes place by the gift of the double power of faith, that is, the unconditional trust and unshakable hope that the power of God's love is victorious in one's own life, and thus the salvific community of those united with God remains in the long run until it reaches fulfillment. It is possible to ground certitude of salvation in *predestination* only when we begin with the original Pauline view in which predestination implies God's universal salvific plan: salvation is mediated absolutely by Jesus Christ and relatively by the church. Faith and love are our personal criteria of salvation. In response to the question of the certitude of salvation, this means: the individual Christian has certitude of salvation primarily when he or she fully confides and hopes in the salvific work of Jesus Christ. At a second level, a Christian has certitude of salvation when that person allows his or her salvation to correspond to the community of the church in word and sacrament. At a third level, a Christian has certitude of salvation by personally experiencing the fact that perseverance in faith and in loving action is given as a gift.

See also FAITH; JUSTIFICATION; PREDESTINATION.

Bibliography
Barnes, Robin Bruce. "The Assurance of Salvation in Luther." *LQ* 3 (1989) 209–22.
Beck, Nestor. *The Doctrine of Faith: A Study of the Augsburg Confession and Contemporary Ecumenical Documents.* St. Louis: Concordia, 1987.

Küng, Hans. *Justification: The Doctrine of Karl Barth and a Catholic Reflection; with a Letter by Karl Barth*. New York: Nelson, 1964.
Vander Schaaf, Mark E. "Predestination and Certainty of Salvation in Augustine and Calvin." *RR* 30 (1976) 1–8.

                                                                                       GEORG KRAUS

Chance. The term *chance* refers to an event or a fact that appears to lack any causally or teleologically definable necessity, or actually is lacking in such. The Greeks called it *týche, autómaton;* and the Romans, *contingens, accidens, casus;* the French word *hasard* stems from the Arabic *azzahar* (dice cube). Chance represents something that is not deducible from any prior state of affairs and can be related to any ongoing process only as something excepted; it can, however, serve as the impetus to a new series of events.

(1) *Biblical Background.* The Bible traces many surprising, unexpected happenings directly back to the sovereign freedom of God as the Creator, governor, savior, and perfecter of humanity and history. God intervenes in the course of things in order to meet the demands of GOD'S CARE regarding both the people and particular individuals (see Wis 8:1; Mt 10:29f.; 1 Pt 5:7); this is never conceived, however, as blind chance, but as the realization of God's eternal redemptive plan (see Rom 8:28), which no human can work out.

(2) *History of Theology.* The Fathers were fond of contrasting God's power over history with pagan "fate" (*fatum*) and its associated fatalism or belief in destiny, and they thereby contributed — often while making use of Stoic concepts — to the development of the Christian doctrine of providence. In Thomas Aquinas's view, there can be neither chance nor destiny for God (*STh* 1, q. 22, a. 2); such phenomena present themselves solely to the finite human mind, whereas God always acts in a goal-pursuing way (*STh* 1, q. 22, a. 1).

(3) *Church Teaching.* Doctrinal office has condemned fatalistic astrology (DS 459f.) and also linked, along with the inherent lawfulness of nature, the free actions of humans to the free providence and world-governance of the Creator who supports them (see. DS 3003, 3025).

(4) *Ecumenical Perspectives.* Reformation theology tends to put emphasis on the absolute unmeritedness of divine acts of grace.

(5) *Systematic Reflections.* Present-day theology of creation has to take a position regarding natural-scientific theories of chance. Whereas B. Spinoza still stressed the merely apparent nature of chance, attributing it to a not yet adequate knowledge of the conditions under which the world-process began (see *Ethica* 1, prop. 33.1), J. Monod has given expression to today's widespread — especially in neo-Darwinian circles — doctrine of evolution, according to which all progress depends upon an interplay between "chance and necessity." All genuine novelty is held to arise out of completely improbable occurrences; humanity itself does not owe its arising to any goal-directed striving inherent in living matter; and no serious predictions can be made about the future conditions of living things. Humanity can best be understood as a "wanderer at

the edge of the universe." While J. Monod's theory is inclined, even with consciously atheistic intent, to posit chance as absolute, there are more possibilities of dialogue, for a biblically based dogmatics, with representatives of modern physics, where, alongside of determined processes, a certain measure of undetermined ones are recognized to which the scientist can do justice only through statistical probability calculations. This measure of CONTINGENCY, however, is conceived in such a way as to leave sufficient room for irreducible novelty and creative subjectivity, and by no means excludes even conceiving God in analogy to a reality thus understood. In particular, comparison between an infinitely creative God and a finitely "creative" humanity, not least relevantly from the viewpoint of play, then makes sense.

See also CREATION: BELIEF IN, AND NATURAL SCIENCE; EVOLUTION; PROVIDENCE.

Bibliography
Monod, Jacques. *Chance and Necessity: An Essay on the Natural Philosophy of Modern Biology.* New York: Vintage, 1971.
———. *The Necessity of Being.* London: Elek, 1973.

ALEXANDRE GANOCZY

Charismatic Renewal. In the traditional Christian churches the aim of the charismatic renewal is to reactivate the Pentecostal gifts of the Spirit (charisms) in fellowship, prayer, the gifts of tongues and prophecy, witness, and the gift of healing.

(1) *Biblical Background.* The biblical basis for the charismatic renewal is the accounts of the Jerusalem community in the Acts of the Apostles and Paul's information on the situation in the community at Corinth (1 Corinthians 12–14).

(2) *History of Theology.* The contemporary movement goes back to the "Pentecostal outbreak" in the United States toward the end of the nineteenth century; this movement was spread by Baptist and Methodist preachers (from 1905 on, in Europe as well). The focus here was on personal election, which is experienced in "baptism in the Spirit" (a description based on Mk 1:8; Jn 1:33) but is not uniformly interpreted. It finds expression in charisms and, as a grace bestowed by the third divine person, is in the first place simply a gift to the individuals concerned. Baptism in water is presupposed, but this, as commonly explained, gives only a foundation to which full purity of heart and the fullness of the Holy Spirit are not added until "baptism in the Spirit." The concentration of the movement on the original Pentecostal experience soon led to departures from the ecclesial communities in which it had started, and the formation of separate "Pentecostal churches." After World War II, these churches spread throughout the world as an independent branch of Reformed Protestantism. Since they have no common organization or unified leadership, they display extensive differences among themselves, but are united not only by their focus on the Pentecostal experience but also by their participation in the tri-

ennial World Pentecostal Conference (the fourteenth took place in Zurich in 1985). From about 1950 on, there was a new wave of Pentecostal awakening in the mainline churches, but this did not lead to new break offs. In the wake of Vatican II, the movement spread to Catholic circles in the United States and in a short time won adherents throughout the Catholic world. Since 1976, this group movement, which found a place alongside other efforts at renewal, has been called "the charismatic communal renewal." Thus, while retaining traditional elements of the Pentecostal movement, it has sought to be broader and deeper; it also makes a claim that has yet to be realized.

(3) *Church Teaching.* Ever since the rejection of the errors of Joachim of Fiore (DS 803–8) and the movements of the various Spirituals with their Franciscan ethos (see DS 866), the magisterium has been reserved toward charismatic outbreaks in various contexts and has rejected them (Wycliffe, Hus, Enthusiasts, and Anabaptists). The modern movement, however, is regarded with a certain degree of benevolence by the authorities; there has as yet been no real magisterial statement on the subject. (See "Pentecostal–Roman Catholic Conversation," in H. Meyer and L. Vischer, eds., *Growth in Agreement: Reports and Agreed Statements of Ecumenical Conversations at a World Level,* Ecumenical Documents 2 [New York: Paulist, 1984].)

(4) *Ecumenical Perspectives.* The charismatic renewal provides one of the few spiritual and, to some extent, theological settings in which Christians regularly meet for prayer and dialogue across the lines of the various confessions and traditions. The modern charismatic renewal was originally one of those revival movements, focused on Christian perfection, that have repeatedly surfaced in the history of the church and, especially since Pietism (Jansenism), have sought to promote a practical Christianity that admits of no compromise. This aim is accompanied by reservations with regard to scientific theology, which is usually replaced by a strict biblical fundamentalism and a moral rigorism. Both of these have led in practice to an almost endless multiplication of groups and to a tendency to reject the ecumenical movement. Only since 1960 has a cautious acceptance of official ecumenism been observable; the disregard for confessional boundaries that is proper to the charismatic renewal appears possible chiefly when such differences are ignored and less once these differences have been adverted to.

(5) *Systematic Reflections.* The tendencies of the charismatic renewal run counter to the traditional Catholic understanding of faith and ministry. The chief obstacle to acceptance of the charismatic renewal is the latter's different understanding of the church. The Pentecostal movement seems to lack both a positive orientation to the church as institution and a consciously developed concept of the church. Conversely, the traditional Christian churches have preserved little sensitivity to the living action of the Spirit and its gifts, unless these are given fixed institutional form (preaching, sacraments, respect for church order, religious life). The charismatic renewal starts at the bottom, in the communities, and in this respect is in agreement with the ecclesial base communities

movement, which likewise seeks to renew the church from below. The universal church as people of God and a unity that transcends communities is not taken into consideration, any more than is church government and its function; as a result, the charismatic renewal looks first of all to individuals and seems, in this tendency, to promote a privatization of Christianity. In keeping with this, there is an enthusiastic type of piety (ecstasy and reception of direct inspiration from the Holy Spirit). This approach may indeed be an answer to the interior religious needs of human beings, to which the mainline churches pay too little heed, but it also calls government and institution into question. The danger of subjectivistic interiority is accompanied by an inclination to activism in the world, by which the gifts of the Spirit are to prove themselves. This inclination, however, can also be the starting point for a conscious and shared responsibility for the world, thus taking charismatics beyond an exclusively private quest for and experience of salvation. The precise motivation still needs to be clarified. The emphasis on practice and experience can further hinder reconciliation between the charismatic renewal and the traditional Christian churches in which faith is articulated not only in preaching but also in theological reflection that uses the intellectual tools provided by the age. The attitude of the charismatic renewal to theological reflection appears problematic, even though some representatives of the renewal seek to find in it an opportunity for the renewal of theology as well. The claim that the charismatic renewal can deepen Christian faith and its outward manifestations is to be taken seriously; the movement is to be judged by this intention.

See also CHARISM/CHARISMS.

Bibliography

Hollenweger, Walter J. *The Pentecostals: The Charismatic Movement in the Churches.* Minneapolis: Augsburg, 1972.

McDonnell, Kilian. *Charismatic Renewal and Churches.* New York: Seabury, 1976.

———. *The Charismatic Renewal and Ecumenism.* New York: Paulist, 1978.

———, ed. *Presence, Power, and Praise: Documents on the Charismatic Renewal.* 3 vols. Collegeville, Minn.: Liturgical Press, 1980.

Mühlen, Heribert. *A Charismatic Theology: Initiation in the Spirit.* New York: Paulist, 1978.

Quebedaux, Richard. *The New Charismatics II.* San Francisco: Harper and Row, 1983.

Sullivan, Francis. *Charisms and Charismatic Renewal: A Biblical and Theological Study.* Ann Arbor: Servant, 1982.

KARL HEINZ NEUFELD

Charism/Charisms. Charism means, first of all, grace; then (in the plural) the capabilities that grace brings with it, as well as the bestowal of these primarily for the good of the believing community, and in a special way the gifts of the Holy Spirit.

(1) *Biblical Background.* In Paul (Romans: six times; 1 Corinthians: seven times) a charism is an effect of grace (Greek: *charis*) in the individual graced person or in the graced community, but the term also brings out the gift-

character of grace (grace as gracious *gift*). In the Pastoral Letters charism already refers to offices (which are gifts of grace) that have been transmitted.

(2) *History of Theology.* Despite the importance of the charisms for the doctrine of office and ministry in the church, they came to be regarded with reserve at a quite early date because they were looked upon as exceptions proper to the period when the church was being established or as special vocations. Groups that appealed to such gifts (e.g., Montanists; Baptists in the Reformation period) were regarded as enthusiasts and were attacked. In these cases, however, the issue was church order rather than doctrine. When special vocations could be integrated into, for example, the variety of religious life, they were respected and to some extent promoted by the church as manifestations of piety. As a result, they hardly provided a subject for dogmatic theology but were dealt with in practical or spiritual theology. Only recently has this attitude changed.

(3) *Church Teaching.* Given this situation, it is not surprising that there are no magisterial pronouncements specifically dealing with the charisms. In their general orientation, the teaching authorities have remained committed to the approach that Paul sketched out in 1 Corinthians 12–14 and that aims at properly ordering the charisms for the building up of the community; they seek, that is, to avert all disorder and may, to this end, even require one to renounce the exercise of a charism. In the last hundred years, the question of the charisms became topical once again by way of the idea of the indwelling of the Holy Spirit: Leo XIII (DS 3328–31) made the transition to this personalist view of grace, which Pius XII picked up and developed in 1943 (DS 3807f., 3814–20). Vatican II tries to connect the individual and the ecclesial charisms, while also formulating the distinction between common and special charisms (*LG* 10–12).

(4) *Ecumenical Perspectives.* The personalist conception of the call of grace makes possible a new understanding of the varied forms that Christianity can legitimately take; this new understanding is also of ecumenical importance. Precisely because it is not possible to exclude the working of the Holy Spirit outside the limits of the institutional Catholic Church (ECUMENISM), it is necessary to look for signs of this activity not only in individual Christians but in other communities as well. Such a quest also presupposes an openness to a possible collaboration of charisms for the building up of the church of Jesus Christ. In this building up, the consciousness of the *one* origin of the charisms plays a decisive role, inasmuch as it imposes the task of making clearly and convincingly visible the radical unity of all authentic following of Christ. The question of the extent to which the "charismatic renewal" can be fruitful ecumenically is still open. It can, however, be said that in principle the movement has awakened a new sense of the eschatological dimension of Christian life, thus giving urgency to ecumenical efforts. To that extent, the charisms are signs calling to a constant focus on the coming of the Lord; they militate against any taking up of residence in this world and demand the overcom-

ing of all divisions and separations, which have their ultimate root in the sinfulness of human beings. At the same time, when Christians look to their common Lord and his Second Coming, they are encouraged to ecumenical commitment as an effort to achieve a credible unity amid recognition of the Spirit-given variety in the living of Christianity. From this point of view, the ecumenical movement itself can be conceived and understood as an effect of the charisms.

(5) *Systematic Reflections.* In theological perspective, the charisms are to be understood fundamentally as signs of the activity of the Spirit or of JUSTIFI-CATION effected and incorporated into the people of God/body of Christ. They serve others and are thus directed to the building up of the church; they presuppose baptism and the special role or commission, given by baptism to each individual, to participate in the life of the faith-community with his or her spiritual gifts. The fact that among these gifts, all of which come from God, the church recognizes some in a special way and by official confirmation turns them into official ministries does not justify a fundamental opposition between office (or ordained ministry) and charism. The controversy that has focused on these last two concepts in recent decades has to a great extent no real basis and rests on a misunderstanding. Paul emphasized the point long ago that as far as the church is concerned all charisms are not of equal importance; with this in mind, he proposed his conception of the ordering of charisms. The idea of order brings with it the question of responsibility and the moral obligation imposed by the charisms. The criterion is always the building up of the church in unity and mutual love, that is, while acknowledging the various charisms at work. Consequently, it is up to individuals to make a responsible judgment on the extent to which they are obliged to use their own charisms and translate them into action. Such a judgment is possible only by means of a process of spiritual discernment that requires an alert conscience and a corresponding formation of conscience. The subject of the charisms must be dealt with today in various theological disciplines, with an eye to practice. Of special interest is experience of the charisms and the possibility of classifying new experiences as charisms by examining their spiritual origin and their significance for the church and the church's task in the world. For, as gifts of the Spirit, the charisms are at the service of the catholic-comprehensive mission of the Spirit-led church. To be distinguished from this is the highly formalized use made of charisms in the history of religions, which empties them of their content; the application of the term can therefore lead to misunderstandings.

See also CHARISMATIC RENEWAL; CHURCH; GRACE; MINISTRY IN THE CHURCH; MONASTICISM/RELIGIOUS LIFE.

Bibliography

Duquoc, Christian, and Casiano Floristan, eds. *Charism in the Church.* Vol. 109 of *Concilium.* New York: Seabury, 1978.

Gelpi, Donald. *Charism and Sacrament: A Theology of Christian Conversion.* New York: Paulist, 1976.

Rahner, Karl. *The Dynamic Element in the Church*. New York: Herder and Herder, 1964.
Sullivan, Francis. *Charisms and Charismatic Renewal: A Biblical and Theological Study*. Ann
    Arbor: Servant, 1982.

KARL HEINZ NEUFELD

Children of God. The fact that we are children of God refers to the inner, personal communion (comparable to the parent-child relationship) that exists between God and humankind and is God's gift of love for our salvation. It is therefore a relationship of love, which God as a person enters into with persons as individuals (including their essentially social condition).

(1) *Biblical Background.* The biblical understanding of being children of God is to be distinguished from mythical ideas in other religions, where stories are told of children literally born of gods. In the Bible, being children of God implies no physical generation by God and no physical divinization, but rather the community and its salvation-history, by which God grants participation in the goods of salvation. The expression "children of God" is peripheral in the Old Testament, while in the New Testament it becomes central. In the Old Testament it undergoes a three-stage development: in the *Pentateuch*, being children of God is regarded from the viewpoint of the election and covenant of the whole people. Thus the people of Israel who are called to be in a covenant are described as God's son (Ex 4:22), that is, fellow members of the same people (Dt 32:19). In three places the king of Israel as representative of the people is given the title Son of God (2 Sm 7:14; Pss 2:7; 89:27f.). The *prophets* develop a universal sense of being children of God, starting with the idea of God as Creator (Is 43:6; Mal 2:10). Or they develop an eschatological understanding of sonship starting with the notion of redemption (Hos 2:1; Jer 3:14). In *wisdom literature* the notion of being children of God is individualized. The individual pious or just person is called a child of God (Wis 2:13, 18; 9:4; Sir 4:10). In the New Testament the social, universal, eschatological, and individual moments are continued but developed in totally new ways. In the Synoptics, being children of God is closely related to Jesus' message of God the Father and God's reign. Thus the Sermon on the Mount (Matthew 5–7) and the story of the Prodigal Son (Lk 15:11–32) emphasize individual communion with God the Father, while the logia and the parables of the kingdom of God give prominence to the social (Mt 5:9, 44f.; 25:34), universal (Mt 5:45; Lk 6:35), and eschatological (Mt 8:11; Lk 20:36) aspects of being children of God. Paul (Galatians 3 and 4; Romans 8 and 9) develops a doctrine of sonship (*hyiothesia*). Sonship for him means we are adopted children. It has a Christocentric character with individual, social, universal, and eschatological consequences. John draws similar conclusions from the notion of being children of God. For him it refers to Christians generally. By rebirth (Jn 3:3–9) or spiritual engenderment (1 John 3–4) the baptized Christian is in the closest communion with God. It is also noteworthy that both the Synoptics and John draw a line between Jesus Christ as Son of God and human beings as children of God. In all

four Gospels, Jesus makes a distinction between *my* Father and *your* Father. John uses two different words: one for the Son (*hyuios*) and another for a child (*teknon*) of God.

(2) *History of Theology.* In the history of dogma the notion of children of God, which was the main way of referring to grace in the New Testament, is of no special significance. In the Scholastic doctrine of grace in particular, it remains completely in the background because grace was regarded almost exclusively as a created entity in human beings: a "thing," which was both abstract and static. In neo-scholasticism, because of the labyrinth of distinctions of created grace, the notion of being children of God — in a living relationship to God — fully disappeared.

(3) *Church Teaching.* Trent officially recognized the biblical thesis in dealing with the Reformers' teaching on justification: a major effect of justification is that we become children of God (DS 1524). Vatican II clearly states: the center of divine grace is that we are children of God (*LG* 9 and 32).

(4) *Ecumenical Perspectives.* The Reformation served to bring out the personal, concrete, and dynamic idea of being children of God as a way of describing the loving relationship between God and humankind that takes place in justification. A greater concentration on this idea of being children of God would enable one to overcome the Catholic-Protestant controversy and to interpret the gift of personal communion with God as the deepest source of personal salvation.

(5) *Systematic Reflections.* Systematic reflection on the biblical testimony leads to many different perspectives (see table, p. 68): (*a*) Basically being children of God is a gift of God as Trinity. Our relationship as children of God is mirrored in the appropriations within the economic TRINITY. In creation the Father gives all human beings their original basis for being God's children. Following the very serious disruption of our relationship with God caused by human guilt, the incarnate Son, Jesus Christ, reestablishes us as children of God by his work of redemption. After the Son's return to the Father, the Spirit grants us final fulfillment as children of God. In other words, the Father made us children of God by creation (Dt 32:5f.; Is 64:7); the Son redeemed the children of God (Jn 1:12; Gal 4:4f.); the Spirit fulfilled — or more exactly, is to fulfill — the children of God (Rom 8:14–16; Gal 4:6). Thus the purpose of every salvific work is to make us children of God and a living community (*koinonía*) with the triune God (Cor 1:9; 2 Cor 13:13; 1 John 3). The motive that is at the basis of this gift is God's love from all eternity for humankind (Eph 1:5; 1 Jn 3:1). (*b*) This loving and totally gratuitous call to become children of God has a whole series of concrete effects. The most important *existential* effects on behalf of individuals are security and freedom. Becoming children of God gives us *security* thanks to God's loving care and mercy. This is regarded as motherly concern in the Old Testament (Is 49:15; 66:13), whereas, in Jesus' outlook, it is God's fatherly (Mt 6:32; Lk 12:7), loving care and mercy, which, according to Lk 15:11–32, goes out to those who are guilty and receives them back

PERSPECTIVES ON BEING CHILDREN OF GOD

(a) BEING CHILDREN OF GOD AS THE EFFECT OF THE TRINITY: THE APPROPRIATIONS		
Father	*Son*	*Spirit*
Creation | Children of God by creation | Original communion of love	Redemption | Redeemed children of God | Renewed communion of love	Fulfillment | Becoming children of God fully | Fully realized communion of love

(b) THE EFFECTS OF BEING CHILDREN OF GOD			
existential	*social*	*ecclesiological*	*eschatological*

– security
– freedom
	– equality of
	   personal dignity
	– universal brother/
	   sisterhood
	– solidarity
		– new life in
		   baptism
		– renewed
		   acceptance:
		   reconciliation
		– love banquet in
		   the Eucharist
			– promise of an
			   inheritance
			– hope of glory

as children. The *freedom* of the children of God is seen formally in the maturity of the adult children, produced by the liberating work of God's incarnate Son. This causes them to conform interiorly to the Spirit of God (Gal 4:1–7; 5:1). Materially speaking, it is seen negatively in their freedom from the slavery of the constraining powers of law, sin, and death (Rom 8:1–11) and positively in their freedom with regard to conscience, the good, and life itself. Thus the Christian as child of God is interiorly free to do the will of the divine Father, to be conformed to the example of his or her brother, Jesus Christ, and to respond to the promptings to love of God's Spirit. Becoming children of God as personal grace also has a *social dimension:* equality of personal dignity, universal brother/sisterhood, and solidarity. As children of God all human beings *are equal in dignity* because they are children of the same Creator (Mal 2:10). Since they are all redeemed children of God in Jesus Christ, all distinctions of race, class, and sex disappear (Gal 3:26, 28; Col 3:11). As children of God in the final fulfillment, all have access to the Father by the unifying power of God's Spirit (Eph 2:18f.). A further social effect of being children of God is *the interior bond of unity with one another as brothers and sisters* (see references to sisters as well as brothers [Rom 16:1; 1 Cor 7:15; Phlm 2; Jas 2:15]). This becomes a characteristic of Christians as children of God (1 Jn 3:10, 16). This love is not restricted to the community of the faithful, because becoming children of God produces a *universal solidarity with all men and women,* and it is visible concretely in love of neighbor (Mt 5:44f.; 25:40; 2 Pt 1:7). Being children of God, which was promised to the people of Israel in the Old Testament, has a new dimension in the church as the new people of God. In it the children of God are called to an intimate community of life based on the unity of the trinitarian God (Eph 4:4–6). The church makes the grace of being children of God visible to the senses, especially in the sacraments. Baptism gives new life to be redeemed and fulfilled children of God. In the sacrament of penance the church renews those whose relationship as children of God has been disrupted by sin. The Eucharist, the communal meal of the children of God with their Father and with one another, actualizes this relationship. Finally, being children of God has *eschatological effects*. It implies the promise of an inheritance and the hope of glory. It thus involves the eschatological tension of the kingdom of God: that is, it is a present, inchoative reality that anticipates a future total realization. As children of God who must become so perfectly, we are beckoned toward the promise of the inheritance of the good things of God, determined in advance by the salvific work of the Son and our brother, Jesus Christ (Rom 8:29; Eph 1:11). On the historical way toward final fulfillment as children of God, the first part of our inheritance of the Spirit of God has been given to us (Eph 1:4). The goal that draws us on is eternal life (Ti 3:7; 1 Jn 2:25). Thus, being children of God on earth, we are determined by the hope of a final completion in a universal community of the love of God (HEAVEN).

See also COVENANT; GRACE; HEAVEN; JUSTIFICATION; KINGDOM OF GOD.

Bibliography
Boff, Leonardo. *Liberating Grace*. Maryknoll, N.Y.: Orbis Books, 1979.
Schmaus, Michael. *The Faith of the Church*. Vol. 6. New York: Sheed and Ward, 1977.

GEORG KRAUS

Chiliasm. By chiliasm (Greek: *chilioi* = a thousand) or millenarianism (Latin: *mille* = a thousand) is meant the expectation of a thousand-year reign during which, even before the end of the world, Christ will rule together with the just who have already been raised from the dead.

(1) *Biblical Background.* The biblical point of departure for chiliasm, which has been diversely interpreted in the tradition, is the picture in Rv 20:1–15, reflecting chiefly Jewish apocalyptic ideas, of an intermediate reign between the first and second resurrections.

(2) *History of Theology.* In the patristic period this biblical message was interpreted in different ways. Until the second half of the fourth century, chiliasm was widely associated in the Western Church with concrete and to some extent sensuous ideas, while the Eastern Church was more reserved. In the fourth century an archaic, crude chiliasm was gradually replaced by a more spiritualist interpretation of the thousand-year reign. Origen rejected chiliasm as Judaism, interpreted the relevant passages of Scripture allegorically, and

allowed, at most, for a spiritual coming of Christ at various periods of history. Other Greek theologians also rejected a literal, earthly interpretation of Rv 20:1–15. In the West, chiliasm gained adherents mainly under the influence of Montanism (e.g., Tertullian, Lactantius, Victorinus of Pettau [d. 304]). Augustine identified the thousand-year reign with the period between Christ's resurrection and his return. The "first resurrection" consists of rebirth in baptism and the effects of grace. The kingdom of Christ is the church of this world that has a symbolic duration of a thousand years. The "second resurrection" is the raising of the body at the end of the world. There is thus a first resurrection in the spirit and a second in the body. Although Thomas Aquinas rejected chiliasm and condemned it as heretical, chiliastic trends revived in the Middle Ages when certain presuppositions were accepted. Thus according to Joachim of Fiore (d. 1202), history runs its course in three phases: reign of the Father, reign of the Son (the present church), and reign of the Holy Spirit. Here the thousand-year reign of the Holy Spirit is identified with the third age, which brings the fulfillment of Rv 7:2 and 14:6; the reign of the Spirit begins therefore around 1260. The Catholic theologians of the Counter-Reformation period rejected as erroneous even a mitigated chiliasm, that is, the acceptance of an interim period in which the risen martyrs and confessors will reign with Christ on earth.

(3) *Church Teaching.* A decree of the Holy Office dated July 21, 1944, stated that even a mitigated chiliasm cannot be taught as certain (DS 3839).

(4) *Ecumenical Perspectives.* The Reformers vigorously rejected chiliasm because it is incompatible with their understanding of the church. In CA 17 it is described as a Jewish view. In the following centuries, chiliasm was taken up by various "enthusiastic" sects, such as the Anabaptists, Bohemian Brethren, Adventists, Mormons, and Jehovah's Witnesses. By way of Pietism, chiliasm also entered Lutheranism.

(5) *Systematic Reflections.* Meanwhile, theologians generally have become convinced as a matter of faith that chiliasm is irreconcilable with the general resurrection on the last day that is clearly attested in the Scriptures and the creeds.

See also ANTICHRIST; RESURRECTION OF THE DEAD.

Bibliography
Cohn, Norman. *The Pursuit of the Millennium.* New York: Harper and Row, 1961.

JOSEF FINKENZELLER

The Christ-Event. The Christ-event refers to the occurrences and actions centered in Jesus Christ, which are important for our salvation.

(1) *Biblical Background.* The New Testament, based on the preaching of the apostles, does not offer an abstract teaching on God and salvation in Christ, but rather "that which we have heard, which we have seen with our eyes, which we have looked upon and touched with our hands" (1 Jn 1:1):

namely, Jesus, "mighty in deed and word" (Lk 24:19), Jesus' rejection, passion, death, resurrection, ascension, sending of the Spirit, and elevation to God's right hand (see, e.g., Acts 2:22–36; 1 Cor 15:3–5). Thus, the Christ-event appears as the fulfillment of God's saving work in salvation-history (Heb 1:1; see Ex 3:14).

(2) *History of Theology.* The patristic period emphasized the event of Christ to combat gnosticism, which reduced it to matter for a timeless speculation (Irenaeus, *Adv. haer.;* also 1 Jn 4:2). In modernity, D. F. Strauss understood it as the mythological veil of a universal truth, whereas G. W. F. Hegel regarded it as the dialectical self-revelation of the concept of the absolute.

(3) *Church Teaching.* The teaching office has continually maintained the event character of REVELATION, as is demonstrated by the early church's creeds. Preaching and the sacraments do not merely recall the Christ-event, but cause it to take place for individuals (*LG* 1–17).

(4) *Ecumenical Perspectives.* In principle there are no differences within the world of Christianity. However, the Reformers took a greater interest in the individual events of Christ's life than the Scholastics, who thought in terms of ontological realities. In post-Reformational developments, historical and philological exegesis led to an increased interest in the Jesus of history. Nevertheless, the link to the Christ of faith was maintained in dogma (Lutheran orthodoxy), affective relations (Pietism), speculative idealism (G. W. F. Hegel), and the pure relationship to existence (extreme kerygmatic theology).

(5) *Systematic Reflections.* Theology is related to the Christ-event as contingent and historical. This event is not just the appearance of a divine idea (pantheism), nor is it a cipher or an ideal of something else besides Christ (existentialism, moralism) or the expression of an idea (Hegel). In our time interest in the Christ-event has led to a *functional Christology,* insofar as the mystery of his person and mission, as well as his relation to God, are revealed in his work. But this in turn poses the question of the ontological conditions of the Christ-event. Access to Christ is historical *and* transcendental because the kerygma proclaims both the significance and the transcendental grounds of the Christ-event.

See also CHRISTOLOGY; MYSTERIES OF THE LIFE OF JESUS.

Bibliography
Kasper, Walter. *The God of Jesus Christ.* New York: Crossroad, 1984.
———. *Jesus the Christ.* New York: Paulist, 1976.

GERHARD LUDWIG MÜLLER

Christocentrism. Christocentrism describes the absolutely central place of Christ in the God/world relationship: Christ is in the middle of Christian faith, sacramental life, spirituality, mysticism, and morality. As mediator between God and humankind, he unites in himself the anthropocentricity of the world and reveals the possibility of theocentric human self-transcendence.

(1) *Biblical Background.* The Christocentrism of the New Testament may

be seen from many perspectives. In a *salvation-history perspective,* Jesus, the Son of God made man, is the fulfillment of Old Testament promises (Mt 1:22; Mk 1:1f.; Lk 2:30f.; Acts 2:36; Jn 1:16; Gal 4:4; Rom 8:3; Heb 1:1; etc.). *Soteriologically* he — in his person and his work — is peace between God and humankind, Jews and Gentiles (Eph 2:16). He is the only way to the Father (Jn 14:6), the one who opened earth to heaven (Jn 1:51), the door to eternal life (Jn 10:2, 10), and the only high priest (Heb 7:25), who enters the temple on our behalf; in his humanity he is the only mediator between God and humankind (1 Tm 2:5), and as exalted Lord in the Holy Spirit (Rom 8:27) he is the advocate before God for us sinners (1 Jn 2:1). The theocentrism of spiritual creatureliness (Acts 17:28; Rom 11:36) reaches objective historical fulfillment in Jesus Christ, the one Lord (1 Cor 8:6; Eph 4:5). Salvation is in his name alone (Acts 4:12). Thus too the kerygmatic-sacramental becoming present of his historical work of salvation happens only in his covenant (Mt 18:19; 1 Cor 5:20; 1 Pt 5:2–4). But, because of God's eschatological, universal self-mediation in Jesus Christ and the Holy Spirit, Christ is also the mediator of creation and the goal of all creation in an all-inclusive cosmological sense (Jn 1:3; Eph 1:21f.; Col 1:16f.) and first born from the dead (Col 1:18; 1 Cor 15:20). He is Lord beyond time and immediately present to every time (Heb 13:8). Paul's mystical view sees him as present within the human heart. Because we have died to the selfishness of the old, sinful Adam in Christ, we no longer live by ourselves. He lives in us. We belong to him in living and dying (Rom 6:6f.; 14:8f.; Gal 2:19f.; Phil 1:21; Col 3:4). The revelation of the Holy Spirit does not go beyond or relativize the one self-proclamation of God in the person and history of Christ (as in spiritualists such as Joachim of Fiore), but universalizes and interiorizes it (Jn 16:13f.).

(2) *History of Theology.* In the history of theology and spirituality, Christocentrism is visible in various projects. The Apologists, in their speculation on the Logos, pointed to Christ's cosmic and historical middle position. Against gnosticism and Middle Platonic emanation theory, Irenaeus and the great theologians of the fourth century emphasized that Christ is not an intermediate being between God and creation, but the mediator of creation to God because of the HYPOSTATIC UNION. The structure of Christocentrism in Christian spirituality was first elaborated by Origen (*De orat.*): through Christ, to the Father, in the Holy Spirit. Because the church comes forth from Christ's saving work and is his body, Christ's mediation is worked out in it. In him and through him as head, the prayers of members of the church for each other work to reveal Christ's mediation. Therefore the ancient church did not feel that prayers to the saints were in competition with Christocentric prayer. The systematic theological difficulties regarding a consistent Christocentrism come from the fact that although Christ's mediation of creation is prior, it is only manifest in the order of redemption. Thus since Origen (*De princ.*) pronouncements regarding creation and the fall come after the teaching on the Trinity and the incarnation. The consequence of this is that the relationship between the economic and

the immanent Trinity — and therefore the Christocentrism of creation — is not clear. Jesus was now understood in categories that were merely moral or existential. Yet there were attempts to fill this gap. Fulgentius of Ruspe (*De fide ad Petrum* 1f.) begins with the Trinity and the incarnation, then treats creation, the fall, and redemption. However, he had practically no successors. In his satisfaction theory, Anselm of Canterbury separates Christology from soteriology. He sees redemption from "below" as expiation made to an offended God by the man Jesus, who was able to achieve this because of his hypostatic union. In the *Sentences* of Peter Lombard, the doctrine of the Trinity and Christology are clearly separated with the result that his teaching on the virtues and the sacraments has almost no relationship to Christ. In the *Summa Theologica* of Thomas Aquinas, the treatise on Christology begins in *STh* 3. His project is clearly theocentric. The shortcomings of systematic Christology, which could no longer use the Christocentrism of the Christian notion of being to combat deism and pantheism, were only partially remedied by the Christ mysticism of the great saints (Bernard of Clairvaux, Hildegard of Bingen, Ignatius of Loyola, Teresa of Ávila, Cardinal Berulle).

(3) *Church Teaching*. The teaching office has maintained the Christocentrism of Christian living in all areas. However, there is hardly any evidence of Christ's mediatory role in creation in pronouncements concerning the doctrine of creation.

(4) *Ecumenical Perspectives*. The material principles of the Reformation ("solus Deus, solus Christus, sola fides, sola gratia": God alone, Christ alone, faith alone, grace alone) represent a strong Christocentrism, but they are limited to the existential realm of soteriology. Creation is presented exclusively as the salvific relationship of the sinner to God, not christologically. K. Barth was the first to undertake a radical Christocentrism when he linked the incarnation with the doctrine of God: the covenant is the intrinsic basis of creation; creation is the extrinsic basis of the covenant (*KD* 3/1:44–377).

(5) *Systematic Reflections*. In large part because of Barth's influence, theology today has tried to return to Christocentrism. This is visible in the way K. Rahner and H. de Lubac overcome the diastasis between nature and grace. They allow nature to be qualified and to terminate in the offer of grace. Of course we must respect creation's own self-mediated effectiveness, which does not contradict its christologically determined origin and tendency toward the trinitarian God of creation. Outside the historical word of God heard in Jesus and his church, pure unbelief and rejection of God must not prevail. Christocentrism must be grounded in the tension between the universal claim and the scandalous particularity of the Christ-event, since Christ is presented as a *universal* yet concrete self-mediation of God in the Incarnate Word, which is the ground, criterion, and goal of humanity as a whole and of particular human beings.

See also CHRISTOLOGY; CREATION; CREATION: THEOLOGY OF; DOGMATIC THEOLOGY; SAINTS: HOLINESS, SANCTIFICATION; TRINITY: DOCTRINE OF THE.

Bibliography

Rahner, Karl. "Christology within an Evolutionary View of the World." In *Theological Investigations*, 5:157–92. New York: Crossroad, 1975.

Segundo, Juan Luis. *An Evolutionary Approach to Jesus of Nazareth*. Maryknoll, N.Y.: Orbis Books, 1988.

GERHARD LUDWIG MÜLLER

Christological Heresies. Christological heresies are those pronouncements by Christians concerning the person and mission of Jesus that contradict the church's profession of faith that Jesus is truly human and truly divine. There are basically three types of christological heresies: those that deny or weaken Jesus' true humanity, those that dispute his divinity, and those that misunderstand the unity of divinity and humanity in the divine person of the Logos.

(1) *Biblical Background.* Already in New Testament times there were threats to the early community's faith that Jesus was raised from the dead by God and established Lord and eschatological judge (e.g., Rom 10:9; 1 Cor 12:3; 1 Thes 5:1–11). These threats were related to individual salvific events: some gnostic interpretations denied the PAROUSIA (2 Pt 3:14); others sought salvation not in Christ but in the powers of the elements (Col 2:9); others denied the coming of Christ in the flesh (1 Jn 4:2; 2 Jn 7) or his divine sonship (1 Jn 4:15). In the face of such explanations or Hellenistic falsifications of their faith in Christ, the authors of the New Testament maintained the soteriological theme ("for us") that determined their faith.

(2) *History of Theology.* This vehement struggle continued in the early church. The church's writers made use of the language and intellectual tools of contemporary philosophy to give an ontological basis to New Testament statements, which were of themselves part of salvation-history and soteriology. This happened especially in connection with the following christological heresies:

Heresies regarding Jesus' human nature: (a) *Docetism.* The term refers to heresies that say Christ the heavenly savior only appeared (*dokeîn:* to appear) to have a body. Ignatius of Antioch fought against this error (*Trall.* 9f.). The teaching office also condemns similar teachings of the Manichaeans and Valentinus, among others (DS 46, 48, 189, 357, 401, 1338, 1340ff.). (b) *Apollinarianism* (after Apollinaris of Laodicea). The human person consists of body, soul, and spirit (*noûs*). In Jesus the *noûs* was replaced by the sinless, divine Logos, which was united with the body and soul of a (now incomplete) human being. Thus there is only one nature composed of divinity and (ensouled) flesh. Behind this heresy stands the conviction that God could not take on sinful flesh. It was first condemned at synods in Antioch (362) and Rome (382) (see DS 74, 146, 148f., 159, 359, 534, 1342). According to church teaching, the incarnation means God assumed a human nature consisting of rational soul and body. A harmful consequence of this was that the formula "one nature [*mía phýsis*] of the God-man," which supposedly goes back to Athanasius, was attributed to Cyril of Alexandria and was used by the Monophysites. (c) *Monophysitism.*

Dioscurus of Alexandria and especially Eutyches (d. ca. 450) speak of God and man in Jesus as a unity of *one* nature. The consequence of this is that Christ's humanity is dissolved into his divinity. Against this, church teaching maintains the true humanity *and* divinity of Christ, and it notes that the principle of unity is not a third beyond the natures, but the divine Logos itself. This is expressed conceptually by the terms *one* (divine) *person* in *two natures* (the divine and human). It is already found in Tertullian (*Adv. Prax.* 27.11) and is developed by the patriarchs Proclus and Flavian and by Pope Leo the Great (DS 291–94). It becomes the church's dogmatic teaching at the Council of Chalcedon (DS 300–303). Later Sergius I of Constantinople sought a compromise between the Monophysites and church teaching by accepting only *one* divine will (Monothelitism) or *one* divine action in Christ (Monenergism). Against this, the Lateran Synod of 649 and the Third Council of Constantinople in 680 affirmed as official teaching of faith that there are *two* wills: the human (including creaturely self-consciousness) and the divine, the former being obedient to the latter (DS 500–522, 553–59).

Heresies regarding the divinity of Christ: (*a*) The *Ebionites,* Cerinth, Marcion, Paul of Samosata, Photinus, and others (see DS 1339 etc.), deny the divine nature (and preexistence) of Christ. (*b*) The *Arians* (after Arius of Alexandria, d. 336) regard the Logos merely as God's most perfect creature who should be called "God," but not by nature, only (as we ourselves) by grace. The background for this is the (Middle Platonic) idea that God, the Creator, can be related to the world only through intermediaries — the most important of which is the Logos. Against this the church since Nicaea (325) has maintained that the Logos is "one in being with the Father" (*homooúsios*) (DS 125f.). The Arians later split into factions: the radical Anhomoians, who defended the dissimilarity (*anhómoios*) of the Father and the Logos; and an intermediate position that included the Homoians (the Father and the Logos are similar = *hómoios*) and the Homoiousians (the two are similar in being = *hómoios in ousía*).

Heresies regarding the hypostatic union of Jesus: (*a*) *Gnostic dualism* (Cerinth, Valentinus). It accepted both a human nature (which came from Joseph and Mary) and a spiritual nature (which came about at Jesus' baptism) of Christ. Against this the early Fathers emphasized the personal unity of both natures (Tertullian, *Adv. Prax.* 27.2; Irenaeus, *Adv. haer.* 3.16.3–9; cf. Ignatius of Antioch, *Eph.* 7.2). (*b*) *Adoptionism.* To maintain strict monotheism (the monarchy of the Father) Jewish Christians of the second century (Ebionites, Theodore of Gerber, Paul of Samosata) explained that the divinity of Christ was the consequence of his adoption by God at his baptism in the Jordan. He is only "virtually" the Son of God (dynamic Monarchianism). *Sabellianism* (after Sabellius, fourth century) is a modalistic variation of this: the three divine persons are merely three modes of revelation, that is, three different relationships that God successively enters into (in creation, redemption, and the sending of the Spirit). The so-called *Patripassionists* (Noetus, Praxeas) could therefore say that the Father suffered on the cross (*Pater passus est*). This teaching was condemned by Pope Dionysius (DS 112–15). (*c*) *Nestorianism* (after Nestorius of Constantinople, who however does not really present this teaching). Nestorianism acknowledged only a moral unity of divinity and humanity in Christ. Thus there are two persons: Mary did not bear God; she is the mother of only the human person of Christ. This teaching was condemned by the Council of Ephesus in 431 (DS 250–264; see also the decisions of the Second Council of Constantinople in the so-called Three-Chapters Controversy of 553 [DS 421–37]). The Council of Chalcedon (451) taught that the unity of the Logos is *in*, not *from*, the two distinct natures (DS 301–3). In the eighth century, Elipandus of Toledo and Felix of Urgel represent an adoptionist way of mediating Nestorianism: Christ is Son in a twofold sense, physically (naturally) according to his divinity and by assuming sonship according to his humanity. Against this the church maintained the single sonship of the Logos: even in his humanity Jesus is "naturally" the Son of God because of the hypostatic union (DS 610–19). A consequence of this is that he is sinless habitually, not just de facto (actually), which however includes preserving his human will in obedience (DS 435). In the Middle Ages there were various condemnations of christological views: in 1177 Alexander III opposed the *habitus* theory of Peter Lombard (*Sent.* 3.6.4), according to which the Logos assumed only a separate body and soul (DS 570). Also at odds with church doctrine is the so-called *assumptus-homo* theory, according to which the Logos assumed a complete human nature and therefore also a human person. Because human nature is in principle open to God, it exists by itself without a person ("anhypostatically") and can be truly realized in the person of the Logos ("enhypostatically") (cf. DS 535). In modern times the Socinians (after L. Sozzini, d. 1562) denied the personal unity of the two natures: Jesus is only man, even though worthy of our worship as the representative of God. This sect was forbidden by state decree (Decree of the Polish Sejm, 1658).

(3) *Church Teaching.* The positions taken by church teaching were introduced individually in the previous section. The basic christological position was developed in conjunction with the first ecumenical councils, Nicaea, Ephesus, Chalcedon, and Constantinople I–III.

(4) *Ecumenical Perspectives.* Because the Orthodox and Reformed churches base themselves on the early church's councils, there are no christological differences that divide the churches; there are, however, different accents. Thus P. Melanchthon objected to the objectivizing, essence Christology of Scholasticism, against which he emphasized a more soteriological position. For M. Luther, the incarnation is identical with Christ's taking on our sins — the "blessed exchange." According to his doctrine of *ubiquitas,* developed in opposition to H. Zwingli, the humanity of Christ also shares in the divine omnipresence. This, however, verges on a Monophysite Christology of unity. The Lutheran Kenotics (G. Thomasius, F. H. R. Frank, J. C. K. Hofmann, F. A. Tholuck, W. Gess) hold that in the incarnation the Logos freed himself from

divinity and assumed the sins of humanity in his relationship to the Father. Liberal Protestantism rejected the divinity of Christ. Dialectical theology (K. Barth) opposed this opinion, thus remaining in unity with the early church's faith in Christ. The views of the Kenotics and of liberal Protestantism are not acceptable according to the Catholic viewpoint. According to J. Calvin, the unity of natures is dynamically grounded in Christ's office of mediator. Christ shares in both natures and thus mediates humanity's communion with God in the Spirit. Furthermore, the Logos also exists for himself, without the humanity (the *extra calvinisticum*), because the unity of natures is grounded in the office.

(5) *Systematic Reflections.* The question of christological heresies in recent times must be examined in conjunction with the christological models. If we are to remain in agreement with the church's teaching at Chalcedon of an ontological Christology, a problem then arises with regard to biblical salvation-history. The revolutionary shift in consciousness from a Greek metaphysics of being and essence to postmetaphysical thinking calls for a new translation. Here especially we must clarify the notion of person that in modern times — as different from antiquity or the Middle Ages — means the person's own experiences in consciousness and self-determination. Nevertheless, it should be pointed out that such a Christology "from below" has reversed the Chalcedonian formula and teaches a human personality in Christ, through which the Son of the living God (his divine consciousness?) exists (see, e.g., P. Schoonenberg). In 1972, however, the Congregation for the Doctrine of the Faith rejected such views as erroneous.

See also CHRISTOLOGICAL MODELS; CHRISTOLOGICAL TITLES; CHRISTOLOGY; GOD'S PERSONAL NATURE; HYPOSTATIC UNION; TRINITY.

Bibliography
Gregg, Robert C. *Early Arianism: A View of Salvation.* Philadelphia: Fortress, 1973.
Grillmeier, Alois. *Christ in Christian Tradition.* 2d rev. ed. London: Mowbray, 1975.
Kelly, J. N. D. *Early Christian Doctrines.* New York: Harper, 1960.
Pelikan, Jaroslav. *The Emergence of the Catholic Tradition (100–600).* Vol. 1 of *The Christian Tradition.* Chicago: University of Chicago Press, 1971.
Schoonenberg, Piet. *The Christ.* New York: Herder and Herder, 1971.
Sellars, Robert Victor. *The Council of Chalcedon: A Historical and Doctrinal Survey.* London: SPCK, 1961.

GERHARD LUDWIG MÜLLER

Christological Models. At present, christological models are ideas that make faith in Christ comprehensible in terms of modernity with its historical, scientific, and technical manner of thinking. Because biblical and official church Christology begins "from above" using statements about preexistence and Easter faith — and this is suspected of being mythological or dependent on Hellenistic metaphysics of essences — many theologians have proposed a Christology "from below," in order to derive the necessary transcendental aspects from the humanity and history of Jesus.

(1) *Biblical Background.* A certain right to explain the Christ-event speculatively using various viewpoints and systems of thought goes back to the New

Testament itself. The Christologies implied by their individual titles are in function of the people being addressed (gentile Christians, Jewish Christians, and Hellenistic Jewish Christians). Here already both ascending and descending Christologies are adequately represented. Paul, the deutero-Pauline writings, and John, each in a different way, begin with the cross, resurrection, and pre-existence of the Son or Logos (Phil 2:5–11; Rom 8:3; Gal 4:4; Eph 1:3–14; Col 1:15–20; 2:9; 1 Tm 3:16; Jn 1:1–18; Heb 1:1–3) and contain only brief glimpses of the earthly life of Jesus (Rom 1:3; Gal 4:4; 2 Cor 5:16). In John, Jesus' whole earthly life is understood as the revelation of his glory. On the other hand, the Synoptics begin with the public historical life of Jesus' words and deeds, in order then to reveal the mystery of his person in the light of the cross and resurrection. Yet already Matthew and Luke could not refrain from adding an introduction that presents Jesus' origins (INFANCY NARRATIVES).

(2) *History of Theology.* After initial attempts at Spirit, Wisdom, or angel Christologies, Logos Christology gained wide acceptance. Because of the need to combat the ideas of the Arians and Apollinarians, according to which the Logos assumed only a human body or a body with a vegetative soul, the early Logos-*sárx* schema was replaced by a Logos-*anthropos* schema. According to this latter, the Logos assumed a complete human nature with a rational soul (with human actions and free will). "What is not assumed is not saved" (Origen, *Disp. cum Heracl.;* Gregory of Nazianzus, *Ep.* 101). The subsequent debates involved in achieving an orthodox Christology were determined both by a Christology of unity (Alexandrian school) and a Christology of difference (Antiochene school). The critical exegesis of the latter school starts with the literal meaning and emphasizes the true humanity of Jesus, thereby running the risk of voluntarism in the verification process. Yet it contributed to the "Chalcedonian compromise" and thus redirected the latent Monophysite tendency of the Alexandrians. In Scholasticism the *assumptus-homo* theory of Abelard came close to Nestorianism, in that the union of the Logos with the "assumed man" is only juridical. According to Peter Lombard's *habitus* theory, Christ took on humanity as a garment. Against this Thomas proposed a subsistence theory. Duns Scotus sees the person as determined not only by its nature, but also by its creaturely relationship to God. The person of Christ is not realized by itself, but in a unique manner by God's Logos. As developed by F. Suárez, this interpretation within the context of the Creator-creature relationship has come down to the present (K. Rahner).

(3) *Church Teaching.* By its very nature, the teaching office of the church cannot attach itself to any one christological model. Thus the two-natures doctrine of Chalcedon is also a profession of faith. The content of faith is maintained without any claim to "clarify" the mystery (DS 301–3). All christological models are to be judged by whether or not they are in union with the church's faith as seen in Scripture and tradition, not whether they correspond to some speculative deduction. In 1140–41 the Council of Sens condemned Abelard's *assumptus-homo* theory (DS 723). In 1951 Pope Pius XII (DS 3905)

condemned its psychologized form (Deodat de Basly, d. 1937), whereby Jesus' spiritual life is a *subiectum sui juris* that does not subsist in the person of the Logos, but is there as "somebody other." The Congregation for the Doctrine of the Faith rejected errors whereby Jesus' humanity would not subsist in the Logos, but in itself as a human person — thus God would be only a revealer present in this human being (*Herder Korrespondenz* 26 [1972] 228f.). In briefs of 1170 and 1177, Pope Alcxander III condemned Peter Lombard's theories on Christ's humanity (DS 749f.).

(4) *Ecumenical Perspectives.* Because the Reformation accepted the councils of the early church, there is no confessional difference concerning belief in the Trinity and Christ. However, because of specific soteriological and existential emphases, important shifts occur due to different speculative and hermeneutical approaches.

(5) *Systematic Reflections.* The christological models of the last fifty years are so numerous and diverse that a complete classification would be impossible. Two of their aims may, however, be mentioned. The first aim has to do with the fact that metaphysical and theological presuppositions of the early church's Christology are no longer comprehensible to modernity. Language about God's incarnation is suspected of being mythological. Therefore, K. Rahner (see *e* below) seeks a way to present Christ as the essential fulfillment of human desires and hopes. W. Welte was in agreement with this project when he emphasized the biblical notion of *event*. Both projects brought out the greater value of functional, relational, and historical statements rather than the early church's ontological and essential reflections. Nevertheless, the question remains whether a human nature without a corresponding personality is incomplete (see W. Pannenberg [*c* below], P. Schoonenberg [*e* below], E. Schillebeeckx, H. Küng, as well as P. Wiederkehr). The second aim regards the question (newly posed by E. Käsemann) about the HISTORICAL JESUS. Using aspects drawn from both aims, we can distinguish the following groups of christological models:

a. Believing Christologies. In the kerygma, Christ is an existential claim that places me before a decision and calls me to the authenticity of my existence (R. Bultmann). Christ is the mediator of faith in God because of his example (G. Ebeling). Christology functions as anthropology once it is divested of content statements. It appears as the concrete fulfillment of faith in the ongoing event of cohumanity (H. Braun). In a dekerygmatized Christology, Jesus is the cipher of true humanness (F. Buri).

b. Cosmological-Evolutionary Project. This project, working within an evolutionary worldview and starting with cosmogenesis and anthropogenesis, views Jesus as the moment of Christogenesis, the inner goal of cosmic and historical development (P. Teilhard de Chardin). K. Rahner adapted and deepened this view in his project of transcendental anthropology.

c. Universal History. W. Pannenberg attacks K. Barth's revelational positivism that allows no correlation of the word of God and human questions concerning salvation, but also R. Bultmann, who recognizes no relationship between the Jesus of history and the Christ of the kerygma, thus separating reality from its existential significance. The particular experience of meaning reaches its truth and fulfillment at the end through the totality of history. Thus it is eschatologically oriented, as is clear in late Jewish apocalyptic, which pictures Yahweh's self-revelation at the resurrection of the dead. Jesus' resurrection is the anticipation of the end of history. In this prolepsis he receives a universal, unsurpassable rank. In the resurrection, Jesus' preexistence is revealed, along with his divinity and power of judgment. Jesus' personality in relation to the Father is manifest in his trusting submission. In it he is both distinct from the Father and in a life-giving relationship with him (see Richard of St. Victor, Duns Scotus, F. Suárez). In this way Pannenberg seeks to avoid misunderstanding the two-natures doctrine as a conjunction of two substances.

d. *Political-Eschatological Reflection.* For J. Moltmann the resurrection is not the proleptic end and totality but the setting-in-motion of the hope of what will be. God is revealed as a God of hope, and faith fixes its present-critical sight on this future as a call to a world-changing action. Thus this reflection is more than just the interpretation of history. A careful examination also demonstrates that Jesus' struggle against those who held political power over the powerless and those without rights was the reason he had to be crucified. The cross has political significance as a criticism of all prevailing power systems, and the resurrection sets loose a dynamism of practical change. But here a trinitarian dimension appears, insofar as Jesus' interior union with God, his Father, makes the cross an event within God. In Jesus' suffering the history of suffering becomes God's suffering. In Jesus' death the Father suffers the infinite pain of love as the identity of life and death. In Jesus' resurrection hope is given of overcoming suffering. Human suffering becomes a part of intratrinitarian suffering, and salvation comes about only with the end of the intratrinitarian history of God in the cross and resurrection. This inevitably poses the question of God's immutability, as well as God's historicity and ability to suffer (see the project of process theology among English and American theologians).

e. *Anthropological Projects.* K. Rahner attempts to avoid the mythological misunderstanding that Jesus is God wandering about on earth. Using transcendental anthropology he seeks to grasp Jesus' relation to God as the one successful case of the Creator-creature relationship. Every anthropology is deficient Christology. Christ experienced his transcendental relationship as absolute self-giving. But the sole reason this opens up only a possibility of union with God is that God's self-sharing in Jesus was done in an absolute way, which can happen only once. Others have only a derived relationship to God in grace, whereas the unity of God with Jesus is ontological. Even though differentiated from the Logos, Jesus' humanity is constituted by the Logos; as realized by the Logos it is united with the Logos. P. Schoonenberg attempts to overcome the (implied) aporia of the two-natures doctrine by turning it upside down. The Logos is no longer a person. It subsists in the human person of Jesus. In this case a man, within the infinity of his transcendental horizon, apparently attains God in such a way that this man coincides with God's infinity. The Logos exists enhypostatically in Jesus' personal being. E. Schillebeeckx would deduce Jesus' uniqueness not from a supernatural "addition," but from the universal human expectation of salvation as expressed in the self-understanding of modernity. Jesus stands in an unbroken unity with the creaturely status of all human beings. He understands his own being and his humanity as radical being-from-God, as being-God's-Son. As related, his being is not diminished, but its finitude is increased. Jesus' relational being as Son is the most radical realization of creatureliness. H. Küng combats the alleged Hellenism of early Christology, although he fails to take into account research that shows this is not so (A. Grillmeier). He tries to establish the uniqueness of Jesus' relationship to God. However, it consists only in his being the advocate, delegate, and representative of the distant God. There is no deeper unity anchored in the eternal sonship of the Logos.

f. Trinitarian Projects. The projects of K. Barth and H. Urs von Balthasar are more difficult to communicate to modern audiences, yet they are more biblical. Barth begins resolutely with the intratrinitarian event. In it Jesus' human reality is eternally joined with the Logos by election and by grace, and it is predestined for the work of redemption and reconciliation. However, only in lowering himself, in the incarnation, cross, and resurrection, does he become for us the revelation of God and the cause of humanity's elevation. Thus in a real sense Christology *in statu exinanitionis* (in the state of emptying) is Christology from above. However, because the humanity remains fully passive (a predicate without a subject) — thus overcoming the teaching of *anhypostasis* — redemption is an event between God and God. Jesus' humanity (with its creaturely freedom) is not the bearer of a human self-gift, but the instrument of revelation. This is an extreme consequence of Barth's predestinational doctrine of grace (see GRACE: DOCTRINE OF). H. Urs von Balthasar also considers the salvation-history of Jesus as intratrinitarian. Only because the poverty, self-denial, and self-sacrifice of the Son exist in God — which thus binds the Son with the Father in the Holy Spirit in mutual love, where the lovers are differentiated — can the Son follow the path of kenosis, from the incarnation to the cross, as already attested in the pre-Pauline hymns that are in immediate proximity to the Christ-event (30–34 C.E.). The radical self-giving of the man Jesus personally includes the radical filial obedience of the Logos. Since he represents the weight of humanity's sins, drawing them into love in the mutual openness of Father and Son (even after he has assumed a human nature), guilt is overcome and a new way of being human *in forma Christi* is made available.

See also CHRISTOLOGICAL HERESIES; CHRISTOLOGICAL TITLES; CHRISTOLOGY; GOD-MAN.

Bibliography
See the bibliography under CHRISTOLOGY: CONTEMPORARY ISSUES.

GERHARD LUDWIG MÜLLER

Christological Titles. Christological titles are used in the New Testament to describe Christ's dignity. As confessions, acclamations, formulas of faith, and hymns, they answer the basic question: "Who do people say I am?" (Mk 8:27 par.).

(1) *Biblical Background.* In the New Testament there are approximately fifty different ways of naming the earthly Jesus or resurrected Lord. The most frequent are Christ/messiah (500 times), Kyrios (350), Son of Man (80), Son of God (75), Son of David (20), followed by servant of God, teacher, and prophet. Encounters with the resurrected Christ lead to the basic belief that the earthly, crucified Jesus is the one who was exalted and is present as the Christ of the church (1 Cor 15:3–5). Paul's Christology of the cross and resurrection is complemented by the Gospels' Christology that begins with the historical Jesus: from an Easter faith, they conclude to the deeper sense of Jesus' message, power, and claims based on his person. The historical question of whether he himself used titles or whether he acted in such a way that they were naturally assigned to him after Easter must remain open because of the mixture of history and kerygma in the Gospels. The most important titles are:

a. Kyrios. The use of this title was certainly a post-Easter reaction to the experience of Jesus' exaltation to the Father as Lord of creation (Phil 2:11) and to his felt presence at the meal of the community, where hope in his powerful return was expressed. There is a debate over whether this title began in gentile Christian communities that made him their cultic deity analogous to those in Oriental mystery religions (W. Bousset, R. Bultmann), or as an antithesis to the Roman title of Lord used in the cult of Caesar (O. Cullmann, based on 1 Cor 12:3). It also undoubtedly has Jewish-Christian roots. In the prayer *"Marana tha"* (1 Cor 16:22), which is of Aramaic origin and can be translated in two ways ("Come, Lord!" and "The Lord has come"), Paul is expressing his conviction that the Lord who is present in the Spirit (2 Cor 3:17) is also the Lord who will come again in the future. The Septuagint translates the divine name, Yahweh, as Kyrios. Whether the title used of Jesus implies a claim to his divinity (K. Berger) or whether the use of the same name is merely a subsequent fact (Conzelmann) is debatable. The first is more likely.

b. Son of God. In the light of later conciliar Christology, this is the most significant title. In the New Testament it was originally linked with salvation-history and soteriology, and only in Paul and John do we find themes that lead to ontological statements about essences. Its origin is not in Hellenistic *theios-aner* ideas (R. Bultmann), but in the experience of the resurrection. The title can have three meanings. First, it can have a messianic sense. Jesus is enthroned as God's Son (see 2 Sm 7:14; Ps 2:7; Lk 1:32); he has been empowered "since" his resurrection (see Rom 1:3f). In the Synoptics he is established as Son of God at his baptism in the Jordan (Mk 1:9–11 par.). In each MIRACLE he shows his divine power (Mk 5:1–20 par.). Speculation also goes backward to Jesus' birth (Mt 1:20; 2:15; Lk 1:31, 35), to his mediatorship of creation (Eph 1:21f.; Col 1:16; Heb 1:2; Jn 1:3), and forward to the completion of creation at the

last judgment (1 Cor 15:28; 1 Thes 1:9f.). Second, the title can have the sense implied by Jesus' unique form of addressing God as "My Father" (Abba). This certainly represents Jesus' actual practice (Mk 14:36; Lk 11:2, 25, 27; 23:34, 36; Mt 26:29; cf. Jn 11:41, etc.). Whether Jesus described himself as "Son" is questionable. But what is more important is his self-understanding in relation to God in his being and mission. Third, the title can be a statement about Jesus' being. Already in Paul we find the idea of Christ's divine sonship through which we are adopted children (Gal 4:4–7; Rom 8:14–17; Eph 1:5). In Christ, God is saving us (Gal 2:19f.; Rom 5:10; 8:3f., 32). John then predicates sonship of Jesus in an absolute sense. The Son is the total revelation of the Father; he is one with him in knowledge and love (Jn 10:30), yet differentiated because within this personal relationship he is sent by the Father. This leads necessarily to statements about his preexistence (Jn 1:1; Phil 2:6; Col 1:15; Heb 1:3; 13:8). A parallel to this Son-Christology in the Synoptics is Jesus' cry of jubilation (Mt 11:25–27; Lk 10:21f.). The Father and the Son are one in mutual knowledge. In accordance with Jewish wisdom literature, Jesus is Sophia, the mediator of divine revelation, the identity of revealer and revelation, the content of which is the Father. It is noteworthy that there are very few New Testament passages in which Christ is either called God (without an article) (Rom 9:5; Ti 2:13) or worshiped in the same way as the Father (Rv 1:6; 5:13; 7:10; 2 Pt 3:18).

c. *Messiah/Christ*. The various expectations of an eschatological savior in Judaism cannot be reduced to a common denominator. When the early church uses the title messiah, the meaning comes from its faith in the resurrected Jesus. At the same time it claims that all the hopes contained in the dynamism of Israel's faith are fulfilled in Jesus, who brings us God's glory. It is implausible that Jesus used this title to refer to himself, although he was condemned to death as a messianic pretender (Mt 15:26). An indirect self-recognition of messiahship is perhaps implied in the hearing before the Sanhedrin (Mk 14:61f.). There is also an indirect messianic claim in Jesus' entrance onto the scene, his preaching of an eschatological kingdom of God, and his behavior.

d. *Son of David*. The fact claimed by this title needs to be verified (genealogies in Matthew and Luke). More important however is its theological truth, and this is connected with the notion of messiah. Jesus is greeted by the people (2 Sm 7:12–16; 1 Chr 17:10–14) as the one who is to come (Is 9:7; 22:22; Jer 23:5; 30:9; Mt 21:9; Lk 1:32). In its pre-Pauline formulation the title functions within the framework of an exaltation Christology and establishes the true humanity of Jesus.

e. *Son of Man*. In the theological research there is a debate over the extent to which Jesus understood himself as Son of Man or as related to such a figure, which he refers to in the third person. There are three categories: first, the Son of Man refers to the *future judge* who comes from heaven (Mk 8:38); second, it means Jesus who must *suffer* and *die* and be raised up on the third day (Mk 8:31; 9:8); or, third, it refers to Jesus acting here on this earth *in the present* (Mk 2:10). Q sees Jesus as the coming Son of Man, recalling that Jesus' sal-

vific action in the coming kingdom of God is fulfilled and confirmed only by the "Son of Man," who is no other than Jesus himself (Mk 14:62). Jesus sees himself as approaching this figure, which emphasizes the eschatological character of the message of the kingdom and its proclamation. At the time of Jesus the term had already lost its corporative meaning: Jesus himself understood it in the sense of an individual figure. Behind this christological title stands a long salvational (Jesus' passion, his coming as judge) and religio-ethical relationship to the Jesus event (discipleship).

f. Ebed-Yahweh (Servant of God). The atoning death of Jesus was soon brought into relationship with the servant songs of Isaiah 53, directly or by allusion (Mt 8:17; 12:18–21; Lk 22:37; Acts 2:23; 8:32f.; Rom 4:25; 8:32; 15:31; 1 Cor 15:3–5; Phil 2:6–12; and Mk 1:11 [see Is 42:1]). To what extent Jesus himself understood his death in this sense is debatable. In a general way, the memory of his proexistent bearing must have suggested interpreting it in the light of God's suffering servant. This is especially clear in the logion on ransom money (Mk 10:45 par.) and in the use of *hyper* (for you) in the words over the bread and the cup (Mk 14:24; Mt 26:28; 1 Cor 11:24; Lk 22:20).

g. Teacher. Jesus' activity as rabbi is well attested. His teaching, however, is characterized by an eschatological claim to power that distinguishes him from other teachers and leads to fatal tensions (Mk 1:22, 27; 2:12; 3:16). In an unsurpassable way he is the new teacher from God whose authority is greater than Moses (Mt 5:17). He becomes the standard for all the teachings of his disciples (Mt 23:8).

h. Prophet. In the history of God's self-revelation Jesus can be seen as the culmination of a lineage that began with the prophets (Hebrews 1) and is now surpassed (Lk 7:16; Acts 3:22; 7:37; Jn 6:14; 7:40–45). In Q (Lk 11:49–52), Wisdom says the prophets will be persecuted and suffer death in Jerusalem, and the people considered Jesus to be a prophet. Yet only after Easter did the disciples understand that Jesus as messiah had to suffer in order to enter into his glory (Lk 24:7, 26, 46; Acts 17:3). The later christological reflections turned to his exaltation and ontology, the more any suggestion that he was "only" a prophet had to be regarded as a falsification of the Christ-event (see heretical Jewish Christianity, Islam, Socinianism, rationalism, liberal theology).

(2) *History of Theology.* Most of the christological titles have been unfruitful for spirituality and theology. The title Christ, which prevailed and practically became part of Jesus' name, points to his messiahship and its relationship to the Old Testament, for the titles Lord (especially in the liturgy) and Son of God were at the center of the struggle to correctly define the mystery of his person. In the sense of an essential oneness with the Father (and the Holy Spirit), it becomes the key to orthodox Christology. The Fathers of the Church take Son of Man as a statement of the true humanity of Jesus.

(3) *Church Teaching.* In the christological debates of the first seven centuries, the teaching office of the church took an interest in the titles as important statements about Christ's true divinity, humanity, and personal unity. Central to this

discussion were the titles Son of God, Incarnate Word, and true God. To describe his humanity received from Mary by which he suffered and died, he is called Son of Man (DS 189, 250, 317, 368, 420, 442, 491, 535, 619, 791).

(4) *Ecumenical Perspectives.* There are no theological controversies regarding the christological titles.

(5) *Systematic Reflections.* With the advent of historical studies, the christological titles have taken on new significance. They lead to Jesus' self-awareness as messiah and his eschatological claims and uncover the implicit christological structures of the pre-Easter Jesus. They give us an insight into the genesis of early christological professions of faith and offer possibilities for developing a dogmatics based on salvation-history and for re-creating the whole of early Christian faith. Thus they open up new horizons for traditional Christology. But this will be realized only when we transform static New Testament title-Christology by using the more comprehensive dynamism of God's self-unfolding in the history and drama of Jesus' life and destiny.

See also CHRISTOLOGY; CONFESSIONS (CREEDS/CHURCHES).

Bibliography
Bousset, Wilhelm. *Kyrios Christos.* Nashville: Abingdon, 1970.
Cullmann, Oscar. *The Christology of the New Testament.* Philadelphia: Westminster, 1963.
Fuller, Reginald H. *The Foundations of New Testament Christology.* New York: Scribner's, 1965.
Goppelt, Leonhard. *Theology of the New Testament.* Grand Rapids: Eerdmans, 1981.
Hahn, Ferdinand. *The Titles of Jesus in Christology: Their History in Early Christianity.* London: Lutterworth, 1969.
Taylor, Vincent. *The Names of Jesus.* London: Macmillan, 1959.
Todt, Heinz Edward. *The Son of Man in the Synoptic Tradition.* London: SCM, 1965.

GERHARD LUDWIG MÜLLER

Christology. Christology is the central treatise of dogmatics. Its content includes the person, mission, and destiny of Jesus Christ, the incarnate Son of God; it starts with his proclamation of the kingdom of God; it takes up his crucifixion, his resurrection, his ascension, and the sending of the Spirit; it then addresses his final coming at the end of time. In speaking about Christ it is always in the light of his salvific action *for us.* Thus SOTERIOLOGY is part of Christology. In what follows we describe only the place and task of Christology within the whole of Christian theology.

(1) *Biblical Background.* The central theme of all the New Testament writings is Jesus Christ: the one who brings about God's eschatological salvation, who is the only mediator between God and humankind, and who is the eternal Incarnate Word of the eternal Father. There are in fact several New Testament Christologies. They all rely on the same basic christological experience, that is, that the same historical Jesus who preaches, is rejected and crucified, is also the resurrected, exalted Lord, who will come again to judge. Paul builds his Christology on the cross and resurrection. The Synoptics work out a Christol-

ogy "from below." Starting with the historical Jesus they develop the mystery of his person and mission in the passion and resurrection. John understands the history of the *verbum incarnatum* (Incarnate Word) as the history of the revelation of his glory in his suffering, humiliation, and exaltation. The different New Testament Christologies must form part of — and be verified in — later post–New Testament theology.

(2) *History of Theology.* The term *Christology* was first used by B. Meissner (*Christologia sacra* [Wittenberg, 1624]). The matter treated begins with the distinction between *theologia* (the intrinsic connection of Christ with the Father in the eternal intratrinitarian process and his birth in time by Mary) and the *oeconomia* (the salvific action of the trinitarian God in the person and mission of Jesus). The period ending in the seventh century was the most important time for Christology, when the trinitarian and christological dogmas were worked out by means of theological debate and conciliar decisions. This period remains normative for all succeeding generations in the church. As a consequence, all church-oriented Christology must deal critically and constructively with the themes that were then introduced (see the key themes in other articles dealing with Christology and the doctrine of God). Although there was never any doubt about the central and fundamental significance of Christ for our relationship to God, at various times there have been difficulties in the presentation of a Christology. Ever since Origen (*De princip.*), the presentation that became normative is: the trinitarian God–creation–the fall–the incarnation–redemption. The discussion of Christology was thus divided into two separate groups: one in connection with abstract speculation on the Trinity and the other concerning the incarnation (in reference to the forgiveness of sin) (CHRISTOCENTRISM). In the West ever since Anselm of Canterbury's SATISFACTION THEORY, a distinction has been made between Christology as the doctrine of the *person* of Christ and soteriology as the doctrine of Jesus' *work* (or his *office,* according to the Reformers). The fact is, however, that this leads to the loss of a unified, comprehensive Christology.

(3) *Church Teaching.* That christological statements are the basis and criterion for what is Christian is demonstrated in the early church's creeds, and these creeds have always been reaffirmed by the church's teaching office (see DS, *Index systematicus:* E). Factually, the second, christological article of faith is both central and quantitatively the most important.

(4) *Ecumenical Perspectives.* Insofar as nearly all Christian churches and ecclesial communities accept the Nicene-Constantinopolitan Creed, we may speak of a basic ecumenical consensus in Christology. It does not exclude different accents. Thus, for example, in Reformed communities, the objective-ontological importance of early church Christologies recedes in favor of their soteriological meaning. In many Evangelical dogmatic manuals, Christology comes before the doctrine of the Trinity.

(5) *Systematic Reflections.* Any contemporary Christology must include the following points: (*a*) It must start with an anthropological formulation of the

question. Important worldviews and philosophies demonstrate that the quest for meaning and salvation belongs to the essence of being human. Thus there is a desire for an absolute bearer of salvation. But such a hope must be related to God as the absolute and transcendent ground of reality, even while it has something to do with the experienced world of history, society, and materiality. By articulating such experiences starting with Old Testament salvation-history, Christology can make Jesus comprehensible as God's absolute word of salvation in a human-historical form. (b) It must begin biblically, that is, with the original experience of the New Testament community that Jesus of Nazareth, the awaited messiah, is the Christ of God, and, as the eschatological self-opening of this God, also the Lord of the church. The New Testament testimony to Christ, with its reference point in the pre-Easter, historical Jesus and the resurrected Christ (the road from an implicit to an explicit Christology), must be fully accepted. (c) It must receive the christological dogmas creatively (DOGMA/DOGMATIC STATEMENT; RECEPTION). Just as the Christology of the early councils did not abandon the biblical testimony, but integrated it in new horizons, so today these councils' dogmatic decisions must provide the impetus for a deeper knowledge of the mystery of Christ. On the one hand, this objective is not met by a merely *functional* Christology. On the other hand, a moralizing Christology can be checked only by the acceptance of ontological and personal categories. This does not mean a metaphysics of universal essences, but a metaphysics of existence: God, through God's free activity within beings, realizes truth, and this truth is known as historical truth in the person and destiny (cross and resurrection) of Jesus. (d) Christology is to be presented within the framework of an existentially and universally historical conception of truth as the mediation of the real relationship between God and humankind, and therefore also as the goal of human history. (e) In a soteriological perspective, Christology must show that personal community with Jesus Christ in faith and discipleship fulfills the desire of humankind for ultimate possession of salvation. The only way to the Father is in living and dying. Thus salvation within the world — in whatever form it is found — is to be understood as the grace of Christ. This also holds true for people who have not known him as savior.

See also GOD: THEOLOGY OF; HISTORICAL JESUS; TRINITY: DOCTRINE OF THE.

Bibliography
Adam, Karl. *The Christ of Faith: The Christology of the Church.* New York: Pantheon, 1957.
Boff, Leonardo. *Jesus Christ Liberator: A Critical Christology for Our Times.* Maryknoll, N.Y.: Orbis Books, 1978.
Bouyer, Louis. *The Eternal Son: A Theology of the Word of God and Christology.* Huntington, Ind.: Our Sunday Visitor, 1978.
Cullmann, Oscar. *The Christology of the New Testament.* Rev. ed. Philadelphia: Westminster, 1963.
Galvin, John. "Christ." In *Systematic Theology: Roman Catholic Perspectives,* edited by Francis Fiorenza and John Galvin, 1:251–324. Minneapolis: Fortress, 1991.
Grillmeier, Alois. *Christ in Christian Tradition.* 2d ed. London: Mowbray, 1975.

Johnson, Elizabeth A. *Consider Jesus: Waves of Renewal in Christology.* New York: Crossroad, 1990.

Kasper, Walter. *Jesus the Christ.* New York: Paulist, 1976.

Lienhard, Marc. *Luther, Witness to Jesus Christ: Stages and Themes of the Reformer's Christology.* Minneapolis: Augsburg, 1982.

Pannenberg, Wolfhart. *Jesus: God and Man.* 2d ed. Philadelphia: Westminster, 1977.

Rahner, Karl. *Foundations of the Christian Faith.* New York: Crossroad, 1978, chap. 7.

Schillebeeckx, Edward. *Christ: The Experience of Jesus as Lord.* New York: Crossroad, 1980.

———. *Interim Report on the Books "Jesus" and "Christ."* New York: Crossroad, 1980.

———. *Jesus: An Experiment in Christology.* New York: Seabury, 1979.

Thompson, William M. *The Jesus Debate.* New York: Paulist, 1985.

GERHARD LUDWIG MÜLLER

OVERVIEW OF THE DEVELOPMENT OF CHRISTOLOGY UNTIL CHALCEDON (451)

Starting point: New Testament

God's Son — born of a woman (Gal 4:4)

God's form — in human likeness (Phil 2:6f)

God's Son — descended from David (Rom 1:3)

The consequence of this: God is neither an enclosed unity (vs. the rigid monotheism of Judaism) nor an absolute transcendence (vs. Platonic teaching on God).

The problems that remain:

(*a*) The meaning of divine sonship (How many gods are there?).

(*b*) How are divinity and humanity related to each other in Jesus?

Theological significance:

We are dealing with human redemption: "Quod non est assumptum, non est sanatum" (What is not assumed is not saved).

The proposed solution:

In the council, the second article represents a functional Christology: the dogmas succeed in developing an ontological Christology by transposing biblical statements into a Hellenistic intellectual horizon.

The Path toward a Solution: 2nd to 5th Centuries		
To (a): How many gods are there?		
Subordinationism	Incarnation Theology	Modalism
It preserves the incomparability of the Father (auto-theós), but also attributes the divine name to the Son: the Son is subordinated.	The concepts of Logos and Son are joined: the Logos (God) is spiritually engendered by the Father (= the Son), and thus is distinguished (as Son) from the Father and yet is in an indivisible unity (both are God).	It clarifies that in Jesus we meet God, but it destroys the distinction Father/Son: the Son becomes a "mode of being" of the Father.
EBIONITES: Jesus as God's messenger.	IRENAEUS: God becomes man so that we might become divine.	DOCETISM: Jesus only appears to be human.
ADOPTIONISTS: God adopted Jesus as God's Son (Paul of Samosata).	TERTULLIAN: from the one substance of God comes the person of the Logos (subordinationist).	SABELLIANISM: the one God is manifested in three revelations (prosopa= masks).
ARIUS: the unbegotten Father made (created) an independent essence (hypóstasis), the Logos, before the beginning of the world.	ORIGEN: the Logos makes possible God's entry into the world so that the world might be divinized (subordinationist and adoptionist). Dogmatic solution: Nicaea (325): Christ is begotten, not made, from the essence (being) of the Father. Solution: monotheism.	PATRIPASSIONISM: because the Father and the Son are only nominally differentiated, the Father suffers on the cross.
To (b): How are divinity and humanity related to one another in Jesus?		
Christological concepts:	Nature (phýsis)=the divine or human aspect of Jesus in the light of their association. Hypostasis (substantia)=the individualizing principle of a reality. Person (prósopon)= the same as hypostasis, but implies a social relationship.	
Anthropological model:	In antiquity, the human being is seen as composed of flesh/body (sárx), soul (psyché), and spirit (noûs). This determines the individuality of human beings. This tripartite schema tends toward a dual schema: spirit+ensouled body= humanity.	
Historical remark:	The solution was made comprehensible by using various models (see what follows). These contain a core of truth and are thus orthodox, but they also include a typical danger, which, in the course of further reflection, leads to excessive and heretical interpretations.	

Christology of Unity	Orthodoxy	Christology of Separation
Emphasizes the unity of God and humanity (the legacy of subordinationism).	Affirms unity in distinction (development of Nicaea).	Emphasizes the unity of God and *humankind* (legacy of modalism).
Philosophical background: the "hierarchical" thinking of the Stoa.		*Philosophical background:* the "realistic" thinking of Aristotle.
School: Alexandrine *Model:* as soul is joined to body in humans, so the Logos and *sárx* are joined in Christ (Logos-*sárx* model).		*School:* Antiochene *Model:* just as human beings consist of spirit and ensouled bodies, so Christ consists of Logos and *anthropos* (Logos-*anthropos* theory).
Advantage: God truly enters into humanity; unity in Christ is assured. *Danger:* divinity impoverishes the humanity; the whole of humanity is not assumed.		*Advantage:* God and humanity are clearly distinguished; Christ's humanity remains intact. *Danger:* the distinction tends to be a separation.

Protagonists and Decisions		
APOLLINARIS: the unity is conceivable only as the unity of essential components of the same nature (Spirit+ensouled flesh=man). Thus Jesus must be Logos+ensouled flesh. But in this case he is no longer a complete man (he lacks a human spirit). *Dogmatic solution:* condemnation, Constantinople (381).	CAPPADOCIANS: in Jesus the Logos permeates his humanity (=spirit, soul, body) (legacy of Alexandrian school). THEODORE OF MOPSUESTIA: Jesus is of the same essence as the Father, yet fully human+united in the same activity to the Logos (legacy of Antiochene school).	
EUTYCHES (MONOPHYSITE): in Jesus there is only one divine nature (*mone physis*).	CYRIL OF ALEXANDRIA: from both natures there is a unity that does not eliminate the difference. *Dogmatic solution:* Ephesus (431): Jesus is God and man; Mary is Mother of God.	

Tendency: a protest against absolutizing a Christology of separation based on a Christology of unity. Chalcedon (451): Jesus is one and the same as divine and human (Cyril), fully divine and fully human, in that both natures (=perfect divinity and perfect humanity) are united in *one hypostasis* (unity). The relationship of the natures to one another is: w/o commingling (*asýnchytos*) or change (*átreptos*) (vs. Eutyches); w/o division (*adi-áiretos*) or separation (*achóristos*) (vs. Nestorius).	NESTORIANISM: the divine and human natures are only spiritually joined. Mary only bore the human person/Christ.	
MONOTHELITES: In Jesus there is only one divine will.	Constantinople (680): Jesus has two wills: a divine and a human. *Tendency:* protest against absolutizing a Christology of unity, on the basis of a Christology of separation. *Solution:* open Christology.	

From: W. Beinert, *Dogmatik Studieren* (Regensburg, 1985), 62–65.

Christology

Contemporary Issues

In the contemporary discussion of Christology, the following issues are at the forefront: the historical Jesus, the relationship of Christology to political and liberation theology, and the uniqueness of Christ in a pluralist culture.

The Historical Jesus

In contemporary Catholic Christology the HISTORICAL JESUS — the picture of Jesus of Nazareth reconstructed through the use of historical-critical methods and derived from the never fully retrievable "real" or "earthly" Jesus — plays a crucial and even criteriological role. This is due in large part to the reevaluation of the classical christological claims during the 1950s and early 1960s that recovered and reintegrated into Roman Catholic theology the constitutive role of the full humanity of Jesus for his identity as God's self-expression and incarnate presence to the world. This reintegration, at first pursued at a more theoretical level, paved the way for the use of the more concrete results of historical-critical exegesis in the Christologies written during the 1970s and 1980s.

However, just as the original "quest for the historical Jesus" ended with A. Schweitzer's critique, so now the post-Bultmannian "new quest" is thought to be exhausted (LIFE OF JESUS RESEARCH). In its place has arisen the "third quest," whose participants display more optimism over how much can be known about Jesus and his historical context (e.g., J. Meier, B. Meyer) and who seek to place Jesus *within* his Jewish context rather than *outside* and *over against* it (as did the "new quest").

Some important results of this recent research are these: recognizing Jesus' mission as directed primarily to the reform of Israel; evaluating his expressed relationship to God as well within the parameters of traditional Jewish monotheism and piety; viewing his message as clearly part of the spectrum of diverse positions of Second Temple Judaism regarding Torah and temple; acknowledging that Jesus' proclamation of the KINGDOM OF GOD, rather than being apolitical, included an implicit critique of the social and political situation of his fellow Palestinian Jews; noting that, while the identity of a messiah was a contested issue during Jesus' life, he rejected both the title and role as inadequate expressions of his mission and self-understanding, preferring instead to function within the categories of prophet and charismatic healer or even (according to some more recent theories) as a wandering sage in the style of the ancient Cynics (CHRISTOLOGICAL TITLES).

One controversial issue has been the relationship between Jesus and the "crisis" he saw confronting Israel. Jesus' preaching of the kingdom of God was his prophetic expression both of God's judgment of Israel and of the fundamental transformation of Israel's situation to be carried out by God and mediated by Jesus' own person. But opinions differ concerning the manner and time frame of the kingdom's arrival. Most assume that Jesus' message can be understood only against the background of first-century Jewish eschatological expectation — not that he expected the imminent end of the physical universe (a too-literal reading of the apocalyptic language used by Jesus and his contemporaries), but rather that he preached the imminent end of the oppressive and negative world order of his time and its transformation into a purified age by the mighty power of God, a power already being felt through Jesus' ministry and which pointed to the future for its definitive fulfillment (see, e.g., E. P. Sanders). More recently others have claimed that Jesus' preaching and lifestyle were fundamentally noneschatological or nonapocalyptic in character and that the portrait of him as the eschatological prophet of an imminent end has been exegetically undermined over the last quarter-century. The "apocalyptic Jesus" is either a misunderstanding rooted in the theological agenda of the original "quest" (M. Borg) or is a later Jewish reformatting of Jesus' more original "sapiential" vision that proclaimed the unmediated presence of God's transformative power through the metaphor of an "ethical kingdom" present to Israel now and not delayed to the future (see J. D. Crossan). Such noneschatological readings of the Jesus material, along with the perception of Jesus as a Cynic sage, have depended on an evaluation of gnostic or gnostic-style extracanonical traditions (such as Q and the *Gospel of Thomas*) as older and thus more authentic than the Jewish narrative traditions reflected in the Synoptic Gospels (an evaluation, however, that has not gone uncontested).

This new research presents several challenges. An important one is respect for the Jewishness of Jesus — the realization that the New Testament presents portraits of Jesus the Jew rather than Jesus the proto-Christian. Such respect will lead to the recognition and diminishment of the various covert types of anti-Semitism that still infect contemporary Christologies (e.g., in discussions of Jesus' relationship to Torah, or the reasons for the death of Jesus). But it will also lead to the necessity of Christology dealing with yet another "ugly ditch," one proposed by some advocates of the "third quest" between Jesus the Jewish reformer and the Christ of the churches. However Christology may bridge this most recent version of the "historical Jesus/Christ of faith" rift, its argumentation must respect not only the legitimacy of the Christian confession of Jewish Jesus as the Christ, but also the legitimacy of the Jewish decision not to commit to the "reform Judaism" of Jesus but rather to choose the Pharisaic option offered in the wake of Jerusalem's destruction in 70 C.E.

Christology and Liberation

Political and liberation theologies agree with critical theory that truth is the justice that is done, the humanizing liberation that is accomplished. Such a theory of truth coupled with the incarnational emphases of the Gospel traditions prevent one from interpreting the transformation promised by the kingdom of God as purely individual or "merely" spiritual and force one to see its political ramifications as well (R. Horsley). God's "kingly rule" and abounding care transform situations of concrete negativity and suffering into ones of positivity and surprising human flourishing beyond any human accomplishment. This action of reversal and the solidarity of God with sinners, the outcast, and the poor are made manifest in the person, behavior, death, and resurrection of Jesus, God's Son. But the kingdom of God is made continually present only through the actualization of its values and the performance of the reversal in emancipatory service to others. Thus, Christology also articulates a call to discipleship and to justice: "following Jesus" implies that the members of the Christian community look critically at their own social, political, and economic situations, discern those dehumanizing aspects, and then act according to the values of the kingdom to reverse negativity and create the space for human flourishing. Inspired by political and liberation theologies, Christology develops the ability to discern and articulate how God's salvation offered through Christ is already at work in the world. Since Christology is intrinsically oriented to justice, it also must be self-critical and work to undo those claims that have promoted injustice in the past (e.g., using Christ's sufferings to promote an attitude of passive victimization, or aligning the "imperial Christ" with the interests of the powerful elites).

Feminist theology provides Christology with another fuller understanding of Christ's significance. R. Radford Ruether's question "Can a male savior save women?" is provoked by the oppression of women and what has been the consistent denial of women's full humanity. Such a situation has many sources, from the pervasive sexism of society to the history of Christology itself, which has served the subordination and oppression of women by being used to support androcentrism and the patriarchalization of church structures. Classical christological interpretations have contributed in a foundational way: they have made the maleness of Jesus into a universal principle, and thus the essential maleness of God is thought to have been revealed, and exclusively male images have been considered the only proper analogies for God. What has broken the hold of sexist Christologies has been the use of the essential hermeneutic of Christology both to retrieve a useful history of Jesus and to view the elements of this history through women's experience to disclose new possibilities of existence (E. Schüssler Fiorenza, E. Johnson, R. Nakashima Brock). This is similar to the critical principle followed by liberation theology. Jesus' address of the kingdom of God to all and especially to the marginalized of first-century Palestinian society, his characterization of God as his compassionate "Abba" rather than as a dominating royal figure, the inclusion of women in his circle of disciples, the testimony of women as the first witnesses to the resurrection, the identification of Jesus as "the Wisdom [*Sophia*] of God" (Mt 11:19) — these and other elements of the Gospel narratives are recalled and used to critique any christological interpretation that would deny the full humanity of women and betray the inclusiveness of God's salvation.

These liberating theologies have influenced Christology by functioning not only as gateways to new understandings but also as correctives to past distorted and destructive ideological uses. They disclose aspects of Christ's significance that had been unavailable to, or even suppressed by, classical Christology. The significance of Jesus as liberator and the interpretation of his life, death, and resurrection as the revelation of God's solidarity with suffering humankind are insights that have forced Christology to widen its focus from dealing with primarily theoretical issues to including issues of Christian praxis and spirituality. Christology thereby becomes an act of faith and discernment, rather than merely an exercise in metaphysical certainty.

The Uniqueness of Christ

Recent theological discussions have questioned the unique MEDIATORSHIP OF JESUS CHRIST when seen in the context of the plurality of religious traditions. This issue has been discussed intensely ever since Vatican II acknowledged that salvation is available to those who belong to faith traditions other than Christianity (*LG* 16). These discussions are characterized by three basic types of responses: exclusivism, inclusivism, and pluralism.

Exclusivism, the response with the longest history, claims that salvation is available only to those who accept the gospel, confess Jesus as the Christ, and become members of the church. *Inclusivist* arguments in various forms make the common claim that while Christ is the definitive revelation of God, salvation is presently available in non-Christian religious communities because "all religious communities implicitly aim at the salvation that the Christian community most adequately commends" (J. DiNoia, *The Diversity of Religions* [Washington, D.C., 1992], 37). *Pluralist* positions, also in various forms, generally argue that a common core or essence is shared by all religions and that they all aim at some sort of salvation or liberation; therefore, no one path to the divine or transcendent reality is more valid than any other. Pluralist arguments are those most critical of traditional claims for Christ as the necessary mediator of salvation and suggest that Christian theology must drop its traditional "Christocentrism" for a more inclusive "theocentrism" or "soterio-centrism" (P. Knitter, J. Hick) if it is to enter into a productive dialogue with other religions.

All three positions have been criticized as flawed responses to the basic christological question. In the light of Vatican II's position, the traditional exclusivist position, associated with the axiom *extra ecclesiam nulla salus* (although the original meaning of the phrase had nothing to do with non-Christians), has been dismissed as imperialist, offensive to those of non-Christian faiths, and contradictory to Jesus' announcement of God's universal love and desire to save all people. While some form of inclusivism (e.g., the argument for "anonymous Christianity") has functioned as the mainstream Roman Catholic theological argument for the last quarter-century, it has been accused both of making the role of Christ as unique mediator ultimately disposable and of assimilating the distinctive salvific aims of other religious practices too closely to that of Christianity, thereby robbing other religions of their identity. Pluralist positions, which are proposed as the most open and adequate theological explanations of the empirical fact of the diversity of religions and religious traditions, seem to be replacing inclusivism as the Christian theological position of choice. But they, too, have been criticized for presupposing a modern, abstract definition of "religion," advocating a reductionist view of God, ignoring or downgrading the historical particularity and different aims of concrete religious practices, and avoiding questions concerning the truth claims of religious traditions.

Christology's developing response to the empirical diversity of religious aims and practices must balance its incarnational understanding of revelation with an expectation that God is able to act in ways and practices different from those espoused by Christians. A growing consensus holds that without Christian belief in the definitive status of Jesus as the mediator of God's presence, Christian identity itself is evacuated, and any standpoint from which Christianity might dialogue with other religions is eliminated. If it is a nonnegotiable for Christian identity and existence that the eternal love of God is neither known nor appropriated abstractly, but only as made available through the historical incarnational particularity of Jesus of Nazareth, then the pluralist option with its essentialism and reductionist ahistoricism is ruled out as a christological strategy. But a belief in incarnation rules out exclusivism as well: a commitment to the God of Jesus, and thus to the perduring historical presence of God's all-inclusive love, denies the human attempt to draw a boundary around God's universal will to save. A recent alternative proposal is an inclusivist "trinitarian Christology" where the definitive particularity of God's revelation through Jesus is retained, and where its salvific effects are played out universally through the activity of the Holy Spirit in diverse particular religious experiences and traditions (G. D'Costa).

Bibliography

Borg, Marcus. *Jesus, a New Vision: Spirit, Culture, and the Life of Discipleship.* San Francisco: Harper and Row, 1987.

Brock, Rita Nakashima. *Journeys by Heart: A Christology of Erotic Power.* New York: Crossroad, 1988.

Crossan, John Dominic. *The Historical Jesus: The Life of a Mediterranean Jewish Peasant.* San Francisco: HarperCollins, 1991.

D'Costa, Gavin, ed. *Christian Uniqueness Reconsidered: The Myth of a Pluralistic Theology of Religions.* Maryknoll, N.Y.: Orbis Books, 1990.

Hick, John, and Paul F. Knitter, eds. *The Myth of Christian Uniqueness.* Maryknoll, N.Y.: Orbis Books, 1987.

Horsley, Richard A. *Jesus and the Spiral of Violence: Popular Jewish Resistance in Roman Palestine.* San Francisco: Harper and Row, 1987.

Johnson, Elizabeth A. *Consider Jesus: Waves of Renewal in Christology.* New York: Crossroad, 1990.

Meier, John P. *The Roots of the Problem and the Person.* Vol. 1 of *A Marginal Jew: Rethinking the Historical Jesus.* Anchor Bible Reference Library. Garden City, N.Y.: Doubleday, 1991.

Meyer, Ben F. *The Aims of Jesus.* London: SCM, 1979.

Ruether, Rosemary Radford. *Sexism and God-Talk: Toward a Feminist Theology.* Rev. ed. Boston: Beacon, 1993.

Sanders, E. P. *Jesus and Judaism.* Philadelphia: Fortress, 1985.

Schüssler Fiorenza, Elisabeth. *In Memory of Her: A Feminist Theological Reconstruction of Christian Origins.* New York: Crossroad, 1983.

ANTHONY J. GODZIEBA

Christ's Descent into Hell. The creed says that after his death Christ "descended into hell" or went into the "kingdom of death" (Sheol, Hades, the underworld). In other words he overcame death as an expression of absence of holiness and as distance from God, and, by his salvific death and resurrection, led the dead into God's universal reign of everlasting life.

(1) *Biblical Background.* The image of a journey by a god or a human being into the underworld is found in many religions as well as in Greco-Roman syncretism. It is the mythical expression of an anthropologically based hope that death is not the last word for humankind. There is no descent of God into the realm of the dead in the Old Testament and intertestamental literature, because of their particular image of God. In his transcendence, Yahweh remains above Sheol; his power is not interrupted by death. But he is no longer active for the dead (Pss 6:6; 81:11f.). Nevertheless, the one who prays is in God's sight (Ps 49:73). In the New Testament, language about the descent into hell is completely determined by Jesus' messianic act of salvation. His atoning death and resurrection, as the beginning of eternal communion with God, determine his relationship to death and the dead of the past. He actually suffered death with all its horror and was buried (1 Cor 15:4; Acts 2:29). Referring to Ps 16:10, Peter says that Jesus was in Hades and was saved from it as one of "God's saints." In order to call upon Christ, no one has to ascend into heaven or descend into the abyss (Rom 10:7; Eph 4:8f.). Jesus' descent and stay — paralleling the experience of the prophet Jonah (Mt 12:40 pars.) in the belly of the whale (an image referring to the abyss of distress, suffering, and fear of death) — are part of the messianic drama. The outcome is the real effectiveness of Jesus, who subdues the power of hell (Rv 1:18). He is Lord of the living and the dead (Rom 14:9). When he died, the graves were opened, "and many bodies of the saints who had fallen asleep were raised" (Mt 27:52). The main texts of the New Testament relating to the descent into hell say that because of his unique death on account of our sins, whereby he restored us to life, Christ also preached to the spirits "in prison" (1 Pt 3:19f.). "For this is the reason the gospel was proclaimed even to the dead, so that, though they had been judged in the flesh as everyone is judged, they might live in the Spirit as God does" (1 Pt 4:6; cf. *1 Enoch* 12–16). The allusion to those who are saved by the waters of the flood is a typological reference to baptism (1 Pt 4:21; cf. Rom 6:3). Thus, the New Testament is aware of Jesus' stay in Hades between his death and resurrection as well as his proclamation or demonstration of God's power, including his power to overcome sin, death, and distance from God.

(2) *History of Theology.* For theology, language about the descent into hell has been significant christologically and soteriologically. The Fathers emphasized the descent in combating the gnostics (cf. Ignatius of Antioch, *Magn.* 9.2; Irenaeus, *Adv. haer.* 5.31, etc.). Jesus' rescue was to have taken place through his preaching, and sometimes they accepted a baptism of the just who had died. The apocryphal texts link the descent into hell to mythological motives: war against Leviathan, Satan enchained and outwitted, the ransom of the just from

Satan's hands. A christological question that is of interest to the Fathers is: In what sense did Christ descend into hell? While the Apollinarians allowed only a descent of the Logos, which in death had departed from the body (without its rational soul), orthodox Christology held that the soul was united to the Logos during the descent. A distinction was made between Sheol, the abode of the just who had died (*limbus patrum*), and Gehenna, the "place" of the damned (Thomas Aquinas, *STh* 3, q. 52, a. 2), where Christ only demonstrated his victory. Catholic apologetics tries to demonstrate that the doctrine of the descent into hell is equivalent to the teaching on PURGATORY. Christian Enlightenment theology (seventeenth/eighteenth century) linked its understanding of the temporality of the pains of hell to the idea of a second opportunity for conversion or to unlimited moral self-development; this, it claimed, was suggested by Christ's descent into hell.

(3) *Church Teaching.* Christ's descent into hell has been mentioned by councils since 270 C.E. using the formula, *Descendit ad inferos* or *ad inferna* (DS 16, 27, 63, 76, 852). It is found in Pope Hormisdas (DS 369) and the Fourth Council of Toledo (DS 485). The Council of Sens (1140–41) condemned Abelard's view that the soul of Christ was only in the underworld through its effects, not in itself (DS 739). According to the Fourth Lateran Council, Christ descended into the world of the dead with his soul, he arose with his body, and he ascended into heaven with his body and soul (DS 801). Benedict XII (DS 1011) and Clement V (DS 1077) condemned the opinion attributed to the Armenians that in the descent into hell Christ abolished hell (of the damned).

(4) *Ecumenical Perspectives.* M. Luther added an existential meaning to the realistic sense of the teaching of the descent: in his passion, Christ experienced opposition and abandonment by God as the wrath of God, and therefore as hell (*WA* 2:690). In a similar way, J. Calvin sees the abyss of death in Jesus' spiritual suffering (*OS* 3.495f.). But he recognizes no descent into hell "after" Christ's death.

(5) *Systematic Reflections.* Today, in any interpretation, all mythological images are to be excluded. What is at stake is how to explain theologically the depth of Christ's death and the extent of its effectiveness. There is no new salvific deed "after" his death. Instead, redemption through his death extends to the whole of humanity in a temporal and spatial sense that encompasses even the past. Only by developing a theology of Good Friday can we succeed in clarifying the meaning of the immortal Christ who voluntarily undergoes the law of death (see DS 294). H. Urs von Balthasar demonstrates the background of such a project in trinitarian theology: in the incarnate Son, God takes the path of extreme self-alienation. The Son goes into the depth of death that is abandonment by God and absolute distance from love and therefore life. In being dead he reveals himself as the mighty one, and, in the resurrection of the crucified one who was buried, he goes beyond the law of the devil, of negativity and of sin, whose wages are death (Rom 5:12; Jn 1:15; Rv 6:8). By his resurrection Christ did not simply dethrone the power of death. He overcame it,

and, in passing through extreme alienation, he definitively included humanity in a dialogue of love with the Father in the Son. Thus the descent is really the event of our salvation.

See also DEATH; HELL; REDEMPTION AND LIBERATION.

Bibliography
Balthasar, Hans Urs von. *Mysterium Paschale: The Mystery of Easter.* Edinburgh: T and T Clark, 1990.

GERHARD LUDWIG MÜLLER

Church. The church is the communion of those who believe in the gospel, have been incorporated into the "body of Christ" by baptism, come together at the table of the Eucharist, and give expression to their faith in witness and service.

(1) *Biblical Background.* The New Testament presupposes the church in many ways. Its writings bear witness to the life and faith not only of individual Christians but also of communities and even the entire church at that time. Furthermore, the majority of the New Testament writings are addressed to communities and through them to the church generally. In addition, many of these writings deal with questions of ecclesiology. In so doing, they emphasize different aspects. Mark understands the church as the continuation of the original group of disciples. Matthew's emphasis is on the church as the "new Israel." As in Mark, so in Matthew the group of disciples is the anticipatory form of the church. According to Luke, the time of the church is the time of the Spirit's activity; in this way Luke integrates the church into his overall conception of the history of salvation. The Fourth Gospel understands the church as the company of believers. The church is intended to be universal, but it also has structures, for example, the Petrine office. Word and sacrament (baptism and Eucharist) bring the church into existence and constantly renew it. In the Pauline letters the church is given names that suggest a promising future: people of God (*ecclesia*), body of Christ, temple of the Holy Spirit. Baptism and Eucharist are celebrated in the church. Charisms mark the church's life, while the task of the apostolic ministry is to organize that life. In the Pastoral Letters the church can be seen at the point where its first stage is behind and it is beginning a lengthy journey through history; ministries and states of life are given their first concrete form. Hebrews describes the church as the journeying people of God. Finally, Revelation situates the church in the light of the eschatological events; here it is seen as a church that is tested and afflicted but also, by God's grace, victorious.

(2) *History of Theology.* The church advances through time as the new people of God. It is a "pilgrim church." Its fundamental activities remain essentially the same: worship, witness, and service. Its form, however, varies. In the first centuries it was a church of the Mediterranean world; from the early Middle Ages to the modern period it was a European church; it is now beginning to take on the characteristics of a world church. For many centuries it presented itself as a "communion of churches." The estrangement between the Church of

the East and the Church of the West formed the background for developments that led to the Church of the West becoming a pope-centered "perfect society" and provided some of the conditions for the schism of the sixteenth century. For some decades now the churches have been trying to eliminate or at least diminish the effects of the various schisms. The restoration, begun by Vatican II, of the early Christian form of the church is an important contribution of the Roman Catholic Church to the ecumenical movement.

(3) *Church Teaching.* In most of its documents Vatican II deals with the nature, structure, and mission of the church. A key word throughout is *mystery* (see, e.g., *LG* 1). The term refers to the origin of the church in the action of the triune God (*LG* 2–4), to the nature of the church as a sacrament (*LG* 8), and, finally, to the impossibility of talking about the church except in a multiplicity of mutually complementary images and concepts (*LG* 6–7). Vatican II emphasizes the "communional" (W. Beinert) aspect of the church. "Communional" refers both to the church's constitutive relationship to the Eucharist and to the fact that it manifests itself in many communities and dioceses that are in "communion" with one another. The church's episcopal structure is connected with this "communional" aspect; Vatican II deliberately strengthened this structure. The church, in which most of the faithful are laypeople, has a variety of relationships to the "world." Vatican II summons the church to dialogue with the world in its multiple forms and to awareness of its missionary and caritative obligations to the world.

(4) *Ecumenical Perspectives.* The characterization of the church as "mystery" touches on questions that are debated in the ecumenical movement and, at the same time, have decisive implications. At issue is the understanding in sacramental terms of the nature and consequently the tasks of the church. In the churches of the Reformation this approach is felt to be alien. The activities of the church are there defined instead in functional terms — that is, they derive their meaning, and limits, from the fact that the word of God becomes audible through them, so that it can be appropriated in faith. The church is made up of human beings who are called together by the word and under its influence have become believers. It is in this kind of fundamental option that the various structures and their theological description are based in the various churches.

(5) *Systematic Reflections.* The church can be traced back not to a single founding statement of Jesus but to the mysteries of his life and especially to the Easter-event; in that light, too, the nature of the church as a mystery of faith can be made clear: (*a*) *Easter origin of the church:* a decisive role in the establishment of the church is played by the agreement of the other disciples with Peter's faith-inspired answer: "You are the Messiah" (see Mk 8:27ff.); the community of disciples hereby establishes itself as a communion of faith. But these words of Peter are (in the view of many exegetes) a response to the postresurrection appearance of the Lord. (*b*) *Origin of the church in the mysteries of Jesus:* the following six events especially are to be taken into account. (i) Incarnation: the church bases its life on faith in the incarnation of God and regards

itself as the sacramental continuation of the incarnation. (ii) Mary's response of faith at the annunciation: like the Mother of God, the church provides a place for the Incarnate Word in the world (see Jn 1:1ff.); MARY is therefore a "prototype of the church." (iii) Preaching of Jesus: because the disciples were included as active partners in Jesus' preaching of the message of the kingdom of God, the church understands itself to be a community called to proclaim the word of God (task of evangelization). (iv) Call of the disciples (with a special position for Peter): the church, as a structured entity (COMMUNITY [GROUP]; MINISTRY IN THE CHURCH), continues the mission given to the disciples. (v) Last Supper of Jesus: the church is essentially a eucharistic table fellowship resulting from the representation of the supper celebrated on the first Holy Thursday. (vi) Death of Jesus on the cross: this is the supreme sign of Jesus' complete self-giving for sinners; the church shares in this movement of "being for others" through the proclamation of God's word and the administration of the sacraments. Through the sending of the Spirit on Pentecost, the church definitively enters upon the journey that leads it through history.

See also DISCIPLESHIP; ECCLESIOLOGY; LOCAL CHURCH; MYSTERIES OF THE LIFE OF JESUS CHRIST; SACRAMENT.

Bibliography
Kloppenberg, Bonaventure. *The Ecclesiology of Vatican II*. Chicago: Franciscan Herald, 1974.
Küng, Hans. *The Church*. Garden City, N.Y.: Doubleday, 1976.
McBrien, Richard P. *The Remaking of the Church: An Agenda for Reform*. New York: Harper and Row, 1973.
Pannenberg, Wolfhart. *The Church*. Philadelphia: Westminster, 1983.
Schillebeeckx, Edward. *Church: The Human Story of God*. New York: Crossroad, 1990.

WERNER LÖSER

Church

Contemporary Issues

The Context of North American Ecclesiology

Despite Roman Catholics' unity in faith and worship, their theological elaborations of beliefs, especially regarding the church, tend to be more and more distinctive today because of the variety of the ecclesial and cultural contexts in which theologies are being formulated. Readers from the North American continent who consult the fifty-one articles in this volume relating to the theology of the church (written by W. Löser) should not be surprised if they are occasionally disoriented by unfamiliar terrain. Theologians on opposite sides of the Atlantic often approach ecclesial topics from different angles. Such differences are positive signs that inculturation and contextualization are being taken seriously within particular churches.

Catholic universities in North America normally require students to enroll in several theology courses, thereby creating a setting for doing theology apart from the seminaries. Graduate programs at North American Catholic universities foster characteristic emphases and interdepartmental cooperation. Newer generations of theology professors who have completed doctoral studies at a variety of other universities research topics according to distinct methodologies. Unlike the German confessional faculties of theology attached to state universities, the North American theological scene is markedly ecumenical. American graduate theology students interact on a daily basis with others including Eastern Orthodox (with roots in Greek, Slav, or Arab cultures), Episcopalians from the Anglican Communion, and Presbyterians, Baptists, Methodists, Mennonites, and others. In the German context, Protestant (*Evangelisch*) dialogue partners are predominantly Lutheran. American ecumenical consortia of theological schools train lay and clerical students in collaborative settings that do not exist in Germany.

American Catholic theology has lost whatever similarities it once had to the teaching methods used at Rome's institutions or mirrored in manuals of theology (frequently written in Latin). It has eliminated vestiges of the thesis method, the use of scriptural proof-texts, and departmentalization of dogmatic theology from pastoral theology. North American theology, by reason of its public and ecumenical character, is not inclined to cite Denzinger, the councils of Trent and Vatican I, or the new Code of Canon Law. Large numbers of American women theologians, lay and religious, as well as lay men, have eliminated theology's earlier dominance by clerics.

North American Catholic ecclesiology, expressed along organic lines, finds somewhat constrictive the formal use of paradigmatic structures such as this volume's five organizational categories (biblical roots, history of dogma, magisterial pronouncements, ecumenical perspectives, and theological elaboration). In North America the large constituency of women theologians would make it unlikely that a volume of this size would draw upon only twelve men, without a single contribution by a woman theologian. To illustrate such contextual differences one could compare the present volume with a similar North American venture entitled *The New Dictionary of Theology,* edited by J. A. Komonchak, M. (Mary) Collins, and D. A. Lane (Wilmington, Del.: Glazier, 1987). In the U.S. publication, one notes greater gender balance, a larger number of collaborators, and a broader diversity in the authors' cultural and educational backgrounds, resulting in notable differences in tone. The bibliographies for the American readership are more international in scope. Because of its broad ethnic diversity, North American theology draws upon Latin American,

African, and Asian perspectives as well as the experiences of basic Christian communities.

North American Emphases

Ecclesiology formulated in North America has developed special interest in several areas among which the following eight are notable:

The Social Setting of Early Christianity

The North American context is characterized by keen interest in how the church and its structure developed in the New Testament and in the pre-Nicene communities. This includes attention to the emergence of "early Catholicism," the rise of monoepiscopacy in the various Mediterranean settings, and expressions of ecclesial communion among churches. In the context of ecumenical dialogue in North America, the role of Peter in the New Testament and the eventual association of Petrine ministry with the church of Rome have been closely studied. American Catholics have drawn upon the pioneering work of exegetes such as R. Schnackenburg regarding the New Testament distinction between Jesus' preaching of the kingdom of God (*basileia tou theou*) and the church (*ekklesia*) that emerged following the resurrection and Pentecost. Typical American contributions to studies on the social setting of the New Testament and early church would be the writings of W. Meeks, A. Malherbe, B. Malina, and R. Horsley. North Americans have effectively used redaction-critical methods to investigate the distinctive characteristics of local churches in Antioch, Jerusalem, Rome, and so on (see the work of R. Brown and J. P. Meier). These studies of diversity allow ecumenists to describe levels of diversity in today's churches that could be compatible with full visible communion of churches. The studies on the social settings of the early church allow one to recognize that specific features of church identity (such as the function of the bishop or presbyter) once perceived as originating in "the mind of Jesus" should more accurately be understood as the result of responsible decisions by the early church under the inspiration of the Holy Spirit.

Use of Models in Ecclesiology

A. Dulles's *Models of the Church* (1st ed., 1974) has had an enormous impact on the way American Catholics study ecclesiology. Dulles identified five models used to understand the nature of the community of faith: church seen as institution, mystical communion, sacrament, herald, servant (and later adding a sixth model, the church as community of discipleship). From among these models the concept of church as sacrament seems to have pride of place in North American Catholic theology. Ecclesiology is typically investigated in close relationship to pneumatology and liturgical worship. North American ecclesiology, as did Vatican II, highlights the church's enhanced self-realization during the celebration of the eucharistic liturgy. From its ecumenical contacts with the Orthodox it has drawn heavily upon the "eucharistic ecclesiology" of the East.

Ecumenical and Other Councils

Prominent North American Catholic theologians tend now, again because of their ongoing ecumenical dialogue with Orthodox and Protestants, to nuance the term *ecumenical councils*. From Y. Congar they have borrowed the insight that in Christian church life there is a *hierarchia conciliorum*. Hence one needs to differentiate the ecumenical councils of the first millennium accepted by both East and West from the later general synods of the West. This distinction was also promoted by Pope Paul VI in his famous letter to Cardinal Willebrands (dated October 5, 1974) commenting on the seventh centenary of the Council of Lyons II (1274), which he described as "the sixth of the general synods held in the West" (see *Documentation catholique* 72 [1975] 63–67). Historical contextualization shows that what appears to be a firm conviction of traditional Catholic teaching, here the number of ecumenical councils, dates in fact only from R. Bellarmine's publication of various conciliar acta in the sixteenth century. Charts like the one in this book that lists the twenty-one "ecumenical councils" would surely be organized in a different way by North Americans who wish to avoid fostering the impression that a council such as the Council of Chalcedon has the same degree of doctrinal importance as, for instance, the various general synods of the West held at the Lateran.

Historical Ecclesiology

North American ecclesiology at its best stresses the interconnectedness of historical settings and doctrinal formulations. In recent years North American Catholic theologians, again through ecumenical consultations, have become more attuned to the historical contexts surrounding the mutual anathemas between Rome and Constantinople formulated in 1054 c.e. or the events giving rise to the Protestant Reformation in Europe. This results in trying to appreciate specific dogmatic elaborations as responses to historical issues that may no longer be controverted.

Reception as an Ecclesiological Theme

North American ecclesiologists have given special attention to the theological notion of "reception," whether it be reception of councils, reception by the faithful of the ordinary magisterium, or, expressed in other ways, the role of the sensus fidelium. By *reception* is meant the wider community of believers' receiving the teachings from councils or the ordinary magisterium in such a way that one's own experience of grace and faith is appropriately incorporated. In this process the faithful sometimes observe a forgotten truth or complementary dimension that needs reclaiming in order for the church as a whole to possess a comprehensive teaching on a particular issue. This bid for greater inclusiveness is sometimes inaccurately labeled as "dissent." But questioning the scope of certain modern formulations of doctrine or disciplinary decisions is not dissent from the ecclesial magisterium, but rather an invitation to those in authority perhaps to reappropriate some forgotten dimensions of the Catholic experience or at least a plea to present complex issues with a greater degree of intellectual modesty. North American ecclesiology recognizes the responsibility belonging to the lay faithful in this matter.

Evangelization

Another area being developed in North American ecclesiology is the church's role in mission and evangelization, which has also played an important role in the modern papacy especially since Paul VI's *Evangelii nuntiandi* (1975). The celebration of the five-hundredth anniversary of the arrival of Europeans in the Americas in 1492 encouraged a reexamination of methods used to Christianize the native people of the Americas. Further, the dramatic political changes in Eastern Europe that followed in the wake of the demise of the Soviet Union engendered a religious freedom that has led to new ecclesiological reflections about mission. There has been lively controversy, especially with the Eastern Orthodox, about the roots and limitations of Uniatism as a form of promoting church unity. In response to the questionable initiatives taken by other Christian churches to expand their presence in regions that for centuries have been predominantly Orthodox, North American theologians have joined in condemnation of proselytism that is judged to be "sheep stealing" and based on an illegitimate understanding of evangelization.

Feminist Insights

As regards ecclesiology, publications by women theologians are far more extensive in North America than in Europe. Most of the articles in European editions of the present volume reflect little rethinking of the doctrinal material from a feminist perspective. Many North American women and men theologians have become highly sensitive to the need for complementary emphases on a "discipleship of equals" for elaborating dogmatics. The experience of women in general and the publications of women theologians such as R. Radford Ruether, E. Schüssler Fiorenza, E. Johnson, and C. LaCugna have received growing and major attention.

North American Resources

Finally, North American theologians have their own favorite theologians who apparently are not always appreciated in other parts of the world. Among these favorites would be B. Lonergan, D. Tracy, A. Dulles, J.-M. Tillard, G. Tavard, E. Kilmartin, M. Hellwig, and P. Granfield; some Latin American theologians could also be added to this list: for instance, G. Gutiérrez and J. L. Segundo. In America since the 1970s there has existed a creative symbiosis between the Canon Law Society of America (CLSA) and other theological organizations, and that relationship has promoted permanent seminars on the church as communion, on the mission of the church, and on the laity in the church. The CLSA has also collaborated with the Catholic Theological Society of America on a text entitled *Cooperation between Theologians and the Ecclesiastical Magisterium* (ed. L. J. O'Donovan, 1982).

These emphases show that North American ecclesiology has achieved maturity and acquired a distinctiveness that needs to be studied in its context.

Bibliography
Brown, Raymond E. *The Churches the Apostles Left Behind.* New York: Paulist, 1984.
Brown, Raymond E., and John P. Meier. *Antioch and Rome: New Testament Cradles of Catholic Christianity.* New York: Paulist, 1979.
Dulles, Avery. *Models of the Church.* 2d ed. Garden City, N.Y.: Doubleday, 1987.
Fahey, Michael A. "Church." In *Systematic Theology: Roman Catholic Perspectives,* ed. Francis Schüssler Fiorenza and John Galvin, 2:3–74. Minneapolis: Fortress, 1991.
Granfield, Patrick. *The Limits of the Papacy.* New York: Crossroad, 1987.
Meeks, Wayne A. *The First Urban Christians.* New Haven: Yale University Press, 1986.
Sullivan, Francis A. *The Church We Believe In: One Holy, Catholic and Apostolic.* New York: Paulist, 1983.
Tavard, George H. *The Church, Community of Salvation: An Ecumenical Ecclesiology.* Collegeville, Minn.: Liturgical Press, 1992.
Tillard, Jean-Marie R. *Église d'églises: L'ecclésiologie de communion.* Cogitatio Fidei 143. Paris: Cerf, 1987.

MICHAEL A. FAHEY

Church and Churches. Church and churches: this phrase implies the question of how the one church of Jesus Christ in the creed is related to the many churches that exist side by side at the level of historical experience.

(1) *Biblical Background.* The New Testament speaks, on the one hand, of the church as one and all-embracing and, on the other, of the many local churches in which the one church concretely manifests itself (see, e.g., Ephesians 4 and the opening formulas of the Pauline letters).

(2) *History of Theology.* In the first centuries the church thought of itself as a communion of churches, each gathered around the eucharistic altar and its bishop, and all linked together by a variety of relationships. As these local churches increased in number, associations were formed: the patriarchates. The patriarchal see of each group was regarded as a directive and organizational center. From the fifth century on, there were five patriarchates: Rome, Constantinople, Alexandria, Antioch, and Jerusalem (the "Pentarchy"). The drifting apart of the Roman patriarchate, on the one hand, and the four eastern patriarchates, on the other, led to divergent developments on the two sides. The East essentially retained the inherited model and developed it in the course of time, so that there are now eight patriarchates as well as a number of "autocephalous churches." Under the governance of the pope, on the other hand, the West-

ern Church developed under the explicit sign of unity. The plural "churches" gradually faded from view, while the singular "church united under the pope" took over. Little room was left within the Roman Church (*ecclesia Romana*) for the development of original forms of the local church. At the Reformation this long-neglected concern explicitly asserted itself, but outside the ancient church. The churches of the Reformation, which have become independent entities, pay homage to the principle of a multiplicity of churches and take the local church as the starting point. The idea of multiplicity as compatible pluriformity is opposed to the Roman principle of exclusive uniformity, especially when both are understood in an exaggerated way.

(3) *Church Teaching.* Vatican II attempts to balance the two principles when it gives increased value, in its own church, to the ideas of the "communion of churches" (*communio ecclesiarum*) and the local church (*LG* 26; *SC* 42) and when, turning to Christendom as a whole, it acknowledges that there are churches and ecclesial communities outside the Roman Church (*ecclesia Romana*) (*UR* 3; 19).

(4) *Ecumenical Perspectives.* The ecumenical movement is based on the insight that the experiential multiplicity of churches must be matched by a no less experiential unity. The World Council of Churches (as well as its regional equivalents: in Europe, the Conference of European Churches; in West Germany, the Association of Christian Churches in West Germany) does not claim to be itself a church, but regards itself as a communion of churches that retain their independence. The same is true of the Evangelical Church in Germany.

(5) *Systematic Reflections.* In view of the possibility, admitted even by Catholics, and indeed the fact, that alongside the Roman Catholic Church there are communities that show the marks of a church, the question arises of how the Roman Catholic Church justifies its simultaneous claim that the church of Jesus Christ "subsists" in it (*LG* 8), whereas the ecclesiality of other communities is marred by "shortcomings" (*defectus*). The answer: not only does the Roman Catholic Church proclaim the word of God and celebrate the sacraments, but it alone has at its disposal the hierarchic instrumentalities that it, being itself a sacramental community, needs in order to manifest and fulfill its nature (of which its unity is a constitutive part). In addition to the episcopal ministry with its apostolic succession and to other institutions, these instrumentalities include especially the papal office. In this context it is important to note that in *LG* 8, immediately after the passage in which the claim of the Roman Catholic Church is set forth, there is another that directs the church to follow the poor and crucified Jesus. Only if it takes this path will its claim be believable and tolerable.

See also CATHOLICITY OF THE CHURCH; ECUMENISM; LOCAL CHURCH; UNITY OF THE CHURCH.

Bibliography
Fries, Heinrich, and Karl Rahner. *Unity of the Churches: An Actual Possibility.* Philadelphia: Fortress; New York: Paulist, 1985.

WERNER LÖSER

Church Law. By church law is meant the totality of the ordinances that are issued by legitimate ecclesiastical authorities and that regulate the life of the church.

(1) *Biblical Background.* Regarding the biblical basis for church law John Paul II speaks as follows in his apostolic constitution *Sacrae disciplinae leges:* "Christ the Lord...did not wish in the least to destroy the very rich heritage of the law and the prophets which was gradually formed from the history and experience of the people of God in the Old Testament, but he brought it to completion (cf. Mt 5:17) such that in a new and higher way it became part of the heritage of the New Testament. Therefore, although in expounding the paschal mystery St. Paul teaches that justification is not obtained by the works of the law but by means of faith (cf. Rom 3:28; Gal 2:16), he does not thereby exclude the binding force of the Decalogue (see Rom 13:28; Gal 5:13–25; 6:2), nor does he deny the importance of discipline in the Church of God (see 1 Corinthians 5 and 6)" (*AAS* 75 [1983] 10).

(2) *History of Theology.* The legal regulations (*canones*) that the church gradually developed were initially assembled in private collections; it was out of these that the *Decretum gratiani* arose in the twelfth century, to become in turn the basis for further collections, which were required especially by the extensive legislative activity of the popes (the decretals) that began at that same period. These led to the *Corpus iuris canonici*, the church's first collection of laws (the name first occurs in Gregory XIII, 1580). By the end of the nineteenth century, church law had become a confusion; its reorganization led to the Code of Canon Law (promulgated on May 27, 1917; in force from May 19, 1918). When John XXIII announced Vatican II he also announced a revision of church law, which was not completed, however, until 1983 (promulgated January 25; in force from the first Sunday of Advent, 1983); the new Code of Canon Law (*CIC*) applies only to the Latin Church.

(3) *Church Teaching.* The official Latin text (*Codex iuris canonici auctoritate Ioannis Pauli PP. II promulgatus*) was published, together with an English translation and the introductory apostolic constitution, by the Canon Law Society of America (Washington, D.C., 1983).

(4) *Ecumenical Perspectives.* Other Christian communities also have their church law, the objectives and enforcement of which are determined by the ecclesiology of each community.

(5) *Systematic Reflections.* The theological objective of church law is described in the apostolic constitution: the church needs its own laws because it is a visible, social community, and in order to accomplish its spiritual functions. The sacramentality specific to the church provides the guidelines for its legislative activity. Church law is therefore law of a special kind: it cannot be imposed by force but is accepted by those subject to it because they have made the commitment of faith and are members of the church.

See also CHURCH; MINISTRY IN THE CHURCH.

Bibliography
Orsy, Ladislas M. *Theology and Canon Law: New Horizons for Legislation and Interpretation.* Collegeville, Minn.: Liturgical Press, 1992.
———. *From Vision to Legislation: From the Council to a Code of Laws.* Milwaukee: Marquette University Press, 1985.

WERNER LÖSER

Collegiality. The word *collegiality* describes an essential dimension of the episcopal ministry: anyone who is a bishop is such by reason of his membership in the communion or college of bishops. Responsibility for the governance of the universal church belongs to this college together with the pope.

(1) *Biblical Background.* The New Testament origin of collegiality is to be seen in the ministry of the "Twelve." The Gospel of Mark speaks frequently of them (Mk 3:14, 16; 4:10; 6:7, 35; 10:32; 11:11; 14:10, 43, and par.), but they are mentioned in other writings too (see Acts 6:2; 1 Cor 15:5; Rv 12:14).

(2) *History of Theology.* In the early church the ministry of bishop was regarded as collegial. The many particular churches, a bishop at the head of each, appeared as a communion of churches due to the sharing of one another's Eucharist and the links that existed among the bishops. The term *college (collegium)* appears first in Cyprian (*Ep.* 68) and is frequently used from then on. The collegiality of the episcopal ministry was shown in the practice of having the ordination of a bishop celebrated by at least three bishops, who represented the college. From the Middle Ages on, the consciousness of collegiality faded. The reasons for this were the shift in emphasis to the "priestly" aspect in the theology of ministry and the growing prominence of the papal office. The relation of the bishop to his own diocese was henceforth regarded as alone important. The Reformers accepted this restricted view of ecclesiastical ministry: the essential thing is assignment to a particular community.

(3) *Church Teaching.* Vatican II gave renewed importance to the idea of collegiality in connection with its reappraisal of the episcopal ministry: the college of bishops, in union with the pope, possesses supreme authority in the church, an authority exercised in councils and other collegial actions (*LG* 22); as members of the college, the bishops have joint responsibility for the universal church; unions of areas within the universal church are specifically mentioned (patriarchates, episcopal conferences) (*LG* 23). There is also collegiality at the level of the local church: priests, in union with their bishop, form a sacerdotal college (*presbyterium*) (LG 28; PO 7f.).

(4) *Ecumenical Perspectives.* In the churches of the Reformation collegial elements survive in their synods. The Lima Report's text on convergence in regard to "ministry" (1982; nos. 26f.) is an effort to recover collegiality at the ecumenical level.

(5) *Systematic Reflections.* Collegiality is one way in which the interplay of multiplicity and unity manifests itself. To the extent that it has its origin in the group of twelve disciples or apostles, it is a sign of the APOSTOLICITY OF THE

CHURCH. Collegiality shows that the church, in which the one faith is brought into being and the one baptism administered, also possesses a single ministry in which, in the course of space and time, many have participated through ordination. These many are thus made aware in advance of their duties toward one another, inasmuch as (as colleagues) they represent, for their part, the internal, sacramentally based organization of the church as body of Christ. Collegiality thus understood must express and prove itself in a fraternal sharing of life and activity.

See also APOSTLE; BISHOP; MINISTRY IN THE CHURCH; POPE; PRIMACY.

Bibliography
Betrams, Williams. *The Papacy, the Episcopacy, and Collegiality.* Westminster, Md.: Newman, 1964.
Suenens, Léon. *Coresponsibility in the Church.* New York: Herder and Herder, 1968.

WERNER LÖSER

Communion under Both Kinds. Behind this rubric is the question whether the reception of the consecrated wine (the chalice for the laity) as well as of the consecrated bread is required for a complete participation in the Eucharist, not only by the celebrating priest but also by the laity who join in the celebration.

(1) *Biblical Background.* In the accounts of institution the New Testament suggests the practice of Communion under both kinds but does not make it compulsory, inasmuch as Jesus Christ gives himself wholly under each of the two kinds. The eucharistic statements in John yield a similar result.

(2) *History of Theology.* Until the twelfth/thirteenth century, Communion under both kinds was everywhere practiced in the church, except in special cases such as the sick, to whom Communion was administered only in the form of bread, or little children, to whom it was given only in the form of wine. The Eastern churches retained the practice of Communion under both kinds (dipping of the bread into the wine), whereas the Western Church dropped it from the thirteenth century on. From the beginning of the fifteenth century on, the question of Communion under both kinds (*communio sub utraque specie*) repeatedly became a matter of dispute. First the Bohemian Brethren, or Hussites, who became known as "Utraquists," demanded Communion under both kinds; later, M. Luther and J. Calvin called for it. During the Reformation period there were also Catholics who urged the chalice for the laity. The theologians of the high Middle Ages, on the other hand, had advised that Communion under one kind is fully valid and sufficient.

(3) *Church Teaching.* The latter view was adopted by the magisterium against the Utraquists as early as 1415 at the Council of Constance (DS 1198–1200). The Council of Trent decreed that only Communion under one kind is necessary for the laity and for priests who are not celebrating, since in such a Communion one receives the whole Christ and participates in his sacrifice (DS 1726–29, 1731–33). Vatican II (*SC* 55) and the liturgical legislation that

followed upon it allow Communion under both kinds in a whole series of instances. In 1970 local ordinaries were given authority to decide in what other circumstances Communion might be given under both kinds. The Code of Canon Law (can. 925) lays down the rule that "Holy Communion is to be given under the form of bread alone or under both kinds in accord with the norm of the liturgical laws or even under the form of wine alone in case of necessity."

(4) *Ecumenical Perspectives.* The permission to have Communion under both kinds doubtless conforms to the teaching and practice of the Eastern churches as well as to the demands of the Reformers; but then it is necessary to justify the continuing regular practice of Communion under one kind.

(5) *Systematic Reflections.* If we look at the Eucharist as a sacrament, that is, as a symbolic action, then its integrity requires the eating and drinking of both the consecrated bread and the consecrated wine. The self-surrender of Jesus as suffering and death "for us" is given especially clear expression in the form of the wine. Thus Communion under both kinds has a profound meaning not only for the celebrating priest (who is in any case obliged to receive under both kinds) but also for the other persons joining in the celebration. It heightens the symbolic power of the sacrament for the individual and the community. On the other hand, there can be no doubt that the Lord gives himself whole and entire under each of the two forms and therefore also gives his salvation whole and entire. Communion under the form of bread alone is therefore dogmatically justified; for practical or disciplinary reasons it will probably continue to be the rule when congregations are large.

See also EUCHARIST; EUCHARIST: ACCOUNTS OF INSTITUTION; SACRAMENT.

Bibliography
Jounel, Pierre. *The Rite of Concelebration of Mass and of Communion under both Species: History, Texts in English, and Commentaries.* New York: Desclée, 1967.

GÜNTER KOCH

Community (Group). Community is the name given to the assembly of Christians in a place or in some other frame of reference. The church manifests itself concretely in a community gathered for prayer, witness, or service.

(1) *Biblical Background.* In the New Testament, the word *ekklēsia* refers either to the universal church (1 Cor 10:32; 11:22; 12:28; 15:9; Gal 1:12; Phil 3:6) or to the local, visible community, in which case the reference may be either to a particular community in distinction from others (Rom 16:1, 6; 1 Cor 4:17; 6:4) or to a house-community (Rom 16:5; 1 Cor 16:19b; Col 4:15; Philemon 2).

(2) *History of Theology.* In the early Christian period Christians were a suspect or even a persecuted minority. Their cohesiveness as a community was sustained by each individual's personal decision of faith. This fact ensured an evident fervor. Once the church became a recognized state religion in the Roman Empire (end of the fourth century) and the number of its members quickly grew, it seemed reasonable to organize the communities into territorial parishes.

This made it possible to carry out a wide-ranging pastoral activity among the peoples making up the church, and this activity was accepted by large sectors of "Christianized society." The parish community and the secular community entered into a symbiotic relationship as economic, social, and cultural entities. The concept of community used to play no role in ecclesiastical parlance as compared with that of parish; quite recently, however, it has come very much to the fore, while "parish," though not disappearing, has become less important.

(3) *Church Teaching.* Vatican II does not propose any explicit theology of the community, but it does lay the foundations for such a theology with its emphasis on the particular churches. Only in *LG* 26 is there a somewhat lengthy passage on the meaning and importance of the community. The documents of the synods of the West German bishoprics frequently speak of the community. The document "Die pastoralen Dienste in der Gemeinde" (Pastoral ministries in the community) (2.3.2) says: "A community is the assembly of those who, in union with the universal Church, believe in Jesus Christ and bear witness to the salvation bestowed through him; this community exists in a particular place or among a particular group of persons; it is established through word and sacrament, united and governed by the servant ministry, and called to glorify God and serve their fellow human beings."

(4) *Ecumenical Perspectives.* In the churches of the Reformation the community principle played an important role from the outset.

(5) *Systematic Reflections.* The emphasis on the community provides a major pastoral opportunity; admittedly, it also brings some danger, inasmuch as more comprehensive ecclesial groupings may disappear from the consciousness of the faithful. The linguistic shifts indicated earlier (see [2] above) reflect large-scale ecclesial and social changes: membership in church and parish has ceased to be something taken for granted by society, while the personal decision of faith, as well as the experiential unity of Christians that manifests itself in manifold relationships, have become the basis and support of communities. The territorial principle is indeed still at work, but it has lost its earlier unchallenged influence. "Basic communities," "personal communities," "religious communities," and other Christian groups and movements not infrequently compete with the parishes.

See also LOCAL CHURCH.

Bibliography
Gustafson, James M. *Treasure in Earthen Vessels: The Church as a Human Community.* New York: Harper and Row, 1961.
Niebuhr, Reinhold. *The Nature and Destiny of Man.* 2 vols. New York: Scribner's, 1963.
Segundo, Juan Luis. *The Community Called Church.* Maryknoll, N.Y.: Orbis Books, 1973.

WERNER LÖSER

Community (Relationship). Community is formed by two or more persons who are linked to each other through a direct sharing of life. Where human persons only interact with one another as freely interchangeable representatives of various functions (role-bearers), one can no longer really speak of community. Community in the theological sense has its origin and ground in an experience of salvation that stems from the initiative of God.

(1) *Biblical Background.* That Yahweh's election of the people Israel acts as community-building is indeed witnessed to in the Old Testament in various ways, yet is not uniformly described. It is first in the New Testament — in Paul and in 1 John — that the idea of community (*koinonía*) becomes a clearly theological concept. Faith means community with Christ and through him with God. From this community with God is founded the community among one another (1 Jn 1:3; 1 Cor 10:14–17). In Acts the faithful in Jerusalem are described as an all-encompassing community of life. In connection with the relief action taken for the needy Jerusalem community there is also already suggested the idea of a community among the communities (Rom 15:26). The metaphor of the table-community in the kingdom of God (Lk 14:15) raises the expectation that all who reach fulfillment in God will form one single community.

(2) *History of Theology.* Under the guiding image of the shared meal, the concept of community in the early church took on central significance for the self-understanding of the church. All the faithful share in the holy elements (*communio in sacris*), above all in the Eucharist, and thus constitute a communion of saints (*communio sanctorum*). Augustine distinguished between the spiritual community in faith and love and the visible church. In the Middle Ages, particular Christian communities (religious orders, confraternities) were formed within the church. The communion of saints became understood as the other-worldly, heavenly number toward which the church was to lead the faithful. Nevertheless, the ideal of a community of love that binds together all Christians continually flared up (church of the Spirit, church of love). The longing for community in the increasingly anonymous modern societies has caused the concept of community to attract renewed attention within theology.

(3) *Church Teaching.* This enlargement of meaning has also found expression in the ecclesial doctrinal language of Vatican II (e.g., AG 19; GS 32, 89).

(4) *Ecumenical Perspectives.* The rediscovery of community as the essential form of Christian existence gives ecumenical theology fresh impulses. In the exchange of theological insights and experiences of faith between ecclesiastically separated Christians community itself happens in faith and love, and this reinforces the desire to find ways toward church unity.

(5) *Systematic Reflections.* Since faith in Jesus Christ is inseparable from love in concrete life, the Christian message of faith constitutes among the faithful a community of mutual love, which in communal recognition and celebration also presents itself as such. The psychological capability of the human person to share in the life of others, however, is limited. When the concept of community is extended to all Christians or indeed to all persons in the world, it can easily become an ideology, in that it inevitably masks the given institutional

structures. Just as the love of neighbor in the sense that Jesus gave it referred to whoever is the neighbor (see Lk 12:27–37), Christian community is to be formed among those whom one encounters. The all-encompassing community in the kingdom of God is already being realized in the coming to being of such concretely limited community. For this reason the concept of community retains a critical function toward ecclesial structures: they exist in order to make community possible.

See also CHURCH; LOCAL CHURCH; LOVE OF GOD–LOVE OF NEIGHBOR; MONASTICISM/RELIGIOUS LIFE; SALVATION; SOCIETY.

Bibliography
Azevedo, Marcello de Carvallio. Basic Ecclesial Communities in Brazil. Washington, D.C.: Georgetown University Press, 1987.
Gager, John G. Kingdom and Community: The Social World of Early Christianity. Englewood Cliffs, N.J.: Prentice-Hall, 1975.
Lohfink, Gerhard. Jesus and Community. Philadelphia: Fortress; Mahwah, N.J.: Paulist, 1982.
Nisbet, Robert A. The Quest for Community: A Study in the Ethics of Order and Freedom. San Francisco: ICS, 1990.
Torres, Sergio, and John Eagleson, eds. The Challenge of Basic Christian Communities. Maryknoll, N.Y.: Orbis Books, 1982.

GEORG LANGEMEYER

Concelebration. In the narrower (sacramental) sense concelebration is the joint celebration of Mass by several ordained priests, with the words of consecration being spoke by all together. Concelebration in the broader (liturgical) sense is the communal celebration of a liturgy under the presidency of a principal celebrant.

(1) *Biblical Background.* The New Testament texts provide no information about concelebration, although it is indeed likely that in instances where we find a group of leaders at the head of a community, they would have celebrated the Eucharist jointly.

(2) *History of Theology.* In any case, still in New Testament times, we find, in the case of Ignatius of Antioch, a bishop and his presbyterium leading the community and presiding at the Eucharist. Until the twelfth century in the West, and until today in the Eastern churches, concelebration was the common practice, although the words of consecration were spoken by one individual, usually the bishop. According to a theological view that is widespread today, such celebrations were indeed concelebrations in the sacramental sense because of the intention that the participating priests had of consecrating. From the twelfth or thirteenth century on, in the Western Church the words of consecration were in some instances (e.g., at the ordination of priests) spoken by all the concelebrating priests. The question is raised whether in this "concelebration" (the term is now used for that situation) anything was added to the act of consecrating. The practice of concelebration subsequently was forgotten in the West; individual celebrants celebrated numerous Masses, often excessively numerous, side

by side in the same church. Only in the modern period was the meaning of concelebration rediscovered, in connection with the liturgical movement (cardinals and bishops concelebrated at the eucharistic congress in Rome in 1922).

(3) *Church Teaching*. In 1956, Pius XII decreed that concelebration requires all the participating priests to join in saying the words of consecration aloud; Roman declarations of 1957 and 1958 confirmed this decree. Vatican II says that in concelebration "the unity of the priesthood is appropriately manifested," and it radically broadens the permission to concelebrate (*SC* 57). The Code of Canon Law (can. 902) says accordingly: "Priests may concelebrate the Eucharist unless the welfare of the Christian faithful requires or urges otherwise."

(4) *Ecumenical Perspectives*. Although it is only in the Russian Orthodox Church that all the concelebrants speak the words of consecration, the revival of concelebration in the West can be the basis for agreement in this area. As far as the churches of the Reformation are concerned, insofar as concelebration helps to prevent an accumulation of private Masses ("Masses off in the corner"), it can help to remove one stumbling block.

(5) *Systematic Reflections*. Concelebration is theologically meaningful. It can show that the Eucharist is the concern of the entire people of God. In this context, concelebration by priests corresponds, in its own way, to the active participation of the faithful. It can show forth in a sensible way the unity and fellowship (*communio*) of the presbyterium and, in given circumstances, of the episcopate as well. Concelebration can signal the end of quantitative thinking about the Eucharist (the more Masses, the more grace). All the concelebrants can share in the infinite value of the one sacrifice of the Mass, which is in no way increased by concelebration. On the other hand, concelebration should not be turned into an ideological statement. Other forms of the Mass, in which one priest celebrates or several join in with him, can be meaningful and even powerful signs.

See also EUCHARIST.

Bibliography
Jounel, Pierre. *The Rite of Concelebration of Mass and of Communion under Both Species: History, Texts in English, and Commentaries.* New York: Desclée, 1967.

GÜNTER KOCH

Concupiscence. *Concupiscence* is the technical theological term for the compulsiveness of the human person. Its origin and depth structure are discussed in modern anthropology on the basis of numerous investigations (comparative ethology, psychoanalysis). In contrast to animals, the concupiscence of the human person is not determined by instinct but rather is regulated through sociocultural controls that originally were always stabilized by religion. Without such regulation the human person would not be able to survive (CULTURE). Because of this need for regulation, the experience of concupiscence frequently has an uncanny, a threatening, or, as it is seen religiously, a demoniacal quality. From this it is understandable that the theological concept of concupiscence is usually set in the context of evil and sin.

(1) *Biblical Background.* The Old Testament knows about the concupiscence of the human person, also with regard to the seduction toward evil; yet concupiscence receives its significance for salvation or damnation through the obedience or disobedience of the human person toward God's electing will (covenant, law). Rabbinic theology later distinguished between a good and an evil drive that are in conflict with each other in the human person. In the New Testament in the writings of Paul concupiscence takes on central meaning for the understanding of sin. The human person becomes aware of it — as the inclination toward evil — through its contrast to God's commandments and prohibitions in the law or in conscience (Rom 7:7–23; cf. 1:24–32). Concupiscence is the means through which sin exercises its inescapable power over the human person. While according to Paul this power of sin arises from within the person in the form of evil desire, according to John, the evil desire is awakened more or less from outside, by the world (1 Jn 2:16f.).

(2) *History of Theology.* Against the belief in fate spread in Hellenism, theology, first of all, had to stress that the decision over good and evil is made through the free will of the human person. The connection between concupiscence and sin was examined thoroughly for the first time by Augustine. Drawing upon the philosophy of Plotinus, he attributed to human reason the directing force over concupiscence. Reason can exercise this function only when it orients itself toward God's absolute truth and goodness. Otherwise it falls prey to the blind, pernicious inclinations of concupiscence. As a consequence of Adam's turning away from God, all human beings have fallen under concupiscence. Because of a misunderstanding of the Augustinian teaching, concupiscence itself was later regarded as evil. Thomas Aquinas then proposed understanding the regulated human concupiscence as creaturely vitality. The blind arbitrariness of concupiscence that overwhelms and debases the human person is first set free with the loss of concordance with the natural order (in modern terms: with the sociocultural orientation).

(3) *Church Teaching.* This view found its ecclesial confirmation in the teaching of the Council of Trent. Concupiscence is not sin in the real sense but rather tends toward evil only as a result of the sinful turning away from God through a person's free will. It makes the human person a servant of passions from which he or she can be freed only with God's help (grace) (DS 1515; cf. *GS* 17).

(4) *Ecumenical Perspectives.* Protestant theology believes that one can interpret Paul's statements on the sinful desire in the human person adequately by understanding concupiscence as a manifestation of sin rooted in the HEART of the person. Following Luther, this theological tradition sees the Thomistic conception of a creaturely, good concupiscence as an evasion before the reality of sin. This reality alone must determine the human person's experience of self before God so that no chance whatsoever remains for self-justification.

(5) *Systematic Reflections.* The crucial question arising today from the dissent between the Catholic and the Protestant traditions is: Does the sociocultural orientation (without which there is no specifically human concupiscence) already in itself lead away from God and toward evil? *Or* does it already convey elements of divine assistance, sparks of the gospel, so to speak, such that the human person concretely is never merely delivered to sin but rather also always already finds himself or herself under God's call to salvation and under the influence of the divine Spirit? In the first case, concupiscence would be the pure manifestation of evil. In the second case, it would be only insofar as it is directed from one's own evil will (personal sin) or from iniquitous and inhuman cultural conditions ("original sin").

See also GRACE; ORIGINAL SIN; SIN AND GUILT.

Bibliography

Irwin, Alexander C. "The Faces of Desire: Tillich on 'Essential Libido,' Concupiscence and the Transcendence of Estrangement." *Encounter* 51 (1990) 339–58.

Miles, Margaret. *Desire and Delight: A New Reading of Augustine's "Confessions."* New York: Crossroad, 1992.

Rahner, Karl. "The Theological Concept of Concupiscentia." In *Theological Investigations,* 1:347–82. Baltimore: Helicon, 1961.

GEORG LANGEMEYER

Confession. Confession is one of the three essential acts of the penitent in the sacrament of penance; it means the confession of sins before God through the mediation of the church, which is represented by a priest who has power of jurisdiction.

(1) *Biblical Background.* It is not possible to provide a strict scriptural proof of the necessity of confession. However, penitential procedures in the New Testament that also display characteristics of an ecclesiastical juridical procedure suggest the necessity of a personal confession of sins. In addition, such passages as Jas 5:16 ("Therefore confess your sins to one another and pray for one another, so that you may be healed") and 1 Jn 1:9 ("If we confess our sins, he is faithful and just; he forgives us our sins") show that the confession of sins was practiced in the church, not simply by individuals apart but as an action in the community. Relationship with God and relationship with the community are seen as closely connected.

(2) *History of Theology.* When the penance laid down by church law in the first centuries of the church was replaced by tariff penance or individual confession, the confession of sins became the decisive action of the penitent in the sacrament of penance, which thus became known simply as "confession." Theologians came to the conclusion that a full confession of "mortal" or serious sins is necessary. In addition, from the High Middle Ages on even great theologians recommended and justified "confessions of devotion," although these are not necessary for salvation and require no complete and detailed confession.

(3) *Church Teaching*. The Fourth Lateran Council (1215) imposed the obligation on the faithful of confessing their (serious) sins at least once a year in the sacrament of penance (DS 812; see 1708). Subsequently, it was chiefly the Council of Trent that concerned itself with the necessity and scope of confession: sacramental confession to a priest is the only way of fulfilling the command of Christ and is "instituted by divine law" (DS 1706). It is necessary "by divine law" to confess each and all mortal sins of which one is aware after a careful examination of conscience (DS 1707). Venial sins can be "profitably" confessed but need not be (DS 1680; see 1707). The magisterium has on numerous occasions recommended devotional confession (e.g., Vatican II, *LG* 11); also recommended is "general confession," that is, the confession of sins that have already been forgiven in the sacrament (see DS 880). According to various magisterial statements, confession must be honest and humble, formally complete, and secret (under the seal of confession).

(4) *Ecumenical Perspectives*. The Eastern churches generally acknowledge the necessity of confession but are often less strict in their practice; moreover, there is a wide variety in the forms of confession. Nonetheless, the Code of Canon Law allows the Catholic faithful to receive the sacrament of penance from ministers of the Eastern churches in case of necessity (can. 844.2). In dialogue with the churches of the Reformation on the confession of sins, Catholics find in many Evangelical Christians a new openness to individual confession, such as Luther himself practiced; but they will hardly find any understanding of the necessity of such confession.

(5) *Systematic Reflections*. Contemporary theological reflection on confession has to take the following points into account: (*a*) The starting point must be acceptance of the fact that the necessity of a confession of serious sins, by the individual and to the church, belongs to the substance of the faith handed down by the church. However, a proper understanding of the Tridentine phrase "of divine law" will allow some leeway when it comes to concretizing this confession. (*b*) If confession is felt nowadays to be a burden and not a liberation, then the need is to make even clearer the ecclesial dimension of sin and of the confession of sins; the need is also to go more deeply into the true nature of serious sin as this affects the person and, at the same time, the community of the church. (*c*) In this connection, people must be educated to go beyond a purely quantitatively complete confession to a qualitative "completeness," by which individuals may present themselves as they are to God and the church. The same principle applies to confessions of devotion. (*d*) Confession can and should be understood as an act of receiving: persons manifest to God their concrete sinfulness (which originates at once in freedom and in compulsion) and their need, in order to receive from God's gracious love an answer that the mediation of the church enables them to hear, namely, forgiveness in the form of new life from God in the liberated community of human beings.

See also ABSOLUTION; FORGIVENESS OF SIN: THE CHURCH AND THE; PENANCE.

Bibliography
Dallen, James. *The Reconciling Community: The Rite of Penance.* New York: Pueblo, 1986.
Dooley, Catherine. "Development of the Practice of Devotional Confession." *Questions Liturgique* 64 (1983) 89–117.
Peter, Carl. "Auricular Confession and the Council of Trent." *The Jurist* 28 (1969) 280–97.
———. "Integral Confession and the Council of Trent." In *Sacramental Reconciliation.* Vol. 61 of *Concilium,* edited by Edward Schillebeeckx. New York: Herder and Herder, 1971.
Tentler, Thomas. *Sin and Confession on the Eve of the Reformation.* Princeton, N.J.: Princeton University Press, 1977.

GÜNTER KOCH

Confessions (Creeds/Churches).

A confession is: (*a*) a didactic text that enunciates a profession of faith (e.g., CA); or (*b*) a church, insofar as it expresses its specific nature by reference to (*a*).

(1) *Biblical Background.* The New Testament provides no basis for a variety of confessions; even the multiformity that the church is there shown as having cannot be taken as such a basis (for a different view, see E. Käsemann).

(2) *History of Theology.* Only since the sixteenth century has it been possible to speak of the formation of confessions, once the communities created at the Reformation became independent churches, each with its dogma, constitution, and manner of life.

(3) *Church Teaching.* The Roman Catholic Church has never regarded itself as a confession, but since Vatican II it has recognized other Christian communities as "Churches and ecclesial communities" (*LG* 8; *UR* 13–24).

(4) *Ecumenical Perspectives.* In the contemporary ecumenical dialogue the recovery of the theological perspectives of the early centuries has led to a broadening of confessional perspectives. The consequence of this could be a relativization of the idea of confessions, but at the same time the confessions are showing an increased concern to maintain their own "identity."

(5) *Systematic Reflections.* Although the church cannot be understood in Roman Catholic theology as a communion of confessions, efforts are being made in the scientific study of confessions to promote ecumenical understanding and agreement.

See also ECUMENISM.

Bibliography
Barth, Karl. *Credo.* New York: Scribner's, 1962.
Kelly, J. N. D. *Early Christian Creeds.* 3d ed. London: Longman, 1972.
Lubac, Henri de. *The Christian Faith: An Essay on the Structure of the Apostles' Creed.* San Francisco: Ignatius, 1986.
Neuner, Joseph, and J. Dupuis. *The Christian Faith in the Doctrinal Documents of the Catholic Church.* Westminster, Md.: Christian Classics, 1975.
Pannenberg, Wolfhart. *The Apostles' Creed in the Light of Today's Questions.* Philadelphia: Westminster, 1972.
Ratzinger, Joseph. *Introduction to Christianity.* New York: Herder and Herder, 1970.
———. *Principles of Catholic Theology.* San Francisco: Ignatius, 1987.

WERNER LÖSER

Confirmation. Confirmation, like baptism and the Eucharist, is a sacrament of initiation, of entrance into the full reality of being a Christian, of full incorporation into the church.

(1) *Biblical Background.* A New Testament basis for confirmation was traditionally found chiefly in the Acts of the Apostles (Acts 8:14–17; 10:44–48; 19:1–7). According to Acts 8:14–17, the people of Samaria had accepted the faith and been baptized in response to the preaching of Philip. The Holy Spirit was given to them, however, only when the apostles Peter and John hurried down and laid hands on them. But according to contemporary biblical exegesis, this passage (and something similar applies to the other two passages mentioned) does not witness to an independent confirmation. The intention of the passage is to show that the primarily private missionary and baptismal activity of Philip becomes fully fruitful only through the intervention of the apostles, and therefore in the unity of the church. In any case, the passage attests to the laying on of hands as a sign of the descent of the Holy Spirit. The text also shows that at least in exceptional cases baptism and the reception of the Spirit could be separated. More important is the general biblical background and the New Testament theology of the Holy Spirit. Especially to be noted in this context is that in the Old Testament and the New Testament individuals receive the Holy Spirit in connection with their call (installation in office, beginning of their public activity): prophets, kings, and Jesus himself. Jesus received the Spirit at his baptism (see Mk 1:9–11 par.), although the Spirit in its fullness certainly dwelt in him from the beginning of his life. The Spirit now enables him to live his messianic vocation (see Is 11:2) and to let himself be fully absorbed by this vocation. Against this background it is legitimate for the church to develop a special sacrament in which individuals say yes to their baptism and allow themselves to be drawn into the service of their innermost human and Christian vocation.

(2) *History of Theology.* It took a long time for the church to reach that point. In the early church, people became conscious only gradually that the rites of imposition of hands or anointing with chrism, which were connected with baptism, could represent an independent sacrament, the administration of which could, if need be, take place long after baptism. In the Western Church, where the two rites mentioned were reserved to the bishop, it was generally the custom until the twelfth century to have this episcopal "completion" of the baptism administered in infancy take place as the sacrament of confirmation between the ages of seven and twelve (age of discretion). Only in the Middle Ages did a special theology of confirmation develop.

(3) *Church Teaching.* That theology was given official expression by the teaching church in the Decree for the Armenians at the Council of Florence (1439–45). The most important statements made there about confirmation are these: it is one of the seven sacraments (DS 1310); it imprints "on the soul an indelible character, that is a certain spiritual sign" (DS 1313); "By confirmation we grow in grace and are strengthened in the faith" (DS 1311); more

SUMMARY OF VATICAN II'S STATEMENTS ON CONFIRMATION

Baptism and confirmation belong closely together	LG 11; SC 71
They unite us with Christ the Head	AA 3
Confirmation links us more perfectly to the church	LG 11; AA 3
It bestows a special strength of the Holy Spirit	LG 11; AA 3
It empowers and obliges us all the more strictly to the apostolate, the fulfillment of the Christian vocation	LG 11; AA 3
Bishops are the original, primary ministers of confirmation	LG 26

PATHS OF THE CURRENT THEOLOGY OF CONFIRMATION

The christological approach	Confirmation as a closer union of grace with Christ as teacher, shepherd, and priest
The ecclesiological approach	Confirmation as a closer integration into the church as the realm of the Spirit's activity and into the church's mission
The approach from individual anthropology	Confirmation as a Spirit-given opportunity, and responsibility, for assuming one's own baptism by a free decision

specifically: in confirmation, "The Holy Spirit is given for strength...in order that the Christian may courageously confess the name of Christ" (DS 1319); the bishop is the ordinary minister (DS 1318); and the matter of confirmation is the anointing with chrism, the form, a formula of administration (DS 1317), which would later be changed by Paul VI. In 1547 the Council of Trent ratified these statements in their essentials and in the process emphasized, above all else, the status of confirmation as an independent sacrament (DS 1628–30). The few but important statements of Vatican II are summed up in the table above. According to Paul VI: "The sacrament of confirmation is conferred through the anointing with chrism on the forehead, which is done by the laying on of the hand, and through the words: Be sealed with the gift of the Holy Spirit."

(4) *Ecumenical Perspectives.* In the Eastern churches confirmation has always remained connected to baptism. The Reformers rejected it as a special sacrament ("Confirmation is a testing, a profession of faith, a reception into the community, a 'blessing'"). A renewed Catholic theology of confirmation that emphasizes the unity of the sacraments of initiation and the character of confirmation as a divinely efficacious sacrament of commitment to service could open up new possibilities of dialogue.

(5) *Systematic Reflections.* The theology of confirmation nowadays follows any one of three paths, depending on which aspect of confirmation is especially emphasized (see table above). These three aspects belong closely together,

although the third must be given special weight today. Confirmation is a dialogical event, a new gracious call of God, mediated through the church, that the person, aided by the Holy Spirit, can and must answer. If the person does not respond with the full self-surrender of faith, God does not on that account withdraw the call; the new opportunity God offers permanently influences the person in the form of the "confirmation character." What God offers is the opportunity of being taken into the service of the kingdom of God, a service that gives life its most intrinsic meaning and at the same time makes this meaning known. In this dialogue individuals find direction and the great perspective that gives meaning to life, inasmuch as the Spirit unites them more closely to Christ and incorporates them more fully into the church. Although baptism already gives them the Holy Spirit without reservation, a growth in interiority (as in love) and in intensity is possible that at the same time gives them new strength, new vital energy and enthusiasm, provided they allow the Spirit to take hold of them. The pastoral question of the proper age for confirmation also depends on the theological approach to which preference is given. Those who stress the element of decision in confirmation will urge a later age than the one customary in Germany (between the eleventh and the thirteenth year), but will then have to consider also the dangers of this solution (a two-class community of the confirmed and the unconfirmed and a loss of opportunities for socialization).

See also INDELIBLE CHARACTER; SACRAMENTS OF INITIATION.

Bibliography
Austin, Gerard. *The Rite of Confirmation: Anointing with the Spirit.* New York: Pueblo, 1985.
Dix, Gregory. *The Theology of Confirmation in Relation to Baptism.* London: Dacre, 1946.
Holmes, Urban T. *Confirmation: The Celebration of Maturity in Christ.* New York: Seabury, 1975.
Kavanagh, Aidan. *Confirmation: Origins and Reform.* New York: Pueblo, 1988.
Rite of Confirmation. Washington, D.C.: National Conference of Catholic Bishops, 1975.
Searle, Mark, ed. *Baptism and Confirmation.* Vol. 2 of *Alternative Futures for Worship.* Collegeville, Minn.: Liturgical Press, 1987.

GÜNTER KOCH

Constitution of the Church. The constitution of the church is the structure in which the church manifests its essential nature.

(1) *Biblical Background.* In the primitive church only the rudiments of constitutional structures were present. The cooperation of charismatics played a decisive role in the beginning (see Romans 12; 1 Corinthians 12; 14). Nonetheless, even in the first generation of the church, a ministry existed (the "apostolic ministry") and thus the starting point for the later "hierarchic constitution of the church," which is already beginning to take concrete form in the New Testament in the Pastoral Letters.

(2) *History of Theology.* To a considerable extent, the understanding and structure of the ecclesiastical ministries make up the constitution of the church

at any given period. The history of the church is therefore in large measure to be seen in the history of ecclesiastical ministries (BISHOP; COUNCIL; POPE; PRIEST) and other institutions that shape the constitution of the church.

(3) *Church Teaching.* Among the types of church constitution that are conceivable and have in fact found embodiment on the ecumenical scene (congregational, synodal, episcopal), the *episcopal* constitution of the church is characteristic of the Roman Catholic Church (as well as of the Orthodox Church and the Anglican Communion). This has, of course, developed in concrete ways and is a hierarchic, episcopal, and papal constitution that has other distinctive elements as well; Vatican II has given a coherent description of the church's constitution (*LG,* chap. 3). It is to be noted in this context that the decrees of Vatican I on the pope are presupposed (and confirmed), that the hierarchy is seen as part of the people of God (*LG,* chap. 2), and that essential elements in the constitution of the church are also contained in *LG,* chap. 4 (on the laity). The Code of Canon Law draws the juridical conclusions from this description (CHURCH LAW): book 2, containing the laws that apply to persons, is entitled "The People of God" and deals with "the Christian faithful" (laity and clergy), "the hierarchical constitution of the church" (from the viewpoints of the universal church and the particular churches), and "institutes of consecrated life and societies of apostolic life" (cans. 204–746).

(4) *Ecumenical Perspectives.* In the Roman Catholic Church the constitution of the church has, amid all changes, remained relatively stable and unified down through the centuries and around the world. This has not been the case in the churches of the Reformation, which implemented a wide range of possible church constitutions. It is not surprising, therefore, that questions of the constitution of the church should be the subject of extensive reflection in Evangelical theology. Divergent ecclesiologies find expression in the various church constitutions. The problems thus raised are a source of special difficulty in the ecumenical dialogue.

(5) *Systematic Reflections.* In the Catholic view, the church's hierarchic constitution is connected with the sacramentality of the church. In *LG* 8 the church's constitution is seen as originating both in the will of Jesus Christ and in the basic nature of the church, which in turn calls to mind the mystery of the incarnation of the Word of God.

See also HIERARCHY; MINISTRY IN THE CHURCH.

Bibliography
Vorgrimler, Herbert, ed. *Commentary on the Documents of Vatican II.* 5 vols. Reprint. New York: Crossroad, 1968–69.

WERNER LÖSER

Contingency. This concept refers to concrete beings insofar as they do not exist necessarily and are dependent for existence on causation. In *logic,* contingency is the fourth category, along with necessity, possibility, and impossibility; it designates the sort of being that lies, as it were, between being possible and not being (able to be). In cultivated everyday language, the word *contingent* is applied to unforeseeable, suddenly intervening, fortuitous, freely arising events and conditions, happenings that are not inferable from anything preceding them. In the terminology of the *natural sciences,* contingency refers to processes that cannot be explained through the lawful workings of a single factor, but only by taking account of a whole complex of factors. *Scholastic dogmatics* adopts from philosophy of divinity the so-called contingency proof of God's existence. This is based on insight into the impossibility of assuming an infinite series of contingent events and entities, and into the corresponding sensibleness of postulating, as a causative and explanatory principle for finite contingent series, the existence of an absolutely necessary being, a "self-existent being" (*esse per se ipsum*), that cannot not be. Biblically based and hermeneutically oriented dogmatics often understands by "contingency" gracelike events within redemptive history and the life history of the believer. The advent of Christ, as a singular and uniquely redemptive event derivable from no prototype preexistent or external to Christianity, can be illumined in this way, as can "overturnings" of the "old creation" in the direction of its eschatological transformation and consummation (RESURRECTION OF THE DEAD). W. Pannenberg has made an attempt, with the help of the two concepts "contingency" and "natural law," to bring about a new dialogue between modern physics and a theology of creation (see CREATION: THEOLOGY OF) oriented toward redemptive history and eschatology.

See *also* CAUSALITY; GOD: PROOFS OF EXISTENCE OF.

Bibliography
Buckingham, Thomas. *Thomas Buckingham and the Contingency of Futures: The Possibility of Human Freedom.* Edited by Bartholomew R. De la Torre. Notre Dame, Ind.: University of Notre Dame Press, 1987.
Platt, David. *The Gift of Contingency.* New York: Peter Lang, 1991.

ALEXANDRE GANOCZY

Contrition. *See* REPENTANCE.

Corporality of the Human Person. The corporality of the human person refers to the fact that human persons discover themselves existing as physical beings and that they actualize their existence in and through their bodies. The body is, on the one hand, the medium of self-presentation and self-realization in the world of one's fellow human beings. On the other hand, it is the medium in which the human person experiences his or her fellow human beings and is acted upon by them and by the world. In this active and passive realization of corporality the human person has the experience of being at one with her or his body and of being distinguished from that body. In general, the consciousness of one's own corporality is characterized by an unfathomable depth.

(1) *Biblical Background.* According to the Old Testament, the human per-

son is a body that is animated through God's breath of life (Gn 2:7). When the breath of life leaves the body, the human person as a whole is dead. It is first under the influence of Hellenism that the immortal spiritual soul and the mortal body are distinguished from one another (e.g., in the Book of Wisdom). The New Testament did not take over this distinction. It knows only the resurrection of the whole human person that in the resurrection of Jesus has become the promise for all. Paul distinguishes between body (*soma*) and flesh (*sárx*). With "body" he characterizes the concrete person. Yet he also uses "body" in an instrumental sense (1 Cor 9:27; Rom 12:1). As a person or as an instrument of the person, the body can be under the influence of the desire of the sinful flesh or of God's Spirit. In the latter case it is the temple of the Holy Spirit (1 Cor 6:19). The Christian community (see COMMUNITY [GROUP]) is also called "temple of the Spirit" and "body of Christ": the Spirit of Christ is embodied in the mutual love of Christians (BODY OF CHRIST).

(2) *History of Theology.* Already in patristic theology the Platonic-Hellenistic view — that the human person consists of soul and body as two essentially different substances — had become dominant. In the cosmic theology of the East, however, the corporality of the human person retained a central salvific meaning as the link between spirit and cosmos (microcosm) that is realized in Christ, the reconciler of heaven and earth, the head of the whole cosmos. Western theology considered the corporality of the human person more as the place of temptation, of atonement, and of testing for the beatific vision of the soul that comes after death. In Scholasticism, Thomas Aquinas then picked up the theme of the instrumental understanding of the body. The soul is the form-giving essential principle of the body (*forma corporis*). Yet shortly afterwards, Duns Scotus emphasized the autonomy of the corporeal, upon which the spiritual soul only imposes a form. While in modern times, under the influence of R. Descartes, the body was assigned to the corporeal world and opposed to the world of consciousness, nevertheless, evolutionary theory, depth psychology, and sociology have promoted the understanding that the intellectual and corporeal elements of the human person are inseparably joined through mutual conditioning and mutual interaction. Theology, however, still conceives itself much more as a humane discipline that regards the corporeal primarily as the expression of the intentions of the human spirit and the instrument for this.

(3) *Church Teaching.* The church teaches that the body belongs essentially to the human person (DS 902; GS 14). Through the body the human person carries "in himself the elements of the material world" and lends them his or her voice to the praise of God (GS 14).

(4) *Ecumenical Perspectives.* The unity of the body and intellect of the human person before God receives even more emphasis in Protestant than in Catholic theology.

(5) *Systematic Reflections.* The theological interpretation of the corporality of the human person usually focuses on the mediating function of the body

from material reality (cosmos) toward the spirit of the human person, which then takes up the material in its relation to the absolute Spirit (see [3]). This is contradicted not only by the experience of the unfathomable character of the corporeal and cosmic element but also by the insight from empirical anthropology that the spiritual-intellectual sphere is deeply rooted in and remains within the biophysical sphere. Perhaps the hierarchical gradation of the spirit over the body that pervades the whole of Western intellectual history must be fundamentally corrected. If the irreducible polarity of spirit and body as it is manifested in the consciousness of the human person is an essential characteristic of her or his creatureliness, then God cannot be conceived only as the absolute Spirit. God is then the absolute origin that transcends the difference of spirit and body. For the theological interpretation of corporality this would mean that also in the unfathomable character of his or her corporeal-cosmic rootedness the human person experiences him- or herself as oriented toward the transcendent mystery of God. The insights of depth psychology into prerational representations and experiences (myths, dreams) would then hold a theological significance that dogmatic theology has only rarely (E. Drewermann) and hesitatingly begun to acknowledge.

See also FLESH-SPIRIT; IMMORTALITY; PERSON; SOUL.

Bibliography
See the bibliography under BODY OF CHRIST.

GEORG LANGEMEYER

Cosmogony. The word *cosmogony* is applied primarily to mythopoetic accounts of the origin of the world. In modern physics and astronomy, it signifies descriptions of the development of the universe out of matter. For the societies in which they are culturally embedded, mythic cosmogonies possess an existential significance that brings the cosmogony into play at decisive moments in the life of the individual: birth, initiation, sickness, marriage, death. The cosmogony is constantly revivified through ceremonial presentation or enactment, with magical activities often being practiced on the basis of belief that knowledge of the origin of a natural phenomenon renders it subject to control or exorcism. Among the prototypes found in cosmogony are: emanation; growth; and formation out of primal matter by God, the gods, or a demiurge, who then, in the myths, engage in verbal or sexual acts by way of a divine struggle against chaos — although in others, contrastingly, a primal undividedness of the male and female world-principles (androgyny) is recognized. Occasionally presupposed as well are theogonies, that is, accounts of the generation of the gods (Hesiod). Cosmogonic myths are extremely ancient, occurring in cultures as different as the Sumerian, Babylonian, Egyptian, Greek, Polynesian, Indo-Vedic, and Aztec. Theologically, they are of interest as contrasts to the biblical accounts of creation.

See also EVOLUTION: THEORY OF, AND CREATION; MYTHS OF CREATION.

Bibliography

Eliade, Mircea. *The Myth of the Eternal Return.* Princeton, N.J.: Princeton University Press, 1971.

Shafer, Byron E. *Religion in Ancient Egypt: Gods, Myths, and Personal Practice.* Ithaca, N.Y.: Cornell University Press, 1991.

Weigle, Marta. *Creation and Procreation: Feminist Reflections on Mythologies of Cosmogony and Parturition.* Philadelphia: University of Pennsylvania Press, 1989.

ALEXANDRE GANOCZY

Cosmology. Cosmology is the philosophical or natural-scientific study of the universe and its history. In the Western cultural sphere, ancient Greek cosmology was of great significance, its impetus lying in many-sided inquiry, beyond the level of mythology, about the ultimate ground of things (*arché* [see BEGINNING]). The philosophers also attempted to identify the primary material of the cosmos: water (Thales), air (Anaximenes), fire (Heraclitus), the four "elements" (Empedocles), or infinite matter (Anaxagoras). Leucippus of Miletus and Democritus had already reduced the universe to "atoms" — that is, the smallest, indivisible unities — and their eternal, autonomous motion in infinite space. Constantly new combinations of atoms were held to give rise to constantly new bodies and worlds. The harmony of the cosmos as an ordered whole was due, according to the Pythagoreans, to eternal mathematical laws; according to Plato, to the ideas and the world-soul; and according to Aristotle, to a concentric structure existing in time, with no beginning or end, but having the earth as its spatially finite center. Ptolemy supplemented the Aristotelian worldview with his theory of the eccentric orbits of the planets. Five centuries before him, to be sure, Aristarchus of Samos (third century B.C.E.) had already postulated the revolution of the earth around the sun. Not until the fifteenth and sixteenth centuries, with N. Copernicus, J. Kepler, and G. Galileo, did the Christian West find its way to acceptance of this heliocentric worldview (originating in philosophy and taken over by physics) and to ultimate abandonment of the geocentrism long defended by the church. Modern natural science is primarily interested in the formation of the cosmos as a developmental dimension of matter. Its cosmology is grounded in physics and astronomy. Its research objective is a system of mathematical formulas to describe the universe in its present state. Currently, two directions can be observed in such cosmologies: one postulates a primal core and primal state of the universe as a unity, which suggests the question of its age; the other regards the cosmos as temporally infinite, and rests content with descriptions of partial processes. The dogmatics of creation comes under challenge from both directions and needs to take a position on the worldview that results from modern natural science and philosophy.

See also BEGINNING; CREATION: THEOLOGY OF; EVOLUTION: THEORY OF, AND CREATION; WORLDVIEW.

Bibliography

Hoyle, Fred. *The Intelligent Universe.* New York: Holt, Rinehart, and Winston, 1984.

Miller, James B., and Kenneth E. McCall, eds. *The Church and Contemporary Cosmology.* Pittsburgh: Carnegie-Mellon University Press, 1990.

Toulmin, Stephen. *The Return to Cosmology: Postmodern Science and the Theology of Nature.* Berkeley: University of California Press, 1982.

Tracy, David, and Nicholas Lash, eds. *Cosmology and Theology.* Vol. 166 of *Concilium.* New York: Seabury, 1983.

Unsold, Albrecht. *The New Cosmos.* 2d rev. and enl. ed. New York: Springer, 1977.

Yourgrau, Wolfgang, and Allan Breck. *Cosmology, History, and Theology.* New York: Plenum, 1977.

ALEXANDRE GANOCZY

Council. A council is a meeting of the leaders of all, or several, of the particular churches; at this meeting they come to binding decisions in matters of faith and Christian life.

(1) *Biblical Background.* The so-called Apostolic Council (Acts 15; perhaps also Gal 2:1–10), which shows points of contact with the Jewish Synedrium or Sanhedrin (see Dt 17:8–13), is regarded as the New Testament prototype of councils.

(2) *History of Theology.* Despite the many traits they have in common, the twenty-one ecumenical councils held thus far (see table) show very great differences, which are due to the different reasons, external and internal, for which they were called.

(3) *Church Teaching.* The position of a council in relation to office in the church was defined most recently at Vatican II (*LG* 22; *CD* 4): convocation, presidency, and confirmation (at least in the sense of acceptance) of its decrees are papal prerogatives (see also *CIC* 338–41).

(4) *Ecumenical Perspectives.* In the churches of the East councils play an important theological role as expressions of joint consultation and decision making in the Holy Spirit. These churches, however, accept only the first four or five as ecumenical; the medieval councils of the West are regarded as local synods. In Protestantism councils are simply means set down in human law for determining whether faith and constitution are in accordance with the Scriptures. In the ecumenical dialogue, councils are taking on a growing importance: the Orthodox churches are planning a "Pan-Orthodox Council," while the call for a "truly universal council" is also being heard in the West.

(5) *Systematic Reflections.* The theological basis for councils is the fundamentally conciliar nature of the church: because the church is a communion (*communio*), qualified members of the church ought to gather, as a group possessing authority, to consult and make decisions in the Holy Spirit for the protection of the Catholic unity of the church. As actualizations of communion, councils belong to the CONSTITUTION OF THE CHURCH, although there is no necessity, to this end, either of councils as we presently have them or of any permanent and unchangeable form of council. RECEPTION of councils is an important phase in the process.

See also CHURCH; COLLEGIALITY; TEACHING OFFICE OF THE CHURCH.

ECUMENICAL COUNCILS

Place	Time	Sessions	Pope	Subjects of Discussion and Decrees
1. Nicaea I	5/20–7/25(?)/ 325		Sylvester I	Profession of faith against the Arians (Father and Son consubstantial) (20 canons)
2. Constantinople I	May–July 381		Damasus I	Profession of faith (Nicene-Constantinopolitan) with confession of divinity of Spirit (4 canons)
3. Ephesus	6/22–7/17/431	5	Celestine I	Divine maternity of Mary (vs. Nestorius) (6 canons)
4. Chalcedon	10/8–11/1/451	17	Leo I	Two natures, one person in Christ (28 canons)
5. Constantinople II	5/5–6/2/553	8	Vigilius	Condemnation of the Nestorian "Three Chapters"
6. Constantinople III (Trullanum)	11/7/680– 9/16/681	16	Agatho, Leo II	Condemnation of Monotheletism (problem of Honorius)
7. Nicaea II	9/24–10/23/ 787	8	Hadrian I	Meaning and legitimacy of image veneration (20 canons)
8. Constantinople IV	10/5/869– 2/28/870	10	Hadrian II	Elimination of the Photian schism (27 canons)
9. Lateran I	3/18–4/6/ 1123		Callistus II	Confirmation of the Concordat of Worms (25 canons)
10. Lateran II	April 1139		Innocent II	Settlement of the ecclesial confusion caused by the schism of Anacletus; renewal of the principles of the Gregorian Reform
11. Lateran III	3/5–19 (or 23) 1179	3	Alexander III	Two-thirds majority for election of a pope (27 chapters)
12. Lateran IV	11/11–11/30 1215	3	Innocent III	Profession of faith vs. Cathars; transubstantiation; annual confession and communion; prohibition of secret marriages (70 chapters)
13. Lyons I	6/28–7/17/ 1245	3	Innocent IV	Deposition of Emperor Frederick II (22 chapters)
14. Lyons II	5/7–7/17/ 1274	6	Gregory X	Regulation of conclaves; union with Greeks; Crusade (31 chapters)
15. Vienne	10/16/1311– 5/6/1312	3	Clement V	Abolition of Order of Templars; poverty controversy; church reform
16. Constance	11/5/1414– 4/22/1418	45		Removal of the Western Schism (3 popes); election of Martin V (11/11/1417); condemnation of J. Huss; Decrees *Sacrosancta* (superiority of pope over council) and *Frequens* (periodicity of councils)
17. Basel-Ferrara-Florence	11/5/1431– 2/24/1443 (with interruptions)		Eugene IV	Union with Greeks, Armenians, and Jacobites
18. Lateran V	5/10/1512– 3/16/1517	12	Julius II, Leo X	Vs. schismatic Council of Pisa; immortality of soul; rejection of doctrine of "double truth"; reform
19. Trent	12/13/1545– 12/4/1563 (3 periods)	25	Paul III, Julius III, Pius IV	Clash with the Reformation; Scripture and tradition; original sin; justification; sacraments; sacrifice of Mass; veneration of saints; reform decrees
20. Vatican I	12/8/1869– 7/18/1870	4	Pius IX	Faith, revelation, papal primacy of jurisdiction and infallibility
21. Vatican II	10/11/1962– 12/8/1965	4	John XXIII, Paul VI	Revelation; church; ecumenism; freedom of religion; liturgical reform (16 documents)

(Data from *LThK* 6:529f.)

Bibliography
Black, Antony. *Council and Commune: The Conciliar Movement and the Council of Basle.* London: Burns and Oates, 1979.
Tierney, Brian. *Foundations of Conciliar Theory.* Cambridge: Cambridge University Press, 1955.

WERNER LÖSER

Covenant. In a theological perspective, covenant is the community of personal partnership between God and human beings that God establishes in history out of unconditional, free love so that human beings can be saved.

(1) *Biblical Background.* Covenant (Hebrew: *berit;* Greek: *diathéke;* Latin: *foedus* or *pactum*), a term employed frequently in the Old Testament, is a major theme there. In the New Testament, covenant — in its few occurrences — is a pivotal notion insofar as the salvific work of Jesus Christ establishes a new covenant. The Old Testament term *berit*, traditionally translated "covenant" (although this is now debated), describes the living history in which God establishes community with humankind in ever-new ways: thus the covenant with Noah (Gn 9:8–17), the covenant with Abraham (Gn 15:7–21), and the covenant with the people of Israel on Sinai. One key characteristic of these great covenants is that the initiative is completely and unilaterally from God: God offers a covenant by grace, without any merit on the part of humankind. The purpose of the covenant is the establishment of a living community between God and human beings that brings them salvation as the highest goal. The Sinaitic covenant involves covenantal behavior on both sides: God is bound totally to human beings, God's conduct being characterized by goodness (mercy) and fidelity; and human beings owe God obedience and fidelity in response to God's directives. Human beings are partners in this covenant, but God remains the absolute Lord of the covenant, the one who guarantees salvation for fidelity to the covenant and condemnation if they break it. In Israel's time of exile, Jeremiah, Ezekiel, and Second Isaiah introduce the idea of a new covenant that is interior and universal. In this new covenant the love of God brings about an inner transformation, a renewal of hearts (Jer 31:33; 32:40; Ez 36:26). It includes all people eschatologically (Is 55:3–5) since the suffering servant of God is a universal mediator of salvation (Is 42:6f.; 49:6). Hosea uses the image of a marriage covenant to describe this covenant of the end-time (Hos 2:21f.). The essential message proclaimed by the New Testament is that in Jesus Christ, God realized the prophets' promise of a new covenant (Acts 3:24–26); the Sinai covenant is positively dissolved since its statements concerning salvation have achieved their eschatological fulfillment in the salvific work of Jesus Christ (Lk 1:68–72). The explicit proclamation of the new covenant is achieved in the Last Supper narrative (SEE EUCHARIST: ACCOUNTS OF INSTITUTION): by means of his words over the cup, Jesus interprets his bloody self-gift on the cross as "the blood of the covenant" (Mt 26:28; Mk 14:24) or as "the new covenant in my blood" (Lk 22:20; 1 Cor 11:25). Paul speaks of the differ-

ence between the outmoded old covenant and the new covenant, using striking antitheses: the opposition of law and gospel, slavery and freedom (Galatians 3–5), the letter that kills and the life-giving Spirit, what is passing and what remains (2 Cor 3:6–18). Hebrews uses ritual categories to develop a theology of covenant (7:1–10:18): Jesus Christ as eternal and perfect priest becomes "the guarantee of a better covenant" (7:22). By means of his once-for-all oblation on the cross, which brings about eternal redemption, he is the "mediator of a new covenant" (9:15).

(2) *History of Theology.* In the history of dogmatics the notion of covenant plays no important role in the early church and medieval theology.

(3) *Church Teaching.* There have been no official pronouncements concerning the theme of covenant.

(4) *Ecumenical Perspectives.* Starting with the Reformation a theology of covenant based on salvation-history becomes extremely significant and is a specific characteristic of Reformed theology. H. Zwingli (d. 1531) lays the foundation for later "covenant theology" (*Foederaltheologie*), according to which there is a single covenant from creation until the final fulfillment. According to J. Calvin (d. 1564), the covenant with the patriarchs is already the gospel covenant and has its fulfillment only in Jesus Christ (*Inst.* 2.9–11). As distinct from the single covenant in Zwingli and Calvin, many Reformers of the following period develop a twofold covenant, and this notion is considered normative in the Westminster profession of faith (1647). According to a promise and fulfillment schema, they distinguish between a temporal covenant of action, which is written in the heart, and an eternal covenant of grace, which is realized eschatologically in Jesus Christ. Thus covenant theology is predominant in Reformed doctrine of the seventeenth century and attains classical proportion in J. Cocceius (d. 1669). After a long interval, K. Barth in the twentieth century renews the idea of a salvation-history covenant, the covenant of an eternal election by grace (*KD* 3/1 and 4/1). The Old Testament and the New Testament are unified in continuing the covenant of grace that was laid down from eternity in the God-man, Jesus Christ, and fulfilled in his eschatological work of reconciliation. The law — in the sequence, gospel then law — is not opposed to, but a part of the gospel. Creation and covenant are in a dialectical relationship, that is, the covenant is the inner ground of creation, and creation is the external ground of covenant. In an ecumenical perspective, it is striking that at present, Lutheran theologians firmly reject Barth's position because it posits an order prior to the gospel and finds a place for the law. But in standard Catholic dogmatics (e.g., *MystSal* 2), Barth's dialectical relationship of the orders of creation and redemption is accepted.

(5) *Systematic Reflections.* The notion of covenant reveals God's grace as a willingness to exist in community: God accepts the relationship to human beings as a living determination of God's self and elevates humanity to partnership in salvific love, even though it is unmerited and unearned. God is so involved with human beings that throughout history God keeps renewing the

invitation to community. However, God gives humanity complete freedom to accept or reject the covenant. The person who responds affirmatively to God's offer of a covenant can rejoice in God's loving partnership and receives the power to follow the covenantal directives that are given on behalf of his or her salvation. Thus the idea of covenant characterizes the relationship of God and humankind as a personal community of life and destiny, while the infinite distance between God and humankind still remains: God is God, and human beings are still creatures. The notion of covenant is significant not only in determining the relationship of God and humankind but also in clarifying the relationship between the Old and New Testaments, for in every dogmatic perspective it yields a summary description of the continuity and difference between the Testaments. Thus, for theories of theological knowledge, the continuity and the difference between Old Testament and New Testament revelation are as follows: the same God who makes known a desire to be in community with human beings in Old Testament covenants also reveals in the incarnation of his son, Jesus Christ, a desire to be in the closest relationship with humankind through a new covenant. Jesus Christ is both the dissolution of and the fulfillment of the Old Testament, for by becoming the bodily realization of the community willed by God, he brings the Old Testament covenant unsurpassably and definitively to its truth. The covenant reveals God's salvific will as soteriological and shows how it continues throughout the history of humankind, reaching an unimaginable new phase in the salvific work of Jesus Christ. Ecclesiologically, the covenant changes from the old to the new people of God; in other words, from Israel to the church. While Israel, as a specific people, had a limited salvific mandate, the church from the beginning is at home with all peoples and is sent as a messenger of salvation to all peoples. In the Old Testament as well as the New Testament there are signs of the covenant that are worthy of reflection, but the New Testament replaces the Old Testament covenantal signs of circumcision and bloody sacrifice with the sacraments of BAPTISM and the EUCHARIST, where the once-for-all covenantal sacrifice of Jesus Christ on the cross is made present (in an unbloody sacrifice). From an eschatological viewpoint, the old covenant is a stage leading to the eternal new covenant, which was initially realized with the coming of Jesus Christ and will be completed by his return (see KINGDOM OF GOD).

See also EUCHARIST; LAW AND GOSPEL; UNIVERSAL SALVIFIC WILL OF GOD.

Bibliography

Borowitz, Eugene B. *Renewing the Covenant: A Theology for the Postmodern Jew.* Philadelphia: Jewish Publication Society, 1991.

Carmichael, Calum M. *The Origins of Biblical Law: The Decalogues and the Book of the Covenant.* Ithaca, N.Y.: Cornell University Press, 1992.

Carroll, Robert P. *From Chaos to Covenant: Prophecy in the Book of Jeremiah.* New York: Crossroad, 1981.

Clifford, Richard. *Deuteronomy: With an Excursus on Covenant and Law.* Wilmington, Del.: Glazier, 1982.

Elazar, Daniel Judah. *Covenant and Polity in Biblical Israel: Biblical Foundations and Jewish Expressions.* New Brunswick, N.J.: Transaction, 1994.

Fuller, Daniel P. *Gospel and Law: Contrast or Continuum? The Hermeneutics of Dispensationalism and Covenant Theology.* Grand Rapids: Eerdmans, 1980.

Keefe, Donald J. *Covenantal Theology: The Eucharistic Order of History.* Lanham, Md.: University Press of America, 1991.

Lohfink, Norbert. *The Covenant Never Revoked: Biblical Reflections on Christian-Jewish Dialogue.* New York: Paulist, 1991.

Longenecker, Bruce W. *Eschatology and the Covenant: A Comparison of 4 Ezra and Romans 1–11.* Sheffield, England: JSOT, 1991.

Murray, Robert. *The Cosmic Covenant: Biblical Themes of Justice, Peace and the Integrity of Creation.* London: Sheed and Ward, 1992.

Nicholson, Ernest W. *God and His People: Covenant and Theology in the Old Testament.* Oxford: Clarendon, 1986.

Poole, David N. J. *The History of the Covenant Concept from the Bible to Johannes Cloppenburg: De foedere Dei.* San Francisco: Mellen, 1992.

GEORG KRAUS

Creation. The word *creation* denotes the exclusively divine activity of originating, forming, and newly forming (Genesis 1; Is 43:1; 45:7), as well as what results from that activity. There is an impulsion toward the perfecting of all created things (Is 41:20; 42:5). Creation has implicit ties to human beings' desire to understand their existence — about where they came from, where they are going, and what for.

(1) *Biblical Background.* The Bible discusses this in the so-called accounts of creation. Of God's own accord and without relying upon any preexisting material, God effects the absolute beginning of the history of nature and humanity. To designate this activity, Gn 1:1 and other texts (Pss 89:48; 104:30; Is 43:1; 54:16; 65:17f.) use the verb *bara,* which can have only God as its subject. It implies commanding speech that, with consummate ease, effects what it states: "God said... and it occurred" (see Ps 148:5) — something from which an analogically personal being can be inferred. Humans make their appearance as beings who are bound to matter (Adam = man of clay, from *'adāmāh* = clay) and imbued with a soul (Gn 2:7). Their life stems from God, the living one. Superior to the animals, humans alone, as male and female beings, are referred to as the "image" of God (Gn 1:27). Called to a special relationship of trust with their Creator, humans nevertheless have the possibility of rejecting that trust, of overstepping the bounds laid down by God, of committing offenses against God and against their social or natural environment as well as themselves, of sinning (see Genesis 3–6; 11:1–9). But God judges them and, at the same time, shows them God's forgiving and newly creating grace (e.g., Gn 6:8; 7:1; 8:21). The cosmos is also part of God's creation. Matter, plants, and animals come into being as nature and develop themselves in accordance with nature's own inherent laws (see Gn 1:11–13, 22, 28). Their function is to subserve the glory of the Creator and the welfare of the human species, but they must not be regarded by the latter as utilitarian objects to be exploited at will

and destroyed. Rather, humanity should watch over nature in the sense of a good shepherd (Gn 1:28f.; cf. 2:15). The New Testament also shares the beliefs about creation just outlined. Jesus, despite anticipating the imminent end, by no means disdains this world. He enjoys its goods (cf. the abusive terms "glutton" and "drunkard" [Mt 11:19]). He has come not "to destroy human beings, but to save them" (see Lk 9:55). At the end of time, "God's creation" is to be subjected to tribulation (Mk 13:19f.). But as long as history continues, God's fatherly care remains in effect for creation (Mt 5:43–45; 6:25–34; 10:29–31). Jesus, in his parables, makes nature a preacher of the coming dominion of God. His farewell meal amounts to a truly Jewish panegyric on the Creator and redeemer of the people (Mt 14:22f.). The risen crucified one appears in the New Testament as the Lord of all creation (Phil 2:5–11). He is called the new, "last [eschatological] Adam" (1 Cor 15:45–49). Through his resurrection in unprecedented bodily form, human beings undergo an exaltation that is pregnant with eternity, and sinners undergo a reconciliation that encompasses all places and times (Col 1:17–20; Eph 1:10). Whoever is in Christ is a "new creation" (2 Cor 5:17). The redeemed community of creatures also encompasses the whole of the cosmos (Rom 8:19–21). The Holy Spirit intercedes for them with pleadings that give cause for hope (Rom 8:23–30).

(2) *History of Theology.* In the course of the history of dogma, the Christian understanding of creation was initially given — counter to gnostic heresies antagonistic to the body and history — a redemptive-historical stamp, primarily by Irenaeus of Lyons (d. 202): creation is the joint achievement of the triune God (*Adv. haer.* 4.20:1–3) and is oriented from the very start toward the goal of Christ, the redeemer (3.22.1); the world and history move, despite the disruptions caused by evil (4.37.1ff.), toward their consummation, or more precisely, toward recapitulation under the one head, Christ (*anakephalaíosis, recapitulatio*) (2.22.4; 3.18.1–7). What the Bible tended to call watchful care, many Church Fathers, influenced by Stoicism, speak of as God's providence (*prónoia*). According to Clement of Rome (d. ca. 100), creation owes its order and beauty to the cosmic fatherhood of the Creator (1 Clem 7:3; 20:8). God's providence enables the seeds to bring forth fruit (24:5). John Chrysostom (d. 407) occupies himself with the ordered lawfulness of creation (*Ad pop. Antioch. hom.,* 9.4). SUFFERING and EVIL acquire from the Creator an ultimate meaning. It was at the time of the Fathers that the doctrines of "creation out of nothing" (*creatio ex nihilo*) and — linked especially to Augustine — of original and inherited sin were developed.

(3) *Church Teaching.* Teaching office set itself initially against tendencies to demonize corporeality. This occurred at a provincial synod of Toledo in 447 (DS 283–86). A similar synod (Braga, 561) called attention to the esteem of human nature that is implicit in the incarnation (DS 454). There, too, a doctrine on angels (DS 455; see ANGEL) and the DEVIL (DS 457) was formulated. The goodness of marriage within the framework of creation was confirmed both there (DS 461f.) and — in opposition to the Albigensians — at the Fourth

Lateran Council in 1215. Centrally important, along with a summary of tradition, was the following declaration: God, "in his almighty power and at the beginning of time, created both orders of creation [i.e., the material and the spiritual] in the same way, out of nothing" (DS 800; for the other declarations, see DS 801f.). In 1546–47, the Council of Trent firmly upheld, against the Lutheran challenge, the Catholic doctrines of original sin (DS 1510–15) and free will (DS 1521, 1554f.).

(4) *Ecumenical Perspectives.* In this area more than any other, attempts to achieve ecumenical unification are needed. The question ultimately comes down to defining the correct relationship between the orders of creation and redemption. Protestant interpreters of the Old Testament (G. von Rad, C. Westermann) and the New Testament (U. Wilckens, commentary on the Letter to the Romans), but also systematic theologians (G. Ebeling, W. Pannenberg, J. Moltmann), have made important contributions to a common Christian doctrine of creation.

(5) *Systematic Reflections.* Theological explication of a religious position on creation for our time has been definitively advanced by Catholic doctrinal office at Vatican II (*GS*). Vatican I still had to focus its attention mainly on errors resulting from improper appropriation of ideas from C. Darwin and G. W. F. Hegel. Repudiated were pantheism (DS 3001), materialism (DS 3023), and evolutionism (DS 3024); advocated were creation of the world through God's "most freely willed decision" (DS 3002), out of God's goodness, for the purpose of God's glorification (DS 3002, 3025), and in view of God's all-protecting and all-governing providence (DS 3003). As a supplement to these declarations, Vatican II put forward a doctrine of creation giving prominence to the bodily and spiritual worth (*GS* 14–18) of the two-sided human person (*GS* 11–13). Creation comes about "out of love" (*ex amore*), out of God's creative love (*GS* 19), which seeks its witnesses even today (*GS* 20–22). Human creativity issues from the blessing conferred by the Creator on God's two-gendered "image" (*GS* 33–37): labor develops and advances God's work (*GS* 34; cf. 67), while progress toward better technology and higher justice corresponds to God's will (*GS* 35). Discordant with creation are manifestations of inordinate self-love (*GS* 37). Human creativity is therefore to be redeemed (*GS* 38) and eschatologically perfected (*GS* 39). Marriage, family (*GS* 48–52), and society (*GS* 23f., 32, 57–94) have significance for the kingdom of God from within God's creation (see *GS* 39).

See also BEGINNING; CREATION: BELIEF IN, AND NATURAL SCIENCE; CREATION: THEOLOGY OF; CREATION NARRATIVES; CREATION OUT OF NOTHING; CREATURELINESS; DEISM; EVOLUTION: THEORY OF, AND CREATION; MYTHS OF CREATION; NATURE; THEODICY; WORLDVIEW.

Bibliography
Daly, Gabriel. *Creation and Redemption.* Wilmington, Del.: Glazier, 1989.
Gilkey, Langdon. *Maker of Heaven and Earth.* Garden City, N.Y.: Doubleday, 1959.
Hayes, Zachary. *What Are They Saying about Creation?* New York: Paulist, 1980.

Moltmann, Jürgen. *God in Creation: An Ecological Doctrine of Creation.* London: SCM, 1985.

Peters, Ted, ed. *Cosmos as Creation: Theology and Science in Consonance.* Nashville: Abingdon, 1988.

Trefil, James S. *The Moment of Creation: Big Bang Physics from before the First Millisecond to the Present Universe.* New York: Scribner's, 1983.

                                                    ALEXANDRE GANOCZY

Creation: Belief in, and Natural Science. The juxtaposed notions of "belief in creation" and "natural science" give expression to a tension-laden relationship arising from the fact that the one identical reality of world and humanity is interpreted and evaluated religiously, as the creation of God, by belief in creation, whereas it is described, under the conditions of the SPACE-TIME SCHEMA, empirically and rationally — and thus in a value-free way — by natural science.

(1) *Biblical Background.* The Bible creates, in a remote but effective manner, favorable conditions for a dialogue between belief in creation and natural science under the assumption that these are complementary approaches to knowing the world. The CREATION NARRATIVES offer an essentially demythologized interpretation of the world. The stars and other forces of nature lose their divine or demonic character: they perform serving functions within the divinely willed natural order. Genesis and the wisdom texts reflect the knowledge of nature that was current at the time of their composition without recording it as revealed truth. The gap between the human creature and its material, vegetable, and animal environment manifests itself not as a separation, but as something that makes possible dealing objectively with that environment. Insofar as the natural sciences aim at doing this, they are acting in the sense of the "commission of creation," which is simultaneously a blessing: to "subdue" the earth (Gn 1:28), that is, to take responsible possession of it. In those words can be glimpsed the foundations of a Christian CULTURE, which virtually thrusts toward the development of natural science.

(2) *History of Theology.* The Fathers were generally under the influence of philosophical cosmologies when, while not failing to appreciate the natural science of their time, they defended Christian belief in creation against competing interpretations of the world and developed it theologically (CREATION OUT OF NOTHING [CREATIO EX NIHILO]; DUALISM; ENTELECHY; GOD'S CARE; PRESERVATION OF THE WORLD; WORLDVIEW). The Christian Middle Ages became the cradle of modern natural science, in no small part through a successful synthesis of the biblical view of nature and Aristotelian realism. Albert the Great, Thomas Aquinas, and the Franciscan school are good examples of this. N. Copernicus, P. Gassendi, J. Kepler, B. Pascal, and I. Newton understood their research work as service to God the Creator.

(3) *Church Teaching.* Doctrinal office did not arrive at a positive evaluation of the relationship between belief in creation and the natural sciences until after both the Inquisition's overreaction to Galileo (see *GS* 36, n. 7; commentary

in *LThK*[2] 3:387) and the apologetic opposition to Darwin had been overcome. Vatican I introduced the fundamental clarification that there can never be a real contradiction between faith and reason "because the same God who reveals the mysteries and instills belief has also given the human soul the light of reason" (DS 3017); faith and reason "assist one another"; the church does not wish to forbid that the sciences "employ their own principles and methods within their area of inquiry" (DS 3019). Vatican II spoke even more unambiguously of the "autonomy of earthly realities" that corresponds to the "will of the Creator" (*GS* 36): "Through having been created themselves, all particular sorts of reality have their fixed distinctiveness,...their own laws and their own orders which humanity must respect by acknowledging the methods peculiar to the particular sciences and technologies."

(4) *Ecumenical Perspectives.* Reformation theology also experienced, and still experiences, instances of conflict between belief in creation and natural science. Luther held fast to Ptolemaic geocentrism, against Galileo's heliocentrism, on the basis of a precritical exegesis. Today, it is fundamentalist streams within Protestantism that oppose current natural-scientific knowledge in the name of belief in creation.

(5) *Systematic Reflections.* Modern theology of creation (see CREATION: THEOLOGY OF), right across confessional boundaries, takes up P. Teilhard de Chardin's concern to bring natural-scientific investigation, description, explanation, organization, and interpretation of the world into reciprocally complementary interrelation on the basis of belief in creation. Its responses rest primarily not on the compelling logic of demonstrable factual conditions, but on the trustworthiness of God as conclusively manifested in Christ. Inasmuch as it thus *interprets* and *evaluates* the beginning, duration, course, and goal of world and history, it recognizes in the cosmic process a mystery of creatively self-communicating agape as well as a drama of the struggle between God-willed good and God-opposed evil (EVIL, MORAL). The natural sciences, by contrast, realize that they are not responsible for answering humanity's existential, ethical, and ultimate questions; their aim is to achieve precise knowledge of objective facts, which they order in accordance with hypothetically derived laws and measure by means of generally valid numerical systems. The drawing of analogies between EVOLUTION and continuous creation, the history of nature and redemptive history, contingency and the working of grace, and HOMINIZATION and the perfection of humans in resurrected life is an important approach for belief in creation today. After the turning point that occurred with relativity theory and quantum theory, which brought rejection of Enlightenment myths like the absolute determinedness of world processes, the total objectivity of observation, the complete certainty and precision of the results of measurement, or the unendingness of progress, the danger of an ideologization of the natural sciences — except perhaps within orthodox Marxism — lessened significantly. The ultimate questions are once again left to religion and philosophy. At the same time, consciousness increases that a humanity empowered with

the natural sciences is capable of doing terrifyingly more than it should do —
thoroughly despoiling its environment, extirpating entire species, and ruining
its own future on earth and in outer space. Nuclear energy and gene technology
give cause for alarm. In this dramatic context, calls are often made for a hermeneutics of belief in creation that does justice to present-day circumstances,
so that *application* of the natural sciences might be subjected to appropriate
ethical norms.

See also CREATION; EVOLUTION: THEORY OF, AND CREATION; FAITH; HERME-
NEUTICS; NATURE.

Bibliography
Barbour, Ian. *Myths, Models, and Paradigms: A Comparative Study in Science and Religion.*
    New York: Harper and Row, 1974.
———. *Religion in an Age of Science.* San Francisco: Harper and Row, 1990.
Brooke, John Hedley. *Science and Religion: Some Historical Perspectives.* New York:
    Cambridge University Press, 1991.
Gerhart, Mary, and Allan Russell. *Metaphoric Process: The Creation of Scientific and
    Religious Understanding.* Fort Worth: Texas Christian University Press, 1984.
Jaki, Stanley L. *Universe and Creed.* Milwaukee: Marquette University Press, 1992.
Kaiser, Christopher B. *Creation and the History of Science.* Grand Rapids: Eerdmans, 1991.
McMullin, Ernan, ed. *Evolution and Creation.* Notre Dame, Ind.: University of Notre Dame
    Press, 1985.
Peacocke, Arthur R. *The Sciences and Theology in the Twentieth Century.* Notre Dame, Ind.:
    University of Notre Dame Press, 1981.
Peters, Ted, ed. *Cosmos as Creation: Theology and Science in Consonance.* Nashville:
    Abingdon, 1988.
Polkinghorne, John. *One World: The Interaction of Science and Theology.* London: SPCK,
    1986.
Russell, Robert John, et al. *Physics, Philosophy, and Theology.* Vatican City: Vatican
    Observatory; and Notre Dame, Ind.: University of Notre Dame Press, 1984.
Schindler, David, ed. *Beyond Mechanism: The Universe in Recent Physics and Catholic
    Thought.* New York: University Press of America, 1986.

ALEXANDRE GANOCZY

Creation

Contemporary Issues

The doctrine of CREATION is a theological response to the foundational question that is at one and the same time religious, philosophical, and scientific:
Why is there anything at all, rather than nothing? The doctrine responds with
the belief that it is GOD who ultimately is the source, ground, and goal of all
things, visible and invisible. In the initial centuries of Christianity's encounter
with Greco-Roman culture the patterns for articulating the "why" for creation

emerged in contradistinction to gnostic DUALISM and pantheism. Against the dualism of the gnostics, Christianity emphasized that the cosmos and all of the matter that comprises it are divinely ordered and good, created by the same loving God revealed in Jesus Christ. Against pantheism, Christianity asserted that God created the cosmos neither from the divine substance nor out of necessity, but freely from nothing.

The biblically rooted traditional theology of creation emphasized God's transcendence over a universe with an intelligible order that is contingent (CONTINGENCY) rather than necessary. These elements contributed inadvertently to the desacralization of nature, characteristic of modernity, to the accompanying rise to hegemony of the natural sciences, to the emergence of a philosophical ATHEISM or secular humanism that presumes that the origins and evolution of the cosmos have an exclusively this-worldly explanation, and to the environmental exploitation that has resulted in our current ecological crisis (ECOLOGY). Questions related to these areas are among the major concerns of creation theology today. Contemporary perspectives on creation, on the whole, are marked by a far less defensive posture toward science than was common prior to Vatican II and by a growing interest in dialogue between theologians and scientists.

Scientific Creationism (Creation Science) and Evolution

The hegemony of the natural sciences is clearly evident in scientific creationism, which claims that there is scientific evidence for the content of Genesis 1–11, specifically the simultaneous creation of the earth and all of its life-forms. Contemporary creation scientists are the ideological descendants of the North American fundamentalists who opposed Darwinian evolution theory. Both take a strong stand for the literal truth of the Bible; both are concerned about the effects of secular ("Godless") humanism on society. There are major differences, however. While the fundamentalists of the era of the Scopes monkey trial (1920s) argued their case against science from the unerring authority of the Bible, creation scientists (1960s–) argue their case for the scientific content of Genesis 1–11 as a theory worthy of treatment equal to that given the theory of biological evolution. To win equal time for teaching creationism as a science in public schools, "balanced treatment" statutes were enacted statewide in Arkansas and Louisiana in 1981. In 1987 the U.S. Supreme Court declared the Louisiana law unconstitutional on the grounds that it seeks to advance a specific religious viewpoint in the name of science.

Although not a Catholic movement per se, scientific creationism has attracted the attention of Catholic laity and theologians. A Catholic theological response to scientific creationism has been succinctly expressed by the Louisiana Catholic Conference: "The Bible teaches certainly that God is creator of all things, and this truth is helpful for salvation. Whatever complex processes may be involved in nature have been left by God for the discovery and wonder

of the human mind. Catholic biblical principles or the teachings of the church
do not require that we take the stories of creation as historical and scientific
accounts; therefore we cannot draw from the Bible any scientific conclusions"
(*Origins* 12 [1983] 604). This statement is predicated on a biblical interpretation that is mindful of the difference in WORLDVIEW between biblical times and
our own. It also recognizes that on an epistemological level scientific theories
and theological doctrines are different.

Cosmology, Creation out of Nothing, and Continuous Creation

Scientific creationism is an attempt to set up an explicit concordist relationship between the content of a scientific theory and belief in a Creator-God.
Concordism has also been evident in theological response to scientific cosmology. Cosmology brings together astronomy and quantum physics in response
to questions about the structure, origin, and evolution of the universe. The big
bang theory, an inflationary model (G. Gamow and others) that depicts the
universe evolving from a singular explosive event roughly fifteen billion years
ago (plus or minus five billion years), is the most widely accepted cosmological theory today. The big bang model is the first occasion that natural science
asserted something that sounds like the beginning of the universe and the birth
of time. Even prior to the wide acceptance of the theory, concordist interpretations by Christian theologians were commonplace. Pope Pius XII (1951) hailed
it for unveiling the secrets of nature and thereby disclosing the creative work of
God. Others regarded it as a proof for CREATION FROM NOTHING (CREATION
EX NIHILO).

Concordist positions, however, are widely regarded as highly problematic today for two major reasons: (1) From the side of science, the big bang (even if
it actually occurred) cannot be assumed to be *the* beginning of time. It could
very well have been preceded by a contraction as part of an infinitely repeat-
able cycle of an oscillating universe. In a strict sense, the big bang does not
refer to the absolute beginning of time; it is a plausible account of the evolution of the universe from a fraction of a second after the initial singularity that
set the expanding universe that we can observe in process. (2) From the side
of theology, creation from nothing is a metaphysical statement and not a scientific or historical one. Made an official doctrine of the church at the Fourth
Lateran Council in 1215 (DS 800), the concept has much earlier roots. The
words "creation from nothing" are found in 2 Mc 7:28 and were applied by
the "Shepherd of Hermas," Irenaeus, Origen, Tertullian, and Augustine in arguments to counter either the Greek pantheistic idea of the coeternity of God
and matter or the moral-metaphysical dualism of the gnostics. None of the
early theologians cited above interpret the Bible in the ways that are widely accepted today. Read in context, 2 Mc 7:28–29 is an eschatological text in which
a mother gives her child reason for resurrection hope in the face of execution,

rather than a protological creation text per se. The Fourth Lateran Council associated creation from nothing with the beginning of time (a problematic area for Thomas Aquinas, *STh* 1a, q. 46). The connection between *creatio ex nihilo* and temporal beginnings is due to the influence of the Vulgate translation of the initial words of Gn 1:1, "In the beginning God created the heavens and the earth," although an alternate translation, "When God began to create the heaven and the earth...," is equally accurate. The difficulties associated with the biblical roots of creation from nothing and its clear metaphysical intent have led theologians to abandon concordist arguments between it and the big bang, to interpret *creatio ex nihilo* as a symbol for the absolute dependence of everything for its existence on God, and to search for other areas of consonance with emphasis on continuous creation.

Continuous creation is a term with many nuanced meanings: the continuous and purposeful support of beings already called into existence (the traditional conserving/preserving/sustaining of divine governance), the incompleteness of the world from the beginning (CONTINGENCY), and the creation of new forms of existence (novelty). Elements of all of these meanings are evident in varying degrees in contemporary theological perspectives on Teilhard's thought, process theology, and anthropic reasoning.

P. Teilhard de Chardin (1881–1955), a Jesuit paleontologist, accepted evolution at a time in which it was held suspect and argued that it had direction and purpose. Teilhard's argument for consonance between evolution and creation faith took the form of a claim for a radial energy, basically psychic in nature, that operates within the evolutionary processes as an intelligence that makes choices among available alternatives. The radial energies of the universe are a manifestation of the "Omega Point" to which all of life is directed. For Teilhard the goal of the universe (God) discloses its meaning. Teilhard's positions, although initially held suspect, influenced *Gaudium et spes* (no. 5) and continue to be a source for Catholic creation theology.

Process theology, like the thought of Teilhard, is receptive to the scientific notion of evolution. Dependent on the philosophical ideas of A. N. Whitehead and C. Hartshorne, process theology affirms continuous creation with emphasis on novelty and preserving care. The central concept of process thought is creativity, the moment-by-moment emergence of an infinite variety of actual occasions of experience that constitutes the whole process of reality, including the very being of God. Process theology understands God to be the source of novelty who, through persuasive love, produces order out of chaos. With this conception of creation, process theology reconciles God with scientific evolution. It envisions God to be the source and stimulus of the evolving cosmos and the evolutionary process to be in harmony with the character and purpose of God.

Continuous creation in new forms of existence is such a strong emphasis in process thought that some process theologians either ignore *creatio ex nihilo* or dismiss it as an archaic symbol. Process theology critiques classical understandings of God because they depict the Creator as a static, preexistent, and transcendent being who suddenly created a world in the beginning out of nothingness but remained totally apart from it. In contrast, process theology, while arguing that God is distinct from creation, emphasizes the immanence of God who exists not before all creation, but with all creation. God is unsurpassably related to the world.

A more recent candidate for theological reflection is the "anthropic principle." In its many differently nuanced "strong" and "weak" versions, the anthropic principle argues that the universe evolving from the big bang, although it could have been very different, is fine-tuned for the appearance of intelligent life. In its strong version, the anthropic principle claims that life and intelligence are a metaprinciple, ultimately responsible for ordering all the fundamental constants of nature in such a way as to make the universe self-aware in human beings. Making intelligence a key factor in the cosmos is a teleological statement that is closely related to classic arguments from design. Members of the scientific community have not reacted favorably to the strong version of anthropic reasoning because the data that support the principles of uncertainty (W. Heisenberg) and of natural selection (C. Darwin) undermine their argument for design. The anthropic principle in its weak form starts from the final observed datum (intelligent human existence now) and reasons back through the chain of properties required to support it. Although more acceptable to the scientific community, it has also received criticism because it reverses conventional scientific reasoning, which starts with an initial situation and then predicts some subsequent development.

A theological consensus on the consonance of anthropic reasoning with creation faith has not yet been reached. Many theologians dismiss it, due to scientific skepticism about its validity. The principle does, however, provide theologians with data for reflection about the cosmos and its delicately balanced processes. Whereas it affirms that the human species is not a mere accident of nature, it points out that humans are an integral part of a finely tuned cosmic process. The principle, therefore, provides a critique of theological anthropocentrism, which places humanity at the center of the universe. Humans may be a privileged outcome of God's creative love; our existence, however, is profoundly dependent on the cosmos as a whole.

Positive theological response to the strong version posits that one cannot argue for the presence of design with intelligence without also positing the existence of a designer (Creator) who intends life to develop in the way it has. An argument for theological consonance with the strong version, however, does not actually further dialogue between science and theology because this version is only marginally scientific, at best. Positive theological response to its weak version affirms purpose in the evolutionary processes of the cosmos. The evolution of the cosmos as we know it is broadly consonant with belief in the existence of divine governance.

Creation and Ecology

One of the newest issues to be addressed in creation theology is ecology. The current ecological crisis, which threatens the future of all life-forms on earth, has brought with it questions not only about the relationship of creation faith to attitudes about earth but also about humanity's place on earth. Criticisms of Christianity have been directed to its indifference to the well-being of non-human nature resulting from its other-worldly emphasis on personal salvation and to the anthropocentrism of the biblical directive for humanity to exercise dominion over the earth (Gn 1:26–28).

Responses to these criticisms have been both apologetic and constructive. Apologetic responses most often base their replies to the environmental crisis on Scripture and tradition. They argue that there are Christian texts that have something positive to offer where ecology or the environment is concerned. The inherent goodness of nature and stewardship are themes most commonly emphasized in the apologetic approach.

Constructive responses to the ecological crisis have taken a number of forms: more explicitly creation-centered revisionist understandings of the world as God's body; an emphasis on the relationality of the TRINITY to the world, cosmic CHRISTOLOGY, the revelatory potential of cosmic processes (REVELATION), and the sacramentality of all of NATURE; ecofeminist revisions of THEOLOGICAL ANTHROPOLOGY; and an ecojustice focus in moral theology.

Bibliography

Barrow, John D., and Frank J. Tipler. *The Anthropic Cosmological Principle.* New York: Oxford University Press, 1986.

Clifford, Anne M. "Creation." In *Systematic Theology: Roman Catholic Perspectives,* edited by Francis Schüssler Fiorenza and John Galvin, 1:193–248. Minneapolis: Fortress Press, 1991.

Frye, Roland Mushat, ed. *Is God a Creationist? The Religious Case against Creation-Science.* New York: Scribner's, 1983.

Haught, John F. *The Promise of Nature: Ecology and Cosmic Purpose.* New York: Paulist, 1993.

McMullin, Ernan. "How Should Cosmology Relate to Theology?" In *The Sciences and Theology in the Twentieth Century,* edited by Arthur Peacocke, 17–51. Notre Dame, Ind.: University of Notre Dame Press, 1981.

———, ed. *Evolution and Creation.* Notre Dame, Ind.: University of Notre Dame Press, 1985.

Moltmann, Jürgen. *God in Creation: An Ecological Doctrine of Creation.* London: SCM, 1985.

Russell, Robert J., William R. Stoeger, and George V. Coyne, eds. *Physics, Philosophy and Theology: A Common Quest for Understanding.* Vatican City: Vatican Observatory, 1988.

Teilhard de Chardin, Pierre. *The Phenomenon of Man.* New York: Harper and Row, 1965.

ANNE M. CLIFFORD, C.S.J.

Creation: Theology of. Theology of creation deals in general with the relationship between the Creator and the Creator's creatures. In the narrower sense of the term — that is, as a classical treatise in dogmatics — it concerns itself centrally today with theological anthropology, cosmology, and theory of history. In recent decades, important Catholic and Protestant dogmatists have developed theologies of creation, each from a particular starting point, and it is these that will be mainly discussed here.

(1) *Biblical Background.* The Bible is the revelatory source of all the essential themes in Christian theology of creation.

(2) *History of Theology.* The Fathers interpret the biblical evidence in a conceptual language that corresponds, in each case, to the particular needs for understanding characteristic of their times.

(3) *Church Teaching.* In opposition to dualistic and modernistic distortions, Catholic doctrinal office has made binding declarations about belief in creation and, at Vatican II, formulated a relatively comprehensive conception of it in view of present-day world realities (see *GS*).

(4) *Ecumenical Perspectives.* Specifically Reformed accentuations were given to traditional theology of creation by M. Luther and J. Calvin. Luther conceives of all of God's activity in the world as something verbal. Initially, God's word *creates* and calls the human creature to God's grace. For fallen humanity, this word becomes the law. Only through the gospel in Christ, however, can the sinner be newly created. Luther keeps the order of creation largely separate from the order of redemption in the face of sin. His doctrine of justification nevertheless also integrates the worldly-earthly things of life — for example, the different vocations — insofar as they have been released by grace. Calvin sees creation in terms of the history of redemption, with pre-Christian (Plato), Old Testament, and New Testament statements about the Creator being regarded as forming a multileveled unity. Decisive to Calvin's theology of creation are the ideas of the old and the new covenants together with an ethical dimension (see *Inst.* 1.1–5, 16ff.). For him, as similarly for K. Barth (*KD* 3/4) later on, the important thing is the sanctification of creaturely activity in all areas of life. Barth further intensifies the Christocentrism of Calvinist theology of creation (*KD* 3/1–4): the incarnate Word of God signifies a constant crisis for God's creatures, but then also a reconciliation. Reconciliation in Christ constitutes the covenant as the meaning-bestowing "inner ground" of creation. In the work of D. Bonhoeffer and F. Gogarten, creation appears as the field of activity for the mature Christian who stands responsibly before God. Much in these ideas forms a constructive contribution to an ecumenical theology of creation.

(5) *Systematic Reflections.* More or less the same applies regarding specifically Catholic models for theology of creation. New pathways were opened by P. Teilhard de Chardin, with his attempt at a synthesis between the natural-scientific, evolutionary understanding of reality and a Christian view of creation centered primarily on the deutero-Pauline cosmic figure of Christ. He rejects the dualism of matter and spirit; in Christ, who is simultaneously both mover

and result of evolutional processes, he sees the unity-conferring meaning of creation. Thus, God both enables and sustains, from within, a development of nature and humanity that otherwise unfolds according to its own laws, advancing toward ever higher stages of complexity and synthesis. K. Rahner's theology of creation, in its general conception, is more than a little related to Teilhard's insofar as it defines God as the transcendental ground of our evolving world (HOMINIZATION); however, instead of a cosmological emphasis, it proceeds under a pronouncedly anthropocentric one. Moreover, Rahner endeavors to define the precise position of theology of creation within general dogmatics: it belongs at the head of a fundamental theology that precedes "special" dogmatics, since it deals with "creatureliness as the enduring basic relationship of humanity to God." Theology of creation is centrally thematic to *theology of God,* inasmuch as God reveals God's nature by being the originator of, and meaning-giver to, our creatureliness; to *theology of grace,* since grace destines human nature as something having the "capacity for obedience" (*potentia oboedientialis*), for the unmerited self-communication of God; to *anthropology,* in which the spiritual creature appears not as "a piece of the world" but as a subject favored with "supernatural existence"; in *Christology,* because Christ is the eschatological, supreme realization of being human, that is, the highest type of creaturely being; and finally to *redemptive history,* which realizes itself as "continuous creation" (*creatio continua*) and gives history in general its true beginning and true goal (*LThK*^{2} 8:471–73). On the basis of this sort of "Christian anthropocentrism," J. B. Metz develops the "theology of the world," including political theology, that was left more or less undeveloped by Rahner. From the Protestant side, J. Moltmann thinks along similar lines when he, too, links up more with K. Barth's legacy than with Thomistic and neo-Kantian approaches. Characteristic of his theology of creation are the following: a striving to adhere to biblical foundations, a thoroughly trinitarian understanding of the Creator, the thesis of the "crucified God," a pneumatologically based perspectivization, and an integration of ECOLOGY with Latin American liberation theology. Another Barth student, E. Jüngel, succeeds in making "God as the mystery of the world" credible — with a view to Hegel's philosophy of history and modern criticism of religion — as God of the eternal, triune agape that is active within creation. W. Pannenberg, in proffering a largely future-oriented, universal-historical theology of creation mindful of human freedom, gives logically consistent development to P. Althaus's idea that we must assume, prior to and outside of the revelation through Christ, a revelation through creation — for instance, in the world religions. The central theme of Jesus' message, namely, the coming dominion of God, provides him with the framework within which God is conceived as the "unifying future of the world," the "creative eschaton," which, from the standpoint of the "end" (i.e., the coming meaningful totality of history) and by force of its immeasurable love, generates everything that was, is, and will be (Pannenberg). A. Ganoczy attempts to reflect on God's creation both from the standpoint of human creativity and — critically and constructively — with a view to that creativity itself; further, in dialogue with modern physics, he attempts to formulate a theology of nature.

See also BEGINNING; CREATION; CREATION: BELIEF IN, AND NATURAL SCIENCE; CREATION NARRATIVES; CREATION OUT OF NOTHING (CREATIO EX NIHILO); CREATURELINESS; DEISM; EVOLUTION: THEORY OF, AND CREATION; NATURE; MYTHS OF CREATION; WORLDVIEW.

Bibliography
Burrell, David B. *Freedom and Creation in Three Traditions.* Notre Dame, Ind.: University of Notre Dame Press, 1993.
Clifford, Richard J., and John J. Collins. *Creation in the Biblical Traditions.* Washington, D.C.: Catholic Biblical Association of America, 1992.
Gilkey, Langdon. *Maker of Heaven and Earth.* Garden City, N.Y.: Doubleday, 1959.
Moltmann, Jürgen. *God in Creation: An Ecological Doctrine of Creation.* London: SCM, 1985.
Pannenberg, Wolfhart. *Theology and the Kingdom of God.* Philadelphia: Westminster, 1969.
Tanner, Kathryn. *God and Creation in Christian Theology: Tyranny or Empowerment?* New York: Blackwell, 1988.

ALEXANDRE GANOCZY

Creationism-Generationism. The terms *creationism* and *generationism* have to do with the theological question about the origin of the human spiritual soul. According to creationism, it is created at or after conception directly by God (*creare*). According to generationism, it is, just as with physical life, generated by the parents (*generare*).

(1) *Biblical Background.* Scripture gives no clear answer to this question. In the Old Testament, however, the idea is dominant that the breath of life (Hebrew: *ruach* = breath, spirit) that enlivens the whole human person comes from God (Gn 2:7). Yet this is true in a similar way for all creatures (Ps 104:29f.).

(2) *History of Theology.* In the early church both views were held. It was with Augustine that generationism first received a plausible theological grounding: it best explained the transmission of the sin of Adam to all human beings (ORIGINAL SIN). Through a different theory of the transfer of the original sin, Thomas Aquinas broke up the connection of original sin and the process of procreation and helped creationism to become generally accepted (see DS 1007). The problem of creationism-generationism arose again in modern times in the discussion about the evolution of life-forms (Darwin) and about philosophical materialism.

(3) *Church Teaching.* According to ecclesiastical teaching, the assertion that the human spiritual soul is duplicated through procreation or comes forth from the sensitive soul is erroneous (DS 3220ff.). Rather, the Catholic faith maintains that souls are created directly by God (enc. *Humani generis,* 1950 [DS 3896]).

(4) *Ecumenical Perspectives.* Following Luther, Protestant theology generally has a stronger tendency toward generationism.

(5) *Systematic Reflections.* The whole of creation, including each individual

human person, is comprised in one indivisible act in God's will for creation. This is not contradicted by the fact that on the creaturely level the whole human person is begotten by one's parents, if the divine act of creation is seen as being at work in and supporting this act of procreation. The expression "to be created directly [*immediately*] by God" then is to be understood as a more specific determination of the way in which the divine act of creation is present with regard to the spiritual soul in the procreative act of the parents. There is an anthropological viewpoint behind this statement: reason and freedom (the spiritual soul) of the human person have their origin in God's act of creation and ground the special relatedness of the human person to God.

See also HOMINIZATION; ORIGINAL SIN.

Bibliography
Gilkey, Langdon. *Creationism on Trial: Evolution and God at Little Rock.* Minneapolis: Winston, 1985.
————. *Nature, Reality, and the Sacred: The Nexus of Science and Religion.* Minneapolis: Fortress, 1993.

GEORG LANGEMEYER

Creation Narratives. In Christian theology, the term *creation narratives* refers to the didactic stories of Genesis 1–11, in which fundamental statements are made about the Creator, the world, and humankind.

(1) *Biblical Background.* According to present-day exegesis, the Bible contains two accounts of creation: (*a*) the earlier (from 1000 to 900 B.C.E.: time of the kings, epoch of moral degeneration) was transmitted in the texts of the so-called Yahwist (J source) and includes Gn 2:4b–4:26; 6:1–8; 7:1–5, 16b, 17, 22f.; 8:6–12, 20–22; 9:18–26; 11:1–9; and (*b*) the later (from ca. 550 B.C.E., during the Babylonian Exile: interest in ceremonial and religious reconstruction) is contained in the so-called Priestly source (P source) and consists of Gn 1:1–2, 4a; 5:1–32; 6:9–22; 7:6–16a, 18–21, 24; 8:1–5, 13–19; 9:1–17; 10:1–32; 11:10–32. These traditions were integrated and reworked by a single editor at the end of the sixth century B.C.E. Regarding (*a*): the main theme of J — which it treats with earthy, pictorial symbolism — is the prehistoric state of human existence, sin, and grace. Its statements apply to humanity as a generic being. Yahweh forms this Adam out of *'adāmāh,* that is, the clay of the ground (2:7), to which he returns after his death (3:19), but which he also has to "cultivate" and "care for" (2:15). His special relation to God, represented by Yahweh's directly blowing the breath of life into his nostrils (2:7), makes him far superior to the animals. His relation to the animals is marked by kinship and difference. He establishes control over them by giving them their names (2:19f.). The relation between man and woman is presented as implying, in a way revolutionary for its time, that they are esteemed as equals. For the man, the woman is "flesh of his flesh": his closest relative (2:23). Thus, by way of an overturning of patriarchal custom, *he* leaves his father and mother in order to cling to his wife (2:24). Sin is kindled by use and enjoyment of goods that are, in themselves,

willed by God (cf. 3:1, 5, 6). Attainment of knowledge forbidden by God, murder of a brother (4:1–16), intermarriage with "the sons of heaven" (6:1–4), and intemperate ambition for accomplishment (11:1–9) are its prototypical instantiations. God's grace responds immediately to sin. The threatened punishment by death (3:3) is not carried out. God "makes leather garments" for the naked, banished human couple (3:21). Noah finds "favor with the Lord" (6:8). Eve, despite the sin, becomes "mother of all the living" (3:20). Regarding (b): in contrast to J, P approaches humankind from the standpoint of God's miraculous act of creating the cosmos. God's word imparts order to chaos (1:2f.) and allows the organic to arise by degrees from the inorganic (1:11–13). The stars, in contrast with their status in mythology, have nothing divine about them, but serve (see 1:15). The Creator confers the blessing of fruitfulness on the animals (1:22; and again, after the flood, 8:17). God makes humankind "in his image," male and female (1:27). God directs to humankind a three-part, commissioning blessing: to multiply and to "fill" the area (cf. the "promised land") allotted to it; to "subdue" the earth (i.e., according to present-day exegesis, to "take possession" of it); and to "have dominion" over the animals in the manner of a good shepherd (1:28). Humans are called to creativity at the cultural level, and thus to imitation of the Creator. They receive support from the charisms of the divine Spirit that are correlative to their work (Ex 35:30–33 [P]). The "seventh day" symbolizes God's loving attentiveness toward creation and humanity's resting before God in homage and gratitude (2:2f.). The covenant is the Creator's gift of grace to the people (Gn 6:18–21; 9:9). The significance of Abraham, as the pre-Jewish father of the nations, is that of the partner in the covenant who adheres believingly to God despite all blows of fate (10:1–33; 11:10–32).

(2) *History of Theology.* The Church Fathers frequently interpreted the accounts of creation, sometimes in a typological vein angled toward Christ, his redemptive work, and Mary as the new Eve.

(3) *Church Teaching.* Doctrinal office, via the Bible Commission, has twice commented on the historicality of what is recounted in Genesis. Whereas the response of 1909 affirms only broadly, without precise detail, the "historical sense of the words" in the accounts of creation (DS 3514), the declaration of 1948 comes close to the notion of "primal history" set out there: it is a matter of fundamental truths that "lie at the basis of the economy of salvation, recounted in pictorial language" (DS 3863; cf. 3898).

(4) *Ecumenical Perspectives.* The accounts of creation scarcely give cause for confessional disputes.

(5) *Systematic Reflections.* Present-day exegesis prefers the term *primal history* to the notion of an account of creation, so as to do justice to the fact that what is portrayed has the character of both a past happening and a basic model. In these statements about the beginnings, expression is given to prototypal aspects like creatureliness, the duality of sex, work, fallibility, the need for liberation — in short, the greatness and wretchedness of human existence.

In the form of a history stretching from Adam to Abraham, Israel's experiences with God and the world at the time of exodus and exile are summarized in the accounts of creation. Creation thus stands in the context of liberation and redemption. The accounts of creation are nevertheless not historical reports but attestation-like expressions or etiologies (Greek: *aitía* = beginning, origin, cause), that is, portrayals intended to make the general experiences of the present theologically understandable by relating them back to the origins (e.g., the fall or Sabbath rest).

See also CREATION; CREATION: THEOLOGY OF.

Bibliography

Anderson, Bernhard W. *Creation versus Chaos: The Reinterpretation of Mythical Symbolism in the Bible*. New York: Association Press; Philadelphia: Fortress, 1987.

Doria, Charles, and Harris Lenowitz, eds. *Origins: Creation Texts from the Ancient Mediterranean*. Garden City, N.Y.: Doubleday, 1976.

Hyers, Conrad. *The Meaning of Creation: Genesis and Modern Science*. Atlanta: John Knox, 1984.

Stuhlmuller, Carol. *Creative Redemption in Deutero-Isaiah*. Rome: Biblical Institute Press, 1970.

ALEXANDRE GANOCZY

Creation out of Nothing (*Creatio ex Nihilo*). As originally conceived, this philosophico-theological expression is an assertion more about the Creator than about what creation was "out of" or where it "came from." It refers to the absolute independence, and sole authorship of the world, of the one God of Christian revelation, who, in effecting the beginning of cosmos and history, is dependent on no preexisting matter and no outside helper, and also contains the ground and motive for the (loving) act of creation solely within God's self. At a later stage in the development of its meaning, creation out of nothing signifies the transition of the emerging world from metaphysically conceived nonbeing into being, or also the "nothingness" attaching to every finite being in view of the Creator's infinite fullness of being.

(1) *Biblical Background.* The Bible nowhere shows an interest in cosmology of a decidedly metaphysical turn. It invokes the formulation "creation out of nothing" at only two places, and then only in an oblique way: 2 Mc 7:28 and Rom 4:17 refer, in the Greek, to the "nonexistent" (in the latter passage, in the plural and with the article: *tà mè ónta*) in order to contrast human dying with the promised resurrection from the dead, or more precisely, to emphasize the need for trust in God's creative omnipotence. In Rom 4:17, the stress is "not on the occurrence of world-creation as such, but on God's ever-present creative force, which manifests itself just as well in his calling the non-existent into existence as in his creating new life for the dead" (U. Wilckens). This idea is essentially consistent with the Hebrew verb *bara* and also with Old Testament evidence that God created heaven and earth with effortless ease, through a spoken command (Gn 1:3–26), and not through laborious construction from primal matter or through strife or procreation, as conceived in myths. The

Old Testament, however, also often represents divine creation as a structuring of chaos (Gn 1:1), a forming out of the "ground" (Gn 2:7, 19) or out of "formless matter" (Wis 11:71), which is, of course, particularly interesting in the framework of an evolutionary view of the world. Regardless of this, divine effectuation of the absolute beginning remains a notion completely beyond experience and thus one that has no analogy. To that extent, *bara* essentially corresponds to the intended sense of "creation out of nothing" (at least in Genesis 1). Elsewhere, the verb refers to specifically divine activity regarding things that already exist (e.g., Ps 104:29f.; Is 41:20; 45:7; 65:17f.). Also to be regarded as "creation out of something" (*creatio ex aliquo*) is that "new creation" that, according to Paul, is represented by the human who "is in Christ" (2 Cor 5:17; cf. Gal 6:15). Death does not annihilate humans, so their resurrection does not occur "out of nothing" (*ex nihilo*) (see 1 Cor 15:53–55).

(2) *History of Theology.* It was Hermas (ca. 150) who first used the expression "creation out of nothing" in a metaphysical sense: "Believe that there is a God who has made everything...out of nothing [*ek toû mé óntos*]" (mand. 1.1; cf. vis. 1.1.6). Irenaeus (*Adv. haer.* 4.20.2) and Origen (*In Io.* 32.9) spoke similarly. These Fathers usually wanted to guard against heathen polytheistic, and especially dualistic, conceptions of the beginning of the world: the beginning was not effected by a demiurge who is more or less subordinate to the (main) god; or: matter is not just as eternal as God. For the Fathers, purely philosophical discussion — beginning with the distinction between an absolute "nothing" (*nihil*), in the sense of being an utter nonpossibility, and a relative "nothing," in the sense of being (so far) a mere nonreality — plays at most a subsidiary role. Such discussion is not undertaken directly until the medieval theologians, when, for instance, they define the Creator as the "first cause" of all possible being and of all being. Closer to the original biblical-patristic orientation are modern approaches that understand the creation of the world through analogies based on forms of personal behavior like self-communication and conferred participation.

(3) *Church Teaching.* Doctrinal office has contented itself with declaring that God "created out of nothing," "at the beginning of time and in the same manner," both the spiritual and the material orders (Fourth Lateran Council, 1215 [DS 800]), and that God "brought forth" all things, "as regards their entire substance, out of nothing," and in fact, "out of his goodness" (Vatican I, 1870 [DS 3002, 3025]).

(4) *Ecumenical Perspectives.* M. Luther, in the framework of his doctrine of justification, imparts an anthropological turn to the way the question is posed: human beings, as sinners, are things of nothingness, and so are their "works." He argues this, in part, as follows: "The creature is made out of nothing, so everything that it can do is nothing" (*WA* 43:178f.). It is important to recognize this, since "out of one who is not first nothing God is also able to make nothing"; God makes nothing "living but the dead, makes nothing pious but the sinful" (*WA* 1:183f.). A modern counterpart to this doctrine reads: "Only

the sinner is the appropriate material for God: that which is nothing before God and out of which God alone can make something" (G. Ebeling, *Dogmatik des christlichen Glaubens I* [Tübingen, 1979], 310).

(5) *Systematic Reflections.* Current research is directed toward precisely distinguishing particular ways of applying the nothing-analogy and toward establishing the relevance of the biblical findings to present-day circumstances.

See also BEGINNING; CREATION; DUALISM.

Bibliography
Cupitt, Don. *Creation out of Nothing.* Philadelphia: Trinity, 1990.
Kelsey, David. "The Doctrine of Creation from Nothing." In *Evolution and Creation,* edited by Ernan McMullin. Notre Dame, Ind.: University of Notre Dame Press, 1985.

ALEXANDRE GANOCZY

Creatureliness. Creatureliness, or createdness, means that all extradivine beings are fundamentally determined by and are radically dependent upon the Creator. From the standpoint of the goal and self-development of humans, this concept refers to their absolute reliance upon God as the originator, redeemer, and consummator of all reality.

(1) *Biblical Background.* The Bible emphasizes that all of material reality was created by the hand of God. It characterizes human creatureliness particularly in terms of the likeness to God of the two-sexed human species (see Gn 1:26).

(2) *History of Theology.* The Patristic doctrine of creation adopted the full substance of the teaching on creatureliness.

(3) *Church Teaching.* The Fourth Lateran Council, which regards as self-evidently valid analogies between God and humans that are based on the principle of creatureliness, nevertheless states more precisely: "No similarity can be asserted between Creator and creature without implicit acknowledgment that there is a greater dissimilarity between them" (DS 806).

(4) *Ecumenical Perspectives.* Protestant dogmatists like K. Barth, E. Brunner, and G. Ebeling give emphasis to the creatureliness of humans in the sense of their radical differentness from God, that is, between Creator and creature, and between grace and sin. Neither bestowed grace nor eschatological consummation annuls the relationship of tension inherent in creatureliness. Humans are not deified as happens in mythology. Even within the person of Christ, his divine and creaturely natures remain unmixed; this is precisely the condition that enables their mutual communication. Particularly in sinners, creatureliness can manifest itself as nothingness.

(5) *Systematic Reflections.* From the Catholic side, H. Urs von Balthasar and H. Küng have declared themselves partly in agreement with the theses on this subject that were formulated by K. Barth in his doctrine of justification. A central theme favored by K. Rahner is the spiritual creature as addressee of the "absolute nearness" of the "absolute mystery," a nearness that, precisely because absolute, by no means cancels out the incomprehen-

sibility of what communicates itself in grace (see Rahner, review of Küng's *Justification*).

Bibliography
Balthasar, Hans Urs von. *The Theology of Karl Barth*. Garden City, N.Y.: Doubleday, 1972.
Barth, Karl. *Church Dogmatics, 3/1–4*. Edinburgh: T and T Clark, 1958.
Küng, Hans. *Justification: The Doctrine of Karl Barth and a Catholic Reflection; with a Letter by Karl Barth*. New York: Nelson, 1964.
Rahner, Karl. *Foundations of Christian Faith: An Introduction to the Idea of Christianity*. New York: Crossroad, 1982.
———. "Questions of Controversial Theology on Justification." Review of *Justification*, by Hans Küng. *Theological Investigations*, 4:189–218. New York: Seabury, 1974.

ALEXANDRE GANOCZY

Creatureliness of the Human Person. The creatureliness of the human person, because of its origin in the creative will of God, is an abiding property of human and also of Christian existence. It is brought to consciousness in various ways: in the accidental and arbitrary character of existence (contingency); as the temporally scattered, split-up nature of existence (finiteness); in the sense of the basic human neediness (for food, shelter, social contact); in the awareness of the historically situated limitedness of the possibilities of existence and its realization ("to be lucky or unlucky"); as insecurity (anxiety) and the experience of being easily led astray.

(1) *Biblical Background.* In a liturgical hymn, the first creation account (Genesis 1) emphasizes the human person as the best of all of God's good works, while the second account (Genesis 2) describes the creatureliness of the human person more or less from the perspective of everyday experience. Human persons are transitory, needy, and susceptible to a pride or hubris that makes them unwilling to recognize their creatureliness and causes them to want to be like God. Therefore, creatureliness expresses itself in the plea for God's life-giving power, help, and mercy (Psalm 90; 104:13–16, 29f.). Psalm 8 combines both accounts of creation: "What is man that you should be mindful of him?" and "You have made him little less than the angels. . . . You have given him rule over the works of your hands" (vv. 5, 6f.). In Ecclesiastes the ephemeral and frail character of creatureliness is elevated to a mystery. The human being becomes silent before God's incomprehensible intention in creation. The New Testament mainly proclaims the new era that has come about through Jesus Christ, yet it presupposes the creatureliness of the human person in the sense of the Old Testament (e.g., Mt 6:19–34; Rom 9:20f.). The divine salvation that God has worked in Jesus Christ, which is usually described as the liberation from the rule of sin or evil, includes the satisfaction and fulfillment of creatureliness: in the reign of God everything that the human being requires as a creature will be given as well (Mt 6:33), and the deficiencies of being a creature will be overcome (see Col 1:15–20; Eph 1:10; 4:8–10).

(2) *History of Theology.* Theology has found it difficult to bring together both aspects of the saving work of Christ: on the one hand, the affirmation

(restoration) of creatureliness (Anselm of Canterbury, Duns Scotus) and, on the other, the elevation of creation — which was ruined by original sin — beyond itself to participation in God's eternal life (Augustine). Thomas Aquinas sought a synthesis in the view that the supernatural elevation of the human person is at the same time a perfection of the created order (nature). Scholastic theology, however, as a whole tends to interpret the redemption from sin and the gift of participation in the life of God as a liberation from the characteristics of creatureliness. This tendency is fully realized by M. Luther, who interprets creatureliness as the nothingness of the human person before God, thus understanding it as already the creatureliness of the sinner.

(3) *Church Teaching.* In contrast, the Council of Trent defended the abiding dignity of the creature, even after sin (DS 1557).

(4) *Ecumenical Perspectives.* In today's theological anthropology two basic approaches can be distinguished, one starting out from the human person as a sinner (O. H. Pesch, W. Pannenberg) and the other starting from the human person as a creature (K. Rahner). This distinction, however, is no longer fully identical with the distinction between Protestant and Catholic theology.

(5) *Systematic Reflections.* The biblical statement that the human being is made from the dust of the earth (Gn 2:7) anticipates in its own way the insight into the evolutionary origin of the human person from the cosmos. Because recent theology has taken the side of the human sciences and their approach, using a historical hermeneutics, it usually interprets the creatureliness of the human person as HISTORICITY that on account of the history of salvation is oriented toward a future freed from natural limitations. Here, however, the abiding rootedness of the human person in the cosmic-natural world is theologically neglected. The redemption through Christ is understood as a liberation from the cosmic-natural situation to pure subjectivity and intersubjectivity in which the natural component serves only as a medium of communication. In this way the tendency within the theological tradition to interpret redemption from sin as a redemption from creatureliness is continued. The equilibrium between nature and history, cosmos and spirit — the reconciliation of heaven and earth in the cross of Christ (Col 1:20; Eph 4:8–10) — disappears from view. At present, the threatening experience of the limits of the realm of intersubjectivity before nature forces theology to give more weight to the abiding aspect of creatureliness.

See also CREATURELINESS; EVOLUTION: THEORY OF, AND CREATION; PEACE; REDEMPTION AND LIBERATION.

Bibliography
Gilkey, Langdon. *Maker of Heaven and Earth.* Garden City, N.Y.: Doubleday, 1965.
Segundo, Juan Luis. *Grace and the Human Condition.* Maryknoll, N.Y.: Orbis Books, 1973.

GEORG LANGEMEYER

Creeds. *See* CONFESSIONS (CREEDS/CHURCHES).

Cross, Theology of the. A theology of the cross examines the cross of Jesus Christ as the free revelation of God's love. God the all-powerful not only has compassion on God's creatures but suffered with them. Thus God takes away the helplessness of suffering by means of redemption.

(1) *Biblical Background.* The starting point of a theology of the cross is God's self-emptying (*kenosis*) in Christ (Phil 2:6–11). The "message about the cross" is "God's power and wisdom" (1 Cor 1:18–31). The emptying does not take away the fact that God is God, but unveils God's being concerned with us by means of Jesus' history and his death on the cross. Old Testament anthropomorphisms already tell us something about God's real concern when they speak about God's compassion, anger, and mercy (Gn 6:6; Ps 78:74; Is 63:10; Hos 11:8; Jer 31:20). In rabbinical literature, God's pain is taken seriously. According to this *theo*-logical perspective, statements about Jesus Christ's being concerned (e.g., his anger [Mk 3:5]; his compassion [Mk 6:34]; his weeping over Jerusalem [Lk 19:41]) have a certain weight and point to him as the revelation of God in his humanity (see Ti 3:4). The "com-passion" of God's Son made flesh is especially clear in his abandonment by God on the cross (Mk 15:34 par.). In Hebrews this dimension of the "weakness" of Jesus Christ is especially emphasized (5:2, 8; see 2:18; 4:15). To this extent we may say that the very humanity of Jesus, his living and dying, is God's "self-presentation."

(2) *History of Theology.* Although the early church espoused the axiom of God's *apatheia* (impassibility and immutability) to correct mythological language used of God, nevertheless the Fathers — in connection with Sacred Scripture — frequently attribute feelings to God such as anger, love, and mercy. Ignatius of Antioch (*Eph.* 3.2; see 7.3) and Melito of Sardis regarded the juxtaposition of these two languages as paradoxical and allowed both to stand. We should note, however, that they are viewing the capacity to suffer in a christological and soteriological context: God is incapable of suffering, *and* God suffers in the Son. The strongest formulation is: "One of the Trinity suffered in the flesh." Its source is unclear, but it is used by the Syrian "Monophysites," Philoxenes of Mabbug (d. 523), and Severus of Antioch (d. 482). In the *Henotikon* of the emperor Zeno (482 C.E.) we first encounter the formula, "The one who was of the Trinity, God the Word, was made flesh." The Fathers — for example, Origen (d. ca. 254) or Gregory of Nyssa (d. 394) — distinguish involuntary and voluntary (allowed or chosen) suffering, which express the freedom, power, and love of God. In Scholastic theology this patristic theme was not developed. According to Thomas Aquinas (d. 1274), the divine action and will are mutable (*terminative,* in the creature), but God is immutable (*entitative,* in being) (*STh* 1, q. 13, a. 7; q. 19, a. 7; *Sent.* 1.30.1). The freely willed (voluntary) suffering of Christ is regarded soteriologically as satisfaction for our sins and ethically as an example of patience. The shift from an incarnational to a cross-centered starting point in Christology/soteriology meant that the cross — the locus of God's revelation and Jesus Christ's knowledge — could once again be considered as possible and recommendable, even in Catholic dog-

matics. This may be seen in Latin American liberation theology, which links a theology of the cross to the concrete sufferings of the poor.

(3) *Church Teaching.* The fact that Jesus Christ freely suffered is stated in creeds and synods (DS 6, 62f., 423, 442, 502): he bore all the bodily disfigurations (DS 189); his suffering was real suffering (DS 325). Referring to Phil 2:7, a Roman synod under Damascus I (382 C.E.) maintained that in the suffering on the cross not God but the Son of God in the flesh endured pain in his soul. Because of the doctrine of two natures, various ways are used to maintain the paradox that the impassible did not disdain to become man (DS 294, 801, 1337). When the formula "one of the Trinity suffered" (DS 367ff.) was being considered, John II (534 C.E.) recognized it as valid (DS 401), and to support the formula "God, who suffered in the flesh," he appealed to the twelve anathemas of Cyril of Alexandria (DS 263). The Second Council of Constantinople (553) defined the neo-Chalcedonian teaching in the sense that the human nature of Jesus subsisted in the hypostasis of the Logos (DS 424–30). Thus we must profess: "Our Lord Jesus Christ, who was crucified in the flesh, is...one of the Holy Trinity" (DS 432; cf. 1337). The Third Council of Constantinople (680–81) explains that the human will of Christ did not disappear but was divinized; it is the enfleshed will of the Logos. Thus the human freedom of Jesus was not destroyed but set free to be itself.

(4) *Ecumenical Perspectives.* Already in the Heidelberg disputations of 1518 (in the context of the doctrine of justification), M. Luther speaks of a *theologia crucis.* More often, however, especially after 1530, he is speaking of its theological basis (in his understanding), the *communicatio idiomatum.* God really shares in the suffering and death of Christ's humanity. In so doing Luther turns away from the Platonic image of an immutable and impassible God and rethinks God, starting with the cross of Christ. J. Calvin and the Reformed theologians, considering the matter in a different way — namely, on the basis of the *extra Calvinisticum* — sought to safeguard the transcendence of the Logos in relation to the humanity of Christ. A controversy arose in the seventeenth century between Lutheran theologians of the Tübingen school and those of the Giessen school over the "doctrine of *kenosis.*" The Tübingen theologians emphasized an "emptying within the veiling" — that is, the Word made flesh did not reveal its divine attributes. Those of Giessen spoke of an "emptying of use." There was no question of a *kenosis* of the divinity of the Logos. The Kenotics of the nineteenth century (G. Thomasius, W. F. Gess, K. T. Liebner, F. H. R. Frank) made the traditional concept of God's immutability a problem when they attempted to think of God *in* history: factually, however, the divinity of Christ was largely abandoned. In Anglican theology of the nineteenth and twentieth centuries there was a whole series of projects to do a theology of the "suffering of God." Among Evangelical theologians today, we would mention especially J. Moltmann, E. Jüngel, G. Koch, and K. Kitamori. K. Barth speaks of "God's triune suffering in Christ."

(5) *Systematic Reflections.* Theology today is reconsidering the statements of

the New Testament and the councils because it regards the cross of Christ as the self-presentation of a free and loving God and therefore as proof of God's might. The suffering of the Son is the final proof of the eschatological love of God. God in Christ is not "a-pathetic," but sympathetic, that is, literally a "com-passionate" God!

See also LOVE; REDEMPTION AND LIBERATION; SUFFERING; THEODICY.

Bibliography

Best, Ernst. *The Temptation and Passion.* 2d. ed. Cambridge: Cambridge University Press, 1990.
Cousar, Charles B. *A Theology of the Cross: The Death of Jesus in the Pauline Letters.* Minneapolis: Fortress, 1990.
Jüngel, Eberhard. *God as the Mystery of the World: On the Foundation of the Theology of the Crucified One in the Dispute between Theism and Atheism.* Grand Rapids: Eerdmans, 1983.
Knox, John. *The Death of Christ.* New York: Abingdon, 1958.
Lienhard, Marc. *Luther, Witness to Jesus Christ: Stages and Themes of the Reformer's Christology.* Minneapolis: Augsburg, 1982.
Matera, Frank J. *Passion Narratives and Gospel Theologies.* Mahwah, N.J.: Paulist, 1986.
McGrath, Alister E. *Luther's Theology of the Cross: Martin Luther's Theological Breakthrough.* New York: Blackwell, 1985.
Moltmann, Jürgen. *The Crucified God.* 2d ed. New York: Harper and Row, 1973.
Persaud, Winston D. *The Theology of the Cross and Marx's Anthropology: A View from the Caribbean.* New York: Peter Lang, 1991.

LOTHAR ULLRICH

Cult. Cult is the explicit adoration of God. It includes all acts of consciousness and all exterior actions whose primary and real intention is to acknowledge God in God's absolute sovereignty and to offer reverence to God. One should distinguish between the *private* cult of individuals or groups (individual piety, popular piety) and the *official* cult (liturgy), as well as between spontaneous *creative* cult and *ritualized* cult. The forms of expression of cult (words, things, and actions) have symbolic character; that is, they are — as in the case of a work of art or of a ceremony — raised above the daily context of purpose and meaning and thus become transparent for the concealed divine reality. Therefore, the ritualized symbols of cult constitute more or less clearly their own sacred realm of reality that is separated from the profane.

(1) *Biblical Background.* Like all religions, that of Israel has a sacred cultic sphere. Gn 2:2f. indicates that the rhythm of work and cultic activity (Sabbath) belongs to the realization of the essence of the human person as creature. What is characteristic for the Old Testament cult, however, is its relationship to the historical events in which Israel had experienced Yahweh's salvific will (the exodus, the conquest of the land, the kingship, the building of the Jerusalem temple). Thus, the biblical understanding of cult is essentially characterized by the commemoration of God's saving deeds and by the expectation — on occasion expressed in the form of pleas and complaints — of future signs of salvation in which God's salvific will that had been experienced in the past will

be confirmed and completed. The New Testament exhibits a remarkable reserve before all cultic understandings, both those of the Old Testament and those of Hellenism. The New Testament sees the Old Testament cult symbols as actually realized and completed in the life, death, and resurrection of Jesus (e.g., Hebrews 4–10). From this point of view, the proclamation of the gospel and the works of love of neighbor (collection for Jerusalem) can be described as cult (Rom 1:9; 2 Cor 9:12). The entire Christian existence is cult — that is, divine service. This indicates, at least, that the New Testament sees cult and concrete daily living as one inseparable unity. In the New Testament communities, nevertheless, basic approaches toward a specifically Christian cult can be found (e.g., 1 Corinthians 11; 14:26–40). The separation between cultic and profane activity is also already indicated in the distinction between the Lord's Supper and ordinary meals (1 Cor 11:27f.). The context, however, stresses the connection between the two table communities (1 Cor 11:20ff.; cf. Jas 2:2f.).

(2) *History of Theology.* In the Eastern Church, the Christian cult developed into a realm of its own with holy pictures, things, and actions (divine liturgy). This realm mediates between profane life and the divine reality and is therefore at the same time the place of adoration and of salvific participation in the divine. In the Orthodox Church, the divine liturgy is considered together with Scripture as sources of dogmatic knowledge. The Western Church, in the midst of the confusion of the tribal migrations, had to strive, above all, to preserve the essentials of the cultic tradition as the heritage of Jesus Christ. Here, cult was seen more under the aspect of the duty of the creature toward God. From this starting point, the dogmatic question arising for Scholasticism was only that of the specific kind of cult that the human person owes to God. In the framework of the doctrine on the virtues, there was a discussion concerning to which virtue cult was to be assigned. This Scholastic view is the background for the distinction usually made in eucharistic doctrine between sacrifice (cult) and sacrament (Communion).

(3) *Church Teaching.* The teaching of the church also distinguishes in its liturgical activity "the work of our redemption" (*SC* 2) and the "completed glorification of God" (*SC* 5). On the whole, however, Vatican II's Constitution on the Liturgy is more concerned with the proclamation of salvation and the saving activity of liturgy.

(4) *Ecumenical Perspectives.* The Protestant churches eliminated all cultic symbolic activity and limited cult to word and song. Recently, however, the cultic character of the Last Supper is being acknowledged. The ecumenical cooperation of Catholic and Protestant theologians with representatives of the Orthodox Church (Lima Report, 1982) has proved itself especially fruitful for a new reflection on liturgical cult.

(5) *Systematic Reflections.* The waning comprehension of the Christian faithful for cult, which is manifested in the rapid decrease of participation in church services, has again made dogmatic theology attentive to the lack of a theology of cult. The theological connection between Christian cult and the practical

DISCIPLESHIP of Christ has not been sufficiently clarified in theological tradition. Two contrary tendencies manifest themselves today. The first would like to see the sense of symbolical cultic actions primarily in their function as a stimulus for Christians toward practical action ("political" liturgies). The other makes cultic actions autonomous as sacramental anticipations of the otherworldly kingdom of God that remain removed from the practical activity of this world and therefore can be conveyed to Christians only through symbolical participation. The truth is probably to be found in the middle: cult and the praxis of daily living are mutually related to each other without one becoming a mere function of the other.

See also DOGMA/DOGMATICS; GLORY OF GOD; GOD'S WILL.

Bibliography
Jasper, David. *Language and the Worship of the Church*. London: Macmillan, 1990.
Rahner, Karl. "On the Theology of Worship." In *Theological Investigations,* 19:141–51. New York: Crossroad, 1983.
Schmidt, H., and David Power. *Liturgy and Cultural Religious Traditions.* Vol. 102 of *Concilium.* New York: Seabury, 1977.

GEORG LANGEMEYER

Culture. Culture is the specifically human way through which persons perceive and shape their reality, that is, their own selves, their fellow human beings, and the world they share. Human beings are creatures who possess and who produce culture. Culture is closely linked with religion yet must be distinguished from it. In the development of most cultures there are tensions that arise between the culture and the religious tradition, taking the form of a critique of the mythos, a kind of Enlightenment, as also was the case with the Western Christian culture. Religion and culture, however, remain related to one another.

(1) *Biblical Background.* The Old Testament interprets culture first of all as an endowment of God's creation that the human person, as God's image, participates in forming (Gn 1:28ff.; 2:8, 18ff.). At the time of the kingdom of Solomon, court circles cultivating wisdom developed basic approaches toward a relatively independent culture (see, e.g., the "worldly" Song of Songs). This was denounced by the prophets as a falling away from faith. The New Testament communities remained reserved toward the cultures in which they lived, at first because of the expectation of the imminent return of the Lord, later because of increasing social and political pressure. Culture therefore belonged to this world, which existed under the rule of evil. Only Colossians and Ephesians at least develop the notion of an incorporation of the Christian faith and the church in the Hellenistic culture.

(2) *History of Theology.* The theological estimation of culture throughout history was always dependent upon the relationship between church and society (see table).

(3) *Church Teaching.* Vatican II treats extensively the relationship between faith and culture. It emphasizes the mandate of creation that Christians have in

THE RECIPROCAL RELATIONSHIPS
BETWEEN CULTURE AND THEOLOGY

Church/Culture	Theology
Before Constantine: persecution of the church	Reception of cultural contents of meaning for the sake of apologetic and missionary work
After Constantine: the linking of church and empire in a cultural unity	Interpretation of the Christian belief in salvation within the Greek-Hellenistic conceptual framework
Middle Ages: church=bearer of culture	Theological interpretation of the church as mother and mediator of salvation and culture
Renaissance: formation of an autonomous "civil" urban culture and the gradual separation from the church	Crisis of Scholastic theology (nominalism); separation of culture and faith (Reformation)
Modern times: an independent, worldly culture; beside it, a Catholic subculture	Handing down and further development of Scholastic theology (neo-scholasticism); apologetic building up of fences before cultural development

common with all human persons (GS 57). The aim, however, is not to create a Christian monoculture. According to the message of the gospel, the church is sent to all cultures. The Christian faith is not bound to any specific culture; rather, it must express itself and give practical witness of itself in every culture (GS 58). Moreover, the inculturation of the one Christian faith in the different cultures of the earth is to be of service toward the unity of humankind and toward a more universal form of human culture that must itself be constituted in a mutual respect toward different cultures (GS 54). In this regard, the autonomy of culture is acknowledged to the degree that it remains open for religion and faith (GS 59).

(4) *Ecumenical Perspectives.* With this view the Catholic Church has again come closer to the Protestant tradition that (despite a contrary phase in the liberal cultural Protestantism of the last century), on the one hand, with Luther sharply distinguishes between the gospel and culture and, on the other hand, stresses the service of Christians to and in their respective cultures.

(5) *Systematic Reflections.* Presently the theological discussion centers on two problems. (*a*) To what degree are Christian theology and practice bound to the late bourgeois culture of modernity, which, as a culture of intellect and educational formation, fancies itself to be relatively independent of socioeconomic conditions and thereby veils the reification of the human person in modern industrial societies (see the critical theory of the Frankfurt school and political theology)? (*b*) The language of Christian faith and the theological tradition

have come into being within the European cultural sphere. In the meantime, however, the church has gained within other cultural spheres a culturally specific character. Do the dogmatic doctrinal decisions of the church, which were all formulated in the context of the problems of the European cultural development, have the same validity claims for the non-European churches as for the church in the European cultural realm? And what would a theological reflection upon the Christian faith look like when it takes into account the irreducible difference of cultures?

See also CATHOLICITY OF THE CHURCH; CREATION; IMAGE OF GOD; MISSION; THEOLOGY.

Bibliography
Geertz, Clifford. The Interpretation of Culture. New York: Basic Books, 1973.
————. Local Knowledge: Further Essays in Interpretive Anthropology. New York: Basic Books, 1983.
Gilkey, Langdon. Society and the Sacred: Toward a Theology of Culture in Decline. New York: Crossroad, 1981.

GEORG LANGEMEYER

D d

Deacon. Deacons are those possessing a ministry, transmitted by sacramental ordination, in which the works of love that accord with the gospel and must be undertaken by the church are entrusted to them in a special way.

(1) *Biblical Background.* The New Testament speaks several times of *diakonoi.* Acts 6:1–6 tells of the appointment of "seven men ... to serve at table"; the apostles prayed and laid hands on them. In Phil 1:1, Paul expressly greets the deacons, and 1 Tm 3:8 speaks of the moral behavior expected of them. In the background are the statements about Jesus Christ himself, who came "to serve and to give his life" (Mk 10:45).

(2) *History of Theology.* Ignatius of Antioch speaks of deacons when he mentions the three degrees of the ecclesiastical ministry. In his *Traditio apostolica,* Hippolytus of Rome passes on the formulary for diaconal ordination. In the early centuries of the church women too were appointed to the office of deacon (deaconesses). From the Middle Ages on, the diaconate was regarded as a stage on the way to the priesthood and ceased to be a self-sufficient degree of orders.

(3) *Church Teaching.* Despite this development, texts of the Council of Trent state that by divine institution the ecclesiastical hierarchy consists of bishops, priests, and deacons (*ministri*) (DS 1768, 1776). In 1947, in connection with the revision of the ordination liturgy, Pius XII mentioned the diaconate as a degree of sacramental orders. Vatican II deals explicitly with the diaconate in *LG* 29, *AG* 16, and *OE* 17. The diaconate has acquired a new importance due to the restoration of the three degrees of ecclesiastical office; it is now no longer exclusively a stage on the way to priesthood, but, in the form of the "permanent diaconate," an independent hierarchical degree. It is transmitted through prayer and the laying on of hands and is a sacrament. Deacons share many tasks with priests (administration of baptism, assistance at marriages, leadership of prayer services, instruction of the faithful, and so on). They cannot, however, preside at the Eucharist or administer the sacrament of penance. Their duties include caritative services in particular.

(4) *Ecumenical Perspectives.* The doctrine concerning the diaconate has been little discussed in the ecumenical dialogue. The Lima Report of 1982 on ministry urges all churches to adopt the threefold ministry and thus implicitly the restoration of the ministry of deacons.

(5) *Systematic Reflections.* The restoration of the permanent diaconate has given urgency to the question of the independent character of the diaconate as compared with the priesthood; no satisfactory answers have thus far been developed either in theory or in practice. The question whether women can exercise the office of deacon, as in the first centuries of the church, has for the time

161

being been answered negatively by church law (*CIC* 1024), but it continues to be raised repeatedly.

See also BISHOP; PRIEST; SACRAMENT OF ORDERS.

Bibliography
Giles, Kevin. *Patterns of Ministry among the First Christians.* Melbourne: CollinsDove, 1989.
Nowell, Robert. *The Ministry of Service: Deacons in the Contemporary Church.* New York: Herder and Herder, 1968.

WERNER LÖSER

Death. From the viewpoint of theology, human death is the definitive end of earthly life, that is, the moment in which all life processes come to an irreversible end. Death, which is to be understood as the term of a lengthy process of dying, marks the beginning of life hereafter, in which the human situation of salvation or damnation is determined by the earthly life that individuals have freely fashioned for themselves before God.

(1) *Biblical Background.* The Scriptures present various ideas of death and the afterlife that cannot be simply harmonized among themselves. As understood in the Old Testament, death is of the very essence of the human being. The living God, who by God's nature possesses life and is the fountain of life (Ps 36:10), gives life as a loan and takes it back in death, so that the whole person, and not just the body, dies. This idea finds etiological expression in the creation story of the Yahwist (Gn 2:4b–7; 3:39). Sheol (Hades, the lower world) serves as an image of death in the Old Testament (and even in the New Testament): Sheol is thought of as located inside the earth and is understood as a mass grave for the human race. To descend into or be buried in Sheol thus means first of all to be delivered up to the radical power of death. While the idea of a survival after death is also connected with Sheol, the shadowy existence that is meant is incapable of awakening any real hope. Only in a later period will life after death be viewed more positively and understood as a time of rewards and punishments (ESCHATOLOGY; INTERMEDIATE STATE). In various passages of the Old Testament death is regarded as a consequence of sin or a punishment for it (Genesis 2–3; Wis 2:23–24; see 1:13–16). The New Testament takes over not only the Old Testament image of the human person but also the associated understanding of death. The Pauline and deutero-Pauline letters, in particular, provide a well-developed theology of death: they explain it, against the background of the prehistory, as a consequence of sin (Rom 5:12; 6:23; 7:13; 8:10; Eph 2:1, 5; Col 2:13). The distinctive element in the New Testament theology of death is its christological and soteriological interpretation. Because the Son of God became a true human being (Jn 1:14; Phil 2:7) and is like us in everything except sin (Heb 2:17; 4:15), he had to die our human death. The death of Christ, which was shown by the resurrection to be a saving death, is understood, on the basis of various images and models, as a death in vicarious expiation for humankind. In his resurrection Christ stripped human death of its power and vanquished it. This thought finds expression first in the

healings of the sick and raisings of the dead in the Gospels, but above all in the unified vision of Christ's death and resurrection as connected with our own future resurrection. Just as death came into the world through the first Adam, so has the power of death been definitively vanquished by Christ, the second Adam (1 Cor 15:21–22). Because Christ arose first (1 Cor 15:23), all who belong to him have through him the guaranty of their own resurrection from the dead. Paul understands the dying of Christians to be a dying with Christ (Rom 6:8), a dying in the Lord (1 Cor 15:18). In baptism we participate in the saving power of Christ's death (Rom 6:3–5). His power that overcomes sin and death becomes ours in the Lord's Supper (1 Cor 11:26). The definitive conquest of death is a blessing of the final age and an object of hope (1 Cor 15:26). Revelation, too, says that at the PAROUSIA of Christ death will be definitively banished (20:14; 21:4).

(2) *History of Theology.* In its encounter with Hellenism and the Greek view of the human person, the Christian tradition also took over the Greek understanding of death, so that death was now understood as the separation of soul from body, and life after death as the continuing existence of a soul now free of the body. But in view of biblical anthropology and the hope of the resurrection of the dead these ideas were reshaped in important ways (HUMAN PERSON: IMAGE OF; SOUL; THEOLOGICAL ANTHROPOLOGY).

(3) *Church Teaching.* Taking the biblical statements about death as its point of reference, the ecclesial magisterium has spoken about death and life after death from various points of views. At the Second Council of Orange (529), death is said, in light of Rom 5:12, to be a consequence of the sin of Adam (DS 371–72). This statement is confirmed by the decree of the Council of Trent (1546) on original sin (DS 1512). In the rejection of the errors of M. Baius (1567), the magisterium expressly says that the immortality of human beings in paradise is a gift of grace and therefore not their natural condition (DS 1978). The medieval decrees of the magisterium on the lot of the human person after death not only presuppose the understanding of death as separation of soul from body; they also understand death to be the end of the human state of pilgrimage, so that earthly life determines what kind of eschatological existence the person will forever have (see DS 856–58, 1000). A declaration of the Congregation for the Doctrine of the Faith entitled "Some Questions of Eschatology" (May 17, 1979) teaches that the bodily glorification bestowed on Mary at her death was a privilege unique to her, so that the situation of other human beings immediately after death must be distinguished from that which will be granted us when Christ appears in glory (*AAS* 71 [1979] 941).

(4) *Ecumenical Perspectives.* On the ecumenical scene, the *total-death theory* held by a considerable number of Evangelical theologians (e.g., P. Althaus, K. Barth, O. Cullmann, W. Elert) has become very important. In the context of a somewhat brusque rejection of the immortality of the soul, this doctrine says that death lays hold of the entire person, therefore soul as well as body. Nothing survives death, not even an immortal soul. All that remains is God's fidelity

to the human being, without any referent on the human side. In its drastic form this doctrine stresses the point that the soul ceases to exist. In a mitigated form it says that the soul lives on after death in a kind of sleep or dream-state. The resurrection of the dead is interpreted in a correspondingly comprehensive and radical way as a new creation based on the memory God retains of the person, as a raising up of the entire person, body and soul.

(5) *Systematic Reflections.* Death is a subject much discussed in contemporary theology. People today have an ambivalent attitude toward death. On the one hand, death has become a taboo subject, something improper, to be hidden away and suppressed from consciousness as far as possible; on the other hand, it has been trivialized and put on display for spectators. Both attitudes are profoundly inhuman because they bring in their train a dehumanization of life. Since the human soul is by its nature an incarnated entity and since death lays hold of the entire person, it affects the soul too, however much the latter may continue to live on after death The soul then acquires, to some extent, a new relationship to the world: it becomes not acosmic but all-cosmic (K. Rahner). Death marks the end of spatiality and temporality as experienced by human beings on earth. Life after death is the definitive form of the life produced by free activity but removed now from the previously known time and space; it is the definitive form, too, of history. In addition, L. Boros understands death as *final option:* that is, at the moment of death human beings are given the possibility of determining their manner of existence in the afterlife by a definitive and fully personal decision. Personal JUDGMENT and PURGATORY are understood as aspects of this final decision at death. Even greater importance attaches to the thesis on the *resurrection* that is proposed in contemporary theology and is defended essentially by the following arguments. Since after death the time known to physics and experienced by us here no longer exists, the last day comes for the individual at death. There is a parousia only in the sense that the individual who has passed through death appears before God or, rather, God appears before the individual. God's coming occurs, therefore, not at the death of the last human being but at the death of each and every person. The earlier mentioned declaration of the Congregation for the Doctrine of the Faith has this thesis in mind. Although the problem of time as it affects human existence after death cannot be resolved speculatively in a satisfactory way, it is not to be forgotten that in the understanding of the Scriptures and ecclesial tradition the last day is essentially an event still to come.

See also ETERNAL LIFE; HEAVEN; HELL; IMMORTALITY; MORTALITY; PASSION AND DEATH OF JESUS CHRIST; PURGATORY; RESURRECTION OF JESUS; RESURRECTION OF THE DEAD; SIN AND GUILT; SOTERIOLOGY.

Bibliography
Aries, Philippe. *The Hour of Our Death.* New York: Knopf, 1981.
Boros, Ladislas. *The Mystery of Death.* New York: Herder and Herder, 1965.
Greeley, Andrew. *Death and Beyond.* Chicago: Thomas More, 1976.

Hellwig, Monika. *What Are They Saying about Death and Christian Hope?* New York: Paulist, 1978.

Rahner, Karl. *On the Theology of Death.* New York: Herder and Herder, 1973.

Richards, Hubert J. *Death and After: What Will Really Happen.* Mystic, Conn.: Twenty-Third, 1987.

JOSEF FINKENZELLER

Decision. Decision (derived from legal language) in the theological sense is the ultimate judicial judgment of God upon human beings, history, and the world. Because of this, human persons in history inevitably find themselves in the situation of decision or judgment. This is not a question of a choice of one from a number of possibilities, but rather of a strict either-or: for or against God.

(1) *Biblical Background.* In the Old Testament, Yahweh's judicial sovereignty over the people plays an important role. In this perspective of its faith in Yahweh, Israel understands the events of its history: as signs of Yahweh's blessing or curse or punishment (see Deuteronomy 28; 29). With his message of the imminent breaking forth of the kingdom of God, Jesus introduced the final and ultimate situation of decision and judgment. Therefore with his message comes the appeal to conversion (Mk 1:15), which does not tolerate any delay or excuse (see the parables of the kingdom of God). At stake is the decision for faith or for unbelief, and in this God's reign as judgment is already realized (cf. Jn 12:47f.). In Galatians and Romans, Paul can therefore contrast the real justification that is received in one's faith in Jesus Christ with the vain attempt to justify oneself before God through good works (fulfillment of the law).

(2) *History of Theology.* The concept of decision was taken up in theological anthropology through the influence of S. Kierkegaard and of existential philosophy. This made it possible to distinguish between human persons' basic attitude toward their existence and their reflected choice between particular possibilities in the realization of their lives. In theology this made possible a clearer distinction between faith and ethics, and between love and the works of love, than was attainable in Scholasticism (faith/love — deeds) and in M. Luther (faith — love/deeds).

(3) *Church Teaching.* One can see a confirmation for this prereflective existential decision in faith and love in the teaching of the Council of Trent that nobody can know for sure whether he or she — through faith and love — is justified (DS 1540f.).

(4) *Ecumenical Perspectives.* Luther had understood faith as an effect of the word of God that is received by the human person in a purely passive way. Protestant theologians therefore stress frequently the priority of God in the decision of faith, while in Catholic theology the predominant idea is that the decision for faith comes at the same time wholly both from God and from the free response of the human person.

(5) *Systematic Reflections.* The concept of decision in its existential sense, which is also called the "fundamental option," carries within it the tendency to

withdraw theological statements on the human person from empirical inquiry; this was also true — yet in other ways — of the metaphysical theology of neo-scholasticism, with its emphasis on supernatural truths. It is rightly emphasized today that the existential decision between faith and unbelief is not made removed from the concrete situation of human praxis but rather in and with it. Thus the choice for the gospel in the time of persecution of the first centuries of the church was often taken as a decision for or against martyrdom. Today in Latin America this decision is phrased in terms of accepting or rejecting the option for the poor (liberation theology). As these examples make clear, the distinction between the decision for or against the gospel and the concretely situated decision must be maintained. The concrete decision for practical discipleship must remain related to the situation that is limited with regard to time and sometimes also place. It has to remain open to the creatural and historical variety of human reality. In contrast, the decision that the gospel calls for is unconditional and ultimate (baptismal pledge). The aim is, therefore, to understand the unconditional decision for the kingdom of God in such a way that in it the diversity present in creation and throughout history comes under the rule of God.

See also FAITH; FREEDOM; JUDGMENT.

Bibliography
See the bibliography under FREEDOM.

GEORG LANGEMEYER

Deism. Today, the term *deism* refers to that theory of natural religion which holds that, subsequent to the act of creation, God exerts no further influence on the world; those who hold the theory present it as a critical standard for all "positive religions" — including primarily Christianity — that make appeal to special revelation.

(1) *Biblical Background.* Deism clearly contradicts the statements of Holy Scripture about the Creator's active care and PROVIDENCE.

(2) *History of Theology.* An important source of deism is the Stoic notion of natural law, according to which religion and morality are determined by God — or the gods — merely in broad outline, whereas the rest of their content is innate in all humans; another source is Epicurean philosophy, which holds that the lives of the gods are unruffled by what happens in the world (*ataraxia*). Deism was developed in the sixteenth century (D. V. Coornhert [d. ca. 1590], J. Bodin [d. 1596]), and its initial flowering occurred in England. According to Herbert of Cherbury (d. 1648), these basic truths are innate in human beings: the existence of God; the obligation to serve God; the duty to be virtuous and pious and to atone for one's sins; and awareness of the dispensation of rewards and punishments. From then on, the mechanistic view of the world (I. Newton [d. 1727]), the rationalism following R. Descartes (d. 1650), and elements of antitrinitarian Socinianism (TRINITARIAN HERESIES) shifted God into

the role of an inactive originator of the cosmos. Deism became, above all, the religion of the Enlightenment: the world was regarded as a necessary unfolding of God, the course of which was determined by immutable natural laws; the only task remaining for religion was to make people conscious of the moral system of the "rational instinct" (Voltaire [d. 1778]) or the innate concept of God (C. Wolff [d. 1754]). The firm philosophical basis for deism was provided, in the postulates of practical reason, by I. Kant.

(3) *Church Teaching.* Vatican I produced an apologia of Christian revelation against deism, stating that the syllabus of Pius IX (1864) had already condemned the proposition that "any active influence by God on human beings and the world" was to be denied (DS 2902). The COUNCIL held that God created the world "out of his goodness," "in order to reveal his perfection through the goods that he communicates to creatures" (DS 3002); even today, God "protects and guides" creation in a way inclusive of the free actions of humans (DS 3003); among the "external proofs of his revelation" are the miracles (DS 3009, 3034), which are by no means unworthy of God's transcendence and not to be understood as interference by the Creator in the affairs of a world that God intended to be autonomous.

(4) *Ecumenical Perspectives.* Within Protestant theology, deism acquired a not insignificant influence on biblical criticism, primarily through the writings of H. S. Reimarus and G. E. Lessing.

(5) *Systematic Reflections.* Today, Christian theology proceeds on the assumption that deism, insofar as it was shaped by a kind of natural-scientific thinking presupposing determinism, has been deprived of its essential support since the turn to quantum mechanics (W. Heisenberg).

See also CREATION; MIRACLE; REVELATION.

Bibliography

Buckley, Michael. *At the Origins of Modern Atheism.* New Haven: Yale University Press, 1987.
Küng, Hans. *Does God Exist? An Answer for Today.* Garden City, N.Y.: Doubleday, 1980.
Lubac, Henri de. *The Drama of Atheistic Humanism.* Cleveland: World, 1963.

ALEXANDRE GANOCZY

Demons. According to ancient Greek popular belief and the literature based on it (Homer), the Greek word *daimónion* (neuter) designates gods and lower deities who influence human destiny through their superhuman, unpredictable, and often cruel powers, and whom people therefore attempt to control through exorcism and magic. The demons represent, in the context of a mythological understanding of reality, the threatening awfulness of the natural environment. Handed down from the Old Testament, but even more from early Judaism, this notion is carried over into the New Testament with an altered content: the demons embody forces of inherently groundless resistance to the coming dominion of God. As "unclean spirits," they concretize the mysterious power of evil in a world created by God as good. Thus creation, in its experienced form, cannot be imagined without the element of the demonic.

(1) *Biblical Background.* The Old Testament refers to desert demons (Lv 16:8–26), night demons (Is 34:14), noonday demons (Ps 91:6), and various other malefic demons (2 Chr 11:15; Is 2:6; Ps 106:6); such references clearly highlight their relation to nature. The prophets protest most vehemently against any interpretation of them in the sense of pagan polytheism, so that, in the end, demons play only a very subordinate role in the Old Testament. Early Judaism, however, occupies itself with demons to a much greater extent: it identifies them with alien idols and sees in them evil spirits, harmers, corrupters, and seducers of humanity. To the question of their origin, the answer is given — among others — that they are rebellious or fallen angels (*1 Enoch* 6–36). Nothing of this is known, however, to original history as recounted in the Old Testament. Only Gn 6:1–4, dealing with marriage between the "sons of heaven" and the daughters of humans, could suggest an interpretation (albeit distorted) along those lines. Still, the monks of Qumran maintain the unshakable lordship of Yahweh over the demons (1QS 3:25). For Jesus, who makes use of such early Jewish modes of expression, demons are "impure spirits" that, causing possession and illness, set themselves against the coming of God's dominion (see Mk 3:22–30). He drives them out, thereby signaling the already approaching kingdom (Lk 11:20 par.). The post-Easter tradition then interprets his death and resurrection as a devastating victory over these powers (see 1 Cor 15:23–28; Col 2:15). Where the evil forces had rent things apart, Christ "made peace" (Col 1:20).

(2) *History of Theology.* Among the Church Fathers, opinion firmed that demons were fallen angels who had succumbed to their lust for the daughters of humans (e.g., Tertullian, *De cultu fem.* 1.2f.; 2.10; Ambrose, *Exp. Ps* 108) — something denied by Chrysostom (*Hom. in Gen.* 2) and Augustine (*De civ. Dei* 15.23) — or whose envy and pride became their undoing (Augustine, *De Gen. ad litt.* 11.14f.). Thus they find themselves in a "state of deferred judgment" (G. Tavard, *HDG* 2/2b:43).

(3) *Church Teaching.* Doctrinal office held fears of a Manichaean-dualistic division within creation and also of a related demonization, in principle, of material creation. Therefore, in 1215, the Fourth Lateran Council declared: "God created the devil and the other evil spirits as good by nature, but they became bad through themselves" (DS 800).

(4/5) *Ecumenical Perspectives/Systematic Reflections.* Ecumenical and recent theological perspectives result, for Catholic dogmatists, from relating the question of demons back to the mystery of evil, which is imagined as something personal only in a very weak analogical sense, and therefore does not release humans from their responsibility for evil deeds. Among Protestant theologians, self-critical comments such as this may be found: "Protestant dogmatics needs to resist the danger of becoming bogged down in an unclear, generalized mood of pessimism and uncritically confusing the 'category' of the demonic with the statements of the New Testament" (G. Gloege, *RGG* 2:4).

See also EVIL, MORAL; KINGDOM OF GOD.

Bibliography
Detweiler, Robert, and William G. Doty. *The Daemonic Imagination: Biblical Text and Secular Story.* Atlanta: Scholars Press, 1990.

ALEXANDRE GANOCZY

Descent into Hell. *See* CHRIST'S DESCENT INTO HELL.

Development of Dogma. The development of dogma is the process carried out throughout history in which the message of revelation is grasped theologically and opened up for faith.

(1) *Biblical Background.* A type of intrabiblical development of dogma is present where new interpretations are given in view of changed situations or addressees, as becomes clear in a comparison of the logia on divorce from Mk 10:11f. (husband and wife can commit adultery) and from Mt 19:9 (only the man can commit adultery); in James's expansion of the Pauline teaching on justification through the works of piety; and in the different characteristics of the four Gospels. Looking at Mt 28:20 and Jn 16:12–15, it becomes clear that revelation is already completed but at the same time must be continually disclosed anew: Christians must now hold on to what Jesus *has* taught; the Spirit recalls the memory of Jesus and *leads* into his truth.

(2) *History of Theology.* In the situation of the early church, naturally, the homogeneity of Christian teaching was emphasized. The Fathers, however, already recognized an organic growth in the understanding of it (Vincent of Lérins, *Commonit.* 23.2, 4, 12). The Middle Ages also did not explicitly confront the question of changes in the faith, although theologians were aware of them (the different length of the creeds, the absence of important elements of faith within them, the debate about the possibility of new formulas of faith). These questions were answered with reference to a tradition alongside Scripture. Only with the Enlightenment and the increased awareness of the historicity of truth did the problem become critical for theology. It arises from the juxtaposition of the following presuppositions: (*a*) revelation is completed; (*b*) there are propositions that the church, as it moves through time, has proclaimed as divinely revealed dogma — the explanation being that they either were not known to be this up until the time of proclamation, or were not formulated as such, or were not verifiable through equivalent statements in the tradition. The problematic was first treated by the Catholic Tübingen school. Afterward, different theories were formed to explain the phenomenon. The most important of these were developed by (*a*) *neo-scholastic theology*: the development of dogma is a process of deduction in which a logical advance in knowledge from obscurity toward clarity takes place. What is controversial here is whether only what is formally implicitly revealed (R. M. Schultes), or

also what is virtually revealed (F. Marin-Sola, M. Tuyaerts), is capable of becoming dogma. (b) J. H. Newman: the development of dogma is the result of an illative sense, through which the validity of an insight is acknowledged in a personal decision. (c) M. Blondel: the development of dogma is the process in which a reality that has been proven in Christian life is passed on and translated anew in concrete action. In this way the knowledge of the contents of faith is also increased. (d) H. de Lubac, H. Urs von Balthasar: the development of dogma is the unfolding of the global Christian faith consciousness under the influence of the Spirit. None of these four attempted solutions has prevailed. Because of the reason mentioned under (5), theologians today are of the opinion that a universal theory for the development of dogma cannot be proposed.

(3) *Church Teaching*. The ecclesial magisterium of the nineteenth and twentieth centuries has substantially contributed to the actualization of these problems through the promulgation of the dogmas of the IMMACULATE CONCEPTION (1854) and the ASSUMPTION OF MARY into God's glory (1950) as well as through the proclamation of the papal dogmas of 1870, all of which are not explicitly found in Scripture. In this fashion the magisterium itself seemed to change from an authority judging dogma to one developing dogma. Vatican I maintains that the meaning of the truths of faith must be retained, but with reference to Vincent of Lérins allows within this limit an increase and development (DS 3020). Vatican II explains that the apostolic tradition "makes progress in the Church with the help of the Holy Spirit" through study, inner reflection, and the preaching of the magisterium (*DV* 8; see *LG* 12; *GS* 62).

(4) *Ecumenical Perspectives*. The Orthodox Church acknowledges the development of dogma in the sense of an increase in dogmatic interpretation but not, however, as a process that touches dogma itself. For Protestantism the problem of the development of dogma is not raised inasmuch as it does not recognize a magisterium similar to that present in Roman Catholicism. Doctrinal developments are considered as historical processes.

(5) *Systematic Reflections*. The problem of the development of dogma results from the historicity of dogma. While dogma, indeed, possesses binding validity, it does not constitute either the completion of or the last word on a dogmatic question. It must, while retaining the intended sense, be translated into new situations, deepened through new insights, and included in the comprehensive perspective of the faith as a whole. This occurs especially by reflecting back upon the spiritual (doxological) and existential significance of the creedal expressions. Because of all this, however, processes of change are inevitably released. They may consist of (a) a magisterial definition, which formally pronounces a statement materially contained in the faith resources (e.g., Mary is the mother of God); (b) making more precise a concept that in its substance is an already recognized element of faith (e.g., the relationship between God the Father and Christ through *homousios*); or (c) the development of elements of faith implicitly contained in the faith resources (e.g., recogni-

tion of the sacramentality of marriage, of the existence of seven sacraments, or of Mary's freedom from original sin). This type of development is the actual test case for the development of dogma. In considering all the various attempts at explanation, one must remember that the expressions of revelation do not form a system of propositions, but rather are moments within a salvific dialogue. While after the coming of Christ they do not increase in a quantitative way (revelation is completed), qualitatively they can and must be elaborated. This happens through the continuing contemplation of the whole faith community upon the message of revelation. This meditation does not involve a transition from what has not been believed to what is believed, but rather a transition from a lesser to a greater certainty that a statement is a revealed truth. This process happens under the influence of the Holy Spirit. It is accomplished by continually looking back to the sources of faith, by responding to the needs of the present situation, and by looking toward a future unfolding of the understanding of the faith. The process can be set in motion through the initiatives of the magisterium, through the SENSUS FIDELIUM (above all through Christian spirituality), through reaction to HERESIES, and through theological reflection. Since the development of dogma is being carried out throughout all of history, and thus is not yet completed, there cannot be a universal a priori theory for the development of dogma that encompasses all the possibilities.

See also DOGMA/DOGMATIC STATEMENT; HISTORY/HISTORICITY; REVELATION; TRADITION.

Bibliography

Blondel, Maurice. *History and Dogma.* New York: Holt, Rinehart and Winston, 1964.

Geiselmann, Joseph. *Tradition.* New York: Herder and Herder, 1976.

Newman, John Henry. *An Essay on the Development of Christian Doctrine.* Notre Dame, Ind.: University of Notre Dame Press, 1989.

Rahner, Karl. "Considerations on the Development of Dogma." In *Theological Investigations,* 4:3–35. New York: Seabury, 1974.

Walgrave, Jan Hendrik. *Person and Society: A Christian View.* Pittsburgh: Duquesne University Press, 1965.

———. *Unfolding Revelation: The Nature of Doctrinal Development.* Philadelphia: Westminster, 1972.

WOLFGANG BEINERT

Devil. The term *devil* (from the Greek *diábolos* = confounder), or *Satan* (from the Hebrew), signifies a (supreme) evil spiritual being, occurring in many religions as well as in Holy Scripture, who usually rules over numerous subordinate demons.

(1) *Biblical Background.* In the Old Testament, hostile earthly figures from the political, judicial, or military sphere can also be called *satan* (1 Kgs 5:18; 11:24f.; Ps 109:6; 1 Sm 29:4), as can even God, to the extent that God appears as the adversary of the sufferer (Jb 16:9; 30:21). As a "son of God" engaged in discussion with God, he provokes the testing of Job (Jb 1:6–2:10); he re-

mains, however, subordinate to God's will (see Zec 3:1f.; Ps 109:6). In 1 Chr 21:1, the devil takes on an independent status; the idea that he is an instrument of divine anger (see 2 Sm 24:1–3) recedes in favor of the notion of an angel who has fallen away from the Creator (see *2 Enoch* 29:4f.) and become God's enemy and a seducer of humanity (*Jub* 10:1–13; *1 Enoch* 6–9). Radical elimination of this thoroughly evil Satan — who also plays an important role in the dualism of the Qumran sect (1QS 3:21–23; 1QM 13:11f.; 1QH 3:28, 36; 11:22) — is provided for at the end of time (*Jub* 23:29; *1 Enoch* 16:1). In the New Testament, mythologically tinged notions introduced by early Judaism are frequently drawn upon in order to allude, with eschatological compellingness, to the power of evil in the world. In the Synoptics, the devil is called "the enemy" (Mt 13:39; Lk 10:19) and "the evil one" (Mt 13:19, 38) — a name that is then used more emphatically, together with "the ruler of this world" (Jn 12:31; 14:30; 16:11), in the Johannine texts (Jn 17:15; 1 Jn 2:13f.; 5:18), allowing the devil to appear, quite consistently, as the opponent of the redemptive work of the Son of God (1 Jn 3:8; see 3:10). The evangelists tell us of Jesus' struggle with the devil. Tempted by him in the desert (Mk 1:12f. par.), he nevertheless overcomes him, being "the stronger" (Mk 3:27), and effects his fall from heaven (Lk 10:18). He who is capable of driving out demons (Mk 3:22f.; Lk 11:20) is also beyond being conquered by the devil-inspired treachery of Judas (Lk 22:3; Jn 13:27). The deutero-Paulines lend a cosmic dimension to the glorified Christ's victory over the devil (Eph 2:2; 6:10–20; see Col 2:9, 15), and Revelation prophesies the devil's total overthrow (Rv 12:7–9). Nevertheless, for the time being, the devil retains the potential for seducing the faithful (1 Cor 7:5; 2 Cor 2:11; Acts 5:3), for thwarting evangelization (1 Thes 2:18), and for inflicting persecution upon God's church (Acts 13:10; 1 Pt 5:8f.; Rv 12:13–17). Before the end of history, he can even unleash the Antichrist against it (2 Thes 2:9; Revelation 13); but he will then still be overthrown and cast into hell (Rv 20:8–10).

(2) *History of Theology.* The Fathers refer to the devil above all as "Satan," "the evil one," and "Lucifer" (following a fairly arbitrary interpretation of Is 14:12 and Jb 41:10). Methodius calls him "Pharaoh," and Basil, "misanthrope" (hater of humanity); many others identify him with the "serpent" of Genesis 3 and 2 Cor 11:3 — a view that has been completely abandoned in modern exegesis. The thesis that the devil is one of the highest (or the highest) of the angels who rebelled against God, or indeed, the highest of all creatures who became, through his arrogance, the lowest (Origen), is very widespread among the Fathers, even though it lacks solid biblical foundations.

(3) *Church Teaching.* Significantly, it was only as a result of dualistic heresies like Priscillianism that doctrinal office was moved to explain that the devil was not a primordial substance that had emerged independently from chaos, thus being the principle of evil, but was originally one of God's good creatures, who had then turned the God-willed good to bad, unnatural purpose (Leo I, 447 [DS 286]). Accordingly, the devil's sin is structurally equivalent

to humanity's: an act of free will (see DS 797). The Synod of Braga, in 561, confirmed this doctrine (DS 457) and rejected the view that the devil is himself a creator who "causes, by his own power, thunder, lightning, and stormy weather" (DS 458) and "the formation of the human body" in the womb (DS 462). In 1215, for the first time with the authority of an ecumenical convocation, the Fourth Lateran Council taught: "God created the devil and other evil spirits good by nature, but they became bad through themselves. Humankind sinned at the instigation of the devil" (DS 800). Otherwise, the devil is mentioned only in comments peripheral to central statements of doctrinal office: as the overseer of the "empire of death" (*imperium mortis*) (DS 291) and of all evil rule in the world (DS 1347, 1511, 1521, 1668), and as the object of a "perpetual punishment" (*poena perpetua*) (DS 801). On the other hand, doctrinal office rejected the drawing of any hasty, strained inferences, on the basis of parapsychological phenomena (DS 2192, 2241–53, 3233), about demoniacal possession. Interestingly, the devil is not mentioned in the teaching on creation of Vatican I and receives at best only marginal mention in that of Vatican II (*LG* 48; *GS* 22; *AG* 9).

(4) *Ecumenical Perspectives.* The Reformation teaching on creation does not essentially deviate from this tradition.

(5) *Systematic Reflections.* Theological explication takes its bearings today, in a demythologized intellectual context, by the concrete manifestations of evil in the world: oppression, injustice, violence, or an egocentric anthropocentrism that irreversibly damages the environment. Correlatively, individualistic fear of the devil, in the sense associated with the Gospels, is superseded. The question about the appropriateness of applying the person-analogy to the power of evil — that is, posing the question of whether evil *as such* is operative only as the evil *one* — cannot be settled by recourse to cheap anthropomorphisms. "The devil is not a personal figure, but a self-dissolving mal-figure, an entity that perverts itself into a mal-entity; he is a person in the manner of a mal-person" (W. Kasper, in W. Kasper and K. Lehmann, eds., *Teufel, Dämonen, Besessenheit* [Mainz, 1978], 63).

See also ANGEL; ANTICHRIST; DEMONS; EVIL, MORAL; HELL.

Bibliography

Kallas, James G. *Jesus and the Power of Satan.* Philadelphia: Westminster, 1968.

Russell, Jeffrey Burton. *The Devil: Perceptions of Evil from Antiquity to Primitive Christianity.* Ithaca, N.Y.: Cornell University Press, 1977.

———. *Lucifer: The Devil in the Middle Ages.* Ithaca, N.Y.: Cornell University Press, 1984.

———. *Mephistopheles: The Devil in the Modern World.* Ithaca, N.Y.: Cornell University Press, 1986.

———. *The Prince of Darkness: Radical Evil and the Power of Good in History.* Ithaca, N.Y.: Cornell University Press, 1988.

———. *Satan: The Early Christian Tradition.* Ithaca, N.Y.: Cornell University Press, 1981.

ALEXANDRE GANOCZY

Dialogue. Dialogue means a conversation between equal partners, in which agreement (consensus) regarding the truth is sought.

(1) *Biblical Background.* The concept as such is not found in the Scriptures, which have nonetheless indirectly influenced the modern understanding of dialogue (see [5]).

(2) *History of Theology.* The theological importance of "dialoguing" became fully clear only in the modern age, not least in the debate with transcendental idealism; elements of dialogue, however, came into play in the past (the dialogue as a literary genre, e.g., Justin, *Dialogus cum Tryphone;* Abelard, *Dialogus inter Philosophum, Judaeum, et Christianum*). Dialogue as a literary form is also the basis of the Scholastic "disputation" (*disputatio*), especially in the heightened form of disputation practiced by Luther. In the Catholic Church, the utterances of the ECCLESIAL MAGISTERIUM were so much emphasized in the modern age that the dialogical quest for and understanding of the truth of faith were downplayed.

(3) *Church Teaching.* According to Vatican II, elements of truth, holiness, and ecclesiality exist outside the Roman Catholic Church. The council could therefore urge dialogue with other churches, religions, and cultures (see especially *UR* 4, 9, 11, 14, 18f., 21, 23; *GS* 3, 19, 21, 25, 40, 43, 56; *AG* 16, 20, 41).

(4) *Ecumenical Perspectives.* The recommendations of Vatican II were implemented especially in dialogues with the other churches and ecclesial communities, in which each is to "treat...the other on an equal footing" (*UR* 9). In the dialogue with the Eastern churches two phases have been distinguished: the "dialogue of love" and the "dialogue of truth." In addition, a distinction is made in the ecumenical movement between dialogues that are *bilateral* (between two churches) and *multilateral* (between several churches), *official* (with a mandate from church authorities) and *unofficial* (without such a mandate), *regional* (at the local or regional level) and *worldwide.* Their goal is communion between the churches. Many ecumenical dialogues have already produced statements of convergence and consensus.

(5) *Systematic Reflections.* It is no accident that in our time dialogical thinking has been fostered by philosophers and theologians who acknowledge their especially close ties with the Jewish-Christian tradition (the "philosophers of dialogue": M. Buber, F. Ebner, F. Rosenzweig; today: J. Heinrichs and J. Splett, among others). To them we owe our special vision of "I" and "Thou," the category of encounter, the priority of action, our specific understanding of language and TIME, and, above all, our understanding of God speaking to human beings (in Jesus) and of human beings speaking to God (PRAYER). From all this it is also clear that the "openness" of ecclesial and theological dialogue is limited by the fact that the truth of faith that is discussed in dialogue is already given through REVELATION and the teaching of the church and does not emerge only from dialogue itself. The consensus that arises out of

WORLDWIDE ECUMENICAL DIALOGUES INVOLVING
CATHOLIC THEOLOGIANS

Commission/confession	Subjects
Anglican–Roman Catholic Conversations	Report of the Preparatory Commission (Malta Report) (1968) Final Report of the Anglican–Roman Catholic International Commission (1981) (In addition to an Introduction and Conclusion, the Report contains: — Eucharistic Doctrine [Windsor Statement], 1971 — Eucharistic Doctrine: Elucidation, Salisbury, 1979 — Ministry and Ordination [Canterbury Statement], 1973 — Ministry and Ordination: Elucidation, Salisbury, 1979 — Authority in the Church I [Venice Statement], 1976 — Authority in the Church: Elucidation, Windsor, 1981 — Authority in the Church [Windsor Statement], 1981) The Theology of Marriage and Its Application to Mixed Marriages (1975) Salvation and the Church (1986)
Disciples of Christ–Roman Catholic Conversations	Report on the International Commission for the Dialogue between the Disciples of Christ and the Roman Catholic Church (1977–81)
Lutheran–Roman Catholic Conversations	The Gospel and the Church (Malta Report) (1972) The Eucharist (1978) Ways to Community (1980) All under One Christ (1980) The Ministry in the Church (1981) Martin Luther — Witness to Jesus Christ (1983) The Unity ahead of Us (1985)
Lutheran–Reformed–Roman Catholic Conversations	The Theology of Marriage and the Problem of Mixed Marriages (1976)
Methodist–Roman Catholic Conversations	Report of the Joint Commission (Denver Report) (1971) Report of the Joint Commission (Dublin Report) (1976) Report of the Joint Commission (Honolulu Report, 1981) Report of the Joint Commission (1986)
Pentecostal–Roman Catholic Conversations	Concluding Report between the Secretariat for Christian Unity and Leading Representatives of Some Pentecostal Churches as well as Participants in the Charismatic Movement in the Evangelical and Anglican Churches (1972–76) Concluding Report of the Second Phase of the Conversations (1984)
Reformed–Roman Catholic Conversations	The Presence of Christ in Church and World (1977) The Church: People of God, Body of Christ, Temple of the Holy Spirit [conversations not yet ended]
Baptist–Roman Catholic Conversations	[Begun in 1984; not yet finished]
Orthodox–Roman Catholic Conversations	The Mystery of the Church and the Eucharist in Light of the Mystery of the Most Holy Trinity (1982) Faith, Sacraments, and Unity (1986; not yet concluded)
Eastern Orthodox–Roman Catholic Conversations	Joint Report of the First Meeting of the Joint Commission of the Catholic Church and the Coptic Orthodox Church (Cairo, 1974) Joint Report of the Second Meeting (Cairo, 1975) Declaration on Christology (Vienna, 1976)
Commission of Faith and Order of the World Council of Churches	Baptism, Eucharist, and Ministry: Statements of Convergence (Lima, 1982)

dialogue must therefore be evaluated once more in the light of the truth of the gospel.

See also ECUMENISM; LANGUAGE; TRUTH OF FAITH.

Bibliography

Fries, Heinrich, and Karl Rahner. *Unity of the Churches: An Actual Possibility.* Philadelphia: Fortress; New York: Paulist, 1985.

Reynolds, Frank, and David Tracy, eds. *Discourse and Practice.* Albany: State University of New York Press, 1992.

See also the bibliography under ECUMENISM.

WERNER LÖSER

Discipleship. Discipleship refers to the group of persons whom Jesus of Nazareth called to communion with himself and gave a share in his mission. This group is the preresurrection prototype of the church.

(1) *Biblical Background.* Whenever in religions and cultures students gather around a teacher, there is discipleship in a general sense of the term. In postexilic Judaism teachers of the law made their appearance and were joined by disciples. The New Testament tells of Jesus of Nazareth calling and sending disciples. The references are either to the group of "Twelve," who are also named individually (Mk 3:13–19 par.), or to a wider circle of persons who follow after Jesus (Mt 8:21), especially the "seventy-two" whom Jesus sends out (Lk 10:1). At times, all who believe in Jesus are called disciples (Jn 2:11; 8:31; 20:29). Jn 6:66 reports that some of Jesus' disciples subsequently left him. The call of disciples by Jesus is one of the best attested elements in the Jesus tradition and displays certain characteristic traits: discipleship has to do less with a doctrine or a skill than with the person of Jesus himself. None of the disciples can take his place; they remain disciples "under" their Lord and teacher. To be a disciple of Jesus means the surrender of one's person to him, and not simply a commitment that is temporary or limited in scope. Therefore the disciples share in the life and death of Jesus (Mt 16:21–23) and are included in his mission (Matthew 10). Consequently, the gathering and sending of disciples by Jesus is an "eschatological phenomenon" that cannot be subsumed under other forms of "following."

(2) *History of Theology.* Discipleship acquires ecclesial significance only as a result of Easter, because only through his resurrection is Jesus exalted as the risen Lord. Discipleship now acquires its full form in the one church as the community called and sent by Jesus. Those who exercise hierarchical ministry are at the service of this church, and the religious communities live within it. In both of these phenomena certain dimensions of the original discipleship emerge. Ministries are characterized by authority to act with Jesus and as he did (on the transmission of authority, see Mt 16:16–18; 18:18; 20:21; on acting with Jesus of Nazareth and as he did, see Lk 9:1–6 par.). The religious communities are made up of men and women who are conscious of a special call to

follow the poor, celibate, and obedient Jesus. The group of disciples in the New Testament is the first and prototypical embodiment of this call.

(3) *Church Teaching.* The theme of discipleship has not been explicitly treated in the documents of Vatican II or in other documents of the ecclesial magisterium. It is, however, dealt with materially and implicitly when statements about the theology of ministry in the church or the theology of religious life are linked to the New Testament origins of ministry or religious life (see, e.g., *LG* 19, 42).

(4) *Ecumenical Perspectives.* There is one Christian church that uses the term "disciples" to express its self-understanding: the Disciples of Christ. An ecumenical dialogue took place from 1977 to 1981 between this body and the Roman Catholic Church.

(5) *Systematic Reflections.* The church can constantly renew itself only by reflection on its origins. For this reason, the idea of discipleship is always relevant, and the church must always be mindful of it.

See also APOSTLE; CHURCH; DISCIPLESHIP, CHRISTIAN; MINISTRY IN THE CHURCH.

WERNER LÖSER

Discipleship, Christian. Christian discipleship *generally* means the orientation of one's own daily living to the way of life of Jesus of Nazareth. The *theological concept* of Christian discipleship includes as its fundamental and essential characteristic faith in Jesus as the Christ, that is, as the unsurpassable bearer of God's salvation for all human beings.

(1) *Biblical Background.* As the Gospels relate, Jesus himself called persons to be his disciples, which meant, first of all, to wander around with Jesus and in word and deed to bring the kingdom of God closer to other people. The post-Easter communities extended this calling to all those who believe in Christ (Mt 28:19; see Acts 6:1, 7). In terms of content, being a disciple of Christ now above all means an "imitation" of Christ's attitude of love (Phil 2:5; sec 1 Cor 11:1). The foundation for this is the sacramental union with Christ in baptism (Rom 6:3–5). This imitation is concretized most clearly in the discipleship of suffering for the sake of the gospel and in martyrdom (2 Cor 4:10f.; Acts 7:55–60; 1 Pt 2:21; Rv 14:4).

(2) *History of Theology.* The praxis of Christian discipleship and the theological meaning given to it have had a lively history (see table, p. 178).

(3) *Church Teaching.* The ecclesial magisterium recognizes in the monastic tradition the special discipleship of Christ, since it is "founded in the teaching and example of the Lord" (*LG* 43) and since this state imitates the form of life of the Lord "more explicitly" than the other Christian groups do (*LG* 44; see DS 1810). At the same time, the magisterium emphasizes the obligation of all Christians to the discipleship of Christ (*LG* 40, 41; *AA* 4). Especially remarkable is the statement that the church itself has to follow the way of the poor,

THE FORMS OF CHRISTIAN DISCIPLESHIP IN HISTORY

1. Time of persecution	Discipleship in the martyr's death; readiness for this as a basic Christian attitude
2. From Constantine until the Middle Ages	Discipleship as the monastic way of life in poverty, celibacy, and obedience: a special position in the church
3. The poverty movements in the Middle Ages	To move around like Jesus without a home or possessions and through word and deed to bring the gospel closer especially to the poor and outcast
4. Late Middle Ages and Baroque: mysticism, *devotio moderna,* Ignatius Loyola (Jesuits)	To reexperience innerly the life and death of Jesus and to realize this spiritually until the mystical death of the soul (new birth from God) and in action as God's instrument ("blind" obedience)
5. Modern times, the Enlightenment	The life and teaching of Jesus as ethical model for the love of neighbor and for the care for the poor and the sick
6. Current situation: political theology, liberation theology	A social-ethical discipleship of Jesus: to commit oneself for human rights and the rights of the underprivileged; nonviolent resistance

persecuted, and serving Lord and to engage itself according to his example above all for the poor and the suffering (*LG* 8).

(4) *Ecumenical Perspectives.* Protestant theology in accordance with Luther follows two concerns: (*a*) to understand faith as a purely receptive act of the discipleship of Christ (DECISION); and (*b*) to value all forms of Christian discipleship as theologically equal.

(5) *Systematic Reflections.* Actually the decisive theological criterion for the discipleship of Christ cannot lie in the greater or lesser assumption of Jesus' concrete way of life. It is, rather, to be sought in the intention of Jesus' way of life, to serve in bringing God's love for humankind and God's salvific will into the world. The discipleship of Christ consists primarily in allowing oneself to be led by the Spirit of Christ that aims toward the future and the fulfillment of all people and that has already begun with the resurrection of Christ (Rom 8:5–30). The way of life that is needed for this in each respective age is to be understood as the discipleship of Christ to which each Christian, corresponding to his or her special capabilities, is called in his or her own specific way. This orientation toward the kingdom of God preserves the discipleship of Christ not only from being misunderstood as an exact imitation of Jesus' actual way of life but also from being reduced to the social-ethical and political level or, in contrast to this, to the inner dimension of the ascent of the soul to God.

See also CHURCH; MONASTICISM/RELIGIOUS LIFE.

Bibliography
Happel, Stephen, and James J. Walter. *Conversion and Discipleship*. Philadelphia: Fortress, 1986.
Schüssler Fiorenza, Elisabeth. *Discipleship of Equals*. New York: Crossroad, 1993.

Georg Langemeyer

Discourse about God. Because the word *God* is intended to designate an absolutely singular and unique reality, the question arises whether discourse about God expresses the reality of merely a human projection or whether it expresses an absolute reality, namely, God.

(1) *Biblical Background.* Holy Scripture, as a total body of writing, is understandable only on the following assumption: if God is spoken *about*, that is possible only *if*, and *because*, God has spoken and is recognizable as God from God's words. This applies not only to the revelation of God's word in a proper sense, but also (according to this revelation) in the sense that, as Creator, God speaks through works and that this speaking reaches humans and can be apprehended by them. The revelation of God's word takes up and articulates this discourse for the sake of the following goal: God's self-communication to humans in the form of life in fellowship with them (*communio*); this relationship is expressed in the profession of faith "The Lord is God" (1 Kgs 18:39 and its context). The New Testament gives a christological formulation of this *communio*: "What we have seen and heard we proclaim now to you, so that you...may have fellowship with us; for our fellowship is with the Father and with his Son, Jesus Christ" (1 Jn 1:3). Jesus' preaching also refers (this is often overlooked) to this fellowship. When Jesus, as one both coming from and moving toward God, speaks about God, he includes humanity in the breaking in of God's kingdom. As a whole, then, biblical proclamation about God emphasizes that God is virtually omnipresent in human life, although not as an object humans take in their grasp and bring under control through discourse. Instead God is the one who, through such discourse, unleashes a dynamic that is centered on God and that leads, through Christ as the "way" and the Holy Spirit as the "gift," to communion with God.

(2) *History of Theology.* In the history of theology, the word *God* was an uncontested term up to modern times (Thomas Aquinas, *STh* 1, q. 23: "That is what everyone calls God," as concluding his proofs of the existence of God). Theologians endeavored, by means of the principles of analogy, to comprehend more precisely the reality behind that term. In the modern age, the danger exists of functionalizing discourse and thereby reducing God to an explanatory principle for the cosmos. In contrast, B. Pascal is prominent in emphasizing the "God of Abraham, Isaac, and Jacob," that is, the living God of the Bible.

(3) *Church Teaching.* Vatican II (*DV* esp. 2) emphasizes the close relationship between word and deed in the history of revelation, thereby opening up understanding of a revealing God and thereby creating the possibility of human discourse about God.

(4) *Ecumenical Perspectives*. Since Reformation spirituality has forcefully focused on the theological significance of the word, it has, among other things, drawn attention to the interrelation between believing and listening. In this connection, the significance of the "word of creation" has not always been preserved (NATURAL THEOLOGY).

(5) *Systematic Reflections*. As a consequence of questions arising in modern philosophy of language, theology should confront problems pertaining mainly to the possibility of disclosure of reality and its verification through human language. This debate has consequences for discourse about God. When logical positivism denies that the word *God* has any sense at all because of its nonverifiability, it must be noted that this position leaves out of account the problem areas of human responsibility and the question of meaning. On the other hand, the debate with critical rationalism has made this clear: God is not a factor in the resolution of inner-worldly problems (in the sense of the *Deus ex machina*). Nor is God so remote from the world and in such a way that the problems could be resolved "as if God were not given" (*ac si non daretur Deus*) (Hugo Grotius). Discourse about God should neither identify nor separate God and world. Also related to this is the fact that believing discourse about God cannot determine the content of the term *God* to the rest of the linguistic community — God should be acknowledged in freedom; hence, discourse about God may only make an appeal for such free decision by bearing witness to God as the God of love and hope. God's love, however, is not only to be proclaimed but also lived out as an example. Discourse about God is, therefore, always anticipatory, for it presents the opportunity for believers to become involved, sincerely and openly, with the difficulties experienced by their contemporaries.

See also ANALOGY; GOD; GOD: POSSIBILITY OF KNOWLEDGE OF; GOD: PROOFS OF EXISTENCE OF; GOD: THEOLOGY OF; REVELATION.

Bibliography

Cobb, John B., Jr., and David Tracy. *Talking about God: Doing Theology in the Context of Modern Pluralism*. New York: Seabury, 1975.

Ferre, Frederick. *Language, Logic, and God*. New York: Harper and Row, 1961.

Gilkey, Langdon. *Naming the Whirlwind: The Renewal of God-Language*. Indianapolis: Bobbs-Merrill, 1969.

McFague, Sallie. *Metaphorical Theology: Models of God in Religious Language*. Philadelphia: Fortress, 1982.

Ramsey, Ian T. *Religious Language: An Empirical Placing of Theological Phrases*. New York: Macmillan, 1963.

Tilley, T. W. *Talking of God: An Introduction to Philosophical Analysis of Religious Language*. Princeton, N.J.: Princeton University Press, 1978.

WILHELM BREUNING

Disposition for Receiving Grace.

In the framework of a theology of grace, the disposition for grace refers to the preparations human beings need in order to be justified. The disposition is a response to the call of God's love and is realized by a total conversion.

(1) *Biblical Background.* In the Bible, conversion (Old Testament: *shub;* New Testament: *metanoein, epistrephein*) manifests our disposition for grace. *Shub* has a negative sense: a *turning away from* sin, and a positive sense: *turning toward* God. When there is a conversion of the whole heart, God rescues and saves us. This is the main content of the preaching of the prophets (Is 30:15; 44:22; Jer 18:8; 25:5; Ez 18:28, 32; Hos 14:2–9; Zech 1:3; Mal 3:7). The initiative for conversion comes from God: "Lead us back to you, O Lord, that we may be restored" (Lam 5:21). Jeremiah and Hosea understand conversion as humankind's response to God's wooing love (using the images from marriage: Jeremiah 3; Hosea 1–3). To describe the human preparation for God's saving action, the Old Testament often uses the notion of seeking God (Dt 4:29; 1 Chr 16:10; 2 Chr 15:4; Pss 9:11; 34:11; Is 51:1; Am 5:4–6). In the New Testament, John the Baptist and Jesus begin their preaching with a call to conversion of the heart (*metanoia*), which leads to participation in the coming kingdom of God (Mt 3:2; 4:17). Mk 1:15 relates conversion directly to belief in the gospel. According to Lk 5:32, Jesus thinks his mission is to call sinners to conversion. In the preaching of the apostles, conversion is the condition for receiving baptism as the forgiveness and the gift of the Holy Spirit (Acts 2:38). This emphasizes the close relationship between conversion and faith (Acts 20:21; see Heb 6:1). The emphasis is on God's initiative. The call to sinners comes from Jesus (Mk 2:17). Every good work that human beings do begins in God (Phil 1:6). Humans are drawn interiorly by the Father (Jn 6:44).

(2) *History of Theology.* The problem of the disposition for grace first becomes acute in the debate between Augustine and Semi-Pelagianism. Augustine emphasizes that the initiative for faith is a free gift of God (*Ep.* 194.30; *De praed.* 1.2). This initial action by God does not, however, exclude human action, but includes it (*Contra Jul.* 1.133). The expression *disposition for grace*, in the sense of a preparation for justification, is introduced by Scholasticism. The Scholastic understanding of a disposition for grace is summarized in the sentence: "To the one who does what he can, God does not deny grace" ("Facienti quod est in se, Deus non denegat gratiam"). The young Thomas understood this axiom in the sense of a positive disposition for grace, that is, as readiness stemming from purely human power (*SK* 2.28; 4.20). He overcomes this Semi-Pelagian position in his later teaching: the human preparation for justification is efficacious because of God's antecedent help, by a special interior movement of God (*CG* 3.149, 156; *STh* 1–2, q. 112, a. 3). This is a habitual, anticipatory disposition for grace (*STh* 1–2, q. 113, a. 8). Peter Aureoli (d. 1322) develops the notion of a negative disposition for grace, and this later becomes important through the Suarcsians. Here that which constitutes the disposition for grace by human power is a setting aside of obstacles to grace by avoiding sin. Neo-scholasticism rejected any positive disposition for grace but permitted a negative disposition.

(3) *Church Teaching.* In opposition to Semi-Pelagianism, the Synod of Orange (529) insists on God's initiative as the beginning of justification. Human

beings do not begin to prepare for justification by their own power, but by the help of grace, namely, through the action of the Holy Spirit (DS 375f.). In its response to M. Luther, the Council of Trent notes: in the case of adults, the beginning of justification comes from a prevenient grace of God through Christ, that is, by his call that summons people apart from their own merit (DS 1525). The four main actions that dispose us for grace (faith, hope, love, conversion) can be done only by means of the preparatory gift and help of the Holy Spirit (DS 1553). In this we are not completely passive, but rather by means of these preparatory acts our God-given free will actively cooperates in assenting to them (DS 1554, see DS 1555–59).

(4) *Ecumenical Perspectives.* Before the Reformation, Luther accepted the cooperation of free will and consequently a positive meritorious disposition for God's grace (WA 4:261f.). After the Reformation, because of his principle of "grace alone" (*sola gratia*), he excluded any disposition for the grace of God (WA 56:503). Basically he denied that human beings have any positive power at all because of the corruption of original sin. Therefore they radically lack freedom in the event of salvation. Thus, over the centuries, the caricatures of polemical theology have been: Lutheranism is deterministic; Catholicism is Semi-Pelagian. Only in present-day theology, due to a reassessment of the biblical understanding of justification, has there been a return to the question of the disposition for God's grace. Lutheran theologians now recognize that the official Catholic teaching always agreed on the primacy of grace. Catholic theologians now acknowledge that according to the confessional writings of the Reformation, there is a role for human freedom in justification. Thus there has been agreement regarding the formulation of the problem of a disposition for grace: the preparation for justification is based solely on grace, although justification itself does not take place without free human acts. Since grace does not exclude the human personality but includes it (here again there is consensus), it can also be said regarding personal decision as part of the disposition that God calls people by grace to the decision that is conversion. But a person who has attained mature freedom may respond affirmatively or negatively.

(5) *Systematic Reflections.* In discussing the disposition for God's grace as a preparation for justification, we are dealing with the way mature adults are justified. The abstract Aristotelian notions used by Scholasticism to define the disposition for grace should be transformed or replaced by biblical expressions, which describe the beginning of a living relationship between God and humankind. In the Bible the preparation for justification is the act of seeking God and a readiness for the fundamental decision of conversion of the whole heart. This preparation for justification is to be seen in the context of the relationship of grace and freedom. Since the grace of God has the absolute initiative in every salvific event and since this grace nonetheless respects human freedom, there is a preparation for justification. In an unearned and unmerited act of love, God sets in motion the preparatory event and then sustains it. The human agent engages his or her created powers and embarks on the path of

preparation. Concretely, in the preparation for justification there is a living interchange between God's loving call and the person's loving response, between God's turning toward humankind and humankind's inclination toward God, and between God's call and the human decision for God.

See also BAPTISM; FREEDOM; GRACE; GRACE: DOCTRINE OF; GRACE: THEOLOGICAL HERESIES; JUSTIFICATION.

Bibliography

Lubac, Henri de. *Augustinianism and Modern Theology*. New York: Herder and Herder, 1969.

———. *The Mystery of the Supernatural*. New York: Herder and Herder, 1967.

GEORG KRAUS

Divine Motherhood of Mary. Since Jesus in his person is God, Mary is called God-bearer or Mother of God. This assertion is drawn from the dogma of the hypostatic union, according to which Christ's human nature is personally united with the divine Logos; Mary as the physical mother provides the human prerequisite for this unification of the divine and the human in Christ. "Mother of God" is the most fundamental and comprehensive honorific title of Mary; it identifies the center of her personhood in terms of salvation-history.

(1) *Biblical Background.* Sacred Scripture does not speak explicitly concerning Mary's divine motherhood. The intrinsic basis for this title is found in Jesus' divine mission and personality. As the understanding about Jesus as the Son of God and the Kyrios (Lord) grew, so also did the appreciation for his physical mother; she was greeted as blessed among women (Lk 1:42) and as "the mother of my Lord" (Lk 1:43).

(2) *History of Theology.* As early as the beginning of the fourth century, Mary was expressly termed Theotókos (God-bearer) in texts of the Alexandrian community. In a creed from out of the turmoil of the Arian controversy, it is stated, among other things: "We know the resurrection of the dead, of which our Lord Jesus Christ was the first-fruits, who took on a body, truly and not merely apparently, from Mary the God-bearer" (Theodoretus of Cyrus, *Hist. eccl.* 1.4.54). In this case the text came from an older rule of faith formulated by an earlier authority. The expression Theotókos could thus have originated in the old Alexandrian community of the early second century (*RAC* 11:1077). It derives from the Christology of the school of Alexandria, which placed emphasis upon the unity of the divine and the human in the person of Christ, and therefore the title God-bearer as fitting only for Mary. The school of Antioch placed greater importance on the integrity of both natures, yet found no correct concept for their union. "Person" as a unifying framework was not yet available; in the circumstances of the Council of Ephesus (431) this function was filled by, among others, the title Theotókos.

(3) *Church Teaching.* In the third general council, the discussion dealt directly with the unity of natures as these relate to Christ as redeemer (DS

250–52). Because of the personal identity of the eternal divine Logos with her Son, Mary can be called God-bearer. The serious concern on the part of the official church, lest this honorary title of Mary lead to an effacement of her mission in salvation-history, is shown by the grave reservations against the title "*Mother of God*"; in its stead, the term Theo*tókos, God-bearer,* had been newly coined in the Alexandrian circles. Its utilization had a distinctly *antimythical* tendency, for indeed in the fourth and fifth centuries the title "Mother of God" was the form of address to a goddess. In fact, in the fourth century there existed the Christian sect of the Collyridians, women who worshiped Mary as a goddess, offered bread to her, and ate thereof. Since there were a considerable number of maternal deities (Cybeles; the Magna Mater [Great Mother], Artemis, Astarte, Demeter, Isis) in the Mediterranean area of that age, by way of differentiation Mary was named Theo*tókos:* "She bore the incarnate Logos of God *according to the flesh*" (DS 252): that is, she is the woman who bore the eternal Logos of God *into time.* This semantic regulation, because of the mythical ambience, was upheld even in eighth-century Latin hymns and is a strong argument against the thesis in the history of religions that the cult of Artemis at Ephesus lies behind the veneration of Mary as bearer of God. A second argument is the origin of the Theotókos title in the Egyptian-Alexandrian area.

(4) *Ecumenical Perspectives.* Mary's divine motherhood is considered as a common Christian heritage. Reformation Christology is oriented toward ancient church councils. Accordingly, Mary is termed the true Mother of God (with support from the doctrine of the communication of idioms) (*BSLK* 806, 1024). To the extent that this determination remains currently in effect, the divine motherhood arouses no ecumenical controversy today.

(5) *Systematic Reflections.* The theological background for the understanding of Mary's divine motherhood is the old distinction between nature and person; there is in addition the belief in the two natures and in the personal unity of Christ, which is clearly stated in the doctrine of the hypostatic union. Since the one divine person of the redeemer is the subject of all christological (both divine and human) statements, Mary can be called Mother of God; for motherhood is a relationship, the object of which is the person and not the nature. The divine motherhood of Mary thus proves to be a statement most intimately ordered to the mystery of the incarnation.

See also HYPOSTATIC UNION.

Bibliography
Boff, Leonardo. *The Maternal Face of God: The Feminine and Its Religious Expressions.* San Francisco: Harper and Row, 1987.
Gebara, Ivone, and María Clara Bingemer. *Mary: Mother of God, Mother of the Poor.* Maryknoll, N.Y.: Orbis Books, 1989.
Hale, Rosemary. "Imitatio Mariae: Motherhood Motifs in Devotional Memoirs." *Mystics Quarterly* 16 (1990) 193–203.
Vollert, Cyril O. *A Theology of Mary.* New York: Herder and Herder, 1965.

FRANZ COURTH

Dogma/Dogmatic Statement. The term _dogma_ refers to a doctrinal statement binding on Christians in which a truth of revelation is interpreted in a contemporary way through ecclesially established forms of speech, related to Christian praxis, and whose core of meaning is thereby preserved (dogma in the narrower sense). A _dogmatic statement_ is a scientific judgment that presents, grounds, or interprets the contents of the Christian faith mediated through the church or is part of the preparatory work for a future dogma (dogma in the wider sense).

(1) _Biblical Background._ The formation of the canon was just as much a dogmatically binding process as the composition of the writings that make up the canon: it had to be clarified once and for all which statements are important for salvation and normative for faith. In the "instructional writings" of the Old Testament the effort to present them as belonging together is clearly recognizable. The New Testament can describe the life of the church as "holding on to the apostles' teachings" or to the "traditions" (Acts 2:42; 1 Cor 11:2; 2 Thes 2:15; 1 Tm 4:16; 2 Tm 1:13). These are expressed in theologically informed _concepts_ such as "light," "life" "cross," and "Son of Man"; in _confessional formulas_ (e.g., Mt 16:16; 1 Cor 12:3; 15:3–5); and above all in the different _presentations of the experience of Jesus_ as the risen and exalted Christ (the passion predictions and Easter accounts). The word _dogma_ itself is found in several places, but it describes political decrees (Lk 2:1; Acts 17:7; Heb 11:23), the Mosaic law (Eph 2:15; Col 2:14), or the decisions of the so-called Council of Jerusalem (Acts 16:4).

(2) _History of Theology._ Etymologically, dogma means opinion, teaching, decision, principle, or decree. It has been applied since the time of the Apostolic Fathers also to the teaching and prescriptions of Jesus and the apostles (Ignatius of Antioch, _Magn._ 13.1; _Didache_ 11:3). Over the centuries the word has thus had a wide spectrum of meanings, and it was not until the nineteenth century that it was accepted as a technical term in Catholic theology. Models for this technical use are found in the usage of Vincent of Lérins (d. before 450), who described _dogma catholicum_ as "what has been believed everywhere, always, and by all" (_Commonit._ 2), as well as in the edict of the emperor Justinian (d. 565), who decreed that the decisions of the early councils as "God's true dogmas" were to become imperial law. The matter itself is rendered in the early church with terms _pistis_ (faith), _ékthesis tês písteos_ (explanation of the faith), _didaskalía_ (teaching), or _homológesis_ (profession). In the Middle Ages one spoke of _doctrina_ (_catholica_), and one called the individual statement _articulus fidei_ (actually: component of the whole faith). Only since around 1850 has the word _dogma_ been taken over into the language of the official church documents, and it has been accepted since then. The theological basis for dogma/dogmatic statements is the church's witness to Christ as the expression of its self-understanding. This needed to be taken down in propositional form for its preaching, catechesis, and apologetics. It was first concretized in the creeds and was then shaped into doctrinal pronouncements primarily by the councils

(see Chalcedon [DS 301]: "We unanimously teach to confess...". It sometimes was rendered in the form of an explicit rejection of a false opinion (see, e.g., Trent [DS 1551] and elsewhere: "Whoever says..., let him be anathema"). While the dogmas of the early church were predominantly antiheretical, those of modern times are to be seen rather as expressions of praise for God's deeds (thus the Marian dogmas of 1854 and 1950). In the twentieth century the historicity of dogma became the main problem of theological epistemology, and indeed not only in principle, but also in view of the necessity of transferring dogmas and dogmatic statements into the new sociocultural contexts (e.g., the situation of the Third World, of women). At Vatican II, therefore, no more dogmas were formally defined; rather pastorally oriented, yet binding expressions of faith were made.

(3) *Church Teaching.* At the Council of Trent the term *dogma* was still employed in an unspecific way in reference to the rule of faith (DS 1505) or to a false statement (DS 1825: *falsum dogma*). For the modern understanding of dogma the formulation of Vatican I became authoritative, whereby all those things are to be believed which are contained in Scripture and tradition "and which by the Church, either in solemn judgment or through her ordinary and universal teaching office, are proposed for belief as having been divinely revealed" (DS 3011; see 3020, 3041, 3073). The factor of historicity, after an initial approach in Vatican II (*GS* 62), has been formally accepted by the magisterium with the declaration *Mysterium Ecclesiae* of the Congregation for the Doctrine of the Faith (Feb. 2, 1975; see no. 5).

(4) *Ecumenical Perspectives.* Dogmas/dogmatic statements are by their very nature ecumenical because they strive to reflect the faith of the whole church. Although they come from a concrete church community, their purpose is to convey understanding to others, and they thus make a contribution toward the removal of the divisions between believers. For the Orthodox Church, dogmas are Christian doctrinal elements that have been established by the early church councils, accepted by the whole church, and adopted in understanding obedience. These doctrinal elements are then to be interpreted by theology, to be witnessed to in the liturgy, and to be assimilated into the faith consciousness. M. Luther and many Reformers with him subject dogmas — which are seen principally as dogmatic propositions from ecclesial authorities — to a strong criticism because they assume that all the articles of faith are already found in Scripture. In practice, nevertheless, the early church dogmas were taken over insofar as they were recognized as being consonant with Scripture. Instead of dogma, *confession* is highlighted as the human answer to the saving message of justification, in which the church finds its identity. This was recorded in the confessional writings, that is, doctrinal writings with an orientation toward preaching. The term *dogma,* which had fallen into disrepute, was rehabilitated in the twentieth century by K. Barth, who saw dogma as a judgment of faith taken over and authorized by the church.

(5) *Systematic Reflections.* Dogmas/dogmatic statements must be understood

against the background of the reality of Christian *doctrine*. This includes the whole complex of truths that are to be believed and that as truths follow from the fact of the resurrection and exaltation of Jesus, from which come salvation and life. Dogma is an excerpt from this: because of reasons conditioned by the contemporary situation, an expression of revelation set down in Scripture must be made intelligible, clarified, or defended. Here the ecclesial magisterium holds responsibility with regard to the actual dogma, while theology bears responsibility for dogmatic statements. From this results the following distinguishing characteristics of dogmas/dogmatic statements. They are *experiential statements:* as explanations of the message of revelation, they take the form and are the coming into language of the Easter experience; therefore, the component of giving praise (Greek: *doxa*) is also always appropriate. They are *concrete statements:* they are an expression of the truth and reality that are recognized by the ecclesial community and are lived out in practice. As a result of this, dogma is also a regulating of language, without which the witness of faith could not be proclaimed or passed on. Dogma therefore has a functional character. Dogmas/dogmatic statements are *statements of the time:* because they are historically conditioned statements, one must interpret them carefully: (*a*) they are conditioned by language; since there is no atemporal or absolute language, every dogma is expressed incompletely, so that the dogma possesses a surplus of meaning beyond its formulation; (*b*) they have a limited horizon; every dogma is primarily related to the situation from which it arose, and thus its contents are never exhausted; (*c*) they are conditioned by the situation; dogma is not the calm academic expression of self-reflection upon faith, but rather is normally a reaction to a specific challenge and therefore incomplete in its treatment, inasmuch as more can still be said about the themes touched upon; (*d*) they are conditioned by a model of thought: because dogma strives to be an illumination of Scripture, it must follow certain models so that what is difficult to understand (a biblical statement) becomes more understandable. In the face of reality, such models, however, always remain undifferentiated in certain ways, such that a lack of intelligibility results. All these conditions are not rooted in the unknowability of truth, but rather in the limitedness of human nature as well as in God's freely given direction in history, as God leads the church on this path into the whole truth. From this also follows that faith can never live only from formally defined dogma (inasmuch as many important elements of faith were never defined in this way). Rather, faith must remain open toward the total revelation that is partially formulated in the dogmatic statement. Every interpretation of a dogma should then respect the conditions mentioned above and the faith as a whole. It is precisely here that the truth of dogma is preserved and its binding character is grounded. With these reflections in mind, one can specify the characteristics of *dogma:* it is (*a*) an expression of the truth of revelation (*b*) in the form of a judgment (proposition) that is (*c*) the infallible expression of faith and therefore (*d*) binding in conscience; each dogma (*e*) arises on account of a specific historical problem. Characteristics of a *dog-*

matic statement: it is (*a*) a true statement that (*b*) more precisely formulates the faith that (*c*) the church confesses; each dogmatic statement is made (*d*) according to a specific historical situation. The intrinsic historicity of both elements as well as their necessity follow from the fact that in their core they are the expression of the faith that is testified to and lived by the whole church. As expressions of life, however, they cannot be captured in a quantitative way, which is why the question about the *number* of binding dogmas cannot be answered.

See also CANON; CONFESSIONS (CREEDS/CHURCHES); DOGMATIC THEOLOGY; ECCLESIAL MAGISTERIUM; HISTORY/HISTORICITY.

Bibliography
Beinert, Wolfgang. *Dogmatik Studieren.* Regensburg: Pustet, 1985.
Dulles, Avery. *The Survival of Dogma.* Rev. ed. New York: Crossroad, 1987.
Hines, Mary E. *The Transformation of Dogma.* New York: Paulist, 1989.
Lindbeck, George. *The Nature of Doctrine.* Philadelphia: Westminster, 1984.
O'Collins, Gerard. *Has Dogma a Future? The Nature of Dogma.* London: Darton, Longman and Todd, 1975.
Rahner, Karl, and Karl Lehmann. *Kerygma and Dogma.* New York: Herder and Herder, 1969.

WOLFGANG BEINERT

Dogmatic Theology. Dogmatic theology is the theological science treating God's self-disclosure through Jesus Christ in the Holy Spirit as expressed in the entire proclamation of the church, including the way in which this self-disclosure is accepted in Christian faith and becomes normative for Christian life.

(1) *Biblical Background.* Dogmatic theology is the central theological subject area and thus is grounded biblically in the same way as theology itself is, namely, *implicitly* through the efforts of the biblical authors to make accessible in their writings the message of revelation to the addressees according to all dimensions (including the rational), and *explicitly,* for example, through 1 Pt 3:15, according to which the Christian should be able to give anyone an account of his or her faith.

(2) *History of Theology.* The material of dogmatic theology is described up until the seventeenth century by using the terms *sacra pagina, institutio(nes), doctrina christiana, sententiae, summa theologica,* and *loci (communes).* The term *dogmatic theology* was used in a technical sense for the first time in 1661 by the Protestant theologian L. F. Reinhart (*Theologia christiana dogmatica*). G. Calixtus in 1662 made a distinction between *theologia dogmatica* and moral theology. The development of the discipline was closely tied to the critique of dogma that, for various reasons, was generated by Pietism, historicism, and the rise of religious studies (E. Troeltsch), and to the accusation of *dogmatism* (rigidity in a system focused on self-security and protection from change). This charge is raised today by critical rationalism (H. Albert), but actually was already made at the time of the Enlightenment. Since the fresh start for Catholic theology begun in the nineteenth century (the Tübingen school; later, Catho-

lic theology between World Wars I and II), the salvation-history approach has dominated. The main problems of modern dogmatic theology are the questions about the fundamental principle of dogmatic theology, about its relationship to the magisterium and to philosophy, as well as above all the tension between remaining true to the faith and being adequate to contemporary needs, a situation that arises as the church crosses over into new cultures with their new modes of thought and problems (e.g., Third World, ecology, feminism).

(3) *Church Teaching.* Dogmatic theology takes a central place in all ecclesially approved plans of study. Vatican II (*OT* 16) proposed a course of study whose contents were filled out by local bishops conferences (e.g., the "Program for Priestly Formation").

CLASSIFICATION OF THE SUBJECTS OF DOGMATIC THEOLOGY

The following treatises are usually offered in the subject area of dogmatic theology in theological faculties.

Name of the treatise	Object
Theological epistemology or foundations	Explanation of the principles and sources according to which dogmatic theology achieves its knowledge; usually joined to an introduction to dogmatic theology.
Doctrine of God	Explanation of the nature of God, as it can be developed from the data of salvation-history.
Doctrine of creation	Explanation of the foundational beginning of salvation-history and theological insights resulting from this.
Theological anthropology	Theology of the human person as summit and caretaker of creation as well as covenant partner with God.
Christology and soteriology	Elucidation of the mystery of Jesus of Nazareth as the consubstantial Son of God and redeemer of the world.
Mariology	Teaching about the mother of Jesus as the personal full realization of God's redemptive deed in Christ.
Pneumatology	Teaching about the nature and activity of the Holy Spirit as the third divine person.
Ecclesiology	Teaching about the church as sign and instrument of the redemptive work of God in history.
Sacramental doctrine	Presentation of the seven individual sacraments as concrete means of realization of the church's mission of salvation.
Doctrine of grace	Demonstration of God's salvation as deed of God's free benevolence.
Eschatology	Teaching of the fulfillment of history in God.

(4) *Ecumenical Perspectives.* Since John of Damascus (ca. 740/750), the Christian East possessed *De fide orthodoxa,* an authoritative systematic presentation of the faith. Only later, in the eighteenth century, did new independent dogmatic works again appear (the first being that of Vincent Damodos in

1730). Because of the overly narrow Catholic understanding of dogma, there existed for a long time in Protestantism an aversion toward the concept "dogmatics," which was then replaced mostly through the terms (used as a general heading) "systematic theology" or "doctrine of faith." Today this antipathy has substantially disappeared, as revealed in works by K. Barth, G. Ebeling, F. Mildenberger, E. Schlink, W. Trillhaas, and others. There is an increasing consensus that not only a systematic but also a binding presentation of faith is necessary.

(5) *Systematic Reflections.* Dogmatic theology has the task of systematically and methodically presenting the meaning of God's activity as disclosed in revelation and in the experience of the church of Christ gained through the ages; further, it has the task of making such revelation and experience applicable to life. Both are expressed fundamentally in all the forms of the life of the church (liturgy, art, piety), above all in propositional form. A few of these are formally defined by the magisterium (dogmas in the narrower sense); usually, however, they are developed from the faith witness of the entire church (dogmas in the wider sense, dogmatic statements). Insofar as dogmatic theology interprets the statements of the faith of the church as discourse about God, it is a theological science that first of all investigates the positive data in a historically critical way. Since dogmatic theology must encompass, order, and develop the content of faith, it is a hermeneutical and speculative science, which by necessity must be free in order to expound the content of faith in a contemporary and understandable way. This happens today through a presentation ordered on salvation-history: dogmatic theology is presented *historically* because God has made God's self experienceable in history. This history is presented as a *saving* history because God's activity is directed toward the salvation of humanity and of the world. Here the question about the essence of God and God's salvation is raised (essential perspective), but also the relationship to life (existential prospect) is considered. Within the theological system dogmatic theology belongs to the section "systematic theology." For pedagogical reasons, dogmatic theology is divided up into several treatises. Their order is neither logical nor binding. However, they generally follow a historical sequence, namely, that of salvation-history, and they do seek to present what is essential. The treatises are often introduced with a separate treatise on epistemology.

See also DOGMA/DOGMATIC STATEMENT; HIERARCHY OF TRUTHS; REVELATION; THEOLOGY.

Bibliography
Beinert, Wolfgang. *Dogmatik Studieren.* Regensburg: Pustet, 1985.
Dulles, Avery. *The Craft of Theology.* New York: Crossroad, 1992.
Fiorenza, Francis Schüssler. "Systematic Theology: Task and Methods." In *Systematic Theology: Roman Catholic Perspectives,* edited by Francis Schüssler Fiorenza and John P. Galvin, 1:1–87. Minneapolis: Fortress, 1991.
Kasper, Walter. *The Methods of Dogmatic Theology.* Glen Rock, N.J.: Paulist, 1969.

Lonergan, Bernard. *Method in Theology.* New York: Herder and Herder, 1972.
Ratzinger, Joseph. *Principles of Catholic Theology: Building Stones for a Fundamental Theology.* San Francisco: Ignatius, 1987.

WOLFGANG BEINERT

Dualism. In the broader sense, dualism signifies a relation of tension between two polar realities that are, however, logical counterparts and mutually dependent; in the narrower sense, dualism means the opposedness of two principles that can be neither derived from nor unified with one another. It became a dogmatically influential concept in the areas of cosmology (God–world), anthropology (soul–body), and theology (grace–law, purity–sin).

(1) *Biblical Background.* In the Bible, there are traces of a relative anthropological dualism, which, however, was diluted in the process of being adopted from the cultural environment (Wis 9:15; cf. 1 Pt 2:11). A corresponding influence was exerted on the New Testament by early Jewish rabbinical maxims about the "evil impulse" and the "good impulse" (Billerbeck 4:470–77) and by Qumran, with its devaluation of the flesh and its doctrine of two antagonistic spirits within human beings (1QS 3:17f.; 4:23f.; cf. 1 Jn 4:6). Here (1QS 3:20f.), as in the apocalyptic writings (2 *Enoch* 30, 15), anthropological dualism is transformed into an ethical dualism that clearly accords with the primarily Johannine polarities "light–darkness" (Jn 3:19–21; 1 Jn 1:7; see also Eph 5:8–10; 1 Thes 5:5–10) and "truth–lie" (Jn 3:21; 1 Jn 1:6). A cosmological dualism is expressed in the notion of spiritual "principalities and powers" that, under the leadership of a "ruler," incite humans to turn against God (1QS 3:20–25; Jn 12:31; 14:30; 2 Cor 4:4; 6:14–16) but are ultimately conquered and judged by God (= turning point of the aeons or world epochs: 1QS 4:19–23; 1QM 5:11; Rom 13:12; Eph 6:10–18). For present times, the cosmos is determined by the duality of what is either "above" or "below" (Jn 1:51; 3:13, 31; 8:23; Col 3:1–3; Eph 4:8–10). Still, early Jewish dualism is made doubly relative in the New Testament by the conviction, in view of redemptive history, that it has already been overcome in Jesus Christ.

(2) *History of Theology.* In ancient times, the radical forms of dualism in the cosmological, anthropological, and theological spheres were gnosticism, Mazdaism, the worldview of Zoroaster, and Manichaeanism. By contrast, the polarities discernible in Plato between body and soul (*Phd.* 82E; cf. Philo, *Legum alleg.* 1.108), the visible and invisible worlds (*Politeia* 517B), and image and idea (ibid., 507A–509C) need not lead — contrary to widespread belief — to any general devaluation of the first component of each, since the first can always serve as the form, or locus, of the presence of the second. What the Fathers had to deal with, in particular, were various forms of gnostic dualism. Justin (*Apol.* 1.26.58), Tertullian (*Adv. Marc.*), and Irenaeus (*Adv. haer.* 2.27.1–4; 3.4.3; 4.27–32) wrote against Marcion (d. ca. 160), who went so far as to postulate a dialectic between two divinities. Exaggerating Paulinism, he opposed gospel to law, merciful love to punitive justice, and the Jewish Old Tes-

tament to the Christian New Testament. In theology of divinity, he recognized an Old Testament demiurge who created matter and a New Testament "alien God" who manifested himself — without being born — in the apparent body of Jesus Christ in order, through the apparent occurrence of the crucifixion, descent into hell, and resurrection, to redeem creation from bondage to the evil demiurge. As opposed to this, Irenaeus places emphasis on the direct creation of matter and flesh by the one God (*Adv. haer.* 1.22.1; 2.11.2; 4.20.1) — or the triune God (4.20.1, 3; 5.6.1) — himself, and on the redemptive recapitulation of the whole of the world and history through a Christ who *truly* became flesh, died, and rose from the dead (4.34.4; cf. 5.22.2). Christology thus becomes a harmonizing surmounter of all opposites.

(4) *Ecumenical Perspectives.* Because of the Christocentric emphasis behind them, the contrastingly formulated pairs of concepts like Luther's "hidden God" (*deus absconditus*) and "revealed God" (*deus revelatus*), Calvin's "predestination to salvation or to damnation," and K. Barth's creation and nullity cannot really be seen as dualistic.

(5) *Systematic Reflections.* Today, theology of creation allows itself to be stimulated by the system-oriented way of thinking established in the latest natural science and tries to take an overall view, in a critical and constructive way, of the most differing spheres of reality when considering any duality.

See also BODY OF CHRIST; CREATION: THEOLOGY OF; INTERMEDIATE STATE; LAW AND GOSPEL; MANICHAEANISM; MONISM; SOUL.

Bibliography
Bianchi, Ugo. *Selected Essays on Gnosticism, Dualism and Mysteriosophy.* Leiden: Brill, 1978.
Rudolf, Kurt. *Gnosis: The Nature and History of Gnosticism.* San Francisco: Harper and Row, 1983.

ALEXANDRE GANOCZY

Ee

Ecclesia ab Abel. *Ecclesia ab Abel* (the church beginning with Abel) is a name given to the church "before Christ"; it was coined by Augustine and repeatedly used after him.

(1) *Biblical Background.* The idea does not occur in the New Testament. According to the latter, the church begins its journey through history with Jesus Christ. At the same time, however, there are a few passages that speak of a "heavenly," eternal existence of the church (Gal 4:26; Rv 21:2; others are less explicit but nonetheless imply this idea, e.g., Heb 12:22). Thus there are at least hints of an existence of the church "before Christ," although not within history.

(2) *History of Theology.* The theologians of the early church emphasize the oneness of grace and the continuity of the divine plan of salvation (against Marcion, the Montanists, and the Manichaeans); they see this oneness and continuity in holy pagans and Jews (e.g., Job) in the time of the former covenant and regard these persons as belonging to the church. Augustine consolidates the notion of a church before Christ by appealing to the sole mediatorship of Christ and the universality of the church; on both counts all the just belong to the church (therefore *ecclesia ab Abel*, not *ab Adam*, Adam having been a sinner; also playing a role in Augustine is the idea in his theology of history that Cain personifies the earthly city [*civitas terrena*] while Abel personifies the city of God [*civitas Dei*]). After Augustine, especially in the Middle Ages, theologians frequently invoked the idea of *ecclesia ab Abel*.

(3) *Church Teaching.* In *LG* 2 Vatican II speaks of the *ecclesia ab Abel* in an eschatological perspective.

(4) *Ecumenical Perspectives.* The Orthodox churches venerate the saints of the old covenant in their liturgy. From this it may be inferred that the idea of a "church before Christ" is not alien to them.

(5) *Systematic Reflections.* The theme of *ecclesia ab Abel* comes up in connection with the question of the church's origin. The church has its source in the triune God (*LG* 2–4) but also in the life and work of the earthly Jesus (*LG* 5). The statement that the church already begins with Abel (*LG* 2) has, therefore, an important function: it is intended to show that there is a way of belonging to the church even for human beings who have never heard and accepted the gospel of Jesus Christ. This is not to be interpreted, however, as invoking a simple universality of salvation, but rather as a limit-possibility for those who, like Abel, live justly to the point of surrendering their lives.

See also HISTORY/HISTORICITY; UNIVERSAL SALVIFIC WILL OF GOD.

Bibliography
Congar, Yves. *The Mystery of the Church: Studies by Yves Congar.* Baltimore: Helicon, 1960.
———. *Sainte Église: Études et Approches Écclesiologique.* Paris: Cerf, 1963.

WERNER LÖSER

Ecclesial Magisterium. The ecclesial magisterium is that authority in the overall structure of the church that has the task of preserving, handing on, and interpreting the elements of faith, when necessary, in a finally binding manner.

(1) *Biblical Background.* The first and the original concern of the community of Christ is the passing on of the Easter experience in the proclamation (*kerygma*) that claims universal validity (Gal 1:9; 2 John 10). There arises from this intention already in the later period of the New Testament a doctrine with a truth claim (1 Tm 2:4f.; 4:3; 2 Tm 2:25; 3:7f.; Ti 1:1, 9). The handing on of this doctrine is entrusted fundamentally to the whole community (Mt 18:15–20; Jn 14:16f.; 15:26; 16:13; 1 Tm 3:15); within the community, however, it is a special task of the apostles (Mt 5:13; Mk 3:14; 16:15; Lk 10:16; 24:47f.; Acts 1:8; 10:41).

(2) *History of Theology.* Seen from the New Testament heritage, the history of the ecclesial magisterium is practically identical with the history of the self-understanding of the church as the bearer of the message of the gospel that is to be proclaimed in its abiding truth. The first millennium saw the undistorted, genuine transmission guaranteed in the accord with the apostolic tradition (which is guaranteed through the apostolic succession) and with the consensus of the whole church. The latter is set down and promoted at synods and above all at the ecumenical councils. These, then, are the points of intersection of the vertical consensus (apostolic succession) and the horizontal consensus in the church. From the ninth century onward, belief in the infallibility of the councils has been explicitly expressed (Abu Qurra [d. 820–25]). The ecclesial magisterium becomes a theological problem only in the second millennium after the schism between the Western and Eastern churches. In the West it is not so much salvation that is highlighted as the *mediation* of salvation and, with this, the question about its bearers. With regard to grace, these are the sacraments; with regard to the truth, it is the ecclesial magisterium. Here, the attention is focused on its highest bearer, the pope. Thomas Aquinas attributes to the pope the right of issuing definitions in a propositional form (*sententialiter determinare: STh* 2-2, q. 1, a. 10). From the thirteenth century (Petrus Johannes Olivi, Guido Terreni), infallibility has been attributed to the pope, and this position was defined dogmatically at Vatican I. In modern times, the ecclesial magisterium was first put into question by the Reformation, then through the passionate appeal to freedom of autonomous reason. The main points of the current discussion are the historicity and the binding character of doctrinal statements as well as the question of how a statement that does not have the claim of being free from error can be received with obedience.

(3) *Church Teaching.* The Council of Trent defined as the object of the ecclesial magisterium the doctrine of faith and of morals (*res fidei et morum*),
whereby it remains open until today what exactly the content of *mores* would
be. Vatican I proclaimed as dogma the infallibility of the papal magisterium
under specific conditions (DS 3074). Vatican II integrates the doctrinal authority of the pope into the context of the self-realization of the entire church.
Infallible doctrinal authority is attributed to the totality of all the faithful (*LG*
12), to the council of bishops with the pope, as well as to the pope alone (*LG*
25); yet this doctrinal authority always remains subordinate to the word of
God (*DV* 10). The Code of Canon Law (749.3) sets down a condition: "No
doctrine is understood to be infallibly defined unless it is clearly [*manifesto*]
established as such."

(4) *Ecumenical Perspectives.* According to the Orthodox understanding,
faith is the unity of all the expressions of life of the church; church teaching
and doctrinal formulations are only one element of faith that always has to
be reintegrated into the context of the others. For this reason, both noninsti-
tutionalized teaching authorities, like the Monastic Fathers and the "Ascetic
Elders," as well as institutional authorities, such as, above all, the ecumenical
council, are integrated in the process of reception of the entire church. In addition to these councils (only the early church councils until Nicaea II [787]
are acknowledged) the five ancient patriarchal sees of Rome, Constantinople,
Antioch, Alexandria, and Jerusalem have special doctrinal authority (pentarchi-
cal principle). Under the influence of the West, in modern times there arose
dogmatic confessional writings (Cyril Lucar, Peter Mogila, Dosítheos). In Protestantism from the start attention was not directed to the authorities but rather
to the sources, that is, to Scripture, which becomes the single and supreme
binding doctrinal authority. An ecclesial magisterium is not compatible with
this. The responsibility for the rightful proclamation is shared fundamentally
by all the faithful on the basis of their universal priesthood. Yet differences
in competence and teaching assignment do exist: thus, the confessional writings, university teachers, ministers, and church supervisory bodies (including
the synods) have special significance. Doctrinal decisions are sought by way
of consensus; in this, the supervisory bodies have a central function. The existence of a communal doctrinal responsibility that goes beyond an individual's
judgment is also manifested in the fact that disciplinary procedures relating to
doctrine are provided for.

(5) *Systematic Reflections.* The occurrence of divine revelation and its acceptance in faith are fundamentally an interpersonal event of communication
between God and human beings in which Christ is attributed the highest authority as the summit of God's self-communication. Yet because revelation is
meant to be universally valid and to be believed by all human beings, steps must
be taken such that its identity be preserved. This happens primarily through
that objectification of communication that we call *doctrine*. It is the task of
the whole church since, as the community of the faithful, it is the bearer of the

message of revelation in history. Yet the church is an ordered structure in which an authorized and authoritative instance exists that in cases of conflict makes the genuine and unabridged identity of the message of revelation known in a way that is binding and free from error: the ecclesial magisterium. Its authority, however, is never absolute: it stands under the word of God, is dependent upon the living interchange with the whole church, and has no additional possibilities of knowing beyond those that these have. Nevertheless, the authority of the ecclesial magisterium stands on its own and is based neither on delegation nor on the legal ratification by the rest of the faithful. In detail, the following holds:

(*a*) Bearer of the ecclesial magisterium:

Officeholder	Their magisterium is	Their statements are
Single bishop	ordinary	possibly not free from error
The (collegial) totality of all the bishops with the pope	ordinary and universal	free from error
The bishops assembled with the pope at an ecumenical council	extraordinary and universal	free from error
Roman pope	ordinary	possibly not free from error
	extraordinary (*ex cathedra*)	free from error

(*b*) Object of ecclesial magisterium:

i. immediate or direct: the content of revelation = *depositum fidei* (all the content of faith that is significant for salvation) = *res fidei et morum* (the basic content of revealed faith and the basic orientation of Christian life). This content can be contained explicitly or implicitly, that is, in images or parables, in revelation.

ii. mediated or indirect: truths that are necessary or helpful for the preservation of revelation. Which specific truths fall under this category is theologically controversial. Usually the following are mentioned (as examples):

- *theological conclusions:* these truths achieve an increase in understanding through the synthesis of a revealed and a natural truth (Christ is a truly human being; to be a truly human being means to have a human will: thus Christ has a human will);

- the *preambles of faith:* all the premises for a justified acceptance of a truth of revelation (existence of God, personality of the human being);

- the *presuppositions of dogma:* presuppositions for the trustworthy proclamation of a truth of revelation (legitimacy of a council or of the pope; in the Jansenist controversy also the content of sentences was designated as a *factum dogmaticum* [DS 2001–5, 2027, 2390]);

- the *canonization of saints* (traditional).

ECCLESIAL FAITH AND THE MAGISTERIUM

Faith of the entire church

Ecclesial magisterium

The magisterium stands in a circle of communication with the faith and the understanding of faith of the entire church. Under the assistance of the Spirit it brings forth from this faith what it presents as revealed truth. The faith consciousness of the whole church for its part receives the decision of the magisterium as corresponding to its faith in a knowledge directed by the Holy Spirit. The relations are thus primarily defined in a pneumatological, not in a juridical, way.

Whether a matter falls under the competence of the ecclesial magisterium is decided by the ecclesial magisterium itself.

(*c*) Quality of magisterial statements:

i. The magisterium speaks *infallibly* when the following conditions are simultaneously fulfilled:

- the teaching authority is exercised either *collegially* by all the bishops with the pope in ordinary or extraordinary form or from the pope alone *ex cathedra* (in his function as supreme teacher with finally binding authority in questions of faith and life);

- there is an express intention to make an infallible doctrinal statement.

By the *collegial exercise* of the ecclesial magisterium is understood the moral agreement of the bishops that a statement is definitively binding for faith. A merely factual agreement is not sufficient; it could also only be the common opinion.

ii. The magisterium speaks *authentically* when it speaks in a binding way and with authority but not with the claim of infallibility. The reasons given are subject to scholarly judgment since authority by itself does not create truth. Such expressions are in principle revisable (statement of the German bishops of Sept. 23, 1967). Their significance is dependent upon their importance for ecclesial life, upon the author (e.g., the pope or papal authorities with general or special approval of the pope; only in the latter case do decrees count as an act of the pope), upon the addressees (e.g., individual groups, the whole church), and upon contemporary circumstances (a defense against certain tendencies).

THE BINDING CHARACTER OF THEOLOGICAL STATEMENTS

Not all magisterial and academic theological statements have the same binding character. Correspondingly, the degree of certainty that applies to their reception varies. Therefore, there has been an attempt to give *theological qualifications* to the individual expressions. Positive qualifications are also called theological *notes,* negative ones theological *censures.* The nomenclature and the classification are not always uniform; the qualification of theological conclusions is especially controversial: Are they *de fide* (articles of faith) or only *theologice certum* (theologically certain)? Today the teaching on qualifications has minor importance; in older dogmatic works it played a larger role.

Quality of the statement	Note	Censure
Formally revealed truth (material dogma)	*de fide divina* [of divine faith]	*haeresis manifesta* [manifest heresy]
Formally revealed and as such truth defined by the magisterium (formal dogma)	*de fide divina definita* [of divine defined faith]	*haeresis formalis* [formal heresy]
Truth taught as revealed by the ordinary magisterium	*de fide* [of faith]	*haeresis* [heresy]
Defined statements from the indirect domain of the magisterium	*de fide ecclesiastica definita* [of defined ecclesial faith]	*propositio reprobata* [rejected proposition]
Statements from the indirect domain of the magisterium	*de fide ecclesiastica* [of ecclesial faith]	*propositio falsa* [false proposition]
Proposition from the direct domain of the magisterium upon which the magisterium has not expressed itself finally, yet whose denial may possibly threaten another truth of faith	*fidei proximum* [proximate to faith]	*haeresi proximum* [proximate to heresy]
Proposition from the indirect domain for which the same is valid	*theologice certum* [theologically certain]	*sententia falsa* [false proposition]
Propositions of academic theology	*sententia communis, probabilis, tolerata, pia* [common doctrine, probable, tolerated, pious]	

(*d*) Modes of expression of the ecclesial magisterium:

i. ordinary magisterium: pronouncements (sermons, catechism, pastoral letters, etc.) of the bishop in his diocese, of the bishops' conferences, of all the bishops outside of the ecumenical council, or of the pope when he does not speak *ex cathedra.*

ii. extraordinary magisterium: dogmatic definitions at an ecumenical council or through the pope speaking *ex cathedra.*

(*e*) Theological character of magisterial statements:

- *foundation:* Scripture as interpreted in tradition;

- *content:* the more precise expression and concretization of statements that are contained in revelation;

- *form:* confession of the faith (see the formulas "credimus, profitemur, confitemur" [we believe, we declare, we confess], etc.);

- *validity claim:* authoritative, if necessary as finally decisive for the protection of the message of revelation. Nonobservance can have as a consequence the exclusion from the ecclesial community.

- *integration with the entire church:* in congruence with all the other authorities and organs of the church, the statement must be oriented toward the salvation of all human beings; this congruence is manifested in the *reception* by the church.

(f) Interpretation of magisterial statements:

- the intention of the statement of the ecclesial magisterium is to be construed (intention, degree, and content of obligation);

- the historical circumstances of the statement are to be considered;

- the interpretation has to be performed in a precise way;

- the statement has to be analyzed in accord with the *analogia fidei* (integration into the connection of the whole faith) and with the hierarchy of truths.

See also APOSTOLIC SUCCESSION; CHURCH; COLLEGIALITY; HIERARCHY OF TRUTHS; INFALLIBILITY; POPE; RECEPTION; SENSUS FIDELIUM.

Bibliography
Curran, Charles, and R. A. McCormick, eds. *The Magisterium and Morality.* Vol. 3 of *Readings in Moral Theology.* New York: Paulist, 1982.
Empie, P. C., T. A. Murphy, and J. A. Burgess. *Teaching Authority and Infallibility in the Church.* Minneapolis: Augsburg, 1978.
O'Donovan, Leo J., ed. *Cooperation between Theologians and the Ecclesiastical Magisterium.* Washington, D.C.: CLSA, 1982.
Sullivan, Francis. *Magisterium: Teaching Authority in the Church.* New York: Paulist, 1983.

WOLFGANG BEINERT

Ecclesiology. Ecclesiology is the name given to the systematically organized theological treatise on the church.

(1) *Biblical Background.* The New Testament writings yield a rich and comprehensive picture of the church (see the other entries in this volume that address ecclesiological issues; see also *MystSal* 4/1:101–221), but they do not yet contain a treatise on ecclesiology.

(2) *History of Theology.* Until the Middle Ages theologians often dealt with the church (in their interpretations of Scripture, especially the Song of Songs, and in sermons, canonical documents, and spiritual writings), but these reflections on the church did not take the form of a systematic treatise. Writers limited themselves rather to the discussion of particular questions, for example, the relation between pope and council. The document *Unam sanctam*

(1302; DS 870–75) led to some descriptions of the church (James of Viterbo; Augustinus Triumphus); in 1440/41 John of Ragusa composed the *Tractatus de ecclesia* (ed. J. Sanjek [Zagreb, 1983]). The first systematic treatise is considered to be John of Torquemada's *Summa de ecclesia* (ca. 1450, with a vast influence on subsequent theology). Since the Reformation, ecclesiology has become increasingly organized and has been developed no longer only canonically but also theologically. When fundamental theology began to develop as a separate branch of theology from the eighteenth century on, it soon took over ecclesiology as indispensable for its apologetic task. On the other hand, DOGMATIC THEOLOGY also claimed ecclesiology as an independent treatise, so that in the history of modern theology fundamental theological and dogmatic presentations of the doctrine of the church have existed side by side.

(3) *Church Teaching*. The ecclesial magisterium has dealt with the doctrine of the church from various dogmatic viewpoints, chiefly in the following documents: Vatican I, *Pastor aeternus* (DS 3050–75; this constitution is only the ninth chapter of a comprehensive *Summa de ecclesia*, which there was not time to adopt in its entirety); Pius XII, encyclical *Mystici corporis* (1943; excerpts in DS 3800–3822); Vatican II, *Lumen gentium* (1964; the first full magisterial statement on ecclesiology). According to the "Plan for Priestly Training" of the German Episcopal Conference (1978), ecclesiology is dealt with in both fundamental theology and dogmatic theology (nos. 83–86).

(4) *Ecumenical Perspectives*. In the Evangelical world ecclesiology is discussed in terms of the corresponding chapters of the confessional documents and therefore dogmatically and not in terms of fundamental theology. Ecclesiology is the field in which, on the whole, theological conversations between the churches and confessions are most difficult. The Faith and Order Commission of the World Council of Churches is working on a study that will, for the first time, have the church as its main subject. The study is entitled "The Unity of the Church and the Renewal of the Human Community."

(5) *Systematic Reflections*. The treatise on fundamental theology is concerned with the church insofar as it is the medium and means of transmitting divine revelation. The dogmatic treatise deals with the origin of the church, its (sacramental) nature, its structure, its tasks, its future. In the course of time, clear changes have taken place in the way in which this treatise has been and is being concretely developed. Various answers are given to the question of the place of the treatise on ecclesiology in Catholic dogmatic theology as a whole. Some dogmatic theologians presuppose that ecclesiology has been exhaustively treated in fundamental theology and therefore do not deal with it again themselves (e.g., F. Diekamp, K. Jüssen, J. Pohle, M. Gierens, J. Gummersbach). B. Barthmann makes ecclesiology a special section after the doctrine on redemption and sanctification and before the doctrine on the sacraments. M. Schmaus places ecclesiology immediately after Christology, to be followed in turn by the doctrine on justification; he also presents the doctrine of the sac-

raments in the framework of ecclesiology. L. Ott subsumes ecclesiology, along with the doctrine of grace and the doctrine of the sacraments, under the doctrine on sanctification. Finally, *Mysterium salutis* integrates the doctrine on the church into a comprehensive concept of theology as salvation-history; it follows directly upon Christology, under the heading of "The Saving Event in the Community of Jesus Christ."

Bibliography
Congar, Yves. *L'Ecclésiologie de S. Augustin à l'époque moderne*. Paris: Cerf, 1970.
Granfield, Patrick, and Avery Dulles. *The Church: A Bibliography*. Wilmington, Del.: Glazier, 1985.
Jay, Eric G. *The Church: Its Changing Image through Twenty Centuries*. Atlanta: John Knox, 1980.
Küng, Hans. *The Church*. Garden City, N.Y.: Doubleday, 1976.
McBrien, Richard P. *The Church: Continuing Quest*. New York: Paulist, 1970.
Schmaus, Michael. *Dogma*. 6 vols. London: Sheed and Ward, 1972ff.

WERNER LÖSER

Ecology. Ecology (Greek: *oíkos* = house) is: (*a*) *biologically*, the study of the relations between living creatures and their environment; and (*b*) *anthropologically*, the study of the relations between humans, as cultural and technical beings, and the world of nature; in this latter sense, it is the object of dogmatic and ethical reflection.

(1) *Biblical Background.* The biblical writings bear the stamp of a state of the world in which nature, culture, and society still appear — despite the fear of yet untamed natural forces — as a living whole in their shared interdependency. Only at particular times did their equilibrium become a problem, as, for example, in the case of a crisis of overpopulation in Mesopotamia that is recognizably mirrored in the Atrahasis epic (seventeenth century B.C.E.) — a work that possibly influenced Genesis 1. The Yahwist account of creation (see CREATION NARRATIVES), with its symbols of the clay of the ground (*'adāmāh*) (Gn 2:4–7), out of which humans (*'ādām*), like the animals, were formed (Gn 2:19), and the garden, which humans were "to cultivate and care for" (Gn 2:15), asserts both humanity's belongingness to its inorganic and organic environment and its appointedness to creativity at the cultural level. Through sin, however, the harmonious relationship between humanity and nature undergoes a rupture from which both sides suffer (Gn 3:14–19). According to present-day exegesis, God's words of blessing in Gn 1:28 are not to be understood in the sense of a license for unlimited increase of population and for arbitrary exploitation of nature. Rather, it is a matter of dealing responsibly with nature, of a protective, "pastoral dominion." The prophets predict that the apocalyptic end of history will see a state of total peace among the animals (Is 11:6–9; 65:25; Ez 34:25–31; Hos 2:20). Jesus' parables, in which nature variously becomes a figurative proclamation of the dominion of God, his speeches about God's caring for humans, plants, and animals (see Mt 10:29–31), his attachment to life to the point of fearing of death, his nonviolence and esteem for

the lowly, create the ideal preconditions for a coming together of ecology and theology.

(2) *History of Theology.* Not a few of the Church Fathers, especially Eastern ones, show that they have real cosmological awareness, and are fond of elucidating their doctrine of providence through references to the unobtrusive wonders of biological processes (e.g., Basil, John Chrysostom).

(3) *Church Teaching.* At Vatican II, doctrinal office takes up the theme of recognition that human beings are a "part of nature" (*GS* 14) and addresses, in the sense of Rom 8:22, the destiny that they share with "all creation." In the same breath, it acknowledges the unique corporal and spiritual worth of humans (*GS* 14) and makes "the future fate of the world" dependent upon the presence, or loss, of human wisdom (*GS* 15). Through the conciliar interpretation of human creativity in the sense of Gn 1:28 (*GS* 34, 67) and through the corresponding legitimation of love of "created things" (*GS* 37), useful approaches are made to a theological ecology.

(4) *Ecumenical Perspectives.* The search for such an ecology is often carried on today through ecumenical collaboration involving theologians of differing confession and even differing religions, with significant contributions being made, in addition to that of Christianity, by Judaism, Islam, Hinduism, and Buddhism.

(5) *Systematic Reflections.* The main areas of focus in this search are: (*a*) a circumspect exegesis and a hermeneutics of the biblical documents that does justice to present-day knowledge (N. Lohfink, E. Zenger, O. H. Steck); (*b*) an integration of the problem-complex of the "limits of growth," as made clear by the Club of Rome in 1972, into the problem-complex of Christian theology of creation (G. Altner, J. Moltmann), with relevant thought also encompassing the viewpoint of human creativity (A. Ganoczy); and (*c*) the gradual construction, on these bases, of a new "environmental ethics" (A. Auer). Ecology becomes more and more a theological topic as a result of insight into the "cocreaturely" interconnectedness of all living creatures at a time when the environment is being progressively destroyed and many species of animals are being extirpated forever.

See also CREATION; NATURE.

Bibliography
Birch, Charles, ed. *Liberating Life: Contemporary Approaches to Ecological Theology.* Maryknoll, N.Y.: Orbis Books, 1990.
Birch, Charles, and John B. Cobb, Jr. *The Liberation of Life.* New York: Cambridge University Press, 1981.
Fox, Matthew. *Creation Spirituality: Liberating Gifts for the Peoples of the Earth.* San Francisco: Harper and Row, 1991.
Küng, Hans. *Global Responsibility: In Search of a New World Ethic.* New York: Crossroad, 1991.
McFague, Sallie. *The Body of God: An Ecological Theology.* Minneapolis: Fortress, 1993.
Moule, C. F. D. *Man and Nature in the New Testament.* Philadelphia: Fortress, 1967.

Ruether, Rosemary Radford. *Gaia and God: An Ecofeminist Theology of Earth Healing.* San Francisco: Harper and Row, 1992.

Spring, David, and Eileen Spring. *Ecology and Religion in History.* San Francisco: Harper and Row, 1974.

Stendahl, Krister. *Energy for Life: Reflections on the Theme "Come, Holy Spirit, Renew the Whole Creation."* Geneva: World Council of Churches, 1990.

ALEXANDRE GANOCZY

Ecumenism. By ecumenism is meant "the initiatives and activities encouraged and organized, according to the various needs of the Church and as opportunities offer, to promote Christian unity" (*UR* 4).

(1) *Biblical Background.* It is the will of Jesus Christ that those who belong to him should "all be one ... so that the world may believe" (Jn 17:21). The New Testament provides the basis not for a multiplicity of confessions but for the unity of the church, insofar as the various writings of the New Testament are to be understood as situationally determined developments of the primitive Christian, christologically oriented confessional texts (e.g., 1 Cor 15:3–5) and therefore are unified not simply by arbitrary decree but by the reality that they attest.

(2) *History of Theology.* Among the many tensions that have nonetheless arisen in the history of Christianity two are exceptionally important: the tensions between the Eastern and Western churches (1054) and the tension within the Western Church (sixteenth century). There have always been efforts to reestablish the experiential unity of the church. Due to basic theological convictions, the Roman Catholic Church for a long time made no contribution (at least officially) to the movement that has gone on for almost a century under the name of "the ecumenical movement" and that led in 1948 to the establishment of the World Council of Churches (WCC) (see sec. 3 below). Individuals and institutions did make their own the concerns of ecumenism and thus paved the way for the decrees of Vatican II (the Una Sancta movement; the Evangelical and Catholic Ecumenical Task Force: Y. Congar, R. Grosche, M. J. Metzger).

(3) *Church Teaching.* After an initial rejection of ecumenism (Pius XI, *Mortalium animos,* 1928: *AAS* 20 [1928] 5–16) the Roman Catholic Church reached ecclesiological decisions at Vatican II that brought the church's entry into the movement. Due to the trinitarian approach in the council's teaching on the church and to its understanding of "communion" (*communio*), not only was there a new awareness of intuitions of the early church that had been retained in all confessions, but relations with the non-Catholic communities were also reformulated (see *LG* 8, 15). *Unitatis redintegratio* stated the resultant principles of a Catholic ecumenism. In the years that followed, the Roman Catholic Church helped actively promote the ecumenical movement at the local, regional, and universal levels. Above all, it engaged in bilateral conversations, of which those with the Lutheran churches, the Anglican Communion, and, in the last few years, the Orthodox churches are especially important. Col-

STRUCTURE OF THE WCC

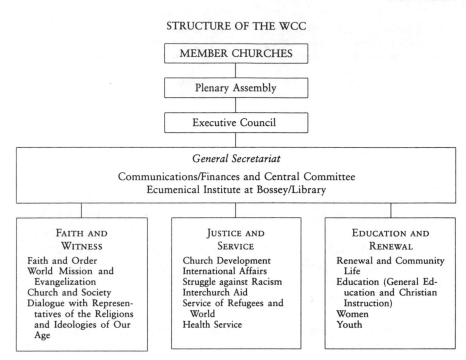

```
                    ┌──────────────────────────┐
                    │     MEMBER CHURCHES      │
                    └──────────────────────────┘
                    ┌──────────────────────────┐
                    │     Plenary Assembly     │
                    └──────────────────────────┘
                    ┌──────────────────────────┐
                    │     Executive Council    │
                    └──────────────────────────┘
```

General Secretariat

Communications/Finances and Central Committee
Ecumenical Institute at Bossey/Library

FAITH AND WITNESS	JUSTICE AND SERVICE	EDUCATION AND RENEWAL
Faith and Order	Church Development	Renewal and Community
World Mission and	International Affairs	Life
Evangelization	Struggle against Racism	Education (General Ed-
Church and Society	Interchurch Aid	ucation and Christian
Dialogue with Represen-	Service of Refugees and	Instruction)
tatives of the Religions	World	Women
and Ideologies of Our	Health Service	Youth
Age		

laboration with the WCC has taken the form, on the one hand, of a "joint working group" of the Roman Catholic Church and the WCC and, on the other, of membership in the Faith and Order Commission.

(4) *Ecumenical Perspectives.* Confessional studies serve ecumenical understanding and agreement. In the seventeenth century such studies were polemical but became irenic in the age of Pietism and the Enlightenment; today, that is, since J. A. Möhler's *Symbolik* (1832), they are characterized by a quest for objective information and solidly grounded cooperation. At the present time, the most noteworthy of these confessional studies are found in the series *Die Kirchen der Welt*, which contains twenty volumes (the twentieth is on the Roman Catholic Church [1986]).

(5) *Systematic Reflections.* The contribution of the Roman Catholic Church to establishment of the desired ecclesial and liturgical communion with other churches consists, on the one hand, in reforms that allow the "communion image of the church," which the council intended, to emerge more clearly and, on the other, in conversions and purifications that permit the Catholic understanding of the church to be grasped in a purer and more credible way.

See also CHURCH; CONFESSIONS (CREEDS/CHURCHES); DIALOGUE.

Bibliography
Achutegui, Pedro S. de. *Ecumenism and Vatican II: Select Perspectives.* Manila: Loyola School of Theology, Ateneo de Manila University, 1972.

Anderson, H. George, and James R. Crumley, Jr., eds. *Promoting Unity: Themes in Lutheran-Catholic Dialogue*. Minneapolis: Augsburg, 1989.

Congar, Yves. *Dialogue between Christians: Catholic Contributions to Ecumenism*. Westminster, Md.: Newman, 1966.

Dionne, Robert. *The Papacy and the Church: A Study of Praxis and Reception in Ecumenical Perspective*. New York: Philosophical Library, 1987.

Fahey, Michael A. *Ecumenism: A Bibliographical Overview*. Westport, Conn.: Greenwood, 1992.

Horgan, Thaddeus D. *Walking Together: Roman Catholics and Ecumenism Twenty-Five Years after Vatican II*. Grand Rapids: Eerdmans, 1990.

Küng, Hans, ed. *The Church and Ecumenism*. Vol. 4 of *Concilium*. New York: Paulist, 1965.

———, ed. *The Future of Ecumenism*. Vol. 44 of *Concilium*. New York: Paulist, 1969.

Leeming, Bernard. *The Vatican Council and Christian Unity: A Commentary on the Decree on Ecumenism of the Second Vatican Council*. London: Darton, Longman and Todd, 1966.

Phan, Peter C. *Christianity and the Wider Ecumenism*. New York: Paragon, 1990.

Rusch, William G. *Ecumenism: A Movement toward Church Unity*. Philadelphia: Fortress, 1985.

WERNER LÖSER

Education. Education refers back to the fact that every human being comes to the world in an unfinished state. Only under the influence of other human beings does he or she learn to speak and to develop into an independent person. In systematic theology this dependence of the human person on education is transferred to his or her relationship to God.

(1) *Biblical Background.* The concept of God's formational activity is not foreign to the Bible. It describes most often the chastisement of the disobedient people or of an individual person that is seen, however, as the expression of God's love. This should lead to repentance and conversion. It is in this sense that Paul characterizes the entire law up until Christ as an educator (disciplinarian) (Gal 3:24). Yet Paul contrasts the Hellenistic educational ideal of worldly wisdom (philosophy) with the foolishness of the cross (1 Cor 1:20–25). Nevertheless, the pedagogical categories of Hellenism find a place in the later writings of the New Testament: grace "trains us to reject godless ways and worldly desires, and to live temperately, justly, and devoutly in this age" (Ti 2:12). In Eph 6:4, fathers are admonished to bring up their children in the discipline of the Lord (*paideía kyríou*).

(2) *History of Theology.* The Church Fathers, especially Clement of Alexandria, interpreted the history of salvation as the education of humankind toward salvation. This view was hardly received into Western theology. In the West, faced with the newly converted, uneducated Germans, the church in the ministry of grace was perceived as the mother and educator of humankind. In the aftermath of the modern Enlightenment, the gospel was interpreted as an educational instrument toward humaneness and reverence before God. Educational institutions (parents, schools, the state) received from this their theological legitimation as organs of the divine formation to salvation.

(3) *Church Teaching.* The church has repeatedly emphasized the divine mis-

sion of parents and teachers to educate, but did not view education itself as a divine working of grace, but rather as a preparation toward it or as an introduction toward a life lived in grace (*GE* 1–3).

(4) *Ecumenical Perspectives.* Protestant theology has usually been more sensitive to the distinction between education and God's saving activity, following the Reformed principle that faith comes only through the word of God.

(5) *Systematic Reflections.* In Catholic theology recently the attempt has been made to interpret "grace" basically as God's educational activity toward the human person (G. Greshake). Without doubt, there exists a link between faith, which is dependent on God's grace, and the education of the human person to the free use of reason, both in view of the decision for faith as well as in view of the life that stems from faith. In practice, it is not possible to make a precise distinction between the proclamation of the gospel or witnessing to it and the formational care offered to the human person. This is why an educational interpretation of the saving activity of God can be valid, as long as it remains clear that it refers to one among other levels of the mediation of salvation.

See also GRACE.

Bibliography
Groome, Thomas. *Christian Religious Education: Sharing Our Story and Vision.* New York: Harper and Row, 1980.
———. *Sharing Faith: A Comprehensive Approach to Religious Education and Pastoral Ministry: The Way of Shared Praxis.* San Francisco: HarperSanFrancisco, 1991.
Scheffler, Israel. *Reason and Teaching.* New York: Bobbs-Merrill, 1973.

GEORG LANGEMEYER

Election. Election by God refers to God's eternal, loving choice at a given time of universal mediators of salvation, especially God's gratuitous call to service of a community or of an individual.

(1) *Biblical Background.* The biblical terms for election are: in the Old Testament, *bahar,* and in the New Testament, *eklegomai.* The Old Testament refers only to a *temporal election;* the New Testament adds to this an *eternal election.* The temporal election is an intrahistorical preference. In the Old Testament as well as the New Testament it generally refers to the collectivity (Israel or the church). Only seldom does it involve an individual. It is always an election for some act of service within salvation-history. Thus in the Old Testament, Deuteronomy (e.g., 7:6–9; 10:14f.; 14:1f.) particularly emphasizes the collective election of the people of Israel. Second Isaiah (e.g., 43:10; 49:6) understands election most clearly as universally salvific. Because of its special covenant with God, the people of Israel has been chosen to be God's witness before all other peoples. In conjunction with the people, individuals are also described as chosen: Abraham (Neh 9:7f.), Moses (Ps 106:23), Aaron (Ps 105:26), the Levites (Dt 18:5; 21:5; 1 Chr 15:2), kings (1 Sm 10:24: Saul; 2 Sm 6:21: David; 1 Chr 28:5–10: Solomon). In the New Testament letters too, election designates the divine call of the community, that is, the church (see 1 Cor 1:2;

Col 3:12, 15). The church exists for the salvific service of all; it has a universal mission (see 1 Pt 2:9). Generally, the Synoptics speak of the elect in the plural: that is, the chosen community (see Mk 13:20, 22, 27; Lk 18:7). The only individual who is called the chosen one is Jesus Christ (Lk 9:35: "God's Son, his chosen"; Lk 23:35: "the messiah of God, his chosen one"). In John, on the other hand, the choice of individuals is prominent: namely, those chosen as disciples by Jesus Christ (e.g., 6:70; 13:18; 15:16, 19). This obviously refers to Jesus' disciples called to the office of apostle. The idea of an *eternal* election, which is absent in the Old Testament, appears explicitly in the New Testament only twice: most clearly in Eph 1:4 ("He chose us in Christ before the foundation of the world"), then again in 1 Pt 1:1f. ("To the exiles who have been chosen... by God the Father"). The Christocentric and ecclesiological aspects are important here: eternal election to salvation is based on Jesus Christ. The object of election is the church or the community of the elect.

(2) *History of Theology.* In the history of theology the opinion of Augustine (d. 430) has predominated. He deals only with eternal election and identifies it — as an *electio ex proposito* (election by plan) (*Ad Simpl.* 1.2.6) — with the predestination of individuals to eternal salvation. This view becomes important in Scholasticism. Thus, for example, Thomas Aquinas (d. 1274) bases predestination on the election as choice of individuals for eternal salvation (*STh* 1, q. 23, a. 4). In the period following, this position remains decisive for Catholic theology.

(3) *Church Teaching.* The magisterium has not made any direct pronouncements concerning the notion of an election by grace.

(4) *Ecumenical Perspectives.* For M. Luther (d. 1546) the question concerning a graceful God is part of the predestination dispute: Do I personally belong to the number of those chosen (*WA* 2:688)? According to Luther an individual gains certainty about being chosen or saved only by faith as unconditional trust in the word and work of a graceful God (*WA* 6:1811). For Calvin, because of his teaching of a double predestination, there is a strict parallel between the election of the individual to eternal salvation and the condemnation of individuals to eternal damnation (*OS* 4.393f.). Eternal election takes place by pure grace (*OS* 4.369). It is a gratuitous election (*electio gratuita: OS* 4.382). In the twentieth century, K. Barth makes the notion of election central in that he treats election by grace extensively as a basic treatise (*KD* 2/2:1–563). Barth tries to overcome Calvin's double predestination by means of a Christocentric and ecclesiological viewpoint. Jesus Christ is God choosing and the one chosen, the one who on the cross represents and takes upon himself the condemnation of all human beings. Therefore he is the only one condemned. The election is primarily in relationship to the community (both Israel and the church), which is called to a universal salvific service and mediates the election-event in Jesus Christ for all individual human beings.

(5) *Systematic Reflections.* Election deals with mediation, not with the establishment of eternal salvation of individuals. Traditional theology misun-

derstood election as individual and particular: as the selection of individuals for eternal salvation. Thus this election — in the sense of an eternal predestination — is reduced in advance to a few human beings. In an authentically biblical view, a systematic distinction is possible between eternal and temporal election. Eternal election consists in the fact that from eternity God chose Jesus Christ as absolute mediator of salvation and the church — in dependence on Jesus — as relative mediator of salvation. This mediatorship of salvation in Jesus Christ and the church is universal; that is, both are destined to mediate eternal salvation for all human beings. The traditional individualistic and particularist narrowing of election is overcome in a Christocentric and ecclesiological election: individuals, and indeed all human beings, are thereby called to attain eternal salvation through Jesus Christ and the church. The election of Jesus Christ and the church is preordered to the election of individuals. Eternal election is intrinsically connected with the universal salvific will of God, for its motive is the universal love of God for humankind. The temporal election of communities or individuals is a call to an intrahistorical service in God's saving plan. Those chosen for the service of salvation are indeed called into a special relationship to God, but most importantly, this freely given gift of God implies a task, a duty, and a test. Thus the temporal election to the service of salvation is neither the basis for obscurity about election, since it is a gratuitous gift, nor a previously fixed, automatic guarantee of eternal salvation, since it is demanded of those chosen that they confirm their contract by fulfilling it.

See also GRACE; MEDIATORSHIP OF JESUS CHRIST; PREDESTINATION; UNIVERSAL SALVIFIC WILL OF GOD.

Bibliography
Berkouwer, Gernt C. *Divine Election.* Grand Rapids: Eerdmans, 1960.
Colwell, John. *Actuality and Provisionality: Eternity and Election in the Theology of Karl Barth.* Edinburgh: Rutherford, 1989.
Kraus, Hans-Joachim. *The People of God in the Old Testament.* New York: Association Press, 1958.
Pannenberg, Wolfhart. *Human Nature, Election, and History.* Philadelphia: Westminster, 1977.

GEORG KRAUS

Entelechy. This concept (*en-tel-echeia:* "that which has a goal in itself") stems from Aristotle and signifies, in his *Metaphysics,* a striving force, inherent in the essence of all things, by virtue of which any particular thing impels itself toward its own goal and perfection (*Meta.* 994a.6ff.; 994b.10ff.). Aristotle calls life "entelechy" as well (*De an.* 2.4.415b.15ff.). According to him, living entities are subject, even at the level of their material components, to the influence of the "form" (*morphē*) that stamps them, maintains itself within them, and renders them capable of self-movement. Thus the immortal world-soul realizes itself within them, in each case in an individual manner, and propels them toward the goal of perfection that has been implanted in them. Aristotelian ontology carries the notion of entelechy to the conclusion that reality as a whole has a goal-directed, *teleo*logical structure.

(1) *Biblical Background.* The Bible shows no special interest in metaphysical questions. It speaks about nature theologically. Out of the wisdom of the Creator, the creatures are imbued with purposiveness (Sir 43:1–33). Thus the earth "brings forth vegetation" (Gn 1:11); the organic world subdivides into species (Gn 1:11–13); and humanity is given a blessing in the form of a commission (Gn 1:28). Israel and the tribes also receive from God their prescribed goals. All perfection is understood as a free promise and gift of grace from God. It cannot be derived from forces immanent in nature, that is, from any sort of entelechy. God can suddenly alter the course of things, can omit perfection here and there.

(2) *History of Theology.* Proceeding biblically in regard to intellectual content, but often Hellenistically in regard to conceptual language, the Fathers combine belief in providence with the idea of the purposefulness, lawfulness, and goal-directedness of history (e.g., Irenaeus, *Adv. haer.* 2.25.1; 2.26.3; Clement of Alexandria, *Strom.* 6.16; Basil, *In hexaem.* 5.1; John Chrysostom, *Ad pop. Ant. hom.* 9.4; 10.2f.).

(3) *Church Teaching.* Vatican I teaches that God is "the ground and goal of all things" (DS 3004) and that God has "subordinated humanity to a supernatural goal, namely, participation in the divine goods" (DS 3005). The word *entelechy* does not belong to the vocabulary of doctrinal office.

(4) *Ecumenical Perspectives.* Entelechy is not an ecumenically significant concept.

(5) *Systematic Reflections.* Today, when dealing with the questions of purposefulness and goal-directedness that are bound up with the notion of entelechy, the Christian doctrine of creation finds itself faced with the task of considering biblical teaching together with the results of modern natural philosophy and science. Here, account must be taken of: I. Kant's opinion that a teleological approach is useful only as a "regulative idea" of reason, in order to understand the "inner purposefulness" of living entities; C. Darwin's doctrine of a purposefulness within organic structures and functions that is, however, largely determined by chance, the struggle for survival, and processes of natural selection; H. Driesch's neovitalism, which assumes, in the area of genetics and heredity, the existence of natural "building plans," thus, to that extent, giving nature a teleological cast; and the approach of system-dynamics, which sees individual processes as being regulated through interaction and feedback mechanisms. If teleology remains a controversial issue in the context of natural objects, it nonetheless retains its credibility in transcendental anthropology. The latter can speak of entelechy in connection with the fundamental referredness of spiritual creatures to God as their ultimate goal. P. Teilhard de Chardin's attempt to view natural evolutionary and mutational processes in synthesis with realization of the divine redemptive plan (*évolution rédemptrice*) is both scientifically and theologically controversial.

See also PROVIDENCE.

Bibliography

Arnold, Uwe. *Die Entelechie: Systematik bei Platon und Aristoteles.* Wien: Oldenbourg, 1965.

Driesch, Hans. *The Science and Philosophy of the Organism.* London: A. and C. Black, 1929.

ALEXANDRE GANOCZY

Eschatology. By eschatology (Greek: *eschatos* = last; the doctrine of the "last things") is meant the statements of faith regarding the final destiny of the individual person and the divinely effected restructuring of humanity and the entire cosmos at the end of time.

(1) *Biblical Background.* Only a few basic trends in the extremely rich and tension-filled development of eschatology in the Scriptures can be mentioned here. It is characteristic of the Old Testament that eschatology is connected with the salvation-history organized by God. Israel exists, in principle, under the law of promise and fulfillment as the basic structure of its faith. God is leading the people to a perfect state that God has planned but that is unknown to human beings. In keeping with the holistic (monistic) picture of the human person, in which the latter is understood as a corporeal-spiritual unit that is responsible for the condition of the earth, Israel's hope is directed to a numerous posterity and the promised land that flows with milk and honey (see the promise to Abraham [Gn 12:1f.]). The introduction of the monarchy is accompanied by the hope that the savior will spring from the Davidic line (2 Samuel 7; Psalms 2; 21; 45; 72; 110). During the exile the preaching of the prophets brings a change in the eschatological hope, which now centers on the "day of Yahweh," which is understood as a day of judgment and salvation that is increasingly seen as universal and cosmic. Especially in Second Isaiah (Isaiah 40–55), the hope is expressed of a complete divine re-creation of the human race and the world: the new heavens and the new earth. Under the influence of Greek teaching on the soul and its IMMORTALITY, the eschatology of the wisdom literature focuses more on the individual person (see Wis 2:23; 3:1, 4; 9:15). A final decisive factor in the eschatology of this period is the hope that God will rescue the individual person from his or her individual death (Pss 46:16; 73:23–26). In the apocalyptic literature from the period of harsh persecution there emerges the hope of a final establishment of God's reign, with the accompanying destruction of kingdoms hostile to God. Dominion and kingship are now transferred to the Son of Man who comes on the clouds of heaven. All human beings must serve him; his dominion will last forever (Daniel 7). Whereas previously the central hope was in large measure focused on a liberation to be accomplished in the near future by an action of God within history, a strictly transcendent eschatology now prevails and with it the idea of a universal and cosmic salvation. It is in this phase of the development of eschatology that belief in the RESURRECTION OF THE DEAD makes its appearance (Daniel and 2 Maccabees). In the New Testament the eschatological expectations of the Old Testament and early Judaism are revised in light of the Christ-event. The eschatology of the Synop-

tic tradition is determined primarily by the concept of the KINGDOM OF GOD, which has come in preliminary form in Jesus and will attain its complete and final form when the Son of Man appears on the clouds of heaven. The urgent EXPECTATION OF AN IMMINENT END and the associated idea of a sudden onset of the kingdom of God are accompanied by the exhortation to conversion, watchfulness, and constant readiness. A basic element in the message of Jesus is the thought that the present life is decisive for salvation in the next world. In a dispute with the Sadducees (Mt 22:23–33 par.) Jesus maintains the resurrection of the dead but departs from the Jewish tradition by revising it on an essential point. In the Gospel of John as we now have it there are two different approaches to eschatology that cannot be automatically harmonized. In the foreground is "realized" eschatology, that is, the idea that salvation and judgment take place in the encounter with Jesus. Those who believe the message of Jesus have everlasting life; they will not be judged; they have already passed from death to life (5:24). Those who do not believe are already judged (3:18); upon them the wrath of God remains (3:36) (JUDGMENT; ETERNAL LIFE). But alongside these statements are others that postpone final salvation or damnation to the last day and attest to the resurrection of the dead (6:39–40). The Eucharist is understood as the sacrament of life and eschatological hope, the sacrament that ensures resurrection on the last day (6:54). A truly cosmic eschatology is to be found in the Book of Revelation, which uses Old Testament language to speak of the resurrection of the dead, the general judgment, and the new heavens and new earth (20:11–21:5). In Pauline eschatology, as in the Synoptics, there is an urgent expectation of an imminent end and an apocalyptic description of the PAROUSIA. The most decisive point in this eschatology is that Paul connects the future resurrection of the dead with the resurrection of Christ, deriving the former from the latter, and in this context offers a detailed reflection on the risen body.

(2) *History of Theology.* In the Christian tradition the varied eschatological statements of Scripture undergo a clear change according to the concrete historical situation. Individual statements, especially of the New Testament, are quite often singled out and given a one-sided interpretation. In the patristic period we find, along with the expectation of the parousia and the problem of its delay, the debate especially between the Greek doctrine of the immortality of the soul and the biblical message of the resurrection of the dead, which is defended against all spiritualizing tendencies. Relevant here is the doctrine of the INTERMEDIATE STATE. In connection with the effort to understand prayer for the dead, especially during the celebration of the Eucharist, and the development of the church's penitential practice, the doctrine of PURGATORY takes form. On the authority of Origen the doctrine of the APOCATASTASIS acquires great importance. When the latter is rejected by the church, the concern that is its basis continues to find expression in various speculations regarding a possible alleviation of the pains of HELL. Finally, a different interpretation is found in the doctrine of CHILIASM, which had arisen in connection with Rv 20:1–15. Al-

though Thomas Aquinas, influenced by Augustine's authority, rejects chiliasm as heretical, chiliastic currents of thought nonetheless become highly important in the Middle Ages in connection with the philosophy and theology of history of Joachim of Fiore and the Franciscan Spirituals. A decisive factor in the further development of eschatology is the varied approaches to the understanding of the immortality of the soul that is separated from the body in death and of the ordination of this soul to the risen body; connected with this is the question of how the risen body is identical with the earthly body. Finally, speculative theology seeks an understanding of HEAVEN as beatific vision and enjoyment of beatitude. In the period of the Enlightenment eschatology was regarded as closely connected with moral theology, insofar as its doctrine of retribution will help attract persons to the good and deter them from evil. The Catholic school of Tübingen was the source of noteworthy stimuli to development in a new direction. These had their basis in the idea of the kingdom of God and in the idealistic view of history. F. A. Staudenmeier (d. 1856) locates eschatology under the generic heading of "The Perfecting of the Church"; that is, he understands eschatology as part of ecclesiology, which in turn is integrated into the doctrine of redemption. In neo-scholasticism, which arose in the second half of the nineteenth century and was promoted by the church, eschatology is limited mainly to a consideration of the several elements making up the "last things," which will occur some day and at present are wholly future. This approach could not provide any inspiration in coping with the varied problems posed by the rise and spread of atheism and Marxism. On the other hand, a decisive role has been played by nineteenth- and twentieth-century eschatological ideas that started in Evangelical theology and then became fruitful also in Catholic theology and led to original approaches.

(3) *Church Teaching.* The doctrinal decisions issued by the church in the course of history, together with their essential content, can be summarized as follows (see also the table): (*a*) The two principal professions of faith: the Apostles' Creed (DS 10f.) and the Nicene-Constantinopolitan Creed (DS 150): return of Christ in glory; judgment of the living and the dead; resurrection of the dead and life of the world to come. (*b*) Faith of Damasus (originated probably in fifth-century Gaul [DS 72]): resurrection in the body (flesh) in which we now live; eternal life or eternal punishment. (*c*) Pseudo-Athanasian Creed (between the end of the fourth and the end of the sixth century [DS 76]): return of Christ; judgment of the living and the dead; resurrection of the dead in their bodies; rendering of an account of earthly life; eternal life or eternal punishment. (*d*) Second Council of Orange (529 [DS 372]): death as consequence of Adam's sin (Rom 5:12). (*e*) Provincial Synod of Constantinople (543 [DS 411]): rejection of the doctrine of apocatastasis. (*f*) Eleventh Council of Toledo (675 [DS 540]): resurrection in the body in which we live, exist, and move. (*g*) Declaration of Leo IX (1053 [DS 684]): real resurrection of the same body (flesh) that is now mine; eternal life. (*h*) Fourth Lateran Council (1215 [DS 800–801]): production of the entire creation by God at the beginning of time; resurrection

of all human beings in the bodies they now have; eternal punishment or eternal life. (*i*) First Council of Lyons (1254 [DS 838–39]): purgatory; heaven or hell for the soul before the resurrection of the dead; last judgment. (*j*) Second Council of Lyons (1274 [DS 856–59]): purgatory; heaven or hell for the soul before the resurrection of the dead; last judgment. (*k*) Constitution *Benedictus Deus* (1336 [DS 1000–1002]): purgatory; immediate vision of God and blessedness of the soul before the last judgment; hell; resurrection of human beings in their bodies; last judgment. (*l*) Council of Florence (1439 [DS 1304–6]): purgatory; clear vision of the one and triune God by the souls of the just before the last day, a vision that differs according to the measure of their merits; differentiated punishment of the souls in hell according to the measure of their demerits. (*m*) Condemnation of the errors of M. Baius by Pius V (1567 [DS 1978]): the immortality granted in paradise was a gift of grace, not a natural condition. (*n*) Condemnation of the errors of the Synod of Pistoia by Pius VI (1794 [DS 2626]): statement on the limbo of children. (*o*) Decree of the Holy Office, July 21, 1944 (DS 3839): statement on mitigated chiliasm. (*p*) Instruction of the Congregation for the Doctrine of the Faith entitled "Some Questions of Eschatology" (May 17, 1979 [*AAS* 71 (1979) 939–43]): continued existence after death of a spiritual element that has consciousness and volition and that the church calls "the soul"; meaning of prayers for the deceased and of the funeral rites; distinction and difference between, on the one hand, the situation of human beings immediately after death and, on the other, the appearance of our Lord Jesus Christ in glory and the bodily assumption of Mary into heaven.

(4) *Ecumenical Perspectives.* From an ecumenical standpoint, it is to be noted that the Orthodox churches interpret the intermediate state and PURGATORY differently than the Latin Church. The churches dating from the time of the Reformation establish an especially close link between eschatology and Christology and reject purgatory as not scriptural.

(5) *Systematic Reflections.* Although Sacred Scripture and Christian tradition contain a variety of eschatological statements, the word *eschatology* was first used by Lutheran theologian A. Calov (d. 1686), who dealt with death, resurrection, judgment, and the consummation of the world under the general title "Sacred Eschatology." F. Schleiermacher's use of the word gave it increasing importance, and it entered the common theological vocabulary. In the course of history eschatology has been subdivided from different points of view and, at the same time, has been connected with other dogmatic treatises. In view of Christian tradition the most important distinction is between general and individual eschatology. General (universal, collective) eschatology deals with the events at the end of history and the world: parousia (Second Coming) of Christ, resurrection of the dead, general (last) judgment, re-creation of the world, and heaven and hell as states of eternal salvation or damnation after the resurrection of the dead. Individual eschatology deals with the death of the human being, individual judgment, the continued existence of the SOUL that is without the body but ordered to the risen body. The principal subjects of discussion

IMPORTANT DOCUMENTS OF THE ECCLESIAL MAGISTERIUM ON ESCHATOLOGY

Document	Main Contents
Creeds of the early church (ca. 150–7th cent.)	Resurrection of the whole person
Lateran IV (1215)	Everlasting retribution according to works (DS 801)
Innocent IV (1254)	Existence of a place of purification (DS 838)
Lyons II (1274)	Prayers for the dead; different punishments (DS 856–58)
Benedict XII (*Benedictus Deus*) (1336)	Definitiveness of death; immediate definitive destiny (DS 1001–2; NR 2306–7)
Florence (1439)	Same as Lyons II (DS 1304–6)
Lateran V (1513)	Individual immortality (DS 1440)
Trent (1563)	Existence of a place of purification; prayers for the dead; sobriety in preaching of things eschatological (DS 1820)
Vatican II (*Lumen gentium*) (1964)	The eschaton is an ecclesiological category
Congregation for the Doctrine of the Faith (1979)	Seven theses, chiefly on the question of the "intermediate state"

in Catholic theology in this area are the intermediate state, the purification in purgatory that is part of that state, and heaven and hell as "places" of reward and punishment in the other world prior to the resurrection of the dead. Also important in contemporary eschatology is the distinction between realized and future eschatology, since the tension between the two brings out the real meaning of eschatology. Eschatology should not be reduced to a purely realized or a purely future eschatology. A realized eschatology, which leaves the dimension of the future out of consideration, does not do justice to the thrust of the gospel and to the claim latent in it. On the other hand, a futurist eschatology is always in danger of forgetting the present and regarding statements about it as statements solely about the future; this causes men and women to flee the present and destroys the future as future. Eschatology has an especially close relation to Christology, insofar as the event of Christ's death and resurrection is the pledge of the eschatological salvation of other human beings. In the course of history, eschatology has played a considerable role in moral theology, especially insofar as it speaks of reward and punishment and thus provides motivation for moral behavior. In our day, meaningful eschatological statements can be made only against the background of the various intraworldly projections of the future (FUTURE). The precise and methodical interpretation of eschatological texts is especially difficult (HERMENEUTICS). As part of dogmatics, eschatology is in principle bound to use the scientific method customary in this discipline; eschatology is, however, subject to additional difficulties that can only be briefly mentioned here. Although SCRIPTURE is the most important source of Christian eschatology, it is necessary to ask, in the interpretation of each individual text, what presuppositions the sacred writer had in making his statement. One such presupposition is the ancient conception of the world (for us outmoded) as horizon of understanding. In addition, eschatological statements are made exclusively in a variety of images that cannot be pieced together to form a total picture, since one and the same image can also be used in a conflicting statement. Thus, fire, for example, is an image for hell and purgatorial purification; it also signifies judgment; and, in the form of light, it becomes, in the description of the brightly lit heavenly banquet hall, the opposite of the outer darkness (Mt 22:13) that describes the lot of the lost. It is only possible to study the individual images for what they intend to say and then to systematize the theological statements derived from the images. In view of the extensive development of eschatological statements in the Sacred Scriptures one must be careful not to remove particular stages of the development from their context and absolutize them, as has been done from time to time in the course of history. What is true of the world picture generally is true in a special way of apocalyptic texts, which must be regarded as a special category of statements. While theology has long since recognized the special character of the category of "space" as found in the ancient world picture, it still has great difficulty in coming to grips with the category of "time" (see TIME). Although nobody denies that time as experienced within the context of the world and measured by physical means does not exist beyond the boundary set by death, there are nonetheless still disagreements in contemporary theology about the understanding of the intermediate state, purgatory, and the relation between the death of the individual person and the resurrection of the dead on the last day. If eschatological statements are read today in the horizon of intraworldly ideas of the future, it follows, on the one hand, that eschatology can no longer disregard questions posed by the natural sciences and, on the other, that in addition to philosophy, various modern scientific disciplines such as sociology, political science, and futurology can be helpful in explaining the meaning of eschatological texts to contemporaries. In addition, it is generally accepted in theology that the real content of eschatological texts of the Bible is not a report on events that will take place later on in the next world but is rather to be understood as a call to structure life and history in the present world. Statements about the future interpret the present in relation to the future.

Bibliography
Hayes, Zachary. *Visions of a Future: A Study of Christian Eschatology.* Wilmington, Del.: Glazier, 1989.

Küng, Hans. *Eternal Life? Life after Death as a Medical, Philosophical, and Theological Problem.* Garden City, N.Y.: Doubleday, 1984.
Mussner, Franz. *Readings in Christian Eschatology.* Derby, N.Y.: Society of St. Paul, 1966.
Ratzinger, Joseph. *Eschatology: Death and Eternal Life.* Washington, D.C.: Catholic University of America Press, 1989.
Van de Walle, A. R. *From Darkness to the Dawn.* Mystic, Conn.: Twenty-Third, 1985.

JOSEF FINKENZELLER

Eschatology: Conceptions of. Conceptions of eschatology are theological approaches in which the basic thrust of eschatology becomes discernible and that make possible, and call for, the interpretation and critique of particular eschatological statements.

(1) *Biblical Background–*(3) *Church Teaching,* see ESCHATOLOGY.

(4) *Ecumenical Perspectives.* Since the nineteenth century and especially in the twentieth there has been a reemergence of eschatology that has produced a series of conceptions of eschatology in the Protestant churches. Some of these need to be presented here. The theory of *consistent eschatology*, also known as *eschatologism*, which arose under the influence of the history-of-religions approach and has been represented by J. Weiss, A. Schweitzer, M. Werner, and others, takes as its starting point the radically eschatological character of the preaching of Jesus and the primitive church. According to this theory, the history of Christianity is due to the postponement of the parousia and the abandonment of the expectation of an imminent end and of the concomitant eschatological interpretation of the message of Jesus. In continuity with the baptist movement, Jesus (in this theory) proclaimed the immediately imminent coming of the kingdom of God and hoped that penitents might by their activity force the coming of the end. Jesus' expectation of being transformed into the heavenly Son of Man was not realized, and therefore he decided to offer himself for death in order to suffer the final hardships that were still to come and thus bring on the parousia. Faced with death, he relied on the sure hope that he would return after death to inaugurate the new order of things. This hope he bequeathed to his disciples. When the early Christians were disappointed in their expectation that the Lord would come soon, they gradually established doctrine and forms of worship and administration with a view to a lengthy future. In our century, eschatology has been given an especially important place in dialectical theology. For K. Barth, eschatology constitutes the main topic and formal principle of theology. He remarks very pithily in his *Commentary on Romans* (1922): "Christianity that is not totally and completely eschatology has totally and completely nothing to do with Christianity." Among the conceptions of eschatology an extremely important one is the approach of R. Bultmann, whose call for a demythologization and existential interpretation of the New Testament has far-reaching implications for traditional eschatology. He argues for a consistently realized eschatology in which statements about the future have no place: "Christian eschatology knows that it hopes, but it does

not know what it hopes for." Christology and eschatology merge, insofar as Christ is the eschatological event, not as one who lived in the past but as the one who at each moment addresses the listener here and now in preaching. Those who commit themselves in faith to the word of preaching obtain true life. This true freedom that faith bestows is itself the "eschaton." Believers do not await a future still to come; rather, the future becomes present in the now of challenge and response. A position radically opposed to Bultmann's is to be found in the approach of O. Cullmann. While eschatology is the essence of New Testament Christianity according to Bultmann, a vision of salvation-history stands at the center for Cullmann. This becomes especially clear in his understanding of TIME. In Greek thought time is conceived as cyclic, that is, as a closed circle marked by a constant return of the same, so that salvation cannot be looked for in time; according to the biblical conception of it, time is linear, that is, it is seen as consisting in the forward-moving interconnection of yesterday, today, and tomorrow. Salvation takes place *in time*. Time and salvation are interrelated. Given this background, the novelty of Jesus' message is clear. In Jewish thinking, the only thing of importance after the creation is the future parousia, which will separate the two aeons; according to the New Testament, however, the center of time lies in the past or, in the case of the Gospels, in the present of Jesus and the apostles. The appearance of Jesus on the scene marks the turning point and center of time: this point is no longer to be identified with the end of world-history, which outwardly may continue for some time yet. In this new vision of time and history, the question of how long this period before the end will last becomes secondary. As a result, the problem of the expectation of an imminent end ceases to be burdensome. For the decisive element in the message of Jesus is to be found not in the question of a short space of time before the parousia but in the emphasis on the center, which is already here. According to J. Moltmann, who in his theology of hope opposes E. Bloch's atheistic philosophy of the future, the existential interpretation of the New Testament misses the very essence of the human person because it overlooks the person's relatedness to history. Nor is it enough to focus one's gaze solely on the saving event that took place in Jesus as the center of time. To be a Christian means rather to deal with present realities in the light of the future. Because the God of the Bible is one who "wholly changes" things, "the assertions of hope in connection with the promise contradict reality as presently experienced. . . . They are intended to shed light not on the reality at hand but on the reality that is coming. . . . They are meant not to carry reality's train but to precede reality with a torch." It is not possible to speak of a faith-inspired existence in radical openness if one regards the world as a piece of machinery or a self-enclosed nexus of cause and effect objectively set over against the human person. "Without a cosmological eschatology it is impossible to give expression to the eschatological existence of human beings." Christian hope is not grounded in a certainty produced by the natural sciences or in empirical facts, but solely in the fidelity of God, who stands by God's promises. Christian faith speaks of a future that is promised by

Christ and grounded in his resurrection. The practical importance of the theology of hope becomes visible in the relation between Christianity and society.
Christian hope unleashes a power that is critical of present circumstances and
spurs to action against them.

(5) *Systematic Reflections.* The reemergence of eschatology in Catholic theology is clear in the much-cited statement of H. Urs von Balthasar: "Eschatology
is the 'storm center' of the theology of our time. It is thence that the storms arise
which threaten, in a fruitful way, the entire land of theology: they rain damaging hail or they bring refreshment." Balthasar calls chiefly for a personalization
and christological structuring of eschatology. "God is the 'last thing' of his creature. When attained, he is heaven; when lost, he is hell; when he searches the
heart, he is judgment; when he purifies, he is purgatory.... But he is all this
in his turning to the world, that is, in his Son Jesus Christ, who is the openness of God and therefore the very essence of the 'last things.' " According to
D. Wiederkehr, eschatology should not be regarded as a self-contained treatise;
rather it must have repercussions on the whole of theology. "The dimension
of the eschatological, of the completion of history by God himself, is not simply one theme among others in the preaching of Jesus; it is *the* dimension by
which even the position and person of Jesus in himself are to be ascertained."
There is no further eschatological "more" beyond Easter. The resurrection of
Jesus is the inauguration and introduction of an event that spreads and extends
to other things. The absolute future is distinguished from any possible intraworldly future by its transcendence, which leaves all creaturely objectives far
behind. In the human person we find an openness to and a longing for the absolute future that is God. But the intraworldly future cannot lead smoothly into
the absolute future. The relation between history and eschatology requires that
"in one or other way, the person who exists in present history must at least be
also the subject of the future and of fulfillment; the contrary would mean the
end of any authentically human historicity, and any relation at all to the future and fulfillment.... Eschatology would no longer be history in any proper
sense, if *nothing* survived, not even in some minimal degree; nor would it be
history any longer if *everything* survived in a maximal way." "A continuous
eschatology will allow the present activity of human beings to lead, along as unbroken a line as possible, to eschatological fulfillment and will thereby enhance
its value. An eschatology of discontinuity, on the other hand, will maintain
the paramount and transcendent nature of fulfillment, but will risk allowing
the present history and earthly accomplishments of human beings to be played
down as unimportant and secondary." K. Rahner is probably the thinker who
has had the most lasting influence on contemporary eschatology. Only the most
important themes can be mentioned here: the interpretation of eschatological
statements, the understanding of death and survival after death, the meaning
of history (see HISTORY/HISTORICITY), the relation between world-history and
salvation-history, the relation between intraworldly and absolute FUTURE, and
the possibility of the self-transcendence of history. Finally, the confrontation

with the various Marxist systems has given rise to a "political theology," developed chiefly by J. B. Metz, and to various kinds of "liberation theology," which differ widely among themselves in their point of departure and their objectives. In his effort to reconcile natural science and faith, P. Teilhard de Chardin (d. 1955) developed, against the background of evolution, an independent theological approach that amounts to a combination of natural and supernatural eschatology. Because the starting point of evolution that is guided by a *Deus evolutor* presupposes a psychoidal, that is, a soul-like spirit in matter, the course of evolution leads to a spiritualization of which the human race is the axis and apex. After the second apex of evolution, namely, the incarnation of the Son of God, anthropocentrism becomes Christocentrism, evolution becomes Christification, and the *Deus evolutor* becomes *Christus evolutor*. The natural and supernatural fulfillment of the world is described as "Omega," which is not only the last letter of the Greek alphabet but also a name of the returning Christ (Rv 1:8; 21:6; 22:13). Appealing to 1 Cor 15:28 and Col 1:15–18, Teilhard assumes that in the course of evolution and the accompanying Christification the human race is led to a supernatural goal, namely, the fulfilling Christ, who incorporates into himself humanity that has been brought home and united, and makes it his mystical body. Teilhard takes the return of Christ, the last day, the end of the world, the resurrection of the dead, and the new heavens and new earth as biblical code-names for these supernatural goals of evolution.

See also ESCHATOLOGY; HERMENEUTICS.

Bibliography

Galvin, John, ed. *Faith and the Future: Studies in Christian Eschatology.* New York: Paulist, 1994.

Murphy, Marie. *New Images of the Last Things: Karl Rahner on Death and Life after Death.* New York: Paulist, 1988.

Mussner, Franz. *Readings in Christian Eschatology.* Derby, N.Y.: Society of Saint Paul, 1966.

Phan, Peter C. *Eternity in Time: A Study of Rahner's Eschatology.* Toronto: Associated University Presses, 1988.

Rahner, Karl. "The Hermeneutics of Eschatological Statements." In *Theological Investigations,* 4:323–54. New York: Crossroad, 1982.

Schillebeeckx, Edward, and Boniface Willems, eds. *The Problem of Eschatology.* Vol. 41 of *Concilium.* New York: Paulist, 1969.

Schüssler Fiorenza, Elisabeth. "Eschatology of the New Testament." In *Interpreter's Dictionary of the Bible.* Nashville: Abingdon, 1976.

Verbeke, Werner, Daniel Verhelst, and Andries Welkenhuysen, eds. *The Use and Abuse of Eschatology in the Middle Ages.* Louvain: Louvain University Press, 1988.

JOSEF FINKENZELLER

Eschatology

Contemporary Issues

Eschatology is the doctrine of the end of time. It deals with the end of individual personal life in the doctrines concerning DEATH, JUDGMENT, PURGATORY, ETERNAL LIFE, HEAVEN, and HELL. On the cosmic level it treats of God's total re-creation of humanity and the world in such notions as PAROUSIA, RESURRECTION OF THE DEAD, and KINGDOM OF GOD. Some of the issues in eschatology that are particularly pressing or are undergoing development today are the following.

Eschatology and Scientific Knowledge

Topics that heretofore were discussed only in the mythic or symbolic language of religion are now being discussed in scientific, "empirical" language. On the individual level descriptions of near-death experiences appear to provide some glimpse over the threshold between life and death. Much harder science has looked back over the process of creation and forward into the future and given cogent this-worldly scenarios for both the beginning and the end of reality. For example, just as the universe preexisted humanity by billions of years, so too is it most probable that the universe will continue after humanity's relatively brief existence. Given this contemporary discussion it becomes incumbent on theology to distinguish clearly the language of faith and what it deals with from the subject matter of science. The end-time in the language of faith is not the mere end or stoppage of time but its goal, finality, and purpose as those can be realized only by a transcending power. This language begins where science leaves off; it transcends and draws up into itself empirical beginnings and endings. Theology provides no empirical information about the end-time, and its credibility requires a clear and firm distinction of itself from a literal or descriptive understanding of the apocalyptic language of fundamentalism (EXPECTATION OF AN IMMINENT END). But at the same time this scientific discussion, which is also intrinsically engaging, provides the context of present-day eschatological thinking. Just as the eschatologies of the past presupposed some worldview as their context, so too contemporary eschatology is beginning to situate its language and claims within a framework of today's scientific imagination. This entails a closer linkage of eschatology with creation science and the doctrine of creation. The closer science binds humanity to nature and the world of which it is a part, the more eschatology as a doctrine of faith will have to consider the future of the planet on which it depends, and the more anthropocentrism will become resituated in a wider theocentric perspective.

Demythologization of Eschatological Statements

Closely related to the context provided by the new scientific discussion of the cosmos is the apologetic exigency to examine critically the foundations of eschatological affirmations. This issue has a bearing on all of the subtopics of eschatology; it defines generically the meaning of these assertions on the basis of their origin and source in Christian experience. In Catholic theology Karl Rahner took the lead in this discussion. Rahner rejects demythologization in the sense of a complete reduction of these assertions to their existential meaning and insists that they refer to a real future. But the future remains mysterious and hidden even in its revelation. The basis of this revelation is the experience of God as love and the saving union with God that is mediated through Jesus Christ. This is eschatology insofar as it also characterizes a definitive self-communication of God and acceptance of the world that reaches to the end-time. God will complete what God started; God will bring to fulfillment what God intended in creation as that is experienced in Christ. The only way human beings can know the future is by extrapolating from what is already contained in the past and the present. In this case that present experience is the recognition of God's saving grace or self-communication historically effected in Jesus. This explanation of eschatological language binds it intrinsically to Christology, existential and historical anthropology, and the doctrine of grace as experienced salvation in the present. Eschatological language depends on religious experience for its meaning and must appeal to such experience in order to communicate and be intelligible. This explanation also distinguishes eschatological language from science as well as relates it positively to science. On the one hand, eschatological assertions are not empirical projections; the predictions of fundamentalist preaching are a childish and sometimes demonic naïveté. But genuine eschatological insight may be nurtured by the religious awe and questioning that the science of the cosmos can engender.

The Social Dimension of Eschatology

In catechesis, popular piety, and the theology of the manuals before Vatican II eschatology was often reduced to the subtopics that have a bearing on personal death and its aftermath. The doctrine thus took on an individualist character insofar as it came to bear directly upon personal spirituality. While the individual dimension of the human person cannot be suppressed and is thus intrinsic to eschatology, it is being transformed by a social perspective on two fronts. First, beneath the question of my personal salvation lies that of the human race as such; the one intrinsically entails the other so that one cannot consider one's salvation apart from others. But today historical consciousness, a

more positive view of the religions of the world, and the new experience of the
UNIVERSAL SALVIFIC WILL OF GOD have raised the question of universal salvation in a new way (APOCATASTASIS). How could God's intention in creation be
thwarted (Athanasius, Anselm)? Granted, human freedom can resist God's will,
but can it defeat God's love? Since the church never declares any specific person
as eternally damned, for such can never really be known, theologians reason-
ably express a hope that all will be saved. Second, the eschatological symbol of
the KINGDOM OF GOD is being employed to express the idea of social salvation
within history. Eschatological concepts not only emerge out of present-day experience but also double back and illumine the present situation. Like a concept
of utopia, that which is imagined on the basis of the experience of salvation in
Christ reveals the sin and imperfection of the present order. Thus political and
liberation theologies have developed the realized and realizable aspect of the eschatological language of the kingdom to further overcome individualism. The
relevance and currency of social eschatological language reflect the new realization of the social constitution of the human person. There is no such thing as
an autonomous individual person; the human person is a social individual constituted in and by his or her relationships. These relationships are constantly
developing and changing over time. In the public forum, these social relationships constitute human history. The doctrines of eschatology affirm that this
movement as a whole has a goal, a purpose, a transcendent meaning-giving
finality. Eschatology therefore provides the individual with a social identity.

Human Freedom, History, and Eschatology

The social relevance of eschatological concepts is not enough to guarantee the
meaningfulness of history. One also has to establish the character of the ontological relationship between history and the end-time. In response to this
question political and liberation theologies have generated slogans such as
"building the kingdom of God." At first sight this phrase appears antithetical to
the fundamental Christian conviction that only God saves. The Gospels insist
that God's kingdom is God's rule and its effects are wrought by God alone. No
human being, nor humanity generally, can effect the kingdom of God, not in the
next world and not in this. In objective terms the problem is often described
in terms of an alternative between a discontinuous and a continuous eschatology (ESCHATOLOGY: CONCEPTIONS OF). A discontinuous eschatology assigns
the total work of effecting the final age of salvation to God. A continuous eschatology postulates some measure of continuity between human freedom and
history on the one hand and the end-time on the other. But the real problem is
new, could not have been foreseen by the New Testament, and calls for a deliberate hermeneutical strategy. With modernity the central significance of human
freedom, which itself defines the distinctiveness of the human, has shifted from
"choice" and from "commitment" to "creativity." With this as a premise, the
problem becomes whether or not this freedom, both personal and corporate,

is ultimately meaningful in its historical creativity. In the view of a discontinuous eschatology it would appear that human creativity is finally meaningless: it has no ultimate meaning because it does not contribute to the kingdom of God; the immediate experience of creativity is in the long run an illusion; the course of human life is a waiting and being tested. By contrast, process theologians and some liberation theologians affirm a real causal connection between human activity and the eschaton. This is not an evolutionary connection and does not entail necessary progress. Nor is the kingdom of God at all visible on the surface of history but will be made visible only in the end. The arguments that are elicited for this view are strengthened by the negative contrast of the ultimate meaninglessness of freedom and history without some causal continuity with final reality. God who created human freedom in God's own image of creativity must, by a fitting consistency, have provided for its effectiveness by the same self-limitation as creation itself. On the analogy of cooperative grace (GRACE: CONTEMPORARY ISSUES), the creativity of human freedom is not competitive with God but unfolds within the framework of God's design and sustaining power.

Eschatology, Church, and Spirituality

Eschatology, the doctrine of the completion and fulfillment of human existence, bends back on life in this world to reveal what it should be. This circular disclosure has a bearing on Christian life in the same measure that an individual's concern and preparation for death is a powerful impulse toward a certain way of life. When spirituality is regarded as a consistent commitment that organizes the whole of one's life, the social dimension of the goal of life and the contribution of each human freedom in grace to that final reality will shape a spirituality of responsibility that transcends individualism. Analogous developments such as these can be found in political and liberation theologies and socially and historically conscious theologians generally. Such a corporate spirituality is most obvious in ecclesiology, for the church is the institutionalization of the faith-life of its people. The church is conceived in the line of Vatican II as having a mission in the world; it is a church with a worldly vocation because the world according to the revelation of Jesus Christ has a final destiny that is divine. This ecclesiology and attendant ecclesial spirituality emphasize the responsibility of the laity in the church's dialogue with the world. It is a church that consciously reflects on its involvement in social issues in the world because it cannot escape such involvement. The MISSION of the church is to be a visible sign or sacramental mediator of the humanizing grace of God. This visibility entails an institutionalization of the values projected as the fulfillment of the end-time within the present life of the church. In doing this it continues the eschatological mediation of Jesus. Such a spirituality underlines the eschatological value of work. Human labor is the exercise of human freedom consistent with the ultimate aim of God's creation. When it is creative according to the values of Jesus, it contributes to the kingdom of God.

Bibliography
Gilkey, Langdon. *Reaping the Whirlwind: A Christian Interpretation of History.* New York: Seabury, 1976.
Hayes, Zachary. *Visions of a Future: A Study of Christian Eschatology.* Wilmington, Del.: Glazier, 1989.
Hellwig, Monika. "Eschatology." In *Systematic Theology: Roman Catholic Perspectives,* edited by Francis Schüssler Fiorenza and John Galvin, 2:349–72. Minneapolis: Fortress, 1991.
Moltmann, Jürgen. *The Theology of Hope: On the Ground and the Implications of a Christian Eschatology.* New York: Harper and Row, 1967.
Rahner, Karl. "The Hermeneutics of Eschatological Assertions." In *Theological Investigations,* 4:323–47. Baltimore: Helicon, 1966.
———. *On the Theology of Death.* New York: Seabury, 1973.

ROGER HAIGHT

Eternal Life. Eternal life is the eternal salvation that God bestows upon human beings after death or after the resurrection of the dead and is identical with the blessedness of heaven.

(1) *Biblical Background.* According to the Old Testament, the living God possesses life by God's very nature and is the fountain of life (Ps 36:10). Every kind of earthly life is governed and bestowed by God. God breathes it in and turns the human entity into a living being (Gn 2:7); in death God withdraws this life. In the Old Testament life is not originally thought of as eternal life but as a quantitative and qualitative abundance of earthly life, that is, as a long, healthy, and happy life. In the later period of Israel's existence the beginnings of a hope for the conquest of death and an eternal life in the transcendent sense gradually make their appearance. Only in the final centuries before Christ does belief in a resurrection of the dead that ensures the entrance of the just into eternal life take definitive hold. In order to understand the New Testament idea of life a distinction must be made between earthly life that is destined for death (*psychē*) and eternal life (*zoē*). In the Synoptics, with a few exceptions (in Lk 12:15 and 16:25, *zoē* = earthly, physical life), eternal life (*zoē*) is understood in a transcendent and eschatological sense, so that it is identical with the KINGDOM OF GOD in its complete and perfect form. The just will enter into eternal life (Mt 25:46). The attainment of eternal life must be the sole concern of human beings (Mt 7:14; 18:8; 19:6; Mk 9:43; 10:17; Lk 10:25; 18:18). Eternal life is promised to the disciple who abandons everything for the sake of Jesus (Mt 19:29; Mk 10:30; Lk 18:30). In the Pauline and deutero-Pauline letters life, in the sense of a blessing of salvation that is both present and eschatological, derives its meaning from the "Christ-reality." The life of the faithful is a grace-

given participation in the life of the risen Christ and a consequence of being justified and made a new creature (Rom 5:18, 21; 6:22; 2 Cor 5:17; Eph 2:5f.). This life, which is given by the action of the Holy Spirit who is bestowed in baptism (Rom 6:3f.; Col 2:12), is hidden with Christ in God. When Christ, our life, appears, we too will appear with him in glory (Col 3:3–4). An extensively developed theology of eternal life is provided by John, for whom life (*zoē*) sums up the whole of salvation. In him the distinction between *psychē* and *zoē* is emphasized in an especially clear way. The good shepherd gives his life (*psychē*) for his sheep (10:15). True love is shown in the giving of one's life (*psychē*) for one's friends (15:13). Eternal life (*zoē*) is given by the Holy Spirit (3:6; 6:63; see 1:13). The true light is connected with the life engendered by the Spirit (1:4). The incarnate Son of God is the one, exclusive, and universal giver of eternal life. He is the bread of life (6:35, 48), the resurrection and the life (11:25), the way, the truth, and the life (14:6). The bread that he gives is his flesh for the life of the world (6:51c). The sole, but all-embracing, presupposition for the reception of eternal life is faith (3:36; 5:24; 6:40, 47; 11:25–26). In keeping with the realized ESCHATOLOGY of John this life is understood as a present blessing of salvation for believers. BAPTISM (3:5–6) and the EUCHARIST (6:51c–54) are the sacraments that bestow it. In Revelation, eternal life is described in apocalyptic images: eating from the tree of life in paradise (2:7), receiving the crown of life (2:10), being led to the springs from which the waters of life flow (7:17; see 21:6; 22:1).

(2) *History of Theology.* In the Christian tradition, after acceptance of the doctrine of the immortality of the soul and development of the doctrine of the INTERMEDIATE STATE, the souls of the just are said to enter into eternal life after death, with the glorified body also sharing in this life after the resurrection of the dead. Statements about eternal life were developed at the speculative level as a result of controversies over the understanding of heavenly beatitude.

(3) *Church Teaching.* In the great confessions of faith the ecclesial magisterium professes its faith in eternal life: "I believe in the resurrection of the dead and the life of the world to come" (Nicene-Constantinopolitan Creed [DS 150]); "I believe in the resurrection of the flesh (the dead) and everlasting life" (Apostles' Creed [DS 10f.]). Although here, in continuity with biblical thought, eternal life is related to the whole person after the last day, the medieval councils stress that the souls of the deceased, after purification if this be needed, immediately obtain the direct vision of God.

(4) *Ecumenical Perspectives.* On the ecumenical scene the doctrine of eternal life has become important in relation to the question of the intermediate state and the connected debate over whether the fullness of salvation is given after death or after the resurrection of the dead.

(5) *Systematic Reflections.* In speculative theology, eternal life is understood not only as expressing the salvation of the soul after death and of the whole person after the resurrection of the dead; it is also understood as supernatural

life and identified with sanctifying grace, which has eternal life as its reward but can also be lost while on earth.

See also HEAVEN; IMMORTALITY; RESURRECTION OF THE DEAD; SOUL; THEO-LOGICAL ANTHROPOLOGY.

Bibliography

Baillie, John. *And the Life Everlasting*. New York: Scribner's, 1933.

Fortman, Edmund J. *Everlasting Life: Towards a Theology of the Future Life*. New York: Alba House, 1986.

Küng, Hans. *Eternal Life*. Garden City, N.Y.: Doubleday, 1984.

Pelikan, Jaroslav. *The Shape of Death: Life, Death, and Immortality in the Early Fathers*. Nashville: Abingdon, 1961.

Peter, Carl J. *Participated Eternity in the Vision of God: A Study of the Opinion of Thomas Aquinas*. Rome: Gregorian University Press, 1964.

Tillich, Paul. *Systematic Theology*. Vol. 3. Chicago: University of Chicago Press, 1971.

JOSEF FINKENZELLER

Eucharist. The Eucharist is the key sacrament of the church and, at the same time, the center of its worship and its self-fulfillment in Christ. Other biblical names for this sacrament, such as "the Lord's Supper" (see 1 Cor 11:20) and "the breaking of bread" (see Acts 2:42), as well as names originating in a later time, such as "Mass," "Holy Sacrifice," "Service," or "Office," bring out the many aspects of this sacrament.

(1) *Biblical Background*. The most important New Testament witnesses to the Eucharist (= thanksgiving; see 1 Cor 11:24 par.; Mk 14:23 par.), which was universally celebrated from the beginning, are the four accounts of the Last Supper or of institution, which make it possible to reconstruct this final meal of Jesus. We learn of the central importance of the Eucharist in the life of the primitive church from the picture given of the latter in the Acts of the Apostles, for example, 2:42–47 ("They held fast to the teaching of the apostles and the communal life, to the breaking of bread and the prayers"). Even though Christians are still taking part in the temple worship, they break bread in the homes of the community; they celebrate the Eucharist in connection with an ordinary meal. Paul makes an important theological statement about the Eucharist in 1 Cor 10:16–21, when he declares that participation in the "table of the Lord" and participation in meals involving sacrifice to idols are incompatible ("Is not the cup of blessing, over which we utter a blessing, a sharing in the blood of Christ? Is not the bread we break a sharing in the body of Christ? The bread is one; therefore we, though many, are one body"). He is emphasizing here, above all, the communion of life that participation in the body and blood of Christ establishes with the Lord and his community. Finally, a section of the great discourse on bread in John 6 constitutes another important passage on the Eucharist. While the discourse for the most part is about the bread from heaven — Jesus himself — which is eaten in faith, Jn 6:51–59 speaks of the Eucharist. The Eucharist establishes a communion between Christ and the

participants in the eucharistic meal: a reciprocal dwelling in each other. Thus it bestows at the same time the gift of God's eternal life, which is granted to the recipients of Communion as a result of the self-giving of Jesus Christ. Even in the form it has in the primitive church, the Eucharist is already more than a simple repetition of the last meal of Jesus. After the resurrection of Jesus it becomes a joyous meal and a sacrifice of thanksgiving for which a rich liturgy soon develops; in the New Testament period the Eucharist is still attached to an ordinary meal.

(2) *History of Theology.* It is possible, however, that the separation of the Eucharist from an ordinary meal and its association with a liturgy of the word go back to New Testament times. The first detailed description is in Justin (d. ca. 165). The most important time for the liturgy is no longer the evening but Sunday morning, which reminds the participants of the resurrection. In the patristic period not only does the eucharistic liturgy undergo further expansion, but a theology of the Eucharist is also developed that is primarily pastoral in its orientation; it reflects on the various aspects of this sacrament, while at the same time keeping sight of its unity. The mystagogical catecheses of Cyril of Jerusalem (348) may be mentioned as an example. Augustine in particular emphasizes an important aspect of the Eucharist: when Christians receive the body of Christ they also receive themselves, in order to become ever more fully what they ought to be, namely, the body of Christ; the Eucharist is a celebration of the whole body of Christ, that is, head and members. The development in the early and high Middle Ages not only leads to progress in the understanding of the Eucharist but also brings imbalances with it. The question of the real presence of Jesus in the Eucharist occupies the limelight. In the ninth and eleventh centuries some theologians proposed an exclusively symbolic understanding of the presence of Christ in the Eucharist (especially Berengarius of Tours [d. 1088]). In response, other theologians and episcopal synods stressed the real presence of the Lord. In response to the one-sided emphasis on the meal aspect of the Eucharist by the sixteenth-century Reformers, the theologians of the Counter-Reformation again stressed the real presence and, at the same time, the sacrificial character of the Eucharist. The energies needed for a new synthesis flagged, and practical piety became in large measure focused on adoration. It was the liturgical movement of our own century that rediscovered the full form of the Eucharist. The theology of the mysteries made it clear that not only Christ himself but also his work of salvation are present in the Eucharist, and that presence gives the faithful a share in the Eucharist's effects, which have to do with everyday life. The liturgy of the word that is associated with the sacrament regained its proper importance. Thus the way was prepared for the teaching of Vatican II on the Eucharist.

(3) *Church Teaching.* One of the first official statements of the magisterium on the Eucharist was the profession of faith in the real, substantial change in the bread and wine, a profession that was imposed on Berengarius of Tours (DS 700). The Waldensians were obliged to profess in addition that only an

ordained priest can celebrate the Eucharist (DS 794). The Council of Florence also included important statements on the Eucharist in its doctrinal decree for the Armenians: the matter of the Eucharist is wheaten bread and wine from grapes, the latter mixed with a little water. The form of the Eucharist is the words of Jesus himself "with which He effected this sacrament." The priest effects it "by speaking in the person of Christ." The effect of the Eucharist is "to unite [the person who receives it worthily] with Christ," as well as an increase of grace, union with the members of Christ's body, and a strengthening in the doing of good (DS 1320–22). The Council of Trent dealt very extensively with the Eucharist; it discussed the decisive questions in its thirteenth, twenty-first, and twenty-second sessions. The first issue was the real presence of Christ (DS 1635–48, 1651–61). The second of the three sessions dealt chiefly with the very controversial issue of the chalice for the laity (DS 1726–34). Finally, the twenty-second session went extensively into the doctrine of the sacrifice of the Mass (DS 1738–59). The most important statement made in this final session was the confirmation of the absolute dependence of the sacrifice of the Mass on the once-for-all sacrifice of the cross: Christ left to the church "a visible sacrifice (as the nature of man demands), by which the bloody sacrifice which He was once-for-all to accomplish on the cross would be represented [repraesentaretur], its memory perpetuated until the end of the world and its salutary power applied for the forgiveness of the sins which we daily commit" (DS 1740). The encyclical Mediator Dei of Pius XII (1947) was the first to bring out clearly the several presences of the risen Lord in the liturgy, the heart of which is the Eucharist (DS 3840). Vatican II not only took over that idea — saying that Christ is present in the liturgical actions, especially in the sacrifice of the Mass in the person of the priest and above all in the eucharistic species — but also added that Christ is present in his word and in the gathered community of believers (see SC 7). The council also speaks of the Eucharist as "the source and summit of the Christian life" (LG 11) and "of all the preaching of the Gospel" (PO 5). Together with the priest, the faithful "offer the divine victim to God and themselves along with it" (LG 11). The Eucharist is a sacrament of the unity of the people of God, a unity that it both signifies and realizes (see LG 11). All in all, the council unifies once more the aspects of the Eucharist that had become separated (it even speaks of "the Lord's Supper" in SC 10) and emphasizes the connection of the Eucharist with the daily life of Christians (SC 10). Also to be mentioned are the encyclical Mysterium fidei of Paul VI (1965), which, among other things, turns once to the question of the substantial change that takes place at the consecration of the Eucharist, and a declaration of the Congregation for the Doctrine of the Faith in 1983 that only bishops and priests have the power "to do again in the eucharistic mystery what Christ did at the Last Supper."

(4) Ecumenical Perspectives. The Reformers' understanding of the Eucharist or Lord's Supper emphasized, above all else, the meal aspect of the Eucharist. The points of disagreement with Rome were their rejection of the sacrificial character of the Mass, their different understanding of the presence of Christ

in the Eucharist, which seemed unacceptable to Luther at least inasmuch as it involves transubstantiation, and their rejection of the idea that only a priest can celebrate the Eucharist. In all these areas a convergence is being sought through ecumenical dialogue, at least with sectors of the Reformation churches. The Catholic Church has rediscovered the meal aspect of the Eucharist; a purified understanding of the sacrificial character of the Eucharist makes the differences seem, here again, not irreconcilable; in the question of the real presence, a vocabulary from the ontology of objects has at least been supplemented on the Catholic side by a vocabulary from a personalist ontology. The greatest difficulties are still those created by the Catholic position that only a priest can validly celebrate the Eucharist. At any rate, the Decree on Ecumenism of Vatican II, at least implicitly, does not deny the salvific value of the Evangelical celebration of the Lord's Supper. In Lima, in 1982, the Commission on Faith and Order of the World Council of Churches produced a statement on "convergences" that shows at least the direction to be taken in at last achieving full eucharistic unity.

(5) *Systematic Reflections.* The focal points in theological discussion of the Eucharist are the following: (*a*) The question of the *real presence:* the decisive point here is that the real presence is being interpreted not only in the categories of an older "ontology of things" but also in the presently available categories of an "ontology of the personal," and that at the same time it is made clear that in the real presence of Christ the church as body of Christ is likewise symbolized and realized. (*b*) The question of the *sacrificial character* of the Mass: in response to misunderstandings both theoretical and practical, the Council of Trent declared that there is no question in the Mass of a repetition of Christ's sacrifice on the cross. The sacrificial character of the Mass consists in making the sacrifice of the cross present, thus effectively applying its fruits of redemption to us and introducing it into the present time and situation. In this way we become contemporaneous with the sacrifice of Christ on the cross. The Eucharist is the sacrifice of the church and the faithful in the sense that when they celebrate it they provide the vessel, so to speak, in which the cross and resurrection of Jesus become present for us in such a way that the faithful can introduce themselves and their world into that sacrifice and encounter with the God of salvation and so experience in Christ the forgiving and life-giving response of the heavenly Father. Also to be taken into consideration here is the aspect of the Eucharist as a sacrifice of thanksgiving; as a meal celebrating a sacrifice of thanksgiving, the Eucharist is an acceptable worship of God. (*c*) The importance of the *meal element*: since the liturgical movement many regard the Eucharist as first and foremost a meal, at which the host, Jesus, unites the guests in a saving way with himself and with one another. The actual sacramental signs of the Eucharist are those of a meal: when bread, the basic food, is distributed it expresses fellowship, as does the wine, which also symbolizes joy and a (shared) fullness of life. Admittedly, the Eucharist is a meal of a special kind, a meal of thanksgiving, blessing, and sacrifice — themes that have expression since the earliest times in prayers and in compositions of praise and

thanksgiving. The Lord's Supper is unique. It is a memorial (*anamnēsis*) of the suffering, death, and resurrection of the Lord, and it also looks forward to the consummation to come; past and future are really and effectively present in the real presence of the Lord himself. (*d*) The question of the *unifying principle*: that which gives the Eucharist its inner unity is not the simple form of a meal, as some maintain. The various aspects of the Eucharist are integrated into something more comprehensive. This J. Ratzinger calls "Eucharist." He is referring to the basic form: the meal that is a sacrifice of thanksgiving in which the Lord himself gives thanks, offers sacrifice, and gives himself as the food and drink of eternal life, thereby making his followers become in a new and deeper way the community that is the church.

See also EUCHARIST: ACCOUNTS OF INSTITUTION; REAL PRESENCE; SACRAMENT OF ORDERS; SACRAMENTS OF INITIATION; THEOLOGY OF THE MYSTERIES.

Bibliography
Léon-Dufour, Xavier. *Sharing the Eucharistic Bread: The Witness of the New Testament.* New York: Paulist, 1987.
Mitchell, Nathan. *Cult and Controversy: The Worship of the Eucharist outside of the Mass.* New York: Pueblo, 1982.
Power, David. *The Sacrifice We Offer: The Tridentine Dogma and Its Reinterpretation.* New York: Crossroad, 1987.
————. *Unsearchable Riches: The Symbolic Nature of Liturgy.* New York: Pueblo, 1984.
Schillebeeckx, Edward. *The Eucharist.* New York: Sheed and Ward, 1968.
Seasoltz, Kevin, ed. *Living Bread, Saving Cup: Readings on the Eucharist.* Rev. ed. New York: Pueblo, 1987.

GÜNTER KOCH

Eucharist: Accounts of Institution. The accounts of institution, also called the accounts of the Last Supper, are the New Testament texts that tell of the final meal that Jesus took with his disciples and in which the Eucharist has its roots.

(1) *Biblical Background.* There are four accounts of institution in the New Testament: Mt 26:26–29; Mk 14:22–25; Lk 22:19–20; 1 Cor 11:24–26 (and the context of each). The versions of Matthew and Mark are closely related to each another (that of Mark coming first), and those of Luke and Paul are likewise closely related (that of Paul being the earlier). These texts all have in common the following two points in particular: (*a*) Christ takes bread and breaks it, offers thanks (praise), and says: "This is my body." Body means here the bodily person. Jesus gives himself. (*b*) Christ takes the cup and says: "This is my blood of the covenant" (Mark; Matthew), or, in a different turn of phrase but with the same meaning: "This cup is the new covenant in my blood" (1 Corinthians; Luke). Here again, blood means the living being with blood in it; in the context there is also the connotation of a bloody death. This self-giving of Jesus is interpreted as a confirmation of God's covenant with Israel (see Ex 24:8) or the establishment of a new covenant (see Jer 31:31–34). In addition, there are phrases that differ in the four accounts, for example, "for you" in con-

nection with the Lord's body (1 Corinthians; Luke); "for many" or "for you" in connection with the Lord's blood (Mark; Matthew). The idea of the suffering servant of God (see Is 53:4–12) comes into play here, as does the veiled announcement of Jesus' death in Mark and Matthew (see Lk 22:16–18); above all, there is the command of repetition, as it is called (only in Paul). From these texts, especially those of Mark and Paul, both of whom had ancient (Jerusalem) traditions at their disposal, it is possible to reconstruct the essential lines of the meal that Jesus celebrated with his apostles before he suffered and died. In view of his death and resurrection — and as it were in anticipation of them — Jesus gave himself to his followers as bread and wine, in order to establish an indissoluble communion with them; it is possible that in doing so he understood his fate in light of the Old Testament theology of the suffering servant of God and the covenant. This meal probably had a Passover meal for its setting (the ritual of the bread coming before the main meal, the ritual of the cup after it). The setting of Jesus' last meal may also have been a so-called Toda meal, which many exegetes have reconstructed for this period; such a meal was a sacrifice of thanksgiving, but this character may be assumed for all Jewish festive meals of a religious kind. Even if the command of repetition is not historical, the apostles must beyond doubt have had the inescapable impression that Jesus intended in his risen life to continue (in a sacramental way) this most profound form of communion.

(2) *History of Theology*. Even in the early period the accounts of institution used in the liturgy showed a certain independence of the biblical accounts. There was evidently an awareness that the important thing was not historical records but the attestation of a living faith. Even later on, changes were made (making the accounts more parallel; introduction of decorative adjectives that promote reverence; addition of "the mystery of faith" [*mysterium fidei*], which is attested from the seventh century on).

(3) *Church Teaching*. The ecclesiastical magisterium has not dealt with the accounts of institution as such, although it has made use of them in support of truths in the doctrine of the Eucharist.

(4) *Ecumenical Perspectives*. Exegetical insights, in particular, regarding the accounts of institution can provide stimuli for ecumenical dialogue. Recent convergence of exegetical opinion can certainly make it understandable that in the rite of bread and wine we have a real self-giving of Jesus and his real presence as a gift to his followers, however this real presence be conceptualized. The aspect of thanksgiving sacrifice, which marks Jesus' last meal (though not all agree on this), can also be helpful in discussion of the sacrificial character of the Eucharist.

(5) *Systematic Reflections*. The preceding makes clear the tasks facing systematic theology. It is quite certain that ontological concepts of Christ's eucharistic presence, concepts little suited for expressing personal presence (among these is the concept of transubstantiation or change of substance; see DS 1642), must be supplemented by concepts derived from an ontology of the

personal (e.g., transignification or change of meaning, and transfinalization or change of purpose). One point must, however, be kept clear throughout: human faith does not *make* Jesus present but *receives* the presence he himself bestows. It is also possible that exegetical insights (and new personalist categories) can lead to a deeper understanding of the sacrificial character of the Eucharist.

See also EUCHARIST; REAL PRESENCE.

GÜNTER KOCH

Evil. Evil is anything that humans experience as flawed, bad, unfortunate, or harmful, or as the cause of want, suffering, mischance, or calamity. It is something negative directed against the human impulse toward life, well-being, happiness, self-realization, wholeness, and meaningfulness. One speaks of *physical* evil when the cause is seen as lying in physical, biological, or other natural processes, and of *moral* (volitive) evil when the cause lies within human responsibility. The latter often results in the former: moral evil harms not only the victim but also ultimately the evildoer as well.

(1) *Biblical Background.* The Old Testament usually refers to evil, whether physical or moral, by the one word *rā'* or *rā'ā* and considers it an inherent part of experienceable history. To the question of the origin of evil, Genesis 3 responds with the protohistorical and etiological story of the "fall." According to it, suffering and in part death, as well as the propensity to further sinning, are consequences of sin, of the turning away from God by a humanity that possesses strong cognitive powers and the capacity for decision. The destructive processes of nature (natural catastrophes) are not specifically discussed. For a long period of time, the theological idea of the all-effectiveness of the Creator predominates here: Yahweh creates light and darkness, well-being and woe (Is 45:7; Lam 3:38; Am 3:6; Prv 16:4). In any case, God turns all manifestations of evil to some purpose, sometimes as punishment (Jer 6:19), sometimes as trial and purification (Ps 66:10ff.). A sign of the divine will that human life should flourish is the anthropomorphic statement that the Lord feels regretful about the woe (Ex 32:14; Jer 26:13, 19) and thus releases humanity from it at the right moment (Gn 48:16). This all-encompassing urge of the Creator to hold fast to creation, despite its being "badly battered" by evil, is expressed in the divine pledge to Noah that God will "never again...strike down all living beings" nor again "doom the earth because of man" (Gn 8:21f.). In the New Testament, one looks in vain for a detailed analysis of the notion of evil; instead, its manifestations are addressed more concretely: suffering, want, persecution, illness, death. Jesus fought against these. He cures the sick and drives out DEMONS (Mk 1:34). He also commissions his disciples to do this (Mk 6:13). He himself does not seek suffering or even death, but he accepts them as consequences of his uncompromising activity on behalf of the kingdom. Jesus seems to resist energetically any overly simplistic linkage between experienced misfortune or infirmity and assumed guilt on the part of oneself or one's parents (see Lk 13:1–5; Jn 9:1–3). Through sufferers, the impoverished, and the dead,

God's redemptive will is to be made visible in a way that imparts hope (Jn 9:3). On the basis of the post-Easter religious conviction that Jesus' suffering, as endured in a spirit of freely willed self-sacrifice and universal representativeness (cf. Is 53:3–6; Mt 26:28), made comprehensible the Creator's unrestricted commitment to humanity, and that he thereby overcame for all time not only the power of death but also that of sin, Paul is able to conceive the relationship between these two powers as being quite close. He begins with reflection on the raised crucified one, who conquered both the ultimate affliction, death, and the evil that codetermines it, the power of sin; from there, he moves to a description of Adamic humanity, in which death, as the "wages of sin" and determined by sin (Rom 6:23), was still able to reign unopposed (Rom 5:17). According to present-day dogmatics, these texts do not justify the assumption that, in the absence of sin, earthly life would have had no natural end (ORIGINAL STATE). At the stage of universal, eschatological participation in the resurrected life of Christ, even death, as the ultimate affliction and "last enemy," is to be destroyed (1 Cor 15:26). On this is based, quite consistently, the hope that, if we suffer with Christ, we will also be glorified with him and find "that the sufferings of this present time are as nothing compared with the glory to be revealed for us" (Rom 8:17f.).

(2) *History of Theology*. The Fathers' treatment of the problem of evil, in the context of confronting gnostic DUALISM and MANICHAEANISM, took on philosophical characteristics. They refused to attribute the origin of affliction to a principle of evil that competes against God. In the case of Augustine, this led to the following chain of argument: God's creation is good; goodness is a quality of all true being; hence, whatever presents itself as "not good" (*malum*) cannot truly *be*. Evil can be understood as a "privation of being and goodness" (*privatio essendi et boni*) (*Conf.* 3.7.12; *De nat. boni* 17), as a nonsubstance (*Conf.* 7.12.18), as contrary to nature (*De civ. Dei* 11.17), and as inherently tending toward nothingness (*De nat. boni* 4). Because the "bad" (*malum*) has no being of its own, it can become actual only in something "good" (*bonum*): the evil feeds on the good (*De civ. Dei* 11.9; 12.3). God, however, is also the Lord over evil and is able to turn it to good purpose (*bene utens et malis*), to enable the good to emerge from it (*Enchir.* 27.100). God's works are thus often good in the very midst of our evil works (*De mus.* 6.30). This is why God permits moral evil at all and makes use of physical evil for the purpose of overcoming itself. God's encounter with affliction on the cross of Christ had redemptive consequences: "Killed by death, he killed death" (*In Evang. Iohan.* 12.10f.). "The old state of things was that human beings die. In order that this not constitute a finality for humankind, the new state of things was effected: that God dies" (*Sermo.* 350.1). This cosuffering, in a spirit of solidarity, of the ultimate affliction of creatures by their Creator offers itself as a source of meaningfulness to all sufferers, and particularly to those who are blameless. Thomas Aquinas systematically expanded the Augustinian theory of a "privation of being and goodness" (*STh* 1, q. 48f.) as well as giving corresponding formulation to the

doctrine of permission (*STh* 1, q. 19, a. 9; q. 48, a. 2 ad 3). Cajetan uses the first to criticize the "privation" theory (*Comm. in STh* 1–2, q. 71, a. 6; q. 72, a. 7).

(3) *Church Teaching.* Doctrinal office initially rejected pessimistic demonization of nature and the human body (DS 461–64), then also rejected systematic identification of suffering with divine punishment (DS 1972, 2470). In a previously unheard of manner, Vatican II placed strong emphasis on human responsibility for the elimination of evil; its criticism was also directed against structural evil in the world: poverty, hunger, oppression, unemployment, war. Christians must fight against this with all available scientific and moral means (*GS* 35). Their victories can then be signs of the greatness of God (*GS* 34). Human beings, even if masters of this creation (*GS* 12; see 22, 24, 29, 34), nevertheless suffer, in the course of their "being-toward-death" (M. Heidegger), a "degeneration of the body" (*GS* 18) and remain at the mercy of natural catastrophes; yet they themselves are also causers of these when, as a result of inordinate self-love, they inflict damaging side-effects on nature (see Rom 8:20). Not only the question of guilt, however, should occupy believers who are oriented toward Christ's cross, but primarily the question of a future that — in the sense of the healing and hallowing activity of Jesus — they have to fashion, by means of both belief and knowledge, into an increasingly humane one (*GS* 15). Never before has Catholic theology of creation directed attention so intensively to human responsibility for the elimination of evil.

(4) *Ecumenical Perspectives.* The Reformers followed the Augustinian tradition but gave extremely clear prominence, even regarding the problem of evil, to the universal sinfulness, and indeed, corruptness, of human nature.

(5) *Systematic Reflections.* A Catholic dogmatics that proceeds hermeneutically guards against any simplistic linkage of evil back to some misdeed.

See also DEATH; EVIL, MORAL; GOD'S PERMISSION; ILLNESS; SIN AND GUILT.

Bibliography
Farley, Edward. *Good and Evil: Interpreting a Human Condition.* Minneapolis: Fortress, 1990.
Hick, John. *Evil and the God of Love.* Rev. ed. New York: Harper and Row, 1979.
Levenson, Jon D. *Creation and the Persistence of Evil: The Jewish Drama of Divine Omnipotence.* San Francisco: Harper and Row, 1988.
Surin, Kenneth. *Theology and the Problem of Evil.* New York: Blackwell, 1986.

ALEXANDRE GANOCZY

Evil, Moral. The concept of volitive evil is a relative one: the evil cannot be conceived or desired without the good; whoever desires it still desires something good in it, as is shown by the example of temptation or self-exoneration. In contrast to afflictive evil, volitive evil is defined as the deliberately pursued opposite of (divinely willed) good. Its place of origin is the human will, which sets up its own judgment as the supreme standard and thereby ignores the order of values prescribed for it. Essential to it is an element of caprice. "The principle behind the good will is: 'Because this is good, I desire it'; that behind the evil will: 'This is good because I desire it'" (K. Hemmerle, *SM* 1:620). From the thus-sanctioned self-will of the individual, volitive evil spreads its effects out into the world, disordering, seducing, and corrupting it.

(1) *Biblical Background.* According to biblical teaching, volitive evil arises from freely chosen acts of human disobedience in relation to the Creator of all good. At the level of primal history, we find that humanity willingly surrenders to temptation by a good that is "delectable," "enticing," and highly promising (see Gn 3:6). Of course, the Creator of everything good, and thus also of freedom to choose, is still the ground of that decision. Hence, Old Testament writers can have Yahweh declare: "I make well-being and create woe" (Is 45:7b), or: "It is I also who have created the destroyer" (Is 54:16); in both instances, the term used is *bara* (see CREATION). Thus Paul, regarding the implication of what Scripture says about God and pharaoh, can write: "Consequently, he [God] has mercy upon whom he wills, and he hardens whom he wills" (Rom 9:18; see also vv. 19–24). On this basis, even present-day theologians do not hesitate to speak of a divine assumption of responsibility for human freedom of choice that extends all the way to the negative consequences of that freedom. Nevertheless, firm belief in a redemptive history that will be fulfilled eschatologically predominates in the Bible in such a way that volitive evil is condemned to being ultimately overcome by God. Until the eschatological separation of the wheat and the weeds, God allows them both to grow (Mt 13:30). Until then, too, the Father allows the sun to "rise on the bad and the good" (Mt 5:45). In the end, however, by virtue of the resurrected crucified one, all the powers of evil, together with death, are subjugated and destroyed (see 1 Cor 15:24–28; 2 Thes 2:8). But even now, the possibility exists for believers to overcome volitive evil through Christ, "who gave himself for our sins that he might rescue us from the present evil age" (Gal 1:4; see Col 1:13; 2:15). In response to the question of what causes humans to do evil, the New Testament did not adopt, in its systematic form, the rabbinically developed doctrine—already hinted at in the Old Testament (see Sir 15:14)—of the "impulse to evil" that God has supposedly implanted, along with an "impulse to good," in every child at birth. Still, the New Testament teaches that evil desires do not spring, for example, from the body, but rather from the "HEART," that is, from the rational and conative center of the person (see Mt 15:18f. par.).

(2) *History of Theology.* Among the Fathers, it was Augustine who occupied himself most intensively with the problem and mystery of evil. He distinguishes between "physical evil" (*malum physicum*) and "moral evil" (*malum morale*), that is, between afflictive evil, which is usually conditioned by nature, and proper, moral evil, for which humans are responsible. He regards both as a "privation of being and goodness" (*Conf.* 3.7.12), which does not, of course, adequately explain their experienceable force. Proper, moral evil does not come directly from God, nor does it come from some primal principle of evil (Manichaeans), but rather from an action by Adam, who perverted the order of goods (see *De nat. boni* 16). By so doing, he brought himself per-

ilously close to annihilation and bequeathed to his progeny a corresponding doom. Formally, according to Augustine, moral evil consists in uncontrolled self-love, which excludes love of God and thus brings devastating, futility-laden consequences for human society (see *De civ. Dei* 14.28). Thomas Aquinas inquired into the ground of the possibility of volitive evil. He discerned this in the tension between human beings' existence and their essence, and between the finitude of human will and the infinitude of the good to which it is called. The will is a particular "inclination" (*inclinatio*) or "appetite" (*appetitus*) that *draws,* but does not force, one toward the good (*De verit.* 22.5). The good forms an infinite horizon for the finite will, so that the latter must will continually more. Only in this way can the subject of the will become what he or she is. Only in this way does one progress toward realization of one's essence. Here, however, one can go astray from oneself by choosing wrongly in the face of the multiplicity of chooseable goods. Thus, as a finite being called to the infinite, one does evil (ibid., 22.6). Disordered, malcontent, and selfish, one snatches at the infinite from within the finite (see also ibid., 24).

(3) *Church Teaching.* Doctrinal office nowhere offers a "solution" to the mystery of volitive evil. It restricts itself to affirming the original goodness of God's creation, to denying the character of a "nature" (*natura*) or a "substance" (*substantia*) to moral evil (see Augustine) (DS 286, 1333), and to condemning the dualistic doctrine that moral evil is the creation of an uncreated adversary of God (DS 455–58, 874). The Fourth Lateran Council declares that God created even the devil as good by nature; that creature "became bad through himself" (DS 800).

(4) *Ecumenical Perspectives.* On the topic of moral evil, there are no particular differences between the confessions.

(5) *Systematic Reflections.* Present-day theology determines its position within the following bounds. A pessimistic anthropology, according to which the majority of humanity would be consigned to evil or humans would be merely the playthings of blind forces (this anthropology being based, for example, on the Augustinian doctrine of the "condemned multitude" [*massa damnata*] and the corresponding notion of PREDESTINATION), is as little favored as an optimistic view of the world that makes evil a necessary factor in the self-development of the world-spirit (B. Spinoza, in part G. W. F. Hegel) or of the classless society (K. Marx). Dualism, too, is avoided. Whereas many modern philosophers (roughly from I. Kant to the neo-Marxists) see volitive evil as lying in contrahuman behavior for which humans themselves are to blame (with consequences like depersonalization, collective delusion, totalitarianism, and lack of confidence in the future), theology views such inhumanity in connection with the opposition to God that fundamentally contributes to it. Dogmatics is currently attempting, through interdisciplinary means, to reach a position on the biological theory of "so-called evil" (K. Lorenz), that is, of the natural aggressiveness in animals and humans that furthers evolutionary change.

See also DEMONS; DUALISM; EVIL; ORIGINAL SIN; PRIMAL REVELATION.

Bibliography

Farley, Edward. *Good and Evil: Interpreting a Human Condition.* Minneapolis: Fortress, 1990.

Hick, John. *Evil and the God of Love.* Rev. ed. New York: Harper and Row, 1979.

Lorenz, Konrad. *On Aggression.* New York: Harcourt, Brace and World, 1966.

Michalson, Gordon E. *Fallen Freedom: Kant on Radical Evil and Moral Regeneration.* New York: Cambridge University Press, 1990.

Ricoeur, Paul. *Symbolism of Evil.* Boston: Beacon, 1969.

ALEXANDRE GANOCZY

Evolution: Theory of, and Creation. Understood broadly, the term *theory of evolution* refers to attempts to describe scientifically the generation and development of something essentially new out of some preexisting thing to which that new thing is tied through a complex play of continuity and change. The theory of evolution that is associated with the name C. Darwin pertains mainly to biology; it attempts to explain the origin and genesis of constantly new and higher species (phylogenesis) in terms of both natural selection (or selective breeding) and their ability to survive in the struggle for existence. It also claims to elucidate the derivation (descent) of humans from highly developed animal species, that is, their HOMINIZATION. Important natural scientists extend the theory of evolution to the development of the cosmos (M. Eigen), to the development of matter to the level of living organisms, and to the development of human cultures.

(1) *Biblical Background.* The theory of evolution, in the scientific sense, is undoubtedly something far removed from the biblical accounts of creation; still, there are analogies between continuous creation and evolution: the successive arising of matter and life, the differentiation of living creatures according to species, the formation of human beings from clay, their relatedness to the animals, their struggle to stay alive, and the cultivation and keeping of the "garden." What the Bible says about the Creator is not inconsistent with the claim that God is the author of potentialities and developmental forces that are immanent in the world. God allows the world to realize itself as such through its own internal laws, inasmuch as God enables and sustains the processes that natural science describes as evolution.

(2) *History of Theology.* In the sphere of biology, the theory of evolution is, at present, largely uncontested. That does not apply, however, to determination of the causes of evolution. For some natural sciences, which take the evolution of the cosmos as their starting point, matter itself possesses an inherent tendency toward the essentially new (cf. entropy) and thus toward self-development through time, so that one can speak of there being a "history of nature" (C. F. von Weizsäcker) even before the appearance of the human species. The so-called red shift of spectral lines, at the level of the largest known galaxies, suggests the conclusion that the universe is constantly expanding and that this process began from a highly concentrated original state. The age of our world-system is estimated at between five and ten billion years. There is

also the big bang theory, that is, the theory that the process of cosmic expansion began with something like an explosion. The thesis that the world is of infinite duration thus ceases to be the only probable one, although the hypothesis of a "perpetual generation of matter" likewise rests on grounds that must be taken seriously (e.g., H. Bondi's "steady-state" theory). Regardless of how cosmic evolution is specifically formulated, the evolution of living creatures appears as one of its constituent aspects, with organic structures standing out, as opposed to the inorganic ones on which they are based, through their greater diversification of attributes. In the evolutionary context, newly appearing living creatures are usually represented as descendants of other similar living creatures, although the boundary between nonliving and living — for instance, in the case of viruses — seems to be very tenuous. Paleontology postulates, on the basis of fragmentary findings and reconstructed series of forms, the existence of continuities of descent. The Darwinian doctrine of spontaneous mutations (which lead, within the genetic inheritance of organisms, to decisive new developments) and also the theory of natural selection (according to which mutations, by increasing the amount of information in the inherited DNA content, lead to the emergence of species more fitted to the struggle for existence, thus ensuring their survival) certainly describe partial causes of evolution, without being able to explain them completely. Other causes have been identified by researchers like P. Kropotkin, M. Eigen, I. Prigogine, and E. Jantsch: these include "more peaceful" factors in a genuine coevolution like symbiosis, mutual assistance, and spiritual processes. The human species, in putting into practice its growing knowledge of nature, exerts both a positive and a negative influence on the course of the world's development. Within the realm of humanity's power lies even the destruction of its own environment.

(3) *Church Teaching.* In his encyclical *Humani generis* (1950), Pius XII took a first step away from unconditional rejection — motivated by religious and humanistic concerns — of the theory of evolution (the fear being that humanity might vanish beneath the mechanics of natural laws and the uniqueness of every individual no longer be recognized): "The Church's doctrinal office does not forbid that the doctrine of evolutionism, as accords with the current state of knowledge in the profane sciences and theology, be dealt with ... by scholars in both fields ... insofar as such inquiry pertains to the generation of the human body out of already existent and living matter; for as regards the soul, the Catholic Faith requires that we adhere to its having been directly created by God" (DS 3896). The text specifies neither what, in detail, is to be understood by "body" and "soul" nor how, in this connection, their unity is to be conceived. Vatican II proceeds from the assumption that present-day humanity has undergone "a transition from a more static understanding of the order of total reality to a more dynamic and evolutional one" (*GS* 5). It turns "development" into an important concept for theology, too, regarding interpretation of anthropological (*GS* 34), sociological (*GS* 44), scientific (*GS* 54), and economic (*GS* 6, 66) processes. In this context, as accords with belief in creation, it

raises the question of meaning (*GS* 3, 26) and the issue of the justice that ought to obtain. Christians are made responsible for the further course of cultural evolution, albeit within the biotechnological sphere.

(4) *Ecumenical Perspectives.* Problems surrounding the theory of evolution and belief in creation hardly play a controversial role in ecumenical dialogue today.

(5) *Systematic Reflections.* Most of the credible forms of the theory of evolution advocated today are not contradictory to biblically revealed belief in creation. In some circumstances, they can even be understood as an elaboration of this belief within the horizon of the natural sciences. This noncontradictoriness rests, to be sure, on a difference in focus between the two areas of inquiry. The theory of evolution presupposes the real world and matter as already existing things; belief in creation relates to the same from the viewpoint of the absolute beginning and the ultimate goal that ought to be realized (ESCHATOLOGY). Belief in creation inquires from the viewpoint of God the Creator and offers, in God's name and primarily on the basis of the advent of Christ, an answer to the question of meaning. It calls attention to the CREATURELINESS of humanity and nature and founds an ethos of cocreaturely "solidarity" and responsibility.

Bibliography
Binns, Emily. *The World as Creation: Creation in Christ in an Evolutionary View.* Wilmington, Del.: Glazier, 1990.
Hulsbosch, A. *God in Creation and Evolution.* New York: Sheed and Ward, 1965.
Lubac, Henri de. *Pierre Teilhard de Chardin: The Man and His Meaning.* New York: Hawthorn, 1965.
McMullin, Ernan, ed. *Evolution and Creation.* Notre Dame, Ind.: University of Notre Dame Press, 1985.
Peacocke, Arthur. *God and the New Biology.* San Francisco: Harper and Row, 1986.
Peacocke, Arthur, and Svend Andersen, eds. *Evolution and Creation: A European Perspective.* Aarhus: Aarhus University Press, 1987.

ALEXANDRE GANOCZY

Examination of Conscience. In teaching on the sacraments the examination of conscience refers not simply to moral self-scrutiny by persons, even if they be Christians, but to a self-scrutiny that is connected by a certain intrinsic necessity with the acts of the penitent in the sacrament of penance.

(1) *Biblical Background.* The Bible provides only a general background here when it urges believers to test their way of life against the norm of the divine will. "I reflect upon my ways; I turn my steps to your decrees" (Ps 119:59); "Let us test our ways and examine them, and turn to the Lord" (Lam 3:40).

(2) *History of Theology.* In the form of a general examination of conscience this interior act is recommended as a regular practice by ascetical writers as early as Basil and John Cassian; later on, as the "entranceway" to the sacrament of penance, it is presupposed rather than being a specific subject of reflection.

(3) *Church Teaching.* As for the magisterium, the Council of Trent makes brief reference to the examination of conscience in connection with the sacrament of penance when it speaks of the obligation to confess all mortal sins "which one remembers after a due and diligent examination (*praemeditatione*)" (DS 1707).

(4) *Ecumenical Perspectives.* Among the Reformers who do not recognize the sacrament of penance as such, the question of the examination of conscience as here understood does not arise. On the other hand, where Evangelical Christians practice confession, this kind of examination of conscience can become a subject of ecumenical conversations.

(5) *Systematic Reflections.* Contemporary theology needs to bring out the dialogical character of the examination of conscience. This examination is not simply a review of objective moral norms and a determination of failures in relation to them. In the examination of conscience persons interiorly enter the presence of the living Thou that is God through prayer and a thankful awareness of their dependence and redemption. The purpose is to let God show them the way to their true selves, as well as beyond themselves and to their fellow human beings, and in the process to recognize in a repentant spirit their departures from this way, so that after being accepted anew by God's forgiving love in the sacrament of penance, they may travel this way once more.

See also SACRAMENT OF RECONCILIATION.

Bibliography
Conn, Walter. *Conscience: Development of Self-Transcendence.* Birmingham, Ala.: Religious Education Press, 1981.

GÜNTER KOCH

Excommunication. Excommunication is an exclusion from participation in various activities of the church.

(1) *Biblical Background.* In the Old Testament the consciousness of being the people chosen by God for the covenant was strong. Those who broke the covenant, that is, sinned, were "excommunicated" from the community (see Leviticus 26). The writings of the rabbis attest to the institution of a ban from the synagogue. The members of the Qumran community lived the covenant in their own fashion; those who sinned were excluded. The New Testament basis for the practice of excommunication is Mt 18:17; it is to be noted, however, that this passage is immediately followed by the giving of the power of the keys and the authority to reconcile (Mt 18:18). Excommunication took the practical form of a curse (see 1 Cor 5:4f.) or the breaking off of personal relations (see Ti 3:10; 3 John 10) or exclusion from the Eucharist (see 1 Cor 10:20f.).

(2) *History of Theology.* The ecclesiastical institution of excommunication was thought out and organized by the canonists in an increasingly careful way as the centuries passed. In the early church this development took place primarily in the area of the church's theology and practice of penance. There again excommunication and reconciliation went together.

(3) *Church Teaching.* Excommunication is described in the Code of Canon Law (can. 1331). It is one of three censures (i.e., medicinal penalties as distinct from expiatory penalties): excommunication, interdict, and suspension. "The application of the punishment of excommunication means that the person is forbidden to take any ministerial role in the celebration of the eucharistic sacrifice or any other liturgical action, to administer sacraments and sacramentals or receive sacraments, to exercise licitly any ecclesiastical offices, ministries, or functions, or perform acts of governance. The punishments are extended when the excommunication is declared or is determined to have been automatically incurred" (*HkKR* 93h).

(4) *Ecumenical Perspectives.* In the Evangelical churches excommunication is practiced in the framework of the application of "church discipline," although for the most part in the form of the "little excommunication" (denial of Communion and official ecclesial activities, deprivation of the rights of membership, etc.). The modalities are set down in the various church orders.

(5) *Systematic Reflections.* The deeper meaning of excommunication is revealed only against the background of an ecclesiology of "communion" (*communio*). This last term designates both the community of the faithful who live in unity amid their multiplicity and through faith and baptism form the body of Christ, and also the eucharistic community gathered around the table of the Lord. Those whose behavior differs in a serious way from that of the community already bring upon themselves an exclusion from the community that is then formalized according to church law. But this exclusion can only be "medicinal," because membership in the body of Christ cannot be cancelled. Consequently, excommunication looks in every case to reconciliation.

See also RECONCILIATION; SACRAMENT OF RECONCILIATION.

Bibliography

Hein, Kenneth. *Eucharist and Excommunication: A Study in Early Christian Doctrine and Discipline.* Bern: Herbert Lang; Frankfurt: Peter Lang, 1973.

Williams, Paul L. *Everything You Always Wanted to Know about the Catholic Church but Were Afraid to Ask for Fear of Excommunication.* New York: Doubleday, 1989.

WERNER LÖSER

Ex Opere Operato. The formula describes the objective way in which the sacraments have their effect: they bestow grace in the recipient "in virtue of the properly performed sacramental action" due to the divine power and authority.

(1) *Biblical Background.* The concept is evidently not to be found in the Bible. It is possible, however, to find a basis there for what the concept says when properly understood: thus baptism is described as having an efficacy that comes from God and not from the faith of the recipients (see Ti 3:5; Jn 3:5); a similar efficacy is ascribed to the word of God, which plays a decisive role in the sacraments (see 1 Pt 1:23; Jn 15:3; Heb 4:12).

(2) *History of Theology.* While the Fathers simply repeat the ideas found in

the Bible and speak, for example, of the maternal womb of baptism, the concept of *ex opere operato* was used from the end of the twelfth century in contrast to *ex opere operantis* ("in virtue of the acting" minister or recipient); it is found first in Peter of Poitiers (d. 1205). The point was to characterize the sacramental action as the sole instrumental cause of grace; the description was aimed also at heretical or schismatic movements that made the efficacy of the sacraments dependent on the faith or even the holiness of the minister or recipient.

(3) *Church Teaching.* In reaction to the stress placed by the Reformers on faith, which, in the form of trust in God, alone justifies even in the sacraments, the Council of Trent introduced the concept of *ex opere operato* into one of its definitions: "If anyone says that through the sacraments of the New Law grace is not conferred by the performance of the rite itself (*ex opere operato*)...*anathema sit*" (DS 1608).

(4) *Ecumenical Perspectives.* This definition became a bone of contention because of the Reformers' understanding of the faith. Yet the concept could provide an opportunity for dialogue if theologians made it clear that the real intent of *ex opere operato* is to show God to be the sole cause of salvation.

(5) *Systematic Reflections.* Such is the abiding significance of *ex opere operato*. This concept need not, and should not, be allowed to exclude the response of faith by the recipient of the sacrament to God's offer of salvation. As a matter of fact, however, this response is somewhat overshadowed. It is probably for this reason that Vatican II, which understands the sacraments to be dialogical events, leaves *ex opere operato* entirely in the background.

See also SACRAMENT; WORD AND SACRAMENT.

Bibliography

O'Neill, Colman E. *"Opus Operans, Opus Operatum": A Thomistic Interpretation of a Sacramental Formula.* Rome: Athenaeum, 1958.

Rahner, Karl. *The Church and the Sacraments.* New York: Herder and Herder, 1963.

———. "The Theology of Symbol." In *Theological Investigations,* 4:221–52. New York: Crossroad, 1966.

Tappeiner, Daniel A. "Sacramental Causality in Aquinas and Rahner: Some Critical Thoughts." *SJT* 28 (1975) 243–57.

                                                                    GÜNTER KOCH

Expectation of an Imminent End. By expectation of an imminent end is meant the idea, presented from several points of view in the New Testament, of the immediate imminence of the end of the world and the concomitant definitive dawning of the kingdom of God or, as the case may be, the imminence of the parousia of the Son of Man and the events of the final age, namely, the RESURRECTION OF THE DEAD and the judgment upon the world.

(1) *Biblical Background.* When it comes to details, a distinction must be made between the expectation of an imminent end of Jesus and the understanding of it in the New Testament writings. The Synoptics say not only that in Jesus the kingdom of God has come in an interim form but also that the

present generation will experience the definitive dawning of the kingdom of God (Mt 10:23; 16:28; Mk 9:1; 13:28–30; Lk 9:27). Because the dawning will occur suddenly (Lk 12:39; 17:24, 27, 29; 21:35), the disciples are exhorted to be watchful and ready (Mt 25:14–30; Mk 13:33–37; Lk 12:35–40; 19:11–27). Jesus explicitly rejects the typically apocalyptic calculation of periods for determining the coming of the end (Mt 24:43, 50; Lk 17:20). Not even the Son of Man, but only the Father knows the day and the hour (Mk 13:32; see JESUS' KNOWLEDGE AND CONSCIOUSNESS). In the post-Easter New Testament communities we find initially an urgent expectation of an imminent end (Rom 8:22; 1 Cor 7:29–32; 16:22; 1 Thes 4:15–17). A change in outlook already makes its appearance in 2 Thes 1:4–7, where the persecutions and afflictions suffered by the community of disciples are understood as a necessary probation before the parousia, but a probation that will be rewarded by participation in the kingdom of God. There is even a warning against an exaggerated expectation of an imminent end as against a false doctrine (2 Thes 2:2–8). The late writings of the New Testament say even more clearly that in the difficult times ahead all the vices will prevail (1 Tm 4:1; 2 Tm 3:1–9). The final hour is marked by a great many false teachers ("Antichrists" [1 Jn 2:18]). Because of disobedience even the church stands under the judgment of God (1 Pt 4:17). The distress and affliction of the community show that the end of all things is at hand (1 Pt 4:7). The expectation of an imminent end appears in its most pronounced form in Revelation, which has for its purpose to comfort the persecuted church of the final days (see especially 1:1 and 22:20). The afflictions that precede the parousia are described in apocalyptic images (see Rv 6:1–8; 12:3; 13:1–18). The growing problem created by the delay in the parousia can be glimpsed in 2 Peter (1:16; 3:3, 8–10). In any case, the coming of the Lord can be hastened by a holy and devout life (2 Pt 3:12). Luke and Acts attempt to solve the problem facing the church by holding fast, on the one hand, to the expectation of an imminent end, and by accepting, on the other, an interim period between the ascension and the return of Christ. This time of the church is understood as a period in which the Holy Spirit is active.

(2) *History of Theology.* In the tradition we find two basic attempts at a solution. After an initial hesitation, the "Great Church" accepted that the parousia belongs to a distant future; at the same time, the doctrines of personal JUDGMENT and an INTERMEDIATE STATE were developed with ever greater clarity. In various sects, on the other hand, from the Montanists to the Adventists, efforts have been made to keep awake the expectation of an imminent end by ever new predictions.

(3) *Church Teaching.* The ecclesiastical magisterium has not taken an explicit position on the expectation of an imminent end.

(4) *Ecumenical Perspectives.* Ecumenically, the question of the expectation of an imminent end has not acquired any special importance because the Bible poses the same problem for the theology of all the major Christian churches.

(5) *Systematic Reflections.* In contemporary theology, an effort is made to remove the tension between the exegetical data on statements about Jesus' expectation of an imminent end and the theological relevance of these. One theory says that the expectation of an imminent end is to be understood not in temporal terms but as a constant readiness on the part of human beings and a timeless immediate presence of God to humankind, so that the eschatological events take effect for individuals at their death. An existentialist interpretation of the message of Jesus makes the expectation of an imminent end refer to the now of decision. Helpful though these and similar theories may be for preaching, they leave unresolved the christological problem of Jesus' own expectation of an imminent end, a problem that takes us into the mystery of the HYPOSTATIC UNION.

See also CHILIASM; KINGDOM OF GOD; PAROUSIA.

Bibliography

Beasley-Murray, George. *Jesus and the Last Days.* Peabody, Mass.: Hendrickson, 1992.

Beker, Johan Christiaan. *Paul's Apocalyptic Gospel: The Coming Triumph of God.* Philadelphia: Fortress, 1982.

Efird, James M. *End-Times: Rapture, Antichrist, Millennium: What the Bible Says.* Nashville: Abingdon, 1986.

Tiede, David Lenz. *Jesus and the Future.* New York: Cambridge University Press, 1990.

Witherington, Ben. *Jesus, Paul, and the End of the World: A Comparative Study in New Testament Eschatology.* Downers Grove, Ill.: InterVarsity, 1992.

JOSEF FINKENZELLER

Experience. By experience is meant, in everyday parlance, the living knowledge gained from practice; in philosophy, a knowledge, gained through contemplation or perception (i.e., empirically, not theoretically), that is the basis for insight; in the science of religions, a becoming conscious of the reality of the divine (the numinous); in theology, a becoming aware of the self-communication of God as the foundation of faith in the context of the spiritual life.

(1) *Biblical Background.* In the Bible, experience is an ever-present reality. It finds conceptual expression in the verb *geuesthai* (taste, savor). Experienced realities are, above all, death (Mk 1:9 par.; Jn 8:32), which those who believe in Jesus will not "taste," and the Holy Spirit (Heb 6:4f.; 1 Pt 2:3).

(2) *History of Theology.* Given what we find in the Bible, it cannot be surprising that from the outset experience characterized Christianity, which, as a church, had originated in the experience of Pentecost. Accordingly, Christian life was seen chiefly as a matter of immediate experience, the rational comprehension of which gradually led to appropriate formulations. Through the action of the Holy Spirit this experience remained related to the figure of Jesus Christ. Comparison with this origin forced theologians to a variety of conceptual schemes, without the problem of experience as such becoming thematic. This is evidenced by the New Testament collection of writings. In this framework, basic experience and the experience of each moment make possible an

understanding of what is known in present-day philosophy and theology as transcendental experience. In addition, there is already at work here the distinction between external and internal experience, as well as the distinction between spiritual and material experience. These distinctions are not absolute, inasmuch as the realities distinguished remain correlative to each other. Historically, in the Middle Ages the distinctions contributed to the problematic of experience; this occurred when the Aristotelian concept of experience entered Christian thought by way of Albert the Great and when Thomas Aquinas and Bonaventure made use of it, each in his own fashion, in order to distinguish between scientific-intellectual knowledge and knowledge based on mystical experience. Experience as a mystical concept was developed in the seventeenth century (J. Sandaeus) and as a result played a key role in Pietism. Experience, understood as a feeling of dependence that arises in the self-consciousness of the devout, became for F. Schleiermacher the foundational principle of his teaching on faith. On the Catholic side, F. von Baader maintained the originality of interior experience. Both men, even if only indirectly, had a certain influence on nineteenth-century Catholic theology. However, only as a result of the growing influence in our time of spirituality, the liturgy, and the mysteries has experience become a central category of theology, whether by way of acceptance or by way of rejection. This state of affairs has not been possible apart from the study and critical analysis of trends in contemporary philosophy. But this difficult task is proving to be a fruitful one.

(3) *Church Teaching.* In the form of interior experience taken as the basis for the certitude of faith, experience was rejected by Vatican I (DS 3033) and during the clash with modernism (DS 3477–82), but this did not mean that the entire realm of experience was banished from theological work. The emphasis at that period was on the theme of certainty regarding salvation, which had already been rejected by the Council of Trent (see DS 1533, 1563ff.), whereas that same council, when dealing with the Eucharist, had fully accepted experience as a source of strength and consolation (see DS 1649, 1674).

(4) *Ecumenical Perspectives.* There is a certain parallelism in theologico-philosophical development (Schleiermacher–Baader; R. Otto–R. Guardini; etc.) that makes experience a problem for the contemporary church. As a result, despite divergent emphases in the several traditions, a common task has been imposed that in practice has already been frequently tackled in the ecumenical movement but of which until now theologians have not been very conscious and which they have not taken up as such.

(5) *Systematic Reflections.* The theological concept of experience has in common with the others that experience signifies an immediate perception by the senses, which makes possible, supports, and safeguards a rational apprehension and description of reality. At bottom, the Christian religion, and therefore Christian theology as well, has as its transcendental foundation the experience of Jesus Christ in the Holy Spirit. Experience thus becomes a fundamental theological concept, the content of which must be disclosed by developing its

comprehensive philosophico-theological meaning. (*a*) Because human beings live in space and time, they attain to self-awareness only as they make their way through reality with its juxtapositions and sequences, that is, "travel" it (German: *erfahren*) or "make trial of it" (Latin: *experiuntur*). This takes place concretely in their contact with human beings, things, and circumstances, which call attention to their meaning and challenge them to take a responsible position toward them. At the same time, this situation calls for their *spiritual* appropriation of what they have experienced. Experience must therefore first be passively accepted (one cannot escape from all experience), but then immediately be actively explored. From this point of view experience is a nonmanipulable challenge to human freedom. It obliges reason to seek understanding. Because experience is based on immediate contact with reality, it is in principle open to all reality, including, for example, the community but also God as the transcendental reality that grounds all else. (*b*) The resultant religious experience confronts human beings with the ultimate ground and goal of being and life. Consequently, the acceptance or rejection of such experience decides whether the person's own existence is to be a success or a failure. There is, however, a difficulty in this area: the forms that mediate religious experience (natural phenomena, culture, history, social or psychological conditions) remain indeterminate and ambiguous in relation to the mediated reality of the divine; furthermore, this experience can hardly be given adequate linguistic expression, since the divine always remains mysterious. Even positive answers to such experiences (wonder, adoration, prayer, etc.) remain partial and fragmentary. (*c*) In the Christian understanding of it, religious experience is inseparable from the action of the Holy Spirit in the human person. The Spirit makes possible an encounter with the salvation offered by Christ and by this means brings about conversion, acceptance of the gospel, and, in this acceptance, faith. The social dimension of Christian experience arises from the fact that the Spirit is at the same time the active ground of the church. The church bears witness to the New Testament message of salvation and interprets it; consequently, the church plays a constitutive part in the occurrence of Christian experience. The action of the Spirit in Christian experience prevents Christian faith from being simply an intellectual acceptance of the message as true and turns it into a vital activity. This is true of the faith of the church as well as the faith of individuals; growth in both of these faiths constitutes the "tradition" in which the divine revelation is transmitted. Vatican II says expressly that the "interior insight which derives from spiritual experience" plays a part in this process (*DV* 8). The specific content of revelation removes the indeterminateness of religious experience and also opens the way for Christians to ever-new experiences. Christian experience is thus a gracious gift directed to beatitude as its goal and also an invitation to new life and activity, to the discovery of new vital possibilities. With an eye on the consummation of things, but related meanwhile to the pilgrim state (*status viatoris*), it leads human beings to a radically new vision of reality.

See also FAITH; HOLY SPIRIT.

Bibliography
James, William. *The Varieties of Religious Experience*. New York: New American Library, 1958.
Proudfoot, Wayne. *Religious Experience*. Berkeley: University of California Press, 1985.
Rahner, Karl. "Experience of the Spirit and Existential Commitment." In *Theological Investigations*, 16:24–34. New York: Seabury, 1979.
Runzo, Joseph, and Graig K. Ihara, eds. *Religious Experience and Religious Belief*. Lanham, Md.: University Press of America, 1986.
Smith, J. *The Analogy of Experience*. New York: Harper and Row, 1973.

KARL HEINZ NEUFELD

Experience of God. In present-day theological language, experience of God refers to contact with the reality of God as the most profound and comprehensive dimension of human relations. This contact emerges from the total human experience of life, including thought and self-reflection.

(1) *Biblical Background.* In the Scriptures the bearers of revelation are primarily the subjects of experiences of God such as calls to prophethood, visions, auditions, and mystical experiences. Even prior to their actual experiences, they enjoy an inner closeness to the God of the covenant. Such experiences enable them to become mediators of the divine message and thereby the medium through which the people of the covenant are to receive directives and interpretations of events. These experiences of God are made accessible in the Psalms and the wisdom texts of the Old Testament. The New Testament writings link experiences of God with the gift and mission of the Holy Spirit as the new form of the presence of the risen Christ. This linkage of experience of God to Christ has significance for a theology of grace and church. It means that the Spirit is a gift both to the church and to its individual members (1 Cor 2:13–16; 12–14; 2 Cor 3:4–18; Gal 5:16–22; see also Rom 5:1–11 and John 14–16). The experience of God and the teaching of the church are thus not alternatives. Though we have such experience only through the belief of the church, such an experience is at the same time the living activity of God in the "hearts" of human beings (Rom 5:5; see Ex 36:26f.), so that "the Spirit itself intercedes for us with inexpressible groanings" (Rom 8:26; see v. 16), and we thereby become so closely tied to the resurrected one that he becomes our vital principle (Gal 2:20; Phil 3:7–14).

(2) *History of Theology.* Given the charismatic disposition of the early church, experience of God was hardly a problem. Theoretically, however, these experiences needed to be clarified in view of the debate with gnosticism, which sought to escape the reality of history through a premature state of perfection. In contrast, Paul emphasized that belief, hope, and love clearly link the Christian to God, but that nevertheless the Christian life is still one of pilgrimage. In antiquity, Augustine, as an eminent theologian of experience of God, emphasized that humans have the center of their desires inalienably in God. However, given their sinful tendencies, their relation to God is over and over again given as a gift of God's love. Thomas Aquinas combines the Augustinian tradition

with the Eastern. Even though grace does not make God's essence manifest, it still signifies a living together with God that becomes symbolically visible in the fruits of the Spirit in belief, hope, and love (*STh* 1, q. 12, a. 13).

(3) *Church Teaching.* Church teaching has not dealt comprehensively with the experience of God. It has, however, rejected the claim of a direct contact with God's nature (DS 3009, 3033). The Council of Trent rejected a Lutheran conception of fiducial belief that identifies the certainty of belief with the certainty of salvation (DS 1533f.).

(4) *Ecumenical Perspectives.* The problem of experience of God became ecumenically controversial in connection with theology of the act of belief. Luther emphasized, on the one hand, the nonintuitiveness of belief, but also taught, on the other hand, that attentiveness to God's word confers a redemptive presence that embraces most profoundly the realm of experience as well. Fiducial belief, in the sense of the Tridentine condemnation, is certainly to be rejected; yet we must recognize that it is in trustful self-abandonment to God that precisely the encounter with God — and, as part of that, also God — is realized.

(5) *Systematic Reflections.* Contemporary discussions center on the question of whether, and how, human experience of God is based on human consciousness or, more technically expressed, is transcendentally grounded. To give content to the idea of God is not within the ability of human consciousness. However, insofar as human persons experience themselves and these experiences are given to them in freedom, they are related to the giver as their Creator. This basic relationship, however, must also be comprehended and lived out. That is not a matter of a single act but is realized in HISTORY as the time granted humanity for God to come to it. Both kinds of encounter (God's love as underlying creation and the historically realized encounter with God's love) stamp the life of the believer in such a way that, despite all the incomprehensibility of God, the believer "knows" and "senses" the one in whom he or she believes. An experience of God is possible, therefore, that transcends all knowledge yet confers most intimate communion with God. Thus God is already active before humans hear externally about God and God's revelation. It is among the primary tasks of fundamental theology to reflect on these interconnections and to clarify them.

See also EXPERIENCE; FAITH; GOD; GOD: ACTS OF; GRACE: DOCTRINE OF.

Bibliography

Lash, Nicholas. *Easter in Ordinary: Reflections on Human Experiences and the Knowledge of God.* Notre Dame, Ind.: University of Notre Dame Press, 1988.

Proudfoot, Wayne. *Religious Experience.* Berkeley: University of California Press, 1985.

Rahner, Karl. *The Foundations of Christian Faith: An Introduction to the Idea of Christianity.* New York: Crossroad, 1978.

WILHELM BREUNING

Extreme Unction. *See* ANOINTING OF THE SICK.

F f

Faith. Faith in theological understanding is the personal, fundamental option in which the human being, through grace and trusting in God's power effective in Jesus Christ, responds in consensus with the church with his or her confession to the saving event of revelation. In contrast to its colloquial meanings (believe = think, suppose, be of the well-founded conviction, agree with an authority, trust in something on the basis of probability), faith in its theological meaning is an absolute assent based on inner certainty.

(1) *Biblical Background.* In Scripture the structure of faith is expressed under different concepts; the decisive explanations are offered in the New Testament (by drawing upon the Old Testament) (see table, p. 250). The content of faith in the Old Testament is the secure trust in God's promises and guidance with relation to God's people Israel. True faith is demonstrated in personal responses: Abraham reacts to Yahweh's instructions in trust, hope, and obedience (Gn 12:22) and thus becomes the "Father of the faith" (Rom 4:11); Moses becomes the liberator of his people in his obedience to God's plan (Ex 3:16f.; see Heb 11:23–31); the prophets in their steadfast trust in God's decrees prove themselves as comforters of Israel (Is 40:27–31). In formulas of faith (such as Dt 26:5–9; Jos 24:2–13) such experiences find their written expression. Individual qualities of faith include fundamental assurance (Is 7:9), obedience (Gn 22:1f.), trust (Gn 15:6; Ps 119:66; Jer 39:18), faithfulness (Is 26:2f.), and hope (Jer 8:15; Ps 119:81f.). In the New Testament, faith is the comprehensive concept for the relationship between God and human beings on the basis of God's saving activity for, in, and through Jesus Christ. It consists of the elements of trust (Mk 11:24), confidence (Mk 9:24), obedience (Rom 10:16; 2 Cor 9:13), and knowledge (Jn 1:18; 6:69; 14:9). In Jesus' preaching faith is the presupposition for his miracles (Mk 6:5f.), for his cures (Mt 9:23f.; Mk 5:34), and for the forgiveness of sins (Mk 2:1–12; Lk 7:48–50). In John, the acknowledgment of Jesus' personal mission is a condition for salvation (Jn 3:15f., 36; 5:24; 6:40, 47). After Easter faith is articulated as the acknowledgment of Jesus as the Christ of God (Rom 10:9f.; 1 Cor 15:2–5; Eph 1:3–13), through which the human being enters into a completely new relationship to God. This relationship is described as a new being in Christ (2 Cor 5:17; Gal 2:20; 6:15), as participation in his destiny (Rom 6:4–11), as the unfolding of new possibilities of knowing (Jn 1:18; 14:9), and as wisdom from above (1 Cor 2:10; 3:1). Above all faith brings about the JUSTIFICATION of the sinner (Rom 1:17; 3:21–31; 4:13; Gal 3:15–18). It is thus really a new foundation of reality (Heb 11:1), in the Johannine vocabulary light (Jn 3:21; 1 Jn 1:5), way, and life (Jn 14:4–6; 17:3; 20:31). It comes into being by listening to the word of God in the

BASIC CONCEPTIONS OF "FAITH"

Hebrew	Greek	Latin	German/English
aman to be sure, reliable, proven *batah* rely on, put hope in *hasah* seek shelter *hakah* remain steadfast, have patience	*pisteúein* trust *hypakoúein* obey *oikodoméin* build up	*credere = cor dare* familiar, trust cordially	*galaubjan* *gelafen* (OE) to cherish something, to become familiar with something

REFERENCES OF THE VERB "BELIEVE"

Credere	Believe	Example
aliquid	something	that God exists.
alicui	someone	God, that God is my salvation.
in aliquem	in someone	in God, who is my salvation.

Whenever one encounters the verb *to believe* in a text, one must take its context into account. With a direct object a *content* of faith is stated; with a dative object a *warrantor* is stated, on whose witness a content is believed. A unique use that is possible only within a theological or religious context is the prepositional use (*believe in*). This use indicates an absolute trust, an unconditional surrender: both qualities in their full sense are possible only toward God.

gospel (Rom 10:14–21), can increase (2 Cor 10:15f.), and must be protected from heretical disputes (1 Tm 4:1; 6:20f.). Although it is grace, it is still, as James stresses, also a moral response on the part of human beings (2:14–26).

(2) *History of Theology.* Any theology of faith must start from its two-dimensional structure that since Augustine (*De Trin.* 13.2.5) has been characterized as *fides qua* (*creditur*), or Thou-faith, and *fides quae* (*creditur*), or That-faith. On the one hand, it is an attitude toward the self-revealing God; on the other hand, it is the acceptance of the profession of the contents of this revelation. Theological reflection on faith therefore is always influenced by reflection on revelation. In Christian antiquity, faith in correspondence with the epiphanic understanding of revelation was seen formally as a personal surrender to the God of Christ, an entrusting that became evident in the everyday praxis of Christian life (faith personally appropriated in ethics). From a material point of view its contents were developed in the CANON, in the rule of faith, in dogmas, in theological works, and in the formation of the ECCLESIAL MAGISTERIUM. A significant factor for this development were heresies, which were countered by imposing a ban (*anathema*): with this, faith inherited a canonical aspect. In the Middle Ages, corresponding to the

prevalent doctrinal-theoretical model of revelation, faith was conceived as an intellectual assent ("hold-to-be-true") to the truths pronounced authoritatively by the ecclesial magisterium. It thus became a topic for reason (Anselm of Canterbury, *Proslog.*, title: "Fides quaerens intellectum" [Faith seeking understanding]), which is capable of offering convincing reasons for it (*Monol.*, prol.; *Cur Deus homo*, praef.). While Scholasticism stressed the rational moment in faith, monastic and, later on, Franciscan theology (Bonaventure) underlined the psychological-affective element. Thomas Aquinas attempted a synthesis: faith is a speculative-intellectual consent to revealed truths, brought about by the person's will. In the nineteenth century the relationship of faith and knowledge was the main point of a debate in which two extremes conflicted with the Catholic view: rationalism (G. W. F. Hegel) dissolved faith into knowledge, and fideism (H. F. R. Lamennais, A. Bonnetty) rejected rationality in favor of a nonrational intuition and inner experience. In connection with the development of the communicative-theoretical model of revelation, J. H. Newman, M. Blondel, and L. Laberthonnière prepared the way for a renewal of the concept of faith: faith appears as the radical response to the love of God. An important special problem was treated under the phrase *Analysis fidei* (analysis of faith): How can the certainty of faith be grounded? If it is based on the pure authority of God, faith is no longer rational; if it is based on a prior knowledge of the contents of revelation, it is no longer free (for the solution, see sec. 5.a.viii, below). In the present day, the main questions treated concern the possibility of a rational foundation for faith, the value of experience for faith, and the validity claims of historical witnesses to faith. Above all in the non-Western churches a lively discussion has begun about the way in which the faith can be articulated in their own cultural and historical contexts.

(3) *Church Teaching.* The ecclesial magisterium has reflected theologically on faith primarily in the last three councils. Against the Reformers, the Council of Trent (DS 1528–34, 1561–64) explained faith as an integrating component of justification — thereby necessary for salvation — which is above all an affirmative act of the intellect. Vatican I (DS 3008–20, 3031–36) underlined the doctrinal-theoretical understanding of faith as the acceptance of the authority of the self-revealing God. This acceptance is effected by the Holy Spirit and is supported by external signs (miracles, prophecies). Vatican II (*DV* 1f., 5) conceives faith as a total personal submission to God, which is grounded christologically and effected by the Spirit.

(4) *Ecumenical Perspectives.* Corresponding to the fundamental agreement of the major church confessions on the understanding of revelation, there also exists a basic consensus in the understanding of faith as *fides qua*. This does not apply to the description of faith with regard to its contents: here the visible unity in the one faith is still a goal to be achieved. At the time of the Reformation, admittedly, differences also arose in relation to faith as *fides qua*. In opposition to the justification by works that he protested against in the old church, Luther underlined the graced character of faith, which is an event influ-

enced by the Spirit that encompasses the whole person. In it, the human being is justified without his or her own previous effort. While being totally grace from the side of God, it is "bold confidence in God's grace" on the side of the human being (FC sol. decl. 4), pure trust (*fiducia*). In comparison to this the importance of *fides quae* is sharply reduced. Yet already Melanchthon and the early Protestant orthodoxy admitted some human cooperation. The existential aspect of faith was later stressed by S. Kierkegaard, K. Barth, and R. Bultmann, while F. Schleiermacher presented a position similar to fideism.

(5) *Systematic Reflections.* Faith is not a spontaneous human act; rather, it is founded in revelation, which only begins to reach its goal when it awakens faith. Its formal structure therefore is: "I believe in God's revelation in Jesus Christ." From this definition and under consideration of the theology of revelation the following theological insights become clear: (*a*) As *fides qua,* faith is: (i) an act that is made possible through God's *grace* (*lumen fidei,* light of faith), insofar as in faith, God grants human beings salvation; (ii) an act that is structured in a *trinitarian* way, insofar as the Father as the initiator of revelation is also the author, the Son as the climax of revelation is also the ground, and the Holy Spirit as Paraclete is also the effecter of the Christian faith; (iii) a *personal* and *comprehensive* act that by way of love moves a human being to new knowledge about his or her self (being related to God), about his or her fellow human beings (destined for salvation), and about history (as different realizations of the one faith) and the universe (as God's creation); in all these aspects, faith as *fides qua* conveys the experience of a liberating final meaningfulness beyond all empirical knowledge (hermeneutical function); presupposed in all this is the credibility of revelation; (iv) a *unified* act, since in all its forms and expressions it remains directed to the one God; (v) an act *supplementing knowledge,* insofar as it leads it beyond its inherent limits to the ultimate transcendental ground of the world, and thus completes it; in this sense, on the one hand, faith offers a ground of meaning for existential reason; on the other hand, faith needs reason as a critical authority for its own credibility and intelligibility; (vi) an *eschatologically* oriented act, as it urges the believer toward the fulfillment of all promises in the eternal communion with God; (vii) a *free* act, insofar as it is a genuine human answer to God's offer of dialogue in revelation; and (viii) a *rational* act, insofar as it is a fundamental decision of the human person who by nature is endowed with reason; certainty in faith comes to the person when the expressions of faith are proved true in life (*analysis fidei*): faith is therefore both a decision and a project that lays claim to, involves, and interprets the whole person and all of his or her reality. (*b*) Since faith is factually related to the word of God and its contents, it objectifies itself as *fides quae* through creedal expressions and formulas of faith. Under this aspect, faith is: (i) acknowledgment of the material propositions of *revelation;* (ii) *ecclesial,* insofar as revelation is always oriented to the community and therefore takes place in the concrete community of the church, which can be defined as the community of all the faithful; (iii) submitted to a *regulation of language,* because the

unity of the community can be articulated only through a common language; and (iv) to be developed *theologically*, because it is a subject for fundamental theology; theology has therefore a mediating position between revelation and faith; it fulfills its task when it analyzes the themes, interests, historical conditions, and thought categories of the expressions of faith, and at the same time attempts, when necessary, to translate them into new forms in order to make them intelligible.

See also DOGMA/DOGMATIC STATEMENT; HISTORY/HISTORICITY; REVELATION; THEOLOGY; TRUTH OF FAITH.

Bibliography

Coventry, John. *The Theology of Faith*. Notre Dame, Ind.: Fides, 1968.

Dulles, Avery. *The Survival of Dogma*. New York: Crossroad, 1971.

Ebeling, Gerhard. *The Nature of Faith*. Philadelphia: Fortress, 1967.

Niebuhr, H. Richard. *Faith on Earth*. New Haven: Yale University Press, 1991.

Tillich, Paul. *Dynamics of Faith*. New York: Harper and Row, 1957.

Walgrave, Jan Hendrik. *Newman the Theologian: The Nature of Belief and Doctrine as in His Life and Works*. New York: Sheed and Ward, 1960.

WOLFGANG BEINERT

Fideism. The term *fideism* refers to those directions in theology that either deny the significance of reason for decisions about religious belief or circumscribe it so strictly that the freedom of belief is no longer ensured.

(1) *Biblical Background.* Holy Scripture presupposes the significance of reason. For example, it characterizes nonrecognition of God as sinful (Wisdom 13 is the relevant Old Testament reference; in the New Testament, Rom 1:18–21 takes the same viewpoint).

(2) *History of Theology.* Fideism is a phenomenon of the nineteenth century. In Catholic theology, its main representative, L.-E.-M. Bautain (d. 1867), advocated the view that human reason is in principle incapable of recognizing religious and metaphysical truths and that their sole source is revelation.

(3) *Church Teaching.* Vatican I expressly condemned this form of fideism (DS 3004, 3026).

(4) *Ecumenical Perspectives.* Among nineteenth-century Protestant theologians, some wanted to oppose "feeling-based belief" to "understanding-based belief" (R. A. Lipsius, F. Schleiermacher, F. H. Jacobi). Under their influence, the Parisian professors A. Sabatier and E. Ménégoz founded a school of thought holding that dogmas and religious concepts are only symbols of religious feeling and embrace no transcendent reality.

(5) *Systematic Reflections.* Fideism directs attention to the specific character of the act of belief but is unable to do justice to it as an authentically human act. As such, the act of belief is free, and the believer must be responsible for it. The theology of revelation "also has, as an intrinsic component and condition of its possibility, the transcendental-unlimited horizon of the human spirit,

which provides the sole perspective from which something such as God can be understood at all" (K. Rahner, *MystSal* 2:409).

See also GOD: POSSIBILITY OF KNOWLEDGE OF; NATURAL THEOLOGY; TRA-DITIONALISM.

Bibliography
Dulles, Avery. *The Survival of Dogma.* New York: Doubleday, 1973.
Mitchell, Basil. *The Justification of Religious Belief.* New York: Macmillan, 1973.
Phillips, D. Z. *Faith after Foundationalism.* New York: Routledge, 1988.

WILHELM BREUNING

Filioque. The term *filioque* comes from the (Western) version of the Nicene-Constantinopolitan Creed and says that the Holy Spirit proceeds from the Father *and the Son*; the intention is to underscore the full divinity and consubstantiality of the third person of the Trinity.

(1) *Biblical Background.* The *filioque* is the result of later theological speculation; we must not expect to find a direct biblical attestation of the point.

(2) *History of Theology.* The term was added to the Great Creed in the Iberian area (after the Fourth Synod of Braga [675]) and made its way throughout Gaul and Italy in the eighth century; as early as 807–9 it was the subject of dispute between Latin and Greek monks in Jerusalem. It was probably not accepted in Rome until about 1000.

(3) *Church Teaching.* Because of disagreements with Eastern theology (see sec. 4, below) the ecclesial magisterium insists that the *filioque* was added "with good reason" (*rationabiliter Symbolo fuisse appositam* [DS 1302]).

(4) *Ecumenical Perspectives.* Since the time when Patriarch Photius of Constantinople made the addition his chief indictment of the Western Church, the *filioque* has been the most important cause of disagreement between Catholicism and Orthodoxy. Although formulas of agreement ("from the Father *through the Son*") have been proposed and to some extent accepted, there has been no real reconciliation of differences. The reason is that divergent conceptions of the intratrinitarian relationships are at work. If the emphasis is placed, as it is in the West, on the consubstantiality of the Spirit with the Father and the Son, the result is a rigorously triadic thinking: the Spirit then owes its being to the combined activity of the Father *and* the Son. If, however, the emphasis is placed, as it is in the East, on the dynamics of the divine life (as manifested especially in the salvation-historical sending of the Spirit beginning on Pentecost), then our gaze focuses primarily on the Father as the exclusive source and root of the divine being and activity. From this principle proceeds the notion of "energies," which can be used to describe the being and activity of the other divine persons.

(5) *Systematic Reflections.* If we leave aside the question of the possibility of additions to the established wording of the profession of faith, the problem of the *filioque* is situated within the problematic of the very doctrine of God. The

question for Western theology is whether the essentialist philosophy that has long prevailed there has not led in fact to a fundamentally unresolved identification of the economic and the immanent Trinity. In the process, the idea of the historicity of salvation has certainly not received its due attention. In the final analysis, however, the issue is access to the essence of God as such. For this reason, as Western theology tries to come to grips with atheism as well as with non-Christian ideas of God, it can scarcely surrender its position. For it asserts not only the oneness of the God of Jesus Christ and of this God's life and activity but also the tri-personed communion in which this one God lives and acts. The seemingly natural unilinear approach to the Trinity that begins with the work of salvation can lead to distorted and false ideas if it is not balanced by an emphasis on the identical being and action of all three persons. If this is safeguarded, the formula is not very important.

See also PROFESSION OF FAITH; TRINITY: DOCTRINE OF THE.

Bibliography

Stylianopoulos, Theodore, and S. Mark Heim, eds. *Spirit of Truth: Ecumenical Perspectives on the Holy Spirit.* Brookline, Mass.: Holy Cross Orthodox Press, 1986.
Vischer, Lukas, ed. *Spirit of God, Spirit of Christ: Ecumenical Reflections on the Filioque Controversy.* London: SPCK, 1981.

KARL HEINZ NEUFELD

Flesh–Spirit. The flesh–spirit problem refers to the difficulty that arises from the difference between the Semitic and Greek/Western linguistic usage with regard to the concepts of flesh and spirit. In Hebrew, the terms *flesh* and *spirit* characterize the whole human person under various aspects. In the Greek-speaking cultural sphere, spirit and flesh are considered as relatively independent realities (substances), which are joined together in the human person.

(1) *Biblical Background.* In the Old Testament the human being is called flesh insofar as he or she is a frail, transient creature. Spirit is the breath of life that is infused into human beings by God and through which they are living beings. In the New Testament, Paul and John take up this manner of speaking in their descriptions of the modes of existence of human beings in faith and in unbelief (e.g., Romans 7; 8; Galatians 5; John 6): "It is the spirit that gives life; the flesh is useless" (Jn 6:63). Here the line distinguishing between the Spirit of God and the spirit of the human person is not always sharply drawn. In some contexts it is clear that it is the human spirit as distinguished from the divine Spirit that is treated (Rom 8:16; 1 Cor 2:11; 1 Jn 4:2f.).

(2) *History of Theology.* Already in the New Testament there begins the argument — based on a Hellenistic interpretation (gnosis) — that the bodily-material element (flesh) has its origin in evil while the psychic-intellectual element (spirit) comes from God and must be freed from the captivity of the flesh in order to be able to return to God. In the long run, gnosticism could be effectively fought only when the original biblical meaning was successfully

transferred into Greek thought and modes of expression. In this effort a graduated ordering evolved — in the West above all through Augustine — according to which the corporeal-material component was valued as the lower plane and the psychic-intellectual component as the higher. Thomas Aquinas, nevertheless, stressed the corporeal-psychic unity of the human person. With regard to the human person considered as a corporeal and intellectual unity, he distinguished between the lower order of nature and the higher order of grace and thus once again came closer to the original biblical distinction. But it was only through historical-critical exegesis that the original sense of the biblical language of flesh and spirit was again made accessible. Existentialist philosophy with its concept of DECISION offered systematic theology the possibility of developing the original biblical sense in a new way.

(3) *Church Teaching.* The Fourth Lateran Council (1215) taught that God created the human person as an essential unity of body and intellect (DS 800; see DS 902, 1440). This teaching became a basic element of the ecclesial doctrine of faith (DS 3002).

(4) *Ecumenical Perspectives.* Orthodox theology took another path: when the divine Logos took on flesh (incarnation), the Spirit of God entered into all flesh and causes the image of God to be illuminated in the material. The opposition of spirit and flesh within the human person is reconciled through the Spirit of God, which pervades both and creates harmony between the invisible soul (spirit) and its physical-material appearance (flesh).

(5) *Systematic Reflections.* In Western theology the view has prevailed that flesh and spirit respectively describe the fundamental attitude of the whole human person toward God. Recently, theology has given attention to the fact that the Bible speaks almost in the same breath of the spirit of the human person and of the Spirit of God in the human person. The basic stance of the human person toward God presupposes or at least includes the understanding that God's Spirit enables the human person to reach this decision from within.

See also HOLY SPIRIT; IMMORTALITY; SEXUALITY; SOUL.

Bibliography
Barclay, William. *Flesh and Spirit: An Examination of Galatians 5:19–23.* London: SCM, 1962.
Cooper, John W. *Body, Soul, and Life Everlasting: Biblical Anthropology and the Monism–Dualism Debate.* Grand Rapids: Eerdmans, 1989.
Spicker, Stuart F., ed. *The Philosophy of the Body: Rejections of Cartesian Dualism.* Chicago: Quadrangle Books, 1970.

                                                        GEORG LANGEMEYER

Forgiveness of Sin: The Church and the. The "power of the church to forgive sins" is a technical term for the fact that God, who alone can forgive sins, authorizes ecclesial ministers to forgive even serious sins in God's name in the form of a judicial act in the sacrament of reconciliation.

(1) *Biblical Background.* New Testament evidence (SACRAMENT OF RECON-CILIATION): a power, validated by God, to forgive sins is given to the church as a whole and, at the same time, to its official representatives who have their mission from Christ.

(2) *History of Theology.* Throughout the varied history of the sacrament of reconciliation, the church has claimed the power to forgive sins; beginning in the Middle Ages it also has engaged in theological reflection on this power.

(3) *Church Teaching.* The Council of Trent teaches that the church has a real power to forgive and retain sins (DS 1703). Sacramental absolution given by a priest is an effective judicial act and not simply a ministry of pronouncing forgiveness (DS 1709).

(4) *Ecumenical Perspectives.* Even though the tradition of confessing to un-ordained monks made its appearance in the Eastern churches, there is no disagreement in principle with the Western Church on the reality of the church's power to forgive sins, except in regard to the strictly juridical definition of this power. The churches of the Reformation, on the other hand, do not ac-knowledge a power of the church to forgive sins. A dialogue on the subject would be possible only once the ministerial character (which does not ex-clude but requires authority) of the church's power to forgive sins were further clarified.

(5) *Systematic Reflections.* This last statement surely points to an important theological task of our day. The sacrament of reconciliation is a "judgment" in an analogous sense: it is a judgment springing from grace, a freely under-taken manifestation of sin that must be met by the comforting words of divine forgiveness, provided no serious obstacles stand in the way. In addition, the sacrament of reconciliation has to be seen in the context of other means of for-giveness (of nondeadly sins) that have been given to the church; not least of these is the Eucharist, but there is also the forgiveness of Christian by fellow Christian. These means, too, when properly understood, are exercises of the church's power to forgive sins.

See also CHURCH; SACRAMENT OF RECONCILIATION; SIN AND GUILT.

Bibliography
Fernández García, Domiciano. *The Father's Forgiveness: Re-thinking the Sacrament of Reconciliation.* Collegeville, Minn.: Liturgical Press, 1991.
Rahner, Karl. "Forgotten Truths concerning the Sacrament of Penance." In *Theological Investigations,* 2:135–74. New York: Crossroad, 1982.

GÜNTER KOCH

Foundations of Theology
Contemporary Issues

Several contemporary issues concerning the foundations of theology and theological method involve the nature of fundamental theology, the critique of foundationalism, the use of metaphors and models within theology, and the significance of social publics and their diverse criteria of truth and practice for theology.

Fundamental or Foundational Theology

The English translation of the Latin phrase *theologia fundamentalis* can be "fundamental theology" or "foundational theology." A different meaning has become attached to each. *Fundamental theology* is the traditional term that was used in neo-scholastic and neo-Thomist manuals. It was used to refer to a branch of theology sharply distinguished from dogmatic theology. In this neo-scholastic framework, dogmatic theology was based upon the teachings of the Catholic Church, and fundamental theology had as its prior task a threefold demonstration: the demonstration of the possibility of revelation, the demonstration of Christian revelation culminating with Christ as the divine legate, and, finally, the demonstration of the Catholic Church as divinely established. It was fundamental insofar as it provided a foundation through philosophical and historical arguments. It was a separate discipline comprising an apologetic philosophy of religion and a demonstration based on historical and exegetical evidence. As prior to dogmatic theology, it provided an independent foundation for it.

The term *foundational theology* refers to a discipline that is not as sharply separated from systematic theology and that relates much more integrally to other theological disciplines and to the faith of the believer. B. Lonergan's development of method in theology has contributed to a new view of foundational theology. His method in theology divides the various theological disciplines not according to different fields or subject matters, but rather according to diverse functional specialties. Foundational theology is a specific functional specialty dealing with the foundations of theology. It elaborates the horizon and standpoint in which religious affirmations have their meaning and value. On the basis of foundations, doctrinal theology selects from alternative formulations of doctrines, whereas systematic theology clarifies the meaning of doctrines. Lonergan relates foundational theology as a functional specialty to religious, moral, and intellectual conversion. Its direct religious affirmations provide the foundations for doctrines, systematics, and communications.

The Critique of Foundationalism

The critique of foundationalism refers to a criticism of certain conceptions of the basis of knowledge. This critique has its origins in North American pragmatic philosophy, especially in the work of C. S. Peirce, W. James, J. Dewey, and W. Sellars. Pragmatic philosophy criticizes Cartesianism as well as positivism for limiting knowledge to secure and certain foundations. Consequently they admit as knowledge only what can give absolute certitude independent of other considerations and standpoints. The pragmatic tradition argues, on the contrary, that knowledge is holistic. It is based not on an appeal to one but to many interrelated elements that need to be interpreted within the context of one another. Theologians influenced by this American pragmatic tradition have also drawn on hermeneutical theory that points to the interpretive nature of experience and to the role of horizons in the interpretation of tradition. They have thereby sought to develop a conception of theology and of the foundations of theology that is not "foundationalist."

The critique of foundationalism concerns the interpretation of the starting point or foundations of theology, be they biblical or experiential. Taking the critique of foundationalism seriously does not mean that one must assume there are no foundations or that in theology one should not appeal to the Scriptures or to religious experiences. Instead the critique suggests that such appeals to foundations do not involve transcendental or positivist foundations that are abstracted from historical conditioning and thereby produce clear-cut evidence and certitude. Rather, the foundations of theology are permeated with historically mediated language, symbols, and social structures.

The theologians seeking to incorporate the critique of foundationalism embrace a broad spectrum of theological opinion. Some use the critique of foundationalism to develop a narrative or confessional method of theology (R. F. Thiemann, W. C. Placher, M. L. Cook). Others, borrowing from L. Wittgenstein's notion of language-game, develop a notion of theology that stresses doctrines as cultural linguistic rules of a particular religious community rather than as expressions of religious experiences or as propositional objective affirmations (G. Lindbeck). Within the philosophy of religion, a "reformed epistemological" approach to religious knowledge interprets the belief in God as a basic belief rather than as a belief resting upon more basic evidence or apologetic reasons (see GOD: CONTEMPORARY ISSUES).

Foundational theology has also been conceived along the lines of a method of reflective equilibrium. This method, originally developed within American pragmatic theories of ethics, underscores that theological judgments entail taking into consideration and seeking to balance diverse elements in judgments open to revision. These elements include the interpretation of a tradition; background theories about human nature, the cosmos, and society; methods of interpretation; and retrodictive warrants drawn from contemporary experiences, practices, and communities of discourse (F. S. Fiorenza).

Models in Theology

North American theological reflection has focused much attention on the function of models in theology. Models have diverse uses. A model is illustrative insofar as it uses an image or visual component to illustrate in a readily imagined way a more abstract function. A model is, thereby, perspectival insofar as the visual image illustrates one aspect of the theory but does not point to other aspects. A model is also explanatory to the extent that it can synthesize diverse and contradictory material in a unified and comprehensible manner. For example, the model of organic growth enabled early nineteenth-century theologians to explain the development of doctrines in a way that reconciled discontinuity with identity. A model is also an analytical tool insofar as it allows one to show that a particular theological view or tradition is based upon a particular model and, therefore, has all its advantages and disadvantages.

Those who use a model must be aware of the limitations of the particular visual object, image, or metaphor underlying the model. The awareness of the limitations of models leads to a call for a pluralism of models, for it acknowledges that other models contribute important illustrative and explanatory perspectives. Within North American Roman Catholic theology, A. Dulles has used models to help understand the various theologies dealing with the church, revelation, ecumenism, and Christology. His analysis of the models of the church that have underlain diverse theological expositions of the church has made a significant and influential contribution to theology. These models are: church as an institution, mystical communion, herald, sacrament, servant, and disciple (see CHURCH: CONTEMPORARY ISSUES). Likewise, revelation has been interpreted diversely as doctrine, as history, as inner experience, as dialectical presence, as new awareness, and as a symbol. The use of models and metaphor has been a central issue within theological proposals for understanding religious language about God (see GOD: CONTEMPORARY ISSUES).

Another influential analysis is D. Kelsey's exposition of the models according to which the Scriptures have authority for diverse Christian communities and theologians. The Scriptures may be viewed as authoritative because they contain basic Christian doctrines; they express the key concepts of biblical theology; they recite God's saving acts in history; they narrate God's identity and agency; they contain images expressive of the divine mystery; and they reveal basic religious symbols expressing divine revelation. In addition, the Scriptures may be seen as the basic beginning or constitution of the church or in their emancipatory function for Christian community.

Pluralism and Publics in Theology

Theological pluralism concerning the foundations of theology is connected not only to diverse models but also with distinct publics. Theological disciplines can be related to distinct publics with their corresponding modes of argumentation and ethical and religious stances. Systematic theology relates to the social reality of the church and seeks to reinterpret the transformative potential of its religious texts and traditions. Practical theology relates to the public of particular social and political movements and displays its religious aspect. Fundamental theologies are concerned much more with the disciplines and criteria of discourse in the academy. D. Tracy's notion of "public" and social realities interprets fundamental theology (in a way that is closer to classic fundamental theology) as providing arguments that all persons, religious or not, can acknowledge as reasonable in principle. Fundamental theology develops the adequacy of truth claims concerning what constitutes argumentation as well as the criteria of claims to truth and meaning in the wider public and academy.

Bibliography

Cook, Martin L. *The Open Circle: Confessional Method in Theology.* Minneapolis: Fortress, 1991.

Dulles, Avery. *The Craft of Theology: From Symbol to System.* New York: Crossroad, 1992.

Fiorenza, Francis Schüssler. *Foundational Theology: Jesus and the Church.* New York: Crossroad, 1984.

Guarino, Thomas G. *Revelation and Truth: Unity and Plurality in Contemporary Theology.* Scranton, Pa.: University of Scranton Press, 1993.

Lindbeck, George A. *The Nature of Doctrine: Religion and Theology in a Postliberal Age.* Philadelphia: Westminster, 1984.

Lonergan, Bernard. *Method in Theology.* New York: Crossroad, 1972.

Maddox, Randy L. *Toward an Ecumenical Fundamental Theology.* Chico, Calif.: Scholars Press, 1984.

Placher, William C. *Unapologetical Theology: A Christian Voice in a Pluralistic Conversation.* Louisville: Westminster, 1989.

Tracy, David, *The Analogical Imagination.* New York: Crossroad, 1981.

FRANCIS SCHÜSSLER FIORENZA

Freedom. *Freedom* is the catchword in which all the needs, wishes, goals, and ideals of humanity today are brought together. Freedom, therefore, has also become a central concept in the theological interpretation of the Christian message of salvation. Here one must distinguish between the freedom *from exterior and interior forces* (liberation) and the freedom *of the will,* which is present with consciousness and reason. The freedom of the will must further be differentiated between *existential* freedom, in which the human person takes a fundamental stance either positively or negatively with regard to his or her existence, and freedom of *choice,* for example, regarding the choice of a job, a way of life, a place of residence. Which type of freedom is intended must therefore always be determined by the context.

(1) *Biblical Background.* When the word *freedom* is used in the Bible, the primary meaning is *liberation.* God liberates human beings, makes them free from exterior needs and inner anxieties. In the New Testament, this is primarily a question of the freedom from sin, freedom from personal guilt and from seductive powers. In a positive sense, freedom is then freedom for God, for love following the example of Jesus Christ. Freedom in judgment and ethical action can result only when it is based on these two meanings.

(2) *History of Theology.* In the Hellenistic cultural sphere, the Christian message of freedom was confronted with the belief in fate expressed in diverse philosophical and religious perspectives. In this situation the freedom of the will had to be emphasized theologically: it is the most precious initial gift of the Creator to human beings. In the West, this led to the first great dispute on the relationship between grace and freedom. The dominating influence of Augustine upon the Western history of theology had the effect that the theological understanding of freedom was unfolded primarily in the context of the doctrine of grace. The relationship between grace and freedom became the crucial theological point of the Reformation, and thus this question moved again into the center of Catholic theology. Only in the present century have the developmental psychological, social, and political aspects of human freedom been able to gain greater theological importance.

(3) *Church Teaching.* The Catholic Church has often defended the freedom of the human person against deterministic tendencies and protected this stance like a dogma (DS 3245). Yet several important consequences of this freedom — for example, freedom of conscience and of religious expression — were explicitly drawn only at Vatican II (*GS* 26, 41, 73; *DH*).

(4) *Ecumenical Perspectives.* Orthodox theology with its understanding of freedom as an indelible endowment from the Creator treats the contemporary ideal of freedom with greater ease than Western tradition. Due to the Augustinian and Reformed doctrinal disputes and to the confrontation with the emancipatory concept of freedom of the Enlightenment, the concept of freedom in the West has become so differentiated and multilayered that it is accessible only to experts. Thus, further conversation on this theme with the Orthodox Church is considered by many to be essential.

(5) *Systematic Reflections.* At the present moment, the most urgent problem consists in expressing theologically the connection between the psychosocial conditioning of freedom and the inner freedom that is experienced in faith in God. In this task, one has to consider both what unites Christian freedom with emancipatory freedom (liberation) and what distinguishes Christian freedom from this secular drive toward liberation. A simple separation between the two would endanger the practical significance of Christian faith; a simple identification would make Christian faith superfluous.

See also DECISION; GRACE; REDEMPTION AND LIBERATION.

Bibliography

Gilkey, Langdon. *Reaping the Whirlwind: A Christian Interpretation of History.* New York: Seabury, 1976.

Henrich, Dieter. *Aesthetic Judgment and the Moral Image of the World: Studies in Kant.* Stanford, Calif.: Stanford University Press, 1992.

Krieger, Leonard. *The German Idea of Freedom.* Chicago: University of Chicago Press, 1972.

GEORG LANGEMEYER

Future. The future, as compared with the past and the present, is time and reality still to come, which human beings face with hope and fear, and which, despite its fundamental inaccessibility, they can and must shape and organize.

(1) *Biblical Background.* Sacred Scripture speaks of the future in the perspective of faith and of hope in the fulfillment of the divine promises. In the Old Testament, Yahweh is the hope of the people (Jer 17:7). Yahweh reveals the divine name: "I am who I am" (Ex 3:14), as a description not of metaphysical essence but of God's active attitude to the chosen people. Israel's faith has its basis, therefore, in its experiences of God's great deeds in history. Hope is directed to the commitments and prophetic promises given by God. The bond uniting past and future is the fidelity of God. The model for the attitude of faith and hope is Abraham, who contrary to all earthly hope trusted in God's promises (Genesis 15). The New Testament likewise reaches back to Abraham as model of faith and hope; the Pauline letters attest to the new christological dimension (Rom 4:1f.; Gal 3:6f., 14). Because the risen Christ is the firstfruits of those who have fallen asleep (1 Cor 15:20), we who have been baptized and have received the gift of the Holy Spirit will also rise (Gal 5:5; see Rom 15:13). In the Synoptic tradition, the hope of an ideal future is found in the idea of the KINGDOM OF GOD, which has come inchoatively in Jesus and will appear in its fullness at the parousia of Christ. This conception of salvation as already given but also still to come obliges Christians to constant readiness and watchfulness (Mk 13:13). In Revelation the future that is brought on by God is described in apocalyptic images as a time of definitive salvation that will embrace the entire universe (Revelation 21).

(2) *History of Theology.* In the church's tradition the hope of an ideal future finds expression in various movements and ideas (APOCATASTASIS; CHILIASM; ESCHATOLOGY: CONCEPTIONS OF).

(3) *Church Teaching.* No explicit position has been taken by the church regarding the future, unless one interprets as such the magisterial statements regarding the movements just mentioned.

(4) *Ecumenical Perspectives.* On the ecumenical scene, the view taken of the future has become important especially in our century, when theologians in the various Christian confessions have presented approaches to hope that in many cases spring from an analysis of atheistic humanism.

(5) *Systematic Reflections.* A theological reflection on the future starts with the fact that the future is fundamentally relative to past and present. Any talk

of the future has *the present as its point of reference*, inasmuch as statements about the future interpret the present in relation to the future; statements about the future are meaningful only when they offer the possibility of preparing for it, entering into some relationship to it, and changing it. The main perduring influence in this area in contemporary discussion has been E. Bloch's philosophy of hope, which understands the human person as a "deficient being" who is marked by openness and a utopian function and whose drives are reflected in a "forward directedness." In their "anticipatory consciousness" human beings must establish utopias for themselves, that is, "desirable futures," and try to make these a reality by their future-oriented praxis. The theology of hope of J. Moltmann is to be understood as a direct response to Bloch's philosophy of the future. Moltmann understands the God of the Bible as the "Wholly Other" and the "Radical Changer," who has promised radical novelty and thus set no limits to human transcendence. The biblical God of the promise is a God of history who sweeps us along with God and who through the resurrection of Jesus Christ has given humanity a "hope against all hope." Christian obedience to mission consists in our changing ourselves and our conditions by anticipating the future of God and thus moving from the past into the future. Among Catholic theologians, K. Rahner, in particular, has distinguished between, on the one hand, an intraworldly future in the form of a utopia that human beings set before themselves as a goal that can be planned and is in principle attainable in history but is for any given age a future still to come, and, on the other, an absolute future in the form of a complete and transcendental consummation of the world that God brings about. In his "political theology," J. B. Metz demands that Christianity be deprivatized and politicized and that the orthodoxy of faith be continually "proven well-founded" in the orthopraxis of activity in the world that is directed to the final age. If it is to be a productive and aggressive eschatology, Christian hope must make it convincingly clear that it is capable of making the eschatological promises operative under the conditions of our present time and thereby validating them. Because of the "eschatological proviso" the activity of human beings in history is relativized, the commitment of those who hope is radicalized, and the hope of Christians becomes a liberating imperative. Christian reception of the Marxist analysis of society has produced, especially in Latin America, various approaches to a "theology of liberation"; in its legitimate forms this theology endeavors to spur action, based on the hope of the Bible, for the deliverance of human beings from their social distress.

See also ESCHATOLOGY; EXPECTATION OF AN IMMINENT END; HISTORY/ HISTORICITY; PAROUSIA; TIME.

Bibliography
Marty, Martin E. *The Search for a Usable Future.* New York: Harper and Row, 1969.
Moltmann, Jürgen. *The Future of Creation.* Philadelphia: Fortress, 1979.
———. *Theology of Hope.* New York: Harper and Row, 1975.

JOSEF FINKENZELLER

Gg

Glory of God. This concept means both (*a*) the divineness of the one God in God's now self-concealing, now self-disclosing self-communicatedness, and (*b*) acknowledgment of God's magnificence (also "beauty") as manifested in creation, redemptive history, and ultimately in Jesus Christ.

(1) *Biblical Background.* In the Old Testament, the notion of the glory of God is expressed mainly through the term *kabod* (from the verb *kbd* = to be weighty, momentous); the Septuagint usually renders it as *dóxa*. The revelatory element is fundamentally bound up with God's actions in God's creations. Yahweh acts in such a way that the divine glory cannot be "given" to any other (Is 48:9–11); Yahweh stands by the divine word in an incomparable manner; none among the gods might have produced works like those of Yahweh, who alone does wondrous things (Ps 86:8–10). The glory of God manifests itself sometimes in helping, sometimes in punishing (Lv 9:6, 23f.); it maintains its unreachable transcendence in the image of fire (Ex 24:17; 40:34f.); it fills "heaven and earth" (Is 6:3), creates astonishment in Israel and the people (Ex 15:1–3; Pss 18:28; 115:1), and allows itself to be seen by Ezekiel, at times as a heavenly vision (1:27f.), at times in the temple (9:3), and primarily in terms of the eschatological (43:3–5). The element of respectful acknowledgment can be found in many calls to give God glory (Is 24:14–16; Prv 3:9; Ps 86:9); not only do "the heavens declare the glory of God" (Ps 19:2), but every believer must give God thanks and "glorify" God's "name forever" (Ps 86:12). According to the Synoptics, reports of Jesus' miracles are frequently concluded with a reference to the glory of God or to God's glorification (Mt 9:8; 15:31; Lk 13:13; 17:15, 18). At Jesus' transfiguration, the *dóxa* shines forth as a phenomenon of light (Lk 9:31f.). Something similar occurs at the conversion of Saul (Acts 9:3). The Johannine Jesus speaks of a reciprocal glorification (*doxázein*) between the Father and the Son (Jn 13:31f.; 17:1–5). In Christ, as Word become flesh or as Son of the Father, the *dóxa* is visibly present (Jn 1:14). According to Paul, Christ is the "Lord of glory" (1 Cor 2:8), the living promise that our "lowly body" will one day be changed "to conform with his glorified body" (Phil 3:21). Human beings are to take part in the *dóxa* that is disclosed by God in Christ (Rom 8:18, 20, 30; 2 Cor 3:18; 4:4–6); in such action, that glory of God is concretized that then finds expression in manifold "doxologies" (Gal 1:5; Eph 3:21; Heb 13:20f.), in hymns (Rv 1:6; 5:12f.; 11:13), and in the genuinely Christian way of life (1 Cor 6:20; see Eph 1:6–14).

(2) *History of Theology.* The Fathers make the glory of God their theme in numerous texts of a doxological turn (*Didache* 8–10), in both a christological and a patrocentric context (*Mart. Pol.* 20f.; see *Barn.* 12:7; *1 Clem.* 19f.;

265

36:1–4; 45:7). Ignatius of Antioch wishes believers to respond to the God who glorifies them by glorifying God in turn (Ignatius, *Eph.* 2.2). According to ancient liturgical custom, glory is bestowed on God the Father "through Christ and the Holy Spirit" (Clement of Alexandria, *Quis dives* 42:2) or "through Christ in the Holy Spirit" (Origen, *De orat.;* Serapion, *Euchol.* 4). The glory of God is increasingly articulated with a view to God's triune nature (J. A. Jungmann, *LThK*² 3:535f.).

(3) *Church Teaching.* Vatican I affirmed: "Whoever denies that the world has been created for the glorification of God is to be excluded" (DS 3025).

(4) *Ecumenical Perspectives.* In Reformation tradition, J. Calvin is regarded as the one who made the "glory of God" the fundamental principle of his theology (similarly to the way that Ignatius of Loyola made it that of his spirituality). He wants the glory of God to become radiant again in the sight of the church (*OS* 1.37, 110, 161), and not be "transferred" to any creature, not even the SAINTS (*Inst.* 2.8.25). Believers glorify God by acknowledging God as their Father (ibid. 3.2.26, with reference to Mal 1:6).

(5) *Systematic Reflections.* Scholastic dogmatics distinguishes: (*a*) the "internal formal" glory of God: God's self-possession in knowledge and love (elaboration in trinitarian terms is often missing here); (*b*) the "external formal" glory of God, whose acknowledgment comes about through creatures; (*c*) the "internal fundamental" glory of God: the perfection of God, whose goodness presses for self-communication; and (*d*) the "external fundamental" glory of God: all instances of creaturely perfection.

See also GOD; TRINITY.

Bibliography
Balthasar, Hans Urs von. *The Glory of the Lord: A Theological Aesthetics.* San Francisco: Ignatius; New York: Crossroad, 1983.

ALEXANDRE GANOCZY

God. The word *God* immediately implies (at least today) the question of whether God exists. Theology, as the reflective study of God's self-disclosure, answers that question positively. It is, however, the task of theology to explain who is referred to by the word *God*. That is decisive for believers if they are to be sure that they believe in the "true" God and also for preaching the faith if God is to become universally recognizable as humanity's ultimate ground of meaning. Hence, the question of God is always related to some specific situation.

(1) *Biblical Background.* (*a*) Biblical thought proceeds from the assumption that the nature of God is not recognizable through the self-initiated efforts of abstract reason and that God must disclose God's self to human beings and their thinking. By recounting the history of creation and redemption, Holy Scripture renders this encounter accessible to the reader and becomes itself its vital center insofar as God's present action is still a choosing (which, since Jesus Christ, has entered upon its unsurpassable final stage). Biblical history thus

leads to a God who is at work throughout the *whole* of world-history and is also "encounterable" there. The biblical term *God* does not, therefore, express what is absolutely unknown in any other context. But it also does not express a "general" idea of God, one derived by abstraction from different religions and worldviews. For the Bible, God is quite concretely the "God of Abraham, Isaac, and Jacob" and (in the New Testament) the trinitarian God (as "Father of our Lord Jesus Christ"). Precisely for that reason, however, the Scriptures remain open to a philosophical conception of God (e.g., God as transcendent Other and indeed all-determining reality). Such a philosophical conception can be a helpful approach on the path to the Father of Christ. (*b*) Inasmuch as the Scriptures locate God within the concrete reality of our existence, they become the basic text for all statements about God. The Scriptures show that, prior to any rational search for a ground of the universe, God is always already *there* — not as one who is merely present, but as one who chooses, encounters, and communicates to God's creatures. Were God not always to meet humans half-way, humans could never encounter God. The original encounter is established from the start insofar as humans are made in the likeness of God (IMAGE OF GOD) (Gn 1:26–2:3; see THEOLOGICAL ANTHROPOLOGY [2]). The way that the Scriptures integrate humanity into creation and its history shows that God can never be found in independence of the one, universal history of the world and humanity. The Scriptures know, of course, that the reality of God is in fact spoken about only within a history of sin characterized by humanity's having entered into rivalry with God, attempting to suppress God's reality or to exploit that reality for its own purposes. Biblical history then recounts, in the history of the choosing of Israel and the history of the incarnation, the way that God wins (back) humanity through God's own free initiative. In this history, God exhibits the divine nature as a love that transcends all comprehension (1 Jn 4:8, 16; regarding the Old Testament, see, for example, Hosea 11): "God is love" is the basic statement about God that is made between all the lines in the Bible. But in that history, Holy Scripture also makes clear the fact, and the way, that God transcends the world. God's very self is love — this is illustrated biblically through the statements about the relations between Father, Son, and Spirit (TRINITY); thus God does not "need" the world, but is there, in freedom and enduring majesty, for the world. From this perspective, it becomes clear that God cannot be adequately conceived on the basis of the world, that is, as its ultimately necessary ground. As absolute love, God is the Ever-greater (see Jn 14:28), and yet God's incomparability does not restrict the communication of the divine love (this is the tenor of Romans; John 15). Worshiping God in freedom therefore confers incomparable dignity (see the basic structure of the Lord's Prayer; see also the Book of Revelation). (*c*) The concrete biblical history of redemption begins with election, promise, and liberation. It reaches its dramatic climax in the crucifixion of Jesus Christ. The Scriptures make visible a "pedagogical" intent on the part of God in the confusion of history, for history, in all its manifoldness, is a unity and totality that, on the one hand, confounds evolutionary explanation through qualitative breaches and, on the other hand, promotes awareness of God's fidelity. Thus the Bible does not give intellectual instruction about God but mediates experience of God out of the covenantal relationship between God and God's people. This is clearly shown in the foundational statement of monotheism in Dt 6:4f.: "The Lord is our God, the Lord alone! *Therefore,* you shall love the Lord, your God, with all your heart." God's divinity is experienced in love for God; the New Testament adds that Christ is the way to this God (Jn 14:6). God and the people of the covenant do not really stand in a relation of partnership: aside from the people's unfaithfulness, the relation is beyond comparison with all other human relationships because the people's love is wholly and utterly dependent on God. One can formulate the following structural law: the closer God is, the more God's incomparability (that is, God's divinity) does not pale but becomes clear. At the same time, this incomparability — which permits recognition of an "individual" God with "attributes" — does not imply an impenetrable and forbidding darkness, but is "good" for the world and human beings. Therefore the Genesis account of the origin of human history acquits God of any responsibility for the sin of humanity. (*d*) Within the history of the covenant, God's name *Yahweh* ("I am who I am" [Ex 3:14]) takes on fundamental significance: God *is there* as one who is there *for us.* In the Exodus passage, the God of deliverance (out of Egypt) is also identified with the God of the fathers (Abraham, Isaac, and Jacob). This identification constitutes Israel's distinctness from all other religions and cults (Canaan, Baal). It makes unambiguous acknowledgment of the "true" God necessary for Israel (see 1 Kings 18–19). This identification is also expressed in the ban on making images, which underscores the incomparability of Yahweh (who, incidentally, creates human beings in God's image). Israelite monotheism, based on the oneness of God, takes on a universal orientation at the moment when Israel's autonomy as a state is shattered; in captivity, Deutero-Isaiah proclaims in a universal sense: "Your God is king!" (Is 52:7). The prophetic message emphasizes that God is right when God passes judgment (Amos). Thus one can be intimidated before God and must fear God, but one need not be anxious, for the Old Testament discerns God's love and goodness even in divine anger. God remains faithful to God's creation and people when acting to defend the divine right. In this knowledge, pious persons in the Old Testament can put probing questions to God that, as in the case of Job, seem almost blasphemous — at those times, namely, when believers become aware that not all suffering can mean judgment as well, that evildoers triumph while believers are oppressed. They also come to experience that God is really faithful (Jb 19:27; Ps 73:23, 26). This becomes definitively experienceable in the New Testament from the perspective of Jesus' death on the cross. Belief in God then finds stability in the imitation of the Lord (a theme of Mark). Moreover, God's love for the poor and the weak also becomes visible here (1 Cor 1:27; Phil 2:6–11). It is an aspect of God's humble and, in the Son, virtually self-abasing love. In this context, poverty is a theological, and not a sociological, attribute, but

God's attachment to the lowly also has social implications for believers. (*e*) In the New Testament, Jesus' person, life, suffering, death, and resurrection impart a new quality to the basic Old Testament revelation of God's presence. God is now *present* in Jesus' relationship with God as his Father, a unique relationship (Mt 11:27; Jn 14:9). God appears both as the genuine Other to Jesus *and* as Father and Son really coinherent. New Testament PNEUMATOLOGY sees the Holy Spirit as mediating between this otherness and presence. Through the Spirit, God externalizes God's life into the Son and man Jesus; in him, one can recognize Jesus as the Son. Whoever, as a Christian, says *God*, refers to this event as a whole that is explicated in theology of the Trinity and of the incarnation. Thus we have the quintessence of the biblical teaching on God: God takes us up into God's own life and becomes, as transcendent God, in Jesus a participant in our human history. Exactly this is what Christians mean when they say *God*.

(2) *History of Theology.* In the history of theology, interest was initially concentrated on exploring the trinitarian mystery of God: How can one acknowledge the *one* God as Father, Son, and Spirit? Thereby, (Greek) philosophical understanding of God was critically integrated into the biblical conception of God. Later on, precisely the movement of philosophical thought constantly made the problem acute. The Enlightenment created a new situation insofar as it forced confrontation with theoretical ATHEISM. In the nineteenth century, rationalism and idealism firstly sought to reduce dogmatics to a rational discipline.

(3) *Church Teaching.* The basic teaching of the church about God is contained in the baptismal creed, which, following Mt 28:19, has a trinitarian structure. This creed is made more precise through the interpolations by the Councils of Nicea (DS 125) and Constantinople I (DS 150). The relationship between God and world was classically formulated at the Fourth Lateran Council (DS 800; ANALOGY). In view of the situation in modern times, Vatican I made explicit the profession of faith in God's existence, creatorship, and separateness from the world (DS 3001–3, 3021–25).

(4) *Ecumenical Perspectives.* Profession of faith in the triune God is part of that "basic consensus" among all Christian confessions by virtue of which they are not completely different from one another. This consensus does not preclude theological emphases peculiar to specific confessions, such as can be found in the pneumatology of the Eastern Church or in Lutheran "theology of the cross" (*theologia crucis*). A specifically Protestant perspective is given prominence by K. Barth, E. Jüngel, and J. Moltmann and a Catholic perspective by H. Urs von Balthasar and W. Kasper among others. For the Christian understanding of God, moreover, Judaism, with its monotheism, is not an archaeological foundation but a living root; to the extent that Islam also shares in this, its relation to Christianity is one of special kinship.

(5) *Systematic Reflections.* In contemporary theology, therefore, (*a*) the question about God has become the center of all areas of theological study in general. (*b*) Moreover, theology can only contribute to making God's self-

manifestation in the course of history, known through the Scriptures, audible and visible as contemporarily relevant redemptive activity; (c) God's manifestation is of ultimate concern even, and especially, to humans today; and (d) persons receive, to be sure, an answer to their profoundest questions. They need, however, to learn that the answer infinitely transcends their questions. Such an approach combines a theology of the Trinity (how God "exists" in God's self) and a theology of the incarnation, which understands the incarnation in the form of a theology of the cross (*theologia crucis*) as God's humble self-sacrifice. A tension therefore emerges in dealing with the tradition concerning the relationship between THEOLOGY and the possibility of a philosophical doctrine about God. One should sharply distinguish between them. One should resist the pressure to sunder the two, especially when one has grasped the *theological* nature of a synthesis such as occurs, for instance, in Thomas Aquinas. When, for example, Thomas understands God as "Being itself" (*ipsum esse subsistens*), he does not place philosophy over the God of revelation. For he thereby wants, on the one hand, to capture — although in a language drawn from philosophy — precisely the radical difference between God and world, which is simply not to be bridged by some notion of being that is formulatable from the human side. However, Thomas is, on the other hand, convinced that, from the side of God as Creator, a connection exists that is beyond human control but that humanity may, and must, accept as the self-goodness of God. In one of his profoundest thoughts, he states: "Thus God is not good because he causes good" (that is also held, for example, by neo-Platonism), "but rather goodness flows from him because he is good. As Augustine says ... because he is good, we exist" (*STh* 1, q. 13, a. 2). If the concept of "Being itself" (*ipsum esse subsistens*), which is intended to capture this, rests historically on a misinterpretation of Ex 3:14 ("I am who am"), then Thomas's interpretation correctly recovers the intended meaning ("I am who am there") in an astonishing way: God, in God's goodness, that is, in God's divinity, is the inscrutable but — since God is freely good — not groundless ground of all that can be: God's "being there" is what is first and last.

See also EXPERIENCE OF GOD; GOD: POSSIBILITY OF KNOWLEDGE OF; GOD: THEOLOGY OF; GOD'S GLORY; GOD'S ONENESS; LOVE; TRINITY: DOCTRINE OF THE.

Bibliography
Araya, Victorio. *God of the Poor: The Mystery of God in Latin American Liberation Theology.* Maryknoll, N.Y.: Orbis Books, 1988.
Balthasar, Hans Urs von. *The Glory of the Lord: A Theological Aesthetics.* San Francisco: Ignatius; New York: Crossroad, 1983.
Hankey, W. J. *God in Himself: Aquinas' Doctrine of God as Expounded in the "Summa Theologiae."* New York: Oxford University Press, 1987.
Kasper, Walter. *The God of Jesus Christ.* New York: Crossroad, 1984.
Lonergan, Bernard. *Philosophy of God, and Theology.* Philadelphia: Westminster, 1973.
McFague, Sallie. *Models of God: Theology for an Ecological, Nuclear Age.* Philadelphia: Fortress, 1987.

Rahner, Karl. *The Foundations of Christian Faith: An Introduction to the Idea of Christianity.* New York: Crossroad, 1978.
Thielecke, Helmut. *The Evangelical Faith.* Vol. 1. Grand Rapids: Eerdmans, 1974.

                                                                                        WILHELM BREUNING

God: Acts of. Theology reflects upon the acts of God from the viewpoint of God's love, freedom, and omnipotence.

(1) *Biblical Background.* Holy Scripture recognizes God, within experience-able reality, as the one "who gives life to the dead and calls into being what does not exist" (Rom 4:17). Thus it is established that God's action is a comprehensive whole that nevertheless always bears directly on the individual creature.

(2) *History of Theology.* In the history of theology, God's action, as such, tends to be taken for granted rather than subjected to direct reflection; and, when such reflection does occur, the focus is usually on isolated questions like the possibility and actuality of miracles. Of importance, however, is the insight — contributed to theology by Thomas Aquinas — that God, as the primary cause, does not act in addition to, nor in disregard of, secondary causes, but as an enduringly exerted creative force. In recent times, Teilhard de Chardin has taken up this idea: "God creates what is self-creative."

(3) *Church Teaching.* Church teaching has dealt with God's action mainly in the course of opposing pantheistic conceptions of God as the mere dynamics of the cosmos. Vatican I stressed God's personal *capacity* for action (DS 3002).

(4) *Ecumenical Perspectives.* The subject matter is not a matter of interconfessional controversy.

(5) *Systematic Reflections.* Theology will have to concentrate above all on the fact *that* God acts; *how* God acts remains as mysterious as God. Today, God's concrete governance of history needs to be made meaningful, that is, interpreted not mythically but from the perspective of the eschatology of both the resurrection of Jesus and the hoped-for resurrection of the dead. The meaningful categories for such an interpretation stem from Rom 4:17: God's action is always creative activity and implicitly — as is quite manifest in the raising of the dead — an ultimate self-communication of this God. All the concrete, particular aspects of God's action point back to this as the source of their meaning.

See also GOD; GOD: ATTRIBUTES OF; EXPERIENCE OF GOD; MIRACLE.

Bibliography
Burrell, David B. *Aquinas: God and Action.* Notre Dame, Ind.: University of Notre Dame Press, 1979.
Gilkey, Langdon. *Maker of Heaven and Earth.* Garden City, N.Y.: Doubleday, 1959.
Hodgson, Peter. *God in History: Shapes of Freedom.* Nashville: Abingdon, 1989.
Thomas, Owen C. *God's Activity in the World: The Contemporary Problem.* Chico, Calif.: Scholars Press, 1983.
Tracy, Thomas F. *God, Action, and Embodiment.* Grand Rapids: Eerdmans, 1984.

                                                                                        WILHELM BREUNING

God: Attributes of. The phrase *attributes of God* refers to predicates or statements about God that are concretely based on God's nature, the events of revelation, and the rules of analogy.

(1) *Biblical Background.* The Bible attributes both direct and indirect predicates of God. These predicates are in part negative, that is, those that negate any kind of limitation in God (e.g., nonfinitude), and in part positive, that is, those that inherently imply no limitation (e.g., magnificence or kindness). Such statements cannot be dismissed in advance as anthropomorphisms: wherever God's greatness and mystery are expressly reflected, God's "existence" also takes on concrete form for us.

(2) *History of Theology.* The doctrine of God's attributes was developed primarily in Scholasticism. Thomas Aquinas made the most profound argument for this theological mode of speaking: despite God's infinitude and transcendence, God is neither alien to nor remote from creation; God affirms the goodness of creation as expressing the reality of God's self that God has also imparted to creation in the act of creation (see *STh* 1, q. 13, a. 11). Scholastic theology denied any limitation or contingency of God. For in God all plenitude is "intermerged," whereas, in creation, it can be realized only as subject to temporal succession and spatial dispersion. Starting out from creation, Nicholas of Cusa, therefore, refers to a "coincidence of opposites" (*coincidentia oppositorum*) in God.

(3) *Church Teaching.* The Fourth Lateran Council drew up a list of important attributes of God (DS 800) that was later reasserted by Vatican I (DS 3001f.).

(4) *Ecumenical Perspectives.* There is no basic difference between the confessions in regard to the attributes of God. Nevertheless, conceptions of God, influenced by the diverse confessions, can still lead to certain forms of one-sidedness. Whereas Reformation theology, influenced by its nominalistic heritage, tends to emphasize especially the darker sides of divine power, Catholic theology is sometimes uncritical regarding metaphysical statements about God. On the other hand, the particular confessional conceptions of God bring a certain enrichment with them: Lutheran theology of the cross proclaims a God who is manifest in what is opposite to God; Orthodox theology emphasizes the magnificence of God and therefore gives prominence to the mystery of Easter.

(5) *Systematic Reflections.* Catholic theological reflection today combines biblical and Thomistic thought by explicating the attributes of God in such a way that God's LOVE becomes the unifying point and also the basis for the predication of many concrete attributes of God. The most important of God's attributes are outlined in the accompanying table.

See also ANALOGY; DISCOURSE ABOUT GOD; GOD; GOD: NAMES OF; GOD: THEOLOGY OF.

GOD'S ATTRIBUTES

Term	Explanation	Theological Significance	Sources
Eternity	The essential atemporality of God as the epitome of utmost relevance and innermost livingness	Statement about God's transcendence, which nevertheless encompasses the origin and future of God's creatures	Liturgies
Fidelity	The absolutely reliable affirmation of creatures through the love of God	Statement about the innermost core of the attitude of alliance on the part of God, who guides creation toward God's and its goal	Ex 34:6; 2 Cor 1:19; Eph 1:4
Graciousness	God's self-communication, out of love, to created reality	Statement about God's universal redemptive activity (GRACE)	Ex 33:19; 34:6; Rom 9–11
Hiddenness	The withdrawnness of God, which can be experienced painfully as God's self-withdrawal, but also joyfully as God's self-disclosing accessibility	Statement of particular relevance today in view of forgetfulness of God (GOD); it implies for believers the tasks of affirming God's apparent absence at the Son's cross as a way of God's love and bearing witness to this in their lives	Is 45:15; 55:8; Mt 11:25; Rom 12:33
Holiness	God's simultaneously fascinating and awe-inspiring divine being	Statement about God's innermost essence as sublime mystery	Is 6:3; Jn 17:11
Infinitude	Negatively, the exclusion of any limitedness; positively, an expression of God's infinite fullness of life	Statement about the unbounded and immemorially existent wealth of God's love	DS 3001
Invisibility	Establishment of the fact that God is not an object included in empirical reality	Statement about the reality of God as something not reachable by empirical means. It must be seen against the backdrop of New Testament theology: God appeared in Jesus Christ and can be recognized in him	Ex 33:18–23; 1 Tm 6:11; DS 800, 3001
Magnificence	Designation of God as the source of all goodness, truth, and beauty; it is the basis of the "splendor" that God's creation has	Statement about the cause of the happiness that God wants to bestow on God's creatures. As shown by the glorification of God through Jesus' death on the cross, it remains recognizable even in suffering	Ex 19:12; 33:21f.; Jn 17:1–8; 2 Cor 3:4–4:6
Mercifulness	God's inexhaustible love for weak and sinful humans	Statement about the faithfulness of God, who never abandons God's creatures and is committed on their behalf all the way to the point of self-sacrifice	Ex 34:6; Rom 9–11; tenor of Jesus' preaching
Omnipotence	Sign of the fact that God is so much the all-determining reality that God's activity is always tied to divine love	Statement about God's absolute independence, which has shown itself in the death and resurrection of Jesus Christ as a way of guiding the world that is aimed at the well-being of humanity	General tenor of the biblical interpretation of the world and history, symbols

Term	Explanation	Theological Significance	Sources
Omnipresence	God's independence, superiority, and nearness to created reality both as a whole and in particular	Statement about the freedom of God, who is at the same time both wholly self-contained and present to creatures	Ex 3:14; Ps 139
Omniscience	Mod of God's knowledge in relation to God's own nature and in relation to the world and history	Statement about the benevolent guidance of God under which the freedom of (free) creatures is not limited but included	Jb 34:21f.; Pss 7:9; 139; Jer 11:20; Wis 1:7; Rom 11:33–36; DS 3001, 3003
Righteousness	Illust nature of God's will in outward morally in which, in judicious God humans just	Statement about God's concern for his creatures, in which as the justifying God, he sent his Son to the cross	Rom 1–11; DS 1579
Unchangeability	The will of God as thing that faithful its remaining to itself and cannot be threatened by any power	Statement about God's fidelity in relation to creation — despite all his weakness and lowliness	DS 800, 3001
Wisdom	The fullness of God's power of knowledge and its exercise, which is distinguished by its directedness toward the concrete and its ability to see the concrete within the whole and to perceive the whole concretely	Statement of God's loving activity in creation, in history which is concentrated as wisdom in Jesus Christ, the crucified and the resurrected (1 Cor 1:24)	Jb 28:19; Pss 8; Prv 1 Wis 7 18, Sir 1:1, Heb 1:3
Wrath	It does not mean the "reverse side" of God's love, but rather, the terror and intensity of the faithfulness included in God's love	Statement of the innermost self-affectedness of God's love for God's creatures (JUDGMENT; HELL)	Amos

Bibliography

Carman, John. *Majesty and Meekness: A Comparative Study of Contrast and the Concept of God.* Grand Rapids: Eerdmans, 1994.

Funkenstein, Amos. *Theology and the Scientific Imagination from the Middle Seventeenth Century.* Princeton, N.J.: Princeton University Press, 1986.

Haughton, Rosemary. *The Passionate God.* New York: Paulist, 1981.

Morris, Thomas V. *Our Idea of God: An Introduction to Philosophical Theology.* Downers Grove, Ill.: Inter-Varsity Press, 1991.

Ward, Keith. *Images of Eternity: Concepts of God in Five Religious Traditions.* Darton, Longman, and Todd, 1987.

Wierenga, Edward R. *The Nature of God: An Inquiry into Divine Attributes.* Cornell University Press, 1989.

Wippel, John F. *Thomas Aquinas on the Divine Ideas.* Toronto: Medieval Studies, 1993.

GOD'S ATTRIBUTES

Term	Explanation	Theological Significance	Sources
Eternity	The essential atemporality of God as the epitome of utmost relevance and innermost livingness	Statement about God's transcendence, which nevertheless encompasses the origin and future of God's creatures	Liturgies
Fidelity	The absolutely reliable affirmation of creatures through the love of God	Statement about the innermost core of the attitude of alliance on the part of God, who guides creation toward God's and its goal	Ex 34:6; 2 Cor 1:19; Eph 1:4
Graciousness	God's self-communication, out of love, to created reality	Statement about God's universal redemptive activity (GRACE)	Ex 33:19; 34:6; Rom 9–11
Hiddenness	The withdrawnness of God, which can be experienced painfully as God's self-withdrawal, but also joyfully as God's self-disclosing accessibility	Statement of particular relevance today in view of forgetfulness of God (GOD); it implies for believers the tasks of affirming God's apparent absence at the Son's cross as a way of God's love and bearing witness to this in their lives	Is 45:15; 55:8; Mt 11:25; Rom 12:33
Holiness	God's simultaneously fascinating and awe-inspiring divine being	Statement about God's innermost essence as sublime mystery	Is 6:3; Jn 17:11
Infinitude	Negatively, the exclusion of any limitedness; positively, an expression of God's infinite fullness of life	Statement about the unbounded and immemorially existent wealth of God's love	DS 3001
Invisibility	Establishment of the fact that God is not an object included in empirical reality	Statement about the reality of God as something not reachable by empirical means. It must be seen against the backdrop of New Testament theology: God appeared in Jesus Christ and can be recognized in him	Ex 33:18–23; 1 Tm 6:11; DS 800, 3001
Magnificence	Designation of God as the source of all goodness, truth, and beauty; it is the basis of the "splendor" that God's creation has	Statement about the cause of the happiness that God wants to bestow on God's creatures. As shown by the glorification of God through Jesus' death on the cross, it remains recognizable even in suffering	Ex 19:12; 33:21f.; Jn 17:1–8; 2 Cor 3:4–4:6
Mercifulness	God's inexhaustible love for weak and sinful humans	Statement about the faithfulness of God, who never abandons God's creatures and is committed on their behalf all the way to the point of self-sacrifice	Ex 34:6; Rom 9–11; tenor of Jesus' preaching
Omnipotence	Sign of the fact that God is so much the all-determining reality that God's activity is always tied to divine love	Statement about God's absolute independence, which has shown itself in the death and resurrection of Jesus Christ as a way of guiding the world that is aimed at the well-being of humanity	General tenor of the biblical interpretation of the world and history, symbols

Term	Explanation	Theological Significance	Sources
Omnipresence	God's independence, superiority, and nearness to created reality both as a whole and in particular	Statement about the freedom of God, who is at the same time both wholly self-contained and present to creatures	Ex 3:14; Ps 139
Omniscience	Mode of God's knowledge in relation to God's own nature and in relation to the world and history	Statement about the benevolent guidance of God under which the freedom of (free) creatures is not limited but increased	Jb 34:21f.; Pss 7:9; 139; Jer 11:20; Wis 1:7; Rom 11:33–36; DS 3001, 3003
Righteousness	Inner quality of God's will in its outward activity, through which, in judicious love, God makes humans just	Statement about God's concern for his creatures, in which, as the justifying God, he commits his Son to the cross (JUSTIFICATION)	Rom 1–11; DS 1529
Unchangeability	The will of God as something that remains absolutely true to itself and cannot be threatened by any power	Statement about God's free dedication to creation — despite all its weaknesses and sinfulness	DS 800, 3001
Wisdom	The fullness of God's power of knowledge and its exercise, which is distinguished by its directedness toward the concrete and its ability to see the concrete within the whole and to perceive the whole concretely	Statement of God's loving activity in creation, especially in history, which is concentrated as wisdom in Jesus Christ as the crucified and the resurrected (1 Cor 1:24)	Jb 28:1–19; Prv 8; 1 Cor 1–2; 2 Cor 3–18; Col 1:15; Heb 1:3
Wrath	This does not mean the "reverse side" of God's love, but rather, the fervor and intensity of the faithfulness included in God's love	Statement of the innermost self-affectedness of God's love for God's creatures (JUDGMENT; HELL)	Amos

Bibliography

Carman, John. *Majesty and Meekness: A Comparative Study of Contrast and Harmony in the Concept of God.* Grand Rapids: Eerdmans, 1994.

Funkenstein, Amos. *Theology and the Scientific Imagination from the Middle Ages to the Seventeenth Century.* Princeton, N.J.: Princeton University Press, 1986.

Haughton, Rosemary. *The Passionate God.* New York: Paulist, 1981.

Morris, Thomas V. *Our Idea of God: An Introduction to Philosophical Theology.* Downers Grove, Ill.: InterVarsity Press, 1991.

Ward, Keith. *Images of Eternity: Concepts of God in Five Religious Traditions.* London: Darton, Longman, and Todd, 1987.

Wierenga, Edward R. *The Nature of God: An Inquiry into Divine Attributes.* Ithaca, N.Y.: Cornell University Press, 1989.

Wippel, John F. *Thomas Aquinas on the Divine Ideas.* Toronto: Pontifical Institute of Mediaeval Studies, 1993.

WILHELM BREUNING

God

Contemporary Issues

Several important issues are at the center of theological reflections about God in the North American and European contexts. Five of these are: the foundations of the religious knowledge of God or apologetic structure of belief in God; the transcendental approach to the philosophy of God; the nature of God's being within process theism; the significance of metaphorical language about God; and the social context and political consequence of God-language.

Apologetic Structure of the Belief in God

The term *Reformed epistemology* refers to an approach to religious knowledge that seeks to develop the heritage of the Protestant Reformation, especially that of J. Calvin. At the forefront is a group of Christian philosophers of religion (among whom A. Plantinga is the most notable) who seek to relate their Calvinist heritage to contemporary philosophical criticism of foundationalism (see FOUNDATIONS OF THEOLOGY: CONTEMPORARY ISSUES). This Reformed approach to religious knowledge examines what counts as a foundation for the knowledge of God and takes issue with evidentialist objections to the belief in God. Such evidentialist objections argue, first, that belief in God is unreasonable or irrational if insufficient reason or evidence exists for it. It argues that unless one has good reasons for belief in God, one should give up such a belief. However, it argues, second, for a very narrow and empiricist understanding as to what constitutes a good reason or proper evidence for God's existence. Such a position is foundationalist to the extent that it limits knowledge to what is based on the foundations of clear evidence.

In response, A. Plantinga has criticized the foundation of such evidentialist approaches and has proposed that belief in God is a *basic belief* because to some extent it is not based upon other evidence. Most believers do not come to their belief in God via apologetic arguments. Moreover, their belief in God as a basic belief has a greater stability than other arguments. Such a basic belief in God is not simply a belief that God exists but is a belief about God's presence and action. Such experiences of God's presence and action constitute the basic belief in God, and as such it has a certain independence of apologetic defenses or argumentative demonstrations of God's existence. Nevertheless, the demonstration that the belief in God is a basic belief is not the same as demonstrating that the belief in God is true. The Reformed approach to religious knowledge asks: What constitutes proper criteria for a basic belief? Such criteria should not be automatically identified with such foundationalist criteria as self-evidence or incorrigibility. Instead they should emerge inductively from below through examples. Roman Catholic theological responses raise the issue of the relation of this Reformed tradition to traditional Roman Catholic natural theology and to the affirmation of Vatican I concerning the demonstration of God's existence. On the one hand, Roman Catholic theology has a more internalist and communitarian view of belief as a virtue. On the other hand, the medieval view relates faith and knowledge much more integrally to one another than neo-scholasticism did; this is because of the latter's sharp distinction between the natural and supernatural (which it owed more to the Enlightenment than to Thomas Aquinas). The more classical understanding is retrieved by K. Rahner. He shows that some existential preapprehension or preunderstanding of the transcendent must underlie the traditional proofs of God's existence if these are to be intelligible and understandable. His own approach develops motifs similar to Bonaventure's approach.

Transcendental Philosophy of God

The transcendental approach to the question of God explores the relation between human knowing, willing, and deciding and religious experience. This approach is evident in the writings of K. Rahner, a German theologian, and B. Lonergan, a Canadian theologian. Both link the dynamism of the human intellect and the question of God. Rahner underscores that analogous language about God should not be understood as a midpoint between the univocal and equivocal use of language, but as language that expresses a much more fundamental transcendental experience, and the transcendental experience is the basis of human language about God. Lonergan connects the question of God with questions of intelligence, deliberation, reflection, and religious experience. In addition to the interpretation of analogous language in relation to focal metaphors, D. Tracy has sought to explore the significance of mystical experience for the interpretation and understanding of God as triune within the Christian tradition.

Process Theism

Whereas the justification of the belief in God is at the center of Reformed epistemology, the nature of God is the focal point of process philosophy and theology. Leading process philosophers A. N. Whitehead (1861–1947) and C. Hartshorne (b. 1897) suggest that the major weakness of traditional theism lies in the inadequacy of its idea of God. Traditional theism used the categories of substance to talk of God. Instead, process theology proposes the categories of event, actuality, or process. Process theology proposes a "bipolar" concept of God that points to a duality in the nature of God in contrast to the emphasis on the divine simplicity or immutability within classical theism. However, Whitehead and Hartshorne understand this bipolar theism differently. Whitehead distinguishes between a primordial and a consequent nature of God. The primordial nature refers to God's creative activity, whereas the consequent nature refers to God's response to worldly events and actualities. Hartshorne distinguishes between the abstract essence (which refers to God as eternal and absolute) and God's concrete actuality that is temporal and relative to worldly decisions and actualities.

Process theism seeks to reaffirm God's presence and activity within the world by rethinking God's agency within the world and to make conceptions of God compatible with science. Process theology reconceives divine causality insofar as it proposes that God's causality should not be understood so much as an external intervening cause, but rather as an aspect of events. God acts and is efficacious in the world in a way that worldly events include God's activity within them. An example of this divine activity is the experience of God's grace in which God is a part of an experience calling us forward. The divine causality entails the internalization of the antecedent by the consequent.

Within North America, there are many diverse interpretations and conceptions of process theism. Leading North American process theologians are J. Cobb, S. Ogden, D. Griffin, M. Suchocki, C. Keller, and L. Ford. Among Roman Catholic theologians, J. Bracken, E. Cousins, and B. M. Lee have appropriated process categories.

Metaphorical Language about God

The shift from reflective and transcendental to linguistic and metaphorical approaches characterizes several important North American contributions to the God-question. This shift represents an important change within theology. Modernism and liberalism considered the experiential to be foundational and language, metaphors, and doctrinal statements to be secondary and derivative, as mere expressions of more basic religious experience. Modernists often claimed that the linguistic elements (metaphors, doctrines, etc.) could be easily interchanged or revised as long as the root experience remained the same.

Recent hermeneutical and linguistic studies have shown that language and experience as well as image and concept are intrinsic to one another. They cannot simply be exchanged as if they were clearly separable. Image and language constitute specific experiences just as specific experiences constitute diverse images and concepts. The result is a new evaluation of metaphorical language. A traditional claim has been that analogical language is properly predicated of God as a transcendental language, whereas metaphorical language is always improper in reference to God. In contrast, it is now noted that since God's goodness is proportionate to God's being, and we do not know God's being, then goodness is metaphorically asserted of God. Moreover, recent analysis contests the traditional devaluation of metaphor to an improper use of language or mere linguistic or poetic embellishment. Instead of understanding metaphors as linguistic conventions used inappropriately, that is, as belonging properly in one context but used in another, some scholars today understand metaphor in its basic and root character as an "unsubstitutionable" image that provides us with a surplus of meaning and that cannot be reduced to some experience.

Where there cannot be a direct description, a metaphor illumines. It serves less as an identity assertion than as an account. To say God is father or God is mother is not to give an essential definition or identity, but to propose indirect language that suggests ways of God's relationship to humans. Where a metaphor gains permanence, it becomes a model, so that a model is a metaphor with stability, permanence, and scope that patterns a particular language about God. There are metaphors from the political realm (king, rule, lord), from personal life (mother, father, friend, lover), from professional roles (builder, baker, shepherd, and counselor), and from the world of nature (light, breath, spirit, ground, depth, force, and energy).

The pluralism and significance of metaphors impact upon the task of theology. It has the function of assessing the limits and potential of traditional metaphors. It seeks to develop metaphors from contemporary individual and social experience both to express and to illumine the Christian faith. The relevance of metaphors and models as applicable to the language about God consists in their ability to illumine the Christian faith and human experience of God. S. McFague has proposed mother, friend, and lover as nonsexist metaphors for God, arguing that such metaphors can link our language about God to basic human relations. The metaphor of the world as God's body serves to heighten an ecological awareness in which nature is not looked upon solely as an object of human domination. Within Roman Catholic feminist theology this sensitivity to metaphorical language has influenced the interpretation of God and of the doctrine of the Trinity. R. Ruether has criticized sexist language, imagery, and conceptions of God and has sought in her more recent work to develop the significance of the metaphor of Gaia. E. Schüssler Fiorenza has developed the significance of Sophia for creation as well as Christology. E. Johnson has shown how traditional views of the incomprehensibility of God and traditional analogical language do not justify the use of exclusively male language for God. Her interpretation of the Trinity has explored the appropriation of multifaceted metaphorical language for each person of the Trinity.

Social and Political Consequence of God-Language

Emphasis on the social context and political consequence of religious metaphors, symbols, and ideas has a long tradition within North American theology. S. Mathews and S. Jackson Case, representatives of the Chicago school at the turn of the century, emphasized the social context of theology. Mathews analyzed Christian history and tradition in terms of distinct social mind-sets and thereby showed the interrelation between Christian images and conceptions of God. In the last two decades, the influence of political and liberation theologies has increased. The social and political significance of the ideas of God has been underscored by African-American theology, womanist theology, and Latin American liberation theology (and by North American Roman Catholic theologians influenced by Latin American liberation theology). A classic and influential book of African-American theology is J. Cone's *A Black Theology of Liberation*. Written when the death-of-God theologies proclaimed the demise of the Christian God and the beginning of a post-Christian era, Cone's book pointed to the emancipatory presence of God and the vitality of belief in God within the communities of oppressed African-American Christians. Such a theology, however, entails a reconception of God as black. Blackness is not only a physiological trait of black people but also an *ontological* symbol for those participating in the liberation of oppressed humans. The God present and active in the lives, stories, and history of oppressed communities is therefore black. D. S. Williams develops a womanist perspective, that is, one of African-American women and their experience of oppression and struggle for emancipation. Within Latin American liberation theology, J. L. Segundo and V. Araya explicate the relation between the understanding of God and liberation theology.

Bibliography

Bracken, Joseph A. *Society and Spirit: A Trinitarian Cosmology.* Selinsgrove, Pa.: Susquehanna University Press, 1991.

Cobb, John B., and David Ray Griffin. *Process Theology: An Introductory Exposition.* Philadelphia: Westminster, 1976.

Cobb, John B., and David Tracy. *Talking about God: Doing Theology in the Context of Modern Pluralism.* New York: Seabury, 1983.

Cone, James H. *A Black Theology of Liberation.* Twentieth anniversary edition. Maryknoll, N.Y.: Orbis Books, 1990.

Delaney, Cornelius F. *Rationality and Religious Belief.* Notre Dame, Ind.: University of Notre Dame Press, 1979.

Evans, C. Stephen, and Merold Westphal. *Christian Perspectives on Religious Knowledge.* Grand Rapids: Eerdmans, 1993.

Johnson, Elizabeth. *She Who Is.* New York: Crossroad, 1993.

Ruether, Rosemary. *Sexism and God-Talk.* Boston: Beacon, 1983.

Tracy, David. "God." In *Systematic Theology: Roman Catholic Perspectives,* ed. Francis Schüssler Fiorenza and John Galvin, 1:131–48. Minneapolis: Fortress, 1992.

Williams, Dolores S. *Sisters in the Wilderness: The Challenge of Womanist God-Talk.* Maryknoll, N.Y.: Orbis Books, 1993.

Zagzebski, Linda, ed. *Catholic Response to Reformed Epistemology.* Notre Dame, Ind.: University of Notre Dame Press, 1993.

FRANCIS SCHÜSSLER FIORENZA

God: Fatherhood of. In the *history of religion,* the idea of God's fatherhood appears in the sense of an originative relationship along the lines of natural begetting or of a caretaking role comparable to that of the father of a family. The *Christian* acknowledgment of God the Father Almighty has its basis absolutely in Christ the Son. Here, "God's fatherhood" refers to the propriety, in doctrine of the Trinity, that enables the first divine person to be the "Father of Our Lord Jesus Christ."

(1) *Biblical Background.* Biblical teaching on creation contradicts the idea of a natural-procreative connection between God and any creature: thus, for example, the king is not "God's son" by descent, but through enthronement (Psalms 2; 45; 89). Still, the Old Testament does recognize a fatherly attitude on the part of God, which is grounded in God's free, loving devotion to God's people and is intimately connected with God's act of choosing them. Jesus' proclamation develops this strand further. At the same time, however, the New Testament establishes the substance of God's fatherhood on a decisively new basis when that concept is used both to designate Jesus' unique, exclusive position in relation to God and to refer back to its ultimate ground. Concretely, God's fatherhood consists first in God's relation to the Son, who — as theology later interprets the preexistence statements in the New Testament — therefore belongs to the very essence of God. With that, however, God's fatherhood is no longer explained primarily by analogy to human fatherhood, but, vice versa, "every" fatherhood has its origin in God (Eph 3:15): the fatherhood that has its trinitarian basis in the relation between the Father and Son is expanded soteriologically. Creation, as a creation in the image of God, has the Son as its goal, and thereby participates in Christ's sonship (Rom 8:29). By way of analogies based on human life, Holy Scripture also contains, alongside statements about God's being the Father, some that readily attribute *motherliness* to God: God is like a nursing mother (Is 49:15), who shows for God's people a love like that of a mother for her child (Hos 11:1–4); God comforts like a mother (Is 66:13); and God appears as a midwife (Is 66:9).

(2) *History of Theology.* The theology of the East in general, and in the West especially Richard of St. Victor and Bonaventure, elucidate the intratrinitarian relationships along the lines that the originlessness of the Father encompasses the Son and the Holy Spirit as proceeding from him. The image of God as Father tended to support representations that depicted God as male, even though the core of intrabiblical theology had the merit to have excluded from God any sexual attributes. At present, feminist theology contests such images and all their implications.

(3) *Church Teaching.* On God's fatherhood in the sense relevant to trinitarian theology, see the article TRINITY: DOCTRINE OF THE. In recent official statements, cautious mention is also being made of God's "motherliness" (John Paul I).

(4) *Ecumenical Perspectives.* All Christians today are united in acknowledging God as Father, in terms of the christological grounding of God's fatherhood.

In the doctrines of the Trinity and of creation, theology cannot dispense with the relational aspects of God, both within God's life and outwardly, that are addressed in the image of God's fatherhood.

(5) *Systematic Reflections.* More decisively than ever before, however, theology should point out today that human fatherhood, as a model of interpersonal relationships, is invalidated if it is used — no matter on what plane — to sanction unbalanced and distorted social relationships. God's fatherhood has no analogies to the sexuality of human fatherhood (nor to any patriarchal ideas that follow from that); rather, it is an image of God's total and radical love, which, in the sphere of human relationships, is reflected just as much in motherliness as in fatherliness.

See also ANTHROPOLOGY: CONTEMPORARY ISSUES; GOD; HUMAN PERSON: IMAGE OF; TRINITY; TRINITY: DOCTRINE OF THE.

Bibliography
Daly, Mary. *Beyond God the Father.* Boston: Beacon, 1973.
Hamerton-Kelly, Robert. *God the Father: Theology and Patriarchy in the Teaching of Jesus.* Philadelphia: Fortress, 1979.
Metz, Johann Baptist, and Edward Schillebeeckx, eds. *God as Father?* Vol. 143 of *Concilium.* New York: Seabury, 1981.
Moltmann-Wendel, Elisabeth, and Jürgen Moltmann. *God: His and Hers.* New York: Crossroad, 1991.
Rahner, Karl. "Theos in the New Testament." In *Theological Investigations,* 1:79–149. Baltimore: Helicon, 1961.

WILHELM BREUNING

God: Mystery of. The notion of the mystery of God expresses that for believers God is a mystery. This quality of mystery is not, however, negative, as a barrier to knowledge, but positive, as a divine quality.

(1) *Biblical Background.* A basic idea in Holy Scripture is that God's intrinsic glory, as love's yes to itself, does not admit of ultimate grounding, nor does it have need of any. At the same time, it realizes that there is room in God's love for a free "yes" to God's creatures (see 2 Cor 1:19f.). In the New Testament, the term *mystérion* (mystery) becomes an expression of God's nongroundable "yes" to God's Son, which also contains the will to provide him with many brethren (Eph 1:4–9; Rom 8:29). Thus the "mystery of Christ" contains the whole fullness of the mystery of God (Col 2:2f.; see in this connection also 1 Corinthians 1; 2). For humans, therefore, the mystery of God does not imply a deficiency of knowledge that ought to be overcome; instead, it expresses the divine being of God.

(2) *History of Theology.* In this sense, tradition teaches something that Anselm of Canterbury formulates as follows: human beings intellectually and profoundly "comprehend" that God is incomprehensible (*Monolog.* 64).

(3) *Church Teaching.* This incomprehensibility (*incomprehensibilitas*) of God is a basic tenet of Christian belief as the Fourth Lateran Council and Vatican I have both asserted (DS 800, 3001).

(4) *Ecumenical Perspectives.* The notion of the mystery of God has special prominence in Orthodox theology.

(5) *Systematic Reflections.* As opposed to intellectualistic reduction of the mystery to that which is not (yet) known, current theology emphasizes the inner positivity of the notion (K. Rahner). This can be illustrated by means of personal analogies: personal "knowing" does not strive to "see through" the other, but aims at "recognizing" the lovingly affirmed uniqueness of the other. Through that, the mystery of the personal encounter is not diminished, but rather, better understood in its infinitude. Similarly, believing communion with God through Christ in the Holy Spirit confers a deeper grasp of God as the irresolvable mystery.

See also EXPERIENCE OF GOD; GOD: POSSIBILITY OF KNOWLEDGE OF; MYSTERY OF FAITH.

Bibliography
Jüngel, Eberhard. *God as the Mystery of the World: On the Foundation of the Theology of the Crucified One in the Dispute between Theism and Atheism.* Grand Rapids: Eerdmans, 1983.
Kasper, Walter. *The God of Jesus Christ.* New York: Crossroad, 1984.
Kaufman, Gordon. *God as Mystery.* Cambridge, Mass.: Harvard University Press, 1993.
Louth, Andrew. *Discerning the Mystery: An Essay on the Nature of Theology.* Oxford: Clarendon Press, 1983.
Rahner, Karl. "The Concept of Mystery in Catholic Theology." In *Theological Investigations,* 4:36–73. New York: Crossroad, 1974.

WILHELM BREUNING

God: Names of. The topic of God's names constitutes the theological problem of how one can appropriately speak about God at all.

(1) *Biblical Background.* In antiquity, a name was generally not, as for us, just an external designation. Instead, it evoked the essence and function of the person named. Therefore, in the Bible the names for God play a significant role. Fundamental is the knowledge that humans cannot, and may not, make for themselves an image of God (e.g., Ex 20:4f.), but that humans have been created in God's image (Gn 1:26). Thus the unnameable God can — even if imperfectly — be named. That also enables God to be addressed and worshiped. In the Old Testament, then, various names for God do, in fact, occur: the pan-Semitic *'el* (the strong one, the master), *'elohim* (as a plural intensive to express divine power), *'adonai* (lord), and *melek* (king). Above all, however, *Yahweh* is the authentic characterization, in a name, of God's essence (Ex 3:14): God is the one who is there, in free devotedness, for God's people. From the time of the later texts in the Old Testament, an increasing reluctance to name God can be detected (Esther; 1 Maccabees no longer contains the word *God*). Late Judaism employs as a substitute *heaven* or *the power*, or makes use of passive constructions. The New Testament sees the development of *Father* as a name for God: it is found already in the Old Testament, but only in relation to Israel (e.g., Ex 4:22f.; Dt 8:5) or to the royal house of David (2 Sam 7:14). The

name *Father* now becomes an expression of Jesus' unique relationship to God (Mt 11:27; Mk 14:36; and frequently elsewhere), but also a name for God that we, together with Jesus, can use to worship and address God: God is *our* Father (Mt 6:9 par.). The prominent use of this name by Jesus is just as much a reference to the trinitarian essence of God as is the circumstance that the New Testament attributes the name *Kyrios* (Lord) to Jesus himself: Kyrios is the term used to translate the name *Yahweh* in the Septuagint.

(2) *History of Theology.* In the history of theology, the problems surrounding God's names are considered primarily by Dionysius the Areopagite. In explicating a negative THEOLOGY, he teaches that the authentic name for God is "the Unnameable." In the Middle Ages, Thomas Aquinas takes up this idea again. The proposition stimulates him to formulate his doctrine of analogy. The nameless God is, to be sure, incomprehensible and incomparable; yet, since God has entered into creation, we can know and thus — even if not adequately — name God. Aquinas interprets Ex 3:14 ontologically: God is the one who exists absolutely (*ipsum esse subsistens*). Nonetheless, Thomas also recognizes God's relatedness to the world: this is founded in God's PROVIDENCE.

(3) *Church Teaching.* Vatican II teaches that there is, among all peoples, a certain perception and recognition of a concealed divine power that is named and expressed in myths, philosophical conjectures, dogmas, and rules for living (*NA* 2).

(4) *Ecumenical Perspectives.* A common profession of faith in the God and Father of our Lord Jesus Christ binds all Christians together spiritually. In many points there is a common theological terminology, which ultimately rests on the biblical understanding of God's name that provides a basis of ecumenical dialogue.

(5) *Systematic Reflections.* Determining the correct nature of DISCOURSE ABOUT GOD on the basis of biblical symbolical thinking and the doctrine of analogy remains a constant task for theology in all ages and cultural contexts.

See also ANALOGY; DISCOURSE ABOUT GOD; GOD; GOD: ATTRIBUTES OF; LOVE.

Bibliography

Braaten, Carl E., ed. *Our Naming of God: Problems and Prospects of God-Talk Today.* Philadelphia: Fortress, 1989.

Burrell, David B. "Aquinas on Naming God." *Theological Studies* 24 (1963) 183–212.

Collins, Mary. "Naming God in Public Prayer." *Worship* 59 (1985) 291–304.

Dewan, Lawrence. "St. Thomas and the Divine Names." *Science et Esprit* 32 (1980) 19–33.

Janowitz, Naomi. "Theories of Divine Names in Origen and Pseudo-Dionysius." *History of Religions* 30 (1991) 359–72.

Pseudo-Dionysius the Areopagite. *The Divine Names and Mystical Theology.* Translated from the Greek with an introductory study by John D. Jones. Mediaeval Philosophical Texts in Translation 21. Milwaukee: Marquette University Press, 1980.

See also the bibliography under GOD: FATHERHOOD OF.

WILHELM BREUNING

God: Possibility of Knowledge of. The question of whether God can be known is bound up with the ways and forms through which God, who is (in principle) withdrawn by virtue of being absolutely the Other, has made the divine knowable. A distinction is therefore drawn between the *natural* knowledge of God, through creation, and the *supernatural* knowledge of God, through revelation.

(1) *Biblical Background.* For Holy Scripture, the knowledge of God is given through God's presence to the people (Ex 3:14), which begins already at creation (Genesis 1) and becomes clear in the choosing (mainly of Abraham). The prophets warn that correct knowledge of God must be attained by rejecting all conceptions that prejudice God's transcendence. From this perspective, the knowledge of God results from a personal relationship with God entailing trust and familiarity with God (Is 11:9; Jer 31:31f.). Ultimately, love rather than understanding leads to knowledge of God. This action of love, however, also requires a conversion in thought. The natural knowledge of God is attested by the affirmation of Wisdom 13 that humans fail to recognize the Creator on the basis of God's creation. The New Testament, in connection with Christology, resumes the Old Testament idea in a new way: because the Son knows the Father and the Father the Son, the Son takes humans up into his familiarity with the Father (Mt 11:27 par.; John 10, 17). The position stated in Wisdom is continued in Rom 1:18–21: precisely because of the natural knowability of God, those humans are inexcusable who suppress the truth through their sins. God's knowability is thus possible within the history of sin as well; it does not become fully actualized, however, until humans allow themselves to be possessed by God's love (Phil 3:12).

(2) *History of Theology.* In opposition to gnosticism, the early Fathers of the Church rejected the ideal of salvation through knowledge. Nevertheless they sought to find in the philosophy and ethics of their time points of contact with the knowledge of God as the Father of Jesus Christ. Clement of Alexandria referred to the "seeds of Logos" in the pre-Christian and non-Christian worlds. Augustine did not deny the natural knowledge of God, but gave greater emphasis to the path of submissive belief (*Conf.* 8). In Scholasticism, Anselm of Canterbury sought to provide a synthesis. Human rationality seeks to comprehend an incomprehensible God. Through their rational approach, however, humans first open themselves wholly to God's loving self-revelation, which culminates in the absurdity of the cross.

(3) *Church Teaching.* With reference to Rom 1:18–21, Vatican I teaches that the natural knowledge of God is a possibility at the same time it points to (DS 3004, 3026) the supernatural knowledge of God (DS 3004f.). Vatican II seeks to tie both possibilities closely together by taking its departure from the ultimate goal as reflective of God's initial intention (*DV* 2; see *GS* 14, 38).

(4) *Ecumenical Perspectives.* In an ecumenical perspective, the Orthodox Church and theology bring out more clearly God's transcendence in contrast to the rationalistic tendencies in Catholic theology. The Reformers asserted espe-

cially that God is known within the context of the history of salvation. Surely one can know God on the basis of creation, but such knowledge of God, as M. Luther pointed out, can become perverted (Large Catechism, *BSLK*, 560). For him, the proper path to God is the theology of the cross (*theologia crucis*): on the cross, in the form of death, which is alien to God, God made known that the innermost divine essence is love; hence, it is by way of the cross that God wants to be recognized.

(5) *Systematic Reflections.* The question whether God can be known is especially explosive today. First, agnosticism is widespread. In addition, there are inner-theological problems about the extent to which a human person can attain positive, and not just negative, knowledge of God (see already *STh* 1, q. 3, prooem.). Moreover, it must be ensured that humans do not misuse God's turn toward humans as a means for their own self-realization and make God a "function" of themselves. In view of the universal knowability of God, believers should be accountable for the credibility of what is believed and proclaimed about God. The credibility of God can be made known effectively only from the history of Jesus Christ as representing God for us. The one who was crucified and resurrected is not a symbol created by humans in need of one, but rather "the power of God and the wisdom of God" (1 Cor 1:24), which acquire increasing persuasiveness in the course of the religious history of the church and other individual members. The theology of the cross provides a criterion for critical assessment of whether God has been known "correctly." In this, the mere notion that God is necessary for the functioning of the world is left behind as insufficient. An important clue regarding God's knowability can be seen in the way that everything we value and love refers us back to a bestowing love. Questions and temptations remain. Yet in accepting God's love and in giving it to other persons, people become increasingly certain that their faith trusts in a reality that they have not created with their own thoughts, but a reality that entrusts itself to humans in all the dimensions of their humanity and rationality.

See also AGNOSTICISM; ANALOGY; EXPERIENCE OF GOD; FAITH.

Bibliography
Bouillard, Henri. *The Knowledge of God.* New York: Herder and Herder, 1968.
Cooke, Bernard. *The Distancing of God: The Ambiguity of Symbol in History and Theology.* Minneapolis: Fortress, 1990.
Kasper, Walter. *The God of Jesus Christ.* New York: Crossroad, 1984.
Kaufman, Gordon. *God the Problem.* Cambridge, Mass.: Harvard University Press, 1972.
Murray, John Courtney. *The Problem of God: Yesterday and Today.* New Haven: Yale University Press, 1964.
Rahner, Karl. *Foundations of Christian Faith: An Introduction to the Idea of Christianity.* New York: Crossroad, 1982.
Rousselot, Pierre. *The Eyes of Faith: With Rousselot's Answer to Two Attacks.* New York: Fordham University Press, 1990.

WILHELM BREUNING

God: Proofs of Existence of. What we call proofs of God's existence are ways of approach that offer a reasoned, reflective basis for conviction about the existence of God and for a more precise definition of God.

(1) *Biblical Background.* In the Bible, initial attempts at proofs of God's existence can be found in those places in the wisdom books that focus on creation and on God's role in establishing a binding covenant. The interest here is not, of course, scientific and methodologically rigorous but is directly enmeshed with lived reality. In the New Testament, Paul recognizes *noûs* (*reason* as autonomous critical judgment, but in whose functioning the "heart" also plays a role) as an organ of knowledge of God (Rom 1:20).

(2) *History of Theology.* In ancient philosophy, intellectual inquiries about God tended to be aimed at making God recognizable as the originator of the cosmos (the world as ordered to a goal and as a harmonious whole). Early Christian theologians adopted these lines of thought, especially the Stoic, Platonic, or Aristotelian. Rather than a cosmological approach to proving God's existence, Augustine emphasized an anthropological approach. He argued that humans, as intellectually active subjects, in the context of their relationship to the world and themselves, encounter God as that which is primary and sustaining. Following this line of thought, Anselm of Canterbury constructed his "ontological argument." Starting from the way that humans conceive of God (as that than which nothing greater can be conceived), Anselm affirmed that the existence of God is the condition of the very possibility of being able to so conceive of God. The problem with this line of thought, however, consists in the logical legitimacy of the shift from thought to being. Thomas Aquinas therefore rejects Anselm's ontological argument. He gives instead five proofs of the existence of God (the "five ways" [*quinque viae*]): the non–self-evidentness of the contingent yet value-imbued reality of the world, along with its all-pervasive finality, point to a primary originator, conferrer of existence, and governor of history. Problematic here is the sort of "necessity" with which the world needs God as its explanation: Is God just the explanatory component of the world or the living God? Thomas Aquinas ends the proofs with the statement: that which imparts life, meaning, and ends "everyone calls God" (*STh* 1, q. 2, a. 3). From this it is evident that he intends to augment understanding of the living God of the Bible. Kant, of course, accused Thomas, like Anselm, of an unguarded leap from thought to reality and interpreted God as a postulate of practical reason. In modern times, anthropological proofs of God's existence take the place of cosmological ones: God is conceived as the condition of the possibility that human beings are able to understand themselves. The problem here is that God can easily appear as a mere function of humanity (and not humanity as a gift from God). A new point of departure is presented by paths that aim to lead from human beings' responsibility for their fellow humans, the world, and the future to a rational account of God as God is believed in and hoped for. Today, the polemics that have been waged against Kant in neo-scholasticism have become largely irrelevant, regardless of whether what is involved in proofs of

PROOFS OF THE EXISTENCE OF GOD

(Outline: Wolfgang Beinert)

Name	Goes back to	Developed by	Central point	Basic argument
Consensus argument	Stoicism	Cicero	Universal validity of human reason	From the consensus among all peoples that God exists it is concluded that this conviction corresponds to reality.
Anthropo-logical argument		Augustine	Eternal truth	The unchanging validity of truth and norms can have its ground only in some really existing truth and norm — God.
Ontological argument		Anselm (*Proslogion*)	Concept of a perfect being	"God" is the greatest thing conceivable. As such, God must exist, for otherwise something greater would be conceivable (that which is greater in our understanding *and* in reality).
Cosmological argument ("Five ways" [*quinque viae*])		Thomas Aquinas (*STh* 1, q. 2, a. 3)		
First way	Aristotle's *Metaph.* 12		Motion	From the movement of things in the world an unmoved prime mover is inferred.
Second way	Aristotle's *Metaph.* 2		Causality	The dependent causes that we see require the existence of an uncaused first cause, since an "infinite regress" (*regressus in infinitum*) is not possible.
Third way	Plato, Avicenna		Contingency	Nonnecessary being is possible only if it owes its existence to necessary being.
Fourth way	Plato, Augustine, Anselm (*Monologion*)		Hierarchy of being	Truth, goodness, beauty, etc. are realized in the world to varying degrees. But then there must be a highest, perfect being that is the cause of these levels of being.
Fifth way	Plato, Stoicism		Finality	From the experienced functionality and purposiveness in the world the existence of a supreme, ordering mind must be inferred. "Coincidence" explains nothing.
Ethico-theological (deonto-logical) argument		Kant, Newman	Practical reason/ conscience	To our moral actions and/or the promptings of our conscience a supreme moral authority must correspond. Without the harmonizing force that can be guaranteed only by God, the physical and moral world-orders would be contradictory.
Transcendental argument		K. Rahner	God as condition of the possibility of conscious human existence	Humans always find themselves oriented toward an absolute. Their existence is meaningful only if that exists as the perpetual Mystery.

God's existence are strict "proofs" or mere "postulates." An exact ("natural-scientific") proof of God's existence would be an internal contradiction, since God is not an object of empirical knowledge. The appeal to God as a postulate, however, does not really prove the existence of God. Hence, instead of proofs of God's existence, we speak today of *traces of God*.

(3) *Church Teaching*. When Vatican I reaffirms that God *can* be known by the light of natural reason (DS 3026), it implies the *mere possibility* of a demonstration by means of argumentation. Vatican I does not prescribe specific forms of argumentation.

(4) *Ecumenical Perspectives*. In the course of the critical debate about Kantian philosophy, controversies arose between Protestant and Roman Catholic theology, but those have become generally passé today. The problem of the relation between faith and reason still, however, persists as a significant ecumenical issue.

(5) *Systematic Reflections*. Roman Catholic theology holds to the possibility, and necessity, of accounting for faith. It does not, however, envisage such accountability to rest on a single, self-contained argument, but seeks to trace out, within the whole of its thought, and along historical avenues, the "rationality" of faith in God. In the process, the essential elements of the classical proofs of God's existence are reappropriated: the cosmological argument is combined with the ethical, while the personal element in the Augustinian position remains valid. Christians recognize and affirm God as a God of hope through reflection on history and on the signs within history that point to God. These signs or traces give evidence that faith in God is not decisionistic, but also draws sustenance from natural elements. Proofs of God's existence help bring about an enlightened faith that does not know everything, but does know to whom it is devoted (see 2 Tm 1:12).

See also EXPERIENCE OF GOD; GOD; GOD: POSSIBILITY OF KNOWLEDGE OF.

Bibliography
Kenny, Anthony. *The Five Ways: Saint Thomas Aquinas' Proofs of God's Existence*. Notre Dame, Ind.: University of Notre Dame Press, 1980.
Küng, Hans. *Does God Exist? An Answer for Today*. New York: Doubleday, 1980.
Morris, Thomas V. *Anselmian Reflections: Essays in Philosophical Theology*. Notre Dame, Ind.: University of Notre Dame Press, 1987.
Swinburne, Richard. *The Coherence of Theism*. Oxford: Clarendon, 1977.
————. *The Existence of God*. Oxford: Clarendon, 1991.

                                                    WILHELM BREUNING

God: Theology of. The Christian notion of God is theological reflection on the inner reality of the God who is recognizable in biblical revelation as the Creator and the Father of Jesus and the goal of all history. In the dogmatic explication of the contents of faith, it is usually the first tract (DOGMATIC THEOLOGY).

(1) *Biblical Background.* Since the Scriptures are the "story" of God's history with Israel and the story of events of Jesus Christ, the Scriptures contain more than a doctrine of God. Indeed the Scriptures therefore challenge theology to make the one God, self-identical in creation and in the history of redemption, recognizable enough so that the Scriptures can be read as the history of this one and only God.

(2) *History of Theology.* Since the early creedal statements of the church began with belief in God, it was natural that systematic theology should begin with the doctrine of God (as Origin had done in *On First Principles* [*Peri Archōn*]). Problematic, however, was the division of theological and trinitarian books of God (treatise "On the One God" [*De Deo uno*]) and the theology of the Trinity (treatise "On the Triune God" [*De Deo trino*]). In the Middle Ages, Peter Lombard included the treatment of the nature and attributes of God in the treatise on the Trinity. Thomas Aquinas places the question about God's nature at the beginning, as part of the question about the nature common to all the divine persons. This course of events has led to the coexistence, up to the present, of two separate treatises. This separation has become problematic today. In Thomas, the matter is arranged merely according to the external succession of things, without consideration being given to the dynamism of the total conceptual scheme. The doctrine of God ought to be centered on the Trinity in a way that preserves the monotheism of the Old and New Testaments, as the revelation of the living God. Neo-scholastic treatises on God could give rise to the impression that a theological treatment of God closely resembles a philosophical exposition; whereas the treatment on the Trinity often remained at a very abstract level that was not readily understandable.

(3) *Church Teaching.* Church pronouncements speak from the standpoint of the interconnection between belief and life, and do not, therefore, independently develop a systematic theology of divinity. In the proclamation of doctrine, however, statements about God are likely to appear at the very start (see GOD, sec. 3).

(4) *Ecumenical Perspectives.* Theology of divinity is part of the common and (aside from some rationalistic attempts to dissolve theology of the Trinity) uncontested basic fund of all Christian theology and thus provides the foundation for a basic consensus among Christian confessions.

(5) *Systematic Reflections.* Christian understanding of God should be an interpretation of the biblical message of revelation from God. This has its center in the fact that God is the Creator and redeemer of all human beings; through this redemptive activity of God in history, however, we come to learn what God intrinsically *is*: "God is love" (1 Jn 4:8, 16). This relation between redemptive history (or what Greek patristics call the economy of salvation [*oikonomia*]) and the understanding of the immanent nature of God (Greek: *theologia*) is a kind of transcendental basic axiom for all of THEOLOGY. Theological exposition of the meaning of God should, as a logical condition of its development, explicate the relation between salvation-history and the nature of

God. It should do so in a "philosophical" way but not simply by taking over into theology philosophical speculation about God, but rather through dialogue and, if need be, critical debate with it. Besides the items in this dictionary, the following individual themes especially belong to present-day theology of divinity: (a) The meaning of professing belief in *God's existence:* theology has as its initial task to elucidate conceptually the belief in God that the church as the people of God professes in such a way that human beings can make the belief in God their own in a freely responsible sense (see Vatican II, *GS* 11–22). Rather than appealing only to the experiences of the average contemporary person or of specific "philosophers of God," theology has to remain conscious that God's pathway to humanity is Jesus Christ. In him, God attests, with both unsurpassable terseness and utmost expansiveness, to God's existence. It is precisely for this reason, however, that the self-attesting God rather than theological reflection is the "good news" of belief. Profession of belief in God's existence is more than an intellectual act; it is the life-response of human beings in their greatness and their wretchedness (B. Pascal). In this context, then, theology is a "bethinking" of the reality of God. (b) The dialectic of *God's transcendence and immanence:* this dialectic is roughly expressed in the biblical statements that God "dwells in unapproachable light" (1 Tm 6:16) but that "in him we live and move and have our being" (Acts 17:28). Mediation takes place here through the Son, as the "way" to the Father (Jn 14:6), and through the Holy Spirit, who "dwells" within us, as the ultimate depths of God (1 Cor 2:10–16). Inasmuch as theology adheres to this dialectic, it can break through an immanentism that regards the universe as nothing but a closed, self-contained system and at the same time ward off atheistic interpretations of the experience of transcendence (E. Bloch) and ward off explanations of belief as flight from the world (Marxism). Positively, theology can show that God's immanence is encountered in the least of the brothers and sisters of Christ and is displayed in love of one's neighbor; God's immanence is thereby a transcending dynamism in which God — even as one who dwells in unapproachable light — is not only the theoretical goal of humanity but also the practical goal in the living out of everyday life. (c) *God's sovereignty:* this concept, derived from categories of modern political science, illumines important aspects of God's power and rule as attested in the Bible. (The Old Testament name for God, Yahweh, is usually rendered in the New Testament as *Kyrios* = Lord.) There is no authority above or alongside God, who holds dominion over all reality. Jesus' message and destiny illustrate, however, that God's sovereignty is not tyranny and caprice, but love, and thus always appeals to freedom. Insofar as Jesus fully realized the love of God and neighbor, Jesus himself became Kyrios (Phil 2:11), in imitation of whom God's power demonstrates its enduring relevance as a manifestation of love that brings bliss and is worthy of adoration. (d) Critical analysis and debate about *false conceptions* of God: (i) *Polytheism:* historically, polytheism in its very diverse forms is a very widespread religious outlook that recurs today in syncretistic modes of thought within the Christian milieu. Christian theology points to the philosophical contradiction of multiple divine principles, but also, in connection with the biblical critique of "idolatry" (e.g., Isaiah 44; Wisdom 13–15), points out that all forms of polytheism imply the fundamental religious error that humans can gain mastery over their fears and wishful fantasies by making absolutes of worldly values. The monotheistic profession of belief in the singularity of God brings the whole of life and all its powers (see Dt 6:5) under the rule of the one Good. As M. Luther emphasized, the reality to which humans give their hearts is the reality that becomes their "God." This emphasis that humans are inherently oriented toward the transcendent provides a basis for seeing (as Vatican II taught [LG 16; NA 2]) polytheistic religions as containing the search for the true God. (ii) *Pantheism:* this exerts its enduring fascination through the idea that all of reality is ultimately a unity and through the desire to become one with that unity. Assuming that any tendency to encroach upon the uniqueness of God is resisted, both of these can be accommodated by Christian theology. On the one hand, Christian theology stresses the transcendence of God, who "is all" (Sir 43:28) and therefore does not need the world to be a divine expression of God's life but can let the world remain world. On the other hand, Christian theology also clarifies the immanence of God, by virtue of which we move in God (Acts 17:28) yet do not merge into God. Theology mediates both of these aspects and thereby avoids pantheism by its notion of ANALOGY.

See also GOD; TRINITY; TRINITY: DOCTRINE OF THE.

Bibliography
See the bibliography under GOD.

WILHELM BREUNING

God-Man. Jesus is called the God-man because the union of the divine and human natures in the hypostasis of the Logos is the ground for his unity as subject in being and action, knowing and willing.

(1) *Biblical Background.* The New Testament does not use the term but teaches what undergirds it. Although the full humanity of Jesus — his bodiliness or affective and spiritual actions — is never in question, nevertheless, in a unique way, Jesus Christ, the bearer of divinity, is likewise the man who humbled himself unto death on the cross (Phil 2:6–11; Rm 1:3; 8:3). He is the Logos who at a given time assumed flesh and saved us (Jn 1:14). Because of the humanity he assumed he is the mediator between God and human beings (1 Tm 1:15; 2:15; 3:16).

(2) *History of Theology.* The term *God-man* (*theanthropos* = *Deus-homo*) was first used by Origen (*Hom. in Ez.* 3.3). The reality it refers to is already found in Ignatius of Antioch, Melito of Sardis, Irenaeus of Lyons, Tertullian, and, naturally, all post-Nicene Fathers, since they state that it was "one and the same" who was eternally with God as impassible Logos and who also in his human nature was born of Mary, suffered in the flesh, died, and is for-

ever exalted at the right hand of the Father. To counter the danger of splitting Christ into two persons united only morally or consciously, Alexandrian theology stresses the unity of the God-man. The principle of unity is in the person of the divine nature that assumes and thereby gives existence to the human nature. Christ is not an *unum* resulting from the conjunction, but an *unus* who is the same in his presence and action in both natures. A final clarification is provided by the teaching of the *enhypostasis* or *subsistence* of the human in the divine nature (Leontius of Byzantium, Maximus the Confessor, John Damascene, Thomas Aquinas).

(3) *Church Teaching.* The church's teaching recognizes Christ as the God-man in calling Mary the Mother of God (Theotókos) (Council of Ephesus [DS 251]); that is, the Logos assumed humanity from her and, in the hypostatic union, appeared as one and the same God-man. The church also makes this recognition by saying that Christ is "consubstantial" (*homooúsios*) with the Father in his divinity and consubstantial (*homooúsios*) with us in his humanity (Council of Chalcedon [DS 301; cf. DS 125]). Therefore he is worthy of praise (DS 259, 431). The Lateran Council of 649 clarified the theandric activity of Christ as a wondrous union of divine and human activity (DS 515).

(4) *Ecumenical Perspectives.* In principle, the Reformation maintained the early church's Christology. But since the humanity of Jesus was seen more as an instrument or means of revelation, and since Jesus also was not considered to be the head of a new humanity who was acting — as relevant to salvation — autonomously and as a creature, the Monophysitism latent in medieval piety was increased. There was always the danger of a dialectical turn to pure humanism in the Enlightenment and in liberal theology. To counter this danger, K. Barth opposed to it an extreme Christology from above. With the loss of the theandric starting point and the modern turn to the subject came the consciousness of speculative idealism with its own view of the God-man. Thus for I. Kant the idea of the Son of God is nothing other than humanity in the eternal plan of creation as the rational essence of the world in its moral perfection. Christ is only the exemplary appearance of the God-man, humankind morally united with the "will" of God. For G. F. W. Hegel, history is the process by which absolute Spirit becomes itself in another, humanity. At the same time, however, humanity also becomes conscious of divinity in the Spirit. The universality of idea must become conscious by the mediation of the particular. This unity is Christ as God-man. The result of this project is not only the surrender of the free event-character of the coming of God but a monism of the dialectical self-constitution of the God-man; and this eventually leads to the self-divinization of humanity in the materialistic sense that dominates the whole self-understanding of modernity. Thus the reality of the God-man is absent, for the concept describes the greatest possible unity and basic distinction of God and created human beings.

(5) *Systematic Reflections.* The Christian recognition of Jesus Christ as God-man is open to the objection that the doctrine of two natures leads to an aporia: insofar as the human nature is reduced only to "personality" (see CHRIS-

TOLOGICAL MODELS, sec. 5). This was not a problem for the early church's Christology, for it held to the integrity of the human nature (body and rational soul with creaturely consciousness, action, and decision) (see the research of A. de Halleux, L. Abramowski, and A. Grillmeier). As long as "person" is understood as openness to the transcendentality of being and to God as its personal ground, the individuality of the human reality of Jesus then consists in its belonging to the person of the Logos. This free and unlimited belonging constitutes its highest fulfillment. The obedient assimilation of human knowledge and will gives the individual human nature its own reality since it is assumed into the person of the Logos. This divino-human unity can be realized only once. From the perspective of the economy of salvation, the human nature of Christ (rather than a hypostatically divided God — resulting in a radically divided man!) is the temporal-historical expression of the Son's eternally knowing himself indebted to the Father. Today the doctrine of the God-man poses the question of our relationship to God in general. As long as language about Jesus' divinity seems mythical to many, the hypostatic union must be explained using an analysis of the transcendental and ontological structure of humanity. A significant question raised by process theology is the extent to which God can suffer. The theology of the early church first had to underline God's absolute transcendence over the world, to which suffering and potentiality belong. At the same time it had to deal with the Greek axiom on the impassibility (*apatheia*) of God: since the God-man is "one and the same," not only the humanity but also the Word suffers in the flesh. Thus the God-man suffers when he assumes humankind's history of suffering and relates to his divinity as God-man. By redeeming in such a way he raises suffering up into the essence of love. Furthermore, for Catholic Christianity the doctrine of the God-man implies a basic idea (M.-J. Le Guillou): it points out that the human, the bodily, and the "secular" are highly significant. This may be seen today in ideas on CREATION, CORPORALITY OF THE HUMAN PERSON, GRACE, the SACRAMENTS, and the apostolic and sacramental structure of the visible CHURCH.

See also CHRISTOLOGICAL HERESIES; CHRISTOLOGICAL MODELS; CREATION; DIVINE MOTHERHOOD OF MARY; HYPOSTATIC UNION; HUMANKIND.

Bibliography
Kasper, Walter. *Jesus the Christ*. New York: Paulist, 1976.
Rahner, Karl. "On the Theology of Incarnation." In *Theological Investigations*, 4:105–20. New York: Crossroad, 1974.

GERHARD LUDWIG MÜLLER

God's Care. The expression *God's care* refers to the religious conviction that God takes loving care of God's creatures. In systematic contexts, it is usually subordinated to the concept of "providence," which signifies the goal-directed, meaningful guidance of world and history by the Creator.

(1) *Biblical Background.* The Bible testifies above all to the active caringness of God for God's chosen people; the word *prónoia* (providence) occurs

for the first time in two Hellenistically tinged passages (Wis 14:3; 17:2). Implicit in the Old Testament conception of the covenant is the knowledge that it entails divine support (Gn 9:9–11, 12–25; Exodus 24). In sovereign power, Yahweh performs marvels for the people (Ex 34:10), shows that Yahweh is to be their Creator (Is 43:1, 15), opens for them a "path in the mighty waters" (Is 43:16), and puts an end to wars (Ps 46:9f.). But Yahweh also cares for individuals, "hemming" them in "behind ... and before" (Ps 139:5), and sustains the lowly (Ps 147:6). "He ... made the great as well as the small, and he provides for all alike" (Wis 6:7). Although good as well as evil, life as well as death, stem from Yahweh (Sir 11:14; see Is 45:7; 54:16), the believer expects that Yahweh's blessing ultimately remains the stronger. It extends to all living creatures; the Creator nourishes them (Ps 136:25) with the same love that has also set God's people free (Ps 136:10–22). Yahweh "governs all things well" (Wis 8:1), has the care of all (Wis 12:13), and God's "providence" is the force that ultimately "guides" even a craft built by humans (Wis 14:3). The New Testament — especially in the words of Jesus attested by the Synoptics — demonstrates the Creator's fatherhood through the care that God shows for both good and bad persons (Mt 5:45), and indeed, even for plants and animals (Mt 6:26–30; see Lk 12:4–7), whose divinely secured flourishing ought to inspire trust in those of little faith: "Your heavenly Father knows that you need ... all" those things (Mt 6:32). Thus an equivalence between the "dominion of God" and "life" (Mk 9:42–48; Jn 3:3–16) is taken for granted. God gives all things "life and breath and everything" (Acts 17:25), but it is quite particularly to the persecuted community that the invitation applies: "Cast all your worries upon him because he cares for you" (1 Pt 5:7). Pauline literature elucidates God's care as a component of the redemptive plan brought to fulfillment in Christ (Gal 4:4; Eph 1:9f.), even if the carrying out of that plan remains an unsearchable mystery (Rom 11:33–36).

(2) *History of Theology.* The Fathers saw themselves confronted by fatalistic tendencies, stemming in part from Stoicism and pagan astrology. Justin repudiates fate, asserting the particular and general providence of the God of Jesus Christ (*Dial.* 1.4; 118.3). Irenaeus sees the motivation for God's creation of the world and history in God's love, which desires a nondivine object of its benevolent actions (*Adv. haer.* 4.14). The world was created for the sake of humans (ibid., 5.29.1), in the interest of their edification and maturation (ibid., 4.37.7).

(3) *Church Teaching.* Doctrinal office condemned astrological fatalism at the provincial Synod of Braga (DS 459). At Vatican I, it declared: "All that God created, he protects and guides through his providence, ... even that which might eventuate from the free actions of creatures" (DS 3003).

(4) *Ecumenical Perspectives.* The Lutheran, and above all Calvinist, doctrine of predestination attempts to emphasize the sovereign freedom of eternal election (see *Inst.* 3.21.6). Calvin's doctrine of so-called twofold predestination — of one person to salvation and of another to damnation (see ibid., 3.21.7) — is no longer advocated today, in its full radicality, by any Protestant theologian.

Worth mentioning is the Puritan religious conviction that God blesses, and caringly follows, the work of God's chosen to such a degree that its fruits intensify their consciousness of being chosen.

(5) *Systematic Reflections*. Theological development of the doctrine of God's care shifted the accent from the biblical notion of caringness to the postbiblical one of providence. Correspondingly, Thomas Aquinas speaks of providence as a purposive ordering of all things that was preexistent in God's mind (*STh* 1, q. 22, a. 1f.) (see M. Weber). Today, in the age of personalism, God's care manifests itself as a revealed reason for making the individual, the lowliest, the destitute, an object of interhuman and social caring, since God wishes to unfold God's love in that way. This is emphasized especially by advocates of Latin American liberation theology.

See also FREEDOM; PREDESTINATION; PROVIDENCE.

Bibliography
Arts, Herwig. *God, the Christian, and Human Suffering*. Collegeville, Minn.: Liturgical Press, 1993.
Bornkamm, Gunther. *Jesus of Nazareth*. New York: Harper, 1960.
Ganoczy, Alexandre. *Schöphungslehre*. Düsseldorf: Patmos, 1983.
Griffin, David Ray. *Evil Revisited: Responses and Reconsiderations*. Albany: State University of New York Press, 1991.
Rad, Gerhard von. *Old Testament Theology*. Vol. 1. New York: Harper, 1962.
Scheffczyk, Leo. *Creation and Providence*. New York: Herder and Herder, 1970.

ALEXANDRE GANOCZY

God's Foreknowledge. The phrase *God's foreknowledge* refers to God's power over the future as seen in relation to the free actions of spiritual creatures.

(1) *Biblical Background*. According to Is 41:21–29, God's foreknowledge is the mark of God's power as contrasted with the nullity of the gods. God knows persons and their prayers even before they come into existence (Psalm 139; see Sir 23:19–20). The New Testament, in the context of election in Christ, speaks of everything working for good for those, as foreknown and predestined, who love God and are called according to God's eternal plan (Rom 8:28–30; see Eph 1:3–14).

(2) *History of Theology*. The history of theology treats the theme of God's foreknowledge in connection with the doctrine of predestination so as to avoid any fatalism that does not take human freedom seriously. In early modern times, the so-called Thomists (D. Bañez, O.P., being the main Thomist representative) and the so-called Molinists (after L. de Molina, S.J.) debated about the way in which God can foreknow the free actions of humans. Despite their astuteness, these adversaries were unable to solve the problem. In the controversies about predestination, God's foreknowledge was clearly distinguished from predetermination to evil.

(3) *Church Teaching*. Vatican I teaches — without further clarification of how this occurs — that everything lies "naked and exposed" before God (see Heb 4:13), "including that which will come about through the free actions of creatures" (DS 3003).

(4) *Ecumenical Perspectives*. In his critical assessment of Calvin's doctrine of predestination, K. Barth has brought out the redemptive character of God's foreknowledge as determinative ordering toward participation in Christ.

(5) *Systematic Reflections*. After lengthy debate, theology has realized that the aporia presented to us by the competing claims of God's foreknowledge and of free action is irresolvable. In a positive vein, however, the doctrine of God's power over the future implies the consoling message that God's boundless goodness does not follow human destinies in a detached way, but participates lovingly in them.

See also GOD: ATTRIBUTES OF; PREDESTINATION; PROVIDENCE; SYSTEMS OF GRACE.

Bibliography
Craig, William L. *The Problem of Divine Foreknowledge and Future Contingents from Aristotle to Suárez*. Leiden: Brill, 1988.
Fischer, John Martin, ed. *God, Foreknowledge, and Freedom*. Stanford, Calif.: Stanford University Press, 1989.
Kenny, Anthony. *The God of the Philosophers*. New York: Oxford University Press, 1979.
Moskop, John C. *Divine Omniscience and Human Freedom: Thomas Aquinas and Charles Hartshorne*. Macon, Ga.: Mercer University Press, 1984.
Rudavsky, Tamar, ed. *Divine Omniscience and Omnipotence in Medieval Philosophy: Islamic, Jewish, and Christian Perspectives*. Boston: Reidel, 1985.
Zagzebski, Linda. *The Dilemma of Freedom and Foreknowledge*. New York: Oxford University Press, 1991.

WILHELM BREUNING

God's Knowledge. The phrase *God's knowledge* refers to the manner in which God's reality is present and known to God.

(1) *Biblical Background*. In many places, the Bible mentions God's knowledge when it extols God's love and act of creation. For a creature, being known by God is its salvation (Psalm 139). Mt 11:27 describes the unity of Father and Son as a perfect reciprocal knowing. According to 1 Cor 2:10, the Holy Spirit knows the depths of God. The reciprocal knowledge of Father and Son is mediated further by the Son: he knows his and his know him (Jn 10:14).

(2) *History of Theology*. Within the history of theology, discussion about God's knowledge emerges, first, in the theology of creation (God, who gives form to creatures, also knows them), then in the theology of the Trinity, which described intradivine life as a knowing relation of the persons to one another. At the same time, it is also implied in the doctrine of the economic TRINITY with its affirmation that creation finds its truth (as freely conferred by God) in God's knowledge. Augustine, in his psychological doctrine of the Trinity, attempts to make a case for the generation of the Son as a living act of cognition.

(3) *Church Teaching.* Vatican I teaches the infinite perfection of the divine power of knowledge (DS 3001).

(4) *Ecumenical Perspectives.* Conviction regarding God's knowledge is common to all religions based on the Bible.

(5) *Systematic Reflections.* In the case of spiritual beings, what we understand by knowledge is a mode of existence, intensified beyond that of mere presentness, in which those beings are present to themselves and possess an openness to all the rest of reality outside them. Knowledge entails a communication reciprocally acknowledged. Human knowledge of created reality, moreover, entails a relation to the Creator. The possibility of attributing knowledge to God lies in the fact that the Creator must possess the pure perfection of every sort of being. Hence, what is involved in asserting that God has knowledge is not just an anthropomorphic transference. Rather, the possibility of speaking of God's having knowledge is grounded in the love that God has for God's creatures, who have been created as knowing beings. Therefore God's knowledge embraces human knowledge as a sharp illustration of God's knowledge. The theological treatment of God discusses God's knowledge in relation to the divine attributes of omniscience, foreknowledge, and wisdom (GOD: ATTRIBUTES OF).

See also GOD; GOD'S ACTION; GOD'S PERSONAL NATURE; GOD'S WILL; LOVE.

Bibliography

Zagzebski, Linda. *The Dilemma of Freedom and Foreknowledge.* New York: Oxford University Press, 1991.

WILHELM BREUNING

God's Oneness. Negatively, this concept expresses the fact that God's essence cannot be realized in a variety of separately existing individuals (against polytheism). Positively, what is meant is God's being one *of a kind,* which is reconcilable with the fullness of life spoken about in the dogma of the Trinity.

(1) *Biblical Background.* The revelation of God's singularity unfolded in Israel from *monolatry* (worship of a single god, also called "henotheism") to *monotheism* as acknowledgment of the uniqueness of God and at the same time of God's relationship to Israel. It receives condensed formulation in "The Lord is our God, the Lord alone" (Dt 6:4). The earliest prophetic pronouncements affirm a significant theological internal connection between the human community of Israel and its religion based on Israel's covenant with the one God. The distinctiveness of this God becomes the decisive criterion for the judgment of other cults. Because God is one, God is neither a sublimation of natural processes or of fertility nor an exponent of a particular culture. Instead God is an incomprehensible (hence the ban on images in Israel) and simultaneously unutterable nearness. This becomes especially clear in Elijah's struggle against the cult of Baal (see 1 Kings 18). The destruction of the state of Israel and the exile decisively deepened Israel's monotheism: God is one also as the God of all peoples (see Is 44:6–20). This brief sketch of the history of Israel's faith in-

dicates that the oneness of God becomes the religious center-point of the Old Testament and, also, the occasion for undivided love of this God (Dt 6:5).

(2) *History of Theology.* Christian theology took over the Old Testament belief in the oneness of God but made more precise its belief in the Trinity that expresses the fullness of divine life thereby. God's oneness is thus not to be understood numerically (in the sense of the number *1*).

(3) *Church Teaching.* The Nicene-Constantinople Creed combines the statement of God's oneness with the First Article about the Father and also links the unity of the divine nature to the first divine person as the origin (DS 150). Direct affirmation of God's singularity is made in several doctrinal documents (e.g., DS 421, 800).

(4) *Ecumenical Perspectives.* The acknowledgment of monotheism is a basic common component not only of all Christian confessions but also of the world religions of Judaism and Islam. As such, monotheism provides the foundation for a comprehensive ecumenism. The trinitarian interpretation of God's singularity is something specific to Christianity.

(5) *Systematic Reflections.* In order to explain God's oneness, theology has usually drawn upon philosophical speculation: God, as the ultimate ground of all reality, can be conceived of only as a single principle. If theology, however, is to proclaim the gospel, it must orientate itself on the biblical account of revelation that asserts God's oneness, for the sake of bringing humans into living communion with this God.

See also GOD; TRINITY; TRINITY: DOCTRINE OF THE.

Bibliography
Hughes, Christopher. *On a Complex Theory of a Simple God: An Investigation in Theology.* Ithaca, N.Y.: Cornell University Press, 1989.
Hurtado, Larry W. *One God, One Lord: Early Christian Devotion and Ancient Jewish Monotheism.* Philadelphia: Fortress, 1988.
Moor, Johannes Cornelis de. *The Rise of Yahwism: The Roots of Israelite Monotheism.* Bibliotheca ephemeridum theologicarum Lovaniensium 91. Louvain: Louvain University Press, 1990.
Schimmel, Annemarie, and Abdoldjavad Falaturi. *We Believe in One God: The Experience of God in Christianity and Islam.* New York: Seabury, 1979.

WILHELM BREUNING

God's Permission. The theological notion of "God's permission" attempts to provide an understandable connection between the existence of evil acts in the created world and the benevolence and omnipotence of the Creator. Its starting point is God's respect for self-motivation in God's creatures, and especially for human freedom of decision. When nature causes affliction and humans do evil, God permits it (*permissio*), or does not prevent it, even if God fundamentally and ultimately desires its opposite, the good and salutary.

(1) *Biblical Background.* The Bible says extremely contrasting things about this penetrating question but gives priority to the moral dimension. On the one

hand, it stresses that God does not delight in wickedness (Ps 5:5), that God made humankind "straight" (Eccl 7:29), and that God would not tempt humans and thus render God coresponsible for their evildoing (Jas 1:13). On the other hand, the Psalmist has God explain: "So I gave them up to the hardness of their hearts; they walked according to their own counsels" (Ps 81:13); and Paul determines, regarding the idolaters, that God "handed them over" to impurity (see Rom 1:24–28). Apart from the promise that God will extract from affliction and evil something eschatologically good and salvation-bringing, and will annihilate death and sin, the Bible nowhere concerns itself systematically with the various ways in which the divine will is realized.

(2) *History of Theology.* Among the Fathers, however, Augustine does this quite searchingly, and arrives more or less at the conclusion that God's position vis-à-vis humans is such that much "comes about — in a miraculous and inexpressible manner — not *without* his will that is nevertheless *contrary* to his will; it would not come about at all if he did not permit it (*sineret*)" (*Enchir.* 26.100). Thomas Aquinas continues this line of reasoning, explaining that it is good that God, in certain cases, should allow (*permittere*) evil acts and not prevent their doers, to whom God has already communicated forbiddance, from carrying them out (see *STh* 1, q. 19, a. 9r ad 3; a. 12r; q. 48, a. 2 ad 3). He bridges the apparent internal contradiction by reference to the larger totality of God's actions.

(3) *Church Teaching.* The Council of Trent rejected the opinion that God properly causes evil actions and even rejected the notion that God does so "just by permitting" such actions, as would apply, for example, to the betrayal by Judas (DS 1556).

(4) *Ecumenical Perspectives.* The Reformers opposed any talk of God's permission. Luther traces both the hardening of pharaoh's heart and the sin of Judas back to God as the only effective causal force, adding, however, that God, as the Deliverer, has such sin firmly in his control (*De servo arbitrio: WA* 18:714f.; see 616f.). Calvin refuses to leave God with only the role of an "inert permitting" in relation to any human action and cites Is 45:7 and Am 3:6, where both well-being and woe are attributed to God's agency. In reality, after all, God's will is as much "hidden" as "manifold" in its wisdom (Eph 3:9f.), and much of it appears bad only to our shortsighted eyes. Indeed, we never grasp the entire economy of redemption, in which both good and evil nonetheless subserve the one, good, ultimate goal. Calvin hints at the possibility of christologically neutralizing the aporia posed by God's permission: "If Christ were not crucified by the will of God, from where, then, is our redemption to come?" (*Inst.* 1.18.3).

(5) *Systematic Reflections.* An attempt to rethink this question, starting out from both J. Calvin and K. Barth, was made by O. Weber; although wishing to show a certain understanding for talk of God's permission, he nevertheless wants to overcome, via theology of the Trinity, the impossible depiction of the relationship between divine and human willing as one that involves two

competing kinds of cause. God by no means rests content with permitting evil time and again, in a process of point-by-point respect for human freedom, but rather, God circumscribes it with God's omnipotence, which, in view of the cross and resurrection of the Son, is inseparable from God's grace. To the ungodly act of the crucifixion there corresponds, in the triune God, not an act of inert observing and permitting, "but one of the free — though in this freedom, merciful — will of God." In it, God is manifested "as the Lord who watches caringly over his creatures" (Weber, *Grundlagen der Dogmatik,* 3rd ed. [Neukirchen-Vluyn, 1964], 1:492). With this the Catholic dogmatist can fully agree.

See also EVIL; EVIL, MORAL; THEODICY.

Bibliography
Barth, Karl. *Church Dogmatics,* 3/3. Edinburgh: T and T Clark, 1960.
Gutiérrez, Gustavo. *On Job: God-Talk and the Suffering of the Innocent.* Maryknoll, N.Y.: Orbis Books, 1987.
Vieth, Richard F. *God, Where Are You? Suffering and Faith.* New York: United Church Press, 1989.
Whitney, Barry L. *What Are They Saying about God and Evil?* New York: Paulist, 1989.

ALEXANDRE GANOCZY

God's Personal Nature. The notion of "personhood in God" refers, firstly and concretely, to the mutual relations of Father, Son, and Holy Spirit in the Trinity, but it also refers to God's essence as knowing and willing in a way analogous to those aspects of human personality.

(1) *Biblical Background.* The Bible leaves no doubt about the fact that knowledge and will are attributes of God (e.g., Ex 33:19; Is 46:10). In the New Testament, Romans 9–11 especially emphasizes God's total freedom.

(2) *History of Theology.* Augustine's psychological doctrine of the Trinity (see TRINITY: DOCTRINE OF THE, sec. 2) provides the best model for understanding the topic of personality in God.

(3) *Church Teaching.* Vatican I teaches expressly that God is complete in God's self and freely created the world out of love (DS 3001).

(4) *Ecumenical Perspectives.* All Christian theologies share in common a conviction regarding God as personal.

(5) *Systematic Reflections.* Recognition of God as personal is an insight gained from knowledge of the human personality. Some modern pantheistic philosophies deny that God is personal on the grounds that the concept applies only to beings whose behavior is contingent. That, however, would mean reducing the divine to the level of a dull and sightless dynamic process, and ultimately denying it altogether. Human beings, as persons, would then be greater than a "God" that lacked the capacity for conscious self-direction. To be sure, God's personhood is infinitely greater and unconditioned: from this arises the belief that God is able — despite its contingent nature — to guide with wisdom the creation that God willed and to lead it to its proper goal.

See also GOD: ACTS OF; GOD'S KNOWLEDGE; LOVE; PERSON; TRINITARIAN
PERSONHOOD OF GOD; TRINITY; TRINITY: DOCTRINE OF THE.

Bibliography
See the bibliography under TRINITY.

WILHELM BREUNING

God's Will. What we designate as God's will is the self-determination of the divine personality through which God determines God's self as love and as the power of that love to fulfill the divine plan for creatures.

(1) *Biblical Background.* In the Bible, God is encountered as exercising will inasmuch as God appears as acting within history. The basic feature of this acting is love, which God is and which God realizes in everything — in creation, in election, in redemption. God is unrestrictedly capable of all that God wills (Jb 42:2; Ps 115:3) because God's will is the supreme and inappealable authority (Rom 9:9–29). God is shown to us as fatherly love (Mt 6:10; Jn 3:16; Rom 5:8), which reaches its peak in the humble surrender of the Son (Rom 8:32). The New Testament indicates, in undeveloped form, that God's will is identical with God's trinitarian essence: the Son appears as both bearer and fulfiller of God's will (Mt 11:27; Mk 3:13; Jn 5:21), and the Holy Spirit distributes God's gifts to each person as it wills (1 Cor 12:11).

(2) *History of Theology.* In the history of theology, detailed reflection on God's will occurred, first, from a christological viewpoint regarding the question about Christ's will (Monothelitism; see CHRISTOLOGICAL HERESIES), and, second, in the context of the doctrine of the Trinity (see TRINITY: DOCTRINE OF THE). It was explained that the three divine persons have only one will, because that is coexistent with God's innermost essence. God's will is the will of the Father, who dispenses God's self wholly; the will of the Son, who receives himself from the Father and in so doing affirms the Father; and the will of the Spirit, who, as fullness of love, receives itself from the Father through the Son and dispenses itself. It is in this intratrinitarian love that the possibility is based, and the actuality realized, of outward direction of God's free will, which nevertheless, as free willing, corresponds wholly to God's essence. This freedom of will in relation to creatures was emphasized primarily in the Middle Ages by Duns Scotus: in principle, it is possible for God to will anything (*de potentia absoluta*), yet God freely binds God's self to the created order once God has chosen it (*de potentia ordinata*) and is therefore not arbitrary. To be sure, the concept of an "absolute capacity" (*potentia absoluta*), in use before Scotus adopted it, is not unproblematic from the perspective of the trinitarian uniqueness of God's essence. In nominalism, the way is prepared for a dangerous interpretation of God's will. Seeking to make God's sovereignty clear, for example, William of Ockham and G. Biel maintained that God, acting *de potentia absoluta,* could even condemn a just person and reward a sinner with blessedness without thereby being unjust. In such spec-

ulation, God's will is no longer seen as love and is no longer tied to the love that God is.

(3) *Church Teaching.* Confronting Monothelitism, the church taught, as a matter for belief, the proposition that the divine persons possess *one and the same* will (DS 172, 501). Vatican I maintained the infinitude of God's will and his freedom in relation to creation (DS 3001f.).

(4) *Ecumenical Perspectives.* During the Reformation, the issue of God's will played a role in the controversy that was generated by nominalism.

(5) *Systematic Reflections.* Contemplation of God's will not only is an object of theological reflection, but is also and especially — as growing out of that — a matter of the life-orientation of those who believe in God. God's will becomes a sustaining religious force when, in the spirit of Jesus' message about the kingdom of God and in imitation of him, we are honestly able to pray: "Your will be done" (Mt 6:10).

See also CHRISTOLOGY; GOD'S KNOWLEDGE; LOVE; TRINITARIAN PERSONHOOD OF GOD; TRINITY.

Bibliography
Balthasar, Hans Urs von. *The Mystery of Easter.* Edinburgh: T and T Clark, 1990.
See also the bibliography under PROVIDENCE.

WILHELM BREUNING

Grace. Grace is the unconditional, free, loving action of the triune God by which God enters into personal communion with human beings in history in order to give them salvation.

(1) *Biblical Background.* The historical, loving action of God for the salvation of humankind, an action that the New Testament calls grace, is also what basically determines God's dealings with human beings in the Old Testament. It is true that in the Old Testament the reality of grace corresponds with other notions. The substantive *hen* (LXX: *charis*) means the freely bestowed personal favor of God (Gn 6:8; Ex 33:12). The verb *hanan* (LXX: *eleein*) signifies "to be gracious," in the sense of "lovingly devote oneself to." This personal, heartfelt devotion of God to humankind, which takes place in unconditional freedom (Ex 33:19), leads to the expectation of concrete gifts of salvation (Pss 4:2; 6:3; 9:14; 41:11; 51:3; 86:16). The substantive *hesed* (LXX: *eleos*), especially in the Psalms, refers to God's sovereign, abundant goods bestowed upon human beings, which are most forcefully demonstrated in God's love in the covenant and God's fidelity (*emet*) to it (Ex 34:6). God's trustworthy friendship with humankind is expressed concretely in the works of creation and in the redemption of the people of Israel (Psalm 136), as well as in the liberation of individuals from a wide variety of tribulations (Psalm 107). *Rahamim* (LXX: *oiktirmos*), the root meaning of which is "to be motherly," emphasizes the heartfeltness and tenderness of God's gift to humankind. This loving mercy is especially felt by the people of the covenant (Is 54:7; 63:7; Jer 16:5; Hos 2:21), as well as by individuals (Pss 40:12; 51:3). In the New Testament, Luke alone among the

Synoptic Gospels uses the word grace (*charis*). However, the reality of grace is present in Jesus' proclamation of a graceful God as Father and in his message regarding the gift-character of God's reign. *Charis* plays a central role in the Pauline corpus (where two-thirds of the 155 uses of *charis* are to be found). For Paul, grace is the very essence of God's universal and eschatological salvific action in Jesus Christ (Rom 5:15, 20f.). In the "grace of the one man, Jesus Christ" (Rom 5:15), by which God "gave up his own Son for all of us" (Rom 8:32), the forthcoming love of God assumes the form of a person. This is "the grace of Jesus Christ" (2 Cor 13:13). According to Paul the most important effect of Jesus Christ's gracious work of salvation is the gift of justification of sinners (Rom 3:21–26). In clear distinction to Judaic justification by works or particularism of salvation, Paul emphasizes the impossibility of meriting grace, its absolute gift character (Rom 3:24; 11:6), and its universality (Rom 4:16; 5:15, 18). In this gratuitous justification, the grace of Jesus Christ brings about the real beginning of the eschatological goods of salvation: becoming children of God (Rom 8:16f.), God's glory (Rom 5:2), and eternal life (Rom 5:21; 6:23). On behalf of the concrete body of Christ, the church, the one grace of God gives various gifts of grace (*charismata*) for the service of salvation (Romans 12; 1 Corinthians 12). All this is summarized succinctly in the deutero-Pauline letters: grace is the love of God for us (Eph 2:4–9; Ti 3:4–7).

(2) *History of Theology*. In the history of dogma we find quite different emphases in the understanding of grace in the Eastern and Western churches. In the Greek Fathers the predominant idea is that the grace of God causes human beings to be divinized (*theíosis, theopoíesis*): "God became man so that human beings could become God" (Irenaeus, *Adv. haer.* 3.19.1). The notion of divinization is constant throughout the many variations given to it by Athanasius (d. 373) in the Arian controversy, or by Gregory of Nyssa (d. 394) in the Pneumatomachian controversy. The result is a trinitarian, salvation-history perspective: grace is identical with the working of a triune God in salvation-history. The divinization of humankind takes place by the indwelling of the three divine persons. In the West, the doctrine of grace in the later works of Augustine (d. 430) becomes the matrix of theology. In dealing with Pelagianism, Augustine establishes two basic positions. The first is that grace is seen predominantly as an *adiutorium*, as a help in the human soul. He thus detaches grace from God and makes it anthropological and psychological, that is, an inner property of the human person. The second is that — to counteract the Pelagian emphasis on the ability of the human will to achieve — he makes the grace of God something opposed to human freedom insofar as he presents the sole effectiveness of grace in the salvific event. Thus grace and freedom become rivals. In opposition to Augustine's claim that in every event of salvation the absolute initiative belongs to the grace of God, there was during his lifetime, in monasteries in the south of France, a countermovement, which was later called Semi-Pelagianism. It claimed that by the power of their own will human beings are capable of initiating the act of faith (*initium fidei*) and persevering

SCHOLASTIC DIVISIONS OF GRACE

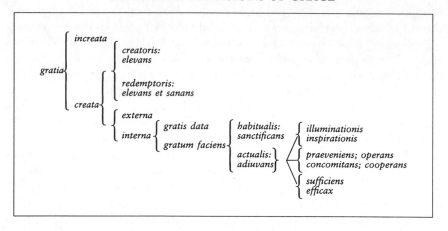

until the end. Grace follows the first step the person makes, or it supports his or her efforts to endure. Scholasticism continues the basic psychological thesis of Augustine. Using an Aristotelian model, Thomas Aquinas (d. 1274) characterizes grace as something essential within the human soul, namely, a lasting, accidental quality (*habitus*) (*STh* 1–2, q. 110). In dependence on Bonaventure (d. 1274) and Duns Scotus (d. 1308), the Franciscan school regards this infused *habitus* of grace as an inner light and as love. The many subdivisions of grace developed by classical Scholasticism continue in Baroque Scholasticism and in the grace controversy between Baianism and Molinism (GRACE SYSTEMS) and are expanded by means of the distinction between sufficient and effective grace. Neo-scholasticism develops the system even further (see table). The meaning of each of these distinctions is as follows: *uncreated* grace (*gratia increata*) is God. *Created* grace refers to the gifts and effects of the grace of God in humankind. Created grace is divided into God's work or the *grace of the Creator* (*gratia creatoris*), which is given to Adam and Eve in paradise as the original state of grace, and the *grace of redemption* (*gratia redemptoris*), which is the grace of Christ that saves fallen humankind. Both of these modes of God's working elevate humankind to a new level of being (*gratia elevans*), where the grace of the redeemer finally heals those who were wounded by sin (*gratia elevans et sanans*). According to the manner by which it is effective, created grace is divided into *external grace* (*gratia externa*), that is, preaching and the sacraments, and *internal grace* (*gratia interna*), which is at work within the soul. External grace is ordered to internal grace as its goal. Internal grace is the central notion and has many subdivisions. The main distinction is between the grace of an office that is given as individual charisms for the service of others, and sanctifying grace, or the grace of justification, which is intended for all to achieve personal holiness. The grace of sanctification is either the *grace of a state,* which as a habitual sanctifying grace (*gratia habitualis sanctificans*) signifies a lasting determination (*habitus*) remaining in the soul, or *actual grace* (*gratia actualis adiuvans*), which is the individual effects conferred by God. Finally, actual grace is subdivided into: the *grace of illumination* or the *grace of inspiration* (*gratia illuminationis, inspirationis*), where God works on the understanding and the will; a *prevenient* or *accompanying grace* (*gratia praeveniens, concomitans*), insofar as God's work precedes or follows through the human activity of the will; and *sufficient* or *efficacious grace* (*gratia sufficiens, efficax*), insofar as God gives the capacity for salvific acts or the ability to complete them. This system of grace prevailed in Catholic theology until Vatican II.

(3) *Church Teaching*. In reaction to the Pelagian claim that human will is fully able to do good and remain free of sin, the Council of Carthage (418) declared that grace is an unconditional necessity for the fulfillment of the commandments. To avoid sin, grace is necessary for strengthening the will (DS 225–27). The *Indiculus* (a list of papal pronouncements on the doctrine of grace) takes a position "against the enemies of divine grace" and "in opposition to the most harmful defenders of free will" (DS 238). Beginning with the damage done to free will by the sin of Adam (DS 239), it emphasizes the principial and ongoing necessity and priority of grace in all our deeds (DS 239–46). Finally, the relationship between grace and freedom is stated positively: "By this help and gift of God, free will is not taken away but made free.... God works in us so that we want and do what he wants, ... so that we too are co-workers with the grace of God" (DS 248). The Council of Ephesus (431) confirms the conclusions of the Western Church in opposition to Pelagianism. In opposition to Semi-Pelagianism, the Second Synod of Orange (529) declares, with regard to the problem of grace and free will: free will, which was weakened by the sin of Adam in every way human beings relate to God, needs the prior grace of God, which is a pure gift and unable to be merited (DS 396). The unconditional priority of grace is also affirmed for the beginning of faith (DS 375). To persevere in good until the end, the help of God is indispensable (DS 380). The Council of Trent takes a middle position between Pelagian overemphasis on free will and the Reformers' overemphasis on grace. Thus in opposition to Pelagianism it emphasizes the unconditional necessity and priority of grace, as well as the inability of human beings to earn it (DS 1525f., 1532, 1551–53). It rejects Luther's position that human free will is totally extinguished and is only a name without content, or that human will is completely inactive or merely passive (DS 1554f.). Furthermore, in opposition to Luther, it says regarding the essence of grace: grace is not only the favor of God but an inherent interior reality infused by the Holy Spirit (DS 1561).

(4) *Ecumenical Perspectives*. M. Luther (d. 1546) identifies grace with the justification of the sinner. Contradicting the basic Scholastic thesis whereby grace constitutes a state of being within humanity, Luther holds that grace is God's benevolence (*favor Dei*) outside human beings that, thanks to a gift that cannot be earned, makes possible God's personal relationship with humanity. Thus — in an exclusivist Christocentrism — Jesus Christ is the grace of God in person. The salvific work of Jesus Christ, which is beyond human beings,

is credited to us as forgiveness of sins by means of faith, which takes place in hearing the word of the gospel (see WA 2:443–618; 8:43–128). In order to ensure the unmeritability of grace alone (*sola gratia*) and to exclude any synergism (cooperation of human beings in the event of salvation), Luther defends the thesis that in salvation the will has been completely corrupted and is totally unfree (see *De servo arbitrio* [1525]: WA 18:600–787). For J. Calvin (d. 1564), as for Luther, grace is justification mediated christologically (OS 3.509–15). In his doctrine of predestination he sees grace specifically as the eternal election of individuals for salvation (OS 3.376f.). To the corrupted but also renewed (by the Holy Spirit) and active free will, Calvin attributes an instrumental activity in the salvific event, which of course is totally subordinate to the sole effectiveness (*Alleinwirksamkeit*) of God (OS 3.315). P. Melanchthon (d. 1560) distinguishes between the *word of God* (as the gospel it grants forgiveness of sins) and the *Spirit of God* (as the gift of the Holy Spirit it renews the heart and sanctifies us). In early Protestant Orthodoxy, the Lutheran tradition teaches a grace of application (*gratia applicatrix*), the efficaciousness of various actions of grace (vocation, enlightenment, justification, rebirth, sanctification) in the step-by-step process of being saved (*ordo salutis*). The Reformed tradition develops the notion of a covenant of grace in which the salvific work of Jesus Christ resurrects (*aufhebt*) the covenant between Creator and creature that was broken by humankind (COVENANT). At the beginning of the twentieth century, the Reformed theologians K. Barth and E. Brunner again make grace a central Christian concept. Barth makes a passionate plea for the triumph of grace in the concrete person Jesus Christ. Brunner underlines the personal character of grace. As the love of God it brings humankind into a living community with God by the unconditional forgiveness of sins. P. Tillich develops a universal concept of grace and distinguishes its three basic forms, namely, the grace of creation, redemption, and providence. In ecumenical dialogue, Evangelical theology in relationship to traditional Catholic teachings insists on the basic positions of the Reformation: grace is God. As a personal relationship it is an inseparable whole. It alone is efficacious in every salvific event. This position rejects the distinction of uncreated and created grace, as well as the characterization of grace as a property (*habitus*) existing in human beings, the division of grace into many categories, and any simultaneous cooperation of humans to bring about salvation. In a positive assessment of questions that are basically biblical, Catholic theology accents a number of new points: grace in its basic essence is, in K. Rahner's language, God's self-sharing; thus grace is efficacious as the event of a personal relationship; in this event, divine grace has the absolute initiative, to which the workings of human freedom are fully subordinate. On the Evangelical side of the dialogue there are new basic insights in constructive response to the Catholic inquiry: grace is not just the benevolence of God as a mere feeling, but God's concrete gift to humans and God's presence that transforms us; we cannot limit grace to individual justification, but must instead be attentive to its ecclesiological and social aspects; grace does not exclude human freedom but frees it for inclusive activity.

(5) *Systematic Reflections.* Grace, as the free, loving action of God for the salvation of human beings, is the central perspective of biblical faith in God. Grace is the very substance of God's positive, personal, and historical relationship to humankind. It is essentially God's love and friendship for human beings (*philanthropia:* Ti 3:4). In an orientation based on the Bible's understanding of grace, the main elements to be established and developed are the following: (*a*) *Trinitarian origin.* To overcome the Scholastic tendency to regard grace as a thing present in human beings (*gratia creata interna*), as well as the Reformation's tendency to situate grace exclusively outside humanity (*iustificatio externa*), theology must once again return to the trinitarian source of salvation-history. According to the New Testament — as the Eastern Fathers correctly emphasize — the living source for all grace is the Trinity's work in salvation-history, or, more precisely, in the trinitarian indwelling of God in human beings. The trinitarian God of love acts with complete freedom in history for the salvation of humankind by means of creation, redemption, and the final completion. In a broad sense we can discern a threefold form of grace: the grace of creation (creative grace), the grace of redemption (redemptive grace), and the grace of fulfillment (consummative grace). In each of these three basic types of grace all three persons work together, even though in a special way we can attribute creation to the Father, redemption to the Son, and fulfillment to the Spirit. At any given time, the trinitarian God confers upon human beings, in the three modes of operation within salvation-history, a specific community of salvation. In creation, they become God's very image and God's sons and daughters; in redemption, they are received back; in the final fulfillment, they are in a lasting, living relationship. This creative, redemptive, and consummative community of God with human beings also implies an indwelling or, in other words, the presence of the trinitarian God in humankind. Thus for humankind grace is participation in the being and life of God. In this trinitarian view of salvation-history, grace is a determination of humanity's being and is given by God from without in a way that is totally unmerited, but which leaves an essential, interior imprint on human beings. (*b*) *Christocentric orientation.* In a narrower sense, New Testament grace is the unconditionally free action of God for the salvation of human beings in the person and work of Jesus Christ. By means of the incarnation of the Son of God in Jesus Christ out of pure love, grace appears as a concrete, historical person. The GOD-MAN, Jesus Christ, who realizes in himself the closest relationship between God and humankind, brings to fulfillment a universal, community-building work of salvation. In his death and resurrection he once and for all mediates real forgiveness of sins and a new creation, which makes possible a new, salvific community of human beings with God. This Christocentric understanding is closely joined with a pneumatological and an ecclesiological perspective. In order to maintain the life of the newly established community between God and humankind, the Father and the Son

send forth the Spirit as love and as personal communication in the hearts of men and women. This means that the Spirit works interiorly as a driving force and an abiding helper to bring to perfection the grace of Jesus Christ. As concrete help in mediating this grace, the divine Spirit calls all human beings who believe to be together in the church. The church is sent to spread the grace of Christ by the salvific work of the gospel and by the sacraments as sanctifying signs. In order that the church might achieve this task, the Spirit of God gives various gifts of grace (*charismata*). (*c*) *Personal character.* By starting with the biblically oriented definition that grace is God's unconditionally free action for the salvation of human beings, two things have been gained. On the one hand, a personal starting point overcomes the main weaknesses of the Scholastic definition of grace. On the other hand, it provides a clearer basis for the traditional formal determination of grace. (The accompanying table compares the Scholastic and biblical views of the basic characteristics of grace.)   In the biblical

Grace: the Scholastic view	Grace: the biblical view
a thing	personal
static	dynamic
accidental	ontic
abstract	historical
spiritualist	of this world
individualistic	communitarian

understanding, all the essential characteristics of grace flow from its personal character. Thus the basic thesis: grace is *personal*. In opposition to grace as a "thing," it is a relationship of love that the triune God enters into with human beings as persons. Grace is *dynamic*. It is continuously happening, and as God's loving action it is a living power that elicits movement in humankind. Grace is *ontic*. It has to do with our being. Since the trinitarian God grants humankind a share in God's being and life, the relationship with God penetrates our very being. Along with this determination of our being God also gives us the divinely oriented forces of faith, hope, and love (THEOLOGICAL VIRTUES). Grace is *historical*. It is a concrete reality in history (see HISTORY/HISTORICITY) with its dimensions of past, present, and future. For humankind the historical effectiveness of love is demonstrated *principally* in creation, redemption, and the final fulfillment and *specially* in the two modes of salvation: law and the gospel, or the old and new covenants (see COVENANT). It is unsurpassably concrete in the person and work of Jesus Christ. For individuals the historical action of God is demonstrated in their vocation (disposition), their justification, and their sanctification. Grace is *communitarian*. It is the salvific action of God by means of a human community (Israel or the church [see COVENANT]). The ELECTION of the old or new people of God mediates salvation for individuals by way of a community. Grace is *of this world*. It is a reality that we can experience fully through sensible signs. It is perceptible. The grace of creation is experienced in

THE PROBLEM OF GRACE AND FREEDOM
Models

Synergism	Monergism	Energism
Thesis: God and humankind both work together at the same level	Antithesis: God alone is efficacious; pure passivity on the part of humanity	Synthesis: God alone is efficacious; covenantal reality on the part of humanity

Model:
Juxtaposition;
Salvation =
   grace+freedom
	Model:
	Opposition;
	Salvation =
	   grace against freedom
		Model:
		Cooperation;
		Salvation =
		   freedom in grace

what is pleasing and beautiful. The grace of redemption is experienced in liberation from bodily or spiritual evil or from socially oppressive forces that violate human laws. The grace of the final fulfillment is experienced as blessed and fulfilling love. Starting with this personal foundation we are better able to grasp the traditional formal attributes of grace: namely, that it is unmerited, necessary, and universal. Grace is *unmerited:* that is, human beings have no claim to the loving action of God. God makes available and dwells in a communion of unconditional love with human beings. By their own achievements they are incapable of earning grace either by their WORKS or by their MERIT. Thus grace is a pure gift. Human beings do not dispose of it, nor can they measure it. Grace is *necessary:* that is, without the action of God human beings cannot be saved. In every salvific event God has the absolute initiative. The beginning, completion, and continuance of the salvific event are dependent on God. Grace is of itself efficacious (*Alleinwirksamkeit*). Human beings cannot act salvifically, prior to or independently of grace, but only within its radius. Grace is *universal:* that is, God's action reaches to all human beings. In God's predestined, universal salvific will God has developed a universal plan of salvation. All human beings have received the offer and have the real possibility of reaching salvation. Grace is *limitless:* from a human perspective it is inconceivable and incomprehensible. (*d*) *Power of liberation.* In order to solve this fundamental problem of the doctrine of grace, two main models have been developed: synergism and monergism. By returning to Jesus Christ both are surpassed (= energism) (see table entitled "The Problem of Grace and Freedom"). The *energism* model takes note of the fact that in Scripture statements are juxtaposed so that, without any explanation, salvation is seen both as the act of God and the act of human beings (see SYSTEMS OF GRACE, sec. 1). This model clarifies the factual unity of grace and freedom by referring to the person of Jesus Christ. In him divine and human activity are united as really working with and in each other. Grace does not exclude freedom but includes it in its autonomy in the salvific event. The principial knowledge behind this is that God is the liberating basis of human freedom. Thus in the work of salvation there is a cooperation, which may be summarized by the formula: *freedom in grace*. In this inclusive relationship, the efficaciousness of divine grace alone is predominant. But it likewise guarantees for human freedom its subordinate, yet independent, efficaciousness. We can explain this inclusivity more precisely as a correlative relationship of both of these unequal realities: God's power and grace increase in direct — not inverse! — proportion to one another. Because God's power allows human freedom to be active, human beings are freer and more active to the extent that they allow divine grace to work within them. Finally, this inclusivity is realized decisively as a dialogical relationship: God respects the freely created or newly freed human being as person and calls him or her to a salvific community of love. The human person is a free partner with God and can respond to God's gracious word of love affirmatively or negatively. In the positive answer there is, by the initiative of grace, a real, historical dialogue of love between God and humankind.

See also CHARISM/CHARISMS; CHILDREN OF GOD; DISPOSITION FOR RECEIVING GRACE; FREEDOM; GRACE: DOCTRINE OF; GRACE: THEOLOGICAL HERESIES; INDWELLING OF THE HOLY SPIRIT; JUSTIFICATION; LAW AND GOSPEL; PREDESTINATION; SALVATION; SYSTEMS OF GRACE; UNIVERSAL SALVIFIC WILL OF GOD.

Bibliography

Boff, Leonardo. *Liberating Grace*. Maryknoll, N.Y.: Orbis Books, 1979.

Küng, Hans. *Justification: The Doctrine of Karl Barth and a Catholic Reflection; with a Letter by Karl Barth*. New York: Nelson, 1964.

Lubac, Henri de. *The Mystery of the Supernatural*. New York: Herder, 1967

Plaskow, Judith. *Sex, Sin and Grace: Women's Experience and the Theologies of Reinhold Niebuhr and Paul Tillich*. Washington, D.C.: University Press of America, 1980.

Schillebeeckx, Edward. *Christ: The Experience of Jesus as Lord*. New York: Crossroad, 1980.

Wicks, Jared. *Man Yearning for Grace: Luther's Early Spiritual Teaching*. Washington, D.C.: Corpus Books, 1968.

———, ed. *Catholic Scholars Dialogue with Luther*. Chicago: Loyola University Press, 1970.

GEORG KRAUS

Grace

Contemporary Issues

Grace is the communication of God's personal self to human beings. God is loving, and this personal acceptance of and presence to human beings is God's salvation. This fundamental notion of grace functions as a metadoctrine in the sense that the loving relationship of God to human beings revealed in Jesus Christ is a concentrated form of all Christian doctrine (GRACE: DOCTRINE OF). Across the history of theology, reflection on grace has dealt with many distinct problems connected to this basic relationship between God and human existence. "Contemporary Issues" refers to only some of the open questions that are receiving attention today. Grace may be systematically understood in terms of the doctrine of the Trinity (GRACE). It has also been portrayed in terms of God's address to human beings through Jesus Christ as God's Word (Luther) or as the action of God in the world appropriate to God as Spirit (Augustine, Rahner). This latter framework is presupposed here.

Grace and Historical Consciousness

Historical consciousness has had a major impact on Catholic theology in the second half of the twentieth century. Vatican II as a phenomenon demonstrated the church's historicity, and many of its teachings display a sense of historicity. Historical consciousness is a reflective sense of being limited by time and space, a consciousness that all beings are in some measure individual, particular, and conditioned by the coordinates of their time, place, and culture. Even classical ideas and values are relative in the sense that every appreciation of them is influenced by the circumstances in which it is held. This historical consciousness has operated as a horizon or deep background for interpreting many of the doctrines of the church. Theology thus gradually becomes contextual or inculturated into a historically conscious society and critically responsive to the experience of such a culture. All of the contemporary perspectives on grace outlined here have their roots in historical consciousness.

Cooperative Grace and History

Cooperative as distinct from operative grace is a notion that was used by Augustine to clarify the relation between God's impulse of grace and human freedom. How can one hold that the prior impulse of God's grace alone causes any and every self-transcending action of a human being that leads toward God and at the same time preserve human freedom? Operative grace initiates a human turning toward God; cooperative grace sustains the human response. For Augustine it was enough that freedom was consent, a going along with the impulse of grace. Whether or not the notion of cooperative grace as it is explained by classical authors is satisfactory today, the notion itself is transformed and becomes particularly relevant in a culture that is historically conscious, activist, conscious of its freedom, and oriented to achievement. History itself is the exercise of human freedom, and despite their obvious failures human beings continually seek an integral emancipation or liberation from anything that binds human freedom in a dehumanizing way. How does God enter into this equation? Underlying political theology, liberation theology, process theology, and more generally many theologies of history lies a concept analogous to cooperative grace. Cooperative grace is God's self-communication and presence that form an a priori horizon for the exercise of human freedom; grace does not compete with human freedom but energizes authentic freedom. This theological construction helps to explain the more classical ideas of PROVIDENCE, ELECTION, and PREDESTINATION in a way that is open to historicity, is not competitive with but supportive of authentic human freedom, and leads it in the direction of the KINGDOM OF GOD. Cooperative grace is the dynamic side of God's self-gift that is captured in the symbol of God as Spirit. It helps to demythologize crude imaginative conceptions of God working in history by understanding God as a divine presence and impulse within human freedom itself.

Grace and Liberation

Another development in the theology of grace, also encouraged by historical consciousness, links grace with liberation by correlating the symbol of salvation with liberation. Grace is God's communication of God's personal self, the effect of which is union with God. But this union with God is not something that is exclusively eschatological; it is a salvation that occurs now, in this world, in one's concrete existence. Moreover the effect of grace that is salvation is not merely an interior relationship with God. Because grace takes up into itself the whole person and every dimension of a person's action, the effects of grace become external and public. Negatively, grace urges resistance against sin, and, positively, it pushes the human person toward a self-transcending love of God and neighbor. A development of this thus far traditional doctrine is that salvation, which is the effect of grace, is being called liberation today by liberation and feminist theologians. This correlation of symbols, however, is incorrectly understood when it is seen as merely a superficial identification of Christian salvation with any emancipation from any social oppression that occurs. Rather these theologians define liberation in an intrinsically Christian manner on the basis of the dynamics of grace to which Scripture and the history of theological reflection give witness. Grace liberates a person from the bondage of sin (Luther); grace opens up human freedom and expands it in the direction of self-transcending love (Augustine). Grace generates actions of love. Grace informs and shapes external and public human actions by the virtues of faith, hope, and love (Aquinas). In other words, this salvation is liberating in this world in a public way insofar as it engenders action that is both liberated and liberating. This is so whether or not this action is explicitly known or characterized by the name Christian. This correlation of the symbol of salvation with liberation through the intrinsic determination of the theology of grace provides it with a certain intelligibility, plausibility, and relevance for contemporary life.

Social Grace

Another present-day development mediated by historical consciousness and socially conscious theologies is a notion of social grace. This concept calls into question certain individualist strains in reflections on grace. The notion of social grace is contingent upon a recognition of the social constitution of human existence that is new insofar as it has been mediated by such social sciences as history, sociology, social anthropology, and linguistics. Human beings exist in and through their social relationships. It is not that various relationships are added on to a common human nature as may be portrayed by some philosophies of substance. Rather what is transcendentally human is to be found within the differences among human beings who are shaped within the social matrix of time, place, and culture. Thus history and society provide another or "second" nature, not second chronologically or in importance, but simply another dimension of human existence. This social nature is a given along with human freedom and learning. Thus on the analogy of the various views of how grace builds on and suffuses human nature developed within the framework of classical Greek philosophy, theologians now also think of grace affecting the social nature or dimension of human existence. Concretely this means that the effects of grace that become external and public through the actions of people influence society; and society, which is constituted by the routinized behavior of its members, has an influence on those who belong to it. On the one hand, the notion of social grace is a heuristic concept: while there is no pure example of social grace, the notion of social grace is a category that provides critical questions about social institutions. On the other hand, some institutions are more clearly and explicitly embodiments of social grace than others. The church, for example, explicitly understands itself as such. But the concept is extended to all public institutions that nurture and enhance human life rather than diminish it.

Grace and Other Religions

Historical consciousness among Christians has generated a new perception of other religions. The element of relativity that accompanies historicity, the obvious fact that Christians are a minority in the world, and the cultural and religious assertions of self-identity outside the West have generated a new, positive a priori attitude toward other religions. Christians have gone well beyond the stages of polemics and objective, neutral study to dialogical interchange with representatives of other religions. Through such dialogue Christian theologians learn much more about other religions than objective study alone can supply, and in the comparison they appreciate better the nature of Christianity. These external events and developments have also generated theological reflection. Particularly relevant here are considerations of the UNIVERSAL SALVIFIC WILL OF GOD and its implications for the theology of grace. For, if God's will for salvation is universal, and that salvation is the effect of God's grace, then

that grace must be universally available and potentially effective. But this requires that it be historically mediated, for everything that affects the human
subject is mediated through the world. From these premises it is inferred that
because of their explicit religious character, the institutions of the various religions are in principle, but not necessarily in fact, the most obvious mediators
or historical bearers of God's grace. This gives the world's religions status as
mediatory of God's grace and thus a place in God's will. In sum, they are willed
by God (K. Rahner). These historical and theological developments continue to
have significant ramifications. They have altered the understanding and practice
of the missiological strategies of the church; dialogue is central when dealing
with peoples of other religious cultures. The "ordinary means of salvation" is
more frequently understood by theologians in a concrete historical and statistical sense rather than in an a priori theological sense. De facto, Christianity
is not the ordinary means of salvation. Theologians are developing methods of
doing specifically Christian theology that are essentially or intrinsically dialogical and comparative. And in all of this Christian theologians are learning a
sense of modesty in their mode of proclaiming the Christian witness.

The Eschatology of Grace

Historical consciousness generates ever-new reflections on the philosophy and
theology of history itself. These inevitably raise the questions of the end of history and ESCHATOLOGY. All knowledge of the future is generated on the basis
of the experience of the past and the present. In theology this general principle
means all religious knowledge of the end-time is based on faith's experience of
God's salvation historically mediated by Jesus and experienced now as God's
gracious gift of God's personal self. On the one hand, eschatological assertions
are extrapolations of the experience of grace. On the other hand, the imaginative projection of the end-time, this statement about fulfilled salvation, bends
back on the present to reveal what is lacking due to sin (ESCHATOLOGY: CON-
TEMPORARY ISSUES). Eschatological reflection builds upon a constant tradition
in the theology of grace that there is a continuity between grace and final fulfillment. A theology of history can exploit the fact that there is also a continuity
between the effects of grace realized in human action and the final reality of
the end-time. Especially the concept of cooperative grace supplies grounds for
arguing against a totally discontinuous eschatology (ESCHATOLOGY: CONCEP-
TIONS OF). By contrast a continuous eschatology based on cooperative grace
provides a new context for understanding traditional doctrines. For example, the theological notions of WORKS and MERIT appear different in this new
setting. So too does Christian SPIRITUALITY when this is understood as an integral Christian life. In liberation and process theologies all actions performed
under the influence of grace are constitutive in a causal way of the KINGDOM
OF GOD.

Bibliography
Haight, Roger. *The Experience and Language of Grace.* New York: Paulist, 1979.
———. "Sin and Grace." In *Systematic Theology: Roman Catholic Perspectives,* edited by
    Francis Schüssler Fiorenza and John Galvin, 2:75–141. Minneapolis: Fortress, 1991.
Rahner, Karl. *Foundations of Christian Faith: An Introduction to the Idea of Christianity.*
    New York: Seabury, 1978.
Schillebeeckx, Edward. *Christ: The Experience of Jesus as Lord.* New York: Seabury, 1980.
Segundo, Juan Luis. *Grace and the Human Condition.* Maryknoll, N.Y.: Orbis Books, 1973.
Stefano, Frances. *The Absolute Value of Human Action in the Theology of Juan Luis
    Segundo.* Lanham, Md.: University Press of America, 1992.

ROGER HAIGHT

Grace: Doctrine of. The doctrine of grace is the dogmatic treatise in which
we reflect systematically on the notion of grace and its theological implications.

(1) *Biblical Background.* In the Bible the rudiments of a systematic reflection on the essence and effects of grace are found only in Paul. Especially in
Romans, Paul explicitly discusses God's gracious activity, how it is objectively
bestowed in the salvific work of Jesus Christ, and how it is subjectively realized
in the justification of sinners.

(2) *History of Theology.* In the history of dogmatics, grace becomes an independent treatise only in the post-Tridentine period. The foundation for this
treatise, which was of central importance in the Western Church, was laid by
Augustine (d. 430). Many of his works in which he combats Pelagianism deal
with the theme of grace (e.g., *De natura et gratia; De gratia Christi et peccato
originali; De gratia et libero arbitrio; De corruptione et gratia*). In Scholasticism
there is no specific treatise on grace. The problems it involves were dealt with
diversely. Thus in Peter Lombard (d. 1160) they are found in the doctrines of
God, creation, redemption, and the sacraments. Thomas Aquinas (d. 1274) situates the question of grace in teachings concerning human activity, that is, with
his ethics. Thus grace is, after law, the second extrinsic principle that sustains
human beings in right actions (*STh* 1–2, q. 109–14). Bonaventure (d. 1274),
operating out of a pneumatological perspective, presents the initial stage of an
independent treatment of grace by including a treatise "on the grace of the Holy
Spirit" between Christology and the sacraments (*Breviloquium* 5). F. Suárez is
the first to develop a complete, comprehensive treatise entitled "De gratia,"
where he proposes a major division of actual and habitual grace. The organization and the themes of this work remain to this day the basic structure for
the Catholic treatise of grace.

(3) *Church Teaching.* There have been no official pronouncements concerning grace as a treatise.

(4) *Ecumenical Perspectives.* The Eastern Church has developed no systematic treatise on grace. Grace is treated as part of salvation-history in the

framework of soteriology. Also, at the beginning of the Reformation, grace was not treated independently. M. Luther (d. 1546) held a personal, Christocentric understanding of grace that is part of his doctrine of justification. For J. Calvin (d. 1564) also grace has no independent role to play. Rather it is based on the redemptive work of Jesus Christ and is realized in the Holy Spirit's work of sanctification. A coherent doctrine of grace is developed by early Protestant orthodoxy: by Lutherans under the heading of the grace of adoption; by the Reformed tradition under the heading of the grace of the covenant. In ecumenical dialogue today between Evangelical and Catholic theologians there is unity regarding the need to change the traditional basic structures for understanding grace. Reacting to the Evangelical criticism that Catholics split up grace and make it into a thing, Catholics have tried to make the treatise on grace more concise and personalized. This follows the structural principle that grace is the triune God's sharing of God's own self with the whole of humankind as persons. In reaction to the Catholic criticism that Evangelicals privatize and spiritualize grace, Evangelical theology has striven to broaden and concretize grace by dealing with its communitarian and this-worldly perspectives.

(5) *Systematic Reflections.* Today the doctrine of grace is in a revolutionary stage. From the viewpoint of a biblical understanding of grace (grace as the unconditional, free action of God for the salvation of human beings), the following basic formal perspectives must be acknowledged: its unity, its historicity, and its personal and social character. Using this formal criterion, the central themes will be those attested to by the Bible: the loving actions of the triune God in history, by which God works for the salvation of humanity, both individual and communitarian. Thus our systematic considerations on grace would be as follows: *fundamentally,* we would reflect on the great historical works of salvation — creation, redemption, and the final fulfillment — as creative, redemptive, and consummative grace. *Specifically,* we would reflect on: God's basic universal plan of salvation as predestined; then God's special historical deeds of salvation, such as the call to each person to be God's very image and child; then election and covenant as God's salvific works in the old and new people of God; finally the justification and sanctification of each individual person. The overall theological connections of these main themes should be studied within a basic trinitarian perspective but should also emphasize christological and pneumatological aspects. Furthermore, there will be protological, anthropological, ecclesiological, sacramental, and eschatological perspectives. By dividing grace into general and specific gracious actions, and by subordinating the remaining traditional questions on grace to this schema, the accompanying "Outline of the Doctrine of Grace" emerges. Finally, using these presuppositions, the question of the place occupied by grace in systematics may now be answered. The graciousness of God's action is a perspective basic to all dogmatic treatises. As a separate treatise the doctrine of grace may stand behind all the other treatises. For in a concentrated overview it

OUTLINE OF THE DOCTRINE OF GRACE

General Doctrine of Grace			
Essence of grace	Unconditional, free love of God for the salvation of humankind	Grace in the broad sense	foundational action of the triune God within salvation-history
Basic biblical characteristic	personal dynamic ontic historical communitarian of this world	The three great works of salvation-history	creation: creative grace; redemption: redemptive grace; the fulfillment: consummative grace
Formal determination	unmerited necessary all-inclusive boundless	Trinitarian present	indwelling: personal community of the triune God with humankind

Special Teachings on Grace			
Grace in the strict sense	Special deeds of the triune God in salvation-history	Relationships: grace and ...	Special problems
Individual foundation	Vocation of each person: – the image of God – child of God	Original plan of salvation	Predestination
		Universality of grace	Universal salvific will of God
Social mediation	Election and covenant: – old people of God (Israel) – new people of God (church)	Human autonomy	Grace and freedom
		Notions of reward	Merit and works
		Basic power of being related to God	Theological virtues – faith – hope – love
Individual realization	Justification and sanctification of each person		

can be demonstrated that all the relations between God and human beings are determined by grace, that is, by the unconditional free action of God.

See also GRACE; GRACE: THEOLOGICAL HERESIES.

Bibliography
Boff, Leonardo. *Liberating Grace.* Maryknoll, N.Y.: Orbis Books, 1979.
Burns, J. Patout. *The Development of Augustine's Doctrine of Operative Grace.* Paris: Études Augustiniennes, 1980.
Duffy, Stephen. *The Dynamics of Grace: Perspectives in Theological Anthropology.* Collegeville, Minn.: Liturgical Press, 1993.

Laporte, Jean-Marc. *Patience and Power: Grace for the First World.* New York: Paulist, 1988.

Lonergan, Bernard. *Grace and Freedom.* New York: Herder and Herder, 1971.

Lubac, Henri de. *Augustinianism and Modern Theology.* London: Chapman, 1969.

Phan, Peter C. *Grace and the Human Condition.* Wilmington, Del.: Glazier, 1988.

GEORG KRAUS

Grace: Theological Heresies. In determining the relationship between grace and nature or grace and freedom, there have been two extreme positions in the history of dogma. On the one hand, Pelagianism or Semi-Pelagianism overemphasize human nature and human freedom. On the other hand, Baianism and Jansenism overemphasize divine grace. The magisterium, which tries to take a middle course between grace and freedom, condemns both of these theological directions as heretical.

1. *Pelagianism and Semi-Pelagianism.* (a) Pelagianism was initiated by the British lay monk Pelagius (d. ca. 425), who around 400 in Rome and later in Palestine was known as a preacher and spiritual guide. He advocated strict Christian moral living and was responsible for an extensive revival movement. The basic tendencies of his theology of grace were used by his disciples Caelestius and Julianus in formulating an extremist system called Pelagianism. Pelagius is responsible for the following statements regarding a theology of grace: by grace God bestowed a naturally good human nature on humanity created in God's image; freedom is a special gift of the grace of creation and gives humanity the capacity and the power to decide between good and evil; thus human beings have the capacity, given to them by the Creator, to live without sin and to attain salvation by the merits of their good works; after the fall of Adam human beings are indeed corrupted by sin, which is Adam's bad example, but there is no original sin; human nature, weakened by its sinful habits, needs special help, and it experiences this help in salvation-history: in the Old Testament by the grace of the law and in the New Testament by the grace of Jesus Christ; the unmerited grace of Jesus Christ becomes effective in baptism, which forgives sins, and after baptism by his teachings, which show the way, give an efficacious example, and promise hope. In the fifth and sixth centuries, in connection with Augustine (d. 430) and his rigorous ideas on grace, a doctrine of grace later (in the sixteenth century) known as Semi-Pelagianism was developed in monasteries of the south of France. Its main representatives are John Cassian (d. 435) and Vincent of Lérins (d. ca. 450). Semi-Pelagianism considers that Augustine undervalued the human factor in salvation-history. For this reason it assigns two independent functions to human freedom: (i) humankind can and must be responsible for the preparatory acts (e.g., prayer) necessary for the beginning of faith (*initium fidei*); and (ii) after receiving grace, the believer, by means of his or her will, can and must persevere in order to reach final salvation. (b) At the instigation of Augustine, the Synod of Carthage rejected Pelagianism as a heresy in 415. It

condemned the Pelagians' denial of original sin (DS 222–24) and clarified the relationship between original sin and grace: the grace of Jesus Christ is efficacious not merely as the forgiveness of sins but also as a help in avoiding further sins. This grace does not merely teach goodness but helps in doing it. It not only makes it easier to do good but is fundamentally necessary for any good action (DS 225–27). At the Council of Ephesus (431) the condemnation of Pelagianism was formally repeated, without further explaining its content. The Second Synod of Orange (529) speaks out against Semi-Pelagianism. It stresses that the beginning of faith, the first step toward salvation, is not due to human initiative but a prior grace of God (DS 373–79, 384, 388). Perseverance in going good until the end is not a human work but a divine work (DS 380). To defend itself against the Reformers' accusation of Pelagianism, the Council of Trent repeated earlier condemnations of it in its decree on justification (1547). With regard to Pelagianism it explained: no human being can be justified by merely human power, without grace. The grace of Jesus Christ should not be limited to the function of making good actions easier (DS 1515f.). The council was equally decisive in its condemnation of Semi-Pelagianism: the beginning of justification is due only to the prior grace of God in Jesus Christ, without any preparatory merit or work on the part of human beings (DS 1525, 1553). Perseverance is a gift of grace (DS 1541).

2. *Baianism and Jansenism.* (a) The Louvain professor M. Baius (d. 1589), using Augustine's doctrine on original sin, regarded human nature as totally corrupt: that is, because of the fallenness of human nature, free will is capable only of sinning. On the other hand, for Baius grace necessarily belongs to human nature and is due to it. Jansenism goes back to the Belgian theologian and bishop C. Jansen (d. 1638). In his main work, *Augustinus*, he demonstrates by means of excerpts from the work of the Doctors of the Church that the systems of grace in Molinism and Congruism, with their emphasis on human freedom, have fallen into heresy. Jansen develops his doctrine of grace as a system of three states of human nature in salvation-history. In paradise, in the state of "sinless nature," humankind had freedom of decision and there was "sufficient grace." "Fallen nature" is the state in which human freedom has been completely destroyed because of original sin and has need of "efficacious actual grace," which acts irresistibly. In the state of "purified nature," which was brought about by the salvific work of Jesus Christ, the grace of Christ reigns, although it produces salvation only for the small number of the predestined. A "second Jansenism" began with the French theologian P. Quesnel (d. 1719), in that he developed Jansen's main theses to their extremes. Thus according to Quesnel, the corruption of fallen humankind makes all the ethical acts of pagans sinful. Grace is irresistible. Jesus Christ did not die for all human beings but only for the predestined. (b) In 1567 Pius V attacked Baianism by condemning seventy-nine sentences of Baius. On the one hand, the Baian claim that grace is due to humankind was rejected (DS 1921). On the other hand, the following statements regarding the damage suffered by human nature were declared he-

retical: without divine grace human free will is capable only of sin (DS 1927); free will has no power to avoid any sin (DS 1928); all the works of unbelievers are sinful and the virtues of the philosophers are mere depravity (DS 1925). With regard to Jansenism, Innocent X condemned the following five sentences as heretical in 1653 (DS 2001–5): (i) some commandments are incapable of being carried out, even by the justified; (ii) grace is irresistible; (iii) human beings do not need interior freedom, but only freedom from exterior constraint, in order to be saved; (iv) human will is incapable of either rejecting or obeying grace; and (v) the death of Jesus was not for all of humankind. In reaction to the papal decision the French Jansenists made the following distinction: these sentences are juridically heretical (*questio iuris*), but in fact (*questio facti*) they are not found in Jansen's *Augustinus*. In 1705 Clement XI declared this distinction to be an untenable subterfuge (DS 2390). In 1713 he condemned 101 sentences of Quesnel. He thereby rejected three types of propositions regarding a theology of grace: (i) propositions that attribute nothing but evil to those outside the grace of Christianity (e.g., DS 2438, 2440, 2459); (ii) propositions that claim that grace is irresistible (e.g., DS 2410–13, 2421, 2430); and (iii) propositions that present grace as particular.

See also FREEDOM; GRACE; NATURE; SYSTEMS OF GRACE.

Bibliography
See the bibliographies under GRACE and GRACE: DOCTRINE OF.

GEORG KRAUS

Guilt. *See* SIN AND GUILT.

Hh

Heart. The word *heart* stands for the holistic center of all the expressions of human life. "Heart" is not easily defined because every definition brings a further differentiation with it: in organic functions (heartbeat), sensual feelings (heart's content), sentiments (warmth of heart), thoughts, desires (attitude of the heart), and so on. Theologically, the heart of the human person is the "place" for total openness before God: only God sees one's heart. From the side of the human person, love "from the whole heart" corresponds to this.

(1) *Biblical Background.* Scripture defines the word *heart* in its whole anthropological range of meaning. According to context, some specific senses can be distinguished. The concept's original, irreducible unity, which generally eludes human reflection, comes above all to bear when it refers to the human person's relationship to God. Only God sees through the heart of the human person. Therefore, only God can judge the human person (e.g., 1 Jn 3:20). Moreover, God has access to the innermost region of the heart, which is neither under the influence of other human persons nor even at one's own disposition. God can harden the heart and make it "blind" (Rom 1:21, 24). God can fundamentally change it (Ez 36:26), inasmuch as God opens it up to the Spirit (Rom 5:5) and allows the divine light to shine in it (2 Cor 4:6). From this renewed heart come forth faith, hope, and love.

(2) *History of Theology.* The Church Fathers followed closely the linguistic usage of Scripture. For the Scholastic method the conceptual distinction and classification of the heart were too undifferentiated. Scholasticism attempted to grasp the depth of the heart that was removed from humankind through metaphysical concepts (nature, supernature). In this way medieval theologians could place God's action upon the human person (grace) above the free self-determination of the human person before God.

(3) *Church Teaching.* There is no special pronouncement on the idea of the heart.

(4) *Ecumenical Perspectives.* Luther, on the other hand, took up the biblical word *heart* in order to express the comprehensive power of sin. Sin is rooted in the human heart that is turned inward upon itself (*cor curvatum in seipsum*) and that is thereby incapable itself of opening up to God.

(5) *Systematic Reflections.* In protest against an overly intellectualistic theology, Christians frequently appeal to the heart, as in the *Devotio moderna* against Scholasticism; in romanticism's theology of feeling, which was opposed to the theology of the Enlightenment; and in the expectations that are frequently attached today to a mystical or pneumatological theology against the current methodically conscious theology. Such protest is justified only when

theology itself is not aware of its intellectualization or does not present this knowledge clearly enough in its formulations. For scientific theology by its nature lays claim above all to the capability to think and reflect. It is "headwork." Because the discussion about the heart eludes conceptual definition and reflection, the reference to the heart in dogmatic anthropology can have only a critical limiting function that points out the shortcomings of every comprehensive systematic attempt at explanation. Theological reflection is not sufficient in itself. It is only one moment in the total realization of the Christian faith, which comes from the heart.

See also CONCUPISCENCE; HUMAN PERSON; IMAGE OF GOD; NATURE AND GRACE.

Bibliography
Minear, Paul S. "A Theology of the Heart." *Worship* 63 (1989) 246–54.
Molin, Lennart. *Hearts and Structures: About Man and Society out of an American Theological Material.* Stockholm: Gummesson, 1976.
Obenhaus, Victor, ed. *Religion and Ethical Issues: Position Guides for Decision Making.* Chicago: Exploration Press, 1991.
Tallon, Andrew. "The Heart in Rahner's Philosophy of Mysticism." *ThS* 53 (1992) 700–728.
———. "The Meaning of Heart Today: Reversing a Paradigm according to Levinas and Rahner." *JRelS* 11 (1983) 59–74.

                                                              GEORG LANGEMEYER

Heaven. Heaven is the definitive and lasting mode of existence proper to eternal salvation; it is given to human beings by God as an unmerited gift after death and any necessary purification; after the resurrection of the dead, the body also shares in it.

(1) *Biblical Background.* In the Old Testament and New Testament the word *heaven* occurs, in the singular and the plural, with a variety of meanings. In the Old Testament, as a part of the picture of the world, heaven is the fixed vault (*firmamentum*) that divides the upper and the lower waters (Gn 1:6) and in which the stars are fastened like lamps (Gn 1:14). "Heaven and earth" is an expression that designates the entire universe (Gn 1:1). Next, and above all, heaven is an image for the dwelling place of God, who sits there on a lofty throne and rules the universe (Dt 26:15; Pss 2:4; 11:4; Is 63:15). But heaven expresses not a localization of God but God's mode of existence and saving power. For this reason Judaism could make heaven a substitute for the real name of God (Yahweh), which no one dared any longer utter. In the New Testament the word *heaven* has in addition a christological and soteriological meaning. Jesus speaks of the heavenly Father, the Father in heaven (Mt 5:16, 45; 6:1, 9; etc.), of the kingdom of heaven (Mt 3:2; 5:10, 19, 20; 7:21; etc.). The Son of Man comes down from heaven (Jn 3:13), comes from heaven (Jn 3:31), and, after carrying out his mission, will be taken back to heaven (Acts 1:9–11); to him all power is given in heaven and on earth (Mt 28:18); at the end of time he will come upon the clouds of heaven with great power and glory (Mt 24:30). The Holy Spirit is sent from heaven (Acts 2:1f.) and is active in the

church and the world. To be in heaven means, therefore: to live in the company of God and Christ. The idea of heaven as communion with God is found in the Synoptics, since ultimate salvation, eternal life, is described as an entering into the kingdom of God or the kingdom of heaven. The idea of heaven as communion with the exalted Lord is found above all in the Pauline letters, which speak of being caught up to meet the Lord (1 Thes 4:17), being with Christ (Phil 1:23; see 2 Cor 5:8), living in union with Christ (1 Thes 5:10), and living with Christ by the power of God (2 Cor 13:4). In the message of Jesus, heaven is understood as a reward for good works in this world (Mt 5:12; 19:21, 29; Mk 10:30; Lk 6:23), although this reward is at the same time a reward that is pure gift (Mt 20:1–16). Finally, the christological understanding of heaven is connected with the vision of the church as a community of saints. The salvation of the individual is not fulfilled until the salvation of the universe and all individuals is complete. In the final analysis, we will not be *in* heaven but rather, as the one Christ, will ourselves *be* heaven. Since the human person, as a being made up of soul and body, belongs to the earth and is responsible for it (see Gn 1:17f.; 2:7f.), definitive salvation requires not only the resurrection of the dead but also an ideal world as the place for perfected human beings; this ideal world is called and described as "a new heaven and a new earth" in Rv 21:1f. In describing heaven as the mode of existence of complete salvation, the New Testament harks back to Old Testament ideas (Ex 24:9–11; Is 25:6) and depicts it chiefly in the image of a banquet (Mt 8:11; Lk 13:29), at which Christ himself is the host who asks everyone he finds keeping watch to come to table (Lk 12:37). The parable of the royal wedding feast (Mt 22:1–14), to which people are invited in from the streets, whereas those first invited come to a terrible end, brings out especially the gift-character of heavenly beatitude. In Rv 21:9–22:5 images of a banquet are combined with the image of the holy city (the new Jerusalem), which in antiquity was a widespread symbol of hope, fellowship, and sure protection. Also found, again inspired by Old Testament passages (Gn 2:4b–25; Ez 36:35; Is 11:6f.; 65:25), are various motifs connected with paradise, such as the eating of the tree of life (Rv 2:7), the image of the water of life (22:1f.), the destruction of the ancient serpent (20:2), and freedom from mourning, tribulation, and death (21:4). Heavenly beatitude is also described in the New Testament as consisting, among other things, in the vision of God (Mt 5:8; 1 Cor 13:12; 2 Cor 3:18; 5:7; see Heb 12:14; 1 Jn 3:2; Rv 22:4), an idea that becomes extremely important in Scholastic theology.

(2) *History of Theology.* Christian tradition continued to preach belief in eschatological salvation in heaven and to explain it theologically. In the process, the word *heaven* became a technical theological term that was not automatically coextensive with the biblical concept. In the Scriptures heaven signifies the manner of existence of the saved after the resurrection, but now it signified definitive salvation both in the intermediate state and after the resurrection of the dead. After the reception of Greek teaching on the soul, the beatitude of heaven was linked to the two powers of the soul, intellect and will, so that it was pos-

sible to speak of a beatifying vision and a beatifying enjoyment. Thus whereas Augustine says that the blessed in heaven embrace the immutable essence of the Creator in vision and love, medieval theology discusses the question whether heavenly beatitude is to be understood more affectively and emotionally as radical love (Scotists) or more contemplatively and intellectually as beatifying vision (Thomists). In fact, the blessedness of heaven is experienced in the depths of the human spirit, where knowledge and volition have not yet separated into two distinct activities. The vision of God is an act of love totally illumined by knowledge and an act of knowledge totally aglow with love.

(3) *Church Teaching.* The doctrine of the beatific vision became the object of various doctrinal statements of the church in the Middle Ages. John XXII held the view that the souls of the elect enjoyed the perfect vision of God only after the resurrection of the dead and had only an imperfect beatitude before then. Benedict XII came out against this view in 1336 (*Benedictus Deus* [DS 1000]) with the teaching that even before the general resurrection the souls of the saints see the essence of God intuitively and face-to-face, without the mediation of any creature. The Council of Florence (1438) adds that heavenly beatitude differs in degree according to the merits of individuals on earth (DS 1305). In its Decree on Justification (1547) the Council of Trent makes this idea its own when it says that the justified can merit an increase of grace, eternal life, and an increase of heavenly glory (DS 1582).

(4) *Ecumenical Perspectives.* The Orthodox churches, on the other hand, emphasize the provisional character of salvation in the intermediate state as compared with the fullness of salvation that is given with the resurrection of the dead. Not a few Evangelical theologians accuse Catholic theology of shifting salvation to the intermediate state to such an extent that the properly biblical statements about salvation are no longer fully respected.

(5) *Systematic Reflections.* In general, contemporary theology emphasizes the point that heaven expresses the complete salvation of the whole person, of the human race, and of the world that has been assigned to the race.

See also ASCENSION OF CHRIST; ETERNAL LIFE; KINGDOM OF GOD; MERIT; PAROUSIA; RESURRECTION OF THE DEAD; SAINTS: HOLINESS, SANCTIFICATION.

Bibliography
Hellwig, Monika. "Eschatology." In *Systematic Theology: Roman Catholic Perspectives,* edited by Francis Schüssler Fiorenza and John P. Galvin, 2:347–72. Minneapolis: Fortress, 1991.
Kreeft, Peter J. *Everything You Ever Wanted to Know about Heaven.* San Francisco: Harper and Row, 1982.
Küng, Hans. *Eternal Life? Life after Death as a Medical, Philosophical, and Theological Problem.* Garden City, N.Y.: Doubleday, 1984.
McDannell, Colleen, and Bernhard Lang. *Heaven: A History.* New York: Random House, 1990.
Mussner, Franz. *Readings in Christian Eschatology.* Derby, N.Y.: Society of St. Paul, 1966.
Ratzinger, Joseph. *Eschatology: Death and Eternal Life.* Washington, D.C.: Catholic University of America Press, 1988.

Richards, Hubert J. *Death and After: What Will Happen?* Mystic, Conn.: Twenty-Third, 1987.

Shea, John. *What a Modern Catholic Believes about Heaven and Hell.* Chicago: Thomas More, 1972.

JOSEF FINKENZELLER

Hell. Hell is the mode of existence of eternal damnation, which according to revelation and ecclesial tradition looms for every human being who dies alienated from God.

(1) *Biblical Background.* In the Old Testament and early Judaism the idea of an otherworldly place of punishment appears primarily in two forms: (*a*) Sheol (the lower world) is no longer understood simply as the place where all the dead sojourn; it is thought of rather as consisting of two separate chambers for the good and the wicked, in which reward is given and punishment inflicted (Lk 16:19–31 presupposes this idea). According to extrabiblical witnesses (4 Maccabees; *1 Enoch*), Sheol is also the final and definitive place of punishment for the ungodly ("Sheol of Damnation"). (*b*) Because of prophetic threats of judgment (Jer 7:32; 19:6; Is 66:24), the Valley of Ben-hinnom, where children were immolated in sacrifice under Ahaz and Manasseh (2 Chr 28:3; 33:6), is regarded in Jewish apocalyptic, from the second century B.C.E. on, as the place where the fire of hell will open up after the final judgment. The New Testament has various images and similes for hell. The Synoptics have the term *gehenna* (a Greek word derived from *gehinnom* = Valley of Hinnom), which signifies the place of eternal punishment that will be opened after the final judgment; it is not intended solely for the devil and his angels (Mt 25:41) but looms for all who were not ready for conversion and spurned the salvation offered by God (Mt 5:29f. par.). John the Baptist (Mt 3:12 par.) and Jesus (Mt 18:8 par.) say that an eternal and inextinguishable fire burns in hell; for this reason it is also called hellfire (Mt 5:22; 18:19) or fiery furnace (Mt 13:42, 50). In other passages the torments of hell are described in the images of wailing and grinding of teeth (Mt 8:12; 13:42, 50; 22:13; 24:51; 25:30; Lk 13:28) or are compared to a worm that never dies (Mk 9:48). When the punishment of hell is described as outer darkness (Mt 8:12; 22:13; 25:30), it is being contrasted with the brightly lit banquet hall of HEAVEN, where the saved are assembled (see Mt 22:1f.). In Revelation (14:10; 19:20; 20:14; 21:8), Old Testament scenes are used (Gn 19:24: destruction of Sodom and Gomorrah by sulfurous fire) to describe the place of damnation as a sea of endlessly burning sulfur. Into it are cast the ANTICHRIST and the false prophet (19:20), the devil (20:10), and, finally, all human beings whose names are not written in the book of life (20:15). Even death and Hades are banished to it (20:14), so that henceforth they can exercise no power. Although Paul does not give a picture of eternal hell, he does speak very plainly of the eternal ruin (1 Cor 1:18; 2 Cor 2:15; 4:3; 2 Thes 2:10) that threatens those who do not obey the gospel (2 Thes 1:9) and that comes upon them as suddenly as labor pains upon a pregnant woman.

(2) *History of Theology.* In Christian tradition the doctrine of hell was accepted from the beginning, although it was also given a new form at certain points. As understood in early Judaism and the New Testament, hell, regarded as preexistent, becomes a place of punishment only after the resurrection of the dead, while other places were assumed to exist for provisional punishment in the INTERMEDIATE STATE; in the first century, however, the idea spread that the wicked are already in hellfire. After the reception of the Greek doctrine of the soul, hellfire was regarded as afflicting the bodiless soul in the intermediate state. No matter what efforts were made to base the eternity of hell on divine justice, the question arose of how this eternity was to be reconciled to the mercy of God. As a result, while in the New Testament kerygma the statements about the universal salvific will of God and the eternity of hell stand side by side unreconciled, the Christian tradition has seen various attempts at a resolution; these continue today. Once the idea of APOCATASTASIS had been rejected, the so-called *misericordia* (mercy) theory won adherents; it says that because God is merciful, it is possible to have a mitigation of the pains of hell. According to John Chrysostom, for example, the good works of those who remain behind on earth can mitigate the pains of hell; Augustine regards as possible an occasional (even weekly, on Sundays) lightening of the punishment. Others take the view that all Christians, even heretics, attain to salvation because the participation in the body of Christ that has its basis in baptism is a guarantee of eternal salvation. Still others limit salvation to those who are baptized in the Catholic Church and persevere in the Catholic faith. The teaching on mitigation was rejected once and for all in the Middle Ages, as a result especially of the disapproval of Thomas Aquinas (d. 1274). From the time of the Fathers down to our own century the explanation of hellfire has occupied an important place. Some (e.g., Origen, Ambrose, and Jerome) take it to be purely metaphorical, while others (e.g., Basil and Augustine) maintain a realistic interpretation, although they also emphasize the differences between hellfire and earthly fire. In this connection, the essence of the punishment of hell is brought out by the distinction between *poena damni* (punishment of exclusion from the vision of God) and *poena sensus* (sensible punishment).

(3) *Church Teaching.* The binding content of the doctrinal decisions of the church in response to various errors depends in each case on the formulation of the question. In addition to the condemnation of the apocatastasis doctrine mention should be made of the Faith of Damasus, which says, in connection with the doctrine of the resurrection of the flesh, that the good receive an eternal reward for their merits while the wicked receive an eternal punishment for their sins (DS 72). The same confession of faith is found in the Pseudo-Athanasian Creed, which says that those who have done evil will go into everlasting fire (DS 76). Similarly, the Fourth Lateran Council (1215) says that at the resurrection of the dead those who have done evil will suffer eternal

punishment along with the devil (DS 801). The Second Council of Lyons (1274) says that immediately after death those who die in mortal sin or even simply in original sin descend into hell, where they suffer different kinds of punishment. Nonetheless, on the day of judgment all will appear, in their bodies, before the judgment seat of God to give an account of their deeds (DS 858–59). The constitution *Benedictus Deus* (1336) presents essentially the same teaching, but it does not mention those who die simply in original sin (DS 1002). According to the Council of Florence (Decree for the Jacobites [1442]), no one can attain to eternal salvation outside the Catholic Church (DS 1351; NECESSITY OF THE CHURCH FOR SALVATION). Finally, there is an implicit reference to eternal damnation in the decree of the Council of Trent on justification (1547), when it rejects the view that the only reason why the just are not damned is that God does not impute unto eternal damnation the evil deeds found even in the just (DS 1539, 1575).

(4) *Ecumenical Perspectives.* On the ecumenical scene it is important to note that the Orthodox churches distinguish between provisional punishment in the intermediate state and definitive punishment after the RESURRECTION OF THE DEAD. In the context of the theory of total death (DEATH), some Evangelical theologians adopt the view that those individuals who were alienated from God in life come to an end in bodily death and do not arise to life, so that their death is a revelation of their nullity.

(5) *Systematic Reflections.* In contemporary theology, the interpretation of statements on hell is discussed from various points of view. Since all eschatological "places" are understood as events and personal encounters with God, so that God as lost is hell for the damned, all questions about the place of hell and about hellfire are to be regarded as settled. There is also agreement on the basic understanding of New Testament statements about hell: these do not provide information about otherworldly factual situations but are meant as kerygmatic efforts to influence our life in this world. It is likely that many theologians of our time also agree that nowhere in Sacred Scripture or in ecclesial tradition is it said that any particular individual is in hell (not even Judas, despite Mk 14:21; Lk 22:3; Jn 13:27). In canonizations the church expresses its belief that certain individuals have surely reached fulfillment in heaven, but it makes no similar statements regarding the damnation of particular individuals. The reality of hell is taken most seriously when each individual becomes aware that "*I* can be lost; therefore *I* hope to be saved for the sake of Christ." A number of theologians also believe that justice is done to the texts of the Bible and the doctrinal pronouncements of the church if one regards hell as an abiding possibility for the pilgrim on earth, in the sense that hell looms for those who in fact die alienated from God. These theologians do not, however, necessarily say that in fact any human being dies in mortal sin.

See also APOCATASTASIS; CHRIST'S DESCENT INTO HELL; FREEDOM; MERCY OF GOD; UNIVERSAL SALVIFIC WILL OF GOD.

Bibliography

Hellwig, Monika. "Eschatology." In *Systematic Theology: Roman Catholic Perspectives,* edited by Francis Schüssler Fiorenza and John Galvin, 2:347–72. Minneapolis: Fortress, 1991.

Küng, Hans. *Eternal Life? Life after Death as a Medical, Philosophical, and Theological Problem.* Garden City, N.Y.: Doubleday, 1984.

Ratzinger, Joseph. *Eschatology: Death and Eternal Life.* Washington, D.C.: Catholic University of America Press, 1988.

Richards, Hubert J. *Death and After: What Will Happen?* Mystic, Conn.: Twenty-Third, 1987.

Shea, John. *What a Modern Catholic Believes about Heaven and Hell.* Chicago: Thomas More, 1972.

Vorgrimler, Herbert. *Geschichte der Holle.* Munich: Fink, 1993.

Walker, D. P. *The Decline of Hell: Seventeenth-Century Discussions of Eternal Torment.* Chicago: University of Chicago Press, 1964.

Walls, Jerry L. *Hell: The Logic of Damnation.* Notre Dame, Ind.: University of Notre Dame Press, 1992.

JOSEF FINKENZELLER

Heresy. Heresy is the conscious, deliberate denial, by the baptized, of truths of faith.

(1) *Biblical Background.* In the Hellenistic world, heresy (from Greek *hairesis* = choice) meant the choice of a particular teaching. According to the New Testament, and especially Acts, groups that have rallied around particular, limited doctrines are living in heresy (see Acts 5:17; 15:5; 24:5, 14; 26:5; 28:22). It may be inferred from Gal 5:20 and 1 Cor 11:8f. that heresy and church are contradictory concepts. This point is made even more emphatically in 2 Pt 2:1, according to which heresy so radically curtails the teaching of the church that alongside the latter there arises a community that the church finds intolerable because it turns the universality of the church into something merely local.

(2) *History of Theology.* In the early church heresy was regarded as a serious offense against the unity of the church. It led to excommunication; reconciliation was achieved through the church's system of public penance. Debates with heretics took the form of theological argumentation. That is how such works as the *Adversus Praxean* of Tertullian or the *Adversus haereses* of Irenaeus came into existence. As the church began to take over public functions in the Roman Empire, its dealings with heretics also took new forms. The instruments of power available to the state were now used against them. The result was forms of persecution of heretics that cannot be justified from the gospel (e.g., the carrying out of death sentences, which were passed by inquisitorial tribunals).

(3) *Church Teaching.* Vatican II does not use the concept of heresy. Since those persons belonging to the non-Christian religions (*NA* 2) and, indeed, all human beings of good will (*LG* 16) can be saved, and since furthermore non-Catholic Christians are described as "separated brethren" (*UR* passim), it must be assumed that the Catholic Church applies the concept of heretic only to

Catholics. According to the Code of Canon Law (can. 1364), heretics incur excommunication.

(4) *Ecumenical Perspectives.* The Reformers also regarded and condemned teachers of false doctrines about the faith as heretics, not only in their confessional documents but also through legal persecution based on the imperial laws against heretics. Today dissociation from heretics is handled by confessional texts (Barmen Theses [1934]) or by procedures for doctrinal discipline (ECCLESIAL MAGISTERIUM).

(5) *Systematic Reflections.* A Catholic is a heretic if he or she refuses assent to one or more truths of faith, not only objectively (*materialiter*) but explicitly (*formaliter*). Heretics are to be distinguished from apostates, who freely and completely repudiate the Christian faith.

See also CHURCH; EXCOMMUNICATION; FAITH; SACRAMENT OF RECONCILIATION; SCHISM; UNITY OF THE CHURCH.

Bibliography
Bauer, W. *Orthodoxy and Heresy in Earliest Christianity.* Philadelphia: Fortress, 1970.
Chesterton, Gilbert K. *Orthodoxy.* Garden City, N.Y.: Doubleday, 1959.
Durham, Barrows. *Heroes and Heretics: A Social History of Dissent.* New York: Knopf, 1967.
Grant, Robert M. *Heresy and Criticism: The Search for Authenticity in Early Christian Literature.* Louisville: Westminster, 1993.
Küng, Hans. *The Church — Maintained in Truth.* New York: Seabury, 1980.
Kurtz, Lester R. *The Politics of Heresy: The Modernist Crisis in Roman Catholicism.* Berkeley: University of California Press, 1986.
Leff, Gordon. *Heresy in the Later Middle Ages: The Relation of Heterodoxy to Dissent c. 1250–1450.* Manchester: Manchester University Press, 1967.
Rahner, Karl. *On Heresy.* Freiburg: Herder, 1964.
Schillebeeckx, Edward, ed. *Dogma and Pluralism.* Vol. 51 of *Concilium.* New York: Herder, 1970.

WERNER LÖSER

Hermeneutics. Hermeneutics (from the Greek: *hermenéuein* = to make something understandable, interpret, translate) is the art and science of the explanation and interpretation of texts.

(1) *Biblical Background.* With regard to hermeneutics within the Bible, see the article entitled SCRIPTURE. An initial guideline for ecclesial hermeneutics is set forth in 2 Pt 1:16–21: the interpretation should follow the apostolic tradition.

(2) *History of Theology.* The problem of interpretation has arisen for the church and its theologians at least since the transition (already begun in the New Testament) from the Jewish cultural sphere into the Greek: the gospel must be made understandable in new ways. Origen was the first to offer some systematic reflections, saying that the historical sense of the Bible is to be deepened through spiritual (allegorical) interpretation. Augustine proposed a hermeneutical theory when he suggested that speech is the symbol (*signum*) for the intended reality (*res*) (*De doctr. christ.*). This theory is extended through

the doctrine of the normative role in interpretation of the rule of faith (Tertullian, Vincent of Lérins). In the Middle Ages these basic approaches were expanded into the doctrine of the fourfold sense of Scripture; at the same time the importance of the ecclesial magisterium as the authentic interpreter of Scripture and tradition increased. This emphasis on the ecclesial magisterium reached its climax at the Council of Trent and at Vatican I. Until modern times hermeneutics was considered to be primarily a theory of the rules for interpretation. This changed with the Enlightenment. The newly awakened historical consciousness raised the question of how texts of Scripture and tradition that are in themselves contingent (because they are historical) can be normative for later eras. Hermeneutics thus becomes the science of historical knowledge, and thereby more a philosophical discipline. F. Schleiermacher expounded hermeneutics as the "art of understanding," developed from both the comprehension of the text and a congenial empathy with the author. W. Dilthey made a distinction between *explanation,* which is obtained scientifically, and *understanding,* which is achieved through hermeneutics. Understanding comes through the analysis of a text that includes the inner correlation of lived experience and of reflection upon it. Dilthey considered this to be the characteristic method of the cultural sciences (*Geisteswissenschaften*) as the sciences of the historical-individual sphere. Through an existential analysis of Being (*Dasein*), M. Heidegger developed the question further and thereby influenced theology. Whereas K. Barth rejected the application of general hermeneutics in theology, R. Bultmann embraced it with his radical program of demythologization. The problem continued to become ever more urgent, not only because the authority of the Bible and dogma was seen to be only formal, but above all because of the fundamental difficulty of human beings within a post-Christian, postmodern period to understand discourse about God and the christological significance of Jesus. From this another meaning of hermeneutics arose, introduced into the conversation by the representatives of the "New Hermeneutic": hermeneutics became the general theory of knowledge, and within theology, it became the "grammar of the faith" (E. Fuchs, G. Ebeling), in which questions were posed about the significance of myth and symbol (M. Buber, P. Tillich, E. Drewermann), about the meaning of narrative (narrative theology), or fundamentally about the meaning of language in the search for an ontological analysis of *Dasein* (H. G. Gadamer).

(3) *Church Teaching.* The Council of Trent emphasized against the Reformers that the magisterium represents the final interpretive authority for Scripture and tradition (DS 1507). Vatican I specified general rules for the understanding of dogmatic texts; these included the use of analogy and the interrelation of the mysteries of faith among each other and with the human person's ultimate end (DS 3016). Vatican II put forward several principles of interpretation for the understanding of Scripture (*DV* 12), which are basically also valid for dogmatic texts.

THE SIGNIFICANCE OF THE HERMENEUTICAL PROCESS
FOR FAITH AND THEOLOGY

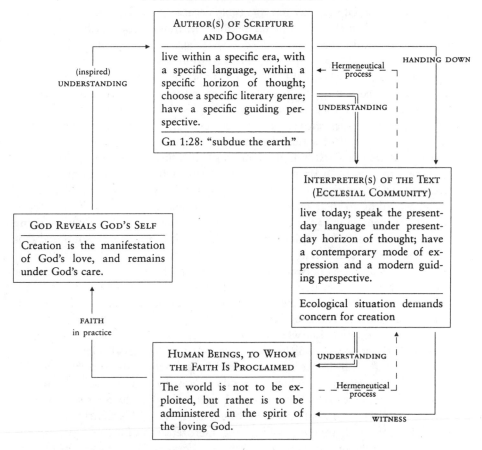

In the hermeneutical process revelation and faith are mediated to each other. The divine revelation (e.g., God's will regarding our behavior toward the world) must be understood

(a) through the inspired author living "at that time" or, in the case of dogma, through the understanding of the dogmatizing church at the time: this comprehension is recorded in the text (e.g., Gn 1:28);

(b) through the interpreter living "today" who appropriates the message of revelation in his or her situation (e.g., the ecological crisis at the end of the twentieth century) and to whom revelation is handed down only through the author. The author's text is accepted as theologically significant (preunderstanding), is taken through the hermeneutical process (What does the text say? How and for what reason does it say it? What does it have to do with me and my experience?) and thereby (better) understood;

(c) through everyone who wants to believe. For this one needs the mediation of the interpreting community of faith: a further hermeneutical process begins. The understanding that results from this makes possible the fulfillment in faith of God's will (care for the world).

In the lived expression of faith a new hermeneutical process begins. The believer experiences that his or her faith proves itself to be truthful, revelation contained in Scripture is seen in a new perspective, and either previous dogma proves its fruitfulness or new dogmas/dogmatic statements are formulated (DOGMA/DOGMATIC STATEMENT, TRUTH OF FAITH).

(4) *Ecumenical Perspectives.* The problem of hermeneutics in modern times has become critical above all through Protestantism. As a result of the rejection of the ecclesial magisterium, the Bible became the only source of faith; the investigation of the Bible's contents became the fundamental task of faith and theology. This shift was accompanied at the same time by a turning away from the previously valid principles of interpretation: the place of the allegorical sense was taken over by an inner principle of Scripture (the doctrine of justification). Hermeneutical research therefore was promoted primarily by Protestant academics. The first theorist was M. Flacius (*Clavis Sacrae Scripturae* [1567]).

(5) *Systematic Reflections.* The starting point for every hermeneutical process is the existence of a text that is considered to be meaningful but that is not immediately understandable. One must thus find out which questions the text seeks to answer. In Scripture and dogmas the Christian community of faith possesses resources that claim universal validity. They must not only be understood according to their thought content (information) but also be developed in view of their significance for salvation in the concrete life of a person living today. Insofar as at the beginning of the process it is already presupposed that these texts have such meaning, the interpreter already always stands within the "hermeneutical circle" between preunderstanding (these texts are significant for me as a Christian) and understanding (the investigation makes clear and concretizes this significance for me). This hermeneutical movement is not, however, actually a "circle," but is closer to being a "spiral" in which one moves toward a more complete knowledge. The hermeneutical process in its theological sense is nothing other than the special case of the dialogical relation between revelation and faith. In the Bible and in dogma (each in specific ways) we encounter God's revelation, which demands an answer in faith. In order to find this answer responsibly, we must carefully examine what the texts say and how revelation relates to our situation. In the concrete case of hermeneutical activity all of the rules apply that are valid for the interpretation of texts in general: one must examine the *text* (literary criticism), the *context*, the *situation of the text* (the author, the problem from the perspective of his or her time, his or her time in the perspective of our time), and the *thought context* (Why do I interpret this text, and from which preunderstanding do I interpret it?). Joined to this are the rules that are linked to the character of the texts as dogmatically important resources: they are to be interpreted taking into account the statements from the other sources of faith (THEOLOGICAL EPISTEMOLOGY).

See also DOGMA/DOGMATIC STATEMENT; ECCLESIAL MAGISTERIUM; FAITH; REVELATION; SCRIPTURE.

Bibliography
Foster, Matthew. *Gadamer and Practical Philosophy: The Hermeneutics of Moral Confidence.* Atlanta: Scholars Press, 1991.
Gadamer, Hans-Georg. *Philosophical Hermeneutics.* Berkeley: University of California Press, 1976.
———. *Truth and Method.* 2d rev. ed. New York: Crossroad, 1989.

Jenrod, Werner G. *Text and Application as Categories of Theological Thinking.* New York: Crossroad, 1988.

Mueller-Vollmer, Kurt. *The Hermeneutics Reader.* New York: Continuum, 1985.

Ricoeur, Paul. *Essays on Biblical Interpretation.* Philadelphia: Fortress, 1980.

———. *Hermeneutics and the Human Sciences.* New York: Cambridge University Press, 1981.

———. *Interpretation Theory: Discourse and the Surplus of Meaning.* Fort Worth: Texas Christian University, 1976.

WOLFGANG BEINERT

Hierarchy. Hierarchy (Greek *hiera archē* = holy origin, sovereignty, order) is the structural order among the holders of office or ministry in the church.

(1) *Biblical Background.* The New Testament attests to the cooperation between office and community, as well as to the cooperation among the various ministries, though only the beginnings of this are perceptible. The concept of hierarchy is not yet present.

(2) *History of Theology.* The most important stimulus to the development of a doctrine of the hierarchy comes from Dionysius the Areopagite, who explained the structure of the heavenly and the earthly cosmos in terms of "hierarchy" (*The Celestial Hierarchy*; *The Ecclesiastical Hierarchy*). In this explanation, triads function as the decisive structural principle. The "celestial hierarchy" consists of three times three groups of angels. The "ecclesiastical hierarchy" consists of, on the one hand, bishops, priests, and deacons, and, on the other, monks, the laity, and catechumens. The ecclesiastical hierarchy derives its priority and symbolic power from the fact that it is an image in which the celestial hierarchy is made present. From the sixteenth century on, a heavy stress has been placed on the ecclesiastical hierarchy as an answer to its relativization in the Reformation. Despite some new emphases, this situation has remained unchanged down to the present time.

(3) *Church Teaching.* Vatican II (especially *LG*, chap. 3) describes the "hierarchical constitution of the Church"; the three-stage ministry (bishop, priest, deacon) is said to go back to apostolic times. It has existed "from ancient times" (*LG* 28) and is therefore of very great and abiding importance. According to *LG* 8, the hierarchical constitution of the church is very closely connected with its sacramentality. The nature of the church as the body of Christ under Christ the head is reflected in its hierarchical structure, the concrete form of which has its roots in the Bible and the early church. The Code of Canon Law deals with the hierarchy in canons 1008–54 under the heading of "Orders" (here there is question only of bishops, presbyters, and deacons). This separate treatment shows that the church makes a distinction between a "hierarchy of orders" and a "hierarchy of offices." This twofold hierarchy is matched by the traditional distinction between the power of orders and pastoral power. The "hierarchy of offices" refers to the entire complex structure, largely developed due to historical circumstance, whereby the authority to govern is exercised in the church. The "hierarchy of orders" refers to the three-stage ministry that is

transmitted by the sacrament of orders. Vatican II tried to show how the "hierarchy of offices" and the "hierarchy of orders" fit together, by stating that orders is the source of authority (*LG* 21), but it did not thereby reduce the ecclesiastical hierarchy to unity.

(4) *Ecumenical Perspectives.* In the Evangelical churches the concept of hierarchy is uncommon.

(5) *Systematic Reflections.* The church now has to face new tasks due to the fact that the "laity" want to be, and ought to be, no longer simply addressees but partners of the hierarchy.

See also SACRAMENT OF ORDERS.

Bibliography
Dulles, Avery. "Institution and Charism in the Church." In *A Church to Believe In.* New York: Crossroad, 1982.
Küng, Hans. *Structures of the Church.* Notre Dame, Ind.: University of Notre Dame Press, 1968.
Pseudo-Dionysius. *The Celestial and Ecclesiastical Hierarchies.* In *Pseudo-Dionysius: The Complete Works.* Edited by Paul Rorem. New York: Paulist, 1987.
Rahner, Karl. *The Shape of the Church to Come.* New York: Seabury, 1974.

WERNER LÖSER

Hierarchy of Truths. This expression is a formula for the fact that while all dogmas are equally binding and while all expressions of faith are true, their importance varies according to how close their content is to the trinitarian and christological foundation of the Christian faith.

(1) *Biblical Background.* For the reader of Scripture it is clear that the fullness of the events and expressions there reported has as its focal point God's revelation in history, which reaches its zenith in Jesus of Nazareth. The New Testament explicitly mentions various fundamental statements upon which faith stands and falls, such as the existence of God and God's role as judge (Heb 6:2) or the resurrection of Jesus (1 Cor 15:17–19). Heb 6:1f. proposes an elaborated catalogue of "basic teachings" (conversion, faith in God, baptism, the imposition of hands, resurrection of the dead, eternal judgment). In the so-called Council of Jerusalem the dispute over the necessity of circumcision for gentile Christians is decided through an appeal to the higher truth of God's universal salvific will that is above the claim of the Jewish law (Acts 15:13–20; see Gal 2:6–10). In the controversy concerning the permissibility of eating meat offered to the idols, Paul places the order of love over Christian freedom (1 Cor 8:1–13).

(2) *History of Theology.* With the increasing development of and reflection on revelation, there arises, under various considerations and with changing formulas, the problem that a materially and qualitatively balanced rule of faith has to be established. The Church Fathers already knew the distinction between the substance of faith, which is recorded in the binding *regula fidei* (rules of faith), and interpretations that assist a deeper understanding and are open to

free debate (e.g., Irenaeus, *Adv. haer.* 1.10.3). Joined to this is the search for a *fundamental dogmatic principle*. With Irenaeus it runs: "The honor of God is the living human being" (*Adv. haer.* 3.20.2). In the Middle Ages, Thomas Aquinas distinguished between "credibilia, de quibus est fides secundum se" (things to be believed because they are themselves of faith) and things "in ordine ad aliud" (in a relation to it) (*STh* 2–2, q. 1, a. 6 ad 1). His fundamental principle is: "sub ratione Dei" (in terms of God) (*STh* 1, q. 1, a. 7). In the period following the Reformation, Catholic theologians considered the attempts of the Protestants to locate a "core of Scripture" (see sec. 4 below) as efforts to reduce the faith, and the Catholic theologians sought to counteract this with an ever-increasing quantitative unfolding of doctrine by way of conclusions ("theology of conclusions"). It was first with the Tübingen school, which proposed as the fundamental principle the teaching of the kingdom of God, that the problem of the hierarchy of truths was again taken up. M. J. Scheeben (*Mysterien des Christentums* [1865]) refers all the truths of faith back to nine fundamental mysteries and these back to the mystery of the Trinity. Among other things, the underlying knowledge of a structured pattern of faith is shown in the attempts to classify the dogmas in propositions that are general and special or necessary and unnecessary for salvation as well as to qualify creedal expressions according to their epistemological degree of certainty (theological qualifications, notes, censures: see ECCLESIAL MAGISTERIUM). This recognition is manifested practically in the considerations that "basic elements of faith" are to be included in the catechism. At the present time it is reflected in the discussion about a new formulation of the creeds and the search for a "short formula of faith."

(3) *Church Teaching.* In modern times the ecclesial magisterium gave decisive impulses to this theme first of all by speaking of a "connection of the mysteries of faith" that presupposes their ordering (Vatican I: DS 3016) and, then, especially at Vatican II (*UR* 11), by stating "that in Catholic doctrine there exists an order or 'hierarchy' of truths since they vary in their relation to the foundation of the Christian faith." In *UR* 12 the trinitarian and christological dogmas are mentioned as this foundation (in close affinity with the fundamental formula of the World Council of Churches [see sec. 4 below]). The decree on "ecumenics" of the communal synod of the dioceses in the Federal Republic of Germany referred back to it (3.2.3).

(4) *Ecumenical Perspectives.* The basic concern of the Reformation was focusing the faith around a center or core in order to bring about a renewal of the church. Luther sees it in the teaching on justification ("homo reus et perditus et Deus iustificans et salvator" [the human person as bound and lost, God as justifying and as savior] [*WA* 40/2:328]), which for him is the "core of Scripture" and the "canon within the canon." As a result of theological controversies, the Lutherans of the sixteenth and seventeenth centuries assembled "fundamental articles" (G. Calixtus: the foundation is the *consensus quinquesaecularis,* i.e., the doctrinal decisions of the first five centuries). At present, the participants in

the ecumenical dialogue — including the Catholic Church (see sec. 3 above) — have recognized that the principle of the hierarchy of truths points out a way toward reconciliation and understanding. The World Council of Churches proposed a "fundamental formula" (1948, enlarged 1961) whose acknowledgment is the presupposition for membership: it understands itself as "the community of Churches which confess the Lord Jesus Christ according to the Scripture as God and Savior and which together strive to fulfill that for which they are called, the honor of God the Father, the Son, and the Holy Spirit." The Malta Report (1972) stated that there is no basic contradiction between the concept of a hierarchy of truths and that of a "core of Scripture."

(5) *Systematic Reflections.* In the formula of the hierarchy of truths, *truths* signify the individual truths of faith as elements of the Christian doctrine; *hierarchy*, that this doctrine has patterns and accents through which faith forms a substantial unity that is expressed in multiple ways and that also justifies a legitimate pluralism in theology. Yet here the point is not so much — as the image of a hierarchy might suggest — a ranking but rather a *rational structure* in which there is a center, a core, a solid foundation. The principle of the hierarchy of truths thus is not a reductionist model or a numerically based principle of selection. Rather, it is a principle of interpretation that is based on the fact that all elements of faith finally elucidate God's revelation as it took place through Jesus Christ in the Holy Spirit for the salvation of human beings. Therefore, faith in its essence is not a system of propositions, although it needs these. Rather, it is the way in which the Christian comes to God in Christ through the work of the Spirit, thus a process that is directed to one singular goal. The core of the Christian faith is thus the trinitarian dogma together with the christological dogma in an anthropological orientation. The recognition of a hierarchy of truths proves itself not only as a fruitful hermeneutical principle within dogmatic theology but also as the means of a missionary-oriented proclamation of faith and as a rule for dialogue in the ecumenical conversation in order to distinguish the binding content of the gospel from traditions that are not generally binding, but legitimate.

See also DOGMA/DOGMATIC STATEMENT; HERMENEUTICS; TRUTH OF FAITH.

Bibliography
Henn, William. *The Hierarchy of Truths according to Yves Congar.* Preface by Yves Congar. Rome: Editrice Pontificia Universita Gregoriana, 1987.
The Notion "Hierarchy of Truths": An Ecumenical Interpretation; The Church, Local and Universal. Two Studies Commissioned and Received by the Joint Working Group between the Roman Catholic Church and the World Council of Churches. Geneva: WCC Publications, 1990.
Valeske, Ulrich. *Hierarchia veritatum.* Munich: Claudius, 1968.

WOLFGANG BEINERT

Historical Jesus.

Historical Jesus. In theology, the term *historical Jesus* refers to what historical criticism can come to know of the pre-Easter Jesus with historical certainty or probability, basing itself especially on the Synoptic Gospels. Thus the modern question concerning the historical Jesus is to be distinguished from the question that has always interested believers regarding the "earthly" Jesus, as opposed to the "exalted Lord."

(1) *Biblical Background.* By means of careful research we can reconstruct the earliest (pre-Gospel) traditions that preserve the message and activity of Jesus, his destiny and his mystery. The purpose of such research is to distinguish the original message of Jesus (*ipsissima vox*), his intentions (*intentio Jesu*), and the facts of his life (*ipsissima facta*) from the post-Easter, faith-inspired writings of the New Testament. An absolutely certain chronology of the life of Jesus is not possible. Nevertheless, despite many peripheral uncertainties due to the different ways of dating things by sources within and outside the New Testament, there is a consensus with regard to the following dates of Jesus' life: he suffered under Pontius Pilate and died on the cross on April 7 (= 15th or 14th Nisan) of the year 30; the two or three years of his public life took place between 27 and 30 C.E.; he was born around the end of the rule of Herod the Great, who died in 4 B.C.E. The geographical area in which Jesus lived and worked was Galilee. His beginnings in Nazareth, well-attested by the New Testament, can be considered as historically certain: first of all because of the "weight" Nazareth had for Jesus himself and the later mission (see Jn 1:45). To what extent he was later "at home" in Capernaum is controversial. Also, the question of whether Bethlehem was the birthplace of Jesus (despite Mt 2:1; Lk 2:4, 11) cannot be answered with historical certainty, given the literary form of the infancy narratives. No exact itinerary — aside from his trip to Jerusalem — can be established for his public ministry. The general consensus today is that John's presentation of three trips to Jerusalem is historically more probable than the Synoptics' references to a single stay in Jerusalem. The central fact of Jesus' baptism by John at the beginning of his *public ministry* is considered to be historically certain because it was so difficult to deal with for later faith-portraits. How could the sinless Jesus receive a baptism for the forgiveness of sins (Mk 1:4)? Jesus' beginnings were in the movement centered around John the Baptist, yet he lived and preached quite differently. He did not follow the Baptist's ascetical lifestyle (Mt 11:18f.; Mk 2:19a). Jesus did not associate with or integrate himself into any of the movements within Judaism at the time (Essenes, Pharisees, Sadducees). He remained an "outsider." In this is revealed the mystery of his person, which is indissolubly linked with the *message of the kingdom* and appears in his *actions*. His preaching — while resembling that of the Baptist in some ways — goes beyond it. What is first is not human action, but the proclamation of God as loving Father. What matters is believing in the unconditional love of God and living from it. The nucleus of his message is *theo*logical: his words concerning God and his relationship to God characterize his message of the kingdom and stand out in relationship to all comparable types of eschatological-apocalyptic preaching. This is demonstrated especially by Jesus' prayer, "Father...may your kingdom come" (Lk 11:2a, c par.). Images of un-

shrunken cloth and new wine (Mk 2:21f. pars.) point to the absolute new beginning that he preaches and that happens with his coming. In the parables of the mustard seed (Mk 4:30–32 pars.) and the yeast (Mt 13:33 par. Lk 13:20) God's kingdom is depicted as continually at work; it is an unstoppable process that has now begun. This newness is a time of joy: God's kingdom turns the present into a feast (Mk 2:19). It is "among you" (Lk 17:2). It happens when people accept it and do God's will. The word on taking by force (Mt 11:12 par. Lk 16:16b), where the kingdom of God suffers (is hindered by?) violence, may belong to this context. It is also a gift, especially to the little ones, the lost, the "poor," who are declared blessed (Lk 6:20b–21 pars.). Whoever strives for it receives everything else as well (Lk 12:31). Thus the command against retaliation becomes understandable (Lk 6:29). When Jesus associates God's kingdom with his *exorcisms* (Lk 11:20 par. Mt 12:28), this may be seen as expressing his function as eschatological mediator of salvation: God becomes Lord among those who are healed and share in God's salvation. The credibility of Jesus' message is seen in his exorcisms or charismatic actions (see MIRACLE), which demonstrate that here there is "more than Jonah" (Mt 12:41f.), "more than a prophet" (Mt 11:9 par.). Thus his message is validated in his deeds as "active proclamation." Two historically certain actions are worth mentioning in this regard. First, Jesus evidently *associated himself with those who were lost, the sinners;* otherwise people would not have complained that he was a "friend of tax-collectors and sinners" (Mt 11:19a par. Lk 7:34a). We may label Jesus a "nonconformist" because, on the one hand, he objected to a legalistic interpretation of the law (e.g., the law of the Sabbath [Mk 2:27]) and, on the other hand, he introduced an intensification of the law (e.g., in commanding love of enemies [Mt 5:43f. par. Lk 6:27f.]). Jesus formulated and practiced the commandment of love in a new way. The second instance is Jesus' *call to discipleship* (Mt 8:21f.; Lk 9:57–62 par.; Mt 10:21 par.): the pre-Easter group of disciples is a "sign for Israel" (see DISCIPLESHIP). Although the pre-Easter basis of the group of Twelve is debated by exegetes, nevertheless the pre-Markan term "one of the Twelve" (Mk 14:34), used in connection with Judas' betrayal, argues for Jesus' choice of "the Twelve." The *apparent failure* of Jesus is historically certain. Although many consider the title on the cross (Mk 15:26: "king of the Jews") as historically probable, the exact circumstances of Jesus' trial and the reason for his condemnation have not yet been clearly explained. However, a more important question is whether we can attribute to the historical Jesus an "*original understanding of his death.*" Any critical attempt to answer this question must bring together the death on the cross and the message of the kingdom and recognize that despite a convergence of arguments only a degree of probability can be reached. The most convincing (although not uncontested) proposal has been that of H. Schürmann. He first notes the dangerousness and powerlessness of Jesus' message of the kingdom, which thus contained the possibility of failure and of his own death. Because of Jesus' eschatological outlook (Mk 14:25), which is definitely related to his Last Supper and can be interpreted as Jesus' hope of resurrection, Jesus' persevering readiness for service even unto death ("dying with persevering proexistence"), despite the failure of his message, now becomes explainable. And this makes understandable that the salvific worth of Jesus, the eschatological mediator of salvation through his death, would be recognizable. The definitive basis for Jesus' message and life, as well as his claim to bring salvation and his whole proexistent death, is his relationship to God, whom he calls Father (Lk 11:2a, c par.). Jesus' relationship to God, concretely realized, is the historical starting point for post-Easter Christology and soteriology.

(2) *History of Theology* and (3) *Church Teaching:* see LIFE OF JESUS RESEARCH.

(4) *Ecumenical Perspectives.* Evangelical dogmatics recognized very early the importance of the question of the historical Jesus and its meaning for Christology (see R. Slenczka). The "new question" concerning Jesus — now the return to the historical Jesus — led to new christological ideas (e.g., in W. Pannenberg) and to basic methodological and hermeneutical considerations concerning the relationship between research on Jesus and Christology, as well as extensive treatment of Jesus' power and his behavior (see G. Ebeling, who speaks of a "return to the origins of Christology").

(5) *Systematic Reflections.* In the view of Catholic dogmatics today, what must be said at the outset is basically that historical-critical research on Jesus can indeed make our faith in Jesus responsible, yet it cannot make it certain: this requires a personal decision on the part of the believer, caused by grace, and in the end this decision is based on the proclamation of the resurrected and exalted Lord, who was also the earthly person who was crucified and can be encountered in the New Testament's faith testimony. The historical Jesus cannot therefore become a "fifth Gospel" or a criterion for the four Gospels. Nevertheless, the question of the historical Jesus has an indispensable function for our modern problematic (in connection with a Christology of Jesus' resurrection) in laying down the foundation of dogmatic Christology and soteriology.

See also CHRISTOLOGY; JESUS' HUMANITY; KINGDOM OF GOD; MYSTERIES OF THE LIFE OF JESUS CHRIST; PASSION AND DEATH OF JESUS CHRIST; SOTERIOLOGY.

Bibliography

Aulèn, Gustaf. *Jesus in Contemporary Historical Research.* Philadelphia: Fortress, 1976.

Bornkamm, Günther. *Jesus of Nazareth.* New York: Harper, 1970.

Braaten, Carl, and Roy Harrisville, eds. *The Historical Jesus and the Kerygmatic Christ.* Nashville: Abingdon, 1979.

Crossan, John Dominic. *The Historical Jesus: The Life of a Mediterranean Jewish Peasant.* San Francisco: HarperSanFrancisco, 1991.

Horsley, Richard A. *Jesus and the Spiral of Violence: Popular Jewish Resistance in Roman Palestine.* San Francisco: Harper and Row, 1987.

Käsemann, Ernst. *Essays on New Testament Themes.* London: SCM, 1964.

Kasper, Walter. *Jesus the Christ.* New York: Paulist, 1976.

Keck, Leander. *A Future for the Historical Jesus.* Nashville: Abingdon, 1971.

Pannenberg, Wolfhart. *Jesus: God and Man.* 2d ed. Philadelphia: Westminster, 1977.
Perrin, Norman. *Rediscovering the Teaching of Jesus.* New York: Harper and Row, 1976.
Robinson, James M. *A New Quest of the Historical Jesus.* London: SCM, 1985.
Schillebeeckx, Edward. *Jesus: An Experiment in Christology.* New York: Seabury, 1979.
Schüssler Fiorenza, Elisabeth. *In Memory of Her.* New York: Crossroad, 1983.
Segundo, Juan Luis. *The Historical Jesus of the Synoptics.* Maryknoll, N.Y.: Orbis Books,
    1984.

LOTHAR ULLRICH

History/Historicity. *History,* colloquially understood, is the course of events that takes place within the limits of space and time (e.g., the history of Rome) or its interpreted presentation (e.g., history as economic history). *Theologically,* it is the taking together of (*a*) the effects and meaning of the accomplishment of God's salvation as it is constituted in space and time through the events of revelation and (*b*) the resulting responses of faith. *Historicity* characterizes the constitution of the human person resulting from this, a creature who is acting in the present, determined through the past, and open to the future, and who must continually find him- or herself in the tension between determination and freedom.

(1) *Biblical Background.* The fundamental biblical conviction is that God does not have a history but is the author and goal of all history (Jdt 9:5f.). In the Old Testament instead of the myths of the surrounding peoples about the origin of the gods (theogonies), there are narratives about human beings with whom God interacts; this is why God can be recognized in history. Here three insights are decisive. (*a*) Because God's saving deeds are demonstrated in time, time is *determined by its content* (Ps 104:27; Eccl 3:1–8). It is time for something. (*b*) Because starting from creation the individual facts are seen in relation to each other, time becomes *salvation-history:* this is professed above all in the summaries Dt 26:5–10 and Jos 24:2–13. (*c*) Because God's saving activity is not completed, but will even surpass itself in the future, time has an *eschatological dimension* (prophets; apocalyptic, where a disaster is the precursor of the new age). With these insights, history appears not as a return of the same (Greek concept of history), but rather as the directed course of events from God toward God. It forms a continuous unity and therefore cannot be divided up into salvation-history and profane history; yet it can be encompassed in its larger connections (see the significance of the succession to the throne of David in 2 Samuel 5–20; 1 Kgs 1:1–2:12; the Deuteronomic History; and the far-reaching periodization of history in Dn 2:7). The New Testament testifies that with the beginning of the kingdom of God through the words, deeds, and death of Jesus Christ time is fulfilled and thus the last age has begun: in him, the time (*kairós* in the Greek) is fulfilled. Thus, he is the midpoint, fullness, and ordering principle of time (Mt 26:18; Jn 7:6; Eph 1:3–14; Col 1:12–23). Since with him, indeed, the kingdom of God has come, but is still not completed, history retains its theological meaning as the intervening period between Easter and the parousia, in which the new creation will be introduced (Matthew 13;

28:20). This history has the distinguishing features that the old and the new aeons remain intertwined in one another (1 Cor 10:11; Gal 1:4; Eph 1:21; 2:7; Heb 6:5) and that within it are found continuity (Mt 1:22; 2:15; 4:14; etc.) and discontinuity (Rom 10:4). In the concrete, this intervening period is the time of the church (Mt 16:18): it is the last age of history, after which comes only its consummation (1 Cor 15:20–28; Revelation).

(2) *History of Theology.* For Christianity, history is a fundamental theological category because its concrete foundation is due to a historical event. This finds its most obvious expression in the reckoning of time from the birth of Christ, introduced for the first time by Dionysius Exiguus in 525; theologically, it is expressed in the historical structure of the creeds (Second Article) and the composition of DOGMATIC THEOLOGY from a salvation-history perspective. The conceptualization of history and historicity is a result of modern theology but has its starting points in theology's own history. From Christ taken as the midpoint, history in antiquity and in the Middle Ages is seen as a sequence of eras that are set in relation to the Trinity. Here the history of Israel (Old Testament) appears as the preparatory development, directed by the Father, to the Christ-event (New Testament), and church history as the Spirit-influenced unfolding of the reality of the incarnation. Among the various and differently developed theologies of history (including those of Hippolytus, Irenaeus, Origen, the Venerable Bede, Rupert of Deutz, and Otto of Freising), which also include heretical variations (Joachim of Fiore), that of Augustine (*De civ. Dei*) exercises the most perduring influence: history is the struggle between the divine and the demonic systems, from which the former will emerge victorious in an eternal fulfillment that transcends history. In the Age of Humanism, the knowledge presupposed by all periodizations of the divine intentions in history is put into question by the historical-critical thinking promoted by the humanists. While for the Enlightenment God's activity is held to be recognizable, it is seen as historically immanent. For Hegel history is the self-interpretation of the absolute Spirit. As a result, the belief in progress takes the place of eschatological expectation. Through historicism a worldview becomes influential according to which all cultural phenomena must be understood from their historical conditions; they are thus unique and therefore relative and are no longer able to be arranged into contexts of understanding. Marxism understands history as the scene of the ongoing class struggle that follows laws of nature. The reaction within Catholic theology to this challenge is mostly apologetic; since the acceptance of Aristotelianism, history is not a scientific category because it does not consider absolute being, but rather the relative individual elements. It was the Catholic Tübingen school that first advocated programmatically the historicity of revelation and faith. At the present, history and historicity acquire far-reaching significance as categories in which the task of the church, now for the first time really becoming spatially universal, can be made clear. This occurs with catchwords and ideas like inculturation, *aggiornamento* (the updating of the church), and the historical shaping of the world in culture, work, politics,

science, and theology. The tension between progress and restoration becomes greater in view of the aporias posed by, for example, questions about peace or the ecological problems.

(3) *Church Teaching.* The history of theology itself is the reason why in Vatican II for the first time the concepts of history and historicity are used and acknowledged by the magisterium. History is considered as salvation-history directed by the Trinity, in which the autonomy of creation is grounded and confirmed. Within this history of salvation the church has the function of a catalyst that from the beginning of the world until its end should lead humanity toward its fulfillment (see *LG* 8f., 48–51; *DV* 2–4; *GS* 10, 38, 40–45). Thus, for the study of theology the guiding theme chosen is "to develop the Mystery of Christ, which affects the whole course of human history" (*OT* 14).

(4) *Ecumenical Perspectives.* The Reformation protested, indeed, with the humanists against the ostensible knowledge of medieval theology about the divine decrees. It did this by emphasizing the hiddenness of God's activity in history, yet the Reformers also recognized history as the place for the unfolding of the kingdom of God. The biblical orientation in Protestantism fostered thinking in terms of salvation-history: already in the time of the Reformation, J. Cocceius (d. 1669) developed a similar concept with his "federal theology." In the confrontation with the Enlightenment in the nineteenth century and above all in the twentieth century, the accent is placed on the infinite qualitative difference between time and eternity, which is why revelation is the "crisis" of all history (S. Kierkegaard, K. Barth); on historicity, which fundamentally determines the human condition (R. Bultmann, for whom then, nevertheless, the revelation in Christ is the end and fulfillment of history); and on history as the most comprehensive and universal horizon of all theology (W. Pannenberg).

(5) *Systematic Reflections.* For methodological clarification, one must distinguish between history (*Historie*) as the report of the sequence of events (the *mere* past) and history (*Geschichte*) as the nexus of events, which presupposes understanding (the *significant* past). From a theological perspective, history is the sphere of encounter between revelation and faith. In this, the former has a historical origin and historical effects, since it addresses itself to people within history; faith, on the other hand, can interpret itself only in history and in the historical community of faith. This has as a consequence that at all times only certain aspects and dimensions of the message of revelation are recognized and accepted (perspectivity of faith). Theological epistemology attempts to interpret the start, course, goal, and structure of history and historicity as the transcendental category of God's activity within the world. A number of particulars can be emphasized in relation to both history and historicity. (*a*) As regards history: (i) history is truly the history of human freedom and at the same time the history of the victorious fulfilling of the divine decree. Because God is the Lord of history, it is fundamentally salvation-history. (ii) Therefore, it is in principle meaningful: it is set up as the space in which God's judgment is accomplished, and, therefore, it is directed toward fulfillment in community

THE DIMENSIONS OF HISTORY
AND THE RELATIONSHIP AMONG THEM

	Past	*Present*	*Future*

=====> = consecutive time of objective history
====== = history as the mere past
· — · — · — = history as the realization of the past in the present and future
· · · · · · = realization of the present in the future

From the present, one can consider history as the closed past (= *Historie*) (======). Actually, however, the present is also formed and determined through what happened yesterday, and this influence also reaches forward into the future, for example, the consequences of Auschwitz for German history (· — · — · —). But just as much, what now happens also has implications for tomorrow, for example, a career decision (· · · · · ·). From this result several possibilities for acting in the present:

	Rejection	*Acceptance*
Past	as guilt: *repentance* as incomplete: *revolution*	as touching and challenging me
Future	as realization of the past: *utopianism* as new: *restoration,* *traditionalism*	as a task for myself

with God. (iii) The direction of meaning in history has become clear and completed in Jesus Christ: since his redemptive deed its orientation toward salvation cannot be reversed. (iv) Nevertheless, until its completion at the end of time, history remains a mixture of salvation and perdition. This is why in its individual moments it can also appear as contradictory and backward; the ideal of eternal progress is not supported by Christian theology. (v) The working of God in history is structured in a trinitarian way: the Father is the author of historical salvation, Christ is its center, and the Holy Spirit makes history the place of the presence of God in Christ. (vi) History is realized as salvation-history not in an individualistic way, but rather in and through the concrete community of the church. (b) As regards historicity: the historicity of human persons is such that in their respective present situations they are determined through the past, which, while being beyond their control, still continues to determine each of them (e.g., as ethnic and family history), as well as through the future, which is just as much a further realization of the past as the unforeseeable new.

Each person is challenged as a historical being in the present to relate to the other two dimensions of time; here several possibilities are imaginable (see the chart, p. 343). An important problem in theological epistemology is the relationship between truth and history. As a historical being the human person can always only approach the truth, but cannot totally grasp it; this is valid above all for the knowledge of the mystery of God in Christ. Since the truth must be pronounced under concrete historical conditions (time, environment, categories of thought, systems of reference, models), the statements regarding the abiding truth change according to these conditions. Already according to the biblical understanding, truth is that which is proved true, that is, that which in history turns out to be what it claims to be (TRUTH OF THE FAITH).

See also FAITH; REVELATION; THEOLOGY.

Bibliography

Bultmann, Rudolf. *History and Eschatology.* Edinburgh: Edinburgh University Press, 1957.

Collingwood, Robin George. *The Idea of History.* Rev. ed., with lectures of 1926–28. Oxford: Clarendon, 1993.

Gadamer, Hans-Georg. *Philosophical Hermeneutics.* Berkeley: University of California Press, 1973.

Koselleck, Reinhart. *Futures Past: On the Semantics of Historical Time.* Cambridge, Mass.: MIT Press, 1985.

WOLFGANG BEINERT

History of Dogma. The term *history of dogma* refers to the theological-historical discipline that researches and describes the process of formation of church doctrine and its effects.

(1) *Biblical Background.* The history of dogma in the strict sense can begin only after the completion of Scripture, because dogma is the elucidation of the biblical message of revelation. In a broader sense, however, one can speak of an intrabiblical history of dogma: Scripture contains a clarification and development of theological thoughts. This is valid in a global sense for the interpretation of the Old Testament through the New Testament. It is also valid for individual questions, as in the expansion of meaning given to the political prophecy of Is 7:14 toward a messianic prophecy in Is 9:5f. and finally to a christological statement in Mt 1:23 (the virginal conception).

(2) *History of Theology.* As long as one conceived dogmas as unchanging formulas, one could not speak of a history of dogma. This approach arose within the framework of the developmental ideal of the Enlightenment at first as a critique of dogma. The original groundwork, however, reaches back into the seventeenth century: the research into sources undertaken by the Maurist Congregation and the work of D. Petau entitled *Dogmata theologia* (5 vols., 1644/50) can be acknowledged as the historical foundation for the history of dogma. In Catholic circles, the history of dogma first found a fixed place in courses of study at the start of the twentieth century. Current problems include the tension between ecclesiastical normativity and the historical relativity

of the ecclesial teaching, as well as the question of what significance the irreversible transition of the church from the Western cultural sphere into other civilizations has for the history of dogma.

(3) *Church Teaching.* On account of the originally critical approach of the history of dogma, the magisterium at first reacted negatively against the underlying idea of development (Vatican I [DS 3020, 3043]). But with the declaration *Mysterium ecclesiae* of 1975 the historicity of dogma was acknowledged, and with it the history of dogma was also awarded full legitimacy.

(4) *Ecumenical Perspectives.* The history of dogma was for a long time the domain of Protestant theology, within which it greatly developed since the beginning of the nineteenth century. It is understood for the most part as a purely historical undertaking with the aim of investigating dogma as a historically effective principle.

(5) *Systematic Reflections.* The basis for the possibility of a history of dogma is the historicity of ecclesial doctrine including its formal dogmas and dogmatic statements. This has its starting point in the Easter experience of the early community and expands and develops itself — not always, of course, in the sense of a steady progress forward — according to contemporary situations. Through this an exchange takes place: the doctrine illumines the situation, and the situation locates the doctrine. Thus dogma and dogmatic statements always effect also an opening up toward a new understanding, whereby precisely in their historical conditionedness they become a subject for modern historical research. The task of the history of dogma is to show this process and the history of its effects, and thereby to open the path toward a deeper understanding of Christian doctrine. It is thus both a historical and a dogmatic discipline. For long periods it runs alongside of the history of theology. Yet it does not focus on the history of dogma and dogmatic statements alone, but also on the description of the origin of all of theology's doctrinal opinions from the viewpoint of the history of ideas. Briefly stated, the history of dogma is the history of the understandings of the faith as they change through history.

See also DEVELOPMENT OF DOGMA; DOGMA.

Bibliography
Cunliffe-Jones, Benjamin. *A History of Christian Doctrines.* Philadelphia: Fortress, 1978.
Harnack, Adolf. *History of Dogmas.* 7 vols. New York: Dover, 1961.
Pelikan, Jaroslav. *The Christian Tradition.* 5 vols. Chicago: University of Chicago Press, 1981–88.
Seeberg, Reinhold. *The History of Doctrines.* 2 vols. Grand Rapids: Baker House, 1977.

WOLFGANG BEINERT

Holiness and Sinfulness of the Church.

Holiness is one of the classical attributes of the church. For a long time there was disagreement as to whether and in what sense sinfulness could be predicated not only of the members of the church but of the church itself.

(1) *Biblical Background.* The most important New Testament passage on the holiness of the church is Eph 5:25–27: Christ, the head of his body, the church, makes it holy. In Revelation the church is at times spoken of as the "bride" (19:7; 21:2, 9; 22:17).

(2) *History of Theology.* For many centuries theologians used the image of the "bride" in order to speak of the holiness of the church. Concretely, this discussion took the form of commentary on the Song of Songs. The "bride" stands over against Christ the "bridegroom" and faces him with faith, hope, and love, with fidelity and self-surrender. But it can happen that the bride is found to be "unfaithful" and that she neglects her Lord and head. She is then sinful, an "unfaithful bride." In the theology of the early and medieval church, the church was then described as a "chaste prostitute" (*casta meretrix*). The important point being made here is that the sinfulness of the church can never completely do away with its holiness, for its holiness comes to it first of all from Christ and is therefore given to it in advance as something it is not free to dispose of — "not free" in the sense that it must comply with this prior gift by its holiness of life. When M. Luther and the other Reformers called attention primarily to the sinfulness of the church because of the church's profoundly unsatisfactory state (the church as "prostitute," "Babylon," etc.), Catholic theologians found themselves forced to respond with an equally one-sided assertion of the holiness of the church. This explains why until very recently hardly anything was said about the sinfulness of the church in Catholic theology.

(3) *Church Teaching.* Vatican II not only spoke explicitly and in detail about the holiness of the church; it deliberately spoke once again of its sinfulness. This is done in language that is admittedly still very cautious: "The Church... clasping sinners to its bosom, at once holy and always in need of purification, follows constantly the path of penance and renewal" (*LG* 8).

(4) *Ecumenical Perspectives.* Insofar as the church itself is an object of ecumenical DIALOGUE, the question of its holiness and sinfulness is always involved, at least materially. Explicit conversations on this theme have thus far been rare (see, e.g., the Roman Catholic–Orthodox conversation, "The Mystery of the Church and the Eucharist in the Light of the Mystery of the Most Holy Trinity" [1982]) but will probably increase in number and importance. The statement "Our Faith — Source of Hope" (Riva del Gardo, 1984) has this to say: the church "is a 'holy Church,' because 'Christ loved the Church and gave himself up for her, in order to purify her with water and the word and to sanctify her' (Eph 5:25ff.; see also Heb 13:12). When Christians are firm in faith, strong in hope, and faithful in love, they are a reflection of this holiness and point the way to the unity which God wills."

(5) *Systematic Reflections.* The holiness of the church finds expression, as in a reality-symbol, in the holiness of its prototype, MARY: by the grace of God she is the "Spotless One" (*Immaculata;* see IMMACULATE CONCEPTION). The holiness of the church is also manifested in the holiness of the saints. The sinfulness

of the church can be understood only as a consequence, reflection, and echo of the sinfulness of individual church members in the universal body of Christ.

See also SAINTS: HOLINESS, SANCTIFICATION; SIN AND GUILT.

Bibliography
Balthasar, Hans Urs von. *Church and World.* New York: Herder and Herder, 1967.
Küng, Hans. *The Council, Reform, and Reunion.* New York: Sheed and Ward, 1962.
Rahner, Karl. "The Church of Saints." In *Theological Investigations,* 3:91–104. New York: Crossroad, 1967.
———. "The Church of Sinners." In *Theological Investigations,* 6:253–69. New York: Crossroad, 1969.
———. "The Sinful Church in the Decrees of Vatican II." In *Theological Investigations,* 6:270–94. New York: Crossroad, 1967.
Vorgrimler, Herbert. *One, Holy, Catholic and Apostolic.* London: Sheed and Ward, 1968.

WERNER LÖSER

Holy Spirit. In the Christian faith, *Holy Spirit* is the name given to the third person of the one triune God. With the Father and the Son, the Spirit realizes the one divine essence.

(1) *Biblical Background.* The Scriptures focus their relevant statements on the action of the Holy Spirit; as a rule, the Spirit's being or nature is expressed only indirectly. According to the Synoptics, the activity and being of Jesus clearly stand under the sign of the Holy Spirit, who descends on the Lord at his baptism by John (Mk 1:10) and, as it were, sends him on his public mission; but the Spirit is also already at work in the conception of Jesus (Lk 1:35; Mt 1:18). According to Acts, the outpouring of the Spirit brings the church into existence (Acts 2:4, 17–21, 38); in it the Spirit is then active in many ways through faith (see 1 Corinthians 12–14 and Romans 8), as is clear especially from what Paul says in his letters. The connection between the action of the Spirit in the church and the work of Jesus Christ is brought out especially in John 14–16. In the process, the person, too, of this Spirit emerges more clearly; finally, the Spirit's divine consubstantiality with the Father and the Son also finds expression in a few formulas (Mt 28:19; 1 Cor 12:4–6; 2 Cor 13:13). Here we have the starting point of the specifically Christian idea of God; its distinctive character remains unmistakable even, and especially, when we take into account what is said in the Old Testament about the operation of the Spirit of God. For this reason, in dealing with the subject of this article there is no need of reviewing the Old Testament writings.

(2) *History of Theology.* The doctrine of the Holy Spirit developed only slowly in the early church, and then in striking dependence on the dogmatic controversies in CHRISTOLOGY. In the West the *De Trinitate* of Hilary of Poitiers and in the East the *De Spiritu Sancto* of Basil the Great were especially important in making the church conscious of the problem. The First Council of Constantinople defined the divinity of the Holy Spirit (DS 150f.). Under the influence of Ambrose (*De Spiritu Sancto*) the divinity was set forth even

more clearly in the *Tomus Damasi* (Rome, 382; DS 152–78). Augustine's *De Trinitate* exerted a decisive influence on later times. When the doctrine of the sacraments received its systematic development, confirmation was understood as the sacrament of the Holy Spirit. The teaching of the Greek Fathers on the INDWELLING OF THE HOLY SPIRIT was revived by D. Petau (d. 1652) and eventually inspired the theology of Leo XIII (DS 3325–31) and Pius XII (DS 3807–15), who spoke of the indwelling of the Holy Spirit in the church. After World War II, H. Mühlen drafted a systematic doctrine of the Holy Spirit that was based on a development of the Scholastic doctrine of relations and made use of modern conceptions of the PERSON. Mühlen understood this doctrine as a structural principle of dogmatics, and one that was to be practically and ecumenically fruitful in the charismatic renewal of Christian communities.

(3) *Church Teaching.* The creed confesses the Holy Spirit to be the Lord and giver of life, who proceeds from the Father and the Son (FILIOQUE) and is equally worshiped and glorified. As the one who speaks through the prophets, the Spirit is explicitly the revealer of the divine saving will and action.

(4) *Ecumenical Perspectives.* The doctrine of the Holy Spirit is not a matter of controversy in the ecumenical movement, but the appeal to it in particular questions often hinders a meeting of minds (GOD; INSPIRATION; SALVATION). On the other hand, a deeper exploration of the doctrine of the Holy Spirit (PNEU-MATOLOGY) could bring a new vision of important points that the confessions have in common.

(5) *Systematic Reflections.* The theological starting point must be the name *Holy Spirit,* since this refers both to the universal phenomenon of "spirit" and to the distinguishing note "holy." The combination of words already shows the difficulty of naming the reality meant. This naming is not possible unless we attend to the connotations of the terms. On the one hand, the name refers to "the Holy One" (= God); on the other, it refers to God's characteristic operations, whether within the divine life or outside it. The concept expresses the mediated and mediating character of this Spirit. Human beings experience it when the Spirit of God bears witness to our spirit that we are the children of God (Rom 8:16). According to the tradition, this testimony is given to human beings with all their powers; that is, it is addressed immediately to the senses, chiefly in the form of light or illumination, and thereby to the heart; in other words, the testimony does not ignore the creaturely conditions of human knowing but transforms them and gives them new potentialities. In this experiential knowledge the Holy Spirit also communicates the content of God's saving revelation. In the process, the Spirit is simultaneously experienced and known as the "gift" (*donum*) of God. Therefore, the Spirit *is* a relationship of love, that is, not only mediation but mediator. The Spirit is therefore closely associated with Jesus Christ and his work, inasmuch as the Spirit enables human beings to understand the historical manifestation of Jesus Christ as the saving action of God in and upon creation and, in addition, prolongs this manifestation in the history that follows upon the establishment of the church at Pentecost. Only in

the Spirit of God as God's gift does history show itself to be the place of God's presence and action for the sake of human beings, that is, only in this Spirit can the truths of the gospel be understood as such. At the same time, the Holy Spirit enables human beings to give the appropriate response of faith to this call. By making Christian existence possible in these two ways, the Holy Spirit shows that it does not link itself in advance to independently existing realities, but rather turns human beings into partners of God by making available both revelation and the response of faith. Therefore access to the Holy Spirit is to be sought via human beings and their experience of faith. For this experience includes that which as a verbalized claim requires existential confirmation. In this sense the doctrine of the Holy Spirit calls for a theological reflection that has an anthropological starting point. The facts that constitute the latter also shed light on the intrinsic connection between spirituality and theology in Christian life. What is meant is not self-analysis but a responsible recording and explanation of the relation, which is always there, in which redeemed human beings are united, through Jesus Christ, with God the Father, who then is shown, through an act of self-revelation, to be the Creator as well. In this experience human beings realize who the Holy Spirit is and what role the Spirit plays in the truth of revelation generally and in each of its aspects.

See also CHURCH; GOD: THEOLOGY OF; HEART; PNEUMATOLOGY; SAINTS: HOLINESS, SANCTIFICATION; WORKS OF THE SPIRIT.

Bibliography
Congar, Yves. *I Believe in the Holy Spirit.* 3 vols. New York: Seabury, 1983.
Del Colle, Ralph. *Christ and the Spirit: Spirit-Christology in Trinitarian Perspective.* New York: Oxford University Press, 1994.
Fortman, Edmund J. *The Triune God: A Historical Study of the Doctrine of the Trinity.* Philadelphia: Westminster, 1972.
Montague, George. *The Holy Spirit: Growth of a Biblical Tradition.* New York: Paulist, 1976.
Welker, Michael. *God the Spirit.* Minneapolis: Fortress, 1994.

KARL HEINZ NEUFELD

Hominization. In biology, *hominization* designates the process through which the human species ultimately differentiated itself, by gradual transformation, from an assumed group of higher animals, namely, the so-called primates.

(1) *Biblical Background.* The biblical accounts of creation suggest an intermingling of God's creative activity and natural processes. According to the Yahwist, humans arose from already existing matter (*'adāmāh* = clay, soil; hence, "Adam") together with the breath of life (Gn 2:7). The Priestly account has it that humans were "made" subsequent to the land animals, but on the same, sixth day (Gn 1:25–27); this suggests the stages of an evolutionary process.

(2) *History of Theology.* The question of hominization was generated by the modern natural sciences and is answered today as follows. Among the *physical* indications of full hominization, according to morphological research, are, above all, an upright carriage that permits free movement of the frontal (or up-

per) limbs, and a relatively large — in comparison to the body — cranial volume that allows space for a large cerebral mass. Among the *psychological* indications are a specific capacity of thought, language, and decision making that issues (as demonstrable from earliest times) in historical consciousness, culture, art, technology, religion, and social institutions. From the side of behavioral research, the question arises of the extent to which human modes of behavior can be unbrokenly *derived* from animal ones. The high degree of attributes common to animals and humans in both the instinctive and psychological spheres (e.g., aggressiveness, body language, hierarchical relationships, abstractive capacity, tradition, learning ability) makes it difficult to draw a precise line, at the prehistorical stage, between prehominids and hominids. Nevertheless, a qualitative difference is recognized and is usually seen as being grounded in conscious apprehension of relationships, conceptual abstraction, reflective judgment, purposeful learning, intentional communication, verbal invention, creation of culture, and historical and religious self-understanding. Neither a certain causal explanation for hominization nor an insight into its concrete course can be provided today, at least not by biology.

(3) *Church Teaching.* On several occasions, doctrinal office has declared itself for the direct creation of individual human souls by God (ontogenesis) (DS 360f., 1007, 2135). Regarding phylogenesis (development of the human species), Pius XII ("On the Human Species" [*Humani generis*], 1950 [DS 3896]) emphasizes that the church's doctrinal office does not forbid elucidating, with the help of a theory of evolution, "the generation of the human *body* out of already existent and living matter"; the Catholic faith, however, requires us to adhere to direct creation of the *soul* by God.

(4) *Ecumenical Perspectives.* Ecumenically, hominization is not a controversial subject.

(5) *Systematic Reflections.* Humankind, by virtue of its spirituality, freedom, and subjectivity, transcends the realm of what can be described in purely empirical terms. Thus natural-scientific observations about hominization do not preclude theological reflection on the becoming human of humankind. Its theme is primarily the relationship between developmental forces immanent in nature and God's transcendent activity with respect to humankind. For any evaluation, the particular underlying anthropological model is decisive. If body and soul are understood neo-scholastically, as dual elements within human beings, then the natural-scientific image of human beings can hardly be theologically integrated. If, by contrast, one understands *soul* as indicating the undisputedly special position of human beings in relation to all other earthly creatures, then theology makes its own original contribution to the hominization problem. One can, with K. Rahner, hold the view that the qualitative leap from the prehuman to the human form of life takes place within the evolutionary process on the basis of "active self-transcendence." This happens, to be sure, through the workings of laws proper to nature, but God supports the process from within; thus one must speak of a direct creation of the human

being (at least regarding the "soul"). Going beyond Rahner, one might well say that, dogmatically, no "division of labor" between nature (as producing the body) and God (as creating the soul) should be assumed; instead, the human being is to be viewed biblically, as a physical, psychological, and spiritual whole, and attention should be directed to the *capacity for God* that is instilled, generically and individually, in humans. It is this that enables them to realize themselves fully — religiously and morally — as human beings. Then, however, one can also speak of a total creation of humans by God. From this perspective, creation and GRACE are conceived in close interrelation: hominization comes about through creative grace. The topic of the PRIMAL REVELATION, that is, the condition of justice and holiness originally intended for humans by God, bears largely on the same thing. In conclusion, it should be noted that paralleling of phylogenetic and ontogenetic hominization must not be taken too far. What humankind as a species inherits from the prehominids is less than what a human child receives, by way of a personally hominized physical, psychological, and spiritual predisposition, from its parents.

See also CREATIONISM-GENERATIONISM; CREATION NARRATIVES; EVOLUTION: THEORY OF, AND CREATION; HUMANKIND; SOUL; THEOLOGICAL ANTHROPOLOGY.

Bibliography
Dewart, Leslie. *Evolution and Consciousness: The Role of Speech in the Origin and Development of Human Nature.* Toronto: University of Toronto Press, 1989.
Goldsmith, Timothy H. *The Biological Roots of Human Nature: Forging Links between Evolution and Behavior.* New York: Oxford University Press, 1991.
Hulsbosch, Ansfridus. *God in Creation and Evolution.* New York: Sheed and Ward, 1965.
Lubac, Henri de. *Pierre Teilhard de Chardin: The Man and His Meaning.* New York: Hawthorn, 1965.
Portmann, Adolf. *The Living Form and the Seeing Eye: Essays in Philosophic Zoology.* Lewiston, N.Y.: Mellen, 1990.
Rahner, Karl. *Hominisation: The Evolutionary Origin of Man as a Theological Problem.* New York: Herder and Herder, 1965.
Teilhard de Chardin, Pierre. *Man's Place in Nature: The Human Zoological Group.* New York: Harper and Row, 1966.
Theissen, Gerd. *Biblical Faith: An Evolutionary Approach.* Philadelphia: Fortress, 1985.

ALEXANDRE GANOCZY

Humankind. In theology, the notion of humankind refers to the unity of all human persons that is intended and grounded by its divine origin. While the term *human person* refers to the characteristics that are equally valid for every human person, the concept of humankind aims at the connection between all human persons. It is a theological term because such a connection cannot be proved empirically and remains philosophically at least doubtful.

(1) *Biblical Background.* In the accounts of creation (Genesis 1, 2), the createdness of all of humanity is declared with the creation of the first human couple. Humankind's unity is presented in the uninterrupted sequence of the generations (e.g., Genesis 5; 10; 11:10–32), which in the New Testament is ex-

tended up to Jesus (Matthew 1; Lk 3:23–38). The history of all of humankind is related to the history of Israel and of Jesus and from this perspective is placed under God's judgment and grace (e.g., Romans 9–11).

(2) *History of Theology.* Under the influence of Greek philosophy, theology and ecclesial teaching interpreted the unity of humankind metaphysically as the one human nature in which all human persons participate. Through Adam's sin the entire human nature and thereby each human person have become guilty. Because God's Son has taken on human nature, all human persons are already destined and called to share in the life of God. The crisis of metaphysics in the intellectual history of the last century caused theology from then on to understand the connection between all human beings as a historical linkage.

(3) *Church Teaching.* This development is reflected in the more recent doctrinal pronouncements of the church. It recognizes in the present situation of worldwide communication and of the continually closer interweaving of economic, political, and cultural networks a sign of the unity of humankind and a positive opportunity for its own mission to gather and to unite all human persons toward the one kingdom of God (*LG* 1; *GS* 42, see 55f.).

(4) *Ecumenical Perspectives.* The tendency generally predominant in Western theology to interpret the unity of humankind in a historical sense might perhaps experience a healthy challenge in the dialogue with Orthodoxy, which sees the one humankind more closely in connection with the cosmos and with the one Spirit of God in creation.

(5) *Systematic Reflections.* The concept of humankind, in the sense of the one humankind, is understood in current theology as a definition of the goal of human history. The unity of humankind is founded by reason of its origin in the unity of the Creator God. The more theoretical question of whether from this a predetermined inner metaphysical or genetic unity (MONOGENISM–POLYGENISM) also must be assumed is still controversial but is increasingly answered negatively. What is more important is the question of how the transcendent unity of humankind in God or in the Spirit of Christ should be realized as a goal of human action within the course of human history. Does not fraternal community, a worldwide communicative interchange, also inevitably lead to the impoverishment of the human variety, toward a humanistic syncretism? In the strivings of the church and of present humankind toward worldwide communication, theology must also remain critically aware of the difference between this communication and that unity which God's Spirit grants and completes precisely in variety.

See also INCARNATION; ORIGINAL SIN.

Bibliography
See the bibliographies under HUMAN PERSON: IMAGE OF; HOMINIZATION; MONOGENISM–POLYGENISM.

GEORG LANGEMEYER

Human Person. The concept of the human person in anthropology comprises the characteristic features of the biological species *Homo sapiens* as they are initially determined by empirical ethology and the experience of the self. In this description it becomes evident that the questioning and searching of the human person for him- or herself extends beyond any possible response that is gained from these applied analyses. Among the characteristics of the human person belongs also the question about the absolute and, in this sense, religion as a relationship between, on the one hand, the human person's conditioned and contingent possibilities and, on the other hand, the beyond. Since in the question of the human person about her- or himself the question of God is also included, the human person is the object of a dogmatic discipline of its own, THEOLOGICAL ANTHROPOLOGY.

(1) *Biblical Background.* Scripture understands itself as a whole (or at least also) as God's response to human persons' questions about themselves. The human person has been created by God (CREATURELINESS OF THE HUMAN PERSON), elevated within creation, and called into service (the IMAGE OF GOD in the human person; DECISION). Therefore, human persons are responsible to God for what they do and do not do (SIN AND GUILT). They are dependent on God's mercy and help (HEART), which according to the witness of the New Testament have been given them in the fullest amount in Jesus Christ. Because of this, human persons are fundamentally characterized by the alternative of whether or not they allow themselves to be led by the Spirit of Christ (FLESH-SPIRIT).

(2) *History of Theology.* The development of the dogmatic teaching on the human person was decisively influenced by the Hellenistic understanding of the human person. According to this, God's pledge of salvation was primarily directed toward the immortal soul. The relationship to fellow human beings and to the world was considered as secondary for the theological characterization of the human person (SOUL). This individualistic and overly spiritualized concept was able to prevail up until the twentieth century in Catholic theology.

(3) *Church Teaching.* The ecclesial magisterium is clearly making efforts to overcome the one-sidedness present in its tradition. Vatican II emphasizes that human persons are created as social beings (*GS* 12) and that they can find their fulfillment only together with others in the "family" of all human persons that is loved by God (*GS* 24, 32). Together with others the human person shares and shapes a common world; its completion is part of the completion of the human being (*GS* 39).

(4) *Ecumenical Perspectives.* Luther, referring back to Paul, had characterized the human person solely in view of his or her relationship to God. According to this view, human persons withhold themselves from God whenever they seek to understand their character through observation of others or through self-experience: they are sinners before God. Insofar as they receive their designation from the word of God (gospel), they are creatures loved by God. Protestant theology therefore prefers a dialectical concept of the human

person that joins in an opposing manner the designation of the human person through God's word with the knowledge that the human person has from him- or herself. The typically Catholic idea of the human person considers the knowledge of the human person of her- or himself (although clouded by sin) a clue toward the Creator's intention of salvation and fulfillment that is revealed in the message of the gospel. Thus, it sees not only a dialectic but also a correspondence between the search of human persons for their characterization and their gracious characterization through God. Today's ecumenical conversation is moving toward a view beyond both of these opposing positions.

(5) *Systematic Reflections.* Anthropology at present does not offer a comprehensive definition of the human person. The various aspects under which the individual disciplines consider human reality cannot be brought under a single denominator. The most adequate approach appears to be to understand the human person as an open process in which an immeasurable number of possibilities can come to be unfolded. The createdness of the human person then signifies that a person is on the way toward fulfillment in God. As soon as human persons no longer follow God's call to fulfillment, as soon as they are no more listeners to God's orientation, they withhold themselves from God. They commit themselves to one or several already known possibilities for development and thus deny themselves their designation toward fulfillment through God. In this case, the dialectic does not consist between the knowledge of human persons of themselves and their designation through God, but rather between that knowledge of themselves which limits itself to what is known and that knowledge which remains open in its questioning.

See also HUMAN PERSON: IMAGE OF; THEOLOGICAL ANTHROPOLOGY.

Bibliography
See the bibliographies under ANTHROPOLOGY: CONTEMPORARY ISSUES; HUMAN PERSON: IMAGE OF; THEOLOGICAL ANTHROPOLOGY.

GEORG LANGEMEYER

Human Person: Image of. The phrase "image of the human person" refers to the views of the human person dominant within a specific historical era or social group, views that orient the thinking and acting of human beings (e.g., the Bible's, the Hellenistic, the workers', or Goethe's image of the human person). The question about the respective images of the human person is important for understanding theological statements (texts) from their sociocultural contexts. The inquirer must pay attention to the fact that this effort of understanding is itself guided by an image of the human person (HERMENEUTICS).

(1) *Biblical Background.* Since Scripture understands the human person fundamentally as being in the image of God, and since it is not permitted to make an image of God, Scripture (insofar as it is understood as the word of God) does not propose an image of the human person. The saving message of the gospel is directed to all human beings with their respective depictions of the human person. Nevertheless, it makes sense to inquire about the images of the

human person found in the Bible — in the Old Testament, New Testament, the Gospels, and so on. For Scripture proclaims the word of God in human testimonies of faith, and these testimonies are shaped by particular images of the human person. Even Jesus' preaching of the kingdom of God is located in the context of a conception of the human person that is shaped by the sociocultural context of the Judaism of his time. What is decisive in his message, however, is not this image of the human person, but rather that God comes to reign in all human beings and therefore in all images of the human person. The kingdom of God, therefore, demands also the conversion to God from any given image of the human person. In this is also implied an openness toward every fellow human being and his or her image of the human person.

(2) *History of Theology.* It is, therefore, not to be regretted that theology reflected upon the Christian salvific message within the framework of the Hellenistic image of the human person and thereby largely cast off the so-called biblical image of the person. What is regrettable is the tendency to hold on to this particular Christian reflection on the human person as *the* Christian image of the person and to defend it against other and newer conceptions of the person. This tendency, to which the magisterium was also susceptible, has contributed to the Western schism and also to the emancipation of modern reason from the tradition of Christian faith.

(3) *Church Teaching.* The ecclesial magisterium today advocates the fundamental independence of the Christian faith from any specific image of the human person and, at the same time, attempts to proclaim the gospel within the current predominant image of the person (CULTURE).

(4) *Ecumenical Perspectives.* The distinction of the Reformers (which, however, was not always maintained in Protestant theology) between the image of the human person formed by human beings and the human person before God (*coram Deo*) can contribute today to the opening up of the conception of the human person in Western Christendom.

(5) *Systematic Reflections.* Theological anthropology is presently confronted with several images of the human person, both within the democratic societies of the Western cultural realm and beyond it in other cultures. It must judge them critically if and to the degree that they presume to give an ultimate definition of the person. It is difficult to evaluate the features of these modern conceptions of the person that are open for the gospel. Thus, in the Western image of the human person, gospel elements such as freedom, solidarity, and personality, which clearly are unrelinquishable, have been developed; yet one should be prepared for the possibility that in other conceptions of the person the same elements might appear under different representations and possess a different status. On the other hand, it could be that through the influence of the gospel upon non-Christian images of the person such elements might appear that scarcely received a chance in the West.

See also HUMAN PERSON; IMAGE OF GOD; THEOLOGICAL ANTHROPOLOGY.

Bibliography

Brueggemann, Walter. *In Man We Trust: The Neglected Side of Biblical Faith*. Richmond, Va.: John Knox, 1972.

Cooper, John W. *Body, Soul, and Life Everlasting: Biblical Anthropology and the Monism-Dualism Debate*. Grand Rapids: Eerdmans, 1989.

Hartt, Julian Norris. *The Lost Image of Man*. Baton Rouge: Louisiana State University Press, 1963.

Krejci, Jaroslav. *The Human Predicament: Its Changing Image: A Study in Comparative Religion and History*. New York: St. Martin's, 1993.

Micks, Marianne H. *Our Search for Identity: Humanity in the Image of God*. Philadelphia: Fortress, 1982.

Pannenberg, Wolfhart. *Anthropology in Theological Perspective*. Philadelphia: Westminster, 1985.

———. *What Is Man? Contemporary Anthropology in Theological Perspective*. Philadelphia: Fortress, 1970.

Stevenson, Leslie, ed. *The Study of Human Nature: Readings*. New York: Oxford University Press, 1981.

GEORG LANGEMEYER

Human Rights and Human Dignity. The term *human rights* refers to those inborn and inalienable rights that pertain to the human person not on the basis of membership in a certain group (race, nationality, church, etc.) but rather because of one's being human. From these rights results the inviolable dignity of the human person. THEOLOGICAL ANTHROPOLOGY is given the task to investigate the relationship between them and God's offer of salvation.

(1) *Biblical Background.* The Old Testament sees the dignity of the human person grounded in being created in the image of God. Its conviction regarding the dignity of every human person shows itself concretely, for example, in the provisions of the law and in the prophetic sayings that interceded for the poor and the oppressed, even if these interventions were first of all limited to the people of Israel. In the New Testament, for example, in the Sermon on the Mount and the parables, the recognition of human rights is extended to all human beings. In Ti 3:4, the ideal concept of Hellenistic (Stoic) humanity, *philanthrōpia,* is taken up when it is said that in Jesus the loving kindness of God toward humanity had appeared in the world. Human rights and the dignity of the human person are founded in God's love for all human beings.

(2) *History of Theology.* While the gospel and theology promoted the consciousness of the dignity of the human person, their influence on the development of human rights remained limited as long as the stratification of medieval society was interpreted as the divine order of creation. Thus, in modern times human rights were first of all proclaimed in protest against the authority of state and church (Declaration of Rights of Virginia [1776]; Declaration of the Rights of Man and Citizen [1789/91]; medieval forerunner: Magna Carta [1215]; Habeas Corpus Act [1679]). Above all, after World War II and its atrocities different catalogues of human rights were drawn up

(United Nations [1948]; European Convention for the Protection of Human Rights and Fundamental Rights [1950]; etc.).

(3) *Church Teaching.* The ecclesial magisterium took a position in this problematic for the first time in connection with the labor question (Leo XIII, *Rerum novarum* [1891], and the later social encyclicals). Against Fascism and National Socialism (Pius XI, *Non abbiamo bisogno* [1931]; *Mit brennender sorge* [1937]) and against war crimes (Pius XII, Christmas messages [1942–44]), the popes interceded for human rights and the dignity of the human person. John XXIII (*Pacem in terris* [1963]) and Vatican II (*GS* 41) explicitly supported human rights. The Code of Canon Law (cans. 208–23) treats the rights of Christians.

(4) *Ecumenical Perspectives.* From the Reformed approach — especially following Luther — the demand for human rights theologically has to be seen primarily as the sinner's attempt at self-justification. Yet in the sense of Christian service to the world, the World Council of Churches has included the promotion of human rights in its program as one of its main tasks (see Declaration of Addis Ababa [1971]).

(5) *Systematic Reflections.* From the standpoint of the gospel, theological anthropology first of all has to uncover critically all the ideological limitations concerning human rights and the dignity of the human person both within and outside the church. Insofar as the human person is open toward fulfillment in God, human rights cannot be listed in an exhaustive catalogue. On the other hand, practical ways of behavior follow from the human person's being created in the image of God that offer a framework for human rights and that ground the dignity of the human person. Thus, the just rule of human beings over other human beings is possible only when the dignity of the governed is respected. The welfare of the community and of each individual member is to be honored (right to marriage, family, association). Above all, being created in the image of God grounds the right to life and to having a future.

See also HUMAN PERSON: IMAGE OF; IMAGE OF GOD.

Bibliography

Hollenbach, David. *Claims in Conflict: Retrieving and Renewing the Catholic Human Rights Tradition.* New York: Paulist, 1979.

Little, David, et al., eds. *Human Rights and the Conflict of Cultures: Western and Islamic Perspectives on Religious Liberty.* Columbia: University of South Carolina Press, 1988.

Moltmann, Jürgen. *On Human Dignity: Political Theology and Ethics.* Philadelphia: Fortress, 1984.

Rouner, Leroy S., ed. *Human Rights and the World's Religions.* Notre Dame, Ind.: University of Notre Dame Press, 1988.

Swidler, Leonard, ed. *Religious Liberty and Human Rights in Nations and in Religions.* Philadelphia: Ecumenical Press; New York: Hippocrene Books, 1986.

United Nations. *For Fundamental Human Rights.* Lake Success, N.Y.: Office of Public Information, 1948.

GEORG LANGEMEYER

Hylomorphism. By hylomorphism is meant the Aristotelico-Scholastic view that everything that comes into existence is composed of matter (*hýle*) and form (*morphé*). The idea was applied to the explanation of the sacraments.

(1) *Biblical Background.* Such a concept is evidently foreign to the Bible. But in baptism at any rate a distinction can be made between action and word, with the two together making up a single symbolic action.

(2) *History of Theology.* Early Scholasticism made use of Augustine's distinction between element and word in order to describe the material (or action) part of the sacrament as *materia* and the words used as *forma*. Once Aristotle became known in the West, these concepts were soon given a strictly hylomorphic meaning: the words have causal power in relation to the matter.

(3) *Church Teaching.* The Decree for the Armenians of the Council of Florence adopts these ideas: "All these sacraments are constituted by three elements: by things as the matter, by words as the form, and by the person of the minister" (DS 1312).

(4) *Ecumenical Perspectives.* Reformation theology explains the efficacy of the sacraments solely by their character as the saving word of God. Hylomorphism is therefore hardly a suitable subject of ecumenical dialogue.

(5) *Systematic Reflections.* At the present time, hylomorphism can still be of help in understanding the sacraments only if one is conscious that its application is analogous. Understanding of the duality-in-unity of material-ritual gesture and word can provide a certain (but by no means exhaustive) insight into the structure of the sacramental symbolic action; it is least able to do so in the sacraments of reconciliation and matrimony.

See also MARRIAGE: SACRAMENT OF; SACRAMENT; SACRAMENT OF RECONCILIATION.

Bibliography
Gill, Mary Louise. *Aristotle on Substance: The Paradox of Unity.* Princeton, N.J.: Princeton University Press, 1989.
McMullin, Ernan. *The Concept of Matter in Greek and Medieval Philosophy.* Notre Dame, Ind.: University of Notre Dame Press, 1963.

GÜNTER KOCH

Hypostatic Union. Hypostatic union means literally *personal union* or *subjective unity.* It describes the unification or union of divinity and humanity in the second divine person, the Son of God.

(1) *Biblical Background.* The two bases of any New Testament Christology are the earthly life of Jesus and his resurrection (ASCENSION OF CHRIST; HISTORICAL JESUS; RESURRECTION OF JESUS). In postresurrectional Christian faith (CHRISTOLOGICAL TITLES) the unity of the two is maintained ("Jesus is the Christ, the Kyrios, the Son of God" [see Acts 2:32, 36; Phil 2:9, 11; Rom 1:3f.; 10:9]), thus expressing the identity (and unity) of subject in the earthly Jesus and the resurrected Christ: the resurrection (or "ascension") definitively reveals who he is. This so-called two-tiered or ascending Christology provides an open-

ended structure for grasping the mystery of the person of Jesus Christ, so that within this framework more distinctions and a deeper understanding of Christian faith were possible — as seen in the New Testament and thereafter. This can be demonstrated by analyzing Rom 1:3f. Its original form was (probably) a simple Jewish-Christian profession of faith in the messiah: one and the same person, Jesus, is, as descendant of David, messiah (the earthly "stage") and, by his resurrection, the enthroned Son of God (the heavenly "stage"). These two "stages" were defined using an un-Pauline (in this case) opposition: *katà sarká — katà pneûma* (cf. 1 Pt 3:18; 1 Tm 3:16a), his earthly and heavenly modes of existence. In the end the "Spirit of holiness" establishes Jesus as "Son of God." Paul's construction excludes any adoptionist misunderstanding: the gospel "concerning [God's] son" (Rom 1:3) precedes Jesus and clarifies that Jesus is already the Son of God in his earthly mode of existence. Through the resurrection he is "Son of God *in power.*" Thus Paul understands this ancient profession of faith in the framework of his own Christology (see Gal 4:4–6; Phil 2:5–11), which is belief in the transhistorical Son of God, who lived historically as a human being and whose power as divine Son — in the same human person — was revealed by the resurrection. There are (now!) three "stages" involved (preexistence, kenosis, exaltation). In other words, the two modes of existence of the incarnate and exalted Son are encompassed in the subjective unity of Jesus Christ as the Son. Paul's testimony is normative because it is original and apostolic. In other words, other ways of understanding the mystery of the person of Jesus remain dependent on Paul, and a return to Jewish-Christian adoptionism is no longer possible.

(2) *History of Theology.* The "*pneûma-sárx* formula" of Rom 1:3 continued to be used by Ignatius of Antioch, the "Shepherd of Hermas," Melito of Sardis, and Hilary of Poitiers. It was gradually separated from the "Logos-sárx formula," which — as we see in Justin, Hippolytus, and Tertullian — is substantially the same and has a scriptural basis in Jn 1:14 (*ho lógos sàrx egeneto:* the Word became flesh). But *pneûma-sárx* is understood "statically" and refers to the "states" (*status*) of humanity (*sárx*) and divinity (*pneûma*) within the same subject: see Ignatius of Antioch, *Eph.* 7.2, where the resurrection is no longer mentioned in this incarnational or descendant Christology. Jesus is "flesh-bearing Kyrios" (Ignatius of Antioch, *Smyrn.* 5.2), not "God-bearing man." In Arianism and Apollinarianism the Logos-*sárx* schema (of the Alexandrians) encountered a crisis. In 325 the Council of Nicaea emphasized the divinity of the Logos (DS 125). Against Apollinarianism it declared the real and complete humanity of Jesus Christ "with a rational soul and a body" (DS 151, 159, 166). Gradually the Logos-*anthropos* schema (of the Antiochenes, Theodore of Mopsuestia, et al.) replaced/supplemented the Logos-*sárx* schema. In the controversy surrounding the patriarch Nestorius (381–451), the Logos-*anthropos* formula was attacked because it was seen as endangering the unity of subject of the Incarnate Word by splitting it into a divine and a human "person" (Cyril of Alexandria's second and third letters to Nestorius were the theme

of the Council of Ephesus in 431 [DS 250f., 252–63]). Cyril's letter (*Laeten-tur*) to John of Antioch, which includes the so-called *Symbolum unionis* (also called *Symbolum ephesinum* [cf. DS 271ff.]), contributed to a unification of Alexandrian and Antiochene Christologies. Eutyches (b. 378) so overempha-sized the Alexandrian "Christology of unity" ("I confess that our Lord comes *from* two natures before the union; after the union I confess *only one na-ture*" = Monophysitism) that, once again, the Son of God's act of becoming *human* disappeared. Flavian (patriarch of Constantinople) reacted by calling a synod (448 C.E.), and the formula he used against Eutyches maintains the "two natures after the incarnation," and indeed, "in one hypostasis and per-son." Leo I, in his letter of 449 to Flavian (the "Tome of Leo"), expressed this as follows: "with the character of both natures unimpaired, coming together in one person" (DS 293; cf. 290–95). In 451 the Council of Chalcedon defined "one person in two natures," using Cyril's letter while respecting the "Tome of Leo" (DS 301f.). To what extent post-Chalcedonian Monophysitism was only verbal is debatable. The so-called neo-Chalcedonianism of the sixth century was, in a narrower historical sense, a temporary phenomenon, insofar as it as-pired to and worked toward a terminological mediation that was equivocal and outdated. But its religious concern remains important for today (see earlier in Cyril: "The divine Logos suffered in the flesh and tasted death" [DS 263]), and it continues in the West especially through the influence of Thomas Aquinas. In the East a peak period for Christology was reached in Maximus the Confessor (d. 662). In the Western Church the Chalcedon "affair" continued, since Chal-cedon's definition was the unquestionable basis of medieval Christology. At the center stood the interpretation of the hypostatic union, discussed in the con-text of metaphysical speculation on being: thus an *essentialist Christology*. The divine and human natures of the person of the Logos are not "commingled" and "divided," but rather they "interpenetrate" one another (*perichoresis*) and are in a certain way "equal." Their relationship to one another and to the Lo-gos is the object of reflection. Only in recent times has Catholic Christology proposed a "relational-trinitarian" explanation of the hypostatic union, which rethinks it in the context of history. The latest christological insights have been dealt with at a theological level in the studies of the International Commis-sion of Theologians ("Selected Questions on Christology") and of the Pontifical Biblical Commission ("Bible and Christology" [1984]).

(3) *Church Teaching*. Chalcedon's creed, which was considered as a deep-ening of Nicaea (DS 125f.) — the decisive council of the early church because of its "fundamental statements on the church's understanding of the incarna-tion" (A. Grillmeier) — was the (provisional) end of a historical process. It emphasizes the unity of subject of Jesus Christ ("one and the same"). In its first section it deals with the two "states" or modes of existence or perfections of Christ and recapitulates the history of Christian belief to that time ("consub-stantial with the Father," "born of the Father" — Nicaea; having a "rational soul and a body" — against Apollinarianism; "mother of God" — Ephesus). In

the second section the unity of subject is attributed to the "person" (*prósopon*) and the hypostasis, and the two states are interpreted as two natures: "one person *in* two natures." In so doing it emphasizes the mystery of this reflexive faith-formula by adding four adverbs: "unconfused, unchangeable, undivided, and inseparable," as negatively formulated equivalents to describe the unity of subject, the person, in relation to the two natures (DS 301f.). Only at the Second Council of Constantinople (553) was the term *hypostatic union* first used (*hénosis kath' hypóstasin, unitio/unitas secundum subsistentiam* [DS 424, 426, 428, 429, 430, 436]). An important "dynamization" of the two-natures doctrine came about in the decisions against Monothelitism or Monenergism at the Lateran Council of 649 under Martin I (DS 501–22) and in 681 at the Third Council of Constantinople (DS 553–59). The background of the Lateran synod was the Christology of Maximus the Confessor. He distinguished the "physical [= natural] will," the basic capacity, which (as a consequence of the two-natures doctrine) is available to both the divinity and the humanity, from the "gnomic will," which is identical to the *liberum arbitrium* and must be attributed to the person. Thus Constantinople III speaks of the free *human* will of the divine Logos because the humanity experiences its fullness in its personal unity with it. "The human will is not taken away, but divinized" (DS 556). In reference to Jn 6:38, the unity of subject is emphasized. The person (the "I" of the Logos) calls the human intellect and will its own because its will is fully united with the Father. Behind this is Maximus's basic insight that "the unity of things is as verifiable as their physical (= natural) difference" (*Opusc. theol.* 8). A greater difference than the one between God and humanity is unthinkable, and nevertheless the two are united in the hypostatic union. Jesus' humanity is fulfilled humanity *because* it is borne by the divine Logos. Thus the free human decisions of Jesus are grounded and fulfilled in it, since it is, through the freedom of the will of the Son, a pure yes to the will of the Father. This basic idea is expressed in the Christology of Vatican II's pastoral constitutions, where Jesus Christ is presented as the church's answer to the questions about being human (esp. *GS* 22). A few of the consequences of the hypostatic union have become dogma: the true divine sonship of the human Jesus (DS 610); the possibility of worshiping Jesus in his human nature united hypostatically with the Logos (DS 431); the so-called *communicatio idiomatum,* according to which things predicated of the divinity or the humanity are ascribed to the one Logos become flesh (DS 255, 295); and Jesus' holiness (sinlessness) (DS 801, 1337).

(4) *Ecumenical Perspectives.* While the doctrine of two states ("states" or stages: Christ's humiliation and his exaltation) had no function in Catholic Christology, it played a great role in Protestantism. Kenosis-Christology (especially in the nineteenth century) represents many attempts to understand two-natures Christology as referring to a dynamic event (in the sense of the doctrine of two states) by which the Logos was emptied of its divinity when it came down, which came close to dissolving the hypostatic union. K. Barth succeeded in bringing together both Christologies. W. Pannenberg, in his criticism

of the two-natures doctrine, developed a Christology that starts with Jesus' resurrection and attempts to reinterpret the hypostatic union in the framework of relational thinking. According to Pannenberg the unity of the human Jesus with the Son of God is only indirectly evident in the personal union of Jesus with God — if we take *person* as a relational term. G. Ebeling calls attention to the reciprocal relationship implied in the basic christological formula *vere deus, vere homo* (truly God, truly man [the one guarantees and interprets the other]) and uses the term *relation* in the sense of a "communication between" God and humankind in order to understand the "together-ness of God and humankind in Jesus" as a "communicative together-ness."

(5) *Systematic Reflections.* In recent Catholic Christology the relational-trinitarian explanation of the hypostatic union has made great advances. Especially noteworthy in this regard are (with important distinctions in details!): D. Wiederkehr, W. Kasper, H. Urs von Balthasar, B. Forte, and J. Ratzinger. The impetus for this new interpretation was a "rereading" of the Fathers and a new appreciation of the historical Jesus. In connection with Augustine's sentence, *ipsa assumptione creatur* (by its assumption it is created [*Contra serm. Ar.* 8.2]), A. Grillmeier points out that the moment Christ assumes (*ipsa assumptione*) humanity in the hypostatic union corresponds with its creation. God creates for "'himself,' i.e., for his Son, a human existence in our world" and can — while remaining fully transcendent — be in our midst. Thus "in the man, Jesus, the *prósopon* of the Son is oriented toward the Father." In his interpretation of John Damascene's doctrine of *perichoresis,* P. Hunermann points out that "the history of Jesus Christ" may be read as "the event of the hypostatic union." Thus the history of Jesus is understood as "the history of the being" or the "history of the constituting" of the hypostatic union, which begins "happening" in the incarnation and continues in every moment of this life until the death and resurrection. Similarly, W. Kasper understands the history and destiny of Jesus as "the history (not the becoming!) of his being, his temporality, and his self-interpretation." In such an interpretation of Jesus' history, the resurrection of Jesus reassumes its central, New Testament significance in Christology, as: "the confirmation, revelation, empowerment, realization, and fulfillment of what Jesus claimed before Easter and of who he in fact was." The new interpretation of the hypostatic union begins with the relationship of the earthly Jesus to God (Abba) and sees in it the revelation of the intradivine relationship of the Son and the Father in the Spirit. Balthasar speaks of an "inversion" or "transfer" of the immanent Trinity into the "economic trinity," that is, into concrete history. In the incarnation of the Son there is a new, yet creaturely realization of the intradivine relationship of the Father and the Son in the Spirit. The doctrine of two natures is explained as a two-relation doctrine: the intradivine relations of the Father to the Son and the Son to the Father in the Spirit are realized in a creaturely relation in the Incarnate Son who receives and gives up his being. The human existence of Jesus is therefore the creaturely fulfillment of sonship (D. Wiederkehr). A divine person is the "subject of a

human history" (B. Forte). The Logos is not just flesh; it became human and had a human history. The "self"-sharing of Father and Son in the Spirit takes place in a creaturely manner in receiving and giving, in obedience and in the love of Jesus Christ. To this extent he is the personal "presentation" (*Auslegung*) of God, who shares freely in love. According to this interpretation we can speak only "indirectly" of the hypostatic union and the two natures. The relationship of Jesus Christ to his Father stands in the foreground (relational-trinitarian interpretation), not the relationship of his humanity to his divinity (essentialist Christology). The unity of Jesus with God expresses his divinity; the relationship of Jesus to his Father expresses his humanity — and thus the abiding distinction of the two is respected. A turn toward "spiritual Christology" is found in J. Ratzinger's trinitarian-relational explanation of the union. In the tradition of Maximus the Confessor, he considers the "continual communication with the Father" as the middle of Jesus' life and person. He understands the christological dogmas as an interpretation of Jesus' prayer, that is, "his living and dying, which was always determined by the Son's dialogue with the Father."

See also CHRISTOLOGICAL HERESIES; CHRISTOLOGY; TRINITARIAN PERSONHOOD OF GOD; TRINITY.

Bibliography

Balthasar, Hans Urs von. *Theo-Drama: Theological Dramatic Theory.* San Francisco: Ignatius, 1988–94.

Grillmeier, Alois. *Christ in Christian Tradition.* 2d rev. ed. London: Mowbray, 1975.

Kasper, Walter. *Jesus the Christ.* New York: Paulist, 1976.

———. *Theology and Church.* New York: Crossroad, 1989.

Principe, Walter H. *Theology of the Hypostatic Union in the Early 13th Century.* Toronto: Pontifical Institute of Medieval Studies, 1963.

Rahner, Karl. "Current Problems in Christology." In *Theological Investigations,* 1:149–200. Baltimore: Helicon, 1965.

Ratzinger, Joseph. *Behold the Pierced One: An Approach to a Spiritual Christology.* San Francisco: Ignatius, 1986.

HISTORY OF THE TEACHING OF THE HYPOSTATIC UNION

1. *The Jewish-Christian formulation**

> "Jesus (is the) Christ
>
> descended from David,   declared Son of God since his
>   resurrection from the dead."

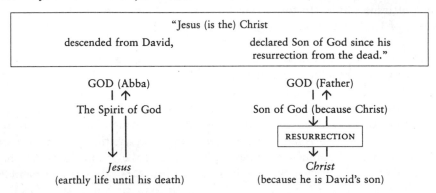

2. *Pre-Pauline precisions of the Jewish-Christian profession**

> "Jesus (is the) Christ,
>
> *descended from David*   *declared Son of God with power*
> *according to the flesh*   *according to the Spirit of holiness*
>   *by rising from the dead.*"

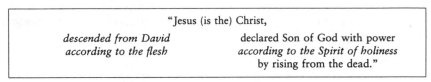

3. *Pauline profession of faith (Rom 1:3f.; ca. 57/58)*
   (Paul set apart for the gospel of God)

> "concerning his Son,
>
> who was descended   and was declared to be
> from David   Son of God with power
> according to the flesh   according to the Spirit
>   of holiness by resurrection
>   from the dead, (by) Jesus
>   Christ, our Lord."

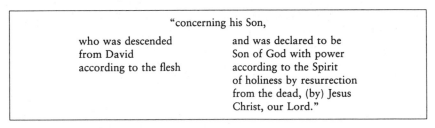

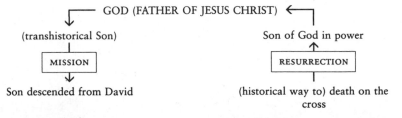

4. Ignatius of Antioch (Ad. Eph. 7.2; ca. 110)

> "There is one doctor,
>
> | | |
> |---|---|
> | who became *flesh*, | of the *Spirit* |
> | took flesh | and unbegotten, |
> | from Mary, | God incarnate, |
> | and in death | genuine life |
> | was seen to be | sprung from God, |
> | capable of suffering, | beyond suffering, |
>
> Jesus Christ."

ONE

in the *flesh* (human state) and in the *Spirit* (divine state)

5. The definition of the Council of Chalcedon (451)

Following the Holy Fathers therefore we all with one accord profess faith in: *"the one identical Son, our Lord Jesus Christ*
– he is perfect both in his divinity and in his humanity;
– truly God and truly man composed of body and rational soul;
– consubstantial with the Father in his divinity, consubstantial with us in his humanity, 'like us in every respect except for sin' (Heb. 4:15);
– in his divinity he was begotten of the Father before time and in his humanity he was begotten in this last age of Mary, the Virgin, the Mother of God for us and our salvation, *the one selfsame Christ, only-begotten of the Father before time*
– in two natures
without any commingling or change or division or separation;
the distinction between the natures is in no way removed by their union but rather the specific character of each nature is preserved;
– and they are united in one person and one hypostasis;
he is not split or divided into two persons;

but there is one selfsame only-begotten Son, God the Word, the Lord Jesus Christ
This the prophets have taught about him from the beginning, this Jesus Christ himself taught us; this the creed of the Fathers has handed down to us."

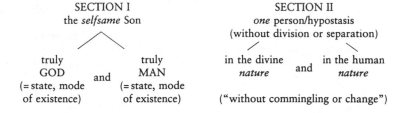

SECTION I	SECTION II
the *selfsame* Son	*one* person/hypostasis (without division or separation)
truly GOD (= state, mode of existence) *and* truly MAN (= state, mode of existence)	in the divine *nature* *and* in the human *nature* ("without commingling or change")

6. Interpretation of essentialist Christology

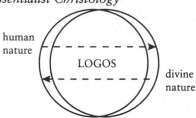

7. Relational-trinitarian interpretation in a historical perspective*

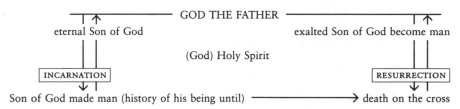

Bibliography

Gray, Patrick T. R. *The Defense of Chalcedon in the East (451–553)*. Leiden: Brill, 1979.

Grillmeier, Alois. *Christ in Christian Tradition*. 2d rev. ed. London: Mowbray, 1975.

Hengel, Martin. *The Son of God: The Origin of Christology and the History of Jewish-Hellenistic Religion*. Philadelphia: Fortress, 1976.

Hultgren, Arland J. *New Testament Christology: A Critical Assessment and Annotated Bibliography*. New York: Greenwood, 1988.

Kelly, J. N. D. *Early Christian Creeds*. London: Longman, 1972.

———. *Early Christian Doctrines*. San Francisco: Harper, 1978.

Pelikan, Jaroslav. *The Emergence of the Catholic Tradition (100–600)*. Vol. 1 of *The Christian Tradition*. Chicago: University of Chicago Press, 1971.

Rahner, Karl, and Wilhelm Thüsing. *A New Christology*. New York: Crossroad, 1980.

Sellers, Robert Victor. *The Council of Chalcedon: A Historical and Doctrinal Survey*. London: SPCK, 1961.

———. *Two Ancient Christologies: A Study in the Christological Thought of the Schools of Alexandria and Antioch in the Early History of Christian Doctrine*. London: SPCK, 1940.

Young, Frances M. *From Nicaea to Chalcedon: A Guide to the Literature and Its Background*. Philadelphia: Fortress, 1983.

LOTHAR ULLRICH

---

*Concerning the reconstruction of 1 and 2 — the two earlier forms of Rom 1:3f. — see H. Schlier. The double arrows in nos. 1 and 7 present the two relationships (the Father's to the Son or Jesus *and* the Son's or Jesus' relation to the Father). The arrows in no. 3 present the "way of the Son" from eternity with the Father, to being sent into history until his death on the cross, then after his resurrection the way "back" to eternity with the Father.

I i

Identity. In recent anthropology, identity characterizes the self-knowledge of the human person or of a group of human persons (self-consciousness). The term reflects the origin of this knowledge: originally, the human person attains to self-consciousness by identifying him- or herself with "that person" who is approached and related to by the human beings around him or her (socialization). This initial identity is transformed through the experiences that the human person has with her or his social surroundings (loss of identity, gain in identity). In faith the Christian gains a new identity that extends beyond social identity, insofar as that person knows him- or herself to be addressed by God as an absolutely unique person.

(1) *Biblical Background.* In the witness of the Old Testament, Israel found its identity as a people in the faith in its election by Yahweh. This is expressed above all through the act of naming. Yahweh gives Jacob the name Israel. On account of this, individual persons are also called by their names through Yahweh or are given new names (prophets, kings). In the New Testament, Christians' experience of gaining a new identity in faith and in baptism is expressed in formulations such as "to receive a new name" or "your names are written in the book of life" (Lk 10:20; Phil 4:3; Rv 2:17; 3:12).

(2) *History of Theology.* In theological tradition the fact of self-consciousness was derived from the essence of the spiritual soul (*anima rationalis*) and was understood as the immediate knowledge of one's own substantial selfhood and personhood. The social mediation of self-consciousness and the problem of identity resulting from this did not yet come into view. In the act of naming performed at baptism, however, the knowledge about the new identity in faith has been preserved.

(3) *Church Teaching.* The term *identity* has not been received into ecclesial doctrinal language.

(4) *Ecumenical Perspectives.* The differences between the churches are not reflected in the discussion of the problem of identity.

(5) *Systematic Reflections.* It is first in modern societies that the finding of one's identity has actually become a problem. The various relatively independent systems of social ordering each demand different identifications. Moreover, different value systems, so-called worldviews, bring their influence to bear (pluralistic society). This explains the widespread tendency to keep one's religious identity vague (partially identified Christians). Theological anthropology must make plausible that the identity gained in Christian faith works against the loss of identity that is caused by the partial identifications demanded by society. It must further make clear that ecclesial identity does not

a priori exclude but rather embraces the openness for other religions and world-views. From this background it is doubtful whether the vague religious identity should be judged only negatively from the point of view of the Christian faith as religious indifferentism, alienation, or sin. It could also be the expression of a critical sensitivity for God's illimitability and sovereignty.

See also PERSONALITY; SOCIETY.

Bibliography
Erikson, Erik. *Identity and the Life Cycle: Selected Papers.* New York: Random House, 1959.
Joas, Hans. *G. H. Mead: A Contemporary Re-examination of His Thought.* Cambridge, Mass.: Polity Press, 1985.
Pannenberg, Wolfhart. *Anthropology in Theological Perspective.* Philadelphia: Westminster, 1985.
Parks, Sharon. *The Critical Years.* New York: Harper, 1991.
Williams, Bernard. *Problems of the Self.* New York: Oxford University Press, 1973.

GEORG LANGEMEYER

Illness. Illness is a disturbance in the functioning of life. Although one can distinguish between physical and mental illnesses, it is always the whole human person who suffers from illness. Ill persons become insecure, isolated from social life, forcibly inactive. At the same time they are given the occasion to reflect on the value of life and are challenged in their will to live. Theologically illness can be seen under different aspects: creatureliness, punishment for sin or a consequence of it, an indication of death and of being delivered to God as the one who judges and fulfills, or the connection between salvation in Christ and healing.

(1) *Biblical Background.* In the Old Testament illness is seen as a withdrawal of Yahweh's life-giving nearness and, as with premature death, is interpreted first of all as a punishment for sin. Later, above all in Job and Ecclesiastes, the connection between illness and sin is put into question. Illness points to God's rule, whose fathoming the creature is not entitled to. It is a proof to be undergone, an endurance test for faith. According to the witness of the New Testament, Jesus also did not recognize any direct connection between illness and sin (Jn 9:2f.; see Lk 13:2–5). Still, illness stands in opposition to the coming of the kingdom of God and belongs to the field of activity of the destructive powers that resist the kingdom. Therefore, Jesus' healings of the sick not only are symbolical signs of the salvation of the human person that the coming kingdom of God brings about but also are in themselves a manifestation of the beginning of the kingdom (Mt 11:2–6). Jesus' proclamation of salvation includes the whole, indivisible human person.

(2) *History of Theology.* The Greek Fathers of the Church and the Orthodox tradition have preferred to interpret sin as an illness of the soul and Jesus as the doctor and have in this way preserved the connection between the salvation and the healing of the whole human person. In contrast, Western theology understood illness as a punitive consequence of sin or as original sin, an occa-

sion for the faithful person to make expiation. In addition, the care for the sick, following the model of Christ, has always been considered a principal duty of the Christian love of neighbor.

(3) *Church Teaching.* The church has not made any explicit statements on the theological significance of illness.

(4) *Ecumenical Perspectives.* In the ecumenical dialogue, illness is also not a central theme.

(5) *Systematic Reflections.* Since current theology gives special attention to the salvific meaning of the life of Jesus, which in the tradition had been neglected in favor of his suffering and death, there has been emphasis on the way in which healing and the overcoming of illness come in direct association with the salvation already experienced in faith. Thus, for example, the invention of penicillin is appealed to as an experience of salvation (Schillebeeckx). In this view the "healing" of social conditions that make human persons ill can be also interpreted as a task of the proclamation of salvation or as an experience of salvation. Nevertheless, not everything that makes a person ill is to be equated with sin or with evil, because the susceptibility for illness is already given in the creatureliness of the human person. Yet the experience of being ill usually brings with it a trial for faith, which is why the church supports the sick with a special sacrament.

See also ANOINTING OF THE SICK; REDEMPTION AND LIBERATION; SALVATION; SIN AND GUILT.

Bibliography
Casey, Juliana M. *Food for the Journey: Theological Foundations of the Catholic Healthcare Ministry.* St. Louis: Catholic Health Association of the United States, 1991.
Muldoon, Maureen H. "A Spirituality for the Long Haul: Response to Chronic Illness." *Journal of Religion and Health* 30 (1991) 99–108.
Rahner, Karl. "Illness." In *The Content of Faith: The Best of Karl Rahner's Theological Writings.* New York: Crossroad, 1993.
Sontag, Susan. *Illness as Metaphor.* New York: Farrar, Straus and Giroux, 1988.

GEORG LANGEMEYER

Image of God. The expression "in the image of God" has become a theological concept to describe the special relationship of human beings to God and the primacy within creation that this implies.

(1) *Biblical Background.* The idea is derived from Gn 1:26: "Let us make the human person in our image, similar to us." The image of God remains in the human person even after the fall into sin (Gn 5:1). In the later period of the Old Testament, the Book of Wisdom, under the influence of Greek religiosity, related the image-of-God theme to the immortality of the soul; this image has been lost through sin (2:23f.). The New Testament recognizes in Jesus Christ the full realization of the image of God in humanity (2 Cor 4:4; Col 1:15). Through faith and baptism, the Christian is remodeled from the image of the original Adam into that of the second Adam (Rom 6:4f.; 1 Cor 15:49; 2 Cor

3:18). The theme of the image of God thus receives in the New Testament a historically dynamic character: the image of God in the creature is directed toward the fulfillment in Christ.

(2) *History of Theology.* The Church Fathers developed these basic approaches, primarily in their efforts to make the gospel understandable to the educated Greeks. Here the theme of the image of God offered itself as a linking concept to the Platonic ontology of images, according to which the world is a copy generated from the eternal divine archetypes (ideas). The religious longings in the Hellenistic culture were concerned with rising from the transitory copies of this world to the eternal divine archetypes. The Fathers of the Church distinguished with reference to Gn 1:26 between being in the image of God ("copy" or "representation"), which makes up the creatural essence of the human person, and likeness to God ("after our likeness"), which first becomes possible through the joining of the divine archetype with the human representation as God took on human flesh. Human persons, following that, can take on the same status with Christ through faith, baptism, and discipleship. The influence of Augustine had the result that this theology of images entered into Scholastic theology with an essential restriction: the image of God became attributed predominantly to the spiritual soul of the human person. Only recently has modern exegesis corrected this limitation.

(3) *Church Teaching.* The ecclesial doctrinal proclamation explained the theme of the image of God as the ability of every human person to recognize and to love his or her Creator as well as to rule over all terrestrial creatures for the greater glory of God (*GS* 12). The image of God in humankind was deformed through sin and became restored in humankind through Christ (*GS* 22).

(4) *Ecumenical Perspectives.* The Reformers rejected the distinction between being in the image of God and having likeness to God. Sin destroyed the image of God in humanity. What remains of it according to Luther is only the superiority of humankind over the rest of creation. The question of the image of God in the sinner unleashed a controversial discussion within Protestant theology in the first half of the twentieth century, in which Catholic theologians were also involved. The reflection back upon the biblical foundations has led in the meantime to an extensive rapprochement of the points of view. The image-of-God theme cannot be adequately specified on the ontological level of a comparison of essential qualities (intellectuality, reason, freedom), and it cannot be reduced to the event of the word (of God) and a response (of faith). A wide spectrum remains open for the ordering of both aspects.

(5) *Systematic Reflections.* Recently the aspect of the sovereignty over nature contained in the concept of the image of God, which up to now was scarcely problematic, has come under discussion. This theme has been accused of being partially responsible for the exploitation of nature and for the modern ecological crisis. It is indisputable that there is a causal connection between the Christian view of the human person as being the image of God and the lifting

of restraints over the use of the forces of nature, previously revered as divine, for human goals. Yet, until the eighteenth century, the sovereignty over nature always stood under the objective aim of the glory of God and in responsibility before the Creator of nature. Thus, the exploitation of nature is also linked to the replacement of Christian faith by a religion of reason alone or by atheism. In view of the modern threat to the ecological equilibrium, theological anthropology raises the question of whether this problem can be sufficiently met if the focus is restricted to the connection — as it is expressed in the theme of the image of God — between humankind's sovereignty over nature and its responsibility before God. The rootedness of the human person within nature and the hope of the Christian in the participation of nature in Christ's glory, which is contained in the faith in the corporeal resurrection of Christ, suggest a cocreatedness with nature, such as comes to expression in the creation psalms or in the "Canticle of the Sun" of St. Francis of Assisi. Only within this "solidarity" of all creation is the task of caring for nature entrusted to the human person (CREATURELINESS OF THE HUMAN PERSON).

See also ECOLOGY; FLESH-SPIRIT; HUMAN PERSON; INCARNATION; NATURE; SOUL; WORLD RESPONSIBILITY.

Bibliography

Atkins, Anne. *Split Image: Male and Female after God's Likeness*. London: Hodder and Stoughton, 1987.

Borresen, Kari Elisabeth, ed. *Image of God and Gender Models in Judaeo-Christian Tradition*. Atlantic Highlands, N.J.: Humanities Press, 1991.

Burghardt, Walter J. *The Image of God in Man according to Cyril of Alexandria*. Woodstock, Md.: Woodstock College Press, 1957.

Gunnlaugur, A. Jonsson. *The Image of God: Genesis 1:26–28 in a Century of Old Testament Research*. Stockholm: Almqvist and Wiksell, 1988.

Merriell, Donald Juvenal. *To the Image of the Trinity: A Study in the Development of Aquinas' Teaching*. Toronto: Pontifical Institute of Mediaeval Studies, 1990.

GEORG LANGEMEYER

Immaculate Conception. The term *immaculate conception* refers to Mary's liberation from original sin at the moment of her own conception in her mother's womb.

(1) *Biblical Background.* This faith conviction cannot rely upon any *direct* scriptural testimony. As with the dogma of the assumption of Mary into God's glory, the only texts that can be utilized here are those that comprise this doctrine *at an undeveloped level.* These sources are especially the ones that regard everything that happens within time as being rooted in God's elective decrees. Such was the calling of the prophets (see Jer 1:5). The same holds true for the New Testament perspective on the church: it has been chosen since before all time to live in a holy and righteous manner under the influence of Christ (Eph 1:3–14). Since God's saving actions match God's eternal decree, the new life in and with Christ is not one stage among many: it is expressly God's choice. Christian existence is willed by God and is always enabled by grace in its spe-

cific character. Paul speaks about the "standard of the faith" that God has given to each person (Rom 12:3). It is in this perspective that the New Testament also sees Mary. According to Lk 1:28, she is the favored one, chosen by God; through her motherhood she is to open up to her Son the way into time. Not only the selection for this service but also the readiness to comply with it is a grace given by God to Mary. She had need of preparation through grace in order to accept and fulfill in faith the physical motherhood of the messiah. When Mary is blessed because of her faith (Lk 1:45), this serves as the outward sign of her inward readiness to be the mother of Christ. This is not further elaborated in the New Testament; it is confined to the basic statement that God's election always includes the appropriate preparation. This is the biblical germ of the dogma.

(2) *History of Theology*. The main driving forces for the dogma's later development issue from considerations in incarnation theology and ecclesiology. One encounters the idea that Mary, by reason of the incarnation of the messiah, had to be sanctified as the temple of God and had to be purified from sin. As Mother of God, a special holiness was proper to her. Irenaeus (*Adv. haer.* 4.33.11) states that Mary became purified by the Holy Spirit at the annunciation. A similar position is found in Augustine (*De natura et gratia* 36, 42), who, by reason of the holiness of Christ, upholds the holiness of Mary: "Because of the honor of the Lord, I do not want there to be the slightest question about her when the discussion turns to sin." Augustine was not yet cognizant of any freedom of Mary from original sin because he placed the essence of original sin in disordered concupiscence and saw sexual desire, absent in Christ alone, as its means of transmittal. Further explanation was still required for the understanding of original sin. Anselm of Canterbury (*De conceptu virginali et de originali peccato* 27), supported by Thomas Aquinas and his school, sees Mary as lacking the grace of the original state. Anselm's approach perceives the sanctification of Mary as an *original* radical bestowal of grace. However, in opposition to this the opinion still existed that it was necessary to speak of Mary's weaknesses out of regard for the universality of Christ's work of redemption. Origen (*In Luc. hom.* 17) held this view: "If she was not perplexed over the Lord at his passion, then Jesus did not die for her sins. If however all have sinned and have need of the Lord's glory, in order to be justified by his grace and redeemed, then Mary too was thoroughly perplexed over him." To connect Mary's sanctification with her need for redemption formed the major controversial question for Scholasticism, a controversy carried on especially between the Dominicans as opponents and the Franciscans as proponents of the dogma. A breakthrough was achieved, after appropriate preliminary work by William of Ware (ca. 1255–60), by John Duns Scotus (d. 1308) with his doctrine of Mary being redeemed in anticipation and therefore first. It asserts that Mary is primarily a member of the humanity that requires redemption: however, for the sake of her Son's honor, from the beginning of her conception she was preserved from the stain of original sin through his redemptive merit and

received into the original communion with God. In this manner the core of the future dogma was addressed. A further impetus is found in the comparison of Eve and Mary in the patristic doctrine and in early Scholasticism. In opposition to sinful Eve stood the obedient and holy new mother of the living. In Mary the holy church stands in contrast to the synagogue and to the pagan world. The less the church experienced itself as the holy and spotless bride of the Lord (Eph 5:27), the more Mary appeared in this image; as a type and representative of the people of god, she becomes a sign that the holy church is present. Finally, the forces of devotion accompanied the development of the dogma out of the complex of revealed truths. From the seventh century in the Eastern Church and from the twelfth century at different places in the West, the feast of the conception of Mary was celebrated, yet its content was not yet fixed in the sense of the later dogma. Thomas Aquinas, who tolerates the feast, does not accept as its content that Mary was holy right from her conception; hence, according to Thomas, on this day there is celebrated "the feast rather of her sanctification than of her conception" (*STh* 3, q. 27, a. 2 ad 3). In line with the ancient living belief, Thomas acknowledges and celebrates Mary as sanctified on account of her motherhood. The forms of veneration toward the immaculate conception increased especially during the seventeenth and eighteenth centuries.

(3) *Church Teaching.* Commencing with these attestations of piety and understanding the definition itself as an act of worshiping God and of honoring Mary, Pius X declared on December 8, 1854, in the bull *Ineffabilis Deus:* "The doctrine that the Blessed Virgin Mary was preserved pure from any fault of original sin at the first instant of her conception through a singular gift of grace and privilege from Almighty God, by virtue of the merits of Christ Jesus, the Redeemer of humanity, is revealed by God and therefore is to be firmly and steadfastly believed by all the faithful" (DS 2803; *NR* 479). Vatican II gives a more concise and a positive formulation: it sees Mary "from the first moment of her conception in the radiance of a singular holiness" (*LG* 56); further, it mentions the dogma's christological point of departure as well as its ecclesiological nexus: Mary is "redeemed in a more sublime manner by virtue of the merits of her Son *and united with him in intimate and imperishable union*"; nonetheless, Mary is also united with all human beings requiring redemption as "Adam's posterity" (*LG* 53).

(4) *Ecumenical Perspectives.* According to Luther, Mary was purified from all sin because of her divine motherhood. She is also a needy and weak creature. Luther's shifting understanding of Mary's freedom from original sin is influenced by his doctrine of grace, alongside his scriptural principle that emerged ever more clearly. For that reason, there are two series of statements, one on Mary's sanctification, and the other on her as a sinner. Current Protestant theology points to the deficient scriptural foundation and sees in the dogma a contradiction of the singular and universal redemptive act by Christ: as in the case of the dogma of the assumption of Mary into God's glory, criticism is aimed here against an improper glorification of the church.

(5) *Systematic Reflections.* Just as with the overview of the history of dogma, a perspective proceeding from incarnation theology and ecclesiology should be examined systematically. The Catholic doctrine of faith in the dogma of Mary's freedom from original sin is concerned with the unconditional primacy of God's sanctifying grace, which it sees realized in Mary as the Mother of God amid any experience of the destructive power of sin; in her, the new Israel is the pure, sanctified bride of the Lord (see Eph 5:26f.). The faith in the primacy of grace, professed with a view to Mary, does not allow us to speak of the sinfulness of the church as being as important as its holiness; there exists an "undialectic precedence of grace over guilt" (K. Rahner, *Schriften* 3 [Einsiedeln, 1967], 167). Therefore Mary, too, as one of the faithful and thus as a type and model of the church, is correctly perceived only when regarded in terms of the grace conferred upon her. Mary as a believer and Mary as full of grace are two aspects necessarily qualifying one another. Without qualification by the theology of grace, Mary as a prototype of the church would be an arbitrary reification by human beings. This thought requires deeper inquiry through incarnation theology; only from that standpoint does it acquire its proper importance. God's decree of the incarnation comprises from eternity the selection of Mary as the human mother of the redeemer. She was chosen for the highest possible personal intimacy, if motherhood indeed is not to be regarded in a narrow biological sense. In this perspective, being redeemed first or in anticipation signifies that Mary has been *chosen and given grace* for the deepest living union with Christ; this expresses in a positive manner what *preservation from original sin* formulates negatively.

See also ASSUMPTION OF MARY; CHURCH; GRACE; ORIGINAL SIN; REDEMPTION AND LIBERATION.

Bibliography
Burgess, Joseph A., H. George Anderson, and J. Francis Stafford, eds. *The One Mediator, the Saints, and Mary.* Minneapolis: Augsburg, 1991.
Cunningham, Agnes. *The Significance of Mary.* Chicago: Thomas More, 1988.
O'Connor, Edward D., ed. *The Dogma of the Immaculate Conception: History and Significance.* Notre Dame, Ind.: University of Notre Dame Press, 1958.
Palmer, Paul F. *Mary in the Documents of the Church.* Westminster, Md.: Newman, 1952.
Rahner, Karl. "The Dogma of the Immaculate Conception in Our Spiritual Life." In *Theological Investigations,* 3:129–40. Baltimore: Helicon, 1967.
———. "The Immaculate Conception." In *Theological Investigations,* 1:201–13. Baltimore: Helicon, 1954.

FRANZ COURTH

Immortality. In theology (and philosophy) immortality means the continued existence of a life that has been transformed by death, whether this continued existence be that of the soul now free of the body or of the entire person in a new and different corporality. While immortality is thus understood basically as the conquest of the power of death, its explanation depends on one's image of the human person (see HUMAN PERSON: IMAGE OF).

(1) *Biblical Background.* The Scriptures on the whole work within the Jewish horizon of thought and present a monistic (holistic) picture of the human being: a distinction is made between a bodily and a spiritual side, but these two cannot be separated. The whole person or rather a shadowy image that detaches itself from the person in death lives on in Sheol. As a result of this holistic vision of the human being the true hope of the people of Israel is the resurrection of the dead, which becomes an article of faith in the last centuries before Christ. In the wisdom literature, which is influenced by Greek thought, immortality beyond death is predicated of the human soul (Wis 3:1–4). This immortality, which is derived from the image of God in the human being, has its foundation in God's creative activity (Wis 2:23); it is bestowed upon the just as a gift (Wis 3:4). Of the wicked, on the other hand, it is said that they forfeit immortality and kill the soul (Wis 1:11). In the main, the New Testament accepts Jewish anthropology and its hope in the resurrection of the dead. Scientific exegesis gives various answers to the question of whether and to what extent the Greek picture of the human person exercises an influence (especially in the interpretation of Mt 10:28) and whether the New Testament teaches an intermediate state and by what anthropological model this is to be explained. Because of the urgent EXPECTATION OF AN IMMINENT END, these questions are not a focus of interest at the time when the New Testament writings come into existence. Immortality is understood rather as a property of God and Christ (1 Tm 1:16); but it can be bestowed on the human person, who is viewed as a unit made up of body and soul.

(2) *History of Theology.* The teaching of Christian tradition on immortality is intelligible only in light of the influence of Greek philosophical teaching on the soul, a conception shaped mainly by Plato and Aristotle. In Plato's dualistic picture of the person a distinction is made between the transitory body and the spiritual soul, which possesses immortality due to its divine origin. As a result of death, understood as the separation of soul from body, and of the judgment that accompanies it, the soul is equipped for the life apportioned to it. Aristotle surmounts this dualism by applying hylomorphism to the relation of soul to body and making the soul the inner formative principle of being and structure that turns the human being into a living, human entity. Being an organic principle, the soul is bound to the body and, like the body, is transitory. The only thing that is immortal is the divine *noûs*, which comes into the human being from without and is not understood to be something individual. At the beginning of the Christian era Philo of Alexandria gives a synthesis of the ideas of diasporan Judaism and the Hellenistic world around it: the human person consists of body and soul; the body is mortal; the soul is immortal in its highest part, namely, the *noûs*, or the divine *pneûma* in the person. But this immortality must be attained through virtue and especially through fear of God. Because the New Testament regards immortality as a divine attribute, the immortality of the soul was accepted only gradually in the Christian tradition and after an initial rejection of it (in Justin, Theophilus of Antioch, Irenaeus). A clear shift

of outlook is visible in Clement of Alexandria and Origen. Tertullian is the first to teach the immortality of the soul as a property of created human nature; he bases the teaching on Stoic ideas of the soul's simplicity and indissolubility. Augustine discusses the immortality of the soul at length in connection with Neoplatonic philosophy. Because of the importance of Greek philosophy and Augustinian theology the doctrine of the immortality of the soul was undisputed in the Middle Ages; it did, however, receive a decisively new form under the influence of Aristotelianism. Thomas Aquinas speaks consistently of the incorruptibility of the soul, whereas, following the Scriptures, he understands immortality to be an attribute of the risen Christ, of the human person in paradise, and of human beings after the resurrection of the dead. When he speaks of the soul as by its nature immortal, he does not mean an "absolute I" but a quality bestowed by God as Creator and thereby granted to the soul as part of its nature. Because the soul is incarnated, it possesses the perfection of its own nature only in union with the body. The soul separated from the body is in a state that is not only imperfect but also, and necessarily, contrary to its nature. Since such a state cannot last forever, the immortality of the soul seems to call for the resurrection of the body, where, in the last analysis, the conquest of death takes place.

(3) *Church Teaching.* Doctrinal statements of the church on the immortality of the soul appear first in the Middle Ages. They presuppose, as their anthropological model, a soul that is free of the body and ordered to a glorified body. It is in this sense that death is understood as the separation of body and soul and that the INTERMEDIATE STATE (PURGATORY, HEAVEN, and HELL) is related to the body-free soul (see DS 838, 902, 1000, 1304–6, 1440). The declaration entitled "Some Questions of Eschatology," which the Congregation for the Doctrine of the Faith published on May 17, 1979 (*AAS* 71 [1979] 941), defends the term *soul,* which has become established in the use of Scripture and in tradition, and understands by it the human "self," which is endowed with consciousness and will and continues to exist after death.

(4) *Ecumenical Perspectives.* The Orthodox churches, the theologians of the Reformation period, and orthodox Lutheran dogmatics hold to the continued existence of an immortal soul after death (although they have a different understanding of aspects of the intermediate state). Many theologians today, however, especially those who accept the total-death theory (e.g., O. Cullmann, K. Barth, W. Pannenberg), object to the Catholic doctrine of the immortality of the soul. They regard it as the "bolt-hole" of Platonism and a granting of dogmatic status to the philosophical heritage of antiquity.

(5) *Systematic Reflections.* In contemporary Catholic theology there is general acceptance of the immortality of the human being in the sense of a continued existence after death. At the same time, however, there is an insistence that various anthropological models can be used to explain this otherworldly existence. The fact that the magisterial pronouncements of the Middle Ages used the model current at the time does not give the latter

any priority; in addition, the Scriptures use almost exclusively a different anthropological model. The controversy between Catholics and Evangelicals on "immortality of the soul or resurrection of the dead" has been toned down inasmuch as an unfounded polemical attitude on the part of Evangelical theologians has gradually been set aside, while the Catholic side has more clearly emphasized that the true Christian hope is for the resurrection of the dead and therefore that the intermediate state is not the definitive state of salvation or damnation. If we prescind from the extreme form of the total-death theory, we see that it is not the fact of human immortality that is disputed but rather the way in which it is to be understood, as is clear especially in the controversies over the total-death theory, resurrection at death, and the intermediate state.

See also CORPORALITY OF THE HUMAN PERSON; DEATH; ETERNAL LIFE; INTERMEDIATE STATE; RESURRECTION OF THE DEAD; SOUL.

Bibliography

Cavarnos, Constantine. *Immortality of the Soul: The Testimony of the Old and New Testaments: Orthodox Iconography and Hymnography, and the Works of Eastern Fathers and Other Writers of the Orthodox Church.* Belmont, Mass.: Institute for Byzantine and Modern Greek Studies, 1993.

Cobb, John B. "The Resurrection of the Soul." *HTR* 80 (1987) 213–27.

Cullmann, Oscar. *Immortality of the Soul; or, Resurrection of the Dead? The Witness of the New Testament.* London: Epworth, 1958.

Jonas, Hans. "Immortality and the Modern Temper." *HTR* 55 (1972) 1–20.

Pieper, Joseph. *Death and Immortality.* New York: Herder and Herder, 1969.

Stendahl, Krister. *Immortality and Resurrection.* New York: Macmillan, 1971.

Sullivan, Lawrence E. *Death, Afterlife, and the Soul.* New York: Macmillan, 1989.

Swinburne, Richard. *The Evolution of the Soul.* New York: Oxford University Press, 1986.

JOSEF FINKENZELLER

Incarnation. The term *incarnation* refers to the basic fact for Christian faith that the trinitarian God assumed human reality in the person of the eternal Word who is the Father's eternal self-expression, so that God, the Creator, could save humankind. Incarnation refers both to the *act* by which the Word of God *assumes* human nature and to the *abiding state* that results from the Word's having assumed human nature.

(1) *Biblical Background.* The New Testament speaks of the incarnation in various ways corresponding to the state of christological reflection and the images being used. Paul sees Christ Jesus as the eternal Son of God, who was sent into the world by God the Father, was born of a woman, and was subject to the law. Although he was without sin, he bore the curse of sin. He accepted our poverty by lowering himself, in obedience to his mission. He was exalted, and he gives us a share in his divine kingdom. Thus he who was in the likeness of God entered into the likeness of created flesh, temptation, and sin (Rom 1:3f.; 2 Cor 5:21; 8:9; Gal 3:13; 4:4, 15; Phil 2:6–11). Finally, he brings us into his own filial relationship to the Father through the Holy Spirit (Rom 8:29; Gal 4:6f.). In a two-stage Christology, the incarnation is part of his condescension.

The deutero-Pauline letters also speak of the revelation of Christ in the flesh (1 Tm 3:16), thus using the epiphany theme to explain the incarnation (2 Tm 1:10; Ti 2:11; 3:4). They describe his existence with God in terms of being the very image of God and the bearer of God's fullness, even before entering the world as man (Col 1:15; 2:9; Heb 13:8; 1 Cor 8:6). The term *incarnation* is based on the Gospel of John. Christ is the eternal Logos, who is with God and thus *is* God (Jn 1:1). He becomes flesh (*sárx*) and is a human person among other human persons, without divesting himself of his divinity (Jn 1:14; 1 Jn 1:1). Thus everyone must confess that the Son of God has come in the flesh (1 Jn 4:2f.; 2 John 7). The statements on preexistence belong to the doctrine of the incarnation. They do not, however, stem from the continuously evolving statements about Christ, but rather describe the intratrinitarian being of the eternal Logos before the incarnation. The birth in time from the Virgin Mary is not the basis of Christ's divine sonship, but a consequence of the incarnation (Mt 1:18–25; Lk 1:26–38).

(2) *History of Theology.* The principal goal of the Christology of the early church was to determine how to view the incarnation correctly, since the mystery of Christ's person is the real condition for his work of redemption. Irenaeus of Lyons was the first to use the term *sárkosis* (incarnation) to describe Christ's going forth (Jn 1:14) (*Adv. haer.* 3.19.2). Because the biblical word *flesh* refers to the fully constituted human person, but also to the person's historical condition, "the Logos became flesh" is interchangeable with "God became man." As a result of misunderstandings on the part of the Arians and the Apollinarians, who claimed Christ assumed only "flesh" (a body) without a rational soul, the Logos-*sárx* schema was gradually replaced by the Logos-*anthropos* schema. Other concerns led to ever-greater precision in the notions of nature and person. In 451, the doctrine of two natures, defined by the Council of Chalcedon, became the criterion for understanding the incarnation. Concretely speaking, however, biblical Christology and soteriological statements are needed to give content to the conceptual framework of a unity of divine and human natures that remain distinct in the hypostasis of the divine Logos. Because redemption was considered to be part of the incarnation, as we see especially in the Eastern Fathers' teaching of divinization, it was sometimes difficult to develop the salvific meaning of the cross. In the liturgy the feast of Christmas was at least as important as Easter. Medieval discussions centered on whether God had become human only because of the redemption (the Thomists) or whether God would have done so regardless of human sins (Scotists). The Enlightenment in its criticism of religion, but also liberal theologians, regarded the incarnation as a myth of a divine Son who came down from heaven. The history-of-religions school, using ideas from Eastern religions, generalized the notion of incarnation and contested the uniqueness and incomparability of the incarnation of God in Christ. For them it was only an outstanding example of a broad religious phenomenon.

(3) *Church Teaching*. The creeds speak of the incarnation as the Son's act of becoming human by the Holy Spirit in Mary the virgin. The incarnation is a work of the whole Trinity (DS 491, 535, 571, 801), which does not contradict the fact that it is attributed especially to the Holy Spirit (APPROPRIATIONS; see the councils). The Son of God freely assumed human nature for our salvation (DS 3274), to redeem all human beings from their sins by his suffering, which he accepted freely and without constraint (DS 423, 442, 502, 1364). In this way he entered into a mystical marriage with the whole of the human race (DS 3274).

(4) *Ecumenical Perspectives*. There is no confessional opposition in the Reformation. However, the Reformers completely subordinate the incarnation to soteriology. M. Luther is more influenced by the Alexandrian school, J. Calvin by the Antiochene Christology of separation. What was assumed in the incarnation was not human nature as such, and then, as a consequence, the guilt and punishment of sin; but rather the incarnation is itself the assumption of concrete, sinful nature. Thus Christ encounters God's wrath and curse in our place. In his human nature Christ has no active function that encompasses and lays open human guilt to God. Thus, in the end, a more precise interpretation of the incarnation remains a focal point of the Catholic–Reformed controversy. The Lutheran Kenotics of the nineteenth century (W. F. Gess, G. Thomasius, H. R. Frank, and others) understand the incarnation in the sense of the Logos's act of giving up divine attributes, rather than the early Lutheran sense of the divine attributes shared in by the Logos's humanity (*genus majestaticum*). Today, many Evangelical systematicians seek to overcome the (suspected) static two-natures doctrine by using dynamic, relational, and personal categories (K. Barth, E. Brunner, H. Vogel, P. Althaus, W. Pannenberg). The danger here is that in so doing they overlook the trinitarian, salvation-history significance of Chalcedon.

(5) *Systematic Reflections*. The incarnation has fundamental significance for an analysis of the relationship of God to the world. The modern divisions of God/world, spirit/matter, interior/world-structured action, and grace/freedom can be overcome only by a deeper, pneumatological understanding of the incarnation. Our encounter with God after the incarnation of the Logos — an encounter that occurs in the church, the word, the sacraments, and grace — involves a relationship to the world. The world in its historicity and materiality does not separate us from God, but binds us to God. In the incarnation, creation in its openness and receptivity to God (*potentia oboedientialis* [obediential capacity]) becomes a basic means of grace for humankind. This does not imply a naive glorification of the world, since the Logos also assumed sin as a contradiction to God. Thus the Logos assumed the disrupted condition of creation enslaved by guilt and, through the cross and resurrection, opened a new horizon of universal hope. A meditation on the incarnation also characterizes (especially in Catholics) an understanding of the CHURCH and the SACRAMENTS.

See also CHRISTOLOGY; DIVINE MOTHERHOOD OF MARY; GOD-MAN; HYPO-
STATIC UNION; JESUS' HUMANITY; PREEXISTENCE OF JESUS CHRIST; SALVATION;
TRINITY.

Bibliography
Bouyer, Louis. *The Eternal Son: A Theology of the Word of God and Christology.*
    Huntington, Ind.: Our Sunday Visitor, 1978.
Goulder, Michael, ed. *Incarnation and Myth: The Debate Continues.* Grand Rapids:
    Eerdmans, 1979.
Green, Michael, ed. *The Truth of God Incarnate.* London: Hodder and Stoughton, 1977.
Grillmeier, Alois. *Christ in Christian Tradition.* 2d rev. ed. London: Mowbray, 1975.
Hick, John, ed. *The Myth of God Incarnate.* London: SCM, 1977.
Kasper, Walter. *Jesus the Christ.* New York: Paulist, 1976.
———. *Theology and Church.* New York: Crossroad, 1989.
Rahner, Karl. "On the Theology of Incarnation." In *Theological Investigations,* 4:105–20.
    New York: Crossroad, 1974.

GERHARD LUDWIG MÜLLER

Indelible Character. The indelible character or seal or mark (*caracter in-delebilis*) is a kind of intermediate effect in baptism, confirmation, and the sacrament of orders; though itself a gracious gift, the character is to be distinguished from the grace that is the proper effect of the sacrament.

(1) *Biblical Background.* A scriptural basis for this doctrine can be worked out only in the light of defined Catholic teaching. An appeal was made chiefly to the idea of the sealing of human beings so that they may bear fruit, a sealing attributed to the Holy Spirit (see 2 Cor 1:21f.; Eph 1:13; 4:30).

(2) *History of Theology.* The doctrine of the indelible character developed out of the realization, which became ever-clearer from the third or fourth century on (controversy over baptism by heretics; clash with the Donatists), that baptism (and therefore confirmation) as well as the sacrament of orders may not be repeated. In justifying this insight of faith, fourth-century theologians, especially Augustine, constructed the beginnings of a theology of the indelible character, although the arguments still took the form rather of appeals to images (e.g., the branding of sheep with the mark of the owner; the tattooing of soldiers with the mark of their general). The theological discussion took on new life in the Middle Ages, and Thomas Aquinas gave the doctrine the fundamentals of its now classic form. The indelible character is a real power in the human person and is the basis for specific relations of the person to Christ and the church. In assimilating the person to Christ it gives, above all, the capability and task of joining him (in a specific function in the sacrament of orders) in living as a Christian, serving God, and bearing witness to the faith. In those who receive one of these sacraments without having the necessary openness to the gracious self-communication of God (that is, who receive it "validly" but not "fruitfully"), the indelible character remains, as it were, the root of the flowering or reflowering of grace when these individuals do open themselves as they should.

(3) *Church Teaching.* This doctrine lies behind definitions of the magisterium such as may be seen in the Council of Florence (DS 1313) or Trent (DS 1609).

(4) *Ecumenical Perspectives.* The doctrine of the indelible character was firmly rejected by the Reformers as not being in accord with the Scriptures. New openings for dialogue on the subject might arise if one were to regard the indelible character less as a primarily objective entity resident in the human being than as God's abidingly effective call to the person.

(5) *Systematic Reflections.* In response to tendencies in contemporary theology to minimalize the doctrine of the indelible character, we can and should explain the meaning of the doctrine in dialogical terms: in the sacraments God calls human beings in an entirely individual and personal way but at the same time as members of the community of Jesus; God does so in a creative way that makes it possible for them to respond in faith. If they do not respond with the due self-surrender of faith, God does not therefore retract God's efficacious call; the continuing new opportunity and responsibility exert an abiding influence in the form of an indelible sacramental seal. It should also be mentioned that, not without reason, many theologians speak of the sacrament of matrimony as bestowing a quasi-indelible character.

See also BAPTISM; CONFIRMATION; MARRIAGE: SACRAMENT OF; SACRAMENT OF ORDERS.

Bibliography

Haring, Nicholas M. "St. Augustine's Use of the Word 'Character.'" *Medieval Studies* 14 (1952) 79–97.

Ruffini, Eliseo. "Character as a Concrete Visible Element in the Sacrament in Relation to the Church." In *The Sacraments in General.* Edited by Edward Schillebeeckx and Boniface Willems. Vol. 31 of *Concilium.* New York: Paulist, 1968.

GÜNTER KOCH

Individual. The individual is the single human person as distinguished from humankind (the human race). The individuality of the human person is determined through several factors: genes, influential persons and events in early childhood, social milieu, personal decisions, and so on. The concept of the individual therefore includes a limitation with regard to the whole of human possibilities for life. It encompasses, rather, what is particular in every human person, that which distinguishes her or him from others, and thus refers to the uniqueness of the person. That is why the terminological distinction between individual and person is not always exact, for example, when a general reference to the problem of the "individual and community" is made.

(1) *Biblical Background.* In the Old Testament the human individual is largely determined by his or her membership in the larger group: clan, tribe, nation. Individual characteristics that threaten the interconnectedness of the group, such as defects of the genital organs, are viewed as signs of Yahweh's curse (Dt 23:2; see Gn 30:22f.). In addition, eminent individuals are seen especially as representatives of the clan, the tribe, or the nation (prophets, kings,

etc.: e.g., 2 Samuel 24). In the New Testament communities all the individual differences (man/woman, pagan/Jew, poor/rich) are superseded in the faith in the one Lord Jesus Christ (e.g., Gal 3:28f.). Yet, at the same time, everyone is to serve this unity according to his or her individual capabilities (charisms). The Spirit of Christ is at once the principle of unity and of individual variety (1 Corinthians 12).

(2) *History of Theology.* In the history of theology the concept of the individual was mostly assigned to the idea of the person. According to the predominant Scholastic definition, the person is the individual rational nature. Modernity conceived individuality above all as the task of becoming an individual personality through religious and cultural formation, to build up an individual world of one's own in the interior realm of consciousness. This ideal contributed a great deal to a theological and spiritual individualism of salvation in the eighteenth and nineteenth centuries ("Save your soul!").

(3) *Church Teaching* and (4) *Ecumenical Perspectives.* In ecclesial teaching as well as in the ecumenical dialogue the concept of the individual (in contrast to that of the person) has no significance of its own.

(5) *Systematic Reflections.* Viewed theologically, the formation of the individual character of the human person is at the same time a gift and a task. The tendency of present theological anthropology to integrate the individual moment into the aspect of the person corresponds to the leveling of the individual element in today's society through the influence of the mass media and mass production. Yet it is difficult to judge theologically interventions into the individual pregiven structures of human existence (sex-change operations, gene manipulation, etc.) under only the aspect of the dignity of the person. Moreover, the neglect of the singular significance of the individual has also a negative practical effect on the recognition and respect of the person. The theological interpretation of the individual variety and the solidarity of human persons on the basis of the human race therefore deserves greater attention.

See also CHARISM/CHARISMS; COMMUNITY (GROUP); CREATURELINESS OF THE HUMAN PERSON; HUMANKIND; PERSONALITY.

Bibliography

Bellah, Robert, et al. *Individualism and Commitment in American Life.* New York: Harper, 1987.

See also the bibliography for PERSONALITY.

GEORG LANGEMEYER

Indulgence. According to the Code of Canon Law an indulgence is "a remission before God of the temporal punishment for sin the guilt of which is already forgiven, which a properly disposed member of the Christian faithful obtains under certain and definite conditions with the help of the church, which, as the minister of redemption, dispenses and applies authoritatively the treasury of the satisfactions of Christ and the saints" (can. 992). There is a distinction between partial indulgences and plenary indulgences. Persons can gain indulgences for themselves or apply them to the dead by way of intercession.

(1) *Biblical Background.* The doctrine of indulgences has no direct basis in the Bible. Now that it has developed, however, it is possible to point to certain convictions of biblical faith to which the doctrine can be traced back: (*a*) the idea that divine forgiveness of a sin does not necessarily do away with its (penal) consequences (see, e.g., 2 Sm 12:10–14; 1 Cor 5:5; 1 Tm 1:20) and that a severe penance can be required; (*b*) the conviction that the church is a solidary community in which there is interaction between sin and grace (see, e.g., 1 Cor 12:25f.).

(2) *History of Theology.* It was not until the eleventh century that the practice and doctrine of indulgences arose in the Western Church. The practice and doctrine do, however, have their roots in the history of the sacrament of reconciliation (penance) in the first millennium. The important thing there is, once again, the conviction that the wiping out of a sin before God does not cause the penal consequences of the sin to disappear, but that these must rather be laboriously cleared away by works of penance; and that in this process the church can aid the penitent. The practice of indulgences began in France and was initially still connected with the sacrament of reconciliation; ensuing theological reflection was at first critical and disapproving, but as time went on it gave increasing endorsement to the practice. According to Thomas Aquinas, in indulgences the church draws authoritatively on the "treasury of the church," which is at its disposal; "treasury of the church" is an often misunderstood image for the merits of Christ and the saints that are "stored up in heaven." Since the thirteenth century indulgences have lost their connection with the sacrament of reconciliation, and the granting of them has been reserved to the pope. Indulgences are still regarded as applicable to the dead by way of intercession. In the later Middle Ages, the granting of indulgences degenerated into a source of income, and one that was often seriously abused.

(3) *Church Teaching.* The official teaching of the church on indulgences was formulated in response to Wycliffe, Huss, and especially Luther, all of whom rejected indulgences; at the same time, however, not very much was said about their theological nature (DS 1266f.; 1647–52; see DS 1447–49). In 1562 the Council of Trent taught that the "salutary" use of indulgences was to be preserved; that the church has the power to grant them; but also that abuses must be eliminated (DS 1835). In 1967 Paul VI reformed the system of indulgences: Jesus Christ himself is the treasury of the church; his redemptive work, with which the good deeds of the saints are connected, still exists and retains its efficacy in God's sight. In indulgences the church is able to draw upon that work through authoritative and efficacious intercession. Not only can indulgences remit the temporal punishments for sin; they can and should also encourage Christians to a renewed life in Christ. The children of God are free to gain indulgences or not gain them. Any specification of days or years has now been eliminated from partial indulgences.

(4) *Ecumenical Perspectives.* The Eastern churches say nothing about indulgences; the churches of the Reformation reject them. The Catholic reform of the system of indulgences may, in combination with anthropological and biblical considerations, provide at least a starting point for dialogue, especially since Luther, too, distinguishes between the justification and the sanctification of human beings.

(5) *Systematic Reflections.* Contemporary efforts at a theological understanding of indulgences (efforts to which K. Rahner has made a substantial contribution) advance along the following lines: (*a*) theologians want to connect indulgences more closely once again with the sacrament of reconciliation; indulgences are not an easier way to the complete conquest of sin. (*b*) The temporal punishments due to sins are no longer understood simply as penal measures that God imposes by a positive act of God's will, but as "painful consequences of sin," disruptions in sinners themselves and in their relations with those around them; these are not automatically eliminated by God's forgiveness (as, e.g., the renunciation of alcohol does not automatically do away with alcoholism and its effects), but must be overcome (through penance) with God's grace. (*c*) The jurisdictional dimension of indulgences is understood to take the form of the prayer of the entire church with Christ its head, a prayer that is certain to be heard and that helps sinners to overcome the effects of sin through interior conversion. (*d*) Indulgences are one important opportunity, among others, that is available for "the free structuring of the Christian life" (W. Beinert), an element in the richness of Catholicism.

See also FORGIVENESS OF SIN: THE CHURCH AND THE; SACRAMENT OF RECONCILIATION.

Bibliography
Campbell, Joseph Edward. *Indulgences: The Ordinary Power of Prelates Inferior to the Pope to Grant Indulgences: An Historical Synopsis and a Canonical Commentary.* Ottawa: University of Ottawa Press, 1953.
Rahner, Karl. "Remarks on the Theology of Indulgences." In *Theological Investigations,* 3:175–202. Baltimore: Helicon, 1983.
Vorgrimler, Herbert. *Sacramental Theology.* Collegeville, Minn.: Liturgical Press, 1992.

GÜNTER KOCH

Indwelling of the Holy Spirit. The indwelling of the Holy Spirit (of God) is the result of the sending of the Holy Spirit or the coming of the divine persons to a human being.

(1) *Biblical Background.* The New Testament distinguishes the presence of God in justified human beings from the universal presence of God in all created things (see 1 Cor 3:15: the human person as temple of God). The concept of indwelling is expressly applied to the Holy Spirit in Rom 8:11 and 1 Tm 1:14. According to Jn 14:16, there is a "staying" and "abiding" of the Spirit; according to 14:23, the Father and Son make their abode in the human person. The Spirit is seen as gift, helper, and advocate. It is the source of rebirth (Jn 3:5f.,

8); Christians must be in the Spirit (Rom 8:9); they should let themselves be guided by it in their way of life (Gal 5:16, 18) so that they may produce fruits of the Spirit (Gal 5:22). The basis for all this is the sending of the Spirit (Jn 14:16f., 26; 16:7–15).

(2) *History of Theology.* While the special closeness and presence of God to God's people that are characteristic of the election of Israel and the covenant with it may indeed be viewed as points of departure for the idea of the indwelling, it is probably more in keeping with the facts to see the indwelling as something given and known only through New Testament revelation. It is no accident that the ancient idea of the indwelling is implicit in the interpretation of revelation as the self-communication of God (see *DV* 2). In the theology of the Fathers, however, the idea of the indwelling was related primarily to the doctrine of the Trinity and later to the doctrine of grace. Only in more recent times has it been called upon to explain the mystery of the church and then to define the essence of revelation. This variety of applications brings out the complexity of the idea of the indwelling and its meaning. There is no disagreement about the fact of the supernatural character of the indwelling of the Holy Spirit as uniting human beings with God in the context of sanctifying grace; the specifics of the concept, however, and its theological explanation are a matter of dispute. The precise relationship of the indwelling of the Holy Spirit to the other themes of theological reflection also needs further clarification and explanation.

(3) *Church Teaching.* In the beginning, the magisterium simply took the idea of the indwelling from the New Testament message and expressed it in some early forms of the profession of faith in the Holy Spirit (DS 44, 46, 48). The Council of Trent mentions it in passing (DS 1678) when describing the impulse to repentance by which the Holy Spirit helps sinners on their way to the sacrament of reconciliation. The idea of the indwelling was first developed by Leo XIII (encyclical *Divinum illud* [DS 3328–31]); Pius XII then took up the same thoughts (encyclical *Mystici corporis* [DS 3807f., 3814f.]). Vatican II speaks of the indwelling in *LG* 7, 9; *UR* 2; *DV* 8; *GS* 22. These statements, however, hardly go beyond what is said in the Bible, even if the context in each case dictates certain emphases.

(4) *Ecumenical Perspectives.* In the ecumenical movement the indwelling of the Holy Spirit can be important in different ways: in collaboration with Orthodoxy the trinitarian aspect will have priority, while as far as the churches of the Reformation are concerned the questions raised by the indwelling in connection with justification and the church seem more important. Since the biblical basis is beyond dispute but the subject has not been explained in a conclusive and coherent way, there is reason to hope that joint efforts will prove fruitful.

(5) *Systematic Reflections.* A theological explanation must begin by coming to grips with the fact that theologians have hitherto predicated the indwelling primarily of God and have only appropriated it to the Holy Spirit. This approach does not seem to do justice to the way the idea of indwelling is clearly

thought of in the Sacred Scriptures. In view, moreover, of the fact that the Holy Spirit is the giver of life, the classic interpretations of the indwelling as either the ground and cause or the goal and reward of the Christian life of virtue likewise call for critical examination. In the tradition, these two possible approaches had already led to quite divergent conclusions (Eastern theology: divinization; Western theology: Christians are children of God through active sanctification). The concept of revelation found in Vatican II now seems to offer a promising point of departure for integrating the various aspects of the Holy Spirit's operation in a convincing way, inasmuch as the Spirit is the hidden agent of the divine "work in the world" (*operatio ad extra*) and effects the communication of divine life. In such a setting the doctrine of the Trinity will take a less schematic form; the life and action of God will shine forth as unity amid living diversity; and human beings will be seen as partners who are existentially one with God while at the same time remaining independent and responsible before God. A further element is incorporation into the communion of the church and participation in its task in relation to the world; the manifestations of the church thus become distinguishable as fruits of the Holy Spirit. The connection between spirituality and theology might thus be made more plausible and effective.

See also CHURCH; GRACE; HOLY SPIRIT; SPIRITUALITY.

Bibliography
Bouyer, Louis. *The Church of God: Body of Christ and Temple of the Holy Spirit.* Chicago: Franciscan Herald, 1982.
Kilian, Sabbas. "The Holy Spirit in Christ and in Christians." *American Benedictine Review* 20 (1969) 99–121.
Rahner, Karl. "Nature and Grace." In *Theological Investigations,* 4:165–88. New York: Seabury, 1974.
———. "Some Implications of the Scholastic Concept of Uncreated Grace." In *Theological Investigations,* 1:319–46. Baltimore: Helicon, 1961.

KARL HEINZ NEUFELD

Inerrancy. By inerrancy is understood the freedom from error of Scripture.

(1) *Biblical Background.* The starting points for the biblical belief in the truth of the word of God are the same as for the doctrine of inspiration.

(2) *History of Theology.* In the history of dogma, the teaching on inerrancy was first put into question in the nineteenth century, as more and more facts from natural science and from religious studies suggested that various positions contained in the books of the Bible were no longer tenable (e.g., the motion of the sun revolving around the earth; see MONOGENISM–POLYGENISM) or were not original (influences of neighboring cultures on biblical statements).

(3) *Church Teaching.* In the face of these challenges the ecclesial magisterium held on to inerrancy (see the encyclicals *Providentissimus Deus* [1893]; *Spiritus Paraclitus* [1920]; *Divino afflante Spiritu* [1943]). Vatican II maintained in *DV* 11 that Scripture teaches the truth of salvation "firmly, faithfully, and without error."

(4) *Ecumenical Perspectives.* The doctrine of inerrancy depends upon the understanding of inspiration; the positions taken on inspiration by the theologies of the various confessions also determine their approaches to this theme.

(5) *Systematic Reflections.* The doctrine of inerrancy is based on the following presuppositions: God can neither err nor deceive; God is the author of Scripture as bearer of the message of revelation and norm for the faith of the church. Therefore, the statements of Scripture must be reliable, insofar as and to the degree that in them and through them the witness to Christ is mediated. These presuppositions also imply that the truth of the Bible does not refer at first to the consistency of its statements, but rather to the undeceivability of the salvation that it proclaims. It is first of all a salvific and not a cognitive truth. Because Scripture presents an inner unity and integrity, it is in its entirety and in all its parts a saving message and trustworthy with respect to salvation. Thus, one cannot limit inerrancy to particular statements or parts of Scripture. One must also remember the human character of the Bible: insofar as it stems from human authors, it shares in the weaknesses of human writing. Scripture is the incomplete and obscure expression of the message of revelation, always in need of interpretation, and therefore to be investigated with all the means that hermeneutics makes available.

See also HERMENEUTICS; INSPIRATION; SCRIPTURE.

Bibliography
Achtemeier, Paul. *The Inspiration of Scripture: Problems and Proposals.* Philadelphia: Westminster, 1980.
Barr, James. *The Bible in the Modern World.* New York: Harper and Row, 1973.
———. *Holy Scripture: Canon, Authority, and Criticism.* Philadelphia: Westminster, 1983.
Brown, Raymond E. *The Critical Meaning of the Bible.* New York: Paulist, 1981.
Newman, John Henry. *On the Inspiration of Scripture.* Edited by J. Derek Holmes and Robert Murray. Washington, D.C.: Corpus, 1967.
Rahner, Karl. *Inspiration in the Bible.* Rev ed. New York: Herder and Herder, 1964.

WOLFGANG BEINERT

Infallibility. Infallibility is a spiritual attribute belonging to the entire church but, under certain circumstances, is possessed in a special way by the college of bishops and the pope; as a result, their doctrinal utterances in matters of faith and Christian life (*fides et mores*) are free of error.

(1) *Biblical Background.* The New Testament manifests a conviction regarding infallibility, not formally (by using the word) but materially: confessional statements (especially in Christology) are made in the conviction that they are unqualifiedly true and valid (e.g., Rom 10:9; 1 Cor 15:3ff.; Gal 1:18; Phil 2:6–11).

(2) *History of Theology.* In the early church the decrees of ecumenical councils were regarded as infallible (e.g., the teaching of Nicaea was regarded as infallible by the Council of Ephesus [DS 265]). Since the Middle Ages the doc-

trine of the infallibility of the pope has been formulated with ever-increasing clarity. This was one object of the Reformers' protests in the sixteenth century.

(3) *Church Teaching.* The infallibility of the pope was defined as a dogma at Vatican I (DS 3065–75). Vatican II confirmed this, but as part of a teaching on the infallibility of the entire church (*LG* 12, 25). More detailed clarifications on the irreformability of infallible propositions are to be found in the declaration *Mysterium ecclesiae* of the Congregation for the Doctrine of the Faith (*AAS* 65 [1973] 396–408).

(4) *Ecumenical Perspectives.* Non-Catholic churches may have thus far refused to acknowledge the infallibility of the pope, but a realization of the importance of binding doctrine is growing.

(5) *Systematic Reflections.* The infallibility of the church and of the church authorities named above is to be understood as an expression of the truth of the faith, to which the church must hold fast if it is to carry out the salvific mission assigned it by Christ. Account must be taken not only of the precisely specified presuppositions for infallible statements (ECCLESIAL MAGISTERIUM, sec. 5) but also of the fact that infallibility extends only to the central content of the statement and not to its manner of expression.

See also COUNCIL; DOGMA/DOGMATIC STATEMENT; ECCLESIAL MAGISTERIUM; POPE; SENSUS FIDELIUM; TRUTH OF FAITH.

Bibliography
Chirico, Peter. *Infallibility: The Crossroads of Doctrine.* Wilmington, Del.: Glazier, 1973.
Ford, John T. "Infallibility: Who Won the Debate?" *Proceedings of the Catholic Theological Society* 31 (1976) 179–92.
Kirvan, John J., ed. *The Infallibility Debate.* New York: Paulist, 1971.
Küng, Hans. *Infallible? An Inquiry.* Garden City, N.Y.: Doubleday, 1971.
Tierney, Brian. *Origins of Papal Infallibility 1150–1350.* Leiden: Brill, 1972.

WERNER LÖSER

Infancy Narratives. Infancy narratives are found in the first two chapters of the Gospels of Matthew and Luke. They could better be described as the "prehistory" (of Jesus) or as a "prologue," because they tell of Jesus' beginnings not out of a biographical interest, but for a theological purpose, in conjunction with major themes found in these two Gospels.

(1) *Biblical Background.* Matthew 1–2 and Luke 1–2 are independent of each other, and therefore their literary form and rhetorical intentions should be judged differently. *Matthew 1–2* tries to prove that Jesus is the promised messiah from God. It is a Jewish-Christian proclamation of the messiah using the Old Testament, which it interprets as referring to Christ. The individual stories are christological lessons. The genealogy (1:2–17) demonstrates that Jesus is the son of David and son of Abraham. As son of David he is the messiah; as son of Abraham, he is a blessing for all peoples (the beginning of Matthew's universalism; see 28:19). However, Jesus is "more than" the son of David and Abraham. The new claim, which begins with the genealogy (1:16b) and contin-

ues in 1:18–25, involves the spiritual origin of Jesus' life and therefore Jesus as Son of God who redeems his people ("Jesus") and is the promised God-with-us ("Emmanuel") (see 18:18; 28:19). In divine providence, God ordained that the promise made to Abraham of salvation for all peoples be wondrously fulfilled in the messiah, Jesus. God's power as Creator is responsible for Jesus' miraculous birth, and through God the Son of the Virgin is in the lineage of David (through Joseph, who not only here but in 2:1–12 is the middle point of the whole narrative!). The meaning of messiahship becomes clear in Matthew 2: the Gentiles are receptive to the coming of the king of the world while the Jewish king is closed to it (2:1–12) (the relationship of Israel to the nations — a central theme of Matthew). But God's power rests upon this child-messiah, from Bethlehem to Egypt to Nazareth. A fulfillment text and a place name conclude each story: 2:13–15 (Hos 11:1; "Egypt"); 2:16–18 (Jer 31:15; "Rama"); and 2:19–23 (Jgs 13:5; "Bethlehem"). The obvious precedent for these stories of the child-messiah is the story of Moses (and Jacob?): yet Jesus, the redeemer of Israel, is greater than Moses. Thus many scholars agree that the literary type of these stories is midrash (= commentaries on the Old Testament) in its haggadic (= theological-ethical) form. Matthew's intention is obvious: here already, at the beginning of the Gospel, we see the dimensions of the history of Jesus. It is about "Jesus," Emmanuel and Son of God from the beginning, who in his precipitous journey is attacked by the world, but is led by none other than God.

Luke 1–2 is a complete prehistory, artfully constructed as a sevenfold wreath of stories that anticipate themes of the Gospel. As a prelude it explains Jesus' beginnings in God, especially in the birth narrative and the temple narrative. It also demonstrates how Jesus' beginnings are connected with those of John the Baptist. Thus there is a double portrait or diptych — of "promise" and fulfillment. The annunciation of John's birth (divided into 1:5–23, 24–25) is followed by the annunciation of the birth of Jesus in two double narratives (1:26–38 and 1:39–56). The "fulfillment" is the news of the birth of John (divided into 1:57–66, 67–79[80]) and the birth of Jesus as a double narrative (2:1–20 and 2:21–39[40]). In the "finale" (2:41–52), we see clearly the interest of the narrative: Jesus is the "Son" (2:49; see already 1:32, 35). A characteristic of Luke's infancy narrative is the use of prophetic voices and canticles (1:42f., 46–55, 67–79; 2:29–32, 34f.) woven into the stories. Here the Christ-event is described as the fulfillment of the Old Testament prophets, and it is therefore typological. The introduction of angels, part of late Jewish apocalyptic, signals the changing of the ages and the time of fulfillment. Angels function as bearers of God's word of revelation and explain the deeper dimension of the event. According to H. Schürmann, early apostolic preaching has created a new literary genre in Luke's infancy narrative, the "confessional history" or "narrative that professes Christ." "In this profession of faith Luke apparently wishes to emphasize the sonship of Jesus (1:32, 35; 2:49–51), which is the basis for his lordship, as well as his soter-function (2:11; cf. 1:16f., 43) based on his Davidic sonship (1:27, 32, 69; 2:4ff.)" (Lk 1:20). But basically the confessional history is related to many holy figures and events of the Old Testament and thus presents an open and complex picture. The temple plays a special role, fulfilling the prophecies of Daniel 9 and Malachi 3. With Jesus' entry into the temple, Yahweh "dwells" among the people. The theological statement of Jesus' divinity is first evident (according to R. Laurentin) in a theological statement concerning Mary (as God's dwelling place, as the personification of the Daughter of Sion, and as antitype of the covenant). For Luke the spiritual origin of Jesus' life (1:35) is not just christological interpretation, but reality: Jesus is the Son of God not by adoption, but by truly coming forth from God.

(2) *History of Theology* and (3) *Church Teaching.* In the transmission of the faith and in pronouncements of the ordinary and extraordinary magisterium, the divine sonship *and* the spiritual origin of Jesus' life ("conceived by the Holy Spirit, born of the Virgin Mary") have been emphasized and defended over and over as teachings of faith (DS 30, 44, 125, 250f., 252, 291–94, 301ff., 422, 427, 503, 801, 852). Regarding other particularities of the infancy narratives there have been no official pronouncements.

(4) *Ecumenical Perspectives.* Exceptions aside (K. Barth), non-Catholic exegetes and systematicians today consider the spiritual origins of Jesus as a theologoumenon that merely expresses the uniqueness of Jesus.

(5) *Systematic Reflections.* Regarding many of the stories contained in the infancy narratives and many of its details, the question must remain open whether they refer to history or whether the literary form suggests a theological actualization. Thus, for example, there are many reasons for saying that the flight into Egypt and the murder of the Holy Innocents in Bethlehem are not historical, and nevertheless both could easily have happened in Herod's time. Likewise, agreement of literarily independent infancy narratives does not lead to certain historical knowledge. For example, the statements of promise can explain why Bethlehem was called the birthplace of Jesus, but there could have been other reasons. Furthermore, the proof from witnesses leads to certainty only with regard to the names of ancestors and places. In any case, historical verifiability should not be the only criterion of truth (not even of the truth of faith). Seen from this viewpoint, the question of the historical origin of the faith tradition that starts with the spiritual origin of Jesus' life does not decide that tradition's facticity and interpretation. It is altogether possible that the story of Jesus' origins does not depend on a historical tradition (e.g., an intimate family tradition, stemming from Mary and Joseph), but is a spiritual meditation or theological reflection of the primitive church, which in apostolic times was familiar not only with progress in knowledge, but also progress in revelation (see the Pauline reformulation of the earlier Jewish-Christian creedal formula in Rom 1:3f.).

See also CHRISTOLOGY; IMMACULATE CONCEPTION; JESUS' HUMANITY.

Bibliography
Brown, Raymond E. *Birth of the Messiah.* 2d rev. ed. Garden City, N.Y.: Doubleday, 1993.
———. *A Coming Christ in Advent.* Collegeville, Minn.: Liturgical Press, 1988.

Brown, Raymond E., et al., eds. *Mary in the New Testament*. Philadelphia: Fortress, 1978.
Fitzmyer, Joseph A. *The Gospel according to Luke (I–IX)*. Garden City, N.Y.: Doubleday, 1981.

LOTHAR ULLRICH

Infant Baptism. By infant baptism (or, more broadly, the baptism of children) is meant the baptism of children who have not attained the use of reason.

(1) *Biblical Background.* Infant baptism is not explicitly attested in the New Testament. It is perhaps implicit, however, in descriptions of the baptism of whole families (1 Cor 1:16) and households (Acts 16:15). A point of departure for the teaching may be seen in Jesus' blessing of children (see Mk 10:13–16 par.: a passage that possibly had as its sociological setting [*Sitz im Leben*] the early Christian celebration of the baptism of young children): with a kind of sacramental gesture Jesus there grants children (including, probably, quite young children) participation in the kingdom of God ("And he took the children in his arms; then he laid his hands on them and blessed them" [Mk 10:16]). The following point also deserves consideration: if, in a sense, baptism replaced Jewish circumcision, then in the Jewish-Christian world it must have been taken for granted that baptism, like circumcision, would be administered to infants.

(2) *History of Theology.* Infant baptism is an ancient, even if not unbroken, tradition of the church; only in modern times has its theological meaning been questioned. Origen (ca. 185–254) was already explicitly tracing the baptism of small children back to an apostolic tradition: the church, he says, "received from the apostles the tradition of baptizing even children" (*In Rom.* 5.9 or 5.1; *PG* 14:1047 or 1010). Admittedly, there was still some hesitation as late as the fifth century: the baptism that remits sins was postponed until young people or adults had "emerged from their worst period."

(3) *Church Teaching.* From the fifth century on the ecclesial magisterium repeatedly and explicitly reaffirmed the legitimacy and meaningfulness of infant baptism: at the Council of Carthage in 418 (DS 223), at the Fourth Lateran Council in 1215 (DS 802), and at the Council of Trent (DS 1514, 1625–27). These statements did not, however, define the strict necessity of infant baptism proper.

(4) *Ecumenical Perspectives.* In the Reformation period there was no disagreement between Catholics and Protestants on the legitimacy and necessity of infant baptism. Both sides opposed the Anabaptists, whose position represented in practice a devaluation of infant baptism. Recent discussion of infant baptism had its start chiefly among Protestants (K. and M. Barth): Does not baptism require a free decision of faith, such as is not yet possible in children? The question was also taken up by Catholic theologians.

(5) *Systematic Reflections.* In the contemporary discussion the following three positions have been adopted and justified: (*a*) infant baptism is meaningless and therefore to be rejected; (*b*) under certain conditions infant baptism

Against infant baptism	For infant baptism	For leaving it to the parents
The freedom of the child should not be influenced in advance	Infant baptism is based on a continuous tradition that has been confirmed by the magisterium	The arguments for and against are of equal weight
By its nature baptism demands a personal response of faith	Decisive traits and values are passed on to the person	Together with a Christian upbringing, infant baptism is a kind of invitation to faith
Many persons baptized as infants remain nominal Christians	Baptism is the beginning of a way that makes demands of the baptized and the community	Infant baptism is not an indispensable element in this invitation
Infant baptism is not attested in the NT	The NT implicitly attests to infant baptism	
God's will to salvation can operate even without baptism	Infant baptism expresses with special clarity the gracious character of salvation and the communal character of faith	

is necessary; (c) the baptism of infants is to be left up to their parents (for the arguments see the accompanying table). For Catholic theologians the starting point must be the position of the ecclesial magisterium that while infant baptism is not appropriate in all circumstances, it is necessary under certain conditions. If the child has no guarantee of a Christian upbringing, a refusal or postponement of baptism may be unavoidable. (In these cases the persons involved must be the object of special attention from the pastor.) If, however, there are at least signs that the child will have a Christian upbringing, or if Christian parents expressly intend this, then the baptism of the child becomes obligatory. The arguments for the possibility and necessity of infant baptism under the conditions described are provided by the biblical starting points and above all by a central tradition that has been confirmed by the teaching church. While we must indeed look upon baptism as a sacrament expressing a response of faith, this can be true even of infant baptism: such a baptism is a creative call of God, who expects that the response will come in the life of the child, but who is also able by God's grace to bring that response into existence; at the same time, such a baptism is the response given by the parents, godparents, and entire community as representatives of the child. Infant baptism can be such a vicarious response because God's self-giving to a human being also occurs through other human beings and because God also communicates God's yes to *this* individual through the yes of the individual's fellow human beings.

Furthermore, God's grace and salvation also take concrete form in the Christian community, the church. Consequently, we may not refuse a child the grace of the Christian community, any more than we may refuse it the love of parents, until such time as it can freely accept it. While the baptism of adults is "normal" in the church to the extent that the church is missionary, infant baptism is normal in Christian communities that are permanently established.

See also BAPTISM; SACRAMENTS OF INITIATION.

Bibliography
Aland, Kurt. *Did the Early Church Baptize Infants?* Philadelphia: Westminster, 1960.
Barth, Karl. *The Teaching of the Church regarding Baptism.* London: SCM, 1948.
Brown, Raymond. "We Profess One Baptism for the Forgiveness of Sins." *Worship* 40 (1966): 260–71.
Covino, Paul F. X. "The Postconciliar Infant Baptism Debate in the American Catholic Church." *Worship* 56 (1982): 240–60.
Fahey, Michael, ed. *Catholic Perspectives on Baptism, Eucharist, and Ministry: CTSA Study.* Lanham, Md.: University Press of America.
Fisher, J. D. C. *Christian Initiation: Baptism in the Medieval West.* London: SPCK, 1965.
Jeremias, Joachim. *Infant Baptism in the First Four Centuries of the Church.* Philadelphia: Westminster, 1960.
Thurian, Max, ed. *Ecumenical Perspectives on Baptism, Eucharist, and Ministry.* Geneva: World Council of Churches, 1983.
Van Roo, William A. *The Christian Sacrament.* Rome: Gregorian University, 1992.

GÜNTER KOCH

Initiation. See SACRAMENTS OF INITIATION.

Inspiration. Inspiration (Latin: *inspirare* = breathe [upon or into]) is the special influence of God upon the origin of Scripture through its human authors; on the basis of this, God must be described as the one actually speaking in Scripture, and Scripture must be understood as the word of God. The manner in which God is considered the author is called *active* inspiration; the way in which the human author experiences this intervention is called *passive* inspiration.

(1) *Biblical Background.* Starting points for a biblical doctrine of inspiration are the relatedness of word and spirit (*ruah*) (as such relatedness appears in, e.g., Is 34:16; 59:21; Neh 9:20, 30; Zec 7:12), the description of the prophets as bearers of the word of God (Is 6:6–13; Jer 1:4–10; 20:7–9; Am 7:12–15), and the conviction of Paul that his words are effected by the Spirit (1 Cor 2:4; 7:40; 2 Cor 4:13). Important texts to consider are 2 Tm 3:14–16 (Scripture is inspired by God), 1 Pt 1:10–12 (men have spoken in the power of the Spirit), and 2 Pt 1:16–21 (there are writings composed under the impulse of the Holy Spirit).

(2) *History of Theology.* From the time of Ambrose and Augustine, the belief in the special dignity of Scripture caused God to be designated as *auctor*, which at first meant *originator*, and then from the time of Gregory the Great meant *literary composer*. In contrast to this, the human author is described as the *scriptor* (scribe). Two theories arose to explain active inspiration. The doc-

trine of *verbal inspiration* states that the individual words of the Bible stem from God; the human being is only the material instrument (like a musical instrument, or a secretary who takes down God's dictation). Beside the Jewish authors Philo and Flavius Josephus, this view was shared by some Fathers of the Church and later by D. Bañez. According to the doctrine of *real inspiration*, the Bible stems from God only in its contents, whether this occurs through subsequent confirmation by the Holy Spirit (*inspiratio subsequens*: L. Lessius [d. 1623], J. B. Franzelin), or through its being protected from errors (*inspiratio concomitans*). When in the time of the Enlightenment it was proven that errors and false statements are found in the books of the Bible, qualifications were added to the theory: only the doctrinal content was inspired (H. Holden, F. Lenormant), or only categorical statements (M.-J. Lagrange). Thomas Aquinas attempted to envision the divine-human relationship such that God can be described as the principal author (*auctor principalis*) and the human author as the instrumental author (*auctor instrumentalis*). In modern times the most common questions are: How do the two "authors" interact with each other? How can the process of inspiration be conceived? How does the church recognize the inspired nature of the individual books of the Bible? And how can the insights of modern exegesis be reconciled with the doctrine of inspiration? An explanation that would be satisfactory for all sides has not yet been found; current theology generally follows the model proposed by Karl Rahner (see sec. 5 below).

(3) *Church Teaching.* The ecclesial magisterium has affirmed the fact of inspiration; the manner of this inspiration is not defined. More specifically, the Council of Trent described God without restriction as the originator of Scripture (DS 1501). In addition, at Vatican I *inspiratio concomitans* and *inspiratio subsequens* were rejected (DS 3006). According to Leo XIII (encyclical *Providentissimus Deus* [1893; DS 3293]), God has given assistance to the human authors (*sacred writers*) in all phases of their activity. Pius XII stressed the true authorship of the human writers (encyclical *Divino afflante Spiritu* [1943]). Vatican II taught that because of inspiration the biblical books "teach that truth which God, for the sake of our salvation, wished to see confided to the Sacred Scriptures" (*DV* 11). Any restriction upon inspiration is rejected.

(4) *Ecumenical Perspectives.* According to the Orthodox view, the authorship of God, interpreted as "real inspiration," extends to all the books of the Bible. The *inspiratio passiva* is understood as an inner illumination bringing about the correct insight and the written transmission of the dogmatic and ethical truths of revelation. Protestantism placed an especially great emphasis on inspiration in order to account for the rejection of the ecclesial magisterium and of tradition, and at the same time to stress against charismatic groups the significance of the written word (in place of the "inner word of the Spirit" that they accented). From this arose in Lutheran Orthodoxy the teaching of an extreme form of verbal inspiration (even the vowel markings of the Masoretic text in the Old Testament are inspired). Today some Protestants reject inspiration.

(5) *Systematic Reflections.* The doctrine of inspiration is the response to the question about the dignity of Scripture as the word of God in human words; it is also a response to the question about the foundation of the canon. When the cooperation of both God *and* human persons in the composition of Scripture is asserted, then this is not in the sense of a competition, but rather analogously: God as originator of Scripture enables the human authorship. God's role as originator follows in general from the divine intention to found the church, and in particular from the normative function of the early church as the community of the apostles and the first bearer of revelation for all further generations of the church. In order to fulfill these tasks, it must be able to determine infallibly what belongs to its fundamental nature. Without doubt Scripture belongs to this essence insofar as revelation and the church's own faith have been recorded in it. If God intended the early church, then God also intended Scripture as the norm for faith: God inspired the human authors (active inspiration), who were thereby chosen and enabled to be norm-giving witnesses to Christ (passive inspiration). Thus, they were not God's instruments or secretaries or merely under God's general influence, but were rather the witnesses, guided by the Spirit, to the revelation of faith in the situation of the early church. They were given a special charism so that in all phases of their activity they were able to grasp and write down the word of God correctly and reliably. As a result of this, inspiration was extended to all the books of the Bible and their whole content, as well as to all human beings who shared in the work of its composition (e.g., also the redactors). The result of this theory, developed above all by K. Rahner, is that inspiration is the ground for the acceptance of a biblical book into the canon. In this act the church witnesses that a writing from the apostolic times is consonant with its essence and normative for it. With regard to the question of the truth of the contents of Scripture, one must reply that it does not have as its goal information dealing with factual truths, but rather a genuine and trust-worthy opening toward a personal encounter with God. Scripture, therefore, does not lie to, deceive, or mislead its readers.

See also CANON; HERMENEUTICS; INERRANCY; SCRIPTURE.

Bibliography

Achtemeier, Paul. *The Inspiration of Scripture: Problems and Proposals.* Philadelphia: Westminster, 1980.

Fiorenza, Francis S. "The Crisis of Scriptural Authority: Interpretation and Reception." *Interpretation* 44 (1990) 353–68.

Rahner, Karl. *Inspiration in the Bible.* 2d rev. ed. New York: Herder and Herder, 1964.

Vawter, Bruce. *Biblical Inspiration.* Philadelphia: Westminster, 1972.

WOLFGANG BEINERT

Institution of the Sacraments.

The question to be discussed under this head-ing is: In what sense can the sacraments be traced back to Jesus Christ and specifically to the earthly Jesus?

(1) *Biblical Background.* There are exegetical as well as historical objections to the idea that Jesus instituted or established each of the seven sacraments by a distinct act of his will. It is true that all seven sacraments are more or less clearly to be found in the texts of the New Testament, but an act of institution is explicitly mentioned only in connection with the Eucharist, baptism, and the sacrament of reconciliation (in the form of a communication of the power to forgive sins). Even here, moreover, it is to be noted that in the case of baptism and to some extent of the "sacrament of reconciliation" (Mt 28:19; Jn 20:23) the words are those of the risen Lord and therefore not the earthly Jesus. It is easiest to speak of a direct, even if implicit, institution in the case of the Eucharist (the command of repetition is certainly from after Easter, but Jesus' intention of instituting the sacrament is obviously clear to the disciples; see also Mk 14:25). Unless one is willing to conclude from the universal practice of baptism from the outset to its direct institution by Jesus, then in this case as in the case of the other sacraments the findings of exegesis make an immediate, direct institution at least improbable. Nonetheless, it can and must be said that the sacraments, as efficacious signs filled with the reality of eschatological salvation, go back to the life and activity of Jesus and therefore to the indications he gave on the path to be taken. As regards Jesus' "institution" of the sacraments we may say the following: (*a*) Jesus regards his activity and his preaching, and especially his miracles, as efficacious signs of the kingdom of God that has arrived in his person (see Mt 11:4–6). Everything that can be heard and seen of Jesus is not simply a sign of a new reality; rather, this reality, namely, definitive, eschatological salvation, has already begun therein. Consequently, in his special symbolic actions, which are in the tradition of the symbolic actions of the prophets, Jesus surpasses all that has gone before. We may unhesitatingly ascribe a sacramental character to the symbolic actions of Jesus (or: to his symbolic words and actions). (*b*) The symbolic actions of Jesus do not simply provide a general background for the sacraments; it is also possible to find in the symbolic actions of Jesus particular points of departure for particular sacraments. The fact that Jesus submitted to the baptism of John would have been a sign that led the primitive church, under the guidance of the Holy Spirit, to introduce *baptism* as an obligatory sacrament. In addition to the *Last Supper* of Jesus, the many other meals that Jesus had previously taken with his friends and with sinners could make known his will to retain salvific ties with his disciples by means of a meal. The *sacrament of reconciliation* has a point of departure not only in the Lord's own explicit words of forgiveness (see Mk 2:5) but also and in particular in the just-mentioned meals taken with sinners: Jesus forgives human beings by drawing them into fellowship with himself. For *confirmation* we may point to those utterances of Jesus that give expression to his own special relationship with the Spirit of God and his intention of bestowing the Spirit (at the baptism of Jesus the New Testament gives symbolic form to the descent of the Spirit). The *anointing of the sick* has its roots in the healing activity of Jesus, which is often accompanied

by symbolic gestures, and in the sending of the disciples in order that they may also heal, using an anointing with oil for this purpose (see Mk 6:13). Finally, there are also historical points of departure for the *sacraments of orders and matrimony*: for example, Jesus calls the Twelve from among the other disciples and empowers and sends them (see Mk 6:6b–13); he also shows his profound concern for the bonds of marriage and locates them in the perspective of the imminent kingdom of God (see Mt 19:3–12).

(2) *History of Theology*. Throughout the church's entire history, theologians have regarded it as obvious that the sacraments must originate in Jesus Christ. Efficacious signs of grace cannot be created by human beings; God alone disposes in sovereign fashion of grace, which is to say: of God's self-communication. There are, however, different interpretations of how the sacraments originated in Christ. Augustine, for example, gives a chiefly mystical explanation: the sacraments sprang, together with the church, from the pierced side of Christ. Thomas Aquinas, on the other hand, prefers to look upon the sacraments as immediately and explicitly instituted by Jesus. In the process he appeals, for a good many of the sacraments, to an unwritten apostolic tradition. Other medieval theologians, for example Bonaventure, are satisfied with a mediate institution for some of the sacraments, that is, an institution by the apostles but at the behest of Jesus. Thomas's view, however, won the day. Even the Reformers adopted it and, for this reason, usually accepted only baptism and the Eucharist as scriptural.

(3) *Church Teaching*. The Council of Trent adopted the same historicizing approach: "If anyone says that the sacraments of the New Law were not all instituted by Jesus Christ our Lord; or that there are more or fewer than seven... *anathema sit*" (DS 1601; *ND* 1311). This relatively cautious formulation does not, however, regard as a binding doctrine of faith the "direct and immediate" institution of the sacraments by the earthly Jesus, to which theologians later committed themselves (see the decree *Lamentabili* [1907; DS 3438f.]).

(4) *Ecumenical Perspectives*. The exegetical realization of the dubiousness of any claim to trace all the sacraments back, by purely historical means, to acts of institution by Jesus may spur the churches of the Reformation to raise anew the question whether later New Testament or even post–New Testament developments may not possibly be responses to the Spirit of Jesus and therefore normative.

(5) *Systematic Reflections*. Theologians today still take it for granted that since the sacraments are efficacious signs of grace, they must have their origin in Jesus Christ. K. Rahner has attempted to resolve the exegetical and other historical difficulties (e.g., the historical changes in many sacraments) by a theory of his own: Jesus instituted the seven sacraments by establishing the universal or root sacrament, namely, the church. The several separate sacraments are the official self-fulfillments of the church, which Rahner calls the "primary sacrament." This theory met with an enthusiastic response but also with criticism, as

for example in the question: Is it, then, easier to show the immediate establishment of the church by the earthly Jesus? Consequently, the (exegetical) task of connecting the sacraments (and the church) with the life and work of Jesus remains indispensable. The data of exegesis can in fact show that the sacraments have a real foundation in Jesus. Rahner's theory is able to show clearly the internal connection between the sacraments and the church as well as between the church and both the earthly and the risen Jesus Christ. Because the church not only goes back to the earthly Jesus but at the same time is and remains the sacrament of the exalted Lord, it is able to carry out in a binding way the intentions of Jesus regarding a symbolic or sacramental communication of salvation and to give form to these intentions in the major situations of human life.

See also CHURCH; SACRAMENT.

Bibliography
Duffy, Regis A. "Sacraments in General." In *Systematic Theology: Roman Catholic Perspectives*, edited by Francis Schüssler Fiorenza and John P. Galvin, 2:181–210. Minneapolis: Fortress, 1991.
Fiorenza, Francis S. *Foundational Theology: Jesus and the Church*. New York: Crossroad, 1984.
Ganoczy, Alexandre. *An Introduction to Catholic Sacramental Theology*. New York: Paulist, 1984.
Schillebeeckx, Edward, and Boniface Willems, eds. *The Sacraments in General*. Vol. 31 of *Concilium*. New York: Paulist, 1968.

GÜNTER KOCH

Intercommunion. Intercommunion is a somewhat vague and indefinite concept that refers, in official discussion, to the question of a full or limited sharing in eucharistic worship or of admission to Communion across the lines of separated churches or ecclesial communities. It can thus include a variety of situations, such as a limited or general admission to Communion (open Communion) by one church, or the agreed reciprocal admission by two or more churches, or, finally, intercelebration, that is, the joint celebration of the Eucharist by ministers of various churches or the exchange of ministers between various churches.

(1) *Biblical Background*. Modern questions of intercommunion are evidently not directly addressed in the New Testament. It must be emphasized, however, that in the New Testament the sharing of the Eucharist is very closely connected with the unity of the community that is the church (see 1 Cor 10:16f.); not only, however, does it establish this unity, but at the same time it attests to its existence (see Eph 4:4f.: "*one* body and *one* Spirit... *one* Lord, *one* faith, *one* baptism").

(2) *History of Theology*. The concept of intercommunion came up for discussion at the very beginning of the ecumenical movement in 1867 and since then has become one of the focal points in the question of the unity of the separated churches; in the process, increasingly nuanced equivalents have come to be used in theological discussion. Attention has therefore rightly and repeatedly

INTERCOMMUNION
Terminological Distinctions (Faith and Order Commission, 1969)
and Catholic Regulations

Term	Meaning	Roman Catholic Regulations
Ecclesial Communion	Complete eucharistic sharing without any differentiation	Not entered into with any other church
Intercelebration	Reciprocal acceptance of ministers of another confession as leaders of eucharistic worship	Not possible
Joint celebration	Ministers of various confessions concelebrate the liturgy	Possible in liturgies of the word, not in liturgies of the Eucharist
Admission to Communion:		
Limited (open Communion)	For pastoral reasons, the faithful from another confession are, by way of exception, allowed to receive Communion, while the faithful of this confession can receive Communion in other confessions	Under certain conditions (a) non-Catholics can be admitted to the Eucharist of the Roman Catholic Church; (b) Catholics can receive the Eucharist in churches in which, in the Roman Catholic view, it is validly administered (= the Eastern churches); see CIC can. 844.1–6
General	All baptized members of other churches, who are also allowed to receive the Eucharist there, are admitted to Communion	Not allowed
Reciprocal (intercommunion in strict sense)	Agreement between two churches to allow all members of each church to receive Communion in the other	Does not exist

been called to the connection between the degree of "eucharistic sharing" (see the Lima Report on convergences) and the understanding of the church. Stimulated by the magisterium (see sec. 3 below), theological discussion of the issues summed up by "intercommunion" is now in full swing. It must be noted that the arguments used in the discussion, and this applies above all to utterances of the ecclesial magisterium, are not always dogmatic in character but pastoral or, as the case may be, disciplinary.

(3) *Church Teaching.* The Catholic Church adopted a fundamental official position at Vatican II. This permits a relatively high degree of eucharistic

sharing with the Eastern churches (*OE* 27). Not so with the churches of the Reformation; these, it is said, "have not preserved the proper reality of the eucharistic mystery in its fullness, especially because of the absence of the sacrament of Orders," although, on the other hand, the Evangelical Lord's Supper is described as a saving reality of faith (*UR* 22). The Ecumenical Directory of 1967 gave further concrete form to this basic attitude, and the Code of Canon Law has drawn the canonical conclusions (can. 844). According to the code, the Catholic Church agrees to intercommunion with the Eastern churches under certain conditions, although this view is not accepted by the Greek Orthodox Church. Other Christians can receive the Eucharist only in emergencies, provided they manifest a Catholic faith in the sacrament. Catholic Christians may not receive the Evangelical Lord's Supper.

(4) *Ecumenical Perspectives.* There is no need of proving that the question of intercommunion is of the greatest importance for the unity of the churches. But further theological and practical clarifications (e.g., in the question of ministry) and developments are needed in order to reach the desired goal. In 1975, nonetheless, the United Evangelical Lutheran Church of Germany allowed Roman Catholic Christians to share in the Lord's Supper and showed an openness in the reverse direction.

(5) *Systematic Reflections.* The chief theological question under discussion is whether the Eucharist must be regarded simply as a sign of an already existing unity and not also as an instrument of unity to be achieved, as the church itself is a "sign and instrument" of union with God and among human beings. Since both aspects are valid and must be constantly brought into balance, eucharistic sharing (hospitality) may legitimately advance a little ahead of the developing unity in theology and practice. But in each case these advances require confirmation from those in charge of church discipline; the latter in turn must remain flexible. The Lima Report of the Faith and Order Commission of the World Council of Churches (1982) contains this cautious statement: "The increased mutual understanding expressed in the present statement may allow some churches to attain a greater measure of eucharistic communion among themselves and so bring closer the day when Christ's divided people will be visibly reunited around the Lord's Table" (Eucharist, no. 33).

See also ECUMENISM; EUCHARIST; SACRAMENT OF ORDERS.

Bibliography
Documents on Anglican–Roman Catholic Relations. Washington, D.C.: USCC, 1976.
Glendon-Hill, Flora. "The Call to Unity: On Growing Together through Worship." *One in Christ* 27 (1991) 49–56.
Larere, Philippe. *Lord's Supper: Towards an Ecumenical Understanding of the Eucharist.* Collegeville, Minn.: Liturgical Press, 1993.
Lebau, Paul. "Vatican II and the Hope of an Ecumenical Eucharist." *One in Christ* 5 (1969) 379–404.
World Council of Churches, Commission on Faith and Order. *Intercommunion: Report of a Theological Commission of Faith and Order.* London: SCM, 1951.

GÜNTER KOCH

Intermediate State. By intermediate state is meant the manner of existence of the individual human person between death and the resurrection on the last day. Although the concept of intermediate state is not tied into any particular anthropological model, it has in fact been thought of almost exclusively in terms of the body-free soul ever since the encounter of Old Testament and New Testament revelation and the Greek philosophical picture of the person. The intermediate state has acquired a special importance in Christian tradition in connection with the doctrine of PURGATORY, because in traditional theology the process of purification is located in the intermediate state and applied to the soul that has been separated from the body in death.

(1) *Biblical Background.* In the Old Testament the concept of an intermediate state results from a linking of the idea of Sheol with the belief in the resurrection of the dead that appears as the true expression of the hope of the people of Israel in the final stage before the Christian era. The intermediate state is found more clearly in extrabiblical Jewish apocalyptic writings (*1 Enoch* and *4 Ezra*), where concern with the rewards and punishments meted out to human beings after death becomes central. Although the impression is occasionally given that this state is a definitive one, there is nonetheless a basic insistence that the intermediate state is relative to the resurrection of the dead and that at the resurrection of the dead their existence in the chambers of Sheol comes to an end. Different answers are given to the question of whether the New Testament provides evidence of an intermediate state. If we take into consideration that the true Christian hope is in the resurrection of the dead and that this hope is linked to the EXPECTATION OF AN IMMINENT END, we may expect that the intermediate state as such will not be a subject of New Testament preaching. This holds first of all for the message of Jesus himself. Some exegetes are of the opinion that Jesus adopted the idea of an intermediate state that had been making its appearances in the intertestamental literature of early Judaism. They give as examples the parables of the foolish landowner (Lk 12:16–21) and of the rich man and poor Lazarus (Lk 16:19–31) and the words of Jesus to the good thief: "Today you will be with me in paradise" (Lk 23:43). Although what is being said in these passages is something different, they are indeed most readily understandable if an intermediate state is presupposed. As regards the letters of Paul, these exegetes cite chiefly Phil 1:23, where Paul expresses his longing to depart and be with Christ. Nothing is said there, however, of how Paul thinks of this union with Christ after death in anthropological terms. Above all, heed must be paid to the fact that in the immediate context of the cited text the resurrection of the dead is stated as the true hope of Christians (Phil 3:20–21). The other passages of the Pauline letters that are occasionally cited — the image of the "bare kernel of wheat" (1 Cor 15:37), the demolishing of the earthly tent and the being clothed with a heavenly dwelling, the leaving of the body and being at home with the Lord (2 Cor 5:1–10) — cannot be interpreted as referring to an intermediate state, since the intention at work in the statements is different.

(2) *History of Theology.* While attestations of the intermediate state are cautious and uncertain in the early patristic period, the hope of the resurrection of the dead after a stay of the soul in Hades is emphasized in the rejection of the gnostic doctrine of the heavenly journey of the soul that has been freed from the body. It is assumed that the souls of martyrs, consecrated virgins, and, later on, all upright Christians are already with God, whereas their bodies will be raised up only on the last day. In the struggle against gnosticism the emphasis is on the deficiencies of the intermediate state by comparison with the future resurrection; in its subsequent development, however, for example in the theology of Augustine and medieval Scholasticism, the intermediate state becomes so important that the biblical hope in the resurrection of the dead takes second place, at least "existentially," to the heavenly beatitude of the soul in the intermediate state.

(3) *Church Teaching.* There is no doctrinal decision of the church that has the intermediate state as its express subject. The medieval utterances of the magisterium on purgatory, the blessedness of HEAVEN, and punishment in HELL before the resurrection of the dead do, however, include the doctrine of an intermediate state for the body-free soul (DS 838, 856, 1000, 1304–6). Again, the declaration of the Congregation for the Doctrine of the Faith entitled "Some Questions of Eschatology" (May 17, 1979) does not mention the intermediate state but presupposes it when it stresses the continued existence of the soul after death and explicitly distinguishes the soul's situation then from its manner of existence after the parousia of Christ.

(4) *Ecumenical Perspectives.* The Orthodox churches accept the doctrine of an intermediate state, but they have a different understanding of purgatory; in addition, they lay great emphasis on the provisional character of rewards and punishments in the intermediate state as compared with the definitive reward and definitive punishment after the resurrection of the dead. Even today, there is still no agreement on the interpretation of the teachings of the Reformers. Some interpreters of Luther think that he rejects the intermediate state, but others think that Luther had in mind the biblical description of death as a sleep and that he understands the intermediate state as a deep, dreamless sleep of a soul without consciousness or feeling; the soul sleeps in the peace of Christ and will, like the body, be reawakened on the last day. According to J. Gerhard (d. 1637), the body reposes in the grave like one asleep and waits for the resurrection, while the soul is already in the same state in which it will be after the judgment, when it is reunited with the body. The souls of the godly are already in heaven and sharing eternal beatitude, while the souls of the wicked are already being punished in hell. J. Calvin likewise relates the biblical expression "sleep" to the body alone. The body lies in the grave and waits to be raised up by God. The soul does not sleep; it lives and enjoys a blessed repose in which it devoutly waits to enter into the glory that the returning Christ will give to it. Many contemporary Evangelical theologians object that Catholic theology shifts salvation and damnation to the intermediate state to such an

extent that the biblically attested manner of salvation and damnation after the resurrection of the dead is pushed too much into the background. The emphatic rejection of the immortality of the soul by various Evangelical theologians takes the ground from under the traditional doctrine of the intermediate state. In the total-death theory (see DEATH) the intermediate state becomes unnecessary or loses its importance.

(5) *Systematic Reflections.* In contemporary Catholic and Evangelical theology the doctrine of the intermediate state is one of the crucial issues in eschatology, as the theory of resurrection at death shows. The main problem is that of time, which after death no longer exists as time experienced in the present life, although the term *intermediate state* seems to presuppose that it does. Nor can the distinction between physical and anthropological time satisfactorily resolve the problems that must be faced.

See also DEATH; IMMORTALITY; RESURRECTION OF THE DEAD; SOUL; TIME.

Bibliography
González-Ruiz, J. M. "Should We De-mythologize the 'Separated Soul'?" In *The Problem of Eschatology*. Edited by Edward Schillebeeckx and Boniface Willems. Vol. 41 of *Concilium*. New York: Paulist, 1969.
Nickelsburg, George W. E. *Resurrection, Immortality, and Eternal Life in Intertestamental Judaism*. Cambridge, Mass.: Harvard University Press, 1972.

JOSEF FINKENZELLER

J j

Jesus' Faith. The faith of Jesus Christ refers to the trust and obedience with which he freely responded to God his Father and through which, as "the pioneer and perfecter of our faith" (Heb 12:2), he opened up for humankind the possibility of believing *in him* (in him or through him to the Father) *as he* believed — that is, the possibility of being his disciple in responding to God with complete freedom.

(1) *Biblical Background.* According to the Old Testament, faith is steadfast reliance on God. It is an existentially necessary attitude for our relationship to God (Is 7:9) and corresponds to God's truth and reliability. The Synoptics do not mention Jesus Christ's faith verbally but refer to it factually in his prayer and in his attitude of trust of and obedience to the Father, the basis of his actions. This is seen, for example, in the "temptations" (Lk 22:28; see Mk 1:12 pars.), in the Garden of Olives (Mk 14:32–42 pars.), in his prayerful relationship with God (Mk 1:35 par.; 6:46 par.; 14:32–42 pars.; Lk 3:21; 6:12; 9:18; 11:1; 23:34), or in Luke's "should" of salvation-history (see 2:49; 4:34; 13:33; 19:5; 22:37; 24:26, 44). John demonstrates Jesus' faithful obedience and intercession in the so-called Priestly Prayer (17:4, along with 19:30 and 4:34; 17:9–19, 20–26). For Paul the faith of Jesus Christ is manifested in his emptying of himself in his death on the cross (Phil 2:8). Henceforth it is possible for us not only to believe in Jesus Christ (*pisteúein eis:* e.g., Gal 2:16b) but also to believe *because of* him (*pistis en:* e.g., Gal 3:26). Christ is the goal ("object") *and* foundation of our faith. The formula "faith of Christ/of the Son of God" (Rom 3:22, 26; Gal 2:16, 20; 3:22; Phil 3:9) hovers between the two: it is a faith that is present in Jesus Christ and at the same time is oriented toward him as its author. The genitive cannot be described as either subjective or objective. It has been called the "mystical" genitive, because this faith expresses both God's fidelity to God's covenant with humankind and human obedience toward God (in Christ). This maintains the basic structure of Old Testament faith and qualifies it christologically as "credere in Deum per Christum et in Christo" (believing in God through Christ and in Christ). According to Hebrews, Jesus Christ is the "pioneer and perfecter of faith" (12:2) not only exemplarily but also soteriologically, that is, as the origin and example of "assurance of things hoped for" in "the conviction of things not seen" (11:1). Here also the faith of Jesus Christ is manifested primarily as obedience (2:17f.; 4:15; 5:7–10; 9:14; 10:5–10).

(2) *History of Theology.* The tradition rarely speaks of the faith of Jesus Christ because faith usually involves knowledge; thus because the beatific vision is regarded objectively, it is impossible to speak of Jesus' faith (see Thomas

Aquinas, *STh* 3, q. 7, a. 3). Nevertheless, the Lord's obedience leads to the faithful obedience of Christians (ibid., ad 2). Some Scholastics recognize in Jesus a *fides lucida* — lucid faith (in opposition to our *fides aenigmatica* [enigmatic faith]) (Alexander of Hales, Nicholas of Cusa: *maxima fides* — maximal faith [*De doct. ignor.* 3.12]). On the other hand, if faith is understood as a personal attitude that is existentially expressed in obedience, the tradition is more open. This is where modern theories begin.

(3) *Church Teaching.* The teaching office takes no direct position on the faith of Jesus Christ. Indirectly there are indications for theological reflection arising from the emphasis on Christ's human freedom (DS 553–59) and Vatican II's personalist understanding of faith (*DV 5*).

(4) *Ecumenical Perspectives.* In contemporary Evangelical systematics, G. Ebeling has made the faith of Jesus Christ the central theme of his Christology. By reason of his power, the earthly Jesus is the indispensable witness of faith who becomes the basis of our faith through the resurrection. Being a disciple of Jesus is therefore identical to faith.

(5) *Systematic Reflections.* As a result of today's systematic theological considerations on the faith of Jesus Christ, two avenues have been opened. (*a*) *An objective, christological-trinitarian aspect.* On the basis of his faith, Jesus Christ is the "place" where access to God is open to us. Faith as trust and total surrender to God was the typical pattern of the earthly existence of Jesus, who lived in essential relatedness to the Father in the Holy Spirit and revealed the trinitarian being of God. The condition of possibility of this manner of existence is the Father's gift and self-sharing in Jesus in the Holy Spirit. This christological-trinitarian aspect points to the unique, unrepeatable character of the faith of Jesus Christ and is indissolubly linked to his person insofar as he is the "pioneer and perfecter of faith." Thus human beings who wish to believe *as* Jesus can do so only through faith *in* Jesus. (*b*) *An existential, soteriological-anthropological aspect.* The faith of Jesus Christ is the ground of possibility of our faith. For Christians faith is possible only by being taken up "in Christ." Imitation means being led by Christ to the Father (*per Christum in Deum*). Thus the faith of Jesus Christ involves his humanness as obedient reception of the possibility and reality of salvation.

See also DISCIPLESHIP, CHRISTIAN; FAITH; HYPOSTATIC UNION; JESUS' HUMANITY; JESUS' KNOWLEDGE AND CONSCIOUSNESS; MYSTERIES OF THE LIFE OF JESUS CHRIST; REPRESENTATION.

Bibliography
Balthasar, Hans Urs von. *Church and World.* Montreal: Palm, 1967.
———. *Test Everything: Hold Fast to What Is Good: An Interview with Hans Urs von Balthasar.* Interview by Angelo Scola. San Francisco: Ignatius, 1989.
Cook, Michael. *The Jesus of Faith.* New York: Paulist, 1981.
Ebeling, Gerhard. *The Nature of Faith.* Philadelphia: Fortress, 1967.
———. *Word and Faith.* London: SCM, 1960.
Pannenberg, Wolfhart. *Jesus, God and Man.* 2d ed. Philadelphia: Westminster, 1977.

Rahner, Karl, and Wilhelm Thüsing. *A New Christology.* New York: Crossroad, 1980.
Sobrino, Jon. *Christology at the Crossroads.* Maryknoll, N.Y.: Orbis Books, 1978.

LOTHAR ULLRICH

Jesus' Humanity. The theological term *Jesus' humanity* refers to the full and integral human nature that the divine Logos assumed and made its own in the incarnation.

(1) *Biblical Background.* The New Testament clearly attests to the humanity of Jesus. He has a true human body (Jn 1:14; 1 Jn 4:2) with a rational soul. All the physical, affective, cognitive, and voluntary actions that are proper to human beings are attributed to Jesus. He is born of a woman (Gal 4:4). He eats and drinks (Mk 2:15; 11:19), is hungry and thirsty (Mk 11:12; Jn 4:7). He becomes tired (Jn 4:6) and sleeps (Mk 4:38). He can be tempted (Mk 4:1; Heb 2:17; 4:14; 5:7). He experiences fear and horror and is deeply distressed (Mk 14:33; Heb 5:7). He has compassion (Lk 7:13). His will can struggle with the will of the Father and be fully one with it in obedience (Lk 22:42). In summary, he is like us in all things except sin (Phil 2:7f.; Heb 2:17f.; 4:15; 5:7f.). He really suffered, died on the cross, and was buried in a tomb (Lk 24:26; 1 Cor 15:3f.). Finally, in Jesus, God's goodness and loving kindness appeared (Ti 3:4).

(2) *History of Theology.* To combat gnosticism, Manichaean dualism, and Docetism, the Fathers emphasized the true incarnation of God in the human and bodily reality of Jesus. He did not merely seem to suffer but really suffered; his body was not apparent but real. Against the Arians and the Apollinarians they had to spell out the completeness of the human nature, including body, soul, and spirit. His human nature would also be incomplete if he did not have active control over a creaturely consciousness and a finite human will, as faculties of the soul (vs. Monothelitism and Monenergism). Gregory of Nazianzus's axiom (*Ep.* 101) is important: "Quod non est assumptum — non est sanatum" (What is not assumed is not saved). Thomas Aquinas emphasized that a human nature is a substantial, not an accidental, unity of a spiritual and a material principle informed by the soul. His precise manner of stating it is: "Verbum assumpsit carnem anima mediante" (The Word assumed flesh by the mediation of the soul) (*STh* 3, q. 6, a. 1). Also, with regard to soteriology: "Christi humanitas via est qua ad Divinitatem pervenitur (homo)" (Christ's humanity is the way by which human beings reach the Divinity) (see *Comp. theol.* 2). In the church's practice, however, the humanity of Jesus sometimes became insignificant in relationship to his divinity.

(3) *Church Teaching.* In refuting the heresies mentioned in sec. 2, the church defended Jesus' true humanity along with his true divinity (DS 291–94, 301–3, 429). He received his humanity from the body of Mary (it was not an ethereal body). His body is a natural body, capable of suffering and death. Thus, according to the rules of *communicatio idiomatum,* it is correct to say: Christ is one of the Trinity. God truly suffered and died (DS 401f., 431–35).

(4) *Ecumenical Perspectives.* The Reformation, of course, defended the humanity of Jesus. However, because of a theory of redemption that depends on a certain idea of God's exclusive powerfulness and effectiveness, the properly human activity of Jesus' humanity (as the head of humankind) was not fully appreciated.

(5) *Systematic Reflections.* At present the humanity of Jesus is not contested but presupposed and taken for granted. Historical-critical research begins with the humanity. The difficulty is to discover indications in the life and behavior of Jesus that are the basis for his unity with God. The humanity of Jesus is not endangered by the doctrine of enhypostasis. The Logos did not take the place of the human personality but assumed it and gave it its basis by realizing it and fulfilling it in its infinite transcendentality, so that the humanity of Jesus appears as the salvific-economic mode of the trinitarian dialogue between the Father and the Son. The special reality of the human Jesus is already manifest in his "Abba" relationship with the Father. Because his life is not just a historical prelude to his act of redemption on the cross, but rather the history in which God's self-sharing takes place and becomes present, Christology should examine further the mysteries of Jesus' life as the expression of Jesus' humanity. At the same time, the question of Jesus' objective knowledge, including his knowledge of himself, can be addressed more impartially when the historicity and finitude of the humanity of Jesus are taken seriously.

See also GOD-MAN; HYPOSTATIC UNION; INCARNATION; MYSTERIES OF THE LIFE OF JESUS CHRIST.

Bibliography
Boring, M. Eugene. *Truly Human/Truly Divine: Christological Language and the Gospel Form.* St. Louis: CBP Press, 1984.
Kuschel, Karl-Josef. *Born before All Time? The Dispute over Christ's Origin.* New York: Crossroad, 1992.
Pollard, T. E. *Fullness of Humanity: Christ's Humanness and Ours.* Sheffield, England: Almond, 1982.
Rahner, Karl. "Dogmatic Reflections on the Knowledge and Consciousness of Christ." In *Theological Investigations,* 5:193–15. Baltimore: Helicon, 1966.

GERHARD LUDWIG MÜLLER

Jesus' Knowledge and Consciousness.

The knowledge and consciousness of Jesus Christ are determined by his immediacy with God and are a given of his basic life-situation, which unfolds humanly in the course of his dealings with God (his Father), his environment, and his lived world.

(1) *Biblical Background.* The New Testament attests the historicity (humanness) as well as the perfection (divinity) of the knowledge and consciousness of Jesus. The perfection is usually referred to incidentally (in statements about his power and unique relationship to God), although it is sometimes expressly developed (see the "signs" and Jesus' revelatory statements in John). The Synoptics preserve important traits of Jesus' human consciousness (progress in

knowledge: Lk 2:52; see 1:80; 2:40; questions that imply openness to learning: Mk 5:9 par.; 5:30 pars.; 6:38; 8:19f., 27, 29 pars., etc.; ignorance about the day of judgment: Mk 13:32 par.; anguish in the face of suffering: Mk 14:33–36 par.). Yet they also attribute to Jesus special wisdom and knowledge that surpass all known forms (see Mk 1:21f. pars.; 11:1–6 pars.; 14:13–15 pars.; 14:18, 25, 27–30 pars.; Lk 2:40, 47). The New Testament applies this particular knowledge and wisdom especially to Jesus' awareness of his mission (esp. Jn 4:34; 5:30, 43; 6:38; 8:42; 16:28), which in turn depends on his singular relationship with the Father (Abba: Lk 11:2 par.; see Mk 14:36 pars.) and his union with the Holy Spirit (see Mt 1:18; 12:28 par.; Mk 1:9–11 pars.; Lk 1:35, etc.). The temptations narrative (Mt 16:22f. par.; 26:51–53; Mk 1:12f. pars., etc.) shows that a "learning process" could be involved. He knows everything because, being led by the Father, he "learns" all in order to reveal the Father and thus accomplish his mission (cf. Jn 16:30 with 5:20; 13:3; 15:15; 17:8).

(2) *History of Theology.* The patristic discussion of Jesus' consciousness is largely determined by the CHRISTOLOGICAL MODELS used (Logos-*sárx* or Logos-*anthropos* schemas) and by the consequences for faith of accepting Jesus' true and complete humanity, including his ignorance, learning, and progressive knowledge (see Tertullian, Phoebadius of Agen [d. after 392], Gregory of Nyssa, Theodore of Mopsuestia, and others). Thus the struggle against the Arians led to an emphasis on Christ's perfect knowledge, because the Arians interpreted the New Testament statements that gave evidence of historicity in Jesus — including his ignorance — as proof that the Logos was created. Many Fathers either are hesitant to speak about Jesus' ignorance (Ambrose) or do not treat his knowledge or consciousness at all (Leo the Great, Gelasius I, Hormisdas) or interpret his ignorance as incapable of being shared (Hilary of Poitiers, Basil, especially Augustine, who attributes beatific vision to the soul of Christ; in the East: Cyril of Alexandria, Maximus the Confessor, John Damascene). Gregory the Great introduces a teaching that substitutes a purely human ignorance in Jesus Christ (*agnoita*), in connection with the heresy of Nestorianism (DS 476). In the Middle Ages, Thomas Aquinas formulates a doctrine of four types of knowledge in Christ: beatific vision (*scientia visionis*), "infused knowledge" (*scientia infusa*), properly human knowledge (*scientia acquisita, experimentalis, intuitiva*), and divine knowledge (*scientia divina*) (STh 3, q. 9–12; q. 15, a. 8). He strongly emphasizes the perfection of Jesus Christ's knowledge: he knows not only all that is but also all that is in any way possible. The knowledge and consciousness of Jesus Christ are understood purely from the viewpoint of his divinity. When the Logos became man, its humanity was perfected in such a way that even its knowledge and consciousness had to be perfect. The historical consequences of this presentation are still visible in papal pronouncements of the twentieth century. In the nineteenth century H. Klee and F. X. Dieringen attempted to do justice to the full humanity of Christ. They did not deny that it was illuminated by grace and possessed beatific vision, but they tried to interpret it historically, starting with the emptying (kenosis). H. Schell

(d. 1906) was the first to make a distinction between knowledge and consciousness. The knowledge of Jesus Christ is human experiential knowledge (of the highest order); his consciousness, as consciousness of self, is the consciousness of the Son, from the beginning of his life, grounded in divine illumination. But even here the historicity of his consciousness is not fully maintained. Between 1949 and 1956 a discussion began within neo-scholasticism concerning how Jesus Christ knew he was the Son of God: by means of the immediate beatific vision of his human soul (the beatific vision theory: P. Galtier) or by a sharing of the consciousness of the Logos in the human soul (the consciousness theory: P. Parente, Thomists). K. Rahner served as a mediator in that he identified the immediate vision of God (not to be understood as conferring happiness unconditionally) with the nonobjective consciousness of Jesus Christ, the Son of God, as an inner moment of the hypostatic union. Christ experienced himself humanly as the Son of God. In this regard it has been observed that, according to the New Testament, the relationship of the human nature of Christ to the Logos that is hypostatically united with it should not lead to an "internal Christology," but rather to the relationship of Jesus to the Father (a relational-trinitarian interpretation in historical perspective: thus, H. Urs von Balthasar, L. Bouyer, B. Forte, W. Kasper, J. Ratzinger, and D. Wiederkehr). When Jesus addresses the Father, he is humanly conscious of his relation as Son.

(3) *Church Teaching.* The teaching office of the church has made no definitive pronouncements concerning the knowledge and consciousness of Jesus Christ. Gregory the Great took a problematic stance against what was called *agnoetas,* but that left practically no room for a real human consciousness in Jesus. Popes and papal officials of the twentieth century have spoken along the lines of Thomas's not uncontroversial position (DS 3432–35, 3645–47, 3812, 3924). On the other hand, Vatican II stressed that the human knowledge of Jesus Christ is an expression of his true humanity (*GS* 22). The Pontifical Biblical Commission (see "Bible and Christology" [1984]) speaks of a "step-by-step" acquisition of "ever more precise consciousness of his mission, from his youth until the cross," as well as of a fully human experience of death.

(4) *Ecumenical Perspectives.* Among Reformed theologians today, W. Pannenberg is involved with the Catholic discussion. According to him, Jesus' personality developed in surrender to the Father. The sonship of Jesus is the fulfillment of this human personality.

(5) *Systematic Reflections.* Any explanation of the knowledge and consciousness of Jesus Christ that would base its research regarding the consciousness problem on dogmatics and exegesis must first question the expressed (and unexpressed) presuppositions of earlier explanations. Today, admitting limits to Jesus' knowledge, and therefore ignorance, is no longer seen as "dishonorable"; it is, rather, a matter of seeing ignorance as a normal condition of human knowledge, just as are readiness to learn and progress in knowledge. What becomes clear at this point is the doubtful usefulness of any perfection principle (but also of an unenlightened "principle of humanity"!). According to

the new thesis of systematic theology, which proposes a relational-trinitarian explanation of the hypostatic union, Jesus' basic human fulfillments are to be situated within the relation to the Father (D. Wiederkehr, W. Kasper, and others). This thesis corresponds better to the New Testament data than the former "internal Christology" thesis. Here the New Testament revelations — and an interpretation of them that maintains the trinitarian doctrine of God and the hypostatic union, as developed by the church's faith — become the basic sources for presenting the knowledge and consciousness of Jesus Christ. Recent areas of anthropological study — personalist thinking, the realization of humanity in dialogue and in relationships, personal identity and its sociological developments, and so on — can be helpful in this task. In this type of presentation, an effort should be made to express the unity of Jesus' mental life while differentiating between his knowledge and consciousness. The starting point is Jesus Christ's *experiential* knowledge, through which his basic situation and his *consciousness of being Son,* as an immediacy to God, develop according to his age (as child, as adolescent, as adult). Within this development, which involves a learning process, the Father shows him his mission. This "revealed knowledge" is the concrete fulfillment of his consciousness of sonship and mission in dialogue with the Father, where his experiences of being with others in an environment and their "reconstruction" are the occasion for or the concrete form of this dialogue in given circumstances. The end result is a unity of Jesus Christ's knowledge and consciousness, a unity that encompasses various aspects but does not create a need to postulate a different manner of knowing.

See also CHRISTOLOGY; HISTORICAL JESUS; HYPOSTATIC UNION; JESUS' HUMANITY.

Bibliography
Brown, Raymond. *Jesus: God-Man.* Milwaukee: Bruce, 1967.
Lonergan, Bernard. "The Subject." In *Second Collection,* 69–86. Philadelphia: Westminster, 1974.
Rahner, Karl. "Dogmatic Reflections on the Knowledge and Consciousness of Christ." In *Theological Investigations,* 5:193–15. Baltimore: Helicon, 1966.

LOTHAR ULLRICH

Joy. Joy is a pleasant subjective feeling. Conceptually, joy belongs to the sentiments. One distinguishes between passing joyful excitements (emotions) and longer-lasting moods. The prevailing tone of joy manifests harmony, that is, a successful bringing together of the various expressions of human life. While joyful excitements are generally able to be stimulated, the fundamental mood of joy cannot be produced. Joy is therefore closely joined with both happiness and good fortune.

(1) *Biblical Background.* According to the witness of the Bible, joy is brought about through the saving and supporting presence of God (Neh 8:10), which is experienced in historical events (Pss 92:5f.; 126), in the law (Ps 119:16), in the temple (Ps 122:1), in prayer (Pss 33:21; 37:4), and in the good things

of daily life seen as gifts of the Creator (Psalm 104). On the basis of the experience of the irrevocable and definitive presence of God in Jesus Christ, joy becomes the characteristic basic attitude of Christians (Phil 4:4). The gospel of Jesus Christ is a message that brings joy (Lk 2:10). The joyful expectation of the fulfillment of salvation perseveres in the inmost being of a Christian even in the sorrow, pain, and anxiety that Christians experience on the way to fulfillment (Mt 5:11f.; 2 Cor 7:4; 1 Pt 1:6–9). For joy is a fruit of the Spirit (Gal 5:22), an anticipatory participation in the glory of Christ (Col 1:12f.). Scripture distinguishes this joy in God from the fleeting pleasure that comes with the desire for individual goods and that perishes with this (1 Jn 1:15–17; see Psalm 73).

(2) *History of Theology.* The joy that cannot be lost and that fulfills the whole human person became, especially through the influence of Augustine, the essence of salvation: the beatifying vision of God (*visio beatifica*). Because of this, in theology the corporeal and cosmic mediation of joy in God dwindled in importance. In modern times the saving significance of joy was displaced through the significance given to FREEDOM. As a reaction to the Enlightenment, the romantic movement then recognized feeling as the genuine place of religious experience and of theological knowing. Against this concentration on emotional religious experience, twentieth-century theology emphasized the seriousness of the decision of faith and of following the cross. Then joy was seen primarily in connection with the promise of future salvation. As joyful expectation it is also already experienceable in hope, yet it continually refers to what has not yet been realized.

(3) *Church Teaching.* The concept of the beatific vision of God — in knowledge and love — has been received into official church doctrine of faith (DS 1000). It stipulates that the fulfillment of the human person consists in the immediate joyful experience of God's self.

(4) *Ecumenical Perspectives.* From its tradition, Protestant theology puts greater stress on the promise of this joy (consolation), whereas Catholic and Orthodox theology understand joy as the beginning of the already present gift of salvation that comes to expression, above all, in liturgical celebration. Yet these different emphases today characterize differing basic theological approaches rather than different denominations.

(5) *Systematic Reflections.* This connection between the joy in God and the salvation of the human person continuously witnessed to throughout the Christian tradition presents theological anthropology today with the task of showing how the whole human person with the variety of her or his possibilities can succeed in finding fulfillment only through being directed by God and toward God. For both the limitations of these possibilities due to historical situations and the finiteness of the span of human life evoke a general mood of sorrow that does not allow an untroubled joy to be the signal of a fulfilled, worthwhile human existence. In faith in the unconditional joy that God's coming to the human person produces, joy in human life becomes an anticipatory manifestation of the fulfillment in God that the human person hopes for.

See also HEAVEN; HOPE; SALVATION; SUFFERING.

Bibliography

Metz, Johann Baptist, and Jean-Pierre Jossua, eds. *Theology of Joy.* New York: Herder and Herder, 1974.

Moltmann, Jürgen. *Theology and Joy.* London: SCM, 1973.

GEORG LANGEMEYER

Judaism and the Church. Judaism and the church are two distinct entities that nonetheless are closely related in a great many ways. Their relationship throughout history has been very tense; today, however, the relationship is entering a more conciliatory phase.

(1) *Biblical Background.* The Jewish people are one of the most astonishing phenomena in the history of humankind. They have behind them a history several millennia long. By about 1000 B.C.E., at the latest, when the monarchy was established, the "twelve tribes" became a people. It was not, however, government by a king that set them apart but their faith in the "God of Israel." This God had united Israel, chosen it for a special covenant, delivered it from slavery in Egypt, and led it into the land God had chosen for it. Thus faith in Yahweh, the God of Israel, and the people and the land are all closely interconnected. Yahweh gave the people the Torah, that is, God's instructions on how to live. The Torah regulates the private and social lives of Jews: circumcision, the Sabbath, the feast days, the dietary laws, the sanctification of everyday life. This list identifies the essential constants of what we know as Judaism. They determine the character and history of the Jewish people. This history has known periods of decline and of progress, periods of suffering and of hopeful joy. In 722 B.C.E. Israel was subjected by the Assyrians and in 586 by the Babylonians. The temple was destroyed; large numbers of the people were deported to Babylon. They returned from there in 538 B.C.E. Since that time the Jewish people have lived in two settings: the land of Israel and the diaspora. In both they have been repeatedly persecuted. The cruel climax of this persecution came in the extermination of the Jews carried out by the German National Socialists. From this period of most profound suffering the Jews arose once again and after World War II established the state of Israel. In the period after the Babylonian exile the Jewish people collected the most important writings in which they had until then interpreted their own existence and made of them the "Scriptures of Israel" (the Christian Old Testament). The life of the Christian church, for its part, is based essentially on the belief that the person and work of Jesus of Nazareth are the new way of salvation that has been opened up by God and cannot be replaced by a better way. This fact led the church at a very early date to separate itself from the context of Jewish life and faith. It developed a trinitarian understanding of God and thus moved beyond the Jewish understanding of God.

(2) *History of Theology.* Although the church at a very early date decisively rejected the temptation of anti-Semitism, when it excommunicated Marcion,

who had given theological justification for it, it has not been guiltless in the persecutions that have constantly afflicted the Jews.

(3) *Church Teaching.* In *NA* 4, Vatican II gave a new description of the church's relation to Judaism. It emphasizes what the church and Judaism have in common and also explains the differences without any accompanying suggestion of anti-Semitism. Any and every persecution of the Jews is criticized and rejected. The document "Jews and Christians," which the Vatican Secretariat for Christian Unity published in 1985, develops these positions and explains them more fully.

(4) *Ecumenical Perspectives.* The persecution of the Jews that reached a fearful climax associated with the name Auschwitz has made a new consciousness and dialogue unavoidable. Meanwhile, there are starting points for a Jewish-Christian dialogue. The various churches have undertaken this dialogue, each in its own manner. On the Jewish side, some theologians have been seeking a rapprochement, as far as this is possible, with the Christian church and its life and practice (S. Ben-Chorin, P. Lapide, D. Flusser, J. J. Petuchowski; among artists: M. Chagall and others). It is not surprising that in this effort there are Jewish boundaries that may not be crossed (rejected are: the Trinity in God; Jesus as the Christ and Son of God; the church as the "new" people of God; faith as the acceptance of the self-communication of God in Jesus). On the other side, Christian theologians are endeavoring to bring out the continuity that remains between Christianity and Judaism despite the new element represented by Jesus and the church. Here the idea of Israel as the first chosen people plays an important role.

(5) *Systematic Reflections.* The rediscovery that Jesus of Nazareth had his origin in Judaism is one of the decisive factors in the relaxation of tension in relations between Judaism and the church. *LG* 9 and *AG* 4, in particular, have defined the close relationship between Judaism and the church in the area of ecclesiology; on the one hand, the concept of "people of God" is developed here, while, on the other, Romans 9–11 is reevaluated.

See also CANON; SCRIPTURE.

Bibliography
Cohen, Martin A., and Helga Croner, eds. *Christian Mission–Jewish Mission.* Ramsey, N.J.: Paulist, 1982.
Fisher, Eugene J. *Faith without Prejudice: Rebuilding Christian Attitudes toward Judaism.* Rev. ed. New York: Crossroad, 1993.
Fisher, Eugene J., and Leon Klenicki, eds. *In Our Time: The Flowering of Jewish-Catholic Dialogue.* New York: Paulist, 1990.
Küng, Hans. *Judaism: Between Yesterday and Tomorrow.* New York: Crossroad, 1992.
Küng, Hans, and Walter Kasper, eds. *Christians and Jews.* Vol. 98 of *Concilium.* New York: Seabury, 1975.
Silva, Antonio Barbosa da. *Is There a New Imbalance in Jewish-Christian Relations? An Analysis of the Theoretical Presuppositions and Theological Implications of the Jewish-Christian Dialogue in the Light of the World Council of Churches' and the Roman Catholic Church's Conceptions of Inter-Religious Dialogue.* Uppsala: Uppsala University Press, 1992.

Thering, Rose. *Jews, Judaism, and Catholic Education: Documentary Survey Report of Catholic Institutions' Implementation of 1965 Conciliar Statement on the Jews, 1974 Roman Catholic Guidelines/Suggestions, 1975 U.S. Bishops' Statement on the Jews; Prepared for the Twentieth Anniversary of the 1965 Promulgation of Vatican II document "Nostra Aetate."* New York: Anti-Defamation League of B'nai B'rith, 1986.

WERNER LÖSER

Judgment. As understood in eschatology, judgment is the final decision of God regarding the definitive salvation or loss of the person and of the human race as a whole. Theologians distinguish between a *general judgment,* or judgment of the entire world on the last day, and an *individual* or *personal judgment* at the death of each person.

(1) *Biblical Background.* In the scriptural passages on judgment account must be taken of the anthropological mode of expression and the analogical character of the term itself, inasmuch as judgment can express not only a condemnation of the person who has incurred guilt in God's sight but also, and above all, the graciousness and mercy of God. According to the Old Testament, God intervenes in the history of God's people to judge, reward or punish, and bring salvation; this history thus becomes a history of salvation, as can be seen especially in the preaching of the prophets on judgment. From Am 5:18–20 on, the "day of Yahweh," which is a name for the final judgment, becomes a regular element in Israel's expectation of the future; according to the witness of the prophets, however, and contrary to popular belief, the "day of Yahweh" will be, even for the chosen people, a day of wrath on which everything unholy will be destroyed (Am 3:2; Is 2:6–21; 13:6; 22:5). The high point in the description of judgment is reached in Daniel 7, where the definitive dawning of the reign of God is connected with the conquest of all kingdoms opposed to God. The Old Testament idea of the judgment is clarified by means of various images and similes: the separation of the animals of the flock (Ez 34:17–22), the harvesting of grain and olives (Is 17:5–6), the divine winepress of wrath (Is 63:1–6), and the smelting furnace (Ez 22:18–22). The important point is that the announcement of judgment is meant to stir conversion and hope and make the hearer aware of the decision that is required. The wrath of God is accompanied by concern for the flock and its salvation, so that the climactic element in the idea of judgment is the rescue and salvation of the people. In the New Testament the idea of God as judge is extended to include the role of the divinely appointed messiah as judge. In the Synoptics a distinction must be made between the preaching of John the Baptist on judgment and what is said of judgment in the preaching of Jesus. The former represents the climax of the Old Testament proclamation of judgment, inasmuch as John preaches not any limited judgment but the final and definitive judgment that God will shortly exercise through God's messiah (Mt 3:10–12). In addition, he combines his preaching of conversion and judgment with a baptism of conversion that is understood as a rite of initiation for a community of those who are ready to repent and will

thereby escape the coming judgment (Mt 3:5–11). The proclamation of judgment is part of the message of Jesus in all phases of his preaching activity: in his clashes with the scribes and Pharisees, in the parables dealing with the kingdom of heaven and the Second Coming, and, above all, in the Sermon on the Mount, in which a new ethic is accompanied by a radicalization of judgment (Mt 5:29–30; see 10:28). When the last judgment is described in the image of the separation of sheep from goats (Mt 25:31–46), a continuity with the Old Testament is established; at the same time, the norm of judgment is declared to be one's concrete neighborly love for the least of the brethren (Mt 25:40, 45). But although the judgment becomes more pointed and radical, the important thing about the message of Jesus is that the proclamation of judgment is integrated into the good news of love for sinners and the savior's concern for them, as is clear from Luke 15, "the gospel within the gospel" (see also Lk 2:8–20). The final judgment is described not only by the image of the separation of sheep from goats but also by the parables of the weeds among the wheat (Mt 13:24–30, 36–43), the net of fish (Mt 13:47–50), and the man who had no wedding garment (Mt 22:11–14). In John the message of judgment takes two forms. In keeping with John's realized ESCHATOLOGY, salvation and judgment occur in the encounter with the message of Jesus, to whom judgment has been entrusted (3:18–19; 5:22, 23, 27; 12:31; see 1 Jn 3:14). In addition there is the idea of a general judgment that is connected with the resurrection of the dead (Jn 5:28–29). In Revelation the images used in describing the judgment are the harvest and the winepress of God's wrath (14:14–20) and the opening of the two books (20:11–15). According to Paul, since all human beings stand under the wrath of God (Rom 1:18–22), all must appear before God's judgment seat in order to receive reward or punishment for their lives on earth (2 Cor 5:10; Gal 6:7–8). Both God (Rom 2:2, 3, 5; 3:6; 14:10) and Christ (Rom 2:16; 1 Cor 4:4; 2 Cor 5:10) are named as judges. Hebrews speaks of judgment with great seriousness (4:13; 9:27; 10:31).

(2) *History of Theology.* In the Christian tradition, the message of final judgment, which is clearly attested in the Bible, was taught and defended from the beginning. From the fourth century on, there is also explicit teaching of an individual or personal judgment that human beings undergo at the moment of death or immediately thereafter and that decides at once the lot of these human beings in the other world. The chief witnesses to this teaching are Augustine, Jerome, and John Chrysostom, although in the patristic period there were still theologians who denied a personal judgment (e.g., Lactantius).

(3) *Church Teaching.* The ecclesial magisterium has professed belief in the last judgment from the beginning, as the creeds of the early church attest: Christ will come to judge the living and the dead (Apostles' Creed [DS 10] and Nicene-Constantinopolitan Creed [DS 150]). Belief in the judgment finds its clearest expression in the Pseudo-Athanasian Creed (DS 76). Similar formulations are found in the Second Council of Lyons (1274 [DS 859]) and the constitution *Benedictus Deus* (1336 [DS 1000]). There is no explicit doctrinal

pronouncement on a personal judgment; this is, however, implicit in the medieval pronouncements of the thirteenth to the fifteenth century that teach that after death and possibly some needed purification, and even before the resurrection of the dead, souls receive reward and punishment (DS 838–39, 857–58, 1305–6), and that explicitly mention the final judgment in connection with the lot of the deceased in the other world (DS 858–59, 1000). No time was available to decide on the draft of a decree on personal judgment that was presented at Vatican I.

(4) *Ecumenical Perspectives.* On the ecumenical scene, the doctrine on judgment has not won an important place, except to the extent that one can point to divergent understandings of death and the intermediate state.

(5) *Systematic Reflections.* The speculative explanation of judgment has for its starting point the fact that human beings are responsible in regard to the moral order, which has its ultimate ground in the holiness of God. The personal judgment is to be understood as a self-judgment that human beings make under the action of God. God's judgment thus takes the form of a self-judgment. Human beings will come to see who and what they are because they see what they have made of themselves. Those who maintain the hypothesis of the final option understand personal judgment to be a moment in the final option that takes place at death.

See also DEATH; HISTORY/HISTORICITY; INTERMEDIATE STATE; PAROUSIA; RESURRECTION OF THE DEAD.

Bibliography

Guardini, Romano. *The Last Things: Concerning Death, Purification after Death, Resurrection, Judgment, and Eternity.* New York: Pantheon, 1954.

Martin, James Perry. *The Last Judgment in Protestant Theology from Orthodoxy to Ritschl.* Grand Rapids: Eerdmans, 1963.

Roetzel, Calvin J. *Judgement in the Community: A Study of the Relationship between Eschatology and Ecclesiology in Paul.* Leiden: Brill, 1972.

JOSEF FINKENZELLER

Justification. Justification is God's saving action through Jesus Christ in the Holy Spirit on behalf of individuals, which graciously bestows upon them freedom from sin and inner renewal. For those justified, this opens a path to eternal salvation by good works and through the community of the church.

(1) *Biblical Background.* Justification is a basic concept in Pauline theology and is rooted in the Old Testament notion of God's righteousness. According to Rom 3:19–21 and Gal 2:15–21, all human beings are sinners and are guilty before God. By the redemptive action of Christ they become purified by grace and justified by faith: their sins are forgiven and they become new persons (Rom 6:4), transformed by the Holy Spirit who dwells in those justified and renews the IMAGE OF GOD in them, making them children of God (Romans 8; Galatians 3). Elsewhere in the New Testament only Jas 2:14–26 is explicitly related to jus-

tification. Against the erroneous thesis that works are unnecessary since faith alone justifies, James emphasizes the need for works of love to perfect faith.

(2) *History of Theology.* Augustine is the first to treat the theme of justification extensively; he does this in his teaching on grace. According to him, justification of sinners is a pure grace, mediated by Christ and based on faith. It grows through works, which faith produces in love. Thus works are merits in which God crowns God's own gifts. The doctrine of justification was again treated in the Middle Ages, in commentaries on the *Sentences* of Peter Lombard (4.17: justification is a synonym for the remission of sins in the sacrament of reconciliation), and was dealt with systematically, especially by Thomas Aquinas (*STh* 1-2, q. 113). The following period dealt with the question of human freedom in justification. Duns Scotus views justification as a free act of unconditional divine acceptance (*acceptatio divina*) without human preconditions. William of Ockham, on the contrary, ascribes absolute freedom to humankind. Despite good works, God by God's absolute power (*potentia absoluta*) is not obliged to justify. Nevertheless human beings should expect that God grants them salvation in the real order of salvation (*potentia Dei ordinata*). M. Luther became acquainted with this theory, which is basically Semi-Pelagian, through G. Biel. It leads to his polemic against the Scholastic doctrine of justification.

(3) *Church Teaching.* The decree on justification of 1547 is one of the most significant pronouncements of the Council of Trent (DS 1520-83). It tries to maintain the basic claims of the Reformation and to defend the tradition against attacks. With the Reformers it emphasizes the universality of sin, the absolute gratuitousness of justification, the mediatory function of faith, and forgiveness of sin as belonging to the essence of justification. It rejects the Reformed position that freedom was destroyed by original sin, that justification is only extrinsically imputed, and that the act of being justified is only punctual. Trent maintains the possibility of human cooperation in grace, the reality of inner renewal and sanctification, and the need for hope and love to achieve eternal life, as well as the growth of grace by means of good works in the event of justification.

(4) *Ecumenical Perspectives.* While the doctrine of justification plays no role in the Eastern churches, it divides the church in the West. In opposing the medieval notion of justification by works, M. Luther bases justification on a threefold "alone": it takes place *solo Christo*, *sola gratia*, *sola fide*. God bestows it by pure mercy. God-given faith grasps the justification of Christ that has been promised (*fides apprehensiva*). Justification is understood as a juridical declaration of justice (the *forensic understanding of justification*) by not imputing our sins and by imputing the justice of Christ, as well as the new being in Christ. Since perfect justification is enduring, human beings remain justified and sinners at the same time (*simul iustus et peccator*) (WA 2:496f., etc.). Finally, Luther explains that after justification, good works mature as the necessary fruits of faith. J. Calvin defines justification as "the acceptance by which God, who accepts us in grace, allows us to be just. And what we say

about this is that it consists in the forgiveness of sins and the accreditation of the justice of Christ" (OS 4.183). Immediately joined to justification is sanctification, from which those good works follow that can be taken as signs of election in the case of individuals. Today there is a broad consensus between the Catholic and the Reformed doctrine of justification. This consensus applies to the basic thesis (justification is by grace alone, by the saving work of Christ, and is appropriated by individuals by their faith) and many details: forensic and effective justification are two sides of the same reality since the declaration of justice brings about actual justice. Justification is a punctual act in its eschatological reality, but also a process that requires works. Since human beings fall into sin after justification they are *simul iustus et peccator.*

(5) *Systematic Reflections.* The message of justification is the central Christian statement regarding the fact that and the way in which humanity once again becomes good before God. Thus it summarizes theologically the doctrine of grace (CHILDREN OF GOD; DISPOSITION FOR RECEIVING GRACE; LAW AND GOSPEL; SAINTS: HOLINESS, SANCTIFICATION; THEOLOGICAL VIRTUES). In justification God, who is love, turns toward sinful humankind in a way that is unearned and unmeritable. Justification is realized in a trinitarian way as the mercy of the Father, the appropriation of the saving work of Christ, and the inner presence of the Holy Spirit. In response to God's call, human beings who are being justified respond by faith, which is both a gift of God and a personal acceptance of justification on their part. In its core, it is a liberating and renewing event. It opens the way to eternal salvation by way of the community of the church and by manifestations of love in deeds (good works). By ethical actions justification also has an effect on society and the world.

See also GRACE: DOCTRINE OF; MERIT; PREDESTINATION; WORKS.

Bibliography

Anderson, H. George, T. Austin Murphy, and Joseph A. Burgess. *Justification by Faith.* Minneapolis: Augsburg, 1985.

Käsemann, Ernst. *New Testament Questions of Today.* Philadelphia: Fortress, 1969.

———. *Perspectives on Paul.* Philadelphia: Fortress, 1971.

Pannenberg, Wolfhart. "The Doctrine of Justification in Ecumenical Dialogue [Lutheran–Roman Catholic]." *Dialog* (Spring 1992) 136–38, 140–42, 144–48.

Reumann, John. *Righteousness in the New Testament.* Philadelphia: Fortress, 1982.

Tavard, George H. "The Doctrine of Justification in Ecumenical Discussions, Ecumenical Trends." *One in Christ* 25, no. 4 (1990) 299–310.

———. *Justification: An Ecumenical Study.* New York: Paulist, 1983.

GEORG KRAUS

K k

Kingdom of God. The kingdom of God, which is the term par excellence for salvation in the Synoptic Gospels, is the future order of things in which God's will reigns unchallenged; it has begun with the coming of Jesus and in its perfect form runs counter to the present aeon.

(1) *Biblical Background.* The idea of the rule of God has its basis in the Old Testament and is further developed in various directions in early Judaism. As Creator of the world and the only true God, Yahweh is also the lord of the world; in a special way, Yahweh is king of Israel. The monarchy that Yahweh establishes is the visible form of this divine rule. The kingship of God will some day extend to the entire world (Is 24:23; Mi 4:7; Psalms 2; 93–99). God's rule, which will incorporate all religious and moral values, is thus an eschatological reality (a reality of the final age) that God will bring about without human assistance (Dn 2:34f.; 7:27). In the period when Israel has no king and is under foreign domination, and in early Judaism, the idea of the rule of God takes on strong political traits. In Pharisaic and rabbinical Judaism at the time of Jesus there are two conceptions of it. According to the first, in which the Shema plays a dominant role, the royal rule of God is the will of God as this finds expression in the law. According to the second, very politically oriented conception, the rule of God has for its purpose to liberate Israel from its subjection to the nations by means of historical and cosmic proofs of God's power and to compel the nations to acknowledge Israel. In the New Testament the expression *kingdom of God* occurs chiefly in the Synoptic Gospels. While Mark and Luke speak of the kingdom of God, this expression is rarely found in Matthew (12:28; 19:24; 21:31, 43). There it is usually replaced by *kingdom of heaven,* "heaven" having become in early Judaism a substitute for the proper name "Yahweh," which people no longer dared to pronounce. The kingdom of God proclaimed by Jesus, and the salvation that it includes, are to be understood as religious. Jesus does not make his own the nationalistic and political elements in the concept of God's dominion. The enemy of the kingdom of God in Jesus' eyes is not, for example, the Roman Empire, but the kingdom of Satan, which is overthrown by Jesus' coming. The kingdom of God that Jesus announces is likewise not a social entity in the modern sense of the term, even though it is obvious that the practice of concrete love of neighbor has extremely important social implications. The kingdom of God is universal insofar as all human beings are meant to meet certain conditions and submit to the kingly rule of God. The kingdom of God is brought about by a free act of God (Lk 12:32; 22:29) and is an unmerited gift for which human beings should pray (Mt 6:10); it is a kingdom that they should seek and for which they should hold themselves in

419

readiness (Mt 24:44; 25:10, 13; Lk 12:31). The only conditions required for entering the kingdom of God, conditions that sum up and include all others, are faith and conversion (Mk 1:15); these conditions, which are to be understood as two aspects of a single human attitude that is decisive for salvation, find their expression in the observance of the twofold commandment of love of God and neighbor; this observance determines entrance into the kingdom of God or exclusion from it (Mt 25:31–46). In its full form, the kingdom of God announced by Jesus is a blessing hoped for at the end of time; at the same time, however, it has begun in his person. The kingdom of God at the end of time coincides with eternal life. The form that the kingdom of God will have at the end of time is depicted especially in the images of a meal, that is, a joyous wedding feast (Mt 22:1–14; Lk 14:15–24), and a harvest (Mt 13:30; Mk 4:29). The beatitudes in the Sermon on the Mount are also stamped with the eschatological character of the kingdom of God. The decisive novelty in the preaching of Jesus is his claim that with his coming the kingdom of God has begun and that this reign of God is connected with his person (Lk 11:20; 17:21). With the appearance of Jesus on the scene the future reign of God has already begun in the midst of an old, unredeemed world. The parables of growth (Mk 4:26–29, 30–32) and the parable of the yeast (Mt 13:33) describe the contrast between the hidden littleness of the beginnings and the magnitude of the final rule of God. The parables of the weeds among the wheat (Mt 13:24–30) and of the fishnet (Mt 13:47–50) show that the church cannot be identified with the kingdom of God, despite the degree to which the two are interrelated (see Mt 16:19–20; 18:18). In John the term *kingdom of God* appears only in the conversation with Nicodemus (3:3, 5). In Acts (1:3; 8:12; 14:22; 19:8; 20:25; 28:23) the future kingdom of God is always meant. The term occurs with that same meaning in the authentic Pauline letters (1 Cor 6:9f.; 15:50; Gal 5:21; Eph 5:5). Paul gives a negative description of the conditions for entrance into the kingdom of God when he lists the vices that are obstacles to unity (1 Cor 6:9; Gal 5:21; Eph 5:5). A different side of the idea of the kingdom of God is found in the Pastoral Letters, where it is identified with the reign of Christ, inasmuch as salvation is mediated through Christ (2 Tm 4:1, 18; see 2 Pt 1:11). A similar concept is found in Revelation when it says that dominion over the world belongs to our Lord and his anointed (11:15).

(2) *History of Theology.* In the course of church history the biblical statements about the kingdom of God have been understood in very different ways and have even been radically misinterpreted, depending on the political situation and on current philosophical ideas. In the beginning, under the influence of the still urgent expectation of an imminent end, the church prays that it may be gathered from the four winds and brought home into the kingdom of God (*Did.* 10:5f.). Origen is convinced that Christ is, in himself, the kingly rule of God (*autobasileia*). The kingdom of God is understood as an interior, spiritual reality in this world, since the kingdom of God exists wherever justice, wisdom, truth, and the other virtues are present. According to Augustine, the church, as

the historical form of the thousand-year reign, is the kingdom of Christ or the kingdom of heaven, but it is also still in conflict and waiting for its completion. The (true) members of the church are already in the kingdom of God; when the time of fulfillment comes, they will form *the* kingdom of God. The political theology at work in the Constantinian revolution and then in the Byzantine Empire understands the imperial reign of peace to be the image and presence of the kingdom of God, to the extent that the monarchy of the emperor represents the monarchy of God. In like manner, Charlemagne understands his rule to be a participation in the kingship of God and Christ. In the Middle Ages, Augustine's ideas are passed on in a, to some extent, coarsened form, when it is claimed that the members of the church are identical with the members of the perfected kingdom of God. During this period an apocalyptic expectation of the kingdom of God is to be seen in the revolutionary criticism of state and church among the Spirituals; this criticism finds particularly effective expression in Joachim of Fiore. In the nineteenth century the idea of the kingdom of God acquires special importance in the Catholic school of Tübingen. According to J. S. Drey, the kingdom of God is "the central idea of Christianity." It has become a reality in Christ and will bring history to its fulfillment in an act of unmerited grace. J. B. Hirscher depicts Christian morality as a "doctrine of the realization of the divine rule in humankind."

(3) *Church Teaching.* There has been no proper magisterial pronouncement of the church on the biblical concept of the kingdom of God.

(4) *Ecumenical Perspectives.* M. Luther held a doctrine of two kingdoms. The worldly kingdom is characterized by law; the essentially invisible rule of God consists in justification by faith in the word of God. While P. Melanchthon identified the kingdom of God and the true church, J. Calvin saw the kingdom of God as coming into existence through a theocracy embracing church and state.

(5) *Systematic Reflections.* The idea of the kingdom of God appears in a completely secularized form in the politico-scientific utopias and philosophical systems of Marxism and socialism. As in biblical eschatology, the future plays the decisive role, but the future here does not come from divine grace and power but is the achievement exclusively of human beings, who are to create an ideal world by their transformative praxis. In "political theology" and the various forms of "liberation theology" an effort is made to respond to these expectations of the future in the spirit of revelation.

See also CHILIASM; CHURCH; EXPECTATION OF AN IMMINENT END; HEAVEN.

Bibliography
Pannenberg, Wolfhart. *Theology and the Kingdom of God.* Philadelphia: Westminster, 1969.
Perrin, Norman. *Jesus and the Language of the Kingdom.* Philadelphia: Fortress, 1976.
Schelkle, Karl Hermann. *Theology of the New Testament.* Collegeville, Minn.: Liturgical Press, 1971.
Schnackenberg, Rudolf. *God's Rule and Kingdom.* 2d ed. New York: Herder, 1968.

JOSEF FINKENZELLER

L l

Laity. As understood in theology, the laity are Christians who belong to the church, the people of God (Greek: *laos theou*), but are not ordained spiritual ministers.

(1) *Biblical Background.* The dignity of the laity is based on their membership in the people of God (1 Pt 2:7–10); for this reason, they can also be described as the faithful, the saints, or the called.

(2) *History of Theology.* The high esteem of the New Testament for the laity was lost as the ecclesial ministries became ever more important and as religious life seemed to offer the way to a more perfect Christianity. The twentieth century brought a renewed reflection on the importance of the laity for the church.

(3) *Church Teaching.* This reflection found expression in Vatican II (*LG,* chap. 4): the "secular character of the laity" is said to be their specifying note.

(4) *Ecumenical Perspectives.* The Reformers opposed the excessive emphasis on the clerical and religious states, both of which they rejected, and emphasized instead the rights that all Christians have due to their baptism.

(5) *Systematic Reflections.* There is no universal spirituality either of the clergy or of the laity. Rather, the basic attitude of love and the practice of the so-called evangelical counsels (poverty, chastity, obedience) find particular expression according to the life situation and special call of individual Christians. Not least for ecumenical reasons Catholic theology has the task of giving careful consideration to the rights and importance of the laity.

See also MONASTICISM/RELIGIOUS LIFE; PEOPLE OF GOD; PRIEST; PRIESTHOOD OF THE FAITHFUL.

Bibliography
Balthasar, Hans Urs von. *Church and World.* New York: Herder and Herder, 1967.
Congar, Yves. *Lay People in the Church.* Westminster, Md.: Newman, 1957.
Newman, John Henry. *On Consulting the Faithful in Matters of Doctrine.* Kansas City: Sheed and Ward, 1985.
Power, David N. *Gifts That Differ: Lay Ministries Established and Unestablished.* New York: Pueblo, 1980.

WERNER LÖSER

Language. Language *in the most universal sense* is the use of constant signs (phonetic sounds, gestures) in order to communicate or the store of such signs. Language in this sense also exists with animals. *Human* language is the system of signs — the foundation of every culture — that serves the meaningful expression of thoughts, of decisions of the will, and of feelings. This is true, above all, for phonetic language. The sequences of sounds (words), which in themselves are polyvalent, receive their concrete meaning only in context. This fact reflects the openness of the human person to go beyond what is given in the senses. This is why language is also able to express what as such exceeds the human power of comprehension and expression: God.

(1) *Biblical Background.* The understanding of language and of word that Scripture presents generally still evidences the unity rooted in the mythical experience of reality between the wording and the thing or event or person. In the word the reality is present. Its potency is shared by the word or by its name (as in a blessing or curse). In the proclamations of the prophets and in the theology of the covenant, the word becomes the medium of Yahweh's electing and judging activity toward Israel and, ultimately, for the creation of the world (Genesis 1). In the New Testament also, the lifework and preaching of Jesus are summarized simply as God's salvific word in which all of God's words to Israel have found their fulfillment (Heb 1:2; 2 Cor 1:19). The language that announces this word of God therefore is not merely the human word, but rather a word that is full of the Spirit and the power of God (1 Thes 1:5; Rom 1:16).

(2) *History of Theology.* As a result of the inculturation of the gospel in Hellenism, the theological meaning of language and of the word changed. From then on, priority was given to the perception of the visible form (image) and the spiritual contemplation of God's eternal plan for salvation. What was now decisive was the visible appearance (epiphany) of salvation, which language pointed toward in the teaching on salvation (see already Ti 2:11, 15). In the theology of both the East and the West this lead to a greater estimation of the visible signs of salvation. To language was attributed a referential and a teaching function.

(3) *Church Teaching.* Even Vatican II understands language and word as something added to the actual events of salvation: as confirmation, teaching, and illumination (*DV* 2).

(4) *Ecumenical Perspectives.* It is the lasting contribution of M. Luther that he rediscovered the irreplaceable significance of language for the announcing of forgiveness and the promise of salvation. Since the beginning of the twentieth century, Protestant theologians have taken up and built upon his theology of the word (e.g., K. Barth, F. Gogarten, G. Ebeling). But Catholic theologians also refer back to him today (see *UR* 21).

(5) *Systematic Reflections.* For the Christian faith language is of essential importance because this faith refers to unique historical events that only through their retelling (in narration and proclamation) can become the foundation of a community of faith. Through scientific research on language, which has had a tremendous upsurge in the twentieth century, new methodological approaches and concrete insights have opened up for theology. Above all the differentiation of language according to its different functions (e.g., informative vs. performative language) has gained importance. A typical example of performative language is the issuing of a command. It does not aim at transmitting information but rather at evoking an effect (speech act). The gospel certainly has to be understood as performative language. It aims at moving the human person

to convert to a life of faith, hope, and love. But it seeks to achieve this through "information" on the historical events in which God's irrevocable, liberating, and fulfilling love for human persons has been experienced.

See also DISCOURSE ABOUT GOD; HERMENEUTICS; REVELATION; THEOLOGY; WORD AND SACRAMENT.

Bibliography
Biderman, Shlomo, and Ben Ami Scharfstein, eds. *Interpretation in Religion*. New York: Brill, 1992.
Ferré, Frederick. *Language, Logic and God*. New York: Harper, 1961.
Herder, Johann Gottfried. *Against Pure Reason: Writings on Religion, Language, and History*. Minneapolis: Fortress, 1993.
Searle, John. *Speech Acts: An Essay in the Philosophy of Language*. New York: Cambridge University Press, 1970.

GEORG LANGEMEYER

Law and Gospel. *Law and gospel* is the Reformation's phrase for the Catholic theme of *law and grace*. It deals with the correct distinction and interrelationship of these two realities of salvation-history. In the law, the salvific will of God is manifested by what is required of human beings. In the gospel, salvation is made available as the unconditional gift of God's love, to which humans respond by acceptance and by bearing fruit.

(1) *Biblical Background.* In the Old Testament, law plays a central role; the gospel is proclaimed as promise. The New Testament revolves around Jesus Christ. From this starting point, the question is posed of the relationship of Jesus Christ to law. In the postexilic view, law, that is, *Torah* (Greek: *nomos*), includes the whole giving of the law to the people of Israel, that is, the ethical, legal, and liturgical writings of the Pentateuch. These behavioral rules are regarded as the immediate revelation of the will of God. The pathway to salvation is obedience to God's directives regarding our actions (see Psalms 1; 19; 37; 119). For the new covenant of the end-time, Jeremiah promises a law written in the heart (31:31–34). In Second and Third Isaiah the notion of gospel makes its appearance as the joyous message of eschatological salvation (Is 40:9; 52:7; 60:6; 61:1). In the New Testament, according to the Synoptics, Jesus dissolves the law by means of his gospel of the KINGDOM OF GOD, insofar as he fulfills it (Mt 5:17–19; Lk 16:16f.). Using the gospel as a criterion, Jesus sharply criticizes the Jewish understanding of the law of his time. In the Sermon on the Mount, he does this by presenting antitheses (Mt 5:31, 33, 38, 43) to the demands of the law or by increasing the depth of its demands (Mt 5:21, 27); elsewhere in his preaching, he does this by freeing people from or deepening the interpretation of Sabbath rest, the laws of ritual purity (Mk 7:1–23), and the temple cult (Mk 11:15–17). Jesus reduces the multitude of the law's prescriptions to a common denominator: the twofold commandment of love (Mt 22:35–40). In Paul the relationship between law and gospel becomes an explicit problem. In Galatians he sees a sharp opposition between law and

gospel. Jesus Christ brought us freedom from the curse of the law (3:10–14), which was meaningful only as a taskmaster preparing for Jesus Christ (3:24f.). Behind this view is Paul's missionary claim that in receiving the gospel the Gentiles are free from circumcision as prescribed by the law (2:2–5). In Romans, Paul sees a dialectical relationship between law and gospel. The law is holy and good (7:12, 16), yet in fact it stands under the reign of sin and is incapable of justifying us before God (3:9–20). Jesus Christ, who is "the end of the law" (10:4), overcomes the justification of the law through justification by faith (10:5f.). Whoever believes in him with a whole heart "is justified and saved" (10:10). Jesus Christ brings us freedom from the law (8:2), and by his Spirit he grants us the freedom of children of God (8:14–16). Christologically, Paul introduces a positive use of the notion of law; that is, he speaks of "the law of the Spirit and of life in Christ Jesus" (8:2) or, briefly, "the law of Christ" (Gal 6:2; 1 Cor 9:21). In practical terms, for Paul, love — springing from faith — is the "fulfillment of the law" (Rom 13:8–10).

(2) *History of Theology.* In the history of dogma until the Reformation, law was always a universal category in its relationship with gospel; that is, the gospel was subordinate to or coordinated with the law. When the Apostolic Fathers used the expression "new law of our Lord Jesus Christ" (*Barn.* 2:6), they were referring to the Christian way of salvation. In opposition to this, Marcion (d. ca. 160) rejected the law and pieced together a New Testament gospel purified of all law. The first person to take a position against this requirement of a lawless Christianity was Justin (d. 165). For him, the new law of Christ reassumed all the natural ethical commandments of the old law, although the Old Testament ritual commandments had been surpassed (*Dial.* 11, 18–23, 46). Irenaeus (d. ca. 202) strengthened this line of argument: Jesus Christ brings about a deepening and fulfillment of the natural law. The twofold command of love, which Jesus made central, was already rooted in the old law (*Adv. haer.* 4.9–17). The groundwork for the basic position of the Greek Fathers of the third and fourth centuries was laid by Clement of Alexandria (d. 215): the same God is author of the law and the gospel (*Strom.* 1.174.3). The law has a graced function in the course of God's historical pedagogy of salvation; that is, the law of Moses is a kind of preschool for the giving of the law of Christ (*Paed.* 3.94.1; *Strom.* 7.86.3). On the basis of the ideal of an education in salvation, the Greek Fathers saw no essential difference, only a difference in degree, between the grace of the law and the grace of Christ. Among the Latin Fathers of the third and fourth centuries, Tertullian's manner of understanding became authoritative. He distinguished three stages of the law: the *law of nature*, which is written in the human heart from the beginning; the *law of Moses*, which was only valid for a time; and the *new law of Jesus Christ,* the fulfillment of the law that is valid for all peoples (*Adv. Iud.* 2–6; *Adv. Marc.* 2.4–7; 4.1–12). Tertullian described the gospel as "our law in the proper sense" (*De mono.* 8). In the Pelagian controversy, Augustine — who grouped the two terms, law and grace — arrived at a specific view of the relationship between the law and the

gospel. He proposed a schema of four successive stages in salvation: the period before the law (the time of Adam); the period under the law (the time of Moses); the period under grace and the fullness of freedom (the time of Jesus Christ); and the eschatological time of fulfillment (*Euch.* 31.118). Concretely this means "the law was given so that grace would be sought; grace is given so that the law will be fulfilled" (*De spir. et litt.* 34). Thomas Aquinas establishes for Scholasticism the classical relationship of grace and law: the new law written in the heart is the grace of the Holy Spirit, which is conferred by faith in Christ (*STh* 1–2, q. 106, a. 1). The old and new laws are related to each other as the imperfect to the perfect (*STh* 1–2, q. 107, a. 1 ad 2).

(3) *Church Teaching.* Trent, which treated the problematic of law and gospel in response to the Reformation, stated: neither the natural nor the Mosaic law has the power to justify (DS 1521). The promises in the time before and under the law are fulfilled in the gracious, salvific work of Jesus Christ (DS 1522). However, once justified, a person is still obliged and, by grace, has the capacity to observe the commandments (DS 1536, 1568). Thus no one should claim that the gospel is the pure and unconditional promise of eternal life that achieves fulfillment apart from observance of the commandments (DS 1570). Furthermore, it must be maintained that Jesus Christ is not only the redeemer but also a law-giver (DS 1571).

(4) *Ecumenical Perspectives.* Once he began his effort to reform the church, M. Luther came to regard the distinction between law and grace as "the greatest genius of Christendom" (*WA* 36:9). Law and grace are "two forms of the word or of preaching" (*WA* 10/1/2:155), in other words, two words of God found both in the Old Testament and in the New Testament. On the one hand, Luther wants the pure gospel (see thesis 62 on indulgences) rather than the written-down legalization of faith of the papal church. On the other hand, he fights for the lasting meaning of the law, which among the Reformers was controversial because of the antinomianism of Agricola. According to Luther the one law has a double use (see *WA* 40/1:519–20): the civil use, which controls political life in the framework of the ten commandments (*usus civilis seu politicus*), and the theological use, which leads human beings to their sinfulness and therefore their dependence on the grace of God in Jesus Christ (*usus theologicus seu elenchticus*). The relationship between law and gospel should be determined in analogy to the christological formula "uncommingled and undivided." In other words, there is a dialectical simultaneity between law and gospel, as in the formula "simultaneously justified and sinner." However, the gospel envelops everything because, faced with the accusations of sin, it brings about gratuitous justification. "The law reveals sins; the gospel reveals grace" (*CR* 21.139). This is how P. Melanchthon succinctly formulates Luther's basic position. And he supplements it by the doctrine of the *third use* of the law, which is to be understood as the commandments' warning in and under the gospel (*CF* 21.405f.). J. Calvin coordinates law and gospel as two steps in the grace of God within salvation-history, the first of which points to the saving

work of Jesus Christ (*OS* 3.398–403). In accord with Melanchthon he speaks of a threefold use or office of law, where the third use, which includes the sanctification of believers, is the main function of the law (*OS* 3.332–40). After the Reformation, the doctrine of law and gospel did not become an essential part of Evangelical theology. With the onset of Lutheran and Reformed Orthodoxy, Luther's evaluation and view of the distinction between law and gospel gradually became meaningless. Only in the beginning of the twentieth century, with the revival of interest in Luther, did the problem once again return to the center of Lutheran theology. This was brought about especially by the controversy begun by K. Barth, who in his *Gospel and Law* (1935) presents the exact reversal of the previous order. According to Barth, the gospel has unconditional priority, for the law is in the gospel, from the gospel, and oriented to the gospel. The law is the necessary form, the content of which is grace. Reacting vigorously against this position, the Lutherans W. Elert and his school emphasize once again the dialectical opposition of the law and the gospel. The law and the gospel are two different words of God: the function of the law is to accuse, whereas the function of the gospel is to rescue us by grace. In present ecumenical discussions concerning the problem of the law and the gospel, the divisions cut across the various denominations. Since Barth and his school in the Reformed Church continue to maintain the inclusive unity of the law within the priority of the gospel, and since most Lutheran systematic theologians defend the dialectical opposition of the law and the gospel, the theme represents a major controversy between the two Evangelical denominations. Catholic ecumenists recognize that from the Catholic viewpoint Luther's view contains nothing capable of dividing the churches, but is rather a beneficial new theme in the history of theology. On the other hand, the majority opinion of Catholic dogmatics follows the basic position of Barth.

(5) *Systematic Reflections.* The problem with regard to the law and the gospel is to define their mutual boundaries and their corelationship. This relationship must receive its orientation from the mainstream of salvation-history in the Old and New Testaments. In the perspective of salvation-history, these two independent historical realities belong together as two phases of a single history, as two expressions of the one grace and love of God, and as historically conditioned paths of salvation of the one human race. Where is the difference and where is the unity of the law and the gospel? The *difference* has its deepest basis in the twofold historical reality of God's love. The love of God is a gift, and it challenges us. In Old Testament law, the will of God as challenging is predominant; in New Testament gospel, the will of God as gracious is foremost. Thus the characteristics of the law, the core of which is the Decalogue, are: the imperative of salvation, instruction, claim, accusation, legal threats, judgment, restriction (obligation), affliction, intimidation. On the other hand, the characteristics of the gospel, the core of which is the nearness of God's reign in the salvific work of Jesus Christ, are: the indicative of salvation, promise, exhortation, acquittal, grace, forgiveness, liberation (freedom), trust, confidence. The

UNITY AND DIFFERENCE OF LAW AND GOSPEL

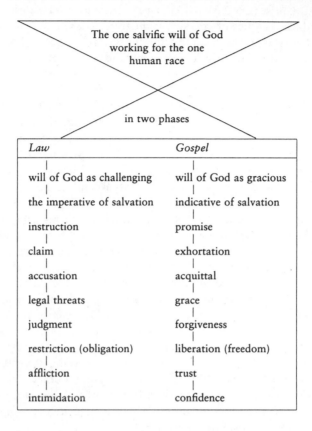

The one salvific will of God
working for the one
human race

in two phases

Law	Gospel
will of God as challenging	will of God as gracious
the imperative of salvation	indicative of salvation
instruction	promise
claim	exhortation
accusation	acquittal
legal threats	grace
judgment	forgiveness
restriction (obligation)	liberation (freedom)
affliction	trust
intimidation	confidence

unity of the law and the gospel is threefold. The law and the gospel have the same author: the one God, the one love of God, and the one salvific will of God at work. Furthermore, the law and the gospel are addressed to the same people: namely, the one human race. Finally, the law and the gospel have the same goal: their intention is the salvation of humankind (see the table "Unity and Difference of Law and Gospel"). How can the tension-filled relationship of the law and the gospel be defined more exactly? We can speak of an inclusive and Christocentric unity. For the most part we are dealing with an *inclusive* unity of the law and the gospel, the law within the gospel. The gospel as an explicit promise of God's grace also embraces the law, which presents only an implicit expression of grace. In the *one* salvific will of God, the law and its demands are subordinate to the gospel and its promise. This inclusion of the law within the gospel also integrates what is demanded by the law, for along with the gift of the gospel comes a task: we must accept this gift interiorly and allow it to bear fruit exteriorly. From the viewpoint of salvation-history there is a *Christocentric* unity with regard to the mutual relationship between the law and the gospel. By means of the gospel, Jesus Christ brings about the end of the law, that is, its fulfillment. Fulfillment, however, means that the law is the historical antecedent of the gospel. On the other hand, the gospel is the synthesis of the law. As synthesis it culminates a three-part development: historically deficient, superseded applications of the law must be set aside; the heart of the law, the Decalogue, remains; the law's lasting demands are elevated to the level of love in which the law is fulfilled.

1. HISTORICAL DEVELOPMENT OF THE COORDINATION

Early church theology	*evangelium* sub *lege*
Marcion	*evangelium* contra *legem*
Greek and Latin Fathers, 3rd–4th centuries	*evangelium* sub *lege*
Augustine	*gratia* in relatione ad *legem*
Thomas Aquinas	*lex* ut forma *gratiae lex nova*
Luther	*simul evangelium et lex* (*simul iustus et peccator*)
Calvin	*lex* in et sub *evangelio*
Barth	*lex* ut forma *evangelii*

2. INCLUSIVE UNITY OF THE LAW IN THE GOSPEL
Gospel as the Fulfillment of the Law

	Law	*Evangelium*
historical protological eschatological	demand preparation	promise fulfillment
ontic	incorporated subordinate serving	inclusive predominant governing
ethical	individual commands	unified twofold commandment of love

3. DIFFERENTIATING LAW AND GOSPEL

Law	Gospel
work of calculating	unconditional grace
merits of salvation as self-justification	salvation as justification by God
the old person	the new person
pride presumption	humility modesty
constraint	freedom

4. MEANING OF THE LAW–GOSPEL DISTINCTION

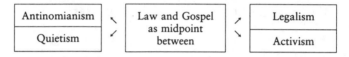

Antinomianism		Law and Gospel as midpoint between		Legalism
Quietism				Activism

5. THE TEACHING OF USE (*USUS*) OF THE LAW IN EVANGELICAL THEOLOGY

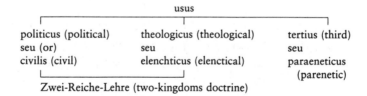

usus

politicus (political)   theologicus (theological)   tertius (third)
seu (or)   seu   seu
civilis (civil)   elenchticus (elenctical)   paraeneticus
                                                                  (parenetic)

Zwei-Reiche-Lehre (two-kingdoms doctrine)

See also GRACE; LOVE OF GOD.

Bibliography
Barth, Karl. *God, Grace, and Gospel*. Edinburgh: Oliver and Boyd, 1959.
Ebeling, Gerhard. "Reflexions on the Doctrine of the Law." In *Word and Faith*, 247–81. London: SCM, 1963.
Elert, Werner. *Law and Gospel*. Philadelphia: Fortress, 1967.
Forde, Gerhard O. *The Law–Gospel Debate: An Interpretation of Its Historical Development*. Minneapolis: Augsburg, 1968.

GEORG KRAUS

Liberation. *See* REDEMPTION AND LIBERATION.

Life of Jesus Research. In a broad sense, life of Jesus research refers to studies that are based on the New Testament sources (and their context) and that present the life of Jesus or a theology of the life of Jesus. This would include all prescientific or unscientific (as judged from today's scientific viewpoint) presentations of Jesus Christ. In a narrower sense, life of Jesus research is historical-critical study of Jesus as developed and used by the fourfold method of historical-critical exegesis.

(1) *Biblical Background.* The New Testament — especially the four Gospels — refers back to Jesus' pre-Easter life, but its interest is theological rather than biographical.

(2) *History of Theology.* In a wider sense there has always been research on the life of Jesus. We could mention Augustine's *De consensu evangelistarum* (ca. 400), the *Meditationes vitae Christi* (thirteenth/fourteenth centuries), Ludolf of Saxony's *Vita Christi* (1470), or R. Guardini's *The Lord* (1937). The purpose of life of Jesus research, carried out in the spirit of the Enlightenment and of rationalism, was to enlist the "Jesus of history in the struggle against dogma" (A. Schweitzer, *Geschichte der Leben-Jesu-Forschung,* 2d ed. [Tübingen, 1913], 4), as we see in Reimarus (d. 1768) or D. F. Strauss (d. 1874), but also to provide a new passageway to Christian faith by means of historical interpretation, as we see in F. Schleiermacher (d. 1834), who was one of the first to give academic lectures on the life of Jesus (the lectures were given between 1819 and 1832). The aporias of liberal research on the historical life of Jesus in the nineteenth century were revealed by A. Schweitzer (d. 1965) in his *Quest for the Historical Jesus.* He points out that "every successive period of theology found its own thoughts in Jesus;...each researcher created him according to his own personality." Thus this type of research failed to reach its goal of producing a decisive version of the life of Jesus: instead, the church's dogma was replaced by the spirit of the times, that is, the worldview or preunderstanding of each researcher. This also applies to Schweitzer's own presentation of Jesus and to other recent authors. The conclusion: a life of Jesus cannot be written. Thus exclusivist kerygmatic theologians (R. Bultmann and his disciples) held that the quest for the historical Jesus was theologically unviable. Nevertheless, since about 1950, there has been a "new quest," a return to the historical Jesus — or the beginning of new research on Jesus — and its concerns are shared by Catholic exegetes (F. Mussner, R. Pesch, R. Schnackenburg, H. Schürmann, W. Trilling, A. Vögtle, and others).

(3) *Church Teaching.* Only with great hesitation has the magisterium become involved in the modern debate, namely, whenever it perceived there was danger to the faith. Thus despite Leo XIII's guarded positive evaluation of modern biblical scholarship in the encyclical *Providentissimus Deus* (1893 [DS 3280–94]), Pius X reacted negatively and condemned it during the so-called modernist crisis in the decretal *Lamentabili* (1907 [DS 3427–38]) and in his

OVERVIEW OF THE QUEST FOR THE HISTORICAL JESUS
(according to F. J. Schierse, *Christologie* [Düsseldorf, 1979], 27f.)

Spirit of the times/worldview	Jesus' intentions
Rationalism	Teach virtue and natural religion
Idealism (D. F. Strauss)	Be the point of coalescence of higher myths, eternal truths
Liberalism (A. von Harnack)	Proclaim pure belief in God the Father and a sublime morality
Eschatological historicism (A. Schweitzer)	Announce the imminent end of the world and the new age (interim ethics)
Modern Judaism	Give liberal explanation of the law and true Jewish piety
Humanism (R. Eisler)	Offer liberation from the Roman yoke
Existential theology (R. Bultmann)	Call humans to a decision for "authenticity"

encyclical *Pascendi* (1907 [DS 3475–3500]). In the encyclical *Divino afflante Spiritu* (1943), Pius XII recommends research on the literal sense of Sacred Scripture and its literary forms (DS 3826–30). Finally, the instruction *Sancta Mater Ecclesia* (1964) of the Pontifical Biblical Commission approves the use of recent exegetical methods for research on the life of Jesus. Vatican II confirms this position (*DV* 19). The document "Bible and Christology" (1984) of the Pontifical Biblical Commission treats life of Jesus research under various methodologies and summarizes its results (see 2.2.1).

(4) *Ecumenical Perspectives.* In present research on Jesus, ecumenical cooperation is presupposed. Different positions regarding factual matters are rarely determined by confessional difference. Nevertheless, in Catholic tradition and Catholic dogmatics, the christological dogma and teachings connected with it (the uniqueness of Jesus' claim, his knowledge about the salvific meaning of his death, the virginity of Mary, etc.) are not regarded indifferently.

(5) *Systematic Reflections.* It must be emphasized here that both liberal nineteenth-century research on the life of Jesus and recent research on Jesus have produced an abundance of positive results, and they have become an essential part of today's scientific exegesis. In the end, it has become clear that there is no access to the historical Jesus except through the New Testament Scriptures. However, these Scriptures are not neutral historical sources but faith witnesses to the earthly Jesus who is the resurrected Christ. Thus in any research on the life of Jesus we must take into account the unresolvable tension and polarity between "history" and "faith." Belief in Christ without reference to the history of Jesus would imply a failure to distinguish such belief from gnosis, mythology, and ideology. Yet any isolated presentation of the his-

torical Jesus remains one-sided and contradicts the New Testament, not only because God legitimated the history of Jesus (his message, praxis, and destiny) through the resurrection, but also because from that time on Jesus (his person and his work) is present in the community in a new way (through the Holy Spirit) and is something qualitatively new. The resurrection alone definitively reveals *who* Jesus *was* and *is*. It should be emphasized that an appeal to the historical Jesus is theologically meaningful, for faith in Christ remains forever linked to the historical reality of Jesus and has, therefore, a fundamental interest in the earthly Jesus. In dogmatics the more recent research on Jesus led to a new consciousness of the basis of Christology and soteriology. Only within the framework given by the New Testament is it possible to develop a "Christology of the mutual correspondence between the earthly Jesus and the resurrected, exalted Christ," where the indispensable function of the historical problematic, as well as the constitutive meaning of the resurrection for such a development, can be determined. In the new research on Jesus, the central problem is to determine the relationship between the pre-Easter history of Jesus and the post-Easter kerygma, so that, aided by our reference to the historical Jesus, we might clarify the reception of the Jesus movement (or its transformation) within the kerygma or the faith tradition. Here the deeper understanding of the pre-Easter Jesus (and early Christian preaching) is decisively dependent on faith that this Jesus is the Christ. It remains to be seen whether the present tools for research on Jesus can be responsibly extended or whether they merely lead to an impasse or to a problematic alternative to new scientific taboos. Concretely we could consider R. Pesch's judgment (which diverges from the consensus of researchers) concerning the tradition of the Lord's Supper and Jesus' destiny; or the attempt by R. and J. Feneberg — which has been disputed by fellow scholars — to write not only a book on Jesus but, by using present research on Jesus, a life of Jesus; or, finally, new questions concerning the "psychology" of Jesus, as seen in H. Schürmann's work on Jesus' *understanding* of death.

See also CHRISTOLOGY; HISTORICAL JESUS; HISTORY/HISTORICITY; SOTERI-OLOGY.

Bibliography
Aulèn, Gustaf. *Jesus in Contemporary Historical Research.* Philadelphia: Fortress, 1976.
Borg, Marcus J. *Meeting Jesus again for the First Time: The Historical Jesus and the Heart of Contemporary Faith.* San Francisco: Harper, 1994.
Carlson, Jeffrey, and Robert A. Ludwig. *Jesus and Faith: A Conversation on the Work of John Dominic Crossan.* Maryknoll, N.Y.: Orbis Books, 1994.
Charlesworth, James H. *Jesus within Judaism.* New York: Doubleday, 1988.
Meier, John P. *A Marginal Jew: Rethinking the Historical Jesus.* New York: Doubleday, 1991.
Schweitzer, Albert. *The Quest of the Historical Jesus.* New York: Macmillan, 1968.
See also the bibliography under HISTORICAL JESUS.

LOTHAR ULLRICH

Limbo. By limbo (Latin: *limbus* = edge, border, ornamental fringe) is meant the place or state of the dead who are not in HEAVEN or HELL or PURGATORY. The

434

limbo of the Fathers (*limbus patrum*) was the place or state of the just who died before Christ but could not reach the beatitude of heaven before his descent among the dead and his ascension. The limbo of children, which alone became important in Christian tradition, is the place or state of infants or of adults who never reached the use of reason and who, once the gospel had been sufficiently promulgated, did not receive the sacrament of baptism and the incorporation into the church that baptism brings.

(1) *Biblical Background.* Sacred Scripture says nothing about a limbo for children.

(2) *History of Theology.* The earliest Christian tradition says nothing explicit about the lot of the unbaptized, but the limbo of children comes to play a very important role in the resistance to Pelagianism. In opposition to the doctrine that baptism is indeed necessary for the attainment of supernatural beatitude (the kingdom of heaven) but not for the attainment of a natural happiness (eternal life), Augustine, appealing to the testimony of Scripture, emphasizes that both baptism and the resultant membership in the church constitute the necessary and the sole way to salvation. The Scriptures and the faith of the church (Augustine argues) know nothing of a natural happiness; therefore, children who die unbaptized go to hell, although they suffer only the mildest possible punishment there. The Scholastic theologians attempt to moderate Augustine's rigorism by postulating for unbaptized children a limbo in which they enjoy a natural happiness; limbo thus differs from hell (in limbo there is exclusion from the vision of God but no sensible torments). Late Scholasticism produces various theories regarding the possibility of justification for the unborn by a divine privilege (W. Durandus, J. Gerson). G. Biel takes the position that a nonsacramental justification comes into play whenever water baptism is impossible. Cardinal Cajetan proposes a substitute for infant baptism, which he explains as a kind of baptism of desire on the part of the parents. Because of the disapproving attitude of the Council of Trent, this doctrine was generally rejected in the post-Tridentine period. In the modern period, H. Klee suggests that God infuses a spiritual light by which children are able to make a personal choice (illumination theory). H. Schell is of the opinion that Christ can justify these children through a kind of quasi-sacrament.

(3) *Church Teaching.* The ecclesial magisterium has never taken an explicit position on the limbo of children, although according to a decree of Pius VI (1794) the concept may not be called a Pelagian fairy tale (DS 2626).

(4) *Ecumenical Perspectives.* The limbo of children plays no part in the ecumenical dialogue.

(5) *Systematic Reflections.* In contemporary theology the doctrine of limbo is controversial. Some theologians regard it as binding because it appears in ecclesial tradition, especially in various catechisms. Most theologians of our time, however, reject the idea of limbo because, on the one hand, it is difficult to reconcile with the universal salvific will of God and, on the other, both the Scriptures and the medieval doctrinal pronouncements of the church acknowl-

edge only heaven and hell as definitive forms of salvation or damnation after a possible period of purification.

See also BAPTISM; NECESSITY OF THE CHURCH FOR SALVATION; UNIVERSAL SALVIFIC WILL OF GOD.

Bibliography
Dyer, George L. *Limbo: Unsettled Questions.* New York: Sheed and Ward, 1964.
Hill, Paul J. *The Existence of a Children's Limbo according to Post-Tridentine Theologians.* Shelby, Ohio: Sacred Heart Fathers, 1962.

JOSEF FINKENZELLER

Local Church. By local church, or particular church (Latin: *ecclesia particularis*), is meant an individual church belonging to a group of local churches or an ecclesial region; such a church is usually a see under the governance of a bishop. To be distinguished from it is a local community, which is the embodiment of the local or particular church in a more or less narrowly circumscribed place (usually a parish).

(1) *Biblical Background.* According to the New Testament the one church of Christ manifests itself in local churches (e.g., 1 Cor 1:2: "The church of God which is in Corinth").

(2) *History of Theology.* In the first few centuries the church existed as a communion of churches (*communio ecclesiarum*), within which groups of local churches (patriarchates) were soon formed that had as their center dominant episcopal sees (Rome, Constantinople, Alexandria, Antioch, Jerusalem). After the separation from the East, where the local church principle continued to be followed without change, the West saw an ever-increasing emphasis on the papal power at its center. The structural significance of the local churches was pushed into the background.

(3) *Church Teaching.* Vatican II strove to establish a balance, based on data from the Bible and the early church, between the universal church and the local churches by depicting the church as a communion in and of the local churches (*LG* 23, 27; *CD* 11). The groupings of local churches are seen as institutions whose importance is clear from historical experience. The Code of Canon Law (cans. 368f.) adopts the teaching of the council; canons 431–59 recognize ecclesial provinces, particular councils, and episcopal conferences as groupings of local churches and ecclesial regions.

(4) *Ecumenical Perspectives.* The East has explicitly preserved the local church principle; the churches of the Reformation have preserved it in their organization.

(5) *Systematic Reflections.* Since the church is today a world church that in fact extends to all parts of the earth and all cultures, the local church principle is of the greatest importance in achieving a balance between the UNITY OF THE CHURCH and the CATHOLICITY OF THE CHURCH; it must therefore be applied and extended.

See also BISHOP; CHURCH; COLLEGIALITY; COMMUNITY (GROUP).

Bibliography

Curran, Charles E., and George J. Dyer, eds. *Shared Responsibility in the Local Church.* Chicago: Chicago Studies, 1970.

Harakas, Stanley. "The Local Church: An Eastern Orthodox Perspective." *ER* 29 (1977) 141–53.

Killian, Sebastian J. *Theological Models for the Parish.* Staten Island, N.Y.: Alba, 1977.

Proceedings of the Catholic Theological Society of America 35 (1980). Articles on the local church by P. Granfield, S. Killian, F. Parrella, and B. Prusak.

Schreiter, Robert. *Constructing Local Theologies.* Maryknoll, N.Y.: Orbis Books, 1985.

Torres, Sergio, and John Eagleson, eds. *The Challenge of Basic Christian Communities.* Maryknoll, N.Y.: Orbis Books, 1982.

WERNER LÖSER

Logos. In the faith-language of the church and its theological reflections, the Logos (*verbum:* word) designates the divinity of the second person, the Son of God, whose "becoming flesh" (= becoming a human being) is the basis for the salvation of humankind.

(1) *Biblical Background.* Logos (in the nominative, absolute sense) appears only in the prologue of John (1:1, 14) and refers to the preexistence of the Logos, its personal association with God, and its divinity (1:1, 2a; see 1:18). The Logos is the mediator of creation on the side of God (1:2f., 10) and — as light and life — salvation for humankind (1:4; see 1:16). The central statement, "And the Word was made flesh" (1:14), is — in its acute oppositeness and synthesis — a most profound statement on the mystery of God's act of becoming human. More than any other sentence in the New Testament, it opened up an extensive history of knowledge and reflection on faith (see "the word of life" [1 Jn 1:1] and parallels in Heb 1:1–4; Col 1:15–20). The sources for Logos theology are first of all the Old Testament and its theology of the Word, especially in early wisdom teachings, but also the Greek philosophical notion of Logos, to which there are parallels, even though the Greek Logos is surpassed by John's statement about the incarnation (see 1 Jn 1:1–3) — a statement that was later used to challenge Greek philosophical opposition to the incarnation. John's Logos must be examined against the background of his whole work, where the idea of revelation is determinative: the Word made flesh, the revealer in person, is Jesus of Nazareth (see 1:45). In another context, Rv 19:11–16 presents the rider on a white horse whose name is "The Word of God" (19:13). He may be linked to Jn 1:1–14, but more probably should be linked with the image of Wis 18:15 and with the prophecy of the Son of Man (Daniel 7), which played an important role in early Christian theology and expressed the expectation of the parousia.

(2) *History of Theology.* After a first use of the concept of the Logos by Ignatius of Antioch (*Magn.* 8.2), the apologists (Justin, Athenagoras, Tatian, Theophilus of Antioch) begin using the Logos teaching of the Stoa and Middle Platonism to explain the mystery of Christ in connection with John 1. Irenaeus sees the incarnation of the Logos as the conclusion of a long series of revelations that began at the creation of the world (*Adv. haer.* 3.18.3). Fur-

ther stages of this reception of the Logos doctrine (and its subordinationism), some of which were not wholly above suspicion, are seen in Clement of Alexandria, Origen, Theognostis, Eusebius of Caesarea, and Arius, who brought about the first public crisis for the Logos doctrine when he regarded the Logos as a creature. Nicaea reacted to this by clearly placing the Son on the side of the Father, because of the baptismal profession of faith. Thus the Logos doctrine was received critically (see Eusebius's profession of faith, which mentions the Logos [DS 40]). Two anti-Arians, Marcellus of Ancyra and Athanasius, make full use of the Logos doctrine in their Christology. According to Athanasius, the Logos is the active principle of Christ's humanity; the body of Christ is the *organon* of the Logos; and the death of Christ implies a separation from the Logos. In Cyril of Alexandria, the characteristics of the Logos doctrine are those that were widely accepted in the East but that led to violent struggles in the history of the reception of Chalcedon. However, at the Second Council of Constantinople (553) and the Lateran Synod of 649, because of the important support of Maximus the Confessor, the emphasis is on the person of the Logos made flesh. In the West the Logos doctrine is developed by Tertullian, Hippolytus, and Novatian. Its Christology is determined by the Logos who is mediator of creation, revelation, and salvation. In Scholasticism, Bonaventure presents a comprehensive theology of the Word, and Thomas Aquinas, who synthesizes Cyril's teaching on the Logos and those of Chalcedon, sees the unity of Christ in the personal being of the Word ("De unione Verbi incarnati" [*STh* 3, q. 2–6]).

(3) *Church Teaching.* Many magisterial documents of various types attest to belief in the Word (made flesh), who is the Son (become man). It is found in creeds (DS 40, 45, 852), in the conciliar texts of Ephesus (DS 250–65), and in the canons of Constantinople II (DS 422–37). Roman synods clarify its usage (DS 178 ["verbum, quia deus"], 502f.). Popes use the notion and make contributions to interpreting it in trinitarian and christological discussions: for example, Dionysius of Rome (DS 113–15), Damasus I (DS 144–47), and Leo I (DS 294, 297, 317f.). In modern times, at the Synod of Pistoia, Pius VI took a stance against the overemphasis on *verbum* rather than "Son." In so doing he appeals to the usage of Scripture, to Augustine, and to Thomas (DS 2698). Vatican II, citing classical texts from Scripture (Jn 1:1–8; Heb 1:1f.; 1 Jn 1:2f.), points out the christological dimension of any theology of the Word or of revelation (esp. *DV* 1–4).

(4) *Ecumenical Perspectives.* In the spirit of the Fathers, Orthodox theologians speak of the Word made flesh (W. Lossky). The Evangelical theologians K. Barth and G. Ebeling offer doctrines of the Logos and a theology of the Word based on the modern problematic. For Barth, Christology is a doctrine of revelation. He begins with the incarnation of the Word but emphasizes the resurrection because the Easter message is the revelation of the Word of God. The Word made flesh is the objective possibility of revelation. Ebeling uses the formula "God's Word in person" to distinguish Jesus' humanity, as the place of God's presence, from other modes of God's presence. In his Christology, he

calls Jesus the Word of God, and he bases this on the dogmatic tradition and on historical considerations.

(5) *Systematic Reflections.* In Catholic dogmatics, a Word theology has a different context. L. Scheffczyk's theology of the Word understands theology as a reality created by the Word — that is, by Christ the perfect Word of God to humankind — within salvation-history and the church. Here God's self-actualization through the Word reaches its goal: the personal Word that is God. The German translation of L. Bouyer's Christology was entitled *Das Wort ist der Sohn* (The Word is the Son), for in fact it is a theology of the Word of God pronounced in the Son, the Word made flesh. J. Alfaro's systematic presentation of the doctrine of the offices of Christ spells out how the basis and function of the Word made flesh are to reveal God. In the outline used for the doctrine of the Trinity, which he sees as proceeding from the model of God's self-sharing, K. Rahner discerns a prior outline of Christology and the doctrine of grace, insofar as the Logos/Son and the Spirit are moments of this one act of God's self-sharing.

See also INCARNATION; PREEXISTENCE OF JESUS CHRIST; TRINITY.

Bibliography
Barth, Karl. *Church Dogmatics,* 1/2 and 4. Edinburgh: T and T Clark, 1956–75.
Bouyer, Louis. *The Eternal Son: A Theology of the Word of God and Christology.* Huntington, Ind.: Our Sunday Visitor, 1978.
Brown, Raymond E. *The Gospel according to John.* Vol. 1. Garden City, N.Y.: Doubleday, 1966.
Kuschel, Karl-Josef. *Born before All Time? The Dispute over Christ's Origin.* New York: Crossroad, 1992.
Lee, Bernard J. *Jesus and the Metaphors of God: The Christs of the New Testament.* New York: Paulist, 1993.
Rahner, Karl. *The Trinity.* New York: Herder and Herder, 1970.
Schnackenburg, Rudolf. *The Gospel according to St. John.* New York: Herder and Herder, 1968.
Wong, Joseph H. P. *Logos-Symbol in the Christology of Karl Rahner.* Rome: LAS, 1984.

LOTHAR ULLRICH

Love. Love is a concept basic to theology insofar as it signifies a reality that (most clearly and most profoundly) displays God's essence. It should therefore also be the supreme motive for all human creative action done in faith.

(1) *Biblical Background.* Even though the word itself is not used, the Old Testament makes frequent reference to God's love in the restrained way in which the Old Testament brings home the fact of God's mercifulness. The prophetic writings exhibit a developed theology of love that focused at first on the people of God (e.g., Hos 11:1–9; Jer 31:20). The notion of a love for all creatures also comes to the fore in the Psalms (e.g., Ps 145:9) and especially in the wisdom literature (e.g., Wis 4:10; 7:28). The New Testament then presents the activity of Jesus (especially in his self-surrender on the cross) as the decisive and unsurpassable revelation of God's love. Pauline and deutero-Pauline letters

explicate this mystery in terms of the notions of reconciliation (Rom 5:8–11; 2 Cor 5:18–21), universal peace (Eph 2:14–18; Col 1:19–21), and grace (Rom 5:5). John summarizes the New Testament theology of love in the statement "God is love" (1 Jn 4:8), which can serve as a concise formulation of the biblical message in general. This all-embracing and unfathomable love of God has implications for us: for one thing, our justification is based on the Trinity (Rom 5:1–11; Gal 5:13–26). In addition, we, then, as justified, have the ethical obligation to respond to this love through the twofold unity of love of God and love of one's neighbor. Again, 1 John gives the most concise formulation of these interconnections: "Let us love one another, because love is of God; everyone who loves is begotten by God and knows God. Whoever is without love does not know God"; this is followed by the statement about God that is cited above (1 Jn 4:7f.; see the larger context: 4:1–21).

(2) *History of Theology.* Theology deepens the knowledge of God's love by interpreting that love, from the standpoint of the Christ-event, as the essential event of the processes of trinitarian life (Augustine). For this life consists of a loving, giving, and receiving that then manifests itself in God's outward-directed activity. The consequence for human responsibility, as the early Church Fathers developed against gnosticism, is that love is the real form of knowledge of God (Evagrius Ponticus calls it the "doorway to knowledge" [*Ad. Anat.*; *PG* 40:1221]). John Chrysostom and Augustine add to this a sacramental-ecclesiological perspective: love as the innermost essence of the self-sacrifice of Christ is the spirit of the church as the body of Christ; for a Christian, then, love of God and love of one's neighbor are identical (*De civ. Dei* 10.5). Theologians in the Middle Ages reflect on the relationship between that love and self-love. Thomas Aquinas sees the two as constitutively interlinked. In contrast, others — for example, Bernard of Clairvaux, as the main exponent — stress that true love must lead away from the subject.

(3) *Church Teaching.* Church teaching has not directly addressed the topic of God's love. Rather it has addressed the nature of love as a divine virtue in the justified. The church has taught that justification is inseparable from the sanctifying love of God and that justification is fully realized only through love on the part of the justified (DS 1530f., 1559, 1561, 1657).

(4) *Ecumenical Perspectives.* From an ecumenical standpoint, a theology of love could provide a standard framework and assist in discernment of the common binding faith in regard to the unification of Christians and the unity of the church.

(5) *Systematic Reflections.* The events of revelation point implicitly toward the need to regard love as the basic determinant of all reality — that of God and therefore also that of creatures. The task of theology, then, can only be to express God as one who loves, and thereby to show that love fulfills basic human relations within every sphere of life: the relationship to God, to oneself, to one's fellow humans, and not least (because of present-day ecological problems) also to the world as something created by, and out of, God's love.

In so doing, of course, theology must take account of the fact that, because of God's hiddenness (GOD: ATTRIBUTES OF), this can often be no longer discerned in particular or universal history. Hence, the assertion that God is love easily presents a temptation, and always presents a challenge, to believers. One can accept such an assertion only if one recognizes that this love finds its paradoxical overintensification in the Son's surrender of himself on the cross. As the most baffling "argument" for God's love, it is also the most convincing. Faith can, therefore, fulfill itself in love only when it leads to a shared community of the crucified one. Only such shared life creates the hope that enables the temptation not only to be borne but also to become fruitful. At the same time, crucified love summons humanity to a shared concern for, and shared realization of, God's original plan — still not abandoned despite all sinfulness — to make humans, through love, into children of God and to allow them to enter into the communion of God's triune life (see Eph 1:4). Such an attitude can help to bring it about that love can actually be made thinkable as the innermost bond of all reality. In this lies the core of the Christian mission — for the individual Christian and for Christianity in general.

See also GOD; GRACE; JUSTIFICATION; TRINITY; TRINITY: DOCTRINE OF THE; UNIVERSAL SALVIFIC WILL OF GOD.

Bibliography
Balthasar, Hans Urs von. *Heart of the World.* San Francisco: Ignatius, 1979.
———. *Love Alone.* New York: Herder and Herder, 1969.
Dodds, Michael. *The Unchanging God of Love: A Study of the Teaching of St. Aquinas on Divine Immutability in View of Certain Criticisms of This Doctrine.* Fribourg: Editions Universitaires, 1986.
Dunne, John S. *Reasons of the Heart: A Journey into Solitude and Back Again into the Human Circle.* New York: Macmillan, 1978.

WILHELM BREUNING

Love of God–Love of Neighbor. The words *love of God–love of neighbor* identify concisely the norm of life for Christians. Love means the perfect, wholehearted turning of the human person to God (love of God) and to his or her fellow human beings (love of neighbor). Dogmatic theology has the goal of showing how faith in Jesus Christ is the necessary foundation for this love and of grasping the inner connection between the love of God and the love of neighbor.

(1) *Biblical Background.* The commandment of the love of God and the love of neighbor is already found in the Old Testament (Dt 6:4f.; Lev 19:18). It has here its foundation in the election by Yahweh. The love of neighbor refers therefore above all to the members of one's people, even when they may harbor hostile intentions against one. It is valid, however, also for the stranger who lives in the land of Israel. In the New Testament the commandment to love one's neighbor is put on the same level with the one to love God (Mk 12:31) and is extended to all human persons, or more exactly, to every human person who

becomes one's neighbor (Lk 10:30–37), with a special emphasis also toward one's enemy. For God also "is kind to the ungrateful and the wicked" (Mt 5:43–48; Lk 6:35). The radicalization of the commandment of love has its ground in God's love for humankind that comes to reign through Jesus. Through the love for one's neighbor the law, the will of God, is fulfilled (Rom 13:10). Everyone who loves lives from the love that comes from God (1 Jn 4:7f.). In the New Testament the love toward God is mentioned relatively rarely. God's love for humankind finds its response in the love of neighbor because God's love has been experienced in the neighbor, in the human life of Jesus (Mt 25:45; 1 Jn 4:9–12, 20).

(2) *History of Theology.* Theology, by and large, has overlooked this biblical interconnection between the love of neighbor and the love of God because it started out from the general experience of God and saw in Jesus Christ primarily the eternal Son of God. Therefore it interpreted love of neighbor as a consequence of love toward God and sought above all to more precisely define the latter: God is to be loved for God's own sake, and everything else — including one's fellow human beings — is also to be loved for God's sake. This, nevertheless, does not mean that the fellow human being may not be loved for himself or herself; for, everyone who loves God also loves everything that God loves and as God loves it. This complete love of God cannot be realized by the human person on his or her own. It flows into the human person's heart through grace (DS 1530). The love of God effected through grace was understood in seventeenth-century France as a completely unselfish love; it excluded any interest of the human person in her or his own salvation.

(3) *Church Teaching.* The ecclesial magisterium rejected this view and thereby granted to the human desire for happiness and fulfillment an indispensable significance within the Christian love of God. The present teaching of the magisterium does not essentially go beyond the tradition, yet it puts more emphasis on the inseparability of the love of God and the love of neighbor when it speaks of the one commandment of love for God and for one's neighbor (*GS* 24; *AA* 8).

(4) *Ecumenical Perspectives.* In Protestant theology the attitude of the Christian toward God is primarily characterized as faith because the human person before God can only be the one who receives (DECISION). "Love" therefore usually means love of neighbor.

(5) *Systematic Reflections.* In the contemporary world the love of neighbor is generally acknowledged at least as an ideal, though as an ideal rarely matched by reality. In contrast, there is no generally acknowledged understanding of God. Theology, therefore, starts out from the love of neighbor. Only where it is a lived reality can it become clear what the love of God can possibly mean. "For whoever does not love a brother whom he has seen cannot love God whom he has not seen" (1 Jn 4:20). The extreme viewpoint that the love of God today cannot mean anything else but love toward one's fellow human beings may be considered as a marginal position in the theological discussion. It overlooks the

fact that the love of one's neighbor in his or her incomparable and irreplaceable uniqueness includes at the same time one's turning to the transcendent ground of this uniqueness. The explicit and conscious acknowledgment of this transcendent ground first enables one to acknowledge the concrete fellow human being as one's unavoidable neighbor or at least helps one over the course of time to take the realization of this knowledge seriously (PERSONALITY). This is precisely the life-witness of Jesus, and based on it Christian faith trusts that love of neighbor ultimately is not merely an illusion. Rather, the love of neighbor has become reality in Jesus through God's love for humankind, and this love can become real again and again.

See also DISCIPLESHIP, CHRISTIAN; FAITH; GOD'S LOVE; HEART.

Bibliography

Burnham, Frederic B., Charles S. McCoy, and M. Douglas Meeks, eds. Love: The Foundation of Hope: The Theology of Jürgen Moltmann and Elisabeth Moltmann-Wendel. San Francisco: Harper and Row, 1988.

Fiorenza, Francis S. "Works of Mercy: Theological Perspectives." In Works of Mercy. Edited by Francis Eigo. Philadelphia: Villanova University Press, 1993.

Rahner, Karl. The Love of Jesus and the Love of Neighbor. New York: Crossroad, 1983.

GEORG LANGEMEYER

M m

Magisterium. *See* ECCLESIAL MAGISTERIUM.

Man. *See* HUMAN PERSON.

Manichaeanism. Manichaeanism is a religion of the gnostic-dualistic type, founded, under the influence of primitive Mandaeism, by Mani (or Manes, born in 216 in Babylonia), and distinguishing radically between God (spirit) and matter and between good and evil.

(1) *Biblical Background.* The biblical accounts of creation completely reject the scission in reality that is characteristic of Manichaeanism.

(2) *History of Theology.* Manichaeanism claimed to go beyond Christianity through truly redemptive knowledge and insight. Although, according to it, the divine-spiritual-good and worldly-material-evil natures stem from the same essence (substance), the "Prince of Darkness" (the devil) and the "Father of Light" nevertheless stand opposed, from all eternity, in irreconcilable hostility. In the struggle between the two, a part of the divine soul falls into matter and becomes mixed with it. To that extent, God is a redeemer who is in need of redemption. The first human couple, engendered by two demons, are of demonic origin; only the soul has the quality of light. Through procreation, the evil imprisonment of the soul is passed on. Liberation is promised only through "illumination," which is brought by Buddha, Zoroaster, Jesus, and Mani. From the second century, Manichaeanism spread rapidly, also influencing many Christians through the radical and uncompromising nature of its doctrines. Significant in the history of theology is its influence on the young Augustine, who believed, until 386, that he had found liberating insight in Manichaeanism. Having become Catholic, he expressly turned against this teaching (*De moribus eccl. cath.; De lib. arb.; C. Faustum; De nat. boni;* et al.).

(3) *Church Teaching.* Under Augustine's influence, doctrinal office adopted an energetic stance. In opposition to Manichaean Priscillianism in Spain, the First Synod of Braga (563) rejected these views: that human souls and angels consist of God's substance; that the devil had no creator and is himself the principle of evil; that human souls, having sinned in heaven, were cast down to earth and bound to a blind destiny; and that marriage, impregnation, and conception are no less the work of the Evil One than is belief in resurrection of the body (DS 455–63). In opposition to the neo-Manichaeanism of Peter of Bruys, the Second Lateran Council (1139) defended the sacrament of marriage (DS 718). Innocent III issued, in 1208, a papal declaration against the Waldensians, who — like the Albigensians, Catharists, Bogomils, and Paulicians — had

443

embraced aspects of Manichaeanism (DS 790–97; see 800, 809). The Council of Florence also condemned Manichaeanism (DS 1336).

(4) *Ecumenical Perspectives.* In the ecumenical sphere, there are no differences regarding the condemnation, in principle, of Manichaeanism.

(5) *Systematic Reflections.* Present-day theology has to face the danger of a renewed influx of dualisms into the areas of spirituality and philosophical outlook.

See also CREATION NARRATIVES; DUALISM.

Bibliography

Boyce, Mary, ed. *A Reader in Manichaean Middle Persian and Parthian Texts.* Leiden: Brill, 1975.

Bryder, Peter. *Manichaean Studies: Proceedings of the First International Conference on Manichaeism, August 5–9, 1987.* Lund: University of Lund, 1988.

Jonas, Hans. *The Gnostic Religion: The Message of the Alien God and the Beginnings of Christianity.* Boston: Beacon, 1963.

Lieu, Samuel N. C. *Manichaeism in the Later Roman Empire and Medieval China.* 2d ed. Tübingen: Mohr, 1992.

Runciman, Steven. *The Medieval Manichee: A Study of the Christian Dualist Heresy.* Cambridge: Cambridge University Press, 1969.

Widengren, George. *Mani and Manichaeism.* London: Weidenfeld and Nicolson, 1965.

ALEXANDRE GANOCZY

Marian Appearances. Apparitions of Mary are expressions of charismatic-mystic endowments belonging to the living history of the church. They are defined as *events immanent to the consciousness,* as so-called *imaginative visions,* and thus as mystical phenomena. In contrast with the so-called corporeal apparitions, in which the sensory effect proceeds from an external object, the Marian appearances are more conveniently defined as psychogenic representations: in them, God works with continuing support upon the life of the human soul and allows it to recognize normally invisible persons (Christ, Mary, saints) or past events (Christ's birth or crucifixion) as being present to the senses (visible and audible).

(1) *Biblical Background.* Sacred Scripture speaks of the apparition of the angel of God in a dream (Mt 1:20; 2:12, 19), of Elijah (Lk 9:8), and especially of the apparitions of the risen one (1 Cor 15:8). Here it is a matter of the *personal encounters* of the crucified and risen one with many people known by name and open to interrogation; in these encounters he allowed himself to be recognized as living. The *similarity* with the Marian appearances is that here the substantial barrier of the reality of God — which is more insurmountable when removed from any kind of human grasp — is opened to some disciples. At the same time, however, the *distinction* is also drawn: it is that the apparitions of the risen one are a constitutive part of the history of revelation in the primitive church and remain constitutive for all further knowledge in faith. The same does not hold true for the Marian appearances.

(2) *History of Theology.* The subsequent history of the faith asks, as does the New Testament earlier (1 Cor 14:37–40), about the criteria for mystic-prophetic gifts. Ever since the *Didache* (11), the principal criterion is the testimony of the prophet's life, oriented toward Jesus' teaching and way of life. It is consistently developed by teachers of the spiritual life. Thomas Aquinas (*STh* 2–2, q. 1, a. 74) sees the positive meaning of such gifts of grace in that they encourage the moral life of the faithful, but he does not hold that they proclaim new realities of revelation.

(3) *Church Teaching.* According to church doctrine, the Marian appearances are to be ranked among private revelations. In their regard, a human faith that adheres to rules of prudence is appropriate. Respectful rejection and critical reserve are possible (DS 3011).

(4) *Ecumenical Perspectives.* Protestant theology does not flatly reject Marian appearances as belonging to the charismatic-mystic endowments of the church. It counts them among those phenomena of Christian religion "that are never completely open to rational interpretation and are capable of creating difficulties both for academic theology's diminution of spiritualistic phenomena as well as for a concept of reality one-sidedly inclined toward classical natural sciences" (D. Rössler, in *RGG* 4:762).

(5) *Systematic Reflections.* Marian appearances (and private revelations in general) are not aimed at an expansion of the doctrine of faith, but rather at the practical conduct of the faithful; they are a prophetic impulse for the heart and the will, in order to concretize in a specific temporal situation the received wealth of revelation with new power. Moreover, they are a charismatic sign of the solidarity transcending ages and nations of all those who belong to Christ. In and with Mary, as she is revealed, the "cloud of witnesses" (Heb 12:1) emerges that surrounds Christian striving.

See also REVELATION.

Bibliography
Beinert, Wolfgang, and H. Petri. *Handbuch der Marienkunde.* Regensburg: Putset, 1984.
Delaney, John J. *A Woman Clothed with the Sun: Eight Great Appearances of Our Lady in Modern Times.* Garden City, N.Y.: Image, 1961.
Rahner, Karl. *Visions and Prophecies.* New York: Herder and Herder, 1963.
Zalecki, Marian. *Theology of a Marian Shrine: Our Lady of Czestochowa.* Dayton: University of Dayton, 1976.

FRANZ COURTH

Marian Veneration. Marian veneration is the appreciative response of the believer to Mary's mission in salvation-history; the veneration directed toward the person of Mary is deemed *absolute,* while the veneration for images and shrines is regarded as *relative.* Veneration for Mary manifests itself in acts of trust, thanks, reverence, invocation, and petition. They shape the liturgy (especially Marian hymns) as well as the wide spectrum of Marian popular piety (including art). Along with these outward forms, Marian veneration expresses itself in the imitation of Mary's exemplarity; it serves as a help and a way toward the imitation of Christ.

(1) *Biblical Background.* In Sacred Scripture, acknowledging Jesus as *Lord* also includes the woman who is at hand at the beginning of his God-endowed life. Lk 1:42 looks with recognition from the Son to the mother and characterizes her for what she is through him: blessed among women and "mother of my Lord." Indeed, the Magnificat (Lk 1:46–55) is an early form of Marian veneration. Before its scope widens (v. 50) to comprise all of salvation-history, it dwells first upon the person of Mary and upon God's salvific actions on her behalf; this establishes that praise is to be rendered her by all generations (v. 48). That early forms of Marian veneration are involved in the salutation of the angel (1:28), in the blessing by Elizabeth (Lk 1:42f.), as well as in the Magnificat (esp. 1:48b) is attested by the argument from form criticism that such a pointed exaltation of Mary can be satisfactorily explained only by an inchoate Marian veneration in the primitive church.

(2) *History of Theology.* The veneration of Mary manifests itself in the post-apostolic period at first in the devout reflection *on* the mother of Jesus. Impetus for development came from the dogmas on Christ and the related understanding of redemption: God became man in Christ, in order that human beings might become like God. Thus the majestic title of Mary as *God-bearer* was objectively established by the christological determination of Nicaea (325). At the Council of Ephesus (431) it served for asserting the redeemer's unity as a subject. The inclusion of Mary in the professing of faith in Christ brought it about that admiration, thanks, and praise were rendered to her in worship and preaching. Along with the dogma on Christ, belief in the resurrection especially shaped the Marian veneration of the early church. Since it was believed that the martyrs and confessors continued to live in Christ, an actual presence was attributed to them beyond their activity on earth. The petition for their intercession flowed from the certainty that those living in ultimate communion with Christ continued to collaborate with him. Against this spiritual background, alongside the pious meditation *on* Mary came *direct invocation of her.* The oldest testimony (around 300) is the prayer "Under Your Protection." The first Marian feasts emerged in the East in the fifth century; in the West, the annunciation, the dormition, the nativity, and the purification of Mary were celebrated in the seventh century. The immediate turning toward Mary finds an especially emphatic form in the hymns of both the Byzantine and the Latin traditions of the early and high Middle Ages. The principal motifs that were developed artistically were the mystery of the incarnation and of Mary's Spirit-caused conception, the events of the visitation and of the presentation of Jesus in the temple, the participation of Mary in the sufferings of Jesus, as well as her original blessedness and her ultimate exaltation. In large measure the guiding concepts for medieval Marian veneration were the doctrine of the ME-DIATION OF MARY as well as the intensified question regarding her preparation for serving as the Mother of God. Forms that continue to function even to-

day are the rosary, pilgrimages, and consecration to Mary. Following Luther's criticism against Marian praise in hymns and against the notion of intercession, the period of the Catholic Reform reinvigorated the medieval veneration of Mary. Marian veneration became characteristic of Catholics. After the turbulence of the Enlightenment and of the French Revolution together with its consequences, the newly awakened dogmatic interest in Mary led to increased veneration of Mary in the nineteenth century; this continued up to Vatican II, then entered into a period of clarification.

(3) *Church Teaching.* In terms of the magisterium, at the Second Council of Nicaea (787) veneration of Mary was defended in connection with the conflict over iconoclasm (DS 600–601). The veneration rendered to images is valid for the prototype that they represent; adoration in the strict sense is reserved to God alone. These ideas were resumed by Trent in its decree on the veneration of images (DS 1823): the veneration of Mary and of the saints, including the petition for their intercession, is good and useful. The council sees the basis for this in the doctrine of the communion of saints (DS 1821). Vatican II (*LG* 66f.) perceives the foundation of Marian devotion to be in Mary's divine motherhood, through which Mary is drawn into the mysteries of Christ. Marian veneration belongs to the tradition of the church since the earliest times; articulated in various forms during the course of history, it is nonetheless not adoration, which is proper only to God and Christ. The standard of authentic Marian devotion is the true faith, "by which we are led to acknowledge the dignity of the Mother of God, and are impelled to a childlike love for our Mother and to the imitation of her virtues" (*LG* 67). In the magisterium, the conciliar veneration of Mary is reinforced by the apostolic letter *Marialis cultus* (1974) of Paul VI.

(4) *Ecumenical Perspectives.* In an ecumenical perspective, the invocation of Mary is particularly disputed on the side of the Reformation churches, on the ground that it encroaches upon Christ's unique position as mediator. In the Protestant understanding, veneration of Mary should not go beyond praise for God's actions of grace become visible in Mary and imitation of her virtues.

(5) *Systematic Reflections.* Beginning from the idea of the body of Christ, one can deduce a systematic presentation of the veneration of Mary. It envisions every believer as involved with irreplaceable responsibility in salvation-history (and thus for the salvation of all). This is true for the patriarchs and prophets as well as for Mary and, with appropriate extension, for every Christian. Inclusion in the one body of Christ (1 Cor 12:12–31) establishes a profound bond and solidarity among all members of the people of God. Homage to Mary and the saints (SAINTS: HOLINESS, SANCTIFICATION) means here respectful acknowledgment of their mission in salvation-history, and intercession means to pray from within the communion of all who belong to Christ. The direct invocation of Mary thus completes nothing else than the certainty of the resurrection, that in union with Christ not even one name goes lost.

See also DISCIPLESHIP, CHRISTIAN; MARY; SALVIFIC SIGNIFICANCE OF MARY.

Bibliography
Agbasiere, Joseph Therese. "The Rosary: Its History and Relevance." *African Ecclesiastical Review* 30 (1988) 242–54.
Brennan, Walter T. *The Sacred Memory of Mary*. New York: Paulist, 1988.
Flicoteaux, Emmanuel. *Lady in the Liturgy*. London: Challoner, 1959.
Greeley, Andrew M. *Myths of Religion*. New York: Warner, 1989.
Madigan, Shawn. "Do Marian Festivals Image 'That Which the Church Hopes to Be'?" *Worship* 65 (1991) 194–207.
Schmidt, H., and David Power, eds. *Liturgy and Cultural Religious Traditions*. Vol. 102 of *Concilium*. New York: Seabury, 1977.
Tripp, Diane Karay. "The Spirituality of the Little Office of the Blessed Virgin Mary and the Office of the Dead." *Worship* 63 (1989) 210–32.

FRANZ COURTH

Mariological Criteria. Mariological criteria of knowledge are those formal, fixed points that shape mariology as a theological discipline. They are fundamentally the same as those that hold true for theology in general; however, in the case of mariology the question concerning the grounding of its content in Sacred Scripture is raised with special emphasis. Through her maternity, Mary is drawn into the event of the incarnation of God in a unique fashion and thereby into the center of the revelation of salvation-history. To the same extent that the incarnation is explicitly discussed in the New Testament, Mary is also mentioned (see Lk 1:43). This development, demonstrated particularly in Mt 1:23–25; Lk 1:5–2:52; 11:27f.; Acts 1:14, yet also Jn 2:1–11; 19:25–27, was addressed by the early Fathers (Ignatius of Antioch, Justin, Irenaeus of Lyons) with growing interest. The later church repeatedly thought over and developed in prayer the mystery of the incarnation and its ramifications. Accordingly, TRADITION as a relative source of theology (and thereby also of mariology) possesses extraordinarily high significance for the question of mariological criteria of knowledge. It makes its appearance in the dogmas of Mary's IMMACULATE CONCEPTION and of the ASSUMPTION OF MARY. It is the task of mariology as a part of systematic theology to connect the statements of these dogmas to the revelation in SACRED SCRIPTURE as the primary and unconditional hermeneutical fixed point.

See also HERMENEUTICS; THEOLOGICAL EPISTEMOLOGY.

Bibliography
Balthasar, Hans Urs von. "The Marian Principle." *Communio* 15 (1988) 122–30.
Greeley, Andrew M. *The Mary Myth: On the Femininity of God*. New York: Seabury, 1977.
Maestri, William. *Mary, Model of Justice*. New York: Alba, 1987.
Ratzinger, Joseph. "'You Are Full of Grace': Elements of Biblical Devotion to Mary." *Communio* 16 (1989) 54–68.

FRANZ COURTH

Mariological Fundamental Principle. The fundamental principle of mariology (also referred to as the fundamental mariological idea) is the comprehensive notion that comprises all other dogmatic statements on Mary as expansions and consequences, and teaches that they are to be understood as an integrated unity. It is the unifying principle for mariology as a separate theological tract; it is an aid for pointing out the intrinsic ordering of Mary toward Jesus and for sketching her position in salvation-history as well as her place in the church. Suggestions for this principle have been: the idea of the divine motherhood (J. Pohle, M. Gierens, C. Feckes), the notion of the new Eve (L. Billot), the idea of Mary as prototype of the church (O. Semmelroth), and the concept of Mary as a member and representative of humanity (H. M. Köster). The last two themes, influenced by ecclesiology, are encountered to a great extent in postconciliar mariology; this approach teaches that Mary is to be seen with all her distinctions in terms of the mystery of the church. The possible danger in this — that is, that all mariological assertions might become depersonalized and dissolved into symbolism — is to be averted by insisting upon the specific personality of Mary within salvation-history; on the basis of the DIVINE MOTHERHOOD OF MARY, this personality belongs to her unalterably. Accordingly, in current discussion the tendency of traditional mariology is verified, namely, to regard the divine motherhood as *the* principle of order. A mariology starting in this fashion is tied in with Christology yet can also be combined with the theology of grace and with ecclesiology insofar as every person is drawn into an irreplaceable responsibility within God's salvation-history. At the root of this lies an image of human beings that neither makes everyone the same nor isolates anyone, but rather binds one firmly as a unique subject in the solidarity of all men and women on their way toward God.

See also MARIOLOGICAL CRITERIA; MARIOLOGY.

Bibliography
Balthasar, Hans Urs von. "The Marian Principle." *Communio* 15 (1988) 122–30.
Cantalamessa, Raniero. *Mary: Mirror of the Church*. Collegeville, Minn.: Liturgical Press, 1992.
Rahner, Karl. *Mary: Mother of the Lord*. New York: Herder and Herder, 1963.
Schillebeeckx, Edward. *Maria: Gisteren, vandaag, morgen*. Baarn: Nelissen, 1992.
Semmelroth, Otto. *Mary: Archetype of the Church*. Intro. by Jaroslav Pelikan. New York: Sheed and Ward, 1963.

FRANZ COURTH

Mariology. Mariology is that branch of theology that presents in methodical order the doctrine of faith concerning the mother of Jesus; it does this in a complete fashion and in relation to the other truths of faith. Particular contact points for mariology are Christology, ecclesiology, the doctrine of grace, and eschatology. The *justification* for this discipline comes from the mariological dogmas (ASSUMPTION OF MARY; DIVINE MOTHERHOOD OF MARY; IMMACULATE CONCEPTION; VIRGINITY OF MARY). Of late this tract has gained further significance inasmuch as popular piety has advanced further into the foreground in the context of liberation theology, and also because of the thematization of Mary by feminist theology. The *sources* of mariology are those of theology in general. In its case, the laws of growth for the doctrine of faith are intensified, with the result that questions of theological HERMENEUTICS are raised with all clarity and rigor concerning mariology.

(1) *Biblical Background.* The biblical foundations of mariology result basically from the position of Mary in the mystery of the incarnation of God. Thus each of the Synoptics as well as the Gospel of John give accounts from their particular perspectives concerning Mary's participation in the incarnation, in the public ministry of Jesus, in Jesus' dying, and in the beginnings of the church.

(2) *History of Theology.* The history of mariology cannot point to any systematic treatise during the period up until the Council of Ephesus (431). The statements about Mary are tightly bound to those about Christ and are formulated in preaching, in liturgical praise, and in acclamations. The pious reflection expressed therein aims to understand Mary through the new people of God, the church, and conversely to interpret the church through Mary, the new Eve. According to pre-Ephesus ecclesiology, the church is the virginal spouse of God and at the same time the mother of many children. Each of its members reflects this basic definition insofar as his or her soul is a virginal womb into which the Logos wants to settle in order to expand its incarnation. In order to bring this out clearly, it helps to look at Mary. She appears as the type of the virginal Mother church as well as of the faithful. This thought was formulated especially by Ambrose and Augustine. The other theological perspective, which in the fourth and fifth centuries helped to make Mary's role clear, was the evolving dogma of Christ and the understanding of redemption coupled with it: "God becomes man in order that man might become like God." Where the incarnation is mentioned, there also is Mary. Her name underscores both the true humanity of the redeemer and his unity as a subject. This perspective corresponded to the systematic interest of Scholasticism, which presented the insights concerning Mary as a unity and gave them a place in the total system of the doctrine of faith. An early mariological synthesis was prepared by Johannes Geometer (d. 990). Through the summas that arose in the twelfth century, the theological comprehensive presentation of Marian doctrine became a fixed custom. Following on this came the work *Summa mariologiae* of Placidus Nigido (Palermo 1602, 2d ed., 1623). Prior to Vatican II, two lines of thought were contrasted in mariology: the so-called *christo-typical* mariology saw the mother of Jesus more under the aspect of her Son and his work of salvation; the so-called *ecclesio-typical* mariology leans more toward the aspect of humanity — since Mary did not collaborate in the Son's work of redemption as such. The opposition between these two lines of thought ceased when Vatican II, following the theology of the early church, taught that Mary is to be regarded in terms of the mystery of both Christ *and* the church. Working from this consideration, it follows that the tract of mariology must be *historically* explicated in a multiple sense. This is true above all because of mariology's structural connection to the historical self-revelation of God with its high point in the coming of Christ. Yet mariology is also historical insofar as it is tied to the historical transmittal

of revelation in the church's life of faith. Finally, mariology is historical because all theological thought is subject to the law of development.

(3) *Church Teaching.* Vatican II was the first council to propound a systematic Marian doctrine (*LG* 52–69). Its principal idea is that Mary, as one redeemed and as a creature of the grace of Christ, is a member of the church; however, as "the mother of the Son of God," as the "highly favored beloved daughter of the Father and the sanctuary of the Holy Spirit" (*LG* 53), she excels over all the faithful. In the view of the council, mariology has to be *theocentric* and *Christocentric;* it must make clear that all declarations of faith concerning Mary "always relate to Christ, the wellspring of all truth, holiness and piety" (*LG* 67). Furthermore, mariology has to be *ecumenically* inclined. Precisely with respect to Marian doctrine, everything is to be avoided "that in word, writing, or action could lead the separated brethren or anyone else to be mistaken concerning the true doctrine of the Church." Both theologians and preachers should "carefully refrain both from any false exaggeration as well as any excessively narrow attitude in reflecting upon the singular dignity of the Mother of God" (*LG* 67). Alongside this negative ecumenical caution, the doctrine on Mary is to be presented in a positive manner so that the "separated brethren" might understand it in its authentic meaning.

(4) *Ecumenical Perspectives.* Among Protestants, mariology as a complete theological tract is viewed with attitudes ranging between rejection and reserve, although individual mariological treatises are not absent. The bases for this reserve are related to Protestantism's theology of revelation (*sola scriptura* [Scripture alone]) and to its Christology (*solus Christus* [Christ alone]). The Eastern Church does not maintain any systematic mariology like the West; it studies Mary in the tracts on Christology, pneumatology, and ecclesiology. Further, the Eastern Church articulates its Marian faith more strongly in the liturgy and cult than in reflective theology. It thereby stands in greater immediate relation to patristic thought, which is normative for it to a very high degree.

(5) *Systematic Reflections.* Although as a consequence of Vatican II the ecclesiological perspective predominates for mariology, there is still no lack of attempts, especially for ecumenical reasons, to subordinate it to the doctrine of grace and justification. As ever, critical points of ecumenical controversy are involved here. The current mariological discussion is evidence of how much there is need for further clarification of the thesis that the question of justification need no longer be divisive among the churches.

See also DOGMA/DOGMATIC STATEMENT; MARIAN VENERATION; MARIO-LOGICAL CRITERIA; MARIOLOGICAL FUNDAMENTAL PRINCIPLE; MARY; MARY: DOGMAS.

Bibliography
Benko, Stephen, ed. *The Virgin Goddess: Studies in the Pagan and Christian Roots of Mariology.* Leiden and New York: Brill, 1993.
Donnelly, Doris, ed. *Mary, Woman of Nazareth: Biblical and Theological Perspectives.* New York: Paulist, 1989.

Govaert, Lutgard. "Newman's Mariology and His Personal Development." *One in Christ* 25 (1989) 359–68.

Johnson, Elizabeth A. "Mary and the Female Face of God." *ThS* 50 (1989) 500–526.

Macquarrie, John. *Mary for All Christians*. Grand Rapids: Eerdmans, 1991.

McSweeney, Bill. "Catholic Piety in the Nineteenth Century." *Social Compass* 34 (1987): 203–10.

Miller, Elliot, and Kenneth R. Samples. *The Cult of the Virgin: Catholic Mariology and the Apparitions of Mary*. Grand Rapids: Baker, 1992.

Newman, John Henry. *Certain Difficulties Felt by Anglicans in Catholic Teaching . . . and in a Letter Addressed to the Duke of Norfolk, on Occasion of Mr. Gladstone's Expostulation of 1874*. London: Pickering, 1876.

O'Meara, Thomas F. *Mary in Protestant and Catholic Theology*. New York: Sheed and Ward, 1966.

Tavard, George H. *The Forthbringer of God: St. Bonaventure on the Virgin Mary*. Chicago: Franciscan Herald, 1989.

FRANZ COURTH

Marriage: Sacrament of. Marriage is one of the seven sacraments of the Catholic Church; by means of it the conjugal union of man and woman is elevated to the order of grace and promised God's special assistance.

(1) *Biblical Background.* Marriage, in which grace and the secular world interpenetrate as they do nowhere else, and, in its root, the sacrament of marriage find support and are given an interpretation even in the Old Testament. The Old Testament shows a development in the direction of monogamy and of a permanent personal relationship between man and woman; both of these are seen as having their basis in the will of God (see Gn 2:18, 23, 24). In the Yahwist story of creation, monogamy, understood as an enduring personal union, is shown as a special concern of God. In the later Priestly story of creation (Gn 1:1–2:4a), man and woman together are the image of God, God's representative on earth to whom jointly God entrusts creation. At the same time, man and woman in their marital union are regarded as an image and sign of God's covenant with God's people (e.g., Hosea 1; 3; Jer 2:3; 31; Ezekiel 16; 23). Despite this high esteem, however, marriage and conjugal fruitfulness are never as it were divinized; they remain created realities. In the New Testament, Jesus defends marriage in sapiential and prophetic language. He sees it in the perspective of the imminent kingdom of God and obliges the married partners to unconditional unity (see Mt 5:32 without the "unchastity proviso"; Lk 16:18). Mark (10:2–12) and Matthew (19:3–9) insert words that are probably originally from Jesus into a debate in which marriage is traced back to God's creative will, which now — at the coming of God's reign — can and must be implemented once again (see Mt 19:11). Accordingly, Jesus not only forbids divorce but once again relates marriage to God's saving will. A basically sacramental understanding of Christian marriage emerges most clearly in the New Testament in Eph 5:21–33: marriage is not simply an imitation of the relation between Christ and the church but is included in this communion of life and love (5:32: "the great mystery"); it participates in it. Despite a number of

rather derogatory remarks (see 1 Corinthians 7), which can be explained by the spirit of the age and by the EXPECTATION OF AN IMMINENT END, Paul is also able to speak convincingly of the sanctifying power of Christian marriage (see 1 Cor 7:14; 1 Thes 4:3–8); Christian marriage is marriage "in the Lord." Finally, a reference to the sacramentality of Christian marriage can also be seen in the saying in Mt 18:19f., which is to be understood as having a more general scope: "Where two or three are gathered in my name, there am I in the midst of them." According to the will of Jesus, marriage is indissoluble (see also 1 Cor 7:10f.). It is indeed possible to speak here of a command about a goal to be sought, provided one realizes that the goal can be attained through the God-given powers bestowed by faith. In the first Christian communities it was, admittedly, necessary also to take into account the concrete circumstances of human lives and decisions, due to which circumstances marriages might fail. As a result, according to the view of many exegetes, in the communities represented by the Gospel of Matthew the innocent party was allowed to remarry after "unchastity," which probably refers to the persistent adulterous conduct of a spouse (Mt 5:32; 19:9: the "unchastity proviso"), a "concession" that has been continued only in the tradition of the Eastern churches. Paul, moreover, allows a spouse who has become a Christian to marry again if his or her still pagan partner wants to separate (1 Cor 7:15f.); this "Pauline privilege" has even been developed further in the Catholic tradition.

(2) *History of Theology.* The theological thought of Augustine exerted a great influence. According to one of his typical devaluations of sexual union, marriage must display three "goods": offspring; fidelity and belief (*fides*); and sacrament. Soon after the emergence of a proper theology of marriage in the Middle Ages, Thomas Aquinas in particular stresses the reciprocal interpenetration of the order of creation and the order of redemption in marriage: the sign of Christ's union with his church, a sign that is effective of grace, is to be seen precisely in the loving union of the spouses (the derogatory attitude toward the sexual realm has also been largely reversed). These viewpoints are later eclipsed by canonical considerations: the essence of marriage is one-sidedly regarded as realized in an exchange of consents, the marital contract (the content of the contract is the right to union aimed at procreation). Marriage and the sacrament of marriage as a personal communion of life are underplayed right down to the modern period. On the positive side is the fact that according to the prevailing tradition and doctrine of the Western Church the spouses administer the sacrament to each other. The indissolubility of a consummated marriage between two baptized persons has been an almost unanimous theological conviction in the Catholic Church since the time of the Fathers, although in practice, especially in the Germanic countries, exceptions were not infrequently made.

(3) *Church Teaching.* The older doctrinal statements of the church do not help very much in explaining the positive content of the sacrament of marriage. They are concerned primarily with indissolubility and defensively emphasize

KEY THEMES ON MARRIAGE EMPHASIZED BY VATICAN II

More personalist view of sacramental marriage:	Dereification of the understanding of marriage
View of marriage as a joint journey of the spouses with Christ:	Dynamic approach to the understanding of marriage
Acknowledgment of the pluridimensionality of the ends or meaning of marriage:	Dehierarchization of the ends of marriage
More positive conception of indissolubility as gift and requirement:	Dejuridicization of the understanding of marriage
More historical view of the actual reality of marriage:	Historicization of the understanding of marriage

the simple fact of sacramentality, this last being always seen as a basic choice against Manichaean views in the church (see DS 794). The positive presentation of the church's teaching on marriage is dependent primarily on Augustine, as at the Council of Florence (DS 1327), where the third good of marriage is simply identified with indissolubility. The Council of Trent upholds the sacrament of marriage; it confirms its basic indissolubility (even when the marriage is not consummated) and asserts, among other things, the power of the church to establish or declare impediments to marriage (DS 1797–1812). Only since Leo XIII and especially in the 1930 encyclical of Pius XI on marriage (*Casti connubii*) has there been any detailed consideration of the "supernatural mystery of marriage" (see DS 3700–3714). The 1918 Code of Canon Law contains the doctrine of the ends of marriage, with "the procreation and rearing of children" being regarded as the primary end. Vatican II has introduced decidedly new emphases in this area (see accompanying table). To begin with, the Dogmatic Constitution on the Church integrates marriage into the ordered universe of the sacraments, looks upon it as a sharing in the love between Christ and the church, puts the mutual support and sanctification of the couple on the same level of value as the good of offspring, and calls the marriage-based family a kind of "domestic Church" (*LG* 11). The Pastoral Constitution on the Church in the Modern World deals extensively with marriage and the sacrament of marriage (see *GS* 48–52). Some important themes in this series were picked up and developed in the apostolic letter of John Paul II on the family (*Familiaris consortio* [1981]); here, just as for that matter in Vatican II, the transhistorical constants of the doctrine on the sacrament of marriage are also emphasized. Since antiquity the indissolubility of consummated sacramental marriages had been defended by the popes (almost) without exception. The Council of Trent presents it as a doctrine of faith required by Christ, although it does so in a formulation that is worded cautiously (because of the practice of the Eastern churches) (DS 1805, 1807). The possibility of a "separation from bed and board" is acknowledged (DS 1808), but any remarriage is excluded.

In cases of failed marriages it is possible to question their validity: the church can issue a binding decision that from the outset no "bond of marriage" in fact existed because of a lack of marital intent or because other conditions required for validity were not fulfilled. The dissolution of the marital bond between baptized partners is possible only in the case of an unconsummated marriage (*CIC* 1142); any other dissolution is possible only in marriages between unbaptized partners, when one of them receives baptism (*CIC* 1143–50).

(4) *Ecumenical Perspectives.* In the Eastern churches divorce is permitted in certain cases, with a new marriage being at least tolerated. In the churches of the Reformation marriage is not numbered among the sacraments; Luther is often cited to the effect that it is a purely secular matter. On closer inspection, however, this does not at all mean that in the Protestant view the created reality known as marriage, when chosen by Christians, has nothing to do with God and God's promise of salvation. It is thus possible to single out some real, objective points of contact between the Catholic view of marriage and that of the Reformers. Differences admittedly remain on a very important aspect of marriage: Protestant doctrine, like that of the Eastern churches, does not accept the absolute indissolubility of a marriage contracted and consummated by Christians.

(5) *Systematic Reflections.* A contemporary theology of marriage must endeavor above all to look for links between doctrine and the concrete experiences of married people. It must show to what extent the sacrament is important for the everyday living of marriage; how, with the grace of God, the married partners can find themselves and God through self-giving to each other; and how at the same time they are to find their place and role in the community, the communion of Christians. In this demonstration, the process or journey character of marriage must be brought in, with its high points and its low points and specifically with the unavoidable crises that must be surmounted in a humanly responsible way and by the power of the sacrament. The nature and meaning of the sacrament of marriage can be illumined by the idea or image of and participation in the relationship of Christ and the church and also by the idea of covenant: God in Christ journeys with the spouses; God is (as Yahweh) there for them, if they open themselves to God. In any case, the categories of personalist thought must be used in explaining the sacrament of marriage. In the process, it is necessary to harmonize the dimension of conjugal communion, of conjugal "friendship," as a primary dimension in the meaning of the sacrament of marriage, as well as the importance of sexuality, with consideration of the essential necessity of being open to children. Also to be harmonized, especially for the contemporary mind-set, are the private aspect of marriage and its communal (ecclesial) aspect, by reason of which marriage is entrusted in a special way to the church as the body concerned with salvation, a concern that extends to more than just a church wedding. One consequence, among others, of this consideration is that just as the married have a responsibility for the community, so the community has a responsibility for the

married. Given the processual character of marriage, consideration must also be given to the period of preparation for the sacrament; this is not simply a time of testing, but can, in its own way, already offer participation in the coming sacrament of marriage. It is clear that the sacrament is not coextensive with the act of getting married; in fact, it is this act that gives rise to the sacrament of marriage as a process and a journey. There is no denying that the journey can be a failure. But even, and especially, an abandoned spouse can bear witness to the love of God, which remains faithful even amid the infidelity of the covenanted partner. Indissolubility as an essential attribute of sacramental marriage must be explained more in terms of its aspect of gift and self-offering (married people *can and ought* to remain together) than in its legal aspect, although we must certainly hold fast to the demand made by marriage as based on the will of Jesus. In practice, however, questions arise that constitute problems for theology: (*a*) the church claims the right to dissolve unconsummated marriages between baptized persons. On what grounds can it ascribe to the mere fact of sexual intercourse, even when this may not be a "human act," the power to turn a conditionally indissoluble marriage into an absolutely indissoluble marriage? (*b*) An indissoluble marriage can be lived out only as a gift and challenge in faith. Is it possible to demand the same kind of indissolubility even of baptized persons who indeed have a real marital will but to whom, as often happens today, the faith is something alien? Is their marriage a sacramental marriage in the full sense? (*c*) When a sacramental marriage fails, it is not possible to act as if there had been nothing there (there remains an indissoluble bond or at least a condition that ought not to be). To what extent can the church tolerate or even recognize a new marital relationship when its abandonment may mean a new sin for the partners (because of the children), even though it is not a sacrament?

See also CHURCH; SACRAMENT.

Bibliography

Albrecht, Stan L. *Divorce and Remarriage: Problems, Adaptations, and Adjustments.* Westport, Conn.: Greenwood, 1983.

Bundage, James A. *Law, Sex, and Christian Society in Medieval Europe.* Chicago: University of Chicago Press, 1987.

Fiorenza, Francis Schüssler. "Marriage." In *Systematic Theology: Roman Catholic Perspectives,* edited by Francis Schüssler Fiorenza and John P. Galvin, 2:305–46. Minneapolis: Fortress, 1991.

Kasper, Walter. *Theology of Christian Marriage.* New York: Crossroad, 1983.

Levinger, George, and Oliver C. Moles. *Divorce and Separation: Contexts, Causes, and Consequences.* New York: Basic Books, 1979.

Mackin, Theodore. *The Marital Sacrament.* New York: Paulist, 1989.

———. *What Is Marriage? Marriage in the Catholic Church.* Ramsey, N.J.: Paulist, 1982.

Rahner, Karl. "Marriage as a Sacrament." In *Theological Investigations,* 10:199–221. New York: Crossroad, 1973.

Roberts, William P. *Commitment to Partnership: Explorations of the Theology of Marriage.* New York: Paulist, 1987.

Schillebeeckx, Edward. *Marriage: Secular Reality and Saving Mystery*. New York: Sheed and Ward, 1965.

Whitehead, Evelyn, and James Whitehead. *Marrying Well: Stages on the Journey of Christian Marriage*. New York: Doubleday, 1984.

GÜNTER KOCH

Mary. Mary is the biblical name of the mother of Jesus (Mt 1:16, 18, 20; 2:11; 13:55; Mk 6:3; Lk 1:27, 30, 34, 38, 39, 41, 46, 56; 2:5, 16, 19, 34; Acts 1:14). It is often mentioned in Luke. Without utilizing the name, other texts refer to the "mother of Jesus" (Jn 2:1, 3), to "his mother" (Mt 2:13, 14, 20, 21; 12:46; Mk 3:31; Lk 2:33, 48, 51; 8:19; Jn 2:5, 12; 19:25) (cf. "your mother" [Mk 3:32 pars.]; also "the mother" [Jn 6:42; 19:26]), and to the "mother of my Lord" (Lk 1:43). Gal 4:4 succinctly states that the Son of God was "born of a woman."

(1) *Biblical Background*. Mark calls Jesus "son of Mary" (6:3), without ever mentioning Joseph as father; this un-Jewish designation is to be understood either as an insult (E. Staufer) or as a cautious reference to the virgin birth (J. Gnilka, *EKK* 2:1, 231f.). Mk 3:32 counts Mary among the relatives (3:31–35), beyond the circle of which Jesus points and expands it out to those who do the will of the Father. The critical tone of this scene is mitigated in Mt 12:46–50 and Lk 8:12–21 insofar as they let pass the negative judgment on the uncomprehending relatives of Jesus and preserve the possibility of drawing his family as well into the new fellowship of God. In the Matthean infancy narrative (1:18–24; 2:1–12, 13–15, 19–23), Mary's virginal conception is evidence of Jesus' divine sonship. Joseph is only the legal father (1:20). Mary has a part in the homage paid to Jesus by the Magi (2:11). "The child and his mother" (2:11, 13, 14, 20, 21) were taken away by Joseph; they are contrasted with him. In comparison with the other two Synoptics, Luke pays special attention to Mary. Departing from Mark, he portrays her as a devout disciple (Lk 8:20f.; 11:27f.). He calls Mary "blessed," the virginal "handmaid of the Lord" (Lk 1:38). On account of the divine majesty of her son, she is the "mother of my Lord" (Lk 1:43). She and not Joseph (Mt 1:21) gives him the name Jesus (Lk 1:31). Because of her faith, Mary is blessed (Lk 1:45); all generations concur in this praise (Lk 1:48). She participates in her son's destiny of suffering (Lk 2:34f.). After Easter she belongs to the praying congregation (Acts 1:14). In John, even more clearly than in Luke, Mary holds a symbolic function. Without having her name mentioned, the mother of Jesus is encountered at the beginning and at the end of his public life. In both instances she is representative of the new community. In Jn 2:1–11 she stands in the place of those who await God's gift of salvation from Jesus. Under the cross (Jn 19:25–27) she represents the community that is commended to John as an authentic witness (Jn 19:35) of the gospel.

(2) *History of Theology*. In the postapostolic age the person of Mary is drawn into the development of the dogma on Christ. Her name is found in

the symbols in connection with the Spirit-caused conception of Jesus. When the Council of Ephesus (431) called Mary "God-bearer" (DS 252), it did so against the background of and in the service of faith in Christ. Further, the name of Mary is involved in the unfolding understanding of salvation-history and of the church. Around the turn from the third to the fourth century, pious meditation *about* Mary became accompanied by *direct invocation.* Moved by faith in the resurrection, the reverent recognition of her soteriological position in Christ's salvific work tended toward direct prayer to Mary. She became venerated in the liturgy and in popular piety; moreover, her veneration turned into a school for living, thus giving the liturgical praise the proper credibility. Praise for Mary in the Middle Ages became outwardly manifest in the works of representative art, in hymns and antiphons, in the rosary (from the fifteenth century), and in Marian pilgrimages. Along with the epoch of Catholic reform, the nineteenth century and early twentieth century were periods of increased Marian devotion and committed mariology. Nonetheless, this was not able to prevent the sundering, characteristic of the twentieth century, of liturgical-biblical and Marian piety. This has led to the shunting of Marian veneration into popular piety and in some ways even into traditionalism.

(3) *Church Teaching.* On the significance that the church's magisterium attributes to Mary, see MARY: DOGMAS.

(4) *Ecumenical Perspectives.* For all its criticism of the late medieval church's superficial Marian cult, the Reformation was not anti-Marian. Mary's virginal conception of Christ was a basic given of its Christology: it emphasized that he was true man and free from original sin. Mary is God-bearer and also a member, indeed even a type, of the church because of her faith. Nonetheless, this distinction did not exclude her sinfulness and weakness. Praise of Mary had to be praise of God and thanks for God's anticipatory grace; direct prayer to Mary contradicts this viewpoint. In the course of the solidifying of denominational differences, praise of Mary became a distinction of Catholicism. For that reason, and also since Sacred Scripture was supposed to be the sole principle of knowledge, a Marian devotion proper to the Reformation could not be developed.

(5) *Systematic Reflections.* Along with the classical questions of theological controversy, various current movements bring the name of Mary again into the center of theological interest. Indeed, feminism and liberation theology display a militant image of Mary. For them, the mother of Jesus is a symbol for both the personal and the societal struggle for liberation. The psychology of religion sees the image of Mary as formed by the male-female structure of the human soul: Mary is an image of God's feminine side. From this perspective, popular piety is given a fresh and positive evaluation. These current inquiries need greater depth to the measure that their symbolic image of Mary conceals the irreplaceable personality of the mother of Jesus in salvation-history and allows her status as a subject to be effaced.

See also CHRISTOLOGY; MARIAN VENERATION; MARIOLOGY; MARY: DOGMAS; SALVIFIC SIGNIFICANCE OF MARY.

Bibliography

Brown, Raymond E., et al., eds. *Mary in the New Testament.* Philadelphia: Fortress, 1978.

Carroll, Eamon R. "Mary in the Apostolic Church: Work in Progress." *One in Christ* 25 (1989) 369–80.

Küng, Hans, and Jürgen Moltmann. *Mary in the Churches.* Vol. 168 of *Concilium.* New York: Seabury, 1983.

Rahner, Karl. *Mary: Mother of the Lord.* New York: Herder and Herder, 1963.

Schillebeeckx, Edward. *Mary: Mother of the Redemption.* New York: Sheed and Ward, 1964.

FRANZ COURTH

Mary

Contemporary Issues

Context

The post–Vatican II church in North America is marked by noticeable diminishment of private devotion and public reflection regarding Mary. This is interpreted theologically as a direct result of the council's spiritual focus on Jesus Christ, along with new emphasis on Scripture and on the nourishment of the Eucharist. With access to God's mercy in Christ through word and sacrament assured, there is no longer a driving need for an approachable mother to mediate with distant divine powers.

Since this result has not occurred around the world, however, there are obviously cultural forces at play as well. The phenomenon is also likely due to the climate of secular culture, a powerful mood wherein the close connection between heaven and earth has broken down. Unlike Christian believers in Latin America and parts of Africa and Asia, North Americans and Europeans live in a post-Enlightenment, postindustrial, postmodern environment marked by a historical and scientific mind-set that leaves very few gaps for God to fill.

If the main religious issue in Western secular culture is whether there is a God at all, and if believers' primary experience of their own loved ones who have died is that they are inaccessible, then it is not surprising that interest in Mary and other holy people of the past has diminished. Existentially, secular culture cannot seem to connect with Mary; such a connection seems irrelevant to the burning religious questions of the day. As a result, traditional mariology is relegated to a marginal position.

Terms

In a very precise expression of the maximalist mind-set of post-Reformation Marian theology, the term *mariology* was coined in the seventeenth century to describe the distinct tract that concentrated on Mary's unique privileges and her universal role in salvation. By contrast, a "theology of Mary" describes a post–Vatican II methodology of connecting Mary with Christ and the church. It "seeks understanding" of this woman in the light of God's gracious kindness that appeared on our earth in Jesus Christ. Who is she? What is her importance in the Christian story? What is her meaning in the community's life of faith?

Critical perspectives that are bringing new insight arise from biblical studies, the spirituality of justice and peace movements, feminist theology, ecumenical dialogue, and systematic theology with a concern for praxis.

Biblical Studies

Contemporary methods of reading the Gospels (as exercised above all in R. Brown, et al., *Mary in the New Testament*) allow the voice of each author to be heard distinctly rather than be submerged in a wider harmonization. As a result the plurality and ambiguity of biblical portraits of Mary become evident. Mark, for example, has a negative view of Mary and the brothers, depicting them as being "outside" the circle of Jesus' true family (3:31–35). Luke's picture, by contrast, is highly positive: Mary is the faith-filled believer, the first to hear the word of God and act upon it (1:26–38). Less clearly categorized are the depictions of Matthew and John, both of whom position Mary as something of an outsider, yet one who plays a significant role in God's plan (see Matthew's genealogy and John's Cana story).

Knowledge of these differences gives impetus to a quest for the historical Miriam of Nazareth. What scholars find is a first-century Jewish woman, probably unlettered, living in a rural village. She is a woman whose faith was shaped by the promise of the Hebrew Scriptures and whose spirituality was centered around religious duties in the home, such as lighting the Sabbath candles. She is the wife of Joseph and the mother of Jesus, in charge of a household comprised of at least six other children: James, Joses, Judas, Simon, and at least two girls, called the brothers and sisters of Jesus (Mark 6:3). Where these brothers and sisters came from is a matter of some debate, but unless one holds to the unlikely proposition that they moved into the household as adults, they were in Mary's care as children. She is someone who did not at first understand her firstborn son's mission, but who, after the tragedy of his execution, was a member of the circle of disciples who believed in him. Elements of this historical picture enable scholars to envision the historical Miriam as a woman of faith, an unconventional woman, a scandal, a member of the 'anawim, a faithful disciple.

Justice and Peace Movements

The spirituality of justice and peace movements discovers Mary in solidarity with those who suffer persecution for the sake of justice around the world. A marginalized, peasant woman, she lived her life under the military rule of a foreign occupying power. Because of the decrees of the powerful state, she had to give birth in a stable far from home. She had to flee with her child from the murderous intent of an evil king. Faithful to his prophetic ministry, her child was cruelly put to death by Roman soldiers.

Through it all she clung to her God in hope, a stance expressed in the great song placed on her lips by Luke. In this Magnificat, Mary prophetically announces the work of God who reverses the fortunes of the rich and poor, siding with the hungry in their need for food. She not only joyfully acclaims this but embodies God's favor in her own life story. Carrying forward this reading, the Pax Christi U.S.A. litany addresses her as oppressed woman, marginalized woman, unwed mother, political refugee, seeker of sanctuary, woman centered in God, widowed mother, mother of a political prisoner, and mother of an executed criminal. In each instance she is claimed as the companion whose presence energizes those who hunger and thirst for justice, for it precisely *this* kind of person for whom God has done great things, as symbol of the redemptive promise for all.

Feminist Theology

Feminist theology mounts a far-ranging reinterpretation of the whole Marian tradition. Guided by the critical principle of the full humanity of women, and having as its goal the mutual participation of women and men in a community of the discipleship of equals, feminist theology analyzes traditional mariology as a creation of the patriarchal imagination that, whether consciously intended to or not, functions to maintain male dominance over women in three ways. First, by dividing Mary from all other women (the Eve–Mary dichotomy) it creates a tool of disparagement since no other woman can ever measure up to Mary's unique prerogatives. Traditionally the exaltation of Mary grew apace with misogyny toward the sexually active, maternal, and public roles of real historical women. Used as a tool of this subordination, the idealized Mary stands out "alone of all her sex," an unreachable norm by which all other women are judged to be deficient.

Second, with its dualistic mentality, patriarchal theology raises up Mary's relation to Christ as a model for the relation of women to men in the church: Christ's preeminence over Mary is the pattern for men's rule over women. Hence not only can women never be fully like Mary, but even if they were the result would be to sediment them in a subordinate position.

Third, the traditional image of Mary personifies the patriarchal ideal of the feminine: nurturing but not challenging, open to receive but not to initiate from her own personal center. As female, her main virtue is humble receptivity to the will of God, the latter invariably imaged as male. A totally devoted mother, bleached of sexuality, lacking critical intelligence and leadership potential, willingly obedient, the official Mary directs the energies of the male celibate culture that created her to the higher, spiritual feminine that elevates the soul, at the same time that it holds forth a set of virtues calculated to suppress women's desire for equality and self-actualization.

In the face of this negative assessment, Christian feminism is searching for new, liberating understandings of Mary. Rather than seeing her in isolation both historically and in the present, it reconnects her to the community of Jesus' disciples. Within this circle of women and men, Mary's unique position as the mother of Jesus does not overshadow her solidarity with other persons of faith. Feminist theology also critically appropriates Mary's representative function as type of the church. Rather than typifying the "feminine" nature of the church that receives grace from an active "masculine" God, Mary represents those subjugated people who have been lifted up by the emptying out of God's power in Jesus, being empowered to become self-actualizing persons in a new, redeemed community. Finally, in contrast with the traditional emphasis on motherhood, virginity, and humble obedience, Mary's story is read so as to highlight her intelligence, initiative, and personal integrity within the framework of her historical vulnerability and limitations. It does not escape notice that once Miriam of Nazareth gives her yes to God, she is never found at home again, according to biblical depiction. As the one whom all generations will call blessed, Mary heralds a revolution in human relationships. Instead of sapping and deflecting the healthy aspirations of women, a feminist theology of Mary can help to build a genuine community of the discipleship of equals.

Ecumenical Dialogue

The Lutheran–Catholic Dialogue in the United States has grappled in new ways with the contentious issues surrounding Mary and the saints (see G. Anderson, et al., *The One Mediator, the Saints, and Mary*). One surprise has been the discovery of the freedom Catholics enjoy with regard to devotion. While the liturgy honors Mary and the saints and while individuals are encouraged to do so, there is no requirement binding on the Catholic conscience to venerate Mary in private prayer or practices of piety. Even granted this freedom, the practice of invocation remains a problem as it seems to denigrate Christ's gracious role as sole mediator. To this it may be answered that just as Christians ask each other to pray for them while alive, such prayer is not forbidden after death. Rather, within a rightly ordered faith it can strengthen the bonds of friendship within the community of saints.

There remains the grave difficulty of the two modern Marian dogmas and their condemnations of those who do not believe in them, more offensive to Protestant Christians for their authoritative, conscience-binding character than for their content. This Lutheran–Catholic Dialogue has concluded that if Lutherans do not condemn Catholics for believing these dogmas, and if Catholics do not force Lutherans to accept them, then they need not be totally church-dividing. The church, it is argued, lived for centuries without them; they are not central to the hierarchy of truths; and, unlike the situation where the pope in each case consulted the sense of the Catholic faithful before moving ahead, the sense of other Christian faithful was not consulted and, indeed, would have given a different answer.

Systematic Theology with Interest in Praxis

Each of the above perspectives locates Mary theologically in the circle of disciples around Christ, using the categories of memory, narrative, and solidarity to express understanding of her meaning. These conceptual tools are not decorative notions brought in to adorn a Christian proclamation that can be better understood by more abstract thought processes. Rather, they are basic categories of human historical consciousness that are important to doing the truth in love in the midst of a conflictual world.

A praxis-oriented approach occasions a paradigm shift from a patronage model of mariology to a community model. The patronage model reflects a social arrangement in which powerful persons can dispense favors to those whom they wish. It seeks Mary and the other saints primarily with petitions for their own blessings or with the request that they obtain blessings from the all-powerful God. An underlying assumption is that Mary or one of the other saints has particular access to God or Christ and, if prayed to correctly, can obtain a benefit for the petitioner from an otherwise unaware or unwilling Almighty. Arising from stress on personal neediness, this model approaches Mary as the most powerful heavenly intercessor.

The *koinonia* (community) model, by contrast, structures relations among the redeemed in Christ along the lines of mutuality: all are companions in Christ. As early Christian writers describe it, other holy persons who are now with God are comrades, fellow disciples, pilgrims with us who follow after the one love. To use a spatial metaphor, the saints and Mary are not situated *between* Jesus Christ and believers, but are *with* their sisters and brothers in the one Spirit. It is not distance from Jesus Christ, nor fear of his judgment, nor impression of his cold disinterest, nor need for grace given only in small portions, nor any other such motivation often found in the patron-petitioner model that impels one to honor Mary or the other saints. Rather, gratitude and delight in this cloud of witnesses with whom we share a common humanity, struggle, and faith commend their memory to our interest.

This is not to say that there is no difference between pilgrims on earth and saints now blessedly with God in heaven. But it is to emphasize that in the light of salvation given by God in Jesus Christ, the relationship between all of the redeemed is fundamentally mutual and collegial. In this model Mary is approached as companion, friend, pilgrim of faith, and sign of hope. She is, in the words of Paul VI, "truly our sister, who as a poor and humble woman fully shared our lot." In communion with her, the community of disciples finds courage for their own journey.

Bibliography

Anderson, George, et al. *The One Mediator, the Saints, and Mary: Lutherans and Catholics in Dialogue.* Vol. 8. Minneapolis: Fortress, 1992.

Brown, Raymond, et al. *Mary in the New Testament.* Philadelphia: Fortress; New York: Paulist, 1978.

Donnelly, Doris, ed. *Mary, Woman of Nazareth: Biblical and Theological Perspectives.* New York: Paulist, 1989.

Elizondo, Virgil. "Our Lady of Guadalupe as a Cultural Symbol: The Power of the Powerless." In *Liturgy and Cultural Religious Traditions,* edited by H. Schmidt and D. Power, 25–33. New York: Seabury, 1977.

Pelikan, Jaroslav, et al. *Mary: Images of the Mother of Jesus in Jewish and Christian Perspective.* Philadelphia: Fortress, 1986.

Ruether, Rosemary Radford. "Mistress of Heaven: The Meaning of Mariology." In *New Woman, New Earth: Sexist Ideologies and Human Liberation,* 36–62. San Francisco: Harper and Row, 1975.

Warner, Marina. *Alone of All Her Sex: The Myth and the Cult of the Virgin Mary.* New York: Knopf, 1976.

Zimdars-Swartz, Sandra. *Encountering Mary: From La Salette to Medjugorje.* Princeton, N.J.: Princeton University Press, 1991.

ELIZABETH A. JOHNSON

Mary: Dogmas. Dogma in general is the *binding form of expression,* accepted by the church, *of the biblical testimony about Christ,* which form became necessary through historical development. Marian dogmas, of course, fall within this definition — they are, then, expositions of what has been revealed about Christ. As such they are never mere theses, but rather are also a response of praise for God's mighty deeds for Mary. Thus the two last Marian dogmas — those regarding Mary's freedom from original sin and her assumption into God's glory — were expressly intended to be acts of worshiping God.

(1) *Biblical Background.* Sacred Scripture perceives a close connection between testimony to Christ and the image of Mary. Thus, the dogma of the DIVINE MOTHERHOOD OF MARY is biblically founded insofar as the confession of Jesus as Lord (Lk 1:43) involves his mother as well. The dogma of Mary's Spirit-caused conception (VIRGINITY OF MARY) is, according to the biblical understanding, a confession of Christ insofar as it expresses that Jesus is the Son of God (Lk 1:31f.). The dogma of Mary's IMMACULATE CONCEPTION dwells on the woman blessed (Lk 1:28, 30) and chosen to be the mother of the redeemer (Lk 1:31–33). The dogma of the ASSUMPTION OF MARY concretizes

THE MARIAN DOGMAS

Designation	Established by the magisterium through	Content
Divine motherhood	Council of Ephesus (431)	Mary can be called God-bearer (*Theotókos*) because of the personal union of Jesus with the divine Logos
Virginity at the Spirit-caused conception of Jesus	Baptismal creeds (from the 3d cent.)	The incarnation of Jesus Christ from Mary surpasses the intrinsic law of generation and birth; it is due to a specific action of the Holy Spirit
Perpetual virginity	Baptismal creeds (starting in the East) (from the 4th cent.)	Mary is permanently reserved to her son; the birth of the redeemer is the beginning of the new creation, which sanctifies and elevates human nature
Freedom from original sin / immaculate conception	Pius IX (1854)	Mary, from the beginning of her existence, is chosen for and blessed in a supremely inward and living bond with Christ; negatively expressed, she is preserved from original sin
Assumption of Mary into the glory of God / physical glorification of Mary	Pius XII (1950)	After the completion of her earthy life, Mary was assumed *entirely* and *without division* into the glory of God, the fulfillment of every earthly thing

the biblical belief in election (Eph 2:5f.) and resurrection (1 Cor 15:20–23) in the person of Mary (see accompanying table).

(2) *History of Theology.* A clear proof within the history of dogma for the nexus between the confessing of Christ and the Marian dogmas is the Council of Ephesus (431): because of the personal identity of the divine Logos with her bodily son, Mary may be called God-bearer (DS 252). The semantic ruling factually established here quickly took its place among the fundamental concepts of Christology as one of the forms of the communication of idioms. Of similar structure is the relation between belief in Christ and the dogma confessing Mary's virginal conception. Starting in the third century, the dogma belonged to the expected content of the symbols. It was utilized for expressing the redeemer's integral humanity and for acknowledging him as God's Son as well. The glory and holiness of the Lord were therefore the driving concern that led toward the development of the dogma of Mary's freedom from original sin; the fact that this is also valid for Christ's work of redemption is an unshakeable pillar for the development of dogma. The dogma of Mary's physical glorification relates to Christ insofar as it asserts the promise, "Wherever I am, my servant

will be there too" (Jn 12:26; see also 17:24), made to the Lord's devout disciple (Lk 8:20f.; 11:27f.). In Scholastic thought, this could only refer to the person's being present in body and soul — that is, whole and undivided.

(3) *Church Teaching.* As much as Pius XII understood the dogmatization of the physical glorification of Mary as being a homage to God, as a confession of Christ, and also as praise of Mary, he nonetheless declined to take any other decisions *ex cathedra:* namely, the then discussed questions on the MEDIATION OF MARY and her coredemptive work were matters that the pope wanted to leave open to free theological debate (see R. Leiber: *StZ* 163 [1958/59] 86). Nor did Vatican II have it in mind "to decide those questions which the work of theologians has not yet fully clarified" (*LG* 54). On the basis of its Christocentric and ecclesiological perspectives, it ordered and formulated anew the traditional doctrine. Its fundamental statement is the confession of the virginal motherhood of Mary (*LG* 52, 61). By reason of this function, she is "enriched from the first instant of her conception with the splendor of an entirely unique holiness" (*LG* 56). Her exaltation was also in conformity to Christ (*LG* 59). The council speaks of the Marian dogmas out of an ecumenical perspective, yet the "separated brethren" should hear the Catholic doctrine correctly and unmistakably (*LG* 67; *UR* 20).

(4) *Ecumenical Perspectives.* For the Eastern Church, the divine motherhood is *the* Marian dogma; subordinate to it is her perpetual virginity. Yet it also confesses Mary's unqualified holiness and her complete exaltation in heaven. In addition, it upholds the meaning of the two last mariological definitions by the Western Church even though it rejects them on formal grounds (as having been proclaimed by the pope). In the Lutheran doctrine Mary has her place in the Christology founded upon the ancient councils. Her name is brought up in order to underscore the true humanity of Jesus Christ. On the basis of the doctrine of the communication of idioms, Mary is called the true Mother of God (FC 8.12.24, in *BSLK* 806, 1024). Relying upon the infancy narratives in the Gospels and the old symbols, the Lutheran confessional writings name Mary as the highly praised, pure, holy virgin (ASm 1.4, in *BSLK* 414; FC 8.24, in *BSLK* 1024). For the Reformed confessional writings as well, Mary's virginal motherhood numbers among the fundamental statements about her. For Mary, the overshadowing by the Holy Spirit means that, as henceforth sanctified, she conceives Christ, and as blessed, gives him life. Through the purifying sanctification by the Holy Spirit, Mary is the pure and holy virgin. Roman Catholic dogmatic development is rejected because of inadequate grounding in Scripture: here the magisterium is said to be turning itself into a source of revelation. Moreover, the two recent Marian dogmas are said to be lacking in basic christological meaning.

(5) *Systematic Reflections.* The systematic treatment can proceed from the common conviction that the biblical testimony on Christ is the fixed center of the Christian confession of faith. Proceeding from this foundation, the effort is made to reach an accord on the question of whether only that can qualify as

biblically based which can be drawn out through strict logical derivation from the wording of individual verses of Sacred Scripture. Cannot a reality also be held to have its foundation in the Bible even though its terminological appropriation of Scripture itself is sketchy and tentative? These questions were answered affirmatively by the Reformers in an indirect way insofar as they called Mary the Mother of God and spoke of her sanctifying and purifying preparation for her singular function in salvation-history. If the concept of dogma appears too narrow and the christological basis of the two most recent Marian dogmas does not seem to have been brought out clearly enough, then the concept of *sign* can be of service as a bridge for the ecumenical dialogue. For the Lutheran P. Meinhold (*Maria in der Ökumene* [Wiesbaden, 1978], 40), Mary is a sign, proceeding from Jesus, "of a humanity engaged in its renewal and advancing toward its fulfillment," a sign "of the radical earnestness and the self-giving love of God," a sign "in the sense of anticipating the consummation," a sign "of that which faith has to hope for." Much would be achieved for ecumenism if the Catholic and Protestant declarations on Mary could find each other in the succinctly conceived notion of sign.

See also CHRISTOLOGY; DEVELOPMENT OF DOGMAS; DOGMA/DOGMATIC STATEMENT; MARIOLOGY; TRADITION.

Bibliography
Graef, Hilda. *Mary: A History of Doctrine and Devotion.* 2 vols. Westminster, Md.: Christian Classics, 1985.
Palmer, Paul F., ed. *Mary in the Documents of the Church.* Westminster, Md.: Newman, 1952.

FRANZ COURTH

Mary: Salvific Significance. *See* SALVIFIC SIGNIFICANCE OF MARY.

Matter. The Latin word *materia* corresponds, in sense, to the Greek *hýle* (wood, building material). The concept of "matter" refers to material substance in general, whether living or nonliving.

(1) *Biblical Background.* The Bible has a deeply positive view of material realities. God, as Creator, brings them forth and arranges them; and from matter (or, more precisely, from "clay" [*'adāmāh*]), God fashions living creatures (CREATION NARRATIVES). To be sure, as bodies (*bāsār, sōma*), humans are seen in the perspective of weakness and transience, but by that very fact are not, in principle, devalued. Beyond death, resurrection and eternal life are promised them.

(2) *History of Theology.* The Fathers, who were influenced by Plato, ascribed to matter the function of pointing toward spiritual realities. In Aristotelian philosophy, which was also appropriated by Christian theology, *hýle* has a dual significance: (*a*) a mere material existent, which is the subject of quantitative measurement and spatio-temporal change ("secondary matter" [*materia secunda*]); and (*b*) the metaphysical element in an existent that enters into

combination with the element of "form" (*morphé*) ("prime matter" [*materia prima*]). The latter implies so-called hylomorphism: matter presents itself as a pure potentiality for the form that actualizes, defines, and enduringly stamps it. From the beginning of the thirteenth century, this theory was employed in dogmatics. According to Thomas Aquinas, all creatures, whether inorganic or organic, are composed of matter and form (*STh* 1, q. 66, a. 2ff.; see q. 115). So, too, are humans, in whom the body, or matter, is enduringly defined by the soul, or form (ibid., q. 76; see q. 91). The fact that humans are thus constituted of body and soul makes it fitting that God sanctifies them through palpable means of grace, SACRAMENTS, consisting of a "matter" (some thing or sign) and a "form" (the corresponding set of words) (*STh* 3, q. 60f.). Regarding the state of ORIGINAL SIN, Thomas distinguishes a "material" element, the inordinate appetitiveness, and a formal, the absence of original justice (*STh* 1–2, q. 82, a. 3). Dogmatics today can no more ignore the results of research into matter by modern physics than it can theories of evolution. For example, when speaking about the world, nature, and history, it has to take into account A. Einstein's theory of relativity, according to which moving bodies must be measured in terms of a complex space–time schema in which the three spatial dimensions are no longer conceivable, as previously, without the fourth, temporal dimension that belongs to them. Similarly revolutionary, at the atomic and subatomic levels, was the effect of quantum theory (see H. Dolch and M. Moser, in *LThK*[2] 7:164). It rendered untenable such certainties of classical physics as unidirectional causality, total determinedness, or absolute objectivity and precision. This enabled the emergence of new analogical possibilities even in the area of the theology of creation, regarding, for instance, the free interplay of nature and grace within redemptive history. Today, the concept of matter seems more complex, enigmatic, and unfixed than ever before. The conditions expected to develop in the course of any physical process can be calculated in advance only with a certain — often very high — degree of probability. They are not unequivocally definable and determined. In this connection, W. Heisenberg introduced the hypothesis of "uncertainty relations" or the "uncertainty principle": many intra-atomic processes cannot be explained in terms of traditional causal laws, but only in terms of "statistical probability," which provides, however, no basis for inferring anything with ultimate precision in specific cases. In addition, he integrated, as constitutive factors, the subjectivity of the observer and the instruments chosen by the observer into the act of knowing observed matter. Claims to absolute objectivity are no longer made, nor to absolute unambiguity, given that, since the discoveries of A. J. Fresnel, A. Einstein, and L. V. de Broglie, such basic phenomena of moving matter as that of light appear to be both corpuscular and wavelike (wave–particle duality). According to M. Eigen, the quantity of matter and energy in the earth's system is subject to positive and negative entropic variations, and this is of decisive significance for the course of EVOLUTION. The analysis of matter provided by quantum physics also leaves scope, however, for renewed reflection, at the physical, biological, psychological, and philosophical levels, on the relationship between matter and spirit.

(3) *Church Teaching.* Doctrinal office has condemned not only spiritualistic demonization of matter and the body (DS 462, 790, 800) but also materialism (DS 3022).

(4) *Ecumenical Perspectives.* This subject is interconfessionally noncontroversial.

(5) *Systematic Reflections.* An attempt at theological reflection on the natural-scientific view of matter is being undertaken today, roughly along the following lines. Nothing prohibits assenting to the proposition, "In the beginning was hydrogen"; for even primal matter has the potential for, and tendency toward, constantly higher evolutionary levels. Matter is a dynamic entity that can "organize" itself and transform itself into increasingly more complex structures. After the leap from inorganic matter to organic, from nonliving to living, a heightened "spontaneity" obtains within evolution, which is never totally determined causally and also unfolds through "uncertain" trials, all the way to the borders of the spiritual and the human. In this connection, according to W. Stegmüller, the materialist principle "All spirit is in fact matter" could be reversed: "All matter is potential spirit." K. Rahner develops approaches by P. Teilhard de Chardin in the direction of proposing that the evolvement of matter into spirit occurs by virtue of a certain self-transcendence of matter, with God, in God's creative power, being assumed by faith as the ultimately supporting factor. Regarding the religious mystery of the "ascension," Rahner speaks, with logical consistency, of a "transfiguration of matter" and of a "persistence of matter in eternity through and beyond such transformation" (Rahner, *Schriften* 7:180).

See also CREATION: BELIEF IN, AND NATURAL SCIENCE; HYLOMORPHISM.

Bibliography
Davies, Paul, and John Gribbin. *The Matter Myth: Dramatic Discoveries That Challenge Our Understanding of Physical Reality.* New York: Simon and Schuster, 1992.
Heisenberg, Werner. *Physics and Philosophy: The Revolution in Modern Science.* London: Penguin, 1989.
McMullin, Ernan, ed. *The Concept of Matter.* Notre Dame, Ind.: University of Notre Dame Press, 1963.
———, ed. *The Concept of Matter in Modern Philosophy.* Rev. ed. Notre Dame, Ind.: University of Notre Dame Press, 1978.
Rahner, Karl. *Hominisation: The Evolutionary Origin of Man as a Theological Problem.* New York: Herder and Herder, 1965.
Simon, Michael A. *The Matter of Life: Philosophical Problems of Biology.* New Haven: Yale University Press, 1971.
Teilhard de Chardin, Pierre. *The Heart of Matter.* New York: Harcourt Brace Jovanovich, 1979.
———. *The Vision of the Past.* New York: Harper, 1966.

ALEXANDRE GANOCZY

Mediation of Mary. The concept refers to Mary's share in mediating salvation within salvation-history; she is bound to this in a special manner as the corporeal mother of the one mediator, Jesus Christ (1 Tm 2:5f.).

(1) *Biblical Background.* The collaboration in question does not exist at the same causal level as does Jesus' redemptive act. Christ alone (*solus Christus*) is the unqualified, true, immediate, and efficacious cause of salvation. The mediation of Mary stands on the level of everyone's creaturely relationship within salvation. For even though salvation and justification are unearned gifts from God to the individual, they nonetheless have a communal, physically concrete form: they are historically mediated and historically lived. In this sense the salvific mediation of everyone, derived and subordinate, yet also to be understood as an instrumental cause (and such is Mary's mediation for us), is a basic law of the people of God (see 1 Cor 12:12–31a).

(2) *History of Theology.* Mary's title as mediatrix was prepared for by earlier forms and usages — in the fifth century by the preposition "through" (*diá, per*) as well as by the verb "to mediate" (*mesiteúein*). The substantive "mediatrix" (*mesítes*) appears in the East in the eighth century; in the West it is common since Anselm of Canterbury. Thomas Aquinas responds to the question, How can the mediation of Mary be reconciled with faith in the one mediator, Jesus Christ? in this way: "In order to bring men into true union with God, (only) Christ is sufficient, ... and therefore Christ alone is the perfect Mediator. . . . Nonetheless, nothing prevents that others also be called mediators between God and men in a limited sense, insofar as they collaborate in uniting men with God by way of preparation or service" (*STh* 3, q. 26, a. 1). This differentiation comprises the two lines of thought proceeding from contrary principles, by which the mediation of Mary was defined before Vatican II. While the so-called *christo-typical* mariology saw the mother of Jesus more under the aspect of her Son and less in relation to the church, the so-called *ecclesio-typical* mariology leans more toward the aspect of humanity — that is, toward Mary's relation to the church — since, it holds, Mary did not collaborate in the Son's work of salvation as such. Vatican II integrates these two lines of thought insofar as it teaches, together with the theology of the early church, that Mary should be regarded in terms of the mystery of Christ and of the mission of the church. The concept of *coredemptrix,* liable to misunderstanding, is left to the side; the title *mediatrix* is given alongside others (advocate, helper, benefactress) and does not function as a systematic concept (*LG* 62). A principal question of preconciliar mariology was whether and to what extent Mary (beyond her contribution to the incarnation) is also the mediatrix of all actual graces. Before the start of Vatican II, it was precisely in this sense that more than five hundred fathers from all over the world called for a definition of the mission of Mary as mediatrix; some fifty had voted for the definition of her coredemption. The council spoke about the mediation of Mary in *LG* 60–62, but without complying with the aforementioned petitions. Above all, it emphasized the confession of Christ, the one media-

tor. Mary's mediating task lies at another level of being, that of the creature facing the Creator: "Indeed, no creature can ever be counted as ranking with the incarnate Word and Redeemer" (*LG* 62). Correspondingly, the mediation of Mary is grounded in Christ's achievement, "relies upon his mediation, depends upon it totally and derives all of its power from it" (*LG* 60). The council regards this *subordinate service of mediation* as perfected in Mary's motherhood, which defines her whole life even unto the cross of her son (*LG* 61); moreover, this mediating work of Jesus' mother goes beyond her historically immanent action in the past and continues without ceasing (*LG* 62). Mary is the spiritual mother of the faithful and of the church. Therefore, a mediation of Mary can be spoken of analogously in all these areas, just as the *goodness* of God does not prevent creation from being *good* in a derived manner. "The Church has no hesitation about acknowledging this kind of subordinate role for Mary" (*LG* 62).

(4) *Ecumenical Perspectives.* For the current, and specifically the ecumenical, discussion on justification (*solus Christus*), it seems advisable to develop the mediation of Mary and its associated cluster of questions on Mary's intercession and assistance from the perspective of the people of God and its solidarity in salvation — that is, from the perspective of the doctrine of the body of Christ (see 1 Cor 12:12–31).

(5) *Systematic Reflections.* The biblical notion of the solidarity of everyone in salvation gains its special New Testament emphasis in that it is believed to reach beyond death. Part of faith in the resurrection is belief that the dissolution of one's earthly frame in death does not mean the dissolution of one's personal identity before God and one's fellow human beings; rather, it leads to an intensification of the communion with the Lord granted in life. The question regarding Mary's mediation, therefore, is to be answered first by pointing to the entire people of God sharing a destiny established by faith in the resurrection. This thought is given sharper focus in that Mary represents a special case of the intercommunicating existence of all who belong to Christ. The breadth of her special motherhood results from her singular relation to the incarnation of the Lord. In the whole history of salvation, to Mary alone was given the task of serving the definitive coming of Christ with her maternity. Since this is the permanent form in which Mary is incorporated into the people of God, it strengthens faith in the resurrection; just as the risen Christ does not cease to continue his work, neither do those who live in ultimate communion with him.

See also MARIOLOGY; MEDIATORSHIP OF JESUS CHRIST.

Bibliography

Burgess, Joseph, et al., eds. *The One Mediator, the Saints, and Mary: Lutherans and Catholics in Dialogue.* Minneapolis: Augsburg, 1991.

Johnson, Elizabeth A. "Lutheran/RC Dialogue (USA) Achieves Statement on the One Mediator, the Saints, and Mary." *EcT* 19 (1990) 97–101.

Meyer, Harding. "The Ecumenical Unburdening of the Mariological Problem: A Lutheran Perspective." *JES* 26 (1989) 681–96, and reply, 697–703.

Stacpoole, Alberie. *Mary's Place in Christian Dialogue.* Wilton, Conn.: Morehouse-Barlow, 1983.

FRANZ COURTH

Mediatorship of Jesus Christ. The mediatorship of Jesus Christ refers to his salvific action as prophet, priest, and shepherd *and* his existence as God-man. Through his *work* ("for all") and in his *person,* God and humankind are linked together, and human beings are linked with one another. The final basis and universal meaning of this mediatorship of redemption come to expression in his mediatorship of creation.

(1) *Biblical Background.* In the New Testament the word *mediator (mesítes)* is found only in 1 Tm 2:5f.; Heb 8:6; 9:15; and 12:24 — in the context of Christ's redemptive death and priesthood. The reality of mediation is present wherever Jesus is spoken of as the exclusive way to God (Jn 14:6; see the "I am" texts: bread of life [6:35, 48, 50]; light of the world [8:12]; the good shepherd [10:11]; the gate [10:9f.]; the resurrection and life [11:25]; and the true vine [15:1, 5]; and see also the texts on Jesus' intercession [John 17; 1 Jn 2:1f.]). According to Jn 1:1–3 (see Heb 1:2), the mediatorship of Jesus Christ has been established from eternity by the mediatorship of the Logos (PREEXISTENCE OF JESUS CHRIST). According to Eph 2:14–18, Christ unites Jews and Gentiles in his crucified body, so that through him we have access to the Father in one Spirit. "Through Christ to God" is Paul's abbreviated form of the mediatorship of Christ, and it is expressed in the pre-Pauline creedal formula of 1 Cor 8:6, where Christ's mediatorship is so universal that creation and the salvation event are comprehended as an inseparable whole. Col 1:12–20 further develops this idea. The Old Testament antecedents are the kingly, priestly, and prophetic mediators of salvation, where reflections on God's servant and representative play a decisive role. An antecedent for the mediatorship of creation is found in the Old Testament or Jewish-Hellenistic presentation of Wisdom. The historical grounds for this may be seen in Jesus' function as eschatological mediator of salvation and his persevering proexistence while he was dying (HISTORICAL JESUS).

(2) *History of Theology.* The Fathers understood Christ's mediatorship universally and as part of salvation-history. Because Christ once became our salvation by dying for our sins, we now have access to the Father through Christ in the Holy Spirit. The incarnation (when Christ becomes mediator), as the beginning of the whole mediative event of salvation, is subordinate to the salvific death on the cross. In the Monothelitist controversy it became clear that the totality of Jesus Christ's mediatorship implied that his free decision for God was based in the divine Logos itself, and thus was able to mediate salvation. Origen emphasized the mediatorship of the Logos, stating that by the very way the Logos was constituted it stands between God and human beings.

As originating in the Father, it is wisdom and the Father's knowledge; in relation to the world, it is word and participation (*De Princ.* 1.2.2f.). The Logos's mediatorship is related to creation and salvation, which consists in preserving the world (ibid., 1.1.3; 1.3.5f.; 2.1.3). It encompasses the whole of history and continues in the church. The problematic nature of the mediate position of the Logos becomes clear with Arius, for whom the Word is still only an "intermediate being" between God and the world. Even in Eusebius, there are stages in his doctrine of God and the Logos when, because of the strong influence of Neoplatonism, he forces the Logos "into the role of a mediator between the uncreated God and the *ousia* (being) of what becomes" (A. Grillmeier). After the Council of Nicaea it becomes evident through Athanasius that the Word is true God and that by truly becoming man he really enters into the human family and is in solidarity with it (*homooúsios hemin; Sent. Dionys.* 10). By reason of the Word's twofold consubstantiality he is no "intermediate being," but a mediator. On the basis of 1 Tm 2:5f., Gregory of Nyssa states clearly against Eunomius: the mediatorship must encompass the true divinity and true humanity (*Ref. conf. Eun.* 142f.). Cyril of Alexandria emphasizes the priesthood of the God-man through which he mediates (see *In Joan.* 11.4 = 17.2). Among the Latin Fathers, Tertullian cites 1 Tm 2:5 and points out the task of the mediator to reestablish humankind in its wholeness by the incarnation (*De res. mort.* 51.2). According to Lactantius, the mediatorship is based on the mediator's divinity and humanity (*Inst.* 4.25). All Augustine's important soteriological themes are centered on the mediatorship (see *Enchir.* 33–35, 41, 48, 92, 108). Among the most frequently cited texts of Scripture is 1 Tm 2:5. Thus Augustine is usually referring to *homo* as the mediator, but he also emphasizes (less often) that Christ as mediator must be God *and* man. Christ's mediatorship of creation is the basis for his mediatorship of salvation (see *Enn. in Ps.* 94.10; 45.14). Augustine sees a special significance in Christ's mediatorship as head of the church, because here Christ is salvifically present and efficacious in grace and the sacraments and because the church reaches out to all men and women, who are thus determined for eternal life. Leo I links the Augustinian predilection for the mediatorship of Christ with the doctrine of two natures and thus points to its profound soteriological meaning: it becomes a doctrine of divinization. Redemption is based on the being of the mediator (DS 293). Thomas Aquinas also regards the mediatorship of Jesus Christ as one of the consequences of the hypostatic union. Here, appealing especially to Augustine and 1 Tm 2:5, he begins with the *man* Jesus Christ as mediator, who by his death reconciled humankind with God (*STh* 3, q. 26). It then becomes understandable why he has to inquire into how Jesus' humanity (for example in the sacraments) is effective. The Thomists refer to a physical mode of effectiveness; the Scotists to a moral mode; L. Billot to an intentional mode. To this day, Catholic dogmatics presents the doctrine of redemption as the mediatorship of Jesus Christ, because this dogma deals with the basic question of salvation as well as the fundamental speculative problem of mediation between God and humankind (W. Kasper).

(3) *Church Teaching.* The most basic statement of belief in the mediatorship of Jesus Christ is that which says that the incarnation and the crucifixion were "for us" and "for our salvation" (DS 125, 150; see 42, 62, 64, etc.). The Council of Florence solemnly declares that Jesus Christ is mediator and considers that the whole life of Jesus has salvific meaning, from his conception to his death. In its decree on original sin, Trent speaks of the "merits of the one mediator" (DS 1513; see also 1523, 1526, 1530, 1560; on the uniqueness of Christ's mediatorship, see also DS 3320, 3370, 3820; *LG* 49, 60). Liturgical formulas like "through Christ, our Lord," are special ways of proclaiming our awareness in faith of Christ's mediatorship. Since Nicaea, Jesus has also been called the mediator of creation (DS 125; see 40, 41, 44, 45, 48, 51, 60, 150, 421, etc.).

(4) *Ecumenical Perspectives.* While the notion of mediator is seldom used by M. Luther, the mediatorship of Jesus Christ plays a large role for P. Melanchthon and J. Calvin. For Melanchthon, mediator is the "principal title of Jesus Christ" (C. H. Ratschow), especially in connection with faithful trust in the mercy of God. Calvin's Christology hinges upon the mediatorship of Christ. Christ is mediator by means of his divine-human person, and thus the basis of the incarnation is his *officium mediatoris.* From his mediatorial function comes Christ's whole work (in the doctrine of three offices). In this schema Christ's obedience is the form of his mediatorship, and reconciliation with the Father by his sacrifice on the cross is its goal. The divine-human person of Jesus Christ was also regarded as mediator in early Protestant dogmatics (see FC sol. decl. 8.47). In recent times, the theme of Jesus Christ's mediatorship has been accepted especially by the dogmatic theology of the Reformed tradition (explicitly by E. Brunner, implicitly by O. Weber). H. Vogel places his Christology under the title of mediator. He considers that the unity of God and humankind in the one person of the mediator, Jesus Christ, is given a basis by the self-revelation of God, "who was, in his Son, a human stricken by the death-curse of our sins"; that is, he uses the theme of representation to view the mediatorship. W. Pannenberg criticizes what he calls the "mediator Christology" (of the Fathers, the Middle Ages, and E. Brunner) and claims that in developing Christology and the Son's mediatorship of creation we should begin not with the doctrine of the Logos but with the concept of revelation.

(5) *Systematic Reflections.* Any theology of the mediatorship of Christ must pay attention to the differentiated unity of creation and redemption. Redemption is eternally in God; the same one who achieved and achieves the work of redemption by mediated salvation is also the mediator of creation. The person and the work cannot be separated. The whole history of salvation in Jesus Christ is a mediation of the salvation-history of his person in his work as prophet, priest, and shepherd. The question of whether he is mediator as Logos, as God-man, or as man can be answered only with respect to him as Son of God, where God and humanity are united, the complete humanity is guaranteed, and he is the personal way to the Father as *Son* become *man.* Because there is an "intercommunication with salvation, as a moment of his being

concretely constituted as man" (K. Rahner), mediatorship may be understood as the Son's entrance into this intercommunication by his incarnation. Human beings alone could not achieve the work of redemption. God achieves it, in God's incarnate Son, who represents us. As the incarnate Son of God, he is really the only mediator, which does not exclude but rather includes other mediations; however, they depend entirely on the foundation of his radical and unique mediatorship.

See also OFFICES OF JESUS CHRIST; REDEMPTION AND LIBERATION; SOTERI-OLOGY.

Bibliography

Carmody, Denise Lardner, and John Tully Carmody. *Christian Uniqueness and Catholic Spirituality*. New York: Paulist, 1990.

Grillmeier, Alois. *Christ in Christian Tradition*. 2d rev. ed. London: Mowbray, 1975.

Kasper, Walter. *Jesus the Christ*. New York: Paulist, 1976.

Pannenberg, Wolfhart. *Jesus, God and Man*. 2d ed. Philadelphia: Westminster, 1977.

Rahner, Karl. "One Mediator and Many Mediations." In *Theological Investigations*, 9:169–84. New York: Herder and Herder, 1972.

White, Vernon. *Atonement and Incarnation: An Essay in Universalism and Particularity*. New York: Cambridge University Press, 1991.

LOTHAR ULLRICH

Membership in the Church. The term *membership in the church* has for its context the Pauline image of the church as the body of Christ; the Code of Canon Law speaks of "the faithful."

(1) *Biblical Background.* In determining membership in the church the New Testament refers primarily to faith and baptism (see Mt 28:19f.; Mk 16:16; Acts 6:7; 1 Cor 12:13; Eph 1:13). Faith finds expression in a confession (see Rom 6:17; 1 Tm 6:16). A vital life with the community is seen as a consequence of membership in the church (see Acts 2:4).

(2) *History of Theology.* There was no systematic discussion of the question of membership in the church until the period of controversy with the churches of the Reformation. According to R. Bellarmine, membership in the church requires the confession of the same faith, communion in the same sacraments, and subordination to the hierarchy. Those who fail to meet any one of these requirements do not belong to the church. They can at best be ordered to the church by an unconscious desire or *votum* (see *Disputationes de controversiis christianae fidei* 3).

(3) *Church Teaching.* In his encyclical *Mystici corporis* (1943) Pius XII described the church in the same terms as Bellarmine (DS 3802). The implied coextensiveness of the church of Jesus Christ with the Roman Catholic Church was abandoned by Vatican II (*LG* 8: the church is not identical with the Roman Church but is "embodied" [*subsistit*] in it, so that elements of sanctification and truth are found outside its social structure); therefore, there are degrees of membership in the church (*LG* 14; *UR* 3; see also *CIC* 204–6).

(4) *Ecumenical Perspectives.* The Evangelical churches distinguish between

metajuridical membership in the church of Jesus Christ and juridical membership in a church. The latter is looked upon as membership in a human, juridically constituted community. For the Lutheran churches, baptism gives membership in the church of Jesus Christ; according to the Reformed churches, baptism points to this membership. Juridical membership in a church is a consequence of baptism, but it remains membership in a corporate body based on human law. When individuals move and take up residence in the area of another church, their earlier membership ceases and they acquire a new one. The distinction between membership in the church of Jesus Christ and membership in a church that is a body based on human law has for a result that at times the second kind of membership is not linked to the reception of baptism (e.g., in the Swedish state church and in some Reformed churches). The Roman Catholic Church (and also the Orthodox churches), on the one hand, and the churches of the Reformation, on the other, disagree on the conditions required for an exceptional or even a regular sacramental sharing (*communicatio in sacris*).

(5) *Systematic Reflections.* Considerable theological and pastoral problems are created by the fact that in many countries of Christendom today the number of the baptized differs greatly from the number of those who believe and participate in the church's life. The concept of membership in the church in the theological and canonical sense is opposed to that of a "partial identification" with the church.

See also NON-CHRISTIANS.

Bibliography
Dulles, Avery. *The Resilient Church.* Garden City, N.Y.: Doubleday, 1977.
Rahner, Karl. "Membership of the Church according to the Teaching of Pius XII's Encyclical 'Mystici corporisi Christi.'" In *Theological Investigations,* 2:1–88. Baltimore: Helicon, 1963.
Ratzinger, Joseph. *Das neue Volk Gottes.* Düsseldorf: Patmos, 1969.
Willems, Boniface. "Who Belongs to the Church?" In *The Church and Mankind.* Edited by Edward Schillebeeckx. Vol. 1 of *Concilium.* New York: Paulist, 1965.

WERNER LÖSER

Merit. In a theology of grace, merit in a strict sense refers to good works by which human beings have a legitimate claim to receive individual salvation or eternal life from God. In a biblical sense, merit may be understood as a reward based on God's promise, that is, as *a reward by grace.*

(1) *Biblical Background.* The word *merit* is not found in the Bible. The basis for the later teaching is the notion of "reward," along with the idea of a double requital or judgment according to works. By reward, however, the Old Testament does not mean any rightful claim, but a recompense by grace (Is 49:4; 61:8). Even the election of the people of Israel is not based on any special achievement but is due to the freedom of God's love (Dt 7:7f.; 9:5f.; Ez 16:1–34; Hos 11:1–4). The mercy of God holds sway in total freedom (Ex 33:19). In the New Testament the Synoptic Gospel writers regard the notion of reward as

an important part of Jesus' message (Mt 5:12; 10:42; 19:29; Mk 9:41; 10:28–31; Lk 6:23, 35; 22:28–30). However, Jesus attacks the Pharisees' calculating righteousness based on works. Reward is always what God does gratuitously and is not based on any claim (Mt 20:1–16; Lk 17:7–10). The most important of Jesus' promises of reward refers to the eschatological goods of God's kingdom (Mt 5:3–12): ETERNAL LIFE (Mt 19:19; 25:46). In Paul also the notion of reward is positive. Even though he firmly denies any possibility of meriting justification (Rom 3:24, 28), he clearly says that the one justified receives the reward of his or her good deeds (1 Cor 3:8, 14; 9:25), that everyone receives recompense at the judgment according to his or her works (2 Cor 5:10), and that the reward for doing good is eternal life (Rom 2:6f.; Gal 6:8f.). However, this is not a juridical claim according to Paul, but grace (Rom 4:4f.).

(2) *History of Theology.* The notion of merit was introduced into Christian theology by Tertullian (d. 220) and brought into relationship with the biblical idea of recompense, in the sense of a rightful, legitimate claim. In the East, the first person who dealt with the question of merit was Origen (d. 253). He warns against regarding eternal life as a reward that we have earned (*In Rom.* 4.1). Although he strongly opposes the Pelagian emphasis on human achievement, he retains the word *merit.* But he explains human merit as the gratuitous work of God: "When God crowns our merits, he crowns nothing else than his gifts" (*Ep.* 194.5.19). Twelfth-century Scholasticism develops a distinction between just merit (*meritum de condigno*) and congruous or fitting merit (*meritum de congruo*). In the first case there is a legitimate claim and therefore a strict equality between achievement and recompense. In the second, the reward is granted freely as something fitting. This is the background for Thomas Aquinas's definition of the doctrine of merit (*STh* 1–2, q. 114), which contains the following basic statements: regarding the *first grace* (justification) there is no merit (a. 5); the one justified can, however, attain eternal life by congruous or fitting merit with the help of God's grace (a. 3); the only justly merited cause of eternal life, however, is the salvific work of Jesus Christ (a. 7) and the efficacious power of the Holy Spirit (a. 3). Late Scholasticism maintains the following view, which scandalizes M. Luther: the moral good works of the unjustified fittingly merit justification. The good works of the justified justly merit eternal life.

(3) *Church Teaching.* The *Indiculus* (431), as a magisterial teaching, preserves the sentence inspired by Augustine: "So great is God's bounty toward all human beings that he wishes his gifts to us to be our merits and to give us eternal reward for what he has bestowed upon us" (DS 248). Likewise, the dialectical formula of the Second Synod of Orange (529) states: "Good works, when they are performed, deserve to be rewarded; however, grace, which is not deserved, precedes our good works" (DS 388). The Council of Trent clearly states: justification can in no way be merited, for both the call to justification (DS 1525) and justification itself (DS 1532) are only by grace without any prior merit. However, it ascribes real merit (*vere promerere*) for achieving eternal life to the one justified (DS 1545–50). Nevertheless, the context suggests that this

merit is the reward of grace. The reason for this and its content are (DS 1582): "By the grace of God and the merits of Jesus Christ" the justified person merits an increase of grace, eternal life, and an increase of glory.

(4) *Ecumenical Perspectives.* The theology of the Eastern Church has no doctrine of merit. In the West, the late Scholastic theory of merit was the most controversial issue of the Reformation. Luther (d. 1546) regarded the notion of merit as the very essence of justification by works or human self-justification. Thus it destroyed trust in God and devalued the salvific work of Jesus Christ. At the same time he affirmed the biblical idea of reward: reward comes from God's promise of grace. The recompense for good works is grace (*WA* 18:693–96). The basic position of Lutheran confessional writings is: justification takes place apart from merit of any kind (CA 4). The faith of the one justified produces good works as its fruit, although these are by no means meritorious (CA 6). Apol. 4, on the one hand, firmly rejects the Scholastic notion of merit. But, on the other, it discusses the notion of recompense in a positive way. Good works bring bodily and spiritual rewards (*praemia*) during and after this life. Eternal life is a recompense (*merces*) because it was promised. In present-day ecumenical dialogue there is still strong disagreement among many Evangelical and Catholic theologians concerning the doctrine of merit. But research has established a basic consensus on both sides regarding the official positions of Trent and the Lutheran confessional writings. Clear agreement has been established on these points: the notion of meriting justification is completely excluded; in the case of those justified, good works produced by grace receive a recompense in the biblical sense — that is, a gratuitous reward because of God's promises and the power of the merits of Jesus Christ. It consists in this-worldly gifts and eternal life.

(5) *Systematic Reflections.* Since the very meaning of merit implies a legitimate claim, as well as an equation of achievement and reward, this notion is hardly apt to describe the relationship between God and humankind. It should therefore be avoided in Christian theology. It is not biblical. As a concept that became part of theology only in the third century, it inevitably developed its own dynamic; that is, it led to a juridical or calculating idea of the relationship between God and humanity, in the sense of a legal claim or commercial achievement. Thus it is not capable of representing adequately the relationship between God and human beings. On the one hand, humankind has no legitimate claim on God: there is no equality of rights because human beings, as created by grace, are fully dependent on God. On the other hand, to equate achievement and reward in the event of salvation is impossible: as finite, humanity can produce only limited achievements, while the eternal life that is promised is completely unlimited. Positively this means: (*a*) in order to maintain the basic truth of the notion of merit, the biblical term of *reward* may be substituted. The basic question is: Do the good actions of human beings have any worth before God? The affirmative answer to this question is the promise that there is a reward by grace. (*b*) The personal perspective is of decisive im-

portance: between God and humankind there is a relationship of personal love. But love does not demand rights, nor does it calculate. It gives freely and likewise awaits a free gift from a Thou; that is, the person who loves in faith hopes for the gift of eternal life from a loving God.

See also FAITH; JUSTIFICATION.

Bibliography
McSorley, Harry. "The Doctrine of Justification and Merit in Roman Catholic Dialogues with Anglicans and Lutherans." *TJT* (1987) 69–78.
———. *Luther: Right or Wrong? An Ecumenical-Theological Study of Luther's Major Work, "The Bondage of the Will."* Minneapolis: Augsburg, 1969.
Sullivan, Jeremiah Stephen. *The Formulation of the Tridentine Doctrine on Merit.* Washington, D.C.: Catholic University of America Press, 1959.

GEORG KRAUS

Millenarianism. *See* CHILIASM.

Ministry in the Church. By ministry in the church is meant the service of leadership in the community that is given to certain persons in the church. It is distinguished from the universal (or common) priesthood of the church and the faithful as a "special ministry" or the "ordained ministry" or, finally, the "hierarchical ministry," and is in the service of the former.

(1) *Biblical Background.* The concept of ministry (or office) is not formally present in the New Testament, but the various elements that characterize it are ready at hand (e.g., DISCIPLESHIP, apostolate, calling and sending, service, imposition of hands, etc.). In the Pastoral Letters the picture of ministry in the church is already taking clear shape.

(2) *History of Theology.* The three degrees of ministry in the church — bishop, presbyter, deacon — are attested as early as Ignatius of Antioch and then in the *Traditio apostolica* of Hippolytus of Rome. From the early Middle Ages on, a restriction of ministerial functions to worship and sacrament is observable. The category of "priest" takes precedence. The Council of Florence described the priestly office as consisting in "the power to offer the sacrifice in the church for the living and the dead" (DS 1326). The Council of Trent confirmed this description and completed it by adding the power to bind and loose. The Reformers laid the emphasis differently: ministry in the church is the ministry of preaching the gospel. In recent decades, the doctrine of the "offices of Jesus Christ" has led Catholic theology to broaden its doctrine of ministry in the church.

(3) *Church Teaching.* The one ministry finds expression in the threefold task of preaching the gospel, administering the sacraments, and providing pastoral care for individuals and the community. Nowadays, this understanding of ministry in the church characterizes all the theological, liturgical, and magisterial documents of the church (see *LG,* chap. 3; *PO; CD; CIC;* Roman pontifical, *Liber de ordinatione diaconi, presbyteri et episcopi* [1963]). Accord-

THE ECCLESIASTICAL MINISTRIES AND THEIR ROLES

Degree of Orders	Manner of Ordination	Roles
Episcopate	Ordination by a bishop as principal consecrator and two (or more) other bishops as coconsecrators. Imposition of hands and prayer (+ preparatory and explanatory words and rites)	Preaching of the gospel; ordination of bishops, presbyters, and deacons; confirmations; governance of a diocese; participation in government of the entire church (with the pope and college of bishops)
Presbyterate	Ordination by a bishop. Imposition of hands and prayer (+ preparatory and explanatory words and rites)	Preaching of the gospel; celebration of the sacraments, especially the Eucharist; pastoral service in a community by commission of the bishop
Diaconate	Ordination by a bishop. Imposition of hands and prayer (+ preparatory and explanatory words and rites)	Preaching of the gospel; celebration of the sacraments (baptism; witness to marriages). Assistance to bishop and presbyters in their pastoral tasks; deployment in the services provided by the Church

ing to *LG* 10, the "hierarchical priesthood" is distinguished "essentially and not only in degree" from the "common priesthood of the faithful." (See the accompanying table.)

(4) *Ecumenical Perspectives.* Despite all the movements that have occurred in the meanwhile, the doctrine of ministry in the church is still a cause of intense controversy between the churches. At issue is the understanding both of apostolicity and of the ecclesiological explanation of the ministry. When it looks at the ecclesial ministries in the churches of the Reformation, the Catholic Church speaks of "deficiencies" (*UR* 22). It considers the removal of these as a prerequisite for the often desired mutual recognition of ministries. In recent decades the ministry has often been the subject of ecumenical dialogues. Among the documents that these dialogues have produced two have drawn special attention: *The Ministry in the Church* (Lutheran–Roman Catholic Conversations, 1981) and *The Ministry* (Commission on Faith and Order, Lima, 1982).

(5) *Systematic Reflections.* The functional explanation of ministry in the church is based, in Catholic teaching, on a sacramental explanation. At the functional level, the ministry is set apart from the community and individual faithful by its "public character" (*UR* 2). At the sacramental level, the ministry is regarded as a structural element of the visible church with its societal constitution. The nature of the church is manifested in its structure. But by its very nature the church originates in Jesus Christ and is constantly referred to him. The ministry "represents" Jesus Christ inasmuch as he is the head of his body, the church (see *LG* 8). The fact that the ministry is transmitted by ordination

(SACRAMENT OF ORDERS) is connected with the sacramentality of ministry in the church.

See also APOSTOLICITY OF THE CHURCH; APOSTOLIC SUCCESSION; BISHOP; COLLEGIALITY; DEACON; OFFICES OF JESUS CHRIST; PRIEST; PRIESTHOOD OF THE FAITHFUL; PROPHET; SACRAMENT OF ORDERS.

Bibliography
Campenhausen, Hans von. *Ecclesiastical Authority and Spiritual Power in the Church of the First Three Centuries.* Stanford, Calif.: Stanford University Press, 1969.
Cooke, Bernard. *Ministry to Word and Sacraments.* Philadelphia: Fortress, 1976.
Grollenberg, Lucas, ed. *Minister? Pastor? Prophet? Grassroots Leadership in the Church.* New York: Crossroad, 1981.
Holmberg, Bengt. *Paul and Power: The Structure of Authority and Power in the Primitive Church as Reflected in the Pauline Epistles.* Philadelphia: Fortress, 1980.
Israel, Bas van, and Roland Murphy, eds. *Office and Ministry in the Church.* Vol. 80 of *Concilium.* New York: Herder and Herder, 1972.
Power, David N. *Gifts That Differ: Lay Ministries Established and Unestablished.* New York: Pueblo, 1980.
Provost, James H. *Official Ministry in a New Age.* Washington, D.C.: Canon Law Society of America, 1981.
Schillebeeckx, Edward. *The Church with a Human Face: A New and Expanded Theology of Ministry.* New York: Crossroad, 1985. Expanded edition of *Ministry: Leadership in the Community of Jesus Christ.* New York: Crossroad, 1981.
Whitehead, Evelyn, and James D. Whitehead. *Method in Ministry.* New York: Seabury, 1981.

WERNER LÖSER

Miracle. A miracle is an event that evokes wonder because something unexpected has happened. In general it is unexplainable in terms of this world and can be regarded as an indication of God's work in the world (even though it is mediated by created, secondary causes). In the biblical history of revelation and in Christian tradition, miracles have a dialogical character; that is, they reveal the personal love of God and concern human salvation. Thus they demand a believing response.

(1) *Biblical Background.* The Gospels abundantly attest to Jesus' miracles. Almost a third of Mark's Gospel consists of stories of miracles. Matthew and Luke use this same material and record additional miracles: in Mt 8:5–11 par. and in Lk 5:1–11; 7:11–17; 13:10–17; 14:1–6; 17:11–19. John records seven miracles, only two of which have no possible Synoptic parallel: the miracle at Cana (2:1–11) and the raising of Lazarus (11:1–46). In the light of this tradition we may say that from the very beginning there has been a firm historical basis for Jesus' miracles. The healings and exorcisms in particular belong to this historical basis, while there is some question concerning the raising of dead people (the daughter of Jairus, the widow of Nain's son). The extent to which nature miracles are historical is debated. In general, the historicity of miracles is proven by their presence in Q (the logia tradition) (e.g., Lk 10:13–15/ Mt 11:21–14). Also, miracles that are "unmotivated" tend to be original (Mk 1:30 pars.), as do those that are openly anti-Jewish and lead to conflict over

the Sabbath (Mk 3:1–6; Lk 13:10–17; 14:1–6). Typically, Jesus connects exorcism of demons with God's power (Lk 11:20/Mt 12:28). This conjunction of eschatology and miracle working is unique: in Jesus' miracles, seen as active proclamation, the kingdom of God is breaking in bodily and physically. He himself is being revealed as the eschatological mediator of salvation. His miracles, clearly directed at the Jewish public, are not overpowering but constitute a call. They presuppose that his message and mission are public and intend to help people believe. When Jesus says, "Your faith has made you well" (Mk 5:34 pars.), it is in connection with a healing miracle. According to John, miracles lead to the revelation of Jesus' glory and to faith in him (2:1–11). In the original epilogue (20:30f.), the lasting meaning of Jesus' signs is that people may believe in Jesus as messiah and Son of God and therefore have life in his name. Nevertheless, individual signs do not prove his divine sonship in isolation from his whole destiny. Already Mark's use of the "Markan secret" (Jesus' command to silence, the nonpublic nature of many miracles, and the disciples' lack of understanding) places the popular Christology of the revealed power of the messiah — seen in the narration of miracles — under the proviso of his death and resurrection. Only in the light of Easter will his miracles be recognized as acts of the Son of God, in a way that is different from during Jesus' earthly life (see Mk 6:1–6). For Matthew the miracles are proofs of Jesus' messiahship (Mt 8:17; cf. Is 53:4; Mt 11:5f./Lk 7:22f.; cf. Is 35:5f.; 61:1).

(2) *History of Theology.* At first biblical miracle stories were handed on uncritically, following the promise and fulfillment schema, and were considered to be proofs of Jesus' messiahship (e.g., Justin, *Apol.* 1.30). Key theoretical reflections on miracles were given by Augustine and Thomas. What is important for Augustine is the miracle's sign or indicative character; thus he gives miracles no special status with regard to their ontological structure: "because leading the entire world is a greater miracle than satisfying five thousand men with five loaves of bread, which strikes people not because it is greater, but because it happens so seldom" (*In Io. Ev.* 24.1, BKV 11:1). As an act of God a miracle helps us recognize God in visible things; thus it points to the divinity of Jesus Christ. Divine miracles happen "to plant in our heart the worship of the one true God and to hold in check worship of the many false gods" (*De civ. Dei* 10.9, BKV 16:86). What is important for Thomas is that miracles are determined by the immediate, transcendent causality of God: God alone can perform miracles. We speak of a miracle "when something happens that is against the natural order" (*STh* 1, q. 110, a. 4) or when "something happens which goes beyond the causes known to us" (q. 105, a. 7). For this reason, although a miracle seen objectively has the "power of proving," nevertheless we need the light of faith to be certain that it is a miracle. Thus the knowledge of the presence of God in the sign is only possible subjectively (*STh* 2-2, q. 1, a. 5 ad 1). This is the background for such seemingly divergent statements as: "Without miracles, I would not be a Christian" (B. Pascal), and "Miracles are not a means against unbelief" (J. H. Newman). In conclusion, we should not overlook the fact that

the church has always recognized miracles in the lives of saints and that even today there are miraculous healings.

(3) *Church Teaching.* In the context of neo-scholastic theology, Vatican I calls miracles "external proofs of revelation," which, in conjunction with "the interior help of the Holy Spirit," are able to demonstrate the credibility of revelation and the reasonableness of faith (DS 3009, 3033). It condemns the denial of miracles and defends their *possibility* and their proof-value for the legitimacy of the Christian religion (DS 3034). Vatican II sees the profound unity of word and work in the revealed events: "The works... show forth and bear out the doctrine...; the words... proclaim the works and bring to light the mystery they contain" (*DV* 2). It also mentions "signs and miracles," but in connection with the "total fact of his [Jesus Christ's] presence and self-manifestation" (*DV* 4), that is, in a christological context. "All the individual miracles are included here in the one and decisive miracle of God, which is Jesus Christ himself" (J. Ratzinger, in *LThK*², Vat. Konz. II, 511).

(4) *Ecumenical Perspectives.* Although the fathers of the Reformation (M. Luther, P. Melanchthon, J. Calvin) had the same understanding of miracles as their Scholastic contemporaries (i.e., as an immediate effect of a first cause, without secondary causality), the situation becomes different after the Enlightenment, for example, with F. Schleiermacher. Religion and miracles are placed on the same plane. In his eyes, Christ is the one miracle, pure and simple, since the kingdom of God is of itself the miracle of Christ. In the twentieth century, the problem of miracles is taken up especially by K. Barth and O. Weber. Barth sees in miracles the revelation of the "otherwise hidden glory of God." Insofar as they are acts of Jesus their intention is to elicit faith. For O. Weber, the Bible understands miracle as a basic form of the "human interiority of God"; Jesus' miracles contain "meaning which comes from him, but is not directed toward him" (U. Mann, *Wunderbare* [Gütersloh, 1979], 70ff.). Documentation concerning parapsychological phenomena and a new understanding of nature are to be taken seriously and are a possible horizon for systematic theological reconsideration of this theme.

(5) *Systematic Reflections.* B. Weissmahr has developed a starting point for a new understanding of miracles. He begins with the fact that God's miraculous work in the world is always mediated by secondary causes: "The more intensively God works in the world, the more the creature itself is at work, and the more independently the creature acts, the more it mediates the activity of God in the world. Consequently, everything that happens in the world is in some way the action of God; however at any given time it is his action *in different ways*" (*Gottes Wirken in der Welt* [Frankfurt, 1973], 143). The things in the world are unique insofar as in every action there is a moment of self-determination and freedom in an analogous sense. "It is sufficient that when God, through the mediation of autonomous inner-worldly causes, happens to bring about some unusual and therefore unexpected events, they are a sign of the personal gift and salvific will of God for human beings" (ibid., 144). How-

ever, it remains true that a miracle cannot be demonstrated unpersonally, but that it is known to faith as taking place personally in an encounter.

See also REVELATION.

Bibliography
Basinger, David. *Philosophy and Miracle: The Contemporary Debate*. Lewiston, N.Y.: Mellen, 1986.
Brown, Colin. *Miracles and the Critical Mind*. Grand Rapids: Eerdmans, 1984.
Detweiler, Robert, and William G. Doty. *The Daemonic Imagination: Biblical Text and Secular Story*. Atlanta: Scholars Press, 1990.
Kee, Howard Clark. *Miracle in the Early Christian World: A Study in Sociohistorical Method*. New Haven: Yale University Press, 1983.
Schüssler Fiorenza, Elisabeth, ed. *Aspects of Religious Propaganda in Judaism and Early Christianity*. Notre Dame, Ind.: University of Notre Dame Press, 1976.
Theissen, Gerd. *The Miracle Stories of the Early Christian Tradition*. Philadelphia: Fortress, 1983.

LOTHAR ULLRICH

Mission. In a broad sense, mission means the fundamental vocation of the church to be the universal sacrament of salvation; in a narrower sense, it means the preaching of the gospel and the establishment of new communities among human beings who have not hitherto belonged to the church.

(1) *Biblical Background*. The classical New Testament text on mission in the narrower sense is the farewell words of Christ in Mt 28:18–20; the classical New Testament model is the groundbreaking decision regarding the mission to the Gentiles (especially Acts 9:32–12:25).

(2) *History of Theology*. The missionary efforts of the church were for many centuries devoted almost exclusively to the European world. Only in the modern period did its mission become worldwide. The modern history of mission can be divided into two main periods, each of these being in turn subdivided into two. (*a*) In the sixteenth to the eighteenth centuries the church's mission was conducted entirely under the ecclesiastico-political sign of the Spanish and Portuguese patronate. From about 1500 to 1650 Madrid and Lisbon were the centers of the worldwide mission. Within this framework the religious orders, especially the Society of Jesus, were able to carry on their missionary activity unhindered. From 1650 on, Rome began to take the leading role: a "colonial" mission gradually became an ecclesial mission; the instrument of this shift was the Congregation for the Doctrine of the Faith, which was established in 1622. The patronal powers allowed their influence to be curtailed only unwillingly and little by little. This first period of the modern history of mission was followed by a time of crisis (the Enlightenment; suppression of the Society of Jesus; lack of missionary personnel). (*b*) The second main period began about 1830 and has extended down to the present: mission was now an exclusively ecclesial matter. Considerable enterprises were undertaken, especially by the missionary orders and the mission societies that supported them. The church acquired a presence in all regions of the world. As late as the first decades

of the twentieth century, a centralist and European understanding of mission dominated: Christianity was identified with its Western form. A new phase began with Benedict XIV's encyclical *Maximum illud* on the missions (1919): the concept of "founding new churches" that would be implanted in the culture (inculturation) replaced the individualistically oriented "conversion of the pagans."

(3) *Church Teaching.* The new concept of mission was consolidated and developed at Vatican II (*LG* 17; above all, *AG*). The goal is "evangelization and the implanting of the church among peoples or groups in which it has not yet taken root" (*AG* 6; for the ecumenical significance of this idea, see *AG* 6, 15, 29, 36). The key concept "implantation of the church" is to be interpreted in light of the new emphasis on the local churches.

(4) *Ecumenical Perspectives.* The church's witness is weakened when it does not speak with one voice in its missionary activity. In order to solve or at least alleviate the problems arising from disunity, a World Missionary Conference was convened in Edinburgh in 1910. From it emerged the International Missionary Council, which was integrated into the World Council of Churches in 1961 and now functions as the Commission on World Mission and Evangelization in the Faith and Witness section.

(5) *Systematic Reflections.* Several conceptions of mission are proposed today; one that is inadequate is that mission should consist simply in dialogue with the cultures. In addition to the conceptions of mission as "conversion of the pagans" and "implantation of the church," there is the conception of it as "evangelization": the church must fill the world with the spirit of the gospel and thereby give it the features of the kingdom of God. In this view, the goal of mission is not ecclesiological but eschatological.

See also APOSTOLICITY OF THE CHURCH; CATHOLICITY OF THE CHURCH; NON-CHRISTIANS; UNIVERSAL SALVIFIC WILL OF GOD.

Bibliography

Benested, J. Brian. *The Pursuit of a Just Social Order: Policy Statements of the U.S. Catholic Bishops.* Washington, D.C.: Ethics and Public Policy Center, 1982.

Clarke, Thomas E. *Above Every Name: The Lordship of Christ and Social Systems.* New York: Paulist, 1984.

Ego, Francis A. *The Works of Mercy: New Perspectives on Ministry.* Villanova, Pa.: Villanova University Press, 1992.

Fiorenza, Francis Schüssler. *Foundational Theology: Jesus and the Church,* chaps. 7 and 8. New York: Crossroad, 1984.

———. "Social Mission of the Church." In *Dictionary of Social Ethics.* Edited by Judith Dwyer. Collegeville, Minn.: Liturgical Press, 1994.

Greinacher, Norbert, and N. Mette. *Diakonia: Church for Others.* Vol. 198 of *Concilium.* New York: Seabury, 1988.

Schillebeeckx, Edward. *The Mission of the Church.* New York: Seabury, 1973.

Senior, Donald, and Carroll Stuhlmueller. *Biblical Foundations for Mission.* Maryknoll, N.Y.: Orbis Books, 1983.

WERNER LÖSER

Models of Unity. Models of unity are structural conceptions of the church unity that is being sought in ecumenism.

(1) *Biblical Background.* It is not possible to find any reflection on models of unity in the New Testament; such reflection became possible only when the churches and communities were separated and then sought to regain their visible unity. Nonetheless, any unity that is to have Christian legitimacy must measure up to the understanding of unity that finds expression in the New Testament.

(2) *History of Theology.* After the failure of the Union of Lyons (1274) the Western Church and the churches of the East attempted a new union at the Council of Florence (1439–45). There they set their sights on an approach that would preserve divergent traditions in liturgy, theology, and law without detracting from unity in faith. Although the Union of Florence did not come to fruition, the conception that the council was promoting served later on as a point of departure. This was the case in, for example, the various unions of groups of Orthodox churches with the Catholic Church. The decrees of the Council of Florence were significant because in them the Roman Catholic Church made it clear that it did not define itself by its Latinness. Lutheran theologian G. Calixtus (d. 1656) took as his point of departure the claim that the "essence of Christianity," which is attested in the consensus of the early church and expressed in the Apostles' Creed, has been preserved through the ages in all the major churches. They are at one, or must again become one, in the "five-centuries-long consensus" (*consensus quinquesaecularis* — the expression actually comes from Calixtus's adversary, Dorsche). This view led Calixtus to an irenic commitment to church unity that aimed at the restoration of a universal church. The conceptions of unity in the Anglican Communion and the Old Catholic Church show points of contact with Calixtus's view.

(3) *Church Teaching.* The Catholic Church, which has not contributed any model of unity of its own to the ecumenical process, can agree to various models of unity, wherever developed, provided they include assent to basic elements of its teaching, especially its ecclesiology (episcopal and papal offices, apostolic succession, etc.).

(4) *Ecumenical Perspectives.* A variety of models of unity are to be seen at present in the ecumenical dialogue. Ever since the meetings of Pope Paul VI and Patriarch Athenagoras I, the Roman Catholic Church and the Orthodox churches of the East have described themselves as "sister churches" (see UR 14). The "communion of sister churches" can be regarded as a first model of unity. Another is called "organic union": various churches enter into a union and in the process surrender their identifying characteristics, so that a new church is formed with a new identity. "United" churches follow this model. "Corporate union" is a key term for a third model. The point here is not a fusion; rather, the participating churches keep their own distinctive character but enter into a communion of faith and life. The efforts of the Catholic Church and the Anglican Communion to achieve union are aimed at a "corpo-

rate reunion." A fourth model is called "conciliar communion" and has been developed in the World Council of Churches. In this model, the local churches are the point of departure. These have baptism and the Eucharist in common, recognize one another's ministries, and work together in witness and service in the world. The one church of Christ is thus understood as a conciliar communion of local churches, which for their part are in fact already united. Certain confessional traditions may be preserved, insofar they do not detract from the basic concept of conciliar communion. A fifth and final model is known as "unity amid reconciled diversity." In this model, the confessional traditions are retained in their essentials. Nonetheless, the churches recognize one another as legitimate expressions of the church of Christ. This recognition leads to communion in baptism and Eucharist, witness and service. It also extends to ministries.

(5) *Systematic Reflections.* Vatican II initiated a revival of early church traditions in theology and liturgy. This creates room for action and decisions that extend the possibilities of encounter even into the realm of what is canonically binding.

See also ECUMENISM; UNITY OF THE CHURCH.

Bibliography
Congar, Yves. *Diversity and Communion.* Mystic, Conn.: Twenty-Third, 1984.
Dulles, Avery. *Models of the Church.* Garden City, N.Y.: Doubleday, 1974.
Dunn, James D. G. *Unity and Diversity in the New Testament.* Philadelphia: Westminster, 1977.

WERNER LÖSER

Monasticism/Religious Life. By monasticism is meant a way of Christian life that is expressly centered on the directives of the gospel, takes concrete form in a "rule," and is characterized by the commitment, under vow, to a life of poverty, celibacy, and obedience (the "evangelical counsels"). Monks who try to live this life in community are called cenobites; those who try to live it in solitude are called eremites.

(1) *Biblical Background.* The call of the disciples to a closer following of Christ is regarded as the biblical point of departure for the "second way" of Christian life. A further basis is the references to the "better part" that Mary has chosen in comparison with her sister Martha (Lk 10:38–42) and to the "counsels," which go beyond the "commandments" (Mt 19:16–30; 1 Corinthians 7). Finally, an appeal is made to the invitation of Jesus in the Sermon on the Mount: "Be perfect as your heavenly Father is perfect" (Mt 5:48).

(2) *History of Theology.* In the early church the greater esteem that Hellenistic culture professed for the contemplative life (*vita contemplativa*) as compared with the active life (*vita activa*) had an influence on the development of monasticism. Once the Christian church was officially recognized and promoted in the fourth century and the increase in the numbers of its members led to a neglect of its essential spiritual character, Christians began to desire new ways of living

Christianity in its purity. The practice of "two ways of Christian life" gradually hardened into one of "two states." These were distinguished in many ways. The "religious state" was defined as higher and more secure by comparison with the "secular state." This teaching is present in a pronounced way in the theologians of the Middle Ages (e.g., Thomas Aquinas, Bonaventure). Appealing to 1 Corinthians 7, the Council of Trent defined the superiority of celibacy for the sake of the kingdom of heaven over marriage (DS 1810). The doctrine of the counsels and the (objective) superiority of religious life were maintained in the utterances of the recent popes.

(3) *Church Teaching.* New emphases are to be seen in the documents of Vatican II (especially *LG,* chaps. 5 and 6) and in the Code of Canon Law (cans. 573–746). The council stresses "the call of the whole Church to holiness" (*LG,* chap. 5) and speaks in this context both of love as the center and sum-total of all Christian life and of the evangelical counsels. With this as basis, it then discusses the distinctive characteristics of religious life (*LG,* chap. 6; practical regulations in *PC*). Thus the differences between the two "ways" and states are relativized.

(4) *Ecumenical Perspectives.* The Orthodox churches have a variety of forms of monasticism. The Evangelical churches have long looked with disfavor on it. Meanwhile, however, new forms of monasticism are beginning to emerge (e.g., the Taizé Community).

(5) *Systematic Reflections.* The spectrum of forms of monasticism is very broad, with the properly monastic forms (withdrawal for prayer) covering only a part of it. For this reason, the concept of monasticism has been replaced by a broader term, "religious life." In the course of time it has also become increasingly clear that while the "evangelical counsels" adopted by religious under vow take a specific form in religious life, they are also components of every Christian way of life in the form, for instance, of moderation of needs, an orderly sexual life, and fitting into the community. The most convincing explanation of religious life today is in terms of "common life" (*vita communis*): poverty is community of property, celibacy is life in communion with one's brothers or sisters, and obedience is the subordination of the individual's life and activity to the life and tasks of the community — all this being looked upon as a following of the poor, celibate, and obedient Christ.

See also DISCIPLESHIP, CHRISTIAN; SPIRITUALITY.

Bibliography
Balthasar, Hans Urs von. *The Christian State of Life.* San Francisco: Ignatius, 1983.
Daly, Robert J., ed. *Religious Life in the U.S. Church: The New Dialogue.* New York: Paulist, 1984.
Huizing, Peter, and William Bassett, eds. *The Future of Religious Life.* Vol. 97 of *Concilium.* New York: Herder and Herder, 1974.
Martelet, Gustave. *The Church's Holiness and Religious Life.* St. Mary's, Kans.: Review for Religious, 1966.
Metz, Johannes Baptist. *Followers of Christ: The Religious Life and the Church.* New York: Paulist, 1978.

O'Malley, J. W. O. "Priesthood, Ministry and Religious Life: Some Historical and Historiographical Considerations." *ThS* 50 (1989) 527–47.

Orsy, Ladislas M. *Open to the Spirit: Religious Life after Vatican II.* Washington, D.C.: Corpus, 1968.

Rahner, Karl. *Further Theology of the Spiritual Life.* Vol. 8 of *Theological Investigations.* New York: Herder and Herder, 1971.

WERNER LÖSER

Monism. By monism is meant (since C. Wolff [d. 1754]) the philosophical, and in part religious, tendency to assume that there is just one kind of reality. It can be understood as the opposite of certain forms of dualism that draw a sharp distinction between, for example, matter and spirit, body and soul, evil and good, or world and God. *Absolute monism* recognizes only one particular substance for all things: spirit (spiritualism, idealism) or matter (materialism) or the divine (pantheism). *Relative monism* traces the many-sidedness of reality back to one general and unifying principle that comprehends all opposites; if this is conceived as a third, necessary, and transcendent thing, then one speaks of *transcendental monism*.

(1) *Biblical Background.* Monistic thinking is scarcely known to Holy Scripture. Rather, the latter recognizes the transcendence of God, who is related in creative freedom and love to a world and humanity that are radically distinct from God.

(2) *History of Theology.* In the Greek cultural sphere, monism was advocated by the Ionian natural philosophers (all things have a fundamental substance in common) and the Stoics (divine interpenetration of all matter). Platonism, by contrast, cannot be subsumed under monism, since for it the primal unity is distinct from, and imparts order to, the cosmic manifold of things. The Fathers, who allowed themselves to be influenced by Stoicism, may well have made individual pronouncements of a monistic cast, but without lending support, on the whole, to theological monism. During the Renaissance, G. Bruno advocated a naturalistic monism. German idealism based its vision of oneness on the "ego" (J. G. Fichte), on a neutral absolute (F. W. J. Schelling), or on the dialectically advancing and unfolding world-spirit (G. W. F. Hegel). In opposition to that, K. Marx developed a materialistic monism. The neo-Kantians gave preeminence to subjective consciousness in order to construct an epistemological monism.

(3) *Church Teaching.* At Vatican I, tendencies toward materialistic (DS 3022) and pantheistic (DS 3023) monism were rejected.

(4) *Ecumenical Perspectives.* There are no monistic tendencies in Reformation theology (unless in its mystics; see J. Boehme) since it gives unusually strong emphasis to the "fundamental distinction" (G. Ebeling) between God and world.

(5) *Systematic Reflections.* Present-day dogmatics appreciates the concern, given that there is one God, to arrive at a conception of the oneness of all re-

ality, but sees this as grounded in the process of dialogue between the triune God, who approaches humanity in words, through grace, incarnately, and redeemingly, and human beings, who respond to God in faith, love, and hope. Of significance to interreligious dialogue are monistic tendencies in Hinduism, Taoism, Confucianism, and Mahayana Buddhism. In the Upanishads, the life-principle (atman) and the godhead (brahman) are posited as identical, and an all-determining nonduality (advaita) is thus maintained.

See also DUALISM; PANTHEISM.

Bibliography
Haeckel, Ernst. *Monism as Connecting Religion and Science: The Confession of Faith of a Man of Science*. London: A. and C. Black, 1895.

                                                             ALEXANDRE GANOCZY

Monogenism–Polygenism. Monogenism and polygenism are the technical terms for the two opposing positions regarding the question of whether all human beings descended from the first human couple (monogenism) or from several couples (polygenism) who appeared more or less simultaneously in different locations (East Asia, Africa).

(1) *Biblical Background.* Scripture does not give a clear answer to this question. According to modern exegetical opinion, the biblical narratives of the creation of the first human couple want to express the belief that God is the Creator of humankind and Lord of human history. In the New Testament the Adam–Christ parallel (Rom 5:12–21; 1 Cor 15:20–22) does refer back to the Old Testament account of creation, but its actual goal is to contrast the new condition of salvation opened up through Christ with the situation of humankind before Christ.

(2) *History of Theology.* In systematic theology monogenism took on special significance in the teaching on original sin. Therefore, the scientific hypothesis that human life had appeared at various locations on earth set off in modern theology a discussion with different suggestions for mediation.

(3) *Church Teaching.* Pius XII expressed the most explicit position of the magisterium with his encyclical *Humani generis* (1950): the church holds fast to monogenism since it is not evident how polygenism could be compatible with the teaching on original sin (DS 3897).

(4) *Ecumenical Perspectives.* For Protestant theology, polygenism is less problematic because Luther did not want to infer the sinfulness of every individual human person from the first sin of Adam.

(5) *Systematic Reflections.* The majority of theologians today see the question of monogenism versus polygenism not as a theological problem but rather as an issue to be solved by empirical or also philosophical inquiry (K. Rahner). Neither original sin nor the theological unity of humankind is linked inseparably with monogenism.

See also HUMANKIND; ORIGINAL SIN.

Bibliography
Kasujja, Augustine. *Polygenism and the Theology of Original Sin Today*. Rome: Urbaniana University Press, 1986.
Rahner, Karl. "Theological Reflections on Monogenism." In *Theological Investigations*, 1:229–96. Baltimore: Helicon, 1961.

GEORG LANGEMEYER

Mortality. In philosophical and theological anthropology, the mortality of the human person does not mean the mere fact that all human persons must die, but rather the transitoriness of human life as it is always in some way implicitly known in a life reflected upon and as it influences the ways in which life is realized.

(1) *Biblical Background.* Scripture acknowledges a beneficial and a pernicious knowledge about human mortality. According to the account of the fall, sin also contains the intention of the human person to gain immortality through his or her own power (Gn 3:4f., 22; see 11:8). This intention is also at the basis of greed (Ps 49:7–10; Lk 12:15–21). The knowledge of one's own mortality can lead to a desperate indulgence of life (1 Cor 15:32). On the other hand, one reads: "Teach us to number our days aright that we may gain wisdom of heart" (Ps 90:12; see Psalms 39; 49). Mortality makes each present moment a unique situation for decision (1 Cor 7:29–31; Rom 13:11f.).

(2) *History of Theology.* For a person in the Hellenistic world, the need for salvation centered around the experience of transitoriness. This need has made a profound impact on the Christian interpretation of salvation. The Fathers of the Church thus prefer to interpret the Christian salvation as deification, that is, as a participation in the immortal divine nature. The Scholastic doctrine of grace saw the meaning of earthly existence primarily in the possibility to earn eternal life after death through the means of grace of the church.

(3) *Church Teaching.* Vatican II describes mortality as the deepest mystery of human existence and, as the Christian answer, emphasizes the hope in eternal life after death (*GS* 18).

(4) *Ecumenical Perspectives.* Within the ecumenical dialogue, Orthodox theology deserves special attention. For from its liturgy it still retains the insight that dying with Christ and being born again with Christ are basic and constant realizations of Christian existence. This is important for the dialogue with Asian religions, especially with Buddhism, whose path of salvation can be interpreted as a total acceptance of transitoriness.

(5) *Systematic Reflections.* Theological anthropology must grapple, on the one hand, with a life-denying surrender to transitoriness (e.g., depression), and, on the other hand, with an attempt to escape by grasping on to possessions and physical life. From the point of view given in Jesus Christ, death and resurrection to new life refer not only to the entire life of the person but also to the daily realization of this life. The freedom of the Christian consists continually in completely letting go of one's life in order continually to receive it anew from

Gòd (see Lk 9:23f.). Christian existence in the memory of the death and resurrection of Christ (baptism, Eucharist), then, has nothing to do with the denial of life and the flight from the world but is, rather, through its very acceptance of mortality, life that has become free for the world that has been given and entrusted to it.

See also DEATH; IMMORTALITY; SALVATION; SIN AND GUILT.

Bibliography
Carse, James P. *Death and Existence: A Conceptual History of Human Mortality.* New York: Wiley, 1980.
Flew, Antony. *The Logic of Mortality.* New York: Blackwell, 1987.
Jonas, Hans. "The Burden and Blessing of Mortality." *Hastings Center Report* 22 (1992) 34–40.

GEORG LANGEMEYER

Mysteries of the Life of Jesus Christ. *Mysteries* is a term that refers to all the events in the life of Jesus Christ to which the New Testament testifies, including his prehistory and exaltation, since in these events the mystery of his person is revealed. Thus they have special salvific significance as part of his whole history and destiny. A theology of the mysteries of Christ's life is therefore a concrete Christology that is also attentive to the underlying systematic-theological ("abstract" or speculative) Christology and soteriology in the unfolding history of dogma and takes into account the problematic and methods used at any given time. It reflects on the biblically attested events in the life of Jesus that are significant for the life of a Christian and spells out their lasting significance for salvation by means of argument and narratives.

(1) *Biblical Background.* Any presentation of the mysteries of Jesus' life as attested by the New Testament should begin by calling attention to and respecting the problematic of the present with its awareness of the historical-critical method. The New Testament writings are testimonies of faith in the earthly Jesus who is the resurrected Christ. What we find in these writings, then, is not just the mysteries of the "life of Jesus," but of the life of Jesus *Christ* — thus the mysteries *of Christ.* Therefore, a concrete Christology of the mysteries of Christ presupposes belief in Jesus as the Christ. But the historical-critical quest for the historical Jesus is important to prevent this faith from becoming gnosis, mythology, or ideology. According to the Synoptics, what is important in the work and message of Jesus Christ is the "mystery of the reign of God" (Mk 4:11 pars.), which breaks in with his arrival on the scene (Lk 10:23ff.; 11:20; see Mt 12:28). The life of Jesus and his message of the *basileia* (kingdom) are inseparably linked and clarify one another. The mystery of God's reign is the mystery of Christ and is spelled out in the mysteries of Christ's whole life including his prehistory (INFANCY NARRATIVES) and his exaltation (RESURRECTION; ASCENSION OF CHRIST). Of special significance are: the baptism, the temptations, the transfiguration, the miracles, his entrance into Jerusalem, and the passion narrative and its individual parts all the way to his crucifix-

ion, death, and burial. In examining how these mysteries are presented, we must be attentive to the particular theology of each evangelist. The New Testament letters do not dwell on the individual mysteries, but speak in general of the "mystery of Christ" (Col 4:3; Eph 3:4). To Paul this means especially the death on the cross and the resurrection. This (as well as Paul's mission [see Gal 4:4; Rom 8:3]) is the starting point for defining the mystery of Christ (see Phil 2:5–11). In treating themes involving faith, Paul at times lists individual salvific events one after another (see Rom 1:3f.; 1 Cor 15:3–5). The Eucharist, which comes forth from mystery or the mystery of Christ, plays a large role in the life of the developing church insofar as the ritual anamnesis of the death (and resurrection) of Jesus Christ is real memory (1 Cor 11:23–25, 26–31; see 10:16–22). Another manner of emphasizing the mysteries of Christ is found in John. He develops his fundamental christological-soteriological concerns in a revelational framework, so that the mysteries of Christ (see his miracles as signs) are the mystery of his person (2:11), and thus his words are revelational (see John 6: the miraculous bread, walking on water, discourse on the bread of life). In John's theology many events have a deeper, symbolic meaning; for example, the washing of feet (13:1–20), Jesus' instructions to his mother and the beloved disciple (19:25–27), and the piercing of his side (19:34).

(2) *History of Theology.* In the patristic period, the central mysteries of Christ were treated in the baptismal catechesis. They were an important part of the great feasts of the liturgical year and were commented on in homilies (see the earliest Easter sermons of Melito of Sardis). An important development is the often exaggerated portrayal of the mysteries of Jesus' *life* in the apocryphal Gospels. Here it should be remembered today that even a "mythical speech form can have its own theological merit" (A. Grillmeier; see DESCENT INTO HELL). The Fathers emphasized the "economy" in the mysteries of Christ. In Origen we already find a spirituality of *Jesus,* developed by means of a contemplation on the mysteries of his life. To combat Arius, who had collected the humility statements of the Gospels, Athanasius, the Cappadocians, and Cyril of Alexandria line up the appearances of divinity in the man Jesus: the baptism of Christ, his victory over the devil in the temptations, and his transfiguration. In Augustine the mysteries of the life of Christ are subordinate to his idea of Jesus Christ's mediatorship. The mysteries, as well as the incarnation, are examples of his humility and his love for us (*De Trin.* 8.5.7). The exemplary character of Jesus' virtuous life is understood as an efficacious basic image "that extends its power to others and becomes a figure" (L. Scheffczyk). To this extent the mysteries of Christ are part of his saving work (see *Enchir.* 53; *In Evang. Iohan.* 108.5). In the context of Chalcedon, the life of Jesus becomes increasingly the "place" to demonstrate the revelation of the true divinity and the true humanity of one and the same Lord (see the Tome of Leo). The orientation provided by the mysteries of the life of Jesus Christ also meant that spirituality and asceticism were discipleship in Christ. In the Middle Ages, the mysteries

of Christ became part of the development of theological systems, as we see for
the first time in the *Elucidarium* of Honorius Augustodensis (d. 1130) and then
in Peter Lombard (d. 1160). Thomas Aquinas (d. 1274) distinguishes speculative Christology from the presentation of the mysteries of Christ. This work
remains important for today and could provide impetus for further considerations (see *STh* 3, q. 27–58). F. Suárez (d. 1619) wrote what is still the definitive
treatise on the mysteries of Christ. The mysteries of the life of Jesus Christ
were always meaningful for spirituality and religious instruction. Worthy of
mention are Benedictine (Rupert of Deutz [d. 1129]) and Cistercian spirituality, the Franciscan movement, Devotio Moderna, the *Spiritual Exercises* of
Ignatius of Loyola (d. 1556), P. Bérulle (d. 1629), and the École Française. In
recent times, because of the influence of H. Urs von Balthasar and K. Rahner,
the mysteries of the life of Jesus Christ have once again become part of systematic theology (e.g., *MystSal* 3/2). A theology of the mysteries of Christ is
rooted in a discursive or narrative Christology and is motivated by catechetical
interests (D. Emeis) or else conceived of as a presentation of the life of Jesus
(R. Guardini).

(3) *Church Teaching.* The mysteries of the life of Jesus Christ are mentioned
in early Christian creeds (DS 125, 150, etc.). In general Vatican II refers to the
words and actions of the Christ-event (*DV* 2, 4). Elements of a theology of the
mysteries of Christ are found in *GS* 22, 32, 38f.

(4) *Ecumenical Perspectives.* In Evangelical theology, modern research on the
life of Jesus had no influence on a theology of the mysteries of Jesus Christ.
G. Ebeling was the first to refer to them.

(5) *Systematic Reflections.* A theology of the mysteries of the life of Christ is
based on the second article of the creed: belief in (*a*) the Son of God, (*b*) who
for us and for our salvation, (*c*) became man. Consequently the mysteries of
Christ have (*a*) a *christo-theo-logical* meaning: in them God reveals who God
is and how God works in history through self-emptying (always in anticipation
of the Easter-event); (*b*) a *christo-soterio-logical* meaning: the relationship of
the Son to the Father and the Holy Spirit is manifest for humankind insofar as
it includes them in the trinitarian community in such a way that discipleship
in Christ makes human beings more human (*GS* 41); (*c*) a *christo-anthropo-
logical* meaning: the mysteries of the life of Jesus Christ clarify what it means
to be human, because the life of Jesus — as the life of the God-man, with all
its earthly limitations — includes the drama of human history and thus (in
Christ's exaltation, which removes all limitations) reveals what God in God's
love intends for human beings.

See also CHRISTOLOGY; HISTORICAL JESUS; LIFE OF JESUS RESEARCH; MEDI-
ATORSHIP OF JESUS CHRIST.

Bibliography

Balthasar, Hans Urs von. *Mysterium Paschale: The Mystery of Easter.* Edinburgh: T and T
    Clark, 1990.

Ebeling, Gerhard. *Dogmatik des Christlichen Glaubens.* 2 vols. Tübingen: Mohr, 1979.
Grillmeier, Alois. *Christ in Christian Tradition.* 2d rev. ed. London: Mowbray, 1975.

LOTHAR ULLRICH

Mystery of Faith. In theology the mystery of faith does not refer to what in the content of faith has not (yet) been grasped, but rather to what is the presupposition and underlying ground of every relationship to God. It thus refers ultimately to God's existence and saving activity itself, insofar as this enters the human horizon of experience through God's REVELATION.

(1) *Biblical Background.* The reality of the mystery of faith is presupposed wherever Scripture speaks about revelation conceptually and concretely: revelation is necessary whenever there are realities that are not normally accessible to human beings and that can become visible (see Jn 1:14; 1 Cor 2:6–10; 1 Jn 1:2) only through a disclosure from God (see Mt 16:17). In the Septuagint, *mystérion* means something concealed that is communicated to chosen persons (wisdom literature) or is the veiled announcement of eschatological events (Dn 2:28f., 47; 4:6). In the New Testament, *mystérion* is the breaking forth of the KINGDOM OF GOD that begins with Jesus. Being recognizable only to the disciples, it thus forms the characteristic that distinguishes them from nondisciples (Mk 4:11 par.). Paul developed this: the content of his proclamation is the "mystery of the hidden wisdom of God," redemption in Christ that is disclosed through the Spirit (1 Cor 2:6–16) and that has as its result the culmination of the whole creation in Christ (Eph 1:9–12; 3:3–6; Col 1:26f.).

(2) *History of Theology.* Since the time of the Church Fathers, either the course of salvation-history (Origen) or (especially) the life of Jesus, whose individual events are significant for salvation (Ignatius of Antioch, *Eph.* 19.1; Leo the Great, *Sermo.* 72.1; in the Middle Ages above all Thomas Aquinas, *STh* 3, q. 27–59), was considered as the mystery of faith. With Tertullian there begins a development in which faith itself is designated as *mysterium* and its sign as a *sacramentum.* The acceptance of the fundamentally mysterious character of faith is reflected finally in the development of negative theology, which recognizes that God must be also described by way of the negation of empirically gained statements, such that theology is *docta ignorantia* ("learned ignorance") (Nicholas of Cusa).

(3) *Church Teaching.* The foundation for the discussion about the mystery of faith is the stance of the Fourth Lateran Council that God is incomprehensible (*incomprehensibilis*) (DS 800). Vatican I teaches the existence of mysteries of faith, which, however, can also be recognized to a certain degree through reason illumined by faith (DS 3015f.). Vatican II in *DV* 2 describes divine revelation as the proclamation of "the mystery [*sacramentum*] of God's will," "that human beings should have access to the Father, through Christ, the Word made flesh, in the Holy Spirit, and thus become sharers in the divine nature."

(4) *Ecumenical Perspectives*. Because of its biblical foundations, the theology of the mystery of faith is well known to all denominations. In Lutheranism it is articulated above all in the teaching about the hidden God (*Deus absconditus*) and in the theology of the cross.

(5) *Systematic Reflections*. The mysterious character of faith is presupposed in the everyday understanding of it; what is understood is an object of knowledge. In the religious sphere the mysteriousness of faith is the sign of the fundamental dependence of human beings on the ground, origin, and goal of their existence, which ultimately remain concealed to them. In the Christian understanding the mystery of faith is the salvific plan of the triune God in history and thereby the foundation of all faith and all theology and the constitutive ground of the principle of the HIERARCHY OF TRUTHS. More specifically, one distinguishes a mystery of faith in an *extended sense* (insights about God that are naturally conceivable, yet that remain blurred because of the analogical character [ANALOGY] of all concepts about God); in the *narrower sense* (insights that are obtained on account of revelation); and in the *strict sense* (*mysteria stricte dicta*: realities whose content even after revelation are not graspable). Among the latter are numbered the Trinity, the incarnation, and the vocation of human beings to divine glory. On account of the inconceivability of God, it must be added that these still remain mysteries even when faith is transcended in the communion of love with God. The mystery of faith is thus in a final understanding the epistemological expression for the infinity of God. It thereby calls forth not only acknowledgment but also prayerful adoration.

See also GOD: MYSTERY OF; MYSTERY OF THE CHURCH; SACRAMENT; THEOLOGY.

Bibliography
Baum, Gregory. *Faith and Doctrine: A Contemporary View*. Paramus, N.J.: Newman, 1969.
Idel, Moshe, and Bernard McGinn, eds. *Mystical Union and Monotheistic Faith: An Ecumenical Dialogue*. New York: Macmillan, 1989.
Rahner, Karl. "The Concept of Mystery in Catholic Theology." In *Theological Investigations*, 4:36–73. New York: Seabury, 1974.
Rousselot, Pierre. *The Eyes of Faith*. New York: Fordham University Press, 1990.

WOLFGANG BEINERT

Mystery of the Church. The term *mystery of the church* is an expression of the church's sacramental nature.

(1) *Biblical Background*. The concept of "mystery" is native to the religions and philosophies of antiquity rather than to the Scriptures. In the latter it occurs chiefly in the apocalyptic writings: a "mystery" is a future event that God foresees but first hides and then reveals (see Dn 2:23f., 47; 2 Thes 2:3ff.; Rv 17:5, 7). In the Pauline and deutero-Pauline writings the concept is firmly linked to the revelation of God in Christ (1 Cor 2:1, 7; Col 1:26; 2:2; Eph 1:9). In Eph 5:32, the union of the church with Christ is said to be a "mystery."

(2) *History of Theology*. In the early church the word *mystery* was used to describe the saving deeds of God, which were said to be hidden in the old covenant, brought to fulfillment in the new, and celebrated now in worship. The concept thus becomes meaningful in the doctrine of the SACRAMENTS and especially in the doctrine of the EUCHARIST. From the Middle Ages down into the twentieth century (Pius XII, *Mystici corporis* [1943]), the church was said, by comparison with the eucharistic body of Christ, to be a "mystical body." H. de Lubac's studies in his *Corpus mysticum* (Einsiedeln, 1969) and *Die Kirche* (Einsiedeln, 1968) proved fruitful for theology.

(3) *Church Teaching*. Vatican II developed the concept "mystery of the church" in its full depth. According to *LG,* chap. 1, the church is a mystery inasmuch as it is a sacrament or "instrument of communion with God and unity among all men" (*LG* 1); because it has its origin in the triune God (*LG* 2–4); inasmuch as it emerged historically from the "mysteries of the life of Jesus" (*LG* 5); because the many biblical images of the church (images that nonetheless add up to a unity) converge in the idea of mystery (*LG* 6f.); inasmuch as, by reason of its sacramentality, it is hierarchically organized and at the same time reaches the limits of creation, even if with descending degrees of fullness. (See also *LG* 39, 44, 52, 63; *UR* 2, 4, 20; *OT* 9, 16; *NA* 4; *AG* 16; *GS* 2, 40.)

(4) *Ecumenical Perspectives*. The sacramentality or "mystery character" of the church is alien to Reformation theology. The latter defines the church in terms of its function of proclaiming the word of God and administering the sacraments. This definition also indicates the limitations of the church.

(5) *Systematic Reflections*. The meaning of the expression *mystery of the church* is not to be derived from epistemological considerations, as though the mysteriousness consisted in our inability to comprehend it, but from theological data. Thus understood, the "mystery" of the church points to the mystery of the self-communicating God.

See also MYSTERY OF FAITH; SACRAMENT.

Bibliography
Congar, Yves. *The Mystery of the Church.* 2d ed. Baltimore: Helicon, 1965.
———. *The Mystery of the Temple.* Westminster, Md.: Newman, 1967.
Dulles, Avery. *Models of the Church.* Garden City, N.Y.: Doubleday, 1974.
Le Guillou, Marie-Joseph. *Christ and Church: A Theology of the Mystery.* New York: Desclée, 1966.
Lubac, Henri de. *The Splendor of the Church.* London: Sheed and Ward, 1979.

WERNER LÖSER

Myths of Creation. The *concept* refers to mythological stories about the origin of the world and humanity, examples of which form part of the cultural heritage of nearly all early peoples. In principle, these myths embody the human impulse to establish control over lived existence in the face of a great number of unknown and untamed forces. Beyond that, they pose the question of truth, inasmuch as they recount "sacred histories" about the origin of everything experienceable (M. Eliade). Through this origin, which occasionally appears as itself divine, the transworldly enters the world and unifies its chaotic multiplicity. Humans, achieve participation in the truth-content and reality-content of the narrative destiny of the gods through ritual reenactment of it. There are many *forms* of myths of creation: auto-narration by a local deity, hymn, epic narrative, and so on. Almost always, the creative gods arise from something preexistent, as, for example, Ptah from the primeval waters of the Nile. According to the Egyptian myths (around 1400 B.C.E.), execution of the acts of creation occurs in a threefold way: (*a*) artistic formation or modeling in clay, (*b*) generative speaking or commanding, and (*c*) procreation, in which either a hermaphroditic god does both the siring and the bearing or a male god enlists the aid of a female. In the Babylonian mythology of the second millennium B.C.E. — for example, in the epic *Enuma Elish* — a fourth manner of execution, the battle, makes its appearance. There, it is reported that a local Mesopotamian deity, Marduk, creates the world by conquering, killing, and dismembering the primal deity (now a sea-dragon, now the primeval waters personified), Tiâmat. In this, he is assisted by a female deity, Ea. It is noticeable that this myth from an advanced civilization, similar to those from Egypt, has a strong cosmological interest. It ascribes a merely subordinate value to humans as individuals and as random members of society: they are there to serve the gods and to relieve them of work. Myths of creation that are older, more primitive, and ultimately closer to nature (such as may, for example, have left traces behind in the "Yahwist" transmittal of Genesis) show a more pronounced interest in humans and their immediate environment. The Bible, it has been shown, adopted aspects of this stock of mythical imagery (see the formation of Adam out of clay; the water symbolism; the image of dividing, separating, for the purpose of differentiation; perhaps even the creative Word), but nevertheless distinguishes itself fundamentally from the myths through its theological statement: the one God is the Creator of the universe; is dependent upon no preexistent material and no assistance; transcends, while encompassing, the differentiation of the sexes; creates not laboriously, but with consummate ease; initiates, with a goal in view, a process of history; does not permit God's creations (e.g., the stars) to be worshiped as gods alongside the true God; and destines humans not to be slaves of the gods but to engage in free creation of culture, engages in dialogue with them, and grants them a covenant with God. All this is said while, finally, no dualistic answer is given to the problem of volitive and afflictive evil. To this extent, the material appropriated by the biblical authors undergoes a "demythologization" that is conscious of its principles and standards.

See also CREATION NARRATIVES; COSMOGONY.

Bibliography
Anderson, Bernhard W. *Creation versus Chaos: The Reinterpretation of Mythical Symbolism in the Bible*. Philadelphia: Fortress, 1987.

Childs, Brevard. *Myth and Reality in the Old Testament*. London: SCM, 1960.
Clifford, Richard J., and John J. Collins, eds. *Creation in the Biblical Traditions*. Washington, D.C.: Catholic Biblical Association of America, 1992.
Eliade, Mircea. *A History of Religious Ideas*. Chicago: University of Chicago Press, 1978–85.
Rad, Gerhard von. *Old Testament Theology*. Vol. 1. New York: Harper, 1962.

ALEXANDRE GANOCZY

Nn

Natural Theology. The combination of "natural" and "theology" refers to the mode of knowledge of God that is conferred along with the very createdness of human beings.

(1) *Biblical Background.* Old Testament wisdom literature explicates the idea that God can be recognized through God's effects in the world. In Rom 1:18–20, Paul takes the natural knowability of God as a basis for the conclusion that nonrecognition and abuse of God are inexcusable. In Acts 17:22–31, Luke describes Paul's appeal to a natural theology for a positive missionary-theological purpose (see also Acts 14:15–17).

(2) *History of Theology.* Likewise, early Christian theology appropriates ideas from Greek philosophy as truths containing the "seeds" of the divine Logos. Since the philosophy of that age was predominantly oriented toward cosmology, Christians contrasted natural theology, as the knowledge of God derived from the "book of Nature," with Christian doctrine as that knowledge that was derived from the "book of Scripture." In general they sought to elaborate the convergence of the two "books." Countering an excessive rational optimism, Augustine emphasized that the human faculty of knowledge has been corrupted by sin. In the Middle Ages, Thomas Aquinas provided an impressive synthesis when he conceived the God who is manifested in nature in the light of the God of the Bible, whose free decision to effect creation is grounded in God's inner "goodness"/love (*STh* 1, q. 13). Thomas's holding together of both elements in his theology was overlooked by his imitative followers when they held that once one had conceived of God as the all-encompassing and necessary cause one had arrived at God. Later, during the Enlightenment, natural theology — understood as rationally attainable truth about God — was advanced as a competing alternative to theology based on revelation, and there was a tendency to transform the latter into natural theology.

(3) *Church Teaching.* Vatican I insists that humans, as created beings, can know God, but declares nothing about the actual possibility, extent, nature, and method of natural theology (DS 3004, 3026). The dogmatic declaration is directed expressly against Catholic currents implying pessimism about reason or salvation (FIDEISM, TRADITIONALISM).

(4) *Ecumenical Perspectives.* Since M. Luther and J. Calvin, Protestant theology has always been skeptical about the possibility of philosophical knowledge of God. In contrast, Roman Catholic theologians have insisted that natural theology does not imply that humans can gain control over God, but it does imply that God, as Creator, is responsive to human appeal by virtue of *God's* will; this is the basis for responsibility on the part of humans. In the

debates within German Protestant theology (K. Barth with E. Brunner, both against liberal theologians) just as in the debates between Protestant and Catholic theologians (K. Barth with E. Przywara and G. Söhngen), the beginnings of an objective convergence emerged. It came to be recognized that responsiveness to humans, as creatures of God, is one of the elements of redemption itself and may, or must, therefore be reflected upon.

(5) *Systematic Reflections.* Today problems emerge about natural theology from the standpoint of philosophies that can hardly be appropriated theologically. In this context it is necessary to insist on the possibility of philosophical knowledge of God. On the other hand, a question arises about the extent to which God is actually demonstrable in the world, given all its confusions and riddles; here, it should be noted that our experience of world and history can still be credibly interpreted as tending toward a hoped-for eschatological goal (W. Pannenberg and W. Kasper). Many of the questions surrounding natural theology also arise from ambiguities in the concept of nature, for nature can be used as the opposite of "spirit," "culture," "the supernatural," or "grace." Catholic theology, however, uses the term *natural theology* to refer to that openness toward God without which human beings could not be human. Taken in that sense, natural theology is reflection on the presuppositions under which belief can be understood at all.

See also GOD: POSSIBILITY OF KNOWLEDGE OF; HISTORY/HISTORICITY; THEOLOGY.

Bibliography
Barr, James. *Biblical Faith and Natural Theology: The Gifford Lectures for 1991.* Oxford: Clarendon, 1993.
Buckley, Michael J. *At the Origins of Modern Atheism.* New Haven: Yale University Press, 1987.
Byrne, Peter. *Natural Religion and the Nature of Religion.* New York: Routledge, 1989.
Lonergan, Bernard. *Insight.* New York: Philosophical Library, 1958.
Long, Eugene Thomas, ed. *Prospects for Natural Theology.* Washington, D.C.: Catholic University of America Press, 1992.
Macquarrie, John. *In Search of Deity: An Essay in Dialectical Theism.* New York: Crossroad, 1985.
McCool, Gerald A. *Catholic Theology in the Nineteenth Century: The Search for a Unitary Method.* New York: Seabury, 1977.

WILHELM BREUNING

Nature. Conceptually, "nature" (Greek: *phýsis,* from *phýein* = to grow, to generate, to be born; Latin: *natura,* from *nasci* = to be born) is a multileveled notion. (*a*) For a long time, theology oriented itself almost exclusively on the concept of nature used in *metaphysics,* seeing it as the constitutive character, the essence, and the fundamental principle of movement and action of a being as a type or individual. (*b*) It then acquired significance for *anthropology.* On the basis of the human and divine nature of Jesus Christ, the nature of human beings became the center of focus. Entelechy and goal-directedness in the world and history are attributed to it, and it is the bearer of a constitutive openness to God, a "natural longing" (*desiderium naturale*) and a "capacity for obedience" (*potentia oboedientialis*) directed toward God. (*c*) In this connection, *theology of grace* in particular speaks of a "supernatural" heightening and perfecting of nature through the unmerited grace of God. (*d*) Today, the concept of nature that is used in the *natural sciences,* and primarily in physics, is predominant. It designates as "nature" all organic and inorganic phenomena insofar as they are the object of sensory experience, rational investigation, and technical manipulation.

(1) *Biblical Background.* In the language of the Bible, the understanding of nature stamped by Greek metaphysics and cosmology plays no appreciable role. The world is seen not as one that has grown out of God, one that issues forth, emanates, from God through generation, but as the reality created by the one God. What Aristotelian physics calls nature is usually called creation in the Bible. The Priestly account of creation expresses its interest in nature by outlining, as original history, the creation of "the heavens and the earth," that is, of the cosmos along with the stars, plants, animals, and human beings, through the sole power of the divine Word (Gn 1:1–2:4a). The Yahwist does the same when he describes the relationship between humans and animals from the viewpoint of their common natural derivation from matter, their connection with the environment, and their being as creatures (Gn 2:4b–24). The wisdom texts emphasize the Creator's well-disposedness toward nature to the extent that they regard (Ps 19:1–9), and praise (Psalm 104), God as the overseer of a cosmos with its own laws. Israel's experiential wisdom forfeits none of its implicit theocentrism when it addresses the world of nature as a great teacher of humanity (see Prv 1:5; 25:23; 30:15, 24–31). The same applies to statements in the wisdom texts about the beauty, order, and purposiveness of the cosmos (see Sir 43:1–32; Jb 9:10; 37:13). This belief in creation by no means excludes "meditation on nature." What is denoted by the material concept of nature has its place in biblical theology. Jesus' nature-based parables, the Pauline inclusion of "all creation" in the drama of slavery and freedom (Rom 8:19–22), and the deutero-Pauline talk of Christ as Lord over the cosmic powers (Col 1:15–20; Eph 1:3–10) can be understood in this context.

(2) *History of Theology.* Numerous Fathers, especially Eastern ones, grant a similar place to cosmology in their theology of creation, without therefore omitting reflection on the metaphysically understood *phýsis* of humanity, God, and Christ. For them, being redeemed often means sharing in the divine nature (see 2 Pt 1:4) or even the "divinization" of human nature.

(3) *Church Teaching.* Teaching office has spoken about nature mainly in the framework of THEOLOGICAL ANTHROPOLOGY. It teaches that the original human state was no mere state of nature, but already a state of grace: a supernatural, unmerited, bestowed sharing of human nature in the divine nature (DS 1921; see 1978); further, that this reprieved human nature was not entirely corrupted by ORIGINAL SIN; and also, that the free will natural to humans was

not fully extinguished but only "weakened" (DS 396, 1521, 1555), so that it remains capable of freely cooperating with, and being supported by, God's justifying grace (DS 1525, 1554). The inception and growth of faith cannot, however, be "a work" (DS 375) or a "gift of nature" (DS 397), neither in the case of pre-Christian believers like Abraham (DS 396) nor in the case of persons on their way to belief in Christ. Only grace is capable of overcoming the power of original sin (DS 1513), of rendering sinners justified (DS 1551), and of bringing about in them the desire for, and realization of, the divine will (DS 374). In relation to salvation, doctrinal office represents human nature — which it usually understands in the sense of Aristotelian-Thomistic metaphysics — as the "conceptual counterpart of grace" (Alfaro, in *LThK*[2], 7:831). In relation to revelation, doctrinal office maintains that, based on the evidence of created things, the natural light of human reason can, in principle, recognize "God, the foundation and goal of all things" "with certainty" (DS 3004); God also, of course, approaches humanity in the "supernatural way" of revelation in Christ (ibid.).

(4) *Ecumenical Perspectives.* It is part of M. Luther's (see *WA* 19:206; 40/1:607; 42:631) and J. Calvin's (*Inst.* 1.2–6) basic concern to reject "natural theology," whereas P. Melanchthon and later Reformed confessional writings (e.g., Confessio Gallicana and Belgica, Art. 2) do not exclude such theology. A similar tension can be observed between K. Barth and E. Brunner. In general, it can be said that many statements of the Council of Trent are directed against a pessimistic evaluation of human nature — more than a little Augustinian in stamp — by the Reformers.

(5) *Systematic Reflections.* Present-day theology of creation is increasingly attempting to integrate even the material concept of nature. In view of the urgent problems posed by the environmental crisis and ecology, the relationships between "nature and practice" and "nature and culture" are being reexamined. Despotic human control over the world of nature, through which nature's independent status and intrinsic value are left fatefully unrecognized, is coming under criticism. The conditions are being sought for the possibility of a new symbiosis between humanized nature and a humanity existing in accord with nature. In the sense of the biblical creation-mandate, but under the conditions of today's industrial and service-oriented society, humanity needs to become the good shepherd of nature in a completely new way. This implies that it abandon the unthinking urge toward destructive mastery of nature and break free of the uncontrolled mechanisms of exponential growth. Without reviving the ancient myth of "Mother Nature," it is in humanity's own interest, properly understood, to perceive nature as a counterpart to human activity whose special character must be respected. Without following the unrealistic slogan "Back to nature!" spiritual beings have to transcend and cultivate nature in a way that accords with it.

See also CREATION; ECOLOGY; ENTELECHY; MATTER; NATURAL THEOLOGY; ORIGINAL STATE.

Bibliography

Carmody, John. *Ecology and Religion: Toward a Christian Theology of Nature*. Ramsey, N.J.: Paulist, 1983.

Dillard, Annie. *Pilgrim at Tinker Creek: A Mystical Excursion into the Natural World*. New York: Bantam, 1974.

Ganoczy, Alexandre. *Schöphungslehre*. Düsseldorf: Patmos, 1983.

Hendry, George S. *Theology of Nature*. Philadelphia: Westminster, 1980.

Pannenberg, Wolfhart. *Toward a Theology of Nature: Essays on Science and Faith*. Edited by Ted Peters. Louisville: Westminster, 1993.

Stewart, Claude. *Nature in Grace: A Study of the Theology of Nature*. Macon, Ga.: Mercer University Press, 1983.

Toulmin, Stephen. *The Return to Cosmology: Postmodern Science and the Theology of Nature*. Berkeley: University of California Press, 1982.

ALEXANDRE GANOCZY

Nature and Grace. The term *nature and grace* refers to the inherent essence of human beings in relationship to God's gratuitous work of salvation.

(1) *Biblical Background.* Nature (Greek: *phýsis*), in relationship to the notion of grace, has only a subordinate role in the Bible (Rom 2:14). In fact nature is seen as part of humankind's creatureliness and its creation in the image of God. In Eph 2:3–5, while nature and grace are both mentioned, nature means humankind's sinfulness.

(2) *History of Theology.* In the history of dogma, the first clear reference to nature and grace is in Tertullian (*De Anima* 21). In opposition to Pelagius (GRACE: THEOLOGICAL HERESIES), Augustine expresses the opinion that human nature has been totally corrupted by ORIGINAL SIN. Thus it is unconditionally in need of grace to do good. Thomas Aquinas regards nature (as perfectible) as open to grace (that which perfects) ("Gratia supponit naturam et perficit illam"). In response to the problem of whether grace can be earned, posed by Luther (d. 1546) and Baius (d. 1589), post-Tridentine Scholasticism proposed the abstract notion of "pure nature" (*natura pura*) apart from grace and distinguished it from other concrete states in salvation-history (see table below). In neo-scholasticism nature is seen as the substratum for an added, accidental, supernatural superstructure (which includes grace). The resulting extrinsicism of grace was contested by the Théologie Nouvelle (H. de Lubac), which emphasized the supernatural condition of concrete humankind. Thus the hypothesis of a *natura pura* became superfluous. K. Rahner was a mediator in the debate that followed. Human nature includes a "supernatural existential," which provides

natura pura	*purely conceptual possibility*
natura elevata	original state of the first man
natura lapsa	state after the sin of the first man
natura reparata	state after redemption by Christ
natura glorificata	state in the final beatific vision

an intrinsic link to grace. The notion of *natura pura* is maintained to assure that grace is unmerited.

(3) *Church Teaching.* The official position of the Council of Carthage (418) condemned Pelagius because he made nature equal to grace. He cheapened the redeeming grace of Jesus Christ by regarding it as merely a help for doing good, and he disregarded the profound sinfulness of human nature (DS 225–30). On the other hand, the Council of Trent rejected Luther's teaching that human nature is totally corrupted by original sin and that by nature human beings can only be sinful (DS 1521, 1555, 1557). The position of Baius was condemned by Pope Pius V in 1567 (DS 1921, 1925, 1927f., 1935–37). To counteract tendencies inherent in the Théologie Nouvelle, Pius XII emphasized that grace is absolutely unmerited (*Humani generis* [1950]). Vatican II avoided the term *supernatural* and replaced the abstract concepts of nature and grace with the concrete notions "humanity and God" and "creation and redemption."

(4) *Ecumenical Perspectives.* Basically, the nature and grace problematic is emphasized in post-Tridentine Catholic theology in order to counteract Luther's pessimistic understanding of human nature. According to M. Luther, the whole human person with all its faculties is so completely corrupted by original sin (*WA* 56:312) that human beings are evil by nature (*WA* 56:236). In particular, original sin brought about the total loss of the divine image. Luther's view of nature and grace is basically dualistic insofar as God's all-effectiveness (*Alleinwirksamkeit*) in salvation-history excludes competition from human effectiveness. Today there is a basic consensus among Evangelical and Catholic theologians that Christianity's understanding of human nature must come from the biblical notions of creation and the divine image. This also overcomes the traditional controversies concerning the divine image. In distancing itself from Luther's theory of a total loss of grace, Evangelical systematic theology recognizes the biblical fact that the divine image always remains fundamental to humankind. In distancing itself from the former division of a natural image that cannot be lost and a supernatural image that can be lost, Catholic dogmatic theology recognizes that the Bible presents the divine image as an indivisible unity.

(5) *Systematic Reflections.* The nature and grace problematic deals with the theological issue of the starting point of divine action in regard to humankind. Basically this starting point is to be seen within our creatureliness or our creation in the divine image, which is likewise a consequence of grace. Since neither of these realities can be lost, humanity is essentially related to God and open to God's saving work. Because Jesus Christ is the eschatologically fulfilled divine image, this type of schema includes a relationship to the God-man. Human nature must also be characterized as related to God historically (in its eschatological orientation) and personally (the whole person as related to God). Thus nature and grace are intrinsically united; that is, grace, as God's personal-historical, loving action, encompasses the personal-historical nature of humankind. Within the sphere of grace, human beings can give their

own answer to God's loving call. The mediation of Christ enables this answer to be concrete, part of salvation-history. In the language of theology this means: instead of nature and grace, we should say "person and grace," to avoid the shortcomings of the traditional exclusive, static, and abstract presentation. Since nature is never without grace and grace as unmerited is already assured in the notion of the absolutely free love of God, the concept of *natura pura* turns out to be superfluous. Likewise, the terms *supernature* and *supernatural* can be abandoned since they inevitably lead to extrinsicist ideas that hide the personal and historical character of grace.

See also CREATION; CREATURELINESS; IMAGE OF GOD; ORIGINAL SIN; REDEMPTION AND LIBERATION.

Bibliography

Lubac, Henri de. *Augustinianism and Modern Theology.* New York: Herder and Herder, 1968.

———. *The Mystery of the Supernatural.* New York: Herder and Herder, 1947.

Rahner, Karl. "Nature and Grace." In *Theological Investigations,* 4:347–82. New York: Crossroad, 1961.

GEORG KRAUS

Necessity of the Church for Salvation. The necessity of the church for salvation means that the salvation accomplished by God in Jesus Christ is historically mediated in and through the church, so that membership in the church is the way to participation in this salvation. This in turn means that there is no salvation outside the church.

(1) *Biblical Background.* The New Testament does not speak explicitly of the necessity of the church for salvation, but its ecclesiology implies the idea (see Mk 16:16). In Acts 4:12, Jesus Christ is said to be the only way to salvation. To the extent that the church belongs to him as his body, it shares in his role as mediator.

(2) *History of Theology.* The Fathers of the Church expatiate on the axiom "Outside the church, no salvation" (*Extra Ecclesiam nulla salus*) (e.g., Origen, *In Jos. hom.* 3; Cyprian, *Ep.* 7: "They cannot have God for Father who do not have the church for Mother"), but they do not exclude the possibility of salvation for the "holy pagans" (CHRIST'S DESCENT INTO HELL).

(3) *Church Teaching.* The documents of the magisterium emphasize the necessity of the church for salvation (Fourth Lateran Council: DS 802; Council of Florence: DS 1351; Boniface VIII, bull *Unam sanctam* [DS 875], declares the necessity of "submission to the Roman Pontiff"), but in more recent times these documents have been concerned primarily to exclude rigoristic interpretations of the axiom (DS 3866–73). Vatican II teaches the necessity of the church for salvation (*LG* 14; *AG* 7), but also acknowledges real possibilities of salvation outside the Roman Catholic Church, not only because of the "implicit desire of baptism" (*votum baptismi*) (DS 1524) but also because the other Christian

churches and ecclesial communities and even the other religions and cultures are ordered in varying degrees to the Catholic Church (see *LG* 15f.).

(4) *Ecumenical Perspectives.* The new understanding of the necessity of the church for salvation has made possible new ecumenical relations with the other churches (CHURCH AND CHURCHES). Each of these in its own way accepts the fundamental principle of the necessity of the church for salvation. The Reformation churches of the Lutheran and Reformed type maintain the principle that "outside the church there is no salvation" (documentation in U. Valeske, *Votum Ecclesiae* [Munich, 1962], 97–99). Of course, by "church" they do not mean the Roman Catholic Church with its societal constitution and its unification under the pope, but rather the "true" (as opposed to the "false") church, the true church being the community of those who hear God's word and accept it in faith. These other churches admit that beyond the boundaries of the church thus understood there arc "traces of the church" (*vestigia Ecclesiae*).

(5) *Systematic Reflections.* The necessity of the church for salvation has its ultimate basis in the divine plan of salvation (Ephesians 1). God wills that human beings be incorporated through faith and baptism into the body of Christ, the church, and in this way attain their salvation. Consequently, the church's missionary activity is in keeping with God's will and the church's own responsibility for the human race. Mission means, on the one hand, the implanting of the church in new regions and, on the other, inviting human beings and leading them to itself (see *LG* 14; *AG* 7).

See also BAPTISM; CATHOLICITY OF THE CHURCH; ECCLESIA AB ABEL; MEMBERSHIP IN THE CHURCH.

Bibliography
Burghardt, Walter J., and William G. Thompson, eds. *Why Church?* New York: Paulist, 1977.
Congar, Yves. *The Wide World My Parish: Salvation and Its Problems.* Baltimore: Helicon, 1961.
Theisen, Jerome P. *The Ultimate Church and the Promise of Salvation.* Collegeville, Minn.: St. John's University Press, 1976.

WERNER LÖSER

Non-Christians.

Non-Christians are human beings who do not believe in Jesus Christ and do not belong to any Christian church.

(1) *Biblical Background.* In connection with the question of the possibility of salvation the New Testament says that "Jews" and "Gentiles" (= all human beings) are deprived of the glory of God and need redemption from their sins (see Romans 3); Christ has dismantled the dividing wall (Eph 2:14). "All of you are 'one in Christ' " (Gal 3:28). God's saving will embraces all (1 Tm 2:4). This will was at work in the establishment of the church as the body of Christ, into which both Jews and Gentiles are incorporated through faith and baptism. In this manner God bestows on them the righteousness that they had previously tried — in vain — to acquire for themselves (see Romans 1–2).

(2) *History of Theology.* In connection with the interpretation of the axiom "No salvation outside the church," which can be traced back as far as Cyprian (d. 258), ever new efforts have been made to think out the possibilities of salvation for non-Christians. Augustine was conscious that a distinction must be made between the dividing line that we can see between Christians and non-Christians and the dividing line that God alone can see. In the Tridentine decree on justification the latter is linked to faith and baptism and thus to membership in the church, but at the same time the council acknowledges the possibility of a baptism "of desire" (*ex voto*) (DS 1524). More recently, K. Rahner introduced the concept of "anonymous Christians." By reason of the "supernatural existential" with which they are endowed, "anonymous Christians" accept the gracious self-communication of God in all their moral decisions and, in so doing, also implicitly affirm the historico-sacramental mediations of salvation. This view, which claims to be one way of interpreting the universal salvific will of God, has not gone unchallenged.

(3) *Church Teaching.* Vatican II introduced needed distinctions into the concept of non-Christians and related these individuals in a variety of ways to the church as the universal sacrament of salvation. It acknowledged religious experiences outside the church (*NA*; see *LG* 16), but at the same time held fast to the necessity of the church for salvation and thus to the duty of mission (*LG* 17; *AG*). The council explicitly discusses the Jews (*LG* 16; *NA* 4), Muslims (*LG* 16; *NA* 3), and Hinduism and Buddhism (*NA* 2).

(4) *Ecumenical Perspectives.* Because Evangelical theology interprets in a radical way the principle of "grace alone (*sola gratia*), faith alone (*sola fides*), and scripture alone (*sola scriptura*)," it has thus far found it difficult to develop a theology of religions. Among Evangelicals, it is chiefly W. Pannenberg who has broken new paths in this area.

(5) *Systematic Reflections.* A new and troubling phenomenon is "post-Christian non-Christians," who are increasing in numbers and creating new tasks for the church.

See also MEMBERSHIP IN THE CHURCH; MISSION; REDEMPTION AND LIBERATION; UNIVERSAL SALVIFIC WILL OF GOD.

Bibliography
Carmody, Denise Lardner. *What Are They Saying about Non-Christian Faith?* New York: Paulist, 1982.
Dawe, Donald G., and John B. Carman. *Christian Faith in a Religiously Plural World.* Maryknoll, N.Y.: Orbis Books, 1978.
D'Costa, Gavin, ed. *Christian Uniqueness Reconsidered: The Myth of a Pluralistic Theology of Religions.* Maryknoll, N.Y.: Orbis Books, 1990.
Rahner, Karl. "On the Importance of Non-Christian Religions for Salvation." Vol. 18 of *Theological Investigations.* New York: Crossroad, 1983.
Theisen, Jerome P. *The Ultimate Church and the Promise of Salvation.* Collegeville, Minn.: St. John's University Press, 1976.

WERNER LÖSER

O o

Offices of Jesus Christ. By "offices" we mean both Jesus Christ's empowerment in the Holy Spirit and the ways he is empowered to mediate salvation, as prophet (teacher, revealer), priest, and pastor (king, Lord).

(1) *Biblical Background.* In the New Testament, the offices of Jesus Christ are seen as the fulfillment of the Old Testament; in addition, the New Testament authors either view the offices as influencing one another mutually or at times place emphasis on one of the offices. The Old Testament expectation of a *prophet*-savior is especially visible in the Mosaic prophet (Dt 18:15–18) and the suffering servant (Is 52:13–53:12). Late Judaism also looked forward to a prophetic irruption (Jl 2:28) or an "eschatological prophet" (see 1 Mc 4:46; 14:41), concretized in the return of Elijah before the day of judgment (Sir 48:10f.). These images are joined with others in depictions of the high priest of messianic times and the kingly messiah. The Synoptics — especially Luke (7:16, 39; 24:19) — and Acts (3:22; 7:37) use a "prophetic Christology." Jesus' teaching is powerful and effective (Mk 1:21f. pars.; 1:27 par.) and results in discipleship (Mt 8:19; Mk 10:27 pars.; see Jn 13:13f.). In Paul (and the deutero-Pauline writings) the revelation of salvation is manifest in Jesus crucified and resurrected (2 Cor 5:4; see Rom 5:8–11; Phil 2:6–11; Col 1:15–20; Eph 1:3–23). According to Heb 1:1–3, the Son is both distinct from the (Old Testament) prophets because he is the eschatological messenger of revelation and also the mediator of creation and redemption (extensively developed as the priestly work of Christ in 4:14–10:18). John concentrates on the "Son (of God)" as eschatological bearer of revelation and life. In the Son, who is God's self-revelation, is found all *doxa* (glory), because the Father who sends and the Son who is sent are one (1:18; 2:11; 10:30; 14:9f.; 17:5, 24). Thus (eternal) life is also linked with belief in the Son of God (20:30; see 1 Jn 1:1–4). Only in the Spirit are "flesh" and the words of Christ salvific (6:63): the "Spirit of truth" makes present the saving revelation of the Son and leads to "the whole truth" (16:13; see 14:16f., 26). The Old Testament *priestly* mediator of salvation has no rigidly fixed form, since the institution of a priesthood was relatively late in Israel. The words on Levites (Dt 33:8–11), according to which mediation of God's will and offering sacrifice are ascribed to a priesthood as an office, receive a messianic explanation just prior to the Christian era. Many Old Testament texts also apply to the priesthood the Davidic idea of kingship and the theological reflections and hopes connected with Zion (2 Samuel 6f.; Is 2:1–5; Mi 4:1–3; see Ps 110:4). In the postexilic period mediation is through the high priest, and this leads to the development of a doctrine of sin (Leviticus 16). This in turn leads to the expectation of two messiahs, a kingly and a priestly

one (Zec 4:1–6a, 10b–14; see Jer 33:14–26), as seen in the intertestamental period (*Testaments of the Twelve Patriarchs;* Qumran). At the same time, there is harsh prophetic criticism of sacrificial rituals (Am 5:21–25; Hos 6:6; Is 1:10–17; Micah; Jeremiah 7) and the priesthood (Am 7:10ff.; Hos 6:9; Is 28:7f.; Jeremiah; Mal 1:10), which also elevates the meaning of covenant and justice above merely external sacrifice (cf. Psalm 51). The New Testament discussion of faith refers variously to these priestly/ritual and prophetic traditions of the Old Testament. On the basis of Jer 31:31–34 (a new covenant), Ex 24:1–11 (the covenant liturgy), and Lv 16:1–34 (liturgy of the day of atonement), Heb 4:10–10:18 develops a theology of Jesus Christ as the only high priest and sacrificial offering of the new covenant. In Christ the Old Testament ideas of priesthood and sacrifice are fulfilled and synthesized. In him is also fulfilled the prophetic criticism of sacrifice: the priest and the sacrifice are identical (7:27; 9:26, 28; 13:12). The means of Christ's sacrifice are his obedience (10:5–10) and his self-gift, which includes his whole life (4:15; 5:7–10; see 2:17f.), from his "entrance into the world" (10:5–10) to his death (9:14). This event is "once for all" (7:27f.; 9:12ff.) and yet "eternal" because of his priestly intercession in heaven at God's right hand (8f.). Thus he is the "mediator of a new [better] covenant" (8:6; 9:15; 12:24). In Pauline soteriology the "word of the cross" (1 Cor 1:18) is seen as a "word of reconciliation" (2 Cor 5:19) and as the "righteousness of God" (Rom 1:16f.), which makes possible our justification through Jesus Christ (Rom 3:21–28; 4:24f.; see 1 Cor 1:30). The key is Jesus Christ "for us" (1 Cor 15:3; Rom 4:25; 2 Cor 5:14f., 21; Gal 2:20; 1 Cor 11:24). Thus the terminology of sacrificial language is used here also (Rom 3:25; 4:25; 1 Cor 5:7; see Eph 1:7; 2:13; Col 1:20) and is linked to Jesus' "self-gift" (Rom 8:32; Gal 2:20; Eph 5:2). According to John, the death of Jesus is the fulfillment of God's revelation and the proof of God's love (13:1; 19:30), and this is seen clearly in his signs (13:1–20). Important references to the salvific meaning of Jesus' death are: the grain of wheat (12:24), the opening of his side (19:34), the lamb of God (1:26–29; 19:36), and the frequent use of "for" ("his life given for" [10:11–15, etc.; see 6:51c; 17:19; 1 Jn 2:2; 4:10]). The Synoptic and Pauline tradition concerning the Last Supper interprets Jesus' death as a vicarious, salvific gift of self and sees Jesus' blood (and therefore his death) as the basis of the new covenant liturgy (Mk 14:24 par. Mt 26:28); alternatively, it sees the gift of his body and blood as fulfilling the prophetic covenant promise (1 Cor 11:23–25 par. Lk 22:19f.; see Jn 6:51c). Together these texts elucidate the eschatological dimension (Mk 14:25; see 26:29; Lk 22:15–18; 1 Cor 11:26) and the idea of atonement through the death of a martyr or through God's servant, and they are part of the "earliest interpretation of Jesus' death" (see Mk 10:45 par. Mt 20:28; Lk 22:37). According to the Old Testament, God shepherds God's flock (Psalm 23; 95:7; Is 40:11; etc.) even when God's earthly kings (shepherds) fail (Jeremiah 23; Ezekiel 34). The Davidic aspirations for a just leader are related to this image (Jer 23:5; see Zec 23:1–6; Ez 34:23f.; 37:24). The promise made to David in the prophecy of Nathan becomes the theme of an eschatological

hope for an ideal lord and kingly mediator of salvation (messiah). This promise was frequently repeated and reinterpreted (see the Royal Psalms: 2; 45; 72;
89; 110; 132; the "Emmanuel cycle" in Is 7:10–17; 9:1–6; 11:1–9; and Zec
9:9f.). The future Lord will be "God's servant" (Ez 34:23f.; Zec 3:8), "God's
anointed one" (Pss 2:2; 89:39, 52), "God's Son" (2 Sm 7:14; Pss 2:7; 110:3; Is
9:5). In the New Testament, because of a Christianized version of the messiah,
the title "Son of God" results in knowledge of the true divine sonship of Jesus
(see Rom 1:3f.; CHRISTOLOGICAL TITLES; HYPOSTATIC UNION), while the pastor
image (and its equivalents) makes possible a deeper understanding of his role
in mediating salvation. It brings together Jesus' earthly concern for the lost (Mt
10:6; Mk 6:34; Lk 15:4–7; 1 Pt 2:25), the salvific act of his death and resurrection (Mk 14:27f. par. Mt 26:31; Heb 13:20), and his eschatological power
(Mk 25:32; 1 Pt 5:4). The inscription on the cross, "king of the Jews" (Mk
15:26 pars.; Jn 18:18), and the trial before Pilate (Mk 15:2 pars.; Jn 18:33–37)
demonstrate the peculiarity of Jesus' kingship: the crucified messiah is exalted
Lord and Christ through his resurrection (Acts 2:32, 36; 5:31; Rom 1:3f.; Phil
2:6–11). According to John, he is the "good shepherd" (10:1–21), who precedes (10:4) and gives his life for his sheep (10:11). Thus the shepherd image
synthesizes the words of the earthly Jesus on discipleship (Mt 8:21f.; 10:26
par.; Lk 9:57–62 par.) and situates the description of Jesus as "leader" (Acts
3:15; 5:31; Heb 2:10; 12:2). It is also related to the journey theme of Luke's
salvation-history as part of a "soteriology of Jesus' life," including his death
and resurrection (Lk 24:26; Acts 10:33–43). The historical basis for the shepherd image is both Jesus' message about the kingdom of God and his whole
life, which point to him as the eschatological mediator of salvation.

   (2) *History of Theology.* In patristic theology there are few references to a
trilogy of offices, even though they are often mentioned individually. Justin is
the first to group them (*Dial.* 86.2), and the trilogy is found in Eusebius of
Caesarea (*Hist. eccl.* 1.3.7–10), Jerome (*Com. in Hab.* 2.3), and Peter Chryso-
logus (*Serm.* 40). In the Middle Ages they are found in Thomas (*Super ad
Hebr.* 1.1.4; *In Ps.* 44.5; *STh* 3, q. 22, a. 1) and Bonaventure (*Lign. vit.* 39;
etc.). In fact, aside from a few exceptions (in commentaries on the *STh*), they
play no role before the end of the nineteenth century. After an initial attempt
(D. Schramm, 1789), the doctrine of the three offices becomes increasingly important (E. Klupfel, B. Galura, F. Walter, G. Philips) and, after M. J. Scheeben,
makes its entry into (neo-scholastic) dogmatic manuals as the principle of division of soteriology. Recent treatments make full use of them (e.g., Alfaro) or
qualify them (e.g., W. Kasper).

   (3) *Church Teaching.* Before the twentieth century, official pronouncements
regarding the offices of Jesus Christ refer to them only individually: to his
priestly office (DS 261, 802, 1740–43) and his pastoral or kingly office insofar as Jesus Christ is described in creeds as the coming judge of "the living and
the dead" (DS 30, 125, 150, etc.), "whose kingdom is without end" (DS 150;
see 41, 42, 44 etc.). The Council of Trent calls him the "redeemer in whom we

believe" and the "lawgiver whom we obey" (DS 1571). In the twentieth century the three offices have been mentioned widely in papal encyclicals (DS 3675ff.; 3847ff.; 3916; see *Mystici corporis*) and in Vatican II (esp. *LG*).

(4) *Ecumenical Perspectives.* In Reformed theology (esp. Calvin) the three offices were first used as a division of soteriology and then became common Christian property. More recently, they are used in different ways by K. Barth, who subordinates the prophetic office to the others, and by G. Ebeling, who in reference to power and powerlessness in the historical Jesus reinterprets the priestly office by regarding Jesus as Word of God, brother of all, and Lord of the world. For W. Pannenberg, Jesus' office is to "call people to God's reign which has already appeared in him," and he speaks of the typological schema of the three offices only to say that Jesus Christ carries within himself all the traditions of Israel by his coming and destiny.

(5) *Systematic Reflections.* Today (despite Vatican II) there is no unified teaching concerning the offices of Jesus Christ in Catholic soteriology, even though any teaching on the offices remains firmly anchored in belief in the redeemer: his incarnation and the paschal mystery are the central events of salvation. In traditional dogmatics the priestly office (usually treated in reference only to Jesus' death) occupied the foreground. In terms of today's problematic, a new grounding of soteriology must rethink the three offices starting with the overall testimony of Scripture, and it must include a "soteriology of the life of Jesus." This means that the offices of Jesus Christ are the eschatological fulfillment of the promises of the Old Testament and that Jesus is the Christ, the eschatological mediatory of salvation (see 1 Cor 15:3–5: "according to the Scriptures"). In his whole life, from the beginning (incarnation) until death and beyond, he is the revealer (prophet, teacher), priest (intercessor), and Lord (shepherd, king) for humankind. Thus no office can ever be assigned exclusively to one "phase" of Jesus' life. Just as the offices of Jesus Christ cannot be divided temporally, so too they cannot be separated from one other. They copenetrate one another and are complementary aspects of the one mystery of salvation in Christ, which is based on the incarnation, realized in the life and crucifixion of Jesus, and eternalized in the resurrection (the exaltation) (see the table under SOTERIOLOGICAL MODELS). Such a doctrine of the three offices, constructed on the basis of salvation-history, reflects on our access to God through Jesus Christ in the Holy Spirit in the ongoing present and is open to the fullness of salvation in the kingdom of God, that is, in eternity.

See also HISTORICAL JESUS; MEDIATORSHIP OF JESUS CHRIST; SALVATION; SOTERIOLOGICAL MODELS; SOTERIOLOGY.

Bibliography

Aulèn, Gustaf. *Christus Victor: An Historical Study of the Three Main Types of the Idea of Atonement.* New York: Macmillan, 1961.

Ban, Joseph D., ed. *The Christological Foundation for Contemporary Theological Education.* Macon, Ga.: Mercer University Press, 1988.

LOTHAR ULLRICH

Offices of the Church. *See* SACRAMENT OF ORDERS.

Oneness of the Church. *See* UNITY OF THE CHURCH.

Ontologism. Ontologism is a position in fundamental theology according to which God, as the ultimate ground of being, is known first as the ontological truth of all things and an immediate light for human knowledge.

(1) *Biblical Background.* The Bible, while emphasizing the tension between the nearness *and* the mysteriousness of God, does not have the problems of a modern epistemology that seeks to engage in ontologism.

(2) *History of Theology.* Ontologism is a nineteenth-century philosophical-anthropological approach that claims its roots are in undeveloped tendencies in Augustine and Bonaventure. Instead they go back to the occasionalism of N. Malebranche. A coherent theory of ontologism was initially developed by V. Gioberti (d. 1852).

(3) *Church Teaching.* In 1861, the Holy Office rejected the "errors of the ontologists" (DS 2841–47), for example, that having immediate knowledge of God is an essential part of human nature (DS 2841). Vatican I did not condemn ontologism, although such condemnation was desired in many quarters.

(4) *Ecumenical Perspectives.* Ontologism acquired no ecumenical significance.

(5) *Systematic Reflections.* Assumption of unmediated insight into the nature of God does not do justice to the creatureliness and historicality of human beings: since humans are subject to these conditions, they require mediation of God's nearness and presence, which is effected most profoundly and most consummately in the incarnation and in redemptive history as stamped by the incarnation. A central concern of ontologism is taken up by transcendental-theological anthropology (e.g., K. Rahner) when it directs attention to the fact that the human state is one of constant referredness to God.

See also GOD: POSSIBILITY OF KNOWLEDGE OF.

Bibliography
McCool, Gerald A. *Catholic Theology in the Nineteenth Century: The Search for a Unitary Method.* New York: Seabury, 1977.

WILHELM BREUNING

Orders. *See* SACRAMENT OF ORDERS.

Original Sin. Original sin (*peccatum originale*) refers to the general imperfect state that, as a result of human sin, has been the lot of every human being since the very beginning of the species.

(1) *Biblical Background.* Composed in the context of the Solomonic crisis in the Yahweh religion, the Yahwist "account of creation" gives expression, in various stories, to an awareness of generally widespread sinning: the first human couple's eating of the fruit of the tree of knowledge that was reserved

for God, an act of disobedience against something divinely commanded (Gn 3:1–24, in which context Adam is seen as a collective personality); the murdering of a brother, through which natural healthy competitiveness issues in an act of evil intemperance (Gn 4:1–16); the intermarriage between the "sons of heaven" and the daughters of man, which is followed by an increase in wickedness on earth (Gn 6:1–7); and the building of the Tower of Babel, an act of insolence in the area of technical capability (Gn 11:1–9). These stories reveal the characteristics of the prototypal act of sinning: turning away from God (and thus from the source of life), greedy seizure for oneself of some good stemming from God (see Jb 15:8), refusal to obey divine commands, making an absolute of self-interest to the point of self-deification, and disregard of the boundaries laid down at creation. Talk of a human "fall" or "decline," out of weakness or under the pressures of fate, seems less suited to characterizing "primal sin," for that is a consciously willed, free act. Some aspects of the theology of original sin, such as radical corruptedness of human nature or biological inheritance of guilt, lie outside the Yahwist field of vision. Also, physical death is not depicted here as a punishment for "primal sin." To be sure, God invokes the threat of punishment by death (Gn 2:17), but God does not carry it out. Here, as elsewhere in the Old Testament, death remains the natural termination of the cycle of life. Ps 51:7 ("Indeed, in guilt was I born, and in sin my mother conceived me") suggests only very remotely the state of affairs denoted by "original sin." In the New Testament, Paul depicts sin as a power structure that he calls *hamartía*. This "reigns" (Rom 5:21; 6:12ff.) within humanity from "Adam" onward; through it, a quite specific mode of physical death "came to all, inasmuch as all sinned" (Rom 5:12), and all are affected as one through an interconnectedness of deeds. *Hamartía* is the power that alienates the world from its constitutive qualities as determined at creation, renders it subject to futility (Rom 8:20), encroaches upon nature as well (Rom 8:19–21), and produces, among heathens, the typical phenomenon of idolatrous worship of the creature "rather than the creator" (Rom 1:23, 25) and, among Jews, that of complacent self-congratulation regarding the law. Nevertheless, concepts like "inherited guilt," "inherited punishment," "inherited death," "doomedness," or "radically corrupted human nature" lie outside Pauline thought. Decisive is the fact that the "one person," Adam, contributes to the ungodly condition of humanity just as do all other humans, and that sins and the consequences of sin keep piling up, so to speak, to burden their existence. In opposition to this power, a greater power intervenes — that of the God who had loved us "while we were still sinners" (Rom 5:8) and made Jesus Christ our reconciler (Rom 5:8–11; 2 Cor 5:19f.) in the "likeness of sinful flesh" (Rom 8:3), so that "where sin increased, grace overflowed all the more" (Rom 5:20). The Johannine tradition also recognizes the power of sin in the world (Jn 8:44; 1 Jn 1:7; 4:7–15, 17), but, according to it, humanity first becomes evil through its deed, and is not so by nature.

(2) *History of Theology.* Cyprian speaks of an "alien guilt" in infants that

has to be expunged through baptism (*Ep.* 64.5). Much influence was exerted by the mistranslation, in the Vulgate, of Rom 5:12 (Greek: *eph' hô pántes hémarton = because* all sinned; Vulgate: *in quo omnes peccaverunt =* in whom [Adam] all have sinned). Thus Ambrose — starting out from the basic principle of Roman law that the conduct of a head of family permanently affects the legal position of the entire family — assumes anticipatory coinvolvement in Adam's sin by all his descendants as a whole: "I am sinful in Adam..., I am dead in Adam" (*lapsus sum in Adam..., mortuus sum in Adam*) (*De excessu fratris* 2.6). Augustine imparts a decisive stamp to the doctrine of original sin. According to him, original sin is transferred via the lustful act of procreation; through that, all humans incur guilt and become condemnable sinners (see *De pecc. et rem.* 1.9–15). In opposition to the Pelagians, who regard the newborn as guiltless, Augustine insists on their inherited sinfulness, seeing this as expressed in their appetitiveness (concupiscence) (ibid., 2.4; *C. Iulianum* 2.3.5). Stained by "paternal guilt" (*Op. imp.* 1.48), they belong to the "condemned multitude" (*Ep.* 186.6.16; *De corr. et gratia* 7.12). Their sole salvation lies in baptism. The problem of the salvation of non-Christian peoples occupies Augustine little. In the Middle Ages, Thomas Aquinas clarified the doctrine of original sin by distinguishing a formal (lack of natural justness) and a material element (evil appetitiveness) (*STh* 1–2, q. 82, a. 3). Eastern patristicism did not develop a theology of original sin.

(3) *Church Teaching.* Teaching office adopted many, but by no means all, of the elements of the Augustinian theory of original sin. The Synod of Carthage (418) rejected the opinions (*a*) that the death of Adam had nothing to do with punishment for his sins (DS 222), (*b*) that the newly born had no natural sin and did not require baptism for remission of sin (DS 223), and (*c*) that the saints were without sin (DS 228). On the positive side, it taught that grace is an indispensable aid to avoiding sins and fulfilling the commandments (DS 225–27). According to the Council of Orange (529), the deciding factor is God's redemptive will. The Council of Trent, in response to the theology of M. Luther (see sec. 4 below), taught that "all of Adam" was "changed for the worse," in body and soul, through his "offense against God," or more precisely, through his loss of the holiness and justness intended by God (DS 1511f.). With that, injury is also done to his descendants, above all whenever sin, the "death of the soul," eventuates (DS 1512). Only the one mediator, Christ, can overcome this condition (DS 1513). Original sin is transferred "through propagation (*propagatione*), not through imitation" (ibid.); it inheres in all, belongs to each, and is expunged through baptism (DS 1514). Further, the point is stressed that concupiscence "originates from sin and disposes toward sin," but is not itself properly sin (DS 1515); the free will is "not lost and extinguished" (DS 1555), but only "weakened" (DS 1521). Vatican II formulated a subtly articulated doctrine of original sin, whereby "corruption of the heart" is seen in an absence from one's existence of the "necessary ultimate orientation" (*GS* 11) and in the tendency to degenerate into a one-sidedly scientific and technical being (*GS* 36).

(4) *Ecumenical Perspectives.* According to Luther, original sin corrupts human nature utterly (see CA 2). Because it displaces free will (*WA* 18:635, 670), humans must despair of their own powers (*WA* 43:178f.; see *WA* 1:183). Original sin and concupiscence become identical.

(5) *Systematic Reflections.* Any theology of original sin must be conscious of the fact that the concept contains two *analogies:* original sin is compared to the notion of *sin* as a sinful deed (since, like that, it contains the element of remoteness from God) and to the notion of *origin* (so as to suggest a preexisting root to which every person newly arrived on earth remains connected). Other analogies clarify the intended meaning today: alienation, fallenness, lack of authenticity. In the background is the factual experience: all humans have, from childhood on, an inclination toward evil (EVIL, MORAL); every evil deed has an intersocial and communicative character; again and again, nexuses of guilt are generated among human beings. Through the theological concept of the primal condition as a state of uncorrupted human existence, the notion of original sin is made still more precise. Present-day dogmatics distances itself decidedly from the theories of Augustine. It puts continued emphasis on the fact of universal sinfulness, but also, with reference to Vatican II (*LG* 16; *NA* 2), on God's comprehensive redemptive plan and on the element of human responsibility, whose psychological and sociological preconditions have been more adequately recognized (the fundamental dividedness of human beings, their collective egoism, their disordered self-love; see here, too, Vatican II, *GS* 8, 13, 37). There is also an awareness of the social consequences of sin. No synthesis has yet been reached; it is being pursued on the basis of a theological anthropology midway between pessimism and naive optimism.

See also BAPTISM; ORIGINAL STATE; REDEMPTION AND LIBERATION; SIN AND GUILT.

Bibliography
Fraine, Jean de. *The Bible and the Origin of Man.* New York: Desclée, 1962.
Ganoczy, Alexandre. *Schöpfungslehre.* Düsseldorf: Patmos, 1983.
Kasujja, Augustine. *Polygenism and the Theology of Original Sin Today.* Rome: Urbaniana University Press, 1986.
McDermot, Brian. *What Are They Saying about Original Sin?* New York: Paulist, 1984.
Rahner, Karl. "The Sin of Adam." In *Theological Investigations,* 11:247–62. New York: Seabury, 1974.
Scheffczyk, Leo. *Creation and Providence.* New York: Herder and Herder, 1970.

ALEXANDRE GANOCZY

Original State. The concept of an "original state" expresses the idea of the human condition, as unimpaired under grace, that was intended for humanity by the Creator "prior to," or apart from, the fact of sin.

(1) *Biblical Background.* In their precritical readings of primal history, the authors of the Old and New Testaments assume that the situation of the first human couple, or of the human species, had been radically changed by the

occurrence, at a certain point in history, of sin. With that, however, they are making not a historical statement but an etiological one: the cause (Greek: *aitía*) of the conditions that now exist is to be uncovered. In this connection, the difference in emphasis between the two "accounts of creation" must be noted. Whereas the Yahwist account brings out very clearly the break between the original state and the sinful state of the first human couple (Gn 3:7–24: awareness of nakedness, fear before God, male-female antagonism, wearisome labor, painful childbirth; yet not a word about loss of immortality!), the Priestly account brings the account of God's six days of activity to a close by simply declaring that "he found it very good" (Gn 1:31) and describing how God then rested (Gn 2:1–4a). The contrast between a very good creation and a world "full of lawlessness" is first broached in the story of Noah (Gn 6:11f.); but it also serves there as a prelude to the great act of grace that is the covenant (Gn 6:18f.). Here, the characteristics of the lost original state are at best indirectly suggested. The New Testament presents Jesus himself as making nothing more than mere allusions to the fall (Mk 10:5–9 par.; Jn 3:5f.; 8:44). Paul, on the other hand, with a view to illustrating the above-mentioned contrast, consciously invokes the notion that death entered history as a result of sin. To be sure, in the two passages that are decisive in this connection (1 Cor 15:21f.; Rom 5:12–21), his main aim is clearly to emphasize the redemption of humankind from sin and death that was effected by Christ. Thus Adam ultimately appears as the subject of a theological subordinate clause that belongs to a main clause centered on Christ.

(2) *History of Theology.* The theology of the original state was developed by Scholasticism. Since there was then scarcely any awareness, in the interpretation of biblical texts, of the distinction between theological intention and historical representation, it interpreted the gifts of the original state quite literally (see Thomas Aquinas, *STh* 1, q. 90–102), sometimes also making use of mythological notions about paradise.

(3) *Church Teaching.* Teaching office speaks of the original state in connection with original sin. It appears as a state of sanctity and righteousness (DS 1512; see 3514), wholeness (DS 1921–26), undiminished freedom of will (DS 1521; see 239, 242, 383), and immortality (DS 1511f.; see 1978, 3514). The concrete form of the last is nowhere made precise. Constantly stressed is the fact that the original state is a heightened one under grace, and thus a supernatural one (DS 1921; see 1901–9, 1923–26, 1978).

(4) *Ecumenical Perspectives.* In the disputation with Protestantism, Catholic theologians distinguished between "supernatural" and "extranatural" (e.g., effortless acquisition of knowledge) gifts under grace of the original state.

(5) *Systematic Reflections.* Present-day dogmatics takes into consideration not only the results of the scholarly exegesis but also the christological-soteriological accentuation of the New Testament comments on Adam. Moreover, it interprets the original state as a statement about the fundamental capacity of humanity to coexist with God in a divinely befitting way. With

that, humanity's responsibility for choosing or rejecting God also becomes most clearly conspicuous. From this perspective, immortality of humans in the original state, for example, would not mean "that the grace of the original state would have prevented the termination of earthly life; rather, this termination would not have had the character of sorrowful death under sin, but would have occurred as an unbroken transitional return of the person into the hands of merciful God" (J. Feiner, *LThK* 10:574).

    See also CREATION NARRATIVES; ORIGINAL SIN.

Bibliography
See the bibliographies under CREATION NARRATIVES and ORIGINAL SIN.

ALEXANDRE GANOCZY

Pp

Parish. *See* LOCAL CHURCH.

Parousia. The parousia is the coming of the exalted Lord in power and glory at the end of time.

(1) *Biblical Background.* In the New Testament the parousia is identified with the "day of Yahweh," which had been expected in the Old Testament. If we look at the New Testament as a whole, we must distinguish between the word *parousía* and the reality that it signifies. (*a*) The Greek word *parousía* signifies, in the Hellenistic period, the visit of a ruler or high official; in the cult of the emperors it signifies the festive arrival of the emperor. Reference is occasionally made also to a parousia of the gods. The New Testament uses the word *parousía* with reference to the Old Testament idea of the emergence of God from hiddenness (see, e.g., the theophanies: Gn 18:1f.; Ex 2:1f.; the visions in which the prophets received their calls: Is 6:1f.; Jer 1:4f.; Ez 1:4f.). In the Synoptics, the word *parousía* occurs only in Mt 24:3, 27, 37, 39. In the Johannine writings it occurs in 1 Jn 2:28. It reaches its highest degree of importance in the Pauline letters, while in the Pastoral Letters it is replaced by the word *epiphany*. The Catholic Letters, too, use the word *parousía* a few times (Jas 5:7, 8; 2 Pt 1:16; 3:4, 12). The expression "return" or "Second Coming of Christ" is at least open to misinterpretation, since it does not bring out the difference between his first coming in poverty and lowliness (Phil 2:7; Jn 1:14; and the infancy narratives in Matthew and Luke) and his appearance in power and glory; in addition, it gives the impression that we are dealing here with something that has happened once before. (*b*) In the Synoptics, statements about the reality signified by the word *parousía* are to be found in the eschatological discourse (Mt 24:1–25:46; Mk 13:1–37; Lk 21:5–36). Mark (13:24–27) uses the stylistic devices of the Old Testament theophany descriptions (see Dt 30:4; Is 13:10; 34:4; Zec 2:10; Dn 7:13) in order to depict the parousia, while in Matthew (25:31–46) the role of the Son of Man as judge emerges more clearly, and in Luke (21:28) the parousia is understood as, among other things, the day of complete redemption and the definitive coming of the royal reign of God. A final characteristic of the Synoptic understanding of the parousia is the idea of the expectation of an imminent end, which is connected with the exhortation to constant vigilance and preparedness, since no one but God knows the day. Although the word *parousía* does not occur in Acts, the reality to which it refers is a main focus of interest inasmuch as the resurrection, ascension (exaltation), and parousia of Christ are regarded as a unity. The same Jesus who was taken up into heaven will come again (1:11); through his Spirit he is at work

519

in the church, which is understood as the time between the ascension and the parousia. The parousia becomes especially important in the Pauline letters in connection with their Kyrios Christology and the urgent sense of an imminent end. The parousia becomes the saving event par excellence because it brings with it the resurrection of the dead and the bestowal of the glorified body. In addition, Paul, like the Synoptics, gives an apocalyptic description of the parousia of the Lord (1 Thes 4:16–17; 2 Thes 1:7–8). The title Kyrios (Lord), which is so characteristic of Pauline Christology, refers to the Lord who has risen and will appear at the parousia, so that *parousía* and *Lord* may be regarded as interchangeable terms, as can be seen in such formulations as the parousia of the Lord (1 Thes 3:13; 4:15; 5:23), hope in the Lord (1 Thes 1:3; 2:19), meeting with the Lord (1 Thes 4:17), and the day of the Lord (1 Thes 5:2; 2 Thes 2:2). In the Pastoral Letters (1 Tm 6:14; 2 Tm 1:10; 4:1, 8; Ti 2:13), *epiphany* (instead of *parousía*) can signify either the coming of Christ at the incarnation or the appearance of the exalted Lord. In these letters the expectation of an imminent end that is so characteristic of the Pauline letters is no longer present and has been replaced by a different eschatological hope (see Ti 2:13; 1 Tm 6:14; 2 Tm 4:1). Although John has primarily a realized ESCHATOLOGY, we find in the postscript chapter the hope of the eschatological coming of Christ (21:22; see 1 Jn 2:28). When John speaks of events connected with the parousia, the expression "last day" is used (6:39, 40, 44, 54; 11:24; 12:48). In Revelation the word *parousía* does not appear, although the reality to which it refers is treated in detail, as can be seen from the beginning (1:1, 3) and end (22:20) of the book. As in the eschatological discourse of the Synoptics, the coming Christ is described with the aid of apocalyptic images and motifs (14:14f.; 19:11f.).

(2) *History of Theology*. In ecclesial tradition hope of the parousia is usually found connected with other eschatological statements, and especially with the doctrine of the resurrection of the dead, the last judgment, and rewards and punishments in the beyond.

(3) *Church Teaching*. In the church's teaching pronouncements the parousia is found in the creeds of the early church (DS 10, 76, 150) and in the doctrinal pronouncements of the Middle Ages (DS 801, 852) that are concerned with the resurrection of the dead and the final judgment and speak in this context of a coming of Christ (in glory). The declaration of the Congregation for the Doctrine of the Faith entitled "Some Questions of Eschatology" (May 17, 1979) distinguishes between the appearance of our Lord Jesus Christ in glory and the situation of human beings immediately after their death (*AAS* 71 [1979] 941).

(4) *Ecumenical Perspectives* and (5) *Systematic Reflections*. In ecumenical discussion and in contemporary theology the parousia has acquired a certain importance due to the thesis of resurrection at death, against which the above-mentioned declaration of the Congregation for the Doctrine of the Faith is directed.

See also EXPECTATION OF AN IMMINENT END; HEAVEN; HELL; JUDGMENT; RESURRECTION OF THE DEAD.

Bibliography
Glasson, T. Francis. "Theophany and Parousia." *NTS* 34 (1988) 259–70.
Moore, A. L. *The Parousia in the New Testament*. Leiden: Brill, 1966.
Nolan, B. M. "Some Observations on the Parousia and New Testament Eschatology." *IThQ* 36 (1960) 283–314.
Perriman, Andrew C. "Paul and the Parousia: 1 Corinthians 15:50–57 and 2 Corinthians 5:1–5." *NTS* 35 (1989) 512–21.
Schnackenburg, Rudolf. *God's Rule and Kingdom*. New York: Herder and Herder, 1963.
———. *The Moral Teaching of the New Testament*. New York: Herder and Herder, 1965.

JOSEF FINKENZELLER

Passion and Death of Jesus Christ. The passion and death of Jesus Christ are the decisive stages of his earthly life that reveal who he is and what he did for the salvation of humankind.

(1) *Biblical Background.* According to the testimony of the New Testament, the passion and death of Jesus Christ are inseparably linked with both his whole earthly life and his resurrection. Jesus' commitment to God and humankind included acceptance of dangers to his life and readiness for death. Thus his death was a self-gift, a "persevering pro-existence unto death" (H. Schürmann). According to Mk 14:25, he hoped for final salvation. Belief in the passion and death of Jesus Christ is expressed in two forms. (a) *In confessional form* (e.g., 1 Thes 4:14; Rom 4:25; 1 Cor 15:3–5; 1 Pt 3:18). Here the cross is closely linked with the resurrection (e.g., Acts 2:23f.; 3:15; 4:10, etc.; Rom 6:5; 8:34; 2 Cor 5:15; Phil 2:6–11; Heb 2:10; 4:14f.; 5:7–10). (b) *In the passion narrative.* At the basis of the Synoptics was probably a pre-Markan tradition (contained in Mk 14:32–16:8) that — referring to the Old Testament (Psalm 22!) in the light of Easter — proclaims that the crucified just person, Jesus, has been raised. Mark composes his whole Gospel as a prelude to the passion and death of Jesus Christ, which is recorded in 14:1–16:18 (see the prophecies of the passion [8:31; 9:31; 10:33f.]; Jesus' understanding of his destiny [10:45]; and the revelation of the mystery of the Son of God [14:62; 15:39]). Matthew views the passion and death of Jesus Christ (26:1–28:10) in their significance for the establishment of the church. The passion is one part of Christ's way to glory (28:16–20). His death (and resurrection) is the beginning of a new world (see 27:51b–53; 28:2–4). For Luke the passion and death of Jesus Christ are phases of the journey to glory that fulfills the divine "ought" (9:22; 13:33; 17:25; 18:32; 22:37; see 24:7, 25f., 44, 46f.). Jesus precedes his disciples on this journey and offers them a path to salvation. Following him (to the cross) has salvific meaning (5:11, 27f.; 9:11, 23, 57, 59, 61; 18:22, 28, 43; 23:26). Their community of destiny with him becomes a community of life (23:43; see 23:47f.). According to John, the passion and death of Jesus Christ (18:1–20:10) are his exaltation and glorification (see 3:14f.; 12:32f.; 17:1, 5, 19). His death proves his love (3:16f.; 13:1–20; 19:30) and has salvific meaning (12:34; 19:34, 36; see 6:51c; 10:11–15:17). All the Synoptics regard the Last Supper narrative as part of the passion. They also interpret the salvific sign of the passion and death

as atonement. A biblical abbreviation of this salvific meaningfulness is the "for us," which can be traced back to the oldest layers of the tradition.

(2) *History of Theology.* The soteriology of the patristic period relates the whole life of Jesus — from the incarnation onward — to redemption through his passion and death. Although as time passed soteriological language became more abstract and universal, some individuals maintained a concrete, spiritual theology of the passion (e.g., Origen, Maximus the Confessor, Augustine, Bernard of Clairvaux, Ignatius of Loyola, M. Luther, L. Chardon). In recent times it has been demonstrated that the eschatological and messianic praxis of Jesus contains a social (or "political") dimension, which should not be isolated from the passion and death. Jesus' life is not just the prelude to his suffering. Latin American liberation theology proposes a concrete, integral theology of the passion and death of Jesus Christ by bringing to light their liberating dimension. This counteracts a quietist interpretation of the cross that is easily misused to maintain power and injustice.

(3) *Church Teaching.* The passion and death of Jesus Christ belong to the essential core of the creed. The individual phases expressly mentioned are: "he suffered, was crucified, died, and was buried" (DS 6, 10, 30, 42 etc.). There is emphasis on Jesus' freedom (DS 6, 62f., 423, 442, 1364) and the reality of his suffering (DS 325), as well as on the fact that he was "crucified for us" (DS 150, etc.). In its decree on the sacrifice of the Mass, the Council of Trent describes the death of Jesus Christ as a sacrifice (DS 1730f., 1743, 1753f.; see 1083, 3316, 3847f.). The fact that the salvific effects of redemption are a result of the passion and death of Jesus Christ was defended in various ways (DS 485, 904, 1523, 1529f., 1741, 3370, 3438, 3805). In GS 22, Vatican II combines various New Testament statements about the passion and death of Christ and also uses the journey theme (see *LG* 3, 5, 7, 9, etc.; *SC* 5f). John Paul II (*Dives in misericordia* [1980]) finds the revelation of God's mercy in the *whole* paschal mystery.

(4) *Ecumenical Perspectives.* Since the turn of the century, Evangelical theologians have discussed Jesus' self-understanding in the passion and death. According to liberal theologians, he saw no salvific meaning in them (W. Wrede, A. von Harnack, J. Weiss). According to others, it is unknown how he regarded his death. In contrast, G. Friedrich claims that he at least considered the possibility of a violent death. According to M. Hengel and P. Stuhlmacher, he attached salvific meaning to it. Beginning from the perspective of Easter, W. Pannenberg and E. Jüngel ascribe a soteriological meaning to the passion and death of Jesus Christ.

(5) *Systematic Reflections.* Exegetical and dogmatic findings point to an inseparable link between the passion and death of Jesus Christ and his life *and* resurrection. Despite the discontinuity of the earthly Jesus and the resurrected Christ, there is also a continuity. It is found first — christologically — in the identity of his person: the crucified Jesus *is* the resurrected, crucified Christ. Furthermore, on this basis the passion and death can also be understood soteri-

ologically. The evident, active proexistence of Jesus as service of humankind is a commitment that comes from God. Thus Jesus himself can be understood as representing God's reign in person. This proexistence is maintained by the dying Jesus in two directions (from God, at the service of humankind) (H. Schürmann). Despite this continuity, however, the death of Jesus is not an "epiphenomenon of the proexistence," just as the life of Jesus is not just a prelude to his death, but has its own salvific worth. The decisive turning point of the last "hour" and the qualitative newness of Jesus' death should not be underestimated. In the death of Jesus, his proexistence for us becomes a definitive reality, and in the resurrection it is established by God. Through the resurrection, Jesus' proexistent life *and* death are unequivocally seen as soteriological and representative, and after Easter this is put into words, using the *hyper*-formula (and its equivalent), and grounded in God, using the ideas of mission and incarnation.

See also CROSS, THEOLOGY OF THE; DISCIPLESHIP, CHRISTIAN; HISTORICAL JESUS; REPRESENTATION; RESURRECTION OF JESUS.

Bibliography
Balthasar, Hans Urs von. *Mysterium Paschale: The Mystery of Easter.* Edinburgh: T and T Clark, 1990.
Boff, Leonardo. *Jesus Christ Liberator: A Critical Christology for Our Times.* Maryknoll, N.Y.: Orbis Books, 1978.
Brown, Raymond E. *The Death of the Messiah: From Gethsemane to the Grave: A Commentary on the Passion Narratives in the Four Gospels.* Garden City, N.Y.: Doubleday, 1994.
Goergen, Donald. *The Death and Resurrection of Jesus.* Wilmington, Del.: Glazier, 1988.
Green, Joel B. *The Death of Jesus: Tradition and Interpretation in the Passion Narrative.* Tübingen: Mohr, 1988.
Lohse, Eduard. *History of the Suffering and Death of Jesus Christ.* Philadelphia: Fortress, 1967.
Neyrey, Jerome H. *The Passion according to Luke: A Redaction Study of Luke's Soteriology.* New York: Paulist, 1985.
Sylva, Dennis D. *Reimaging the Death of the Lukan Jesus.* Frankfurt: Hain, 1990.

LOTHAR ULLRICH

Peace. In German, *Friede* (peace) is closely related etymologically to *Freiheit* (freedom) and *Freude* (joy). In English, from the Latin root of the word *peace* (*pax*) comes also the word *pact*. These references suggest a wider range of meaning for the word than is often recognized. Today peace means either, on the one hand, the opposite of war or conflicts in the social and political spheres or, on the other hand, the subjective feeling of rest, relaxation, and contentment. The more original meaning comprises all areas of life. Peace signifies the interconnection of the conditions of life in which human existence and living with others can flourish in every respect. Theologically, peace in this sense is a gift from God. Peace is thus the quintessence of salvation.

(1) *Biblical Background.* The more comprehensive meaning of peace is found above all in the Old Testament *shālōm,* which is able to take on the most

varied concrete expressions and therefore became the most common word of greeting among Jews. A strict separation between the profane and the religious meanings cannot be made. The flourishing of human life depends on the relationship to Yahweh and on Yahweh's covenant with Israel (e.g., Lev 26:3–13). Since Israel has broken this covenant, its peace, its productive way of life, has been disrupted (Jer 6:14). For the prophets, peace is the object of eschatological hope in Yahweh's faithfulness to the covenant (e.g., Ez 34:25–31). The New Testament builds on this hope when it recognizes Jesus as the bearer of the eschatological peace (Lk 19:38). Christians' greeting of peace among one another represents at the same time the peace with God that has been experienced in their faith in Christ (Rom 5:1), the willingness to live in peace with one another (Rom 12:18), and the hope for the ultimate peace of the kingdom of God (Rom 15:13; Heb 12:14).

(2) *History of Theology.* In the course of the history of theology this wide range of meaning for the idea of peace has been diminished and fragmented. Under the influence of Stoic philosophy the idea of peace of mind was developed. This consists in the untroubled conscience of the human person who lives in agreement with the divine will and is more or less immune from the disturbances in the exterior peace of the world. The Emperor Constantine's ending of the time of persecution granted a theological significance to the peace between the church and society. In the confusion of the period of the tribal migrations and later in the fighting between the feudal lords within the empire, the main accent in the concept of peace became the contrast to war. In the nineteenth century, the subjective dimension of peace (i.e., peace of mind) was once more spotlighted, taking prominence over a sober rationalism. While today the subjective meaning of peace has been thoroughly secularized (we speak of "wanting" peace), the theological meaning — influenced by the experience of two world wars and in view of the armaments race with its weapons of global annihilation — emphasizes peace in contrast to war and violence.

(3) *Church Teaching.* The official expressions of the church with regard to peace are thus found above all in connection with war and violence (the encyclical *Pacem in terris* [1963]; GS 77–82). Beyond this, Vatican II offers starting points for a theology of peace in the comprehensive biblical sense (LG 78; see 83–90).

(4) *Ecumenical Perspectives.* In the ecumenical conversation, the worldwide discussion on peace brings the separated Christian communities closer to each other. For this discussion calls to mind the common task of giving witness in the world to the gospel's message of peace by means of a lived community of peace.

(5) *Systematic Reflections.* The threat of the use of atomic weapons has become global and touches the basic survival of humanity. This threat encompasses the human person in all areas of life and thereby produces existential anxiety. In this situation, the original, more comprehensive meaning of peace comes again into view. Theology can develop the Christian-ecclesiastical, the

political-social, the subjective-emotional, and the eschatological aspects of this peace with God. Here any one-dimensional explanation is to be avoided, since this would bring with it the danger that the gospel's comprehensive message of peace has been cut short.

See also SALVATION.

Bibliography
Küng, Hans, and Jürgen Moltmann, eds. *A Council for Peace.* Edinburgh: T and T Clark, 1988.
Moltmann, Jürgen. *Creating a Just Future: The Politics of Peace and the Ethics of Creation in a Threatened World.* Philadelphia: Trinity, 1989.
Rahner, Karl. "The Peace of God and the Peace of the World." In *Theological Investigations,* 10:371–88. New York: Herder and Herder, 1973.

GEORG LANGEMEYER

Penance. Penance, understood as a way of life and an attitude and as a virtue, is the turning, sustained by God's gracious condescension, of the whole person from sin and to God and God's will. Contrition is the heart of penance. There is both extrasacramental and sacramental penance, the latter being found not only in the sacrament of reconciliation, in BAPTISM, and in the ANOINTING OF THE SICK, but also in the EUCHARIST.

(1) *Biblical Background.* The Old Testament is familiar with the active turning from sin and to God, or conversion, that is expressed in the term *penance.* It knows it, first of all, as an external cultic and ritual practice of penance (see Jl 1:13f.). Sin and penance are here clearly seen as involving the community or even the entire people. To meet the danger that cultic-ritual penance may become simply external, the prophets emphasize the need of interior conversion (see Jl 2:13), which must find expression in acts of love for the neighbor (see Is 58:5–7). Despite all the human cooperation involved, penance is not the independent action of human beings but God's gracious gift (see Is 44:22). In the New Testament, the idea of penance is expressed essentially in the term *metanoia* (conversion, change of mind), which signifies a new direction bestowed by God and affecting the entire person; conversion has a once-for-all character but must, of course, be continued throughout life as the ever-new ratification and deepening of what happened in the past. Even if, as recent exegetical findings claim, an explicit call to *metanoia* was not part of the original preaching of Jesus, the central New Testament texts on penance, such as Mk 1:15 and Acts 2:38, certainly capture the intention of Jesus: the faith that Jesus calls for in the kingdom of God that is dawning in his person implies a conversion. Acceptance of God's great offer and active rejection of sin go together, although the acceptance of God's self-gift by which sin is forgiven has priority.

(2) *History of Theology.* Penance plays an important part in the history of Christian preaching and theology. The Latin word for penance, *paenitentia* or *poenitentia,* which is connected with the idea of punishment, emphasizes, often

in an excessive way, the aspect of atonement and reparation in penance: the divine order that has been disturbed by sin must be restored through works of penance. Also discussed is whether penance is a special virtue or simply a collective term for an important aspect of all the virtues. Thomas Aquinas, for example, regards it as a special virtue.

(3) *Church Teaching.* Magisterial statements have concerned themselves chiefly with contrition as the heart of penance. However, in his apostolic letter *Reconciliatio et paenitentia* of 1984 John Paul II deals with penance specifically and in a comprehensive way in its relation to Christian life.

(4) *Ecumenical Perspectives.* The churches of the Reformation likewise regard it as self-evident that the faith in God's promise, which brings about justification and the forgiveness of sins, sets up an opposition to sin. But faith here is pure receptivity, so that it is difficult to see how penance can be an active renunciation of sin. At any rate, Luther agrees that the grace of justifying faith sets human beings on the path of a new kind of activity. Thus the difference between this and the Catholic understanding of penance is not so great, provided the latter, in keeping with its own central tradition, likewise recognizes that the human "activity" of penance owes its existence solely to grace.

(5) *Systematic Reflections.* This is the real issue: penance is to be seen as a grace-supported response to God's gracious condescension through Jesus Christ in the Holy Spirit and not, for instance, as a condition that human beings must fulfill in order to receive God's forgiveness. In keeping with the testimony of the New Testament, penance is the once-for-all conversion of believers to God, although they must persevere in this conversion and deepen it in their lives and especially in their relationships with the community. More important here than the emphasis on conflict and the struggle against sin is the insistence on an ever-new turning to God, a turning that can take concrete form in the turning to the neighbor. In this process penance can take various forms: the faith-inspired acceptance of the word of God, reparation, "works" of love of neighbor, prayer, the acceptance of suffering imposed on one, heeding the advice of fellow Christians, self-conquest, and finally — and at times indispensably — the sacrament of reconciliation.

See also REPENTANCE; SACRAMENT OF RECONCILIATION; SIN AND GUILT.

Bibliography
Fitzgerald, Allan. *Conversion through Penance in the Italian Church of the Fourth and Fifth Centuries: New Approaches to the Experience of Conversion from Sin.* Lewiston, N.Y.: Mellen, 1988.
Rahner, Karl. *Penance in the Early Church.* New York: Crossroad, 1982.
Schlick, Jean, and Marie Zimmermann. *Penance and Reconciliation: International Bibliography 1975.* Strasbourg: Cerdic Publications, 1984.
Tertullian. *Treatises on Penance: On Penitence and On Purity.* Westminster, Md.: Newman, 1959.
Werbick, Jürgen. *Schulderfahrung und Busssakrament.* Mainz: Matthias-Grünewald, 1985.

GÜNTER KOCH

People of God. "People of God" is one of the names for the church of Jesus Christ. To distinguish the church from the Israel of the Old Testament it is also called "the new people of God."

(1) *Biblical Background.* The church is expressly called people of God in 1 Pt 2:9f. (see also Rom 9:25f.; 2 Cor 6:16; Ti 2:14). The chief equivalent is the Pauline concept of "church" (*ekklēsia*, which originally meant a gathering of the people).

(2) *History of Theology.* In the early church, "people of God" was a common designation for the church (it is central in Augustine), but from the Middle Ages on it yielded place to the concept of BODY OF CHRIST. In the twentieth century it once again became a focus of theological reflection. M. Koster, *Ekklesiologie im Werden* (1940), gave the dogmatic stimulus for extensive exegetical and canonical study.

(3) *Church Teaching.* Vatican II accepted the results of that study: people of God is its usual name for the church (see *LG* 9 and passim).

(4) *Ecumenical Perspectives.* The antihierarchical tendencies of the Reformation were especially favorable to the idea of the people of God. However, the concept also has an important place in ecumenical dialogues on ecclesiology.

(5) *Systematic Reflections.* As understood by Vatican II, "people of God" signifies the unity and equality (based on faith and baptism) of all members of the church, as well as the continuity of the church with the people of God in the old covenant, a continuity that does not deny discontinuity (the church is the "new" people of God). At present, the theology of the people of God is being further developed in a "theology of the people," which reflects on the Christian "base."

See also PRIESTHOOD OF THE FAITHFUL.

Bibliography
Boff, Leonardo. *Ecclesiogenesis*. Maryknoll, N.Y.: Orbis Books, 1976.
Boff, Leonardo, and Virgil Elizondo. *The People of God amidst the Poor*. Edinburgh: T and T Clark, 1984.
Congar, Yves. *Lay People in the Church*. Westminster, Md.: Newman, 1957.
Coriden, James A., ed. *We the People of God: A Study of Constitutional Government in the Church*. Huntington, Ind.: Canon Law Society of America, 1968.
Dahl, Nils Alstrup. *Das Volk Gottes: Eine Untersuchung zum Kirchenbewusstsein des Urchristentums*. Oslo: Dybwad, 1941.
Rahner, Karl. "People of God." In *Sacramentum Mundi: An Encyclopedia of Theology,* edited by Karl Rahner with Cornelius Ernst and Kevin Smyth, 4:400–402. New York: Herder and Herder, 1969.

WERNER LÖSER

Person. Person is an analogical concept. In the Christian doctrine of God it describes the three realities to which the divine substance or divine nature belongs equally but which are nevertheless to be distinguished according to the specific origin and specific mission of each.

(1) *Biblical Background.* The biblical basis of this doctrine consists of ex-

plicit formulas (Mt 28:19; 2 Cor 13:13) and the overall structure of the self-manifestation of Jesus Christ, who refers everything to the Father and announces the sending of the Spirit. It is not yet possible, however, to speak of a clear and binding doctrine of faith on the tripersonhood of God.

(2) *History of Theology.* Tertullian (*Adv. Prax.* 6.1; 8; 18.2) introduced the concept of person into Christian theology in order to illustrate the Christian idea of God (TRINITY; INCARNATION). When the ecumenical councils of the fourth and fifth centuries were endeavoring to explain the being and salvation-historical mission of the Son and the Spirit in their relation to the Father, the term *person* won out against the then controversial Greek equivalents *prósopon* and *hypóstasis*, especially in the documents of the popes (DS 144, 284, 293, 295). In the theology of the Trinity, person alone expresses the differences between Father, Son, and Holy Spirit within a single divine nature; in Christology, person has been used from Chalcedon on (DS 302) to express the unity of Christ in contrast to the diversity of the divine and human natures. The theological concept of person did not arise out of philosophical discussion of a (univocally understood) "essence" of God, but out of inferences drawn from God's action in the history of salvation (the economic Trinity) to God's intradivine being. In the beginning, the concept had a primarily defensive function and was hardly thought out and refined in all its ramifications: person meant a someone to whom certain effects were ascribed. It was Boethius and, following him, the medieval thinkers who turned the word *person* into a philosophical term that was increasingly applied also to human beings. In the modern period, the anthropological use of the concept of person pushed the original theological understanding of it into the background and in fact even became opposed to it. In modern philosophy person is associated with the freedom and autonomous self-disposal of human beings; the "person" is the center out of which the actions of a human being emerge. As a result, not only was an opposition drawn between God and human beings (claim to autonomy; individualism), but the application of person to the Trinity was excluded: its application would mean that in God there are three centers of action and therefore three gods (tritheism). No reconciliation of the classical-theological understanding of person with the modern understanding has as yet been achieved.

(3) *Church Teaching.* The history of theology shows clearly that the term *person* is an indispensable linguistic rule for stating the basic dogmas of the Trinity and Christology.

(4) *Ecumenical Perspectives.* The concept of person in its classical usage belongs to the basic stock of shared Christian thought and language. The explanation and deeper understanding of the term in view of the problem created by modern thought are tasks to be undertaken by all involved in the ecumenical movement.

(5) *Systematic Reflections.* An attempt at a theological explanation against the background of the situation created by the history of dogma (see sec. 2 above) begins with the question of what is meant by describing the Father, Son,

and Holy Spirit as divine persons. The analogy of relationships within a family gives a first hint as to the meaning of the relationship between the first and second divine persons. The New Testament, however, already departs from this analogy when it places the Holy Spirit in a unique relationship both to the Father and to the Son. The analogy now is of spirit as distinct from matter, that is, as principle of life in the most general sense. The Holy Spirit is a person insofar as it makes mediation possible and brings it to pass. Human beings experience such a mediation when they discover themselves to be partners of God, that is, when they understand their own being as persons in relation to the mediating personal being of one who is greater and other and who establishes them in their human finiteness as well as, simultaneously, in the transcendence bestowed on them. The experience raises the question of this partner whom they know to have established them in freedom and to have endowed them with their own freedom. They must therefore understand their relationship to God as a contrast between infinite and finite conditioned freedom, between absolute and contingent self-disposal. Human beings are therefore from the outset and by their very nature called to a partnership toward which they must freely take a stance. The power to do this they can connect only with creation, although they know that at every point the partnership has been wounded by sin and warped in its effectiveness. It is only redemption and a new creation that restore it to them anew and enable them to bring it to fulfillment, so far as it lies in them. This salvation-historical relating of their own existence back to its source confronts human beings, in their effort to understand themselves, with truths that lie outside themselves and that are regarded as the work of God the Father and the work of the Son but are at the same time to be considered effects of the Spirit. This becomes clear to them when they understand themselves in relation to their salvation and come to a decision thereon, insofar as they cannot, from this point of view, ascribe to themselves the really operative reasons for their own behavior but are compelled to interpret them as grace. The acceptance of the divine offer and call, as well as their own response to the pledge of divine grace, can only be characterized as fruits of that Spirit who has been given to us and through whom the love of God is poured out in our hearts (see Rom 5:5). The partnership between God and human beings is thus not a relationship subsequently added on, but exists from the moment when human beings are established as historically free by divine freedom. The partnership is hopelessly endangered when human beings reject it by sin; it is elevated to a new level by the incarnation of the Son of God, and human beings acquire it as their own through the mission and indwelling of the Holy Spirit. The personhood of human beings is distinct from the divine personhood, even though it must be maintained that in God's case, too, there is true personhood. The distinction makes it clear that personhood is realized in different ways and is not to be understood in a schematic and univocal way as a universal concept. This has consequences for the use of the word in relation to God. If personhood means the autonomy of self-disposing freedom in relationality, then various emphases are possible that take into account the metaphorical language of the New Testament and can help to a better understanding of the interpretations given in the classic doctrine of the Trinity but found today to be quite unsatisfactory. In this view, the Father would be the fundamental autonomy of God, while the Son would express the self-disposing freedom of this God, and the Spirit the concrete relationality that is proper to this God. The connection between the three is evidently such that no one of the three is conceivable without the others, while, on the other hand, each has such a specific autonomy that it cannot be regarded simply as a mode or aspect of being. The description "property constitutive of a subject" may be suggested, which does not, of course, replace the biblical names Father, Son, and Holy Spirit, but does explain their personality to contemporary thought in such a way that no erroneous ideas will be connected with the names. As far as the properties of the three are concerned, the personhood of each divine person is realized in a different way that is determined by the position of that person in the entire structure of relations. One difficulty regarding this manner of speaking comes from the traditional teaching that the activity of God outside God's self (*operatio ad extra*) must be common to all the divine persons and that specific aspects of this activity can be attributed (appropriated) only in a figurative sense to one or other of the persons. A debate has developed on this point but has not produced any unambiguous result. It may be taken as certain that it is possible to speak of the personality of God as such only because, and to the extent that, human beings experience the divine activity as emerging from a *single* source. For the sake of the dialogue with philosophy as well as the dialogue with other monotheistic religions (Judaism, Islam), this is a point that must not be relinquished, although it must be made clear that talk of God as a person has a different meaning than the description of the Father, the Son, and the Holy Spirit as persons. In the contemporary intellectual context, however, the appropriation of creation to the Father, of redemption to the Son, and of sanctification to the Holy Spirit may no longer do full justice to the truths mentioned. It would serve as a basis only for a figurative knowledge of the divine persons, and this cannot be regarded as adequate in light of the biblical testimony. A solution of this difficulty is made possible by a deeper reflection on the role of the Holy Spirit, who concretizes relationality in the area both of the divine activity outside God and of the intradivine being; that is, the Spirit realizes in its person the relational character of the relation between Father and Son but also that between Creator and creation, redeemer and redemption, grace-giver and graced (human being/Christian). In this way, mediation would be proper (and not simply attributed) to the Spirit as person, just as the Father would in the proper sense be the original source. This mediation determines the life of God in the three divine persons and the life of God with the world in various activities. Conversely, in this light person may be defined as the independent reality that realizes itself in intellectual mediation and, in addition, exercises freedom and self-disposal. The key word *mediation* always includes communion and a certain history (to be more fully defined) as inseparable elements in the work of mediation.

See also APPROPRIATIONS; CHRISTOLOGY; GOD'S PERSONAL NATURE; HUMAN PERSON; HYPOSTATIC UNION; TRINITARIAN PERSONHOOD OF GOD; TRINITY.

Bibliography
LaCugna, Catherine. *God for Us: The Trinity and Christian Life.* San Francisco: Harper, 1991.
McLean, George F. *The Human Person.* Washington, D.C.: American Catholic Philosophical Association, 1979.
Moingt, Joseph. *Théologie trinitaire de Tertullien.* 4 vols. Paris: Aubier, 1966–69.
Muller, Max, et al. "Person." In *Sacramentum Mundi: An Encyclopedia of Theology,* edited by Karl Rahner with Cornelius Ernst and Kevin Smyth, 4:404–19. New York: Herder and Herder, 1969.
Murphy-O'Connor, Jerome. *Becoming Human Together: The Pastoral Anthropology of St. Paul.* Wilmington, Del.: Glazier, 1982.

KARL HEINZ NEUFELD

Personality. The word *personality* refers to the uniqueness of each individual human person; that uniqueness is based on the fact that the human person knows him- or herself as distinct from all the other human persons and from everything in general and takes a stance toward him- or herself and everything else. Therefore, on the one hand, consciousness and freedom belong to human personality; on the other hand, personality is based on the relation to the other, above all, to other human beings. One has to distinguish between personality as a disposition that all human persons share on the basis of their biological-psychic nature (HUMAN PERSON) and personality as a realization of existence. Personality is therefore a dynamic concept, a characterization that has to be realized in the course of human life.

(1) *Biblical Background.* In Scripture the concept of person does not appear in this sense. In the New Testament, person describes the individually characteristic features and status of the human person. Statements such as "God shows no partiality" (Gal 2:6; Rom 2:11; passim) may seem to downplay this dimension, but they actually mean that God takes seriously every human person in his or her uniqueness. The election of Israel and the call to salvation in Christ address the human person in her or his original and singular responsibility.

(2) *History of Theology.* The theological concept of the person was first developed in the trinitarian doctrine (see TRINITY: DOCTRINE OF THE) and in CHRISTOLOGY and was defined by the early councils. This development both inspired and burdened the efforts of Scholasticism to reach a conceptual determination of personality. The task was to find a definition of the essence of the person that would apply both to the divine persons and to the personality of the human person (ANALOGY). In this effort to find the quality that makes a being endowed with intellect (*natura rationalis*) into a person, some put more emphasis on being self-subsistent (subsistence, independence), others on being in relation (*relatio,* relatedness). On the other hand, the modern concept

of the person defines personality by starting from human consciousness and through the elements of self-possession and self-determination, which in their finiteness (limited by time and world) point toward the absolute divine consciousness (K. Rahner). Dialogical personalism (F. Ebner, M. Buber) corrects or completes this concept of personality through the element of the relationship to one's fellow human beings (I-thou relation). The human person discovers him- or herself as a person through the other. In his relationship to fellow human beings, he or she becomes a person. Theologically, however, Scholasticism's metaphysical concept of the person retains its meaning insofar as the designation of the human person to become a person in the human community before God is given by God in creation and is the basis for the workings of grace.

(3) *Church Teaching.* Church teaching grounds the personality of the human person in the person's being created in the image of God (*GS* 12) and being called to share a communal salvation (*GS* 24). It therefore belongs to the core of the church's mission to "save the human person" (see *GS* 3), that is, to enable the "personalization" of the human person in the increasingly dense net of social interconnections (*GS* 6).

(4) *Ecumenical Perspectives.* Protestant theology usually contrasts the human being's self-understanding as a person with a purely theological determination of personality drawn from the word of God. The human being first becomes a person when he or she is addressed by God's word. Yet at present Protestant theology also searches for a more differentiated determination of the relationship between the theological and the anthropological concept of personality.

(5) *Systematic Reflections.* In current theology the concept of the person has gained fundamental importance. It pervades and links all the individual questions of dogmatics. Political theology, however, suspects this concept of covering up the dependence of the human person and of theology in general on social structures and of promoting a reduction of Christian practice to the realm of interiority or of private sociability. The non-European theologies (India, Africa) find that the religious experiences of their cultures are not sufficiently included in personalistic theology. As regards Scripture, the question arises whether the statements about the unity (*unio*) with God or with Christ and about the unity in the Spirit have been interpreted sufficiently in relation to the notion of community (*communio*). For personhood, in distinction to unity, the relation to the other is essential. It remains problematic whether the concept of personality can integrate all the dimensions and aspects of the human being or whether it is just one beside other fundamental characteristics of the human person (INDIVIDUAL; HUMAN PERSON).

See also COMMUNITY (RELATIONSHIP); GOD'S PERSONAL NATURE; IDENTITY; IMAGE OF GOD; PERSON; TRINITARIAN PERSONHOOD OF GOD.

Bibliography
Astley, Jeff, and Leslie J. Francis, eds. *Christian Perspectives on Faith Development: A Reader.* Grand Rapids: Eerdmans, 1992.

Auer, Johann. *Person: Ein Schlussel zum christlichen Mysterium.* Regensburg: Pustet, 1979.
Brown, Laurence B. *Religion, Personality, and Mental Health.* New York: Springer, 1994.
Schavan, Annette, and Bernhard Welte. *Person und Verantwortung: Zur Bedeutung u. Begrundung von Personalitat.* Düsseldorf: Patmos, 1980.

GEORG LANGEMEYER

Pneumatology. Pneumatology is the dogmatic discipline that deals with the nature and action of the Holy Spirit as the third divine PERSON.

(1) *Biblical Background.* The New Testament does not have an independent doctrine of the Holy Spirit. There is, however, a series of scattered starting points in John (especially 14–16) and Acts, but also, and even earlier, in the letters of Paul; each of these gives a glimpse of a particular representation of the Spirit. These various statements are connected with other statements about the way in which God's saving will is implemented — especially in creation, the incarnation, and sanctification.

(2) *History of Theology.* Prior to any sketch of the history of dogma, attention must be called to the problem posed by the concept of pneumatology. As a theological term it has played a role for barely a generation now; previously it was used in philosophy, although against a theological background. In general, pneumatology means the doctrine of angels and demons; in a more restricted use, it means the metaphysical doctrine of the soul as a spiritual substance or the psychological doctrine of the soul's spiritual functions. Philosophical pneumatology has been in crisis ever since the Enlightenment and German idealism, because its theological background was in the final analysis a gnostic doctrine of angels and demons and had to do therefore with created spirits. Dogmatic pneumatology proper arose as a reaction against fourth-century Macedonianism or Pneumatomachianism, which seems to have thought of the Holy Spirit as a supreme angel and a creature (*ktisma*) or as a being intermediate between God and creatures. The Council of Constantinople (381) condemned this position. Like the heresy just mentioned, the tritheistic doctrine of God proposed by Joachim of Fiore (d. 1202) seems to have originated in gnosticism: Joachim connected the last of the three ages of the world with the Holy Spirit. Despite the condemnation of this teaching at the Fourth Lateran Council (1215), it exerted an influence, via the Franciscan Fraticelli, down to the "Inner Light" movement of the Reformation period (T. Müntzer). The inner enlightenment of the person, interpreted as an immediate effect of the Holy Spirit, served as the key to the belief in the Spirit that the Anabaptist movement continued but that the official churches combated all the more vigorously since these movements were professedly antihierarchical and anti-institutional. Despite their constant appeal to the Holy Spirit, these groups, too, did not develop a pneumatology proper; other concerns were more important to them. Nevertheless, German idealism's philosophy of spirit is truly in continuity with that tradition, so that any attempt at a theological pneumatology today cannot avoid coming to grips first with this current of modern thought and its concept of spirit. The contri-

butions of S. Kierkegaard may be of special importance in tackling this task, but they do not adequately fulfill it any more than do the proposals of the twentieth-century theologians who align themselves with Kierkegaard. At the same time, a critical clarification of the concept is indispensable if equivocations and misunderstandings are to be avoided. Particularly in its application to the Holy Spirit as third divine person the concept of pneumatology needs an unambiguous, communicable, and intelligible content that will give it an unmistakable meaning in modern speech. Such a prospect is dubious as long as the concept is applied without being tested and new meanings are added to it. But the required testing faces difficulties with which present-day theological thinking is confronted all along the line: the relationship of philosophy and theology; the role of language; access to and a starting point for statements about a religious content whose ideational and real content are not antecedently obvious; and the fact that the elements that differ among or are common to designations alone make it possible, even in theology, to stimulate reflection and render it inevitable. Thus the concept of pneumatology raises difficulties that also weigh upon the content of pneumatology. Nor will it be possible to surmount these difficulties simply by returning to the biblical concept of spirit and the concept of the Holy Spirit found in the tradition, without an examination of the history and present understanding of those concepts.

(3) *Church Teaching*. The church's teaching on the Holy Spirit took shape in response to heretical denials of it (see sec. 2 above); the fundamental statement of it is found in the third article of the Nicene-Constantinopolitan Creed. Vatican II has outlined the beginnings of a pneumatology from an ecclesiological perspective (see *LG* 12f., 15, 22, 27f., 39f., 44).

(4) *Ecumenical Perspectives*. Among the Christian churches it is above all the communities in the Reformation tradition that insistently call for reflection on pneumatology. This might well give rise to new thinking throughout the whole of Christian theology.

(5) *Systematic Reflections*. There seems to be agreement today that pneumatology cannot be simply one theological discipline among others, but must be a pervasive dimension of theological thinking. We must "come to Christology from a general pneumatology" (K. Rahner, *Schriften,* 14, 56) if we are to discover the meaning of a special pneumatology. There is, however, this difficulty, that pneumatology is not alone in being offered as a key to the whole of theology; other theologies — ecumenical, trinitarian, political, and liberation — are also proposed for this function. All of theological truth is to be understood and presented "pneumatologically." But what would a nonpneumatological vision of Christian theology possibly be? Like faith, theology is by its nature necessarily linked to the Holy Spirit, since knowledge of the faith is possible only "in the Spirit," who alone permits us to say: "Jesus is Lord!" (1 Cor 12:3). Given this presupposition, pneumatology can consist only in bringing to explicit awareness a characteristic of theology that is always present. But how can such an awareness be achieved in a way that does justice to the object, that is, without

unduly thrusting the proper content of a particular statement of faith into the background or even causing it to be forgotten? The need is rather that the pneumatological awareness should cause this content to emerge even more clearly and convincingly. Would a supplementary thematic treatment of the Holy Spirit serve this purpose? In light of this difficulty, the absence of a pneumatological treatise or the alleged neglect of pneumatology by faith and theology seems less a deficiency or an unfortunate omission than a circumstance that is due, at least to some extent, to the subject itself and that as such has a positive significance. The Scriptures, the creeds, and theology do indeed have statements about the Holy Spirit, though these seem to be inseparably connected with other truths of salvation; in any case, like other statements they have their own specific character, which calls into question the attempt to combine them into a systematic doctrine of the Holy Spirit. According to the evidence of revelation and faith, the Spirit of God is essentially to be known by certain effects that are directly important for salvation and must accordingly be taken into account in reflection on the Holy Spirit. It therefore seems possible to speak about the Holy Spirit, who is by its nature a mediator and thus remains closely linked to the origin and purpose of its mediation (see Jn 16:13f.), only if the focus of attention is on the saving acts and the being of God. It is a legitimate concern of a possible pneumatology that these saving deeds should meanwhile be seen, more clearly than has been customary, as the reality and effect of the Spirit of God. This pneumatology will have all the greater importance and lasting value, the more seriously it takes the specific difficulties it faces and the more convincingly it is able to respond to them.

See also CHRISTOLOGY; GOD: THEOLOGY OF.

Bibliography
Anderson, James B. A Vatican II Pneumatology of the Paschal Mystery: The Historical-Doctrinal Genesis of Ad Gentes I, 2–5. Rome: Editrice Pontificia Universita Gregoriana, 1988.
Congar, Yves. I Believe in the Holy Spirit. 3 vols. New York: Seabury, 1983.
Menzies, Robert P. The Development of Early Christian Pneumatology: With Special Reference to Luke–Acts. Sheffield, England: JSOT, 1991.
Mühlen, Heribert. A Charismatic Theology: Initiation in the Spirit. New York: Paulist, 1978.
Rosato, Philip Joseph. The Spirit as Lord: The Pneumatology of Karl Barth. Edinburgh: T and T Clark, 1981.

KARL HEINZ NEUFELD

Pope. The bishop of Rome is called pope inasmuch as, being the successor of Peter, he holds the highest office of governance and teaching in the universal church.

(1) Biblical Background. The classical text that was regarded as the biblical foundation of the papacy is Mt 16:16–18. Here Peter's confession of the messiah is followed by the promise to Peter and the giving of the power of the keys. Contemporary exegetes note that in addition to this text other passages of the Bible attest to Peter's eminent place in the group of disciples. The call of Peter

is recounted several times (Lk 5:1–11; Jn 1:40–42). Jesus prays for Peter that his faith might not fail (Lk 22:31f.), because it would be his task to strengthen his brethren. Jesus rescues Peter as he is sinking (Mt 14:28–31). Peter meets the risen Lord (Lk 24:34; 1 Cor 15:3–5), who also gives him the office of shepherd (John 21). Peter has a special place in the "council" of Jerusalem (Acts 15). He is the first to turn to the Gentiles in order to convert them to Christ (Acts 10:1–11:18). Thus Peter appears in the New Testament as the representative, the spokesman, of the disciples or apostles. The New Testament recognizes a "Petrine function."

(2) *History of Theology.* Rome is the city where Peter (and Paul) suffered martyrdom and were buried. Consequently (see *1 Clement 5–6*) the Church of Rome, and with it the bishop of Rome, had a special place (*1 Clement 59; 63*; Irenaeus, *Adv. haer.* 3.1–2; Tertullian, *De praescr. haeret.* 36.1–4; etc.) in the communion of churches. When the patriarchates came into existence (from the fourth century on), no one denied that Rome was the "primary see" (*prima sedes*), that is, ahead of Alexandria and Antioch. This continued to be the case when Jerusalem and Constantinople were added to the list of patriarchates. In the first centuries the idea of primacy was associated first and foremost with the Church of Rome, but from the fourth century on it became increasingly linked to the person of the bishop of Rome. The latter claimed to be the successor of Peter and applied Mt 16:18 to himself. In the following period, various factors led to an ever-greater strengthening of the papacy. Even before the estrangement and finally the separation of the Eastern and Western churches, the pope regarded himself not only as the bishop of Rome and patriarch of the West but as head of the universal church. The collapse of the western Roman Empire created a vacuum that it became necessary for the pope to fill. In the long period thereafter, the pope asserted his position against all challenges (Conciliarism, the Reformation, Gallicanism, Febronianism, etc.). He was regarded as the guarantor of the church's freedom from the state and as the visible center of the church's unity.

(3) *Church Teaching.* The climactic point in magisterial teaching on the pope was reached when his primacy of jurisdiction and his infallibility were declared dogmas at Vatican I (DS 3050–75). Vatican II confirmed these, but also placed them in a more comprehensive ecclesiological context when it said that the pope is "the perpetual and visible source and foundation of the unity both of the bishops and of the whole company of the faithful" (*LG 23*).

(4) *Ecumenical Perspectives.* The churches of the Reformation have long rejected the papal office on grounds both of principle and of history. There are some today who are thinking of acknowledging it as a ministry of unity, though not as an institution that is an essential element in the constitution of the church. The Orthodox churches are unable to recognize the pope as possessing a primacy of jurisdiction over the universal church, although they are willing to acknowledge the "patriarch of the West" as possessing a "primacy of honor."

(5) *Systematic Reflections.* The Roman Catholic Church regards the papal office as an essential element in the constitution of the church (by "divine law" [*iuris divini*] and not simply by "human law" [*iuris humani*]). One problem the claim must answer is that the papacy took shape only in the course of the church's history. In response it may be pointed out that on its journey through history the church produces from within itself the institutions it needs in order to be able to act according to its nature in the context of new situations. In order to protect its freedom and to manifest and preserve its unity, the church needed the papal office when emperor and empire were trying to immobilize the church and when the church's growth and implantation in new cultural settings began to threaten its unity.

See also CONSTITUTION OF THE CHURCH; ECCLESIAL MAGISTERIUM; INFALLIBILITY; PRIMACY; UNITY OF THE CHURCH.

Bibliography
Brown, Raymond E., Karl P. Donfried, and John Reumann. *Peter in the New Testament: A Collaborative Assessment by Protestant and Roman Catholic Scholars.* Minneapolis: Augsburg, 1973.
Granfield, Patrick. *The Limits of the Papacy.* New York: Crossroad, 1987.
——. *The Papacy in Transition.* Garden City, N.Y.: Doubleday, 1980.
Tillard, Jean M. R. *The Bishop of Rome.* Wilmington, Del.: Glazier, 1983.
See also the bibliography under PRIMACY.

WERNER LÖSER

Prayer. Prayer is the form of expression in which human beings disclose their religious orientation; it presupposes another being that is experienced as a person. Prayer usually takes the linguistic form of direct address; its principal expression, as the word itself indicates, is petition, but the prayer of praise and thanksgiving is no less important.

(1) *Biblical Background.* Prayer is explicitly attested in the Bible beginning with the lament of Cain (Gn 4:13f.), but especially in a multiplicity of forms in the Book of Psalms, which is also the real prayer book of Christianity. The Psalms show praise and adoration, thanksgiving and petition, to be the typical forms of Israelite prayer. Although Jesus criticizes, sometimes sharply, certain practices and postures of prayer, he nonetheless unreservedly takes the Old Testament heritage as his point of departure, while once again directing it, in a decisive way, exclusively to God, whom he insistently addresses as "Abba" (Father). As a result, the relationship to God takes on a new and more profound character that manifests itself in the Our Father, which is presented as a model for prayer (Mt 6:9–13; Lk 11:2–4). Christian prayer is to be supported by an attitude of unshakable trust. Christians address their prayer to the Father in the name of Jesus (Jn 15:7), but they do so in the power of the Spirit whom Jesus sends to them (Rom 8:15; Gal 4:6) and without whom they cannot confess their faith in the Lord (1 Cor 12:3). The practice of prayer is the strongest and most effective of the bonds uniting the Old Testament and the New Testament.

(2) *History of Theology.* Because the practice and teaching of prayer are found everywhere in the history of religions, it is very difficult to trace a development; any attempt to do so can be made only with reservations. For this reason, the following discussion is limited to Christian prayer. A doctrine of prayer is to be found primarily in Christian practice itself, which clearly continues Jewish practice, as both private prayer and official liturgical prayer attest, but which at the same time is clearly intended to be the prayer of Jesus Christ and makes use of, for example, the Psalms with this understanding. The clash with gnosticism and Montanism forced a disapproval of the elitist prayer of individuals and of spontaneous prayer. This led to an emphasis on the universal necessity and possibility both of formulas of prayer and of fixed texts for prayer. The dogmatic controversies that occurred in the imperial church influenced prayer and, specifically, the understanding of the doxology. When monasticism arose, it developed a special relationship between the prayer of the church and personal prayer. The latter led in the Middle Ages to an increasing emphasis on affective and meditative prayer, whereas liturgical prayer underwent hardly any development at all. Among the people there was a gradual growth of devotions that emphasized petition and responsorial prayer (litanies). By way of the "Exercises movement" that began in the century of the Reformation and continued to spread, broader circles came into contact with a revitalized traditional practice of prayer, and new emphases were placed in the understanding of prayer (seeking the will of God; finding God in all things; being "contemplative in action" [*contemplativus in actione*]). In our own century (in the liturgical movement), reflection on the liturgy (A. Schott) and tradition of the early church has brought a new impetus to the practice of prayer.

(3) *Church Teaching.* The ecclesial magisterium has repeatedly rejected false views of prayer, but, remarkably, it has done so only at a relatively late date and in two characteristic periods: (*a*) in the fourteenth and fifteenth centuries: rejection of the ideas of Meister Eckhart (DS 950–80); defense of vocal prayer and rejection of Wycliffe's assertions (DS 1169–76); defense of special intercessions; (*b*) toward the end of the seventeenth century: rejection of the quietism of M. Molinos and F. de Fénelon (DS 2181–92, 2201–69, 2351–74); proper understanding of contemplative and meditative prayer. The Council of Trent insisted that it is possible to make satisfaction for sins by prayer (DS 1713). These various declarations have to do only with specific points and limit themselves strictly to the rejection of false views. The areas under consideration are "divine worship" and the Christian "striving for perfection," or, in other words, the practice of Christian life; there seems to be no doctrinal disagreement here either with the Orthodox churches or with the groups and churches making up the Protestant Reformation.

(4) *Ecumenical Perspectives.* Against this background it is understandable that prayer should play a decisive role in ecumenical collaboration; it is no accident that the whole idea of ecumenism arose in prayer groups. Those involved, however, accepted this common basis and possibility as something obvious and

belonging to the practical level, rather than as something consciously reflected on, that is, without reckoning with the possibility of a divergent understanding of prayer.

(5) *Systematic Reflections.* A developed theology of prayer is still a desideratum. A contemporary reflection on prayer will take as its starting point modern biblical theology, which can show that in the final analysis all talk of God is and should be doxology. But this demand has to do with a goal that seems presently to have been attained only inchoatively, and the presuppositions of which must first be clarified. In the New Testament, prayer — both the prayer of Jesus and the prayer of the newly established church — is an answer to the saving action of God and to the personal, existential call that this action issues to humankind, the church, and individuals. But this structure is not to be overemphasized nor taken too schematically, since call and response are so interwoven that the very quest for a relationship with God and for the clarification of this relationship already has the character of prayer on the human side and that, consequently, prayer ranges from the petition of the searcher to the praise-filled adoration that refuses to turn back and includes within itself the other forms of prayer. This means, however, that prayer is an expression of the history of human beings with God and therefore finds utterance in keeping with the path that human beings are traveling. The various forms of prayer have their irreplaceable role and cannot be used arbitrarily. The parallelism, already emphasized in Christian antiquity, between prayer and faith (*lex orandi, lex credendi*) becomes especially clear here. The starting point of prayer is the human condition and the stimulus of praying with others. The intention repeatedly discernible in the Old Testament of improving the experientially hopeless present situation by means of prayer is connected with very concrete expectations and formulates prayer accordingly, applying sensible and affective powers with the help of categories borrowed directly from life. Such a procedure is fully justified even though the experience of prayer gradually deepens; it demonstrates the sacramental character of human prayer. Just as deliberate prayer does not do away with spontaneous prayer, so too vocal prayer retains its place alongside forms of meditation and contemplation. In any case, Christian prayer is an activity or attitude of the spirit and therefore is not turned in on itself but is open to the broader dimensions of the vital relationship between God and human beings. Finally, prayer should spring from the hearts of believers and produce the turning to God that is appropriate in each situation in which human beings realize themselves. Only rarely are they able to turn directly and unmediatedly to God; prayer can, therefore, also be directed immediately to Jesus, although when this is done God is always intended. In this context prayer to the saints also has its place, for at bottom such prayer only gives concrete expression to the fact that inasmuch as Christian prayer is the prayer of the church it is essentially also the prayer of the members of the church for one another (see Rom 8:26f.). Prayer therefore leads to commitment to the neighbor; such commitment can, when the situation arises, be a more credible witness to Christianity than formulas

of prayer (see Mt 7:21–23). Christian tradition retains this insight in the formula "active contemplation" (*activus in contemplatione*), which is one of the foundations of the modern idea of the apostolate. At the same time, communal prayer is practiced in the prayer of the hours (in religious orders but also in the breviary of diocesan priests).

See also HOLY SPIRIT; SAINTS: HOLINESS, SANCTIFICATION; SPIRITUALITY.

Bibliography
Balthasar, Hans Urs von. *Prayer*. New York: Sheed and Ward, 1961.
Ebeling, Gerhard. *Prayer*. Philadelphia: Fortress, 1966.
Heiler, Friedrich. *Prayer: A Study in the History and Psychology of Religion*. New York: Oxford University Press, 1958.
Rahner, Karl. *Happiness through Prayer*. London: Burns and Oates, 1958.

KARL HEINZ NEUFELD

Predestination. Predestination refers to God's loving decree from eternity by which God establishes a historical order of salvation to enable all human beings to reach eternal salvation. The salvific goal of this historical plan of salvation is the eternal glory of the children of God. The path of salvation is the absolute mediator of salvation, Jesus Christ, and the relative mediation of the church, as well as FAITH and LOVE as criteria of salvation.

(1) *Biblical Background.* The notion of predestination is found exclusively in the New Testament (Paul). The verb *to predestine* (*proorízein*) is used six times and — with the exception of Acts 4:28 — only in the Pauline and deutero-Pauline letters (Rom 8:29, 30; 1 Cor 2:7; Eph 1:5, 11). The word *predestination* can suggest: *purpose* or *design* (*próthesis* [see Rom 8:28; 9:11; Eph 1:11; 3:11; 2 Tm 1:9]) and *eternal election* (see Eph 1:4). The *loci classici* are Rom 8:28–30 and Eph 1:13–14. The object of eternal predestination is not the individual but a salvific order, including the clearly announced goal of salvation for all human beings. Rom 8:30 speaks of a divine salvific plan. Eternal predestination, then, has to do with the fact that the historical path for each person who is to be saved consists in being called and justified for glory. What is determined in advance is that this salvific path is by way of the mediator Jesus Christ and the church, which depends on him (Eph 1:14–14; 2:10; 3:9–11). From the human side the criteria of salvation are faith (Eph 1:13) and love (Rom 8:28). The final goal is our eternal glory with God (Rom 8:18; 1 Cor 2:7; Eph 1:18). Johannine texts regarding predestination regularly mention the preestablished goal of "eternal love" (3:15; 6:40; 12:50). The classical theology of a double predestination to salvation or damnation is based on Romans 9–11. However, in this context what is important is the role within salvation of the large group, not individual destiny. Neither here nor elsewhere in the Bible is there any question of predestination to eternal damnation. The destiny of the individual is decided only at the last judgment (see Lk 20:17f.; 1 Pt 2:7f.; etc.).

(2) *History of Theology.* In the history of dogmatics, Augustine (d. 430) was the first to develop a systematic doctrine of predestination on the basis

of his anti-Pelagianism and his doctrine of original sin. To safeguard the all-effectiveness of grace he teaches that predestination is "the prior knowledge and prior preparation of God's good deeds by which we are most certainly saved since many are always being saved" (*De dono persev.* 14.35). From the mass of those lost by original sin (*massa damnata*) only a few are singled out for eternal life. Predestination is also unmerited (its *gratuitousness*), infallible (its *infallibility*), and intended only for a small part of humankind (its *particularity*). Lucidus (d. after 474) speaks of a double predestination. In the ninth century Gottschalk (d. 869) agrees with this, while Hinkmar of Rheims rejects it. For Thomas Aquinas predestination is a special case of divine providence, "a plan which is in the Spirit of God to preordain a few to eternal salvation" (*STh* 1, q. 23, a. 2; see in general 1, q. 22f.; 3, q. 24). The free will of the one predestined is a secondary cause of that person's salvation. Christ is the prototype and cause of predestination. Reprobation (*reprobatio*) is an explicit act of the divine will. It is the recognition of human guilt and of damnation as a punishment of this guilt. The infallibility of predestination led to controversies: between Duns Scotus (predestination is guaranteed by a prior decree of God's will) and William of Ockham (there is nothing prior because predestination is God's prevision of future contingent events) or the debate at the University of Louvain in 1465–75. The Baroque period and then neo-scholasticism distinguish between a predestination to grace, which takes place without foreknowledge of human merit (*ante praevisa merita*), and a predestination to glory. According to the Thomists, this happens apart from any merit. According to the Molinists, it takes place with foreknowledge of merit. Jansen (d. 1638) and Quesnel (d. 1719) held to an extreme particularism in predestination: only the elect are given grace.

(3) *Church Teaching*. The magisterium first intervened against the heresy of predestination in the fifth century. At the Synod of Arles (473), Lucidus had to renounce the following theses: Jesus Christ did not suffer death for the salvation of all; God's foreknowledge powerfully constrains some human beings to eternal damnation; some are predestined to eternal death, others to eternal life (DS 332f., 335). In condemning Gottschalk, the Synod of Quierzy (853) teaches that there is only positive predestination to salvation (DS 621). Both the Synod of Orange (529; DS 397) and Trent (against Zwingli and Calvin) reject predestination to evil (DS 1556, 1567); no one can know whether he or she is predestined without a special revelation (DS 1540).

(4) *Ecumenical Perspectives*. The Eastern Church hands on the patristic teaching, which was fairly clear until Augustine: namely, that our predestination to eternal salvation is the consequence of God's nonconstraining foreknowledge of freely willed human action. In the Reformation the doctrine of predestination was central. M. Luther (*De servo arbitrio* [1525]) considers absolute predestination as one of the main pillars of his doctrine of justification. In his eyes the unconditionality of predestination follows from God's all-effectiveness and the total corruption of human beings due to original sin.

God brings about salvation and damnation unconditionally. The doctrine of predestination is one of the main characteristics of the Reformed Church. According to J. Calvin (*Inst.* [1559]), God predestines a part of humankind to salvation, another part to rejection; thus God causes not only all the good actions of the elect but also the evil actions of the damned. K. Barth modifies the teaching of double predestination (*KD* 2/2). Jesus Christ is our double predestination: in him each of us is chosen, and because he, representing all human beings, takes upon himself our condemnation — he is the only rejected one — there is no longer any condemnation. The mediation of election is through the church. In ecumenical dialogue today there is a consensus that predestination is part of early preaching. Since it belongs to the plan of salvation-history, it is to be interpreted christologically and ecclesiologically and is universal in scope. There is still disagreement over the doctrine of double predestination.

(5) *Systematic Reflections.* The perspective of Catholic dogmatics today, with its biblical orientation, is as follows: double as well as single predestination are precluded. There is no temporally prior, absolute predestination of individuals to eternal salvation or damnation. The final decision regarding the eternal destiny of individuals takes place only at the last judgment. The notion of predestination contains a protologically determined, historical plan of salvation, which is universal, Christocentric, and ecclesiological. The universal love of God has from eternity determined that eternal salvation is available to all human beings as their final goal. The concrete realization of eternal salvation takes place by means of a mediation: that is, Jesus Christ, the absolute mediator, by his universal work of salvation brings about salvation, and the church — dependent on him — is a relative mediator in its salvific service of salvation. Finally, individuals have an active role to play in bringing about salvation by their gifts and their commitment of faith and love. Predestination is the good news insofar as it grounds the salvation of humans in the universal, absolute, unshakable, and faithful love of God and thus grants believers a final certainty concerning their eschatological hope.

See also DIVINE PROVIDENCE; GRACE; HELL; JUSTIFICATION; UNIVERSAL SALVIFIC WILL OF GOD.

Bibliography
Barth, Karl. *Church Dogmatics*, 2/2. Edinburgh: T and T Clark, 1957.
Baudry, Leon, ed. *The Quarrel over Future Contingents (Louvain, 1465–1475)*. Boston: Kluwer, 1989.
Brosche, Fredrik. *Luther on Predestination: The Antinomy and the Unity between Love and Wrath in Luther's Concept of God*. Stockholm: Almqvist and Wiksell, 1978.
Lonergan, Bernard. *Grace and Freedom*. New York: Herder and Herder, 1971.
Muller, Richard A. *Christ and the Decree: Christology and Predestination in Reformed Theology from Calvin to Perkins*. Durham, N.C.: Labyrinth, 1986.
Rainbow, Jonathan Herbold. *The Will of God and the Cross: An Historical and Theological Study of John Calvin's Doctrine of Limited Redemption*. Allison Park, Pa.: Pickwick, 1990.

GEORG KRAUS

Preexistence of Jesus Christ. The phrase "preexistence of Jesus Christ" refers to the existence of the eternal Son, Jesus Christ, who is consubstantial with the eternal Father, before his incarnation for our salvation and before the creation of the world. It states and defends the fact that while the salvation of humankind is inseparably joined with the history and destiny of Jesus Christ, the incarnate Son of God, this salvation cannot be deduced from the history of humankind and the world. Rather it is grounded in God eternal.

(1) *Biblical Background.* The pre-Pauline formula "one God, one Lord" (1 Cor 8:6), expresses Jesus Christ's mediatorship of creation and redemption and presupposes his preexistence. When Paul speaks of the "sending of the Son" (Gal 4:4f.; Rom 8:3f.; etc.), he presupposes that the Son existed before the incarnation. Using Old Testament wisdom images he interprets the "spiritual rock" (1 Cor 10:4) as the preexistent Christ (see 1 Cor 1:30; 2:7f.). Finally, in Phil 2:6–11, preexistence is part of exaltation Christology. Thus a two-stage Christology (condescension–exaltation) becomes a three-stage Christology, explaining the salvation-history of the suprahistorical, preexistent Son of God who was exalted as Lord and is worthy of divine worship (or: whose sonship is revealed in power [see Rom 1:3f.]). John speaks of preexistence *directly* in 1:1–3; 17:5, 24, and *indirectly* when he employs the general model of the Son of Man's coming down and going up or in the notions of his coming, being sent, and returning to the Father. According to 1 Tm 3:16, the basis of Christ's reign over the world is not his exaltation but his preexistence. Col 1:15–20 is a hymn to Christ's mediatorship of creation and redemption. Here his preexistence and mediatorship of creation are part of a soteriology that encompasses the world. Heb 1:1–3 views the Son as the very image of God who created the world and holds it in existence through the Son. Here too his mediatorship of creation is connected with wisdom literature. The Son is the eschatological Word of God to us (1:2) and "has destroyed the defilement of sin" (1:3). Col 1:15–20 and Heb 1:1–3 are evidently related to Old Testament and Jewish–Hellenistic wisdom themes (the image of God, the firstborn of all creation, the beginning, reflection, imprint).

(2) *History of Theology.* A tendency is already noticeable in the Apostolic Fathers (based on Philippians 2) to emphasize the preexistence instead of the exaltation in order to ground Jesus' lordship (Ignatius; *Diog.*; 1 *Clem.* 16:2; the anti-Arian emphasis of Athanasius, *Or. c. Arianos* 1.4; *Or. 3 c. Arianos* 39). Col 1:15–20 is also a key text for the patristic presentation of the preexistence (see Justin, *Apol.* 1.63.15), especially for Origen, who describes the "firstborn" as the uncreated (*C. Cels.* 6.17) and considers the divine begetting or the title of Son as the basis for this relationship (*C. Cels.* 7.16.65; *In Ioan.* 28.16, etc.). Thus we may speak of a "preexistence Christology" in the Fathers, for example, in Justin, according to whom the messiah receives his being in his preexistence. Here he is already the anointed one because he is God (*Dial.* 45.4; 48.2; 87.2; 96.1). Some Fathers employ a "Spirit Christology" and thus use the term *pneûma* for the preexistent Christ (Ignatius, *Magn.*

15.2; Hippolytus, *C. Noet.* 16; Clement of Alexandria, *Paed.* 2.19.4; Tertullian, *De or.* 1.1; *Adv. Prax.* 26.4). Lactantius speaks of a twofold birth (*Epit.* 38.2; *Inst.* 4.8.1–2): by God before the foundation of the world — thus the divine and preexistent Son — and "in the flesh as a human being during the reign of Augustus." For Leo I the twofold birth, "the eternal birth" and the "temporal birth," expresses the preexistence and incarnation of the "equally eternal Son" of the Father for the redemption of humankind (*Ep. ad Fl.* c. 2 [DS 291]). Hilary of Poitiers clearly distinguishes between preexistence, kenosis, and exaltation (*De Trin.* 9.6). This leads to a problem because the statements of the Fathers are related not only to the divinity but also to the person of the earthly Jesus of Nazareth. Their conceptual distinction between the *verbum incarnandum* and the *verbum incarnatum* (*incarnandum* = "to be incarnate"; *incarnatum* = "incarnate") points to a solution that was spelled out in the Middle Ages by Bonaventure and others: creation *and* redemption are grounded in the eternal mystery of God.

(3) *Church Teaching.* In the conciliar decisions of the early church the creed affirms preexistence by referring to the firstborn (see Jn 1:18), consubstantial Son of the (eternal) Father and mediator of creation. Thus Nicaea: "Begotten, not made, of one substance with the Father, through whom all things were made" (DS 125). Any hint that there was a time when he was not is rejected (DS 126). Constantinople I repeats this and expands it: he was born of the Father "before all time" (DS 150). Belief in the triune God implies belief in the incarnation of the eternal, preexistent Son of God. It was customary, as we see in Leo I (DS 290–95) and Chalcedon (DS 301), to speak of the two births of the one Son and thus to emphasize that he who "existed before time" (the preexistence) and is eternal became man "in time" (DS 357, 504, 536, 572, 681, 852). Some creeds also add to "only begotten Son" (from Jn 1:18) the "firstborn before all creation" (from Col 1:15) (DS 40, 50f., 60).

(4) *Ecumenical Perspectives.* Alongside clear adherence to the preexistence of Jesus Christ because of the early church's trinitarian faith (e.g., K. Barth), there have also been attempts in Evangelical theology to reject preexistence as a Hellenistic deviation (A. von Harnack) or a mythological idea from the history of religions, or to demythologize it (i.e., interpret it existentially: R. Bultmann). This leads to studying Christology as only a function of human belief, namely, an anthropology (H. Braun) or a framework for nontheistic theology (D. Sölle). With some qualifications we could then call this a soteriology without a Christology.

(5) *Systematic Reflections.* The preexistence of Jesus Christ is an indispensable element of any Christology done "from above" because the preexistence of Jesus Christ guarantees that the redemption of humankind is accomplished by God. It should be noted that in systematic theology, the preexistence of Jesus Christ should never be seen in isolation, but should rather be part of the important contexts where it acquires concrete meaning and becomes more precise, as we see in the New Testament and the tradition. The concrete history of

Jesus and his exaltation reveal who he truly is "from the beginning," "before all time," and "before the foundation of the world": namely, the Son, who is eternal wisdom and mediator of creation. Furthermore, the Christ-event has a universal dimension. Christ is the redeemer of the whole world, and — as eternal Word with the Spirit standing at God's side — he participated in the creation and foundation of the world. As *verbum incarnandum* he exists from eternity in order to enter time as *verbum incarnatum,* and by becoming flesh he brings the message of the one whose profound love he alone knows and by whom he was sent. When we consider that the incarnation is also the "emptying" (kenosis), then the condition for the possibility of the concrete history of Jesus and his crucifixion — on the basis of the preexistence — is God: the personal relations in God by themselves are self-gift and emptying (H. Urs von Balthasar), and the preexistent Son is the lamb who was slain since the foundation of the world (see Rv 13:8; 1 Pt 1:19f.). The preexistence of Jesus Christ points to God's eternity as power over time and shows that through the Son from eternity, God is a God of history and is for humankind in the freedom of love: one God who is God through self-giving.

See also CHRISTOLOGY; LOVE; MEDIATORSHIP OF JESUS CHRIST; SALVATION; TRINITY.

Bibliography
Hengel, Martin. *The Son of God: The Origin of Christology and the History of Jewish-Hellenistic Religion.* Philadelphia: Fortress, 1976.
Kasper, Walter. *Jesus the Christ.* New York: Paulist, 1976.
Küng, Hans. *Justification: The Doctrine of Karl Barth and a Catholic Reflection; with a Letter by Karl Barth.* New York: Nelson, 1964.
Kuschel, Karl-Josef. *Born before All Time? The Dispute over Christ's Origin.* New York: Crossroad, 1992.
Schüssler Fiorenza, Elisabeth. "Wisdom Mythology and the Christological Hymns of the New Testament." In *Aspects of Wisdom in Judaism and Early Christianity.* Edited by Robert Wilken. Notre Dame, Ind.: University of Notre Dame Press, 1975.

LOTHAR ULLRICH

Preservation of the World. This concept serves to express the fact that God's creative power relates to creatures not just as a one-time impetus to their arisal and development, but as something continuously operative behind their endurance and being. For this, theological tradition introduced the term *continuous creation* (*creatio continua*). It refers to God's eternal activity, which encompasses everything that God originated in time and thereby sustains in being or life.

(1) *Biblical Background.* The Bible hardly enters into ontological deliberations like, for example, those of speculative theology, for which created things would "fall back" into nonbeing if God did not constantly sustain them in being. The Old Testament thinks about creation in concrete terms. The story of the flood attests to the Creator's vow that God will "never again...strike down all living beings" (Gn 8:21b) nor, "as long as the earth lasts," allow the cycle of

"seedtime and harvest" to cease. The world owes its existence to God's grace. Significantly, the same verb, *bara,* is used both for this divine activity and for the act of creation; thus the belief is evidenced that God constantly brings life to living things on earth (Ps 104:30), to humans (Ps 89:48), and to the people (Is 43:1) — along with which, however, God also brings not only well-being but woe (Is 45:7). The postexilic texts gratefully record the preservation of Israel and the possibility of its reestablishment in the homeland. In the wisdom texts, which are partly Hellenistic in cast, an ontological interest is combined with the more concretely life-related one: "And how could a thing remain, unless you willed it; or be preserved, had it not been called forth by you?...O Lord and lover of life" (Wis 11:25f.). In the New Testament, Jesus speaks of God's care. Paul and his school speak of the fact not only that all things "are" (1 Cor 8:6) through Christ, the eternal Son of God, and "were created through him and for him" (Col 1:16), but also that "in him all things hold together" (Col 1:17) and that he sustains "all things by his mighty word" (Heb 1:3). At one point, Luke expresses the biblical and redemptive-historical conviction that God allows "all peoples to go their own ways" and gives them nourishment (Acts 14:16f.), and at another, the Hellenistic proposition about the divine sphere in which "we live and move and have our being" (Acts 17:28).

(2) *History of Theology.* The early Fathers had to confront the Aristotelian challenge that the matter contained in the universe was eternal and the function of the prime mover exerted only once, which implied that there would be no need for divine sustainment of the world, as well as the Epicurean claim that the world owed its existence to the free interplay of eternal atoms. The Stoic notion of God as the omnipotent, all-supporting, paternal sustainer of the universe, or as the "Pantocrator," was appropriated in the course of this debate and combined with the biblical doctrine of creation. This is seen in Clement of Rome, who calls God the Father of the cosmos and of the epochs (*1 Clem.* 19:2; 35:3), by which he implies an ongoing fatherhood; it is in this sense that the baptismal vows also formulate belief in the "Father almighty, Creator of all things visible and invisible," and in Christ, whose kingdom will "exist without end" (DS 125). Irenaeus teaches the unerring directedness of history toward Christ, its goal (*Adv. haer.* 2.34.2f.; 3.22.1). Clement of Alexandria understands the world unequivocally as a process of continuous creation (*Strom.* 6.16). John Chrysostom takes up the "Pantocrator" concept (*In Ep. ad Hebr. hom.* 2.3) in order to see in God's continuous creative activity the cause of the ordered lawfulness and beauty of the cosmos (*Ad pop. Ant. hom.* 9.4; 10.2f.). He also touches on the difficult problem of EVIL and moral evil (see EVIL, MORAL). Augustine attributes to divine sustainment of the world the fact that created things do not fall into oblivion (*De Gen. ad litt.* 5.20.40).

(3) *Church Teaching.* At Vatican I, in what it said about God's providence and in opposition to the tendencies of DEISM, doctrinal office indirectly formulated the Catholic teaching on the world: God does not withdraw after

having created the world, but vigorously "protects and guides" all created things (DS 3003).

(4) *Ecumenical Perspectives.* M. Luther declared: "He did not create the world in the way that a carpenter builds a house and then departs, but he remains with it and sustains everything, for otherwise it would be incapable of either existing or enduring" (*WA* 21:521). J. Calvin thought that, since God is no demiurge who acts arbitrarily and for the moment, only belief in God's sustainment of the world would do God justice (*Inst.* 1.16.1).

(5) *Systematic Reflections.* Thomas Aquinas contributed to the theological explication of this matter mainly through the following thesis: "The sustainment of things by God does not come about by means of some new kind of activity, but by continuance of that activity through which he confers being" (*STh* 1, q. 104, a. 1). Seen from the viewpoint of God, this is eternal and transtemporal, but from that of humanity, temporal and historical. Today, dogmatics emphasizes that sustainment of the world is an aspect of redemptive history, namely, realization of what the Creator intends by means of a nature with its own inherent laws and a free humanity that God transcendentally enables, supports, and allows to develop toward self-understanding. It also testifies to God's faithfulness to the divine plan for ultimate fulfillment. An evolutive WORLDVIEW by no means contradicts this view of things.

See also HISTORY/HISTORICITY; PROVIDENCE.

Bibliography
Löfgren, David. *Die Theologie der Schöpfung bei Luther.* Göttingen: Vandenhoeck und Ruprecht, 1960.
Pannenberg, Wolfhart. *Systematic Theology.* Vol. 2. Grand Rapids: Eerdmans, 1994.

ALEXANDRE GANOCZY

Priest. The name *priest* (Greek: *presbýteros* = elder) is applied, in a broad sense, to all ordained ministers of the church who in their persons, words, and actions render present the priestly ministry of Christ and thus contribute to the building up of the church. Understood in a narrower sense, a priest is one who possesses a specific degree of the sacrament of orders and as such is distinguished from bishops and deacons.

(1) *Biblical Background.* Jesus Christ, whose life and work found their summation and completion in his death on the cross "for us," is several times called a priest in Hebrews (5:6; 7:17, 21; 10:11f., 21). His priestly ministry ("sacrifice") sums up all the priestly activity found in the various religions and in Israel, brings it to an end, and transcends it. The apostles accomplished a priestly ministry when they rendered the priestly ministry of Jesus Christ present in word and sacrament and pastoral care. They thus became God's instruments in building up the church as a "priestly people" (1 Pt 2:5, 9). The official ministers of the church are given various titles in the New Testament; "priest" (Greek: *hiereús*) is not one of them. To be sure, the elements for the

later development of priestly ministry as such are ready to hand in the New Testament.

(2) *History of Theology.* Beginning in the early Middle Ages, the understanding and consequently the practice of the ecclesiastical ministry were gradually narrowed. The category of "priest" was heavily emphasized. The episcopate was henceforth understood to be simply a higher honor, since the essential priestly tasks had already been entrusted to the minister in ordination to the priesthood. The diaconate became simply a stage on the way to the priesthood. The duties of the priest that could be derived from the concept of sacrifice overshadowed the duties of preaching and pastoral care. The idea of sacrifice as applied to the priest's action contained elements stemming from the pre-Christian religions. This restricted understanding of the priesthood was one reason for the protest of the Reformers, but their reaction led only to a hardening of positions.

(3) *Church Teaching.* The understanding of priesthood maintained by Vatican II (*LG* 28; especially *PO*) changed the situation. The content of the concept of priest is here brought into line with the concept of presbyter in the Bible and early church. Priesthood is a degree of sacramental ordination within the three-stage ministry (episcopate, presbyterate, diaconate). Along with other priests, who together make up the presbyterium, a priest works under the orders of the bishop. The priestly ministry is said to have several dimensions: preaching, sanctification (through the administration of the sacraments), direction of the community and individuals. The celebration of the Eucharist has a central place. There is a strong emphasis today on the idea that the priestly office is one of service; it is described as a "ministry" (*ministerium*) (*LG* 24; *PO*).

(4) *Ecumenical Perspectives.* The emphasis on the priesthood as being a sacrificing priesthood met with rejection by the Reformers. To the extent that this emphasis has been moderated by locating the priestly ministry within a more comprehensively understood ecclesiastical ministry, many earlier controversies have lost their edge in the ecumenical movement. As a result, there are more points of contact than before in ecumenical conversations on the ecclesiastical ministry.

(5) *Systematic Reflections.* A priest is a "representative" in two ways: he represents Jesus Christ to the community, and he represents the church. In a derivative sense he is a "mediator," without in any way detracting from the abiding sole mediatorship of Jesus Christ (1 Tm 2:5; *LG* 14).

See also BISHOP; DEACON; MINISTRY IN THE CHURCH; SACRAMENT OF ORDERS.

Bibliography
Brown, Raymond E. *Priest and Bishop: Biblical Reflections.* New York: Paulist, 1970.
Cooke, Bernard. *Ministry to Word and Sacraments: History and Theology.* Philadelphia: Fortress, 1976.
Donovan, Daniel. *What Are They Saying about the Ministerial Priesthood?* Mahwah, N.J.: Paulist, 1992.

Kilmartin, Edward J. *Church, Eucharist, and Priesthood: A Theological Commentary on "The Mystery and Worship of the Most Holy Eucharist."* New York: Paulist, 1981.

Küng, Hans. *Why Priests?* Garden City, N.Y.: Doubleday, 1972.

O'Meara, Thomas F. *Theology of Ministry.* New York: Paulist, 1983.

Osborne, Kevin. *Priesthood: A History of the Ordained Ministry in the Roman Catholic Church.* New York: Paulist, 1988.

Rahner, Karl. *The Priesthood.* New York: Herder, 1973.

———. "Priestly Existence." In *Theological Investigations,* 3:239–62. New York: Crossroad, 1967.

Ratzinger, Joseph. "Priestly Ministry." *Emmanuel* 76 (1970) 442–53, 490–505.

Tavard, George H. *A Theology for Ministry.* Wilmington, Del.: Glazier, 1983.

Wister, Robert J. *Priests: Identity and Ministry.* Wilmington, Del.: Glazier, 1990.

WERNER LÖSER

Priesthood of the Faithful. The priesthood of the faithful (or universal priesthood or, in Catholic parlance, common priesthood) means the participation of the entire church and of all who belong to it through faith and baptism, as well as through confirmation and the Eucharist, in the priesthood of Jesus Christ.

(1) *Biblical Background.* The concept of the priesthood of the faithful does not occur as such in Scripture. On the other hand, the people chosen by God is often described as a priestly people. In the Old Testament, Ex 19:6 ("You shall belong to me as a kingdom of priests") is especially important. In the New Testament, relevant texts are to be found in 1 Peter and Revelation. In 1 Pt 2:5, the community is spoken of as a "spiritual house" that is to become a "holy priesthood," and 1 Pt 2:9 says that the community is "a chosen race, a royal priesthood." Rv 1:6 and 5:9f. say that by the power of his death on the cross Jesus Christ has made human beings of every nation into "priests and kings before God."

(2) *History of Theology.* The patristic and medieval tradition refers continually to the priestly character of the baptized. The authors were thinking less of cultic functions or sacramental empowerments than of the spirituality implicit in the concept of "priest." The baptized are to offer the "spiritual sacrifice" of a devout life. The doctrine of a universal priesthood acquired a new and momentous importance among the Reformers, especially M. Luther. In some of his writings between 1520 and 1525 this doctrine is emphasized in an especially decisive way. Controversies with the left wing of the Reformation led him, from 1525 on, to lay greater emphasis on the special ministry in the church. In the reform-oriented writings of 1520 (*The Babylonian Captivity of the Church; Christian Freedom; To the Christian Nobility of the German Nation*) as well as in *The Formation of Ministers of the Church* (1523) Luther derived all priestly powers and responsibilities from baptism. He attacked the Roman Catholic Church and its hierarchical priesthood that is based on the sacrament of orders. This emphasis of Luther (and the other Reformers) on a universal priesthood caused the Roman Catholic Church to focus all the more decisively and exclusively on the hierarchical priesthood. Until the twentieth

century, the priesthood of the faithful was not a matter discussed in Catholic theology. The "liturgical movement" and related new departures then prepared the way for the revolution that bore its full fruit in Vatican II. The conciliar documents speak explicitly of the "common priesthood" (*sacerdotium commune*) of the entire people of God and its members.

(3) *Church Teaching.* Appealing especially to 1 Pt 2:5, 9, the council attributes a common priesthood to the church as people of God and body of Christ. Individual Christians share in this priesthood insofar as they are members of this people and body. The common priesthood finds expression in communal prayer, the celebration of the sacraments, missionary witness, and service to human beings (see *LG* 9, 10, 26, 34; *SC* 14, 48; *AA* 3; *PO* 3; *AG* 15). Although the common priesthood of the church and the faithful is heavily emphasized, the hierarchical priesthood retains its independent place in the church.

(4) *Ecumenical Perspectives.* The prominence given to the common priesthood or priesthood of the faithful is of great ecumenical importance. The Roman Catholic Church was long regarded as a "church of the official priesthood" and the churches of the Reformation as churches of universal priesthood. Now that the Roman Catholic Church is placing greater emphasis on the priesthood of the faithful, it is tackling concerns that in the past seemed to be peculiar to the churches of the Reformation. There is reason to suspect, however, that the difference in vocabulary (universal priesthood versus common priesthood or priesthood of the faithful) expresses a difference of understanding that will not easily be rectified.

(5) *Systematic Reflections.* The participation of the church and its members in the priesthood of Jesus Christ finds expression in the common priesthood of the faithful; for the church is his body, and he is its Lord and head. Because of its common priesthood, the church, which becomes concrete in each community, is not only the addressee and object of actions by possessors of the special priesthood, but also the subject of a priestly life of prayer, witness, and service. The dealings of Christians with one another must reflect this fact.

See also COMMUNITY (GROUP); MINISTRY IN THE CHURCH; OFFICES OF JESUS CHRIST; PRIEST.

Bibliography
Congar, Yves. *Lay People in the Church.* Westminster, Md.: Newman, 1957.
———. "My Pathfindings in the Theology of the Laity and Ministries." *The Jurist* 32 (1972) 169–88.
———. *Priest and Layman.* London: Darton, 1967.
Rahner, Karl. *The Shape of the Church to Come.* New York: Crossroad, 1974.

WERNER LÖSER

Primacy. Primacy is the name given to the highest and broadest authority in the church. This authority resides in the pope.

(1) *Biblical Background.* The New Testament basis for the doctrine of pa-

pal primacy is to be found in the collection of texts that speak of Peter. The giving of the power of the keys to Peter (Mt 16:18) has always been regarded as especially probative.

(2) *History of Theology.* While the community in Rome was initially regarded as possessing the primacy within the communion of churches, this role became increasingly attached to the person of the bishop of Rome.

(3) *Church Teaching.* According to Vatican I, the pope has full, supreme, ordinary, and immediate power of jurisdiction over the whole church (DS 3064). Vatican II confirmed this teaching but placed it in a broader setting by adding its own revised version of the doctrine on the episcopal office (*LG* 18, 22, 24). In their own dioceses bishops likewise have a "proper, ordinary, and immediate authority" that comes to them not from the pope but from their episcopal ordination. It follows from this that the primacy of the pope must be described in the context of the leadership responsibility of the bishops: the church is governed either by the pope alone or by a COUNCIL with the pope at its head (see "Prefatory Note of Explanation" 3f. [in appendix to *LG*]). It is obvious that this statement reflects a tension that is not easily resolved.

(4) *Ecumenical Perspectives.* The Orthodox churches reject the papal primacy of jurisdiction but are willing to attribute to the pope a "primacy of honor." The churches of the Reformation likewise reject the primacy of jurisdiction. Some Lutheran theologians, however, have said that they could approve giving the pope, "by human law" (*iure humano*), a role as unifier.

(5) *Systematic Reflections.* The key to a contemporary understanding of the primacy of the pope is to be found in the formula: in the service of unity. In the future it will be very important that this service not seek to introduce a uniformity in all manifestations of the church's life, but rather a unity in multiplicity. To this end, new forms must be developed in which the primacy can find expression.

See also BISHOP; COLLEGIALITY; POPE.

Bibliography
Dionne, Robert. *The Papacy and the Church: A Study of Praxis and Reception in Ecumenical Perspective.* New York: Philosophical Library, 1987.
Empie, Paul C., and T. Austin Murphy, eds. *Papal Primacy and the Universal Church.* Minneapolis: Augsburg, 1974.
Miller, J. Michael. *The Divine Right of the Papacy in Recent Ecumenical Theology.* Rome: Gregoriana, 1980.
———. *What Are They Saying about Papal Primacy?* New York: Paulist, 1983.
Misner, Paul. *Papacy and Development: Newman and the Primacy of the Pope.* Leiden: Brill, 1976.

WERNER LÖSER

Primal Revelation. This notion pertains to a thesis in speculative theology according to which the first human — in the ORIGINAL STATE and therefore prior to the "fall" — is supposed to have received special moral-religious knowledge from the Creator. Among the contents of original revelation were usually cited those expressed in Genesis 1–3: consciousness of CREATURELINESS, the conditions for concord with God, the possibility of wrongdoing, the consequences of sin, and even the promise of a redeemer.

(1) *Biblical Background.* Included among the themes in the Old Testament is that of those righteous Gentiles (e.g., Job) who, by their piety, sometimes virtually shame the chosen people (Jer 2:10f.), are capable of recognizing Yahweh's great deeds (Ps 126:2; Dn 2:47), join Israel in worshiping Yahweh at the messianic fulfillment of time (Is 2:2f.; Zep 3:9f.), and are consequently to be granted salvation (Is 25:6ff.; Jer 16:19). The New Testament similarly testifies that Gentiles are called to the kingdom (*basileia*), since the messiah is "a light for revelation" to them, too (Lk 2:32). Jesus praises the faith of the Canaanite woman (Mt 15:28) and more than once contrasts righteous non-Jews with unrighteous Jews. But nowhere in the previously cited Old and New Testament texts is the fact that outsiders are capable of being saved associated with, in the sense of following causally from, an original revelation intended for the first human. Paul, however, expresses a vivid awareness of the possibility that people who have never received any revelation in the sense of the Jewish "law" can still have knowledge of God: "Ever since the creation of the world, his invisible attributes of eternal power and divinity have been able to be understood and perceived in what he has made. As a result, they have no excuse" (Rom 1:20; see 2:14–16).

(2) *History of Theology.* The Fathers know nothing of an original revelation as such, but they incorporate what the concept signifies insofar as they speak, in Platonic terms, of the fragments (*lógoi spermatikoí*) of the revelation of Christ that are scattered like seeds among all peoples. When the question arose, at the time of discovery of previously unknown parts of the world in the sixteenth century, about whether it was possible for heathens to be saved, theologians like A. Steuchus (*De perenni philosophia* [Lyon, 1540]) and M. de Medina (*De recta in Deum fide* [Venice, 1563]) responded with the thesis of original revelation. In the nineteenth century, representatives of the Catholic Tübingen school (J. S. von Drey, J. A. Möhler, F. A. Staudenmaier) saw a possibility of salvation for heathens in the framework of God's historico-educative plan.

(3) *Church Teaching.* Teaching office rejected the French traditionalist thesis that original revelation was absolutely necessary in order to fructify a natural reason that otherwise remained passive regarding the matter of knowledge of God (DS 3026). It explicitly teaches that biblically certified revelation (DS 3004f.) is the sole way in which the truth that brings salvation "can be recognized easily, with firm certainty, and without any admixture of error" (DS 3005) by all human beings in their sin-conditioned state. On the other hand, it also adheres to the proposition that "God, the ground and end of all things, can be recognized with certainty, on the basis of created things, by the natural light of human reason" (DS 3004, 3026). Knowledge of God that is attained outside the "supernatural" way is therefore possible. In which manner, "since when," and just where are left without binding definition.

(4) *Ecumenical Perspectives.* This topic is not ecumenically controversial.

(5) *Systematic Reflections.* According to our current state of knowledge, no explicitly thematic and consciously conceptualized original revelation can be demonstrated in, or inferred from, human history. It would appear to follow, however, from the dogma of the UNIVERSAL SALVIFIC WILL OF GOD, that this would confer upon every human being sufficient grace for justification; and this grace can be assumed to be accompanied by a certain knowledge of God, even if it is not necessarily to be thought of as propositional and reflective. The universality of the phenomena of RELIGION and piety points in this direction.

See also TRADITIONALISM.

Bibliography
Geiselmann, Joseph Rupert. *The Meaning of Tradition.* New York: Herder and Herder, 1966.
Rahner, Karl, and Joseph Ratzinger. *Revelation and Tradition.* New York: Herder and Herder, 1966.

ALEXANDRE GANOCZY

Profession of Faith. "Profession of faith" means either the act of professing the faith or the text in which the faith of the church finds verbal form (a creed). Act and text go together and point to each other. The text of the profession can be understood as the form of the act of professing.

(1) *Biblical Background.* In the New Testament, confessional statements are the earliest verbal form taken by the Christian kerygma. These statements occur as acclamations (e.g., 1 Cor 12:3) or formulaic summations of the gospel (e.g., 1 Cor 15:3–5; Rom 1:3f.; 10:9) or hymns (e.g., Phil 2:6–11; Eph 2:14–16). These confessions or professions (*homologiai*) are the point of departure and abiding center of the New Testament writings, provided the latter are understood as developments of the confessions in relation to various situations.

(2) *History of Theology.* The church's professions of faith soon took a trinitarian form. The place where these were originally used was the baptismal liturgy. Related to them in content were the "rules of faith," which played a role chiefly in theological controversy. The following professions of faith achieved universal importance and became obligatory: the Apostles' Creed (DS 30), which is attested from the third century and which, because of its conciseness, wealth of motifs, and supposed composition by the apostles, became the most widely used in the West; the Great Creed (Nicene-Constantinopolitan Creed [DS 150]), which was a reinforcement, ordered by the Council of Constantinople (381), of the creed of Nicaea (325) and which was given ecumenical recognition at the Council of Chalcedon (451) and was and is used in both West and East with varying frequency; the Athanasian Creed (the Pseudo-Athanasian Symbol "Quicumque" [DS 75f.]), a doctrinal document that came into existence around 500 and was more important in theology than in the liturgy. New versions of the profession of faith have from time to time been suggested (e.g., Thomas Aquinas) or produced (Paul VI, 1968; "Short Formula of Faith," ca.

1970) on the grounds that the present one was incomplete or was supposedly not understood by the people.

(3) *Church Teaching.* The church's early professions of faith are part of its body of doctrine; the Apostles' Creed and the Great Creed are also used in the liturgy. The Great Creed is professed when a person assumes an ecclesiastical office (*AAS* 59 [1967] 1058). New versions (see sec. 2 above) neither can nor are intended to replace or suppress the officially recognized professions of faith.

(4) *Ecumenical Perspectives.* The churches of the Reformation accepted the creeds of the early church into their collections of confessional material. By adhering to these creeds, the churches express their continuity with the early church. In the ecumenical movement a considerable effort is being made at present to reclaim the Great Creed as a common "expression of apostolic faith today." During the sixteen-hundredth anniversary of the Council of Constantinople (1981) many churches and their representatives emphasized the permanently binding importance of its creed, an importance that needs to be further investigated for ecumenical purposes. The World Council of Churches is working on a joint study of the profession of faith of 381.

(5) *Systematic Reflections.* The professions of faith make it clear that Christian faith is a participation in the "faith of the church." It is also a faith that by its very nature refers to a God who has communicated God's self to humankind in the mysteries of faith that are listed in the creed.

See also FAITH; MYSTERY OF FAITH.

Bibliography
Kelly, John N. D. *Early Christian Creeds.* London: Longman, 1972.
Lubac, Henri de. *The Christian Faith: An Essay on the Structure of the Apostles' Creed.* San Francisco: Ignatius, 1986.
Orsy, Ladislas M. *The Profession of Faith and the Oath of Fidelity: A Theological and Canonical Analysis.* Wilmington, Del.: Glazier, 1990.
Ratzinger, Joseph. *Introduction to Christianity.* New York: Herder and Herder, 1969.

WERNER LÖSER

Prophecy. Prophecy is the gift, given to one called, of interpreting a given situation of salvation or disaster in light of its decisive causes (which however are not readily accessible to everyone) and thus of opening up a perspective on the future by gesture or utterance. A prophet is therefore a seer or speaker, who speaks in the name of God.

(1) *Biblical Background.* Although prophecy can exist outside the world of Judeo-Christian revelation, it acquired its clearest form in the relevant documents of the Old Testament and New Testament. In the Old Testament it developed on the basis of the covenant and law of Moses. It becomes a perceptible historical reality in connection with the Old Testament monarchy and therefore in a political context. A more detailed picture becomes possible, however, only with the help of the documentation provided by the writing prophets. Until the exile both true and false prophecy are to be found. Prophets always

appeal to Yahweh and communicate Yahweh's word; that is, prophets speak
from an experience that has brought them into direct contact with the reality and presence of God. "Thus says Yahweh" is the stereotyped formula of
Old Testament prophecy. On the other hand, no preexilic prophet appeals to
the Spirit. In the postexilic period, the positive concept of prophecy becomes
universal, but the phenomenon itself fades away; the prophets are increasingly
displaced by the scribes. Prophecy becomes a definable thing of the past. In the
New Testament there is a revival of prophecy in the persons of John the Baptist and Jesus himself. Of all the figures of Israelite tradition it is that of the
prophet that most resembles Jesus in his appearance on the scene and in his
discourses and actions. At the same time, however, there are references to false
prophets. In early Christianity prophecy is regarded as a charism (1 Cor 14:1),
but the role of prophets in the community is not entirely clear. An explicit linking of Old Testament prophecy with the Spirit of Christ is to be found in 1 Pt
1:11, while 2 Pt 1:21 explains all prophecy as due to a movement of the Holy
Spirit. These thoughts probably reflect a Christian explanation of prophecy that
presupposes the New Testament concept of the Holy Spirit.

(2) *History of Theology.* Prophecy acknowledged as such seems not to have
occurred after the New Testament period. Wherever a claim to prophecy was
made, as in gnosis and Montanism, the church raised objections to it. Until
the modern age, on the other hand, there was no disagreement about the fact
of Old Testament prophecy or about the fundamental understanding of it; any
discussion, especially with Jews, was concerned with its correct interpretation.
In post-Reformation apologetics prophecy was regarded, along with miracles,
as a proof of the supernatural character of Christian revelation; in the process,
however, prophecy was narrowly conceived as a miraculous prediction of the
future. Understood in the same way, it was also listed among the motives of
credibility in the analysis of the act of faith. It was only modern Old Testament
exegesis that made readers aware that they had too narrow an understanding
of prophecy. At the same time, studies in the history of religions challenged
the apologetic use of the phenomenon. Nowadays the phenomenon is linked to
mystical experience and explained in its light. In any case, prophecy serves to
counteract a purely institutional understanding of ministry.

(3) *Church Teaching.* The statement of the creed that the Holy Spirit spoke
through (the law and) the prophets (DS 41f., 44, 46, 48, 150) is binding doctrine. The apologetic use of the phenomenon of prophecy was defended by the
Syllabus (DS 2907), Vatican I (DS 3009), and decisions of the Pontifical Biblical Commission (DS 3505f., 3528). Vatican II sees the faithful exercising a
prophetic role through their sense of the faith (*LG* 12); this gift thus belongs
in principle to all Christians.

(4) *Ecumenical Perspectives.* In ecumenical dialogue reflection on the gift of
prophecy can lead to a "rereading" of the truths of faith on the basis of the
present-day understanding of reality: prophets have always understood their
role to be that of giving new currency to the data of faith in their own time.

(5) *Systematic Reflections.* Jesus Christ is the decisive factor in the Christian understanding of prophecy. The latter is the gift of judging in accordance with the saving will of God that has been definitively revealed in Jesus. In other words, prophecy is the discernment of spirits as being the factors that determine our reality. Prophecy thus makes possible right decisions and the recognition of the "signs of the times" (*GS* 4), and this not only for individuals but for the church as a whole. Prophecy can therefore be understood also as a public witness to the faith in light of the demands of the age. To the extent that prophecy is understood as a direct communication of revelation, Christ is unquestionably the prophet par excellence. Then this immediate prophecy must be distinguished from a mediate prophecy that transmits the saving event. This distinction, however, sheds light on only one side of the dependence of mediated prophecy on the occurrence of prophecy par excellence in Jesus Christ, an occurrence that has its model in the making of the covenant through Moses, who is the point of reference for all prophets. There is another side: in these mediations the New Testament saving event itself and as such becomes present and puts its stamp on each concrete moment, so that the definitive revelation is communicated over and over again to human beings through new and unique figures who are not interchangeable. This mediate prophecy, which is at one and the same time the presence of the fundamental prophetic event and its communication at particular points in space and time, makes possible an authentic salvation-historical growth of Christian faith without derogating from the figure of Jesus Christ and its importance. The possibility of all this is conceivable only as an effect of the Holy Spirit, who not only bestows a general theological faith as a response to the revelation or self-communication of God but also determines the concrete form of this response of faith, the form, that is, in which alone it can and ought to be given by individuals in their particular circumstances. The challenge of revelation already takes this concrete situation into account, without the fullness and definitiveness of God's self-revelation being thereby impaired. The concreteness shows up even more strongly in the response of faith. The explanation, communication, and acceptance of salvation, all closely connected as the action of the Holy Spirit, are to be looked upon as Christian prophecy. As a gift of the Spirit (see 1 Cor 14:1), Christian prophecy is characterized by the power to make the original revelation present and by the power to apply it in a concrete historical situation, this application being found through an indispensable discernment of spirits. Only then may we say with Vatican II: "The whole body of the faithful who have an anointing that comes from the holy one (see 1 Jn 2:20 and 27) cannot err in matters of belief" (*LG* 12).

See *also* CHARISM/CHARISMS; PROPHET; SENSUS FIDELIUM.

Bibliography
Benoit, Pierre, and Paul Synave. *Prophecy and Inspiration: A Commentary on the "Summa Theologica" II–II, Questions 171–178.* New York: Desclée, 1961.
Koch, Klaus. *The Prophets.* 2 vols. Philadelphia: Fortress, 1983–84.

Petersen, David L., ed. *Prophecy in Israel: Search for an Identity*. Philadelphia: Fortress, 1987.
Rad, Gerhard von. *Old Testament Theology*. Vol. 2. New York: Harper, 1962.
Wilson, Robert R. *Prophecy and Society in Ancient Israel*. Philadelphia: Fortress, 1980.
See also the bibliography under PROPHET.

KARL HEINZ NEUFELD

Prophet. A prophet is a proclaimer of God's word who is moved by the Spirit of God. He or she is distinct both from the priest, to whom the temple worship is entrusted, and from the king and shepherd, who leads and cares for those entrusted to him.

(1) *Biblical Background.* Prophets play a very important role in the Old Testament. They are not, however, a uniform phenomenon: there are prophets who are part of an organized personnel (1 Chr 25:1) and prophets who are independent; there are groups of prophets (1 Sm 19:20; 2 Kgs 4:38; 6:1) and individual prophetic figures (2 Samuel 7; 12; 1 Kings 17–19; 2 Kings 1–9; 13); there are prophets of salvation (Second Isaiah) and prophets of doom (Amos); there are the earlier prophets whose words and deeds are recorded in the historical books of the Old Testament (Abraham, Moses, etc.; see Nm 11:24–29; Dt 18:18; 34:10) and the writing prophets (Amos, Hosea, Isaiah, Micah, etc.); finally, there are true and false prophets (see Jer 20:9; 23:16; Am 3:8). The New Testament makes frequent reference to the Old Testament prophets: they point ahead to Jesus, the messiah, and, as martyrs, prefigure him. In the early part of Jesus' own story prophetic figures make their appearance: Zechariah, Elizabeth, Simeon, Anna, John the Baptist. Jesus himself is at times called a prophet (Mt 21:11, 46; Mk 6:15; 8:28; Lk 7:16, 39; 24:19; Jn 4:19; 6:14; 7:40; 9:17; Acts 3:22f.; 7:37). It is characteristic of Jesus that he is not only a prophet but also a shepherd or king (John 10; 19) and priest (see Hebrews). In the first Christian community prophecy was regarded as one of the most important charisms. This importance is frequently attested: Acts 13:1, 15, 22, 32; Rom 12:6f.; 1 Cor 12:28f.; 14:1; Eph 2:20; 3:5; 4:11; Rv 11:18; 16:6; 18:24.

(2) *History of Theology.* In the early church of the postapostolic period the charism of prophecy was still widespread (*Didache*; *Hermas*). At the same time, however, the phenomenon of "false prophets" also spread (Montanism); in these persons there was a contradiction between their doctrine and their life, and the extraordinary manifestations accompanying prophecy became excessive. In the struggle against false prophets prophecy itself fell into a certain disrepute in the church generally, although it lived on in the saints. Led by the Holy Spirit, these men and women interpret the word and will of God, especially by their lives, in a way that is relevant to their situation. In reaction against the one-sided emphasis on the priestly ministry in the late Middle Ages, the Reformers emphasized the ministry of preaching; the result, however, was simply a hardening of previous positions.

(3) *Church Teaching.* Vatican II made use of the doctrine of the three of-

fices of Jesus Christ for its ecclesiology. As a result, in its theology of ministry the ministry of sanctification and governance is accompanied by the ministry of preaching, which is often called "the prophetic office" (*munus propheticum*). But the council also speaks of a prophetic role for the laity and the whole people of God (*LG* 12, 31, 35; *AA* 3). In this context, mention is made of the charisms that are bestowed upon each individual for the good of the whole.

(4) *Ecumenical Perspectives.* The revaluation of the prophetic is ecumenically important inasmuch it meets a concern of the churches of the Reformation (especially the Free Churches).

(5) *Systematic Reflections.* It is in keeping with the church's nature as an image of the triune God that in it the institutional and the prophetic should exist side by side in a unity amid tension.

See also CHARISM/CHARISMS; MINISTRY IN THE CHURCH; OFFICES OF JESUS CHRIST; SAINTS: SANCTIFICATION, HOLINESS.

Bibliography

Aune, David E. *Prophecy in Early Christianity and the Mediterranean World.* Grand Rapids: Eerdmans, 1983.

Davies, Philip R., and David J. A. Clines. *Among the Prophets: Language, Image and Structure in the Prophetic Writings.* Sheffield, England: JSOT, 1993.

Horsley, Richard A. *Bandits, Prophets, and Messiahs: Popular Movements in the Time of Jesus.* New York: Harper and Row, 1985.

Petersen, David L. *The Roles of Israel's Prophets.* Sheffield, England: JSOT, 1981.

Rahner, Karl. *The Dynamic Element in the Church.* New York: Herder and Herder, 1964.

Sawyer, John F. A. *Prophecy and the Prophets of the Old Testament.* New York: Oxford University Press, 1987.

WERNER LÖSER

Protology. "Protology" means the theory (usually developed speculatively) of the beginning, origin, or ORIGINAL STATE, that is, of that which God had intended for humanity as the "first" — something with which, of course, original sin, as a rejection of this "first" that can be experienced at all stages of history, becomes involved. The term itself was formulated by analogy with the term "eschatology."

(1) *Biblical Background.* This analogy rests on the biblically documented religious insight that the grace that God intended for humanity at the very beginning will not be realized, in full form, until the very end, that is, eschatologically. Hence, for example in Paul, the protological statement about Adam's sin and the mortality that it brings about (Rom 5:12) corresponds to the eschatological statement about Adam who prefigures the coming Christ (Rom 5:14). Quite consistently, he calls Christ the "last [*eschatos*] Adam" (1 Cor 15:45b) and describes him as the victor over sin and death, as the one who died sinless and was raised by God. By virtue of a similar christological recursion, various New Testament texts speak of Christ's participation in the creation of the world and humanity: "Jesus Christ, through whom all things are and through whom we exist" (1 Cor 8:6; see Phil 2:6; Col 1:15–20; Eph 1:4; Heb 1:2f.; Jn 1:1f.).

(2) *History of Theology.* The contribution of the Church Fathers to protology consists mainly in the development of the "creation out of nothing" (*creatio ex nihilo*) doctrine with regard to redemptive history (Irenaeus) or the fall (Augustine).

(3) *Church Teaching.* For determinations on protology by doctrinal office, see CREATION OUT OF NOTHING (CREATIO EX NIHILO) and CREATION.

(4) *Ecumenical Perspectives.* There is no record of theological controversy in the area of protology.

(5) *Systematic Reflections.* Today, there are two main types of protologico-eschatological speculation. In the first, which starts (in a supralapsarian way) with creation "before the fall," final perfection tends to be treated as a new creation that grants humanity full self-development in Christ and his Spirit; the second starts (in an infralapsarian way) with the sinful state of the human species "after the fall" and regards salvation as the regaining of the forfeited original state. K. Rahner often speaks of the subject matter of protology as the condition of the possibility of all redemptive perfection.

See also BEGINNING; ESCHATOLOGY.

Bibliography
Beinert, Wolfgang. *Christus und der Kosmos: Perspektiven zu einer Theologie der Schöpfung.* Freiburg: Herder, 1974.
Rahner, Karl. "Grundsätzliche Überlegungen zur Anthropologie und Protologie im Rahmen der Theologie." In *MystSal,* 2:406–20. Einsiedeln: Benziger, 1965.

ALEXANDRE GANOCZY

Providence. "Providence," in the dogmatic sense, signifies God's planning will, by which God creates the world and especially the spiritual and personal history of humanity for the sake of the goal God predetermined.

(1) *Biblical Background.* In the Old Testament, the concept of providence occurs only in Jb 10:12 and Wis 6:7; 14:3; 17:2. The phenomenon itself is a central idea: God guides history but in such a way that the independent and free human actions are not annulled. In the postexilic period, the idea is extended to apply to individuals as well (e.g., Jer 1:5; Jb 5:19–21). The benevolence of God's providence is made manifest by Jesus in the New Testament when Jesus shatters the rigid scheme of doing and faring, sin and punishment. He states of the man born blind that neither he nor his parents had sinned (thus there is no question of his having deservedly "incurred" the blindness), but that "the works of God" were to "be made manifest in him" (Jn 9:3). God's providence is not theoretically explained, but a way to catch sight of the divine love holding sway within it is indicated: "But seek first his kingdom and his righteousness, and all these things will be yours as well" (Mt 6:33). Paul turns that idea in the direction of pious trustfulness: "We know that in everything God works for good with those who love him" (Rom 8:28). Eph 1:3–14 outlines God's plan of salvation.

(2) *History of Theology.* The historical roots of belief in God's providence lie in Greek philosophy, already as a principle in the pre-Socratics, but first in verbal form in Herodotus (3.108.2). It then becomes the "basic dogma" of Stoicism. As a result of biblical and philosophical stimuli, a richly developed theology of providence is found in the Fathers of the Church, so that denial of God's providence (*prónoia*) is equated with atheism (Clement of Alexandria, *Strom.* 6.122). In this connection, the Fathers decisively preserve the idea of human freedom and responsibility. Augustine gives a profound and speculative meaning to the doctrine of providence; following his line, Thomas Aquinas defines God's providence as a "plan [*ratio*] for the directing of things toward the goal that preexists in the divine mind" (*STh* 1, q. 22, a. 1). In modern times, the idea of God's providence exerts an influence — by way of Augustine, *De civ. Dei* — on the theology of history (J.-B. Bossuet). During the Enlightenment, God's providence was viewed as a rational truth that was identified with the idea of a meaningful order of history and of the cosmos (G. W. Leibniz: God has created the best of all possible worlds).

(3) *Church Teaching.* Countering atheistic and dualistic explanations, Vatican I expounds God's providence as God's way of governing the world and protecting God's creatures (DS 3003).

(4) *Ecumenical Perspectives.* J. Calvin's teaching on predestination has a theologically controversial bearing on the doctrine of God's providence. However, since its elaboration by K. Barth, there are no longer any essential differences between it and Catholic thinking.

(5) *Systematic Reflections.* The backdrop to belief in providence is the manner of God's encounter with God's creatures in their concrete history. That should not be imagined as God's making calculating use of a mere rationality of ends and means, but should be seen as the holding sway of God's universal love. This rules out any resolution of the topic through speculative thought: the substance of belief in providence is that humans should, in loving obedience, allow the loving God to work the divine will and rule. They thereby become active participants in the play of events that is overseen by God's providence. This providence now appears not only as a will to an end but also as an accompaniment for creatures along the way. All of this does not exclude but rather — in view of Christ's cross — allows that belief in providence includes doubt in a special way and shares quite intensely in the essential opacity of faith. But because Jesus Christ, as the crucified and resurrected one, is the way for us, God's providence nevertheless also ultimately discloses itself as the working of God's love. Belief in providence is thus neither fatalism nor passivity, but enables the highest kind of activity in the form of devotion to the God of providence.

See also GOD'S FOREKNOWLEDGE; LOVE; PREDESTINATION.

Bibliography
Fackenheim, Emil. *God's Presence in History: Jewish Affirmations and Philosophical Reflections.* New York: New York University Press, 1970.

Gilkey, Langdon. *Reaping the Whirlwind: A Christian Interpretation of History*. New York: Seabury, 1976.

Hodgson, Peter. *God in History: Shapes of Freedom*. Nashville, Abingdon, 1989.

Scheffczyk, Leo. *Creation and Providence*. New York: Herder and Herder, 1970.

WILHELM BREUNING

Purgatory. As understood in ecclesial tradition, purgatory is the process of purification, in the other world, that frees persons from every defect and makes it possible for them to enter into the fulfillment of heaven.

(1) *Biblical Background.* No one denies today that there is no passage in Scripture that can with certainty be interpreted as referring to a purgatory. The biblical idea of Sheol (lower world, kingdom of the dead) does not signify a state of purification but rather the radical power of death and a continued shadowy existence of human beings in the beyond; at a later stage of development, Sheol is a place of rewards and punishments for human beings. Several passages of Scripture have traditionally been offered as proofs of purgatory. The frequently cited passage in 2 Mc 12:40–45 does indeed attest to belief in the resurrection of the dead, but not to a purification in the other world. There is just as little ground for interpreting Mt 12:32 as a reference to purgatory. More difficult is Mt 5:25–26, a passage that played an important role in patristic theology; it speaks of a prison from which no one emerges until the last farthing has been paid. In contemporary exegesis the prison is understood as referring not to purgatory but to hell. A comparable view is to be taken of 1 Cor 3:10–15. In the immediate context, the fire mentioned there is not a purifying fire but the fire of judgment on the last day or the Christ of the parousia who will appear in majesty and exercise his role as judge. On the other hand, it must be noted that this passage, together with Mt 5:25–26, played an important part in the development of the doctrine of purgatory.

(2) *History of Theology.* A proper doctrine of purgatory is first developed in the patristic period, on the basis of the biblical promises of salvation and references to their fulfillment. In this process the celebration of the Eucharist and the development of the sacrament of reconciliation play an important part. Prayer for the dead is attested from the second century on. In the third century the custom arises of praying for the departed during the Eucharist. Finally, there is general acceptance of the practice of offering the sacrifice of the Mass for them. In the *Apostolic Constitutions*, prayers for the dead, which had earlier been couched in general terms, become more specific and move in the direction of a doctrine of purgatory, since God, friend of human beings, is there asked to release the soul, which God has now taken, from every voluntary or involuntary sin. The *Euchologion* of Serapion (fourth century) implores God not to remember the sins and errors of the deceased. Even more important for the development of the doctrine of purgatory is the penitential process, which until the sixth century was allowed only once in a person's life. In the Western Church the process was in large measure penal in character, inasmuch as fulfill-

ment of the penance imposed was meant to earn the forgiveness of sin. In time of persecution, however, the penitent was reconciled to the church before completion of the penance, because people were convinced that the penance still to be performed could be completed in the other world. In the East, on the other hand, the penitential process was understood as a matter of spiritual pedagogy or else as medicine and therapy, inasmuch as the overcoming of sin with the help of the priest who imposed the penance and acted as a physician of the soul was interpreted as the healing of a sickness of the soul. This process of recuperation and purification can also continue after death. These differences in the understanding of the penitential process led to divergent understandings of purgatory. In the Western Fathers the purification between death and resurrection is penal in nature (thus Tertullian, Cyprian, Augustine); in the Eastern Fathers it is understood as a process of maturation (Clement of Alexandria, Origen, and especially John Chrysostom).

(3) *Church Teaching.* The teaching pronouncements of the church in the Middle Ages and early modern period are directed against the doctrine of the Orthodox churches on purgatory and against the denial of purgatory by the Reformers. The Second Council of Lyons (1274; DS 856) and the Council of Florence (1439; DS 1304) teach that the souls of those who have died repentant and in a state of charity but have not yet done appropriate penance for their sins are cleansed by purifying punishments. These punishments can be mitigated by the intercessions of the living faithful in the forms of the Mass, prayer, almsgiving, and other pious works that the faithful perform for one another in accord with the institutions established by the church. The expression "fire of purgatory" (*ignis purgatorius*) is deliberately avoided. The basic focus of the Latins finds expression in the term "purifying punishments" (*poenae purgatoriae*). The doctrine common to the two great churches consists by and large in the idea of purification in general and, above all, in the reference to the Eucharist and the intercessory prayer of the church. Completely excluded from this common belief is the idea of indulgences for the dead, which the Orthodox reject. The decree of the Council of Trent on purgatory (1563; DS 1820) takes as its starting point the fact that once serious sin is forgiven and eternal punishment is remitted not all temporal punishments are thereby set aside in every case. Consequently, in addition to the possibility of the remission of temporal punishment in this world there is also a purification in the other world; here the church can aid the souls of the deceased through intercessory prayer and especially through the Mass. It is to be observed that the Council of Trent appeals for justification of its teaching on purgatory to the Scriptures generally and to the patristic tradition, without citing even a single specific passage of Scripture.

(4) *Ecumenical Perspectives.* In the ecumenical dialogue purgatory has acquired a certain importance inasmuch as the Orthodox completely reject the idea of a purification in the other world through punishment and expiation, as well as a purifying fire and indulgences for the dead, while the Reformers reject the whole idea of purgatory. As was pointed out above, the church's doc-

trinal pronouncements do not speak of a purifying fire, nor do they mention indulgences for the dead. The binding doctrine of the church consists, therefore, in the simple statement that there is a purgatory, the detailed explanation of which is left to the theologians.

(5) *Systematic Reflections.* The expression "fire of purgatory," which arose in the West in the twelfth century in connection with 1 Cor 3:15, can lead to several misunderstandings, since, on the one hand, it almost inevitably localizes the process of purification and, on the other, it does not attend sufficiently to the multiple symbolic meanings of the image of "fire" as this appears in the Scriptures. At the level of speculative explanation, the purification in the other world is to be understood as the love-inspired desire to be liberated from the last defects that are still an obstacle to the full vision of God. Only to the extent that this growth in love of God is painful may we speak of suffering in purgatory. The assumption that there are additional punishments imposed by God is neither necessary nor meaningful. In Western theology, the object of the purification is usually said to be the temporal punishments for sin that still remain after the forgiveness of the person's guilt. But it must be observed that the distinction between guilt and sin was unknown for a long time, and even the medieval theologians took the view that the purification in the other world had to do with venial sin and temporal punishment. In any case, "temporal punishment" must be understood as a consequence flowing from the very nature of sin and causing suffering, and not as a punishment that God imposes by positive law. In contemporary theology, various explanations of purgatory have been essayed. K. Rahner, for example, accepts the understanding just given of guilt and punishment and considers purgatory to be a process in which, after death, the multileveled human reality is integrated into the basic option that the person made during life. Because of the loving communication that goes on between all who are linked together in Christ, this process can be supported by the intercession of people on earth. In the context of his final-option hypothesis, L. Boros explains purgatory as the quality and intensity of the final choice of God that takes place in death.

See also DEATH; EUCHARIST; INDULGENCE; PRAYER; SACRAMENT OF RECONCILIATION.

Bibliography
Boros, Ladislas. *The Mystery of Death.* New York: Herder and Herder, 1965.
Catherine of Genoa, Saint. *Purgation and Purgatory: The Spiritual Dialogue.* New York: Paulist, 1979.
Lanne, Emmanuel. "The Teaching of the Catholic Church on Purgatory." *One in Christ* 28 (1992) 13–30.
Le Goff, Jacques. *The Birth of Purgatory.* Chicago: University of Chicago Press, 1984.
Rahner, Karl. "Purgatory." In *Theological Investigations,* 19:181–93. New York: Crossroad, 1983.

JOSEF FINKENZELLER

Q q

Quest for Meaning. In philosophical language, "meaning" (*Sinn*) signifies the purpose, end, and value inherent in something. From the theological perspective, then, the question of meaning signifies the question about the end, purpose, and value of human beings and their lives as posed in the context of discourse about God as Creator and redeemer.

(1) *Biblical Background.* In representing and proclaiming both universal and individual history as redemptive history, the Bible testifies to the meaningfulness of that history, but it does not pose the question of meaning as such. That holds true even of instances in which God's actions become impenetrable to humans (Job).

(2) *History of Theology.* The question of such meaning has become a problematic issue only in the modern era. With the collapse of the medieval conception of the world and its all-embracing "ordo," with the expanded view of the world that resulted from geographical and natural-scientific discoveries, and ultimately with the psychoanalytical experience of the fathomlessness of the modern psyche, modern humankind has become radically conscious, as never before, of insecurity and of being threatened. In the present-day world, with its wholly new sorts of challenge (the ecological issue, the problems of biogenetics, the nuclear threat), this consciousness has acquired unprecedented dimensions. The attempts at autonomous self-grounding of humanity that were undertaken in the nineteenth and twentieth centuries (e.g., in existentialism) are seen as having foundered.

(3) *Church Teaching.* The pastoral constitution *Gaudium et spes* of Vatican II addresses the various modern problems surrounding the topic of meaning: it formulates the question of meaning (esp. GS 10) and explains that the church shares in humanity's joy, hope, anxiety, and sadness (GS 1), but also knows a response: "Through Christ and in Christ...the riddle of pain and death, which overpowers us outside his Gospel, is clarified" (GS 22; see, as a whole, the first main section, nos. 11–45).

(4) *Ecumenical Perspectives.* Important contributions toward surmounting the question of meaning in the modern context can be gained from the Lutheran doctrine of justification insofar as it pregnantly stresses that meaning is a *gift from God.* Humans must not, therefore, place central focus on the question of meaning and draw conclusions about it in accordance with their own view of things.

(5) *Systematic Reflections.* That humans can and should ask about the meaning of life is part of the dignity of the human person. The question of meaning can become an irresolvable dilemma and a source of agonizing despair

when one has lost all sense of direction, when one suffers because of the injustice in the world, and when one can no longer even begin to comprehend the course of worldly events. In such situations, Christian theology has an urgent obligation to make understandable God's call to blessed life with God (HEAVEN) as an actual goal even for humans today. In so doing, theology becomes a theology of hope that derives its legitimation from the fact that God bestows the meaning of life, which is thus not an object to be achieved through effort. It should demonstrate that this world holds in store not only disappointments but also fulfillments that warrant hope for an ultimate meaning.

See also GOD; GOD: POSSIBILITY OF KNOWLEDGE OF.

Bibliography
Dupré, Louis K. *The Other Dimension: A Search for the Meaning of Religious Attitudes.* Garden City, N.Y.: Doubleday, 1972.
Hill, William J. *Search for the Absent God: Tradition and Modernity in Religious Understanding.* New York: Crossroad, 1992.
Kaufman, Gordon. *God the Problem.* Cambridge, Mass.: Harvard University Press, 1972.
Lonergan, Bernard. *Insight.* New York: Philosophical Library, 1958.
Tillich, Paul. *Systematic Theology.* Vol. 1. Chicago: University of Chicago Press, 1951.
———. *The Courage to Be.* New Haven: Yale University Press, 1952.
Wuthnow, Robert. *Meaning and Moral Order: Explorations in Cultural Analysis.* Berkeley: University of California Press, 1987.

WILHELM BREUNING

Rr

Real Presence. "Real presence" refers to the real and abiding presence of Jesus Christ in the gifts of bread and wine that have been consecrated at the Eucharist.

(1) *Biblical Background.* The doctrine of the real presence goes back to the New Testament accounts of the Last Supper, at which, in the ritual of the bread and wine, Jesus gave his entire personal reality to the disciples, with the intention of giving himself in the same manner to the faithful after his death and resurrection. The two other important eucharistic texts of the New Testament, 1 Cor 10:16–21 and Jn 6:51–59, also give unambiguous support to the conviction of faith that Jesus gives himself in the consecrated gifts of bread and wine and does not intend simply to keep the memory of himself alive.

(2) *History of Theology.* Until about the ninth century the theological conviction regarding a real presence of the Lord in the Eucharist was undisputed. Concepts were used that point to a change of bread and wine into the body and blood of the Lord. When bread and wine were called "symbols," "types," or "antitypes" of Christ's body and blood, these terms were accompanied by a conviction of a genuine real presence on the basis of the idea of participation or, as the case might be, of a transformative action of the Holy Spirit. This period of unquestioning acceptance of the real presence was followed, especially in the West, by prolonged theological controversies in which theologians sought to safeguard the mystery of the real presence with the aid of sometimes quite sophisticated philosophical distinctions and various theories of the change that ranged from a purely symbolic understanding (bread and wine *signify* the body and blood of Christ) to an overly literal historical interpretation (bread and wine *become identical* with the body and blood of the earthly Jesus). Two questions were regarded as important. The first was: Is Christ present in different ways in the consecrated bread and the consecrated wine? As a result of this question, a distinction came to be commonly accepted in the Middle Ages: the flesh of Christ is present in the bread and his blood in the wine "in virtue of the words spoken" (*vi verborum*); "by concomitance" (*per concomitantiam*) — that is, as a necessary consequence — the entire corporeal Christ, in whom divinity and humanity are united, is present in both kinds and indeed in each of their parts. The second question was: What internal happening leads to the real presence, and how are we to understand the relation between the continuing forms of bread and wine and the invisible but real presence of Christ? In this context the concept and term *transubstantiation* (change of substance) were developed beginning in the twelfth century. Behind this concept lies the philosophical idea that everything in this world has an inner, invisible essence

566

or *substance* that makes it be what it is. On the other hand, form, appearance, and so on, are *accidents* — that is, they are attached in a nonessential way to the inner substance. At the consecration of the Eucharist this inner substance is completely transformed, and only the outward manifestations of the bread and wine remain. Luther responded to this theory with a doctrine of *impanation* or *consubstantiation*, which had sometimes been defended in the past and which was also intended to preserve the real presence: the body and blood of Christ coexist with the still present substances of bread and wine and can therefore be received in faith.

(3) *Church Teaching.* In the teaching of the church the real presence is set down as a binding doctrine by the Fourth Lateran Council (1215), where it is already linked to the concept of transubstantiation (DS 802). The same had been the case with the profession of faith demanded of Berengarius of Tours in 1079 (DS 700). The dogmas of the Council of Trent are decisive. Its most important definitions are the following. (*a*) In the Eucharist "the body and blood, together with the soul and divinity, of our Lord Jesus Christ and, therefore, the whole Christ is truly, really, and substantially contained" (DS 1651; ND 1526). (*b*) A "wonderful and unique change of the whole substance of the bread into His body and of the whole substance of the wine into His blood" takes place; this change "the Catholic Church very fittingly calls transubstantiation" (DS 1652; ND 1527). (*c*) The whole Christ is contained in each of the two species or kinds and in each part of each species (DS 1653). (*d*) The body and blood of Christ remain after the consecration and may and should be worshiped with the adoration given to God. In his encyclical *Mysterium fidei* (1965) Paul VI once again emphasized the indispensability of the concept of transubstantiation as a safeguard of the real presence, but he also acknowledged the legitimacy of concepts that complement transubstantiation and further explain it (ND 1577–80).

(4) *Ecumenical Perspectives.* Despite differences in terminology and emphasis there is a large measure of agreement with the Eastern Church as regards the real presence. There is disagreement only about when the consecration takes place. In the Western Church the eucharistic consecration is identified with the words of institution; in the Eastern Church it is identified rather with the epiclesis or invocation of the Holy Spirit on the bread and wine, although even here the words of institution precede. Meanwhile, however, the Western Church has also come to assign a great importance to the epiclesis by introducing it into the new eucharistic prayers. A greater agreement in this matter is possible to the extent that in the Eastern Church the consecration is not exclusively attributed to the epiclesis. Since the real presence is clearly maintained in the theology of M. Luther, a further agreement is possible here, provided that certain terms and concepts are not absolutized and that attention is focused rather on the meaning that these convey. A continuing difficulty is created by Luther's view that the real presence is given only during use or reception (*in usu*). Given the heavy emphasis on symbolism in the other Reformers (bread and wine *signify*

the body and blood of Christ), a rapprochement is possible only if there could be agreement that the symbols have a reality content due to the action of God.

(5) *Systematic Reflections.* An effort is being made in contemporary theology to explain the real presence rather in the categories of a personalist ontology. It is becoming clearer that the meaning that human beings give to things decides at least in part what things are and mean. As a result, theologians have sought to explain the real presence with the help of the concepts of transignification (change of meaning) and transfinalization (change of purpose) instead of transubstantiation; in so doing, they have certainly provided a useful complement to the older concept. If the ecclesial magisterium still gives priority to the concept of transubstantiation, its intention is to emphasize the indispensability of a truth that in principle can and must also be expressed in new concepts: it is not human "thinking it to be so" that turns bread and wine into the body and blood of the Lord; rather it is God's creative word that has this effect. Bread and wine become a new reality through the words of institution when spoken by a priest with the authority of Christ. Human belief does not *make* Jesus Christ but *receives* him as he gives himself.

See also COMMUNION UNDER BOTH KINDS; EUCHARIST; EUCHARIST: ACCOUNTS OF INSTITUTION.

Bibliography
Duffy, Regis. *Real Presence: Worship, Sacraments, and Commitment.* San Francisco: Harper and Row, 1992.
Fink, Peter. "Perceiving the Presence of Christ." *Worship* 58 (1984) 17–28.
Schillebeeckx, Edward. *The Eucharist.* New York: Sheed and Ward, 1968.

                                                                GÜNTER KOCH

Reason. Reason is the human ability to think and know. It starts out with sensory perception and operates in the medium of language. Yet it also goes beyond and transcends empirically given sensation and language through its openness to everything — otherwise a translation into other languages would not be possible.

(1) *Biblical Background.* Scripture shows little interest in the actual achievements of reason. Knowledge in the biblical sense comes closer to what we colloquially describe as "common sense": practical life experience and worldly wisdom that for the Israelites, nevertheless, included in the first place the fear of God. According to Paul, the rational wisdom of the Greeks is actually an obstacle to salvation because it judges the cross of Christ as foolishness (1 Cor 1:19–27). Yet faith is not oriented against reason itself but rather avails itself of reason in order to realize itself in a manner that fosters the call to salvation (1 Cor 14:19f.).

(2) *History of Theology.* Christian theology has understood itself as reasoned knowledge in the service of faith. Because Scholasticism considered human reason as being created in the image of God, it was convinced that it is possible to grasp the divine reasons for the plan of creation and salvation.

In contrast, in the late Middle Ages there arose a deep skepticism with regard to the theological possibilities of knowing (nominalism), which also influenced the Reformation. Modern reason established itself first of all as the arbiter in the controversies between the confessions (religion of reason). Then, however, under the influence of the exact sciences, it came more and more into contradiction with revealed faith and with faith in God in general. The relationship between faith and reason, therefore, became the central theme of theology in the last century.

(3) *Church Teaching.* Vatican I took an explicit stance on the relationship between faith and reason. (*a*) There is a difference between knowledge from faith and knowledge from reason. (*b*) Even the knowledge from faith cannot completely understand God's essence and saving work; they remain a mystery. (*c*) Nevertheless, ultimately there can be no contradiction between faith and reason because God is the origin of both (DS 3015–17).

(4) *Ecumenical Perspectives.* Protestant theology puts greater emphasis on the sinful perversion of reason and opposes to it faithful listening to the word of God (*sola scriptura*). However, the problem of understanding (HERMENEUTICS) has led today to a substantial reduction of the confessional differences.

(5) *Systematic Reflections.* At the moment, theology stands between two fronts. Against a scientifically oriented reason that dominates life in society, it must disclose the aporias of a concept of humanity founded upon reason alone. Against an increasingly popular irrational religiosity, it must make clear the religious openness of reason and the necessity of reasoned judgments in matters of faith and in the praxis of faith.

See also FAITH; LANGUAGE; MYSTERY OF FAITH; REVELATION.

Bibliography
Gadamer, Hans-Georg. *Reason in the Age of Science.* Cambridge, Mass.: MIT Press, 1983.
Green, Ronald. *Religion and Moral Reason: A New Method for Comparative Study.* New York: Oxford University Press, 1988.
Hollis, Martin, and Steven Lukes. *Rationality and Relativism.* Cambridge, Mass.: MIT Press, 1982.
Pannenberg, Wolfhart. "Faith and Reason." In *Basic Questions in Theology,* 2:46–64. Philadelphia: Fortress, 1971.
Putnam, Hilary. *Reason, Truth, and History.* New York: Cambridge University Press, 1981.
Tracy, David. *Dialogue with the Other: The Inter-religious Dialogue.* Grand Rapids: Eerdmans, 1990.

GEORG LANGEMEYER

Reception. Reception (from Latin *recipere* = record, take over, receive) is the process in which the community of faith acknowledges a decision of the church authority as true, binding, and fostering faith and makes this its own.

(1) *Biblical Background.* Insofar as according to biblical conviction human beings are dependent on the gracious saving activity of God, which they experience and make their own in FAITH through the message of revelation, this acceptance of God's salvation can be regarded from the human perspective as

a process of reception. It is explicitly stated that faith in the gospel is an act of receiving (1 Cor 11:23; 15:1–3; Gal 1:9–12).

(2) *History of Theology.* The formation of the biblical canon and the acceptance of church tradition are processes of reception. Up until 1234 the veneration of the saints was also based on reception. For the history of dogma the question became relevant because of the history of the councils: it often required a very long time until a regional or universal church gathering was acknowledged as binding. This happened, for example, for Nicaea (325) at Constantinople (381); the Council of Constantinople for its part was first recognized in Rome in 519, and the Second Council of Nicaea (787) only in 1053. On the other hand, many local synods through their reception gained importance for the universal church, for example, Antioch in 269 (against Paul of Samosata), Carthage in 418 (against the Pelagians), and Orange in 529 (doctrine on grace). In many cases reception occurred selectively: from the "Tome of Leo" (DS 290–95) the Council of Chalcedon took over only the dogmatic section; the *filioque* (and the Son) of the Nicene-Constantinopolitan Creed was not accepted by Eastern Christianity; in modern times Pope John XXIII's encyclical *Veterum sapientia* (promoting Latin as the language of theological instruction) was ignored by the local churches. The path for an impartial theological reflection was for a long time blocked because of the movements called Conciliarism and Gallicanism, which demanded a legally prescribed acceptance of the decisions of the ecclesial magisterium as the presupposition for their validity.

(3) *Church Teaching.* The magisterium rejected reception in the sense of a constitutive ratification of its decrees (DS 2281–84, 3074). Vatican II spoke of papal acts of reception (*LG* 22; *CD* 4).

(4) *Ecumenical Perspectives.* The question of reception plays a very important role in the Orthodox Church. The Slavic theology of the nineteenth century (A. S. Chomjakov [d. 1860]) represented the view that conciliar decisions are dogmatically binding only when the whole church has acknowledged them. Today a modified opinion — namely, that the decrees must correspond to the faith of the entire church — is held to be correct. Reception is the coming to consciousness of the knowledge that a decision is in agreement with the faith of the church. It is thus a conclusion, not a legally binding act. In current ecumenical discussion the pressing question has become whether and to what degree the processes of reception can serve as models for agreement among the churches (Louvain 1972, discussion over the Lima Report of 1982).

(5) *Systematic Reflections.* Theological discussion on reception is still in its beginnings. It is, however, clear that reception is an essential process in and for the church, insofar as it describes the way in which Christ's message of revelation is mediated to the living faith of Christians and is adopted by it. Insofar as faith is a dynamic process, the practice of reception occurs continually. It is above all of important practical significance regarding the influence of official church decisions: through their reception or nonreception it becomes clear whether they really contribute to the building up of faith. The reason for the

possibility of reception stems from the fact that the faithful are subjects of the Spirit-directed activity of the church, which not only is hierarchically structured but is also a brotherly and sisterly community of the children of God (*communio*). Reception is therefore not a simple act of obedience, but rather a consent arising from the community's own judgment. Nevertheless, because the ecclesial authority possesses its own right, reception cannot legitimize in the juridical sense an official act such that the act would not be valid without it. It is rather a sign that it is a genuine expression of the church's faith.

See also CANON; CHURCH; COUNCIL; ECCLESIAL MAGISTERIUM; SENSUS FI-DELIUM; TRADITION.

Bibliography
Carter, David. "Catholics, Methodists, and Reception." *One in Christ* 28 (1992) 3:232–47.
Dionne, Robert. *The Papacy and the Church: A Study of Praxis and Reception in Ecumenical Perspective.* New York: Philosophical Library, 1987.
Jauss, Hans Robert. *Toward an Aesthetic of Reception.* Minneapolis: University of Minnesota Press, 1982.

WOLFGANG BEINERT

Reconciliation. Reconciliation, along with redemption and liberation or salvation, is a basic soteriological category that describes God's act of salvation through Jesus Christ in the Holy Spirit. It is based entirely on God's love and mercy and reaches its climax in the death of Jesus, as his free act of obedience and his gift of himself in the place of fallen sinners. Through this death humankind ("the world") as guilty is released from a situation where it could not save itself by its own efforts and is granted peace. This comprises forgiveness of sins, a life in righteousness and freedom, and the capacity for a covenant of justice before God and one's fellow human beings.

(1) *Biblical Background.* In the Old Testament, reconciliation, atonement, and forgiveness (all linked through the root *kpr* or its equivalents) are viewed in the context of the covenant between God and the chosen people, who are crushed by sin but remain true to God in covenantal justice (and behavior). Especially in the area of cult (e.g., the cultic theology of atonement of the priestly tradition), there is a concentration on this communitarian justice according to the covenant: thus, in impossible situations, a life that had been forfeited and could not otherwise be saved is "ransomed." The blood (= life; see Lv 17:10–12) of the sacrificial animal is, as it were, an "existential representation," a symbolic living gift of the one offering it. This is expressed in the ritual of the "day of atonement" (Leviticus 16). It is also seen (in noncultic terms) in the vicarious suffering of God's servant (Is 52:13–53:12) and in texts where God directly ransoms the one whose life was forfeited (Is 43:3f.; Jb 33:24; Ps 49:8, 16). This Old Testament structure of cultic and communitarian justification by the covenant is used (and surpassed) in the New Testament, especially by Paul, to demonstrate that the cross of Christ is the source of universal salvation: the death of Jesus Christ is an atonement for sin. God demonstrates God's

covenantal justification by wiping out the sins (of all). Consequently, faith in the crucified one overcomes the way of the law and the Israelite atonement ritual (Rom 3:5, 23–26; see Rom 8:3; Gal 2:5–21). Therefore, the "message of reconciliation" (2 Cor 5:19b) summarizes for Paul (now in noncultic, personal language) the whole salvific work of God through Jesus Christ ("In Christ, God was reconciling the world [and us, through Christ] to himself" [2 Cor 5:19a or v. 18; see Rom 5:10f.; Eph 2:16; Col 1:20, 22]), and other formulations express the basic structure of reconciliation. (a) The *initiative* for reconciliation lies in the mercy and love of God (Rom 5:8–11; 2 Cor 5:14–21; see Rom 8:35, 39; Col 1:19ff.; Eph 2:16). (b) Reconciliation is grounded in the *self-gift of the Son* (Rom 8:3, 31; Gal 1:4; 2:20), which becomes concrete in his death or his blood poured out (Rom 3:23–26; 5:9f.; see Col 1:20; Eph 2:14, 16). (c) Reconciliation effects an *exchange* (1 Cor 1:30; see 2 Cor 5:21; 8:9; Gal 3:13f.). (d) Reconciliation changes the state of enmity (Rom 5:10; see Col 1:21; Eph 2:14, 16b) and *establishes peace* (Rom 5:1; see Col 1:20; Eph 2:15). (e) Reconciliation is mediated by the "service of reconciliation" (2 Cor 5:18) and gives a capacity for reconciliation (5:20) and therefore for covenantal justification. This basic structure is capable of integrating other New Testament statements on redemption and is therefore the basic form of the Christian teaching on reconciliation. Its midpoint is the element of "exchange," grounded in the expression "for us" or "for our sake" (1 Cor 2:6; the Last Supper tradition; Mk 10:45). According to John, the basis of the Son's self-gift is the love of God (3:6f.; see 1 Jn 4:10): it is a free gift (Jn 10:17f.), made out of love (15:13). The exalted Jesus is universal salvation (Jn 12:32). Together with the Spirit he gives full power to forgive sins (20:22). Jesus' self-gift is the measure for the disciple's willingness to give of self (1 Jn 3:16). Hebrews depicts Jesus as the high priest and his salvific work as a priestly service of reconciliation (referring to and fulfilling Leviticus 16) (4:14–10:18). All initiatives come from the Son, who as high priest expiates the sins of the people (2:17) and proclaims his obedient and free gift of himself (10:5–7), from the moment he enters into the world (all this is described as a prayerful process). Because of this freely willed decision, human beings are sanctified once and for all by the offering of his life (10:10), that is, concretely, by his blood as an offering "through the eternal Spirit" (9:14). In him the offering and the priest are identical (9:12). As truly human the Son shares the destiny of all humans and is capable of representing us (2:9–18; 4:5; 5:1–10). Through his offering once for all he realizes his mediatorship (8:6; 9:15; 12:24) so that all are made holy and have access to the goods of salvation in faith, hope, and love (10:19–24, etc.). This cultic explanation of God's salvific work through Christ in the Holy Spirit also involves the idea of a way (2:1), of the search for the land of peace and community with God (4:1–11), of hope as a firm guide that helps us attain the land of the promise (6:13–20), and of the wanderings of God's people to the future city (13:14). Along this way Jesus is the "pioneer" (2:10; 12:2). In the prophecies of the passion in the Synoptics (Mt 17:22 pars.; Mt 20:18f. pars.), the "self-gift of the Son" is a "handing over" (by God). In the

Last Supper tradition the death of Jesus is understood as the establishment of the eschatological covenant (Lk 22:20 par.; 1 Cor 11:25; see Jer 31:31) and an atoning covenant liturgy (Mt 26:28; Mk 14:24 par.; see Ex 24:8), whose background is Isaiah 53 or the vicarious atonement of martyrs. Traces of Is 53:10f. may already be visible in pre-Pauline formulas (Rom 4:25; 8:32; Gal 1:4; 1 Tm 2:6; see HISTORICAL JESUS).

(2) *History of Theology.* In the history of theology the doctrine of reconciliation has been handed on in combination with other themes (martyrdom, the practice of penance, the Eucharist as memorial of the sacrifice of the cross) and developed by means of language that was cultic (priest, offering, atonement), legal (reparation, merit), and personal (being-for, intercession, proexistence, representation, community/solidarity). In the patristic period its center was the *admirabile commercium* (see the "exchange-formulas" in the *Letter of Diognetus* and in Irenaeus, Cyprian, Athanasius, and others). Here the incarnation is understood as the beginning of the kenosis unto death that, however, brings reconciliation only in the paschal mystery (the cross, resurrection, and sending of the Spirit). It is a *commercium caritatis* = exchange of love (Augustine, *C. Faust.* 5.9). In Anselm's satisfaction theory, the medieval doctrine of reconciliation reaches a high point. Thomas moderates it in some ways through the character of Christ as head of the church or through a notion of humanity that links reconciliation to the idea of merit and reparation (*STh* 3, q. 48, a. 1; a. 2 ad 1; q. 49, a. 1.3 ad 3); Thomas also moderates it by stressing the perfect love of Christ for God and humans (*STh* 3, q. 46, a. 3; q. 47, a. 3 ad 3; q. 48, a. 2f.; *CG* 3.158). M. Luther (in agreement with his contemporaries and a long theological tradition) radicalizes Anselm's satisfaction teaching, making it a teaching on vicarious suffering of punishment, by taking literally the description of Christ's exchange with the sinner in 2 Cor 5:21, which states "for our sake he made him to be sin." Other interpretations are that he became "an offering for our sins" (DS 599) or took on "sinful flesh" for us and therefore death, the punishment of sin (Thomas Aquinas, *STh* 3, q. 46, a. 4 ad 3). Variations on the teaching of punishment suffered vicariously have been present over the centuries and remain to this day in Reformed theology (J. Calvin, K. Barth, W. Pannenberg, J. Moltmann) as well as in Catholic theology (Erasmus, Cajetan, A. Salmerón, M. Blondel, J. Danielou, G. Martelet, H. Urs von Balthasar). Here the unavoidable question has to do with God's "righteousness" and the image of God that lies behind such a teaching. Thus some theologians return to Anselm and emphasize Jesus' representation as the establishment of new freedom (G. Greshake), or they underline the idea of solidarity (K. Rahner). Others situate their explanation of the atonement theme in the intratrinitarian event (H. Urs von Balthasar, N. Hoffmann). A complete "exoneration" of God is found in R. Schwager's scapegoat theory, worked out in dependence on R. Girard, according to which humankind diverts its evil onto Christ the scapegoat: his cross is the revelation of and final victory over the scapegoat mechanism. Thus language concerning God's wrath or a judge who punishes proves to be

problematic, and it may be asked to what extent such God-language is merely anthropomorphic and should be explained allegorically (as it was already by the Fathers), existentially, and anthropologically (God's love is "unbearable" by sinners and thus experienced as wrath), or in the sense of the scapegoat mechanism (R. Schwager).

(3) *Church Teaching.* Outside the basic statement in the creeds that Jesus Christ "was crucified for us" (DS 42, 62, 64, 150, etc.), there are few official pronouncements concerning the sacrificial death of Jesus and the priesthood of Christ (DS 261, 539, 3678) except in declarations concerning the Eucharist (DS 802, 1083, 1739f., 1743, 1753f., 3316, 3847f.; see Vatican II: *SC* 5–10, 47; *LG* 10, 26, 28, 34). In connection with the doctrine of original sin a statement was made that Christ reconciled us with God (DS 1513), and Trent mentions incidentally that he achieved satisfaction before the Father for us or for our sins. In connection with the doctrine of justification, the reconciling power of his suffering (and death) is described as that which Christ merited (DS 1523, 1529f., 1560; see 1534, 1576, 1582). Reconciliation with God and forgiveness of sins for each individual believer become concrete in BAPTISM and the SACRAMENT OF RECONCILIATION. The idea of atonement has been taken up more recently in Pius XI's encyclical on the Sacred Heart of Jesus (*Miserentissimus redemptor* [1928]) and in Pius XII's *Haurietis aquas* (1956). John Paul II's encyclicals *Redemptor hominis* (1979) and *Dives in misericordia* (1980) and his apostolic decree *Reconciliatio et paenitentia* (1984) touch upon fundamental dimensions of the doctrine of reconciliation.

(4) *Ecumenical Perspectives.* The doctrine of reconciliation has been the heart of dogmatics from the beginning of the Reformation until today, especially in the Lutheran tradition (see G. Ebeling). For this reason, a given theologian's position toward the doctrine is an indication of her or his dogmatic orientation.

(5) *Systematic Reflections.* Any teaching on reconciliation should respect the preestablished basic structure set down by biblical testimony. It should also take into account the cultic, legal, and personal links within any of its interpretations or categories and allow them to be decisively modified and surpassed by the Christ-event as a whole and the crucifixion of Jesus in particular. The "message of reconciliation" and the "message of the cross" spell the end to every sacrificial cult, every kind of self-justification, every duplicitous "arrangement." Yet they open up the possibility of new life in self-surrender, a new justice and a newly grounded personal relation between God and humankind and among humans themselves. However, this possibility is realized actively/passively, starting with God on the cross, and it brings about atonement because sin and death are thereby overcome. Thus reconciliation is grounded in God, who perseveres in love for the sinner and enters a particular situation and changes it fundamentally, making possible new community with God. The question concerning the condition of possibility of atonement on the cross ultimately returns to the trinitarian mystery of God.

See also COVENANT; CROSS, THEOLOGY OF THE; MEDIATORSHIP OF JESUS
CHRIST; REDEMPTION AND LIBERATION; REPRESENTATION; SALVATION; SATIS-
FACTION THEORY; SOTERIOLOGY.

Bibliography
Balthasar, Hans Urs von. *Theo-Drama: Theological Dramatic Theory.* San Francisco:
    Ignatius, 1988ff.
Bloesch, Donald G. *Jesus Is Victor! Karl Barth's Doctrine of Salvation.* Nashville: Abingdon,
    1976.
Dillestone, F. W. *The Christian Understanding of Atonement.* Philadelphia: Westminster,
    1968.
Fiorenza, Francis Schüssler. "Redemption." In *The New Dictionary of Theology,* edited by
    Joseph A. Komanchack et al., 836–51. Wilmington, Del.: Glazier, 1988.
Hengel, Martin. *The Atonement.* Philadelphia: Fortress, 1981.
Pannenberg, Wolfhart. *Systematic Theology.* Vol. 2. Grand Rapids: Eerdmans, 1994.

LOTHAR ULLRICH

Redemption and Liberation. Redemption and liberation are basic soteriological categories of the saving work of God through Jesus Christ in the Holy
Spirit for and in humankind. Humans must receive and cooperate with this
work using their God-given freedom.

(1) *Biblical Background.* In the Old Testament *redeem* and *liberate* are almost synonymous (see *yasa* or *hosi* — lead out, liberate [slaves]; *padah* — the
buying back or redeeming of slaves; *goël* — redeemer; in family law, reestablish-
ing a previous relationship). In being led out of Egypt, the people experienced
and reflected on God's saving deed (Ex 15:21: the whole structure of Exodus
1–15 involves the "rescue" theme) — God's liberation of Israel (Mi 6:4; Dt
15:15; Ex 6:6f.; 15:13; Ps 77:16, etc.). Thus the Israelites belong to Yahweh as
"servants" (Lev 25:55) and "slaves," and they should not oppress their brothers and sisters (Lev 25:42ff.). Yahweh's saving deed is a motive for following
God's commandments (Ex 20:2; Dt 5:6) and an ethical imperative for the Israelites' behavior toward foreigners (Ex 20:20; 23:9; Dt 10:19; 15:15: 24:18).
Especially in Deutero-Isaiah the new exodus (from Babylon) is described as
Yahweh's act of liberation (e.g., Is 43:1–4), and redemption is seen as forgiveness of transgressions (44:21–23). Both are definitive (see the "eschatological"
prophecy about a basic change of structures [Is 55:3–5; Ezra 34; Jer 31:31–
34]). Yahweh is always the one who acts. However, Yahweh empowers and
expects action from those who are redeemed and liberated. In connection with
the experience of the exodus (esp. Lev 25:42, 55) there is a direct line from
the eschatology of the prophets to the New Testament's conviction that when
we all become children of God (as a possibility and an imperative), every kind
of social discrimination disappears (Gal 3:25ff.; see 1 Cor 12:13; Col 3:11). In
the New Testament the terminology of redemption and liberation is centered
on the proclamation of the truth that makes us free (John). The key images
and concepts are "buying back"; "ransom money"; freedom from death, sin,
and the law; our freedom to live for God and Christ; and our ability to love

and fulfill the commandments (Paul). But the main message is Jesus' kingdom made concrete in his life, which prepares and calls us to discipleship (including conversion and faith) (the Synoptics). According to John, the reality of the redemption is completely determined by the Word made flesh, the Son of God, who brings grace and truth (1:14). His saving gifts are life and light (1:4; 3:15, etc.; see 1 Jn 1:1–4). Here John's proclamation of life may be understood as his interpretation of the message of the kingdom. The gift of life as well as the gift of the Spirit are joined with Jesus' gift of himself in his death (see 7:39; 10:11; 19:34; 1 Jn 2:2; 4:10). In the framework of John's "realized eschatology," he is expressing the liberating effect of truth for the believer (8:31f., 36). Paul speaks in various ways of the saving work of God through Jesus Christ in the Holy Spirit. Among the most prominent concepts he employs are reconciliation and justification; but he also uses the terms *salvation* and *liberation* (see the summary in 1 Cor 1:30: God made Jesus Christ "our righteousness [see 2 Cor 5:21], sanctification [see 2 Cor 8:9], and redemption [see Gal 3:13f.]"). Thus his teaching on redemption is also his "gospel of freedom," as seen in central texts such as Gal 4:4–6 (the sending of the Son to redeem those who stood under the law and longed for sonship); Gal 5:1–13 (we were freed and called to freedom in order to serve one another in love); Rom 6:15–23 (we were freed from sin and death); Rom 7:1–6 (we were freed from the law); and Rom 9:1–17 (we were freed in order to live in the Spirit as sons). The Spirit engenders freedom (2 Cor 3:17), and creation itself "will be set free to obtain the liberty of the children of God" (Rom 8:21). This freedom depends on Jesus, who gave himself for our sins (Gal 1:4), just as justification is through redemption by Jesus Christ in his expiating blood (Rom 3:24f.; see Eph 1:7; Col 1:14). The Spirit is the first "installment" of our redemption (Eph 1:14). Redemption and liberation create a new relationship of humankind to God through Jesus Christ in the Holy Spirit, which should determine the whole life of God *and* human beings in faith, hope, and love (see 1 Corinthians 13). Hebrews first deals with "eternal redemption," which is worked "through the blood" of the high priest, Christ, "once for all" (9:12). Even the incarnation is seen in relation to the death of the Son, who thereby "destroyed" death and the devil and "delivered" all those who had fallen into death (2:14). The "pioneer [*archegos*] of salvation" (2:10) or of "faith" (12:2) is Jesus Christ (in the context of his suffering and crucifixion). This can be seen as a reference to the liberating actions of Jesus during his lifetime, when he went before his own disciples. The Vulgate's translation, *auctor* (author, founder), offers an important indication. Even as an image it goes back to an original fact: *because* Jesus achieved a "breakthrough" by the power of the Spirit, the door to salvation has been opened and remains linked to him. In Acts this title (3:15: "author [*auctor*] of life"; 5:31: "leader" [*princeps*]) is brought into relationship with the resurrection or exaltation of Christ and (in 5:31) with the title "savior" (*soter, salvator*). Behind this is Luke's theology of salvation-history, in which the important developments and steps in the divine salvific plan are presented as a theology of the "way"; its whole trajectory includes the parousia, as the completion of salvation (Lk 21:28), and the death of Jesus (Lk 24:26; see 24:46ff.). But there is a soteriological emphasis (as in the Synoptics generally) on the liberating message of the kingdom and Jesus' life. The life of Jesus should be examined on its own merits, not just as the "prelude to the passion." It was lived wholly in the service of God's sovereign authority. In this respect Mk 1:15 should be considered as programmatic (see HISTORICAL JESUS). Peace, freedom, justice, and life are the horizon of the perennial question within which Jesus' message of the kingdom and his life are to be considered. What he proclaims in word becomes real and knowable in his signs and MIRACLES. We are dealing with the realization of a holistic human salvation: corporeal and spiritual health through the forgiveness of sins and the healing of disease (Mk 2:1–12 par.; see Lk 13:10–17). His exorcisms enable us to experience the liberating nature of God's power (Mt 12:28; Lk 11:20 par.). Jesus speaks in a special way of God when he teaches people a new type of behavior that frees them from "powers" that enslave them and destroy their humanity (the commandment of love as liberation from the need for retribution [Lk 6:27f. par.]), when he reminds them of God's PROVIDENCE as liberation from worry (Lk 12:24, 27, 28), or when he insists on faith as liberation from one's own powerlessness (Lk 17:6) and from the drive to self-righteousness (Lk 16:15; 18:9–14a). God's sovereignty is a gift, as is clear in God's forgiveness (Mt 18:23–25; Lk 15:11–32; see Mt 6:12; Lk 11:4 par.). It allows no discrimination: the poor are declared blessed (Mt 5:3 par.); the outcasts are healed (Lk 17:11–19); Jesus mixes with tax collectors and sinners (Mt 11:19a; see Lk 7:34); he blesses children (Mk 10:13–16 pars.); and he affirms the role of women (Mk 10:2–12; Lk 16:18 pars.). In the context of praxis and soteriology we also see the mystery of Jesus' person, his relationship to God, whom he calls Abba. With this starting point his passion and crucifixion can also (but not only) be seen as consequences of his actions during his lifetime.

(2) *History of Theology.* The doctrine of the redemption according to the Greek Fathers can be understood (according to G. Greshake) within the framework of the Greek notion of *paideia* (education, in the sense of formation). In the discussion of Christology and the Trinity, it became increasingly a personal and conceptual instrument that emphasized freedom. Thus the ancient notion of *paideia* was Christianized by orienting it toward freedom and the personality of God and human beings. In Latin Christianity, the subjective aspect plays a greater role in the doctrine of the redemption (Augustine): thus the question of the "liberation of freedom" (by grace). Finally, modernity's turn to the subject and its preoccupation with freedom prepare the ground for understanding redemption as liberation and for taking an interest not only in soteriology but also in soterio-praxis in connection with Jesus' life praxis (H. Kessler, D. Wiederkehr). In liberation theology this basic theme has been developed by J. Sobrino and L. Boff. At this point, however, the basic problem encountered by liberation theology (as well as political theology) is the kind and manner of the relationship between politics, ethics, and redemption. Its Chris-

tology addresses, among other things, the question of whether the category of discipleship is the only or the decisive principle of Christology/soteriology.

(3) *Church Teaching.* Regarding soteriological questions the teaching office has until now been very discreet, so that no theory of redemption has been defined. The magisterium has always dealt with basic faith statements regarding the incarnation of the Son of God "[for us and] for our salvation" (DS 40, 125, 150, etc.) and regarding his death on the cross "for the redemption of sinners" (DS 59) and "for the salvation of either the world" (DS 48) or humankind (DS 491, 1337). At times there have been more complete formulations that put together various aspects (DS 492) and speak expressly of the "liberation [*liberatio*] of humankind" (DS 533). The merits and satisfaction of Jesus' death (DS 1529, 1690), which in a way correspond with the redeeming power of his suffering and death (without however defining the satisfaction theory), have also been mentioned. Only in recent times has an expanded soteriology been outlined that uses the this-worldly effects of the redemption and takes into account the Christian's responsibility for the world (see esp. GS 41). Official statements on liberation theology and the theme of liberation or freedom have been made in two instructions of the Congregation for the Doctrine of the Faith (*Libertatis nuntius* [1984]; *Libertatis conscientia* [1986]) and by the general meeting of Latin American bishops at Medellín (1968) and Puebla (1979).

(4) *Ecumenical Perspectives.* The ideas of redemption in the Enlightenment, in rationalism, in speculative idealism, and in liberation theology are quite different, but they all converge in the conviction that the experience of modernity and the traditional doctrine of redemption must be brought together. Redemption is now seen primarily (or exclusively) as a "moment in and of the history of subjective freedom" (G. Greshake; see E. Kant, F. C. Baur, F. Schleiermacher). This also holds true for recent projects: see J. Moltmann's formula, "Emancipation is the immanence of redemption; redemption is the transcendence of emancipation." Here perhaps the claim to totality of emancipation is not taken seriously enough. Redemption and the history of emancipation cannot simply be divorced or combined "in the sense of an abstract teaching of two kingdoms." Despite the density of the issue, Evangelical theology — more than Catholic theology — has attempted to think through the coherence of redemption and human emancipation.

(5) *Systematic Reflections.* The sensitive point within modern teachings on redemption is the question of an alternative to (or a mediation of) redemption or emancipation: Should it be "theo-soterics" or "auto-soterics" (M. Seckler)? At stake here is not only soterio-praxis and the realization of redemption, but what is to be called salvific and what is the goal of redemption. The distinction between an *instrumental* and a *final* understanding of theo-soterics (the realization of redemption) is helpful here. Redemption can be realized only by God in Jesus Christ through the Holy Spirit. Understood *finally,* redemption and salvation are possible only *in God,* yet — understood *instrumentally* — they must be brought into view and mediated by a combination of human fulfillment and

divine salvation. This understanding is basic in setting forth goals. We are dealing with God's *self*-mediation that basically "constitutes, enables, and demands co-operative praxis" (M. Seckler). God's righteousness, truth, love, and peace become real in human actions: thus human commitment is necessary. However, the theo-soteric principle remains, "so that salvation and human fulfillment are *in* God and *from* God. They are withdrawn from the will to dispose of oneself, as well as from self-sufficient power of achievement" (M. Seckler). This must be distinguished from "theo-soteric theories" in which there is a theo-soteric principle. The one is not identical with the other. The status of every theo-soteric theory is historically provisional. Thus dialogue or complementarity between theories is of decisive significance.

See also CHRISTOLOGY; CROSS, THEOLOGY OF THE; GRACE; RECONCILIATION; SALVATION; SOTERIOLOGICAL MODELS; SOTERIOLOGY.

Bibliography
Boff, Leonardo. *Jesus Christ Liberator: A Critical Christology for Our Times.* Maryknoll, N.Y.: Orbis Books, 1978.
Boff, Leonardo, and Clodovis Boff. *Salvation and Liberation: In Search of a Balance between Faith and Politics.* Maryknoll, N.Y.: Orbis Books, 1978.
Gutiérrez, Gustavo. *A Theology of Liberation.* Maryknoll, N.Y.: Orbis Books, 1973.
Sobrino, Jon. *Christ at the Crossroads.* Maryknoll, N.Y.: Orbis Books, 1978.
———. *Jesus in Latin America.* Maryknoll, N.Y.: Orbis Books, 1987.

LOTHAR ULLRICH

Religion. Defining "religion" from a history-of-religions perspective is difficult because of the many concrete forms of religion. Nevertheless, one can discern in the sorts of behavior that one calls religion a basic, familiar aspect: how humans behave in relation to "God." The following does not seek to present a descriptive account capable of evoking consensus among religious scholars, but rather to consider, from the standpoint of the God of biblically founded Christian belief, how types of religious behavior are to be assessed as ways from and toward God.

(1) *Biblical Background.* Basic to the biblical understanding of religion is the divine initiative, namely, the creation of humans in the image of God, the self-disclosure of God in a "definitive" redemptive history. This understanding results in criteria for distinguishing the "true" God. The covenant with Israel (the religious origin of Judeo-Christian monotheism) has its origin in a widespread Near Eastern religious-historical context and crystallizes around the norm "The Lord alone!" and the response to love God with all one's heart, all one's soul, and all one's strength (Dt 6:4f.). This norm forms the criterion in Israel for deciding between true and false religion, worship of God or worship of idols. It also provides the foundation for the Christian understanding of redemption through Christ. Christ, God's way to us and simultaneously our way to God (see Jn 14:6), forms the criterion by which Christian belief assesses religion. In both the Old and the New Testaments, such assessment has a strik-

ingly wide range. It moves between the following poles: on the one hand, God, who is constantly active as Creator, can be heard and worshiped even outside of the history of revelation (see the universalism in the history of the patriarchs in Genesis as well as in Acts 17:16–30); on the other hand, other religions are criticized most radically because they contribute to perversion of the relation to God (e.g., Wisdom 13–15; Rom 1:18–23).

(2) *History of Theology.* In the history of Christian mission, the negative assessment of other religions has been dominant, but, despite its severity, it has not become a basic principle. This negativity has resulted in part because missionary theology has often forged links not with other religions but rather with ethical and philosophical doctrines of God. The missionaries themselves, in contrast, have integrated elements of the local religion into Christian practice.

(3) *Church Teaching.* Vatican II signifies a turning point whose consequences are still not measurable. Although it continues the theological affirmation of the tradition, it ventures the idea — new in this form — of a *preevangelization (praeparatio evangelica)* that occurs in and through the history of religion. This basic but still controversial idea does not ultimately imply a more optimistic relation to the *cultural* history of religions, but rather, a more logically consistent view of God's will for salvation. This idea entails that human beings are not saved in a way that just bypasses their religions. God's grace, ultimately the grace of the cross, is at work in every concrete situation where humans live out their creaturely existence with an orientation toward God. In this, the various religions — despite the undoubted validity of Romans 1 — also have a positive function (*LG* 16; *NA* 1–3).

(4) *Ecumenical Perspectives.* The attempt by K. Barth and, following him, D. Bonhoeffer to effect a radical separation between religion and Christian faith failed to gain wide acceptance even in Protestant circles. "Faith" is a form of religion. If the biblical God is the true God, then the biblical God presents the normative form.

(5) *Systematic Reflections.* Christianity, then, does not make such a separation. It must bear witness in the mode of love — and that means in the mode of continually renewed attempts at dialogue — to the God whose self-revelation has been as the only God, the God who "deserves" to be loved with all one's heart, all one's soul, and all one's strength. This witness is to be borne as *evangelion,* that is, as the news that brings joy and liberation. In this lies the consummation of "true" religion, which, for that reason, can reject nothing in the various religions that is "true and holy" (*NA* 2).

See also UNIVERSAL SALVIFIC WILL OF GOD.

Bibliography
Berger, Peter. *The Sacred Canopy.* Garden City, N.Y.: Doubleday, 1967.
Hick, John. *An Interpretation of Religion: Human Responses to the Transcendent.* New Haven: Yale University Press, 1989.
Lawson, E. Thomas, and Robert N. McCauley. *Rethinking Religion: Connecting Cognition and Culture.* New York: Cambridge University Press, 1990.

Paden, William E. *Interpreting the Sacred: Ways of Viewing Religion.* Boston: Beacon, 1992.
Proudfoot, Wayne. *Religious Experience.* Berkeley: University of California Press, 1985.
Smith, Wilfred Cantwell. *The Meaning and End of Religion.* San Francisco: Harper and Row, 1978.
Tracy, David. *Blessed Rage for Order: The New Pluralism in Theology.* New York: Seabury, 1975.
———. *Plurality and Ambiguity: Hermeneutics, Religion, Hope.* San Francisco: Harper and Row, 1987.

WILHELM BREUNING

Repentance. Repentance, which is the heart of confession and the crucial act of the penitent in the sacrament of reconciliation, is a renunciation in mind and will (and, desirably, in feeling as well) of one's sins and a turning to God and to what God wills. Perfect contrition (*contritio*) is motivated primarily by love of God. Imperfect contrition ("attrition" [*attritio*]) is motivated primarily by a (morally estimable) fear of God as well as by a realization of the harm done by sin and the punishment it merits, and by fear of these effects. As understood in Christianity, all contrition is made possible by the loving concern of a God who is ready to forgive, that is, by grace.

(1) *Biblical Background.* In the New Testament, "contrition" as well as "repentance" translate the Greek word *metanoia*. But in both the Old Testament and the New Testament, a number of other words or phrases are also used to describe the same reality. "Return" (see Zec 1:3), "a remorseful spirit, a broken and contrite heart" (see Ps 51:19), and "a sorrow according to God" that leads to a change of spirit (see 2 Cor 7:9f.) are some descriptions that find compressed parabolic expression in the decision of the prodigal son to return home (see Lk 15:18).

(2) *History of Theology.* Theological reflection on repentance begins in the Middle Ages. From the twelfth century on a distinction is made between contrition (*contritio*) and attrition (*attritio*), although initially each of these terms is defined in quite different ways. Durandus de S. Porciano (d. 1334) is the first to distinguish them by the motive at work, and this approach determines the subsequent development: on the one side, the grace-given love of God, and, on the other, rather the fear of God, linked to a proper self-love, are the distinguishing motives. Later on, a fierce controversy arose, which was ended by the ecclesial magisterium (1667), between the "contritionists," who required at least an inchoative love of God as the motive for repentance, even in the sacrament of reconciliation, and the "attritionists," who thought this was not necessary.

(3) *Church Teaching.* At the Council of Trent the ecclesial magisterium describes repentance as "the sorrow of the soul and the detestation of the sin committed, together with the resolve not to sin any more" (DS 1676; ND 1622). In saying this, it certainly lays too much emphasis on the emotional aspect of contrition. In opposition to the position of the Reformers, the council insists that repentance "implies not only cessation from sin and the re-

solve and beginning of a new life, but also the hatred of the old" (DS 1676; ND 1622). The council takes over the distinction between perfect contrition ("contrition ... perfect through charity" [*contritio caritate perfecta*]) and imperfect contrition. The former reconciles human beings to God even before the actual reception of the sacrament, which must be at least implicitly intended; the latter justifies only in the sacrament of reconciliation (see DS 1677f.; 1705). Imperfect contrition is nonetheless "a gift of God and a prompting of the Holy Spirit," which prepare the way for grace (DS 1678; ND 1624).

(4) *Ecumenical Perspectives.* According to the Reformers, contrition does not justify, but only the forgiving word of God. This leads, admittedly, to a "hostility" toward sin. Justification and the will to continue sinning are incompatible. The Catholic tradition (of which Catholics must become fully conscious once more) that any justifying contrition has its basis in God's gracious condescension is possibly not too far removed from the view of the Reformers.

(5) *Systematic Reflections.* Theological reflection on repentance will have to take into consideration the following points in particular. (*a*) Repentance is a dialogical experience in which God speaks the first word, the word expressing God's readiness to forgive; human beings may, must, and can respond to this word by turning to God and turning away from sin with mind, will, and, if possible, feeling as well. (*b*) In the response of repentance, which God makes possible, conversion to God is structurally (but not necessarily temporally or psychologically) to the fore. It is only in the light of God's forgiving love that the character of sin as a "straying from the way" becomes fully clear, as does God's will as the way out of self-destruction into true self-fulfillment. (*c*) Repentance as an act also has a complex and processual character that is supported from the outset by God's grace and that therefore includes a love of God that is God's gift, provided that the contrition is religiously motivated and is not a purely human annoyance at one's own failure and its consequences. It is not possible to determine with complete clarity whether contrition is perfect or imperfect; rather one must trust that God is breathing God's love into it and thus making it perfect.

See also CONFESSION; SACRAMENT OF RECONCILIATION; SIN AND GUILT.

Bibliography
Fitzgerald, Allan. *Conversion through Penance in the Italian Church of the Fourth and Fifth Centuries: New Approaches to the Experience of Conversion from Sin.* Lewiston, N.Y.: Mellen, 1988.
Osborne, Kenan B. *Reconciliation and Justification: The Sacrament and Its Theology.* New York: Paulist, 1992.
Rahner, Karl. *Penance in the Early Church.* New York: Crossroad, 1982.
Suttner, Ernst. *Busse und Beichte.* Regensburg: Pustet, 1972.
Tentler, Thomas N. *Sin and Confession on the Eve of the Reformation.* Princeton, N.J.: Princeton University Press, 1977.

GÜNTER KOCH

Representation. Representation is a structural law of salvation-history, where one person is able to bring about the salvation of another or be in his or her place. It is based on the universal salvific will of God and is manifested in human solidarity as a being-with and being-for others. Its criterion and apex are the person and work of Jesus Christ.

(1) *Biblical Background.* In the Old Testament, representation is especially evident in the universalist perspective on salvation of the Yahwist and the songs of the suffering servant in Second Isaiah. The programmatic formula of Gn 12:1–3 indicates that in Abraham the election of one person is for the salvation of all: this particular election becomes universal salvation (see Jn 18:18; 26:4). This is concretized when Abraham asks a favor of God (Gn 18:23–33). It points to the possibility that the few can save the many (18:32), even though this possibility is frustrated by the Sodomites. In Is 52:13–53:12, the person of the servant of God demonstrates that God's plan of salvation is achieved by the servant's vicarious suffering and death for the many. He obediently and freely endured suffering for the sake of sinners and gave his life as expiation for them. Second Isaiah probably represents a prophetic expectation similar to the portrait of Moses in Deuteronomy, where Moses' basic attitude is to represent his people before God. Thus he dies outside the promised land for the sake of the people (Dt 3:23–28; 4:21f.). Moses soon becomes the type of the prophet who is to come (Dt 18:18). Other important indications concerning the representational role of prophets are found in Ez 13:5; 20:30; Zec 12:10–13:1. In late Judaism, the atoning suffering and death of martyrs are regarded as vicarious or representational (Dn 3:40; 2 Mc 7:38). However, only in the life and death of Jesus Christ do we see clearly the salvific effects of one person for the many or in place of the many. According to 1 Tm 2:1–6, Jesus' representation is based on the universal salvific will of God, and this has consequences for the community's representational service of interceding for all human beings. Jesus' representation as a gift for all is centered on his death (see Rom 4:25; 8:22; Gal 1:4; 2:20; cf. 1 Cor 15:3b). Thus the sins of the world are expiated forever (Rom 6:10; 1 Pt 3:18; Heb 7:27; 9:12; 10:10). Christ's act of changing places with sinners is evident in places where the context is quite different (Gal 3:13f.; 2 Cor 5:21f.; see 2 Cor 5:14f.; 8:9). The "substitution" of Christ's situation for our own is for our good and comes from God (2 Cor 5:21f.) or from Christ himself (Gal 3:13f.; 2 Cor 5:14f.; 8:9). It is noteworthy that this representation concerns solidarity in salvation — that is, we are not only redeemed from guilt and sin but freed for a new life of righteousness and holiness (Rom 5:10, 17; 1 Cor 1:30; 2 Cor 5:15, 21b; 8:9; 13:10; Gal 2:20), which is to be realized by following Christ as a service (Mk 10:41–45 pars.; see Lk 22:24–27; 1 Pt 2:21–25). Finally, we must examine the Last Supper tradition (Mt 26:26–28; Mk 14:19–24 par.; Lk 22:29f. par.; 1 Cor 11:23ff.), where the death of Jesus is understood as an atoning covenant liturgy (Mark par. Matthew) or the establishment of the new covenant (Luke par. Paul). In both traditions, the background is the vicarious suffering of the servant of God or the martyr. The

active proexistence of Jesus in his earthly life has its own salvific value, in which we participate through baptism (Mk 1:9–11 pars.). It is service to humankind and to God. Jesus presents himself as one who serves (Lk 22:27; see Jn 13:1–20) and demands the same of his disciples (Mk 9:35 pars.). This involves service to those in need (Mt 5:42 par.; 25:31–46; Lk 6:30f., 36, 38f.; 10:30–35), an invitation (Mk 2:17), and a seeking out (Lk 15:4–10, 11–32) and an acceptance of sinners (Lk 7:36–47; 19:1–20), and it overcomes guilt (Mk 18:23–35; Lk 6:37, 41f.). This proexistence is completely theocentric (Mt 6:24; Mk 12:17f.; 12:30 pars.; Lk 11:2) so that there is an in-breaking of God's reign in the work and words of Jesus (Lk 10:23f.; see 10:9; 11:20). In Christ's death his substitution is completed; in his resurrection — and the whole proexistence of Christ as redemptive existence from God — it is confirmed. Paul, who pours himself out for the community (2 Cor 12:15; see Col 2:1; Eph 3:13) and goes to his death (2 Cor 4:12), demonstrates in exemplary fashion the power of Christian discipleship and the law of representation. For this reason he can also encourage the community to give of themselves (Gal 2:20; 6:2; Phil 2:5–11) and to intercede for everyone (1 Tm 2:1).

(2) *History of Theology.* The Fathers express the law of representation with the term *admirable exchange* (*commercium caritatis* [exchange of love]) (Augustine, *C. Faust.* 5.9): Christ became man so that humans could become children of God (e.g., Irenaeus, *Adv. Haer.* 3.19.1; Gregory of Nyssa, *Or. cat.* 32). In the Fathers' theology of penance and martyrdom, both intercessory prayer for penitents and the death of saints have a salvific effect on the community (see, e.g., Ignatius of Antioch, *Trall.* 13.3; *Eph.* 8.1). The notion of representation reappears in the Middle Ages in the SATISFACTION THEORY. But it becomes embroiled in the crisis resulting from abuses in the theory and practice of the sacrifice of the Mass, as well as the practice of absolution, ideas on merit, and the inadequately understood doctrine of the *thesaurus ecclesiae* (treasury of the church). On the other hand, representation finds expression in spirituality — in a mysticism of suffering and ideas on expiation — and, especially since the seventeenth century, has remained alive in devotion to the Sacred Heart of Jesus. Further, a theology of representation has found new life in connection with ecclesiology, especially with regard to the meaning and mediatory role of the church in a secularized and non-Christian world (H. de Lubac, Y. Montcheuil, Y. Congar, H. Urs von Balthasar, J. Ratzinger). H. Urs von Balthasar, K. Lehmann, H. Schürmann, and others explain that representation is the heart of soteriology, while K. Rahner and others argue rather from "solidarity of intercommunication of all people in salvation," which stresses the irreplaceable decision of each individual, but also maintains the salvific effectiveness of one for the many or for others. The real problem for a theology of representation is in explaining the correct relationship of solidarity and representation.

(3) *Church Teaching.* To this day the teaching office has developed no theology of representation. The creed maintains that the incarnation of God's Son

was "for us and for our salvation" and his crucifixion was "for us" (DS 150, etc.). Thus it states its fundamental and unique effectiveness for salvation. But its mode and manner are not further explained. Nor are there any definitive pronouncements on the doctrine of vicarious atonement. The Council of Trent speaks of it (DS 1529, 1690) and Pius XII defends it (DS 3891). The idea of vicarious atonement is used in the encyclicals on the Sacred Heart (Pius XI, *Miserentissimus redemptor* [1928]; Pius XII, *Haurietis aquas* [1956]; see also Pius XII, *Mystici corporis* [1943]). There are important elements of representation in Vatican II's theology of priestly ordination (the priest acts *in persona Christi capitis* [in the person of Christ the head] [*PO* 2, etc.]) and in the teaching on the church as universal sacrament of salvation (*LG* 9, 26, 48), as well as in its Christology (*GS* 22). It has always been deeply embedded in the liturgy (the prayers of petition and the anamnesis, which recalls Christ's death for our salvation [third eucharistic prayer] or for the salvation of the whole world [fourth eucharistic prayer]).

(4) *Ecumenical Perspectives.* The doctrine of the representative function of Jesus Christ's suffering has (despite many protests) been part of Evangelical theology from the beginning of the Reformation until today (M. Luther, J. Calvin, K. Barth, J. Moltmann, W. Pannenberg). In his teaching on election, K. Barth developed a theology of representation based on his original interpretation of double predestination, and it has had a strong influence in Catholic theologians such as H. Urs von Balthasar and J. Ratzinger. According to E. Brunner, Christ's role as mediator is identical with his actions and suffering as representative. In this way his understanding of mediation corresponds to the solidarity between humanity and God, based on the incarnation. D. Sölle, on the other hand, understands Jesus as the representative of the *absent* God (Jesus represents God to us and us to God) and in immediate relationship to the practice of love of one's fellow human beings. According to D. Bonhoeffer, representation, as the central principle of Christian living, is the substitutional act of assuming guilt: in unconditional being-for-another, intercession, mutual forgiveness, and ethical responsibility.

(5) *Systematic Reflections.* Basic to any theology of representation is belief in the incarnate Son of God who became man "for us," lived, worked, suffered, was crucified, and was raised from the dead. His solidarity (*coexistence, community-with*) with all men and women was lived out as *proexistence* (supportive and constitutive existence), in place of all humans and for them unto death, and is grounded in his *preexistence,* in the mystery of God. The original community and representation are grounded in the Trinity itself, so that representation "is never just a substitute, but rather a constant relational reality between personal freedoms" (E. Salmann). The solidarity of God with humankind, revealed and realized in Jesus, and Jesus' representation of us are the basis for a new solidarity. They also make representation possible among human beings. At this point we might ask whether a theology of representation need be so closely joined with Barth's teaching on election, even though this

rediscovery proved to be hermeneutically fruitful, or whether it could not be grounded in God's universal salvific will or the divine life and being itself (thus L. Scheffczyk). A theology of representation becomes increasingly significant for Christian and ecclesial existence in a non-Christian world, and thus for a theology of the diaspora and of mission. But it is also helpful within the church (e.g., for a spirituality of CHARISM/CHARISMS, the priesthood, etc.). In order to counterbalance individualism and collectivism, much can be gained from regarding representation as a way of enabling and grounding true freedom and responsibility for the individual and society, even philosophically and ethically (see L. Winner and the ethics of E. Levinas).

See also DISCIPLESHIP, CHRISTIAN; MEDIATORSHIP OF JESUS CHRIST; SALVATION; UNIVERSAL SALVIFIC WILL OF GOD.

Bibliography
Balthasar, Hans Urs von. *Theo-Drama: Theological Dramatic Theory.* San Francisco: Ignatius, 1988ff.
Barth, Karl. *Church Dogmatics,* 2/1. Edinburgh: T and T Clark, 1957.
Brunner, Emil. *The Mediator: A Study of the Central Doctrine of the Christian Faith.* Philadelphia: Westminster, 1947.
Cullmann, Oscar. *Christ and Time: The Primitive Christian Conception of Time and History.* Philadelphia: Westminster, 1964.
Kasper, Walter. *Jesus the Christ.* New York: Paulist, 1976.
Rahner, Karl. "One Mediator and Many Mediations." In *Theological Investigations,* 9:169–84. New York: Herder and Herder, 1972.
Sölle, Dorothee. *Christ the Representative: An Essay in Theology after the Death of God.* Philadelphia: Fortress, 1967.

LOTHAR ULLRICH

Resurrection Narratives. Resurrection narratives are the New Testament testimony to the resurrection or the raising of Jesus, developed either formally in a narrative — as in the Easter kerygma — or as professions of faith using argument or reflection.

(1) *Biblical Background.* In the single-member profession of faith in Jesus risen ("God raised Jesus from the dead") or in speaking of God ("God who raised Jesus from the dead" [1 Thes 1:10; Gal 1:1; 1 Cor 15:15; Rom 4:24; 10:9; Acts 2:32]), we find the oldest testimony to the resurrection of Jesus. The so-called resurrection formula corresponds to this (see 1 Thes 4:14b). The resurrection formula contains a direct christological statement, whereas the confession "Jesus is risen" is indirect: Jesus lives; God caused him to be alive, elevated him, and made him the definitive mediator of salvation. This becomes clearer in the multiple-member formulas concerning Jesus' resurrection, where the resurrection is seen in relationship to: (*a*) his death and its salvific meaning (1 Thes 4:14; Rom 4:25; 8:34; 2 Cor 5:15); (*b*) the present power and mediation of the salvation brought about by the elevated, crucified one (Rom 1:3f.; 10:9; see 1 Thes 1:9f. and the *maranatha* in 1 Cor 16:22 or Rv 22:20); (*c*) conversion or baptism (Rom 6:3f.; Col 2:12f.) and the present and future life of

the baptized (Rom 6:8–11; 1 Thes 4:14ff.). Thus, (d) the relationship to the appearances as the disciples' encounters with the risen one is particularly important, because Jesus himself gave testimony and revealed himself to them and, according to the New Testament, awakened in them their Easter faith (Lk 24:34; Acts 13:30; 1 Cor 15:3–5; see 1 Cor 15:8; Gal 1:1, 12, 15f.). In 1 Cor 15:3–5 (6–8) we find a four-member creedal formula that is a very ancient witness to the resurrection. It originated in early, Greek-speaking Jewish Christianity and was taken over by Paul in Damascus or Jerusalem (Gal 1:18f.) a few (three to six) years after the death of Jesus (vv. 6a–7 are pre-Pauline; vv. 6b and 8 are Pauline additions). According to Scripture, the death and resurrection of Jesus are salvific events: Jesus died "for our sins"; he arose "on the third day." These are not historical data but theological expressions of a salvific turning point brought about by God. The indications about the burial and the appearances, as beliefs, are part of the salvific event of death and resurrection. The appearances are the "place" where this eschatological, salvific deed of God is revealed to concrete people. Thus it is clear that (a) access to the resurrection of Jesus is only through the testimony of witnesses to whom the Lord himself has made a revelation; and (b) the Easter experience (of the witnesses) and the Easter reality (of the risen one) are not simply identical. The Greek word *ophthe* with the dative (v. 5; see Lk 24:34; Acts 13:30) is to be translated neither as a passive (he was seen) nor as a theological passive (God made him ... visible), but as a middle form: *he let himself ... be seen,* or *he was made ... visible,* or *he appeared.* When we realize that (a) in the Septuagint this expresses God's self-manifestation (e.g., Gn 12:7; Ex 3:2) or the manifestation of God's salvation in the present, and that (b) even apart from 1 Cor 15:8, Paul describes his encounter with the resurrected Jesus as a "seeing" (1 Cor 9:1) or as a "revelation" (Gal 1:15f.; see 2 Cor 4:6) and as "being grasped by Christ" (Phil 3:8–12), then we may distinguish four basic elements of the appearances: (a) they refer to the self-proclamation or self-revelation of the resurrected crucified one; (b) the subject responsible for what occurs is Jesus, who demonstrates he is living in unity with God and is recognized as the crucified one; that is, the appearances are not anonymous "happenings" that elicit reflection, but rather "meetings" as objective-subjective events happening from without — that is, from Jesus, and leading to a personal encounter; (c) the appearances reveal the present salvation of Jesus living in a completely new oneness with God; and (d) they concern concrete persons (Peter, James, Paul) or groups (the Twelve, five hundred brethren) who come to believe in the crucified and resurrected one. On the one hand, this implies conversion and forgiveness (Paul); on the other hand, the personal Easter experience does not remain private but includes service and mission insofar as the appearances establish the church and in a way "legitimate" the believers' testimony (this is certainly true for Peter, the Twelve, James, and Paul). The *Easter stories* in the Gospels (see the accompanying diagram) develop the Easter kerygma and the appearance stories narratively, corresponding to the theology of the earliest Gospel. In the Gospels

THE RESURRECTION AND APPEARANCES OF JESUS:
HISTORICALLY VERIFIABLE FACTS

The following overview (a modified version of H. Kessler, *Sucht den Lebenden nicht bei den Toten* [Düsseldorf, 1985], 158) demonstrates to what extent we can attain historical knowledge of the resurrection of Jesus. The event itself is not immediately accessible (the "x" factor). The testimony of the early community has been handed on in several levels of the New Testament: in various formulas, in relatively late claims that the risen Jesus was seen (appearances), and in reports about the "empty tomb." The evidence clearly indicates the importance of the appearances, which were first of all experienced, then developed extensively in narratives. The different traditions are first combined in the second century, in the so-called canonical ending of Mark (Mk 16:9–16). Paul's testimony (1 Cor 15:3–5), which was written down around 50 C.E., actually goes back to twenty years earlier (his visit with the apostles), thus to within two to four years of the original event, the "x" factor. (In this overview texts of the New Testament are repeated several times to draw attention to the amalgamation or linking together of the various traditions.)

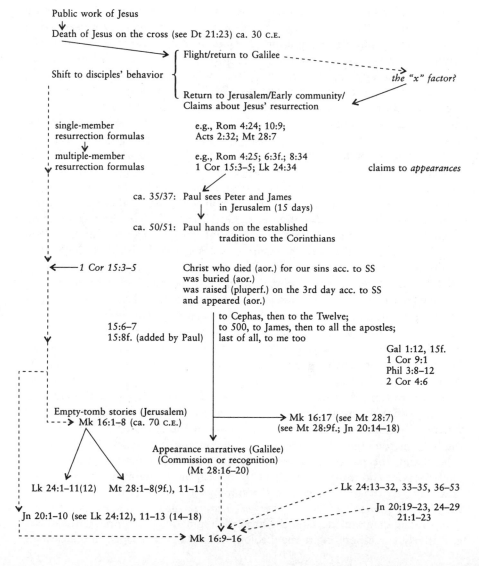

the traditions involving appearance stories that refer to Galilee were increasingly combined with an empty-tomb story tradition, stemming from Jerusalem. Thus it is no longer possible to harmonize the different levels. This impossibility of a later harmonization also holds true for the *appearance stories:* there is no exact depiction of the course of events. Nevertheless, belief in the resurrected crucified one has to be described in language and in various ways. The resurrection itself as eschatological event is indescribable and without analogy. The appearances are its historical halfway point, the "passage" to the historical world. What happened is attested to as a faith experience and developed narratively in a series of images that correspond to theological aspects. Beyond the basic elements already mentioned there is also an apologetic theme dealing with doubt and proof of identity (see Mt 28:17; Lk 24:36–43; Jn 20:19f., 24–29). The particular tradition of the women who visit the tomb on the first of the week and find it empty is found in all the Synoptics (Mk 16:1–8 pars.) and in a modified form in Jn 20:1–13. In the Synoptic *empty-tomb stories* the meaning of the empty tomb is clarified by the Easter kerygma (Mt 27:5; Mk 16:6; Lk 24:6). The Easter message is given by the appearance of an angel (as *angelus interpres?* [interpreting angel]) in or at the empty tomb. The original form could have been a pre-Markan narrative unit (Mk 16:5, 6, 8a) that wished to present the message of the resurrection realistically. To what extent the historicity of the empty tomb is thus handed on is debated, even among Catholic exegetes. Even if we consider it as more probable, the emptiness of the tomb and the disappearance of the body may be interpreted in many ways and are no "proof" of the resurrection. Only in connection with the Easter kerygma and the appearance stories is the empty-tomb tradition a "signpost," that is, an indication pointing to the centrality of Easter faith, which underscores the reality of the resurrection. Certainly, according to what can be stated or reconstructed historically, the empty tomb is a constitutive part of Easter faith (see diagram).

(2) *History of Theology.* In the early church the resurrection and its revelation or experience were seen in relation to the Sunday liturgy or the ending of the fast at Easter time or in the Eucharist. In sermons and writings the Fathers and medieval theologians assimilated the New Testament testimony to the resurrection and made it available to their audiences or reflected on it (e.g., Augustine, *Tract. in Io.*; *De consensu evangelistarum*; Thomas Aquinas, *STh* 3, q. 55). Our present-day problematic, influenced by the Enlightenment and historical-critical exegesis, is however basically different. Nevertheless, many traditional solutions can be meaningful today in interpreting the resurrection: for example, pointing out that the appearances can be received only in faith (Origen, *C. Celsum* 2.64f.; Chrysostom, *Acts Hom.* 1.4; Thomas Aquinas, *STh* 3, q. 55, a. 2 ad 1) or Thomas's insight concerning the angel at the tomb as mediator of revelation — it points to the impossibility of seeing the resurrection itself and thus underlines its necessary revelational character (*STh* 3, q. 2).

(3) *Church Teaching.* There have been no official pronouncements that bear directly on the appearances. The Second Council of Constantinople (DS 434)

opposed a one-sided explanation of Jn 20:22, 28. Pius X, speaking against rationalistic Enlightenment exegesis, emphasized that the resurrection was not a gradual deduction from other data by Christian consciousness (DS 3436). Vatican II (*DV* 19), referring in general to the tradition of the four Gospels, speaks of the "fuller understanding which they, instructed by the glorious events of Christ and enlightened by the Spirit of truth, now enjoyed." Also pertinent to the appearances is what *DV* 12 says about being attentive to literary forms in interpreting Scripture. The expression "on the third day" (according to Scripture) is found in several professions of faith (DS 10f., 30, 125, 150). Beyond scriptural texts themselves, there have been no further official statements on this passage. Thus exegetical explanations today (without explaining the temporal assertion, but rather in soteriological statements) may determine its systematic interpretation.

(4) *Ecumenical Perspectives.* Protestant exegesis/systematic theology has treated the modern problematic of the appearances, but such treatment is dependent on various hermeneutical premises. For example, D. F. Strauss (d. 1874), influenced by rationalism and idealism, actually dissolves resurrectional faith by treating the resurrection — and therefore the appearances — from a purely historical perspective; K. Barth (d. 1968), in contrast, holds that the historical-critical method is inappropriate for understanding the resurrection as a revelational event. W. Pannenberg's project of universal history and his historical understanding of the resurrection through historical-critical research place a burden on it that it cannot bear. The existential interpretation of R. Bultmann (d. 1968) and his disciples is in danger of making the resurrection so dependent on the Easter faith of the disciples that the two become identical. Thus the Easter-event, seen historically, is reduced to a visionary experience. The systematic views of the resurrection in recent Evangelical dogmatics are more balanced. Thus G. Ebeling speaks of the grounding experience of Easter faith and points to the appearances, which are distinguished from the basic event of the resurrection and refer to Jesus as the basis of faith. E. Schlink distinguishes between the grounding of the resurrectional message by means of the appearances of Jesus after his death and the confirmation by the work of Jesus as exalted Lord. The two are inseparably bound and interact in the transmission of the Easter appearances.

(5) *Systematic Reflections.* In exegetical and systematic discussions, the research and reflections concerning the beginning of Easter faith have more and more regarded the appearances from a historical-critical perspective. With regard to the consensus of this research (disregarding many differences and questions regarding details) in relationship to the historical-critical facts about the events after the death of Jesus, see the accompanying diagram. According to the overwhelming testimony of the New Testament, the Easter appearances were the historically understandable beginning that sparked the enormous dynamic movement of the early church. Thus far all historical attempts at clarification that try to go behind the appearances and that examine the ba-

sic elements involved have been unfruitful and are largely conjectural. Another question is how later generations came to believe in the crucified-risen Jesus. The original Easter experience is qualitatively unique. The "initial experience of a breakthrough" cannot be repeated; yet later experiences enter into the new community of the church's believers as the inner-historically manifest signs and mediums of the ongoing presence of the Lord. Thus mediated, they become part of an immediate personal encounter with the Lord. This situation is already mirrored in the redactional reworking of the Emmaus story (Lk 24:13–35; see Jn 20:24–29). Easter faith relies on and is only possible in the tradition of the community. This faith lives from its Easter message and is proclaimed in the celebration of the Lord's Supper and the solidarity of believers. It becomes real in each person's believing "yes" to the resurrected-crucified one. This is rationally responsible because of the credibility of the apostolic testimony to Easter.

See also RESURRECTION OF JESUS.

Bibliography
Alsup, Joseph E. *The Post-resurrection Appearance Stories of the Gospel Tradition: A History-of-Traditions Analysis.* London: SPCK, 1975.
Balthasar, Hans Urs von. *Mysterium Paschale: The Mystery of Easter.* Edinburgh: T and T Clark, 1990.
Brown, Raymond E. *The Virginal Conception and the Bodily Resurrection of Jesus.* New York: Paulist, 1973.
Evans, C. F. *Resurrection and the New Testament.* London: SCM, 1970.
Fuller, Reginald. *The Formation of the Resurrection Narratives.* New York: Macmillan, 1971.
Kasper, Walter. *Jesus the Christ.* New York: Paulist, 1976.
Schillebeeckx, Edward. *Jesus: An Experiment in Christology.* New York: Crossroad, 1979.
Schmaus, Michael. *The Faith of the Church.* Vol. 4. New York: Sheed and Ward, 1972.

LOTHAR ULLRICH

Resurrection of Jesus. In Christian faith the resurrection of Jesus Christ refers to God's creative salvific act at the moment of the death of Jesus of Nazareth whereby the general resurrection of the dead already takes place in this particular event: he is manifested as messiah and Son of God, and the possibility of definitive community with God is now made available to each and every human being.

(1) *Biblical Background.* The New Testament testimony to the resurrection of Jesus (the Easter faith) should not be separated either from the eschatological message of the Old Testament that, starting with faith in Yahweh, develops a hope of resurrection (Dn 12:2; 2 Mc 7:9, 14; 12:43f.) and immortality (Wis 3:1, 4) or from the testimony to Christ and God in the whole New Testament. Of particular importance is the inseparable connection between the death on the cross (the passion), on the one hand, and the resurrection and historical life of Jesus, on the other. The unconditional claim of the prepaschal Jesus to God's power and his relationship to God his Father included openness to accept threats to himself because of this claim and thus readiness for death. Thus his death was not mere fate but a gift, and he could hope to be saved

(Mk 14:25). The resurrection of Jesus reveals his definitive oneness with God, who already demonstrates divinity in the dying Jesus insofar as God legitimates Jesus' claim of lordship by a new creative act that reveals the new quality of the eschatological and definitive lordship of God's Son. The New Testament testimony to the resurrection is formalized as the Easter kerygma or Easter faith, and it plays a decisive role in the formation of creeds (Rom 10:9). It may be spelled out narratively (the Easter story) or by means of reflective arguments (see 1 Cor 15:12–58). Various wordings are used to communicate the resurrection: "He is risen" (1 Thes 4:14); "God raised him up" (1 Thes 1:10; Rom 10:9); "He was raised" (1 Cor 15:4; passive tense assuming the name of God and identical to "He was reawakened"); "He was made alive [in the spirit]" (1 Pt 3:18); "He lived again" (Rom 14:9); "He entered into his glory" (Lk 24:26); "[He] is exalted" (Phil 2:9; Acts 2:33; 5:31); "[He is] glorified" (Jn 7:39; 12:16; 17:1); and "He departed/was going to the Father/God" (Jn 13:1, 3). All these metaphors express a unique event that is without analogy and therefore indescribable. These metaphors attempt to put into words God's creative action in the death of Jesus crucified. According to the testimony of the New Testament, there is no doubt about the reality of the resurrection of Jesus: the one who died on the cross lives by the power of God. He is alive in the present, is able to enter into a personal relationship with us, and calls us to serve him. The New Testament develops three aspects of the resurrection. (a) Through it God demonstrates creative power and fidelity to the covenant since God is the one "who raised Jesus from the dead" (Rom 4:24; 8:11; 2 Cor 4:14; Gal 1:1; Eph 1:20; Col 2:12). Christian belief in God is defined by the resurrection of Jesus (see Rom 4:17). Faith in the resurrection of Jesus is a statement of the creative power and fidelity of God that cannot be deterred by death (the resurrected Christ is the first of many brothers to awaken from the dead; see 1 Cor 15:20; Col 1:18; Rom 8:29). (b) The resurrection of Jesus clearly reveals who Jesus is: namely, messiah and Kyrios (Acts 2:32, 36; see 5:30f.; Phil 2:9, 11) and Son (Acts 13:33; Rom 1:3f.; see Gal 1:16). Here Old Testament images (Pss 2:7; 110:1; 2 Sm 7:14) play a significant role. (c) In later developments in the history of dogmatics we find the general structure of a so-called high or two-tiered Christology (katà sarká–katà pneûma [Rom 1:3f.; 1 Pt 3:18; 1 Tm 3:16a]): in the resurrection of Jesus, the salvation of Christ is open to all human beings through the Spirit (Rom 4:25; 8:11; 1 Cor 15:45; see Jn 7:37ff.) through baptism (Rom 6:4; see Col 2:12f.; 3:1–4; Eph 2:6) and through faith (Gal 2:20; 3:26f.), so that the believer or the baptized is a new creature in Christ (2 Cor 5:17; Gal 6:15). Whoever believes in Christ will live because Christ is the resurrection (Jn 11:25ff.; see 6:39f.). Christians have been freed and called to freedom (Gal 5:1, 13); wherever there is the Spirit of the Lord, there is freedom (2 Cor 3:17). Thus the resurrection of Jesus initiates the gathering of the church as the people of God of a new covenant. The working of the Spirit proves this (1 Cor 12:14; see Acts 2). Forgiveness of sins (Jn 20:23), baptism (Mt 28:19; see 1 Cor 12:13), the Lord's Supper (1 Cor 10:16f.; 11:20, 23–29), and words and acts of reconciliation (2 Cor 5:18ff.) constitute it. In the threefold relationship to God (the Father), to the Son, and to the Spirit, the resurrection of Jesus is also the revelation of a trinitarian God. After the resurrection of Jesus, we can speak about God only in relationship to the resurrected crucified one, the Son, and the Spirit, through whom he was raised up and can be experienced.

(2) *History of Theology*. The early church's belief in the resurrection of Jesus is solidly grounded in its liturgical life: "Sunday" (Justin, *Ap.* 1.67.7), the "lord's day" (Ignatius, *Magn.* 9.2), the "eighth day" (*Barn.* 15.8f.) as the memory of the resurrection of Jesus; midnight prayer services or vigils as references to the resurrection of Jesus (*Apost. Const.* 8.34; Pseudo-Athanasius, *De Virginitate* 20); the Easter liturgy and the Easter homilies (e.g., Melito of Sardis); the baptismal liturgy as the original site for the development of creeds (e.g., Hippolytus, *Apost. Trad.* 21ff.); the celebration of the Eucharist as the memory of the death and resurrection of Jesus (ibid., 4); and the Eucharist as a profession of the living resurrection of Jesus (Ignatius, *Eph.* 20; *Smyrn.* 5.1). The reality of the resurrection of Jesus is unquestioned in the early church, but it is not the central theme of Christology. This role is reserved for the incarnation. Consequently, Eusebius of Caesarea understands the resurrection of Jesus as a new incarnation (*Dem. ev.* 3.4), and ever since Paul of Samosata any exclusively resurrectional Christology has been considered dubious. Christ has not become divine with the resurrection, although the resurrection proves his divinity and the truth of his teaching (see Asterius Sophistes, *Hom.* 8.10). It was especially during the gnostic controversy — because the gnostics claimed that the future resurrection of the dead had already taken place in the resurrection of Jesus — that the incarnation and because of it the resurrection of the flesh were emphasized. Emphasis was laid on the unity of the whole Christ and his work, including the resurrection. This view was continued by Scholasticism and remained important in dogmatic manuals until recently. However, the soteriological moment of the resurrection of Jesus was not lost sight of as the cause of our resurrection and our justification (e.g., in Thomas Aquinas, *STh* 3, q. 56, a. 1f.). Only recently, because of new awareness of the centrality of the cross and resurrection of Jesus in the New Testament, has there been a corresponding shift in Christology (e.g., in W. Kasper).

(3) *Church Teaching*. The resurrection of Jesus is part of the church's basic faith, handed on in the creeds (DS 6, 10–30, 40–64, 72, 76, 125, 150, 801, 852, 1338). The creeds emphasize the reality of bodiliness (DS 681, 791, 801, 852, 1338) and reflect the viewpoint that faith in the resurrection of Jesus is deduced only from other data (DS 3436f.). Many creeds speak of the resurrection as self-validating in order to underline the activity of Jesus on the basis of his divinity. Against the background of a fully developed doctrine of the Trinity and in light of the unity of all its *ad extra* activity, it is stated that the whole Trinity causes the resurrection because of the intradivine relations.

(4) *Ecumenical Perspectives*. In recent Evangelical systematic theology the resurrection of Jesus has become increasingly important as the basis of any

Christology/soteriology. Thus, for example, K. Barth joins the doctrine of two natures (divinity and humanity of Jesus as two aspects of one person) with the doctrine of two states (God's abasement, humankind's elevation). Jesus Christ is "Lord as servant" in the abasement and "servant as Lord" in the elevation. Jesus' obedience on the cross and God's fidelity in the resurrection correspond to each other in this project of a resurrection Christology. In a special way, W. Pannenberg's Christology is a "Christology of the resurrection of Jesus." The claim of the earthly Jesus is confirmed by the resurrection; it is an anticipation of the end of history and the eschatological self-revelation of God. G. Ebeling begins his Christology/soteriology with a liturgically framed reflection (Christmas, Good Friday, Easter) on the "main christological data." He sees the resurrection of Jesus as the drawing of humans into the life of God. The elevated one remains the crucified one; what the resurrection of Jesus changed in relation to the time of the earthly Jesus is the knowledge and certitude of his togetherness with God. E. Schlink — in the context of a long discussion of the project of Christology — claims that "no Christology can go behind the resurrection to knowledge of Jesus as eternal Son of God" (*Ökumenische Dogmatik* [Göttingen, 1983], 272), and other Evangelical systematicians consider the resurrection of Jesus as an insufficient basis for Christology (e.g., C. H. Ratschow, *Jesus Christus* [Gütersloh, 1982], 247).

(5) *Systematic Reflections.* Because the resurrection of Jesus has become part of systematic Christology, the latter is now faced with a new situation. On the one hand, a reflection is needed that sees the unity of divinity and humanity in Jesus in relation to Jesus' oneness with God without regarding the resurrection as the beginning of the *Deus vere* (true God) or the surrender of a *homo vere* (true man); and, on the other hand, this reflection must clarify the fact "that Jesus becomes what he already is both before and during his earthly existence" (H. Urs von Balthasar, "Mysterium Paschale," in *MystSal* 3/2:273). The resurrection does not change Jesus' stance before God but rather reveals his definitive unity as a human being in union with God. Thus his perduring relationship to the world is included in a divine manner. This is also the heart of the lasting problem of the bodiliness of the resurrected crucified one: he really is totally with God, and at the same time he is with us. The *manner* of his corporal relation to the world can then be spelled out by means of various models of thought or by images: Pauline ones, clarified by modern anthropological categories (as in W. Kasper and H. Kessler), or natural-philosophical considerations (e.g., in neo-scholasticism, with or without reference to Thomas, as in L. Scheffczyk). A systematic theology of the resurrection of Jesus will then have to define its relationship to all the themes of dogmatics: as the definitive revelation of the Trinity, as the incipient fulfillment of the reality of creation and the clarification of the meaning of history, as the beginning of the church and the basic power of its proclamation of the word and celebration of the sacraments, and as the revelation of a new humanity and ground for hope in the eschatological fulfillment of individuals and of the world.

See also CROSS, THEOLOGY OF; HISTORICAL JESUS; RESURRECTION NAR-
RATIVES.

Bibliography
Balthasar, Hans Urs von. *Mysterium Paschale: The Mystery of Easter.* Edinburgh: T and T
    Clark, 1990.
Barth, Karl. *Church Dogmatics,* 4/1 and 2. Edinburgh: T and T Clark, 1961.
Brown, Raymond E. *The Virginal Conception and the Bodily Resurrection of Jesus.* New
    York: Paulist, 1973.
De Surgy, P. *The Resurrection and Modern Biblical Thought.* New York: Corpus, 1970.
Fiorenza, Francis Schüssler. *Foundational Theology: Jesus and the Church.* New York:
    Crossroad, 1984.
O'Collins, Gerald. *Interpreting the Resurrection: Examining the Major Problems in Stories
    of Jesus' Resurrection.* New York: Paulist, 1988.
———. *The Resurrection of Jesus Christ: Some Contemporary Issues.* Milwaukee: Marquette
    University Press, 1993.
Pannenberg, Wolfhart. *Jesus, God and Man.* Philadelphia: Westminster, 1968.
Perkins, Pheme. *Resurrection: New Testament Witness and Contemporary Reflection.* Garden
    City, N.Y.: Doubleday, 1984.
Rahner, Karl. "Dogmatic Questions on Easter." In *Theological Investigations,* 4:121–33.
    New York: Crossroad, 1966.
———. "Jesus' Resurrection." In *Theological Investigations,* 17:16–23. New York: Cross-
    road, 1981.
Schillebeeckx, Edward. *Interim Report on the Books "Jesus" and "Christ."* New York:
    Crossroad, 1980.
———. *Jesus: An Experiment in Christology.* New York: Crossroad, 1979.
Schmaus, Michael. *The Faith of the Church.* Vol. 4. New York: Sheed and Ward, 1972.
Stanley, David M. *Christ's Resurrection in Pauline Soteriology.* Rome: Biblical Institute Press,
    1961.
Wilckens, Ulrich. *Resurrection: Biblical Testimony to the Resurrection.* Atlanta: John Knox,
    1978.

                                                              LOTHAR ULLRICH

Resurrection of the Dead. The resurrection of the dead (the flesh) is the definitive perfecting of the entire human person in all its dimensions at the end of
time, and is connected with the parousia of Christ.

(1) *Biblical Background.* Because the God of the old covenant is the living
God in whom all life has its ground, and because in Semitic thinking (HUMAN
PERSON: IMAGE OF) the human person is understood in a holistic (monistic)
way, the hope of Israel is directed by and large not to a disembodied existence
of the soul but to the promised land and, ultimately, to the resurrection of the
dead. It is surprising that despite this fundamental outlook of the Old Testament, clear testimonies are to be found only in the last centuries before Christ.
As a rule, critical exegesis does not accept Hos 6:1–2 and Ez 37:1–14 as evidence for the resurrection of the dead. Also disputed are various passages in the
Isaian "Apocalypse" (24–27, especially 26:19; see also Is 53:9–12). Generally
accepted as testimonies to the resurrection of the dead are Dn 12:2–3, where
death is understood as a sleep and the resurrection of the dead as an awakening,
and 2 Mc 7:9, 14, where the resurrection of the dead is explained as a reward

for fidelity to the law and martyrdom. Even these passages probably do not assume a general resurrection of the dead. When 2 Mc 7:11 speaks of a recovery of the bodily limbs sacrificed in martyrdom, the resurrection of the dead is probably being understood as a kind of return to the present life. Extrabiblical Jewish apocalyptic (1 *Enoch, Psalms of Solomon, 2 Apocalypse of Baruch*) likewise provides clear testimonies to the resurrection of the dead, but the wording of the passages relates this only to the just. In the *Psalms of Solomon,* sinners are expressly excluded from the resurrection of the dead. Various intentions are at work in the New Testament testimonies to the resurrection of the dead. The Synoptics have only one passage that speaks explicitly of the resurrection of the dead: the debate between Jesus and the Sadducees, who in contrast to the Pharisees denied, among other truths, the resurrection of the dead (Mt 22:22–33 par.). Because the Sadducees accept only the Pentateuch, Jesus argues for belief in the resurrection of the dead by an appeal to Ex 3:6. He thus supports the Pharisees' belief in the resurrection but corrects it insofar as he understands the life initiated by the resurrection of the dead to be not a more intense continuation of earthly life but a life in a different form of corporeality, which is expressed in such phrases as "being like angels" and "no more marrying." The Synoptics do not speak directly of a resurrection of the wicked; in fact, Lk 14:14 refers expressly to the resurrection of the just. A general resurrection of the dead emerges, however, from various passages on judgment (Mt 11:22; 12:36, 41) and especially from the description of the final judgment (Mt 25:31–46). In Johannine references to the resurrection of the dead two strata of the Gospel must be distinguished. According to the realized ESCHATOLOGY that is peculiar to the Fourth Gospel, the awakening of the human person from spiritual death takes place in encounter with Christ (Jn 5:25). In a second stratum of the Gospel there are clear attestations of a general resurrection of the dead on the last day (Jn 5:28–29; see Rv 20:13–15). In the discourse on bread in John 6 we find not only faith in the resurrection of the dead (6:39, 44); in addition, this is connected with the eating of the Eucharist, which is understood as a pledge of the resurrection of the dead (6:54). For the primitive community in Jerusalem and the churches of the New Testament, faith in the resurrection of the dead was part of the Christian kerygma from the outset (Acts 4:2; 17:18, 32; 24:14; 26:8). The author of Hebrews regards it as an elementary doctrine of the faith (6:2). Paul provides a detailed theology of the resurrection of the dead and of the risen body; at the same time, he gives a christological justification of both, insofar as he emphasizes the indissoluble connection between the resurrection of Christ and our resurrection (1 Cor 15:13–14, 22, 23; 1 Thes 4:14; Rom 8:11, 29). He explains the difference between the earthly body and the risen body by means of a number of images and comparisons. Thus he contrasts corruptibility and incorruptibility; weakness and strength; the earthly and the celestial body (1 Cor 15:36–49). As God by God's creative power causes a splendid plant to arise in place of the seed that is sown in the soil, so God will raise up a glorious body after the earthly body is laid in the grave.

(2) *History of Theology.* In the church's tradition the resurrection of the dead has been understood from the beginning to be the specifically Christian hope; after the encounter of theology with Hellenism and the adoption of the Greek teaching on the soul, it was stressed in response to all the forms of hostility to the body that made their appearance in the Docetists, gnostics, Manichaeans, and, in the Middle Ages, the Waldensians and Cathars. The defense of the resurrection of the dead had both an anthropological and a christological dimension. The whole human person will obtain salvation; the flesh, too, is capable of enjoying salvation. The salvation of the human person has its exemplar and pledge in Christ, the incarnate Son of God who has been raised bodily from the dead. Irenaeus, for example, stresses the redemption of the entire human being in light of the mystery of Christ, arguing that the Word of God would never have become flesh if the flesh were not capable of being redeemed. Tertullian calls the flesh the crucial and chief element in salvation. The liturgy confesses the same faith, especially in its commemoration of the deceased during the Eucharist. Down into the Middle Ages the question of the identity of the earthly body with the risen body confronted the Christian tradition with a well-nigh insoluble difficulty. (If one prescinds from the teaching of the school of Origen, according to which the risen body will have the ideal form of a sphere, the emphasis in the tradition was on the complete identity of the two bodies.) Thus we find even in Thomas Aquinas (d. 1274) the idea that the risen body will be composed primarily of matter from the earthly body, although the formation of the risen body from a different matter is not excluded. During that period the identity of the risen body with the earthly was seen, by and large, as due to the "informing spiritual soul." In the thirteenth and fourteenth centuries this doctrine developed to the point of saying that the spiritual soul was enough to ensure the identity of the risen body with the earthly body (see especially Durandus [d. 1334]).

(3) *Church Teaching.* The ecclesial magisterium bears witness to the resurrection of the dead in various professions of faith that speak of the resurrection of the dead (Nicene-Constantinopolitan Creed) or the resurrection of the flesh (*carnis resurrectio*) (Apostles' Creed). The Pseudo-Athanasian Creed (between the end of the fourth and the end of the sixth century) says that at the Second Coming of Christ all will rise in their bodies (DS 76). The "Faith of Damasus" (which probably originated in fifth-century Gaul) declares that we shall arise in the flesh in which we now live (DS 72). The Eleventh Council of Toledo (675) says that we shall arise in the body in which we now live, are, and move (DS 540). A profession of faith from the year 1053, under Leo IX, expresses faith in the resurrection of the same flesh that we now have (DS 684). The Fourth Lateran Council (1215) says the same against the Cathars: all human beings will arise with the same bodies that they now have (DS 801). In evaluating these doctrinal decrees of the church a distinction must be made between the objective statement about the identity of the earthly and risen bodies and the philosophical and theological theory that determines the form the state-

ment takes. In the fight against a spiritualistic interpretation of salvation the emphasis on the identity of the two bodies often took an exaggerated form.

(4) *Ecumenical Perspectives.* In the ecumenical dialogue the resurrection of the dead plays no part, inasmuch as the main non-Catholic Christian churches accept the unanimous tradition and profess it.

(5) *Systematic Reflections.* The medieval question of the identity of the earthly and risen body takes a different form today: it is well known that the earthly body itself undergoes a constant change of its material components; its identity derives solely from the person who possesses the body or, rather, is this body. Resurrection of the body means, therefore, that the whole person with his or her entire life's history will exist once again in God's presence. A debated question in contemporary theology is whether the resurrection of the dead is to be understood solely as an event of the last day or whether it already occurs at the death of each individual. This question is connected with that of the intermediate state. The Congregation for the Doctrine of the Faith has intervened in the debate to the extent of pointing out that the manifestation of Christ in glory must be distinguished from the situation of other human beings immediately after death and that the bodily glorification of Mary is a privilege granted to her alone ("Declaration on Some Questions of Eschatology," May 17, 1979 = *Origins* [1979]).

See also HEAVEN; HELL; INTERMEDIATE STATE; PAROUSIA; RESURRECTION OF JESUS.

Bibliography
Cullmann, Oscar. *Immortality of the Soul; or, Resurrection of the Dead? The Witness of the New Testament.* New York: Macmillan, 1958.
Nickelsburg, George W. E. *Resurrection, Immortality, and Eternal Life in Intertestamental Judaism.* Cambridge, Mass.: Harvard University Press, 1972.
Rahner, Karl. "The Resurrection of the Body." In *Theological Investigations,* 2:203–16. New York: Crossroad, 1963.
Stendahl, Krister. *Immortality and Resurrection.* New York: Macmillan, 1971.

JOSEF FINKENZELLER

Revelation. Revelation in its *colloquial* meaning is the unexpected experience of a significant fact. In a *religious-studies* perspective, it is the appearance or influence of the divine in the world. In the *Christian theological* sense, it is the radical and total self-communication of God as the absolute mystery, a self-communication that occurs in history through words, deeds, and events and that reaches its climax in Jesus Christ. This divine self-communication is mediated through the Holy Spirit and unfolds its efficacy for salvation when it is accepted in faith by human beings.

(1) *Biblical Background.* Scripture is the literary expression of the experience that God, who as such is concealed (Is 45:15), has made God's self known many times and in various ways in the history of Israel and in the first Christian generation but finally and unsurpassably in Jesus of Nazareth (Heb 1:1f.),

who is God's image (*icon:* 2 Cor 4:4; Col 1:15). The Old Testament did not develop its own concept of revelation but elaborated various categories in which the reality is itself expressed. The revealing activity of God shows itself above all (*a*) in inner experiences of God (inner voices, visions, oracles, dreams: e.g., Nm 22–24; Is 1:1; 6:1–13; 1 Sm 10:17–27; Gn 20:6); (*b*) in historical experiences that are grasped conceptually in the categories of promise/fulfillment, slavery/freedom, perdition/salvation (e.g., Dt 26:5–9) and that have high points like the calling of Abraham in prehistory, of Moses in Israel's process of becoming a people, and of the prophets in the stabilization of Israel; (*c*) in the experience of the word of God that reveals God's self as the God of human beings, the God of the people (Ex 6:7; 8:6; 9:14, 29; Ez 7:9; 21:10, passim); (*d*) in the experience of the covenant through which Israel, as the unique people from the very beginning, is made God's people (Gn 17:1–14). The content of this manifold revelation is above all: Yahweh is the God of Israel (Dt 6:4), lord of history (Ex 3:6; Hos 12:10; 13:4), Creator of the world (Psalm 104), person (Ex 3:6–17; 20:2), and initiator of the covenant (Genesis 17). The fundamental attitude of the human person is the recognition of God's glory (*kabod*) (Is 6:3; Pss 19:2; 72; 97; Is 42:8), which calls forth love (Dt 6:5) and faithfulness toward God who, as the one who is to come, will bring history to perfection (Is 25:6–8; 52:7–10). Thus history, as the place of the proclamation of the divine will, also becomes the place of decision for faith in God. The New Testament proclaims that the self-communication of God that started in the Old Testament has reached its final completion in Jesus as the Christ. In this, the final word about the understanding and the realization of human existence has been spoken by God. As in the Old Testament, various extraordinary phenomena, which go back to God as their author and which illuminate God's decrees, are reported, such as dreams (Mt 1:20; 2:12), visions (Mt 17:1–9; Acts 7:55f.), miracles (Mt 11:2–6; 12:28; Jn 2:11), and, above all, the Easter appearances (Mt 28:9f., 16–20; Mk 16:9–20; Lk 24:13; Jn 20–21). Yet they all refer to Jesus, whose preaching of God's kingdom has itself a revealing quality (Jn 17:6, 26) because he alone knows the Father (Mt 11:27), so that whoever has seen him, has seen the Father (Jn 14:9). He is thus revealer and revelation at the same time (see Jn 8:12; 11:25; 14:6), the fulfillment of all the Old Testament promises (according to the New Testament interpretation of the passion of Jesus), and the source of salvation for the new covenant (Acts 2:14–36). Above all Paul interprets this experience theologically: Christ is the content (Rom 3:21–23; Gal 1:16; Eph 3:4f.; 1 Tm 3:16), the summary (Rom 3:25; 16:25f.; 1 Cor 15:28; Eph 1:10; 3:9–11; Phil 2:6–11; Col 1:15–20), and the perfection of divine revelation (2 Cor 1:20; Eph 3:6). In this, Christ is, at the same time, the manifestation of divine love (Jn 1:1–5; Rom 8:31–39; 1 Jn 4:9, 16) and the beginning of the justification of human beings (Rom 1:16–18; 3:21–24). John underlines especially the disclosure of the glory of God through Jesus (Jn 1:14; 2:11; yet see also Lk 2:9–14; 9:32; 24:26). Finally, Jesus is portrayed like Yahweh as the one who is yet to come (Ti 2:13). Drawing upon allusions in the

Old Testament (Jl 3:1–5), the New Testament emphasizes that the disclosure of God is mediated through God's Spirit (Acts 2:14–21; 1 Cor 2:9f.; see Jn 14:26; 15:26; 16:13). In the church, which is filled with the Spirit, the faithful have the task of witnessing to and passing on revelation (Acts 10:41; 1 Cor 9:1; Gal 1:15f.; 1 Jn 1:1). That this experience of revelation is focused on Jesus and his relation to the Father and to the Holy Spirit is expressed in the confessions in which Jesus is identified with God (see Mt 1:23; Jn 1:1–18; Col 1:25–27; Rv 19:11–16). Together with the references to the Holy Spirit, it is God's trinitarian essence that is disclosed as an essentially new revelation.

(2) *History of Theology.* In the history of theology up until now, three models for the understanding of revelation have principally been developed: (*a*) the *epiphanic model* is rooted in Scripture and is developed in the early church. According to it, God's self-manifestation in history is as judge and giver of grace. The whole event of salvation is interpreted as the actualization of God's constitutive self-disclosure which has reached its summit in Christ. Thus, the Church Fathers and the early councils and canons — up until the Council of Trent — used terms for revelation (*revelare, inspirare*) that are also used for the interpretation of Scripture. (*b*) The *doctrinal-theoretical* model was promoted by the focus on the conceptual form of the contents of revelation (dogmas). The model was formed within Scholasticism and celebrated its triumph in the nineteenth century. Here revelation is a process of planned actions: God communicates in an exceptional way specific truths capable of being expressed in propositions that otherwise could not be acknowledged by reason. To this intellectual mediation of salvation corresponds faith as an act of intellectual submission. With this concept Catholic theology had sought to answer the challenges of modernity. Modernity had denied historical revelation, either because it rejected any this-worldly activity of God except the act of creation (deism), or because one considered all of God's activity to be knowable through reason (the Enlightenment), or because one held that only sensorially experienceable phenomena are accessible to human beings (empiricism, rationalism). The concept of divine revelation is therefore viewed as a conservative strategy of immunization and as an imposition upon the autonomy of human reason. B. Spinoza, G. E. Lessing, I. Kant, and D. Diderot are the protagonists for theses of this kind. As an extreme reaction to this, there arose movements of irrationalism according to which revelation is an experience solely of feeling (F. Schleiermacher and R. Otto). For FIDEISM and TRADITIONALISM, human reason without revelation cannot grasp ethical and religious truths, and, therefore, there must have been a primordial revelation present at the beginning (H. F. R. de Lamennais, L. E. M. Bautain, and A. Bonnetty). Semirationalism attempted to find a mediating position according to which revelation, once it has happened, can be fully recognized through reason (A. Günther and J. Frohschammer). In reaction to this, Catholic theology, drawing back on Scholasticism, developed the fundamental theological treatise on revelation. It distinguishes natural revelation (= recognizing God by using reason to consider the course of creation) and

supernatural revelation. The latter is based on the infallible authority of God, who communicates truths that are attested to by miracles and that lead to the knowledge of many truths that are written down in Scripture and tradition. The truths are infallibly interpreted by the church as the proximate authority for human beings. Revelation thus becomes the content of church teaching that is transmitted externally to human beings in an authoritative form (extrinsic concept of revelation). After Vatican I (see sec. 3 below) had, more or less, sanctioned this concept, theology at the turn of the twentieth century had to find a new starting point, for modernism had opposed this extrinsicism with its concept of revelation as an articulation of the religious need that is inherent in the subject (psychological immanentism). J. A. Möhler, S. Drey, M. J. Scheeben, and J. H. Newman had already stressed the mysterious character and the dynamic quality of revelation. M. Blondel sought a new approach between neo-scholasticism and modernism with his "method of immanence" (knowledge of revelation has to be initiated from outside, yet it remains a possibility of reason). (c) Out of this arises the *communicative-theoretical model*. According to this model, revelation is God's historical self-communication to human beings through which the redeeming and liberating reality of God becomes present, which brings human beings into salvation-bringing community with God and with one another. Since revelation is communication, it must be able to be elucidated before the questions of reason. Revelation and reason, thus, are not opposed to each other. Essential contributions to this development came from R. Guardini (introduction of the personalist category), H. Urs von Balthasar (revelation as a presupposition of all theistic thinking), K. Rahner (revelation as objectification of God's gracious self-communication), and the Théologie Nouvelle (emphasis on the historical character of revelation). Vatican II (see sec. 3 below) took up this new model. At the present, specific aspects or themes of the concept of revelation are taken as starting points for new theological proposals (*promise* in the theology of hope, *liberation* in the theology of liberation, *historicity* in process theology).

(3) *Church Teaching.* On account of circumstances in the history of theology, the concept of revelation has been explicitly treated by the magisterium only in modern times. This happens for the first time in a detailed way at Vatican I (DS 3004–7, 3026–29). Against rationalistic views, the magisterium teaches the supernatural and freely given quality of revelation and the subordination of reason to it. Against irrationalistic tendencies, it emphasizes the possibility of reason grasping revelation and making a decision upon it. In positive explanations the doctrinal-theoretical model is taken over. Further, it is emphasized that revelation is completed and is to be passed on by the church in an unchanged way (DS 3070). Vatican II then offers the first comprehensive conciliar presentation of a theology of revelation (*DV*). The conceptualistic-intellectualistic understanding of revelation of Vatican I is replaced by a personal-soteriological view of revelation that accepts the communicative-theoretical model: revelation is an event of encounter between

God and the human person in which the triune God is subject, content, and goal. It is a reality that encompasses words and deeds, activity and doctrine, knowing and willing, and that is structured in a sacramental way: the words interpret God's activity. While revelation has come to completion in Christ, the Christ-event continues to be interpreted in the life, the teaching, and the cult of the church; revelation thus receives an eschatological orientation. In summary, revelation is the real self-communication of God through which the human person is affected in his or her whole existence as God's covenant partner: revelation does not convey something otherwise unknowable, but rather salvation.

(4) *Ecumenical Perspectives.* Revelation is a shared category among Christians and the common denominator of Christian self-understanding, the place of understanding common to all Christians. Therefore, no fundamental differences exist between the Christian theologies. Orthodoxy views natural revelation in nature, history, and conscience as the more comprehensive concept, and the supernatural revelation in Scripture is considered a special case of this. Besides this exterior or objective revelation that is completed, there is the interior revelation (grace-filled insight) that has not yet come to an end. The transmission of exterior revelation takes place in the church both orally and in writing (in tradition and in the Fathers of the Church). From its beginning Protestantism has emphasized the personal moment of revelation — Luther experienced it as God's breaking through the sinful self-enclosure of the human person, a breaking through that occurs through the law (the revelation of the sinfulness of the human being and his or her condemnation by God) and the gospel (the revelation of God's pardon and forgiveness). While for the liberal theology of the nineteenth century revelation was the ideal that enabled the human being to satisfy the desires of his or her spiritual nature, the theology of the twentieth century has accented the dogmatic meaning of revelation as the principle of knowing (K. Barth), as the disclosure of the meaning of history (W. Pannenberg), and as the provocation of the existential decision of the human person (R. Bultmann).

(5) *Systematic Reflections.* The modern debate has shown that revelation is a fundamental and transcendental theological concept that distinguishes Christian from non-Christian convictions and specifies what is Christian. This is to say: revelation is the reality that is decisive for the position of Christianity in relation to the other religions (an exclusive understanding of revelation: there are no common points; an inclusive understanding of revelation: a moral life directed by reason and conscience is always already Christian; a salvation-history understanding of revelation: God brings the plan for salvation that begins in creation through the other religions, but that plan comes to fulfillment in Christianity). This reality, then, is the ground and the norm of ecclesial structures, of the proclamation and the contents of Christian doctrine, and of its theological interpretation. In dogmatic theology revelation is thus the fundamental principle of knowing. On the one hand, on account of its rootedness in a his-

REVELATION AS EPISTEMOLOGICAL PRINCIPLE OF THEOLOGY

Object	Supernatural revelation
Condition of the possibility	Essential inaccessibility of God; spiritual nature of the human person
Motive	God's free act of love
Realization	Through word and deed in the framework of the covenant with human beings; the summit is the Christ-event
Addressee	The free, self-transcending human person
Acceptance	Faith
Dogmatic significance	Basic hermeneutical rule for all theological knowledge
Domain	(a) Truths that either are indispensable for the understanding of faith (*praeambula fidei*) or directly concern faith and Christian life (*res fidei vel morum*) (b) Historical events with theological significance (*facta dogmatica*)
Communication	(a) According to the intention, *direct* or *indirect* (b) According to the explicitness, *formally explicit*, or *implicit* or *virtual* (to be disclosed only theologically)

torical event with a universal and absolute validity claim (God's trinitarian self-communication in history), revelation needs continuous interpretation in order to realize this claim. This happens concretely in the church, which is not only the addressee but also the proclaimer of revelation through Scripture, tradition, the magisterium, the sensus fidelium, and theology. On the other hand, the church with all its elements and aspects continues always to be bound to the claim of revelation so that this becomes the critical court of appeal: only what is supported and legitimized by it has validity and authority in the church. This connection is expressed in the talk of the completion of revelation in the generation of the apostles: because Christ is the final and unsurpassable self-expression of God, there can later occur no new public constitutive revelation. Private revelations are therefore never obligatory (*DV* 4). The church has the task of faithfully preserving the content of revelation (*depositum fidei*). However, since the process of the proclamation and appropriation of revelation takes place in the context of human experience, both individually and collectively, revelation continues through history. Dogmatic theology analyzes revelation especially as God's word that is freely communicated and therefore is expressed in historically concrete forms; that brings about salvation and therefore is not only teaching but also life; that possesses a sacramental structure and thus realizes itself in God's activity as a saving word and that interprets the deed through the word as a saving deed; that, finally, is also a critical interpretation of reality and thereby validates God's claim. Accordingly, revelation occurs wherever God is at work in history, thus also as "natural revelation" in the reality of creation. Yet this is fully recognized as revelation only in God's grace in a "supernatural" way.

See also CHURCH; DOGMA/DOGMATIC STATEMENT; DOGMATIC THEOLOGY; ECCLESIAL MAGISTERIUM; FAITH; HISTORY/HISTORICITY; MYSTERY OF FAITH; THEOLOGY; TRADITION.

Bibliography
Dulles, Avery. *Models of Revelation*. Garden City, N.Y.: Doubleday, 1983.
Fries, Heinrich. *Revelation*. New York: Herder and Herder, 1969.
Niebuhr, H. Richard. *The Meaning of Revelation*. New York: Macmillan, 1960.
Rahner, Karl, and Joseph Ratzinger. *Revelation and Tradition*. New York: Herder and Herder, 1966.
Thiemann, Ron. *Revelation and Theology*. Notre Dame, Ind.: University of Notre Dame Press, 1985.

WOLFGANG BEINERT

S s

Sacrament. A sacrament is a significant symbolic action that at least points to a religious reality. The seven sacraments of the Catholic Church do not simply point to this religious reality (grace, salvation), but, in their administration, which is a process of communication between minister and recipient, and ultimately between God and a human being, they simultaneously communicate this saving reality to believers.

(1) *Biblical Background.* In the New Testament all the sign-actions that are later indicated by the term *sacrament* occur with greater or lesser (e.g, confirmation) clarity, but there is no Greek word that applies to them as a group. It is important to note, however, that the Latin word *sacramentum* is a translation of the Greek *mystērion* and is to be found from the second/third century on in the Old Latin versions of the Bible. As a result, meanings of the biblically important term *mystērion* (*mysterium*) may have found their way into the later concept of sacrament. What is the meaning of *mysterium*, which occurs twenty-seven times in the New Testament (twenty in Paul alone)? In continuity with the eschatological and apocalyptic thinking of the late Old Testament, the *mysterium* in Mk 4:11 is the "mystery of the kingdom of God" (the reign of God that God causes suddenly to break into history) that is revealed to believers. For Paul and those who follow him the *mysterium* is a reality in God: God's eternal, hidden plan of salvation (e.g., 1 Cor 2:1, 7); this takes shape in history as salvation for all in Jesus Christ (cp. 1 Cor 1:23 with 1 Cor 3:7; Col 2:2). Finally, the *mysterium* of God is fulfilled in the church of Jesus Christ, which is united to him as his body and his bride (see Eph 5:32). It can be said, then, that in the New Testament *mysterium/sacramentum* has a theological, a christological, and an ecclesiological dimension, all of which were to come together in the later, more specific concept of sacrament and to play a normative role in its meaning. The same holds for the universalist aspect (salvation not limited to a few chosen persons) that attached to the concept of *mysterium* in the New Testament.

(2) *History of Theology.* If *sacramentum* is a translation of *mysterium*, an unavoidable question arises: What is the connection between the Christian doctrine of the sacraments and the "mysteries" of antiquity? Various answers are given. Some influence of the cultic practices associated with the mysteries and of the philosophical thought behind them is undeniable. On the other hand, the Christian understanding of the sacraments cannot be derived from that practice or thought. The mysteries of antiquity were nature-centered and exclusive. The gods of the ancient mystery cults were themselves subject to the cycle of becoming and passing away, with the result that participation in their lot by way of

605

the mysteries promised only a natural salvation. The salvation brought by Jesus Christ was established at a particular point within history and yet it transcends this history. In the mystery cults salvation was meant only for the initiated (the *mystēs*) or, as the case might be, only for the educated; Christian salvation is meant for all. Tertullian (d. after 220) played an especially important role in the development of the concept of sacrament. He was probably the first consciously to apply "sacrament" to baptism and, with the help of this concept, to whose secular meaning he also appealed, to develop a kind of baptismal theology that became a contribution to the general doctrine of the sacraments. In its secular use the word *sacramentum* at that time meant an oath of fidelity to the flag, an oath of service, and a monetary pledge. With the aid of this concept Tertullian brought out the moral self-commitment that responds to God's saving act, a dialogical aspect, which, however, soon disappeared for a long time. In any case, for centuries "sacraments" included not only baptism and the Eucharist but many other rites and signs, as well as doctrines and services. Augustine (d. 430) made an important contribution to the doctrine of the sacraments. Inspired by Neoplatonism and the Bible, he saw in all the things and occurrences of the sensible world signs and reflections of a higher spiritual reality that has its foundation in the mind of God. Of these sensible things the one whose referential character is clearest is the word. The failure to understand the referential character of the material world is due to sin. In the history of salvation God has established new and clearer signs, which become part of the lives of believers especially through baptism and the Eucharist. These are sacraments of the divine reality of grace. Sacraments have two elements in their structure: a material element and the explanatory word; only when the two are combined can sacraments become fully effective: "Word is added to element and the result is a sacrament [*accedit verbum ad elementum et fit sacramentum*]" (*In Evang. Iohan.* 80.3). A sacrament is thus a "visible word" (*verbum visibile*). But Augustine does not make the effect of the sacrament (*res sacramenti*) depend solely on the human believer's understanding of the sign; it is Christ who, as the real administrator of the sacrament, effects God's grace in the recipient. Sacramental symbolism is accompanied by sacramental realism in a unity-in-tension that was not to be subsequently maintained, any more than was the Augustinian unity-in-tension of the individual and ecclesial effects of the sacraments. The concept of sacrament was further developed in the twelfth century and found to be verified in our present-day seven sacraments (previously there were thought to be five or twelve or as many as thirty sacraments). An important criterion for a sacrament is institution by Jesus Christ. Thomas Aquinas exerted a decisive influence on the doctrine of the sacraments. As a follower of Aristotle he was interested in the makeup of reality from matter and form and in the question of cause and effect. According to Thomas, even the sacraments are composites of a sensible element and a verbal element. They are as it were (physical) instruments through which God in Christ (with the help of the minister) effects his grace in human beings to the extent that the latter do not place any interior obstacle in the way. The advantages of this doctrine are: (a) it brings out the exclusive causality of God in the order of salvation; (b) in contrast to Augustinian Platonism, God's salvation lays hold of human beings in all dimensions of their lives (the material, too, has its proper value). Disadvantages: (a) the symbolic aspect of the sacraments and their aspect as appeals to the person are overshadowed; (b) the faith response of the recipient seems less important. The doctrine of the sacraments did not receive any decisive new stimuli until the recent past in the theology of the mysteries and the emphasis on the dialogical character of the sacraments.

(3) *Church Teaching.* It is chiefly the sacramental theology of St. Thomas that is reflected in the documents of the ecclesial magisterium. Thus in the Decree for the Armenians of the Council of Florence (1439): "Our sacraments both contain grace and confer it on those who receive them worthily" (DS 1310; ND 1305). "All these sacraments are constituted by three elements: by things as the matter, by words as the form, and by the person of the minister conferring the sacrament with the intention of doing what the church does" (DS 1312; ND 1307). Surprisingly, nothing is said of the recipient. The Reformers (see sec. 4 below) regard the sacraments as simply a special form of proclamation and, in the main, accept only baptism and the Eucharist as sacraments, on the grounds that these alone were instituted by Christ. In contrast, the Council of Trent (1547) maintains that "all true justification either begins through the sacraments, or, once begun, increases through them, or when lost is regained through them" (DS 1600; ND 1310). Of the canons issued by Trent the most important are the first (the seven sacraments were instituted by Christ [DS 1601; ND 1311]), the sixth (the sacraments contain the grace that they signify and confer it on those who place no obstacle in the way [DS 1606; ND 1316]), and the eighth (grace is conferred by the performance of the rite [*ex opere operato*] [DS 1608; ND 1318]). Vatican II has initiated a new synthesis of sacramental realism and sacramental symbolism. "The purpose of the sacraments is to sanctify men, to build up the body of Christ, and, finally, to give worship to God; because they are signs, they also instruct. They not only presuppose faith, but by words and objects they also nourish, strengthen, and express it; that is why they are called 'sacraments of faith' " (SC 59; ND 1335; see SC 61). In addition to the new emphasis on the sign aspect of the sacraments, the following points made by Vatican II are important: (a) the sacraments are seen as having the entire liturgy for their context; (b) they have a dialogical character; (c) individual and ecclesial meaning are kept equally in view; (d) the effect of the sacraments comes from the paschal mystery; (e) symbolic and instrumental action are interconnected; (f) the effects of grace produced by the sacraments also relate to the situations of the present life and history.

(4) *Ecumenical Perspectives.* There is still no full agreement with the churches of the Reformation regarding the sacraments and how they are to be understood. But rapprochements are in sight. Since Vatican II, the Catholic Church has emphasized the proclamation aspect of the sacraments as well as

their efficacy. They express faith and strengthen it. For Protestants the question arises of whether it is legitimate to assign solely to the word the responsibility for the proclamation that leads to faith and justification, and whether this must not rather be applied also to signs and symbols, which have a whole language of their own. In this context, greater emphasis needs to be placed on contemporary insights into the action of symbols, which lay hold of the depths of the person and at the same time create communication. Does the testimony of the Bible prevent us from seeing symbols in the service of proclamation? Although this is certainly not the only possible way of looking at the sacraments, there are Catholic theologians who view the sacraments as the highest form of the word that brings forgiveness and salvation (K. Rahner). This is another point of departure for a fruitful dialogue. A final source of progress can be found in the revival of a theological distinction regarded as valid since the Middle Ages: the distinction between "principal sacraments" (*sacramenta maiora*) and secondary or situation-linked sacraments (*sacramenta minora*). A growing agreement on the principal sacraments can create an atmosphere of calm in which to reflect on a possible role, in faith and salvation, for the situation-linked sacraments in the life of the individual (e.g., confirmation as an effective renewal of baptism) or of the ecclesial community (e.g., the sacrament of orders as a handing on of ministry with the promise of effective divine aid). There is extensive agreement with the Eastern churches on the understanding of the sacraments; this agreement has been further reinforced by the influence of the theology of the mysteries. Differences with regard to particular sacraments (e.g., the sacrament of reconciliation and the anointing of the sick) are less important by comparison. A dialogue with the Eastern churches on sacramental theology can bring important stimuli to the West.

(5) *Systematic Reflections.* (a) There is agreement among theologians today that the individual sacraments may not unconditionally be brought under the umbrella of the secondary concept of sacrament. There is need of seeing, more clearly than in the past, not only what the sacraments have in common but also what is specific to each. (b) There is also widespread agreement that the administration of the sacraments needs to be explained, much more than in the past, in personalist categories (which include both the individual and the communal-ecclesial aspects). In this context, such concepts as dialogue, encounter, and communication (expressed in the interaction of minister and recipient) have become important. Also relevant here is the concept of actualization (of the paschal mystery), which makes possible both personal inclusion and personal-communal participation. (c) Another point that is widely acknowledged is the importance of the connection between the doctrine of the sacraments, Christology, and ecclesiology, a connection that can be made clear precisely with the aid of the concept of sacrament: sacraments are saving encounters with God through Christ, the primal sacrament, in the church, the universal sacrament. (d) Finally, there are widespread efforts to bring home the realism of significant or symbolic actions in a more fruitful way. Various paths are being followed to

this end, but these need not be mutually exclusive. Some of these paths include: efforts at anthropological explanation of the symbolic sacramental event and its language, in relation, for example, to the basic situations, the nodal points of human life and social existence; the placing of greater emphasis on the results of modern theories of communication; or taking as the starting point the importance of festivity and celebration in human life and society. (*e*) It is generally acknowledged that God in God's salvific activity does not overlook the "natural" patterns of symbolic interactions but makes use of them and effects salvation through them, while at the same time far transcending them.

See also CHURCH; EX OPERE OPERATO; HYLOMORPHISM; INDELIBLE CHARACTER; INSTITUTION OF THE SACRAMENTS; MYSTERY OF FAITH; SACRAMENTAL SIGN; SACRAMENTAL THEOLOGY; SACRAMENTS AS SEVEN IN NUMBER; THEOLOGY OF THE MYSTERIES; WORD AND SACRAMENT.

Bibliography
Ganoczy, Alexandre. *An Introduction to Catholic Sacramental Theology.* New York: Paulist, 1984.
Lee, Bernard. *Alternative Futures for Worship.* 7 vols. Collegeville, Minn.: Liturgical Press, 1987.
Rahner, Karl. *The Church and the Sacraments.* New York: Herder and Herder, 1963.
Schillebeeckx, Edward. *Christ, the Sacrament of Encounter with God.* New York: Sheed and Ward, 1963.
Semmelroth, Otto. *Church and Sacraments.* Notre Dame, Ind.: Fides, 1965.
Vorgrimler, Herbert. *Sacramental Theology.* Collegeville, Minn.: Liturgical Press, 1992.

GÜNTER KOCH

Sacramentals. Sacramentals are symbolic actions that have been established by the church and that, in virtue of the intercession and faith of the church as well as the faith of the recipient and possibly of the minister, attest in a sensible way to God's saving action and at the same time apply it. They have traditionally been divided into consecrations, blessings, and exorcisms.

(1) *Biblical Background.* It used to be said that the sacraments were instituted by Jesus Christ, while the sacramentals were instituted by the church as a kind of imitation of the sacraments; today, however, this distinction runs into exegetical difficulties. The INSTITUTION OF THE SACRAMENTS can in some cases be traced back only indirectly to the historical Jesus, while, on the other hand, Jesus certainly blessed and exorcised. These and other symbolic actions attested by the New Testament can be regarded as providing a general New Testament background for both the sacraments and the sacramentals, although the sacraments, of course, can already be seen there, in an at least inchoative way, as immediate saving gifts of God to the church.

(2) *History of Theology.* The church had already developed a large number of the rites known as sacramentals in the first millennium, often in connection with the liturgies of baptism and the Eucharist. A more precise theological explanation came in the period beginning in the twelfth century, as the spe-

cial nature of the sacraments and their identification as seven in number were definitely decided. While the sacraments have their effect in virtue of the properly performed sacramental rite (EX OPERE OPERATO), the sacramentals produce their effect *ex opere operantis (ecclesiae)*, that is, in virtue of the action of the church or, as the case may be, also of the recipient and of the minister, who, according to current law, must usually be a cleric, although for some sacramentals the minister may be a layperson (*CIC* 1168f.).

(3) *Church Teaching.* It was chiefly in response to the Reformers (see sec. 4 below), who looked upon the sacramentals as attempts at human self-redemption, that the ecclesial magisterium took a position on the liturgical sacramentals (thus the Council of Trent: DS 1613, 1746, 1757, 1775; ND 1323, 1551, 1561, 1718): such signs are in accordance with human nature and are meant to call the heart to the things of God. Vatican II makes the following points regarding the sacramentals (*SC* 60f.): they have been instituted by the church and are effective in virtue of the church's intercession; they prepare human beings to receive the effects of the sacraments; like the sacraments, they draw their power from the paschal mystery; they sanctify concrete human life, even, and specifically, in its material aspects; they help the faithful to make everything in their lives serve their salvation and give praise to God.

(4) *Ecumenical Perspectives.* The fact that Vatican II brought the sacramentals closer, in many respects, to the sacraments, was probably a response to the Eastern churches' understanding of them. The fact that the efficacy of the sacramentals is seen as dependent on the Easter-event as well as on the faith-inspired openness of the recipient might be a point of departure for dialogue with the churches of the Reformation. Luther, be it noted, still accepted as a self-evident practice the signing of oneself with the cross (which is a sacramental in a broader sense); blessings, too, play a significant role in the churches of the Reformation.

(5) *Systematic Reflections.* A basic requirement in dealing with all the kinds of sacramentals is both to avoid any magical interpretation and at the same time to bring out their anthropological significance. Special requirements attach to the several categories of sacramentals. While consecrations represent a special transfer of the object or person into the possession of God, this transfer should not be interpreted as a sacral separation from the "profane": consecrated persons and buildings should attest, and be of service to, precisely the universality of redemption through Christ. The same holds for blessings and the use of blessed objects: they are meant to be helps in apprehending and perceiving the redemptive power of Christian faith in all the situations of life. Exorcisms, which are directed against evil forces or the devil, offer greater difficulties today. Experiences that people can well have even, and especially, today provide possible approaches to the understanding of exorcisms: people feel themselves entangled in evil, possibly even fascinated by evil; they come up against walls of hatred and contempt for human beings. Does there not lurk in the background an evil force before which the individual feels helpless? In cer-

tain cases, the church can, by its use of exorcisms, confess the greater power of God in an effective and sensible way, and thus create space for it.

See also SACRAMENT.

Bibliography

Chupungco, Anscar J. *Liturgical Inculturation: Sacramentals, Religiosity, and Catechesis.* Collegeville, Minn.: Liturgical Press, 1992.

Palmer, Paul F. *Sacraments and Forgiveness: History and Doctrinal Development of Penance, Extreme Unction and Indulgences.* Westminster, Md.: Newman, 1959.

GÜNTER KOCH

Sacramental Sign. It is in the nature of sacraments that they take the form of significant or symbolic actions involving minister and recipient.

(1) *Biblical Background.* The New Testament attests to such symbolic actions in an especially clear way for baptism, the Eucharist, the anointing of the sick, and the sacrament of orders; in the case of these sacraments, a verbal component is discernible along with the visible action. For the other sacraments, these must be inferred.

(2) *History of Theology.* In the patristic period Augustine in particular reflected on the distinctive nature of a sacramental sign. He identifies it as a twofold structure made up of material element and explanatory word, with the word playing the leading role: a sacrament is a "visible word" (*verbum visibile*) that, as a sign, points to the higher spiritual and indeed divine reality and at the same time bestows this reality. While this approach is influenced by the Neoplatonic spirit, Aristotelian influence manifests itself in the next decisive contribution to the understanding of sacramental signs: that of Thomas Aquinas in the Middle Ages. In keeping with hylomorphism, sacramental signs are composed of a sensible element and a verbal element. Thus they are as it were instruments that God, aided by the minister, uses to effect grace in the recipient. The instructional aspect plays a lesser role here, as does the interior response of the recipient. Modern efforts at understanding sacramental signs seek to revive both the instructional aspect and the dialogical aspect.

(3) *Church Teaching.* Magisterial pronouncements on sacramental signs have turned chiefly to Thomas's understanding of them. Especially typical is a statement of the Council of Florence in its doctrinal Decree for the Armenians: "All these sacraments are constituted by three elements: by things as the matter, by words as the form, and by the person of the minister conferring the sacrament with the intention of doing what the church does" (DS 1312; ND 1307). The striking thing here is that the minister is directly incorporated into the sacramental sign, while the recipient is simply forgotten. When Vatican II describes the sacraments as "sacraments of faith" (SC 59), this "forgetfulness about the recipient" is overcome, and sacramental signs acquire an additional dimension; there is a new awareness of their communicative and interactive character.

(4) *Ecumenical Perspectives.* The Reformers clung strictly and, to some extent, one-sidedly to Augustine's understanding of sacramental signs. A sac-

MINISTER AND RECIPIENT OF THE SACRAMENTS

Sacrament	Minister	Recipient
Baptism	Ordinary ministers of (solemn) baptism are bishops, priests, and deacons; in an emergency anyone can baptize who intends to do what the church does.	Any human being not yet baptized. Of adults faith is to be required, which includes sorrow for past sins.
Confirmation	The original minister is the bishop. Priests to whom authority has been given can be extraordinary ministers.	Any baptized person who has not been confirmed can and should receive confirmation. The state of grace is a necessary presupposition for fruitful reception.
Eucharist	Bishops and priests. Men and women commissioned by the church can distribute the consecrated species.	The baptized who are in the state of grace. Mature Christians celebrate the Eucharist along with the minister. The church allows children who have attained the initial use of reason to receive communion (in the Eastern churches communion is distributed even to newly baptized infants in the form of the wine).
Reconciliation	In addition to the bishop, priests possessing the power of orders and jurisdiction. The first of these is given by ordination; jurisdiction must be given in accordance with the relevant norms of law.	Baptized sinners, who must have attained the use of reason and whose basic condition of life is not contrary to reason's requirements (e.g., persons living in concubinage). The fullness and validity of the sacrament depend on the three acts of the penitent: contrition, confession, and satisfaction, insofar as these acts are possible for them.
Anointing of the sick	Bishops and priests.	The baptized who are in (even in a somewhat remote) danger of death because of illness or the weakness of age. If the person is unconscious, only the probability is required that the Christian would desire, if he or she could, to receive the sacrament with faith.
Orders	The bishop; usually with two coconsecrating bishops when ordaining another bishop. The ordination of a bishop is permitted only by papal mandate.	Baptized males. The degrees of orders can be received only in this sequence: diaconate, presbyterate, episcopate.
Matrimony	Each of the partners is minister to the other. The priest or deacon normally required for validity is simply a designated witness and representative of the church.	Each of the partners receives the sacrament from the other.

rament is a visible word that awakens in the recipient the response of justifying faith. To that extent, the minister and, above all, the recipient play a direct part in the placing of the sacramental sign. Since the Catholic Church, without neglecting other indispensable components, is also once more taking seriously this element of the tradition, there are real points of departure for ecumenical dialogue. Conversely, the Evangelical side must think out anew the importance for faith of (not purely verbal) symbolic interactions (on anthropological as well as other grounds).

(5) *Systematic Reflections.* An important contemporary theological insight is that both the minister and the recipient of the sacrament, together with their interaction, are part of the sacramental sign. The tradition of the faith already makes this clear as far as the minister is concerned. The efficacy of the sacraments does not depend on his orthodoxy and holiness (however much he is called upon to participate with faith); he is the sign of Jesus Christ and his church, who through him effect divine salvation. Recipients are required to participate actively (*actuosa participatio*), thereby giving expression not only to their interior encounter with Jesus Christ but also to their membership in the body of Christ. All this takes place in the sacramental sign in the narrower sense. For it is important to observe that the sacramental signs (except in the case of emergency baptism) have for their setting the liturgy, which again brings out that these signs are dialogical, mediations of a salvation that includes the community, and at the same time acts of divine worship. The following contribute to the sacramental sign: (*a*) a material sign (except in reconciliation and marriage), for example, water, oil, bread; (*b*) use of the material element in a contextualized action (e.g., washing, anointing), whereby the effectiveness of the sign is intensified (e.g., purification, strengthening); (*c*) the meaning of the overall action (e.g., a meal as expression of festivity, joy, and communion); (*d*) definition of the action by words (formula of administration); the action is thus made transparent in relation to Christ and his saving work in all the dimensions of time. All the sacraments efficaciously symbolize: (*a*) the encounter with Christ and his saving work in the past, today, and at the consummation, and, as a result, a new or intensified union with God and God's salvation; (*b*) a new unity among human beings, peace (that extends to the whole of creation), love, acceptance (in the form also of forgiving love), meaning, consolation, and hope that reaches beyond death. In addition, the particular signs of the several sacraments are related to special aspects of salvation. In summary: sacraments effect salvation by symbolizing it. God uses the "natural" meaning of the symbols, but over and above this effects salvation in those who give the response of receptive faith.

See also HYLOMORPHISM; SACRAMENT.

Bibliography
Ganoczy, Alexandre. *An Introduction to Catholic Sacramental Theology.* New York: Paulist, 1984.
Rahner, Karl. *The Church and the Sacraments.* New York: Herder and Herder, 1963.
———. "Theology of Symbol." In *Theological Investigations,* 4:221–52. Baltimore: Helicon, 1966.
Schillebeeckx, Edward. *Christ, the Sacrament of Encounter with God.* New York: Sheed and Ward, 1963.

GÜNTER KOCH

Sacramental Theology. Under this heading is included not only the teaching on the sacraments in general and in particular, but also, and even more, the theoretical scientific question of the relation between a dogmatic reflection on the sacraments and other theological disciplines, of the place of this sector within dogmatics as a whole, and of the internal structuring of a dogmatic reflection on the sacraments.

(1) *Biblical Background.* The Bible speaks only of the individual sacraments and this in specific contexts; accordingly, only the ultimate foundations of a doctrine and theology of the sacraments are provided.

(2) *History of Theology.* Until the Middle Ages, only individual sacraments or groups of sacraments, especially the SACRAMENTS OF INITIATION, were discussed, in a variety of contexts. Once the concept of a sacrament was developed, there was discussion not only of the individual sacraments (*de sacramentis in specie*) but also of the sacraments generally (*de sacramentis in genere*); the foundation was thus laid for the later distinction between general and special sacramental teaching. Once dogmatics (DOGMATIC THEOLOGY) became part of the scientific Scholastic enterprise, the doctrine and theology of the sacraments were introduced as a special treatise; however, there has been until the present only the beginnings of a theoretical scientific reflection on the (material) doctrine and theology of the sacraments, or no such reflection at all. In the traditional dogmatics of the schools the doctrine and theology of the sacraments have occupied a relatively large place (as much as a third).

(3) *Church Teaching.* Like dogmatics in general, the doctrine and theology of the sacraments are prescribed for all ecclesiastically approved courses of theological studies.

(4) *Ecumenical Perspectives.* In the outlines of systematic theology that are followed by the churches of the Reformation, the sacraments recognized in those churches have a quite variable place. A theoretical scientific reflection on the decisions thus made has, here again, begun only recently. The same is true of theology in the Eastern churches. It can be said that reciprocal stimuli are definitely at work here.

(5) *Systematic Reflections.* (a) The dogmatic theology of the sacraments stands in an especially close relationship with fundamental theology, on the one hand, and pastoral theology, moral theology, canon law, and liturgical science, on the other; dogmatic sacramental theology exercises a critical function in relation to all of these. But the relationship is also reciprocal (see table). (b) Today the doctrine and theology of the sacraments are usually seen as closely connected with ecclesiology. K. Rahner even regards general sacramental theology as an intrinsic part of ecclesiology. He would assign the individual sacraments to various locations within an "anthropology of the life of the redeemed who live in the church." The German bishops' *Plan of Priestly Formation* (1978) lines the treatises up this way:

- Ecclesiology
- Doctrine of the sacraments
- Doctrine of grace

In this lineup it is necessary to consider also the intrinsic connection between the doctrine and theology of the sacraments and the other dogmatic treatises (especially Christology and soteriology, as well as eschatology). In the *Mysterium salutis* enterprise, sacramental theology is integrated, on the one hand, into ecclesiology (sacraments in general, Eucharist, marriage, sacrament of orders) and, on the other, into eschatology in the section entitled "Interim Period and Consummation of the History of Salvation" (baptism, confirmation, penance, anointing of the sick). In locating sacramental theology it must be kept in mind that the various criteria used in fitting the sacraments in do not permit any completely convincing combinations. (*c*) In regard to the internal structuring of a separate treatise on sacramental theology the question arises whether general sacramental theology is correctly placed before the theology of the individual sacraments. Those who adopt this order must be careful not to reduce the specific form and function of the individual sacraments to a common level. In general, in dealing with the individual sacraments, one must not limit oneself to the questions suggested by general sacramental theology but approach each sacrament from the viewpoint of its specific place.

See also CHURCH; SACRAMENTS; SACRAMENTS OF INITIATION.

RELATION BETWEEN DOGMATIC THEOLOGY AND OTHER DISCIPLINES

Fundamental theology	Reflects on the human conditions for the possibility of a sacramental mediation of salvation; e.g., on the significance and efficacy of symbolic action.
Dogmatic sacramental theology	Presents the sacraments, in the light of the sources of the Christian faith, as concrete situational ways in which the church as universal sacrament is realized.
Pastoral theology	Considers how faith and the community of faith can best be developed with the aid of the sacraments and in the conditions of our age.
Moral theology	Considers how individuals and the Christian community need to encounter the sacraments and what norms and impulses the sacraments provide for the moral life.
Canon law	Presents the laws currently governing the sacraments; in the new *CIC* these laws are correlated no longer, as in the past, with the laws governing objects, but with the church's ministry of sanctification. It asks whether the dogmatic theology of the sacraments can entail new juridical consequences.
Liturgical science	Sees the sacraments, in their liturgical setting, as essential parts of the church's worship, inquires into the laws governing their structure and form, and asks whether they do justice to the dogmatic theology of the sacraments.

Bibliography
Ganoczy, Alexandre. *An Introduction to Catholic Sacramental Theology.* New York: Paulist, 1984.
Schillebeeckx, Edward, and Boniface Willems, eds. *The Sacraments in General.* Vol. 31 of *Concilium.* New York: Paulist, 1968.
Vorgrimler, Herbert. *Sacramental Theology.* Collegeville, Minn.: Liturgical Press, 1992.
See also the bibliography under SACRAMENTS.

GÜNTER KOCH

Sacrament of Matrimony. *See* MARRIAGE: SACRAMENT OF.

Sacrament of Orders. The sacrament of orders, one of the seven sacraments of the church, is that by which ministers of the church (bishops, priests, deacons: the three stages of sacramental ordination) are appointed in a sacramental manner to their authorized ministry.

(1) *Biblical Background.* Even if it is not possible to speak of a formal institution of the sacrament of orders by the historical Jesus, the ecclesial ministry that is transmitted by ordination does go back to him: he summoned men to a special kind of following that was not required of all; he gave them — especially the Twelve — a share in his own mission (see Mk 3:13–15; 6:6b–13; Lk 10:1). After the death and resurrection of Jesus, the Twelve (or the Eleven with Matthias chosen to join them) realize that they have received a new authorization, along with other witnesses to the appearances of the risen Jesus, to proclaim him and the redemption that he had accomplished. Paul associates himself with them, for he regards himself as likewise one who saw Christ (see 1 Cor 15:8) and as an apostle chosen by Christ or God (see Rom 1:1). His consciousness of being an apostle finds especially forceful expression in 2 Cor 5:20: "So we are ambassadors for Christ, since God is making his appeal through us; we entreat you on behalf of Christ, be reconciled to God." Here, as elsewhere in the New Testament, the word *hiereus* (priest) is never used to describe the Christian minister. Only the corresponding verb is used by Paul in describing the authorized ministry of preaching as the exercise of a priestly ministry (see Rom 15:16). He evidently did not understand this office in terms of a cultic priesthood or as directly analogous either to the Jewish priesthood or to any pagan priesthood; it was something that had to be understood in the light of Jesus Christ and his eschatological activity. The further development of the New Testament ministry in the apostolic and postapostolic generation took different forms and in the process borrowed from the secular structures of office to be found in the given environment (see the group of seven in Acts 6:1–7; the presbyters of Acts 11:30, etc.; the numerous ministries and charisms in the Pauline communities, which regarded the apostle as their leader). It is hardly possible now to reconstruct this development in detail. We know concretely that in the Pastoral Letters bishops (overseers), deacons, and presbyters (elders) are listed together (1 Tm 3:1–13; 5:17). The manner in which ministry was transmitted is important for the question of the sacrament of orders. We do not

MINISTRY AND APPOINTMENT TO MINISTRY
IN THE NEW TESTAMENT

Development of Ministry	Appointment to Ministry
The disciples, especially the Twelve, share in Jesus' mission of proclaiming the imminent reign of God	Jesus' call to follow him, and sending of the disciples
As apostles, the witnesses to the appearances of the risen Lord, especially the Twelve and Paul, establish the ministerial structure of the church	The appearances of the risen Lord – an immediate call by God or Christ to the office of apostle
Numerous ministries arise in the communities; of these, the ministries of presbyter, bishop, and deacon increasingly stand out	Appointment by the apostles or communities – increasing practice of and transmission by laying on of hands

know whether during this first phase it was transmitted in every instance by a special rite. At an early point we do, however, find in the Acts of the Apostles the rite of laying on of hands, combined with prayer. There was an Old Testament precedent for this (see Nm 8:10; 27:18–20; Dt 34:9); in early Judaism the teachers of the law appointed their students to their office by a laying on of hands. In Acts 6:6 we are told of the appointment of the seven: "They had these men stand before the apostles, who prayed and laid their hands on them." This does not necessarily mean, however, that the imposition of hands was regarded as a sacramental sign in the present-day theological understanding of the term. The Pastoral Letters, however, contain something closer to this last: "Do not neglect the gift that is in you, which was given to you through prophecy with the laying on of hands by the council of elders" (1 Tm 4:14; see 2 Tm 1:6; 1 Tm 5:22). In the rite of the laying on of hands, a gift of interior grace, corresponding to the ministry transmitted, is given in a symbolic manner.

(2) *History of Theology.* Ignatius of Antioch (d. ca. 117) plays an important role in the history of the understanding of ministry and ordination. According to him, in both practice and theory a bishop stands at the head of a large community; around the bishop are a number of priests, who are also joined by deacons. According to the *Apostolic Tradition* of Hippolytus of Rome (d. 235), these three ministries are transmitted by the laying on of hands, with the bishop as sole ordainer. Later on, Rome adopted a rite of ordination in which the laying on of hands and prayer were supplemented by the anointing of the hands and, soon after, also the handing over of sacred vessels (for priests: a paten with bread on it and a chalice containing wine); these further rites even came to be of primary importance. Only in post-Tridentine theology, beginning with R. Bellarmine (d. 1621), did the imposition of hands and prayer come to the fore again as the decisive rite of ordination; as a result, it must be said that in the sacrament of orders a striking change in the sacramental symbolic ac-

tion had occurred. Post-Tridentine theology, in its effort to come to grips with the Reformers' rejection of the sacrament of orders, reflected explicitly on the sacramentality of orders; careful consideration was given to its external sign, its interior grace, and its institution by Christ, which was regarded as having taken place at the Last Supper. From the end of the second century on, the number of ministries and degrees of orders varied (in the sixteenth and seventeenth centuries the subdiaconate was still regarded as a sacrament; even the four "minor orders" could be described as sacraments). The sacramentality of episcopal ordination, on the other hand, had long been controverted; priestly ordination was regarded as the perfect example of the sacrament of orders.

(3) *Church Teaching.* The series of magisterial utterances begins with the doctrinal Decree for the Armenians at the Council of Florence (1438–45) (DS 1326). This decree specified the matter (handing over of the "instruments" proper to each degree of orders), the form (a formula for the transmission of the ministerial power), the minister (a bishop), and the grace-effect ("The effect is an increase of grace so that one may be a suitable minister of Christ" [ND 1705]). The teaching of the Council of Trent (1563) (DS 1763–78) is directed against the Reformers' rejection of the sacrament of orders. In this teaching there is an emphasis on the Latin words *sacerdotium* (priesthood) and *sacerdos* (priest), the Greek equivalents of which are foreign to the New Testament. This emphasis signals the predominance of a cultic priesthood approach to the church's ordained ministries, which are here seen as epitomized in the priesthood (i.e., presbyterate). The priesthood is distinguished by the "power of consecrating and offering the true body and blood of the Lord and of remitting and retaining sins"; it is not reducible to "the bare ministry of preaching the Gospel" (DS 1771; ND 1714). Furthermore, orders is a true sacrament, instituted by Christ, that communicates the Holy Spirit and imprints an indelible character. The ecclesiastical hierarchy consists, by divine ordinance, of bishops, priests, and ministers (deacons). Bishops are superior to priests and distinguished by the power to confirm and ordain (see DS 1776f.). What is principally in view in these statements are questions of the power to govern, but the answer is certainly being given against the background of a sacramental understanding of the three degrees of orders. In 1947 Pius XII decreed that the sole matter of the orders of diaconate, presbyterate, and episcopate is the laying on of hands; the form is the words, in the accompanying preface of consecration, that determine the application of the matter (DS 3859f.). Vatican II came to some important conclusions regarding the sacrament of orders. The following general statement displays emphases that differ from those of Trent: "Those among the faithful who have received Holy Orders are appointed to nourish the Church with the word and grace of God in the name of Christ" (*LG* 11). Chapter 3 of *LG* deals with the hierarchical constitution of the church and especially with the episcopal office. With regard to the degrees of orders it says that "through episcopal consecration, the fullness of the sacrament of Order is conferred" (*LG* 21; ND 1739). By way of ordination this episcopal pleni-

tude is shared by presbyters, who "depend on the bishops in the exercise of their power" (*LG* 28; ND 1740). "At a lower level of the hierarchy stand the deacons, upon whom hands are imposed 'not unto the priesthood, but unto a ministry (of service)'" (*LG* 29; ND 1741). In these several statements the sacramental character of episcopal consecration is settled, and the diaconate is restored as a permanent institution (and not simply a transitional step to priest-hood). All these ministries participate in the threefold ministry or office of Jesus Christ. The laity, too, share in these three offices, but "the common priesthood of the faithful" and "the ministerial or hierarchical priesthood" "differ from one another in essence and not only in degree" (*LG* 10; ND 1738).

(4) *Ecumenical Perspectives.* Once Luther and, in a less brusque manner, Calvin had rejected a distinct sacrament of orders as unbiblical, the Catholic Church and the churches of the Reformation differed and have continued to differ in their understanding not only of the ministry but of the way in which the ministry is transmitted. The churches of the Reformation deny any place to the idea of a succession in the apostolic office (*successio apostolica*), which is essential to the Roman Catholic and Eastern churches' understanding of the ministry and of the church itself. The ecclesiastical ministry is regarded as pri-marily a ministry of preaching; in the Reformed churches it is also a ministry of governance. A certain rapprochement, which has already found expression in various consensus documents, has resulted from the new Catholic emphasis on the element of preaching in the ministry (see *LG* 11) and the new Evangelical understanding of the mission aspect of the ministry, an aspect that cannot have the community as its ultimate source and that at the same time includes an ef-ficacious promise of divine assistance that is possibly to be linked to the rite of ordination. With regard to the degrees of orders, account must be taken of the fact that even in some churches of the Reformation there are not only ordained pastors but an episcopal office. The restoration of the permanent diaconate is a new link to the practice of the Eastern churches.

(5) *Systematic Reflections.* The primary point to be taken seriously is that the New Testament priesthood is not a more perfect continuation of Old Testament–Jewish or pagan priesthood. Rather it is a participation in the of-fices of Jesus Christ. The lack of the word *hiereus* in the New Testament is an indication that the cultic-sacerdotal element should not be described as the unqualifiedly central effect of the sacrament of orders, although, on the other hand, this element, looked upon as a participation in the eschatological high priesthood of Jesus Christ (see Hebrews), should not be ignored. This raises the question, much discussed today, of the principal element in the understand-ing of ministry (service of the word, pastoral office, or "sacerdotal" activity?). The inner unity of priestly service can be seen in the special mission given by Christ (J. Ratzinger): priests (deacons analogously; bishops a fortiori) are "rep-resentatives" of the one who sends them, as well as of those to whom they are sent. The ministry is thus to be defined in light of the comprehensive nature of Christ's "official" mission (G. Greshake); given the situation of the age, it

would seem that the pastoral aspect of the ministry as service of the oneness of the community should be emphasized (W. Kasper). Priesthood, then, is a special, official authorization to make Christ visible and audible as Lord of the church, especially through word and sacrament. In addition, those ordained are authorized by the irreversible call given by ordination (the seal of ordination, or the indelible character of orders), which at the same time is a promise of God's helping grace. The question, also much discussed, of the source of ministry — an immediate mission by Christ or a special participation in the mission of the entire church — is probably to be answered in the form of a synthesis such as G. Greshake offers (a trinitarian synthesis). It might also be said that the ordained are immediately sent by Christ when they are given, in a specific and official way, a participation in the mission of the church. This would make it clear that even the ordained derive their fundamental dignity and "basic spiritual image" from the membership in the church that they share with the other baptized and confirmed, to whom at the same time they officially represent the Lord of the church. There are no dogmatic reasons for the position taken by the Roman Catholic Church in obliging its priests to follow the celibate way of life. The question whether the present-day lack of priests makes some change in this position urgently necessary must remain an open one despite the official rejection of it by the church. The tradition casts a unanimous vote against the ordination of women as priests. The question whether this rejection has a basis in the faith or is simply sociologically conditioned must be answered by the ongoing dialogue of faith within the church. With regard to the degrees of orders, other questions call for further reflection: Are priests simply representatives of the bishop and participants in his fullness of ministry, or are they also independent representatives of Christ the shepherd and head (see *LG* 28)? How does the college of presbyters share, in principle and in practice, in the government of a diocese? What authority to lead does the bishop have in virtue of his ordination, and what in virtue of a special conferral of jurisdiction? What is the specific character of the deacons in relation to presbyters but also in relation to lay ministers in the church?

See also APOSTOLIC SUCCESSION; BISHOP; DEACON; MINISTRY IN THE CHURCH; OFFICES OF JESUS CHRIST; PRIEST; PRIESTHOOD OF THE FAITHFUL; SACRAMENTAL SIGN.

Bibliography
Donovan, Daniel. *What Are They Saying about the Ministerial Priesthood?* Mahwah, N.J.: Paulist, 1992.
Ganoczy, Alexandre. *An Introduction to Catholic Sacramental Theology.* New York: Paulist, 1984.
Mitchell, Nathan. *Mission and Ministry: History and Theology in the Sacrament of Order.* Wilmington, Del.: Glazier, 1982.
Poschmann, Bernhard. *Penance and the Anointing of the Sick.* New York: Herder and Herder, 1964.
Power, David N. *The Christian Priest: Elder and Prophet.* London: Sheed and Ward, 1973.

———. *Ministers of Christ and His Church: The Theology of the Priesthood.* London: Chapman, 1969.

Vorgrimler, Herbert. *Sacramental Theology.* Collegeville, Minn.: Liturgical Press, 1992.

GÜNTER KOCH

Sacrament of Reconciliation.

The sacrament of reconciliation is one of the seven sacraments of the church; in it reconciliation takes sacramental form, that is, sinful human beings are reconciled with God and at the same time with the church and thus receive forgiveness of their sins.

(1) *Biblical Background.* According to the New Testament, Jesus himself forgave sins (see Mt 9:2; Mk 2:5), while at the same time he called his listeners to penance, to a complete conversion, a radical change of mind (see Mk 1:15). According to Matthew, John, and Paul, the post-Easter church believed that the power of Jesus to forgive sins had passed to the Christian communities or their representatives. In Mt 16:19 the Lord grants Peter a power to bind and loose that is valid even in heaven. He grants the same power to the entire community in Mt 18:18. In this context we already find (vv. 15–18) an early Christian penitential process as part of the rules given for the community in Matthew 18. This penitential process, which displays stages of correction, ends, should all else fail, in the exclusion, valid in God's sight, of sinners from the community, but also allows for their restoration ("loosing"), which is likewise valid in God's sight. A similar authority is given to the disciples in Jn 20:23: "Whose sins you forgive, they are forgiven them; whose sins you retain, they are retained." A corresponding penitential process is also attested for the Pauline communities. Speaking of one guilty of unchaste behavior, Paul urges the community: "Expel the evildoer from your midst!" (see 1 Cor 5:9–13). Under what might be called the internal guidance of Paul the community is to pronounce this sentence of exclusion, so as "to hand this person over to Satan for the destruction of his flesh, in order that his spirit may be saved on the day of the Lord" (1 Cor 5:3–5). Here again, the exclusion has at the same time a medicinal character (see 2 Cor 2:5–11): as the New Testament sees it, the sinner is to be saved and reconciled, although this hope may not always be made fully clear. A motive for exclusion that is at least equally important in the New Testament is the protection of the holiness of the community, which the sinner has wounded. These New Testament roots of the sacrament of reconciliation have a marked ecclesial character: sin and the forgiveness of sin deeply affect the community, and the community itself takes an active part in the appropriate penitential process.

(2) *History of Theology.* The history of the sacrament of reconciliation is characterized by profound changes and is rich in aspects and perspectives. It can be presented schematically only in a greatly simplified form. The most important distinction to be made is between the "canonical ecclesiastical penance" of the early church and the "tariff penance" with private confession that took over from the sixth century on. It is to be noted, finally, that in the Eastern

Church the sacrament of reconciliation developed in ways significantly different from the Western Church. Beginning with Tertullian at the end of the second century we have clear evidence of canonical penance, a process in which the community continued to be involved, even though the decisive functions had passed into the hands of the church's ministers. This ecclesiastical penance was provided only for very serious sins (apostasy, murder, adultery) and was allowed only once in a lifetime. The confession of sins to the bishop and, in a more general form, to the community was followed by an often very lengthy period of penance during which severe penances were imposed that in certain circumstances might be lifelong. Once the period of penance was completed, the penitent was received back into the community by the laying on of the hands of bishop or presider. Here again the community participated through their intercession. The conviction was that reconciliation with the community meant reconciliation with God and forgiveness by God ("peace with the church = peace with God" [pax cum ecclesia = pax cum Deo]). In the course of time, the severity of ecclesiastical penance caused people not to receive this sacrament until the last possible moment before death. "Tariff penance," which originated in the Irish–Anglo-Saxon world and, despite resistance, came to be accepted throughout the entire Western part of the church, provided for repeated absolution. Penitential books set down detailed forms of satisfaction to be imposed on the penitent in each specific circumstance. Many abuses became common in the fulfillment of these penances. Out of tariff penance, meanwhile, there developed the type of private confession familiar to us, in which severe penances were replaced by simpler, more hidden ones. The confession of sins now became the crucial act of the sacrament of reconciliation. In the East, meanwhile, private confession to a spiritual director (usually a monk who did not have to be a priest) became a common practice, alongside ecclesiastical penance, by the end of the fourth century. Theological discussion of the sacrament of reconciliation among the Scholastics centered on such questions as, for example, whether absolution by a priest is the basis for removal of guilt before God. Thomas Aquinas said that it is, but he also introduced into his answer the earlier insight into the power of contrition to wipe sins away: true contrition (he says) involves a desire for the sacrament and, in this way, wipes away sins.

(3) *Church Teaching.* The theology of Thomas Aquinas became part of the church's teaching. The Council of Florence (Decree for the Armenians [1439]) regards the acts of the penitent — contrition, confession, satisfaction — as the "quasi-matter" of the sacrament; "the form ... is the words of absolution spoken by the priest.... The effect ... is absolution from sins" (DS 1323; ND 1612). In response to the (quite varied) attacks of the Reformers on the sacrament of penance the Council of Trent (in 1551) developed a comprehensive "Doctrine on the Sacrament of Penance" as well as fifteen canons (DS 1667–93 and 1701–15) that had a decisive influence on the subsequent period. The following statements, given in an abbreviated form, are especially important:

- The sacrament of penance (reconciliation) is a sacrament instituted by Christ and may be repeated (DS 1701).

- The church possesses a real power to forgive and retain sins (DS 1703).

- Even what is called imperfect contrition is a preparation for reception of the sacrament (DS 1705).

- Only sacramental confession to a priest fulfills Christ's command and was "instituted... by divine law" (DS 1706).

- It is necessary "by divine law" to confess each and all mortal sins in the sacrament of penance (DS 1707).

- Christians are obliged to confess their (serious) sins once a year (DS 1708).

- The sacramental absolution given by a priest is an efficacious judicial act and not a mere ministry of declaring forgiveness (DS 1709).

- Priests alone possess the power (even if they are in the state of mortal sin) to bind and loose (DS 1710).

- The entire punishment is not always remitted by God along with the sin (DS 1712).

In this teaching the ecclesial (social) dimension of sin and penance was largely lost. It comes to the fore again in Vatican II: "Those who approach the sacrament of penance obtain pardon from the mercy of God for their offences committed against Him. They are, at the same time, reconciled with the church whom they have wounded by their sin, and who, by her charity, her example and her prayer, collaborates in their conversion" (LG 11; ND 1667). The recovery of the communal aspect of sin and forgiveness is also reflected in the new Rite of Penance (1973); the formula of absolution, after referring to God's saving action, goes on to say: "May He grant you pardon and peace through the ministry of the Church. And I absolve you..." (ND 1671). The rite provides for three ways of celebrating the sacrament of reconciliation:

- Celebration of reconciliation of individual penitents.

- Celebration of reconciliation of several penitents with individual confession and individual absolution.

- Celebration of reconciliation of several penitents with general confession and general sacramental absolution. In this case, each individual must confess his or her sins when opportunity offers.

In his apostolic exhortation on reconciliation and penance (*Reconciliatio et Paenitentia* [1984]), John Paul II gives renewed approval to the rite but very firmly insists that the third form be used only by way of exception and in difficult pastoral circumstances (to be judged by the bishop).

(4) *Ecumenical Perspectives.* The various Reformers differed in their attitude to the sacrament of reconciliation. They did not want it to be considered
a sacrament, but Luther retained confession, even for himself. He understood
it as a testimony to the justifying and forgiving grace of God in response to
the personal confession of sins, for which no special authorization is required.
This kind of individual confession is once again being practiced today in many
Evangelical circles. In ecumenical dialogue it is necessary on both sides to take
into account the ecclesial dimension of sin and the forgiveness of sin. On the
Catholic side, greater emphasis should be placed on the analogical nature of
the judicial character of the sacrament of reconciliation: the act is an authoritative assertion of grace and thus in fact a "ministry of the church" in rendering
present the Christ who forgives sins.

(5) *Systematic Reflections.* There is no denying that the practice of individual confession has fallen on hard times. There are various reasons for this. In
this area systematic theology is engaged in the following tasks and can devote
even greater energy to them:

- Relating the sacrament of reconciliation to the properly understood penitential character of Christian life.

- Seeking a synthesis of the private and the ecclesial aspects of reconciliation
  and penance.

- Showing possibilities of further development of the sacrament of reconciliation in light of our present knowledge of the range of historical forms it
  has taken.

The forgiveness of sins and reconciliation do not take place only in the sacrament of reconciliation. The grace-supported conversion of the person to God
that occurs once and fundamentally, in baptism, in every Christian life must
become a basic determinant of that life. This existential fulfillment of baptism as a thankful acceptance of God's forgiveness and of reconciliation with
other human beings takes numerous forms. The sacrament of reconciliation is
one way that is very helpful and, in the case of serious sin, necessary. God's
forgiveness can certainly be given directly in response to every act of "perfect" contrition, but the social aspect of all sin requires the participation of the
church (which again can take many forms) and, in the case of mortal sin, the
sacrament of reconciliation. Many theologians consider peace with the church
to be the effective sign (*sacramentum et res*) of peace with God. Admittedly,
the definitions of the Council of Trent hardly seem to allow any further major
developments in addition to individual confession. But a proper interpretation
of the Tridentine decrees must take into account the apologetic intentions of
the council. In the view of not a few theologians, a confession that is as concrete as possible while remaining general would satisfy the requirements of the
council and thus permit a truly communal celebration of the sacrament. Here,
of course, pastoral considerations must also play a decisive role.

See also ABSOLUTION; CHURCH; CONFESSION; CONTRITION; PENANCE; SIN AND GUILT.

Bibliography
Dallen, James. *The Reconciling Community: The Rite of Penance.* New York: Pueblo, 1986.
Fink, Peter, ed. *Reconciliation.* Vol. 4 of *Alternative Futures for Worship.* Collegeville, Minn.: Liturgical Press, 1987.
Ganoczy, Alexandre. *An Introduction to Catholic Sacramental Theology.* New York: Paulist, 1984.
Gula, Richard. *To Walk Together: The Sacrament of Reconciliation.* New York: Paulist, 1984.
Kennedy, Robert, ed. *Reconciliation: The Continuing Agenda.* Collegeville, Minn.: Liturgical Press, 1987.
Neunheuser, Burkhard. *Baptism and Confirmation.* New York: Herder and Herder, 1964.
Rahner, Karl. "Forgotten Truths concerning the Sacrament of Penance." In *Theological Investigations,* 2:135–74. Baltimore: Helicon, 1963.
Schillebeeckx, Edward, ed. *Sacramental Reconciliation.* Vol. 61 of *Concilium.* New York: Herder and Herder, 1971.

GÜNTER KOCH

Sacraments

Contemporary Issues

A proper understanding of sacraments requires that a doctrinal approach, which examines sacraments as vehicles of grace entrusted by Christ to the church, be complemented by one that recognizes them to be liturgical actions of the church as well. This requirement stems from three sources: a newfound appreciation of the link between the law of faith and the law of prayer ("Ut lex orandi statuit legem credendi" [Prosper of Aquitane]); the 1983 Code of Canon Law, which treats sacraments under the heading "The Sanctifying Mission of the Church"; and especially Vatican II's Constitution on the Sacred Liturgy (*SC*), which presents a rich vision of the church at prayer and includes within its scope all of the church's sacraments.

SC locates the origin of sacraments within the unfolding plan of God, whose desire to sanctify the human race issued forth in the incarnation of God's Son. Sent by the Father and anointed by the Spirit, Jesus had the mission of proclaiming the good news of God's constant and transforming love. To this mission he was faithful even unto death. Jesus' death on the cross not only was that act of the God-man that broke the bonds of sin and death and established a new covenant between God and humanity but was also the birth of the church: "For it was from the side of Christ as he slept the sleep of death upon the cross that there came forth the wondrous sacrament of the whole Church" (*SC* 5). Empowered with the Spirit sent by the Father at the Son's request, the church has been given the mandate to continue Christ's saving work until he comes again.

Sacraments are those actions of the church, and of Christ in the church, by which the saving work of Christ continues to unfold in human life and history (SC 6). The agency of Christ is primary: "Christ, indeed, always associates the Church with himself in this great work in which God is perfectly glorified and men and women are sanctified" (SC 7). Yet this action of Christ continues to take human form in and through the action of the church. Every liturgical celebration is, of its very nature, "an action of Christ the Priest and of his Body, which is the Church" (ibid.). The human form of sacraments is determined by, and in turn determines, the effect that Christ wishes to bring about in those who enact them. Sacraments are signs that are perceptible to the senses, and as human signs each has its own meaning and dynamic. Yet through these signs human sanctification is made manifest, and in ways proper to each of these signs human sanctification is brought about (ibid.).

Sacraments are effective for human sanctification, and the mode of their effectiveness is related to their nature as signifying actions. The human actions that comprise the church's sacraments signify the action of Christ in human life, and by signifying they achieve their effects. Sacraments involve participants in a world of images that are presented to human consciousness and that carry with them specific affections, which in turn call forth specific human behavior. When images of God, of oneself, and of others are rooted in the revelation of Jesus Christ, the affections that are proper to those images are the affections of Christ himself, and the behavior they summon forth is the behavior that shaped Christ's own life. Sacraments also involve participants in the Christlike behavior itself. In the liturgical action, the church not only listens in the liturgy of the word to God's revelation about a particular aspect of human life but also enacts that revelation in response to the word proclaimed. Both the images presented through Scripture and the behavior enacted in response appeal to the human heart to be converted to the affections that are proper to both.

Sacraments are indeed vehicles of God's grace. Grace, however, does not impose itself upon the human heart, but is always and only a free offer of God's own self to the human person. The offer of grace respects human freedom and can therefore present itself only in the form of an appeal. Conversion of heart is the human response to that appeal.

SC offers a threefold purpose for the celebration of sacraments. They are transforming actions that aim to "sanctify men and women" (SC 59). They are formative actions that aim to "build up the Body of Christ" (ibid.). And they are prayerful actions that engage the church in Christ's own prayer to the Father and thus "give worship to God" (ibid.). Through the proclamation of Scripture and the various actions and prayers that follow, sacraments have a teaching function (ibid.), and by engaging participants fully and actively in their ritual enactment, sacraments take the faith that the participants already have, and that the sacraments themselves presuppose and express, and nourish and deepen it. As liturgical actions, however, sacraments require the full and active participation by all of the faithful for their effectiveness to be true.

Doctrinal theology has been content to view sacraments in terms of the proper minister and the recipient, with little regard for the assembled church that enacts the sacramental ritual. This in turn has fostered a minimalist view of sacraments looking only to what was required for valid and licit celebration. The prayers and actions of the assembled church were not included as essential to the celebration, and the minister's role as presider over the church's prayer was not attended to.

SC is clear that all sacraments are communal actions requiring the full and active participation by all of the faithful and that through such participation all of the faithful are effected when sacraments are celebrated (*SC* 14). Indeed, the communal celebration of sacraments is considered normative. As liturgical actions, sacraments are not private functions, but are celebrations belonging to the church—the holy people united and ordered under their bishops (*SC* 26). Sacraments involve the whole church and have effects on the whole church. Preference is therefore given to communal celebrations of sacraments over forms that are private or semiprivate (ibid.).

Doctrinal theology considers the minister of the sacrament, in all cases except marriage and emergency baptism, to be a bishop, priest, or deacon empowered and designated as such through ordination. Liturgical theology must consider that in any sacrament there are many ministers and many ministries, and that, even in the case of marriage, the bishop, priest, or deacon serves first and foremost as presider of the liturgical assembly. In such capacity, the bishop, priest, or deacon serves in the person of Christ and addresses prayers to God in the name of the whole church and of all present (*SC* 33). Doctrinal theology also considers the recipient of the sacrament and the effects of the sacrament on, for example, the one baptized, ordained, or absolved. Liturgical theology must ask about the effect of the sacrament on the whole assembled body and must consider the *recipient* as likewise performing a ministry to the assembled body. There are no spectators at the church's sacraments.

In the sacraments of the church Christ continues his saving action in the world. In order to do this, Christ is himself present and active within the liturgical celebrations of the church. Each sacramental ritual is an action of the assembled church, and this assembly of the church is already a mode of Christ's presence. Each sacramental ritual begins with the proclamation of the word, and this too is a mode of Christ's presence: "It is he himself who speaks when the holy Scriptures are read in the Church" (*SC* 7). Christ is also present in the person and ministry of the presiding priest such that, for example, "when anybody baptizes it is really Christ himself who baptizes" (ibid.). And while Christ is uniquely present in the Eucharist in the form of consecrated bread and wine, a mode of presence that has no equal in the other sacraments, in each of the other sacraments there is an analogous transformation into Christ that needs to be recognized. Both baptism and orders involve a conformity to Christ identified as the sacramental character. Marriage involves a transformation of two persons into an intimate unity that is grounded in, and that in turn portrays, the unity of Christ and the church. The absolution of penance and reconciliation restores baptismal conformity to Christ, and the anointing of the sick transforms illness from sickness unto death to sickness unto new life in Christ.

At the heart of all of the sacraments is their relationship to the saving action of Jesus Christ carried out once for all upon the cross. The cross is the final surrender of Christ in obedience to the Father. In the person of Jesus, humanity itself is offered to the Father in a total act of love. The cross is also the Father's acceptance of Jesus' total obedience: "Into your hands I commit my spirit" (Luke 23:46); "Therefore God has highly exalted him" (Phil 2:9). In the person of Jesus humanity is embraced in a new covenant of love by God. The Holy Spirit, sent by the Father at Jesus' own request (Jn 14:16), is that embrace of love, the transforming action of God unleashed into the world "to complete his work on earth and bring us the fullness of grace" (eucharistic prayer 4).

The mystery of the cross, which includes within itself the exaltation of Christ by the Father and the sending of the Spirit into the world, comes to expression in the church's sacraments and is itself the source of their saving power. SC puts it succinctly: it is "through the liturgy, especially, that the faithful are able to express in their lives and manifest to others the mystery of Christ and the real nature of the true Church" (SC 2). The Eucharist is most clearly the sacrament of Christ's sacrifice, and the doctrinal tradition in Catholic theology has given ample notice of this fact. A liturgical theology of sacraments is invited to expand this sacrificial theme and explore it as the inner nature of all of the church's sacraments. It is this mystery, present as the inner truth of all sacraments, that gives them both their essential liturgical structure and indeed their own sanctifying power.

The mystery of Christ has as a first essential element the initiative of God. It is to this initiative, which is the mandate of the incarnation, that Jesus was totally obedient. In the sacraments this initiative is always expressed by the liturgy of the word. The remaining elements of the mystery of Christ, namely, the obedience of Christ, the exaltation of Christ by the Father, and the formation of the church through the sending of the Spirit, come to expression in the three essential parts of the eucharistic liturgy: offering, consecration, and communion. In the offering, which is explicitly expressed as the anamnesis of the eucharistic prayer (e.g., "In memory of his death and resurrection we offer . . . " [eucharistic prayer 2]), and which is still the inner core of the presentation of gifts (intercession, collection, offering of bread and wine), the mystical body of Christ, head and members, enacts once again that obedience that governed Jesus' whole life and sealed the sacrifice of his death. In the consecration, which is the transforming action of God directed not only to the food but to the church, the exaltation of Christ, again head and members, is ritually expressed. And in the communion, which is prayed for in the eucharistic prayer in the second epiclesis (e.g., "May all of us who share in the body and blood of Christ be brought together in unity by the Holy Spirit" [also eucharistic prayer 2]), and which is enacted in the actual partaking of the eucharistic food, the sending of the Spirit to transform the church and indeed to transform the whole of creation is brought to ritual expression. In word, offering, consecration, and communion the mystery of Christ is expressed, the saving work of Christ is made present, and the fruit of Christ's own sacrifice is unfolded in the life of those who participate.

This same mystery of Christ comes to expression for those who are entering the church in the sacraments of initiation (baptism, confirmation or chrismation, and Eucharist) and constitutes the inner unity that exists among the three. Christian initiation begins with an action of God exciting in the person a desire to enter the church. This action of God, named in doctrinal theology "prevenient grace," has as its first response an approach to the church in the form of inquiry. When the process of initiation begins formally, this action of God remains in the forefront, presented now in all its details in the books of Scripture that guide the catechumens. The catechumenate is a prolonged liturgy of the word, a process that continues until the next action of God and the church calls the catechumens to the Easter sacraments. The analogue of offering, consecration, and communion is found in the sacraments of baptism, confirmation, and first Eucharist.

The water bath of baptism is the sacrament of communion with Christ. Entrance into the water and emersion from it is the primary symbol through which the person enters into the dying and rising of Christ (Paul) and is born again into the life of the risen Christ (John). By such union with Christ the spiritual deficiency that is original sin is removed, and, in accordance with the prophecy of Ezekiel and Jeremiah, God's own heart is placed within us. Within the sequence of the initiation sacraments, baptism represents the offering of a human life with Christ to the Father. The life of the baptized is placed into the obedient offering of Christ.

In the discipline of the church, two patterns of initiation stand side by side. When infants are baptized, the act takes on the tones of promise on the part of the parents, sponsors, and indeed the whole community of the church. The gathered assembly renews its own baptismal commitment by professing its faith, and it is into that faith that the child is baptized. The promise made by all is to pass on to the child the faith of the church into which he or she is baptized. Though confirmation and first Eucharist are usually not administered to infants in the West, the prayer and gesture of the postbaptismal anointing serve to express both the element of consecration and the fact of communion that the remaining initiation sacraments contain: "The God of power and the Father of our Lord Jesus Christ has freed you from sin and brought you to new life through water and the Holy Spirit [offering]. He now anoints you with the chrism of salvation [consecration], so that, united with his people [communion], you may remain forever a member of Christ." In the pattern employed for adults, unless pastoral reasons suggest otherwise, these are confirmed and admitted to first Eucharist at the time of baptism.

Liturgical theology can shed some light on an issue that doctrinal theology could not resolve. Unlike the churches of the East, which employ chrismation or confirmation as the only postbaptismal anointing, the West inherited the anomaly of two anointings. In attempts to understand the difference, Western theology named the postbaptismal anointing within the baptismal ritual as anointing into the priesthood of Christ, with the anointing of confirmation considered to be the anointing of the Spirit. The distinction was at best tenuous. When seen through the lens of liturgical theology, this distinction becomes even more questionable. While the two anointings remain in force in the case of infant baptism, when an adult is confirmed immediately after baptism the postbaptismal anointing is omitted. The suggestion is that this first anointing within the baptismal rite is rendered unnecessary when confirmation itself is conferred.

The traditions of both East and West illustrate that within the unity of the initiation sacraments it is necessary to employ an anointing associated with the water bath of baptism. However it is interpreted, this anointing carries with it God's response to the obedience of Christ. The transformation and exaltation of Christ are offered to those who are baptized into Christ. A separate gesture is required because the gift of the transforming Spirit is a response to Christ's obedient death freely made by the God who raised Jesus to new life. The action of baptism is something that the church does. The church places a human life within the mystery of Christ. The action of the anointing is, in contrast, something that the church receives. God sends the Holy Spirit upon the church and places God's own heart within the baptized.

For the newly baptized, their baptism and anointing are echoed within the Eucharist in which they participate for the first time. Their initiation is brought into the presentation of gifts, and their own transformation into Christ is renewed in the consecration of the eucharistic food. First Eucharist completes the initiation sacraments by establishing communion in Christ with the people of the church. Henceforth every eucharistic celebration will renew the fullness of their baptism, confirmation, and first Eucharist.

The mystery of Christ governs the two sacraments of healing, the sacrament of reconciliation and the anointing of the sick. In each of these as well the initiative of God that guided Jesus' own life is brought forward in the liturgy of the word. In reconciliation, God's interpretation of sin is set forth. In God's eyes sin is already forgiven and disharmony is already reconciled. Thus penitents are invited to set in motion the fullness of the Christ mystery by placing even their sins into the offering of Christ. Confession, in whatever form the acknowledgment of one's sins may take, is a particular expression of one's baptism: all of human life is placed with Christ in his offering to the Father. Even one's sin can become matter for worship. The words of absolution are effective words that transform sin into nonsin. The forgiveness of God offered to the sinner who confesses is a particular expression of that anointing that claimed the baptized for God.

In its earliest form, the sacrament of reconciliation concluded with the restoration of the sinner to the communion of the church. Restoration to Eucharist was its proper completion. Only later, when participation in the Eucharist lost the tones of communion with others in Christ and became more the baptismal communion with Christ, did the sacrament of reconciliation change as well. Then it became an act that had to be carried out before participation in the Eucharist; no longer was participation in the Eucharist its proper completion. The postconciliar reform has brought us closer to restoring the Eucharist as the fullness of the sacrament of penance at least by coupling the note of reconciliation with the note of forgiveness. These are not precisely the same thing. Forgiveness marks the decision of God in relation to the sinner; reconciliation with the church follows from this. In regard to sin, then, the mystery of Christ unfolds as confession (offering), absolution and forgiveness (consecration), and reconciliation with the church (communion).

In the sacrament of the sick the mystery of Christ unfolds in a similar vein. This sacrament, however, is presented as more than a liturgical act. It is offered as a rich pattern of pastoral care. While the hope presented in the Scripture is for healing, possibly physical but in any case spiritual, the deeper message presented by God through the ministry of many caregivers is *companionship*. The person who is sick is cared for by God. The ritual does not offer any explicit act of offering or surrender in an act of worship of God. This is, however, the silent aim of the sacramental act, that the person who is sick join this sickness and the possible journey to death that it may involve, to his or her baptismal gift with Christ to God (offering). Sickness is a manifestation of the fragility of life, and yet even in its fragility this human life belongs to God. The anointing expresses this claim of God once again (consecration), and while the oil has the nature of soothing balm, it also serves to reenact in the midst of human fragility the promise of transformation and exaltation first enacted through the postbaptismal chrismation or confirmation. Within the mystery of Christ the aim of this sacrament too is union with the church (communion), either restoration to the church on earth or passage to the communion of saints in heaven.

This same ritual movement is enacted once again when some of the baptized are selected for the ministerial priesthood of the ordained. Though the prayers differ for deacon, presbyter, and bishop to specify the distinctions of ministry within the sacrament of orders, the essential movement is the same for each. By their own willingness and by the consent of the assembled church, candidates for orders are presented (offering) to the presiding bishop for ordination. By the laying on of hands and the solemn prayer of consecration, the transforming Spirit is invoked upon the person that the person be empowered for ministry and faithful in the ministry that the church will assign (consecration). The ordained deacon, priest, or bishop, who is taken from among the faithful of the church for sacred duties, is then reunited to the church in the ministerial relationship (communion).

A rich theology of marriage emerges when this sacrament too is viewed as an act of the whole church bringing the mystery of Christ to expression. Doctrinal

theology has been content to see in the exchange of marriage vows the administration of this sacrament by the married couple themselves. In this the West
has understood marriage differently from the East, where the blessing of the
couple by the priest is taken to be the sacramental act. Liturgical theology must
begin with the sacrament of marriage as a liturgical act of the church and recognize the place of the bride and groom, of the deacon, priest, or bishop presider,
and indeed of the whole assembly. The aim of this sacrament is to establish
the newly married couple as a sacrament of Christ's relationship to his church.
This ministry of the couple to the whole church is, like the ministry of the ordained, a new relationship to the church itself (communion), and it too requires
an offering and a consecration. The exchange of wedding vows is in fact a presentation of the love of husband and wife to Christ and a uniting of that love
with Christ's own love of Abba. But the assembled church is not present simply
to witness this act; the assembly joins with the bride and groom in this act of
presentation (offering). The nuptial blessing emerges as a far more significant
act than its current placement as an embolism to the Lord's Prayer would suggest. It is a solemn blessing upon the husband and wife that their own human
love may faithfully become for the church a sign of the union of Christ and the
church. "Christ abundantly blesses this love. He has already consecrated you
in baptism and now he enriches and strengthens you by a special sacrament"
(ritual of marriage, introduction). The liturgy links the baptismal consecration
with the action of Christ blessing this love (consecration).

By bringing the mystery of Christ to ritual expression, all sacraments, though
each in different ways, present to human life the saving action of Jesus Christ.
Through the sacraments as liturgical acts "the work of our redemption is accomplished" (SC 2). This work of our redemption consists always and only
in our being united to Christ in his own perfect offering of self to Abba, and
receiving in return that life-giving and transforming Spirit through which Jesus
was raised from the dead and established as firstborn of the church. Union with
Christ in his offering is union with Christ in the consecration with which God
transformed him. It is likewise a union in Christ (communion) of all who believe and are united both in sacrament and in fact to the person of Jesus Christ.
The sacramental life of the church consists in this, constantly to renew the saving mystery of Christ in the lives of its members and through such renewal
constantly to renew the church itself.

Bibliography
Duffy, Regis. "Sacraments in General," "Baptism and Confirmation," "Penance," and
    "Anointing of the Sick." In *Systematic Theology: Roman Catholic Perspectives,* edited by
    Francis Schüssler Fiorenza and John P. Galvin, 2:181–211. Minneapolis: Fortress, 1991.
Fink, Peter E. *The New Dictionary of Sacramental Worship.* Collegeville, Minn.: Liturgical
    Press, 1990.
———. "Three Languages of Christian Sacraments." *Worship* 52 (1978) 561–75.
———. *Worship: Prayer and the Sacraments.* Washington, D.C.: Pastoral Press, 1991.
Lee, Bernard, ed. *Alternative Futures for Worship.* 7 vols. Collegeville, Minn.: Liturgical
    Press, 1987.

Power, David. "Eucharist" and "Order." In *Systematic Theology: Roman Catholic Perspectives,* edited by Francis Schüssler Fiorenza and John P. Galvin, 2:259–304. Minneapolis: Fortress, 1991.

———. *Worship: Culture and Theology.* Washington, D.C.: Pastoral Press, 1990.

See also the bibliography under SACRAMENT.

PETER E. FINK, S.J.

Sacraments: Institution of. *See* INSTITUTION OF THE SACRAMENTS.

Sacraments as Seven in Number. Implicit in the words "seven in number" is the question whether and in what sense it is a matter of Catholic faith that there are no more and no fewer than seven sacraments, despite the fact that the determination of seven came only at a relatively late point in history.

(1) *Biblical Background.* The New Testament does not recognize the sacraments as being seven in number, any more than it uses the term *sacrament* for those symbolic actions effective of grace that are later designated by this name. It does indeed bear material witness to all seven sacraments, but no distinction is made between these and other symbolic actions (e.g., the washing of feet).

(2) *History of Theology.* Whereas Augustine (for instance) generally applies the cultic concept of sacrament only to baptism and the Eucharist, it was extended in the early Middle Ages to the other sacraments and to various anointings insofar as these were parts of consecratory rites. The number of sacraments varied from five to twelve, and even to thirty. The concept of sacrament was developed beginning in the twelfth century and then limited to our present seven. Shortly afterward, theologians began to give prominence to the "seven, no more, no less" and to bring out its inner meaning. The teaching of Thomas Aquinas became especially important in this area. He supports the position with theological considerations in which he establishes an analogy between the seven sacraments and the development of individual and social human life (conception, physical and mental growth, nourishment, two threats to bodily and spiritual integrity, and society's need of leadership and regeneration). Thus the sacraments constitute an organic unity in the service of the supernatural life; the heart of this unified system is the Eucharist. In the Eastern churches, too, the sacraments as seven in number have played a role since the thirteenth century, probably under the influence of Western theology. However, the sacraments in question are not in every respect the same as in the West (e.g., the sacrament of reconciliation administered in the form of individual confession differs in a more than minor way from "monk's confession," that is, confession to monks who are not priests). The Reformers generally accepted only baptism and the Lord's Supper, or sometimes reconciliation and ordination (P. Melanchthon), as sacraments.

(3) *Church Teaching*. At the level of magisterial utterances, the number seven plays a role as early as the Second Council of Lyons in 1274 (DS 860). In 1647 the Council of Trent issued a definition regarding it: "If anyone says that the sacraments of the New Law were not all instituted by Jesus Christ our Lord; or that there are more or fewer than seven...*anathema sit*" (DS 1601; ND 1311). At the same time, however, the following view is rejected: "If anyone says that these sacraments are so equal to one another that one is not in any way of greater worth than another, *anathema sit*" (DS 1603; ND 1313).

(4) *Ecumenical Perspectives*. Provided it is not overly inflexible, the emphasis on the sacraments as seven could lead to new possibilities of agreement with the Eastern churches and with the churches of the Reformation (see sec. 2 above). Thus since the Middle Ages a distinction has been made between principal sacraments (*sacramenta maiora*), namely, baptism and the Eucharist, and secondary sacraments (*sacramenta minora*). Theologians are once again recognizing that each sacrament is to be explained not primarily in terms of the formal concept of sacrament, but according to its specific role in salvation. Furthermore, they are seeing that the distinction between sacraments and sacramentals is not as absolute as was long claimed.

(5) *Systematic Reflections*. Theologians today see more clearly than in the past that the conviction about the sacraments being seven in number was historically conditioned and how, for example, the high esteem felt for seven as the perfect number played a part in the rise of the doctrine. In any case, it is already possible to come up with a different number if we take the stages of the sacrament of orders as separate sacraments. The number seven cannot, therefore, be said to be intrinsically necessary. Since, however, the Catholic Church (and, to a lesser degree, the Eastern churches) regard the seven sacraments as highly important in fact and in the history of doctrine, there is no persuasive reason for calling the number into question. Before we ask, for example, whether the church might not be able to institute new sacraments for new situations in contemporary life, we must devote more attention to the urgent theological and pastoral task of fully relating the seven sacraments to the reality of contemporary life and, if need be, of developing them further.

See also SACRAMENTALS; SACRAMENTAL THEOLOGY; SACRAMENTS.

Bibliography
Duffy, Regis. "Sacraments in General." In *Systematic Theology: Roman Catholic Perspectives,* edited by Francis Schüssler Fiorenza and John P. Galvin, 2:181–211. Minneapolis: Fortress, 1991.
Ganoczy, Alexandre. *An Introduction to Catholic Sacramental Theology.* New York: Paulist, 1984.
See also the bibliography under INSTITUTION OF THE SACRAMENTS.

GÜNTER KOCH

Sacraments of Initiation. The sacraments of initiation are those sacraments that together incorporate human beings into the church and its life and thus into the fullness of being a Christian: namely, baptism, confirmation, and Eucharist.

(1) *Biblical Background.* A distinction must be made between the *concept* of initiation (incorporation or insertion), which does not occur in the New Testament any more than does the concept of sacrament, and the *reality* expressed by this term. Initiation and its associated concepts play hardly any role in the New Testament, probably because they were freighted with meanings derived from pagan religions: rite of acceptance into the religious and social world of adults, or into secret societies and mystery cults. In fact, however, baptism in the New Testament is an incorporation into Christ and the church (confirmation was not yet separated out from baptism in the New Testament period). The Eucharist, too, has an initiation aspect (as the fulfillment of baptism).

(2) *History of Theology.* The controversy that the early church carried on with the mystery cults led to many material and terminological borrowings in the service of a theological understanding of the sacraments of baptism and the Eucharist. In the process, especially from the fourth century on, elements from the terminological and conceptual field of "initiation" were also accepted, although with a new meaning. More important is the fact that the intrinsic connection between baptism, confirmation (which achieved independence from baptism only after a lengthy development), and the Eucharist was realized, implemented, and also made the subject of theological reflection (see the mystagogical catecheses of Cyril of Jerusalem [d. ca. 387]). These three sacraments were administered together to both adults and children. In the Eastern churches they are still administered together today, even to infants (Communion with a little of the consecrated wine), whereas in the West their unity was lost sight of from the Middle Ages on and was rediscovered only in recent decades. Prior to Vatican II the term *initiation* was applied to these three sacraments in, for example, *L'Église en prière,* ed. A.-G. Martimort (Paris, 1961) (Eng. trans.: *The Church at Prayer: An Introduction to the Liturgy,* 4 vols., rev. ed. [Collegeville, Minn.: Liturgical Press, 1986–88]).

(3) *Church Teaching.* Vatican II adopted the concept of initiation; for example, in the Constitution on the Liturgy, where it is expected that the rite of confirmation will be so revised that "the intimate connection of this sacrament with the whole of Christian initiation may more clearly appear" (*SC* 71); or in the decree on the church's missionary activity where the actual phrase "the sacraments of Christian initiation" appears (*AG* 14). The mandate given by Vatican II has been carried out in the new Roman Ritual, where the unity of the three sacraments finds expression in the title "Rite of Christian Initiation of Adults." Finally, *CIC* 842.2 has this programmatic statement: "The sacraments of baptism, confirmation, and the Most Holy Eucharist are so interrelated that they are required for full Christian initiation."

(4) *Ecumenical Perspectives.* The recognition of the inner unity of the sacraments of initiation undoubtedly opens up new possibilities for dialogue with the churches of the Christian East, where this unity has never been broken (see

sec. 2 above). In regard to the churches of the Reformation, there is question rather of joint reflection on how the sacraments of initiation together form a process of introduction into the faith, of decision for faith, and of life based on faith, especially since in the case of infant baptism the inner unity of the sacraments of initiation does not and need not mean the administration of all three on the same occasion, as in the Eastern churches.

(5) *Systematic Reflections.* The theological need here is to gain a deeper insight into the internal unity of the sacraments of initiation, with special emphasis on the close connection of baptism and confirmation. If, as intended, the three sacraments of initiation are administered in a single celebration when adults are being baptized, it must be realized, here too, that a journey into faith — which itself is part of the initiation — must lead up to this celebration, just as the sacraments of initiation must be the point of departure for a journey of faith in which the initiation is constantly made present and deepened. Even in the case of infant baptism, the sacraments of initiation are to be seen as interconnected saving events on a journey of faith; from this fact, however, it is hardly possible to give dogmatic answers to pastoral questions (such as: the proper age for confirmation; the proper sequence: confirmation and first Communion or vice versa).

See also BAPTISM; CONFIRMATION; EUCHARIST.

Bibliography

Austin, Gerard. *Anointing with the Spirit: The Rite of Confirmation: The Use of Oil and Chrism.* New York: Pueblo, 1985.

Dix, Gregory. *The Theology of Confirmation in Relation to Baptism.* London: Dacre, 1946.

Kavanagh, Aidan. *Confirmation: Origins and Reform.* New York: Pueblo, 1988.

Lampe, G. W. H. *The Seal of the Spirit: A Study in the Doctrine of Baptism and Confirmation in the New Testament and the Fathers.* London: SPCK, 1967.

Riley, Hugh M. *Christian Initiation: A Comparative Study of the Interpretation of the Baptismal Liturgy in the Mystagogical Writings of Cyril of Jerusalem, John Chrysostom, Theodore of Mopsuestia and Ambrose of Milan.* Washington, D.C.: Catholic University of America Press, 1974.

Schillebeeckx, Edward, and Boniface Willems, eds. *The Sacraments in General.* Vol. 31 of *Concilium.* New York: Paulist, 1968.

Wainwright, Geoffrey. *Christian Initiation.* Richmond: John Knox, 1969.

GÜNTER KOCH

Saints: Holiness, Sanctification. In the New Testament all Christians are saints since, in Jesus Christ and the Holy Spirit, they have a share by grace in the holiness of God. In Catholic usage those Christians are called saints who, by loving God and their neighbor, have lived their Christian faith in an extraordinary and exemplary manner and have been given the title of saint by the official church. *Holiness* as a state originally refers to God's very being. In a derived way it refers to participation by grace in God's holiness. *Sanctification* is the process of becoming holy. It originates in the vocation of those sanctified by grace to realize the gift of participation in holiness by loving God and neighbor.

(1) *Biblical Background.* In the Bible the word *holy* (or *holiness*) originally refers to the essence of God. Human beings were holy in only a secondary way, by graciously sharing in God's holiness. Ritually, persons or things were called holy because of their service or significance for God. In the Old Testament, the words *holy* (*kadosh*) and *holiness* (*kodesh*) mean "separated from the unclean or profane" (1 Sm 21:5; Ez 22:26). God is called simply "the Holy One" (Nm 16:5; Jb 6:10; Prv 9:10) or is given threefold praise as holy (Is 6:3). Thus holiness refers to God's very being. This holiness is also revealed as an ontic or ethical reality. The holiness of God is essentially the same as God's immeasurable grandeur (Ex 15:11; Ps 99:3; Hb 3:3). Ethically, God's holiness is identical with God's unblemished perfection and righteousness (Lv 19:2; Is 5:16). By means of the holiness that comes from God, Israel is a "holy people" (Ex 19:6). To the "holy one of Israel" (Ps 89:19; Is 12:6) God sets down a condition: "You must be holy, as I am holy" (Lv 11:45). In order to maintain their ritual communion with the holy God, certain persons and things are regarded as ritually holy. In the New Testament, God's holiness unfolds in a trinity. God is addressed as "holy Father" (Jn 17:11). The Son of God, Jesus Christ, is called "the holy one of God" (Mk 1:24; Lk 4:34; Jn 6:69) or simply the "holy one" (Acts 3:14; 4:27; 1 Jn 2:20). The Spirit of God is often referred to as the "Holy Spirit." Those who are "baptized in the Holy Spirit" are called "saints in Christ Jesus" (1 Cor 1:2), and the church, which is presented as the new people of God, is called "the holy priesthood" (1 Pt 2:5) or "the holy race" (1 Pt 2:9). The triune God produces holiness in all the members of the church (1 Thes 5:23; 1 Cor 1:30; 6:11). Thus all Christians are called "saints" (e.g., Acts 9:13; Rom 8:27; Eph 1:1). Or, more precisely, those "called to holiness" (Rom 1:17) have the task of becoming holy by a blameless life (Eph 1:4; 1 Thes 4:3; 1 Pt 1:15). Likewise those called in Christ have received the hope of obtaining definitively a share in the glory of God (Eph 1:18; Col 1:12; 2 Thes 2:13f.). In the New Testament there are no statements concerning ritually holy persons or things. Rather, true service of God consists in Christians' presenting themselves as a "living sacrifice, holy and acceptable to God" (Rom 12:1f.), by means of a perfect life according to the will of God.

(2) *History of Theology.* Beginning in the second century, martyrs have been considered and honored as saints, and in the fourth century others also (ascetics, bishops, rulers) were added. The title "saint" was at first granted by popular devotion, but since the tenth century it has involved a papal procedure. From the third century on, saints have been regarded as intercessors before God (Tertullian, Origen, Cyprian). In Scholastic dogmatics, saints are treated as part of eschatology. In response to the criticism of the Reformers, neo-scholasticism developed the treatise "De cultu sanctorum." Today work goes on to develop a basic theology of the saints.

(3) *Church Teaching.* The magisterium distinguishes between worship due to God alone (*latria*) and veneration of the saints (*proskynesis, dulia*) (DS 601). The goal of the latter must be God's honor, although the saints may be called

upon as intercessors (DS 675, 1821, 1824). Vatican II began a basic reflection on holiness and the saints: people attain sainthood in everyday situations and vocations by loving God and neighbor (*LG* 39–42). It also defended the legitimacy of venerating and calling upon the saints (*LG* 50).

(4) *Ecumenical Perspectives.* In the Eastern Church the veneration of saints is of major importance. Recognizing someone as a saint is the result of a process of canonization by a bishop. Because of the excesses of popular piety, where, for example, assistance was seen as coming directly from the saint, M. Luther at first undertook a moderate reform of the veneration of saints with a Christocentric emphasis. In his work "Epistle or Instruction on the Saints" (1522) he develops the position that CA 21 formulates in a definitive way: the saints should be considered as witnesses of grace for the strengthening of faith and their good works as examples to imitate. But calling upon the saints as intercessors is biblically unwarranted, since Jesus Christ is the only mediator and intercessor. Calvinism radically rejects any form of veneration of the saints. The Lutheran churches continue the liturgical remembrance of "biblical saints' days" and publish calendars with the feast days of exemplary witnesses of faith, for example, in 1984, the ecumenical "evangelical calendar of feast days." Today there is a strong movement to emphasize the positive meaning of the saints in connection with an ecclesiological "communion of saints." But their role as intercessors is still denied. Recently, Catholic and Protestant theology have come closer to each other in how they relate justification and sanctification. Justification and sanctification are not clearly separate acts of God so that a priority could be granted to either sanctification (Catholic position) or justification (Evangelical position). Rather justification entails sanctification as the declaring just of the sinner and is therefore the foundation of holiness in concrete life.

(5) *Systematic Reflections.* Following Vatican II, Catholic dogmatics views holiness according to a number of perspectives. It is *theocentric* (trinitarian). GOD in God's very being (sovereignty and glory) and in God's actions (goodness and perfection) is simply the Holy One (saint) and because of this holiness is characterized as three persons who share love: the Father, the Son, and the Holy Spirit. Thus holiness is closely related to love. Moreover, holiness is a *personal* reality in that it originally determines the personal being of God and, in a derived way, makes human beings persons. In the context of COVENANT this implies participation in divine holiness. From this comes the duty to become holy by loving God and neighbor. Holiness is a *social* reality since it involves the individual as member of the holy people of the covenant (Israel, the church). Holiness is also a *universal* reality. Because Jesus Christ has reestablished the goodness of creation, every creature is called to the service of holiness. As an *eschatological* reality, holiness involves a tension between a not yet fully realized participation and the goal of unlimited participation in the holiness of God. The implication of this for the definition and veneration of saints is as follows: by baptism all Christians are ontically holy and called upon to realize this holiness. For the church the veneration of saints is entirely legitimate and im-

portant. For individual Christians, however, it is neither a duty nor a necessity for salvation, but it is part of the freedom of individual piety. The intercessory function of saints must be integrated into the uniqueness and particularity of Christ's mediatorship. On the basis of the solidarity of the saints in the eschatological "communion of saints," all members — those already perfected and those who are still being perfected — are united with one another before God.

See also HOLINESS AND SINFULNESS OF THE CHURCH; JUSTIFICATION; LOVE OF GOD–LOVE OF NEIGHBOR.

Bibliography
Beinert, Wolfgang. *Die Heiligen heute ehren.* Freiburg: Herder, 1983.
Brown, Peter. *The Cult of the Saints: Its Rise and Function in Latin Christianity.* London: SCM, 1981.
Butler, Alban. *Butler's Lives of the Saints.* Edited by Michael Walsh. Rev. ed. San Francisco: HarperSanFrancisco, 1991.
Coulson, John. *Saints: A Concise Biographical Dictionary.* New York: Hawthorn, 1958.
Cunningham, Lawrence. *The Meaning of Saints.* San Francisco: Harper and Row, 1980.
Gallup, George. *The Saints among Us.* Harrisburg, Pa.: Morehouse, 1992.
Kenneth, Brother. *Saints of the Twentieth Century.* Rev. ed. London: Mowbray, 1987.
Nicholl, Donald. *Holiness.* London: Darton, Longman and Todd, 1981.
Reed, Olwen. *An Illustrated History of Saints and Symbols.* Bourne End, England: Spurbooks, 1978.
Sherry, Patrick. *Spirit, Saints, and Immortality.* Albany: State University of New York Press, 1984.
Valentine, Mary Hester. *Saints for Contemporary Women.* Chicago: Thomas More, 1987.
Weinstein, Donald. *Saints and Society: The Two Worlds of Western Christendom, 1000–1700.* Chicago: University of Chicago Press, 1982.

GEORG KRAUS

Salvation. Salvation, a central theological theme, refers to the fulfillment of the human desire for an ultimate truth and goodness in freedom and love. This is achieved in history through an act of God that redeems, frees, and rescues. In the deepest sense salvation is God's presence among human beings, the fulfillment of their transcendence, by which they as spiritual-personal creatures are referred to their author and the goal of goodness. An integral part of salvation is the categorial structure of human relationships in a personal world of history and nature. Stated negatively, salvation is the absence of abandonment by God and the absence of hate, destruction, doubt, exploitation, hunger, distress, sickness, and death.

(1) *Biblical Background.* Although the Old Testament notion of salvation has been contrasted with the New Testament notion — which is supposedly spiritual and interior — the Old Testament conception is by no means restricted to material goods. Already in the Old Testament salvation is linked to God. Israel's hope for rescue in the face of enemies, disease, death, and every kind of danger, mentioned frequently in the Psalms, is rooted in the basic experience, starting with exodus, that Yahweh is a God who saves. Yahweh *is* the God who promises blessings. Because of Yahweh there is a history of the sal-

vation of Israel, the people of the covenant. Concrete images of salvation, such as long life, rich posterity, good pastures and fields, and so on, are immediately related to God's blessing. They are visible expressions of God's favor. Salvation is threatened by sin. The prophets' preaching of a return to Yahweh through repentance and penance includes the hope of an eschatological kingdom where God rules in peace and where there is righteousness for all peoples and the gift of new life, even for the dead in the underworld (Isaiah 66). Here the figure of an eschatological, messianic mediator of salvation emerges, who is *God's servant* (Isaiah 42–53) and *the Son of Man* (Dn 7:13). A hope begins of a new, interior covenant between God and humankind — a covenant written upon the hearts of the people of Israel (Jer 31:31). In the New Testament, Jesus proclaims the coming kingdom of God. It is visible where diseases, that is, physical and mental suffering, are being overcome (Mk 4:23 par.). Jesus' appearance unveils God's salvific will, which encompasses all men and women (Lk 3:8; Rom 5:18; 1 Tm 2:4) in the totality of their existence in time and eternity. His rejection by Israel leads to his crucifixion. In Jesus' destiny the salvific will of God prevails, so that by the cross and resurrection of Jesus, God definitively offers salvation (Lk 3:6; Acts 4:12). The gospel, faith, and baptism bind us to Jesus, the mediator between God and humankind (1 Tm 2:5), the pioneer of salvation (Heb 2:10), and the author of life (Acts 3:15). The history of salvation is fulfilled through the *coming of Christ* in the fullness of time (Gal 4:4; Eph 1:10). As the new Adam (Rom 5:15; 1 Cor 15:21f.), he overcomes the law, sin, and death — the expressions of our distance from God — and brings grace and life for all. But the christological structure of salvation has a future, eschatological dimension. Christians are related to it by their basic attitudes and the dynamism of hope (1 Thes 5:8). Communion with Christ binds us to his suffering and death (Phil 3:10). Thus suffering is not simply the absence of salvation, but also a way to salvation (1 Pt 3:14; Heb 2:10).

(2) *History of Theology.* Salvation as an all-encompassing viewpoint touches all the themes of theology. Thus the exact interpretation of salvation — what it is, how it is realized and acquired — gives a particular imprint to any theological project. In the East, salvation is understood as the divinization of humankind in grace. Through the long process of salvation-history, God educates, transforms, and renders human beings like unto God (see Clement of Alexandria, Origen). In the West, beginning with Augustine's struggle against Pelagianism, salvation is regarded as forgiveness of sins. Due to the influence of the Reformation (see sec. 4 below), the dialectic of salvation and human action is seen rather in terms of an alternative: salvation by God's hand *or* by deeds of free self-realization, salvation as pure transcendence *or* as manifested in immanence, salvation of the transcendent soul *or* good fortune understood materially. (The Enlightenment and the critique of religion by L. Feuerbach, K. Marx, F. Nietzsche, and S. Freud emphasize the second element of these three alternatives. The basis for this is the objection that the doctrine of

supernatural salvation makes of religion an empty promise to those who are exploited and who therefore are incapable of self-liberation.)

(3) *Church Teaching*. Salvation is a key to the church's teaching. According to Vatican II, the church itself is understood as the sacrament of salvation in Christ for the world (*LG* 1, 9, 48, 59; see *SC* 5, 26; *AG* 1, 5; *GS* 42, 45). It exercises its service of salvation in preaching and the SACRAMENTS (DS 1604–8; 2536; *LG* 11). Of particular significance for salvation are baptism and baptism of desire (DS 1529, 1604, 1618), or the sacrament or desire of penance on the part of those who have fallen after baptism (DS 1672, 1706, 1579). Although salvation comes only from the grace of God, human beings are empowered to cooperate, since grace sets in motion a new morality (DS 225–30, 373–97, 1520–83). Since there is grace outside the church (DS 2429), salvation is possible for innocent atheists and adherents of other religions who do not know Christ (*LG* 16; *GS* 22). The basis for the universality of salvation is the incarnation: according to the creed, "He came down from heaven for us and for our salvation" (DS 125).

(4) *Ecumenical Perspectives*. The Reformation began with M. Luther's personal question about a graceful God. Consequently, there is a heavy concentration on the soteriological in describing the content and act of faith. Justification by grace and human participation are seen as antithetical. The result of this is that faith becomes an immanent and conscious acceptance of forgiveness, and salvation consists in the interior experience *pro me* (for me) of Christ's redemption. Thus soteriology is individualized and becomes unworldly. The ecclesiastical community and secular society are under the law of God, but they are not the place where we experience salvation (see the doctrine of two kingdoms). Today Catholic–Reformed dialogue concentrates on the question of how salvation is appropriated (JUSTIFICATION; PREDESTINATION; RECONCILIATION).

(5) *Systematic Reflections*. Present theological ideas of salvation are largely determined by the effort to respond critically to the Marxist objection. Thus the salvation proclaimed by Jesus' message of the kingdom of God that sets us free must be understood as overcoming structural injustice and power. This has been the project of political theology and liberation theology. By taking advantage of the findings of psychology and sociology for pastoral care, we have become more aware of the medical, social, cultural, and political dimensions of salvation. Salvation is also sanctification and so must take place in the areas of experience of self and interpersonal relations. Instead of a purely religious and interior view of salvation, Vatican II calls attention to the duty of the church to serve the world (*GS* 36), although the relationship between salvation and the world is not always clear. Nevertheless, the theological dimension of salvation should not be understood as a play of opposites. Our personal relationship to God is universal. God in Christ is the salvation of humankind. Human beings are persons, not just a network of relationships. Thus the theological definition of salvation is transcendental in character. Humans are personally related

to God in the dialogical events of sacramental life in the church as community and in prayer. While eternal life is now hidden from us, it really is present. In death it will be revealed fully, when we are raised up to God. However, salvation is also experienced in the relationships that constitute everyday existence. Thus part and parcel of the service of Christians and the church is to work for changes in anything within the political or social orders that is mere pretense and not conducive to being human (this might involve, e.g., service, charity, support of certain social legislation, and political involvement to bring about a democratic and constitutional government). However, the conditions of human living can never be changed to the point where there would be a definitive "paradise on earth." Suffering and death remain. The Christian accepts unavoidable suffering (incurable disease, the loss of loved ones, persecution because of faith, the struggle against one's own irresponsibility) by imitating the crucified Lord. In him, through a process of purification, testing, and living of hope, the Christian finds meaning because Christ leads us to a deeper community with God, from whom alone everything may be expected. In the cross, Jesus deprived death of its meaning as distance from God and contradiction to life and transformed it into the possibility of a final surrender to the Father who received, fortified, and elevated him. Henceforth the cross is the way to resurrection in the kingdom of God, my salvation (Ps 51:14). Here the Christian is not saved *from* the world, but rather *with* him or her the world is redeemed in the new heaven and new earth of the kingdom of God.

See also CHURCH; GRACE; REDEMPTION AND LIBERATION; SIN AND GUILT; SOTERIOLOGY; UNIVERSAL SALVIFIC WILL OF GOD.

Bibliography
Corrington, Gail Paterson. *Her Image of Salvation: Female Saviors and Formative Christianity.* Louisville: Westminster, 1992.
Davies, Douglas James. *Meaning and Salvation in Religious Studies.* Leiden: Brill, 1984.
Edwards, Denis. *What Are They Saying about Salvation?* New York: Paulist, 1986.
Gutiérrez, Gustavo. *A Theology of Liberation.* Maryknoll, N.Y.: Orbis Books, 1973.
Hultgren, Arland J. *Christ and His Benefits: Christology and Redemption in the New Testament.* Philadelphia: Fortress, 1987.
Kettler, Christian D. *The Vicarious Humanity of Christ and the Reality of Salvation.* Lanham, Md.: University Press of America, 1991.
Martin, Dale B. *Slavery as Salvation: The Metaphor of Slavery in Pauline Christianity.* New Haven: Yale University Press, 1990.
McIntyre, John. *The Shape of Soteriology: Studies in the Doctrine of the Death of Christ.* Edinburgh: T and T Clark, 1992.
Nicolson, Ronald. *A Black Future? Jesus and Salvation in South Africa.* Philadelphia: Trinity, 1990.
Sloyan, Gerard Stephen. *Jesus: Redeemer and Divine Word.* Wilmington, Del.: Glazier, 1989.
Snook, Lee E. *The Anonymous Christ: Jesus as Savior in Modern Theology.* Minneapolis: Augsburg, 1986.
Viladesau, Richard. *Answering for Faith: Christ and the Human Search for Salvation.* New York: Paulist, 1987.

GERHARD LUDWIG MÜLLER

Salvific Significance of Mary. The salvific significance of Mary comprises and evaluates Mary's specific involvement in salvation-history; it goes beyond the theme of the mediation of Mary to the extent that, along with the question concerning the distinct causality of salvation, the question of her importance also arises. Mary's significance for salvation can be discussed from the perspectives of incarnation theology, ecclesiology, and eschatology.

(1) *Biblical Background.* The New Testament shows a growing understanding of the mother of Jesus and of her place in salvation-history. Gal 4:4 mentions the mother of Jesus (not the father) as the mediatrix of his human existence. Mk 6:3 speaks of Jesus (uncommonly among Jews) using the name of his mother (he is "the son of Mary"), without at all mentioning Joseph as father. Mt 1:20–23 sees the virginal conception of Mary as pointing to the divine sonship of Jesus. "The child and his mother" appears as a set term (Mt 2:11, 13, 14, 20, 21). Mary shares in the homage rendered to her son by the Gentiles (Mt 2:11). Matthew modifies his Markan prototype concerning the lack of faith of Jesus' relatives (Mk 3:20f.) and counts his mother and brethren among the believing disciples (Mt 12:46–50). While in the Matthean infancy narratives Joseph is the protagonist, in Luke it is Mary; Luke pays increased attention to her person and significance. He terms Mary "blessed" (Lk 1:28) and the virginal "handmaid of the Lord" (Lk 1:38); because of the divine majesty of her son, she is the "mother of my Lord" (Lk 1:43); for her faith she is called "blessed" (Lk 1:45); all generations agree in her praise (Lk 1:48). Even more clearly than Matthew, Luke portrays Mary as a devout disciple (Lk 8:20f.; 11:27f.), who suffers with Jesus at his rejection and death (Lk 2:34f.); he shows her praying in the midst of the young church (Acts 1:14). Since Luke (1:28, 35, 43) portrays Mary as the new Israel, as the daughter of Zion, he lays the biblical foundation for the patristic view of Mary as a type of the church. The same holds true in John. Here Mary is found both at the beginning and at the end of Jesus' public ministry. This has a symbolical and theological meaning. In Jn 2:1–11 Mary is a representative of those who await God's gift of salvation from Jesus, who ask for it, and who are filled with it to overflowing. According to Jn 19:25–27, Mary represents the community of salvation, which is commended to John as the guarantor and witness (Jn 19:35) for the gospel. This double symbolism is reason for speaking of a "privileged role" of Mary in the thought of the Johannine school (J. Wanke, "Maria im vierten Evangelium," *ThJb*[L] [1983] 124).

(2) *History of Theology.* Mary's ancillary cooperation in the incarnation of the Logos and her role in opening up understanding for the church were upheld with positive appreciation by the postapostolic church. Starting with Justin (*Dial.* 100) and Irenaeus (*Adv. haer.* 3.22), this was done by comparing Mary and Eve. Soon it became part of the general theological treasury of the patristic age to interpret the church, as humanity renewed in Christ, in terms of Mary, the new Eve, and likewise to understand Mary in terms of the new people of God. These relationships of Eve–Mary and Mary–church have re-

mained favorite aids even to the present for defining Mary's salvific significance. Entwined with these considerations are also reasons for a moral image of Mary that portrays the mother of Jesus as an example and stimulus for the Christian life. The degree to which the patristic age valued the salvific significance of Mary is shown by the Council of Ephesus (431): with the aid of the assertion of Mary's dignity as God-bearer, it declared the redeemer's unity as a subject (DS 252). The perfected integration of Mary into the dogma of Christ clearly manifests that mention of her belongs to authentic proclamation of Christ. Accordingly, since the third century the early church embodied the name of Mary into the symbols (DS 10ff.) and has regarded her as God's elect and as accepted into service for the incarnation in a unique manner. Along with her historically imminent significance as the mother of Christ, rooted in the past, from the third/fourth centuries she was also recognized for her meaning to the present. The direct appeal made to her in prayer is an expression of this. This thrives on the devout certainty that Mary is with God and there maintains her place as mother. It is as a consequence of this faith that her further honorific titles are to be understood: lady, queen, patroness. Augustine writes on her universal motherhood: "She is mother of [the Head's] members, who are ourselves; for she has cooperated through her love so that believers are born in the church, who are the members of this Head" (De s. virg. 1.6). Mary's current salvific significance is understood in analogy to her service as God-bearer.

(3) *Church Teaching.* Vatican II was the first council to issue a complete and extensive statement on Mary's function and significance for salvation. *LG* 52–69 declares that Mary stands in organic relation both to the mystery of Christ and to that of the church, in which she is involved as a creature of the grace of Christ. As in the perspective of the early church, Mary is held by the council to be a "preeminent and totally singular member of the church as well as its type and clearest model in faith and love" (*LG* 53). Under this christological and ecclesiological aspect, the traditional Marian statements are reassembled and reordered by the council. The ambiguous term *coredemptrix* was not included; the title *mediatrix* occurs alongside others (advocate, helper, benefactress) and is not developed as a systematic idea (*LG* 62).

(4) *Ecumenical Perspectives.* Protestant theology acknowledges a subordinate salvific significance of Mary as the mother of the eternal Word of God. With M. Luther, it sees in Mary a sign of God's work of grace for the sake of the sinner and a model of Christian virtues; the idea of Mary as a *type of the church* or as *mother of the church* is also approached. Rejected are any direct invocations of Mary as well as any causal understandings of Mary's mediation in salvation. The problem of mediation, which includes the question concerning human chances and possibilities in the bestowal of salvation and in its dispensation through the community, requires further clarification through theological controversy.

(5) *Systematic Reflections.* The systematic presentation of Mary's salvific significance can proceed from the biblical conviction that God seeks the indi-

vidual in and for the community of the people of God and claims each one specifically. This law, that every human being is involved with inalienable responsibility in God's history of salvation, attains in Mary, the human mother of the eternal Word, its finest concretization. Her historical motherhood is the immediate temporal beginning that God chose in order to turn human history into *God's own* history through Christ in an unsurpassable manner. The belief in Mary's physical glorification underscores that one's personality in salvation-history endures and is fulfilled by God. If one sees Mary in this perspective of salvation-history, which includes causal and typological notions, then the Pauline image of the body of Christ that has many members takes on specific outlines (see 1 Cor 12:12–31). Starting with this dogmatic foundation, further and still current questions concerning Mary's salvific significance can be approached, such as Mary and woman, Mary and liberation movements.

See also ASSUMPTION OF MARY; CHRISTOLOGY; MEDIATION OF MARY; REDEMPTION AND LIBERATION.

Bibliography

Allchin, A. M. "*Redemptoris Mater:* An Anglican Response." *One in Christ* 23 (1987) 324–29.

Beinert, Wolfgang, and H. Petri. *Handbuch der Marienkunde.* Regensburg: Pustet, 1984.

Corrington, Gail Paterson. "The Milk of Salvation: Redemption by the Mother in Late Antiquity and Early Christianity." *HTR* 82 (1989) 393–420.

John Paul II, Pope. *Redemptoris Mater (Mother of the Redeemer): Encyclical Letter.* Introduction by Joseph Cardinal Ratzinger and commentary by Hans Urs von Balthasar. San Francisco: Ignatius, 1988.

Philippe, Pierre Paul. *The Virgin Mary and the Priesthood.* Staten Island, N.Y.: Alba House, 1993.

FRANZ COURTH

Satisfaction (Penitential). In the doctrine on the sacraments, satisfaction (also called "[the] penance") is one of the three acts of penitents in the sacrament of reconciliation. It is a commitment, supported by divine grace, to make reparation for sin or the effects of sin in relation to God, to the sinners themselves who have been wounded by their sins, and to their fellow human beings.

(1) *Biblical Background.* The overall witness of the Bible allows the inference that when God forgives human beings their sins God does not always deliver them from all the effects of their sins but permits these to remain as a salutary punishment (see Gn 3:14–19; Nm 20:10–12; 2 Sm 12:13f.) and that God allows human beings to cooperate actively, through works made possible by grace, in overcoming sin and its effects (e.g., by fasting and works of charity: see Is 58:1–12; Mt 6:16f.; by almsgiving: see Tb 4:7–11; Mt 6:3f.; and by prayer: see Jb 42:8; Mt 6:5f.). Thus there is a biblical background for the role of satisfaction in the sacrament of reconciliation.

(2) *History of Theology.* The role of satisfaction has undergone profound changes in the history of the sacrament of reconciliation and in theological re-

flection: from the system of canonical penance, in which the performance of penance, and this specifically as penal, was supremely important, down to a modern theological understanding that integrates satisfaction more firmly into the total context of repentance and the sacrament of reconciliation (e.g., as active contrition) and emphasizes its medicinal character.

(3) *Church Teaching.* The Council of Florence makes satisfaction, along with contrition and confession, the matter of the sacrament of reconciliation (DS 1323). The Council of Trent devotes a separate chapter to defending "the necessity and fruit of satisfaction" (satisfaction is in keeping with the divine justice and goodness; it helps to heal human beings and conforms them to Christ, on whose satisfaction theirs is entirely dependent; it is imposed by the priest as a safeguard and aid for the future and a punishment for the past [DS 1689–92]); the council states in its canons that the imposed works of satisfaction, if properly understood, obscure neither the grace of God nor the benefit of Christ's death (DS 1713f.).

(4) *Ecumenical Perspectives.* Disagreement with the churches of the Reformation, while extending to the entire understanding of penance and repentance, is focused on the understanding of satisfaction: the Catholic conception must face the question of whether it places justifying human works in competition with the message of God's gracious forgiveness, which alone justifies.

(5) *Systematic Reflections.* In order to correct misunderstandings that in fact existed in the past, it must be made emphatically clear that it is God who at every point accomplishes works of satisfaction in human beings and that God alone graciously allows human beings to be God's free collaborators. For their own healing and the healing of relationships with their fellows that have been damaged by sin, human beings are permitted to participate in the work of Christ that alone makes satisfaction and heals.

See also CONFESSION; GRACE; INDULGENCE; REPENTANCE; SACRAMENT OF RECONCILIATION.

Bibliography
See the bibliographies under CONFESSION; REPENTANCE; and SACRAMENT OF RECONCILIATION.

GÜNTER KOCH

Satisfaction Theory. The satisfaction theory was proposed by Anselm of Canterbury (1033/34–1109) in his work *Cur Deus homo* (1098) as a manner of defining our redemption by Jesus Christ as representative satisfaction (*satisfactio*).

(1) *Biblical Background.* Concerning its biblical background, see the articles referred to in the list of cross references at the end of this article.

(2) *History of Theology.* The occasion for the satisfaction theory was the problem of "unbelievers" (Jews and Muslims), for whom the incarnation and death of God's Son, who redeems us from sin, were obstacles and were meaningless. This apologetic motive leads Anselm to use *sola ratione* (by reason

alone), a procedure that he explains beforehand while also listing four premises that "all hold as true": (1) humankind was made for happiness; (2) happiness cannot be possessed in this life; (3) no one passes through this life without sins; and (4) no one can attain happiness without forgiveness of sins (1.10). Thus, on the basis of these premises alone and *remoto Christo* (apart from Christ — Anselm proceeds by supposing "that the Incarnation of God and what we say of that man [Christ] never occurred [1.10]), he seeks to explain to "unbelievers" the meaning of the incarnation and of the death of God's Son. He also objects to a one-sided "ransom theory," according to which the death of Jesus would be the price of redemption paid to the devil. He objects to the theory because belief in the incarnation and the salvific death of the Son of God would then be exposed to ridicule: Isn't it a powerless God who can show love only in this way (1.6)? Isn't God a monster "if he so derives delight from, or has need of, the blood of the innocent, that he neither wishes nor is able to spare the guilty without the death of the innocent" (1.10)? Beyond the presuppositions already mentioned, Anselm's argument involves four additional ones, without which it is difficult to understand his proposal today. (1) Anselm bases the argument on a teleologically oriented theory of creation: humankind is created for God — is created in order to know, love, and "listen" to God. Therein lies salvation for humankind *and* "God's honor" (*honor Dei,* later also called *gloria Dei externa* — the external glory of God). (2) "God's honor" (as *gloria Dei externa*) is a concept that involves mediation and is used in the framework of medieval thinking to understand God's relationship to what is outside God (this external glory must be distinguished from the "intrinsic honor of God," God's glory and holiness that can in no way be touched by creation [see 1.15]). (3) Humankind owes God — as creator and Lord — "honor," worship, recognition, and obedience: this is the created order as *ordo iustitiae* (the order of justice — for Anselm, the legal metaphor is a concrete formulation of the relationship of humankind to God understood teleologically). Here it should be noted that *iustitia* (justice) and *veritas* (truth) are expressions of the *rectitudo* (rectitude) of creation. Thus they presume that law is grounded in being or creation. (4) God's honor, according to the then-contemporary sociocultural context, was understood as grounding the order of freedom, law, and peace. Thus the king, who was the apex of the social order, had a political and social function for the whole. Beginning with *these* presuppositions, Anselm is able to view sin, which is a refusal to recognize God and grant the obedience which is God's due, as the destruction of the order of the world (likewise, it could be said that by disrupting order the sinner denies God recognition and obedience; later Thomas would argue similarly: "God is offended by nothing more than what we do against our own good" [*CG* 3.122]). Thus the sinner is guilty before God. *Satisfactio aut poena* (satisfaction or punishment) can wipe out guilt, that is, reestablish order (1.15). *Poena* as eternal punishment is, however, not a possibility for Anselm. In this case the creature would not attain its goal. If God is to truly perfect creation, only satisfaction remains as a means to reestablish the order and reconcile the world with God. Within the limits of his presupposition, Anselm shows that human beings are profoundly trapped in sin and therefore *only God* can achieve satisfaction. However, on the other hand, only a human being, acting freely, *should* achieve satisfaction (already Anselm is dealing with how the race must "rise and be lifted up by itself" [2.8]). Therefore, *only* a God-man can represent all human beings before God by his death, which was fully "guiltless" before God because Jesus Christ was without sin and therefore not worthy of death. By his gift of self out of love and obedience, Jesus Christ restored the order of creation, that is, he made satisfaction. Here we should recall that, according to Anselm, Jesus' death cannot be isolated from his life but is "the freely maintained obedience of a lifetime." Thus the God-man reconstitutes the order of creation in freedom, so that a space of reconciliation, peace, and freedom is opened in which human beings can become disciples of Jesus. Following Anselm, the discussion of the satisfaction theory has ranged over a broad spectrum, from critical agreement (e.g., the Victorines, Alexander of Hales, Bonaventure, and Thomas, down to those Catholic theologians today who regard the satisfaction theory as the classical soteriological interpretation of Jesus' death), through critical reserve (which has increased in recent times: e.g., F. Hammer, J. Ratzinger, H. Urs von Balthasar), to rejection (e.g., H. Kessler). In these discussions the notions of satisfaction and expiation are often imprecise, which leads to the following questions: To what extent is the axiom *aut satisfactio aut poena* (either satisfaction or punishment) valid or able to be grounded? Does the *iustitia Dei* assume an overly prominent role in the satisfaction theory? Aren't sin and redemption viewed too "extrinsically"? Is the satisfaction theory sufficient to explain the death of Jesus? Isn't the principle of the "exchange" being obscured, so that the unguilty, dying redeemer is completely without contact with the sins of humankind? Isn't the organic unity with everything else too weak and only "exemplary"? In any critical reexamination, these and similar questions would have to be considered, as demonstrated by G. Greshake's explanation of the satisfaction theory.

(3) *Church Teaching.* There have been no definitive magisterial pronouncements on the satisfaction theory. The Council of Trent mentions satisfaction twice (DS 1529, 1690), and Pius XII defends it (DS 3891).

(4) *Ecumenical Perspectives.* The Reformers (esp. M. Luther) emphasize Christ's representative suffering of punishment, which radicalizes the satisfaction theory. But basically they return to Anselm's option for satisfaction (rather than *poena*). During the Enlightenment, at least its early phase (e.g., the Socinians), because of the emphasis on the autonomy of the self-conscious subject, a fundamental questioning of the satisfaction theory began to emerge (E. Kant). Its place within the framework of the doctrine of reconciliation becomes henceforth a problem of mediating between the medieval understanding of *ordo* and modern subjectivity (F. Schleiermacher, A. Ritschl).

(5) *Systematic Reflections.* The satisfaction theory is part of reinterpreting the covenant biblically: God remains true to creation and therefore true to the

covenant with humankind. The covenant binds human beings to "covenantal behavior" and establishes them in a freedom that is not "violated" by God but respected in the satisfaction by Jesus Christ and made newly available for humankind. Thus redemption can be understood as the "freeing of human freedom by the representation of the one free person" (G. Greshake). Anselm takes seriously the weight of sin and its profound unhumanness, as negative folly leading to Christ's overabundant fullness of salvation. At the same time, however, this points to the way opened by God's love, by which sin is overcome: Jesus' life and death reveal a radical obedience that is representative (in our place) and normative (as a call to discipleship). The "all-inclusive 'yes' of Christ" provides the basis "for the possibility of sinners saying 'yes'" (H. Urs von Balthasar).

See also COVENANT; INCARNATION; JESUS' HUMANITY; RECONCILIATION; SALVATION; SOTERIOLOGICAL MODELS.

Bibliography
Anselm, Saint. *Cur Deus Homo: Why God Became Man, and the Virgin Conception and Original Sin.* Albany: Magi Books, 1969.
Balthasar, Hans Urs von. *Mysterium Paschale: The Mystery of Easter.* Edinburgh: T and T Clark, 1990.
Fiorenza, Francis. "Critical Social Theory and Christology." *Proceedings of the Catholic Theological Society of America* 30 (1975) 63–110.
McIntyre, John. *St. Anselm and His Critics: A Re-interpretation of the "Cur Deus Homo."* Edinburgh: Oliver and Boyd, 1954.

LOTHAR ULLRICH

Schism. Schism (Greek: *schisma* = division, separation) is a deliberate separation from the unity of the church, or the state of separation, or the community that is formed as a result of the separation. Unlike heresy, the separation here is not based on doctrinal differences.

(1) *Biblical Background.* The term *schism* is rarely attested in the extrabiblical literature, but when it occurs it means a division within a cultic community. According to John, the coming of Jesus led to a division among his hearers. The division was caused by diverse judgments regarding his origin (7:43), his deeds (9:16), and his words (10–19). According to 1 Corinthians 1–4, there were schisms in Corinth. These endanger Christian unity in thought and speech, as well as the shared celebration of the Supper (1 Cor 11:18). The schisms result from attachments to certain individuals (1 Cor 1:12). Paul labors to overcome these divisions.

(2) *History of Theology.* In the theology of the early church schisms are seen as resulting from disputes and a lack of love; they are therefore to be overcome by peaceableness and love. While the concept was originally applied primarily to quarrels within a local community, in the Middle Ages the tendency was to apply it to the universal church, schism now meaning separation from the pope. In the sixteenth century schism means separation from the church as such; consequently, all members of non–Roman Catholic ecclesial communities are

convicted of both heresy and schism. It is not possible to draw up a complete list of schisms. Among the best known and most momentous are the schisms of the Novatians and Donatists in the third and fourth centuries, the Acacian in the fifth and sixth, the "Eastern schism" in the eleventh (also known as the Photian schism because in the East Photius was regarded as the patron of anti-Roman polemics and in the West as the key cause of the schism), and finally the "Western schism" that occurred in the fourteenth century in connection with the question of the legitimate pope.

(3) *Church Teaching.* According to the Code of Canon Law (can. 1364), schism is an offense that brings automatic excommunication as its punishment.

(4) *Ecumenical Perspectives.* Evangelical church law contains no punishments for schismatics, but Evangelical theology regards separation from the church and the formation of separate communities as a serious disruption of unity.

(5) *Systematic Reflections.* The meaning given to the concept of schism reflects the self-understanding of the church at a given period. Now that the ecclesial character of non-Catholic communities has been rethought at Vatican II, schism, if the term is used at all, is defined as it was in the early church.

See also HERESY.

Bibliography

Congar, Yves. *After Nine Hundred Years: The Background of the Schism between the Eastern and Western Churches.* New York: Fordham University Press, 1959.

Dawson, Christopher. *The Dividing of Christendom.* New York: Sheed and Ward, 1965.

Nichols, Aidan. *Rome and the Eastern Churches: A Study in Schism.* Edinburgh: T and T Clark, 1992.

Tierney, Brian. *Foundations of the Conciliar Theory: The Contribution of the Medieval Canonists from Gratian to the Great Schism.* London: Cambridge University Press, 1968.

Ullmann, Walter. *The Origins of the Great Schism: A Study in Fourteenth-Century Ecclesiastical History.* Hamden, Conn.: Archon, 1967.

WERNER LÖSER

Scripture. Scripture is the written expression of the word of God communicated in revelation, an expression that has arisen from the faith of the church and that has been ever since the norm for that faith. It is therefore the highest source of theological knowledge.

(1) *Biblical Background.* The significance of Scripture for Christianity can be developed from the New Testament. The original form for the proclamation of the event of Christ was the spoken word. As the distance from the events surrounding Jesus increased, a self-presentation of the faith of the church in written form proved necessary for missionary work, apologetical defense, liturgy, and theological reflection. The model for this was the Scripture of the Jews (in the translation of the Septuagint), which was acknowledged as authoritative (Acts 1:16; 17:2, 11 and elsewhere) and which was viewed as the indispensable presupposition for understanding these events (Lk 24:27, 32, 45; Jn 2:22; 20:9; Heb 1:1f.). Jesus himself had emphasized its normative character

(Mt 5:17–19; Jn 10:35) yet at the same time claimed his own authority over it (Mt 5:21–48): he wanted to uncover anew its character as the message of God's revelation (cf. Mt 19:4–8 to Gn 1:27; 2:24; or Mt 21:12f. to Is 56:7). With the help of typology, Paul outlined the relationship of the church to the Jewish Scripture: the latter had already pointed toward what was to be accomplished in Jesus; it therefore becomes the *Old* Testament, which is fulfilled in the *New* (in Rom 5:12–21, Christ is the new Adam; in 1 Cor 10:1–4, the passage through the Red Sea and the feeding with manna are seen as references to baptism and the Eucharist). With this, the New Testament is at the same time the superseding of the Old Testament (Heb 8:13). Yet this also makes possible in principle the interpretation of Scripture: this is already present within the Old Testament (the prophets speak of a new covenant and a new exodus in remembrance of earlier events [Jer 31:31–34; Ez 16:60; 20:41–44]) and is practiced within the New Testament (cf. Lk 4:16–30 to Is 61:1f.; 29:18; 58:6). Preliminary rules are set forth in 2 Pt 1:16–21. The normative status of the New Testament is suggested in Jn 20:30f. and 1 Jn 1:1–3.

(2) *History of Theology*. From the beginning the books that later on were collected together in the canon were considered as Scripture (i.e., as books of divine origin and divine dignity); these, however, were to be taken together with the Word of God in the flesh and the Word of God in the Eucharist (Origen). By the time of the Arian controversy it became evident that the meaning of Scripture can be preserved only if terms that are not contained in Scripture are introduced into church proclamation (the deity of Jesus can be expressed in the thought horizon of the fourth century only through the concept *homousios* = of the same being): thus dogma became necessary for the interpretation of Scripture. For Scripture itself Origen, borrowing from the hermeneutics of antiquity, developed the doctrine of the threefold sense of Scripture; John Cassian (d. around 430) extended it to the teaching of the fourfold scriptural sense (see the accompanying table), which was followed until the end of the Middle Ages. In the theological instruction of the Middle Ages the meanings of the senses of Scripture were captured in the refrain "*Littera* gesta docet, quid credas *allegoria. Moralis* quid agas, quo tendas *anagogia*" (The literal teaches facts; the allegorical, what you believe; the moral, what you do; the anagogical, what you strive for). This theory made it possible to interpret the Bible with regard to the various situations of Christian existence, and under this aspect it is still important today. In this way Scripture becomes the impulse for the realization of the various aspects of Christian existence through theological reflection. Because the inherent danger of subjectivism within this method was soon recognized, the Fathers of the Church bound interpretation to the ecclesial rule of faith. Drawing upon the guidelines of Tyconius, Augustine proposed hermeneutical rules (*De doctr. christ.* 3.30–37). In the tension between historical and allegorical exegesis, the Alexandrian school in antiquity and monasticism in the Middle Ages tended toward the allegorical sense, while the Antiochene school and, later on, Scholasticism

THE DOCTRINE OF THE FOURFOLD MEANING OF SCRIPTURE

Name	Latin name	Meaning	Example: "Jerusalem"
Literal sense	littera, historia	literal, historical interpretation	City in Israel
Allegorical sense	allegoria	interpretation with regard to faith = dogmatic interpretation	Image of the church
Tropological sense	tropologia, sensus moralis	interpretation with regard to Christian love = moral theological interpretation	Image of the human soul
Anagogical sense	anagogia	interpretation in view of hope = eschatological interpretation	Image of heavenly glory

tended toward literal interpretation. In the age of humanism, the production of philologically correct editions paved the way for early attempts at a critical examination of Scripture. Through the Reformation, the Bible received new and up until then rarely known consideration (see sec. 4 below). The Enlightenment developed historical-critical interpretation: in order to bring attention to bear on the specific passages of the various texts, all the stages of their development were uncovered, and the history of their effects was investigated. The father of this method was the Catholic priest R. Simon (d. 1712); the first representatives were the Protestants J. S. Semler (d. 1791) and H. S. Reimarus (d. 1768), whose writings were edited by G. E. Lessing. In the nineteenth century, liberal exegesis in following this method dedicated itself to the reconstruction of the life of Jesus (D. F. Strauss, F. C. Baur, A. Schweitzer). K. Barth protested against it, because for him, Scripture is the witness of faith to revelation. R. Bultmann radicalized this view with his theory of demythologization: the content of Scripture must be freed from cosmological imagery in order for it to be clearly recognized as God's existential appeal to human beings. In the Catholic sphere the Biblical Movement has fostered the study of Scripture since 1920. Today the principle debate focuses around the relationship between historical-critical and dogmatic interpretation.

(3) *Church Teaching.* The ecclesial magisterium at the Council of Trent insisted against the Reformers that Scripture cannot be interpreted against the teaching of the church handed down in the tradition (DS 1507). According to Vatican I (DS 3007), the ecclesial magisterium becomes the positive norm of Scripture; Scripture is here subordinated to the magisterium. Since 1905 the Pontifical Biblical Commission has released various decisions wherein authentic interpretations for individual passages are proposed (DS 3372f., 3394–3400, 3505–28; in addition, 3503, 3561–93, 3628–30, 3750f., 3792f., 3999). After a cautious opening begun with Leo XIII (in the encyclical *Providentissimus Deus* 1893 [DS 3286]), Pius XII in his 1943 encyclical *Divino afflante Spiritu* (DS 3825–31) permitted and recommended the use of the historical-critical

method in exegesis. Vatican II stressed the priority of Scripture over all other sources of knowledge for the church and theology. The magisterium is subordinate to Scripture, and theology should orient itself toward Scripture (*DV* 10, 12, 21, 24).

(4) *Ecumenical Perspectives.* Scripture is the fundamental source of knowledge for all the Christian churches. In 1961 the Ecumenical Council of Churches therefore enlarged its fundamental formula to state that only those churches could be members that "confess the Lord Jesus Christ as God and Savior *according to Holy Scripture.*" Differences mainly arise concerning the ordering of the other sources of theological knowledge to Scripture. The Orthodox Church sees tradition as a source that completes Scripture; yet, Scripture, in the infallible interpretation of the church, has precedence over tradition. Philological and historical exegesis is permitted. The Reformers of the sixteenth century, especially the Lutherans, took Scripture as the only authentic foundation for faith (*sola Scriptura:* Scripture is *norma normans non normata* [the norm-giving norm that is not under any other norm]). It interprets itself (*sui interpres*), whereby for Luther the teaching on justification became the inner-biblical criterion ("what compels Christ" [*WA DB* 7:384]; with this, he founded a "canon within the canon"). This principle introduced a separation from tradition and the ecclesial magisterium, and that separation was sharpened by the theology of Scripture of the early Protestant Orthodoxy of the sixteenth and seventeenth centuries. This viewed Scripture as the literal recording of the word of God (verbal inspiration) and taught its *sufficientia* (Scripture is identical with revelation, thus there is no binding character to tradition), *auctoritas* (authority as inspired), *perspicuitas* (understandability for all Christians, thus a magisterium is superfluous), and *efficacia* (relevance for every Christian even without theological explanation). Pietism promoted textual criticism, since for it Scripture is the only foundation of life and of doctrine (J. A. Bengel [d. 1752]). The promotion of the historical-critical method has been primarily a work of Protestant theologians. Today there exists considerable agreement with Catholic theology about its significance and the criteria for its interpretation.

(5) *Systematic Reflections.* In Scripture the word of God is not expressed in an immediate way, but rather is mediated through human forms of communication (e.g., reports, Gospels, poems, confessions). It is the foundation and safeguard of the church's proclamation of faith and therefore its highest and ultimate constitutive norm (*norma normans non normata*), by which every statement of faith must be justified. The word of the church is the proclamation of the word of God *as* the word of Scripture. Yet in this hermeneutical circle Scripture is also bound to the church: it owes its origin to the decision of the church on the formation of the canon, and it unfolds its effects in the history and interpretation of the church. Thus, one has to add: Scripture is the word of God *as* word of the church. What has to be clarified theologically is: (*a*) the question within the Bible of the relationship between the Old and New

PROCESS OF THE EXEGESIS OF BIBLICAL TEXTS

1 *Textual criticism*	Inquiry into the original wording
2 *Literary criticism*	Determination of the author, of possible redactors, of the unity and layers of the text
3 *Linguistic analysis*	Uncovering of the meaning, structure, aim, and horizon of the speech action of the text
4 *Form and genre criticism*	Clarification of the life situation from which the text originates
5 *Thematic criticism*	Investigations of the motifs, themes, and traditions that have been set down within the text
6 *Tradition criticism*	Inquiry into the traditions received in the text
7 *Redaction criticism*	Examination of the process in which the different layers of the text have been composed or have been joined together
8 *Dating questions*	When was the text produced?
9 *Particular and overall interpretation*	What does the text mean in itself and in its context?
10 *Theological criticism*	Investigation of the material for its systematic-theological importance

Testaments; and (*b*) the exegetical question about correct interpretation. The explanation of the first issue begins with the understanding that for Christianity, Christ is the actual "meaning" and the center of Scripture; he is witnessed to directly in the New Testament. For this reason the Old Testament is *superseded* by the New Testament, insofar as it is understood as the prehistory to the Christ-event; it is *universalized* insofar as it develops from a book for Judaism to a book for all humanity; and it is *fulfilled* insofar as in the New Testament it is received in a way that discloses its meaning. The explanation of the second issue begins with the understanding that Christian theology has always held on to the precedence of the historical sense of the text. Already because of this point, but especially also because of the proven fruitfulness of historical-critical exegesis for unfolding the meaning of the text, one cannot return to a stage before it (for the individual steps, see the accompanying table). Yet theology just as much must remain aware of the fact that Scripture contains more than exegesis can disclose. Scripture is first of all a book of life and of faith, whose deeper levels are completely developed only through the analogy of faith, which is provided in the ecclesial community and in which God's overall plan of salvation becomes evident. The church can thus be understood as a community of contemplation that recognizes and receives in faith the content of revelation that has been set down in Scripture through the centuries. This content is grasped in increasing measure under the illumination of the Holy Spirit and is concretized by historical challenges (today, e.g., through the ecological problem). The insights and experiences gained in this process must necessarily remain consonant with Scripture, even if they go beyond the word of Scripture in their formulation and concretization (see the formation of the dogmas of the immaculate conception and the assumption of Mary into God's glory).

See also CANON; DOGMA/DOGMATIC STATEMENT; HERMENEUTICS; INERRANCY; INSPIRATION.

Bibliography
Brown, Raymond E. *The Critical Meaning of the Bible*. New York: Paulist, 1981.
Curran, Charles, and Richard McCormick. *The Use of Scripture in Moral Theology*. Vol. 4 of *Readings in Moral Theology*. New York: Paulist, 1984.
Evans, Gillian R. *The Language and Logic of the Bible: The Earlier Middle Ages*. New York: Cambridge University Press, 1985.
———. *The Language and Logic of the Bible: The Road to Reformation*. New York: Cambridge University Press, 1985.
Fitzmyer, Joseph. *Scripture and Christology: A Statement of the Pontifical Biblical Commission with a Commentary*. New York: Paulist, 1986.
Grant, Robert, with David Tracy. *A Short History of the Interpretation of the Bible*. Philadelphia: Fortress, 1989.
Kelsey, David. *The Uses of Scripture in Recent Theology*. Philadelphia: Fortress, 1975.
Neuhaus, Richard John. *Biblical Interpretation in Crisis: The Ratzinger Conference on Bible and Church*. Grand Rapids: Eerdmans, 1989.
The New Jerome Biblical Commentary. Englewood Cliffs, N.J.: Prentice Hall, 1968.
Smalley, Beryl. *The Study of the Bible in the Middle Ages*. Oxford: Oxford University Press, 1952.

WOLFGANG BEINERT

Sensus Fidelium. The sensus fidelium is a charism, given to all members of the church, of interior affinity with the object of faith; in virtue of this charism the church as a whole, which expresses itself in the consensus of faith, recognizes the object of faith and confesses it in its life, in constant agreement with Sacred Scripture, tradition, and the magisterium of the church.

(1) *Biblical Background.* According to 1 Pt 2:9, the proclamation of the glorious deeds of God is the function of the priestly people of God. To this end they possess the "mind of Christ" (1 Cor 2:16), the "eyes of the heart" (Eph 1:18), and the Spirit who leads them into the entire truth (Jn 14:17; 16:13). The faithful have an understanding that is the work of the Spirit (Col 1:9).

(2) *History of Theology.* In defending the truth of Christian doctrine, the Fathers appeal to the witness of the faithful (Jerome, *Adv. Vigilant.* 5; Augustine, *C. Julian.* 1.7, 31; *De praed. sanct.* 14.27), to whom they attribute a Christian, Catholic, and ecclesial sense (*sensus*) (e.g., Vincent of Lérins, *Commonit.* 2; Eusebius, *Hist. eccl.* 5.28). Thomas Aquinas speaks of an innate affinity (*connaturalitas*) of the faithful with the matters on which they must pass judgment; this affinity is a gift of the Holy Spirit (*STh* 2–2, q. 45, a. 2). M. Cano re-

gards the sensus fidelium as a source of theological knowledge. In more recent times, J. H. Newman and M. J. Scheeben in particular saw that the steadfast character of the teaching of faith has its direct basis in the body of the faithful as a whole. Historical facts contributed to this conviction: it was clear that in the fourth century, for example, ecclesial orthodoxy was saved not by those in office but by the ordinary faithful. Discussion of the Marian dogmas of 1854 and 1950, which cannot be derived directly from the Bible, greatly stimulated reflection on this subject. The questions raised today have to do mainly with discerning the sensus fidelium and with its theological status.

(3) *Church Teaching.* The ecclesial magisterium has as a rule emphasized its own competency and the obligation of the faithful to obey; this led to the idea of an opposition between the "teaching" church and the "listening" church. But the Council of Trent in its day already recognized a "universal understanding of the church" as guarantee of orthodox belief in opposition to error (DS 1637). Vatican II assigns a special importance to the *sensus fidei:* this "sense" is an error-free expression of the participation of all the faithful in the prophetic office of Christ (*LG* 12); therefore, for the good of the church and its service to the world, the bishops should also pay heed to the manifestations of the laity's faith and life (*LG* 37).

(4) *Ecumenical Perspectives.* In the Eastern churches in particular there has always been a lively awareness of the importance of the sensus fidelium; this awareness finds expression in all areas of the church's life and is especially clear in the reception of the decrees of councils. Because the churches of the Reformation reject an ecclesial magisterium and are convinced that the Scriptures are to be understood in terms of themselves, they have developed a doctrine of a comprehensive priesthood of all the faithful, to whom the confession of faith owes its origin.

(5) *Systematic Reflections.* Theological reflection on the sensus fidelium is only beginning. In the process whereby the church gives expression to its faith, the sensus fidelium comes into play after the religious predisposition (*instinctus fidei*), which precedes the process leading to faith, and after the individual's insight of faith (often called the *sensus fidei* to distinguish it from the sensus fidelium), and before the common expression of faith (*consensus fidelium*), which is the result of the sensus fidelium. The sensus fidelium is a charism that flows from the gift of the Spirit in baptism and confirmation and is an expression of the presence of the grace and truth of Jesus Christ in the church, which consists essentially of the totality and community of all believers. The sensus fidelium is thus a basic means of understanding the faith and as such exercises a truth-finding and truth-attesting function that has as its special characteristic that it takes into account the faithful's experience of the world. It is therefore a criterion of theological understanding. To the extent that the magisterium does not establish the faith but preserves and communicates it as handed down by the community, it is subordinate to the sensus fidelium; to the extent, on the other hand, that the magisterium possesses its own apostolic commission to

provide authentic interpretation and issue final decisions in matters of faith, it takes precedence over the sensus fidelium and ranks higher. Moreover, the presence of the truth and grace of Christ manifests itself not only in the sensus fidelium and the magisterium but also in Sacred Scripture, tradition, and theology; the sensus fidelium is therefore always related to these theological *loci*. The expressions of faith differ in fullness and form. It is therefore not easy to determine the part played by the sensus fidelium in the consensus. It is present in the total complex of confessions and attestations of faith, in forms of spirituality and ethical and political behavior, and in artistic expressions. The faith and lives of the saints are especially important.

See also FAITH; TRUTH OF FAITH.

Bibliography
See bibliography under FAITH.

WOLFGANG BEINERT

Sexuality. Sexuality is a basic component of human behavior and experience. It manifests itself differently according to the stage of life, but it remains present from childhood until old age. Its theological interpretation is strongly influenced by each respective culture.

(1) *Biblical Background.* In the Old Testament, sexuality is always taken into account whenever the relation between God and the human person is treated. The two accounts of creation (Genesis 1; 2) offer two different theological interpretations. According to Genesis 1, Yahweh's blessing is bestowed on sexuality in view of the value of having numerous descendants (Gn 1:27). According to Genesis 2, the contact of body and mind ("one flesh" [Gn 2:26]) serves for the stabilization of the human creature, who is lonely and helpless when alone. Israel's neighbors offered very attractive religious interpretations of sexual feeling. In Israel, therefore, such interpretations were viewed as an endangering of covenant faithfulness. Nudity was forbidden, and the cultivation of shame was viewed as protection against the endangerment to faith brought by the sexual instinct. In the New Testament, the sexuality of the human person only occasionally comes into view, when it causes concrete problems in the community. The Old Testament's defensive attitude toward sexual desire still seems to have an effect (Mt 19:12; Mk 12:25; 1 Cor 6:12–7:40). Yet the individual statements have to be interpreted against the background of Jesus' proclamation of the breaking forth of God's rule in (the whole of!) creation.

(2) *History of Theology.* While the Eastern theology of icons elevated sexual desire to the symbolic level by interpreting it as the creatural expression of the human longing for salvation through participation in the divine, Augustine steered Western theology toward the connection between sexuality and sin, by explaining the transfer of original sin through the uncontrolled lust of procreation. In contrast, Thomas Aquinas considered the sexual instinct as a good gift of creation, yet restricted it to the purpose of procreation according to the

animal nature that human beings and animals share. Under the influence of personalism in our century, the integration of sexuality into a personal relationship has become a new and important theme (e.g., in the discussion about the aims of marriage).

(3) *Church Teaching.* Ecclesial statements on the sexuality of the human person mostly deal with the moral problems of the permissibility and sinfulness of ways of sexual behavior (see *GS* 51).

(4) *Ecumenical Perspectives.* Protestant and Catholic theology today both try to come to grips with the tradition formed by Augustine.

(5) *Systematic Reflections.* The Enlightenment's drive toward emancipation extends to sexuality. A fundamental interpretation of sexuality that extends beyond the problems of moral theology therefore becomes necessary. Sexuality is to be interpreted theologically, first of all, as an expression of creatural neediness. This refers human persons in all the realms of reality of their existence to their fellow creatures. Physical and intellectual contact with one's fellow persons is experienced as pleasurable: as the promise of the joy of an enriching existence. Human existence, therefore, cannot succeed if sexual desire is only just tolerated or even refuted. It has to be affirmed fully in the frame of creatural neediness. Sexual need leads to the distortion of existence only when all the joy of a fulfilled existence is expected *from it alone.* And since human existence can come into perfection only under God's reign, such a distortion is at the same time sin. Only if the sexual need develops in agreement with the other bodily and intellectual needs does the creatural neediness of the human person correspond to the Creator's intention of preservation and fulfillment. Only then is God's reign at work also in the sexuality of the human person.

See also FLESH–SPIRIT PROBLEM; JOY; ORIGINAL SIN.

Bibliography
Cahill, Lisa. *Between the Sexes: Foundations for a Christian Ethics of Sexuality.* Philadelphia: Fortress, 1985.
Green, Ronald M. *Religion and Sexual Health: Ethical, Theological, and Clinical Perspectives.* Dordrecht and Boston: Kluwer, 1992.
Kosnick, Anthony, ed. *Human Sexuality: New Directions in American Catholic Thought.* New York: Paulist, 1977.
Nelson, James B. *Embodiment: An Approach to Sexuality and Christian Theology.* Minneapolis: Augsburg, 1979.
Whitehead, Evelyn, and James Whitehead. *A Sense of Sexuality: Christian Love and Intimacy.* Garden City, N.Y.: Doubleday, 1989.

GEORG LANGEMEYER

Sin and Guilt. In theology, sin and guilt characterize the intentional transgression against God's will. Sin comprises the deed (to commit a sin), whereas guilt refers to the transgressor (to be guilty). Thus, they presuppose insight and free decision. Beyond this, guilt has also a purely anthropological sense: for example, responsibility for breaking the law or violating a valid norm (feeling of guilt).

(1) *Biblical Background.* The Old Testament has numerous words for sin. It does not, however, distinguish between the intentional and the inadvertent trespassing of a norm, nor between sin and punishment or consequence (e.g., for the people or the coming generations). It sees sin and guilt in connection with the history of Israel. Yet, throughout, sin and guilt are understood theologically. They are an offense against the election of Israel and the divine covenant even if they concretely refer to fellow human beings or to things. In Judaism the conviction arises that all human persons sin, either on account of an evil drive that is effective from birth or because of demonic powers that rule an era (a key theme of apocalyptic literature). According to the witness of the gospel, Jesus also considered all human persons as sinners who have to convert themselves to God's will. Sin and guilt culminate in a pride that makes persons believe they do not need conversion (Mt 23:28). A reflection on sin and guilt is found in Paul and John. According to both, sin and guilt have at the same time the character of a free deed of the will and the character of an evil fate, whether as the power of sin in the person (Paul) or as the sin of the world (John). Nobody can escape from sin and guilt without God's mercy and help.

(2) *History of Theology.* In the history of theology, sin and guilt are closely linked with the interpretation of redemption through Christ and the interpretation of grace. Basically, one can say that the Greek Fathers of the Church saw them encompassed by the economy of salvation, that is, by God's eternal plan for salvation. They are an illness of the will in the face of God's salvific work. Only obstinate unbelief is a sin unto death, because here finally one shuts oneself off to this work. The Latin Fathers of the Church, on the other hand, sought to grasp sin and guilt with legal concepts, viewing them as signifying an injustice against God that destroys the saving relationship to God. This relationship can be restored only by God. Every freely willed serious offense against God's commandment brings about as its consequence death and damnation. From this perspective, Scholasticism worked out the distinction between mortal and venial sin, that is, between a sin that separates from God and a sin that weakens or endangers the saving relationship to God. Characteristic for Western theology is the focusing on the individual relationship of the single human person to God and on the degree of guilt.

(3) *Church Teaching.* The ecclesial magisterium confirmed this view against the Reformers (DS 1544; 1680–82). Vatican II, however, stressed especially the social dimension of sin and guilt (*SC* 109; *LG* 11; *GS* 25).

(4) *Ecumenical Perspectives.* In the understanding of sin and guilt there are differences that continue to exist between Catholics, Protestants, and Orthodox; these become obvious in their different confessional praxes. In its basic approach, the Protestant doctrine of sin is even more individualistic than the Catholic since it makes every human person totally responsible for sin before God. This is why Orthodox theology can serve as a stimulus to both to reconsider the social and cosmic interwovenness of the human person in sin and guilt.

(5) *Systematic Reflections.* The theological view of sin and guilt is gradually being changed by the modern experience and insight that everything inhuman first and especially receives its threatening character through its psychosocial network that, on the one hand, is objectified in structures that go beyond the individual and that, on the other hand, are already prestructured in the depths of the psyche. This modern perspective enables a new understanding of the uncanny and demonic element in sin and guilt and also allows the inhuman actions of the individual, which often appear far too human, to be grasped in their theological meaning. For only if one sees how this far too human factor contributes to the web of the superindividual inhuman bondage does it become obvious that it is in contradiction to God's salvific will and love for humankind. This also makes clear, however, that forgiveness and the overcoming of sin and guilt are possible only in another network, namely, in the concretely lived Christian community (church) that at the same time works for transformation in the world. The theology of sin thus also criticizes any shifting of guilt to a scapegoat as well as any form of flight from of the evil world of the "others" into the inner realm of the individual.

See also DEATH; PENANCE; SACRAMENT OF RECONCILIATION; SALVATION.

Bibliography

Fenn, Richard K. *The Secularization of Sin.* Louisville: Westminster, 1991.
Hulsbosch, A. *God in Creation and Evolution.* New York: Sheed and Ward, 1965.
Ricoeur, Paul. *Symbolism of Evil.* New York: Beacon, 1967.
Schoonenberg, Piet. *Man and Sin: A Theological View.* Notre Dame, Ind.: University of Notre Dame Press, 1968.

GEORG LANGEMEYER

Society. Society is the totality of the structures of meaning and corresponding patterns of behavior that determine life in a social framework. Societal structures necessarily develop whenever a social configuration exceeds the size of a small group. Social determinations of human life and of human interaction are theologically significant because (*a*) the message of the gospel is addressed to socially determined human beings; (*b*) Christian communities live in societies; and (*c*) parish communities and the church as a whole by reason of their size have themselves a societal status.

(1) *Biblical Background.* The Old Testament grounds the norms for the society of ancient Israel in its election through Yahweh and then anchors them in the law of the covenant. The prophetic proclamation interprets the influence of foreign cultures on Israel brought about after its loss of sovereignty as God's punishment and discipline. In apocalyptic literature, the society of whatever empire dominated the land of Israel at the time is seen as the sphere of Satan's power that thereby prevents the realization of the law of Yahweh in that era. Jesus did not fundamentally reject either the Jewish or the Roman society, but rather placed them under the criterion of the salvific will of God. According to the New Testament, societal structures that are formed within the New

Testament communities, therefore, are to be put completely in the service of the salvific message. Because the society of the Roman Empire presented itself to the Christian communities as foreign and increasingly hostile, it is unmasked in the New Testament as the realm of the influence of evil powers. Nevertheless, at the same time society is to be distinguished from its members, whom Christians should treat with respect and with concern for their salvation (e.g., 1 Pt 2:12, 17).

(2) *History of Theology.* The theological interpretation of the relationship between society and faith depends strongly upon historical developments (see table).

Society	Theology/Church
After Constantine's conversion: society of the empire	– The divine order of creation, which is subordinated to the order of salvation
Modern times: dissolution of the bonds between church and empire, autonomous societies	– Church = the *societas perfecta* founded by God; theological criterion for worldly societies
Present day: secularized societies	– Acknowledgment of autonomy; service of Christians in the humane development of society

(3) *Church Teaching.* At Vatican II, the church acknowledged the relative autonomy of society (*LG* 36) yet at the same time emphasized the Christian mission and responsibility for its humane construction (*GS* 3, 26), since societal conditions have a certain influence upon the positive or negative development of the human person toward independence (*GS* 25).

(4) *Ecumenical Perspectives.* The discussion about the relationship between Christian faith and society at present has led to a polarization in Protestant as well as in Catholic theology.

(5) *Systematic Reflections.* The core of the discussion regards the connection between societal conditions, individuals' capability of performing actions for which they are responsible, and the decision of faith for the message of the gospel (DECISION; FREEDOM). If this connection is an intrinsic one, then the proclamation of the gospel and Christian discipleship directly imply the task to change conditions in society that fundamentally hinder or make impossible personal freedom and the ability to be the subject of one's activity. This enables the gospel to be proclaimed as a call to faith with a social dimension (J. B. Metz; liberation theology). If, on the other hand, the freedom of the person is only externally influenced by society, then the gospel is directed primarily to the inner freedom of the human person. In this case the community/church, which gathers together in the name of the kingdom of God, is in principle independent from its respective society.

See also CHURCH; COMMUNITY; LOCAL CHURCH.

Bibliography

Clifford, James. *The Predicament of Culture: Twentieth-Century Ethnography, Literature, and Art.* Cambridge, Mass.: Harvard University Press, 1988.

Clifford, James, and George E. Marcus, eds. *Writing Culture: The Poetics and Politics of Ethnography.* Berkeley: University of California Press, 1986.

Farley, Edward. *Good and Evil: Interpreting a Human Condition.* Minneapolis: Fortress, 1990.

Metz, Johannes Baptist. *Faith in History and Society: Toward a Practical Fundamental Theology.* New York: Seabury, 1979.

GEORG LANGEMEYER

Soteriological Models. A soteriological model is an attempt to put into words the salvific Christ-event as it is known in the living experience and tradition of faith and as it is responsibly reflected on theologically to determine whether it is coherent with or opposed to ongoing life and thought, which are the contemporary "context" of faith.

(1) *Biblical Background.* All post-Easter soteriological models, as expressed in various forms of speech from the Old Testament and the late Jewish horizon of expectation or from the Hellenistic context, have their historical roots in Jesus' message of the *basileia* (kingdom, reign), his life practice, his claim as mediator of salvation, and his proexistent death (HISTORICAL JESUS), and are therefore based on Jesus' relationship to God. But, on the other hand, they are also grounded in the resurrection of Jesus, which is a divine confirmation and a qualitative new beginning. In the New Testament three dominant models of soteriology emerge: a "soteriology of the life of Jesus" (Synoptics: especially the journey theme in Luke), a theology of the cross (Paul, Hebrews, the Last Supper tradition), and a revelational schema ("realized eschatology") (John). These models correspond approximately to the offices of Jesus Christ as shepherd, priest, and prophet and may be grouped into three basic soteriological categories: redemption/liberation, reconciliation/forgiveness, and salvation/ransom. They do not exist in isolation from one another but are focal points that complement and limit one another. The "soteriology of the life of Jesus" of the Synoptics also encompasses the prophet-Christology and son-Christology (INFANCY NARRATIVES; see Mk 1:1; 15:39) and the Last Supper tradition. Paul's cross-centered soteriology also expresses the revelational character of the cross, the (preexistent) Son whom God sent, and the title of Kyrios (related to the titles of shepherd and king). Also Paul refers to the older formula "according to the flesh" (Rom 1:3f.) before proposing (1:16f.) and developing (1:18–8:39) his gospel of the righteousness of God. The revelational schema of John, which is characterized by the Word made flesh (1:14), is complemented by the sacrifice theme and the shepherd image. Thus any of these soteriological models may dominate while also accepting the rest of the faith tradition, resulting in complementary soteriologies that are open to one another (see accompanying table). The New Testament's understanding of faith is authoritative for every post–New Testament soteriological model and is confirmed by later history.

SOTERIOLOGICAL MODELS

I. *New Testament basis:* the inner axis of the New Testament's understanding of faith: the human history of Jesus and the salvation of humankind are based on the real divine sonship of Jesus.

Soteriological Categories	Salvation/Ransom	Reconciliation/ Forgiveness	Redemption/ Liberation
Basic NT model	Dominant: revelational schema, incarnation (Jn) Complementary: shepherd, gift of one's life	Dominant: theology of the cross (Paul, Last Supper tradition, Heb) Complementary: incarnation (mission), Kyrios	Dominant: soteriology of the life of Jesus (Syn.), journey theme (Lk-Acts), leader (Acts, Heb) Complementary: prophet, Son of God
Clarifications: complementary of the doctrine of three offices	Dominant: teacher/ prophet Complementary: shepherd, priest	Dominant: priest Complementary: shepherd, prophet	Dominant: shepherd Complementary: prophet, priest

II. *The history of theology:* the inner axis of the christological doctrine of redemption is the history of human freedom, realized by the Christ-event.

Soteriological Categories	Salvation/Ransom	Reconciliation/ Forgiveness	Redemption/ Liberation
Period	Patristic	Medieval	Modern
Typical representatives	Athanasius (d. 373) Augustine (d. 430)→ Maximus Confessor (d. 662)	Anselm of Canterbury (d. 1109) Thomas Aquinas (d. 1274) Martin Luther→ (d. 1546)	F. Schleiermacher (d. 1834) H. Kessler (b. 1938) J. Sobrino (b. 1938)
Typologies of – Protestant theology in the 19th century – G. Aulèn (1930) – G. Greshake (1973)	mystical *Christus victor* *paideia* in the framework of ancient Greek cosmic thought	juridical *Christus victima* inner grace of the individual, based on a legalistic representation of the order of God and humankind	moral/subjective *Christus exemplar* inner moment of the history of modern subjectivity

Key to the table: the salvation that Jesus brought is interpreted by the New Testament as salvation/ ransom, reconciliation/forgiveness, or redemption/liberation. One of these terms appears as the basis of the model or as *dominant*, while the others are also present or *complementary*. The models were further developed in the history of dogma. For each period there are typical representatives: Augustine and M. Luther have a lasting effect (indicated by an arrows). Modern theology has attempted to qualify the individual models theologically. The overview mentions a few examples.

The inner axis of New Testament thought, as expressed in the main soteriological models, is the basis of Jesus' human history — and therefore of the salvation of humankind — in God. This continues in the trinitarian and christological decisions of the early church.

(2) *History of Theology.* In the history of dogma and theology various typologies of the soteriological models were developed. In the nineteenth century, Protestant theology treated in a somewhat abbreviated way the link between Jesus as bringer of salvation and those redeemed; it saw this link as mystical (ontological-sacramental, physical); as juridical, because of the legal metaphor in Anselm's satisfaction theory; and as moral, because ethically mediated. While G. Aulèn sought to determine soteriological models on the basis of their dominant images of Christ (victorious Kyrios, the crucified as victim, and Jesus who exhorts exemplarily), G. Greshake calls attention to the common intellectual horizons of antiquity, the Middle Ages, and modernity (see table). The theologians referred to in the table are examples of the three periods. Augustine and M. Luther also introduce new periods. Here it is evident that any typology is approximative, and each soteriology is richer than the typology it represents. The soteriological models of the Fathers were based on the soteriological implications of the doctrine of the Logos, insofar as the real revelation of salvation is the incarnation of the Logos, through which humankind is "divinized" *and* "educated" by the incarnate one's teaching and example (the Apologists, Irenaeus, Tertullian, Clement of Alexandria, Origen, Cyprian, Lactantius, Council of Nicaea, Athanasius, Hilary, Gregory of Nyssa, Augustine, Cyril of Alexandria). Other statements found here are: in Origen, Jesus' priesthood is the kenosis of the Logos. Clement speaks of the priesthood of the God-man. Augustine speaks of Jesus' death as *sacrificium reconciliationis:* sacrifice of reconciliation (in his exegesis of 2 Cor 5:21); his death is an offering (*hostia*) for sins (*De Trin.* 4.12.15), brought forth by a holy and righteous priest in full freedom (4.13.16). In the Middle Ages, the salvific meaning of Jesus' death, his priesthood, and the salvation of each individual stood in the foreground. This "soteriology of justification" is found in Anselm, Thomas, M. Luther, and the Council of Trent, among others. However, Thomas develops his whole soteriology with the hypostatic union in mind, on the basis of which Jesus is priest by means of his humanity (as the *instrumentum coniunctum* of the word [*STh* 3, q. 22]) and mediator (q. 26): the suffering of Jesus (and his death [see 3, q. 26, a. 3]) — seen as merit and expiation or offering (q. 48) and based on his love and free obedience (3, q. 47, a. 3 ad 3; q. 48, a. 2f.) — is the cause of our salvation. Thomas also speaks of the exalted Christ's power to judge (q. 58), and, in his commentary on John, he refers to the incarnate Word as revealer (c. 1, 1.4; c. 6, 1.2; etc.). This establishes a framework that was the soteriological model of dogmatic manuals until recently (and determined the doctrine of the three offices). Only recently has the life of Jesus been placed in the foreground: his salvific work is interpreted as liberation and the office of shepherd as emancipation (political theology, liberation theology).

Thus H. Kessler makes it clear that the emancipatory starting point of his soteriological model is completely open to incarnational and stauro-paschal themes that complement it. In Evangelical theology this trend began with the Enlightenment (E. Kant, F. C. Baur, F. Schleiermacher). The inner axis of the Christian doctrine of redemption proceeds in the direction of freedom and human personality, which are in and from God. The important stages along this path are Augustine, Maximus, Anselm, and the most recent soteriological models.

(3) *Church Teaching.* Official pronouncements have contributed to various soteriological models, yet no one model has been espoused or canonized. Thus the church's official soteriology remains open. What has been emphasized is the redemptive power of the suffering and death of Jesus (DS 485, 904, 1523, 1529f., 3438, 3805) and the merits of Jesus (for the salvation of each individual [DS 1523, 1530, 1560, 3329]). We should take note of the soteriological implications of the trinitarian and christological definitions of the early church (DS 125, 150, 556ff.): if *God* had not become *man,* we would not be redeemed. If the Holy Spirit is not *God,* baptism does not bring salvation. Only as a free human being could Jesus redeem us, yet the free decision of the *human* will of Jesus for God is itself grounded in the *divine Logos.* Thus each soteriological model must explain that salvation is based on God, at the same time as it expresses the more secular effects of redemption as liberation (freedom, justice, peace, well-being). (See the documents of Medellín [1968], Puebla [1979], and the two instructions of the Congregation for the Doctrine of the Faith on liberation theology: *Libertatis nuntius* [1984] and *Libertatis conscientia* [1986].)

(4) *Ecumenical Perspectives.* See sec. 2 above.

(5) *Systematic Reflections.* The starting point for a soteriological model is one of three themes: the incarnation (incarnational starting point), the cross (and resurrection) (stauro-centric or paschal starting point), or the life of Jesus (practical-emancipatory starting point). On the basis of the New Testament and in the light of the history of theology, it may be stated that no soteriological model developed from one of these three starting points should be isolated, but rather it should be complemented by the others. Cultural contexts differ, and there is a need to develop specific soteriological models that are congruent with each. However, the tradition of the faith also implies a crisis for every context. Thus the original truth may stand in contradiction to a given context. Accommodation and contradiction, coherence and contestation determine every soteriological model.

See also KINGDOM OF GOD; OFFICES OF JESUS CHRIST; REDEMPTION AND LIBERATION; RESURRECTION OF JESUS; SALVATION.

Bibliography
Aulèn, Gustaf. *Christus Victor: An Historical Study of the Three Main Types of the Idea of Atonement.* New York: Macmillan, 1961.
Bloesch, Donald G. *Jesus Is Victor: Karl Barth's Doctrine of Salvation.* Nashville: Abingdon, 1976.

Fiorenza, Francis Schüssler. "Christian Redemption between Colonialism and Pluralism." In *Reconstructing Theology*, edited by Rebecca Chopp and Mark Taylor, 269–302. Minneapolis: Fortress, 1994.

———. "Redemption." In *The New Dictionary of Theology*, edited by Joseph A. Komanchack et al., 836–51. Wilmington, Del.: Glazier, 1988.

McIntyre, John. *The Shape of Soteriology: Studies in the Doctrine of the Death of Christ.* Edinburgh: T and T Clark, 1992.

Schelkle, Karl Hermann. *Theology of the New Testament.* Collegeville, Minn.: Liturgical Press, 1971.

LOTHAR ULLRICH

Soteriology. As a dogmatic treatise, soteriology describes the doctrine of the redemption (Greek: *soteria*) of all human beings by the atoning death of Jesus Christ on the cross. Because of the reality it deals with, soteriology contains all the themes of Christian theology. Thus it is more than a topical treatise. There is a distinction between the objective act of Christ's redemption and its subjective reception by believers, which is treated in the doctrine of grace (GRACE: DOCTRINE OF).

(1) *Biblical Background.* In the New Testament, statements concerning the person and work of Christ are inseparable. He reestablishes the relationship between humans and God that was disrupted by sin by taking our sins upon himself although he was sinless. By his death, our sins are buried with him; in his resurrection, sin is overcome (Rom 4:25; 8:3; 1 Cor 5:21; Gal 3:13; Heb 4:15). He overcame the legacy of death in Adam and thus gained for us new life with God; he makes us brothers and sisters in the Holy Spirit, and through grace he makes it possible for us to share in his relationship of being Son of the Father (Rom 8:29; Col 1:18; Eph 1:5). The whole public work of Jesus, the bearer of eschatological hope of salvation, is summarized in the New Testament *hyper* (for us) formula. Especially at the Last Supper, the death of Jesus is seen as the external expression of his proexistence. Trustfully and obediently he gives his life "for the many," for the forgiveness of sin (Mt 26:28; Mk 14:24; Lk 22:20; Jn 19:29; 1 Cor 11:25; 15:3; 1 Pt 1:24; see Is 53:11f.). The representative, atoning death of Jesus is explained using various images, most inspired by the Old Testament: ransom from the slavery of sin, justification, purification, and redemption by Christ's blood (Rom 5:9; 1 Cor 6:20; Eph 1:7; Col 1:14; Heb 9:14; 13:11f.; 1 Pt 1:19; 1 Jn 1:7; Rv 5:9); the gift of his life as ransom for the many (Mk 10:45; Gal 1:4; 1 Tm 2:6; see the song of the suffering servant [Isaiah 53]); self-sacrifice of atonement through his blood (Rom 3:25); or expiation for our sins (Rom 3:25–30; 8:3; Gal 1:4; 1 Pt 3:18; 1 Jn 2:2; 4:10; Heb 2:17; 1 Tm 2:6). This central act of Jesus and its result are found in the New Testament in various theological concepts: justification of the sinner by grace through faith (Rom 3:28; 5:9; 8:30; 1 Cor 6:11; Gal 2:16f.; Ti 3:7); forgiveness of sins (numerous texts); reconciliation (Rom 5:11; 11:15; 2 Cor 5:18f.; Eph 2:16; Col 1:20f.; Heb 2:17; 1 Jn 2:2; 4:10); liberation or rescue (Acts 2:21; Rom 5:9; 6:18; Col 1:13; Ti 3:5; 4:10); healing (Jn 17:17; Rom 6:22; 1 Thes

4:3, 7; 1 Cor 6:11; Heb 2:11; 10:10; 13:2); redemption (Lk 1:68; 2:38; 4:19; 21:28; Rom 3:24; 1 Cor 1:30; Eph 1:7; Col 1:14; Heb 9:15); a new and everlasting covenant (Mt 26:28; Mk 14:24; Lk 22:20; 1 Cor 11:25) whose high priest and mediator is Christ (Heb 8:6; 9:15; 12:24); communion and peace with God and human beings (Jn 1:3; 16:33; Acts 10:36; Rom 5:1; 14:17; 1 Cor 1:9; 2 Cor 13:13; Eph 1:3, 20; 2:14); participation in divine life and nature (Rom 8:29; Eph 1:17f.; 2 Pt 1:4); being reborn to new life (Jn 3:5; Ti 3:5); being a new creation (2 Cor 5:17; Gal 6:15; Eph 4:24). John also considers the sacrificial death of Christ as the reason for redemption (Jn 1:29; 10:11; 12:24, 33; 15:13; 19:34). Jesus' exaltation and the revelation of the Father's glory in the Son both happen at Jesus' death. God so loved the world that God gave up the Son in death, so that all who believe in him might have eternal life (Jn 3:16; 1 Jn 4:9f.). The believer appropriates the gifts of redemption by conversion, faith, baptism, the Eucharist, discipleship in the here and now through the gift of the Spirit, righteousness, and divine sonship (Mk 13:11; Gal 3:2f.; 4:6f.; Rom 8:12–17). The firstfruits of future redemption are already given and anticipate a full revelation at the parousia: namely, bodily resurrection (Jn 5:25; 1 Cor 15:12) and eternal life; the glory of the children of God (Rom 8:17; 1 Jn 3:1f.); the vision of God (1 Cor 13:12; 1 Jn 3:2); the communion of the saints (Eph 1:10; Heb 12:22–24; 1 Thes 4:14); the new heaven and new earth (Is 65:17; 6:22; Rv 21:1), along with a final victory over death, Satan, and the powers and forces of evil (Rom 21:4; 1 Cor 15:25f.).

(2) *History of Theology.* The patristic teaching is characterized by an inner unity of *theologia* and *oeconomia* (THEOLOGY). God is the subject of redemption. God acts through Christ. In Christ the world is reconciled with God. Because of the hypostatic union there is in Christ a harmonious interaction of the movement from God to humankind (grace, love) and from humankind to God (sacrifice, obedience). In Christ, God assumes humanity as a whole. In him the whole of creation is "recapitulated" and integrated. The incarnation was meant to bring human beings into a likeness and conformity with Christ and ultimately — in overcoming sin and disobedience through the grace of Christ — to divinize them (Irenaeus, *Adv. haer.* 3.18.1). The cross and resurrection are by no means subordinated to the incarnation, as a widespread misconception of the "physical" doctrine of redemption would have it. Rather the trinitarian background of salvation-history already manifests God as the goal of the whole movement. The goal is reached only by the condescension of the Son, who assumed concrete human nature in its distance from God and its fallenness, in other words by his obedience unto death in the *forma servi* (Phil 2:7). Thus he overcame the root of Adam's sin, namely, pride and disobedience, the outward expression of which is the mortality of the body. In his resurrection he is the new Adam. In him there is new life for all who are in the *forma Christi,* that is, those who enter into the "body" of the new humanity through the obedience of faith, discipleship with the crucified one, and hope of resurrection. The well-known themes of patristic soteriology (the devil who is overcome by Christ,

the ransom of sinners from the devil's power) are only popular ways of illustrating the theory of redemption as mediation of divine life, and this in turn should be interpreted in terms of God's universal plan of salvation. A wholly different type of project was developed by Anselm of Canterbury (*Cur Deus homo*) in conjunction with his satisfaction theory. By using arguments (*rationes necessariae:* necessary reasons), he hoped to make revelation rationally comprehensible. Here juridical categories are primary — and this falls in line with the tendencies of Western, Roman culture since Tertullian. Sin is an infinite offense to the honor of God. However, no individual human being can achieve satisfaction of God's righteousness. This can only be achieved representatively by the God-man. Because of the hypostatic union, the human acts of Christ (his obedience, suffering, and death) have infinite worth (merit) and can satisfy God and achieve reconciliation. With variations in certain details, this manner of conceiving things remains predominant in the West. The Enlightenment's criticism of Christianity, starting with a crude version of the satisfaction theory, asks whether it is compatible with God's goodness to subject the Son to a gruesome death so that God's wrath or grievances could be placated. The dignity of moral freedom seems to be contradicted by an arrangement in which satisfaction is procured by someone who represents us (E. Kant). This perspective radically contests the unity of humankind even as something negative (ORIGINAL SIN), as determined transcendentally by its relationship to God. It argues that sins are a weakness of nature or a structural shortcoming of society and can therefore be overcome psychologically and sociologically. Suffering and death are decreased by an evolutionary development in which matter becomes more complex. Thus the work of Christ can be understood only in moral or political categories, at the expense of its central theological components (liberal theology).

(3) *Church Teaching.* The teaching office of the church espouses no particular theory of redemption. The most important statements were in the first centuries during the great christological controversies. The controversies over Pelagianism and the Reformation concerned the subjective side of redemption. The basis for the objective act of redemption is God's mercy and salvific will. Because of the hypostatic union, the Son is mediator between God and humankind in his priestly, kingly, and prophetic offices (DS 261). Though sinless he took upon himself the weaknesses of human nature for the sole purpose of redeeming humankind from the reign of sin, the devil, and death. In his divine nature he overcomes guilt (DS 291f., 209) since he truly died a human death (DS 539). Because of his obedience unto death, he earned for us an infinite reward, overcoming by himself the sin of Adam and its consequences (DS 1513) and bringing about a new righteousness, eternal life, and reconciliation (DS 1522f.). The merits of his suffering are infinite and encompass all men and women, since he gained sanctifying grace and justification for all. Thus he achieved satisfaction before the Father (DS 1529). Although Christ offered himself only *once* on the altar of the cross as a bloody sacrifice, he maintains the presence of this sacrifice in his church in sacramental form, where, as victim

and priest, he offers to the Father expiation and petitions, praise, thanksgiving, and worship (DS 1739–43, 1751–54). Human beings share in redemption only through faith, hope, and love, as well as by baptism and penance (DS 1520–83). They are able to mature in grace, and, as members of the body of Christ, by means of their new moral activity, they achieve merits by their life of grace and make satisfaction for their sins. This does not contradict the complete sufficiency of the sacrifice on the cross, but presupposes it. Jesus' objective work of salvation is fulfilled in the incarnation; in Mary's conception by the Spirit; in Jesus' birth, suffering, death, descent among the dead, resurrection, and ascension; and in the sending of the Spirit (see the creeds).

(4) *Ecumenical Perspectives.* The Reformation produced new emphasis on the idea of satisfaction. According to Reformation thought, the incarnation is not the assumption of human nature whereby Christ also becomes the head of a new humanity and brings its free actions to the Father. There remains no room for such notions as sacrifice, atonement, and merit. The incarnation belongs to the office of Christ. As divine he is the bearer of satisfactory action — hidden in his assumed, human flesh. The cross is actually a relationship of God to God in the form of an alienation for the sake of our sins. Thus human beings can only receive salvation as a gift and be one with the crucified God in faith, on the level of their consciousness. They are not graced and empowered for their own action as members of Jesus' humanity. This has no meaning for the acceptance of salvation and growth in grace. This has consequences for the Christian's relationship to the world and anthropology and results in the distinctive characteristics of the various denominations.

(5) *Systematic Reflections.* Today we must reexamine what is behind the satisfaction theory and draw conclusions from the wider perspective of the biblical and patristic views of salvation-history, Christology, ecclesiology, pneumatology, and sacramental theology. Grace must be understood by means of dialogical thinking as a life-revealing word and a liberating action of God. Only in this way will it be compatible with the modern problematic of freedom. When salvation is seen as the sharing of divine life that of itself brings human beings into a communion with God, grace can be seen as the condition of possibility and the very content of human freedom. God's historical action demonstrates that the theological perspective is not just a theory that would become practice only in social and political relationships. On the contrary, since salvation addresses human beings in all their relationships, it is concretized in all reaches of life. To this extent, the projects of political theology and liberation theology find their relative place in the satisfaction theory: humankind's history of suffering must be related to the passion of Jesus. The MYSTERIES OF THE LIFE OF JESUS CHRIST establish a connection to the experience of salvation in the concrete life-paths of Christians.

See also GRACE; INCARNATION; JUSTIFICATION; REDEMPTION AND LIBERATION; RESURRECTION OF JESUS; SALVATION; SATISFACTION THEORY.

Bibliography
See the bibliographies under SALVATION; SATISFACTION THEORY; and SOTERIOLOGICAL MODELS.

GERHARD LUDWIG MÜLLER

Soul. The soul in the theological sense is the uniform basis of life of the whole human person in her or his unity of mind and body. Joined to the concept of the soul is the theological statement that the human person's life as such ultimately comes from God and therefore belongs to God and is not at the human person's disposal. God alone is the Lord of life. From this follows the responsibility of human persons before God for their own lives (their souls) and the lives of their fellow human beings (care of souls).

(1) *Biblical Background.* In Scripture the soul frequently means as much as "life" or the living human person. The soul can also characterize the subject of the expressions of life, above all of the intellectual and spiritual expressions. As such, the soul is subject to divine judgment (reward and punishment) and is the receiver of eternal life. Though a Greek-Hellenistic influence can be felt marginally (in Wisdom and the later letters of the New Testament), the eternal life of the soul is always considered as God's saving gift and includes the resurrection of the body.

(2) *History of Theology.* The Greek-Hellenistic concept of the soul is based on the experience of the contrast between the spatio-temporal corporeal world perceived by the senses (a world that arises and passes away) and the world of thoughts and judgments that are valid independently of space and time. These two heterogeneous realms of being are joined in the human person, who consists of a transitory body and an eternal, immortal soul. In this view, salvation consists in the liberation of the soul from the bondage of the transitory corporeal world. Theology succeeded in distinguishing and in keeping the Christian faith free from this concept of salvation. The whole human person with body and soul has been created by God as good. Yet the conceptual distinction between the soul and the body as the two individual substances of which the human person consists has influenced theological thinking until the present. It was only in High Scholasticism (Thomas Aquinas) that the soul was again interpreted as the one form-giving life principle of the whole human person. Under the influence of modern rational philosophy (R. Descartes), however, the contrasting nature of soul and body (consciousness and matter) once more became influential in theology and in piety.

(3) *Church Teaching.* The magisterium rejected the derivation of human being from several partial principles (e.g., spirit, soul, body) and maintained the unified basis of life of the whole human person: the soul is the form-giving principle of the body (*anima forma corporis* [DS 902]). It also rejected as false Renaissance speculations that denied the existence of the individual soul and its individual immortality (DS 1440; see GS 14).

(4) *Ecumenical Perspectives.* Protestant theologians find fault with the

teaching on the immortality of the soul because it did not originate in the Bible but rather in Greek philosophy. Recently, this teaching is also an object of discussion in Catholic theology.

(5) *Systematic Reflections.* In empirical anthropology today the concept of soul hardly plays a role. In theology also it is mostly replaced by "human person" or "person." However, the underlying experience of the difference between intellectual thinking and willing, on the one hand, and sensual perception, on the other hand, remains a phenomenon that is theologically significant.

See also DEATH; CORPORALITY OF THE HUMAN PERSON; HUMAN PERSON; IMMORTALITY; INTERMEDIATE STATE; PERSONALITY; RESURRECTION OF THE DEAD.

Bibliography
Bremmer, Jan N. *The Early Greek Concept of the Soul.* Princeton, N.J.: Princeton University Press, 1983.
Brotzman, Ellis Robert. *The Plurality of "Soul" in the Old Testament, with Special Attention Given to the Use of Nepes.* Ann Arbor: University Microfilms International, 1987.
Davis, Charles. *Body as Spirit: The Nature of Religious Feeling.* New York: Seabury, 1976.
Fiorenza, Francis, and Johann B. Metz. "Der Mensch als Einheit von Leib und Seele." In *MystSal,* 2:584–636.
The Human Body. Statements on the human body by popes, selected and arranged by the monks of Solesmes. Boston: St. Paul Editions, 1960.
Molnar, Thomas Steven. *Philosophical Grounds.* New York: Lang, 1991.
Owen, Derwyn. *Body and Soul: A Study on the Christian View of Man.* Philadelphia: Westminster, 1956.
Rosenstock-Huessy, Eugen. *Applied Science of the Soul.* San Francisco: Golden Phoenix, 1984.
Sullivan, Lawrence E, ed. *Death, Afterlife, and the Soul.* New York: Macmillan, 1989.
Swinburne, Richard. *The Evolution of the Soul.* New York: Oxford University Press, 1986.
Tilby, Angela. *Science and the Soul: God, Self, and the New Cosmology.* New York: Doubleday, 1993.

GEORG LANGEMEYER

Space–Time Schema.

The "space–time schema" corresponds to the general experience that all objects and events appear, to their observer, as a reality that can be organized in terms of spatial (height, width, and length as dimensions of space) and temporal (what is past, present, or future) standards. These categories perform an ordering function. They enable visualization, narration, and other modes of spoken, written, plastic, and symbolic representation.

(1) *Biblical Background.* In the Bible, there is no religiously binding revelation about the space–time schema. Only temporally conditioned things are stated. The three-tiered, geocentric worldview characteristic of the ancient Orient serves as the setting for the course of history, which God creates and guides toward redemption. God's presence is referred to imagistically as "dwelling" (Jb 23:8–10; Jer 7:4–12), even if it knows no bounds. God's activity in the world is compared to a "coming" or a "coming again." Eschatologically, God appears as the Lord and Creator of a certain kind of future. The time of human beings and God's eternity stand in sharp contrast to each other (see

Ps 90:4). Yet the Eternal has attributes of the living (Dt 12:7) and the omnipresent (1 Kgs 8:27). When the heavens and earth were created, God already *is*. Unlike the gods, Yahweh is both present at all times and places (Ps 139:5–13) and absolutely beyond them. Yahweh "hems them in," as it were, from all sides (Ps 139:5). Human beings, by contrast, are bound to the temporal, spatial, cognitive, and volitional finitude characteristic of them. They are mortal and corruptible. Their mortality is transformed into immortality and their corruptibility into incorruptibility only through the grace of the creative redeemer (1 Cor 15:53). Their salvation is realized when, in being conformed to the raised crucified one, they are led over the bounds of the space–time schema and into eternal glory (Rom 8:18–30, and esp. Rom 38f.: "Nor present things, nor future things, nor powers, nor height, nor depth, nor any other creature will be able to separate us from the love of God in Christ Jesus our Lord").

(2) *History of Theology.* Among the Fathers, Augustine, with his psychological theory of time, is particularly prominent. According to him, time is essentially human time, since it is understandable only within our consciousness of passing and enduring (*Conf.* 11.20). The world, whose center is humanity, was created by God not in time, but along with time. Time has existed only since the world has existed (ibid., 11.30). To our eyes, space unfolds itself temporally; in God's eyes, however, all things that have come into being appear simultaneously. God views creation as a reality that is linked to God's eternity and supported by it, even though radically different from it. Thus the principle holds true that the world was "not created *in* time but *with* time" (*De civ. Dei* 11.6). In any case, there is no sense at all in speaking of a time, or also a space, as existing "before the creation of the world." Time is always time, and space is always space *for* something that was created. In the tradition stemming from Augustine (Boethius, Thomas), eternity is strictly distinguished from "infinite time" (see *STh* 1, q. 46, a. 2; q. 57, a. 3). The former is beyond all measurement, while the latter can be thought of as a reality divisible, in its constant succession from earlier to later, into infinitely many temporal intervals. Nicholas of Cusa "held that a world infinite in space and time, as corresponds to the infinitude of God, was a work particularly appropriate to the perfection of the Creator" (W. Pannenberg). Thus the existence of different kinds of infinitude is postulated.

(3) *Church Teaching.* Doctrinal office adheres to the proposition that God created the world "at the beginning of time" (DS 800, 3002); hence, it must not be thought that "the world exists from eternity" (DS 952) or that it is as eternal as the Son of God (DS 953; see 951). Eternity must, then, remain exclusively an attribute of God, even if — in the case, for example, of Thomas Aquinas and Nicholas of Cusa — the possibility of a spatio-temporally infinite cosmos is assumed. A combination of both ideas was intimated by the Provincial Synod of Cologne in 1860: "The world did not exist from eternity, but was created by God in time (N.B.: less ambiguous, Augustine: 'with time'). The act through which he willed the existence of the world was in God from eternity — where

there is no successiveness and no awaiting — but it first took effect in time, or better, at the beginning of time" (NR 308).

(4) *Ecumenical Perspectives.* The space–time schema is not a particular object of controversy in the interconfessional sphere.

(5) *Systematic Reflections.* Present-day theology of creation is not uninterested in A. Einstein's theory of relativity, which put an end to the total dominance of two rigid schemes of interpretation: Euclidian geometry with its strictly intuitable three-dimensionality, and the Newtonian concept of "absolute space," which is supposed to remain constantly the same apart from relatedness to other things and without regard for the time factor. The curvature of space (analogous to the surface of a sphere) — which was initially assumed hypothetically by Einstein but later confirmed by repeated experiments beyond the earth's atmosphere — restricts the range of the first-named scheme's validity. A similar fate befalls the second-named scheme, insofar as Einstein has shown that the three dimensions of space correlate with time, as a "fourth dimension," to form a seamless structure of relativity. Both of Einstein's proposals bring with them increased insight into the enormous complexity of cosmological reality and also into the constantly innovative dynamics of that reality. From this viewpoint, the proposals are not incompatible with a historical, and redemptive-historical, understanding of that unity of space and time that forms our world in its biblically revealed relationship with the eternal Creator.

See also INTERMEDIATE STATE; JUDGMENT; WORLDVIEW.

Bibliography
Pannenberg, Wolfhart. "Contingency and Natural Law." In *Toward a Theology of Nature: Essays on Science and Faith.* Edited by Ted Peters. Louisville: Westminster, 1993.
Ray, Christopher. *Time, Space, and Philosophy.* New York: Routledge, 1991.
Salmon, Wesley C. *Space, Time, and Motion: A Philosophical Introduction.* 2d ed. Minneapolis: University of Minnesota Press, 1980.
Sklar, Lawrence. *Philosophy and Spacetime Physics.* Berkeley: University of California Press, 1985.
Swinburne, Richard, ed. *Space, Time, and Causality.* Boston: Reidel, 1983.
Trusted, Jennifer. *Physics and Metaphysics: Theories of Space and Time.* New York: Routledge, 1991.

ALEXANDRE GANOCZY

Spirituality. Spirituality means the personal relationship of a human being with God, along with all the attitudes and modes of expression that this relationship includes. The reality conveyed by "spirituality" is also described as "piety."

(1) *Biblical Background.* In the Old Testament the group known as the "just" includes the great variety of people leading a "spiritual life" under the sign of the history of God's covenant with Israel. In the New Testament and especially in Paul these persons are called "saints." They are characterized by an effort to live out the election/grace bestowed on them by God by seeking God's

will in humility, patience, service to the brethren, and so on. This can be done, concretely, in an almost incalculable variety of ways. The inspiration, possibility, and motives for such a life are ascribed to God and the Spirit of God who acts in human beings and prepares them from within for the external challenge of the message of salvation. Involved, therefore, is the whole range of religious volition, which rises to consciousness in the person as a fruit of the Spirit and is exercised in prayer, sacrifice, and service.

(2) *History of Theology.* As far as its linguistic form is concerned, the word *spirituality* could have the same meaning as *pneumatology.* Both are collective terms. Only in recent centuries was "spirituality" given the meaning it developed in France, starting in the seventeenth but especially during the nineteenth century: spirituality as signifying the numerous new breakthroughs that occur in a life devoted to God, more intense Christian forms of life, new methods of prayer, new commitments and ways of service. Spirituality thus understood was considered to be a distinguishing mark of a few people, who, it was supposed, received a special call. In revivalist movements, too, spirituality was not infrequently regarded as something inaccessible to the uninitiated. It was only the emphatic recall of the *one* Spirit (see 1 Cor 12:4) that spurred the search for what is common to all and the understanding of this as the decisive element. This led to a new awareness that spirituality plays a decisive role in every Christian life, beginning with the person's call and baptism (Rom 1:6; 1 Cor 1:24ff.; 7:20; Gal 3:27). At the same time, spirituality, which had originally been understood in a heavily literary and cognitive way, was extended to the other human powers; that is, feeling, veneration, and enthusiasm became important. Here, however, the question immediately arose of the criteria of spirituality and the distinction between true and false spirituality, as did the task of ordering and imparting spirituality (1 Cor 11:31; 12:10). Since the concern is always with lived Christianity, it was natural to take as basic norm the story of the Jesus-event as narrated in the Gospels. From this point of view spirituality is the following of Christ, that is, the acceptance and implementation of the vocation of Jesus Christ in the life of the individual and of the ecclesial community (Jn 13:15). In contrast to earlier currents of piety, this concentration on the person of the Lord, along with the criterion of discernment, has allowed the center of Christian spirituality to emerge into clear consciousness once more (Jn 6:29; 8:12).

(3) *Church Teaching.* In the course of history the magisterium has repeatedly come out against false and one-sided spiritualities; on the other hand, rarely has it spoken explicitly of spirituality as such. It did so in the thirteenth century when dealing with the mendicant orders viewed as a "movement of Spirituals" (DS 842f.) and with the radical groups that emerged from them (DS 866) and that rejected the institutional church, its sacraments, offices, and decrees (DS 911f., 930): spirituality here turned into opposition to the visible church. In response, the magisterium emphasized its intrinsic relation to the visible church in a unity amid tension.

(4) *Ecumenical Perspectives*. For the very reason that in spirituality the group and the individual live out their concrete relationship with God, there is antecedently a certain freedom that even the officials of the church must respect: "Do not extinguish the Spirit" (1 Thes 5:9). Conversely, this Spirit manifests its identity by its respect for the ecclesial institution and tradition. These two statements also describe the fundamental model at work in the ecumenical movement: the freedom of the Spirit and a joint acceptance of what is necessary. The differences between ecclesial communities and groups may be traced back not least to different spiritualities; in any case, it is becoming increasingly difficult in many instances to determine accurately the compelling reasons behind a separation. It is not enough, however, to regard confessional differences as simply different spiritualities. For the power of spiritualities to create differences seems hardly to be balanced by an equally effective force working for unity. For this reason, there is need to stress the connection of spiritualities with the normative truth of the gospel and of faith. This is certainly proving to be the most difficult obstacle to unification. All the same, the fact that spirituality is related to the truths of the gospel and faith and that such statements of truths have a living spirituality as their proper context may be able to pave the way for a consensus not only on the necessity of binding propositions of faith but also on the central contents of these propositions.

(5) *Systematic Reflections*. A theological description of spirituality begins with the express gift of the Spirit, which, according to Christian belief, is communicated in baptism as a grace. At this point of origin the institutional and spontaneously personal aspects of spirituality are closely linked. For the spiritual life must be lived in and with the church, regardless of the fact that spirituality always has a unique and special form corresponding to the personal salvation-history of the individual or of a small group/religious order. Spirituality provides the conscious framework of Christian existence; it is not, however, entirely reducible to theoretical and rational terms; rather, because it is not to be wholly captured by any theory, it brings us into the presence of the mystery dimension of Christian life. In this sense, the real meaning ("relevance") of theological reflection depends on spirituality. The latter mediates between the realms of primordial experience and theological explanation; it could therefore satisfy the demand for a new linkage of theology and spirituality (R. Guardini), of which a great deal is said but which rarely becomes a reality. An example would be the work of K. Rahner, which shows how the experience of a life of faith gives rise to discourse and leads rational discourse in turn to new experiences. Such a spirituality no longer permits us to deal with the truth of faith solely in the isolation of speculative thought. Language aims at understanding and the latter in turn at ideas that do justice to reality and the times. In this sense, the linkage of theological reflection with spirituality shows that we are taking seriously the historical dimension of Christianity and therefore also the possibility of mission and deeper understanding

as well as of bridging the gap between the data of faith and the human sense of ongoing life.

See also DISCIPLESHIP, CHRISTIAN; GRACE; PNEUMATOLOGY.

Bibliography

Dupré, Louis, and Don E. Saliers, eds., in collaboration with John Meyendorff. *Christian Spirituality: Post-Reformation and Modern.* New York: Crossroad, 1989.

Egan, Harvey D. *What Are They Saying about Mysticism?* New York: Paulist, 1982.

McGinn, Bernard. *The Presence of God: A History of Christian Mysticism.* Vol. 1: *The Foundations of Mysticism.* New York: Crossroad, 1991.

McGinn, Bernard, and John Meyendorff, in collaboration with Jean Leclercq. *Christian Spirituality: Origins to the Twelfth Century.* New York: Crossroad, 1985.

Raitt, Jill, ed., in collaboration with Bernard McGinn and John Meyendorff. *Christian Spirituality: High Middle Ages and Reformation.* New York: Crossroad, 1987.

World Spirituality: An Encyclopedic History of the Religious Quest. New York: Crossroad. This is an ongoing, multivolume series that deals with the history of spirituality in various traditions.

KARL HEINZ NEUFELD

Spirituality

Contemporary Issues

The term *spirituality* refers both to experience and to an academic discipline. The ways in which the term refers to life-experience will be noted first. Then we trace the emergence of the academic field that studies this spiritual experience.

Spirituality as Experience

Paul's letters describe any reality under the influence of the Holy Spirit as "spiritual." There are spiritual blessings, spiritual gifts, spiritual persons. When Paul distinguishes spiritual from natural persons, he does not mean to contrast the spiritual to the material or evil. He simply distinguishes those who act under the Spirit's influence from those who do not.

This theological denotation for the words *spiritual* or *spirituality* continued until the twelfth century when other meanings arose. In philosophy, the spiritual was opposed to the material. In church law, *spiritual* referred to ecclesiastical goods whereas *temporal* designated secular things. In the seventeenth century, *spirituality* came to refer to the interior life of Christians, but also carried overtones of dangerous enthusiasm or even heresy. A preferred term was *devotion,* which carried the sense of careful and prompt good action. By the eighteenth century, *spirituality* referred to the life of perfection that could lead to mysticism, in contrast with the "ordinary" life of faith. By the nineteenth and twentieth centuries, *spirituality* meant the interior life of those striving for perfection. Since the 1950s the meaning of *spirituality* has expanded beyond a Christian or even a religious denotation.

Today, the term *spirituality* can refer to human experience in three ways. First, it refers to a general human capacity for self-transcendence, for movement beyond mere self-maintenance or self-interest. Some philosophical, psychological, or anthropological discussions would use this term. For example, when Jungian psychologists speak of masculine or feminine spirituality they use the term in this generic sense. Second, the term *spirituality* can refer to a religious dimension of life, to a capacity for self-transcendence that is said to be actualized by the Holy, however that may be understood. Third, it may refer to a specific type of religious experience such as Jewish, Christian, Muslim, or Buddhist.

Self-transcendence is central to the meaning of spirituality. This does not mean that one escapes being oneself or attending to oneself or caring for oneself. Rather, one acts out of the center of oneself in a way that "reaches out" in love, freedom, and truth to others and to one's own capacities. And one does this within the horizon of whatever one imagines or judges to be ultimate. One's spirituality depends on one's ultimate value. If that ultimacy is God revealed in the death and resurrection of Jesus and known in the power of the Holy Spirit poured out in the community, then one has Christian spirituality. If that ultimacy is the individuated self, then one has humanistic spirituality. In summary, self-transcendence is central to the full range of spirituality, nonreligious as well as religious.

Although the definition of spirituality may be generic, there is no "generic spirituality." All spiritual experience is concrete and shaped by the particularities of experience. These would include, for example, symbol and story, boundary of social awareness, mode of knowing and feeling, gender and race. Consequently, there is no generic, uniform Catholic or Protestant spirituality. Spirituality as experience has all the complexity and richness of each person's history, personality, and social location.

Spirituality as an Academic Field

Until the High Middle Ages all theology was spiritual theology in the sense that it was reflection upon life "in the Spirit." All theology arose in monastic or pastoral settings as an attempt to convey the experience of faith expressed in Scripture, liturgy, private prayer, communal life, or pastoral care.

When the university rather than the monastery became the primary home of theology, the "sacred science" gradually moved away from its explicit foundation in spiritual experience and focused on a foundation in philosophy, logical argumentation, or even in controversy. Reformation theology of the Eucharist, for example, seldom aimed to explicate the religious experience of union or division in Christ; rather it tried to expose contradictions in its opponents' use of Scripture.

Explicit reflection upon religious experience did continue in monastic and pastoral settings, but this was not considered academically reputable. For example, Julian of Norwich gave years of careful attention to her experience of the Trinity and described this in her book *Revelations*, yet this was not studied in the religious academy until recently. Throughout history many careful and even systematic accounts of the spiritual life were written outside of formal theology in many different literary genres: religious rules, commentaries on Scripture, autobiography, letters of spiritual advice, poetry, sermons. In the eighteenth and nineteenth centuries academic credibility did come to the study of the spiritual life, but it came only by admitting this field through the side door of moral theology. Using principles from dogmatic theology and Scholastic vocabulary, ascetical and mystical theology emerged as subdivisions of "morals." Ascetical theology studied "the purgative way" of ordinary Christians up to the phase of development known as "infused contemplation" or "mysticism." Mystical theology studied the spiritual life from the onset of "the illuminative way" of passive contemplation up to the "unitive way" characteristic of great sanctity. As each field of study mirrors the culture that nourishes it, so this forerunner of academic spirituality reflected its culture's assumptions about the hierarchy of spiritual stages, the elitism of Christian perfection available primarily to celibate religious, and the certitude of dogmatic conclusions about God and "man."

When Scripture and tradition were studied with a more critical method, the inadequacy of these earlier assumptions became clear and there gradually emerged a new academic discipline. Spirituality is a young discipline that studies not only Christian but all spiritual experience precisely *as experience*. That is, it aims to understand spirituality in all its concreteness, in all its complex interaction with its social, cultural, and cosmic setting.

Although spirituality as an academic field is young, and scholars debate its distinctive nature and methodology, some clarity has emerged. Spirituality as an academic discipline is the field of study that attempts to investigate in an interdisciplinary way spiritual experience as such, that is, as spiritual and as experience. Also, spirituality is understood as descriptive and critical rather than prescriptive and normative. Scholars agree that spirituality is ecumenical, interreligious, and cross-cultural. Another characteristic of spirituality is wholeness. That is, every aspect of human spiritual experience is integral to the discipline: bodily, psychological, historical, political, aesthetic, intellectual, and social.

Turning from characteristics of spirituality to its practice involves attention to its particular *object*, its *methodological style*, and its *objective*. These distinguish it from other disciplines. The object of spirituality is spiritual experience in its individuality, in its messy particularity.

No one method fits spirituality because its interdisciplinary nature calls for the use of all the methods needed for the understanding of its object. Yet a participative style of methodology fits spirituality in a way that is similar to that of psychology and anthropology. That is, it deals with material that cannot be understood, in the sense of personally appropriated, except through personal experience or involvement with research data.

This participative style presents a problem regarding the appropriate objectivity of the discipline, and members of the academy have raised serious questions that reveal their mistrust of spirituality. Some wonder whether spiritual practice may replace research, while others suspect that evangelization may be a hidden agenda in degree programs in spirituality. Any response to these concerns needs to deal with academic spirituality's conviction that only when a researcher is critically aware of her or his actual commitments and assumptions, and acts to make them assist rather than prevent insight, can the researcher be objective. It is attention to this level of experience that characterizes the researcher in spirituality.

Another aspect of the practice of spirituality is the tendency for serious studies to move in a pattern of three phases. Phase one is descriptive, intending to surface the data associated with the experience being investigated. Phase two is analytical and critical, leading to an explanation and evaluation of the subject. In this phase theological, human, and social sciences are very important. A final phase is synthetic and/or constructive, leading to the kind of personal knowledge that deeply shifts the scholar's own horizon on the experience studied as well as on the wider world.

Spirituality has a threefold objective. Although most people will associate spirituality primarily with practical assistance toward a life of greater self-transcendence, the first goal of this discipline is knowledge about the particular spiritual experience being studied. Only then can this academic discipline move well to the second and third goals: developing the researcher's own spirituality and fostering the spirituality of others. This triple goal may contrast with the goal of the "hard sciences," but is common to the social sciences, such as psychology, and to the humanities, such as art and philosophy, which aim to liberate humanity from a narrow horizon and free humans for mature relationships.

Bibliography
Schneiders, Sandra M. "Spirituality in the Academy." *ThS* 50, no. 4 (1989) 676–97.
Wolski Conn, Joann. "Spirituality." In *The New Dictionary of Theology*, edited by J. Komonchak et al., 972–86. Collegeville, Minn.: Liturgical, 1987.

JOANN WOLSKI CONN

Suffering. *Suffering* is the generic term for everything that produces the feeling of pain. The beginning of human life is marked with suffering (the primal scream). The history of humanity is a chain of immense suffering. Every human achievement is paid for with suffering. The reality of suffering is, therefore, the most serious argument against the existence of God. The question of suffering pervades all of theology.

(1) *Biblical Background.* According to the Old Testament, suffering has come into God's originally good creation as a consequence of sin (Gn 1:31; 3:16–19). God sends suffering as a punishment, as a penance, and finally as vicarious atonement on the part of the just person for the sins of the people (Is 53:4–12). Job gives a different response to the question of suffering: through suffering the faith of the just man is tested. According to the witness of the Gospels, Jesus rejected a direct connection between sin and suffering (Lk 13:2f.; Jn 9:3). In his activity for the coming kingdom of God, he opposed suffering in all forms. According to the New Testament, in the kingdom of God all suffering will be overcome. Nevertheless, Jesus finally delivered himself up to suffering including his death on the cross. In the New Testament communities, therefore, suffering counts as a special grace that leads Christians to the glory of the resurrection (e.g., 1 Pt 2:20). This view is due not only to the focusing of faith on the suffering, death, and resurrection of Christ but also to the situation of persecution in which the Christians lived.

(2) *History of Theology.* Two reactions to human suffering, patience in suffering and compassion with the suffering of others, characterized theological thinking in later times. The overcoming of suffering remains by and large the object of hope for the next world. The connection between suffering and sin was underlined in Scholastic theology through speculations over the kind of suffering in PURGATORY and HELL.

(3) *Church Teaching.* The ecclesial doctrine of faith also sees suffering, on the one hand, in connection with sin and, on the other hand, with the taking up of the cross (*LG* 8, 41).

(4) *Ecumenical Perspectives.* After the experiences of suffering in World War II (e.g., Auschwitz), the question of suffering has become a new challenge for all Christian theologians alike.

(5) *Systematic Reflections.* The renewed reflection on the salvific meaning of Jesus' praxis of relieving suffering (e.g., healings of the sick), on the one hand, and the efforts of society to alleviate suffering, on the other hand, make possible today a more nuanced theological response to the question of suffering. The discipleship of Jesus includes not only the carrying of the cross but also the liberation of the human person from suffering. Theological criteria need to be developed for explaining the necessity of the one aspect just as much as for the other. Suffering can be unavoidable (*a*) because of the creatureliness (CONTINGENCY) of the human person: the realization of values is often possible only through renunciation, and the search for what is right necessarily runs the risk of error; and (*b*) because of the sinful condition of the human person:

ultimately, Christian love has nothing to set against the lack of love in sin except suffering because of it. Thus, the following of the cross does not consist in bearing any kind of pain, but rather in the defenselessness of love before this lack of love. This is why the final response to the question about suffering has to be seen in God's own love. Before the immeasurable suffering of human beings, the justification of this love as God's own cause must remain the subject of Christian hope.

See also CONTINGENCY; CROSS: THEOLOGY OF THE; DEATH; DISCIPLESHIP, CHRISTIAN; EVIL; ILLNESS; PASSION AND DEATH OF JESUS CHRIST; THEODICY.

Bibliography
Crenshaw, James L., ed. *Theodicy in the Old Testament.* Philadelphia: Fortress, 1983.
Gutiérrez, Gustavo. *On Job: God-Talk and the Suffering of the Innocent.* Maryknoll, N.Y.: Orbis Books, 1987.
Lewis, C. S. *The Problem of Pain.* New York: Macmillan, 1962.
Morris, David B. *The Culture of Pain.* Berkeley: University of California Press, 1991.
Rahner, Karl. "Why Does God Allow Us to Suffer?" In *Theological Investigations,* 19:194–208. New York: Crossroad, 1983.
Richard, Lucien. *What Are They Saying about Suffering?* New York: Paulist, 1992–93.
Scarry, Elaine. *The Body in Pain: The Making and Unmaking of the World.* New York: Oxford University Press, 1985.
Sölle, Dorothee. *Suffering.* Philadelphia: Fortress, 1984.

GEORG LANGEMEYER

Synod. In its original meaning the term *synod* (Greek: *synodos* = assembly) is a synonym for council; it means secondarily an assembly of the bishops of regional churches who exercise their ministry of governance collegially (synod of bishops; episcopal conferences) or the designated members of a local church under the leadership of the bishop (diocesan synod). In what follows, *synod* refers to the secondary forms.

(1) *Biblical Background.* The biblical basis is found in what is said about the church as people of God (1 Peter 2) and about the "apostolic council" (Acts 15).

(2) *History of Theology.* Synods of various kinds have been held throughout the entire history of the church. Their character depends in each case on the contemporary state of the church's self-understanding and on the prevailing balance of power within the church and in the political world.

(3) *Church Teaching.* The regulations of the Code of Canon Law are normative for the modern secondary forms of synod. According to canons 342ff. a synod of bishops is an assembly of bishops who are called or sent as representatives of regional groups of churches and then form a "consultative body"; that is, they advise the pope in the exercise of his authority and therefore do not exercise their own collegial authority. The episcopal conference, whose importance has grown steadily in the course of time, is likewise a synodal body. According to canons 447ff. it is a permanent institution (see CD 38), a grouping of bishops of a given nation or territory who "jointly exercise cer-

tain pastoral functions on behalf of the Christian faithful of their territory."
Its powers are limited by the laws governing the universal church and by the
inalienable responsibility that each bishop has for his own diocese. As a permanent institution it has developed into a very effective instrument for synodal
government of the church. Next, as part of the internal organization of the local churches there is the diocesan synod (see *CIC* 460ff.), that is, an assembly of
selected priests "and other Christian faithful of a particular church" who assist
the diocesan bishop with their counsel. Lastly, there are also synods of groups
of local churches (e.g., the Joint Synods of the Sees in the German Federal
Republic, 1971–75), in which officials and laity take part.

(4) *Ecumenical Perspectives.* Synods play an important role in all churches:
in Orthodoxy they are an essential element in the constitution of the church; in
Protestantism they provide a constitutional counterweight to the officials who
govern the churches.

(5) *Systematic Reflections.* As understood in Catholicism, synods are supplementary aids to the government of the church. It is likely that in the future they
will have to be given greater importance as a way of enabling all Christians to
take an active part in the life of the church.

See also COLLEGIALITY; CONSTITUTION OF THE CHURCH; COUNCIL; PEOPLE
OF GOD.

Bibliography
Broucker, José de. *The Suenens Dossier: The Case for Collegiality.* Notre Dame, Ind.: Fides
    Publishers, 1970.
Coriden, James, ed. *The One and Future Church.* Staten Island, N.Y.: Alba House, 1971.
Lettmann, Reinhard. "Episcopal Conferences in the New Canon Law." *Studia Canonica* 14
    (1980) 347–67.
Orsy, Ladislas. "Episcopal Conferences: Their Theological Standing and Their Doctrinal
    Authority." *America* (November 8, 1986) 282–85.

                                                            WERNER LÖSER

Systems of Grace. Systems of grace are attempts to make comprehensible
the relationship of divine grace and human freedom by using some speculative
principle of unity.

(1) *Biblical Background.* The Bible does not contain any such systems. Instead we find immediately juxtaposed statements in which salvation appears
to be an act of God and an act of human beings. Thus in the Old Testament
conversion is: an act of God (Lam 5:21; Jer 31:18) and a human act (Zec 1:3;
Hos 14:2). In the New Testament it is the overall course of salvific events (Phil
2:12f.); according to Romans, love (11:19–23), guilt (9:30–10:21), obduracy
(11:7–11), and belief/disbelief (11:19–23) are caused by God and by human
beings; in Jesus' preaching the simultaneity of divine and human activity is presupposed. Thus we conclude: in the Bible human freedom is an autonomous
reality in relationship to divine grace. There is no contradiction between the

activities of grace and freedom, nor is there any clarification of how these two work together simultaneously.

(2) *History of Theology.* In post-Tridentine Catholic theology, the relationship between these two realities becomes the center of speculative interest. Two opposing systems of grace emerge (= the grace controversy): *Molinism* (begun by L. de Molina, S.J. [d. 1600], continued by Jesuit theologians) seeks a solution to the problem by using the notion of God's *scientia media*. This "mediate knowledge" is distinct from God's natural knowledge (*scientia naturalis*), by which God knows pure possibilities, and God's free knowledge (*scientia libera*), by which God grasps realities. Through it God knows in advance the continually free actions of human beings (*futurabilia*). As a foreknowledge it respects both God's sovereignty and human freedom. *Bañezianism* (begun by D. Bañez, O.P. [d. 1604], continued by Dominican theologians) seeks an answer to the problem by using the notion of God's *praemotio* or *praedeterminatio physica*. In a "physical prior motion," distinct from a mere moral influence, God causes all human actions naturally. God does not thereby remove freedom but grounds it. As a freedom that makes possible predestination, this preserves God's all-powerfulness as well as free human actions. The weakness in both systems of grace is that they seek to level out any system of mediation that uses a different principle of unity than the one they have established.

(3) *Church Teaching.* The vehemence of the grace controversy caused the magisterium to intervene in 1597. But it was only in 1607, after much controversy, that Paul V granted the freedom to teach the Molinist and the Bañezian positions (DS 1997). It was renewed by Benedict XIV in 1748 and extended to Augustinianism (DS 2564f.).

(4) *Ecumenical Perspectives.* Neither the Eastern Church nor the Reformed churches have systems of grace. Moreover, systems of grace play no role in ecumenism.

(5) *Systematic Reflections.* The systems of grace, which had already lost their creative strength at the end of the eighteenth century, were continued by the schools of the individual orders until the middle of this century. Today they are no longer presented. Critical reevaluation of the systems of grace reveal their basic positive concerns. However, the impossibility of continuing such speculative systems with regard to the relationship of grace and freedom has now been accepted. The main reason for this is the incomprehensibility of the mystery of God and the insufficiency of human knowledge. The basis for all further reflections on the possibility of unifying divine and human action in the salvific event can only be the biblical data, which reveal their factual simultaneity. From this we may conclude: the event of salvation is wholly God's act and wholly the act of human beings. The two are not in competition, nor does one exclude the other. While we may agree to an inclusive coordination of autonomous human actions with God's all-effectiveness, nevertheless the mysterious ways in which the divine and the human cooperate cannot be completely clarified by means of any thought system.

SYSTEMS OF GRACE

I. Main Systems

	Molinism	Bañezianism
Key Term	Scientia media (= mediate knowledge)	Praemotio physica (= physical prior movement)
Emphasis	Human Freedom	God's all-powerfulness
	Accent on sufficient grace	Accent on efficacious grace
	Trust in God's universal salvific will	Necessity of predestination for individuals
	Predestination after knowing human merits in advance (post praevisa merita)	Predestination before foreknowledge of human merits (ante praevisa merita)
Problems	Threatens divine sovereignty and all-powerfulness	Threatens human freedom and responsibility

II. Attempts at Mediation

Name	Representatives	Principle of Unity
Congruism	F. Suárez, R. Bellarmine	Gratia congrua: grace is efficacious because it is congruent with what human beings freely will
Codeterminism	B. Mastrius, Franciscan theologians	Decretum condeterminans: the decision of God that determines human will is simultaneous with free human acts (decretum condeterminans)
Sorbonne system of grace	W. de Ysambert, N. Tournely, A. de Liguori	Prayer: sufficient grace gives prayer its freedom; it mediates efficacious grace in difficult actions regarding salvation
Augustinianism	E. Noris, G. L. Berti	Gratia victrix: efficacious grace is the joy awakened in us by God that, in free human decisions, proves victorious

See also FREEDOM; GRACE; GRACE: THEOLOGICAL HERESIES.

Bibliography
See the bibliography under GRACE.

GEORG KRAUS

T t

Teaching Office of the Church. *See* ECCLESIAL MAGISTERIUM.

Temptation. Temptation is the incentive to evil under the simulation of the good. In temptation one single creatural value appears more important to the human person than the total orientation of his or her creatural reality toward the will of God.

(1) *Biblical Background.* According to the witness of Scripture, the human person can be exposed to temptation in every situation of life. Even the mediators of salvation, Abraham, Moses, and Jesus himself, were led into temptation (Heb 4:15). Since God is the unrestricted Lord of all, temptation also ultimately proceeds from God: God tests the covenant faithfulness and the faith of the human person. Holding fast in the face of temptation brings the human person closer to God. Concretely, however, temptation starts out from creatural realities, from evil desire, and from the goods of the world whose seductive power is experienced as personified in Satan and his subservient spirits (demons). Sinners cannot free themselves from the web of these powers. But the faithful may trust that God allows no temptation that is too much of a challenge for faith (Lk 11:4; 1 Cor 10:13; Jas 1:13f.). In Scripture, temptation has also another meaning: the human person tests God through continued sinning; that is, he or she plays with God's mercy and grace and risks losing definitively God's goodwill.

(2) *History of Theology.* Theology has seen the ground for the fact that human persons remain accessible to temptation their whole lives long in the human capacity for striving. On account of original sin, the human person's spontaneous sentiments are no longer integrated in the basic orientation of the will. Depending on whether the will gives in to temptation or resists it, the seductive power of the temptations increases or decreases. Therefore, the intensity and the frequency of temptation can be culpably generated.

(3) *Church Teaching.* According to church teaching, however, temptation through spontaneous desire as such is not yet sin (DS 1515); with God's help, the faithful can overcome it without fault (DS 1536f.).

(4) *Ecumenical Perspectives.* From its tradition, Protestant theology sees in temptation a symptom of sin, that is, of the self-centeredness of the human heart. Under the viewpoint that the concrete situation that becomes a temptation for the individual is always one that is caused through human fault, the opposing points of view can be brought closer to each other.

(5) *Systematic Reflections.* The current theological discussion deals especially with the temptation to which the human person is exposed through social and economic structures. These leave their mark upon the basic motivation of

the free will more or less from the moment of birth (FREEDOM). Here the close connection between temptation and sin is manifested.

See also CONCUPISCENCE; DEMONS; DEVIL; SIN AND GUILT.

Bibliography
See the bibliography under CONCUPISCENCE.

GEORG LANGEMEYER

Theodicy. The term *theodicy* (Greek: *theós* = God; *díke* = judgment) refers (*a*), in the broader sense, to the philosophical study of God, and (*b*) to the attempt to defend God's goodness and justness in view of the evil and suffering that are found in creation.

(1) *Biblical Background.* The Old Testament does not contain the word *theodicy,* but it does deal with the question that it implies. The best example of this is the Book of Job. The innocent sufferer wishes to determine, by a process of disputation with God, the reason for his sufferings (Jb 12–14; 17:23). Reference to the fact that, on the whole, the natural order functions well is unable to satisfy him (38–40) — nothing remains but to fall silent before the Creator (40:3–5) and to hope for the coming act of redemption (42:1–6). Similarly, the wisdom texts look forward to the prospect of other-worldly compensation from an ultimately just God (Wis 3:13–4:16; Pss 16:10; 49:15f.). The New Testament repeatedly rejects any automatic explanation of suffering as punishment by God (see Lk 13:1–5; Jn 9:1–3); even death has its cause solely in the guilt of Adam (Romans 5).

(2) *History of Theology.* The question, posed over and over again throughout history, about the reconcilability of the unpropitious state of creation with a benevolent and omnipotent God was already discussed in Greek philosophy. According to Plato, God is not the origin of evil; for evil lacks being, and only that which has being comes from God (*Polit.* 617E). Epicurus, by contrast, in his criticism of religion and with regard to the issue of God's universal causality, formulated the following series of propositions (*Epicurea,* ed. Usener, Frag. 374), which were recorded by the Christian philosopher Lactantius: if God is *unable* to eliminate evil, God is powerless; if God *does not want* to eliminate it, God is grudging; if God both *does not want* and *is unable* to eliminate it, God is powerless and grudging; *that* God might both want and be able to eliminate it is contrary to general experience (*De ira Dei* 13). The Fathers of the Church testified unanimously that God cannot be made responsible for evil. A christological answer was provided by Augustine. The theodicy question took on special importance in the Enlightenment. G. W. Leibniz, with whom the concept of "theodicy" originated (1697), accounts for the existence of evil through the finitude of the world, which is nevertheless still the best possible one (*Essais de théodicée* [1710]). I. Kant initially concurred with that but later declared the resolution of the question of theodicy to be a matter of pure belief. F. W. J. Schelling reopened the possibility of a philosoph-

ical approach; for him, evil constitutes merely the irrational element in reality, while in God, it is the negative phase of God's self-realization, whose overcoming provides the substance of history. For G. W. F. Hegel, the self-developing reality of the world-spirit is a theodicy in process: the course of history, in progressing toward the constantly higher, justifies God wholly. Naturally, such a totalistic perspective on history takes little account of the happiness or misery of the individual. In this connection, Darwin's biological theory of evolution can be seen as an attempt at dedramatization of physical evil (if not, as in K. Lorenz, of "so-called evil"). Physical evil (for instance, pain) can also be helpful to an organism; indeed, it even can be a condition for the emergence of higher forms of life. Sharply opposed to these philosophical or natural-scientific forms of optimism, which are brought together in Marxism, is the pessimism of A. Schopenhauer. According to him, evil is an integral part of a world that is inherently bound to matter; anyone who affirms that world through action or love is caught up in suffering. This can be overcome only by attaining release from the world: theodicy is transformed into cosmodicy, which is then rejected.

(3) *Church Teaching.* Teaching office has no explicit position on the subject of theodicy.

(4) *Ecumenical Perspectives.* In his tract *On the Bondage of the Will* (*De servo arbitrio*), M. Luther points out the irreconcilability between such questioning and authentic belief. God does not have to offer self-justification before the forum of reason-seeking understanding; we have simply to be worshipful of God's mysteries ("It is not for us to investigate, but rather to adore, his mysteries" ["Nec nostrum est quaerere, sed adorare mysteria eius"] [*WA* 18:712]). Belief must trust God to bring about good even through volitive and afflictive evil (see *WA* 56:331).

(5) *Systematic Reflections.* Correspondingly, it is a fact that, in recent decades, it has been predominantly Protestant theologians who have dealt most intensively with the theodicy question: K. Barth, J. Moltmann, E. Jüngel, and D. Sölle. They all seek a christological, or, more precisely, a trinitarian, response. On the cross of his beloved Son, the true human being, God took on responsibility for all the suffering, affliction, and evil in history. Given this most intimate bond, in the one Holy Spirit, with the crucified Son, God can be characterized as the "crucified God." God thereby justifies both sinful humanity and the world filled with suffering. Through this divine act, which once again lends meaning and an eschatological future to tormented creation, there is accomplished an anthropodicy (N. Berdyaev) and a cosmodicy (S. Bulgakov). Inasmuch, however, as God justifies the existence of humanity and the world, God also accomplishes self-justification. Yet that is no purely juridical or logical act, but a creative one. Accordingly, present-day dogmatics is right to move beyond an exclusively theoretical preoccupation with theodicy and toward more pastoral modes of activity. For in the end, it is concrete persons who reproach God with questions about the meaning of their suf-

ferings. They are helped more by patiently attendant love than by rational explanation.

See also EVIL; EVIL, MORAL.

Bibliography
Barth, Karl. *Church Dogmatics,* 3/1. Edinburgh: T and T Clark, 1958.
Griffin, David Ray. *God, Power, and Evil: A Process Theodicy.* Philadelphia: Westminster, 1976.
Harper, Albert W. J. *The Theodicy of Suffering.* Toronto Studies in Theology, vol. 52. San Francisco: Mellen Research University Press, 1990.
Jüngel, Eberhard. *God as the Mystery of the World: On the Foundation of the Theology of the Crucified One in the Dispute between Theism and Atheism.* Grand Rapids: Eerdmans, 1983.
Leibniz, Gottfried Wilhelm. *Theodicy: Essays on the Goodness of God, the Freedom of Man, and the Origin of Evil.* Edited by Austin Farrer. La Salle, Ill.: Open Court, 1985.
Lewis, C. S. *The Problem of Pain.* New York: Macmillan, 1962.
Moltmann, Jürgen. *The Crucified God.* 2d ed. New York: Harper and Row, 1973.
Sölle, Dorothee. *Suffering.* Philadelphia: Fortress, 1984.
Surin, Kenneth. *Theology and the Problem of Evil.* New York: Blackwell, 1986.
Tilley, Terrence W. *The Evils of Theodicy.* Washington, D.C.: Georgetown University Press, 1991.

ALEXANDRE GANOCZY

Theologians. Theologians are those believers who distinguish themselves by their scientific competence in questions of faith. They are more exactly classified according to the criteria of orthodoxy, ecclesiastical recognition, personal holiness, and time period (see accompanying table). In theological epistemology, consensus among them possesses the rank of a principle of knowledge.

(1) *Biblical Background.* Within Scripture, teachers, those who communicate the knowledge of divine realities, have positions of great importance: Moses is considered to be the first teacher in Israel (Ex 24:3, 12; 34:32). The task of instruction was assigned to the priests (see the vocabulary of Deuteronomy 4–11). The authors of the wisdom literature understood themselves as teachers (e.g., Eccl 12:9; Jb 33:33; Ps 51:15). The sayings of the prophets also were fit into a doctrinal tradition (Is 8:16; Jer 36:4–6). In the New Testament, Christ is clearly *the* teacher (e.g., Mt 23:8; Jn 13:13), who passes on his teaching mission to the church (Mt 28:19f.). This is fulfilled by the apostles (Acts 4:18; 5:21, 42; 13:16) but also by charismatic teachers (Acts 13:1; Eph 4:11), who above all in the later period of the New Testament take on greater importance (1 Tm 4:13, 16; 5:17; 6:2–5), especially in the fight against false teaching (Rom 16:17; Eph 4:14; 1 Tm 1:3; 6:3; 2 Pt 2:1; Rv 2:14f., 24). They communicate the teaching of Jesus personally, that is, in the context of specific categories of thought and interpretation that are linked with their persons and their audience.

(2) *History of Theology.* In the first millennium the theologians were most of the time identical with the holders of church offices. Theologians first appeared as their own "guild" in the twelfth century with the acceptance of Aristotelian

	Orthodoxy	Ecclesial recognition	Holiness of life	Membership in the early church
Church Father	+	+	+	+
Church Apologist	0	0	0	+
Doctor of the Church	+	+	+	−
Theologian	+	+	0	−

Symbols:
+ = necessary;   0 = not necessary;   − = no criterion for the classification

scientific theory in the West and with the formation of the universities: the *magistri* were the academically trained specialists who explained the contents of faith rationally, who used arguments and possessed great authority — hence Christians appeal to their writings. Thomas Aquinas distinguishes between the pastoral magisterium (*magisterium cathedrae pastoralis*) and the teaching magisterium (*magisterium cathedrae magistralis*) (e.g., *Quodlib.* 3.4.1[9]; *C. impugnantes* 2). In the thirteenth and fourteenth centuries, the theological faculties often became the ultimate doctrinal authority (above all the Sorbonne in Paris). On the other hand, beginning in the fifteenth century, theologians were understood to be totally subordinated to the papal magisterium. This led in the nineteenth and twentieth centuries to the delegation model, according to which theologians were merely to explain and defend the official church (papal) pronouncements. Today the model of a cooperative partnership has gained increasing importance in the discussion. As regards authority, the Fathers of the Church possess special significance in the history of theology — that is, the great (mostly bishop) theologians of the time up until around 636 in the West (= d. Isidore of Seville) and around 749 in the East (= d. John of Damascus). Polycarp is described as the "Teacher of Asia and Father of Christians" (*Mart. Pol.* 12.2); Alexander of Jerusalem called Pantaenus and Clement of Alexandria "our Fathers and teachers" (Eusebius, *Hist. eccl.* 6.14.9). Also the bishops of the great councils such as the "318 Fathers of Nicaea" or the important charismatic monastic figures were considered to be binding teachers of faith for the entire church. "Following the Holy Fathers" became the formula appealed to at church gatherings (e.g., DS 265, 300f., 1510). In recent times, the patristic movement active in the so-called "theology between the wars" of the twentieth century has studied the decisive contribution of the Church Fathers to the elucidation of the faith.

(3) *Church Teaching.* The formula of appeal cited above shows the influence of theologians on the ecclesial magisterium and on the teaching of Trent (DS 1507) and Vatican I (DS 3007) that Scripture is to be interpreted according to the unanimous witness of the Fathers and the appeal back to the constant consensus of the theologians (DS 2879). Vatican II, in whose work theologians

played an extraordinary role, expressed the expectations of the church toward the theological faculties (*GE* 11).

(4) *Ecumenical Perspectives.* In ecumenical conversations, theologians have made a substantial contribution toward the rapprochement already achieved. The appeal to the Fathers of the Church as witnesses of the undivided Christendom has also contributed to it. Within the various confessions, the Fathers of the Church have played an especially important role within the Orthodox Church. This is manifest in the liturgy: the seventh Sunday after Easter is called "Sunday of the Holy Fathers"; since 1981, the second Sunday in June is dedicated to the memory of the Fathers of the First Council of Constantinople (381). In protest against the subordination of the theologians under the central papal authority during the late Middle Ages, M. Luther proclaimed the precedence of theological research over against the official church doctrinal decisions. In the history of the Reformed churches, this resulted in an overemphasis on the competence of the theological professors.

(5) *Systematic Reflections.* The unanimity of the Fathers of the Church over certain elements of faith is indisputably an important criterion for their being considered as tradition. For, in addition to their special temporal proximity to the New Testament, they had a substantial share in the doctrinal decisions that had universal church significance, such as the formation of the canon, the composition of the creeds, the formation of the liturgy, even the development of rational theology, all of which characterize the self-understanding of the Christian faith. But the consensus of later generations of theologians also has a high critical epistemological value. For theologians are witnesses to contemporary faith, prophetic bearers of ecclesial tradition, competent researchers and teachers. For the interpretation of their writings the general rules of hermeneutics are to be applied, in particular the analysis of their historical position, their category of thought, their authority within theology, and their agreement with the opinion of other theologians. Their authority is basically the same as that of other believers, but is distinguished by its expertise in the subject matter. Insofar as this knowledge is allowed to be employed in the church for the church, it can be described as a CHARISM that has as its task the investigation, further development, and actualization of the elements of faith. Under this aspect, the consensus of theologians is a distinct source of the knowledge of faith that, of course, cannot be separated from the other sources (THEOLOGICAL EPISTEMOLOGY). In this regard special tensions arise here with the ecclesial magisterium. Supported by the studies of the International Theological Commission of 1975 and remarks from leading representatives of the magisterium (Cardinal J. Ratzinger: *Herkorr* 38 [1984] 360–68), including Pope John Paul II (speeches in Cologne and Altötting, 1980), there is a movement to uphold the position that in cases of conflict, at first all possibilities for dialogue and for the finding of consensus are to be exhausted, because faith always requires the support of understanding and the teaching authority that of argumentation, just as theologians cannot dispense with previous magisterial teaching

and the acknowledgment of the magisterium's competence for making binding decisions.

See also ECCLESIAL MAGISTERIUM; HERMENEUTICS; THEOLOGY; TRADITION.

Bibliography
Brown, Raymond E. "Scholars against the Church: Fact or Fiction?" In *The Critical Meaning of the Bible,* 45–63. New York: Paulist, 1981.
O'Donovan, Leo J., ed. *Cooperation between Theologians and the Ecclesiastical Magisterium.* Washington, D.C.: CLSA, 1982.
Ratzinger, Joseph. *Principles of Catholic Theology: Building Stones for a Fundamental Theology.* San Francisco: Ignatius, 1987.

WOLFGANG BEINERT

Theological Anthropology. Theological anthropology is the subdiscipline of dogmatic theology that treats the statements of the Christian doctrine of faith on the human person, studies their inner connection, and makes this connection accessible to men and women today.

(1) *Biblical Background.* The biblical message from God, Creator of the world and Lord of history, expresses how human persons in faith in this God experience and understand themselves: as beings created, chosen, transformed, and called to responsibility. This anthropological component of the Bible can be taken up and elaborated under three different aspects (see table).

BIBLICAL ASPECTS OF THEOLOGICAL ANTHROPOLOGY

Anthropological statements of Scripture	*Anthropological aspects*
1. Basic definitions of the human person	Being in the image of God, sinfulness, being called to salvation, etc.
2. Scripture as God's word to the human person	The human person as respondent and dialogue partner of God
3. Scripture as testimony of the word of God in human language and on the basis of historical experience	Deepening and transformation of human self-understanding through divine revelation

(2) *History of Theology.* The theological teaching on the human person developed in the context of individual theological subsections, above all in the doctrine of creation, in Christology (human nature of Christ), and in the doctrine of grace. In this process, the idea of the SOUL taken over from Greek philosophy and the biblical statement of the human person's being in the IMAGE OF GOD took on major significance. The soul, although immortal and "capable" of the divine, had to be understood theologically as an individually created entity that only through God's grace could participate in the divine. Similarly, with regard to being in the image of God, it was necessary to distinguish between the resemblance evidenced in creation and the likeness to God or deification wrought by grace. Only in our century has it been recognized

SYSTEMATIC ASPECTS
OF THEOLOGICAL ANTHROPOLOGY

Theological characterization of the human person	Anthropological statement
Creatureliness of the human person	Creature
Hamartiological definition	Sinner
Soteriological definition	Redeemed through Christ
Ecclesiological definition	Member of the church of Christ
Eschatological definition	Called to eternal life

that it is necessary to join together the scattered anthropological approaches and to elaborate them into an independent theological anthropology (K. Rahner). This necessity results from the intellectual process of modernity in which a turn took place from a metaphysics that encompasses the human person and the world to subjectivity. Anthropology became the fundamental discipline. It soon, however, split up into an empirical (scientific methods) and a philosophical anthropology (hermeneutical method). Theological anthropology at first drew upon the latter (philosophy of consciousness and existential philosophy).

(3) *Church Teaching.* Church teaching follows the first of the three biblical aspects mentioned in the table on p. 691. It speaks of the human person in connection with creation, redemption, and so on. Vatican II, however, pays attention to the second aspect when it demands that theology as a whole should be oriented in a pastoral and missionary way (*OT* 16; *AG* 39; *GS* 62).

(4) *Ecumenical Perspectives.* Protestant theology was already instructed by M. Luther to read all of Scripture with a view toward the concrete human person (the second biblical aspect in the table). In its tradition, it has therefore already produced several outlines for the systematic connection between anthropology and theology (e.g., F. Schleiermacher).

(5) *Systematic Reflections.* Under the first biblical aspect, five characterizations of the human person are treated today in theological anthropology (see table of systematic aspects). This enumeration, however, is not satisfactory, since theological anthropology must make these characterizations understandable from their inner connection. The most recent outlines therefore start out from the second or the third biblical aspect. Under the second aspect, starting out from the word of God, the human person is first of all defined as the sinner in need of this word and then is verified as such in human self-experience and in empirical anthropology (O. H. Pesch). Under the third aspect, from the philosophical experience of the self (K. Rahner) and from empirical anthropology (W. Pannenberg), one tries to point out the historical and religious dimensions of human experience. From this one seeks to comprehend the specific experience and definition of the human person that Scripture gives witness to. A comparison of both conceptions shows that they approach from oppo-

site poles the relationship of mutual conditioning that exists between theology and anthropology. In starting one's theological approach from the word of God one accepts that a preunderstanding of what the *word of God* could mean for the human person unreflectedly enters into the theological definition of the human person and makes appear as purely biblical characterizations that actually are only *one* possible interpretation of the biblical witness (HUMAN PERSON: IMAGE OF; PERSONALITY). To start one's basic approach in current (empirical and philosophical) anthropology therefore appears, at least according to today's theoretical standards, as the methodically clearer path. It brings with it, nevertheless, the danger that it reduces the unique and incomparable experience of God and of the human person, the biblical revelation, to what is generally plausible anthropologically (ANTHROPOCENTRISM). This danger, however, is dwindling at present, since the human sciences, on account of their heterogeneous methodological approaches, do not arrive anymore at a universally valid definition of the human person. Consequently, they leave the horizon of human experience and especially of religious experience open for the appearance of the historically unique within the ongoing process of becoming human that characterizes the individual and humankind as a whole.

See also CHRISTOLOGY; CREATION: DOCTRINE OF; DOGMATIC THEOLOGY; GRACE: DOCTRINE OF; HUMAN PERSON.

Bibliography
Brueggemann, Walter. *In Man We Trust: The Neglected Side of Biblical Faith.* Richmond: John Knox, 1972.
Moltmann, Jürgen. *Christian Anthropology in the Conflict of the Present.* Philadelphia: Fortress, 1974.
Moltmann-Wendel, Elisabeth, and Jürgen Moltmann. *Humanity in God.* New York: Pilgrim, 1983.
Pannenberg, Wolfhart. *Anthropology in Theological Perspective.* Philadelphia: Westminster, 1985.
———. *What Is Man? Contemporary Anthropology in Theological Perspective.* Philadelphia: Fortress, 1970.
Rahner, Karl. *Foundations of Christian Faith: An Introduction to the Idea of Christianity.* New York: Crossroad, 1982.
Schoonenberg, Peter. *God's World in the Making.* Techny, Ill.: Divine Word, 1964.

GEORG LANGEMEYER

Theological Epistemology. Theological epistemology is the discipline that treats the character and methodology of theological knowledge. Other designations include *theological foundations, fundamental theology, fundamental dogmatics,* or (above all among Protestants) *prolegomena.*

(1) *Biblical Background.* A developed theological epistemology presupposes an advanced state of reflection about the scientific nature of theology itself. The problematic is basically present wherever there is reflection upon the nature of revelation faith. This happens in the New Testament in Rom 10:14 (How do human beings come to faith?) and Gal 1:11f. (the apostolic proclamation stems from a revelation).

SURVEY OF THE PROCESS OF THEOLOGICAL KNOWING

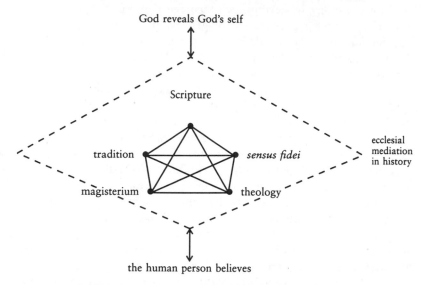

Faith expresses itself in the concrete in dogma, liturgy, spirituality, art, forms of life, etc.

(2) *History of Theology.* Against the attacks of gnosticism in the time of the Church Fathers, TRADITION was presented as a source of theological knowledge (Irenaeus, Vincent of Lérins). In the introductions to the medieval summas and "sentence commentaries," the authors investigated the nature and scientific character of theology, the relationship of faith and knowledge, and the types of theological judgment. The first theoretical investigations were provided by P. D'Ailly and J. Gerson in the late Middle Ages. The father of theological epistemology is considered to be M. Cano (d. 1560) with his work *De locis theologicis* (published posthumously in 1563) in which he gives information about where and how one can locate the object of a theological statement. Under the heading *ratio,* he places philosophy, history, and natural reason; under the title *auctoritas,* he places Scripture, tradition, the faith of the whole church, councils, the Roman Church, the saints, and the Scholastic theologians. The most significant modern work comes from M. J. Scheeben (*Theologische Erkenntnislehre* [1874] = *Gesammelte Schriften* 3 [Freiburg, ³1959]). Today this discipline receives special importance in view of the contestation of Christianity as a revealed religion and the general theoretical academic considerations in relation to theology.

(3) *Church Teaching.* References to ways of theological knowing are found in the documents of Vatican I (DS 3016: reason, reasoning from analogy, nexus of the mysteries of faith, and connection with the ultimate goal of human beings) and Vatican II (*DV* 12 for exegesis; *OT* 16 for dogmatic theology; *UR* 11 for ecumenism).

(4) *Ecumenical Perspectives.* In Orthodox theology, the primary valid source for dogmatic theology is the revelation contained in Scripture and tradition (above all that of the first seven ecumenical councils and of the formulas of faith of the Church Fathers) whose contents were adopted by the faith consciousness of the whole church. In addition there are creedal dogmatic texts that have a lesser epistemological value (the circular letter of 866 of the Patriarch Photius to the episcopal sees of the East; the synodal decisions concerning Hesychasm from 1341, 1347, 1351; the profession of faith of 1440/41 of Markos Eugenikos of Ephesus; the profession of faith of 1455/56 of the Patriarch George Scholarius; the synodal decree against the creed of 1638 of Cyril Lucar; the profession of faith of 1643 of Peter Mogila; the decisions of the synods of Constantinople of 1642, 1672, 1691, 1722, 1727, 1836, 1838, 1895; the profession of faith of 1671 from the patriarch of Jerusalem Dosítheos; the different statements on ecumenism from 1920, 1952, 1961; etc.). In the West, the Reformation advanced the formation of theological epistemology: for the Reformers it was important, with their critique of tradition and the ecclesial magisterium, to ground faith from Scripture alone; for the Counter-Reformation, theological epistemology was important in order to preserve the traditional faith. Today theological epistemology has special significance in the ecumenical dialogue for the further treatment of the "basic differences" that possibly exist between the denominations.

(5) *Systematic Reflections.* The basic question of theology and therefore also of its cognitive theory is: How can God's revelation be mediated to the faith of contemporary human beings? In addition an answer is needed for the question: How do we know what God has communicated? The basic theological response is: through the mediation of the community of faith with all its resources. Here are included all the "source data" (*loci*) for theological argumentation: Scripture, tradition, the magisterium, the sensus fidelium, and the consensus of theologians. These are used to grasp the content of revelation, which faith then interiorizes in different forms (through reception of dogmas, liturgy, spirituality, art, various forms of life, etc.). Because theological propositions are also logical judgments, principles from logic, hermeneutics, linguistic philosophy, and companion disciplines are also added to the epistemological principles of theology. In the systematic structuring of theology, theological epistemology is treated either as the last treatise of fundamental theology (as part of the theological research into foundations) or as the first treatise of dogmatic theology (as reflection on the basic questions of this discipline).

See also CHURCH; RECEPTION; REVELATION; THEOLOGY.

Bibliography

Farley, Edward. *The Fragility of Knowledge.* Philadelphia: Fortress, 1988.

Fiorenza, Francis Schüssler. *Foundational Theology: Jesus and the Church.* New York: Crossroad, 1984.

————. "Systematic Theology: Task and Methods." In *Systematic Theology: Roman Catholic Perspectives,* edited by Francis Schüssler Fiorenza and John P. Galvin, 1:1–88. Minneapolis: Fortress, 1991.

Murphy, Nancey. *Theology in the Age of Scientific Reasoning.* Ithaca, N.Y.: Cornell University Press, 1990.

Pannenberg, Wolfhart. *Theology and the Philosophy of Science.* Philadelphia: Westminster, 1976.

Tracy, David. *The Analogical Imagination.* New York: Crossroad, 1981.

————. *Plurality and Ambiguity: Hermeneutics, Religion, Hope.* San Francisco: Harper and Row, 1987.

Van Huyssteen, Wentzel. *Theology and the Justification of Faith.* Grand Rapids: Eerdmans, 1989.

WOLFGANG BEINERT

Theological Virtues. The theological virtues (also called divine virtues) are the gratuitously given powers of faith, hope, and love, which produce a loving relationship to God in those who are justified. They are called *virtues* because they describe a lasting attitude. They are called *theological* or *divine* because they are given by God and lead immediately to God.

(1) *Biblical Background.* In the Bible the triad of faith, hope, and love is found only in the letters of the New Testament. The most important texts are: Rom 5:1–5; 1 Cor 13:7, 13; Gal 5:5f.; Eph 4:2–5; Col 1:4f.; 1 Thes 1:3; 5:8; Heb 6:10–12; 10:22–24; 1 Pt 1:21f. Beyond this, faith and love are often grouped (e.g., 1 Cor 16:13f.; Eph 1:16; 3:17; 2 Thes 1:3; 1 Tm 6:11; 2 Tm 3:10; Ti 2:2; 1 Jn 3:23), or sometimes faith is joined with hope (e.g., Rom 4:18; 15:13; Ti 1:1f.; Heb 11:1). The central text, Rom 5:1–5, points to what all three have in common: they are gifts of God for our relationship to God. Sometimes they have specific functions: faith, given in justification, is the beginning of our personal relationship to God. Hope gives endurance to our relationship to God. The gift and effects of these three forces for relating to God as Trinity are attributed especially to the Holy Spirit. The Spirit of God is the driving force of faith (2 Cor 4:13). Through the Spirit, the love of God is poured out in our hearts (Rom 5:5). By the power of the Spirit, hope awaits full justification (Gal 5:5). The unity of faith, hope, and love is seen concretely as the living, mutually coeffective working of all these basic powers: faith is efficacious in love (Gal 5:6) and is the assurance of things hoped for (Heb 11:1). Hope stands firm in faith (Rom 4:18; Heb 6:11f.) and trustful in love (Rom 5:5). Love is a source of power for faith and hope (1 Cor 13:7). Of all these, love is greatest for it never passes (1 Cor 13:8) but develops fully in our final communion with God (1 Cor 13:12).

(2) *History of Theology.* The "holy triad" (Clement of Alexandria, *Strom.* 3.51.1) is highly cherished and has many practical applications in the Eastern Fathers of the Church. Cyril of Jerusalem (d. 386) makes it a leading theme in his catecheses. In the Western Church, Augustine calls faith, hope, and love the building blocks of religion (*Ench.* 2f.) and the major goal of all catechesis (*De cat. rud.* 4.8). Gregory the Great (d. 604) is the first person to apply the philo-

sophical notion of "virtue" to faith, hope, and love, which are "of the greatest value" (*Mor.* 27.46). In early Scholasticism, the school of Abelard treats the virtues of faith, hope, and love extensively. Peter Lombard (d. 1160) brings them together in a systematic schema (*Sent.* 3.23–32), which continues into the sixteenth century. The term *theological virtue* (*virtus theologica*) first appears at the beginning of the thirteenth century. Thus, following the tradition of the Scholastic summa, Thomas Aquinas too has a treatise on the theological virtues (*STh* 1–2, q. 62). In post-Tridentine theology, faith, hope, and love are seldom discussed in dogmatics, but always in moral theology. Today dogmatics treats faith, hope, and love as the immediate and lasting effects of justification.

(3) *Church Teaching.* In opposition to Semi-Pelagianism, the Synod of Orange (529) emphasizes that faith (DS 375) and love (DS 387, 395) are gifts of God's prior grace. The Council of Trent stresses that this gratuitousness applies to all three (DS 1553). Likewise, Trent claims that the biblical image of a pouring out, which was used for faith and love at Orange (DS 397), applies to all three and demonstrates that faith, hope, and love are inherent within us (DS 1530). In response to Luther's teaching on JUSTIFICATION by faith alone (*sola fide*), Trent emphasizes that faith, hope, and love belong together: in justification they are all poured out simultaneously as its immediate and lasting effect (DS 1530). It is true that faith, as the foundation and source of every act of justification, is the beginning of salvation (DS 1532), but it leads to complete salvation only in closest conjunction with hope and love (DS 1531). With regard to terminology it is noteworthy that when Trent speaks of faith, hope, and love, it does not use any of the philosophical concepts that had been attacked by Luther, that is, neither the notion of virtue nor the notion of *habitus.*

(4) *Ecumenical Perspectives.* According to M. Luther, the Scholastic use of the philosophical concepts of virtue and *habitus* in discussing faith, hope, and love led to a theological error. Virtue, which is a human achievement, falsely leads to justification by works. *Habitus,* as a factual state and a condition over which we have control, excludes the free, living, gratuitous action of God. Furthermore, according to Luther the basic meaning of faith, which alone justifies, is endangered when the Scholastics teach that faith is given by love (*fides caritate formata*). He reverses the thesis: love is not the form of faith, but faith is the form of love (WA 39/1:318). Because Luther made the triad problematic, it has played practically no role in Evangelical theology. The ecumenical dialogue of our time has succeeded here too in setting aside historically conditioned misunderstandings. Thus, in many Evangelical dogmatic treatises, there are sections that treat positively the close relationship of faith, hope, and love. On the other hand, Catholic dogmatics tends to find substitutes for the notion of virtue. Thus faith, hope, and love are described as basic powers, basic stances, basic or lifetime accomplishments of the Christian (see table, p. 698).

(5) *Systematic Reflections.* The traditional notion of theological virtues as applied to faith, hope, and love could best be replaced by the notion of basic

FAITH, HOPE, AND LOVE AS BASIC POWERS
WITHIN OUR RELATIONSHIP TO GOD

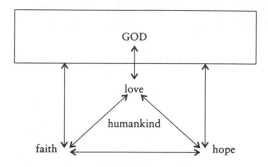

- The theological virtues come from God and lead to God.
- They affect the whole person and work together.
- Love, which is the fullness of communion with God who is love (1 Jn 4:8), remains in the final fulfillment.

powers within our relationship to God. Thus faith, hope, and love have the following characteristics. (*a*) They refer to God in two ways: as their *ground* and their *goal*. (*b*) They are the immediate effects of justification in humanity; in other words, they are anthropological forms of justifying grace. (*c*) They are a supportive foundation for our relationship to God, since they remain throughout life and thus are the basic sources of all that we express in life in relating to God. (*d*) They are a living dynamism in the Christian, first as the driving force that comes from God, second as a striving that ends in God. (*e*) Faith, hope, and love form an inseparable unity. They are essentially united by their divine origin and orientation. They are effectively united as a single dynamic principle of salvation, which unfolds in three concrete forms. (*f*) In the context of this unity they have specific functions: in justification, faith produces the beginning of salvation; in concrete acts of love, love produces the historical realization of salvation; in our trust in God's promise, hope produces our endurance along the path to completing our salvation. (*g*) They are effective in their mutual dependence on complementarity: faith produces acts of love and gives confident hope its firm foundation; love is the living expression of faith and the concrete strength of hope; hope gives to faith a final goal and to love its endurance. (*h*) In the end, faith and hope cease, but love remains forever. Since God is visible and is experienced immediately in everlasting life, faith and hope have fulfilled their task of leading us to communion with the hidden and distant God. However, love reaches its full realization in eternal life since it is experienced as the desired communion, without temporal or spatial limitations, with God who is love and since it is enjoyed forever as the undisturbed happiness of a loving communion with God.

See also FAITH; HOPE; LOVE.

Bibliography
Bars, Henry. *Faith, Hope, and Charity.* New York: Hawthorn Books, 1961.
Ratzinger, Joseph. *To Look on Christ: Exercises in Faith, Hope, and Love.* New York: Crossroad, 1991.
Schlitt, Dale M. "Toward a New Christian Understanding of Faith, Hope and Love." *Église et Theologie* 3 (1989) 385–406.
Wadell, Paul J. *Friends of God: Virtues and Gifts in Aquinas.* New York: Lang, 1991.

GEORG KRAUS

Theologoumenon. A theologoumenon is a theological statement that has not been formally pronounced by the ecclesial magisterium, yet which arises from the insight into the connections resulting when the truths of revelation are brought into contact with concrete historical experience. It expresses the perspective in which the elements of faith are interpreted in a concrete historical context.

WOLFGANG BEINERT

Theology. Theology in the Christian understanding is the scientific — that is, methodical and systematic — disclosure and development of the reality of divine revelation grasped in faith with the aim of making this reality as understandable as possible to human thinking.

(1) *Biblical Background.* Scripture does not offer systematic and theoretical reflections on the concept of theology but does furnish important elements toward this. Unlike the Greeks, the Old Testament does not orient knowing and understanding toward a timeless idea but rather refers them to an existential relatedness to persons; knowing is a form of personal love (Gn 4:1; Dt 33:9; Jer 31:34). This becomes even more evident in the New Testament: knowing is a spiritual perception and acknowledgment of persons (Mt 13:11; 1 Cor 2:19; Col 1:9; 2:2) on the basis of divine grace (Lk 24:45; Jn 7:39; 16:7; 1 Jn 2:14; 5:20), which opens up new dimensions (Rom 8:16f.; 1 Cor 2:11–16; Phil 3:8–10; Col 2:2). The person of Jesus of Nazareth and his destiny demand special intellectual reflection, which is carried out above all by Paul (e.g., Rom 1:1–11:36; 1 Corinthians 2; 15) and John (e.g., Jn 1:1–14) but is visible in the whole New Testament. This is necessary not only so that one's faith can be reassured but also so that one may give an account of it and bear witness to it (1 Pt 3:15). Together with an unwavering adherence to the fundamental contents (e.g., Jesus as messiah, redeemer, the fulfillment of the Old Testament promises), what is characteristic is a large spectrum in their interpretation (e.g., Jesus especially as a miracle worker [Mark], the new Moses [Matthew], the savior [Luke], or the preexistent Logos [John]). In this way there appear various theological conceptions that complete one another.

(2) *History of Theology.* The fundamental problem of theology evidenced in the history of dogma is the relationship between faith and reason, which stand in a permanent tension. If one tries to resolve this in the direction of faith, irra-

tionalism is the consequence. If one resolves this in favor of reason, rationalism (gnosis) is the result. The theologians of the early church sought to counteract the gnostic heresy through an integral reflection that beside understanding also takes into account willing and acting. Concepts used in this undertaking include *(epi)gnosis* (knowledge), *cognitio* (knowledge), *scientia* (knowledge), *sophia* (wisdom), and *sapientia* (wisdom). While in the Christian East the moment of the will was emphasized to a greater degree and led to a mystical-spiritualistic theology, in the West the practical-ethical moment gained the upper hand. The formation of theology in today's sense as an academic discipline with university rank began in the Middle Ages. Taking over the Aristotelian theory of science, Thomas Aquinas explains theology as the science of faith whose supreme principle is the divine revelation from which reason is able to draw conclusions. Theology is defined conceptually as *doctrina (christiana, divina, sacra)* (Christian, divine, and sacred doctrine), *institutio divina* (divine institution), *Scriptura* (Scripture), and *sacra pagina* (sacred page). Modernity puts this understanding into question in the name of the autonomy of reason, which is regarded as the primary scientific authority. Further, the modern perspective holds that since theology claims a suprarational certainty, it is actually a strategy of immunization of an ideological kind (K. Popper, H. Albert). In response, theology seeks to show its anthropological significance in systematic-theoretical reflection and refers explicitly to the historical dimension of its work. The definition of theology, then, has varied throughout history; in this process, the individual definitions emphasize important essential elements. While for Plato theology is the rational interpretation of myths and for Aristotle it is the contemplation of beings in Being, the term is employed in the Christian vocabulary since the fourth century as the announcement of God's inmost being (in contrast: *oikonomia* as the announcement of God's saving activity). Dionysius the Areopagite calls theology the way in which God is expressed in language; he distinguishes the *kataphatic (positive* theology: God is just) from the *apophatic (negative* theology: God is not just in the way in which human beings are just) and *mystical* theology (*speculative* theology: God is just in an infinite way). For Augustine theology is "ratio sive sermo de Deitate" (an account or discourse on the divine nature) (*De civ. Dei* 8.1). The Franciscan school with Bonaventure describes theology as a station on the way to the real knowledge of God that is wisdom (*sapientia* = tasting, perceiving of God). For an overview of the historical development of theology, see the table at the end of this article.

(3) *Church Teaching.* The ecclesial magisterium acknowledges the independence of academic theology even if, naturally, it considers it especially under the aspect of theology's relationship to the magisterium. Against fideism and rationalism, Vatican I points out both the proper claim and the limits of reason (DS 3016): although reason cannot obtain complete insight into the mysteries of faith, it is still able to reach a certain understanding due to the correspondence (ANALOGY) between them and natural knowledge; reason does this by demonstrating the connection of the truths of faith with one another and with

the existential goal of the human person. Vatican II supports the freedom of theological research (*UR* 4, 17) and demands an ecumenical orientation (*UR* 9–11) for a theology that is to be biblically oriented (*DV* 23f.). It also advocates a contemporary presentation of the faith (*GS* 44, 62; *AG* 22, 39) and proposes, above all, an outline of the study of theology (*OT* 15f.) with a special consideration of philosophy.

(4) *Ecumenical Perspectives.* The formation of different Christian confessions and denominations is the result not only of theological differences but also of divergent theological methods. Within the situation of a divided Christianity, theology must therefore be oriented essentially in an ecumenical direction, that is, to question and to consider all Christian traditions but also to reconsider the different standpoints with a view toward reconciliation. In the Orthodox Church theology is understood as ministry within the church for the interpretation and the deepening of dogmas and of the divine plan for salvation, as well as for the vitalization of the activity of the community of faith. It is essentially dogmatic theology and has a strongly spiritual component as *theoria* (contemplation of the divine mysteries). Reformed theology — which came into being in protest against the rationalism of late Scholasticism — took shape primarily as an exegetical undertaking that, according to M. Luther, acquires existential meaning for the faithful in the threefold process of prayer, reflection, and contestation (*oratio, meditatio, tentatio* [WA 50:658ff.]). P. Melanchthon and then Lutheran Orthodoxy, however, again took up the medieval understanding of theology. With the beginning of the Enlightenment, Reformed theology became subject to the same questioning as Catholic theology.

(5) *Systematic Reflections.* Faith, as an existential realization of life, is always also called upon to seek the rational understanding of the contents of revelation. Reason is confronted with statements that stand in contrast to empirical experience (e.g., Jesus is God *and* human being; the crucified *dead* person *lives*). This empirical experience is thus broadened in faith; reason is thereby confronted with new realities that are to be penetrated intellectually. From this there results a fundamental tension that forms the enduring poles of theological work insofar as they are to be mediated without lessening the tension (see table, p. 702). While theology up until modern times began its analysis from the pole of "God," current theology often takes the opposite route. From the characteristic task of theology results a fourfold framing of the question that has become the foundation for its scholarly ordering (see table entitled "Classification of Theology"). More precisely, the following statements are true: (*a*) as with every other academic discipline, theology has presuppositions and a preunderstanding. Among these belong especially the acceptance of the existence of God as the fundamental ground of all reality, the existence of revelation as God's proclamation with a universal validity claim that is set down in Scripture, and the existence of the ecclesial community of faith as the bearer of the mediation of revelation. (*b*) The method of operation of theology is rational, discursive, and argumentative. (*c*) On account of the historicity of

POLES OF THEOLOGICAL WORK

| God
Transcendence
Theonomy
Permanency | Human person
Immanence
Autonomy
Relativity |

Dangers

| Essentialism
Objectivism
Neglect of history
Disregard for the
   secular world | Existentialism
Subjectivism
Historicism
Anthropocentrism,
   secularism |

CLASSIFICATION OF THEOLOGY

Framing of the question	*Path for the solution*	*Subject area*	*Subject*
What is the historical ground of faith?	Critical questioning of Scripture as the basic document of revelation	Biblical theology	Introductory disciplines; OT exegesis; NT exegesis
How has faith been expressed throughout history?	Critical examination of all (including the forgotten) interpretations of revelation	Historical theology	Church history (of the early church with patrology, of the Middle Ages, and of modernity); history of dogma
In what do the significance and the unity of the witnesses to revelation consist?	Integration of the individual expressions of faith into faith as a whole	Systematic theology	Fundamental theology; dogmatic theology; moral theology; Christian social teaching; canon law;* philosophical-theological propaedeutic
How is the message of revelation to be witnessed to and announced in the present?	Orientation of the expressions of faith toward the life situation of the addressees	Practical theology	Religious education; catechetics; pastoral theology; liturgical studies;* homiletics

In the table above, only the most important subject areas within academic theology are given. The areas marked with an asterisk cannot be clearly assigned to only one subject group: canon law also has a practical-theological significance, liturgical studies also have systematic significance.

revelation and faith, theology itself is also historical, insofar as it mediates both elements. (*d*) The historicity of theology brings about its plurality: the content of revelation is given historically and is in itself inexhaustible. The theologian can interpret it always only from her or his limited subjective perspective and must witness to it in a pluralistic anthropological context. Theology must interpret the Christian truth in an unabridged and undistorted manner, yet it can do so only in a variety of sentences, categories of thought, models, and under differing horizons. (*e*) Because faith is mediated through the church, the church community and its witness to faith expressed in Scripture, in tradition, and in the testimonies of the faithful (in liturgy, spiritualities, art, etc.) form a criterion of theological reflection. (*f*) In order to make the faith of the church accessible to the thought of its time, theology requires an appropriate degree of freedom in church and society. (*g*) If the university strives to be the "house of learning" in which the whole of reality is to be reflected upon, it must also allow room to consider the ground of all reality in a scholarly way. From this, theology raises the claim of being a university discipline. (*h*) From the nature of theology the following presuppositions for theological work ensue: since theology is the development of faith from its own presuppositions, the theologian must be a believer; since theology investigates the faith of the church as the mediator of revelation, the theologian must have a sensitivity for the church; since theology works according to scholarly rules, the theologian needs systematic competence; since revelation in its universal validity also has to be mediated in each specific age, the theologian has to think and work in a way that is mindful of his or her contemporary setting.

See also CHURCH; ECCLESIAL MAGISTERIUM; FAITH; GOD; HISTORY/HISTORIC-ITY; REVELATION; THEOLOGIANS.

Bibliography
Congar, Yves. *A History of Theology.* Garden City, N.Y.: Doubleday, 1968.
Dulles, Avery. *The Craft of Theology: From Symbol to System.* New York: Crossroad, 1992.
Evans, Gillian R. *Old Arts and New Theology: The Beginnings of Theology as an Academic Discipline.* Oxford: Clarendon, 1980.
Evans, Gillian R., et al. *The Science of Theology.* Grand Rapids: Eerdmans, 1986.
Farley, Edward. *Theologia: The Fragmentation and Unity of Theological Education.* Philadelphia: Fortress, 1983.
Fiorenza, Francis Schüssler. "Systematic Theology: Task and Methods." In *Systematic Theology: Roman Catholic Perspectives,* edited by Francis Schüssler Fiorenza and John P. Galvin, 1:1–88. Minneapolis: Fortress, 1991.
Haight, Roger. *Dynamics of Theology.* New York: Paulist, 1990.
Lonergan, Bernard. *Method in Theology.* New York: Crossroad, 1972.
Ratzinger, Joseph. *Principles of Catholic Theology: Building Stones for a Fundamental Theology.* San Francisco: Ignatius, 1987.

WOLFGANG BEINERT

SURVEY OF THE EPOCHS OF THE HISTORY
OF THEOLOGY AND DOGMA

This outline intends a first general categorization of names and facts which are mentioned again and again in the individual articles.

Cent.	Era	Main representatives	Characteristics
1–7	Early church		
1/2	Apostolic Fathers	1 Clement, Ignatius, Polycarp, Barnabas, Hermas, Didache	Paraenesis; Christocentrism; eschatological orientation; allegorical method
2	Apologists	Aristides, Tatian, Athenagoras, Justin, Theophilus, Diognetus	Confrontation with Greek philosophy (different forms of Platonism), first results in Christology
2/3	Formation of systematic theology	Tertullian, Clement of Alexandria, Origen, Irenaeus of Lyon, Hippolytus	Formation of the rule of faith against gnosticism, montanism, and millenarianism; attempt at the synthesis of reflection on faith; development of theological terminology; allegorical method
3/4	Origin of the theological schools	Alexandrians: Athanasius, Cyril of Alexandria	Speculative-spiritualistic thinking; emphasis on the divinity of Jesus
		Cappadocians: Basil, Gregory of Nazianzus, Gregory of Nyssa	Development of Christian mysticism; trinitarian theology
		Antiochians: Theodore of Mopsuestia, Cyril of Jerusalem, John Chrysostom	Positive-empirical theology; historical-critical exegesis; emphasis on the humanity of Jesus
4/5	Flourishing of the patristic age	Augustine, Jerome, Ambrose, Leo the Great, Hilary of Poitiers, Ephraem Syrus	In the East, elaboration of the trinitarian and christological dogmas against the heresies of Arianism, monophysitism, and Nestorianism; in the West, a more practical orientation: laying of the foundation for the soteriological dogmas against the Donatists and the Pelagians
6/7	Late patristic age	Gregory the Great, Isidore of Seville, Maximus the Confessor, Pseudo-Dionysius, Boethius, John of Damascus	The results of previous theological work are systematized and made accessible in collections of sayings
8–15	Ecclesiastical Middle Ages		WEST
8/9	Carolingian theology	The Venerable Bede, Alcuin, John Scotus Erigena, Walafrid Strabo	Further mediation of patristic theology to the Middle Ages; practical orientation; debates over the doctrines of the Eucharist and of predestination
11/12	Monasticism	Bernard of Clairvaux, Rupert of Deutz, Hugo and Richard of St. Victor	Elaboration of the ascetic-contemplative elements of the patristic tradition

Cent.	Era	Main representatives	Characteristics
11/12	Early Scholasticism	Anselm of Canterbury, Gilbert de la Porrée, Anselm of Laon, Peter Abelard, Peter Lombard	Reflection on the content of faith from inner and necessary grounds (*fides quaerens intellectum*); the place of patristic *auctoritas* is taken over by argumentative reasoning (*quaestio*); controversy on universals, eucharistic doctrine, and soteriology are focal points
13	High Scholasticism	Albert the Great, Alexander of Hales, Thomas Aquinas	Adoption of the philosophy of Aristotle to illuminate the contents of faith; conceptualistic and intellectualistic theology; elaboration of great syntheses in the summas
		Bonaventure, Duns Scotus	In the Franciscan tradition, theology is carried out in a mystical-voluntaristic way (primacy of the will)
14/15	Late Scholasticism	William of Ockham, Gabriel Biel	Faith and knowledge diverge; positive reflection with an individualistic strain becomes prominent
16–20	Church in the modern period: *Catholic theology*		
16	Reformation and Counter-Reformation	Cajetan de Vio, G. Contarini, R. Bellarmine, J. Sadoleto, Ambrose Catharinus	The Reformers proclaim the Bible practically as the only norm of theology and reject the magisterium and tradition; central importance is given to the teaching on justification (Luther) and predestination (Calvin); in response, a demarcation in controversial theology and apologetics
17	Baroque Scholasticism	G. Vázquez, F. Suárez, Gregory of Valencia, M. Cano, D. Petau	Theology as the metaphysics of the truths of faith; laying the foundation for theological methodology; division of theology into disciplines
18/19	Neo-scholasticism	F. Kleutgen, C.-R. Billuart, C. Schrader, J. B. Franzelin, G. Perrone	Restorative thinking without system-building power; defensive positivism of the magisterium; struggle against the Enlightenment
19	Renewal movements	Catholic Tübingen school (J. A. Möhler, S. Drey, J. E. Kuhn); J. H. Newman; M. J. Scheeben; H. Schell; A. Gardeil, P. Rousselot, M. Blondel	Insight into the fundamental historicity of theology; debate with German idealism and rationalism In the controversy over modernism, elaboration of the problem of subjectivity
20	Theology between the wars	Théologie Nouvelle (H. de Lubac, J. Daniélou, H. Bouillard), R. Guardini, G. Söhngen	Productive reception of the non-Scholastic theological traditions (biblical, patristic, ecumenical, liturgical); in exegesis and dogmatic theology, use of the historical-critical method; discussion with the human sciences
20	Theology of Vatican II and postconciliar theology	K. Rahner, H. U. von Balthasar, Y. Congar, J. B. Metz, E. Schillebeeckx	Theological elaboration of the theology of Vatican II; anthropocentric, practical, ecumenical orientation; development of regional and contextual theologies; orientation toward salvation-history; debate with existentialism and Marxism; discussion of the results of scientific theory and linguistic philosophy

Cent.	Era	Main representatives	Characteristics
16–20	Church in modern times: *Protestant theology*		
16/17	Lutheran Orthodoxy	M. Chemnitz, L. Hutter, J. Gerhard, G. Calixtus, A. Calovius, D. Hollaz	Systematization of Lutheran theology on the basis of confessional writings and the early church tradition with the inclusion of neo-Aristotelian philosophy: many confessional disputes
17/18	Pietism	P. J. Spener, A. H. Francke, N. L. von Zinzendorf	Concentration of theology on the question of salvation with a deferment of the philosophical problems; experience emphasized as the basis of faith; reception of mystical elements
18	Enlightenment	E. Herbert of Cherbury, M. Tindal, J. Carpzov, S. J. Baumgarten, J. S. Semler, H. S. Reimarus	Under the influence of the philosophical systems of the 17th/18th cents., of natural science and jurisprudence (H. Grotius, S. Pufendorf), the explanation of the world starts out from the principles of human reason (rationalism), which is ranked on the same level with revelation; ethics becomes the core of Christianity
19	Theology of the 19th cent.		In discussion and debate with the contemporary philosophical systems, quite different tendencies are developed that range from strict confessionalism to atheism
		F. Schleiermacher	Christian truth is founded in Christian self-consciousness; therefore, dogmatic theology becomes the descriptive account of this self-consciousness
		The Hegelians, P. Marheineke, K. Daub, D. F. Strauss, L. Feuerbach	Under Hegel's influence religion is seen as a phenomenon of the human spirit; with the "left-Hegelians" this leads to the denial of the divinity of Christ or even of God's existence (as a projection of human beings)
		Neo-Lutherans (F. J. Stahl, T. Kliefoth, W. Löhe, A. F. C. Vilmar)	Strict confessional orientation with special stress on ecclesiology (institution)
		Erlangen school (A. Harless, G. Thomasius, J. C. K. Hofmann)	Points out correspondences between Scripture and individual experiences of salvation; conservative character; biblical theological research
		S. Kierkegaard	Christianity is considered as the existential discipleship of Christ in suffering and doubt
		Liberal Protestantism (Tübingen school: F. C. Baur, H. J. Holtzmann; A. Ritschl, A. von Harnack, W. Herrmann)	Definitive introduction of historical-critical exegesis, the concept of a general revelation is declined; dogmatic theology is only a historical description of faith
		M. Kähler, A. Schlatter	Theology oriented to the Bible and to salvation-history
		History of religions school (E. Troeltsch, J. Weiss, A. Schweitzer, H. Gunkel)	Within the history of humanity Christianity is only the highest form of a personal religion

Cent.	Era	Main representatives	Characteristics
20	Theology of the present	Dialectical theology (K. Barth, E. Thurneysen, E. Brunner, F. Gogarten)	In protest against the liberal and the history-of-religions forms of Protestantism, the absolute otherness of God and God's proclamation is emphasized
		Existential theology (R. Bultmann, P. Tillich, E. Käsemann, G. Ebeling, J. Moltmann)	With different focal points, for these theologians Christianity is a call to human existence that has to be translated into today's thinking in a radical way

CHRISTIAN EAST

In contrast to Western theology, in Eastern theology it is not possible to separate precisely either eras or theological currents from one another. A constant feature of Eastern theology is the preservation and transmission of the patristic heritage (above all that of John of Damascus). However, one can note the different impulses of individual theologians.

Cent.	Era	Main Representative	Characteristics
11/14	Mystical theology	Simeon the New Theologian, Gregory Palamas	Only apophatic ("negative") theology can be expressed about the unutterable God
17	Discussion with Western thinking	Cyril Lucar, Peter Mogila, Dositheus	Attempt at a critical reception of Roman Catholic and Reformed positions
19	Slavic theology	A. S. Chomjakov, Philaret of Moscow	Unfolding of Orthodox ecclesiology; concept of reception
20	Neo-patristic theology	W. Lossky, G. Florovsky, J. Meyendorff, A. Schmemann	Dogmatic theology founded on the basis of the theology of the Church Fathers with stress on ecclesiology and eucharistic doctrine

Theology of the Cross. *See* CROSS: THEOLOGY OF THE.

Theology of the Mysteries. The term *theology of the mysteries* refers to the attempt made since the 1920s to use the concept of "mystery" in order to explain the saving event that takes place in the sacraments.

(1) *Biblical Background.* In the New Testament the term *mystery* (*mysterium*) epitomizes the saving action of God in Christ as this is made present in the church (SACRAMENT).

(2) *History of Theology.* Odo Casel, a Benedictine monk (1886–1948) who was an expert in biblical and patristic theology as well as in the mystery religions of antiquity, adopted the term *mystery* in order to explain the interior

saving event that takes place in baptism and the Eucharist and in the other sacraments as well. In the sacraments the saving work of Christ, especially his death and resurrection, becomes present in the form of a cultic mystery. The sacraments are "the presence of the divine work of salvation under the veil of symbols"; those who join in the celebration enter together into this saving work, the paschal mystery, and are thereby assimilated to the lot of Jesus Christ and so saved. A multifaceted controversy subsequently arose regarding the way in which the saving work becomes present. Many of Casel's exegetical explanations and especially his attempt to explain the Christian cultic mystery in light of the mystery cults of antiquity were quite rightly rejected. His basic insight, however, has continued to be one of the most fruitful theological ideas of our century.

(3) *Church Teaching.* Vatican II made the paschal mystery one of its key concepts. The paschal mystery is the source from which "all sacraments and sacramentals draw their power" (*SC* 61); human beings are grafted into it in baptism, and it is celebrated in the Eucharist by the power of the Holy Spirit (see *SC* 6).

(4) *Ecumenical Perspectives.* The theology of the mysteries opens up new possibilities of agreement especially with the churches of the East, in which, in continuity with the tradition of the Fathers of the Church, the idea of a Spirit-mediated sacramental participation in God's saving work in Christ plays a large role. The symbols contain the reality that they represent, and when the faithful celebrate them, they are incorporated into this reality.

(5) *Systematic Reflections.* The basic idea in the theology of the mysteries, namely, the "rendering present" of Christ's saving work, is undoubtedly a fruitful one. It calls, however, for a further development or supplement, and this it soon received: the sacraments bring not only a participation in a saving event but also an "encounter" with the God of salvation through Jesus Christ in the Holy Spirit, as well as a communion of Christians with one another. In this encounter both the past saving work of Christ and his return that brings it to completion are present and operative.

See also SACRAMENT.

Bibliography
Brown, Raymond E. *The Semitic Background of the Term "Mystery" in the New Testament.* Philadelphia: Fortress, 1968.
Casel, Odo. *The Mystery of Christian Worship.* Westminster, Md.: Newman, 1962.

GÜNTER KOCH

Time. *External* time is temporal duration experienced as quantitative and measurable by physical means (movement, rotation of the earth, atomic clocks); here we perceive before and after, past, present, and future. In addition to this cosmocentrically determined duration of things temporal there is a qualitative, *interior* (event-) time that is more important theologically and is defined in anthropological terms; it is in this time that human beings make decisions whereby they "fulfill" quantitative time, which is by its nature empty, and thus determine the value of their temporal life.

(1) *Biblical Background.* In the Sacred Scriptures of the Old Testament and New Testament there is basically no reflection on time in a "natural," abstract form. External time is understood rather as a condition for the possibility of the interior temporality of existence. The focus is not on the empty flow of time but on the response of human beings to the divine offer of a unique time of salvation. The Hebrews are always concerned with time that has a content, time that is something qualitative because identical with its content. Time that is decisive at the religious level is decided by God and given to human beings; it can be a time of grace or of judgment. For everything that happens under the heavens there is a time appointed by God (Eccl 3:1–8). The eternal God, who exists above all time, is at work in the human history that God has organized and turns it into a salvation-history. God brings the lifetime of the individual to an end in death and on the day of Yahweh brings history itself to an end (JUDGMENT). The New Testament understanding of time is determined by the Christ-event. The activity of Christ is dependent on God's "plan for time" (see Mk 1:15; Gal 4:4) and on the "striking of the hour" set by God (Mt 26:45; Mk 14:35; Jn 2:4; 7:30; 17:1). The time of salvation that has been arranged by the Father reaches its fulfillment in the activity of Jesus, so that there can be no time of salvation beyond the Christ-event. Time is a gift that God gives to human beings; the task of working out their salvation is linked to this gift. Just as Jerusalem did not recognize the time of grace (Lk 19:44), so Christians can allow the time given to them once only to slip by unused. They must be vigilant because they do not know when the time will come (Mk 13:33). Especially in the Pauline and deutero-Pauline letters we find clear reminders that we must profit by the time of salvation (Rom 13:11; Gal 6:9–10; Eph 5:15–17; Col 4:5).

(2) *History of Theology.* In Christian tradition, the biblical statements about the time fulfilled by Christ and the time allotted to other human beings are preached to new generations, as can be seen in the understanding of the liturgy as a memorial of the saving actions of Christ, in the prospect of the PAROUSIA, and in the understanding of DEATH and of the personal and general judgments.

(3) *Church Teaching.* The ecclesial magisterium provides no explicit pronouncements on how time is to be understood. The relevant pronouncements in its teaching on creation and eschatology do, however, presuppose a particular theological understanding of time. Thus the statement of the first article of the creed on God as Creator of heaven and earth is expanded at the Fourth Lateran Council (1215 [DS 800]) and Vatican I (DS 3002) by the assertion that at the beginning of time God brought forth the entire creation. The message here is that, on the one hand, the eternal God and Creator exists above time and, on the other, that time and the creation of the world go together. The equivalence of "eschatological" and "belonging to the last days" shows that

the relevant events and modes of existence come at the end of, or after, time as we experience it in this world.

(4) *Ecumenical Perspectives.* Although the basic theological understanding of time is not a matter of ecumenical discussion, the problems involved in the concept become visible when the understanding of death (total death; resurrection at death) and of the INTERMEDIATE STATE comes under discussion.

(5) *Systematic Reflections.* The problem of time is discussed from various points of view in speculative theology. One subject, among others, is the distinction, mentioned earlier, between cosmocentric time and anthropocentric time, each of which shapes human existence in its own way. Human beings live in time and are at its mercy; they cannot think except in the intuitive forms of space and time; they plan their future; they make use of time; they fill up the time allotted to them and at death bring home the harvest of time. The earthly life of Christians is understood as a pilgrimage during which they accrue merits and demerits that lead to rewards and punishments in the hereafter.

See also ESCHATOLOGY; ESCHATOLOGY: CONCEPTIONS OF; HISTORY/HISTORICITY.

Bibliography
Rahner, Karl. "Theological Observations on the Concept of Time." In *Theological Investigations,* 11:288–308. New York: Seabury, 1974.
Ricoeur, Paul. *Time and Narrative.* 3 vols. Chicago: University of Chicago Press, 1984–1988.

JOSEF FINKENZELLER

Title. *See* CHRISTOLOGICAL TITLES.

Tolerance. Tolerance is the attitude of acceptance and sometimes also of respect for the convictions and ways of life of people who think differently. It is grounded ethically in the human dignity and in the freedom of conscience of every human person. It can, moreover, be the correct response before the question of truth because all human knowledge of the true and good is limited and historically conditioned.

(1) *Biblical Background.* The concept of tolerance can be grounded in the biblical view that every human person is made in the image of God, that each person's conscience is the ultimate standard of her or his responsibility toward God; above all, the concept can be grounded in the commandment of the love of neighbor. Yet, practically, Israel's belief in election and also the universal Christian belief in salvation apparently could assert themselves only through intolerance with regard to other religions: "If anyone comes to you and does not bring this doctrine, do not receive him in your house or even greet him" (2 John 10).

(2) *History of Theology.* Roman law in principle assured tolerance to every religion that was not dangerous to the state. As soon as Christianity was also granted this tolerance (Edict of Milan, 313), it began to fight the other religions,

supposedly out of obedience to the one indivisible truth and God's salvific purpose. As a consequence of the close association of church and empire, the claim to the absoluteness of Christianity could again and again be used to serve political purposes (subjection of the Germans and the Slavs, colonization of the new world). Unfortunately, the church for its part, supported with theological justification, also used the power of the state to bring about the unity of faith through force (fighting of heretics). In the Christian West, the concept of tolerance came into effect for the first time as a demand of reason in view of the senseless wars of religion. Church and theology frequently valued the demand for religious tolerance as a profession of indifferentism before the divine truth.

(3) *Church Teaching.* Today the Catholic Church advocates that "our respect and charity" are also to be granted to those who "think and act differently from us in social, political, and religious matters." But this should not make one indifferent toward the true and the good. One must distinguish between the error, which is always to be rejected, and the person who errs (*GS* 28; see *AG* 11).

(4) *Ecumenical Perspectives.* In the ecumenical dialogue, the problem of the tolerance of Christians among each other very soon leads to the contested central question about the necessity and justification of a supreme binding magisterium (pope).

(5) *Systematic Reflections.* Dogmatically, the demand for tolerance has no difficulties, if it is a question of tolerance toward those human persons who hold other religious convictions and practices. Also tolerance toward the so-called partial truths of the others that can be brought in unison with the Catholic truth is not a serious problem; in practice, however, more often than not it is felt to be an especially arrogant intolerance. Tolerance becomes a serious problem when the gospel's claim to absoluteness and its representation through the Catholic Church are at stake. Here, theology will refer to its basic insight that the absolute truth can be grasped only in a way that remains restricted by human limits and by historical perspectives. This truth can be made binding by the magisterium only with these limitations. The other religious convictions, therefore, can be understood as other historical perspectives on the absolute truth whose reference to the universal salvific meaning of Jesus indeed becomes clear only in the light of the gospel. Also the church expresses this salvific meaning of Jesus for all human persons only in a limited way, that is, within the limits of its concrete experienced history. Consequently, the convictions of the other Christian communities and also of the non-Christian religions can make God's universal salvific will known in a way that the church from its own historical tradition does not yet know. In this way, tolerance toward all other religious convictions results precisely from the gospel's claim to absoluteness that the church advocates. It is only within this basic tolerance that the critical dialogue, which has as its guide the revelation of God's love for humankind in Jesus Christ, is also possible and sometimes, indeed, necessary.

See also CONFESSION; CONSCIENCE; DOGMA/DOGMATIC STATEMENT; ECU-

MENISM; HUMAN RIGHTS AND HUMAN DIGNITY; IMAGE OF GOD; LOVE OF
GOD–LOVE OF NEIGHBOR; MEMBERSHIP IN THE CHURCH; TRUTH OF FAITH.

Bibliography
Ferguson, Thomas P. *Catholic and American: The Political Theology of John Courtney Murray.* Kansas City: Sheed and Ward, 1993.
Geffré, Claude, and Jean-Pierre Jossua. *True and False Universality of Christianity.* New York: Seabury, 1980.
Locke, John. *A Letter concerning Toleration.* Edited by John Horton and Susan Mendus. New York: Routledge, 1991.

GEORG LANGEMEYER

Tradition. The term *tradition* refers to the subject, the process, and the content of the transmission of faith through which is made possible the identity, the continuity, and the productive unfolding of the message of revelation in the community of faith. Here one must make distinctions with regard to

- *the process of handing on tradition:*
  the process (*tradere*) or *traditio activa;*
  the content (*tradendum, traditum, depositum*) or *traditio obiectiva;*
  the subject (*tradens*) or *traditio subiectiva;*

- *the origin:*
  the binding contents of revelation (*traditio divino-apostolica, Traditio*);
  ecclesial formulations and mediations of the contents of revelation
    (*traditiones*);

- *the contents:*
  the overall presentation of Christianity (*traditio realis*);
  the representation of Christianity in teaching and proclamation
    (*traditio verbalis*) as part of the actual tradition;

- *the relationship to Scripture:*
  the identity of Scripture and tradition (*traditio inhaesiva*);
  the completion of Scripture through tradition (*traditio constitutiva*);
  the interpretation of Scripture through tradition (*traditio interpretiva
    seu declarativa*).

(1) *Biblical Background.* In Scripture the significance of tradition for revelation and faith becomes evident, on the one hand, in the process of the origin and development of Scripture itself; oral traditions became written ones, and then, within the Bible, those written traditions were applied to later events (e.g., in the descriptions of the formation of the covenants, in the use of the exodus experience to interpret the Babylonian captivity, in the transformation of the imminent expectation of Christ's return between 1 Thes and 2 Thes or of the theology of the law from Paul to James). On the other hand, the significance of tradition shows itself in the behavior of Jesus himself, insofar as he proclaims the law and the prophets of the Old Testament tradition to be normative and

interprets them critically from the viewpoint of the will of God (Mt 5:17–48; 15:1–20; Mk 7:5–13). Since the New Testament authors recognize the necessity of passing on the contents of the Christ-event (verifiable, e.g., in verbs like *send, give witness, proclaim, fight for the received faith, hand on*), they take over as elements of tradition confessions (Rom 1:1–4; 4:24f.; 10:9; 1 Pt 3:18), liturgical formulas (1 Cor 11:23–26), hymns (Eph 5:14; Phil 2:5–11; 1 Tm 2:5f.; 1 Pt 1:20), and, above all, the accounts of the Last Supper and of Easter (1 Cor 11:23; 15:3). In the later New Testament period, the Pastoral Letters explicitly develop the aspect of the handing on of the teaching (1 Tm 1:18; 4:11; 2 Tm 1:13f.; 2:2).

(2) *History of Theology.* In the early church the concept of tradition originates from the necessity of preserving the identity of the Christian faith against heresies. Tertullian and Irenaeus appeal to the preservation of the apostolic tradition through the uninterrupted link between the bishops and their churches. Among the specific moments in the establishment of tradition are the determination of the canon (separation of the apostolic from the nonapostolic writings); the formation of rules of faith, of creeds, and of dogmas (setting down of the binding contents of faith); and the origin of theology (analysis and critique of tradition). From the fourth century onward, the Fathers of the Church become authorities. Basil raises the question about whether there is a *traditio constitutiva* (constitutive tradition) (*De Spir. sancto* 27.66). For the time that follows, this becomes just as significant as the definition of Vincent of Lérins (434) concerning what belongs to the Catholic faith, namely, that which has been believed everywhere, always, and by all (*Commonit.* 2). For the Middle Ages, the acceptance of tradition does not pose a problem: for much of the period, the Bible, patristic theology, canons from the councils, and papal decretals are grouped together as "Holy Scripture" and are regarded as revelation and as inspired. In the late Middle Ages, however, a critical analysis proves to be necessary in order to distinguish between *Traditio* and *traditiones*. It does not succeed insofar as it persists in construing the relationship of natural tension between the two as a contradiction (Henry of Ghent, J. Wycliffe, J. Huss); this point becomes the problem of the following time period (see sec. 4 below). Under the heading "Scripture–Tradition" it becomes an ardently discussed question in the period after the Council of Trent (see sec. 3 below). Three attempted solutions are offered (see chart, p. 714, nos. 1–3). After the opening up of the debate at Vatican II (see sec. 3 below), theology concentrates on the essence of tradition. Here, above all, the discussion focuses on the problem of the critique of tradition, the relationship between the bearers of tradition today (magisterium/sensus fidelium/theology), and the productive realization of the elements of tradition for the present (problem of hermeneutics).

(3) *Church Teaching.* The Council of Trent maintains against the Protestants that the Christian truth and way of life are contained "in written books *and* unwritten traditions" ("in libris scriptis *et* sine scripto traditionibus"), both of which are to be "received and venerated with the same sense of loyalty and

THE RELATIONSHIP OF SCRIPTURE AND TRADITION

(1) Tradition is an autonomous source of knowledge (two-source theory):

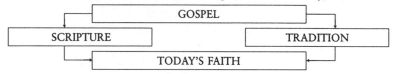

(2) Tradition explains Scripture, which is materially sufficient in itself:

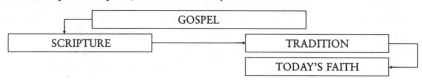

(3) Tradition is related to Scripture and only in a relative sense adds to it:

(4) Tradition and Scripture are means for the mediation of revelation that historically and objectively condition and support each other:

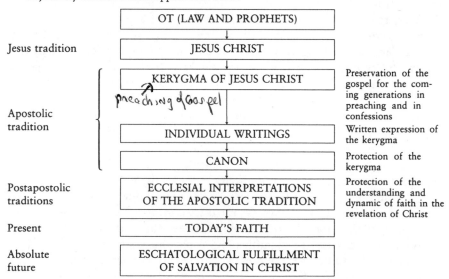

	OT (LAW AND PROPHETS)	
Jesus tradition	JESUS CHRIST	
Apostolic tradition	KERYGMA OF JESUS CHRIST *preaching of Gospel*	Preservation of the gospel for the coming generations in preaching and in confessions
	INDIVIDUAL WRITINGS	Written expression of the kerygma
	CANON	Protection of the kerygma
Postapostolic traditions	ECCLESIAL INTERPRETATIONS OF THE APOSTOLIC TRADITION	Protection of the understanding and dynamic of faith in the revelation of Christ
Present	TODAY'S FAITH	
Absolute future	ESCHATOLOGICAL FULFILLMENT OF SALVATION IN CHRIST	

reverence" ("*pari* pietatis affectu ac reverentia" [DS 1501]). Vatican I repeats this teaching (DS 3006) with a clearly more open formulation (DS 3011: "in verbo Dei scripto *vel* tradito" [contained in the word of God, written *or* handed down]). Vatican II turns the attention away from the determination of the relationship between Scripture and tradition to the essence of tradition (*DV* 7–12). In a sacramental and holistic understanding it sees revelation as one integral event that is mediated not through two sources but rather through two modes of transmission. In this perspective, life, teaching, and cult together make up tradition, which, on account of its apostolic origin and its reception in the whole church, must be actualized in the church.

(4) *Ecumenical Perspectives.* In the Orthodox Church, tradition has the rank of a *traditio constitutiva,* insofar as it is of apostolic origin. As tradition in the narrower sense, it is contained in the creeds, the consensus of the Church Fathers, and the decisions of the first seven ecumenical councils. As tradition in the wider sense, it is found in the individual writings of the Fathers, in the decrees of local synods, and in the early liturgies and ecclesial rites. In the debates of the late Middle Ages, M. Luther and the movement he started join the side of the critics of tradition. For a long time Luther indeed acknowledges the decisions of the first four ecumenical councils as binding (from which the conviction of the *consensus quinquesaecularis* [the consent of the first five centuries] developed), yet later he tends to evaluate the Bible as the exclusive resource of faith. If at all, tradition is acknowledged as *traditio inhaesiva.* On account of the historical controversies, tradition is one of the main themes of the present ecumenical dialogue (Montreal, 1963; Malta, 1971; Roman–Catholic/Reformed Dialogues, 1977). Here a far-reaching agreement on the significance of tradition and its relation to Scripture has been achieved.

(5) *Systematic Reflections.* Tradition is the precondition for the identity of the individual and of the community, a reality that becomes clear, for example, in the necessity of received language. It does not merely serve the conservation of what is past but rather within the critical process of reception serves, above all, to make possible self-realization in the present and in the future. It thus possesses an element that helps create freedom and is an indispensable hermeneutical concept. This is especially true for Christianity since it is grounded in a historical event with a universal validity claim (the Christ-event) that continually and in a lively manner must be witnessed to and handed on. On account of this continual testimony, the history of the interpretation of revelation also belongs to its contemporary assessment, above all, because the community of faith lives under the influence of the Holy Spirit. Tradition in the theological sense is thus the continuing process of the self-communication of God in the Christ-event through the Holy Spirit in the medium of the proclamation of the church; therefore, it is an important criterion of knowledge for theology. This *Traditio* (*divino-apostolica*) appears only in the (human) *traditiones.* Since these as historical phenomena are conditioned by their time, they are not always correct or comprehensive (see, e.g., the opinions of the church on women,

witches, the relationship between the human person and the natural environment, and the relationship to civic authority in the course of history), and they can be received only after critical examination. The principle of tradition is a principle of truth, not of habit (Tertullian, *De virg. vel.* 1.1). Criteria can be named: the traditions must be expressions of the apostolic tradition passed on in Scripture; they are valid not in their form but rather as bearers of meaning; they have to be valid for the entire church; they have to be eschatologically oriented (directed toward the mystery of fulfillment in God). As to the relationship between Scripture and tradition, which was controversial for a long time, agreement has been fundamentally reached that they are not two sources with different contents but rather means for the mediation of revelation that mutually condition and support each other; in this process, tradition, historically, is the more comprehensive reality (see chart, no. 4).

See also APOSTOLIC SUCCESSION; CANON; ECCLESIAL MAGISTERIUM; HERMENEUTICS; SCRIPTURE; THEOLOGIANS.

Bibliography
Congar, Yves. *Tradition and Traditions: An Historical and a Theological Essay.* New York: Macmillan, 1967.
Cook, Martin. *The Open Circle: Confessional Method in Theology.* Minneapolis: Fortress, 1991.
Geiselmann, Josef. *The Meaning of Tradition.* New York: Herder and Herder, 1966.
Mackey, James P. *The Modern Theology of Tradition.* New York: Herder and Herder, 1963.
Rahner, Karl, and Joseph Ratzinger. *Revelation and Tradition.* New York: Herder and Herder, 1966.
Shils, Edward. *Tradition.* Chicago: University of Chicago Press, 1981.

WOLFGANG BEINERT

Traditionalism. In the broadest sense, *traditionalism* means adherence to what has been handed down (being tied to tradition); in the narrower sense, this word is used to refer to defense of a rigid, mechanistic structure of tradition, often with a fundamentalistic (as opposed to a historical) understanding of tradition; finally, in the history of dogma, traditionalism refers to an antirationalistic direction in nineteenth-century philosophy and theology. The last meaning is the subject of discussion here.

(1) *Biblical Background.* See sec. 1 of GOD: POSSIBILITY OF KNOWLEDGE OF.

(2) *History of Theology.* Whereas the tradition of mainline theology holds to the position that belief is rational, the nineteenth century, particularly in France, witnessed an extreme reaction against the rationalistic constructions of the Enlightenment. The main representatives of this direction were J.-M. de Maistre, L. de Bonald, H.-F.-R. Lamennais, and, a generation later, A. Bonnetty. Many of its representatives combined traditionalism with an ecclesiastical integralism. (Traditionalism in the narrower sense especially makes the authority of the pope an element of order.) In a moderated form, traditionalism is represented by the Catholic Tübingen school of J. S. von Drey. This school accentuates the

significance of handing down a living tradition about God in history and the church. The basic tenets of traditionalism are: a conviction that human reason is incapable of attaining knowledge of moral and religious truths and must therefore receive them exclusively from outside itself through the word; a conviction that this word is grounded in an "original revelation" that has to be handed on uninterruptedly from the first human beings to the present day; and a conviction that humanity can accept this tradition only on the basis of authority (that of God or of conviction general to the human race).

(3) *Church Teaching.* Church teaching has repudiated traditionalism in its extreme form insofar as Vatican I affirmed the possibility of natural knowledge of God (DS 3004, 3026).

(4) *Ecumenical Perspectives.* Some similarities to strict traditionalism are evident in Reformation standpoints that pessimistically judge the religious potentialities of reason.

(5) *Systematic Reflections.* Paradoxically, dogmatic traditionalism undermines traditionalism in the broadest sense. What is handed on loses its carrying capacity for transmission of God's word insofar as human beings no longer feel that it speaks to them inwardly. It thus forfeits its plausibility and is no longer able to convince. In contrast, theology should maintain that God speaks to humans externally in such a way that they become receptive to being spoken to inwardly. In this manner belief can also remain an authentically human act.

See also BELIEF; FIDEISM; GOD: POSSIBILITY OF KNOWLEDGE OF; PRIMAL REVELATION; TRADITION.

Bibliography
Fitzer, Joseph, ed. *Romance and the Rock: Nineteenth-Century Catholics on Faith and Reason.* Minneapolis: Fortress, 1989.
McCool, Gerald A. *Catholic Theology in the Nineteenth Century: The Search for a Unitary Method.* New York: Seabury, 1977.
O'Meara, Thomas F. *Roman Idealism and Roman Catholicism: Schelling and the Theologians.* Notre Dame, Ind.: University of Notre Dame Press, 1982.
Thiel, John E. *Imagination and Authority: Theological Authorship in the Modern Tradition.* Minneapolis: Fortress, 1991.

WILHELM BREUNING

Trinitarian Heresies. The term *trinitarian heresies* refers to inadequate, heretical attempts to explain the mystery of the divine Trinity. They lead to dissolution of either the oneness or the threefoldness of God.

(1) *Biblical Background.* Naturally, trinitarian heresies first arise along with the development of the relevant doctrine. Since the heterodox representatives of trinitarian belief claim to be supported by the Bible, the church's rejection of their positions is, at the same time, also part of the history of the interpretation of biblical belief in God.

(2) *History of Theology.* Since Christian trinitarian belief must avowedly preserve both the oneness and the fullness of the divine life, trinitarian heresies stray from the church's integral belief by emphasizing either the singularity

or the triplicity of God. Accordingly, trinitarian heresies divide into two main groups. (a) *Monarchianism,* in its different variations, attempts to preserve the oneness and singularity of God by claiming that God's expressions as Father, Son, and Holy Spirit within the history of creation and redemption are simply modes of God's appearing (Latin: *modi,* hence also *modalism*), and allow no conclusions to be drawn about intradivine life. Its concern is to achieve simple and uncomplicated explication of faith; in reality, however, it strikes the very nerve of Christian faith, which sees the real relatedness of Christ to the Father and the inherent operation of the Spirit as corresponding to the intradivine life processes. The main representatives of Monarchianism are Noetus of Smyrna and Praxeas in the second century, and Sabellius (hence, too, *Sabellianism*) in the third. They led the theology of the Catholic Church to supplement the emphasis on God's oneness by also elucidating more profoundly the real distinctions between the Father, Son, and Holy Spirit. (b) *Subordinationism* in its various forms attempted to make the threefoldness understandable by conceiving the Trinity as an order of levels. Underlying subordinationism is the Platonic view of the cosmos, as well as early christological speculation. The christological concern was to make intelligible the Son's function as mediator. That seemed easily possible under the philosophical assumption that reality is a multileveled hierarchy in which God is unapproachably positioned at the very "top." Christ, as mediator, is to be seen as occupying a position where he is, to be sure, situated above all the rest of worldly reality, yet is clearly subordinated (*subordinatus*) to God (the Father). For theology of the Trinity, that means: *God,* in the strict sense of the term, can be predicated only of the Father (as the originless Origin). The Logos/Son is, at best, a "second God" (*deúteros theós*) because he is the initiator of all creatures, but he is not really *God.* The main representative of subordinationistic thought is Arius (hence the term *Arianism*). His system met with great success not only because of its apparent plausibility but also because of its suitability to the political ideology of strict monarchy. Thus the emperors were prone to embrace it. Arianism had a sequel in Pneumatomachianism ("struggle against the Holy Spirit"), although this met with little response. It raised the question whether, and to what extent, the Holy Spirit is also *God.* All these controversies led the orthodox theology of the ancient church to acknowledge quite clearly the divine sonship of Jesus and thereby to ensure at the same time also the reality and universality of redemption. For redemption has really occurred only if God has effected it. Modern heresies in the doctrine of the Trinity are rooted in rationalistic attempts to dissolve the mystery; they have not helped theology to achieve further increases in depth of understanding.

(3) *Church Teaching.* The definition of the Son's consubstantiality with the Father (*homousios*) at the Council of Nicea (DS 125) and of the divinity of the Holy Spirit at the First Council of Constantinople (DS 150) has secured the faith against the trinitarian heresies of the Old Church.

(4) *Ecumenical Perspectives.* Today, the doctrine of the Trinity is the fixed

theological property of all confessions, although it still needs to be developed more deeply and more closely related to life.

(5) *Systematic Reflections.* In the face of all attempts at overclarification, theology has to endure the tension that is constitutively inherent in trinitarian dogma. Only that ensures the spiritual meaning of the central Christian mystery.

See also TRINITY; TRINITY: DOCTRINE OF THE.

Bibliography
Kelly. J. N. D. *Early Christian Doctrines.* 2d ed. New York: Harper and Row, 1960.
Pelikan, Jaroslav. *The Emergence of the Catholic Tradition.* Vol. 1 of *The Christian Tradition.* Chicago: University of Chicago Press, 1971.
Prestige, George L. *Fathers and Heretics: Six Studies in Dogmatic Faith.* London: SPCK, 1968.
———. *God in Patristic Thought.* 2d ed. London: SPCK, 1968.
Rausch, William, ed. *The Trinitarian Controversy.* Philadelphia: Fortress, 1980.

WILHELM BREUNING

Trinitarian Personhood of God. In theology of the Trinity, the notion of "persons in God" refers to the Father, Son, and Holy Spirit insofar as they each wholly live the one divine life, yet are distinct in relation to one another according to whether they transmit or receive that strictly (= numerically) *one* life.

(1) *Biblical Background.* What the concept "persons in God" intends is derived from New Testament revelation, but the concept itself is not biblical.

(2) *History of Theology.* The concept of person has its origin in "prosopographic" exegesis, that is, in the attribution of all specific scriptural texts to specific persons, to God the Father, to the Son, or to the Holy Spirit (they speak "in the person" of the Father, etc.). Underlying this is the meaning (assumedly stemming from the Etruscan) of "person" as *mask*, out of which evolve the meanings: *role, grammatical person,* and *individual as possessing knowledge and will.* Tertullian deliberately uses the word in a theological sense. In the doctrine in theology of the Trinity, the term *person* signifies, anti-Monarchianically, that which is proper to Father and Son in salvation-history *and* in divine immanence. The corresponding Greek term is actually *prósopon,* but the theological work centers on the concept of *hypóstasis.* Later, these two concepts become merged. A decisive development takes place in the fourth century: since *nature (usia)* was reserved for the life that was common to the divine persons, a word had to be found to express their distinctness. The Cappadocians use the concept of *hypóstasis* (persona) for this. They conceive the differences as the way in which the (undifferentiated) nature *(usia)* is lived differentiatedly in intradivine giving and receiving. Consequently, they conceive each person from the standpoint of the other persons in God. Augustine takes up this conception and works out that the relations arising from the originative event render the persons distinguishable: the Father, as the one who generates the Son and

brings forth the Spirit, is the *Origin* without origin; the Logos, as the one who receives and is related to the emergence of the Spirit, is the *Son;* and the *Spirit* is the one who arises from the Origin through the Son. Thomas Aquinas expresses this theology in the formula: the persons in God are *subsistent* (= existent in their relatedness to a "self") *relations.* This theological concept of person can, in principle, also be used not only for the Trinity but also in Christology, angelology, and anthropology. However, because of its connotation of "being-for-itself," this conception has limited use in regard to the Trinity.

(3) *Church Teaching.* The concept of person, which the theology of the Trinity has elaborated, is not included in the Chalcedonian creed. It is, however, normatively used as a way of speaking in the church's teaching (DS Index systematicus B.2).

(4) *Ecumenical Perspectives.* There is no ecumenical debate about the notion of persons in God.

(5) *Systematic Reflections.* In contemporary theology, K. Barth and K. Rahner have called attention to the weakness (recognized already by Augustine) of the notion of person. Since it is defined on the model of human personhood (a conscious, free center of action and impulses as a self-contained source of actions), it almost necessarily evokes the tritheistic misunderstanding (three divine psychological centers). As a replacement, Rahner suggests "distinct modes of subsistence"; with that, he is close to the fourth-century sense of *hypóstasis.* The difficulties could, however, be better overcome were one to understand the concept of person as basically relational: *love,* as relatedness to some other, belongs essentially to personhood. The supreme, trinitarian form of love (and thus, of person) could then make manifest the fact that relatedness to God belongs essentially to human personhood.

See also PERSON; PERSONALITY; TRINITARIAN HERESIES; TRINITARIAN PERSONHOOD OF GOD; TRINITY; TRINITY: DOCTRINE OF THE.

Bibliography
Kasper, Walter. *The God of Jesus Christ.* New York: Crossroad, 1984.
Pannenberg, Wolfhart. *Systematic Theology.* Vol. 1. Grand Rapids: Eerdmans, 1991.
See also the bibliography under TRINITY.

WILHELM BREUNING

Trinity. *Trinity* is the linguistic term for the *one* God of the Bible who has been revealed through the incarnation of the Son in Jesus and the sending of the Holy Spirit and who has called humanity to life in communion with God.

(1) *Biblical Background.* The Old Testament is pervaded by conviction of God's vitality and fullness of life. Thus it already speaks of God's "Spirit" in order to designate divine inwardness and also God's self-expression as a gift to humanity (see, e.g., Ez 34:27). Actual revelation of the Trinity is distinctively characteristic of the New Testament, which announces that "the Word" becomes "flesh" in Jesus of Nazareth (Jn 1:14) and that he, as the resurrected and exalted Lord, sends the Spirit. But the New Testament does not develop a

pure love. The Council of Nicaea (325) affirms, contrary to Arius, that the Son clearly belongs on the level of being occupied by God. He is "consubstantial with the Father" (*homousios*), and therefore not a creature (no matter how elevated a one). The following historical period achieved a proper understanding of *homousios*. This achievement was due especially to Athanasius and the three so-called Cappadocians (Basil, Gregory of Nazianzus, Gregory of Nyssa). Their theology surmounts the Greek understanding of God at the decisive point. According to them, the Son is not an intermediary entity between an (in principle wholly) unreachable God and the world; instead, he is mediator *as* Son. Moreover, he does not have lower status in divinity than the Father, even though he receives his sonship from the Father. Hence, God (the Father) — and this is the really decisive aspect of this conception — is no longer seen in terms of an absolutely autarchical being that lives only for God. Instead, God is characterized in and through God's movement toward the Son. The Son is characterized by being shown to be the one who has received himself wholly from the Father. The oneness of the Father and Son is the Holy Spirit. It is rationally intelligible to conceive the absolutely distinguishing quality of the divine as self-contained Origin without origin: the Arian Eunomius represents this doctrine. But the church's theology of the Trinity rejects this: that the Father is without origin culminates not in his autarchy, but in his being the origin *for* the Son and Spirit. Thereby, God is clearly acknowledged in faith as love. The *third phase* of the doctrine of the Trinity attempts to resolve a problem that resulted from the foregoing conception: if Father, Son, and Spirit "have" but a single nature, then their mutual real distinctness must also be linguistically expressible. Were the "three" to live the one life of God merely as one nature rendered various by the individual bearers (just as the species *humanity* is realized in different human individuals), then Father, Son, and Spirit would be (numerically) three Gods (tritheism). In the second half of the fourth century, the Cappadocians responded that the Father lives the one and same life of God as one who *gives,* the Son as one who *receives,* and the Spirit as one who *proceeds* from the Father "through" the Son. The distinctness thus lies in the sphere of the *relations* that, as "contraries," impart to one another precisely the strictly *one,* commonly shared element of divine life. Conceptually, this peculiarity of there being "bearers" of the one nature was designated "hypostasis." The term stems from Neoplatonism, in which it characterizes the individual levels within the hierarchic system of reality; thus it has a subordinationistic connotation. Origen also uses it in that way. In contrast to such tendencies, the Council of Nicaea had spoken only of *one* divine hypostasis (DS 126). In the doctrine of the Trinity, however, it now acquires a wholly new quality: it can be conceived in the plural, as "three hypostases," only if the original divine relationships are also strictly conceived, on the basis of the dogma of Nicaea, as "of one nature." The life *processes* that emerge from the one life of God are expressed in language as follows. The Father is the Origin without beginning. The life

theology of the Trinity; rather, it wants to state that, through the living, acting, and dying of the Lord, through his rising and his sending of the Spirit, we become included in the life of God. Moreover, the New Testament explicates Jesus' oneness with, and simultaneous distinctness from, his Father (e.g., Jn 10:30; 14:9). Jesus is not the Father, but he has received himself, including his sonship, entirely from the Father. It becomes clear that this relationship mirrors the intradivine life (PREEXISTENCE OF JESUS CHRIST). Through his glorification at Easter, those who are his also become drawn into this relationship; this occurs through the Holy Spirit as the mysterious bearer of the love that has come to perfection between Father and Son (Jn 7:37–39; 14:1–16:15; also, concentratedly, in Paul: Romans; 1 and 2 Corinthians; Galatians). Instructive is the naming of the Father, the Son, and the Holy Spirit in the baptismal formula in Mt 28:19.

(2) *History of Theology.* The trinitarian baptismal vows are also the first dogmatic foundation for the transmittal of trinitarian belief; their contents are taken up into the eucharistic prayer as contained in the doxology of the High Prayer. On these bases, and through lengthy endeavor, theology works out, conceptually and linguistically, the contents of this belief. First, it is emphasized that *God* is a single living process; hence, what is called God can be nothing but a single quality. That is called *essence, nature,* or *substance.* The innermost essence of God, however, according to biblical revelation, is a copresence and intertwinement of giving, receiving, and oneness that must be designated as the working of divine love. In the fourth century, the connection finally becomes clear: that God cannot be conceived as absolute self-realization. For God is the Origin without origin as much as God is the receiving that correlates with giving. This relational structure is captured by the concept of *person.* The doctrine of the Trinity explicates it in greater detail as such: the unbegotten Father generates the Son and, through him, brings forth the Spirit; God, as Son, receives himself and the breath of the Spirit from the Father; as Spirit, the Spirit flows from the Father and Son "back" into the oneness of Father and Son, and is thus simultaneously the place from which God, in God's self, is open for communion with the creatures that, out of freely acting love, God has called into being. In the course of critical confrontation with trinitarian heresies an additional conceptual clarification took place. The theology of the ancient church made the distinction — and appropriate mutual classification — between "theology" (= the trinitarian being of God in God's self) and "economy" (= the communication of intratrinitarian life to creatures). Contemporary theology refers to the "immanent" and the "economic" Trinity. K. Rahner put forward the principle that the immanent Trinity is the economic one, and vice versa (*MystSal* 2:328). The leading motif of Rahner's conception is the mystery of Christ. The absolute surrender of the Son on the cross (Rom 8:32) allowed but one conclusion: in the Son, God has offered God's self; the Spirit leads us, in fact, into the most intimate unity of life with God (see 1 Cor 2:20).

(3) *Church Teaching.* The history of the doctrine relies on the significance of

beliefs encountered in the early Christian professions of faith (DS 125, 150): the Son is consubstantial (*homousios*) with the Father; the Spirit is worshiped along with the Father and Son. The phrase "one Essence in three Persons," which was developed in the fourth century, appears in later documents of doctrinal office (e.g., DS 421).

(4) *Ecumenical Perspectives.* The trinitarian profession of faith belongs to the cornerstone of Christianity and is the basis for any Christian consensus. The "basis formula" of the World Council of Churches (1948) maintains such a centrality for the trinitarian profession of faith. A difference exists between the Western and Eastern churches regarding the emergence of the Spirit: the East has not accepted the added phrase in the Nicene-Constantinopolitan Creed according to which the Holy Spirit proceeds from "the Father and the Son" (*ex Patre Filioque*). The formula of union of the Council of Florence (DS 1331) asserted that the Father is the Origin without origin; that the Son, in relation to the Spirit, is the "Origin from the Origin"; and that, in this way, Father and Son are the *one* Origin of the Spirit. Today, an attempt at mediation is made through the formula that the Spirit emerges *from* the Father *through* the Son. This formula, from early Eastern theology, has the advantage of being more concrete than the *filioque* (Y. Congar).

(5) *Systematic Reflections.* In the age of liberalism and rationalism, faith in the Trinity occupied a rather marginal position in theology. Today, it has been shifted to the center. God appears in trinitarian theology as love, not in absolute self-relatedness but in total other-relatedness. With the help of a phenomenology that understands spiritual processes in terms of living polarity, and even more because of the interconnectedness of love, freedom, and personality, theology begins to understand God as the *event of love*. That God really is this event can be recognized only from revelation; accordingly, the Trinity remains the innermost and primary MYSTERY OF FAITH. However, the human openness to love allows us to draw near to this mystery and releases praise and adoration. With that, the nature of the relation between the immanent and the economic Trinity is clarified: the economic presupposes the immanent as the one complete in itself. The "economy" is grounded in God's free surrender, which led to the Son's incarnation. Through that, God has actually and wholly communicated God's self as the immanent Trinity: God is revealed as an overflowing mystery that dispenses more than we can ask and are permitted to expect.

See also GOD'S ONENESS; TRINITARIAN HERESIES; TRINITARIAN PERSONHOOD OF GOD; TRINITY: DOCTRINE OF THE.

Bibliography

Grillmeier, Alois. *Christ in Christian Tradition.* 2d ed. London: Mowbray, 1975.
Hill, William. *The Three-Personed God.* Washington, D.C.: Catholic University of America Press, 1983.
Hodson, Leonard. *The Doctrine of the Trinity.* Rev. ed. London: Nisbet, 1960.

Johnson, Elizabeth. *She Who Is: The Mystery of God in a Feminist Theological Perspective.* New York: Crossroad, 1992.
Jüngel, Eberhard. *God as the Mystery of the World.* Grand Rapids: Eerdmans, 1982.
Kasper, Walter. *The God of Jesus Christ.* New York: Crossroad, 1984.
Kelly, J. N. D. *Early Christian Creeds.* London: Longman, 1972.
LaCugna, Catherine. *God for Us: The Trinity and Christian Life.* San Francisco: Harper, 1991.
Lonergan, Bernard. *The Way to Nicea: The Dialectical Development of Trinitarian Theology.* Philadelphia: Westminster, 1976.
Peters, Ted. *God as Trinity: Relationality and Temporality in the Divine Life.* Louisville: Westminster, 1993.
Rahner, Karl. *The Trinity.* New York: Herder, 1970.
Richardson, Cyril. *The Doctrine of the Trinity.* Nashville: Abingdon, 1958.
Welch, Claude. *In This Name: The Doctrine of the Trinity in Contemporary Theology.* New York: Scribner's, 1952.

WILHELM BREUNING

Trinity: Doctrine of the. The doctrine of the Trinity elaborates the concepts in which the New Testament revelation of the triune God can be formulated as a profession of faith, presents this revelation in its interconnectedness, and renders its meaning recognizable as the center of Christian belief.

(1) *Biblical Background.* Holy Scripture has no theology of the Trinity in the sense just described. It is, however, the foundation of such, because it speaks, in the New Testament on the basis of Old Testament monotheism, of God as Father, Son, and Holy Spirit; and also contains first approaches to discourse about this mystery when it makes statements about the relationship of Father and Son and of both to the Spirit.

(2) *History of Theology.* Theology of the Trinity, in the proper sense, starts out historically from the problem of how Old Testament (and philosophical) monotheism can be brought into harmony with the biblical revelation that God is Father, Son, and Spirit. Above all, the teaching about the Trinity attempts to represent Jesus' distinctness from the Father in such a way as to preserve the oneness of God, and it has sought to differentiate that teaching from inadequate conceptual positions. The *first phase* of the theological development seeks to make clear, against modalistic Monarchianism, that the trinitarian interpretation of the history of creation and redemption does not just describe a mode of God's *outwardly directed activity*, but that, in it, *God's inner life itself* is revealed to us. This point is affirmed by the distinction between *oikonomia* (God's outwardly directed activity) and *theologia* (God's inner life). The decisive *second phase* of the theological development takes place in the critical dispute with the Arians. The starting point of the Arians is a Hellenistic understanding of God. The Greeks were able to imagine a hierarchy of being ranged in a structure of descending and ascending levels away from and toward God. Arius installed the Son on one such very high but created level. Such a conception was comprehensible to Greek thought, but is unable to do justice to the statements of the Bible; it is unable to con...

process that constitutes the Son is called _generation_. The life process that con-stitutes the Spirit is termed _procession_ (_ekpóreusis_) in the East and _spiration_ (_spiratio_) in the West ("procession" or _processio_ is used in the West for both Son _and_ Spirit). In this connection, just how Father and Son are related to the emergence of the Spirit remains a point of controversy between East and West. In a _fourth phase_ of doctrine of the Trinity, there is above all a search for analogies or "models" that could, to a certain extent, represent the intra-trinitarian life processes. Augustine develops a so-called _psychological theory of the Trinity_ out of the phenomenology of human spiritual life. In the states of knowing and loving, he sees humans as involved in a relation to themselves that simultaneously goes beyond themselves. Knowing is linked to generation, and loving to spiration. To be sure, this model fails to make understand-able just why divine persons are constituted from that. In the Middle Ages, Richard of St. Victor devises an analogy from the phenomenology of love: he presents God as the loving (Father), beloved (Son), and cobeloved (Spirit) in the sense of a consummation of the dialogue of love between Father and Son. Thomas Aquinas follows the Augustinian line; he also emphasizes, above all, the theology of relations. The problem arising there is how the abstract, formal structure of a relation is to be conceived concretely as love. Resolution of this was attempted mainly by Bonaventure, who stood in the Greek and Victorine traditions.

(3) _Church Teaching_. In addition to the creeds of the ancient church (DS 125, 150), important doctrinal statements explicating the doctrine of the Trin-ity come from the following ecclesiastical church councils and synods: the Synod of Toledo (675; DS 525–532); the Fourth Lateran Council (1215) with the profession of faith drawn up against the Albigensians and Catharists (DS 800) and the condemnation of Joachim of Fiore (DS 803–6); and the Union Council of Florence (1442; DS 1330f.).

(4) _Ecumenical Perspectives_. Today, there are no controversies between Christian confessions about the central content of faith concerning the doctrine of the Trinity. It is thus a part of the basic Christian consensus.

(5) _Systematic Reflections_. Trinitarian theology represents the most difficult chapter in Christian dogmatics. The major and enduring difficulty does not lie merely in the fact that the doctrine deals with the innermost mystery of the life of God, before which human thought shows itself to be inadequate. The difficulty stems from the fact that all the concepts available for a doctrine of the Trinity derive from a mode of thinking oriented toward the objectifiable reality proper to individual objects, whereas the reality proper to God, as the God of one nature in three persons, must be seen as a loving process of giving, receiving, and flowing. For that reason, all analogies, models, and paradigms can be criticized. Conversely, however, by using them, the doctrine of the Trin-ity is able to render at least something of the fertility and life of that mystery intuitable to faith and the life of faith.

OUTLINE OF TERMINOLOGY USED IN THEOLOGY OF THE TRINITY

According to the teaching of the church, three series of statements must be kept firmly in view in theology of the Trinity:

1. God is the Father; God is the Son; God is the Holy Spirit. These are statements about God's essence: God is triune (*Deus est Trinitas*). Therefore, they are reversible:

2. The Father is God; the Son is God; the Holy Spirit is God. At the same time, however, the element of distinctness is also to be preserved. This leads to the series of statements:

3. The Father is not the Son and not the Holy Spirit; the Son is not the Father and not the Holy Spirit; the Holy Spirit is not the Father and not the Son.

Theology of the Trinity attempts to clarify conceptually the internal coherence of these statements. In the course of the history of dogma, this has resulted in the development of its own specific terminology. The most important terms in that are:

Spiration	spiratio	Term for the life process in God that allows the Holy Spirit to be recognized in its individuality. A distinction is made between – active spiration: an activity of Father and Son (= through the Son); – passive spiration: the Spirit as the "result" of that activity.
Procession	processio	Term for the life process in God out of which the individuality of Son and Spirit become recognizable. Accordingly, there are two processions: – of the Son from the Father (generation); – of the Spirit from the Father and Son (= through the Father) (= spiration).
Nature	natura	Term for the *one* divine essence.
Notion	notio	Refers to those life processes in God that make clear the "individuality" of the three persons as relations. They are materially identical with the proprieties.
Perichoresis	circum-incessio	In Latin terminology (see "circumincessio"), the "result" is seen as something tending toward the static (*sedere* = to sit). The concept "perichoresis" makes clear that God's essence, right down to its innermost and deepest ground, is *love*.
	circum-incessio	Concept for intradivine life implying that the three divine persons, in their relational interconnectedness, wholly merge with one another in an interpenetrative way (*cedere* = pass over into something).
Person	persona (*hypostasis*)	Term for what differentiates the Father, Son, and Spirit within the unity of the one divine essence (TRINITARIAN PERSONHOOD OF GOD). The person is the subject of the divine life processes.
Propriety	proprietas	Term for the relative contrasts between the divine persons that are grounded in their particular ways of giving and receiving the divine essence. Thus they ground the individuality of the persons. Altogether, there are five proprieties (or notions). We recognize – the Father by his being originless, generative, and breathing; – the Son by his being generated and breathing; – the Spirit by its being breathed.
Relation	relatio	Term for the positions that the divine persons occupy with respect to one another within the one divine life. It conveys nothing material about the concept *person* (Thomas Aquinas therefore refers to the divine relations as "subsistent relations" [*relationes subsistentes*]), but indicates the relevant mode of being as a person. Accordingly, there are four relations: active and passive generation, and active and passive spiration. These pertain to the various persons as follows: – Father: active generation, active spiration; – Son: passive generation, active spiration; – Spirit: passive spiration.

All of this implies the following concise formulation of the church's teaching on the Trinity: in the Trinity, "there are five notions (proprieties), four relations, three persons, two processions, one nature, and *no proof*" ("Sunt quinque notiones, quattuor relationes, tres personae, duae processiones, una natura, nulla probatio"). Even the concepts are unable to dispel the mystery, but they do make it clear as such.

See also DISCOURSE ABOUT GOD; FILIOQUE; GOD; GOD: THEOLOGY OF; GOD'S ONENESS; TRINITARIAN HERESIES; TRINITY.

Bibliography
See the bibliography under TRINITY.

WILHELM BREUNING

Truth of Faith. The term *truth of faith* refers to the unfolding of reality given through faith.

(1) *Biblical Background.* The biblical understanding of truth is first of all formed from the Old Testament term *emet* (from *aman* = stand firm, be constant, stand the test), which can be rendered most closely with *faithfulness* but which actually intends the fundamental, entire relationship between God and human beings and which is very often taken together with terms such as *hesed* (grace) and *shālōm* (peace) (see, e.g., Dt 9:7; 32:4; Pss 25:10; 26:3; 111:7). The Greek sections of the Old Testament and the New Testament employ *alétheia* (from *a-* [negation] and *léthe* [forgetfulness]). Here this connotes the disclosure of being, the unfolding of a reality. This Greek term is often used in the New Testament with the Hebrew content. Truth is thus essentially that which has perduring existence and remains valid: God's faithfulness (Rom 3:3–7; 15:8), the revelation of God (Jn 8:40, 45f.; 14:6; 16:7), the gospel (Gal 2:5, 14; Eph 4:21), and correct teaching and faith (2 Cor 4:2; Gal 5:7; Col 1:5; above all in the Pastoral Letters: 1 Tm 6:5; 2 Tm 2:18; 3:8; 4:4; Ti 1:14). All this is vouched for by the person of Jesus, who as the truth in person is the revelation of the truth of God (Jn 14:6; see 2 Cor 1:20; Rv 3:14). Where there is the Spirit of truth, Jesus and thus the truth of faith are present (Jn 16:13; 2 Jn 1–6; 3 John 8). From the personal character of truth comes the criterion by which one can recognize it: love (Mt 7:21; 25; Jn 3:21; Gal 5:6; Jas 2:14–26; 1 Jn 4:20).

(2) *History of Theology.* From its beginning, the history of dogma has been characterized by the opposition and mediation between theological and philosophical understandings of truth, a history that cannot be further traced here. Clement of Alexandria had already tried to reconcile the Old Testament with the Greek concept of truth when he named God as the "measure for the truth of all that exists" (*Protrept.* 6). For Augustine, the Son is the truth because as the Word he reveals the Father — in this way the connection to the philosophy and the theology of language is grounded (*De Trin.* 7.3). In Scholasticism, the problem plays a roll in the grounding of theology as a science: for Thomas Aquinas, God is the absolute truth and the foundation of all truths. Faith is then assent to the highest truth for its own sake. Modern discussion about truth shows the mutual referentiality of philosophy and theology. After Catholic theology had reacted defensively for a long time, it is today more open to the theoretical academic discussion with its questions about the historicity of truth or the possibility of the verification of theological statements.

(3) *Church Teaching.* Vatican I saw in the absolute truth of God the basis for

the absolute certainty of faith that relies on this truth (DS 3005, 3008, 3010). Vatican II anchored the truth of faith in Jesus Christ (*DV* 2) and in the Holy Spirit (*DV* 8, 20), who leads the church into it (*LG* 4, 9). Therefore, it is fundamentally historical: it is to be searched after (*GS* 59; *DH* 3) and can also be found outside of ecclesial structures (*LG* 8; *UR* 3; *GS* 92; *AG* 9).

(4) *Ecumenical Perspectives.* The question about the truth of faith is the decisive issue of ecumenical dialogue because unity is possible only in the truth. Here there is at present a widespread consensus that not all corollaries and developments of the one divine truth belong in the same manner to the unrenounceable truth and as a result of this must be affirmed by all. On account of the hierarchy of truths, individual church communities can acknowledge such explanations of the faith made by others as legitimate, without accepting these as their own (see Common Synod of the Catholic Dioceses in West Germany, *Ecumenical Decree* 3.2.3 and 3.3.2). The question about the truth of faith stands in a decisive way behind the pathos of the Lutheran Reformation: the word of God alone is accepted as a source of truth; the theological truth is thereby sharply contrasted with philosophical truth — the relation between the two became an ongoing problem for Protestant theology.

(5) *Systematic Reflections.* For insight into the truth of faith dogmatic theology is always referred back to philosophy but is not dependent on it. Dogmatic theology is not primarily concerned with the correctness of an assertion but rather with the encounter with the reality of God who is disclosing God's self in history. The experiences resulting from this are formulated in statements that are true if they can make plausible that the trust that is expressed in the experience is justified. A statement of faith is thus true when its content proves itself — this, however, takes place in time; that is, it is a historical process. From this follows, first of all, that the truth of faith is not exhausted in its formal profession, but rather, enacted as a truth of life, it must become transformed in praxis. The disclosure of reality brought about in faith is directed toward a transformation of reality; orthodoxy is directed toward orthopraxis. The new reality for its part opens up new dimensions in the knowledge of faith. From the historicity of truth follows, also, that the truth is eschatological: it can never be absorbed in theological propositions and dogmas, but rather remains open to the absolute future of God. Every article of faith is a recognition of the divine truth, toward which the fullness of truth moves (Thomas of Aquinas, *STh* 2-2, q. 1, a. 6). Because, however, after Easter this future is no longer totally empty and open, but rather is decided, dogma and dogmatic statements are also, with all their conditionality, always already a real and true development of the divine reality. They are true, even if they are not the full truth. Clearly, insofar as dogmatic theology claims to be academic, it must establish its validity claims also in academic discourse. Dogmatic statements must be grounded with arguments and be verifiable. Here the presupposition is merely that decisions and agreements experienced as true can be rendered in true statements. Actually, all the sciences are founded on decisions that can be legitimatized only on the basis of

trust: in the natural sciences all possible cases can never be checked, while in the human sciences understanding presupposes a preunderstanding (hermeneutical circle). Yet then dogmatic theology is also entitled to claim faith as the criterion of knowledge for the reality of God. The verification occurs in the praxis of the individual believer as well as in the praxis of the community of the church that is defined by this faith.

See also DOGMA/DOGMATIC STATEMENT; FAITH; HERMENEUTICS; HIERARCHY OF TRUTHS; HISTORY/HISTORICITY; REVELATION.

Bibliography
Baum, Gregory. *Faith and Doctrine: A Contemporary View.* Paramus, N.J.: Newman, 1969.
Baum, Gregory, et al. *The Infallibility Debate.* Edited by John J. Kirvan. New York: Paulist, 1971.
Kasper, Walter. *Dogma unter dem Wort Gottes.* Mainz: Matthias-Grünewald, 1965.
Ratzinger, Joseph. *Principles of Catholic Theology: Building Stones for a Fundamental Theology.* San Francisco: Ignatius, 1987.

WOLFGANG BEINERT

U u

Unity of the Church. Unity is an essential property of the church, by reason of which the church is internally united despite all the diversity in the manifestations of its life and is but a single church amid the multiplicity of ecclesial communities.

(1) *Biblical Background.* According to the New Testament, the church manifests itself in the many individual communities; at the same time, however, it is understood to be a single universal church. "In each local church it is the one church that is present" (H. Schlier). The unity of the church is proved by the care Christians have for one another. Therefore Paul urges participation in the collection for Jerusalem (2 Corinthians 8–9). The unity of the church is reflected in the names for the church: the "Israel of God" (Gal 6:16), the "people of God" (1 Pt 2:8f.), the "temple of God" (1 Cor 3:16f.), the "body of Christ" (Eph 1:22), the "bride of Christ" (2 Cor 11:2). The church is one because it is the work of the one God in the one economy of salvation. God forms the one church through one baptism, one Lord's Supper, and one gospel to which human beings respond with one and the same faith. The one church is served by a ministry that is one. The unity of the church is expressed in the liturgical gathering of its members, but also in common witness and service (Eph 4:2–4).

(2) *History of Theology.* In the first centuries of the church's history unity took the form of a communion of churches (*communio ecclesiarum*). The break with the Eastern Church, as well as various factors at work within the Western Church, caused the latter to develop an understanding of unity in which the almost exclusive starting point was the pope at the apex of the pyramid. This conception found magisterial expression chiefly in the papal dogmas of Vatican I. According to the encyclical *Satis cognitum* (Leo XIII, 1896; *ASS* 28 [1895–96] 708–39), unity was understood at that time to entail both exclusiveness and uniformity. The only image used was the "body of Christ." This exclusively christological explanation of unity corresponded to the likewise exclusive emphasis on the papal office as the principle guaranteeing the unity of the church.

(3) *Church Teaching.* Vatican II aimed at restoring the early church's image of itself. Exclusiveness gave way to an "inclusiveness," inasmuch as all churches, religions, and cultures are regarded as participating, in descending degrees, in the one Catholic Church; uniformity gave way to "complexity," each particular church having the responsibility for developing, within the framework of what all have in common, a distinctive image of its own in response to its situation. This understanding of unity as "inclusive" and "complex" has its ground in the unity and multiplicity of the divine Trinity.

(4) *Ecumenical Perspectives.* As long as the church is divided, its life contradicts its own divinely established and inalienable unity. The goal of the ecumenical movement is to enable the world once again to experience the unity of the church in a deeper way. Admittedly, the churches and communities that take part in the movement have divergent ideas of the concrete form to be taken by the unity for which they are striving.

(5) *Systematic Reflections.* As the second millennium of its history nears its end, the Catholic Church has become a world church. It is trying to find its appropriate way in each of the cultures in which it exists. As time passes, the process of "inculturation" is leading to so great a diversity in the church that the task of preserving its internal unity is taking on new dimensions.

See also CHURCH; ECUMENISM; FAITH; MINISTRY IN THE CHURCH; MODELS OF UNITY.

Bibliography
Congar, Yves. *Diversity and Communion.* Mystic, Conn.: Twenty-Third, 1984.
Fries, Heinrich, and Karl Rahner. *Unity of the Churches: An Actual Possibility.* Philadelphia: Fortress; New York: Paulist, 1985.
Hastings, Adrian. *One and Apostolic.* London: Darton, Longman and Todd, 1963.
Küng, Hans. *The Church.* Garden City, N.Y.: Doubleday, 1976.

WERNER LÖSER

Universal Salvific Will of God. The universal salvific will of God is God's fundamental loving intention to save all human beings. The opposite of this would be theories of a limited or particular salvific will, where God predestines only part of humankind to be saved (particular predestination).

(1) *Biblical Background.* The Old Testament lays the foundation for what the New Testament then reveals definitively in Jesus Christ: God wills the salvation of all human beings. In the Old Testament, although there is a certain tension due to covenantal particularism (namely, the particular covenant of God with the people of Israel), nevertheless there are also clear indications pointing to a universal salvific will, especially in the Book of Genesis (Noah's covenant that includes the whole of humankind [Gn 9:8–17]; Abraham's covenant which promises blessing for all peoples [Gn 18:18]); in the prophets Isaiah, Jeremiah, and Second Isaiah, who proclaim an eschatological, universal salvation (see, e.g., Is 24:13–16; 25:6–8; Jer 16:19–21; Is 45:20–22); and in the enthronement psalms 96 and 98, which praise God as the king of salvation for peoples of the earth. In the New Testament, the idea of a universal salvific will (expressed by the terms *bulē, thélema, próthesis, eudokeía*) is predominant. It is true that the historical Jesus thinks he is "sent only to the lost sheep of the house of Israel" (Mt 15:24), but in his powerful deeds (Mt 8:11) and parables (Mt 13:38) he shows that God, the Father of all human beings, is concerned about the salvation of all. In postpaschal apostolic preaching, Jesus is proclaimed as the Christ, who mediates the salvific plan of God by his death and resurrection for the salvation of all human beings. In the Synoptic Gospels

(the words over the cup: Mt 26:28; Mk 14:24; Lk 22:20), as well as the letters (e.g., Rom 5:8; 1 Cor 15:3; 2 Cor 5:15; 1 Tm 2:6; 1 Jn 2:2), we find the "for" formula: Jesus is crucified "for" the salvation of all human beings. In a single sentence, 1 Tm 2:4–6 concisely summarizes the universal salvific will of God. According to the apostolic view, knowledge of Jesus Christ as the universal mediator of salvation leads to the fact that the community of Jesus Christ, the church, is sent out on a universal mission. This mission is unlimited in scope (Mt 28:19; Mk 16:15).

(2) *History of Theology.* In the history of theology, the universal salvific will of God was often contested by various forms of particular predestination. The Greek and Latin Fathers maintain the notion of God's universal salvific will. In the West, particularism first makes its appearance in the doctrine of original sin and predestination in the late works of Augustine (d. 430). Because of original sin, the whole of humankind is a condemned mass (*massa damnata*), from which God by eternal predestination elected a few to be saved. Against this position, Prosper of Aquitane (d. ca. 455) in his "Call to All Peoples" emphasizes God's universal salvific will. The Saxon monk Gottschalk (d. 869) proposes a double predestination, and with it the peculiar idea that Jesus Christ died not for all, but only for the predestined. The Scholastics (esp. Thomas Aquinas [d. 1274], *Sent.* 1, d. 41, 46; *STh* 1, q. 19) distinguish a twofold grace and salvific will: sufficient grace (*gratia sufficiens*) is universal, while efficacious grace is particular. God's antecedent will (*voluntas antecedens*) to save us is universal, while God's consequent will (*voluntas consequens*) is particular. In modernity, Jansenism represents a particularist form of the salvific work of Jesus Christ (GRACE: THEOLOGICAL HERESIES).

(3) *Church Teaching.* Against all forms of salvific particularism, the magisterium (on the basis of 1 Tm 2:4) has always emphasized the universality of God's salvific will — that is, God wills the salvation of all human beings without exception, even if in fact not all will be saved (DS 623f.). The Council of Trent firmly condemns Calvin for laying aside the salvific will of God (DS 1556). The magisterium takes an equally decisive position against the particularist claims of Jansen and Quesnel, who claimed that Jesus Christ died for the salvation of only the predestined (DS 2006, 2432). Positively, the magisterium's teaching is based on the universal salvific will of God and emphasizes the possibility of salvation for all, starting first with the theory of a desire (*votum*): thus, according to the Council of Trent, a non-Christian can attain salvation by means of an explicit *votum* (desire) for baptism (baptism of desire) (DS 1524). Using the notion of implicit desire for membership in the church (*votum ecclesiae*), a document of the Holy Office of 1949 extends the possibility of salvation to include non-Christians. The one who is hampered by invincible ignorance of the true religion, but lives in perfect love and supernatural faith, has an implicit desire for the church and therefore can be saved (DS 3870, 3872). Finally, Vatican II — referring back to the universality of divinely bestowed cer-

titude (CERTITUDE OF SALVATION) — expands this idea and speaks clearly of the possibility of salvation for all non-Christians, even "atheists" (LG 16).

(4) *Ecumenical Perspectives.* In the Reformation, Calvin (d. 1564) spoke explicitly of a particularism of salvation. According to his teaching of double predestination, it is the eternal will of God that only a part of humankind be saved. In opposition to this particularism of salvation on the part of Calvin and early Reformed theology, not only Catholics but also Lutheran theology emphasize the universalism of salvation. In the twentieth century, the Reformed tradition's particularism of salvation has been corrected by representatives from its own ranks. K. Barth, in his teaching on election by grace, presents an unlimited universalism of salvation. E. Brunner emphasizes God's loving will that chooses all human beings in Jesus Christ. In the Catholic tradition, K. Rahner's widely known universal theory of anonymous Christianity greatly strengthens the idea of God's universal salvific will. Vatican II, using this same idea, states clearly that salvation may be attained by non-Christians. Since the biblical universality of salvation also continues in Reformed theology, there is today an ecumenical consensus concerning God's universal salvific will.

(5) *Systematic Reflections.* The notion of God's universal salvific will demonstrates God's grace as God's benevolence, which is directed toward all human beings without exception. Concretely it implies a universal salvific plan, which is expressed in the historical actions of God for the salvation of all. This salvation-history, seen in an extraordinary way in the divine salvific works of the Old Testament and the New Testament, makes salvation available to all human beings. Thus it is certain that in Jesus Christ each person is called to salvation. The individual Christian, trusting in the salvific work of Jesus Christ, has certain hope that he or she will attain salvation. The community of Christians — the church — has the task of announcing and mediating the salvific work of Jesus Christ for all humankind (MISSION). This biblical understanding of God's universal salvific will excludes two later theories: any eternally decreed predestination of a few people to damnation, as well as APOCATASTASIS — the salvation of all at the final judgment. Nevertheless, a major problem is revealed by the question: How is it possible that some fail to be saved if God wills the salvation of all? To solve this problem, it is necessary to be aware of the dialectic between the love of God and the FREEDOM of humanity. The universal salvific will of God means that salvation is offered to individuals. Salvation is not caused automatically. It is not a necessary reality. God's personal loving will respects human freedom; it courts human love. But it does not force anyone to be saved. Thus a distinction must be made between the *objective salvific will* of God, which applies to everyone, and *subjective acceptance*, which implies that individuals can refuse. A second question is: How is the axiom of God's salvific will to be reconciled with the traditional Catholic axiom that there is no salvation outside the Catholic Church (DS 802, 870, 1351)? Concretely, is salvation possible for non-Catholics and non-Christians? The exclusivist explanation that all human beings outside the church are condemned has been

officially excluded by magisterial teaching: there is grace outside the church (DS 2429); eternal salvation is available to non-Christians in the case of invincible ignorance (*ignorantia invincibilis*) of the true religion (DS 2866, 3870). Positively, salvation is possible for non-Christians by means of an implicit desire for MEMBERSHIP IN THE CHURCH, expressed by faith and love (DS 3870, 3872). All human beings who seek God and live according to their conscience can attain salvation (Vatican II, *LG* 16). Thus the only remaining explanation of the ecclesiological axiom is an inclusive one, and this is best expressed by the positive formula: *per ecclesiam salus* — salvation is through the church. In a more restricted way, consequently: within the church there is certainty of salvation. In a broader sense this means: the church has been given a universal commission to perform a salvific service for all human beings. Thus the church has a unique meaning in mediating salvation, and at the same time the possibility of salvation remains open to non-Christians.

See also ELECTION; FREEDOM; GRACE; HISTORY/HISTORICITY; NECESSITY OF THE CHURCH FOR SALVATION; ORIGINAL SIN; PREDESTINATION; SALVATION.

Bibliography
Barth, Karl. *Church Dogmatics,* 2/2 (see also 4/3). Edinburgh: T and T Clark, 1957.
Brunner, Emil. *Dogmatics.* Vol. 1. London: Lutterworth, 1949.
Hick, John, and Paul Knitter. *The Myth of Christian Uniqueness: Toward a Pluralistic Theology of Religions.* Maryknoll, N.Y.: Orbis Books, 1987.
Küng, Hans. *The Church.* Garden City, N.Y.: Doubleday, 1976.
Rahner, Karl. "Anonymous Christianity and the Missionary Task of the Church." In *Theological Investigations,* 11:161–78. New York: Seabury, 1974.
———. "Christianity and the Non-Christian Religions." In *Theological Investigations,* 5:115–34. New York: Seabury, 1975.
———. "The One Christ, and the Universality of Salvation." In *Theological Investigations,* 16:199–224. New York: Seabury, 1979.
Sachs, John R. "Current Eschatology: Universal Salvation and the Problem of Hell." *ThS* 52 (1991) 227–54.

GEORG KRAUS

V v

Virginity of Mary. The virginity of Mary means that the incarnation of Jesus Christ out of Mary surpasses the intrinsic laws of generation and birth and is owed to a specific intervention of the Holy Spirit. It is an outward sign that God has effectively established the new creation bound to the person of Jesus Christ. Tradition looks beyond the incarnation and speaks of a threefold virginity of Mary: (a) the *virginitas ante partum:* Mary conceived Jesus through the power of the Holy Spirit and without cooperation of any man; (b) the *virginitas in partu:* the birth of Jesus is a gladdening beginning and sign of the redemption under way, for Mary's personal fulfillment; (c) the *virginitas post partum:* even after becoming Joseph's wife and after Jesus' birth, Mary is forever the Virgin Mother of God, devoted to her Son, without bringing any more children into the world. In summarizing these aspects, first the East and then the universal church speak of Mary as *ever Virgin (aeì parthénos).*

(1) *Biblical Background.* Sacred Scripture mentions the fatherless conception of Jesus in two places. Mt 1:18–25 directly excludes Joseph's paternity (v. 18); the child that Mary carries has been conceived by the Holy Spirit (v. 20). A similar report is found in Lk 1:26–38: Mary's promised maternity is to be attributed to the power of the Holy Spirit (v. 35); her pregnancy without a father, unthinkable in human terms, is something God alone accomplishes (v. 38). It is currently discussed whether and to what extent Mary's Spirit-caused pregnancy is to be understood as symbolic imagery or also as a physically real occurrence. The historical-critical examination refers to the Haggadic structure of the infancy narratives in the Gospels, based upon which one cannot judge the historicity of the events. In contrast, systematic theology holds that the historical-critical method achieves only a more or less high degree of probability, and therefore may not exclude formally and fundamentally the physically real factor; genuine certainty of faith can be obtained only from tradition and from the Marian mystery as a whole perceived in the context of the incarnation. The same positions are also found in the exegetically disputed questions regarding to what extent the "brothers and sisters" (Mt 12:46 pars.; 13:55f. pars.; Jn 2:12; 7:3, 5, 10; 20:17[?]; Acts 1:14; 1 Cor 9:5; Gal 1;19) in the New Testament are to be considered as cousins of Jesus.

(2) *History of Theology.* Although the historical-critical exposition of Sacred Scripture might leave fundamental questions open, the acceptance of Mary's virginity by the Fathers is unequivocal. As early as Ignatius of Antioch (ca. 110) it is given considerable theological importance: he speaks of Mary as a guarantee of Jesus' complete humanity. At the same time he sees the virgin birth as causally connected to the divinity of Christ (*Eph.* 7.2) and belonging to the

center of the Christian mystery of faith (*Eph.* 19.1). The same tendency is evident in the Apologists as well as in the other patristic writers. The controversy of the first postapostolic epoch is a touchstone for the high value placed by the early Christians upon Mary's virginity. In stressing the singularity of Jesus' fatherless conception especially in controversy with gnosticism, the Fathers made clear that for them it was a matter of a salvific event to be upheld at any cost, and not a replaceable image.

(3) *Church Teaching.* A similar testimony is provided by the symbols (*Symbola*) of the early church. As early as the beginning of the third century, a candidate for baptism in Rome had to respond to this question: "Do you believe in Jesus Christ, the Son of God, who was born by the Holy Spirit, from the Virgin Mary . . . ?" (DS 10). In an expansion of the Nicene Creed concerning the divine mission of Christ, an argument is made in the Council of Constantinople (381) for strongly emphasizing the integral humanity of the redeemer. Accordingly, the incarnation is specified as "by the Holy Spirit from Mary the Virgin" (DS 150). The Incarnate Word is true man with a particular history, whose beginning, brought about by the Spirit, was arranged by the intervention of God, dominating history. Since the third century, the confession of the fatherless, Spirit-achieved conception of Jesus belonged to the expected content of the creeds. This tradition is maintained intact by Vatican II. Basing itself upon the Creed of Constantinople, it confesses the incarnation of the Son of God by the Holy Spirit and from the Virgin Mary (*LG* 52). As ever, Mary holds the honorific title of being the Ever-Virgin Mother of the Lord (*LG* 15, 52, 69). As does tradition, the council holds Mary to be ever a virgin (*LG* 52, 69). Accordingly, in the revised *Missale Romanum* the virginity and the divine maternity are by far the most common honorific designations for Mary.

(4) *Ecumenical Perspectives.* Together with the symbols of the Old Church, the Reformers confess the virginity of Mary. The Schmalkald Articles (1.3, in *BSLK* 414) mention the incarnate Son of God as "conceived by the Holy Spirit without collaboration of any man and born from the pure, holy, and ever virgin Mary." The Apostolic Dispute (1892–94), however, makes it plain that this view has altered, albeit with opposition. Today the question, as to whether this declaration is merely symbolic or whether it also requires a physical factor, is useful as a point of discussion upon which the opinions among Protestant Christians can legitimately vary ("Maria — Evangelische Fragen und Gesichtspunkte," *US* 37 [1982] 184–201, esp. 187).

(5) *Systematic Reflections.* That the confession of the virgin maternity of Mary is not merely figurative but is to be understood as an event in salvation-history can be established in two steps. The received tradition carries predominant dogmatic weight. In this connection, it is clearly presupposed that the church is sustained by the Spirit of God and led into the truth of revelation precisely in formulating the principal statements of its response in faith, namely in the symbols. In these it expresses its firm certainty of faith; this certainty cannot be outweighed or displaced by historical probability. Another reason for

the fatherless conception by Mary is its character as a sign of the singularity of the divine and human person of her Son: through him a new beginning in salvation-history was thought to be provided by God. Also indicative of this event is that it makes plain human beings' inability to accomplish their own salvation; they can only accept it in an actively receptive manner. In this perspective the virginal motherhood of Mary is comparable to the appearances of the risen one and to the empty tomb as the outer signs of the transcendental event of the resurrection of the crucified one; it is also comparable to the created world as the sign of the supernatural event of creation. Both comparisons illustrate how the element of historical event and the element of transhistorical divinity intertwine with each other. Mary's perduring virginity is also to be concluded based upon its contribution to the incarnation, since this contribution is thereby expanded and clarified. By this is meant, on the one hand, that Mary was perpetually reserved to her Son; on the other hand, that the birth of the redeemer is the start of the new creation, which uplifts and sanctifies human nature. Since every birth from the fall into sin (see Gn 3:16) lies under the sign of pain and even of death, the special element of *this* birth is found in that it is a new and death-overcoming beginning. This spiritual and dogmatic overview surpasses historical-biological considerations as well as moral-ascetic ones; it upholds its believing certainty in Mary's Spirit-achieved divine motherhood, which is the heart of the Marian mystery.

See also DIVINE MOTHERHOOD OF MARY; ECCLESIAL MAGISTERIUM; SALVIFIC SIGNIFICANCE OF MARY.

Bibliography
Beinert, Wolfgang, and H. Petri. *Handbuch der Marienkunde.* Regensburg: Pustet, 1984.
Brown, Raymond E. *The Virginal Conception and Bodily Resurrection of Jesus.* New York: Paulist, 1973.
Brown, Raymond E., et al., eds. *Mary in the New Testament.* Philadelphia: Fortress, 1978.
Courth, Franz. "Historisch oder theologisch — eine falsche Alternative." *ThG* 68 (1978) 283–96.
Rahner, Karl. "Mary's Virginity." In *Theological Investigations,* 19:218–31. New York: Crossroad, 1983.
———. "Virginitas in Partu." In *Theological Investigations,* 4:124–62. New York: Crossroad, 1974.
Riedlinger, H. "Zum gegenwärtigen Verständnis der Geburt Jesu aus der Jungfrau Maria." *ThG* 69 (1979) 22–61.

FRANZ COURTH

Visibility of the Church.

To say that the church is visible means that it is a structured entity and concrete society (in opposition to an invisible, hidden church).

(1) *Biblical Background.* The New Testament contains the basis for later discussion but no developed statements about the visibility of the church. The basis consists chiefly in the images that the New Testament, appealing in many cases to passages of the Old Testament, applies to the church: "people of God"

(1 Pt 2:9–10), "body of Christ" (1 Corinthians 12; Colossians; Ephesians), "temple of the Holy Spirit" (1 Cor 3:16; 6:19) (for other images see *LG* 6).

(2) *History of Theology.* The history of the problem begins with Augustine, who correlates visible church/body/merely external membership, on the one hand, and invisible church/soul/interior membership ("according to the heart"), on the other. This conception, which bears the clear mark of Platonism, implied to many theologians that it is more important to belong to the invisible church. Appealing to this value judgment, individuals and groups distanced themselves from the visible church (in the Middle Ages the Albigensians and Cathars; in the modern period the Jansenists). The main body of the church countered by laying all the greater emphasis on the importance of the church's visibility. After J. Wycliffe and J. Huss had played off invisibility against visibility, the question became all the more acute in the sixteenth century, as various Reformers developed the doctrine of the "hidden" church to which only those belong who are predestined for salvation. In response, the Counter-Reformation theologians (e.g., R. Bellarmine) insisted on the visibility of the church, in which persons are incorporated by faith, baptism, and entry into the visible association.

(3) *Church Teaching.* From the time of Huss's condemnation (DS 1205–10) down to the present (e.g., Pius XII, *Mystici corporis* [1943]), the magisterium has held uncompromisingly to the visibility of the church. Vatican II derives this visibility from the sacramental nature of the church (*LG* 3, 8; *GS* 40, 44).

(4) *Ecumenical Perspectives.* As the history of the problem makes clear (see sec. 2 above), the visibility of the church is a matter of dispute among the confessions, to the extent that visibility refers to the hierarchical and sacramental structure of the church.

(5) *Systematic Reflections.* Catholic theology must use the idea of sacramentality (SACRAMENT) to show that visibility of the church is necessary for its spiritual role and character, so that no contrary picture of the church can be constructed. On the other hand, the proper coordination of the two "sides" must be maintained: the visibility of the church is in the service of its spiritual mission.

See also ATTRIBUTES OF THE CHURCH; MEMBERSHIP IN THE CHURCH.

Bibliography
Congar, Yves. *Diversity and Communion.* Mystic, Conn.: Twenty-Third, 1984.
Hastings, Adrian. *One and Apostolic.* London: Darton, Longman and Todd, 1963.
Lubac, Henri de. *The Splendor of the Church.* San Francisco: Ignatius, 1986.
McBrien, Richard P. *Catholicism.* Minneapolis: Winston, 1981.

WERNER LÖSER

W w

Witness. In theological usage, witness is the communication of a directly perceived reality to another person, so that the latter may likewise have access to it; the person communicating is also called a witness. The truth of the witness or testimony is shown by the fact that the one witnessing stands up for it in his or her own person.

(1) *Biblical Background.* In the New Testament, *witness* is used both for what Jesus says about God (see Jn 3:11, 32f.; 18:37) and for what God (Jn 5:31–40), the Spirit (1 Jn 5:6–12), and human beings (e.g., John the Baptist: Jn 1:7f., 15, 19, 32f.) say about Jesus. The disciples of Jesus are called to give a witness that is based above all on the Easter-event as the key reality of faith (Lk 24:48; Acts 1:8).

(2) *History of Theology.* In the early church, the term *witnesses* was applied without qualification to those who gave witness by their deaths, that is, the martyrs (Greek: *martyria* = witness; *martyr* = the one witnessing). When the period of persecution had passed, preaching and a credible Christian life were regarded as ways of witnessing to Christ, so that the saints became witnesses in a special sense by reason of their following of the Lord.

(3) *Church Teaching.* Vatican II emphasizes the obligation of all the baptized and confirmed to give Christian witness so that the church may effectively carry out its mission (*AG* 11).

(4) *Ecumenical Perspectives.* The ecumenical importance of the idea of witness finds significant expression in the title "Faith and Witness," which the World Council of Churches has given to its first area of activity.

(5) *Systematic Reflections.* The theological concept of witness includes the existential identification of the person witnessing with the truth being attested. Where such testimony occurs, witnesses beget (new) Christian life, that is, a readiness in the hearers likewise to commit themselves existentially to the word of God and to make the word a reality by their faith, with the help of grace.

See also DISCIPLESHIP, CHRISTIAN; SAINTS: SANCTIFICATION, HOLINESS.

Bibliography
Boff, Leonardo. *God's Witnesses in the Heart of the World.* Chicago: Claret Center for Resources of Spirituality, 1981.
Brox, Norbert. *Zeuge und Märtyrer.* Munich: Kösel, 1961.
Haring, Bernhard. *My Witness for the Church.* New York: Paulist, 1992.

WERNER LÖSER

Word and Sacrament. This formula points to the problem, discussed since Vatican II, of the relationship between the preaching of the (biblical) word of

God, on the one hand, and the administration of the sacraments, on the other, in the saving activity of the church.

(1) *Biblical Background.* On the salvific efficacy of the sacraments, see SAC-RAMENT. The Bible is even more explicit in attributing salvific power to the word of God and its proclamation. This word instructs regarding grace and salvation, calls for a life in accordance with God's will, and gives believers a share in salvation. It is an efficacious word. This efficacy is already brought out in the Old Testament: "Is not my word like fire, says the Lord, and like a hammer that crushes rocks?" (Jer 23:29; cp., e.g., Is 55:10f.). According to the Priestly story of creation God made the world by God's word (Gn 1:1–2:4a). In the New Testament, Jesus Christ is the one, comprehensive word of God (see Jn 1:14). The good news that he is and that he has brought, and whose proclamation he entrusts to his disciples, awakens faith and bestows grace and salvation: the gospel "is a power [*dynamis*] of God that rescues everyone who believes" (Rom 1:16; cp. Heb 4:12f.). Many passages of the New Testament attest to this "dynamic" character of the word, a character that certainly does not prescind from the content of the word but does go beyond a simple communication of meaning: "You are already cleansed by the word which I have spoken to you" (Jn 15:1; cp. 1 Pt 1:23).

(2) *History of Theology.* In the history of theology the relationship between word and sacrament has been discussed chiefly in passing, as when, for example, Augustine speaks of a sacrament as a "visible word" (*verbum visibile*). On the other hand, the biblical idea of God's word possessing a salvific efficacy remained vital for a long time, especially since parts of the biblical word of God (prophetic promises; the Our Father) were at times described as "sacraments." Increasingly, however, and especially in reaction against the excessive stress placed by the Reformers on the importance of the word, the revealed word came to be seen as simply a communication of objective truths that God was setting before humankind as an object of faith. It was only in connection with Vatican II that Catholic theologians developed a theology of the word and began to reflect on the relationship between word and sacrament. As they did so, the tendency was either to understand the word and its proclamation in light of the sacraments and therefore to regard it as a quasi-sacrament (O. Semmelroth) or to look upon the sacraments as the highest form of the effective ("exhibitive") word (K. Rahner). In either approach, that which is specific to word or sacrament easily gives the appearance of being a defect. Other theories (e.g, W. Kasper) seek to avoid one-sidedness by taking a conciliatory position in which word and sacrament are ordered to one another due to their relation to the basic situation and the many situations of human existence. The efficacy of the word of God is also often explained by means of the "speech act" theory (W. L. Austin): utterances can be simply informative or they may be performative, that is, they effect what they say (e.g., the closure of a meeting by the words of the chairperson).

(3) *Church Teaching.* There are no explicit statements of the magisterium

on the relationship between word and sacrament. The Council of Trent seems indeed to attribute all salvific efficacy to the sacraments, through which "all true justification either begins... or, once begun, increases... or, when lost, is regained" (DS 1600; ND 1310). But it also says of faith, which comes from hearing the word of God (see Rom 10:17), that it is "'the beginning of man's salvation,' the foundation and root of all justification" (DS 1532; ND 1935). Vatican II frequently emphasizes the efficacy of God's word: for example, "There is such force and efficacy in the word of God that it constitutes strength and support for the church, and for her children it provides strength of faith, the food of the soul and a pure and unfailing source of the spiritual life" (DV 21; ND 255). Also emphasized is the dialogical and personal character of the word of God (see DV 8).

(4) *Ecumenical Perspectives.* In the theology of the Reformers all salvation comes from the word of God, its proclamation, and faith (*solo verbo — sola fide*). The sacraments are special (but not the highest!) forms of the word-event that brings salvation. The Catholic rediscovery of the "saving power of the word" can be the basis for a rapprochement in this area. There must, however, be a corresponding new appreciation among Evangelicals of the specific value of symbolic actions as authentic mediations of revelation and therefore of salvation; there are signs that this change is taking place.

(5) *Systematic Reflections.* Word and sacrament have from the beginning been fundamental elements in the church's mediation of salvation. Despite their affinity (both are signs) neither can be reduced to the other. A starting point for determining their interrelationship might be the situation-relatedness they have in common: the proclamation of the word brings salvation to human beings so that they can make it a reality in any given situation; when the sacraments are received and entered into with faith, they bring the good and bad situations of life, the conscious and the unconscious, that which is within the control of human beings and that which is not, into effective contact with God's renewing word, while in their character as communicative symbols they establish a communion in salvation from and with Christ. In the sacraments, word and sign are brought into the closest possible connection. The special meaning the sacraments have as symbolic gestures needs to be further clarified from the anthropological point of view; the same is true of the efficacy of the word, which even at the human level does not simply inform and mediate meaning but also makes present and effects encounter between human beings (an encounter that in certain circumstances is creative).

See also FAITH; REVELATION; SACRAMENT.

Bibliography

Cessario, Romanus. "Christian Satisfaction and Sacramental Reconciliation." *Communio* 16 (1989) 186–96.

Cooke, Bernard. *The Distancing of God: The Ambiguity of Symbol in History and Theology.* Minneapolis: Fortress, 1990.

————. *Ministry to Word and Sacraments: History and Theology*. Philadelphia: Fortress, 1976.

Ebeling, Gerhard. *The Word of God and Tradition*. Philadelphia: Fortress, 1968.

Kilmartin, Edward. *Christian Liturgy I: Theology*. Kansas City: Sheed and Ward, 1988.

Power, David. *Unsearchable Riches: The Symbolic Nature of Liturgy*. New York: Pueblo, 1984.

GÜNTER KOCH

Works. In a theology of grace, works are the good deeds of love that, after justification, grow out of faith and are the measure of how we will be judged.

(1) *Biblical Background.* In the Old Testament the notion of works is usually used in praise of the glorious works of God's creation. When the term is applied to human beings, its primary meaning is our creative work and only rarely works as moral actions. Tobit summarizes the most important good works in the Old Testament perspective (Tb 3:13–19; 12:6–9) and also emphasizes that "the Lord himself gives all things" (Tb 4:19). In the New Testament the notion of works rarely refers to the work of creation. More often it means the saving work of Jesus Christ and very often the ethical works of baptized Christians. Throughout the New Testament we see the basic requirements and the great importance of good works (e.g., Mt 5:16; Acts 9:36; Rom 13:3; Eph 2:10; Col 1:10; Jas 2:17; 1 Pt 2:12). They are gifts of God (2 Cor 9:8; Phil 1:6) or of Jesus Christ (Col 3:17; 2 Thes 2:17). Their significance is twofold: on the one hand, they are part of service to the honor of God who is the giver of all good gifts (Mt 5:16; 2 Cor 9:8; 1 Pt 2:12). On the other hand, they are of decisive importance at the last judgment, where we will be judged according to our works (Rom 2:6; 2 Cor 5:10), more precisely, our works of love (Mt 25:31–46). When Paul emphasizes justification by faith alone (Rom 1:17; 3:28) and firmly rejects justification by the works of the law (Rom 3:20; Gal 2:16), he means works "in the sense that the law and its obligations elicit the hidden desires of those who do not believe, works of unrighteousness, and works of self-justification" (H. Schlier, *Der Römerbrief,* 2d ed. [Freiburg, 1979], 117). In Paul, the negative work of the law must be clearly distinguished from good works, which he explicitly affirms (Rom 13:3; Phil 1:6) and closely links with faith. Faith works through love (Gal 5:6). Justification by faith produces good works as its fruit (Rom 7:4; 2 Cor 9:10). James also sees that the necessary consequence of a living faith is good works: faith without the works of love is dead; it is only perfected by works (2:14–26).

(2) *History of Theology.* In the history of dogma, the theological problem of good works first came into prominence with Augustine. In opposition to Pelagianism he claims that good works are not humanity's own achievement, but come from the gratuitous work of God. In opposition to Semi-Pelagianism he emphasizes that the beginning of faith is not a person's good works, but only the gratuitous action of God's love. In early and late Scholasticism, Semi-Pelagian notions reappear in regard to the determining of our disposition

(DISPOSITION FOR RECEIVING GRACE): good works such as prayer and compunction are described as the cause of our readiness for justification. Overall Scholasticism holds that: the basis of justification is "faith informed by love" (*fides caritate formata*); grace increases with good works in the one justified; in certain ways good works are meritorious. The good works of non-Christians and sinners are viewed negatively by M. Baius (d. 1589), who holds that all works of unbelievers are sinful, and by P. Quesnel (d. 1719), who regards even the prayers of sinners as sinful.

(3) *Church Teaching.* In opposition to Semi-Pelagianism, the Second Synod of Orange (529) explains that all the human works that prepare us for justification are gifts of grace (DS 376) and that the beginning of every good work is inspired by God (DS 397). In opposition to M. Luther, Trent defends the positive value of good works (DS 1535, 1574, 1582) and the possibility of increasing grace by good works (DS 1539, 1575). On the other hand, it reconfirms Luther's basic claim: the power of Christ works all that is good in those justified; that is, it precedes, accompanies, and follows their works (DS 1546). Despite the great value of good works, the Christian should not glory in himself or herself, but only in God (DS 1548). The positive worth of the good works of non-Christians and sinners is underlined in papal pronouncements against Baius (DS 1925) and Quesnel (DS 2459).

(4) *Ecumenical Perspectives.* Luther and the other Reformers strove passionately to safeguard grace and the honor of God against the then prevailing view of holiness through works, which implies self-justification by means of good works. Luther subordinates good works to two principles: "by grace alone" (*sola gratia*) and "by faith alone" (*sola fide*). Thus good works by grace necessarily increase with faith and should not lead to self-glorification, but only to the praise of God (see also the acknowledgment of this position in CA 4, 6, and Apol. 4, 20). In response to the question, "Why should we do good works?" the Reformed Heidelberg Catechism (q. 86) gives three reasons: to thank and praise God for his blessings, to ascertain that our faith is increasing, and to win over our neighbor to Christ. In present-day Evangelical theology (where justification by faith alone is presupposed) faith is closely joined to ethical action. There is a broad ecumenical consensus between Evangelical and Catholic theology, based on the following common elements: faith alone justifies, but it must be active through good works of love, for the final judgment is based on our works. Faith is the real basis; good works are the cognitive basis for salvation.

(5) *Systematic Reflections.* Dogmatically the problem of good works is closely related to the themes of GRACE, JUSTIFICATION, FAITH, LOVE, and JUDGMENT. Recent thinking in Catholic theology leads to the following statements. (*a*) *Grace and works.* Good works are by no means a person's own achievement by which he or she becomes powerful and can claim salvation as something merited. Rather they are inspired and supported by the grace of God. (*b*) *Justification and works.* Good works do not play a causative role either in preparing for or realizing justification. Justification takes place independently of them and

only as a result of faith, which is God's gift. (*c*) *Faith and works*. Faith, which justifies independently of works, is necessarily active after justification in good works. There is an inner unity between the gift of salvation (an indicative) and the task of salvation (the imperative of salvation): the inchoative gift of justification in faith must be confirmed and become fruitful in deeds. (*d*) *Love and works*. The faith of the one justified is efficacious in love; thus the good works of faith are ultimately loving actions. Without the motivation of love the works of faith are useless. (*e*) *Judgment and works*. At the last judgment good or evil works are the criteria for the salvation or damnation of each individual person. Only believers who have proved themselves as doers of the word by works of love of God and neighbor can stand before the judge, Jesus Christ, in this judgment according to works.

See also FAITH; JUDGMENT; JUSTIFICATION; LOVE; MERIT; THEOLOGICAL VIRTUES.

Bibliography

Küng, Hans. *Justification: The Doctrine of Karl Barth and a Catholic Reflection*. Philadelphia: Westminster, 1981.

McSorley, Harry. "The Doctrine of Justification and Merit in Roman Catholic Dialogues with Anglicans and Lutherans." *TJT* 13 (1987) 69–78.

Pesch, Otto Hermann. *Theologie der Rechtfertigung bei Martin Luther und Thomas von Aquin: Versuch eines systematisch-theologischen Dialogs*. Mainz: Matthias-Grünewald, 1967.

Sullivan, Jeremiah Stephen. *The Formulation of the Tridentine Doctrine on Merit*. Washington, D.C.: Catholic University of America Press, 1959.

Tavard, George H. *Justification: An Ecumenical Study*. New York: Paulist, 1983.

GEORG KRAUS

Works of the Spirit. By "works of the Spirit" is meant those effects that have the Holy Spirit as their source and make it possible for the Spirit to be known as such by human experience.

(1) *Biblical Background*. Since the Scriptures do not provide any unequivocal concept of the Spirit, it is not easy to organize in a systematic way the effects attributed to it. Viewed as the breath of life, the "Spirit of the Lord" is first and foremost a power by means of which Yahweh can lay hold of human beings and endow them with gifts, either transitorily or permanently (see Jgs 3:10; 6:34; 11:29; 13:25; 14:6; but also Nm 24:2; 1 Sm 10:5–13, and Nm 11:17, 25; 27:18; Dt 34:9; 1 Sm 16:13), for heroic deeds, for divine utterances (prophecies, blessings), or even for an office (prophet, king). The effect is of the psychic order, but is related to the covenant and its maintenance. In promises of future transformation (see esp. Is 11:1–3) the Spirit can be perceived as a power active in the area of morality, as the effect on human beings of salvation attained. In the Old Testament we already find prayers for the granting of this power. The Spirit also shows itself at work as God's power in the New Testament, in healings and signs, in teaching and prophetic insights and visions. The Acts of the Apostles and the letters of Paul associate the work of the Spirit not only

with these transitory effects but also with permanent tasks or offices (see 1 Cor 12:28: prophets, teachers) and especially with the apostolic office. The special effect that is sanctification is expressed in the idea of a baptism of fire (Mt 3:11; Lk 3:16f.) and in the Pentecostal outpouring of the Spirit (Acts 1:8; 2:3f.). In addition to personifications of the divine power, we find in Paul and John the beginnings of a conception of the Holy Spirit as an active person.

(2) *History of Theology.* The tradition understands miracles and signs and the so-called gifts of the Spirit, or charisms, as works of the Spirit. In early creeds the Spirit's action is identified concretely with the gift of life (DS 3), the incarnation (DS 10 etc.), consubstantial divinity (DS 29), assistance (DS 41), and locutions through the prophets (DS 41). Following Is 11:1–3, the tradition acknowledged "seven gifts" of the Spirit that are constant, whereas the charisms were viewed as special gifts given for the period when the church was being founded. The possibility of a working of the Spirit outside the boundaries of the organized church was not taken seriously.

(3) *Church Teaching.* The ecclesial magisterium distinguished between the work of the Spirit in salvation-history (inspiration, incarnation, descent of the Spirit on Jesus at his baptism, abiding of the Spirit in Jesus — therefore the Spirit is in a special way the "Spirit of Christ"), its work in the life of the church (as "soul of the church," the Spirit unites it and assists it in matters of faith and government), and its work in the grace life of the faithful (origin of created grace, the "seven gifts" and charisms, the indwelling; the Spirit enlightens the faithful in justification and the exercise of the virtues and is active in the sacraments).

(4) *Ecumenical Perspectives.* The ecumenical movement is viewed as the result of a working of the Spirit that is not confined within the confessional bounds of one or another church. Consequently, there are ways in which the churches can be reconciled under the impulse of the Spirit.

(5) *Systematic Reflections.* The work of the Spirit as experienced in the ecclesial community or in personal life is the basis for a full knowledge of revelation and salvation-history as well as a truly Christian life. The multiplicity of biblical testimonies and of experiences in the course of Christian history calls for a coherent explanation and an objective integration of the work of the Spirit into a comprehensive theological vision. Theologians are therefore faced from the outset with the task of discernment, which cannot be tackled without appropriate criteria. On the work of the Spirit depends the possibility of a theological and spiritual epistemology that experiences its decisive criteria and the evidence for these as based on the act of faith itself. Certain experiences and insights present themselves expressly as the work of the Spirit but also show the natural existence of human beings to be the work of the Spirit (because of creation). In principle, therefore, the work of the Spirit always has a twofold structure (the explicit work of the Spirit, and the reality, in which this explicit work of the Spirit occurs, as itself the result of a nonexplicit work of the Spirit). The task of discernment arises directly out of this situation. Another reason why the char-

acteristic twofold structure applies is that the work of the Spirit always has to be determined in light of what expressly qualifies as the work of the Spirit, and that only with this as a starting point does it become perceptible in the taken-for-grantedness of created reality. For this reason an isolated treatment of the explicit work of the Spirit is impossible; in other words, a consistent thematization of it would of its nature lead astray, since it would exclude what is also the real work of the Spirit. Conversely, the work of the Spirit is relevant to all areas and themes of faith, insofar as there is question of their revealed character and insofar as a judgment of discernment of spirits is indispensable for every decision Christians make regarding state of life or individual actions.

See also CHARISM/CHARISMS; CHURCH; GRACE; HOLY SPIRIT; INSPIRATION; MINISTRY IN THE CHURCH; SACRAMENT.

Bibliography
Burns, J. Patout, and Gerald M. Fagin. *The Holy Spirit*. Wilmington, Del.: Glazier, 1984.
Gunkel, Hermann. *The Influence of the Holy Spirit: According to the Popular View of the Apostolic Age and the Teaching of the Apostle Paul: A Biblical-Theological Study*. Philadelphia: Fortress, 1979.
Rahner, Karl. *The Dynamic Element in the Church*. New York: Herder and Herder, 1964.
Sneck, William Joseph. *Charismatic Spiritual Gifts: A Phenomenological Analysis*. Washington, D.C.: University Press of America, 1981.

KARL HEINZ NEUFELD

World Responsibility. World responsibility in the theological sense is the responsibility of the human person for the formation and conservation of the material world before God, the creator and fulfiller of the world.

(1) *Biblical Background.* The classical citation for the human commission to the world is Gn 1:28: "Fill the earth and subdue it." As the image of God in the world (Gn 1:27), the human person shares in God's creative activity and in God's care for the preservation of creation. The New Testament's proclamation of Jesus' resurrection with its statement on the embodied glory of Jesus also refers to the material world (Rom 8:19–22). This completion of the whole world in Jesus Christ is seen in the New Testament as God's deed both under the aspect of the conservation of the world as well as under the aspect of the transformation of the world (Col 1:16f.; Rv 21:1).

(2) *History of Theology.* Until modern times theology understood the responsibility of the human person toward the world as the unfolding of the natural order of being that had been fixed in the divine plan of creation. The transformation of the world largely remained reserved for God's fulfilling action at the end of the world. It was first with the anthropocentric experience of the world in modern times that theology considered the world in its formation in history as the object of human responsibility (ANTHROPOCENTRISM). Yet this Christian responsibility to the world was expressed first of all in the theological criticism of the scientific-technical transformation of the world whose autonomy was postulated without God. It is only in our century that theology has

also interpreted this secularization of the world in a positive way as the consequence of the liberation of the human person through the gospel (F. Gogarten, J. B. Metz).

(3) *Church Teaching.* Today the church acknowledges the functional autonomy of worldly reality (*GS* 36). Its transformation toward the common good of humankind corresponds to the divine plan of creation (*GS* 34) and will to fulfillment (*GS* 39). The church exercises its responsibility to the world in a practical way through the missionary witness of Christians for the gospel (*AG* 36) and, above all, through the activity of the laity in their respective professions in the world (*LG* 36).

(4) *Ecumenical Perspectives.* Protestant theology in modern times at first fluctuated between openness to the world (liberal Protestantism) and a retreat to the interior relationship to God (Pietism). Today, there are no essential differences between the Protestant and the Catholic grounding of the world responsibility of Christians.

(5) *Systematic Reflections.* The theological view of the responsibility to the world today is undergoing a far-reaching change that has been brought about by the threat of the environmental crisis and the nuclear arms race to the world as the biosphere for humanity. A more critical perception of the responsibility for shaping the world that basically affirms technical progress as a fulfillment of the divine mandate of creation and condemns only interests that are improper (e.g., political or economic competition) is probably no longer sufficient to prevent the threatening disaster. The motif of the hope for fulfillment, which urges the transformation of the world toward the kingdom of God, must be supplemented by the motif of the preservation of God's creation, the reconciliation of heaven and earth in Jesus Christ (Col 1:20) (CREATURELINESS OF THE HUMAN PERSON).

See also CREATION; ECOLOGY; IMAGE OF GOD; LAITY; MISSION.

Bibliography
Gutiérrez, Gustavo. *A Theology of Liberation.* Maryknoll, N.Y.: Orbis Books, 1973.
Küng, Hans. *Global Responsibility: In Search of a New World Ethic.* New York: Crossroad, 1991.
Metz, Johannes Baptist. *The Emergent Church: The Future of Christianity in a Post-Bourgeois World.* New York: Crossroad, 1981.
———. *Theology of the World.* New York: Herder and Herder, 1969.
Rahner, Karl. "The Function of the Church as a Critic of Society." In *Theological Investigations,* 12:229–49. New York: Crossroad, 1974.

GEORG LANGEMEYER

Worldview. "Worldview" signifies a multitude of conceptions about reality as a whole. In principle, these are characterized by concrete intuitability, even if — as in modern physics — they are lent a high degree of abstractness by increasing mathematization. A worldview is always culturally, and usually also religiously, conditioned and is linked in each instance to some body of knowledge about nature. The most ancient worldviews rest on mythic foundations, while the most recent result from knowledge gained in philosophy and the natural and human sciences.

(1) *Biblical Background.* The Bible combines a primitive worldview with an elevated religious belief in the one God, Yahweh, who constantly directs creation as an integral part of redemptive history. The Old and New Testaments reflect the idea of a three-leveled structuring of the world: heaven, earth, and a subterranean region. Heaven, in the form (reflecting the model of Oriental house-roofs) of a "firmly compacted" dome, a "firmament," rests on pillars that are high mountains and at times abodes of God (Jb 26:11; Is 14:13). It divides the heavenly waters from the earthly ones (Gn 1:7) and contains the greater and lesser "lights," the sun, the moon, and the stars (Gn 1:14–16). The earth is a disk, which likewise rests on pillars. Beneath it are concealed the fountains of the great abyss (Gn 7:11; Ex 20:4). The subterranean region not only is the locus of these dangerous waters, which the Creator commands at will, but is simultaneously Sheol, the dwelling place of the dead, for whose shadowy existence no hope remains but that of grace-given intervention by the living in this realm of death. Thus heaven, earth, and the netherworld are essentially arenas for the playing out of redemptive — and also, for the time being, of profane — history.

(2) *History of Theology.* Alongside these biblical models, the worldview of the Fathers was increasingly oriented toward the philosophical cosmologies of the Platonic, Aristotelian, and Stoic traditions. To the Fathers, the medieval theologians, and even the Reformers, geocentrism appeared as self-evident: the earth that was inhabited by human beings, and made special by the incarnation of the Son of God, could not but be the center of the universe. Only with painful slowness did the heliocentrism of N. Copernicus, J. Kepler, and G. Galileo gain acceptance. The question about the infinitude of the universe also remained controversial for a long time (being answered affirmatively by Nicholas of Cusa and G. Bruno). To this was added the difficulty of determining the relationship between a knowledge-furthering mathematization of empirically perceptible nature (Galileo, R. Descartes) and a religious outlook oriented, from the standpoint of God, toward values like the world's ultimate goal, perfection, and meaningfulness. The worldview of classical physics (I. Newton, P. S. Laplace) was inclined toward a mechanistic determinism capable of dispensing completely with the idea of a divine first cause.

(3) *Church Teaching.* Doctrinal office, while not having taken a position directly on the topic of a worldview, has nevertheless rejected modern DEISM (DS 2902, 3003) and materialism (DS 3022), as well as pantheism (DS 2901, 3001, 3023f.).

(4) *Ecumenical Perspectives.* In the general search for a worldview that adequately corresponds to reality, there are no oppositions today between confessions.

(5) *Systematic Reflections*. When dealing with the problem of a world-view, present-day dogmatics shows consideration for the autonomy of natural-scientific research insofar as this does not claim infallibility and exclusive validity for its body of partial knowledge. Dogmatics often engages in interdisciplinary dialogue with the modern physics that has emerged along the lines of relativity theory (A. Einstein) and quantum theory (M. Planck). Such physics has, to be sure, appropriated the mechanistic concept from classical physics without a break, and has continued the mathematization process in a consistent way, but without positing these as absolutes. It increasingly dispenses with concrete intuitability and directs its attention mainly toward functions and relations within nature. Modern physicists no longer attempt to construct worldviews in the proper sense but rather attempt to develop models of observed processes that can then, pursuant to the viewpoint selected, be systematized into "world-models." They no longer adhere to "dogmas" of classical physics like mechanistic causality, the determinedness of processes, absolute objectivity, and the unambiguousness of proofs. They replace them with the following new insights: natural processes are partially undetermined; they depend on complex interactions and feedback-mechanisms; the observing subject influences the observed results in the objective sphere (see W. Heisenberg's uncertainty relations); measurements of spatial and temporal phenomena can never be absolute in character and are meaningful only with regard to some particular reference system (as set out in Einstein's relativity theory); and a given reality can be described from differing perspectives that are mutually complementary (see the wave–particle duality in the explanation of the phenomena of light; the principle of complementarity). An analogy to the complementarity principle in physics is found in the interdisciplinary attempt to interpret the one, selfsame reality of the cosmos once in terms of the Christian, redemptive-historical worldview, then again from the standpoint of physics, of biology, of psychology, and so on, without these different observational approaches contradicting one another or being mutually exclusive. The attempt of C. F. von Weizsäcker to give physics, philosophy, and religious understanding a hearing in the framework of a "history of nature," so as to do justice to the multidimensionality of the finite reality of the world, is a sign of the present-day search for comprehensively integral thought and action. An important philosophical contribution to a specifically modern worldview was made by existentialism (E. Husserl, M. Heidegger, J.-P. Sartre), which understands reality primarily as the world of humans, and understands humans from the perspective of their "being-in-the-world," that is, their mode of self-projection into their concrete world, social surroundings, and natural environment. In addition, the ecological crisis heightens an awareness, which also extends into the sphere of a specifically Christian worldview, of responsibility for the future.

See also COSMOLOGY; CREATION; CREATION: BELIEF IN, AND NATURAL SCIENCE; MYTHS OF CREATION; SPACE–TIME SCHEMA.

Bibliography
Dilthey, Wilhelm. *Pattern and Meaning in History: Thoughts on History and Society.* New York: Harper, 1971.
Kaufman, Gordon D. *Relativism, Knowledge, and Faith.* Chicago: University of Chicago Press, 1960.
Schweiker, William, ed. *Worldviews and Warrants: Plurality and Authority in Theology.* Lanham, Md.: University Press of America, 1987.
Smart, Ninian. *Worldviews: Crosscultural Explorations of Human Beliefs.* New York: Scribner's, 1983.

ALEXANDRE GANOCZY

Abbreviations

Books of the Bible

Acts	Acts of the Apostles
Am	Amos
Bar	Baruch
Bel	Bel and the Dragon
1 Chr	1 Chronicles
2 Chr	2 Chronicles
Col	Colossians
1 Cor	1 Corinthians
2 Cor	2 Corinthians
Dn	Daniel
Dt	Deuteronomy
Eccl	Ecclesiastes
Eph	Ephesians
Est	Esther
Ex	Exodus
Ez	Ezekiel
Ezr	Ezra
Gal	Galatians
Gn	Genesis
Hb	Habakkuk
Heb	Hebrews
Hg	Haggai
Hos	Hosea
Is	Isaiah
Jas	James
Jb	Job
Jdt	Judith
Jer	Jeremiah
Jgs	Judges
Jl	Joel
Jn	John
1 Jn	1 John
2 Jn	2 John
3 Jn	3 John
Jon	Jonah
Jos	Joshua
Jude	Jude
1 Kgs	1 Kings
2 Kgs	2 Kings
Lam	Lamentations
Lk	Luke
Lv	Leviticus
Mal	Malachi
1 Mc	1 Maccabees
2 Mc	2 Maccabees
Mi	Micah
Mk	Mark
Mt	Matthew
Na	Nahum
Neh	Nehemiah
Nm	Numbers
Ob	Obadiah
Phil	Philippians
Phlm	Philemon
Prv	Proverbs
Ps	Psalms
1 Pt	1 Peter
2 Pt	2 Peter
Rom	Romans
Ru	Ruth
Rv	Revelation
Sir	Sirach
1 Sm	1 Samuel
2 Sm	2 Samuel
Song(Sg)	Song of Songs
Sus	Susanna
Tb	Tobit
1 Thes	1 Thessalonians
2 Thes	2 Thessalonians
Ti	Titus
1 Tm	1 Timothy
2 Tm	2 Timothy
Wis	Wisdom
Zec	Zechariah
Zep	Zephaniah

Documents of Vatican II

AA	Apostolicam actuositatem
AG	Ad gentes
CD	Christus dominus
DH	Dignitatis humanae
DV	Dei verbum
GE	Gravissimum educationis
GS	Gaudium et spes
IM	Inter mirifica
LG	Lumen gentium
NA	Nostra aetate
OE	Orientalium ecclesiarum
OT	Optatam totius
PC	Perfectae caritatis
PO	Presbyterorum ordinis
SC	Sacrosanctum concilium
UR	Unitatis redintegratio

Documents of the Magisterium

CT	Catechesi tradendae
DM	Dives in misericordia
ES	Ecclesiam suam
RH	Redemptor hominis
RM	Redemptoris mater

ta Apostolicae Sedis

nuarium Historiae Conciliorum

chivio di Filosofia

chiv für Reformationsgeschichte

chives de Philosophie

chives de Sciences Sociales des Religions

née Théologique

gustinianum

lica

letin of the John Rylands Library

ical Theology Bulletin

ische Zeitschrift

olic Biblical Quarterly

iviltà Cattolica

munio

ilium

enical Trends

enical Review

ios Biblicos

et Vie

erides Theologicae Lovanienses

Théologiques et Religieuses

lical Quarterly

lische Theologie

can Studies Annual

ger Zeitschrift für Philosophie und Theologie

anum

p Journal

Theological Review

lical Studies

Reference Works and Key Texts

Apol.	Apologia Confessionis Augustanae (1531), in *BSLK* 139–404.
ASm	Schmalkaldische Artikel (1537), in *BSLK* 407–68.
BKV	*Bibliothek der kirchenväter,* ed. O. Bardenhewer et al., Kempten, 1911–30.
BSLK	*Bekenntnis-schriften der evangelisch-lutherischen Kirche,* Göttingen, 1986.
BThW	*Bibeltheologisches Wörterbuch,* ed. J. Bauer, Graz, 1976.
CA	Augsburg Confession.
Cath	*Catholicisme,* ed. G. Jacquemet, Paris, 1948ff.
CChrCM	*Corpus christianorum, continuatio mediaevalis,* Brepols, Turnhout, 1966.
CChrSG	*Corpus christianorum, series greca,* Brepols, Turnhout-Louvain, 1977.
CChrSL	*Corpus christianorum, series latina,* Brepols, Turnhout, 1953.
CG	Thomas Aquinas, *Summa contra Gentiles.*
CIC	*Codex iuris canonici.*
CR	*Corpus Reformatorum,* Berlin, 1834ff.; Leipzig, 1906ff.
CSCO	*Corpus scriptorum christianorum orientalium,* Rome, 1903.
CSEL	*Corpus scriptorum ecclesiasticorum latinorum,* ed. Academy of Vienna, Vienna, 1866.
DAFC	*Dictionnaire apologétique de la foi catholique,* ed. D'Alès, Paris, 1909–31.
DBS	*Dictionnaire de la Bible, supplément,* Paris, 1928.
DS	*Enchiridion symbolorum, definitionum et declarationum de rebus fidei et morum,* ed. H. Denzinger and A. Schönmetzer, 36th ed., Freiburg im Breisgau, 1965.
DSp	*Dictionnaire de spiritualité,* ed. M. Viller, Paris, 1937.
DThC	*Dictionnaire de théologie catholique,* ed. E. Vacant, Paris, 1937.
DTI	*Dizionario teologico interdisciplinare,* Turin, 1977–78.
EB	*Enchiridion biblicum: Documenta ecclesiastica Sacram Scripturam spectantia,* Naples-Rome, 1961.
EC	*Enciclopedia cattolica,* Vatican City, 1945–54.
EF	*Enciclopedia filosofica,* Novara, 1979.

EKK	*Evangelisch-katholischer Kommentar zum Neuen Testament,* Neukirchen, 1969ff.
EKL	*Evangelisches Kirchenlexikon,* ed. H. Brunotte and O. Weber, Göttingen, 1956–61.
EO	*Enchiridion oecumenicum,* ed. S. J. Voicu and G. Ceretti, Bologna, 1986–88.
ER	*Encyclopedia of Religions,* ed. M. Eliade, New York-London, 1987.
ETF	*Enciclopedia di teologia fondamentale,* ed. G. Ruggieri, Turin, 1987.
EV	*Enchiridion vaticanum,* Bologna, 1966.
FC	Formula Concordiae (1528/29), in *BSLK* 735–1100.
FC sol. decl.	Formula Concordiae, Solidae Declaratio (1528/29), in *BSLK* 829–1100.
GDR	*Grande dizionario delle religioni,* ed. P. Poupard, Assisi, 1988.
GLNT	*Grande lessico del Nuovo Testamento,* Italian translation of *TWNT,* Brescia, 1965–90.
HDG	*Handbuch der Dogmengeschichte,* Freiburg, 1956.
HFTh	*Handbuch der Fundamentaltheologie,* ed. W. Kern, H. J. Pottmeyer, and M. Seckler, Freiburg, 1985–88.
HKG	*Handbuch der Kirchengeschichte,* ed. H. Jedin, Freiburg, 1962.
HkKR	*Handbuch des katholischen Kirchenrechts,* ed. J. Listl, H. Müller, and H. Schmitz, Regensburg, 1983.
HWP	*Historisches Wörterbuch der Philosophie,* ed. R. Eisler, Basel, 1971.
Inst.	Calvin, *Institutes of the Christian Religion.*
KD	Karl Barth, *Die kirchliche Dogmatik,* Zurich, 1932–70.
LThK	*Lexikon für Theologie und Kirche,* ed. J. Hofer and K. Rahner, Freiburg im Breisgau, 1956–65.
MystSal	*Mysterium salutis,* ed. J. Feiner and M. Löhrer, Brescia, 1967–78.
NCE	*New Catholic Encyclopedia,* New York, 1967–74.
ND	N. Neuner and J. Dupuis, eds., *The Christian Faith in the Doctrinal Documents of the Catholic Church,* rev. ed., Staten Island, N.Y., 1982.
NDL	*Nuovo dizionario di liturgia,* ed. D. Sartore and A. M. Triacca, Rome, 1984.

NDM	*Nuovo dizionario di* Rome, 1985.
NDS	*Nuovo dizionario d* Rome, 1985.
NDT	*Nuovo dizionario* Rome, 1977.
NDTB	*Nuovo dizionario* and A. Girlanda,
NHThG	*Neues Handbuch* Munich, 1984–8
NR	N. Neuner and *Urkunden der L*
OS	Calvin, *Opera s*
PG	*Patrologia grae*
PhW	*Philosophisches*
PL	*Patrologia latin*
PO	*Patrologia orie*
RAC	*Reallexikon fi*
RGG	*Die Religion* ed., Tübinge
SChr	*Sources chrét*
SM	*Sacramentur*
STh	Thomas Aq
TRE	*Theologisch* Berlin-New
TWAT	*Theologisc* G. Botterw
TWNT	*Theologise* and G. Fri
WA	M. Luthe
WA DB	M. Luthe Weimar,
WKL	*Weltkirc* and H.

Journals

AAS

AHC

ArchFil

ARG

ArPh

ASSR

ATh

Aug

Bibl

BJRL

BTB

BZ

CBQ

CivCatt

Comm

Conc

EcT

ER

EstBibl

EsVie

Et

EThL

ETR

EvQ

EvTh

FrSA

FZPT

Greg

HeJ

HTR

IBS

IKZ	*Internationale kirchliche Zeitschrift*
IPhQ	*International Philosophical Quarterly*
Ir	*Irénikon*
IThQ	*Irish Theological Quarterly*
JAAR	*Journal of the American Academy of Religion*
JES	*Journal of Ecumenical Studies*
JRelS	*Journal of Religious Studies*
JThS	*Journal of Theological Studies*
KuD	*Kerygma und Dogma*
Lat	*Lateranum*
LKD	*Literatur des katholischen Deutschlands*
LQ	*Lutheran Quarterly*
MS	*Medieval Studies*
MSR	*Mélanges de Science Religieuse*
MT	*Modern Theology*
MThZ	*Münchener theologische Zeitschrift*
NRTh	*Nouvelle Revue Théologique*
NT	*Novum Testamentum*
NTS	*New Testament Studies*
NZSTh	*Neue Zeitschrift für Systematische Theologie*
PhJ	*Philosophisches Jahrbuch der Görres-Gesellschaft*
RAMy	*Revue d'Ascétique et de Mystique*
RB	*Revue Biblique*
RBén	*Revue Bénédictine*
RCT	*Revista Catalana de Teologia*
RdT	*Rassegna di Teologia*
REB	*Revista Eclesiástica Brasileira*
RET	*Revista Española de Teología*
RFNS	*Rivista di Filosofia Neo-Scolastica*
RHPhR	*Revue d'Histoire et de Philosophie Religieuses*
RR	*Reformed Review*
RSLR	*Rivista di Storia e Letteratura Religiosa*

RSPhTh	*Revue des Sciences Philosophiques et Théologiques*
RSR	*Recherches de Science Religieuse*
RThom	*Revue Thomiste*
RThPh	*Revue de Théologie et de Philosophie*
RTL	*Revue Théologique de Louvain*
RUnOtt	*Revue de l'Université de Ottawa*
Sal	*Salesianum*
ScCatt	*La Scuola Cattolica*
ScE	*Science et Esprit*
SJT	*Scottish Journal of Theology*
SNT	*Schriften des Neuen Testaments*
StCatt	*Studi Cattolici*
StTh	*Studia Theologica*
StZ	*Stimmen der Zeit*
Teol	*Teologia*
ThD	*Theology Digest*
Theol	*Theology*
ThG	*Theologie und Glaube*
ThJb(L)	*Theologisches Jahrbuch* (Leipzig)
Thom	*The Thomist*
ThPh	*Theologie und Philosophie*
ThPQ	*Theologisch-praktische Quartalschrift*
ThQ	*Theologische Quartalschrift*
ThR	*Theologische Rundschau*
ThS	*Theological Studies*
TJT	*Toronto Journal of Theology*
ThS	*Theological Studies*
US	*Una Sancta*
ZAW	*Zeitschrift für die alttestamentliche Wissenschaft*
ZKTh	*Zeitschrift für die katholische Theologie*
ZNW	*Zeitschrift für die neutestamentliche Wissenschaft*
ZThK	*Zeitschrift für Theologie und Kirche*

List of Translators

Paul Duggan translated the articles written by Franz Courth.

Peter Kenny translated the articles written by Wolfgang Beinert and Bernhard Georg Langemeyer.

David Kipp translated the articles written by Wilhelm Breuning and Alexandre Ganoczy.

Matthew O'Connell translated the articles written by Werner Löser, Karl Heinz Neufeld, Günter Koch, and Josef Finkenzeller.

James Zeitz translated the articles written by Gerhard Ludwig Müller, Lothar Ullrich, and Georg Kraus.

Index of Subjects

Bold-faced numbers refer to pages on which an entire article is devoted to a given subject.